W9-DFD-558

Vilfredo Pareto

The Mind and Society

A TREATISE ON GENERAL SOCIOLOGY

by Vilfredo Pareto

Translated by Andrew Bongiorno and Arthur Livingston with the advice and active cooperation of James Harvey Rogers.

Edited by Arthur Livingston

Four volumes bound as two

Volume One: Non-Logical Conduct

Volume Two: Theory of Residues

Published through the sponsorship of The Pareto Fund

Philip E. Allen, Founder and President

New York San Francisco

DOVER PUBLICATIONS, INC.

NEW YORK NEW YORK

Published in the United Kingdom by Constable and Company Limited, 10 Orange Street, London W. C. 2.

This new Dover edition, first published in 1963, is an unabridged and corrected republication of the work first published by Harcourt, Brace and Company, Inc., in 1935.

The first edition of this work appeared in four separate volumes; in this Dover edition the four volumes are bound as two.

Manufactured in the United States of America

Dover Publications, Inc.
180 Varick Street
New York 14, N. Y.

The Mind and Society

A TREATISE ON GENERAL SOCIOLOGY

by Vilfredo Pareto

Volume One: Non-Logical Conduct

Editor's Note

Vilfredo Pareto's *Trattato di Sociologia generale* appears in this English edition as the realization of dreams and efforts that extend over fifteen years. My first moves towards the introduction of this work to the English-speaking world go back to 1920 and they were successful in the sense that from that date an eventual publication of the *Trattato* in English in some form or other was assured. I had published what I believe to be the first American note on Pareto November 25, 1915 (*Nation*), and the second in 1916 (*International Year Book*). These two articles were anterior to Professor Robinson's now famous footnote on Pareto in his *Mind in the Making,* 1921. I reviewed Pareto's *Trasformazione della democrazia,* with allusions to the *Trattato* in the New York *Herald,* April 19, 1922, and gave what I believe to have been the first American course on the *Trattato* in Will Durant's Labor College in New York in the autumn of that same year. I introduced Pareto for the first time to large audiences at meetings of the Foreign Policy Association in New York in December, 1923, and in Philadelphia, January, 1924, and lectured on him again at Columbia in the summer of 1924 and during the spring of 1925. An article called "The Myth of Good English" which I published in *Century,* August, 1925, and which Edward Valentine Mitchell, of Hartford, included in his *Essays of 1925,* made explicit reference to Pareto's theory of group-persistences. Disregarding the much writing and lecturing that I did on Pareto between 1925 and 1930, I will note that an article I published in *Nation,* May, 1926, in view of a certain resonance that it chanced to obtain in the West, I at the time regarded and still regard as the beginning of the Pareto vogue in America. To summarize, and saving correction, the enterprise that finds its completion in these volumes was at least five years old at the time of the opening of Professor Henderson's epoch-making seminar in Harvard; eight years old when Mr. Aldous Huxley first called public attention to Pareto in England; thirteen years old at the time when the Pareto vogue burst upon us in full force as the result of Mr. Canby's notes in the *Saturday Review of Literature,* and of Mr. DeVoto's brilliant, spirited and effective campaign in that same review and in *Harper's,* 1933.

I must beg the reader's forgiveness for mentioning these facts just here in this form. I do so only because a voluminous Pareto literature already exists in which they are differently, and sometimes fantastically, recounted.

This enterprise in publishing has been promoted since 1920 on the assumption that there is no priesthood of learning from which the profane are to be forever excluded by reticence on the part of those who know. It is my faith, which I assert as a faith, and perhaps *quia absurdum,* that the general public is interested, and has an interest, in objective thinking apart from sentiment, and in the methods by which the rational state of mind can be cultivated in the face of the countless pitfalls that environment, temperament, the struggle for life, strew in our way. I believe—again an act of faith—that the work that is here offered to the public is the greatest and noblest effort in that direction to which literary history can point.

That faith betrays itself, to the extent of the capacities of four words, in the title which I have ventured to give this work in preference to the original title. I am aware that there are other points of view from which Pareto's masterpiece may be envisaged (I even share some of them) and for which the original title would better serve. But from the outset the chief purpose in this enterprise has been to make the *Trattato* accessible to the general public to which it belongs. I have called it "The Mind and Society" because it illumines the whole relation of thought to conduct, and of thought to sentiment, and the relation of the individual in all his mental processes to the society in which he lives. That particular stress may not reflect Pareto's original stress and intent. It certainly represents his objective achievement.

This edition is a reproduction without any abbreviations or omissions of the last, the 1923, edition of the *Trattato* in its Italian original. One or two explanations will be in point, however.

The division into volumes is quite arbitrary and is based on typographical considerations only. The Italian original is in three volumes. M. Boven's French translation is in two. The larger units in the treatise are the chapters. The smaller unit is the paragraph, for which I retain a peculiar system of numbering that Pareto used, with one variation or another, in many of his writings. Strange as it may appear to the general reader this device justifies itself once one reflects that the inductive and deductive portions of the exposition are closely related, that the theory is built up systematically like an architectural structure in which the parts are all mutually explanatory and where a cross-reference is now and again most useful.

Pareto first expounded the subject matter of these volumes in the form of lectures that were delivered orally and taken down stenographically. Many traces of that origin survive in the body of the printed Italian text. In this translation I eliminate them. Pareto also makes frequent remarks as to the mechanism of his book or as to his manner of developing his thought. Such comments I regularly throw into footnotes, and in so doing I merely generalize a device that Pareto used to an extent himself. Pareto's original contains a number of repetitions. These too I eliminate, barring exception, inserting cross-references if anything is to be gained by them. In cases where substantial departures from Pareto's text are made, I warn and explain in footnotes.

There has been some public speculation of late as to the whys and wherefores of the many delays that have occurred in the appearance of "The Mind and Society." As a venture in publishing this enterprise has been replete with surprises, difficulties, paradoxes, from its very inception fifteen years ago. As a bookmaking enterprise it has consumed some 9,000 hours of my personal toil spread over the last five years. Nearly half of that has gone into editing the bibliographical material in the notes. Unimportant, from any ordinary point of view, as such problems were, it really seemed that if, in a spirit of textual fidelity, one were compelled to reprint references such as *"F. H. G.,* XIV, 378," or "Antonio in *Melissa,"* one might as well know what they meant, even if Pareto himself never knew or had known and forgotten. I have therefore in many respects amplified Pareto's bibliographical apparatus, and indeed quite generally used a reference system that is all my own, and which, within the limits of human frailty, should be exact.

I believe that up to this time I must be the only person, not excluding Pareto himself, who has ever made a careful reading of his notes throughout in the shape in which he left them. One reason for that belief is that actually as a result of gross misprinting they are often unreadable in the garbled forms in which they appear in the Barbera or the Boven editions (try, for instance, in those volumes, the quotations from St. Peter Damian, or, even, one or two of those from Tacitus). I believe it has been worth the trouble to open this treasure store of enjoyment and learning by making these texts available in English; and I will further add that ninety percent of them at least are from books of the first order, books that made their marks in their day and that still tower above the surface of the vast intellectual production of the ages. The trait was characteristic of Pareto's method of work. In solving the problem of the library, which confronts every scholar, he made for the great beacons of culture, disregarding monographic minutiae.

In the notes in this edition the translations of quoted texts are, as a rule, mine whatever the English translations I may mention in the references. This procedure was adopted for purely practical reasons, and not in any spirit of disrespect for such magnificent versions as Friedländer's, for instance, of "The Guide of the Perplexed," or many others that I might mention. I simply found in practice that it was better to translate the notes with Pareto's specific comment and stress in mind, if I were to spare the reader many editorial notes that would have been otherwise required to make things fit together accurately. An example would be the use I have actually made of the Bostock-Riley version of Pliny in one or two paragraphs. The utility of the double references that I often make will, I think, be self-evident. In addition to serving as a double check on possible misprints, they should prove useful to readers who may care to see ampler contexts of interesting quotations either in the originals from which they were taken or in standard translations. Where Pareto quotes from English writers the originals are, of course, restored.

In solving these thousands of bibliographical problems, finding these hundreds of books, identifying exact references, correcting texts on the originals and checking the translations, I would still be nowhere save for the devoted assistance of Mr. Charles H. Tutt and Miss Elisabeth Abbott, to whom I must extend my sincerest appreciation for their rapid, accurate and ingenious researches on hundreds of points. I must also thank Miss Abbott for her painstaking work in twice copying and proofreading my manuscript; Mr. Gaudence Megaro for valuable researches on a number of points, and the indispensable Miss Isabel Lord for the relentless war she has waged (and doubtless could still wage) on my typographical and other inconsistencies. Presuming to speak now in behalf of Paretan studies in America, I would still have to add many words of appreciation for two gentlemen whose names a code of ethics, which they perhaps too rigorously enforce, keeps from appearing in this note. Their diplomacy and courage have helped this enterprise over many barriers that without them would truly have seemed insuperable. It is with deep regret that I find myself restricted to this indirect allusion.

Another regret is that this edition must go to press without a critical introduction to Pareto from some outstanding American scholar. Pareto, however, was most averse to any introduction that should attempt to summarize, epitomize or otherwise interpret his thought. He left directions covering the point with his heirs and the prohibition was included formally in our agreement with them.

ARTHUR LIVINGSTON

Contents

VOLUME I

the non-logical inclinations of people. They show a multiple evolution. A first encounter with the necessity of making a sharp distinction between the logico-experimental truth of a doctrine and its social utility or any other utility that it may have. The logical form human beings give to non-logical actions.

Chapter III. RATIONALIZATION OF NON-LOGICAL CONDUCT 171

If non-logical actions are of such great importance how have the many men of talent who have concerned themselves with human societies failed to perceive them? They have perceived them, now taking them into account implicitly, now considering them under other names without arriving at any general theory, now noting the particular case without grasping its general bearing. Examples from various authors. The imperfection, from the scientific standpoint, of ordinary language tends to promote logical interpretations of non-logical conduct. Examples. Human beings are somehow prone to shun considering non-logical actions and therefore to disguise them with logical vestments of one sort or another. Classification of the devices that are used for that purpose. Comment on the various categories. The attitude of practical men towards non-logical conduct.

Chapter IV. THEORIES TRANSCENDING EXPERIENCE 231

The ordinary terms "religion," "morality," "law." Do they correspond to anything definite? Study of the term "religion." The terms "natural law" and "law of nations." Type-doctrines and deviations from them. The materials that go into theories and the nexuses by which they are brought together. Examples. The use sociology makes of facts. The unknown has to be explained by the known. The present helps to an understanding of the past and to some lesser extent the past to understand the present. Probability of the conclusions that science reaches. Classification of propositions that add something to the uniformity that experience reveals, or which ignore it. Studv of abstract entities known independently of experience.

Biographical Note

Vilfredo Federico Damaso Pareto was born in Paris, July 15, 1848. He died at Céligny, near Geneva, Switzerland, August 19, 1923. His birth in Paris was incidental, though his mother was a Frenchwoman, Marie Mettenier, and his father, the Marquis Raffaele Pareto, had become a naturalized French citizen. The Paretos were Genoese, and since the days when Napoleon Bonaparte conferred a coronet on Vilfredo Pareto's grandfather, Agostino, the family had been distinguished as conspirators in the cause of Italian independence, and as statesmen. Furious Liberals and Mazzinians, they fought for Italy against Austria and for an Italian republic against Cavour and the monarchists. The Marquis Agostino represented the Republic of Genoa at Vienna in 1815. The Marquis Lorenzo, an uncle of Vilfredo, was involved in the conspiracy of Santarosa, went on to ministerial honors under Charles Albert of Savoy, and was President of the Italian Senate under Victor Emmanuel II. In 1856 an aunt by marriage of Pareto's, an Irishwoman, hid Mazzini in her house and sewed him into a mattress when the police came to arrest him. The Marquis Raffaele himself was in exile in Paris at the time of Vilfredo's birth.

Before the Corsican adventurer made nobles of the Paretos, the family had for generations been prominent in the mercantile bourgeoisie of Genoa. Actually Paretos are numerous all along the two Rivieras into Catalonia. A Bartolommeo Pareto was famous as an astronomer in Catalonia in the days of Columbus.

Vilfredo Pareto left Paris for Turin when he was eleven years old, his father, who was an engineer of note, having accepted a post in the railways under the first great administrator of the new Italy, Quintino Sella. The young man seemed to have inherited his father's talents as a mathematician, but he was just as brilliant in the classics and in history. He completed his elementary education at Turin and graduated from the celebrated Polytechnic Institute in that city at the age of twenty-two. His dissertation dealt with "the index functions of equilibrium in solid bodies." Adepts in mysteries of that sort recognized already in that treatise the germ that was to produce such wonders as Note 2022 [1] in the treatise hereafter following.

Faced with the problem of a career, Pareto followed his father through the famous Breach in Porta Pia into a post in the railways at Rome. He was to work four years as a consulting engineer in the new capital of the kingdom. In 1874 he passed into the employ of the Banca Nazionale of Florence, which selected him as general superintendent of three iron mines that it owned in the Valley of the Arno. He held this post for six years. They were the critical years of his career. As a manager of an important business enterprise he was drawn into the question of free-trade and protection and first began to interest himself in economic questions. On the theoretical side he became impressed with the fact that there was a great deal of "literature" and very little "science" in the political economy that was practised and especially preached in those days. On the practical side he became disgusted with the restraints that a government puts upon free initiative when bureaucracy begins to regulate and manage business. He stood for parliament for the district of Pistoia on the free-trade platform and was defeated.

In Florence during these years he made decisive friendships—Domenico Comparetti, the revered and greatly beloved author of *Virgil in the Middle Ages,* Arturo Linacher, a learned classicist, Sydney Sonnino, the statesman, Giustino Fortunato, the biographer of Giordano Bruno. They were all members of a company of brilliant minds that foregathered in the salon of Emilia Toscanelli-Peruzzi, one of the most charming hostesses of that era in the life of Florence. At this time, too, Pareto fell under the spell of Auguste Comte's writings, and began seriously to ponder the problems of scientific sociology. On his father's death in '82, his mother came to live with him and he retired with her and his wife—for he was now married—on the small competence that was left him, to Villa Rosa in Fiesole, with the idea of preparing himself for a professorship in economics. For twelve years he knocked in vain at the doors of academic Italy, though the papers he read before the Academy of the Georgiofili attracted wide attention. His great friend during this period was the economist, Maffeo Pantaleoni, who figured in the next decisive change in Pareto's life. Pareto had had a poor opinion of Léon Walras, the great Swiss economist. Pantaleoni not only opened Pareto's eyes to the merits of Walras but opened the eyes of Walras to the merits of Pareto. Invited to nominate his own successor to the chair of political economy at Lausanne in 1894, Walras designated Pareto.

Pareto bade farewell to his country with a certain bitterness, which manifested itself in a consistent scorn for such honors as, in the days of his greatness, it would willingly have accorded him. Already he had conceived that utter contempt for plutocratic democracy which finds its completest expression in "The Mind and Society." He was convinced that ten men of courage could at any time march on Rome and put the band of "speculators" that were filling their pockets and ruining Italy to flight. During the great years in Switzerland he scanned the heavens continually for any signs of the certain cataclysm, and thought he saw them, now in 1904 when the Czar's visit to Italy was cancelled in deference to a Socialist protest, now in 1914 when all northern Italy rushed into the wild orgies of the "Red Week." When, in 1922, the unspeakable Facta was frightened by the March on Rome into one of the most abject surrenders known to history, Pareto was able to rise from a sick-bed and utter a triumphant "I told you so!"—the bitter exultance of the justified prophet, not the assertion, and by far, of a wish.

As the "Socialist Systems" followed on the Cours and the Manuale on the "Socialist Systems," Pareto moved to the forefront in social science in Europe as one of the founders, if not the founder, of mathematical economics and of mathematical sociology, and the measure of that eminence was furnished by the jubilee which was celebrated in his honor by his colleagues in science in 1917. Meantime he had acquired a quite different sort of fame in both Italy and France by a long list of trenchant comments on European and world affairs which he contributed to newspapers in Paris, Rome, Turin and Genoa. Noteworthy in this regard was his association with the group of the *Indépendence* in Paris, headed by Georges

Sorel. In 1907 he had inherited a considerable fortune from a parallel branch of his family. He had already settled in the villa at Céligny with which his later years were associated. Born gentleman that he was, he was famous among his friends for his indifference to the exteriors that go with wealth and fame. There is a legend that the whole *Trattato* was written in one pair of shoes and one suit of clothes, and anecdotes abound in that sense. Giving a lecture before a convention of scientists at Geneva, Pareto was interrupted from the floor by a patronizing cry from Gustav Schmoller, an economist of the then German Strassburg: "But are there laws in economics?" Schmoller had no personal acquaintance with Pareto at the time. After the lecture Pareto recognized his heckler on the street and sidled up to him in his shabby clothes and in guise of a beggar: "Please, sir, can you direct me to a restaurant where one can eat for nothing?" "Not where you can eat for nothing, my good man," the German replied, "but here is one where you can eat for very little!" "So there *are* laws in economics!" laughed Pareto as he turned away.

At the time of his death Pareto had accepted a royal appointment to the Italian Senate, and was nominally economic delegate of Italy to the League of Nations. Pareto married twice, the first time unhappily. His second wife was a Frenchwoman, Jane Régis, to whom "The Mind and Society" was dedicated.

A. L.

WORKS

Cours d'économie politique professé à l'université de Lausanne (2 vols., Lausanne, 1896-97)
Les Systèmes socialistes (Paris, 1902-03)
Manuale di economia politica (Milano, 1906)
Manuel d'économie politique, translation and revision of *Manuale* (Paris, 1909)
Le mythe vertuiste et la littérature immorale (Paris, 1911, new ed., 1920)
Trattato di Sociologia generale (1st ed., 2 vols., Florence, 1916; 2nd ed., Florence, 1923)
Traité de Sociologie générale (2 vols., Paris, 1917)
Fatti e teorie (Firenze, 1920)
Trasformazione della democrazia (Milano, 1921)

FOR ARTICLES SEE INDEX IN VOL. IV

THE MIND AND SOCIETY

Volume I: Non-Logical Conduct

CHAPTER I

The Scientific Approach

1. Human society is the subject of many researches. Some of them constitute specialized disciplines: law, political economy, political history, the history of religions, and the like. Others have not yet been distinguished by special names. To the synthesis of them all, which aims at studying human society in general, we may give the name of *sociology.*

2. That definition is very inadequate. It may perhaps be improved upon—but not much; for, after all, of none of the sciences, not even of the several mathematical sciences, have we strict definitions. Nor can we have. Only for purposes of convenience do we divide the subject-matter of our knowledge into various parts, and such divisions are artificial and change in course of time. Who can mark the boundaries between chemistry and physics, or between physics and mechanics? And what are we to do with thermodynamics? If we locate that science in physics, it will fit not badly there; if we put it with mechanics, it will not seem out of place; if we prefer to make a separate science of it, no one surely can find fault with us. Instead of wasting time trying to discover the best classification for it, it will be the wiser part to examine the facts with which it deals. Let us put names aside and consider things.

In the same way, we have something better to do than to waste our time deciding whether sociology is or is not an independent science—whether it is anything but the "philosophy of history" under a different name; or to debate at any great length the methods to be followed in the study of sociology. Let us keep to our quest for the relationships between social facts, and people may then give to that inquiry any name they please. And let knowledge of such relationships be obtained by any method that will serve. We are interested in the end, and much less or not at all interested in the means by which we attain it.

3. In considering the definition of sociology just above we found it necessary to hint at one or two norms that we intend to follow in these volumes. We might do the same in other connexions as occasion arises. On the other hand, we might very well set forth our norms once and for all. Each of those procedures has its merits and its defects. Here we prefer to follow the second.[1]

4. The principles that a writer chooses to follow may be put forward in two different ways. He may, in the first place, ask that his principles be accepted as demonstrated truths. If they are so accepted, all their logical implications must also be regarded as proved. On the other hand, he may state his principles as mere indications of one course that may be followed among the many possible. In that case any logical implication which they may contain is in no sense demonstrated in the concrete, but is merely hypothetical—hypothetical in the same manner and to the same degree as the premises from which it has been derived. It will therefore often be necessary to abstain from drawing such inferences: the deductive aspects of the subject will be ignored, and relationships be inferred from the facts directly.

Let us consider an example. Suppose Euclid's postulate that a straight line is the shortest distance between two points is set before us as a theorem. We must give battle on the theorem; for if we concede it, the whole system of Euclidean geometry stands demonstrated, and we have nothing left to set against it. But suppose, on the contrary, the postulate be put forward as a hypothesis. We are no longer called upon to contest it. Let the mathematician develop the logical consequences that follow from it. If they are in accord with the concrete, we will accept them; if they seem not to be in such accord, we will reject them. Our freedom of choice has not been fettered by any anticipatory concession. Considering things from that point of view, other geometries—non-Euclidean geometries—are possible, and we may study them without in the least surrendering our freedom of choice in the concrete.

3 [1] In the first chapter of my *Manuale* I examined with special regard to political economy several subjects that are touched upon here with regard to sociology.

If before proceeding with their researches mathematicians had insisted upon deciding whether or not the postulate of Euclid corresponded to concrete reality, geometry would not exist even today. And that observation is of general bearing. All sciences have advanced when, instead of quarrelling over first principles, people have considered results. The science of celestial mechanics developed as a result of the hypothesis of the law of universal gravitation. Today we suspect that that attraction may be something different from what it was once thought to be; but even if, in the light of new and better observations of fact, our doubts should prove well founded, the results attained by celestial mechanics on the whole would still stand. They would simply have to be retouched and supplemented.

5. Profiting by such experience, we are here setting out to apply to the study of sociology the methods that have proved so useful in the other sciences. We do not posit any dogma as a premise to our research; and our statement of principles serves merely as an indication of that course, among the many courses that might be chosen, which we elect to follow. Therefore anyone who joins us along such a course by no means renounces his right to follow some other. From the first pages of a treatise on geometry it is the part of the mathematician to make clear whether he is expounding the geometry of Euclid, or, let us say, the geometry of Lobachevski. But that is just a hint; and if he goes on and expounds the geometry of Lobachevski, it does not follow that he rejects all other geometries. In that sense and in no other should the statement of principles which we are here making be taken.

6. Hitherto sociology has nearly always been expounded dogmatically. Let us not be deceived by the word "positive" that Comte foisted upon his philosophy. His sociology is as dogmatic as Bossuet's *Discourse on Universal History*. It is a case of two different religions, but of religions nevertheless; and religions of the same sort are to be seen in the writings of Spencer, De Greef, Letourneau, and numberless other authors.

Faith by its very nature is exclusive. If one believes oneself possessed of the absolute truth, one cannot admit that there are any other truths in the world. So the enthusiastic Christian and the pugnacious free-thinker are, and have to be, equally intolerant. For the believer there is but one good course; all others are bad. The Mohammedan will not take oath upon the Gospels, nor the Christian upon the Koran. But those who have no faith whatever will take their oath upon either Koran or Gospels—or, as a favour to our humanitarians, on the *Social Contract* of Rousseau; nor even would they scruple to swear on the *Decameron* of Boccaccio, were it only to see the grimace Senator Bérenger would make and the brethren of that gentleman's persuasion.[1] We are by no means asserting that sociologies derived from certain dogmatic principles are useless; just as we in no sense deny utility to the geometries of Lobachevski or Riemann. We simply ask of such sociologies that they use premises and reasonings which are as clear and exact as possible. "Humanitarian" sociologies we have to satiety—they are about the only ones that are being published nowadays. Of metaphysical sociologies (with which are to be classed all positive and humanitarian sociologies) we suffer no dearth. Christian, Catholic, and similar sociologies we have to some small extent. Without disparagement of any of those estimable sociologies, we here venture to expound a sociology that is purely experimental, after the fashion of chemistry, physics, and other such sciences.[2] In all that follows, therefore, we intend to take only experience [3] and observation as our guides. So far as experience is not contrasted with observation, we shall, for love of brevity, refer to experience alone. When we say that a thing is attested "by experience," the reader must add "and by observation."

6 [1] [Senator René Bérenger (1830-1915), a *bête noire* of Pareto and one of the villains in this long story, was president of the French *Fédération des sociétés contre la pornographie,* and was the author, among other things, of a *Manuel pratique pour la lutte contre la pornographie* (Paris, 1907) and of a *Rapport* (to the French Senate, 1895) . . . *sur la prostitution et les outrages aux bonnes mœurs.*—A. L.]

6 [2] For greater detail on this point, see Sensini, *La teoria della rendita,* and Boven, *Les applications mathématiques à l'économie politique.*

6 [3] [In Italian the word *esperienza* contains the meaning of "experiment" as well as "experience" and the word "experience" is so used in this translation, barring specification to the contrary.—A. L.]

When we speak of "experimental sciences," the reader must supply the adjective "observational," and so on.

7. Current in any given group of people are a number of propositions, descriptive, preceptive, or otherwise. For example: "Youth lacks discretion." "Covet not thy neighbour's goods, nor thy neighbour's wife." "Love thy neighbour as thyself." "Learn to save if you would not one day be in need." Such propositions, combined by logical or pseudo-logical nexuses and amplified with factual narrations[1] of various sorts, constitute theories, theologies, cosmogonies, systems of metaphysics, and so on. Viewed from the outside without regard to any intrinsic merit with which they may be credited by faith, all such propositions and theories are experimental facts, and as experimental facts we are here obliged to consider and examine them.

8. That examination is very useful to sociology; for the image of social activity is stamped on the majority of such propositions and theories, and often it is through them alone that we manage to gain some knowledge of the forces which are at work in society—that is, of the tendencies and inclinations of human beings. For that reason we shall study them at great length in the course of these volumes. Propositions and theories have to be classified at the very outset, for classification is a first step that is almost indispensable if one would have an adequate grasp of any great number of differing objects.[1] To avoid endless repetition of the words "proposition" and "theory," we shall for the moment use only the latter term; but whatever we say of "theories" should be taken as applying also to "propositions," barring specification to the contrary.

9. For the man who lets himself be guided chiefly by sentiment—for the believer, that is—there are usually but two classes of theories: there are theories that are *true* and theories that are *false*. The terms

7 [1] ["Narration," *narrazione,* is a technical term with Pareto, used for a recital of facts *seriatim* quite apart from any interpretation, organization or "thought."—A. L.]

8 [1] The classification that is barely suggested here will be amply dealt with in later chapters.

"true" and "false" are left vaguely defined. They are felt rather than explained.

10. Oftentimes three further axioms are present:

1. The axiom that every "honest" man, every "intelligent" human being, *must* accept "true" propositions and reject "false" ones. The person who fails to do so is either not honest or not rational. Theories, it follows, have an absolute character, independent of the minds that produce or accept them.

2. The axiom that every proposition which is "true" is also "beneficial," and *vice versa.* When, accordingly, a theory has been shown to be true, the study of it is complete, and it is useless to inquire whether it be beneficial or detrimental.

3. At any rate, it is inadmissible that a theory may be beneficial to certain classes of society and detrimental to others—yet that is an axiom of modern currency, and many people deny it without, however, daring to voice that opinion.

11. Were we to meet those assertions with contrary ones, we too would be reasoning *a priori;* and, experimentally, both sets of assertions would have the same value—zero. If we would remain within the realm of experience, we need simply determine first of all whether the terms used in the assertions correspond to some experimental reality, and then whether the assertions are or are not corroborated by experimental facts. But in order to do that, we are obliged to admit the possibility of both a positive and a negative answer; for it is evident that if we bar one of those two possibilities *a priori,* we shall be giving a solution likewise *a priori* to the problem we have set ourselves, instead of leaving the solution of it to experience as we proposed doing.

12. Let us try therefore to classify theories, using the method we would use were we classifying insects, plants, or rocks. We perceive at once that a theory is not a homogeneous entity, such as the "element" known to chemistry. A theory, rather, is like a rock, which is made up of a number of elements. In a theory one may detect descriptive elements, axiomatic assertions, and functionings of certain entities, now concrete, now abstract, now real, now imaginary; and all such things may be said to constitute the *matter* of the theory. But there are other things in a theory: there are logical or pseudo-logical arguments, appeals to sentiment, "feelings," traces of religious and ethical beliefs, and so on; and such things may be thought of as constituting the instrumentalities whereby the "matter" mentioned above is utilized in order to rear the structure that we call a theory. Here, already, is one aspect under which theories may be considered. It is sufficient for the moment to have called attention to it.[1]

13. In the manner just described, the structure has been reared—the theory exists. It is now one of the objects that we are trying to classify. We may consider it under various aspects:

1. *Objective aspect.* The theory may be considered without reference to the person who has produced it or to the person who assents to it—"objectively," we say, but without attaching any metaphysical sense to the term. In order to take account of all possible combinations that may arise from the character of the *matter* and the character of the *nexus,* we must distinguish the following classes and subclasses:

Class I. Experimental matter
I*a*. Logical nexus
I*b*. Non-logical nexus
Class II. Non-experimental matter
II*a*. Logical nexus
II*b*. Non-logical nexus

The subclasses I*b* and II*b* comprise logical sophistries, or specious reasonings calculated to deceive. For the study in which we are engaged they are often far less important than the subclasses I*a* or II*a*. The subclass I*a* comprises all the experimental sciences; we shall call it *logico-experimental*. Two other varieties may be distinguished in it:

I*a*1, comprising the type that is strictly pure, with the matter strictly experimental and the nexus logical. The abstractions and

12 [1] We shall discuss it at length in Chapter IV (§ 467).

general principles that are used within it are derived exclusively from experience and are subordinated to experience (§ 63).

I*a*2, comprising a deviation from the type, which brings us closer to Class II. Explicitly the matter is still experimental, and the nexus logical; but the abstractions, the general principles, acquire (implicitly or explicitly) a significance transcending experience. This variety might be called *transitional*. Others of like nature might be considered, but they are far less important than this one.

The classification just made, like any other that might be made, is dependent upon the knowledge at our command. A person who regards as experimental certain elements that another person regards as non-experimental will locate in Class I a proposition that the other person will place in Class II. The person who thinks he is using logic and is mistaken will class among logical theories a proposition that a person aware of the error will locate among the non-logical. The classification above is a classification of types of theories. In reality, a given theory may be a blend of such types—it may, that is, contain experimental elements and non-experimental elements, logical elements and non-logical elements.[1]

2. *Subjective aspect*. Theories may be considered with reference to the persons who produce them and to the persons who assent to them. We shall therefore have to consider them under the following subjective aspects:

a. Causes in view of which a given theory is devised by a given person. Why does a given person assert that $A = B$? Conversely, if he makes that assertion, why does he do so?

b. Causes in view of which a given person assents to a given theory. Why does a given person assent to the proposition $A = B$? Conversely, if he gives such assent, why does he do so?

These inquiries are extensible from individuals to society at large.

3. *Aspect of utility*. In this connexion, it is important to keep the

13 [1] There are theories that are logico-experimental in appearance but which substantially are not of that character. For an interesting and very important example of such pseudo-logico-experimental theories, see §§ 407 f. Strictly speaking, such theories should be placed in the non-logico-experimental group.

theory distinct from the state of mind, the sentiments, that it reflects. Certain individuals evolve a theory because they have certain sentiments; but then the theory reacts in turn upon them, as well as upon other individuals, to produce, intensify, or modify certain sentiments.

I. *Utility or detriment resulting from the sentiments reflected by a theory:*
I*a*. As regards the person asserting the theory
I*b*. As regards the person assenting to the theory
II. *Utility or detriment resulting from a given theory:*
II*a*. As regards the person asserting the theory
II*b*. As regards the person assenting to it.

These considerations, too, are extensible to society at large.

We may say, then, that we are to consider propositions and theories under their *objective* and their *subjective aspects,* and also from the standpoint of their individual or social *utility*. However, the meanings of such terms must not be derived from their etymology, or from their usage in common parlance, but exclusively in the manner designated later in § 119.

14. To recapitulate: Given the proposition $A = B$, we must answer the following questions:

1. *Objective aspect.* Is the proposition in accord with experience, or is it not?

2. *Subjective aspect.* Why do certain individuals assert that $A = B$? And why do other individuals believe that $A = B$?

3. *Aspect of utility.* What advantage (or disadvantage) do the sentiments reflected by the proposition $A = B$ have for the person who states it, and for the person who accepts it? What advantage (or disadvantage) does the theory itself have for the person who puts it forward, and for the person who accepts it?

In an extreme case the answer to the first question is yes; and then, as regards the other question, one adds: "People say (people believe) that $A = B$, because it is *true*." "The sentiments reflected in the proposition are beneficial[1] because true." "The theory itself is beneficial because true." In this extreme case, we may find that data of logico-experimental science are present, and then "true" means in accord with experience. But also present may be data that by no means belong to logico-experimental science, and in such event "true" signifies not accord with experience but something else —frequently mere accord with the sentiments of the person defending the thesis. We shall see, as we proceed with our experimental research in chapters hereafter, that the following cases are of frequent occurrence in social matters:

a. Propositions in accord with experience that are asserted and accepted because of their accord with sentiments, the latter being now beneficial, now detrimental, to individuals or society

b. Propositions in accord with experience that are rejected because they are not in accord with sentiments, and which, if accepted, would be detrimental to society

c. Propositions not in accord with experience that are asserted and accepted because of their accord with sentiments, the latter being beneficial, oftentimes exceedingly so, to individuals or society

d. Propositions not in accord with experience that are asserted and accepted because of their accord with sentiments, and which are beneficial to certain individuals, detrimental to others, and now beneficial, now detrimental, to society.

On all that we can know nothing *a priori*. Experience alone can enlighten us.

15. After objects have been classified, they have to be examined, and to that research we shall devote the next chapters. In Chapters IV and V we shall consider theories with special reference to their accord with experience and observation. In Chapters VI, VII, and

14 [1] [Pareto's doctrine of utility takes Bentham's utilitarian theory as its point of departure. Bentham used the adjective "useful" as corresponding to "utility," the opposites being "harm" and "harmful." Pareto uses "useful" (*utile*) quite regularly. In this translation I have found most convenient the terms "utility," "beneficial," "detriment" and "detrimental," alternating, on occasion, with "advantage," "advantageous," "disadvantageous."—A. L.]

VIII we shall study the sentiments in which theories originate. In Chapters IX and X we shall consider the ways in which sentiments are reflected in theories. In Chapter XI we shall examine the characteristics of the elements so detected. And finally in Chapters XII and XIII we shall see the social effects of the various elements, and arrive at an approximate concept of variations in the forms of society—the goal at which we shall have been aiming all along and towards which all our successive chapters will have been leading.[1]

16. From the objective standpoint (§ 13), we divided propositions or theories into two great classes, the first in no way departing from the realm of experience, the second overstepping it in some respect or other.[1] If one would reason at all exactly, it is essential to keep those two classes distinct, for at bottom they are heterogeneous things that must never be in any way confused, and which cannot, either, be compared.[2] Each of them has its own manner of reasoning and, in general, its own peculiar standard whereby it falls into two divisions, the one comprising propositions that are in logical accord with the chosen standard and are called true; the other comprising propositions which are not in accord with that standard and are called false. The terms "true" and "false," therefore, stand in strict dependence on the standard chosen. If one should try to give them an absolute meaning, one would be deserting the logico-experimental field for the field of metaphysics.

The standard of truth for propositions of the first class lies in experience and observation only. The standard of truth for the second class lies outside objective experience—in some divine revelation; in concepts that the human mind finds in itself, as some say, without the aid of objective experience; in the universal consensus of mankind, and so on.

15 [1] In some other book we might carry the investigation begun in this one further and investigate the particular forms of the various social phenomena of which we shall here have found the general forms.

16 [1] Pareto, *Manuale,* Chap. I, § 37.

16 [2] *Ibid.,* Chap. I, § 41: "Fatuous and silly is the claim of certain individuals that the faith they hold is 'more scientific' than the faiths of other people. Faith and science have nothing in common, and a faith can contain neither more nor less of science."

There must never be any quarrelling over names. If someone is minded to ascribe a different meaning to the terms "truth" and "science," for our part we shall not raise the slightest objection. We are satisfied if he specifies the sense that he means to give to the terms he uses and especially the standard by which he recognizes a proposition as "true" or "false."

17. If that standard is not specified, it is idle to proceed with a discussion that could only resolve itself into mere talk; just as it would be idle for lawyers to plead their cases in the absence of a judge. If someone asserts that "*A* has the property *B*," before going on with the discussion we must know who is to judge the controversy between him and another person who maintains that "*A* does not have the property *B*." If it is agreed that the judge shall be objective experience, objective experience will then decide whether *A* has, or does not have, the property *B*. Throughout the course of these volumes, we are in the logico-experimental field. I intend to remain absolutely in that field and refuse to depart from it under any inducement whatsoever. If, therefore, the reader desires a judge other than objective experience, he should stop reading this book, just as he would refrain from proceeding with a case before a court to which he objected.

18. If people disposed to argue the propositions mentioned desire a judge other than objective experience, they will do well to declare exactly what their judge is to be, and if possible (it seldom is) to make themselves very clear on the point. In these volumes we shall refrain from participating in arguments as to the substance of propositions and theories. We are to discuss them strictly from the outside, as social facts with which we have to deal.

19. Metaphysicists generally give the name of "science" to knowledge of the "essences" of things, to knowledge of "principles." If we accept that definition for the moment, it would follow that this work would be in no way scientific. Not only do we refrain from dealing with essences and principles: we do not even know the meaning of those terms (§ 530).

Vera, Hegel's French translator, says,[1] "The notions of science and absolute science are inseparable. . . . Now if there be an absolute science, it is not and cannot be other than philosophy. So philosophy is the common foundation of all the sciences, and as it were the common intelligence of all intelligences." In this book we refuse to have anything whatever to do with such a science, and with those other pretty things that go with it. "The absolute (in other words, essence) and unity (in other words, the necessary relations of beings) are the two prime conditions of science." Both of them will be found missing in these volumes, and we do not even know what they may be. We seek the relationships obtaining between things within the limits of the space and time known to us, and we ask experience and observation to reveal them to us. "Philosophy is at once an explanation and a creation." We have neither the desire nor the ability to explain, in Vera's sense of the term, much less to create. "The science that knows the absolute and grasps the innermost reason of things knows how and why events come to pass and beings are engendered [That is something we do not know.], and not only knows but in a certain way itself engenders and brings to pass in the very fact of grasping the absolute. And indeed we must either deny science, or else admit that there is a point where knowledge and being, thought and its object, coincide and are identified; and a science of the absolute that arose apart from the absolute, and so failed of achieving its real and innermost nature, would not be a science of the absolute, or more exactly, would not be science at all."

20. Well said! In that we agree with Vera. If science is what Vera's terms describe it as being—terms as inspiring as they are (to us) incomprehensible—we are not here dealing with science. We are, however, dealing with another thing that Vera very well describes in a particular case when he says, p. 214, note: "Generally speaking, mechanics is just a miscellany of experiential data and mathematical formulae." In terms still more general, one might say: "a miscellany of experiential data and logical inferences from

19 [1] *Introduction à la philosophie de Hegel*, pp. 78-89.

such data." Suppose, for a moment, we call that non-science. Both Vera and Hegel are then right in saying that the theories of Newton are not science but non-science; and in these volumes I also intend to deal with non-science, since my wish is to construct a system of sociology on the model of celestial mechanics, physics, chemistry, and other similar non-sciences, and eschew entirely the science or sciences of the metaphysicists (§§ 503,[5] 514[2]).

21. A reader might observe: "That granted, why do you continually harp on science in the course of your book, since you use the term in the sense of non-science? Are you trying in that way to usurp for your non-science a prestige that belongs to science alone?" I answer that if the word "science" ordinarily meant what the metaphysicists say it means, rejecting the thing, I would conscientiously reject the word. But that is not the case. Many people, nay, most people, think of celestial mechanics, physics, chemistry, and so on as sciences; and to call them non-sciences or something else of the sort would, I fear, be ridiculous. All the same, if someone is still not satisfied, let him prefix a "non-" to the words "science" and "scientific" whenever he meets them in these volumes, and he will see that the exposition develops just as smoothly, since we are dealing with things and not with words (§ 119).

22. While metaphysics proceeds from absolute principles to concrete cases, experimental science proceeds from concrete cases, not to absolute principles, which, so far as it is concerned, do not exist, but to general principles, which are brought under principles still more general, and so on indefinitely. That procedure is not readily grasped by minds accustomed to metaphysical thinking, and it gives rise to not a few erroneous interpretations.

23. Let us note, just in passing, the preconception that in order to know a thing its "essence" must be known. To the precise contrary, experimental science starts with knowledge of things, to go on, if not to essences, which are entities unknown to science, at least to general principles (§§ 19-20). Another somewhat similar conception is widely prevalent nowadays in the fields of political economy and sociology. It holds that knowledge of things can be acquired only by tracing their "origins"[1] (§§ 93, 346).

24. In an attenuated form the preconception requiring knowledge of "essences" aims at demonstrating particular facts by means of general principles, instead of deriving the general principle from the fact. Just so proof of the fact is confused with proof of its causes. For example, observation shows the existence of a fact *A;* and we go on and designate *B, C, D . . .* as its probable causes. It is later shown that those causes are not operative, and from that the conclusion is drawn that *A* does not exist. The demonstration would be valid if the existence of *B, C, D . . .* had been shown by experience and the existence of *A* inferred from them. It is devoid of the slightest value if observation has yielded *A* directly.

25. Close kin to the preconception just mentioned is the difficulty some people experience in analyzing a situation and studying its various aspects separately. We shall have frequent occasion to return to this matter. Suffice it here to note that the distinctions drawn above in § 13 will not be recognized by many people; and if others do indeed accept them theoretically, they straightway forget them in actual thinking (§§ 31-32, 817).

26. For people of "living faith" the various characteristics of theories designated in § 13 often come down to one only. What the believer wants to know, and nothing else, is whether the proposition is true or not true. Just what "true" means nobody knows, and the believer less than anybody. In a general way it seems to indicate accord with the believer's sentiments; but that fact is evident only to the person viewing the belief from the outside, as a stranger to it—never to the believer himself. He, as a rule, denies the subjective character of his belief. To tell him that it is subjective is almost to insult him, for he considers it true in an absolute sense. For the same reason he refuses to think of the term "true" apart from the meaning he attaches to it, and readily speaks of a truth different from experimental truth and superior to it.[1]

23 [1] Pareto, *Manuale,* Chap. I, § 33.

26 [1] With that state of mind also we shall deal at length in chapters following.

27. It is idle to continue discussions of that type—they can only prove fruitless and inconclusive—unless we know exactly what the terms that are used mean, and unless we have a criterion to refer to, a judge to render judgment in the dispute (§§ 17 f.). Is the criterion, the judge, to be experience and observation, or is it to be something else? That point has to be clearly determined before we can go on. If you are free to choose between two judges, you may pick the one you like best to decide your case. But you cannot choose them both at the same time, unless you are sure in advance that they are both of one mind and one will.

28. Of that agreement metaphysicists enjoy an *a priori* certitude, for their superexperimental criterion is of such majesty and power that it dominates the experimental criterion, which must of necessity accord with it. For a similar reason theologians too are certain *a priori* that the two criteria can never fail of accord. We, much more humble, enjoy no such *a priori* enlightenment. We have no knowledge whatever of what *must* or *ought to* be. We are looking strictly for what *is*. That is why we have to be satisfied with one judge at a time.

29. From our point of view not even logic supplies *necessary* inferences, except when such inferences are mere tautologies. Logic derives its efficacy from experience and from nothing else (§ 97).[1]

30. The human mind is synthetic, and only training in the habit of scientific thinking enables a few individuals to distinguish the parts in a whole by an analytical process (§ 25). Women especially, and the less well-educated among men, often experience an insurmountable difficulty in considering the different aspects of a thing separately, one by one. To be convinced of that one has only to read a newspaper article before a mixed social gathering and then try to discuss one at a time the various aspects under which it may be considered. One will notice that one's listeners do not follow, that they persist in considering all the aspects of the subject all together at one time.

29 [1] This is not the place to deal with the question. We note the point in passing just to avoid misunderstandings.

31. The presence of that trait in the human mind makes it very difficult for both the person who is stating a proposition and the person who is listening to keep the two criteria, the experimental and the non-experimental, distinct. An irresistible force seems always to be driving the majority of human beings to confuse them. Many facts of great significance to sociology find their explanation in just that, as will be more clearly apparent from what follows.

32. In the natural sciences people have finally realized the necessity of analysis in studying the various aspects of a concrete phenomenon—the analysis being followed by a synthesis in getting back from theory to the concrete. In the social sciences that necessity is still not grasped by many people.

33. Hence the very common error of denying the truth of a theory because it fails to explain every aspect of a concrete fact; and the same error, under another form, of insisting on embracing under one theory all other similar or even irrelevant theories.

Let *O* in Figure 1 stand for a concrete situation. By analysis we distinguish within it a number of facts: *c, e, g. . . .*

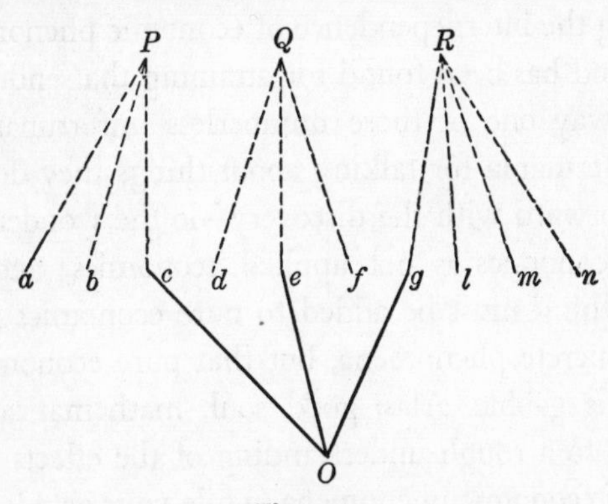

Figure 1

The fact *c* and others like it, *a, b . . .* are brought together under a certain theory, under a general principle, *P*. In the same way, *e* and facts like *e* (*d, f . . .*) yield another theory, *Q;* and the facts *g, l, m, n . . .* still another theory, *R,* and so on. These theories are worked out separately; then, to determine the concrete situation *O,* the results (*c, e, g* . . .) of the various theories are taken together. After analysis comes synthesis.

People who fail to understand that will say: "The situation *O* presents not only the fact *e* but also the fact *c;* therefore the theory *Q* has to account for *c.*" That conclusion is erroneous. One should say—and it is the only sound conclusion: ". . . therefore the theory *Q* accounts for only a part of the situation *O.*"

34. *Example:* Let *Q* stand for the theory of political economy. A concrete situation *O* presents not only an economic aspect, *e,* but the further aspects *c, g* . . . of a sociological character. It is a mistake to include, as many have included, the sociological elements *c, g* . . . under political economy. The only sound conclusion to be drawn from the facts is that the economic theory which accounts for *e* must be supplemented (*supplemented,* not replaced) by other theories which account for *c, g.* . . .

35. In political economy itself, the theories of pure or mathematical economics have to be supplemented—not replaced—by the theories of applied economics. Mathematical economics aims chiefly at emphasizing the interdependence of economic phenomena. So far no other method has been found for attaining that end.[1]

36. Straightway one of those numberless unfortunates who are cursed with the mania for talking about things they do not understand comes forward with the discovery—lo the wonders of genius! —that pure economics is not applied economics, and concludes, not that something must be added to pure economics if we are to understand concrete phenomena, but that pure economics must be replaced by his gabble. Alas, good soul, mathematical economics helps, at least, to a rough understanding of the effects of the interdependence of economic phenomena, while your gabble shows absolutely nothing!

37. And lo, another prodigious genius, who holds that because many economic phenomena depend on the human will, economics must be replaced by psychology. But why stop at psychology? Why not geography, or even astronomy? For after all the economic factor

35 [1] Pareto, *Manuale,* Chap. III, § 228.

is influenced by seas, continents, rivers, and above all by the Sun, fecundator general of "this fair family of flowers and trees and all earthly creatures."[1] Such prattle has been called *positive* economics, and for that our best gratitude, for it provokes a laugh, and laughter, good digestion!

38. Many economists have been inclined to bring each and every sort of economic theory under the theory of *value*.[1] True, nearly all economic phenomena express themselves in terms of *value;* but from that we have a right to conclude that in isolating the various elements in such phenomena we come upon a theory for value—but not that all other elements have to be squeezed into that theory. Nowadays people are going farther still, and value is coming to be the door through which sociology is made to elbow its way into political economy. Perhaps we ought to be thankful that they are stopping at that, for no end of other things might be pushed through the same door: psychology, to explain why and how a thing, real or imaginary, comes to have value; then physiology as handmaiden to psychology; and then—why not?—a little biology to explain the foundations of physiology; and surely a little mathematics, for after all the first member of an equation has the same value as the second and the theory of value would not be complete without the theory of equations; and so on forever. In all of which there is this much truth: that the concrete situation is very complex and may be regarded as a compound of many elements *A, B, C*. . . . Experience teaches that to understand such a situation it is best to isolate the elements *A, B, C* . . . and examine them one by one, that we may then bring them together again and so get the theory of the complex as a whole. That is just what logico-experimental science does. But those who are unfamiliar with its methods grope blindly forward, shifting from *A* to *B,* from *B* to *C,* then every so often turning back, mixing things up, taking refuge in words, thinking of *B* while studying *A,* and of something else while studying *B.* Worse yet, if you are looking into *A* they interrupt to remind you of *B;*

37 [1] [The allusion is to Foscolo, *I sepolcri,* vv. 4-5.—A. L.]
38 [1] Pareto, *Manuale,* Chap. III, § 226; *Systèmes socialistes,* Vol. I, pp. 338 f.

and if you answer on *B,* they are off to *C,* jumping about now here, now there, prattling ever beside the point and demonstrating one thing only: their helpless innocence of any scientific method.

39. Those who deny scientific status to political economy argue, in fact, to show that it is not adequate to explain concrete phenomena; and from that they conclude that it should be ignored in such explanation. The sound conclusion would be that other theories should be added to it. Thinking as such people think we should have to say that chemistry ought to be ignored in agriculture, since chemistry is inadequate to explain everything about a farm. Moreover, engineering schools would have to bar pure mathematics, for it stands to applied mechanics almost as pure economics stands to applied economics.

40. Further, it is difficult, in fact almost impossible, to induce people to keep mere knowledge of the laws (uniformities) of society distinct from action designed to modify them. If someone is keeping strictly to such knowledge, people will insist at all costs that he have some practical purpose in view. They try to find out what it is, and, there being none, one is finally invented for him.

41. In the same way, it is difficult to induce people not to go beyond what an author says and add to the propositions he states others that may seem to be implicit in them but which he never had in mind (§§ 73 f., 311). If you note a defect in a given thing *A,* it is taken for granted that you are condemning *A* as a whole; if you note a good point, that you approve of *A* as a whole. It seems incredibly strange to people that you should be stressing its defects if you are not intending to condemn it as a whole, or its excellences if you are not approving of it as a whole. The inference would be somewhat justified in a case of special pleading, for after all it is not the business of the advocate to accuse his client. But it is not a sound inference from a plain description of fact, or when a scientist is seeking scientific uniformities. The inference would be admissible, further, in the case of an argument not of a logico-experimental character but based on accord of sentiments (§ 514). In fact, when one is trying to win the sympathies of others by such an argument,

one may be expected to declare one's own sympathies; and if that is not done explicitly, people may properly assume that it is done implicitly. But when we are reasoning objectively, according to the logico-experimental method, we are not called upon to declare our sentiments either explicitly or by implication.

42. As regards proofs, a person stating a logico-experimental proposition or theory (§ 13, I*a*) asks them of observation, experience, and logical inferences from observation and experience. But the person asserting a proposition or theory that is not logico-experimental can rely only on the spontaneous assent of other minds and on the more or less logical inferences he can draw from what is assented to. At bottom he is exhorting rather than proving. However, that is not commonly admitted by people using non-logico-experimental theories. They pretend to be offering proofs of the same nature as the proofs offered for logico-experimental theories; and in such pseudo-experimental arguments they take full advantage of the indefiniteness of common everyday language.

As regards persuasion, proofs are convincing only to minds trained to logico-experimental thinking. Authority plays a great part even in logico-experimental propositions, though it has no status as proof. Passions, accords of sentiment, vagueness of terms, are of great efficacy in everything that is not logico-experimental (§ 514).

43. In the sphere of proof, experience is powerless as against faith, and faith as against experience, with the result that each is confined to its own domain. If John, an unbeliever, denies that God created Heaven and Earth, and you meet him with the authority of the Bible, you have made a nice round hole in the water, for he will deny the authority of the Bible and your argument will crumble. To replace the authority of the Bible with the authority of your "Christian experience" is a childish makeshift, for John will reply that his own experience inclines him not in the least to agree with you; and if you retort that his experience is not Christian, you will have reasoned in a neat circle, for it is certain that if only that experience is Christian which leads to your results, one may conclude without fear of contradiction that Christian experience leads to your results—and by that we have learned exactly nothing.

44. When one asserts a logico-experimental proposition (§ 13, I*a*), one can place those who contradict in the dilemma of either accepting the proposition as true or refusing credence to experience and logic. Anyone adopting the latter course would be in the position of John, the unbeliever just mentioned: you would have no way of persuading him.

45. It is therefore evident that, aside as usual from sophistical reasonings made in bad faith, the difference as regards proofs between theories that are logico-experimental (I*a*) and theories that are not lies chiefly in the fact that in our day in Western countries it is easier to find disbelievers in the Koran or the Gospels; in types of experience, whether Christian, personal, humanitarian, rational, or of whatever other kind; in the categorical imperative; or in the dogmas of positivism, nationalism, pacifism, and numberless other things of that brand, than it is to find disbelievers in logic and experience. In dealing with other ages and countries the situation may be different.

46. We are in no sense intending, in company with a certain materialistic metaphysics, to exalt logic and experience to a greater power and majesty than dogmas accepted by sentiment. Our aim is to distinguish, not to compare, and much less to pass judgment on the relative merits and virtues of those two sorts of thinking (§ 69).

47. Again, we have not the remotest intention of bringing back through the window a conviction we have just driven out by the door. We in no wise assert that the logico-experimental proof is superior to the other and is to be preferred. We are saying simply—and it is something quite different—that such proof alone is to be used by a person concerned not to abandon the logico-experimental field.[1]

48. The extreme case of a person flatly repudiating all logical dis-

47 [1] The remark is really tautological and would hardly be worth making if it were not so frequently forgotten by people who mix experience and faith, reasoning and sentiment.

cursion, all experience, is rarely met with. Logico-experimental considerations are commonly enough ignored, left unexpressed, crowded aside, by one device or another; but it is difficult to find anyone really combating them as enemies. That is why people almost always try to demonstrate theories that are not objective, not experimental, by pseudo-logical and pseudo-experimental proofs.

49. All religions have proofs of that type, supplemented as a rule by proofs of utility to individual and society. And when one religion replaces another, it is anxious to create the impression that its experimental proofs are of a better quality than any the declining faith can marshal. Christian miracles were held to be more convincing than pagan miracles, and nowadays the "scientific" proofs of "solidarity" and humanitarianism are considered superior to the Christian miracles. All the same, the man who examines such facts without the assistance of faith fails to notice any great difference in them; for him they have exactly the same scientific value, to wit, zero. We are obliged to believe that "when Punic fury thundered from the Thrasimene" the defeat of the Romans was caused by the impious indifference of the consul Flaminius to the portents sent of the gods. The consul had fallen from his horse in front of the statue of Jupiter Stator. The sacred chickens had refused to eat. Finally, the legionary ensign had stuck in the ground and could not be extricated.[1] We shall also be certain (whether more or less certain, I could not say) that the victory of the Crusaders at Antioch was due to the divine protection concretely symbolized in the Holy Lance.[2] Then again it

49 [1] Cicero, *De divinatione,* I, 35, 77: "On that occasion the standard-bearer of the First Spears found he could not move his ensign from where it was; and nothing could be done about it, though many came to his assistance. But when the thing was reported to Flaminius he, as was his usual habit, paid no attention; and so, within three hours, his army was cut to pieces and he himself was slain." [The literary allusion in "Punic fury" is to Carducci, *"Alle fonti del Clitumno"* (*Poesie,* p. 803).—A. L.]

49 [2] Michaud, *Histoire des croisades,* 1877 ed., Vol. I, p. 94: "Many of the Crusaders attributed the victory they had won over the Saracens to the discovery of the Holy Lance. Raymond d'Agiles avers that the enemy dared not approach battalions in the midst of which the miraculous weapon could be seen glistening." *Idem, Bibliothèque des croisades,* Vol. I, pp. 33-34: "Raymond d'Agiles adds that none of the men fighting about the Holy Lance suffered any harm. 'If someone objects,' he con-

is certain, in fact the height of certitude, because attested by a better and more modern religion, that Louis XVI of France lost his throne and his life simply because he did not love to the degree required his good, his darling, people. The humanitarian god of democracy never suffers such offences to go unpunished!

50. Experimental science has no dogmas, not even the dogma that experimental facts can be explained only by experience. If the contrary were seen to be the case, experimental science would accept the fact, as it accepts every other fact of observation. And it in truth accepts the proposition that inventions may at times be promoted by non-experimental principles, and does so because that proposition is in accord with the results of experience.[1] But so far as demonstration goes, the history of human knowledge clearly shows that all attempts to explain natural phenomena by means of propositions derived from religious or metaphysical principles have failed. Such attempts have finally been abandoned in astronomy, geology, physiology, and all other similar sciences. If traces of them are still to be found in sociology and its subbranches, law, political economy, ethics, and so on, that is simply because in those fields a strictly scientific status has not yet been attained.[2]

51. One of the last efforts to subordinate experience to metaphysics was made by Hegel in his *Philosophy of Nature,* a work which, in all frankness, attains and oversteps the limits of comic absurdity.[1]

52. On the other hand, in our day people are beginning to repudiate dogmas that usurp status as experimental science. Sectarians of the humanitarian cult are wont to meet the "fictions" of the religion they are combating with the "certainty" of science. But that "certainty" is just one of their preconceptions. Scientific theories are

tinues, 'that the Vicomte Héracle, standard-bearer to the Bishop, was wounded, that was because he had handed the banner to another person and had moved some distance away.' "

50 [1] Pareto, *Manuale,* Chap. I, §§ 45, 51.

50 [2] Experiment is helpful even in mathematics. As is well known, modern analysis has discredited by experimental data a number of theories that were considered certain on the basis of sense-perceptions of space.

51 [1] Pareto, *Systèmes socialistes,* Vol. II, pp. 71 f.; *Manuel,* pp. 35, note 1; 14, note 1.

mere hypotheses, which endure so long as they accord with the facts and which die and vanish from the scene as new investigations destroy that accord. They are then superseded by new ones for which a similar fate is held in store (§ 22).

53. Let us assume that a certain number of facts are given. The problem of discovering their theory may be solved in more than one way. A number of theories may satisfy the data equally well, and the choice between them may sometimes be determined by subjective considerations, such as preference for greater simplicity (§ 64).

54. In both logico-experimental (I*a*) and non-logico-experimental theories, one gets certain general propositions called "principles," logically deducible from which are inferences constituting theories. Such principles differ entirely in character in the two kinds of theories mentioned.

55. In logico-experimental theories (I*a*) principles are nothing but abstract propositions summarizing the traits common to many different facts. The principles depend on the facts, not the facts on the principles. They are governed by the facts, not the facts by them. They are accepted hypothetically only so long and so far as they are in agreement with the facts; and they are rejected as soon as there is disagreement (§ 63).

56. But scattered through non-logico-experimental theories one finds principles that are accepted *a priori*, independently of experience, dictating to experience. They do not depend upon the facts; the facts depend upon them. They govern the facts; they are not governed by them. They are accepted without regard to the facts, which must of necessity accord with the inferences deducible from the principles; and if they seem to disagree, one argument after another is tried until one is found that successfully re-establishes the accord, which can never under any circumstances fail.

57. In order of time, the grouping of theories as given in § 13 has in many cases to be reversed. In history, that is, non-logico-experimental theories often come first, the logico-experimental (I*a*) afterwards.

58. The subordination of facts to principles in non-logico-experimental theories is manifested in a number of ways:

1. People are so sure of the principles with which they start that they do not even take the trouble to inquire whether their implications are in accord with experience. Accord there must be, and experience as the subordinate cannot, must not, be allowed to talk back to its superior.[1] That is the case especially when logico-experimental theories (I*a*) begin to invade a domain that has been pre-empted by non-logico-experimental theories.

2. As that invasion gains headway, progress in the experimental sciences finally rescues them from the servitude to which they were regarded as sternly subject. They are conceded a measure of autonomy; they are permitted to verify the inferences drawn from traditional principles, though people continue to assert that verification always corroborates the principle. If things seem not to turn out that way, casuistry comes to the rescue to re-establish the desired accord.

3. When finally that method of maintaining the sovereignty of the general principles also fails, the experimental sciences are resignedly allowed to enjoy their hard-won independence; but their domain is now represented as of an inferior order envisaging the relative and the particular, whereas philosophical principles contemplate the absolute, the universal.

59. No departure from the experimental field and therefore from the domain of logico-experimental theories (I*a*) is involved in the resort to hypotheses, provided they are used strictly as instruments in the quest for consequences that are uniformly subject to verification by experience. The departure arises when hypotheses are used as instruments of proof without reference to experimental verification. The hypothesis of gravitation, for instance, does not carry us outside the experimental field so long as we understand that its implications

58 [1] For example, Zeller well notes of Heraclitus, *Philosophie der Griechen,* Vol. I, p. 658 (Alleyne, Vol. II, p. 95), that when that philosopher is carried to hypotheses which conflict with the known testimony of the senses, he concludes not that his hypotheses are false, as an empiricist would do, but that the senses are deceptive, that reason alone gives trustworthy knowledge.

are at all times subject to experience, as modern physics always assumes. It would carry us outside the experimental field were we to declare gravitation an "essential property" of "matter" and assert that the orbits of the stars must of necessity comply with the Newtonian law. That distinction was not grasped by writers such as Comte, who tried to bar the hypothesis of a luminous ether from science. That hypothesis and others of the kind are to be judged not intrinsically but extrinsically, that is, by ascertaining whether and to what extent inferences drawn from them accord with the facts.

60. When any considerable number of inferences from a given hypothesis have been verified by experience, it becomes exceedingly probable that a new implication will likewise be verified; so in that case the two types of hypotheses mentioned in §§ 55 and 56 are inclined to blend, and in practice there is the temptation to accept the new inference without verifying it. That explains the haziness present in many minds as to the distinction between hypotheses subordinate to experience and hypotheses dominating experience. Still, as a matter of practice there are cases where the implications of this or that hypothesis may be accepted without proof. For instance, certain principles of pure mechanics are being questioned nowadays, at least as regards velocities to any considerable degree greater than velocities practically observable. But it is evident that the mechanical engineer may continue to accept them without the slightest fear of going wrong, since the parts of his machines move at speeds which fall far short of any that would require modifications in the principles of dynamics.

61. In pure economics my hypothesis of "ophelimity" (§ 2110) remains experimental so long as inferences from it are held subject to verification on the facts. Were that subordination to cease, the hypothesis could no longer be called experimental. Walras did not think of his "exchange value" in any such manner.[1] If one drops the

61 [1] Boven, *Les applications mathématiques à l'économie politique,* pp. 106 f.: "First a few definitions of Walras. Interesting his definition of *'value'*: [*Éléments d'économie politique pure,* p. 44.] 'Exchange value is the property possessed by certain things whereby they are not obtained or disposed of gratuitously, but are bought or sold, received or given, in certain quantitative proportions in exchange

hypothesis of ophelimity, as is possible by observing curves of indifference (§ 2408 [1]) or by some other device of the kind, one is excused from verifying experimentally the implications of a hypothesis that is no longer there.

62. Likewise, the hypothesis of value remains experimental so long as value is thought of as something leading to inferences that are experimentally verifiable. It ceases to be experimental when value is taken as a metaphysical entity presumably superior to experimental verification (§ 104).[1]

63. In the logico-experimental sciences, if they are to be kept strictly such, so-called general principles are, as we said above (§ 55), nothing but hypotheses designed to formulate syntheses of facts, linking facts under theories and epitomizing them. Theories, their principles, their implications, are altogether subordinate to facts and possess no other criterion of truth than their capacity for picturing them. That is an exact reversal of the relations between general principles and experimental facts that obtain in non-logico-experimental theories (§ 13, Class II). But the human mind has such a predilection for theories of that sort that general principles have often been seen to recover sovereignty even over theories aspiring to status as logico-experimental (I*a*). It was agreed, that is, that principles had a quasi-

for other things.' This 'property possessed by certain things' smacks of the domain of physics or metaphysics. It is not the same thing as price. . . . One gets the impression that Walras finds it hard to explain just what his 'property' is. He goes round and round it, qualifies it, classifies it, suggests the conditions under which it is to be met with, how it behaves; but he never shows it except under a blurred glass."

62 [1] Pareto, *"L'économie et la sociologie,"* in *Scientia,* Bologna, 1907, No. 2: "The term [value] has finished by designating some mystical, metaphysical entity or other that may mean anything, since it has come to mean nothing at all. William Stanley Jevons in his day [1882] saw that the term was giving rise to endless misunderstandings and proposed banishing it from science [see *Theory of Political Economy,* p. 81]. Meantime matters have grown worse, if possible; and use of the term 'value' may in future serve to distinguish economic treatises that are not scientific from treatises that are. [In a note:] In a volume on economics recently published we find that 'price is a concrete manifestation of value.' We are already familiar with the incarnations of Buddha. To them we are now asked to add the incarnations of Value. Using that sort of language we might say that a cat is a concrete manifestation of 'felinity,' water a concrete manifestation of the 'liquid principle.' But what is the liquid principle? Alas, nobody knows!"

independent subsistence, that only one theory was true, while numberless others were false, that experience could indeed determine which theory was true, but that, having done that much, it was called upon to submit to the theory. In a word, general principles, which were lords by divine right in non-logico-experimental theories (§ 16), became lords by election, but lords nevertheless, in logico-experimental theories (I*a*). So we get the two subclasses distinguished in § 13; but it is well to note that oftentimes their traits are implicit rather than explicit, that is, general principles are used without explicit declaration as to just how they are regarded.

64. Steady progress in the experimental sciences eventually brought about the downfall of this elective sovereignty as well, and so led to strictly logico-experimental theories (I*a*1), in which general principles are mere abstractions devised to picture facts, it being meantime recognized that different theories may be equally true (§ 53), in the sense that they picture the facts equally well and that choice among them is, within certain limits, arbitrary. In a word, one might say that we have reached the extreme of Nominalism, provided that term be stripped of its metaphysical connotations.

65. For the very reason that we intend to remain strictly within logico-experimental bounds, we are not called upon to solve the metaphysical problem of Nominalism and Realism.[1] We do not presume to decide whether only the *individuum,* or only the *species,* exists, for the good reason, among others, that we are not sufficiently clear as to the precise meaning of the term "exist." We intend to study things and hence *individua,* and to consider species as aggregates of more or less similar things on which we determine ourselves for specified purposes. Farther than that we choose not to go just

65 [1] Familiar the language in which Boëthius, translating Porphyry, states the problem, *Isagogen Porphyrii commenta* I, 10 (Vienna, p. 159; Berlin, p. 25): *"Mox de generibus et speciebus, illud quidem sive subsistant sive in solis nudis intellectibus posita sint, sive subsistentia corporalia sint an incorporalia, et utrum separata a sensibilibus an insensibilibus posita et circa haec consistentia, dicere recusabo."* ("Next, as regards genera and species, I must be excused from deciding whether they are real or are mere conceptions of the mind, whether they are corporeal or incorporeal realities, and whether they are real apart from objects or are attributes of objects inseparable from them.")

here, though without prejudice to anybody's privilege of going beyond the point at which we stop.

66. The fact that we deal with *individua* by no means implies that a number of *individua* taken together are to be considered a simple sum. They form compounds which, like chemical compounds, may have properties that are not the sum of the properties of their components.

67. Whether the principle that replaces experience or observation be theological, metaphysical, or pseudo-experimental may be of great importance from certain points of view; but it is of no importance whatever from the standpoint of the logico-experimental sciences. St. Augustine denies the existence of antipodes because Scripture makes no mention of them.[1] In general, the Church Fathers find all their criteria of truths, even of experimental truths, in Holy Writ. Metaphysicists make fun of them and replace their theological principles with other principles just as remote from experience. Scientists who came after Newton, forgetting that he had wisely halted at the dictum that celestial bodies moved *as if* by mutual attraction according to a certain law, saw in that law an absolute principle, divined by human intelligence, verified by experience, and presumably governing all creation eternally. But the principles of mechanics have of late been subjected to searching criticism, and the conclusion has been reached that only facts and the equations that picture them can stand. Poincaré judiciously observes that from the very fact that certain phenomena admit of a mechanical explanation, they admit also of an indefinite number of other explanations.

68. All the natural sciences to a greater or lesser extent are approximating the logico-experimental type (I*a*1). We intend to study sociology in just that fashion, trying, that is, to reduce it to the same type (§§ 6, 486, 514 [2]).

69. The course we elect to pursue in these volumes is therefore the following:

1. We intend in no way to deal with the intrinsic "truth" of any

67 [1] For his arguments see § 485.

religion or faith, or of any belief, whether ethical, metaphysical, or otherwise, and we adopt that resolve not in any scorn for such beliefs, but just because they lie beyond the limits within which we have chosen to confine ourselves. Religions, beliefs, and the like we consider strictly from the outside as social facts, and altogether apart from their intrinsic merits. The proposition that "*A must*[1] be equal to *B*" in virtue of some higher superexperimental principle escapes our examination entirely (§ 46); but we do want to know how that belief arose and developed and in what relationships it stands to other social facts.

2. The field in which we move is therefore the field of experience and observation strictly. We use those terms in the meanings they have in the natural sciences such as astronomy, chemistry, physiology, and so on, and not to mean those other things which it is the fashion to designate by the terms "inner" or "Christian" experience, and which revive, under barely altered names, the "introspection" of the older metaphysicists. Such introspection we consider as a strictly objective fact, as a social fact, and not as otherwise concerning us.

3. Not intruding on the province of others, we cannot grant that others are to intrude on ours.[2] We deem it inept and idiotic to set up experience against principles transcending experience; but we likewise deny any sovereignty of such principles over experience.[3]

69 [1] Pareto, *Manuale,* Chap. I, §§ 39-40.

69 [2] *Ibid.,* Chap. I, §§ 42-48.

69 [3] These volumes were already in type when an article by Adrien Naville appeared in the *Revue de théologie et de philosophie,* Sept.-Oct., 1915, excellently urging against the theories of Bergson ideas similar to those above. The conclusions of a thinker of Naville's distinction are well worth noting. Says he, p. 18: "As regards the theory of the two truths and the case made against science, I have come to the conclusion that science is limited, relative, in part conventional, that it is immersed in mystery, and leaves open a whole world of questions partaking of the nature of transcendental speculation; but that meantime in its own domain and in the fields where it pronounces judgment, there is no authority higher than its own." Just previously Naville had said, p. 3: "A strange development has taken place in our day: The sovereignty of science has been brought under fire, and not by backward minds stifled in routine, not by partisans of ignorance and of a dogma concerned to endure for ever unchanged, but by most wide-awake, most open-minded, most active intelligences. Science is being called to the bar by very enlightened and

4. We start with facts to work out theories, and we try at all times to stray from the facts as little as possible. We do not know what the "essences" of things are (§§ 19, 91, 530) and we ignore them, since that investigation oversteps our field (§ 91). We are looking for the

very daring innovators. . . . Not that the cult of science has entirely disappeared. One might even say that it has become wide-spread and that worshippers of science are more numerous today than fifty years ago. The masses at large are professing for science a reverence that seems to be on the increase [§ 2392] and their leaders are encouraging that attitude in them. . . . But if science has maintained all its prestige for those who move on the lower or middle planes of the intellectual world, the case is different with those who dwell on the summits. These latter have grown mistrustful of science—they are talking back, criticizing, drawing up an indictment and demanding an answer." After reviewing a number of such criticisms, Naville continues, p. 16: "M. Bergson . . . is one of the severest critics that science has ever had. Not that he despises the thing, by any means; he vaunts its merits as loudly as anyone, but only on condition that science attend to its own business, which is, one might say, to formulate the truth that is useful and not the truth that is true. The truth that is true can be obtained only by procedures that are altogether different from the procedures of science."

So by plain observation of facts and without any preconceived theories, Naville is led to note a particular case of a phenomenon of which we shall state the general theory in Chapter XII (§§ 2339 f.); and in the same way he goes on to note other particular cases of the same thing, p. 6: "That there are two truths [Two? There are an infinite number of truths: *quot homines tot sententiae!*]—the one profound, philosophy, the other less profound and, in a word, less true—is a thesis that has frequently turned up in the course of history." From the standpoint of logic and experience, this notion of a number of different truths is a vagary without head or tail, a hotchpotch of meaningless words; but from the standpoint of sentiments and the social or individual utility of sentiments (§§ 1678 f.) it expresses, be it only by combating one error with another, the discrepancy between experience and the dogma that non-logical actions originate exclusively in outworn, absurd, and pernicious prejudices (§ 1679). Says Naville, pp. 7-8: "In Western Europe it [the theory of the two truths] came to the fore with particular aggressiveness in the latter centuries of the Middle Ages. Its appearance marked the decline and heralded the demise of Scholasticism. Scholasticism had been an alliance between Church doctrine and philosophy. There were two Scholasticisms in Europe, the one Christian, the other Judaic. . . . When Greek came to be known and acquaintance with Aristotle to be intimate, the Church had to decide whether to turn her back on Greek science and thought or accept them as auxiliaries and allies. She adopted the latter course, and the alliance was Scholasticism. The Jewish synagogue did likewise. . . . All the same, the alliance between Church doctrine and philosophical speculation had not been struck on a footing of equality. The Church claimed the upper hand—she was mistress; and philosophical research, free within certain limits, was not expected to overstep them. Towards the close of the Middle Ages the number of emancipated minds progressively increased, and then the theory of the two truths came quite generally to the fore in university circles, notably at Paris and at Padua."

At that time the theory served as a bridge between the theology of sentiment and

uniformities presented by facts,[4] and those uniformities we may even call laws (§ 99); but the facts are not subject to the laws: the laws are subject to the facts. Laws imply no *necessity* (§§ 29, 97). They are hypotheses serving to epitomize a more or less extensive number of facts and so serving only until superseded by better ones.

5. Every inquiry of ours, therefore, is contingent, relative, yielding results that are just more or less probable, and at best very highly probable. The space we live in seems actually to be three-dimensional; but if someone says that the Sun and its planets are one day to sweep us into a space of four dimensions, we shall neither agree nor disagree. When experimental proofs of that assertion are brought to us, we shall examine them, but until they are, the problem does not interest us. Every proposition that we state, not excluding propositions in pure logic, must be understood as qualified by the restriction *within the limits of the time and experience known to us* (§ 97).

6. We argue strictly on things and not on the sentiments that the names of things awaken in us. Those sentiments we study as objective facts strictly. So, for example, we refuse to consider whether an action be "just" or "unjust," "moral" or "immoral," unless the things to which such terms refer have been clearly specified. We shall, however, examine as an objective fact what people of a given social class, in a given country, at a given time, meant when they said that *A* was a "just" or a "moral" act. We shall see what their motives were, and how oftentimes the more important motives have done their work unbeknown to the very people who were inspired by them; and we shall try to determine the relationships between such facts and other social facts. We shall avoid arguments involving terms lacking in exactness (§ 486), because from inexact premises only inexact conclusions can be drawn.[5] But such arguments we

the theology of reason, and its indirect consequences were favourable to experimental science. Today the theory is serving as a bridge between the theology of reason and the theology of sentiment; and it may again turn out to be to the benefit of experimental science by demonstrating experimentally the individual and social utility of non-logical conduct. And see §§ 1567-79.

69 [4] Pareto, *Manuale,* Chap. I, §§ 4 f.

69 [5] As always we use the terms "exact," "exactness," in the sense designated in §§ 108 and 119 [1]. They are applied to terms that designate things with the closest

shall examine as social facts; indeed, we have in mind to solve a very curious problem as to how premises altogether foreign to reality sometimes yield inferences that come fairly close to reality (Chapter XI).

7. Proofs of our propositions we seek strictly in experience and observation, along with the logical inferences they admit of, barring all proof by accord of sentiments, "inner persuasion," "dictate of conscience."

8. For that reason in particular we shall keep strictly to terms

approximation possible. The chemist does not reject the term "water" for pure water—as pure, that is, as can be obtained with the means at present at our command; but he would reject it as a designation for sea-water. The mathematician knows very well that there is no number that, when multiplied by itself, gives 2—which is, in other words, the square root of 2; but he does not scruple to use a number as approximate as is required for the calculation he has in hand, say the number 1.414214; yet he would refuse to use the number 5 for the same computation. Mathematicians have proceeded as though a square root of 2 (in general, an irrational number) existed. They have now come to recognize the necessity of using instead two classes of real numbers, the first containing all rational numbers with squares less than 2, the second, all rational numbers with squares larger than 2. The example is noteworthy on two accounts:

1. It illustrates the *continuous development* of science, by showing how in a science as perfect, as exact, as mathematics improvements in the direction of greater perfection and exactness have still been possible. Similar improvements might be mentioned in mathematical series, and in many mathematical demonstrations.

2. It is an example of *successive approximation* in the sense of gradual progress towards greater and greater exactness. The mathematicians of antiquity wisely avoided the risk of losing their way among such niceties, and modern mathematicians have just as wisely gone into them. The ancients were paving the way for the moderns; the moderns are paving the way for their successors. Hipparchus, Kepler, Newton, Laplace, Gauss, Poincaré, represent successive approximations in celestial mechanics. Hegel reached the absolute in one bound; but there is this difference between his speculations and the theories of those scientists: With Hegel's theories one could not locate a star, however indefinitely—he leaves one in the fix of a mathematician taking 100 as the square root of 2; whereas with scientific theories one may determine those locations roughly and with closer and closer approximation, being in the position of the mathematician utilizing some value such as 1.414214 as the square root of 2. We are trying to follow in sociology the path trodden before us by astronomers, physicists, chemists, geologists, botanists, zoologists, physiologists, in short, by all natural scientists of modern times; and to avoid, so far as within us lies, the road that led the Church Fathers to denying the existence of antipodes, and Hegel to prattling about mechanics, chemistry, and other similar sciences—and which is generally followed by metaphysicists, theologians, and men of letters in studies that they pretend deal with facts of nature but which in reality are a mere hotchpotch of sentiments.

corresponding to things, using the utmost care and endeavour to have them as definite as possible in meaning (§ 108).

9. We shall proceed by *successive approximations*. That is to say, we shall first consider things as wholes, deliberately ignoring details. Of the latter we shall then take account in successive approximations (§ 540).[6]

70. We in no sense mean to imply that the course we follow is *better* than others, for the reason, if for no other, that the term "better" in this case has no meaning. No comparison is possible between theories altogether contingent and theories recognizing an absolute. They are heterogeneous things and can never be brought together (§ 16). If someone chooses to construct a system of sociology starting with this or that theological or metaphysical principle or, following a contemporary fashion, with the principles of "progressive democracy," we shall pick no quarrel with him, and his work we shall certainly not disparage. The quarrel will not become inevitable until we are asked in the name of those principles to accept some conclusion that falls within the domain of experience and observation. To go back to the case of St. Augustine: When he asserts that the Scriptures are inspired of God, we have no objection to the proposition, which we do not comprehend very clearly to begin with. But when he sets out to prove by the Scriptures that there are no antipodes (§ 485), we have no interest in his arguments, since jurisdiction in the premises belongs to experience and observation.[1]

71. We move in a narrow field, the field, namely, of experience

69 [6] Pareto, *Manuale*, Chap. I, § 14. I have given many illustrations of the method of successive approximations in my *Cours* and *Manuale*. For sociology a good example is available in Marie Kolabinska's *La circulation des élites en France*. The writer wisely centred on the main elements in her problem, disregarding the secondary. That method is the only one that can be followed if one is to construct a scientific theory and steer clear of the divagations of that ethical literature which is still passed off as sociology. Many further examples of successive approximations will be found in these volumes.

70 [1] Hence also we refrain from passing any judgment on the conflict now raging on the matter of divine inspiration between Catholic orthodoxy and the Modernists. The subject lies outside the field in which we choose to remain. We must, however, remark that the interpretation of the Modernists has really nothing to do with the positive sciences.

and observation. We do not deny that there are other fields, but in these volumes we elect not to enter them. Our purpose is to discover theories that picture facts of experience and observation (§ 486), and in these volumes we refuse to go beyond that. If anyone is minded to do so, if anyone craves an excursion outside the logico-experimental field, he should seek other company and drop ours, for he will find us disappointing.

72. We differ radically from many people following courses similar to ours in that we do not deny the social utility of theories unlike our own. On the contrary we believe that in certain cases they may be very beneficial. Correlation of the social utility of a theory with its experimental truth is, in fact, one of those *a priori* principles which we reject (§ 14). Do the two things always go hand in hand, or do they not? Observation of facts alone can answer the question; and the pages which follow will furnish proofs that the two things can, in certain cases, be altogether unrelated.

73. I ask the reader to bear in mind, accordingly, that when I call a doctrine absurd, in no sense whatever do I mean to imply that it is detrimental to society: on the contrary, it may be very beneficial. Conversely, when I assert that a theory is beneficial to society, in no wise do I mean to imply that it is experimentally true. In short, a doctrine may be ridiculed on its experimental side and at the same time respected from the standpoint of its social utility. And *vice versa.*

74. In general, when I call attention to some untoward consequence of a thing *A,* indeed one very seriously so, in no way do I mean to imply that *A* on the whole is detrimental to society; for there may be good effects to overbalance the bad. Conversely, when I call attention to a good effect of *A,* great though it be, I do not at all imply that on the whole *A* is beneficial to society.

75. The warning I have just given I had to give, for in general people writing on sociology for purposes of propaganda and with ideals to defend speak in unfavourable terms alone of things they consider bad on the whole, and favourably of things they consider good on the whole. Furthermore, since to a greater or lesser extent they use arguments based on accords of sentiment (§§ 41, 514), they are induced to manifest their own sympathies in order to win the sympathies of others. They look at facts with not altogether indifferent eyes. They love and they hate, and they disclose their loves and their hates, their likes and dislikes. Accustomed to that manner of doing and saying, a reader very properly concludes that if a writer speaks unfavourably of a thing and stresses one or another of its defects, that means that on the whole he judges it bad and is unfavourably disposed towards it; whereas if he speaks favourably of a thing and stresses one or another of its good points, on the whole he deems it good and is favourably disposed towards it. That rule does not apply to this work; and I shall feel obliged to remind the reader of that fact over and over again (§ 311). In these volumes I am reasoning objectively, analytically, according to the logico-experimental method. In no way am I called upon to make known such sentiments as I may happen to cherish, and the objective judgment I pass upon one aspect of a thing in no sense implies a similar judgment on the thing considered synthetically as a whole.[1]

76. If one person would persuade another on matters pertaining

75 [1] I am going to register just one exception at this point, and after all it is more apparent than real, since it aims at clearer explanation, by an example, of the objective fact here in point. I shall have occasion hereafter to speak unfavourably, very much so, of certain acts by Athenian demagogues. Now I do not imagine the reader is especially concerned to know my global personal attitude towards the ancient Athenian republic. However, if I may be allowed to state it, I will say that I do not think anyone admires or loves the Greek mind more than I do. I shall poke fun at the "goddess Science," yet the fact stands that I have devoted my life to experimental science. One may ridicule the democratic humanitarianism of this or that French politician and still hold the scientists of that country in highest esteem, and even regard the republican form of government as perhaps the best for France. One may note the licentiousness of certain emancipated women in the United States and still cherish the deepest reverence for the many admirable wives and mothers who are to be found in that country. Finally, to point the finger of scorn at the hypocrisies of German sex-reformers is not inconsistent with admiration for their mighty nation and reverence for German scholarship. I deem it superfluous to note similar contrasts in the case of my own country, Italy. That is my whole confession. I urgently beg the reader to be convinced that this exception will have no counterparts. These volumes should be read not for something that is not there—a statement, namely, of my personal sentiments—but exclusively for reports on objective relationships between things, between facts, and between experimental uniformities.

to experimental science, he chiefly and, better yet, exclusively, states facts and logical implications of facts (§ 42). But if he would persuade another on matters pertaining to what is still called social science, his chief appeal is to sentiments, with a supplement of facts and logical inferences from facts. And he must proceed in that fashion if his idea is to talk not in vain; for if he were to disregard sentiments, he would persuade very few and in all probability fail to get a hearing at all, whereas if he knows how to play deftly on sentiments, his reputation for eloquence will soar (§ 514).[1]

77. Political economy has hitherto been a practical discipline designed to influence human conduct in one direction or another. It could hardly be expected, therefore, to avoid addressing sentiment, and in fact it has not done so. All along economists have given us systems of ethics supplemented in varying degree with narrations of facts and elaborations of the logical implications of facts. That is strikingly apparent in the writings of Bastiat; but it is apparent enough in virtually all writings on economics, not excluding works of the historical school, which are oftentimes more metaphysical and sentimental than the rest. As mere examples of forecasts based on the scientific laws of political economy and sociology (to the exclusion of sentiment), I offer the following. The first volume of my *Cours* appeared in the year 1896, but had been written in 1895, with statistical tables coming down not later than the year 1894.

1. Contrarily to the views of ethical sociologists, whether of the historical school or otherwise, and of sentimental anti-Malthusians, at that time I wrote with reference to population increase: "We are therefore witnessing rates of increase in our day that cannot have obtained in times past and cannot continue to hold in the future."[1] And I mentioned in that connexion the examples of England and Germany. As for England, there were already signs of a slackening. Not so for Germany, where there were as yet no grounds, em-

76 [1] This topic is touched upon just incidentally here. It belongs to our study of the objective aspect of theories (§ 13) and will be amply developed in due course.

77 [1] *Cours*, § 198.

pirically, for arriving at any conclusions whatever. But now both countries show a declining curve.[2]

2. With specific reference to England, after determining the law of population increase for the years 1801-91, I concluded that popu-

77 [2] *Ibid.*, § 196: "It is therefore quite evident that the population of the three countries considered cannot continue to increase indefinitely at the present rate." The three countries were Norway, England-Wales, and Germany. As regards Norway, the annual rate of geometric increase, which was 13.9 per cent for the period 1861-80, fell to 5.7 per cent for the period 1905-10. For England-Wales and Germany the figures are as follows:

	PERCENTAGE OF INCREASE	
YEARS	*England-Wales*	*Germany*
1880-85	11.1	7.1
1885-90	13.4	10.7
1890-95	11.5	11.3
1895-1900	11.5	15.2
1900-05	10.6	14.7
1905-10	10.4	13.7

"It is evident that after reaching a maximum in the years 1895-1900, the rate of population increase in Germany is now [1910] on a descending curve. The falling-off in rate is more clearly apparent still from the annual statistics of births per thousand:

	PERCENTAGE OF INCREASE		
YEARS	*Norway*	*England-Wales*	*Germany*
1875	31.2	35.4	40.6
1885	31.3	32.9	37.0
1895	30.5	30.3	36.1
1900	29.9	28.7	35.6
1905	27.4	27.3	33.0
1910	26.1	25.1	31.1 (for 1909)

"The falling-off in the rate of population increase in Germany is especially notable in the large cities, where wealth has appreciably increased:

	NUMBER OF BIRTHS PER 1000 INHABITANTS	
GERMANY	*1902*	*1912*
Munich	35.1	21.9
Leipzig	31.5	22.1
Dresden	31.5	20.3
Cologne	37.8	26.7
Magdeburg	29.2	22.8
Stettin	35.3	22.7
Danzig	34.7	27.6"

That substantiates what I wrote in my *Cours*, § 198: "It is therefore evident that forces limiting increment in population must have interfered with the genetic tendency in times past, or will do so in the future."

lation could not continue to increase at the same rate. And the rate has in fact fallen.[3]

3. "The gains made by certain Socialistic ideas in England are probably the result of an increment in the economic obstacles to population increase."[4] The soundness of that conclusion is even more apparent now. Socialism has progressed in England, while a falling-off has been observable in the other countries in Europe.

4. In Chapter XII we shall see a verification of a sociological law that I used in my *Systèmes socialistes.*

5. The second volume of my *Cours* was published in 1897. At that

77 [3] *Ibid.*, § 211 [1]. If P is the population in the year t, reckoning from the year 1801, we get:

$$\log P = 6.96324 + 0.005637t.$$

That yields the theoretical law of population for the years 1801-91. The following figures are given in my *Cours:*

YEARS	POPULATION (IN MILLIONS)		
	Real	*Estimated*	*Difference*
1801	8.892	9.188	+ 0.296
1811	10.164	10.294	+ 0.130
1821	12.000	11.912	— 0.088
1831	13.897	13.563	— 0.334
1841	15.914	15.443	— 0.471
1851	17.928	17.583	— 0.345
1861	20.066	20.020	— 0.046
1871	22.712	22.795	+ 0.083
1881	25.975	25.953	— 0.022
1891	29.001	29.551	+ 0.550

The greatest difference, in other words the maximum error, arising in the application of the formula is 0.550. Using the formula to estimate population for the year 1910, we get 37.816, while the actual population was 35.796. The difference is + 2.020, a figure much greater than the maximum error. That proves that population is no longer following the law observable for the years 1801-91, and that it is increasing at a slower rate.

77 [4] *Ibid.*, § 211 [2]. The remark has to be taken in connexion with matter preceding, §§ 179-80: "Movements in the transformation of personal capital are in part dependent on the economic movement. It must not be forgotten that we have not shown their explicit dependence on the economic situation, but merely their dependence on variations in it. [In a note:] If the economic situation is characterized by a function F of any number of variables that are functions of the time t, then we have shown that the numbers of marriages, births, and to a certain extent also deaths, are a function of $\frac{dF}{dt}$; but we have not shown that such numbers are explicit functions of F."

time it was an article of faith with many people that social evolution was in the direction of the rich growing richer and the poor, poorer. Contrarily to that sentimental view, the law of distribution of income led to the proposition [5] that "if total income increases with respect to population, there must be either an increase in the minimum income, or a decrease in inequality in incomes, or the two things must result simultaneously." Between 1897 and 1911 there was an increase in total income as compared with population, and what in fact resulted was an increase in minimum income and a decrease in inequality in incomes.[6] A counter-proof, furthermore, is available in the fact that my *Cours* is defective in those sections into which sentiment was allowed to intrude.[7]

78. A person often accepts a proposition for no other reason than that it accords with his sentiments. Such accord, indeed, usually makes a proposition more "obvious." And from the standpoint of social utility in many cases it is perhaps well that that be so. But from the standpoint of experimental science, such accord has little value and often none whatever. Of that I shall give many examples.

79. Since I intend in these volumes to take my stand strictly within the field of experimental science, I shall try to avoid any appeal to the reader's sentiments whatsoever and keep to facts and implications of facts.[1]

80. When a writer is "doing literature" or addressing sentiments in any way at all, he finds it necessary, in deference to them, to choose between the facts he uses. Not all of them rise to the dignity of rhetorical or historical propriety. There is an aristocracy of facts reference to which is always commendable. There is a commonalty of facts reference to which incurs neither praise nor blame. There is a proletariat of facts reference to which is at all times improper

77 [5] *Ibid.*, § 965.

77 [6] A definition of "decrease in inequality in incomes" is given in *Ibid.*, § 965 [1]. See also my *Manuel*, pp. 389 f., and Sensini, *La teoria della rendita*, pp. 342-53, and especially p. 350, § 185.[4]

77 [7] A criticism of the passages may be found in the introduction to my *Manuale*, where the various errors are duly noted.

79 [1] That is why there will be so many notes with quotations. Their design is to keep the body of facts vividly present before the reader's mind.

and reprehensible. So amateur entomologists may find it pleasant to catch bright-coloured butterflies, just routine to catch flies and wasps, loathsome to lay hand to dung- and carrion-beetles. But the naturalist knows no such distinctions, nor do they arise for us in the field of social science (§§ 85, 896).

81. We keep open house to all facts, whatever their character, provided that directly or indirectly they point the way to discovering a uniformity. Even an absurd, an idiotic argument is a fact, and if accepted by any large number of people, a fact of great importance to sociology. Beliefs, whatever their character, are also facts, and their importance depends not on their intrinsic merits, but on the greater or fewer numbers of individuals who profess them. They serve furthermore to reveal the sentiments of such individuals, and sentiments are among the most important elements with which sociology is called upon to deal (§ 69-6).

82. The reader must bear that in mind, as he encounters in these volumes facts which at first blush might seem insignificant or childish. Tales, legends, the fancies of magic or theology, may often be accounted idle and ridiculous things—and such they are, intrinsically; but then again they may be very helpful as tools for discovering the thoughts and feelings of men. So the psychiatrist studies the ravings of the lunatic not for their intrinsic worth but for their value as symptoms of disease.

83. The road that is to lead us to the uniformities we seek may at times seem a long one. If that is the case, it is simply because I have not succeeded in finding a shorter. If someone manages to do so, all the better; I will straightway leave my road for his. Meantime I deem it the wiser part to push on along the only trail as yet blazed.

84. If one's aim is to inspire or re-enforce certain sentiments in men, one must present facts favourable to that design and keep unfavourable data quiet. But if one is interested strictly in uniformities, one must not ignore any fact that may in any way serve to disclose them. And since my aim in these volumes is no other, I refuse out of hand to consider in a fact anything but its logico-experimental significance.

85. The one concession that I can make—and really it is not so much a concession as a grasp at some method for securing a far greater clearness by removing from the reader's eyes any veil that sentiment may have drawn across them—is to choose from the multitude of facts such as, in my judgment, will exert least influence upon sentiments. So when I have facts of equal experimental value before me from the past and from the present, I choose facts of the past. That accounts for my many quotations from Greek and Latin writers. In the same way, when I have facts of equal experimental value from religions now extinct and religions still extant, I give my preference to the former. But to prefer a thing is not to use it exclusively. In many many cases I am constrained to use facts from the present or from religions still existing, sometimes because I have no other facts of an equivalent experimental value, sometimes in order to show the continuity of certain phenomena from past to present. In such connexions I intend to write with absolute freedom; and the same frankness I maintain against the malevolence of our modern Paladins of Purity, for whom I care not the proverbial fig.[1]

86. In propounding this or that theory an author as a rule wants other people to assent to it and adopt it—in him the seeker after experimental truth and the apostle stand combined. In these volumes I keep those attitudes strictly separate, retaining the first and barring the second. I have said, and I repeat, that my sole interest is the quest for social uniformities, social laws. I am here reporting on the results of my quest, since I hold that in view of the restricted number of readers such a study can have and in view of the scientific training that may be taken for granted in them, such a report can do no harm. I should refrain from doing so if I could reasonably imagine that these volumes were to be at all generally read (§§ 14, 1403).[1]

85 [1] See in this connexion, Pareto, *Le mythe vertuiste*.

86 [1] Running, as it does, counter to the general trend in the social sciences, this work will be severely criticized by all individuals whose minds are closed to innovations from a habit of drifting with that current. They state the problem of judg-

87. Long ago in my *Manuale,* Chap. I, § 1, I wrote: "It is possible for an author to aim exclusively at hunting out and running down uniformities among facts—their laws, in other words—without having any purpose of direct practical utility in mind, any intention of offering remedies and precepts, any ambition, even, to promote the happiness and welfare of mankind in general or of any part of mankind. His purpose in such a case is strictly scientific: he wants *to learn, to know,* and nothing more. I warn the reader that in this *Manual* I am trying exclusively to realize this last purpose only. Not that I underrate the others: I am just drawing distinctions between methods, separating them and indicating the one that is to be followed in this book. Anyone differently minded can find plenty of books to his liking. He should feast on them and leave this one alone, for, as Boccaccio said of his tales [*Decameron,* X, *Conclusione*], it does not go begging a hearing of anybody."

Such a declaration seems to me clear enough, and I confess that I could not express myself in plainer terms. Yet I have been credited with intentions of reforming the world, and even been compared to Fourier! [1]

ing a theory in the terms: "Is it in accord with the theories I consider good?" If the answer is yes, they classify it with the good theories, if no, with the bad. It is obvious enough that being at variance with all such theories, this one of mine will certainly be bad. It may find a warmer welcome among young people whose minds are not yet clogged with the preconceptions of orthodox science and among people who state the problem of judging a theory in the terms: "Is it in accord with the facts?" I must have made it sufficiently clear by this time that that is the only accord I seek, and that I have no interest whatsoever in anything else.

87 [1] In the year 1909 and with the *Manuale,* which had appeared in 1906, before his eyes, Professor Gide, *Histoire des doctrines économiques,* p. 623, was able to write: "The Hedonists [Among whom Gide counts V. Pareto—on what grounds, he only knows] are very reticent as regards the possibilities of realizing their economic world. On the other hand they are very positive, in fact a little too much so, as regards the virtues of their method, not being exempt on that score from a dogmatic conceit that reminds one of the utopian Socialists. One seems to be listening to Fourier when one reads that 'what has already been discovered in political economy is nothing as compared with what may be discovered hereafter'—by the mathematical method, of course." Gide ascribes his quotation to one "V. Pareto, [*"Le nuove teorie economiche"*], *Giornale degli economisti,* September, 1901." Even if the quotation were exact, M. Gide might at least have noted that V. Pareto had changed his views, as is apparent enough from his *Manuale.* But it is not exact, for M. Gide is thinking of *practice,* whereas I was thinking strictly of *pure theory!* A

88. In general, this method of studying the social sciences is not grasped by literary economists, the cast of their minds being against any such thing. Then again they often discuss books and other writings that they know only at second hand, and which they have never read, or never read with the care required for understanding them. Finally, the person who has always had some practical purpose in view can hardly be convinced that anyone can have a purely scientific aim; or if he does understand it for a moment, he immediately forgets. I have therefore little hope that the cautions I have voiced in this chapter will effectually prevent theories which I do not hold from being ascribed to me, similar warnings having failed on past occasions, though endlessly repeated. Yet it seems best to me to follow the maxim "Do what you ought, follow what may." Only I must beg my reader's pardon for certain repetitions that have no other justification, and which may appear superfluous—as they in fact are for anyone consenting to read what I say with moderate attention.

good guess would be that M. Gide had not read the article from which he quoted. My article says, p. 239: ". . . Now the outstanding trait in the new economic theories is that they are the only ones so far to have given us a general picture of the economic phenomenon as a whole. The picture is just approximative, much like a sphere offered as a model of the Earth. All the same we know of nothing better." On p. 241, as to "the equations of pure economics," I clearly state that they are of service only as instruments for study, much as it is of service to know, for instance, the dimensions of the terrestrial ellipsoid. On p. 242: "Pure economics, one may say, has indeed found the tool for its researches, but it has hardly begun to use it. Practically everything along that line is still to be done; and economists really devoted to the progress of their science ought to set about doing it." I was speaking of science, pure science, and not of practical applications, as Gide's allusion to Fourier would insinuate. I conclude, p. 252, with the quotation that Gide detached from its context—with a remodelling to boot: "We are in the first stages of the new science, and what it has already achieved is nothing as compared with the results it may achieve hereafter. The present state of pure economics is not even comparable to the state of astronomy after the appearance of Newton's *Principia.*" The parallel I drew was with an abstract science, astronomy, not with a concrete science. In the rest of his article Professor Gide continues to ascribe to me opinions and theories that I have never held and which I have even disputed as directly opposite to theories actually mine. For further details see my article, *Économie mathématique,* in the *Encyclopédie des sciences mathématiques* [Meyer, Vol. I, pp. 1094-1120, *s. v. Anwendungen der Mathematik auf Nationalökonomie;* Molk, Vol. I, pp. 591-640] and in *Giornale degli economisti,* Nov., 1906, p. 424.

89. This is not the place to add further details touching my manner of regarding economic theories.[1] The reader will find excellent and ample expatiations on that point in the works of Sensini and Boven already referred to.

90. We saw (§§ 13, 63) that our subclass of logico-experimental theories (I*a*) was divisible into two varieties, in one of which general principles were mere abstractions from experimental facts, while in the other they aspired more or less explicitly to an existence of their own not strictly dependent on mere abstraction from facts. The two varieties are often distinguished as based on the *inductive* or the *deductive* methods. But that is not exact. They differ not in the method they use, but in their respective criteria of truth for propositions and theories. In the strict type, I*a*1, whether propositions are obtained by induction or by deduction or by a mixture of the two, they are always subordinate to experience; whereas in the deviation from the type, I*a*2, they tend explicitly to dominate experience. When a general principle is corroborated by facts in large numbers as, for instance, the principles of Euclidean geometry or of universal gravitation are, the two varieties are not very sharply distinguished, for after all the experimental verification may often be taken for granted.

91. But if the gap between the two varieties is very marked, a difference appears that is the better seen in a comparison between theories which are logico-experimental (I*a*) and theories which are not. In the former procedure is gradual. One starts with facts and reaches this or that abstraction, thence going on to a more general abstraction, becoming more and more circumspect, more and more cautious, the farther one gets from direct experience. In non-logico-experimental theories, a deliberate leap is taken away from direct experience, as broad a leap as possible, and the farther one gets from direct experience, the greater the assurance, the greater the reckless-

89 [1] An altogether estimable person once asked whether my science were "democratic"! It has been said, in black and white, that it was "socialistic"; and then again that it was "reactionary." The science interested strictly in uniformities (laws) among facts is nothing of any of those sorts and can in no way be so labelled. It is just a quest for uniformities, and that is the end of it. Personally, I was a free-trader in my *Cours;* but in my *Manuale* I dropped that cloak, and I remain divested of it when dealing with science.

ness. One is bent on knowing the "essences" of things, the only kind of knowledge worthy of the name of "science," direct experience and its implications being mere "empiricism," and as such held in poor esteem (§ 530).

92. Working out a chemistry, for example, on that system, the first problem would be to know what "matter" is. Knowing that, we should know its chemical properties. The modern chemist, instead, following the methods and procedures of logico-experimental science, studies chemical properties directly, and gets more and more general properties or abstractions from them.

The ancients thought that in imagining cosmogonies they were studying astronomy. Modern scientists study the movements of the stars directly, and go no farther than required for establishing uniformities in such movements. Newton found that a certain hypothesis, the so-called hypothesis of universal gravitation, was all that was required for discovering the equations governing the movements of the stars. But what is gravitation? Neither he nor his successors in celestial mechanics took the trouble to go too deeply into that question. Not that the problem was not worth considering; but celestial mechanics can dispense with a solution of it. So long as its equations hold, it matters little how they are obtained.

93. Errors that are ancient history for the more advanced sciences recur or have their modern counterparts in the more backward sciences. So the theory of evolution has in some cases played a rôle in sociology similar to the rôle once played by cosmogony in astronomy. It was generally held that the only way to determine uniformities in social phenomena was to know the history of the latter and trace them back to their origins (§§ 23, 346).

94. For the theories that are to be elaborated in these volumes we cannot avoid going back to a distinction between the objective and the subjective phenomenon. However, we do not need to go beyond that and solve the problem as to the "reality of the external world," assuming (but not granting) that that problem has some exact meaning (§ 149).

95. Solve it as you will, the two great categories mentioned still stand, even if under different names. It may well be that a sheet of paper with engravings on it and a genuine bank-note of the Bank of England are both mere thoughts of the mind; but if you dine at a London restaurant and try to pay your bill with the first of those thoughts, you will soon notice that just as "one thought is of another born," that thought will present you with a whole litter of offspring: first the thought of a policeman, which, whether objectively real or not, will hale you before the thought of a judge, which will introduce you to the thought of a well-barred jail, where you will meet a thought that the English call "hard labour," and which, according to all reports, is not the pleasantest thought in the world. All that will convince you that the two sheets of paper certainly belong to two sharply distinguished categories, since they give rise to differing facts—or differing thoughts, if you prefer.

Similarly, when we assert that to know the properties of sulphuric anhydride one must appeal to experience and not, as Hegelian metaphysics would have it, to the "concept" of sulphur or even of oxygen, we are not in the least intending to set an external world over against an internal world, an objective reality over against a subjective reality. We can state the same proposition in a jargon that recognizes the "existence" of nothing but thought. We can say, that is, that to get the concept of sulphuric anhydride, it is not enough to have the mere concepts of sulphur and oxygen and meditate upon them. We could do that for century on century without getting concepts of sulphuric anhydride that would gibe with the concepts supplied by chemical experiment. The ancient philosophers thought that they could replace observation and experience in just that way, but they were entirely wrong. Chemistry is learned in laboratories and not by philosophical meditations, even of the Hegelian brand (§ 14). To get the concept, or concepts, of sulphuric anhydride we must first have the many concepts acquired through the concept otherwise known as experience—burning sulphur in oxygen or in air, and collecting the concept of sulphuric anhydride in the concept of a glass container—finally bringing all such concepts together to get the concept of the properties of sulphuric anhydride. But such a jargon would be prolix, tedious, ridiculous; and just to avoid it we use the terms "subjective" and "objective." For the logico-experimental purposes we have in view no other terms are required.

96. In the same way and for the same reason it is enough for us to know that social facts reveal certain uniformities which are connected by ties of interdependence.[1] We are not called upon to go to the trouble of finding out whether and just how that result yielded by observation can be reconciled with what is called free will (if indeed the latter phrase has any meaning). Such problems transcend the limits of our investigations.

97. And we shall also neglect to inquire whether scientific laws have the trait of "necessity" (§ 528). On that point observation and experience can tell us nothing. They can only reveal certain uniformities, and those only within the limits of the time and space to which our observation and experience extend. Every scientific law, therefore, is subject to that qualification; and if, for considerations of brevity, it is omitted, the statement of every scientific law must nevertheless be taken as prefaced by the restriction: *within the limits of time and space known to us* (§ 69-5).

In like manner we hold aloof from debates as to the necessity of the conclusion in a syllogism. The syllogism of the text-books on logic, for example, "All men are mortal; Socrates is a man; therefore Socrates is mortal," from the experimental standpoint must be stated thus: "All men of whom we have had any knowledge have died; what we know of Socrates induces us to classify him with such men; therefore it is *very probable* that Socrates is mortal."

That probability is greatly enhanced by other circumstances which we shall specify farther along (§§ 531, 556); and it is therefore greater, enormously greater, than the plausibility of a syllogism that might have been drawn before the discovery of Australia: "All the swans we have ever known have been white; a bird of unknown

96 [1] ["Interdependence" is a technical term with Pareto—see our Index. The same concept is expressed in English by the words "correlation," "interrelation." —A. L.]

colour that has all the characteristics of the swan must be classed with the swans; therefore that bird will probably be white" (§ 526). People reasoning on essences may sometimes substitute certitude for probability, even very great probability. But we know nothing about essences and accordingly lose our certitude.

98. To assert, as some assert, that a miracle is impossible as violating the recognized constancy of natural laws is to reason in a circle and offer an assertion as proof of itself. If a miracle could be proved, the constancy of natural laws would at once go by the board. The kernel of the question therefore lies strictly in the proof of fact. We might add that such a proof has to withstand a scrutiny all the more severe, the farther it carries us outside the circle of known facts. If someone were to assert that the Sun is one day to carry its planetary system to a locality where the laws of chemistry, physics, and mechanics are different from the laws at present known, we could make no objection. We could only remind the prophet that the burden of proof rests upon the person making the assertion. As we have already stated (§ 29), we admit of no exceptions to this rule, even for the laws of logic.

99. Scientific laws are for us, therefore, nothing more than experimental uniformities (§ 69-4). From that point of view there is not the slightest difference between the laws of political economy or sociology and the laws of other sciences. The differences that do exist are of an entirely different character, lying chiefly in the greater or lesser complexity with which effects of the various laws are intertwined (§ 1792). Celestial mechanics has the good fortune to be able to deal with the effects of a single law (uniformity). And that is not all, for the effects might be such as seriously to interfere with the discovery of the uniformity they manifest. But by a most happy circumstance, the mass of the Sun is much greater than the masses of the various planets, so that the uniformity is disclosed under a simple though not strictly exact form by assuming that the planets move around a fixed Sun; whence we can go on to rectify the error involved in the first approximation.[1] Chemistry, physics, mechanics,

99 [1] We shall see something remotely similar in the case of sociology (Chapter XII).

are likewise able to deal with separate laws, or at least, by one device or another, to isolate effects;[2] but then again, there are cases where the complex is hard to unravel. Such cases grow more numerous in biology and geology, and most of all in meteorology. It is with these latter that the social sciences are to be classed in this respect.

100. Another difference in scientific laws lies in the possibility or impossibility of isolating their effects by experiment, which is here to be distinguished from observation. Certain sciences, such as chemistry, physics, mechanics, and biology, can and do make extensive use of experiment. Certain others can use it but sparingly; others, such as the social sciences, little if any; still others not at all, as for instance, celestial mechanics—at least as regards the movements of the heavenly bodies.

101. Economic and social laws as well as the laws of the other sciences never suffer any genuine exception.[1] To speak of a uniformity that is not uniform is to say a thing which has no meaning. What is commonly called an exception to a law is really the superposition of the effect of another law upon its own normal effects. From that standpoint all scientific laws, even the laws of mathematics, suffer exceptions. All bodies on the surface of the earth tend to move toward the centre; but a feather caught by the wind moves away from the centre, and a balloon filled with hydrogen rises in the air. The chief difficulty in a great many sciences lies in finding ways to unravel tangles of many different uniformities.

102. To that end, it often helps to consider not the individual phenomena actually observed but average situations where the effects of certain laws are attenuated and those of others are emphasized. We cannot predict, for example, what the temperature on the tenth of June in some future year is going to be; but we can come pretty close to the mean temperature for the month of June, and closer still to

99 [2] Pareto, *Manuale,* Chap. I, § 20.

101 [1] Pareto, *Manuale,* Chap. 1, § 7. There are still professors of political economy who keep repeating parrot-like that economic laws have exceptions, while physical laws do not. Such "the ignorance that tormenteth them"! Not even with a spyglass could one find a physicist to class among unexceptionable physical laws the law that bodies diminish in volume as they cool.

the mean temperature over a three months' period for a number of years. No one can tell whether John Doe will live or die next year; but we can tell, approximately, how many people out of a hundred thousand of John Doe's age will die. Who can tell whether a given grain of wheat sown by a farmer will sprout and yield a return? But we can predict with reasonable probability the crop an acre of wheat will yield, and even better the average yield over a specified period of years.

103. We must not forget that such averages are largely arbitrary, that they are formulated by ourselves for purposes of our own, and that therefore we must avoid the error of thinking of them as objective things having an existence independent of the facts. One often finds them going about under different names as metaphysical entities, used by scholars to fix on something at least that is constant in the flux of fact.

104. In political economy, for instance, we find that the wholesale prices of commodities differ in almost every transaction. To get a theory we have to have something less variable, something more constant, than that. Scientifically we consider averages, we strike medium curves (interpolations).[1] Metaphysically, people have used an entity called value taken as a constant cause of variations in price. This second manner of reasoning easily leads astray, since it deprives averages of the status they have scientifically and gives them another that is altogether imaginary (§ 62). This statement, however, implies no criticism of early economists for using the term "value." But it was a notable step in advance when "exchange value" came to be distinguished from "utility value." Further progress derived the far more exact concept of "final utility" from the concept of "utility value"; and going on in that fashion, general theories of the economic equilibrium were finally attained. There is nothing unusual about such a course. It is the course the natural sciences have all followed (§§ 69[5], 106). But just as it is no longer possible in our day to study celestial mechanics with the tools of Ptolemy or even of

104 [1] One of the many forms of the method of successive approximations (§§ 69-9, 540).

Kepler, so political economy can no longer be handled with the indeterminate concept of value.[2]

105. In a first approximation we may be satisfied with knowing that, roughly, we have discarded certain effects of minor importance as compared with others of major importance. But it is wiser to get at the earliest possible moment a fairly exact picture of what the terms "minor" and "major" imply, and to know approximately what has been discarded and what has been kept. It will be all the better to determine, if we can, the limits of the variations between the situation as it really is—the facts—and the picture which our averages or theories give us of it. In mathematics, it is already something to know that the fraction 22/7 expresses the approximate relationship of the circumference of a circle to the diameter. It is better yet to know that the actual ratio is greater than 22/7; still better to know that the error is less than 0.015, or that the true ratio lies between the fractions 22/7 and 333/106. It is a good thing to know that prices are not numbers varying haphazard. It is better yet to know that there is some relation between them and the tastes of human beings and the difficulties lying in the way of obtaining commodities. It is even better to have some notion of what that relation is, and better still to have the concept more exact and know the relative importance of the situation pictured by the theory, as compared with the real situation, and to know just what aspects it ignores.

106. A concrete situation cannot be known in all its details; there is always a remainder, which is even physically apparent at times.[1] We can have only approximate concepts of concrete phenomena. A theory therefore can never account for all particulars. Divergences are inevitable, and the best we can do is reduce them to a minimum. And in this connexion too we are once more carried back to our successive approximations. Science is a continuous development; that is to say, every theory is supplanted by another which corresponds

104 [2] Pareto, *Manuale,* Chap. III, §§ 29-30, 35.

106 [1] Pareto, *Manuel,* p. 10. To humour the Hegelians we might say: "It has been observable that the concept of a thing which people have at a given moment is supplemented, as time goes by, with new concepts, and the series of additions, so far as we can tell, must be infinite."

more closely to the real facts. The theory of yesterday has been perfected today; the theory of today will be improved on tomorrow; that of tomorrow, on the following day; and so on. Such the story that is to be read on every page of the history of the sciences, and no one can suppose that it will not continue to be the story for a long long time to come. Since no theory absolutely commands acceptance, of the theories among which we are free to select we shall prefer the one that diverges least from facts of the past, which best enables us to foresee the facts of the future, and which, in addition, embraces the greatest number of facts.

107. In astronomy the theory of epicycles, which some people are at present trying to rehabilitate on sentimental grounds, satisfies the requirement of adequately picturing facts of the past as such facts are known to us. By multiplying the number of epicycles as often as is required, every movement of the stars that observation reveals can be represented; but we cannot, or cannot so well, foresee future movements, as is possible with the theory of gravitation. The latter theory, furthermore, utilizing the general law of mechanics, embraces a greater number of facts. Hence it is certainly to be preferred, as in fact is customary, to the theory of epicycles. But the choice is made for those reasons, or for others of the kind, not for metaphysical considerations as to the "essence" of things.

108. The facts among which we live have their influence upon us, and as a result our minds acquire certain attitudes which must not be too violently in conflict with those facts. Such attitudes go on to give form and manner to language. Some small amount of information as to external facts we can derive, therefore, from knowledge of the processes of the human mind and from language. But that small amount is small indeed, and once a science is at all advanced, more errors than truths are obtained in that fashion (§§ 113 f.).[1]

108 [1] That influence—nothing very definite, to tell the truth—of the facts upon our minds makes up such truth, experimentally speaking, as there is in theories ascribing a scientific status to intuition. Intuition serves about as much towards knowledge of reality as a poor, sometimes a very poor, photograph of a place serves towards knowledge of that place. Sometimes intuition supplies just a fanciful illusion, and not even a poor photograph, of reality.

The terms of common speech are lacking in definiteness, and it cannot be otherwise, for precision goes only with scientific exactitude. Every argument based on sentiment, as all metaphysical arguments are, must of necessity use terms lacking in exactness, since sentiments are indefinite and the name cannot be more definite than the thing. Such arguments, besides, actually rely on the lack of exactness in everyday language to mask their defects in logic and carry conviction (§ 109). Logico-experimental arguments, being based instead on objective observation, tend to use words strictly to designate things and therefore to choose them in such a way as to avoid ambiguities and have terms as exact as possible. Moreover, they eventually equip themselves with a special, technical language and so escape the indefiniteness of common parlance.

As already noted (§ 69-8), our purpose being to use logico-experimental reasoning exclusively, we shall exert every endeavour to use only words that are as far as possible precise and strictly defined, and which correspond to things unequivocally and without ambiguities (§ 119), or better, with a minimum of error.

A word designates a concept, and the concept may or may not correspond to a thing. But the correspondence, when it is there, cannot be perfect. Even if the word corresponds to a thing, it can never correspond to it exactly, in an absolute manner. It is always a question of a more or a less. Not only are there no such things, in the concrete, as geometric entities such as the straight line, the circle, and so on, but not even chemical substances that are *absolutely* pure, not even the species with which zoologists and botanists deal, not even an individual body designated by a name—for it would be further necessary to specify at just what moment it is considered: a piece of iron does not remain identical with itself if it is subject to changes in temperature, in electrical tension, and so on. In a word, the "absolute" has no place in logico-experimental science, and we must always take in a relative sense propositions that in the dress of ordinary parlance seem absolute; and in the same way too, we must make quantitative distinctions where common speech stops at the qualitative (§ 144[1]). That much being clearly grasped, any misunderstanding is impossible; whereas to express ourselves always with absolute exactness would be to wallow in lengthy verbosities as useless as they would be pedantic.

We may say, then, that we are carried outside the logico-experimental field entirely whenever we reason in terms which do not lie in that field; and that we are carried partially outside it whenever we reason in indefinite terms which correspond to experimental entities only in part (Chapter X). This last proposition must be taken in the sense that if our terms have that minimum of indefiniteness which corresponds to the present state of knowledge, they take us so little outside the experimental field that we may overlook the extrusion. Though there are no chemical substances that are absolutely pure, the laws of chemistry are valid, in very close approximation, for the substances that our methods of analysis designate as pure.

109. People in the vast majority use common everyday language. A few scientists use scientific language in their specialties, outside of which they reason as badly as the plain man—and often worse. Human beings are prompted to acquire such knowledge as they have from common speech by two sorts of motives: first, because they assume that a word necessarily corresponds to a thing, whereby the name becomes everything and sometimes even acquires mysterious properties; and, second, because of the great ease with which a "science" can be so constituted, each person carrying within himself all that is required for that purpose, without going to the pains of long, difficult, and tedious researches. It is much easier to talk about antipodes than to go out and see if they are really there. To discuss the implication of a "principle of fire" or "damp" is much more expeditious than to prosecute all the field studies that have made up the science of geology. To ruminate on "natural law" is a much more comfortable profession than to dig out the legal codes of the various countries in various periods of history. To prattle about "value" and ask when and under what circumstances it is said that "a thing has value" is much less difficult than to discover and comprehend the laws of the economic equilibrium.

In view of all that, one readily understands how the history of the sciences down to our time is substantially a history of the battles that the experimental method has had to fight and still has to fight against the methods of introspection, etymology, analysis of verbal expression. Defeated and put to rout in one place, the latter method bobs up in another. If it cannot fight in the open it dissembles, flattening out like a snake in the grass, and so succeeds in making its way into the very camp of the adversary under guise of something else.

110. In our day the method has been largely banished from the physical sciences, and the advances they have made are the fruit of that proscription. But it is still strutting about in political economy and more blatantly still in sociology; whereas if those sciences would progress, it is imperative that they should follow the example set by the physical sciences (§ 118).

111. Belief that the facts of the universe and their relationships could be discovered by introspection was general in a day gone by, and it still remains the foundation of metaphysics, which seeks a criterion of truth outside experience. In our day it found its complete expression in the lunacies of Hegel's *Philosophy of Nature*. One need hardly observe that mankind has never discovered the puniest uniformity in the facts of nature in that fashion (§§ 50, 484).

112. The positivism of Herbert Spencer is nothing but a metaphysics. Though Spencer asserts the relative nature of all knowledge, he still speaks of the relations of knowledge to "absolute reality."[1] He asserts the existence of an Unknowable, but claims, by an amusing contradiction, to know at least something about it.[2]

113. In all the rustle and bustle of our daily lives we cannot of course speak in the manner or with the severity of the logico-experi-

112 [1] *First Principles,* § 46. "Thought being possible only under relation, the relative reality can be conceived as such only in connexion with an absolute reality; and the connexion between the two being absolutely persistent in our consciousness, is real in the same sense as the terms it unites are real." All of Spencer's writing is packed with such concepts.

112 [2] Here is an example selected at random: *Ibid.,* § 48: "Such being our cognition of the relative reality, what are we to say of the absolute reality? We can only say that it is some mode of the Unknowable, related to the Matter we know as cause to effect." There are people who will tell you they understand that.

mental sciences (§§ 108-09), and we are therefore led to ascribe great importance to words. Whenever we are able to give a name to a thing, it succeeds by that sole fact in finding a place in a class of objects of which the properties are known, and its properties therefore also become known. Furthermore—and it is the point that really matters—the thing is viewed in the light of the sentiments the name arouses, and it is to its advantage, therefore, to have a name that awakens favourable sentiments and to its disadvantage to have a name inspiring unfavourable sentiments.[1]

In practical life it would be difficult, nay impossible, to do otherwise. We cannot go to the bottom of all the multifarious questions that are at every moment arising—we cannot test everything in the crucible of doubt. Once we admit that a man's hat is his, that is the end of it; he puts it on his head and goes his way; and we could not, before permitting him to take it, debate the real nature of property, nor settle the problem of individual or collective property or other problems of the kind.

In civilized countries civil and penal laws have an exact terminology; and so in order to pass judgment upon an act one must first know the name by which it can be designated. Ordinary speech too has maxims in large numbers, which, save for exactness, in which they are usually wanting, are like the articles in a code of law; so for maxims too the name to be given to an act or a thing is of great importance. The legislator uses terms in the meanings they commonly have among the people for whom he is legislating. He need not wait for scientists to agree upon a definition of the term "religion" before he makes laws governing sacrilege, religious freedom, and the like. We talk of numberless things offhand, never exactly defining their nature and traits. Practical life evolves in the approximate. Science alone aims at the precise.

Within the sphere of that approximate we get theorems that correspond to facts so long as they are not extended beyond the scope, at times very limited, within which they are valid. Ordinary language crystallizes and preserves them, and it is there that we can

113 [1] Of that we shall give many examples in the pages that follow.

recover and use them, but always with the reservation that, roughly approximative and true only within certain limits (which as a rule are unknown to us), they become false outside those limits (Chapter XI). Such theorems are theorems of words rather than of things; and we can therefore conclude that in practical life, for purposes of influencing others, and oftentimes in the early beginnings of the sciences, words are of great importance, and that it is by no means a waste of time to quarrel over them.

114. But as regards investigations in experimental science our conclusion must be precisely opposite. Such researches envisage things exclusively, and can therefore derive no advantage from words. They can, however, incur great harm, whether because of the sentiments that words arouse, or because the existence of a word may lead one astray as to the reality of the thing that it is supposed to represent (§§ 366-67), and so introduce into the experimental field imaginary entities such as the fictions of metaphysics or theology; or, finally, because reasonings based on words are as a rule woefully lacking in exactness.

115. So the more advanced sciences develop languages of their own as a result both of coining new terms and of giving special meanings to terms of ordinary parlance. The "water" of chemistry, the "light" of physics, the "velocity" of mechanics, have senses very different from the meanings of those identical words in everyday usage.

116. A simple device often serves to determine whether an argument is of the variety that relies on sentiment or on the assistance of the more or less vague notions stored up in the vernacular, or of the variety peculiar to experimental science. It is sufficient to substitute plain letters of the alphabet, *a, b, c* . . . for the key-words in it. If the argument loses cogency, it belongs to the first class; if it retains its full vigor, it belongs to the second (§ 642).

117. Like other sciences, political economy began by using terms from the vernacular, trying merely to give them meanings somewhat more exact; and so it became enriched with the wealth of experience accumulated in everyday language—a capital by no means inconspicuous, for economic operations make up a large fraction of human activity. But then gradually, as political economy progressed, that advantage waned, and the drawbacks involved in the use of such terms became more and more irksome. Jevons in his day very wisely dispensed with the word "value," which from being stretched in this, that, and every direction, and from having countless meanings, ended by having no meaning at all (§ 62 [1]); and he proposed a new term, "rate of exchange," of which he gave an exact definition (§ 387).

118. Literary economists did not follow him along that road; and they are to this day still dilly-dallying with speculations such as "What is *value?*" "What is *capital?*" They cannot get it into their heads that things are everything and words nothing, and that they may apply the terms "value" and "capital" to any blessed things they please, so only they be kind enough—they never are—to tell one precisely what those things are. If their arguments partook of experimental science, they would continue to hold even if blanks were used for the terms "value" and "capital"; for the name being taken away, the things still stand, and it is in things alone that experimental science is interested.[1] But since such arguments are primarily rhetorical, they are strictly dependent on words capable of arousing the sentiments that are useful in convincing people; and that is why literary economists very properly are so much concerned

118 [1] In my *Manuale* I showed that economic theories can just as well be elaborated without mention of the terms "value," "price," "capital," and the like. Literary economists cannot see it that way; and to an extent they are right, since for them the term "capital," let us say, designates not a thing but a sum of sentiments, and naturally enough they want to keep a term to designate that sum. To humour them, the thing might be called "objective capital," and the complex of sentiments "subjective capital." Then one could say: "Economic theories concerned exclusively with investigating relationships between economic facts have nothing to do with the concept 'subjective capital.' They may or may not, as they choose, utilize the concept 'objective capital.'" And going on: "Economic theories that aim at making converts and thereby at achieving some practical result can turn the concept of 'subjective capital' to good account, converts being made by appeals to sentiment. For that reason it is the wiser part for them to create a confusion between the notions of 'objective capital' and 'subjective capital,' so that the scientific argument will not avail against the sentimental argument." At some few points such theories approximate the concrete more closely than the theories of pure

about words and much less about things. Anyone asking what value *is,* what capital *is,* what income *is,* and the like, shows by that mere fact that he is concerned primarily with words and secondarily with things. The word "capital" certainly exists for him. What he is in doubt about is what it means, and he sets out to discover that. This procedure might be justifiable on a reasoning developed as follows: "There is something unknown that acts upon language and gives rise to the word 'capital.' *Since ordinary words are exact copies of the things they represent,* we can understand the thing by studying the word. So by finding out what capital is, we shall come to know the thing unknown." The fallacy in the justification lies in the proposition italicized. It is false. For more convincing proof one need simply substitute for the term "capital" some scientific term such as "water," and see whether the most painstaking inquiry as to what it is that is called water will ever reveal the properties of the chemically pure substance known by that name.

In science the course followed is the exact opposite: first one examines the thing and then hunts up a name to give it. First one considers the substance formed by combining oxygen and hydrogen, and then a term is sought to designate it. Since the substance in question is present in great quantities in the vaguely defined thing that the ordinary vernacular designates as water, we call it water. But it might have been called otherwise—"lavoisier," for instance—and all of chemistry would stand exactly as it is. We would simply say

economics, for they inject into the concept of "subjective capital" sociological notions that have no place in scientific economics. But they still have the fatal defect of being entirely devoid of exactness. If one would get closer to the concrete, instead of introducing sociological concepts implicitly and as it were by stealth, it would be better to advance them openly: that would make at least a certain amount of definiteness unavoidable. All such things can be better seen from Sensini's *La teoria della rendita.*

The concept "subjective capital" becomes of prime importance to sociology, which is in fact directly concerned with the sentiments expressed in such terms; and since the concrete phenomenon is both economic and sociological, anyone studying it in applied economics inevitably encounters notions analogous to "subjective capital." That is why, in my *Manuale,* I examined concrete phenomena not only from the strictly economic standpoint, but also as regards the manners in which they are conceived by the individuals involved in them (see the caption *Veduta soggettiva* in the index to the *Manuale*).

that the liquid present in rivers and in the sea contains great quantities of lavoisier. Literary economists and sociologists do not understand such things, for they are wanting in the mental attitude and the training required for understanding them.

119. In these volumes we intend to keep strictly to the logico-experimental method (§ 108) and deal exclusively with things. Words therefore are of no importance whatever to us; they are mere labels for keeping track of things. So we say, "Such and such a thing we are going to call *A*"; or, "We suggest calling it *A*." We do not say—an entirely different matter—"Such and such a thing is *A*." The first proposition is a definition, and we are free to word it as we choose. The second is a theorem, and requires demonstration; but before we can prove it we have to know exactly what *A* is (§ 963).

To avoid in these volumes the danger, ever threatening in the social sciences, that meanings of words will be persistently sought not in the objective definitions supplied but in common usage and etymology, we would gladly have replaced word-labels with letters of the alphabet, such as *a, b, c* . . . or with ordinal numbers; and that we have done for some parts of our exposition (§ 798). We have refrained from doing so more often in fear lest our argument become altogether too tedious and obscure. So here we follow the example of the chemist who continues using the term "water" but gives it an exact meaning.[1]

We too shall use terms of ordinary parlance, explaining exactly what they are to represent. We accordingly urge the reader to keep strictly to such definitions and never to try to guess from etymology or common usage the meanings of the technical terms that he finds in these volumes. The reader will shortly be meeting the terms "residues" and "derivations" (§ 868). If he desires to know what they mean, let him refer exclusively to the definitions we furnish. If he

119 [1] One should here recall the points alluded to in § 108. There is nothing absolute in logico-experimental science. Here the term "exact" means "with the least possible margin of error." Science tries to bring theory as close to the facts as possible, knowing very well that absolute coincidence cannot be attained. If, in view of that impossibility, anyone refuses to be satisfied with approximate exactness, he had better emigrate from this concrete world, for it has nothing better to offer.

were to seek their meaning in etymology or common acceptation, he would be certain to find things very different from the things we label with them. If anyone does not like them, he may feel quite free to replace them with others—we shall never quarrel on that score. And he will see that with his own terms, or better yet, using letters of the alphabet or numerals, all our arguments will stand just the same.

Anyone finding these explanations superfluous must be patient. My excuse is that similar explanations ever and anon repeated for my term "ophelimity" did not prevent literary economists from seeking its meaning in etymology; while others, who must truly have had a deal of time to waste, began wondering whether "desirability" would not have been a better name.[2] Nor could I silence such idle prattle by showing that we could very well do without "ophelimity" and all other similar terms in developing economic theories.[3]

120. In these volumes I shall use, for the reasons just stated, a number of terms that are also used in mechanics. I must accordingly make clear the exact senses in which I use them.

121. Let *A, B, C* . . . stand for certain things that have a capacity for influencing an economic or social situation. We may consider the situation either at a moment when the action of such things is not yet exhausted, or at a moment when it is entirely spent. Let *A*, for instance, stand for an individual's desire to drink wine, and *B* for a fear he has that it may injure his health. The man drinks one glass of wine, then a second, and then he stops, because after the second glass the fear effectively curbs the thirst. After the first glass the movement is not complete: the thirst is still effective in spite of the fear. Not even the fear has completed its work, because it has not yet quenched the individual's desire for drinking wine. It is evident that when we are considering a situation we have to specify

119 [2] Pareto, *Manuel*, p. 556, note 1.

119 [3] For other misconceptions arising from lack of exactness in language and from the prattle of literary economics, see my *Manuel*, pp. 219, note 1; 246, 329, note 1; 333, note 1; 391, note 1; 414, 439, note 1; 544, note 1; 636, note 1; 638, note 1; but especially, Sensini, *La teoria della rendita*, and Boven, *Les applications mathématiques à l'économie politique*.

whether we are considering it at a time when the things *A, B* have not completed, or at a time when they have completed, their action.

In mechanics there is an analogous situation—analogous, notice, not identical—where two forces are acting upon a physical point. So instead of speaking of two *things, A, B,* that have a capacity for influencing an economic or a social situation, we may for the sake of brevity speak of two *forces, A* and *B.*

122. The intermediate stage in which the individual has drunk the first glass of wine and is about to drink another, in which, that is, the work of *A* and *B* is not yet completed, is described in mechanics by saying that an equilibrium has not yet been attained. The stage in which both the thirst and the fear have completed their work, so that the individual ceases drinking, is described in mechanics by saying that an equilibrium has been attained. By analogy, not from identity, we may likewise use the term *equilibrium* for an economic or a social situation.

123. But an analogy is not a definition; and we should be deliberately exposing ourselves to ready and frequent error were we satisfied with such an analogy to represent the social or economic equilibrium. We are therefore called upon to give an exact definition of the economic or social equilibrium in question; and the reader will find it in Chapter XII.

124. Keeping to the definition of the thing, we can change the term at will and the arguments will stand just the same. For example, instead of calling *A* and *B* "forces," we might call them "influences" ("operative things") or even "things *I.*" The state defined above we might call τέλος, or even "state *X,*" instead of "equilibrium." In which cases all the arguments in which we have used the terms "forces" and "equilibrium" would still hold.

125. It is therefore a monumental stupidity to say, as one critic said, that when I speak of a state of equilibrium, I am thinking of a state which I consider *better* than another state, equilibrium being better than lack of equilibrium!

126. By similar analogy we can use other terms from mechanics in economics and sociology. Suppose we are considering a society in which private property exists. We may propose to study the possible forms of such a society, premising always the condition that private property exist. In the same way other relationships supply other conditions that we may assume or not assume as premises. Similar situations are met with in mechanics, and there the conditions in question are known as *ties* (*vincula*). By analogy, we can use that term in economics and sociology as well.[1] However, if there were no other analogies with mechanics it would be useless to do that, and better in particular not to use the term "tie."

127. Suppose we are considering a system of material points maintained by certain *ties,* and upon which certain forces *A, B, C* . . . are acting. The successive positions of the points will be determined by the resultant of the forces as modified by the ties. Now take a given group of individuals. Certain conditions prevail, such as private property, freedom (or slavery), technical training, wealth, scientific knowledge, religion, and so on. Active also in the group are certain individual desires, interests, prejudices, and the like. The successive states of the group may be assumed as determined by these latter elements working in conjunction with the conditions (the ties) premised.

128. So by analogy—never from identity—we can call the group a social or an economic system and say that certain forces are acting upon it, which determine the position of the points in the system in conjunction with the ties. Considerations of brevity solely and strictly counsel the use of such terms, and as always they may be replaced by others at pleasure.

129. A transition from one state to another is called a ***movement*** in mechanics, and it may be so called in sociology also. In mechanics, if we assume that ties and forces are determined, movements in the system are likewise determined. So in sociology, if we assume conditions and active influences as given, the various successive states of

126 [1] [Pareto's word was *vincolo,* "bond." The *vincolo* is a force that conditions the operation of another force. The term *vinculum* itself has a certain currency in technical sociologies. In most connexions it can well be translated as "condition," or "check," and more generally as "correlation," or even as "premise." In deference to the baroque quality of Pareto's own term, I render it regularly as "tie."—A. L.]

the group are determined. Such movements are called *real* in mechanics, and may be so called in sociology.

130. If, for theoretical purposes, we assume as suppressed some tie in a mechanical system, some condition in a sociological group, the mechanical system will show movements different from the real, and the sociological group will attain states other than those it really attains. Such movements are called *virtual* in mechanics, and *virtual* they may be called in sociology. For example, a person investigating what society would be like if private property were to be abolished is making a study in virtual movements.

131. We can think of the "ties" and "forces" in the social system as summed together; and if we designate the aggregate by the term "conditions," the so-called theory of determinism could be stated by saying that the state of a system is wholly determined by "conditions" and can therefore change only with a change in "conditions."[1]

132. Science has no dogmas, and so cannot and must not accept determinism *a priori;* and so far as it does accept it, it must, as always, do so strictly within the limits of the time and space that have been investigated. With that premise solidly established, experience indicates that in many cases social situations seem really to be determined by "conditions" and change only with changes in "conditions." In such cases we therefore recognize determinism, but without in the least precluding that there may be other cases where it cannot be granted.[1]

133. From the standpoint of the deterministic hypothesis, we are now called upon to solve a problem that is continually arising in one

131 [1] Here, accordingly, the term "conditions" has a different and more comprehensive meaning than it had in § 126.

132 [1] Naville, review of Bergson, *Op. cit.,* p. 11: "I am well aware that determinism has its fascination for the scholar and affords great satisfaction to the scientific mind. [More exactly, "to the theology of Reason."] Determinism is the belief [That word alone should serve to give warning that we are overstepping the boundaries of experimental science.] that everything can be explained, and what the scientist wants is explanations. Determinism is the conviction that all phenomena can be understood, associated, that is, with other phenomena that envelop and produce them. . . . But however natural the inclination [to determinism] may be, it proves nothing, and not all scientists succumb to it."

form or another in history and sociology. According to determinism, whatever happens cannot happen otherwise; and so the terms "possible" and "impossible" as used in ordinary language have no meaning, since only that is possible which happens, and what does not happen is impossible. We do not choose to quarrel over words; so if anyone is inclined to throw such terms overboard, let us do so by all means. All the same, after they have been dispensed with we are still confronted with the different things that were designated by them, and for which it will be expedient to find other designations.

John Doe did not have his dinner yesterday, but speaking in ordinary terms, it was "possible" for him to dine. He did not cut off his head; but it was "impossible" for him to cut off his head, then glue it on again and be alive and well today. It may well be that from the standpoint of determinism the two things are equally impossible; but it is also evident that they are different kinds of things, and it would be a grave misfortune if we were unable to designate the different classes to which they belong. Suppose, for the moment, we label the first class (I) and the second (II). It is at once apparent that the difference between (I) and (II) lies in the fact that cases like (I) have been often enough observable, whereas no case like (II) has ever been seen.

134. To be more exact: in both cases we are dealing with "virtual" movements; and in declaring them both impossible, determinism is merely calling them virtual as opposed to real movements. But there is more than one class of virtual movements. There is a class of virtual movements that take place when we assume as absent a certain tie which was not absent at the time the real movement in question was observed, but which has been found absent on other occasions, when real movements equivalent to the virtual movement have been observable. That movement therefore belongs in the class we have called (I) and which, in ordinary language, is a class of possible things. There is another class of virtual movements that would take place only if we assumed as absent a tie which has never been found absent, so that real movements equivalent to such virtual movements have never been observed. These belong to the class we have called (II), which in ordinary terms is a class of impossible things. Having so supplied exact definitions of the things that the terms "possible" and "impossible" designate, there can be no objection to using them even with the hypothesis of determinism.

135. Of what conceivable use can the study of virtual movements be if they are things foreign to the domain of reality and only real movements actually occur? The advantages are, in chief, two:

1. If we are considering virtual movements that have not been real because of the presence of ties which have been found absent on other occasions—if, in other words, we are considering movements that are virtual in some cases but are observable as real in others—knowledge of the virtual movements may help to foresee what the real movements are going to be like. Such, for instance, are forecasts as to the effects of a certain piece of legislation or of some other practical measure.

2. Consideration of virtual movements may help towards isolating and determining the character and peculiarities of a given social state.

136. The propositions "*A* determines *B*" and "If there were no *A* there would be no *B*" state the same fact, in the one case as a function of *A,* in the other in terms of a virtual movement. The propositions "In such and such a state society has a maximum of *A*" and "If society departs from that state, there will be a diminution in *A*" express the same fact, in the first case as a description of the state, in the second in terms of a virtual movement.

137. In the social sciences, virtual movements are to be resorted to with great caution, for very very often we have no means of knowing what the consequences of suppressing some condition, some tie, would be. If a person says, "If the Emperor Julian had continued very long on the throne, the Christian religion would not have survived," he is assuming that the death of Julian was alone responsible for the triumph of Christianity. And if one answers, "If the Emperor Julian had continued longer on the throne, he might have retarded, but could not have prevented, the triumph of Christianity," one is assuming that there were other conditions present which made that triumph certain. In general, propositions of this second variety are more often verifiable than are propositions of the first kind. In many cases, that is, social developments are determined by the concurrent action of large numbers of conditions; so that the removal of any one of them disturbs the course of events but slightly.

138. Conditions, furthermore, are not independent. Many of them influence each other. Nor is that all. The effects of conditions react in turn upon the conditions themselves. In a word, social facts—that is to say, conditions and effects—are *interdependent,* and modifications in one of them react upon larger or smaller numbers of the others, and with greater or lesser intensities.

139. That is why attempts to remake history by conjecturing what would have happened had a certain event never occurred are altogether fatuous. We have no way of determining all the changes that would have taken place on a given hypothesis if the hypothesis had come true. What would have happened had Napoleon won at Waterloo? Only one answer is possible—"We do not know."

140. We can get something a little better by keeping to effects that are very immediate in a very limited field, and progress in the social sciences will tend gradually to enlarge those very restricted confines. Every time we succeed in discovering some hitherto unknown relation between social facts, we are a little better prepared to know what the effects of certain changes in the social situation will be; and pushing on along that road we make new advances, however slight, towards realizing the purpose of determining the probable course of social developments in the future. Therefore no study that aims at discovering some uniformity in the relations of social facts can be called useless. It may be useless at the present time and continue to be so in any near future; but we cannot be sure that the day will not come when, taken in conjunction with other discoveries, it will contribute towards forecasting probabilities in social evolution.

141. The difficulties in discovering social uniformities are great because of the great complexity of social phenomena. They are immeasurably increased, and in fact become insuperable, when uniformities are sought not with the one and undivided intent of discovering them, but with the purpose, explicitly chosen or tacitly set by sentiment, of justifying a preconception, a doctrine, a faith. Just such impediments account for the present backward state of the social sciences.

142. The man entirely unaffected by sentiments and free from all bias, all faith, does not exist; and to regard that freedom as an essential prerequisite to profitable study of the social sciences would amount to saying that such study is impossible. But experience shows that a person can as it were divide himself in two and, to an extent at least, lay aside his sentiments, preconceptions, and beliefs when engaged in a scientific pursuit, resuming them afterwards. That was the case with Pasteur, who outside his laboratory was a devout Catholic, but inside kept strictly to the experimental method. And before Pasteur one might mention Newton, who certainly used one method in discoursing on the Apocalypse and quite another in his *Principia*.

143. Such self-detachment is more readily achieved in the natural sciences than in the social sciences. It is an easy matter to look at an ant with the sceptical disinterestedness of experimental science. It is much more difficult to look at human beings that way. But even if complete success in such an effort is impossible, we can at least try to succeed in part, and reduce the power and influence of sentiments, preconceptions, beliefs, to a minimum. Only at that price can progress in the social sciences be achieved.

144. Social facts are the elements of our study. Our first effort will be to classify them for the purpose of attaining the one and only objective we have in view: the discovery, namely, of uniformities (laws) in the relations between them. When we have so classified kindred facts, a certain number of uniformities will come to the surface by induction; and after going a good distance along that primarily inductive path, we shall turn to another where more ample room will be found for deduction. So we shall verify the uniformities to which induction has carried us, give them a less empirical, more theoretical form, and see just what their implications are, just what picture they give of society.

In general we have to deal with things that vary by imperceptible degrees, and our picture of them approximates reality the more closely in proportion as it is drawn in *quantitative* terms. That fact if often recognized by saying that as sciences progress, they tend to become more and more quantitative. But that is much more difficult than to study merely qualitative differences. In fact, the first forward step lies always in a rough quantitative approximation.[1]

It is no difficult matter to distinguish day from night with tolerable accuracy. Though there is no precise instant at which day ends and night begins, we can after all roughly say that there is a qualitative difference between them. It is more difficult to divide such periods of time into parts. We manage to do so approximately by saying "shortly after sunrise," "towards noon," and the like; and with more or less success—less rather than more—the night used to be divided into "watches." When clocks came to be available, it was possible to get quantitative measurements of time, the exactness increasing with improvements in clocks and becoming very considerable with the modern chronometer.

For a long time people were satisfied with knowing that the death-rate was higher among the aged than among the young, no one as usual knowing very definitely where youth ended and old age began. Then something more was learned; statistics were made available, very imperfect statistics at first, then better ones, now fairly good ones—and they are steadily improving. For a long time there was very little of the quantitative about political economy.

144 [1] The terms "quality," "quantity," "qualitative," "quantitative," will at all times be used in these volumes not in any metaphysical sense but in the sense commonly used in chemistry in contrasting qualitative with quantitative analysis. The one shows, for instance, that a given substance is an alloy of gold and copper; the other shows the weight of gold and the weight of copper present in a given weight of the alloy. Whenever we note the presence of a certain element in a sociological complex, we are stating a *qualitative* proposition. When we are in a position to designate, however roughly, the intensity of that element, our proposition becomes *quantitative*. Unfortunately no scales are available for weighing the things that are dealt with in sociology, and we shall generally have to be satisfied with designating quantities by certain indices that increase or diminish with the thing itself. An interesting example of that method applied to political economy is provided in my use of indices of ophelimity (see my *Manuale,* Appendix).

Then it became quantitative in pure economics—in theory at least. For sociology we shall try as far as we can to replace qualitative considerations with considerations of quantity. Imperfect, very imperfect, as they may be, they will at any rate be a little better than the qualitative. We shall do what we can, our successors will do better—and so science advances!

In these volumes we shall confine ourselves to a very general picture—something like a sphere offered as a model of the Earth. That is why I call this a *general* sociology. Details will still be left for future study—much as oceans, continents, and mountains have to be drawn in on the sphere of the Earth. Such studies would make up a *special* sociology. Incidentally, however, we shall examine not a few special themes in the course of these volumes; for we shall be meeting them all along the path we shall have to traverse in getting our picture of society in general.

CHAPTER II

Non-logical Conduct[1]

145. So far we have stated our attitude in writing these volumes and the field in which we intend to remain. Now we are to study human conduct, the states of mind to which it corresponds and the ways in which they express themselves, in order to arrive eventually at our goal, which is to discover the forms of society. We are following the inductive method. We have no preconceptions, no *a priori* notions. We find certain facts before us. We describe them, classify them, determine their character, ever on the watch for some uniformity (law) in the relationships between them. In this chapter we begin to interest ourselves in human actions.[1]

146. This is the first step we take along the path of induction. If we were to find, for instance, that all human actions corresponded to logico-experimental theories, or that such actions were the most important, others having to be regarded as phenomena of social pathology deviating from a normal type, our course evidently would be entirely different from what it would be if many of the more important human actions proved to correspond to theories that are not logico-experimental.

147. Let us accordingly examine actions from the standpoint of

[1] [Pareto, following Bentham, invariably uses the word "actions" (*azioni*) where ordinary English parlance uses "conduct" or "behaviour." Such phrases as "logical actions" and "non-logical actions" often lead to syntactical and other paradoxes in Pareto's text that have contributed not a little to his occasional obscurity. For mere convenience *azioni* is rendered here by "conduct," "behaviour," "acts," "actions," more or less interchangeably. The literally-minded reader can always recover the feel of the original Italian by understanding those words as "actions" with constructions in the plural. More troublesome still to the translator is Pareto's use of the phrase "non-logical actions" for "the sentiments (or "impulses" or "residues") underlying non-logical actions," or for "the principles of non-logical actions." There is no extricating him from that situation, and in it as a rule I leave him.—A. L.]

145 [1] Originally written in French, this chapter was in part translated into Italian by the *Rivista italiana di sociologia,* and published in that review, May-August, 1910.

their logico-experimental character. But in order to do that we must first try to classify them, and in that effort we propose to follow the principles of the classification called natural in botany and zoology, whereby objects on the whole presenting similar characteristics are grouped together. In the case of botany Tournefort's classification was very wisely abandoned. It divided plants into "herbs" and "trees," and so came to separate entities that as a matter of fact present close resemblances. The so-called natural method nowadays preferred does away with all divisions of that kind and takes as its norm the characteristics of plants in the mass, putting like with like and keeping the unlike distinct. Can we find similar groupings to classify the actions of human beings?

148. It is not actions as we find them in the concrete that we are called upon to classify, but the elements constituting them. So the chemist classifies elements and compounds of elements, whereas in nature what he finds is mixtures of compounds. Concrete actions are synthetic—they originate in mixtures, in varying degrees, of the elements we are to classify.

149. Every social phenomenon may be considered under two aspects: as it is in reality, and as it presents itself to the mind of this or that human being. The first aspect we shall call *objective,* the second *subjective* (§§ 94 f.). Such a division is necessary, for we cannot put in one same class the operations performed by a chemist in his laboratory and the operations performed by a person practising magic; the conduct of Greek sailors in plying their oars to drive their ship over the water and the sacrifices they offered to Poseidon to make sure of a safe and rapid voyage. In Rome the Laws of the XII Tables punished anyone casting a spell on a harvest. We choose to distinguish such an act from the act of burning a field of grain.

We must not be misled by the names we give to the two classes. In reality both are subjective, for all human knowledge is subjective. They are to be distinguished not so much by any difference in nature as in view of the greater or lesser fund of factual knowledge that we ourselves have. We know, or think we know, that sacrifices to Poseidon have no effect whatsoever upon a voyage. We therefore distinguish them from other acts which (to our best knowledge, at least) are capable of having such effect. If at some future time we were to discover that we have been mistaken, that sacrifices to Poseidon are very influential in securing a favourable voyage, we should have to reclassify them with actions capable of such influence. All that of course is pleonastic. It amounts to saying that when a person makes a classification, he does so according to the knowledge he has. One cannot imagine how things could be otherwise.

150. There are actions that use means appropriate to ends and which logically link means with ends. There are other actions in which those traits are missing. The two sorts of conduct are very different according as they are considered under their objective or their subjective aspect. From the subjective point of view nearly all human actions belong to the logical class. In the eyes of the Greek mariners sacrifices to Poseidon and rowing with oars were equally logical means of navigation. To avoid verbosities which could only prove annoying, we had better give names to these types of conduct.[1] Suppose we apply the term *logical actions* to actions that logically conjoin means to ends not only from the standpoint of the subject performing them, but from the standpoint of other persons who have a more extensive knowledge—in other words, to actions that are logical both subjectively and objectively in the sense just explained. Other actions we shall call *non-logical* (by no means the same as "illogical"). This latter class we shall subdivide into a number of varieties.

150 [1] As we have already said (§§ 116 f.), it would perhaps be better to use designations that have no meanings in themselves, such as letters of the alphabet. On the other hand, such a system would impair the clarity of our argument. We must therefore resign ourselves to using terms of ordinary speech; but the reader must bear in mind that such words, or their etymologies, in no way serve to describe the things they stand for. Things have to be examined directly. Names are just labels to help us keep track of them (§ 119).

151. A synoptic picture of the classification will prove useful:

GENERA AND SPECIES	HAVE THE ACTIONS LOGICAL ENDS AND PURPOSES: *Objectively?*	*Subjectively?*
CLASS I: LOGICAL ACTIONS		
(The objective end and the subjective purpose are identical.)		
	Yes	Yes
CLASS II. NON-LOGICAL ACTIONS		
(The objective end differs from the subjective purpose.)		
Genus 1	No	No
Genus 2	No	Yes
Genus 3	Yes	No
Genus 4	Yes	Yes

SPECIES OF THE GENERA 3 AND 4

3α, 4α	The objective end would be accepted by the subject if he knew it.
3β, 4β	The objective end would be rejected by the subject if he knew it.

The ends and purposes here in question are immediate ends and purposes. We choose to disregard the indirect. The objective end is a real one, located within the field of observation and experience, and not an imaginary end, located outside that field. An imaginary end may, on the other hand, constitute a subjective purpose.

152. Logical actions are very numerous among civilized peoples. Actions connected with the arts and sciences belong to that class, at least for artists and scientists. For those who physically perform them in mere execution of orders from superiors, there may be among them non-logical actions of our II-4 type. The actions dealt with in political economy also belong in very great part in the class of logical actions. In the same class must be located, further, a certain number of actions connected with military, political, legal, and similar activities.

153. So at the very first glance induction leads to the discovery that non-logical actions play an important part in society. Let us therefore proceed with our examination of them.

154. First of all, in order to get better acquainted with these non-logical actions, suppose we look at a few examples. Many others will find their proper places in chapters to follow. Here are some illustrations of actions of Class II:

Genera 1 and 3, which have no subjective purpose, are of scant importance to the human race. Human beings have a very conspicuous tendency to paint a varnish of logic over their conduct. Nearly all human actions therefore work their way into genera 2 and 4. Many actions performed in deference to courtesy and custom might be put in genus 1. But very very often people give some reason or other to justify such conduct, and that transfers it to genus 2. Ignoring the indirect motive involved in the fact that a person violating common usages incurs criticism and dislike, we might find a certain number of actions to place in genera 1 and 3.

Says Hesiod:[1] "Do not make water at the mouth of a river emptying into the sea, nor into a spring. You must avoid that. Do not lighten your bowels there, for it is not good to do so." The precept not to befoul rivers at their mouths belongs to genus 1. No objective or subjective end or purpose is apparent in the avoidance of such pollution. The precept not to befoul drinking-water belongs to genus 3. It has an objective purpose that Hesiod may not have known, but which is familiar to moderns: to prevent contagion from certain diseases.

It is probable that not a few actions of genera 1 and 3 are common among savages and primitive peoples. But travellers are bent on learning at all costs the reasons for the conduct they observe. So in one way or another they finally obtain answers that transfer the conduct to genera 2 and 4.

155. Granting that animals do not reason, we can place nearly all their so-called instinctive acts in genus 3. Some may even go in 1. Genus 3 is the pure type of the non-logical action, and a study of it as it appears in animals will help to an understanding of non-logical conduct in human beings.

154 [1] *Opera et dies*, vv. 757-58.

Of the insects called Eumenes (pseudo-wasps) Blanchard writes that, like other Hymenoptera, they "suck the nectar of flowers when they are full grown [but that] their larvae feed only upon living prey; and since, like the larvae of wasps and bees, they are apodal and incapable of procuring food, they would perish at once if left to themselves. What happens, then, may be foreseen. The mother herself has to procure food for her young. That industrious little animal, who herself lives only on the honey of flowers, wages war upon the tribe of insects to assure a livelihood for her offspring. In order to stock its nest with victuals, this Hymenopteron nearly always attacks particular species of insects, and it knows how to find such species without any trouble, though to the scientist who hunts for them they seem very rare indeed. The female stings her victims with her dart and carries them to her nest. The insect so smitten does not die at once. It is left in a deep coma, which renders it incapable of moving or defending itself. The larvae are hatched in close proximity to the provisions that have been laboriously accumulated by the mother, and find within their reach a food adapted to their needs and in quantities sufficient for their whole life as larvae. Nothing is more amazing than this marvellous foresight; and it is altogether instinctive, it would seem. In laying her eggs every female prepares food for young whom she will never see; for by the time they are hatched she will long since have ceased to live."[1]

155 [1] *Histoire des insectes,* Vol. I, p. 71. But there is something else. Fabre made interesting observations of these insects and others of the kind. He succeeded in determining that the number of caterpillars prepared to feed the larva varies from five to ten, according as the insect is to be female or male. Since the egg is laid after the provisions have been stored, Fabre believes that the mother knows beforehand the sex to which the egg is to belong (*Souvenirs entomologiques,* Ser. 2, pp. 72-73). He reverts to the matter of the sex of the egg in his third series (pp. 384 f.). Fabre managed to discover how the larva of the Eumenis is fed: *Ibid.,* Ser. 2, pp. 78-79: "The egg is not laid on the food: it is hung from the ceiling of the dome by a filament rivalling the thread of a spider's web in fineness. . . . The larva has hatched and is already of some size. Like the egg, it hangs by the back from the ceiling of its home. . . . The worm is now at table! Head down, he feels about over the soft belly of one of the caterpillars. With a wisp of straw I touch the game gently, before it has been bitten. The caterpillars begin wriggling, and the larva beats a hasty re-

Other Hymenoptera, the Cerceres, attack Coleoptera. Here the action, subjectively non-logical, shows a marvellous objective logic. Suppose we let Fabre speak for himself. He observes that, in order to paralyze its prey, the Hymenopteron has first to find Coleoptera either with three thoracic ganglia very close together, contiguous in fact, or with the two rear ganglia joined. "That, really, is the prey they need. These Coleoptera, with motor centres situated so close together as to touch, forming a single mass and standing in intimate mutual connexions, can thus be paralyzed at a single thrust; or if several stings are needed, the ganglia that require treatment will at least lie together under the point of the stinger." Further along: "Out of the vast numbers of Coleoptera upon which the Cerceres might inflict their depredations, only two groups, the weevils and the Buprestes, fulfil the indispensable conditions. They live far from infested and noisome places, for which, it may be, the fastidious huntress has an unconquerable repugnance. Their numerous representatives vary in size, proportionate to the sizes of the various pirates, who are thus free to select their victims at pleasure. They, more than all others, are vulnerable at the one point where the stinger of the Hymenopteron can penetrate with success: for at that point the motor centres of the feet and wings are concentrated in such a way as to be readily accessible to the stinger. These three thoracic ganglia of the weevil lie very close together, the last two touching. In the Buprestes the second and third ganglia blend in a single bulky mass a short distance from the first. Now it is the weevils and the Buprestes precisely, to the absolute exclusion of all other prey, that we find hunted by the eight species of Cerceres that lay in stores of Coleoptera." [2]

treat." It crawls back into a sort of sheath: "The covering of the egg is its tunnel of refuge. It still keeps its cylindrical form, prolonged a little perhaps by the special labours of the new-born larva. At the first signs of peril from the pile of caterpillars, the larva draws into its sheath and climbs back to the ceiling where the wriggling mob cannot reach it." Later on, when the worm has grown stronger and the caterpillars weaker, the worm drops to the floor.

155 [2] *Ibid.*, Ser. 1, pp. 67-79. Another truly extraordinary example is supplied in Fabre's Ser. 4, pp. 253-54. The Callicurgus hunts a certain spider, the Epeiron. The Epeiron "has under his throat two exceedingly sharp needles with drops

156. For that matter, a certain number of actions in animals evince reasoning of a kind, or better, a sort of adaptation of means to ends as circumstances change. Says Fabre, whom we quote at such length because he has studied the subject better than anybody else:[1] "For instinct nothing is difficult, so long as the act does not extrude from the fixed cycle that is the animal's birthright. For instinct also nothing is easy if the act has to deviate from the rut habitually followed. The insect that amazes for its high perspicacity will an instant later, when confronted with the simplest situation foreign to its ordinary practice, astound for its stupidity. . . . Distinguishable in the psychic life of the insect are two wholly different domains. The one is instinct proper, the unconscious impulse that guides the animal in the marvellous achievements of its industry. . . . It is instinct, and nothing but instinct, that makes a mother build a nest for a family she will never know, which counsels a supply of food for an unknowable posterity, which steers the dart toward the nerve-centre of the prey . . . with a view to keeping provisions fresh. . . . But for all of its unbending, unconscious cleverness, pure instinct, all by itself, would leave the insect disarmed in its perpetual battle with circumstance. . . . A guide is necessary to devise, accept, refuse, select, prefer this, ignore that—in a word, take advantage of the usables occasion offers. Such a guide the in-

of poison on the points. The Callicurgus is lost if the spider pricks him, and meantime his operation in anaesthesia requires the unfailing precision of the surgeon's knife. What is he to do in a perilous situation that would ruin the composure of the coolest human operator? The patient has first to be disarmed and then dealt with! And, in fact, there is the stinger of the Callicurgus darting forward from the back and driving into the mouth of the Epeiron with minutest precautions and untiring persistence! Almost at once the poisonous hooks fold up lifeless and the dread prey is powerless to harm. The belly of the Hymenopteron then stretches its bow and drives the stinger home just behind the fourth pair of legs, on the median line, almost at the juncture of belly and cephalo-thorax. . . . The nerve ganglia controlling the movements of the legs are located a little higher than the point pricked, but the backward-forward thrust enables the weapon to reach them. This second stroke paralyzes the eight legs all at once. . . . First, to safeguard the operator, a prick in the mouth, a point terrifyingly armed and to be dreaded more than all else! Then, to safeguard the offspring, a second thrust into the nervous centres of the thorax, to end all movement!"

156 [1] *Ibid.*, Ser. 1, pp. 165-66; Ser. 4, pp. 65-67.

sect certainly has and even to a very conspicuous degree. It is the second domain of his psychic life. In it he is conscious and teachable by experience. Not daring to call that rudimentary aptitude intelligence, a title too exalted for it, I will call it *discernment*."

157. Qualitatively (§ 144 [1]), phenomena are virtually the same in human beings; but quantitatively, the field of logical behaviour, exceedingly limited in the case of animals, becomes very far-reaching in mankind. All the same, many many human actions, even today among the most civilized peoples, are performed instinctively, mechanically, in pursuance of habit; and that is more generally observable still in the past and among less civilized peoples. There are cases in which it is apparent that the effectiveness of certain rites is believed in instinctively, and not as a logical consequence of the religion that practises them (§ 952). Says Fabre: [1]

"The various instinctive acts of insects are therefore inevitably linked together. Because a certain thing has just been done, another must unavoidably be done to complete it or prepare the way for its completion [That is the case with many human actions also.], and the two acts are so strictly correlated that the performance of the first entails the performance of the second, even when by some fortuitous circumstance the second may have become not only unseasonable, but at times even contrary to the animal's interests."

But even in the animal one detects a seed of the logic that is to come to such luxuriant flower in the human being. After describing how he tricked certain insects that obstinately persisted in useless acts, Fabre adds: "But the yellow-winged Sphex does not always let himself be fooled by the game of pulling his cricket away. There are chosen clans in his tribe, families of brainy wit, that, after a few disappointments, perceive the wiles of the trickster and find ways to checkmate them. But such revolutionaries, candidates for progress, are the small minority. The rest, stubborn conservators of the good old-fashioned ways, are the *hoi polloi*, the majority."

This remark should be remembered, for the conflict between a tendency to combinations, which is responsible for innovations, and

157 [1] *Ibid.*, Ser. 1, pp. 174-77.

a tendency to permanence in groups of sensations, which promotes stability, may put us in the way of explaining many things about human societies (Chapter XII).

158. The formation of human language is no whit less marvellous than the instinctive conduct of insects. It would be absurd to claim that the theory of grammar preceded the practice of speech. It certainly followed, and human beings have created most subtle grammatical structures without any knowledge of it.

Take the Greek language as an example. If one chose to go farther back to some Indo-European language from which Greek would be derived, our contentions would hold *a fortiori,* because the chance of any grammatical abstraction would be less and less probable. We cannot imagine that the Greeks one day got together and decided what their system of conjugation was to be. Usage alone made such a masterpiece of the Greek verb. In Attic Greek there is the augment, which is the sign of the past in historical tenses; and, for a very subtle nuance, besides the syllabic augment there is the temporal (quantitative) augment, which consists in a lengthening of the initial vowel. The conception of the aorist, and its functions in syntax, are inventions that would do credit to the most expert logician. The large number of verbal forms and the exactness of their functions in syntax constitute a marvellous whole.[1]

158 [1] Albert Dauzat well says, *La langue française d'aujourd'hui,* pp. 238-39: "The whole field is today under the dominion of a principle that holds the allegiance of the vast majority of philologists, namely, that linguistic phenomena are unconscious. [Another way of expressing what we mean by "non-logical actions."] Almost universally accepted in the domain of phonology—transformations in sounds have long since ceased to be ascribed to individual caprice—the principle is nevertheless meeting the same opposition in the field of semantics that [phonetic] laws were generally arousing not so long ago. M. Bréal [*Essai de sémantique,* p. 311; Cust, pp. 279-81] assigns a very definite rôle to individual volition in the evolution of word-meanings. . . . This [Bréal's] theory, which would have found practically no adversaries fifty years ago, is today rejected with virtual unanimity by philologists, who readily subscribe to the axiom stated by V. Henry [*Antinomies linguistiques,* p. 78] that 'any explanation of a linguistic phenomenon which to any extent whatever assumes exercise of conscious activity on the part of a speaking subject must be *a priori* discarded and held null and void.'" But that is an exaggeration. Scientific terminology is nearly always a product of conscious activity, and some few terms in ordinary language may have similar origins. On the other hand,

159. In Rome, the general invested with the *imperium* had to take the auspices on the Capitol before he could leave the city. He could do that only in Rome. One cannot imagine that that provision had originally the political purpose that it eventually acquired.[1] "As long as the extension of existing *imperia* depended exclusively upon the will of the *comitia,* no new ones carrying full military authority could be established except by taking the auspices on the Capitol—consequently by performing an act that lay within urban jurisdiction. . . . To organize another [taking of auspices] in defiance of the constitution would have implied transgressing bounds held in awe even by the *comitia* of the sovereign People. No constitutional barrier to extraordinary military usurpations held its ground anywhere near as long as this guarantee that had been found in the regulation as to a general's auspices. In the end that regulation also lapsed, or rather was circumvented. In later times some piece of land or other situated outside of Rome was 'annexed' by a legal fiction to the city and taken as though located within the *pomerium,* and the required *auspicium* was celebrated there."

Later on Sulla not only abolished the guarantee of the auspices, but even rendered it inapplicable by an ordinance whereby the magistrate was obligated not to assume command till after the expiration of his year of service [as a magistrate]—at a time, that is, when

Bréal's objection does not disturb the fact that a large number of phenomena are conscious only in appearances, the activity of the subject resolving itself into non-logical behaviour of our varieties 2 and especially 4. Darmesteter, *La vie des mots,* pp. 86, 133: "In all such changes [in the meanings of words] one finds, at bottom, two concurrent intellectual elements, the one principal, the other secondary. In the long run, as the result of an unconscious detour, the mind loses sight of the first and thinks only of the second. . . . So the mind passes from one idea to quite another under cover of one same physiological fact—the word. Now this unconscious development, which shifts the stress from the principal detail to the secondary, is the law, no less, of transformations in the mental world. . . . So in spite of the family relationships that developments in a language may establish between words, words most often lead lives of their own and follow their respective destinies all by themselves. When human beings speak, they are by no means 'doing etymology.'" Nothing could be truer; and that is why people often go astray in trying to infer the meaning of a word from its etymology or, what is worse, trying to reconstruct the unknown history of a remote past on an etymological basis.

159 [1] Mommsen, *Römisches Staatsrecht,* Vol. I, p. 100.

[being in his proconsular province] he could no longer take the urban auspices. Now Sulla, a conservative, obviously had no intention of providing for the overthrow of his constitution in that way, any more than the older Romans, in establishing the requirement of auspices taken in the *Urbs,* were anticipating attacks upon the constitution of the Republic. In reality, in their case, we have a non-logical action of our 4α type; and in the case of Sulla a non-logical action of our 4β type.

In the sphere of political economy, certain measures (for example, wage-cutting) of business men (entrepreneurs) working under conditions of free competition are to some extent non-logical actions of our 4β type, that is, the objective end does not coincide with the subjective purpose. On the other hand, if they enjoy a monopoly, the same measures (wage-cutting) become logical actions.[2]

160. Another very important difference between human conduct and the conduct of animals lies in the fact that we do not observe human conduct wholly from the outside as we do in the case of animals. Frequently we know the actions of human beings through the judgments that people pass upon them, through the impressions they make, and in the light of the motives that people are pleased to imagine for them and assign as their causes. For that reason, actions that would otherwise belong to genera 1 and 3 make their way into 2 and 4.

Operations in magic when unattended by other actions belong to genus 2. The sacrifices of the Greeks and Romans have to be classed in the same genus—at least after those peoples lost faith in the reality of their gods. Hesiod, *Opera et dies,* vv. 735-39, warns against crossing a river without first washing one's hands in it and uttering a prayer. That would be an action of genus 1. But he adds that the

159 [2] Pareto, *Cours,* § 719: ". . . while the business man aims at reducing costs of production, involuntarily he achieves the further effect of reducing selling prices [That is not the case with monopolies.], competition always restoring parity between the two prices." And *cf. Ibid.,* §§ 151, 718. Pareto, *Manuale,* Chap. V, § 11. *Ibid.,* Chap. V, § 74: "So competing enterprises get to a point where they had no intention of going. Each of them has been looking strictly to profits and thinking of the consumer only in so far as he can be exploited; but owing to the successive adjustments and readjustments required by competition their combined exertions turn out to the advantage of the consumer."

gods punish anyone who crosses a river without so washing his hands. That makes it an action of genus 2.

This rationalizing procedure is habitual and very wide-spread. Hesiod says also, vv. 780-82, that grain should not be sown on the thirteenth of a month, but that that day is otherwise very auspicious for planting, and he gives many other precepts of the kind. They all belong to genus 2. In Rome a soothsayer who had observed signs in the heavens was authorized to adjourn the *comitia* to some other day.[1] Towards the end of the Republic, when all faith in augural science had been lost, that was a logical action, a means of attaining a desired end. But when people still believed in augury, it was an action of genus 4. For the soothsayers who, with the help of the gods, were so enabled to forestall some decision that they considered harmful to the Roman People, it belonged to our species 4α, as is apparent if one consider that in general such actions correspond, very roughly to be sure, to the provisions used in our time for avoiding ill-considered decisions by legislative bodies: requirements of two or three consecutive readings, of approvals by two houses, and so on.

Most acts of public policy based on tradition or on presumed missions of peoples or individuals belong to genus 4. William I, King of Prussia, and Napoleon III, Emperor of the French, both considered themselves "men of destiny." But William I thought his mission lay in promoting the welfare and greatness of his country, Louis Napoleon believed himself destined to achieve the happiness of mankind. William's policies were of the 4α type; Napoleon's, of the 4β.

Human beings as a rule determine their conduct with reference to certain general rules (morality, custom, law), which give rise in greater or lesser numbers to actions of our 4α and even 4β varieties.

161. Logical actions are at least in large part results of processes

160 [1] Cicero, *De legibus*, II, 12, 31: "If we are thinking of prerogative, what prerogative more extreme than to be able to adjourn assemblies and councils called by the supreme authorities, the highest magistrates, or to annul their enactments if they have already been held? And what more important than that business in course should be postponed if a single augur cries, *Alio die!*?"

of reasoning. Non-logical actions originate chiefly in definite psychic states, sentiments, subconscious feelings, and the like. It is the province of psychology to investigate such psychic states. Here we start with them as data of fact, without going beyond that.

162. Thinking of animals, let us assume that the conduct *B* (I) in Figure 2, which is all we are in a position to observe, is connected with a hypothetical psychic state *A* (I). In human beings that psychic state is revealed not through the conduct *B* (II) alone, but also through expressions of sentiments, *C*, which often develop moral, religious, and other similar theories. The very marked tendency in human beings to transform non-logical into logical conduct leads them to imagine that *B* is an effect of the cause *C*. So a direct relationship, *CB*, is assumed, instead of the indirect relationship arising through the two relations *AB*, *AC*. Sometimes the relation *CB* in fact obtains, but not as often as people think. The same sentiment that restrains people from performing an act *B* (relation *AB*) prompts them to devise a theory *C* (relation *AC*). A man, for example, has a horror of murder, *B*, and he will not commit murder; but he will say that the gods punish murderers, and that constitutes a theory, *C*.

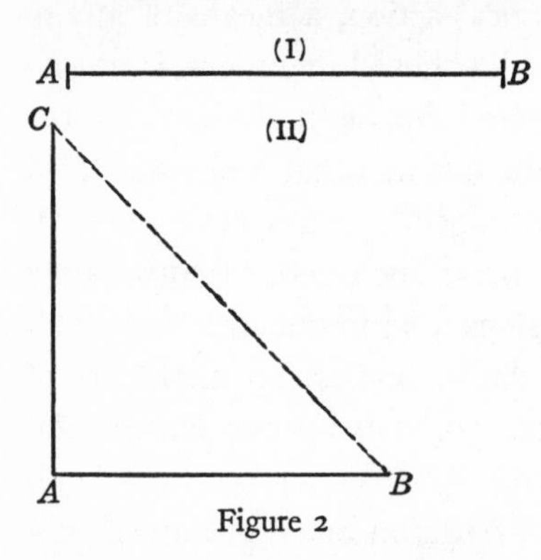

Figure 2

163. We are thinking not only of qualitative relations (§ 144[1]), but of quantitative also. Let us assume, for a moment, that a given force impelling a man to perform an act *B* has an index equivalent to 10 and that the man either performs or refrains from performing the act *B* according as the forces tending to restrain him have an index greater or smaller than 10. We shall then get the following alternatives:

Case 1. The restraining force of the association *AB* has an index greater than 10. In that situation it is strong enough to keep the man from performing the act. The association *CB,* if it exists, is superfluous.

Case 2. The restraining force of the association *CB,* if it exists, has an index larger than 10. In such a case, it is strong enough to prevent the act *B,* even if the force *AB* is equivalent to zero.

Case 3. The force resulting from the association *AB* has, let us say, an index equal to 4; and the force resulting from the association *CB* an index equal to 7. The sum of the indices is 11. The act, therefore, will not be performed. The force resulting from the association *AB* has an index equal to 2, the other retaining its index 7. The sum is 9; the act will be performed.

Suppose the association *AB* represents a person's aversion to performing the act *B*. *AC* represents the theory that the gods punish persons who commit the act *B*. Some people will abstain from doing *B* out of mere aversion to it (Case 1). Others refrain from it only because they fear the punishment of the gods (Case 2). Others still will forbear for both reasons (Case 3).

164. The following propositions are therefore false, because too absolute: "A natural disposition to do good is sufficient to restrain human beings from doing wrong." "Threat of eternal punishment is sufficient to restrain men from doing wrong." "Morality is independent of religion." "Morality is necessarily dependent on religion."

Suppose we say that *C* is a penalty threatened by law. The same sentiment that prompts people to establish the sanction restrains them from committing *B*. Some refrain from *B* because of their aversion to it; others in fear of the penalty *C;* still others for both reasons.

165. The relationships between *A, B, C* that we have just considered are fundamental, but they are far from being the only ones. First of all, the existence of the theory *C* reacts upon the psychic state *A* and in many many cases tends to re-enforce it. The theory consequently influences *B,* following the line *CAB*. On the other hand, the check *B,* which keeps people from doing certain things, reacts upon the psychic state *A* and consequently upon the theory *C*, following the line *BAC*. Then again the influence of *C* upon *B* influences *A* and so is carried back upon *C*. Suppose, for instance, a penalty *C* is considered too severe for a crime *B*. The infliction of such a penalty (*CB*) modifies the psychic state *A*, and as a consequence of the change, the penalty *C* is superseded by another more mild.

Change in a psychic state is first disclosed by an increase in certain crimes *B*. The increase in crime modifies the psychic state *A*, and the modification is translated into terms of a change in *C*.

Up to a certain point, the rites of worship in a religion may be comparable to the conduct *B*, its theology to the theory *C*. The two things both emanate from a certain psychic state *A*.

166. Let us consider certain conduct *D* (Figure 3), depending upon that psychic state, *A*. The rites of worship, *B*, do not influence *D* directly, but influence *A* and consequently *D*. In the same way they influence *C* and, *vice versa*, *C* influences *B*. There can in addition be a direct influence *CD*. The influence of the theology *C* upon *A* is usually rather weak, and consequently its influence upon *D* is also feeble, since the influence *CD* is itself usually slight. In general, then, we go very far astray in assuming that a theology, *C*, is the motive of the conduct, *D*. The proposition so often met with, "This or that people acts as it does because of a certain belief," is rarely true; in fact, it is almost always erroneous. The inverse proposition, "People believe as they do because of this or that conduct," as a rule contains a larger amount of truth; but it is too absolute, and has its modicum of error. Beliefs and conduct are not, to be sure, independent; but their correlation lies in their being, as it were, two branches of one same tree (§ 267).[1]

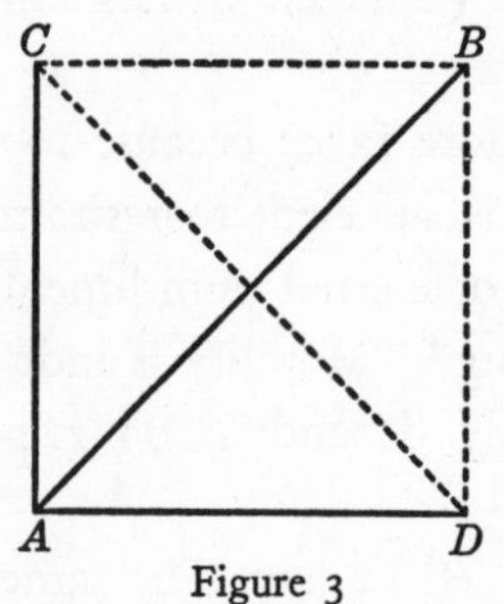

Figure 3

167. Before the invasion of Italy by the gods of Greece, the ancient Roman religion did not have a theology, *C*: it was no more than a

166 [1] This theme will be amply developed in Chapter XI.

cult, *B*. But the cult *B,* reacting upon *A,* exerted a powerful influence on the conduct, *D,* of the Roman people. Nor is that the whole story. The direct relation, *BD,* when it existed, looks to us moderns manifestly absurd. But the relation *BAD* may often have been very reasonable and very beneficial to the Roman people. Any direct influence of a theology, *C,* upon *D* is in general weaker even than its influence upon *A*. It is therefore a serious mistake to measure the social value of a religion strictly by the logical or rational value of its theology (§ 14). Certainly, if the theology becomes absurd to the point of seriously affecting *A,* it will for the same reason seriously affect *D*. But that rarely occurs. Only when the psychic state *A* has changed do people notice certain absurdities that previously had escaped them altogether.

These considerations apply to theories of all kinds.[1] For example, *C* is the theory of free trade; *D,* the concrete adoption of free trade by a country; *A,* a psychic state that is in great part the product of individual interests, economic, political, and social, and of the circumstances under which people live. Direct relations between *C* and *D* are generally very tenuous. To work upon *C* in order to modify *D* leads to insignificant results. But any modification in *A* may react upon *C* and upon *D*. *D* and *C* will be seen to change simultaneously, and a superficial observer may think that *D* has changed because *C* has changed, whereas closer examination will reveal that *D* and *C* are not directly correlated, but depend both upon a common cause, *A*.

168. Theoretical discussions, *C,* are not, therefore, very serviceable directly for modifying *D;* indirectly they may be effective for modifying *A*. But to attain that objective, appeal must be made to sentiments rather than to logic and the results of experience. The situation may be stated, inexactly to be sure, because too absolutely, but nevertheless strikingly, by saying that in order to influence people thought has to be transformed into sentiment.

In the case of England, the continuous practice of free trade *B* (Figure 3) over a long period of years has in our day reacted upon

167 [1] Pareto, *Manuel,* pp. 134-35, 520 (§ 62).

the psychic state *A* (interests, etc.) and intensified it, so increasing obstacles in the way of introducing protection. The theory of free trade, *C,* is in no way responsible for that. However, other facts, such as growing needs on the part of the Exchequer, are nowadays tending to modify *A* in their turn; and such modifications may serve to change *B* and so bring protection about. Meantime modifications in *C* will be observable and new theories favourable to protection will come into vogue.

A theory, *C,* has logical consequences. A certain number of them are to be found present in *B*. Others are absent. That would not be the case if *B* were the direct consequence of *C,* for if it were, all the logical implications of *C* would appear in *B* without exception. But *C* and *B* are simply consequences of a certain psychic state, *A*. There is nothing therefore to require perfect logical correspondence between them. We shall always be on the wrong road, accordingly, when we imagine that we can infer *B* from *C* by establishing that correspondence logically. We are obliged, rather, to start with *C* and determine *A,* and then find a way to infer *B* from *A*. In doing that very serious difficulties are encountered; and unfortunately they have to be overcome before we can hope to attain scientific knowledge of social phenomena.

169. We have no direct knowledge of *A*. What we know is certain manifestations of *A,* such as *C* and *B;* and we have to get back from them to *A*. The difficulties are increased by the fact that though *B* is susceptible of exact observation, *C* is almost always stated in obscure terms altogether devoid of exactness.

170. The theory we have been thinking of is a popular theory, or at least, a theory held by large numbers of people. The case where *C* is a theory framed by scientists is in some respects similar, yet in other respects different.

Unless the theory *C* is coldly scientific, *C* is affected by the psychic state of the scientists who frame it. If they belong to the group that has been performing the acts, *B,* their psychic state has—save in the very rare case of an individual not given to following the beaten path—something in common with the psychic state of the members of the group; and consequently *A* still influences *C*. That is all the case can have in common with the preceding case. If scientists are dealing with the conduct of people belonging to groups entirely different from their own—say with some foreign country, or some very different civilization, or with historical matters going back to a remote past—their psychic state, *A′* (Figure 4), is not identical with *A*. It may differ now more, now less, or even in some particular case be altogether different. Now it is the psychic state that influences *C*. So *A* may affect *C* very little, if at all. If we ignore all influences from *A* or *A′*, we get interpretations of the facts, *B*, that are purely theoretical. If *C* is a strict and exact principle and is applied to *B* with faultless logic and without ambiguities of any kind, we get scientific interpretations.

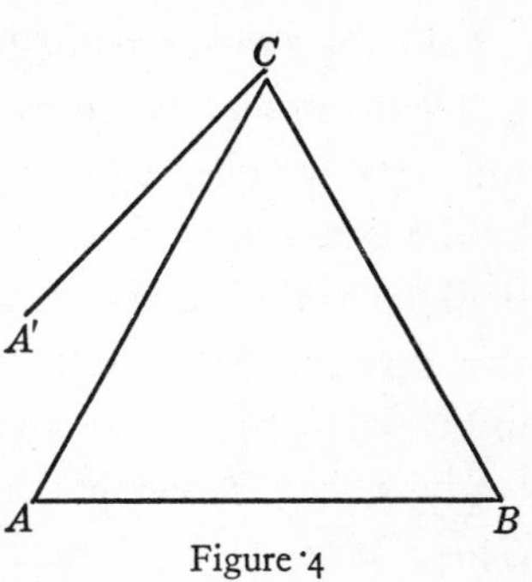

Figure 4

171. But the class of theories that we are here examining includes others. *C* may be an uncertain principle, lacking in exactness, and sometimes even a principle of the experimental type. Furthermore, it may be applied to *B* with illogical reasonings, arguments by analogy, appeals to sentiment, nebulous irrelevancies. In such cases we get theories of little or no logico-experimental value, though they may have a great social value (§ 14). Such theories are very numerous, and we shall find them occupying much of our attention.[1]

172. Let us go back to the situation in Figure 3, and to get better acquainted with that subject, which is far from being an easy one to master, let us put abstractions aside and examine a concrete case. In that way we shall be led to follow certain inductions which arise spontaneously from the exposition of facts. Then we can go back to the general case and continue the study of which we have just sketched the initial outlines.

171 [1] Here we come by induction to many points beyond which we choose not to go for the present. We shall resume our advance from them in chapters to follow, and there devote ourselves specially to many things that are merely signboarded here.

There is a very important psychic state that establishes and maintains certain relationships between sensations, or facts, by means of other sensations, *P, Q, R*. . . . Such sensations may be successive, and that, probably, is one of the ways in which instinct manifests itself in animals. On the other hand they may be simultaneous, or at least be considered such; and their union constitutes one of the chief forces in the social equilibrium.

Let us not give a name to that psychic state, in order, if possible, to avoid any temptation to derive the significance of the thing from the name we give it (§ 119). Let us continue to designate it simply by the letter *A*, as we have done for a psychic state in general. We shall have to think of the state not only as static, but also as dynamic. It is very important to know how the fundamental element in the institutions of a people changes. *Case 1.* It may change but reluctantly, slowly, showing a marked tendency to keep itself the same. *Case* 2. It may change readily, and to very considerable extents, but in different ways, as for instance: *Case 2α*. The form may change as readily as the substance—for a new substance, new forms. The sensations *P, Q, R* . . . may be easily disjoined, whether because the force *X* that unites them is weak, or because, though strong, it succumbs to a still stronger counter-force. *Case 2β*. Substance changes more readily than forms—for a new substance, the old forms! The sensations *P, Q, R* . . . are disjoined with difficulty, whether because the force *X* that unites them is the stronger, or because, though weak, it does not meet any considerable counter-force.

The sensations *P, Q, R* . . . may originate in certain things and later on appear to the individual as abstractions of those things, such as principles, maxims, precepts, and the like. They constitute an aggregate, a group. The permanence of that aggregate, that group, will be the subject of long and important investigations on our part.[1]

173. A superficial observer might confuse the Case 2β with Case

172 [1] It will develop in Chapter VI, when induction has carried us some distance ahead, and we are in a position to replace it with deduction. For the present it would be premature to deal with the problem as it deserves.

1 (§ 172). But in reality they differ radically. Peoples called conservative may be such now only with respect to forms (Case 2β), now only with respect to substance (Case 1). Peoples called formalist may now preserve both forms and substance (Case 1), now only forms (Case 2β). Peoples commonly said to have "fossilized in a certain state" correspond to Case 1.

174. When the unifying force, *X*, is quite considerable, and the force Y—the trend toward innovation—is very weak or non-existent, we get the phenomena of instinct in animals, and something like the situation in Sparta, a state crystallized in its institutions. When *X* is strong, but *Y* equally strong, and innovations are wrought upon substance with due regard to forms, we get a situation like that in ancient Rome—the effort is to change institutions, but disturbing the associations *P, Q, R . . .* as little as possible. That can be done by allowing the relations *P, Q, R . . .* to subsist in form. From that point of view, the Roman people may be called formalist at a certain period in its history, and the same may hold for the English. The aversion of those two peoples to disturbing the formal relations *P, Q, R . . .* may even tempt one to call them conservative. But if we fix our attention on substance, we see that they do not preserve but transform it. Among the ancient Athenians and the modern French, *X* is relatively feeble. It is difficult to assert that Y was more vigorous among the Athenians than among the Romans, more vigorous among the French than among the English from the seventeenth to the nineteenth century. If the effects in question manifest themselves in different ways, the difference lies in the strength of *X* rather than in the strength of *Y*.

Let us assume that in the case of two peoples Y is identical in both and *X* different in both. To bring about innovations, the people among whom *X* is feeble wipes out the relations *P, Q, R . . .* and replaces them with other relations. The people among whom *X* is strong allows those relations to subsist as far as possible and modifies the significance of *P, Q, R. . . .* Furthermore, there will be fewer "relics from the past" in the first people than in the second.

Since X is feeble, there is nothing to hinder abolition of the relations P, Q, R . . . now considered useless; but when X is strong, those relations will be preserved even if they are considered useless.

These inductions are obtainable by observing manifestations of the psychic state A. As regards Rome we have facts in abundance—to begin with, religion. There is now no doubt: (1) that the earliest Romans had no mythology, or at best an exceedingly meagre one; (2) that the classical mythology of the Romans was nothing but a Greek form given to the Roman gods, if not an actual naturalization of foreign deities. Ancient Roman religion consisted essentially of an association of certain religious practices with the conduct of life—it was the perfect type of the P, Q, R . . . associations. Cicero could well say [1] that "the whole religion of the Roman people comes down to cult and auspices (§ 361), with a supplement of prophecies originating in portents and prodigies as interpreted by the Sibyl and the haruspices."

175. Even in our day numerous and most variegated types of the associations P, Q, R . . . are observable. In his *Au pays des Veddas*, pp. 159-62, Deschamps says that in Ceylon "the astrologer plays a part in every act of the native's life. Nothing could be undertaken without his counsel; and . . . I have often seen myself refused the simplest favours because the astrologer had not been consulted as to the day and hour auspicious for granting them." When a piece of ground is to be cleared or brought under cultivation, the astrologer is first consulted, receiving offerings of betel leaves and betel nuts.[1] "If the forecast is favourable, gifts of the leaves and nuts are repeated on a specified day, and an 'auspicious hour' (*nàkata*) is chosen for cutting the first trees and bushes. On the appointed day, the cultivators of the plot selected partake of a repast of cakes, and rice and milk, prepared for the occasion. Then they go forth, their faces

174 [1] *De natura deorum*, III, 2, 5.

175 [1] Bell, *Superstitious Ceremonies Connected with the Cultivation of Alvi or Hill Paddy*, quoted by Deschamps, *loc. cit.* [Paddy is rice. I fail to find any record of just this article by H. C. P. Bell, who was secretary of the Royal Society of Ceylon, and wrote extensively on the rites of the rice cultivators in that colony during the '80's.—A. L.]

turned in the direction designated as propitious by the astrologer. If a lizard chirps at the moment of their departure or if they encounter along the way something of evil omen—a person carrying dead wood or dangerous weapons, a 'rat-snake' crossing the path, a woodpecker—they give up the idea of clearing that particular piece of land, or, more likely, the idea of visiting it that day, picking another *nàkata* and starting over again. On the other hand, if good omens—a milch cow, a woman nursing a child—are encountered, they proceed cheerily and in all confidence. Once on the ground, an auspicious moment is awaited, then the trees and brush are set on fire. Two or three weeks are allowed for the ground to cool, then another *nàkata* is set for the final clearing of the land. . . . On a *nàkata* designated by the same astrologer, a man sows a first handful of rice as a prelude." Birds and also rain may play havoc with the seeding. "To avert such mishaps a *kéma* or magic brew called *navanilla* (nine-herbs?) is made ready. . . . If the *kéma* proves ineffectual, a special kind of oil is distilled for another charm. . . . At weeding-time a *nàkata* is sought of the same fortune-teller. When the rice-blossoms have faded the ceremony of sprinkling with five kinds of milk takes place." They go on in the same way for each of the successive operations till the rice is finally harvested and barned.[2]

176. Similar practices are observable to greater or lesser extents in the primitive periods of all peoples.[1] Differences are quantitative not

175 [2] In Greece and Rome also conduct was largely governed by oracles, presages, and the like. In course of time many such practices became purely formal. Cicero, *De divinatione,* I, 16, 28: "In olden times hardly any business of importance, even of a private nature, was transacted without consulting omens, as witness the 'nuptial auspices' even of our day, which have lost their old substance and preserve just the name (*re omissa nomen tantum tenent*). Nowadays auspices on important occasions are obtained, though somewhat less generally than was once the case, by inspections of entrails. In the old days they were commonly sought of birds."

176 [1] They still endure among half-civilized peoples, such as the Chinese, and they have not disappeared even in our western countries. Matignon, *Superstition, crime et misère en Chine,* pp. 4-8, 18-19: "Superstition, as I am about to describe it, has nothing to do with religion." Going on, Matignon explains the mysterious entity that the Chinese call *fong-choué,* literally, "wind-and-water": "One might in a general way regard it as a sort of topographical superstition. For the Chinese, any given point in the Middle Empire is a centre of forces, of spiritual influences, as to the nature of which they have very vague and ill-defined ideas, and which no one

qualitative. Preller[2] observes that in Rome parallel with the world of the gods was a family of spirits and genii: "Everything that happened in nature, everything that was done by human beings from birth to death, all the vicissitudes of human life and activity, all mutual relationships between citizens, all enterprises . . . were under the jurisdiction of these little gods. Indeed they owe their existence to nothing but those thousands of social relationships with which they are to be identified."[3] Originally they were mere associations of ideas, such as we find in fetishism. They constituted groups, and the groups were called divinities or something else of

understands, but which are all the more respected and feared on that account. [Matignon then tries to explain the facts by the beliefs. He does not succeed, because the facts are not consequences of the beliefs (logical actions), but the beliefs consequences of the facts (non-logical actions)]. The *fong-choué,* accordingly, seems to be something vague, mysterious, obscure, difficult, not to say impossible, of interpretation [As was the case with divination in Greece and Rome]. And nevertheless, in Chinese eyes, that body of fiction becomes science. [Is, in other words, a logical veneer sprinkled lavishly over their non-logical conduct. As regards funerals:] the astrologer must have fixed on a propitious day and especially by long and sagacious investigation, have gone into all aspects of the engrossing problem of the *fong-choué*. . . . In building a house, the Chinaman must not only consider the *fong-choué* of his neighbours, but also of his own house. A millstone, a well, the junction of two walls or two streets, must not be on a line with the main entrance. . . . That is not all. The *fong-choué* may be satisfied with the site and alignment of a building; but how about the use to which it is to be put? *X* builds a house for a rice-shop. But it develops that the *fong-choué* was inclined to favour a tea-shop. There is no further doubt. *X* and his rice business will soon be in the hands of the receiver. . . . The *fong-choué* superstition is exceedingly tenacious [Merely because it is an expression of the psychic state *A* of the Chinese, and nothing else]. It is the one that holds out longest against Christianity. And then again, what Chinaman, even though considered a good Christian, has altogether abandoned his *fong-choué?*" The situation is a general one. See §§ 1002 f.

176 [2] *Römische Mythologie,* p. 66.

176 [3] Marquardt, *Römische Staatsverwaltung: Sacralwesen,* pp. 12-19, gives a list of these gods. It must be very incomplete, for we may reasonably assume that large numbers of names have failed to come down to us. For some of the gods in question see our § 1339. Just a sample here, pp. 12-13: "Potina and Educa, who teach the child to eat and drink; Cuba, who protects the child while it is being carried from cradle to bed; Ossipago, 'who hardens and strengthens the bones of little children'; Carna, who strengthens the muscles; Levana, 'who lifts the child from the floor'; Statanus, Statilinus, and the goddess Statina, who teach the child to stand upright; Abeona and Adeona, who hold him up when he first tries to walk; Farimus and Fabulinus, who help him to talk." Marquardt goes on to list the divinities protecting adolescence, matrimony, and other various circumstances of life, and he adds, p. 15: "The business of the gods just listed was to protect persons;

the sort. Pliny soundly remarks that the god population was larger than the population of men.[4] When the tendency to give a coating of logic to non-logical conduct developed, people tried to explain why certain acts were associated with certain other acts. It was then that the rites of the cult were referred to great numbers of gods, or taken as manifestations of a worship of natural forces or abstractions. In reality we have the same situation here as in § 175. The psychic state of the Romans *A* (Figure 2) gave rise, through certain associations of ideas and acts, to the rites *B*. Later on, or even simultaneously in some instances, the same psychic state expressed itself through the worship *C* of abstractions, natural forces, attributes of certain divinities, and so on. Then, from the simultaneous existence of *B* and *C* came the inference, in most cases mistaken, that *B* was a consequence of *C*.

but there was a whole series of other gods who watched over the manifold activities of men and the scenes of such activities." Marquardt is mistaken in asserting, p. 18, that "originally at least, as Ambrosch has shown [*Ueber die Religionsbücher der Römer, rem.* 121], the thousands of names registered in the *indigitamenta* [ritual catalogues and calendars] were mere designations for the various functions (*potestates*) of relatively few divinities." That is the old abstraction idea. The proofs adduced for it are inadequate. They are stated by Marquardt as follows, pp. 18-19: "1. *Indigitare* meant to offer a prayer to one or more divinities, not in general terms but with specific reference to the divine capacities of which help was asked. The god was addressed several times, each time one attribute or another being added to his name." The various attributes mentioned corresponded at times to a number of gods who had been fused into a single personality. At other times they may have been different aspects of the same god. But that does not prove that Potina, Educa, Cuba, and so on, were abstract capacities of one same divine person. "2. In the second place, pontifical law forbade offering one victim to two gods at the same time." M. Brissaud, Marquardt's French translator, himself shows that that argument is baseless, *Le culte chez les Romains,* Vol. I, p. 24: "There has been no doubt either that some of the names listed were surnames of well-known gods." The fact that some gods had surnames does not prove that all the names catalogued in the *indigitamenta* were surnames, and much less, as Marquardt suggests in a note, p. 18, that they "represented the various attributes of divine Providence." Otherwise one would have to conclude that the various surnames of the Roman Emperors represented various attributes of a single personality.

176 [4] *Historia naturalis,* II, 5, 3 (7) (Bostock-Riley, Vol. I, p. 21): "Wherefore the population of celestials can be seen to be greater than the population of mortals, since individuals make gods for themselves, each one his own (*totidem*), adopting Junos and genii; and peoples [abroad] take certain animals as gods, and even obscene things and things that it is not the part of decency to mention, swearing by smelly onions, garlics, and the like."

177. The view that acts of cult are consequences of a worship of abstractions, whether considered as "natural forces" or otherwise, is the least acceptable of all and must be absolutely rejected (§§ 158, 996).[1] Proofs without end go to show that human beings in general proceed from the concrete to the abstract, and not from the abstract to the concrete. The capacity for abstraction develops with civilization; it is very rudimentary among primitive peoples. Theories that assume it as fully developed in the early stages of human society fall under grave suspicion of error. The ancient Romans, a people still uncivilized, could not have had a very highly developed capacity for abstraction, as would have been necessary if they were to perceive in every concrete fact, sometimes an altogether insignificant fact, a manifestation of some natural power.

Had such a capacity for abstraction existed, it would have left some trace in language. In the beginning, probably, the Greeks did not possess it in any higher degree than the Romans. But they soon acquired it and brought it to remarkable development; and abstraction has left a very definite imprint on their language. Using the article, they are able to turn an adjective, a participle, a whole sentence, into a substantive. The Latins had no article. They could not have availed themselves of that device. But they would certainly have found some other had they felt the need of doing so. On the contrary, it is well known that the capacity for using adjectives substantively is more limited in Latin than in Greek or even in French.[2]

177 [1] We cannot accept what Marquardt says, *Op. cit.*, pp. 6-7: "The gods of the Romans were mere abstractions. In them they worshipped those forces of nature to which the human being feels himself at all times subject, but which he can manage to control by scrupulous observance of the altogether external prescriptions laid down by the state for honouring the gods." The terms have to be inverted. To assure success in their undertakings the Romans meticulously observed certain rules which, spontaneous at first, eventually came to be used by the state. When, in course of time, people wondered how the rules arose, they imagined they saw forces of nature worshipped in them. Marquardt himself, for that matter, stresses the preponderant importance of the material acts and the scant importance of the abstractions, p. 7: "Religious practice required material paraphernalia of the simplest sort; but the rites themselves bristled with difficulties and complications. The slightest irregularity in a ceremony deprived it of all effectiveness."

177 [2] Antoine, *Syntaxe de la langue latine*, p. 125: "The capacity for using adjectives substantively is much more restricted in Latin than in Greek and even than

Probably there is some exaggeration in what St. Augustine says as to the multitude of Roman "gods"; but making all due allowances for overstatement, there are still plenty left who seem to have been created for the sole purpose of accounting logically for the association of certain acts with certain other acts.[3]

in French. Latin avoids the substantive even when it is available and tends to replace it with a paraphrase; for example, 'hearers': *animi eorum qui audiunt;* instead of *auditorum.* For the adjective to be turned into a substantive, it must result distinctly from the arrangement of the words in a sentence and from the sentence as a whole that the adjective designates not the quality, but a definite person or thing possessing the quality." That is the exact opposite of the process which is alleged to have taken place in the little gods considered as qualifying abstractions. Riemann-Goelzer, *Grammaire comparée du grec et du latin,* p. 741, note: "In the beginning the adjective was not distinct from the substantive . . . the substantive derived from the adjective: before coming to substance, people first saw an object only in its modes, in its apparent and striking attributes: a ζῷον was a 'living thing,' an *animal* was a 'thing endowed with life.' Only at a comparatively late date, in an advanced state of civilization when the mind had become capable of conceiving of the object independently of its attributes, were substantives distinguished from adjectives." We cannot, therefore, assume the contrary: namely, that abstract beings, such as Providence, were first conceived, and that the modes whereby they manifested themselves were imagined later. Observation shows that people went from modes to beings—beings most often imaginary.

177 [3] *De civitate Dei,* VI, 9: "If a man assigned two nurses to a child, the one just for giving him his food, the other his drink, the way two goddesses Educa and Potina were appointed to those offices, would we not say that he was mad and that in his own house he was acting like a clown? Some maintain that Liber is derived from *liberare: quod mares in coëundo per eius beneficium emissis seminibus liberentur;* and that Libera, who they also say is Venus, performs the same service for women: *quod et ipsas perhibeant semina emittere,* and therefore the same male organ is set up in the temples to Liber, and the female likewise to Libera. . . . When the male unites with the female, the god Jugatinus presides. Be it so. But the bride has to be taken to the groom's house, and that is the business of the god Domiducus. There is the god Domitius to see that she stays there; and the goddess Maturna that she abide with her husband. What more is needed? Mercy, I pray, on decency! Let concupiscence of flesh and blood do the rest under the secret tutelage of modesty! Why crowd the bedchamber with a throng of gods, when even the 'best men' [paranymphs] have seen fit to withdraw? And yet it is so filled not that the thought of their presence may inspire higher regard for chastity, but to the end that through their concert the maiden, afraid as befits the weakness of her sex of what is in store, may be deprived of her maidenhood without mishap. And that is why the goddess Verginensis is there, and the father-god Subigo, and the mother-goddess Prema, and the goddess Pertunda, and Venus, and Priapus. And why all that? If the groom needed the help of the gods in everything he did, would not one of the gods or one of the goddesses be enough? Was not Venus enough all by herself? She was already there, summoned, they say, because without her influence a

St. Augustine, *loc. cit.,* says that Varro, speaking of the conception of man, gives a list of the gods. He begins with Janus; and, reviewing in succession all the divinities that take care of a man, step by step, down to his extreme old age, he closes with the goddess Nenia, who is naught but the mournful litany chanted at funerals of the aged. He enumerates furthermore divinities who were not concerned with a man's person directly, but rather with the things he uses, such as food, clothing, and the like.

178. Gaston Boissier says in this connexion:[1] "What first strikes one is the little life there is in these gods. No one has gone to the trouble of making legends about them. They have no history. All that is known of them is that they have to be worshipped at a given moment and that, at that time, they can be of use. The moment gone, they are forgotten. They do not have real names. The names they are given do not designate them in themselves, but merely the functions which they fulfil."

The facts are exact, the statement of them slightly erroneous, because Boissier is considering them from the standpoint of logical conduct. Not only did the gods in question have very little life—they had none at all. Once upon a time they were mere associations of acts and ideas. Only at a date relatively recent did they get to be gods (§ 995). "All that is known of them" is the little that need be known for such associations of acts and ideas. When it is said that they have

maid cannot cease to be a maid. . . . And, forsooth, if the goddess Verginensis is there that the maid's girdle be loosed; if the god Subigo is there *ut viro subigatur;* if the goddess Prema is there, *ut subacta ne se commoveat comprimatur*—what, pray, is the goddess Pertunda doing there? Shame on her! Out with her! Let the groom do something himself, I say! *Valde inhonestum est ut quod vocatur illa* (the thing that takes the name from her) *impleat quisquam nisi ille!* But that is perhaps tolerated because she is said to be a goddess not a god. For if the deity were believed a male and called Pertundus, out of respect for his bride the groom would cry for help against him in louder voice than woman in childbirth against Sylvanus. *Sed quid hoc dicam, cum ibi sit et Priapus nimius masculus, super cuius immanissimum et turpissimum fascinum sedere nova nupta iubebatur more honestissimo et religiosissimo matronarum?"* St. Augustine is right, with plenty to spare, if such acts are to be judged from the logical standpoint; but he does not observe that they were originally non-logical acts, mechanical formalities, which eventually found their place among ceremonies of divine worship.

178 [1] *La religion romaine,* Vol. I, p. 5.

to be "worshipped" at certain moments, a new name is being given to an old concept. One might better say that they were "invoked"; or better yet, that certain words were brought into play. When a person pronounces the number 2 (§ 182) to keep a scorpion from stinging, will anybody claim that he is worshipping the number 2 or invoking it? Are we to be surprised that the number 2 has no legend, no history?

179. In the *Odyssey,* X, vv. 304-05, Hermes gives Ulysses a plant to protect him from the enchantments of Circe—"black at the root, like milk in the flower. The gods call it moly. Difficult it is for mortals to tear from the ground, but the gods can do all things."

Here we have a non-logical action of the pure type. There can be no question of an operation in magic whereby a god is constrained to act. To the contrary, a god gives the plant to a mortal. No reason is adduced to explain the working of the plant. Now let us imagine that we were dealing not with a poetic fiction but with a real plant used for a real purpose. An association of ideas would arise between the plant and Hermes, and no end of logical explanations would be devised for it. The plant would be regarded as a means for constraining Hermes to action—and that really would be magic—or as a means of invoking Hermes, or as a form of Hermes or one of his names, or as a means of paying homage to "forces of nature." Homer designates the plant by the words *φάρμακον ἐσθλόν*, which might be translated "healing remedy." Is it not evident, one might argue, that there is a resort to natural forces to counteract the pernicious effects of a poison? And so on to all the rank tanglewood of notions that might be read into Homer's story! [1]

179 [1] The idea is not altogether hypothetical. That blessed weed has a whole literature all its own! Eustathius, *Commentarii ad Homeri Odysseam,* Vol. I, p. 381, offers us our choice between two interpretations. The one is mythological. The giant Pikolous, in flight after his battle with Zeus, landed on Circe's island and attacked her. The Sun rushed to the rescue of his daughter and slew the giant. From the blood that was spilled on the ground there sprouted a plant which was named *μῶλυ* after the terrible fight (*μῶλος*) the giant had offered. The blossom is milk-white because of the bright sun; and the root black because the giant's blood was black, or because of Circe's terror. Hephestion tells more or less the same story.

If that interpretation is not to your liking, Eustathius has another ready—alle-

180. The human being has such a weakness for adding logical developments to non-logical behaviour that anything can serve as an excuse for him to turn to that favourite occupation. Associations of ideas and acts were probably as abundant at one time in Greece as they were in Rome; but in Greece most of them disappeared, and sooner than was the case in Rome. Greek anthropomorphism transformed simple associations of ideas and acts into attributes of gods.

gorical, this time [*Op. cit., loc. cit.*]: *μῶλυ* is education; the root is black, to symbolize ignorance; the flowers milk-white, to symbolize the splendours of knowledge. The plant is difficult to pull up because learning is an arduous achievement. Now all we need is that some pupil of Max Müller shall bob up and tell us that that plant with the black root and the white blossoms, which mortals are unable to pull up, and which has beneficent effects, is the Sun, which rises from the darkness of the night, is brilliantly luminous, cannot be disturbed by any human act, and gives life to the earth.

Pliny, *Historia naturalis,* XXV, 8 (4) (Bostock-Riley, Vol. V, pp. 87-88): "Most celebrated of plants, according to Homer, is the one that he believes was named moly [*Allium magicum,* "witch-garlic," according to Littré, in the notes to his translation of Pliny] by the gods themselves, the discovery of which he credits to Mercury and which he represents as efficacious against deadly poisons [Bostock-Riley: "Against the most potent spells of sorcery"]. It is said that a plant of that name still grows today about Lake Pheneus and at Cyllene in Arcady. It is like the plant mentioned by Homer. It has a round black root, about the size of an onion, with leaves like the squill. It is hard to pull up. [Bostock-Riley: "There is no difficulty experienced in taking it up"]. Greek writers say its blossom is yellow, but Homer describes it as pure white. I once met a physician whose hobby was botany, and he told me that the 'moly' also grew in Italy; and some few days later he brought me a specimen from Campania that he had pulled up with great difficulty from a rocky soil. The root was thirty feet long; and that was not the whole of it, for it had broken off." Theophrastus, *Historia plantarum,* IX, 15, 7 (Hort, Vol. II, pp. 294-95): "The *moly* is found at Pheneus and in the Cyllene region. They also say that it is like the plant Homer mentions. It has a round root, like an onion. The leaves are like the squill. It is used as an antidote and in magic rites. It is not as hard to pull up as Homer says." All of these writers take Homer's *μῶλυ* for a real plant. [Littré's note identifying the moly as "witch-garlic" is not his own but derives from Antoine Laurent Fée, biographer of Linnaeus, who edited Pliny's botany for the French translation of Pliny that was published in 1826 by François Étienne Ajasson de Grandsagne.—A. L.]

In the Middle Ages the mandrake enjoyed a very considerable prestige. Mercury has vanished, but Satan is on hand to replace him. O'Reilly, *Les deux procès de condamnation de Jeanne d'Arc,* Vol. II, pp. 164-65: "Jeanne was in the habit of carrying a mandrake on her person, hoping thereby to procure fortune and riches in this world. She believed, in fact, that the mandrake had the virtue of bringing good fortune. *Q.* What have you to say [about the charge] as to the mandrake? *A.* That is false, absolutely. (Abstract of examinations relative to Charge 7): Thurs-

Says Boissier:[1] "Other countries no doubt felt the need of putting the principal acts of life under divine protection, but ordinarily for such purposes gods well known, powerful, tried and tested of long experience, were chosen, that there might be no doubt as to their efficacy. In Greece the great Athena or the wise Hermes was called upon that a child might grow up competent and wise. In Rome there was a preference for special gods, created for particular purposes and used for no others." The facts are exact, but the explanation is altogether wrong, and again because Boissier is working from the standpoint of logical conduct. His explanation is like an explanation one might make of the declensions in Latin grammar: "Other countries no doubt felt the need of distinguishing the functions of substantive and adjective in a sentence, but ordinarily they chose prepositions for that purpose." No, peoples did not choose their gods, any more than they chose the grammatical forms of their languages. The Athenians never came to any decision in the matter of placing their children under the protection of Hermes and Athena, any more than the Romans after mature reflection chose Vaticanus, Fabulinus, Educa, and Potina for that purpose.

181. It may be that what we see in Greece is merely a stage, somewhat more advanced than the one we find in Rome, in the evolution from the concrete to the abstract, from the non-logical to the logical. It may also be that the evolution was different in the two countries. That point we cannot determine with certainty for lack of documents. In any event—and that is the important thing for the study in which we are engaged—the stages of evolution in Greece and in Rome in historical times were different.

182. In virtue of a most interesting persistence of associations of ideas and acts, words seem to possess some mysterious power over

day, March 1. Questioned as to what she did with her mandrake, she answered that she had never had one, that she had heard that there was one near her house, without having seen it. It was, she had been told, a dangerous and wicked thing to keep. She did not know what it might be used for. Questioned as to the place where the mandrake of which she had heard was, she answered that she had heard it was on the ground near a tree, but she did not know where. She had heard that it was under a walnut-tree."

180 [1] *La religion romaine*, Vol. I, p. 4.

things.[1] Even as late as the day of Pliny the Naturalist, one could still write:[2] "With regard to remedies derived from human beings there is a very important question that remains unsettled: Do magic words, charms, and incantations have any power? If so, it has to be ascribed to the human being. Individually, one by one, our wisest minds have no faith in such things; but in the mass, in their everyday lives, people believe in them unconsciously.[3] [Pliny is an excellent observer here, describing a non-logical action beautifully.] In truth it seems to do no good to sacrifice victims and impossible properly to consult the gods without chants of prayer.[4] The words that are used, moreover, are of different kinds, some serving for entreaty, others for averting evil, others for commendation.[5] We see that our supreme

182 [1] Here we come by induction upon a matter that will be studied deductively and at length in Chapter VI—and we shall meet it in other places also. Other similar cases, which we need not specify, will occur in this present chapter. Just here we are exploring the material before us, now in one direction, now in another. In chapters to follow we shall complete investigations that are merely labelled here for future reference.

182 [2] *Historia naturalis,* XXVIII, 2 (3) (Bostock-Riley, Vol. V, pp. 278-80). This quotation will be of use to us elsewhere. We transcribe it therefore somewhat fully. [Translations of this passage present wide differences. I note in brackets important variations between Pareto's version and that of Bostock-Riley.—A. L.]

182 [3] The Latin reads: *"In universum vero omnibus horis credit vita, nec sentit.* Dalechamps paraphrases (Leyden, 1669, Vol. III, p. 161): *Credit vulgi opinio valere verba nec certa cognitione et rerum sensu id persuasum habet."* Cicero too bars any rational process. *De divinatione,* I, 3, 3: "And the ancients, in my judgment, established such practices rather under admonition of experience than at the dictates of reason." *Cf.* § 296[3].

182 [4] The Latin reads: *"Quippe victimas caedi sine precatione non videtur referre nec deos rite consuli."* The difficulty lies in the verb *referre.* Gronov well paraphrases (Leyden, 1669, Vol. III, p. 798): *" 'Sine precatione non videtur referre [Id est, nihil iuvare putatur, nihil prodesse vulgo creditur] caedi victimas, nec videtur deos rite consuli.' Quo significat necessario preces adhibendas."* [Bostock-Riley follow Gronov: "It is the general belief that without a general form of prayer it would be useless to immolate a victim."—A. L.]

182 [5] Text: *"Praeterea alia sunt verba impetritis, alia depulsoriis, alia commentationis [commentationis* for *commendationis]."* *Impetritum* is a technical term of augury and designates a request made of the gods according to ritual. Cicero, *De divinatione,* II, 15, 35: "How comes it that a person desiring to ask an omen of the gods (*impetrire*) sacrifices a victim appropriate to his need (*rebus suis*)?" Valerius Maximus, *De dictis factisque memorabilibus,* I, 1, 1: "Our forefathers provided that fixed and solemn ceremonies should be entrusted (*explicari voluerunt*) to the learning of pontiffs, assurances of success (*bene gerendarum rerum auctoritates*)

magistrates pray with specified words. And in order that no word be omitted or uttered out of its proper place, a prompter accompanies from the ritual, another person repeats the words, another preserves 'silence,' and a flutist plays so that nothing else may be heard. The two following facts are deservedly memorable. Whenever a prayer has been interrupted by an invocation or been badly recited, forthwith, without hands being laid to the victim, the top of the liver, or else the heart, has been found either missing or double. Still extant, as a revered example, is the formula with which the Decii, father and son, uttered their vows,[6] and we have the prayer uttered by the Vestal Tuccia when, accused of incest, she carried water in a sieve, in the Roman year 609. A man and a woman from Greece, or from some other country with which we were at war, were once buried alive in the Forum Boarium, and such a thing has been seen even in our time. If one but read the sacred prayer that the head of the College of the Quindecemviri is wont to recite ["on such occasions" —Bostock-Riley], one will bear witness to the power of the prayer as demonstrated by the eight hundred and thirty years of our continued prosperity [Bostock-Riley: "by the experience of eight hundred"]. We believe in our day that with a certain prayer our Vestals can arrest the flight of fugitive slaves who have not yet crossed the boundaries of Rome. Once that is granted, once we concede that the gods answer certain prayers or allow themselves to be moved by such words, we have to grant all the rest."[7]

Going on, *loc. cit.,* 5(3), Pliny appeals to conscience, not to rea-

to the observation of augurs, prophecy to the books of the soothsayers of Apollo, and exorcisms of unfavourable omens (*portentorum depulsiones*) to the lore of the Etruscans. By ancient custom, divine influences are invoked, in case of a commendation through a prayer; when something is requested, through a vow; when a favour is to be paid for, by a thanksgiving (*gratulatione*); when information is sought either of entrails or of lots, through a petition (*impetrito,* that is, by an observation of omens); when a solemn rite is called for (*cum solemni ritu peragendum*) by a sacrifice, wherewith also the significance of portents and lightning bolts is carefully observed."

182 [6] Livy, *Ab urbe condita,* VIII, 9, 6-8; X, 28, 14-18.

182 [7] The Latin reads: "*Confitendum sit de tota coniectione.*" Gronov paraphrases (Leyden, 1669, Vol. III, p. 798): "*Perinde est ac si dixisset: de tota lite, de tota quaestione* (we have to surrender "on the whole issue")."

son, that is, he emphasizes, and very soundly, the non-logical character of the acts in question: "I would appeal, too, for confirmation on this subject, to the intimate experience of the individual [Bostock-Riley translation]. . . . Why do we wish each other a happy new year on the first day of each year? Why do we select men with propitious names to lead the victims in public sacrifices? . . . Why do we believe that odd numbers are more effective than others [8]—a thing [Bostock-Riley] that is particularly observed with reference to the critical days in fever. . . . Attalus [Philometor] avers that if one pronounces the number *duo* [9] at sight of a scorpion, the scorpion stops and does not sting." [10]

183. These actions, in which words act upon things, belong to

182 [8] See §§ 960 f. for just a titbit from the endless amount of nonsense connected with numbers. Note Pliny's effort to justify a non-logical fancy—the influence of a day on a fever—by logic.

182 [9] Such data are abundant. For example, Thiers, *Traité des superstitions,* I, 6, 2 (Avignon, Vol. I, p. 415; Amsterdam, Vol. I, p. 101): "To stop a snake by the following conjuration (Mizauld, *Centuriae,* II, no. 93): 'I abjure thee by Him who created thee to stop, and if thou dost not, I curse thee with the curse whereby the Lord God did exterminate thee.'" It is evident that the basic fact in the situation is the feeling that it is possible to act on certain animals by means of certain definite words (element *a* in § 798); the secondary fact is in the words themselves (element *b* in § 798). The basic fact belongs to a very populous class of facts comprising the sentiments which induce human beings to believe that things can be influenced by means of words (genus I-γ of § 888). It is interesting that though Thiers considers certain superstitions absurd, he does not think of them all that way (Avignon, Vol. I, Preface, pp. viii-ix [Amsterdam, Vol. I, p. ii, publisher's note *Au lecteur,* quoting Thiers to the same general effect]): "I have quoted superstitions entire when I felt that there could be no harm in doing so and when it seemed in a way necessary not to abbreviate them if they were to be correctly understood. But I have often used dots and *etc.'s* for certain words, letters, signs, and other things, with which they have to be equipped in order to produce the effects desired of them, because I was afraid of inspiring evil in my effort to combat it."

182 [10] Cicero, *De divinatione,* I, 45, 102: "The Pythagoreans noted the words not only of gods but also of men, calling such things 'omens.' And our forefathers thought words very important, and began everything they did by uttering the formula 'May it be good, fortunate, propitious, successful.' At ceremonies conducted in public there was always the request for silence (*faverent linguis*), and proclamations of religious festivals contained an injunction of abstinence from quarrels and brawls. When a colony was receiving the lustration from its head, an army from its general, the People from the Censor, the individuals who led the victims to sacrifice had to have auspicious names; and so in enlisting men for the army the consuls made sure that the first soldier taken had a good name."

that class of operations which ordinary language more or less vaguely designates as magic. In the extreme type, certain words or acts, by some unknown virtue, have the power to produce certain effects. Next a first coating of logic explains that power as due to the interposition of higher beings, of deities. Going on in that direction we finally get to another extreme where the action is logical throughout—the mediaeval belief, for instance, that by selling his soul to the Devil a human being could acquire the power to harm people. When a person interested strictly in logical actions happens on phenomena of the kind just mentioned, he looks at them contemptuously as pathological states of mind, and goes his way without further thought of them. But anyone aware of the important part non-logical behaviour plays in human society must examine them with great care.[1]

184. Let us suppose that the only cases known to us showed that success in operations in magic depended on the activity of the Devil. Then we might accept the logical interpretation and say, "Men believe in the efficacy of magic because they believe in the Devil." That inference would not be substantially modified by our discovery of other cases where some other divinity functioned in place of the Devil. But it collapses the moment we meet cases that are absolutely independent of any sort of divine collaboration whatsoever. It is then apparent that the essential element in such phenomena is the non-logical action that associates certain words, invocations, practices, with certain desired effects; and that the presence of gods, demons, spirits, and so on is nothing but a logical form that is given to those associations.[1]

The substance remaining intact, several forms may coexist in one individual without his knowing just what share belongs to each. The witch in Theocritus, *Idyllia,* II, vv. 14-17, relies both upon the con-

183 [1] In this, as in other cases, induction has led us to the threshold of an investigation that we shall have to prosecute at length hereafter. Here we shall still go groping along trying to find some road that will take us to our destination—knowledge of the nature and forms of human societies.

184 [1] Here again we get one of the many situations considered in § 162. The logical form serves to connect *C* with *B*.

tributions of gods and upon the efficacy of magic, without distinguishing very clearly just how the two powers are to function. She beseeches Hecate to make the philtres she is preparing deadlier than the potions of Circe, or Medea, or the golden-haired Perimede. Had she relied on Hecate alone, it would have been simpler for her to ask the goddess directly for results that she hoped to get from the philtres. When she repeats the refrain "Wry-neck, wry-neck (*ἰυγή*, a magic bird), drag this man to my dwelling!" she is evidently envisaging some occult relationship between the bird and the effect she desires.[2]

For countless ages people have believed in such nonsense in one form or another; and there are some who take such things seriously even in our day. Only, for the past two or three hundred years there has been an increase in the number of people who laugh at them as Lucian did. But the vogue of spiritualism, telepathy, Christian Science (§ 1695 [2]), and what not, is enough to show what enormous power these sentiments and others like them still have today.[3]

184 [2] Samples of the kind are available for all peoples and in any quantity desired—one has only the embarrassment of choice. The charms imparted by Cato seem to have nothing whatever to do with gods: they function all by themselves. *De re rustica,* 160: "In cases of sprain, a cure may be obtained by the following charm. Take a green stick four or five feet long. Split it in two down the middle, and have two men hold [the two pieces] at [your] hips. Then begin to chant: *In alio s.f. motas vaeta daries dardaries astataries dissunapiter,* and keep on till ["the free ends" (Harrison)] come together [in front of you]. Brandish a knife (*ferrum*) in the air over them. Take them in your hand at the point where they touch on coming together and cut them off, right and left. Bind [the pieces] to the sprain or fracture and it will heal." Pliny mentions this magic formula given by Cato and adds others; *Historia naturalis,* XXVIII, 4 (2) (Bostock-Riley, Vol. V, p. 283): "Cato has handed down to us a magic cure for sprained limbs, and M. Varro one for gout. They say that Caesar, the dictator, after a serious accident in a carriage, was accustomed, before taking his seat in one, to repeat a rigmarole three times to make sure of a safe ride, and we know that many people nowadays do the same."

184 [3] Lucian, *Philopseudes* (Lover of Lies), 14-15 (Harmon, Vol. III, p. 343). A hyperborean magician summons a certain Chrysis to do the pleasure of her admirer, Glaucias. " 'At length the hyperborean moulded a clay Eros, and ordered it to go and fetch Chrysis. Off went the image, and before long there was a knock at the door, and there stood Chrysis! She came in and threw her arms about Glaucias's neck. You would have said she was dying for love of him; and she stayed

185. "Your ox would not die unless you had an evil neighbour," says Hesiod (*Opera et dies,* v. 348); but he does not explain how that all happens. The Laws of the XII Tables deal with the "man who shall bewitch the crops" [1] and with the "man who shall chant a curse" without explaining exactly what was involved in those operations. That type of non-logical action has also come down across the ages and is met with in our day in the use of amulets. In the country about Naples hosts of people wear coral horns on their watch-chains to ward off the evil eye. Many gamblers carry amulets and go through certain motions considered helpful to winning.[2]

186. Suppose we confine ourselves to just one of these countless non-logical actions—to rites relating to the causation or prevention of storms, and to the destruction or protection of crops. And to avoid any bewilderment resulting from examples chosen at random here and there and brought together artificially, suppose we ignore anything pertaining to countries foreign to the Graeco-Roman world. That will enable us to keep to one phenomenon in its ramifications in our Western countries, with some very few allusions to data more

on till at last we heard the cocks crowing. Away flew the Moon to Heaven, Hecate disappeared underground, all the apparitions vanished, and we saw Chrysis out of the house just about dawn.—Now, Tychiades, if you had seen that, it would have been enough to convince you that there was something in incantations.' 'Exactly,' I replied. 'If I had seen it, I should have been convinced: as it is, you must bear with me if I have not your eyes for the miraculous. But as to Chrysis, I know her for a most inflammable [and not very fastidious] lady. I do not see what occasion there was for the clay ambassador, and the Moon, no less, or for a wizard all the way from the land of the hyperboreans! Why, Chrysis would go that distance herself for the sum of twenty shillings. It is a form of incantation that she cannot resist. She is the exact opposite of an apparition. Apparitions, you tell me, take flight at the clash of brass or iron, whereas if Chrysis hears the chink of silver, she flies to the spot.' " (Fowler translation.)

185 [1] The text is given in Pliny, *Historia naturalis,* XXVIII, 4 (2): *"Qui fruges excantassit . . . Qui malum carmen incantassit . . ."* See also Seneca, *Naturales quaestiones,* IV, 6-7, and our § 194.

185 [2] Even nowadays love-philtres are still concocted by processes not materially different from the methods used of old. A court decision handed down at Lucera and examined by Attorney Vittorio Pasotti in the *Monitore dei Tribunali,* Milan, Aug. 9, 1913, recites that three women took human bones from a cemetery for the purpose of compounding a philtre that would induce a man to marry a certain woman. [From 1916 ed.]

remotely sought.[1] The method we adopt for the group of facts we are about to study is the method that will serve for other similar groups of facts. The various phenomena in the group constitute a natural family, in the same sense that the Papilionaceae in botany constitute a natural family: they can readily be identified and grouped together. There are huge numbers of them. We cannot possibly mention them all, but we can consider at least their principal types.

187. We get many cases where there is a belief that by means of certain rites and practices it is possible to raise or quell a storm. At times it is not stated just how the effect ensues—it is taken as a datum of fact. At other times, the supposed reasons are given; the effect is taken as the theoretically explainable consequence of the working of certain forces. In general terms, meteorological phenomena are considered dependent upon certain rites and practices, either directly, or else indirectly, through the interposition of higher powers.

188. Palladius gives precepts without comment. Columella adds a touch of logical interpretation, saying that custom and experience have shown their efficacy.[1] Long before their time, Empedocles,

186 [1] Quite deliberately we choose, for our first example, a group of facts that, in our day at least, have little social importance. For that reason they do not arouse any sentiments likely to disturb the scientifically objective work to which we are trying to apply ourselves. Sentiments are the worst enemies the scientific study of sociology has to fear. Unfortunately we shall not always be able to side-step them in just this way. Later on the reader will have to do his part in holding his sentiments in hand.

188 [1] Palladius, *De re rustica,* I, 35: "Many things are said [to be good] for hail. A millstone is covered with a red cloth. Also, an ax stained with blood may be shaken in threat at the sky. Also, whitevine [briony, *alba vitis*] may be strung about the whole garden, or an owl may be nailed up with outspread wings, or the working-tools may be greased with bear-fat. Some people keep a supply of bear-suet beaten (*tusum*) in olive-oil on hand, and grease the sickles with it at pruning-time; but this remedy must be applied in secret, so that no pruner will know of it. It is reported to be of such efficiency that no harm can be done by any storm or pest (*neque nebula neque aliquo animali possit noceri,* taking *possit noceri* as an impersonal construction). It is also important that nothing that has been profaned be used." Pliny, *Historia naturalis,* XXVIII, 23, 1: "In the first place hail-stones, they say, whirlwinds, and lightning even, will be scared away by a woman uncovering her body while her monthly courses are upon her [Bostock-Riley, Vol. V, p. 314];

according to Diogenes Laertius, *Empedocles,* VIII, 2, 59 (Hicks, Vol. II, pp. 373-75), boasted that he had power over the rain and the winds. On one occasion when the winds were blowing hard and threatening to destroy the harvests, he had bags of ass's skin made and placed on the mountains and in that way, trapped in the bags, the winds abated (*loc. cit.,* 60, quoting Timaeus). Suidas makes this interpretation a little less absurd by saying that Empedocles stretched asses' skins about the city. Plutarch, *Adversus Colotem,* 32 (Goodwin, Vol. V, p. 381), gives an explanation still less implausible (though implausible enough) by having Empedocles save a town from plague and crop-failure by stopping up the mountain gorges through which a wind swept down over the plain. In another place, *De curiositate,* 1 (Goodwin, Vol. II, p. 424), he repeats virtually the same story, but this time mentioning only the plague. Clement of Alexandria credits Empedocles with calming a wind that was bringing disease to the inhabitants and causing barrenness in the women—and in that a new element creeps in, for the feat would be a Greek counterfeit of a Judaic miracle; and so we get a theological interpretation.[2]

and that so the violence of the heavens is averted; and out at sea tempests may be lulled in the same way, even though the woman is not menstruating at the time." Columella, *De re rustica,* I, 1 (Zweibrücken, Vol. I, p. 23).

188 [2] *Stromata,* VI, 3 (*Opera,* Vol. II, pp. 243-52; Wilson, Vol. II, pp. 321 f.). Clement mentions other cases also. The land of Greece suffering from a great drought, the Pythoness prescribed that the people should resort to prayers by Aeacus. Aeacus went up on a mountain and prayed, and soon it rained copiously. For the same incident, see Pindar's scholiast, *Nemea,* V, 17 (Abel, Vol. II, p. 155); Diodorus Siculus, *Bibliotheca historica,* IV, 61, 1-2 (Booth, Vol. I, pp. 272-73); Pausanias, *Periegesis,* I, *Attica,* 44, 9. In the same connexion Clement recalls that Samuel also made it rain (I Kings, 12: 18). Going back to the Greeks, Clement relates how at Chios Aristeus obtained winds from Jove to temper the heat of the dog-days; and that fact is also vouched for by Hyginus, *Poeticon astronomicon,* II, 4, 5 (Chatelain, p. 17). Clement does not forget that at the time of the Persian invasion the Pythoness advised the Greeks to placate the winds (Herodotus, *Historiae,* VII, 178). Then comes the story of Empedocles; and Clement is back with his Bible again, quoting Ps., 83; Deut. 10:16, 17; Isa. 40:26. Then he remarks: "Some say that pestilences, hail-storms, wind-squalls, and other similar calamities are caused not only by natural perturbations, but also by certain demons, or by the wrath of wicked angels." He continues with the story of the officials appointed at Cleonae to prevent hail-storms, and discusses the sacrifices used for that purpose (§ 194). Then he tells about the purification of Athens by Epimenides and mentions other similar stories.

189. It is evident that here we have, as it were, a tree-trunk with many branches shooting off from it: a constant element, then a multitude of interpretations. The trunk, the constant element, is the belief that Empedocles saved a town from damage by winds; the ramifications, the interpretations, are the various conceptions of the way in which that result was achieved, and naturally they depend upon the temperaments of the writers advancing them: the practical man looks for a pseudo-experimental explanation; the theologian, for a theological explanation.

In Pausanias we get a conglomerate of pseudo-experimental, magical, and theological explanations. Speaking of a statue of Athena Anemotis erected at Motona, Pausanias writes, *Periegesis,* IV, *Messenia,* 35, 8: "It is said that Diomedes erected the statue and gave the goddess her name. Winds very violent and blowing out of season began devastating the country. Diomedes offered prayers to Athena; whereafter the country suffered no further ravages from the winds." *Ibid.,* II, *Corinth,* 12, 1: "At the foot of the hill (for the temple is built on a hill) stands the Altar of the Winds, whereon, one night each year, the priest sacrifices to the winds. In four pits that are there he performs other secret ceremonies to calm the fury of the winds, and likewise chants magic words that are said to come down from Medea." *Ibid.,* 34: "I record this fact also, whereat I marvelled greatly while among the Methanians. If the south-east wind ["the Lipz"] blows in from the Saronic Gulf when the vines are budding, it dries up the buds. So, as soon as the wind begins to blow, two men take a white-feathered cock, tear it in two, and run around the vineyards in opposite directions, each carrying half of the cock. Coming back to the point at which they started, they bury it. Such the remedy they have devised against that wind."

Pomponius Mela mentions nine virgins who dwelt on the "Isle of Sena" and who were able to stir up the winds and the sea with their chants.[1] In the *Geoponicon,* compiled by Cassianus Bassus,

189 [1] *De situ orbis,* III, 6, 3: "On [the Isle of] Sena [Sizun, Léon] in the British sea off the shores of Brittany (*Osismicis adversa litoribus*) there is a celebrated oracle of a Gallic divinity, where the priestesses are said to be nine in number and

I, 14, several methods of saving the fields from hail are mentioned; but the compiler of that collection explains that he has transcribed them only to avoid seeming disrespectful to things that have come down from the forefathers. His own beliefs, in a word, are different.

190. One branch shooting off from this nucleus of interpretation overlying non-logical behaviour ends in a deification of tempests. Cicero, *De natura deorum,* III, 20, 51, has Cotta meet Balbus with the objection that if the sky, the stars, and the phenomena of weather were to be deified the number of the gods would be absurdly great. In this case the deification stands by itself; in other examples, it bifurcates and gives rise to numerous interpretations, personifications, explanations.[1]

191. Capacity for controlling winds and storms becomes a sign of intellectual or spiritual power, as in Empedocles; or even of

sanctified by perpetual chastity. They are called 'Barrigenae' (variant, Gallicenae) and are supposed to be endowed with remarkable abilities to raise winds and high seas with their incantations, to turn into any animal they choose, cure diseases usually considered incurable, and see and predict the future; though they will perform such favours only for mariners who have made special voyages for the purpose of consulting them." Reinach deals with this text in *Cultes, mythes et religions,* Vol. I, p. 199, *Les vierges de Sena.* He thinks that Mela was repeating information derived from Greek traditions: "Whatever Mela's immediate source in what he says of the Isle of Sena, there is reason to suppose that the substance of his story is very ancient. I believe I detect traces of it in the *Odyssey* itself, that prototype, as Lucian was to say in his time, of all the geographical romances of antiquity." That may well be; or it may also be that both the stories in the *Odyssey* and the others had a common origin in the notion that it is possible to influence winds, a notion that was variously elaborated and explained as time went on.

190 [1] There are Latin inscriptions with invocations to the "divine" winds. *Corpus inscriptionum Latinarum,* Vol. III-I, nos. 2609-10, p. 308 (Orelli, *Inscriptionum collectio,* no. 1271): *"Iovi O.M. tempestatum divinarum potenti leg. III Aug. dedicante."* Maury, *Histoire des religions de la Grèce antique,* Vol. I, pp. 166-69: "The winds were also worshipped by the primitive peoples of Greece, but that cult, which plays such an important part in the Rig-Veda, had noticeably weakened among the Hellenes. The winds continue, of course, to be personified, but they are worshipped only on special occasions and in certain localities. . . . Among the Chinese, worship of winds and mountains was associated with worship of streams (Biot, *Le Tchéou-li,* Vol. II, p. 86). When the Emperor drove over a mountain in his chariot, the driver offered a sacrifice to the mountain's genius (*Ibid.,* Vol. II, p. 249). . . . The ancient Finns also addressed the winds as gods, especially north and south winds, the cold ones in formulas of disparagement."

divinity, as in Christ quelling the tempest.[1] Magicians and witches demonstrate their powers in that fashion; and Greek anthropomorphism knows lords of winds, storms, and the sea.

192. Sacrifices were made to the winds. The sacrifice is just a logical development of a magical operation like the use of the white cock just described. In fact for that ceremony to become a sacrifice, it need simply be stated that the cock is torn in twain as a sacrifice to this or that divinity.

Virgil has a black sheep sacrificed to the Tempest, a white sheep to the fair Zephyr. Note the elements in his action: 1. *Principal element:* the notion that it is possible to influence the winds by means of certain acts. 2. *Secondary element:* logical explanation of such acts, by introducing an imaginary being (personified winds, divinities, and the like). 3. *An element still more secondary:* specification of the acts, through certain similarities between black sheep and storms, white sheep and fair winds.[1]

193. The winds protected the Greeks against the Persian invasion

191 [1] Matt. 8:23-27. The disciples, in wonder at the cessation of the storm, exclaim: "What manner of man is this that even the winds and the sea obey him!"

192 [1] *Aeneid,* III, 115: "Let us appease the winds, and strike out for the realms of Gnosus." And III, 118: "So saying, he made the due sacrifices on the altars: a bull to Neptune, and a bull to thee, fair Apollo; a black sheep to Hiems [god of storms] and a white sheep to the favouring Zephyrs." Servius annotates (Thilo-Hagen, Vol. I, pp. 364-65): *"due* [*meritos*]: appropriate to each god. . . . The kind of victim should correspond to the character of the divinity, for the victim is sacrificed either for its oppositeness to the gifts of the god, as, for instance, a pig to Ceres, the pig being destructive to crops; or a he-goat to Liber, the goat being harmful to grape-vines; or indeed by way of similitude, as black sheep to the nether gods, and white sheep to the gods of Heaven, black sheep to the Tempests and white to Fair Weather. . . . 'A black sheep to Hiems,' etc. Aeneas performed the sacrifices in the proper order, first averting evil influences, the more readily to allure the good ones."

Aristophanes, *Ranae,* vv. 847-48, plays upon this custom and calls for a black lamb to sacrifice as a shelter from the hurricane which Aeschylus is about to stir up through his chaffing at Euripides: *"Dionysus:* Quick, boys, a black-fleeced ewe! A hurricane is upon us!" The scholiast notes (Dübner, pp. 299, 530, 701): *"Black ewe:* because that is the sacrifice offered to the storm, Typhon, that the hurricane may cease; a black *ewe:* since that is the sacrifice offered to Typhon when the storm is in the form of a tornado. . . . *Black* and not white because Typhon is black."

and in gratitude the Delphians reared an altar to them at Pthios.[1] It is a familiar fact that Boreas, son-in-law to the Athenians by virtue of his marriage to Orithyia, daughter of Erechtheus, dispersed the Persian fleet, and therefore well deserved the altar that the Athenians reared in his honour on the shores of the Ilissus.[2]

Boreas, good fellow, looked after other people besides the Athenians. He destroyed the fleet of Dionysius, as the latter was voyaging to attack the Thurii (Tarentines). "The Thurii therefore sacrificed to Boreas and elected that wind to citizenship [in their city]; assigned him a house and a piece of land, and each year celebrated a festival in his honour."[3] He also saved the Megalopolitanians when they were besieged by the Spartans; and for that reason they offered sacrifices to him every year and honoured him as punctiliously as any other god.[4]

The art of lulling the winds was known to the Persian Magi also. Herodotus relates, *Historiae,* VII, 191, in connexion with the tempest that Boreas raised to help the Athenians and which inflicted heavy losses on the Persian fleet: "For three days the storm raged. The Magi sacrificed victims and addressed magical incantations to the wind, and sacrificed further to Thetis and the Nereids. Whereupon the winds ceased on the fourth day—unless it be that they fell of their own accord." Interesting this scepticism on the part of Herodotus![5]

193 [1] Herodotus, *Historiae,* VII, 178.

193 [2] Herodotus, *loc. cit.,* 189. At a later date one gets an interpretation that clears the episode of the supernatural element and explains it logically—a particular instance of a procedure that is general. Scholiast on Apollonius, *Argonautica,* I, v. 211 (Wellauer, Vol. II, p. 13): "Heragoras [read Hereas] says in his *Megarica* that Boreas, ravisher of Orithyia, was not the wind [of that name] but [a human being] son of Strymon." And *cf.* Carl Müller's note on this scholium in his *Fragmenta historicorum Graecorum,* Vol. IV, p. 427. Still to be found are similar interpretations for other similar cases in which, according to the Athenians, Boreas was of help to them. But that is very easy: there must have been no end of individuals named Boreas!

193 [3] Aelian, *De varia historia,* XII, 61.

193 [4] Pausanias, *Periegesis,* VIII, *Arcadia,* 36, 6 (Dindorf, p. 411).

193 [5] Herodotus has some doubts also as to the aid lent by Boreas to the Athenians. He cautions that he does not know that Boreas really scattered the Barbarian fleet in answer to the prayers of the Athenians. He does know that the

194. The notion that winds, rains, tempests, can be produced by art of magic is a common one in ancient writers.[1] Seneca discusses the causes of weather at length and derides magic. He does not admit the possibility of forecasting the weather by observation, regarding observation as just a preparation for the rites commonly

Athenians assert that Boreas helped them at that time and that he had done so on previous occasions: *Historiae,* VII, 189: *οἱ δ'ὦν 'Αθηναῖοι σφίσι λέγουσι βοηθήσαντα τὸν Βορέην πρότερον καὶ τότε ἐκεῖνα κατεργάσασθαι.*

194 [1] Tibullus, for example, *Delia,* 2, vv. 51-52, mentions a witch at whose pleasure clouds vanish from the sky and snow falls in summer:

> *"Cum libet haec tristi depellit nubila caelo,*
> *cum libet aestivo convocat orbe nives."*

And Ovid, *Amores,* I, 8, vv. 5, 9-10: "She knows the arts of witchcraft and the chants of Circe (*Aeaeaque carmina*). . . . At her pleasure clouds gather over the whole sky, at her pleasure bright day shines forth from the whole orb of Heaven." In Ovid's *Metamorphoses,* VII, v. 201, Medea boasts: "The clouds I bring and drive away, the winds I raise and hush." And Seneca makes her say in *Medea,* vv. 754, 765: "Rain I called forth from dry clouds. . . . The waves began to moan, and wildly did the sea rage, though there was no wind." And see his *Hercules Oetaeus,* vv. 452 f. Lucan, *Pharsalia,* VI, vv. 440-61, describes the arts of a witch of Thessaly at length. It is noteworthy that her powers availed not through grace of the gods but against their will, compelling them. In Thessaly, says Lucan:

> "*. . . plurima surgunt*
> *Vim factura deis . . .*"

(". . . many a plant grows that can force the hand of the gods.") At the command of the Thessalian witch, *Ibid.,* vv. 467-77:

> *"Cessavere vices rerum, dilataque longa*
> *haesit nocte dies; legi non paruit aether,*
> *torpuit et praeceps audito carmine mundus,*
> *axibus et rapidis impulsos Iuppiter urguens*
> *miratur non ire polos. Nunc omnia conplent*
> *imbribus et calido praeducunt nubila Phoebo,*
> *et tonat ignaro caelum Iove; vocibus isdem*
> *umentes late nebulas nimbosque solutis*
> *excussere comis. Ventis cessantibus aequor*
> *intumuit; rursus vetitum sentire procellas*
> *conticuit turbante Noto . . ."*

("The natural changes cease to function. Daylight lingers as night is lengthened; the atmosphere follows not its laws. Under the incantations of the witches the swift-whirling firmament comes to a stop and Jupiter notes with surprise that the heavens cease to turn on their axes. Now they [the witches] drench the earth in rain and make clouds appear under a hot sun: there are peals of thunder that Jove knows nothing of. So with their magic words (*vocibus*) they dispel the canopy of watery vapour and cause the tresses of the storm-clouds to vanish. Now the sea lashes wild

performed for averting storms.[2] He says that at Cleonae there were public officials known as "hail-observers." As soon as they gave warning of the approach of a storm, the inhabitants rushed to the temple and sacrificed some a ewe, others a fowl. Those who had nothing to sacrifice pricked a finger and shed a little blood, and the clouds moved on in another direction. "People have wondered how that happens. Some, as befits educated people, deny that it is possible to bargain with hail-stones and ransom oneself from storms by trifling gifts, granted that gifts sway even the gods. Others suspect that the blood may contain some property that is able to banish clouds. But how can so little blood contain a force of such magnitude as to work far up in the skies and be felt by clouds? How much simpler to say that it is stuff and nonsense. All the same the officials entrusted with forecasting storms at Cleonae were punished when through oversight on their part the vines and the crops were damaged. Our own XII Tables forbid anyone's laying an enchantment on another's crops. An ignorant antiquity believed that clouds could be compelled or dispelled by magic. But such things are so manifestly impossible that no great schooling is required to know as much."

Few writers, however, evince the scepticism of Seneca, and we have a long series of legends about storms and winds that come down to a day very close to our own.

195. The Roman legions led by Marcus Aurelius against the Quadi chanced to be caught by a shortage of water, but a storm came

though there is no wind or lies smooth and calm under the blasts of Notus which it has been forbidden to heed.")

Philostratus, *Vita Apollonii,* III, 14: Coming to the place where the Brahmans dwelt, Apollonius and his companions "beheld two jars of black stone, one the jar of rain and the other the jar of the winds. If India is suffering from a drought, the one containing the rain is opened, and it sends clouds and rains over all the land. If there is too much rain, the jar is closed, and the storm ceases. The jar of the winds works, I should say, something like the bag of Aeolus. If it is opened, one of the winds gets out, and it blows where it is needed and dries the land."

194 [2] *Naturales quaestiones,* IV, 6-7: "I cannot refrain from alluding to the plenteous idiocies of our own Stoics. They say that there are individuals who are expert at observing the clouds and predicting when it is going to hail, the which they are able to do by long experience in noting such colours in the clouds as hail quite frequently (*totiens*) follows."

along just in time to save them. The fact seems to be well authenticated.[1] So then, the why and wherefore of the storm has to be explained; and everybody does so according to his individual sentiments and inclinations.

It may be a case of witchcraft. Even the name of the magician is known—in such cases one can be very specific at small cost! Suidas says he was one Arnuphis, "an Egyptian philosopher who, being in attendance on Marcus Aurelius, the philosopher, Emperor of the Romans, at the time when the Romans fell short of water, straightway caused black clouds to gather in the skies and a heavy rain to fall, wherewith thunder and frequent lightning; and those things he did of his science. Others say that the prodigy was the work of Julian the Chaldean."[2]

Then again pagan gods may have a hand in it—otherwise what are gods good for? Dio Cassius, *Historia Romana,* LXXII, 8 (Cary, Vol. IX, pp. 27-29), says that while the Romans were hard pressed by the Quadi and were suffering terribly from heat and thirst, "of a sudden many clouds gathered and much rain fell, not without divine purpose, and violently. And it is said of this that an Egyptian magician, Arnuphis by name, who was with Marcus, invoked a number of divinities[3] by magic art, and chiefly Hermes Aërius, and so brought on the rain."

Claudian believes that the enemy was put to flight by a rain of fire. And the cause? Magic, or else benevolence of Jove the Thunderer.[4] Capitolinus knows that Marcus Antoninus "with his prayers

195 [1] We need not inquire here whether the legion called the Fulminata got its name from that episode. The question is irrelevant to our present purposes. Even if the story of the storm were itself not true, the example would serve quite as well, since we are interested not in the historical fact but in the sentiments disclosed by the stories, true or false, that grew up around it.

195 [2] *Lexicon, s.v.* Ἄρνουφις.

195 [3] Strictly "demons"; but the pagan δαίμωνες must not be confused with the Christian "demons" (§ 1613).

195 [4] *Panegyricus de sexto consulatu Honorii Augusti,* vv. 342-49 (*Carmina,* Vol. II, p. 98):

> ". . . *nam flammeus imber in hostem decidit . . .*
> *tunc contenta polo mortalis nescia teli*
> *pugna fuit, Chaldaea mago seu carmina ritu*

turned the thunderbolts of heaven against the war machines of the enemy and obtained rain for his soldiers who were suffering from thirst." [5] With Lampridius the episode is further elaborated and assumes new garb. Marcus Antoninus has succeeded in making the Marcomanni friendly to the Romans by certain magical practices. The formulas are withheld from Elagabalus in fear lest he be desiring to start a new war.[6]

armavere deos, seu, quod reor, omne Tonantis
obsequium Marci mores potuere mereri."

("For a storm of fire descended upon the enemy. . . . Then a battle knowing no mortal weapon was fought by Heaven alone: for either Chaldean chants by magic rite had armed the gods; or else, as I believe, the character (*mores*) of Marcus merited all deference from the Thunderer.") Note the ethical elaboration. Boreas interposes on the basis of a mere family relationship with the Athenians. The Thunderer intervenes here not as a favour to Marcus, but in view of his good character. Such transformations are general.

195 [5] *Marcus Antoninus Philosophus,* 24, 4. The case of a storm favouring one of two belligerents as a result of magic or by divine goodwill is to be noted in countries widely separated and under such conditions as to preclude any suspicion of imitation. In *The Chinese,* Vol. II, 1806, p. 112; 1836, pp. 117-18, Davis transcribes a passage from the *History of the Three Kingdoms:* "Lew-pei took occasion to steal upon Chang-paou with his whole force, to baffle which the latter mounted his horse, and, with dishevelled hair and waving sword, betook himself to magic arts. The wind arose with loud peals of thunder, and there descended from on high a black cloud, in which appeared innumerable men and horses as if engaged. Lew-pei immediately drew off his troops in confusion, and giving up the contest, retreated to consult with Choo-tsien. The latter observed, 'Let him have recourse again to magic; I will prepare the blood of swine, sheep, and dogs.' . . . On the following day, Chang-paou, with flags displayed and drums beating, came forth to offer battle, and Lew-pei proceeded to meet him; but scarcely had they joined before Chang-paou put his magic in exercise; the wind and thunder arose, and a storm of sand and stone commenced. A dark cloud obscured the sky, and troops of horsemen seemed to descend. Lew-pei upon this made a show of retreating, and Chang-paou followed him; but scarcely had they turned the hill when the ambushed troops started up and launched upon the enemy their impure stores. The air seemed immediately filled with men and horses of paper or straw, which fell to the earth in confusion; while the winds and thunder at once ceased, and the sand and stones no longer flew about."

195 [6] *Antoninus Heliogabalus,* 9, 1-2 (Magie, Vol. II, p. 125): "Desiring to make war upon the Marcomanni (Marchmen) whom Marcus (Aurelius) Antoninus had very handily (*pulcherrime*) subdued, he [Elagabalus] was told by certain individuals that Marcus had arranged through Chaldean magicians that the Marcomanni should for ever be friendly and devoted to the Roman People, and that that had been done by reciting certain chants, with a rite. When he asked what the chants

Finally the Christians claim the miracle for their God. On the passage from Dio Cassius (LXXII, 8) quoted above, Xiphilinus (Cary, *Dio,* Vol. IX, pp. 29-33) notes that Dio wittingly or unwittingly, but he suspects wittingly, misleads the reader. He surely knew—since he mentions it himself—all about the "Thundering Legion," the Fulminata, to which, and not to the magician Arnuphis, the rescue of the army was due! The truth is as follows: Marcus had a legion made up entirely of Christians. During the battle, the praetor's adjutant came and told Marcus that there was nothing which Christians were unable to obtain by prayer and that there was a legion of Christians in the army. "Hearing which, Marcus urged them to bestir themselves and pray to their God. They prayed, and God heard their prayer immediately and smote the enemy with lightning, whereas the Romans He comforted with rain." Xiphilinus adds that a letter of Marcus Aurelius on the incident was said to be in existence in his time. The letter, forged by people more distinguished for piety than veracity, is also alluded to by other writers; and Justin Martyr goes so far as to give its authentic text.[7]

were or where they could be found, he was not told; for it was certain that he was inquiring about the spell in order to undo it for the purpose of bringing on a war."

195 [7] *Apologia,* I, 71 (Migne, p. 439A, Davie, p. 55). The Emperor Marcus is writing to the Senate, and the forger makes him say of the Christians: "They prayed to a god unknown to me, and straightway water fell from the sky and to us it was ice-cold, but to the enemies of the Romans it was a hail of fire." The miracle grows and grows and gets prettier and prettier! The incident and the letter are mentioned by Tertullian, *Apologeticus,* V, 6; and Eusebius, *Historia ecclesiastica,* V, 1-6. Eusebius does not state that the Emperor requested the Christians to pray—they knelt and prayed of their own accord before the battle. The enemy was surprised at the spectacle. But a more astounding thing then occurred: a hurricane arose and put the enemy to flight, while a gentle rain refreshed the Romans. Zonaras, *Epitome historiarum,* XII, 2 (Migne, Vol. 134, pp. 1003-06), on the other hand, repeats by and large the story of the Pseudo-Justin. Orosius, *Historiae adversus paganos,* VII, 15 (Browne, p. 126), says: "The tribes had risen in insurrection, barbarous in their cruelties and countless in their multitudes, to wit: the Marcomanni, the Quadi, the Vandals, the Sarmatae, the Suebi—in fact almost all Germany. The army having advanced to the frontiers of the Quadi, it was there surrounded by the enemy, and found itself in imminent danger from thirst, but more in view of a shortage of water than because of the foe. Whereupon certain of the soldiers began to pray in great earnestness of faith and publicly to call upon the name of Christ; and straightway a rain fell in such abundance as to refresh the Romans bounteously and with-

196. So the legend expands, widening in scope and gradually approximating a veritable novel. But not only the external embellishments increase in number. Concepts multiply in the substance itself. The nucleus is a mechanical concept.[1] Certain words are uttered, certain rites are performed, and the rain falls. Then comes a feeling that that has to be explained. A first theory assumes the interposition of supernatural beings. But then the interference of such gods has also to be explained, and we get a second explanation. But that explanation too bifurcates according to the supposed reasons for the intervention, foremost among which stands the ethical reason, so introducing a new concept that was altogether absent in the magical operation proper. This new concept enlarges the scope of the whole procedure. Rain was once the sole objective of the rite. Now it becomes a means whereby the divine power rewards its favourites and punishes their enemies, and then, further, a means for rewarding faith and virtue. A final step is to move on from the particular case to the general. It is no longer a question of a single fact, but of a multiplicity of facts, all following a certain rule. This

out damage, whereas the Barbarians were terrified by a rapid succession of thunderbolts and large numbers of them were killed, so that he [Marcus Aurelius] put them to rout." See also Nicephorus Callistus, *Ecclesiastica historia,* IV, 12; Cedrenus, *Historiarum compendium,* I, 250, 15-22 (Bekker, Vol. I, p. 439); Gregory of Nyssa, *Oratio II*[a] *in laudem XL martirum* (*Opera,* Vol. III, pp. 758-72).

196 [1] It appears in virtually naked form in the case of the "pluvial stone" in Rome, which needed only to be moved about the streets to produce rain. Festus, *De verborum significatione,* I, *s.v. Aquaelicium* (London, Vol. I, p. 84): "[This term] is used when rain-water is attracted by certain rites, such as dragging the 'pluvial stone' about the streets of the city as used to be done, according to legend, in days gone by." And *Ibid.,* XI, *s.v. Manalis lapis* "flowing stone" (London, Vol. I, p. 383): "The 'flowing stone,' so called, was a certain stone that lay outside the Porta Capena near the temple of Mars. In times of excessive drought this stone was carried about the streets inside the city, whereupon rain at once ensued. They called it the flowing stone because the water began flowing." So then, all that was required was to drag the stone about the city, and the rain came down at once. *Cf.* Nonius Marcellus, *De compendiosa doctrina,* 15, *s.v. Trulleum* (Mercier, p. 547); Fulgentius, *Expositio sermonum antiquorum ad Chalcidium grammaticum* (Müncker, Vol. II, pp. 169-70): "Labeo, who compiled and annotated the Etruscan rituals of the gods Tages and Bacitis, writes as follows: 'If the flesh of the liver is of a sandarac red, it is time for the flowing stones to be scraped and cleaned (*verrere*).' He means those cylinder-shaped stones which our forefathers used to drag about their properties to break a period of dry weather."

leap is taken by Tertullian. After telling the story of the rain secured by the soldiers of Marcus Aurelius, he adds: "How often have droughts not been stopped by our prayers and our fasts!" [2]

Other cases of the same kind could be adduced; which goes to show that the sentiments in which they originate are fairly common throughout the human race.[3]

197. In Christian writers it is natural that logical explanations of the general law of storms should centre about the Devil. Clement of Alexandria records the belief that wicked angels have a hand in tempests and other such calamities (§ 188 [2]).[1] But, let us not forget,

196 [2] *Ad Scapulam,* 4 (*Opera,* Vol. III, pp. 46-52; English, Vol. I, p. 51): *"Marcus quoque Aurelius in Germanica expeditione Christianorum militum orationibus ad deum factis imbres in siti impetravit.* Quando non geniculationibus et ieiunationibus nostris etiam siccitates sunt depulsae?"

196 [3] Pausanias, *Periegesis,* VIII, *Arcadia,* 38, 4 (Dindorf, pp. 414-15). The author is speaking of the spring called Hagnus on Mount Lycaeus: "When a drought has lasted for a long time and the sown seed and the trees have begun to suffer, the priest of the Lycaean Zeus offers prayers and sacrifices to the water according to the established forms and then stirs the water in the spring with an oak-branch—on the surface, not deep down. As the water is stirred a mistlike vapour rises. Soon the vapour becomes a cloud, and attracting other clouds causes rain to fall on the land of the Arcadians." We shall see (§ 203) that witches caused rain and hail by somewhat similar means, the differences being as follows: 1. The Devil of the Christians takes the place of the pagan divinities (each people of course introducing the beings deified in its own religion). 2. In Pausanias the operation is primarily beneficent. It may be so among Christians; but in general it is a wicked thing. (Deified beings usually exert influences appropriate to their individual characters and the Devil is by nature wicked.) In the present case we see an imaginary fact explained in various ways. The sentiments corresponding to the fact are evidently the constant element, the explanations the variable element.

197 [1] *Stromata,* VI, 3 (*Opera,* Vol. II, p. 247B; Wilson, Vol. II, pp. 319-23). The Dominican Inquisitors, Sprenger and Krämer, who wrote the *Malleus maleficarum,* debate learnedly and at length as to whether the Devil must always work with the magician, or whether they can function separately. *Pars* I, *quaestio* 2 (Summers, p. 12): "Whether it is sound doctrine to hold that the Devil must always co-operate with the sorcerer in an act of witchcraft, or whether the one can produce that effect without the other, as the Devil without the sorcerer, or *vice versa."* As proof that the human being could do without the Devil or, in general terms, the "lower" without the "higher" power, some cited the fact vouched for by Albertus Magnus that sage-leaves when rotted in a certain manner and thrown into a well [Summers, "running water"] could bring on a storm. The *Malleus* has no doubts on the point, but explains it. It begins by distinguishing different effects, such as *ministeriales, noxiales, maleficiales, et naturales* [Summers, p. 14: "beneficial, hurtful, wrought by witchcraft, natural"]. The first are produced by good angels, the second by

that is just an adjunct, by way of explanation, to the basic element—the belief that it is possible to influence storms and other calamities of the kind by certain rites. Victorious Christianity had to fight for its interpretations first with ancient pagan practices and later on with magical arts that in part continued the pagan and in part were new. But great the need of escaping storms! And powerful the thought that there were ways of doing so! So in one manner or another the need was covered and the thought carried out.[2]

198. In mediaeval times individuals endowed with such powers were known as *tempestarii,* and even the law took cognizance of them. Nevertheless the Church did not recognize this power of producing storms without a struggle. The Council of Braga in the year 563 (Labbe, Vol. VI, p. 518) anathematizes anyone teaching that the Devil can produce thunder, lightning, tempests, or drought. A celebrated ecclesiastical decree denies all basis in fact to fanciful tales about witches.[1]

wicked angels, the third by the Devil with the help of sorcerers or witches, the last by influences from celestial bodies. That much clear, it is easy to see how the sage has the effects it has without the help of the Devil [Summers, p. 16]: "And thirdly, as to the sage that has been rotted and thrown into a well, it is to be said that a 'noxial' effect can ensue without the participation of the Devil but not apart from the influence of a celestial body."

197 [2] St. Gregory of Tours, *De sancto Nicetio Treverorum episcopo,* 5 (*Vitae Patrum,* XVII, *Opera,* p. 1083B), tells of an incident that happened to St. Nizier. One day a man called on the Saint to thank him for having saved his life at sea under very perilous circumstances, in the following terms: "A short time since, while in a ship on my way to Italy, I found myself amid a multitude of heathen, and in that great throng of uncouth individuals I was the only Christian. One day a tempest arose and I began to call on the name of God that by His intercession He should cause the tempest to abate. The heathen for their part were praying to their own gods, some beseeching Jove, some calling on Mercury, in loud voice, others begging help now of Minerva, now of Venus. Since we were in grave peril of death, I said to them: 'Gentlemen, pray not to those gods, for they are not gods but devils. If ye would save yourselves from this present perdition, call upon St. Nizier, that he secure you salvation of the mercy of God.' Whereupon with one loud voice they cried, 'God of Nizier, save us!' and straightway the sea subsided, the winds abated, the sun came out, and the ship sailed on whither we were bound."

198 [1] *Decretum Gratiani, pars* II, *causa* 26, *quaestio* 5, *canon* 12 (Friedberg, Vol. I, pp. 1030-31): The witches' sabbath is declared a fraud: "Wherefore the priests through the Churches entrusted to them shall preach to God's people in all urgency that they should know that all such things are altogether false and that

St. Agobard wrote an entire book "against idiotic notions current as to hail and thunder." Says he: "In these parts nearly all people, noble or villein, burgher or rustic, old or young, believe that hail and thunder can be produced at the will of men. They therefore exclaim at the first signs of thunder and lightning: 'Raised air!' Asked to explain what 'raised air' is, they will tell you, some shamefacedly as though conscious of sin, others with the wonted frankness of the ignorant, that the air has been stirred by the incantations of individuals known as 'tempestuaries' and that that is why they say 'raised air.' We have seen and heard many people possessed of such stupidity and out of their heads with such lunacy as to believe and say that there is a certain country called 'Magonie' whence ships sail out on the clouds and return laden with the grain which the hail mows and the storms blow down, and that the 'tempestuaries' are paid by such aerial mariners for the grain and other produce delivered to them. We have seen a great crowd of people—blinded by such great stupidity as to believe such things possible—drag four persons in chains before our court, three men and a woman, alleging that they had fallen from one of those ships. They had been held in chains for several days till the court convened; then they were produced, in our presence, as I said, as culprits worthy to be stoned to death. Nevertheless, after much parley the truth prevailing, the accusers were, in the prophet's words, confounded like thieves caught in the act." [2]

such phantoms are inflicted upon the minds of the faithful not by a divine but by an evil spirit. . . . For who of us is not carried outside himself in dreams and nocturnal visions and does not see in his sleep things never seen while waking? And who could be so stupid and so weak of mind as to think that all such things which take place only in the spirit take place in the body also?" The decree was taken from Reginon, *De disciplinis ecclesiasticis et religione Christiana,* II, 364 (*Opera,* p. 352). It is possibly a fragment of a capitulary of Charles the Bald. Baronio, *Annales ecclesiastici, anno* 382, XX, quotes a decree of Pope Damasus: "Likewise to be excommunicated are all such as attend to spells, auguries, fortune-telling and all other superstitions; and under the same condemnation are especially to be punished women who by the Devil's deception imagine they are carried about at night on the backs of animals and go travelling in company with Herodias."

198 [2] *Contra insulsam vulgi opinionem de grandine et tonitruis* (*Opera,* pp. 147-48). In comment on the passage, Baluze writes: "Girard, Archbishop of Tours, mentions 'tempestuaries' by name in the third section of his statutes: 'Relative to

St. Agobard demonstrates from Holy Writ the error of believing that hail and thunder are at the beck and call of human beings. Others, on the contrary, will likewise show by Scripture that the belief is sound. Yes and no have at all times been produced from Scripture with equal readiness.

199. Doctrines recognizing the powers of witches were mistrusted by the Church for two reasons, at first because they looked like survivals of paganism, the gods of which were identified with devils; then because they were tainted with Manicheism, setting up a principle of evil against a principle of good. But owing to the pressure of the popular beliefs in which the non-logical impulses involved in magic expressed themselves, the Church finally yielded to something it could not prevent, and with little trouble found an interpretation humouring popular superstition and at the same time not incompatible with Catholic theology. After all, what did it want? It wanted the principle of evil to be subordinate to the principle of good. No sooner said than done! We can grant, to be sure, that magic is the work of the Devil—but we will add, "God permitting." That will remain the final doctrine of the Catholic Church.

200. Popular superstitions exerted pressure not only upon the Church but also upon secular governments; and they, without bothering very much to find logical interpretations, set out with a will to punish all sorts of sorcerers and witches, "tempestuaries" included.[1]

spellbinders, enchanters, soothsayers, fortune-tellers, dream-readers, *tempestuaries* and rigmaroles against frosts (? *brevibus pro frigoribus*), and relative to witches and such females as deal in signs and portents of various kinds, that they may be prohibited and public punishment inflicted (*publicae poenitentiae multentur*).' "

200 [1] Eunapius relates, *Vitae philosophorum ac sophistarum, Aedisius, Sopater*, Wright, pp. 383-85, that one year it came to pass that, favourable winds failing, ships could not get to Byzantium with their grain. The famished inhabitants were being entertained in a theatre with scant success and loudly protested to the Emperor Constantine that the philosopher Sopater was the cause of the famine, since "he had shackled the winds with his transcendent science." Constantine was convinced, and ordered the man executed. Suidas, *Lexicon, s.v.* Σώπατρος Ἀπαμεύς, says that the philosopher in question was killed by Constantine "so as to make evident to all that he, Constantine, was no longer a devotee of the Hellenic religion." This version accords with the other, Suidas explaining the "convinced" of Eunapius! *Codex Theodosianus*, IX, 16, 5 (Haenel, p. 869): "Many individuals do not hesitate to disturb the elements by art of magic nor to upset the tranquillity (*vitas*) of inno-

201. Whenever a certain state of fact, a certain state of belief, exists, there is always someone on hand to try to take advantage of it; and it is therefore not surprising that Church, State, and individuals should all have tried to profit by the belief in witchcraft. St. Agobard reports that blackmail was paid to "tempestuaries,"[1] and Charlemagne, no less, admonishes his subjects to pay their tithes to the Church regularly if they would be surer of their crops.[2]

cent citizens and annoy them by fatuous talk (*ventilare*) about evoking ghosts of the dead (*manibus accitis*), on pretence that they can overcome their enemies by witchcraft. Since such individuals are unnatural monsters (*naturae peregrini*), may a deadly pest destroy them." The same law appears in the *Codex Justiniani,* IX, 18, 6 (*Corpus iuris civilis,* Vol. II, p. 596; Scott, Vol. XV, p. 33). And *cf. Codex legis Wisigothorum,* VI, 2, 3 (Canciani, Vol. IV, p. 133): "Sorcerers and storm-compellers who are said to bring hail upon vineyards and grain-fields by certain incantations, and those who disturb the minds of people by conjuring up devils, wheresoever discovered and arrested by a magistrate or by a local representative or attorney [of the Crown] shall be publicly lashed with two hundred lashes, and with their hair clipped in derision they shall be forced, if unconsenting, to march around the ten estates next adjoining, that others may profit by their example." *Capitulare seculare anni 805: De incantoribus et tempestariis,* 25: "As to enchantments, fortune-telling and divinations, and individuals who cause storms or practise other witchcraft, it is the pleasure of the Council that wherever such are arrested, the archbishop of that diocese shall provide for their subjection to a most searching examination to see whether, perchance, they confess to the crimes they have committed."

201 [1] *Op. cit.,* 15: "Such idiocy is no small part of disloyalty to the Church, and meantime the evil has so spread abroad that in many places there are wretches who say they not only know how to cause storms but also how to protect the inhabitants of a locality from storms. They have a tariff (*statutum*) as to how much farmers shall give of their crops, and they call it their 'canon.' There are many people who never pay their tithes to the Church of their own accord, and never give alms to widows and orphans or the other poor; and no matter how often such things are preached and published to them, no matter how urgently they are exhorted, they still refuse. But what they call the 'canon' they pay to those who they think protect them from storms, without any preaching, admonition, or exhortation—strictly of their own accord, the Devil prompting, of course."

201 [2] *Karoli Magni capitularia,* 28, *Synodus Francofurtensis,* June 25, *anno Christi DCCXCIV* (*Monumenta Germaniae historica, Legum,* Vol. I, p. 76): ". . . and every man shall pay the legal tithe to the Church out of his property; for we learned of experience in the year of the great famine that abundant harvests came to naught because devoured by devils, and voices were heard in upbraiding." One of these wicked demons, who was possessing a maiden, was exorcized on relics of St. Marcellinus and St. Peter, and gave a clear explanation of the trouble: "I am," he said, "a satellite and disciple of Satan and was for a long time door-man in Hell. But for some years past, along with eleven companions, I have been ravag-

202. In the Middle Ages and the centuries following there was a veritable deluge of accusations against sorcerers for stirring up storms and destroying harvests. Humanity lived in terror of the Devil for generation after generation. Whenever people spoke of him, they seemed to go out of their heads, and, as might be expected of raving lunatics, spread death and ruin recklessly about.

203. The *Malleus maleficarum* (*Hammer for Witches*) of Sprenger and Krämer gives a good summary of the doctrine prevailing in the fifteenth century, though it was also the doctrine of periods earlier and later:

"That demons and their disciples can work such enchantments on lightning and hail, having received power therefor of God, and namely through His authorization of devils or their disciples, is attested by Holy Writ, Job 1 and 2 . . . whereof St. Thomas in a note on Job writes as follows:[a] 'We must confess that, God permitting, demons may effect disturbances in the air, raise storms, and cause fire to fall from the sky. Though corporeal nature in assuming its forms does not obey the commands of angels, whether good or bad, but only God the Creator, nevertheless, as regards local motion, [corporeal] nature is susceptible of obedience to spiritual nature, as may be seen in human beings, who, by sole power of the will, which is subjective in the soul, are able to move their members to the end of performing desired actions. Therefore motion—which, by its nature, not only good but also wicked angels can effect—is alone possible, save it be forbidden of God.' "[b] The disquisition on

ing this kingdom of France. Grain and wine, and all the other fruits which come of the Earth for the use of mankind, we have destroyed as we were bidden." This intelligent demon expatiates at length on what was back of it all. The devastation was, he said, "due to the wickedness of this people and the many iniquities of its rulers." And, the tongue falling where the tooth scratched, he did not forget the tithes: *"Rari sunt qui fideliter ac devote decimas dent." Cf.* Eginhard, *Historia translationis sanctorum Christi martyrum Marcellini et Petri,* V, 50 (*Opera,* Vol. II, pp. 284-86; Wendell, pp. 66-67).

203 [a] [*In librum beati Job expositio,* I, *lectio* 4 (*Opera,* 1570 ed., Vol. III, p. 3, 2C).]

203 [b] [So Pareto. Summers: "Therefore, whatever can be accomplished by mere local motion, this not only good but also bad spirits can by their natural power accomplish, unless God should forbid it."—A. L.]

the power of demons runs on and finally the authors of the *Malleus* give an example: "In [Nider's] *Formicarius,* [V, 4, f. R2], we are told of a man who was seized by a judge and questioned touching his manner of procedure in raising storms and whether it were an easy matter to do that. He answered: 'It is easy enough to make it hail, but we cannot inflict damage at will because of the surveillance of good angels.' And he added: 'We can harm only those who are without succour of God. Those who take care to carry the sign of the Cross we cannot harm. Our procedure is as follows: First in the field [in question] we pray, by a magic formula, to the Prince of all the demons to send us one of his servants to smite whither we point. The demon comes. Thereupon at a cross-roads we sacrifice a black fowl to him, tossing it high in the air. The demon takes it and obeys. He brings on a storm and hurls hail-stones and lightning-bolts, but not always on the spots we have designated, but whither God permits.' "[1] The writer continues with other stories as plausible as they are marvellous. We will touch briefly here on just one of them which is told by another writer.

The daughters of witches often have the powers their mothers have.[2] "Hence it may happen and has been known to happen . . . that a girl under the age of puberty, eight or ten years old, has produced hail and tempests." And the author gives an example (Summers, p. 144): "In Swabia a peasant with his daughter, hardly eight years old, was once looking at the grain in the fields. And considering the drought, and sorrowful, he wished for rain, saying: 'Alas, when is it going to rain?' The child, hearing her father's words, said in the simpleness of her soul: 'Father, if you would have rain, I will make it rain right soon!' And the father: 'How in the world can you make it rain?' 'Certainly I can, and not only can I make it rain: I can also make it hail and storm.' 'And who taught

203 [1] *Pars* II, *quaestio* I, *cap.* XV (Summers, pp. 147-48): "As to the manner in which sorcerers customarily raise tempests and hail-storms and hurl thunderbolts at human beings and cattle."

203 [2] *Ibid., Pars* II, *quaestio* I, *cap.* XIII (Summers, pp. 140-44): "As to the manner in which midwives who are witches do still greater harm, either killing children or pledging them to the Devil by enchantments."

you that?' 'Mama, but she told me not to tell anyone!'" The conversation continues; and finally "the father led his daughter to a brook. 'Make it rain,' he said, 'but only on our field.' The girl then put her hand into the water, and in the name of her master, according to her mother's teaching, stirred it about. And lo! the rain fell, and only upon her father's field! Seeing which her father said: 'Make it hail, but only upon one of our fields.' When the girl did that too, the father was convinced from what he had seen, and reported his wife to the judge. She was seized, convicted, and burned; and her daughter, baptized anew and consecrated to God, no longer had powers to work her art."

Though Del Rio quotes the *Malleus,* and another authority still, he tells the story somewhat differently, especially as to the way in which the rain was caused. Here we catch these legends in process of formation. Probably not all of this story was invented. Some such incident occurs. It is then amplified, commented upon, explained, and from it, as from a little seed, there comes an abundant harvest of fantastic and grotesque fiction.[3]

204. Del Rio gives a long list of highly reputable writers who maintain that sorcerers can produce hail and storms; and whose names,

203 [3] Del Rio, *Disquisitiones magicae,* II, 11 (Louvain, Vol. I, p. 155; Cologne, p. 139): *"Recentiora exempla nuperi scriptores protulerunt: Addam duo, unum lepidum* [He calls "amusing" a story that ends in the death of two women at the stake!] *horrendum alterum. In ditione Trevirensi rusticus fuit qui cum filiola sua octenni* caules plantabat in horto. Filiolam forte collaudavit, quod apte hoc munus obiret. *Illa sexu et aetate garrula se nosse alia facere magis stupenda iactat. Pater quid id foret sciscitatur: 'Secede paullum,' inquit, 'et in quam voles horti partem subitum imbrem dabo.' Miratus ille: 'Age, secedam,' ait.* Quo recedente, scrobem puella fodit, in eam de pedibus (ut cum Hebraeis loquar pudentius) aquam fundit, eamque bacillo turbidat, nescio quid submurmurans. *Et ecce tibi subito pluviam de nubibus in conditum locum. 'Quis,' inquit obstupefactus pater 'te hoc docuit?' 'Mater,' respondet, 'huius et aliorum similium peritissima.' Zelo incitatus agricola post paucos dies,* invitatum se ad nuptias simulans, uxorem cum gnata festive nuptiali modo exornatas in carrum imponit, in vicinum oppidum devehit, et iudici tradit maleficii crimen supplicio expiaturas. *Hoc mihi fide dignissimorum virorum narratio suggessit. Ubi notandus modus scrobiculam faciendi et quod in eam ieceris bacillo confutandi."* Just for a comparison, I quote the passage in the *Malleus* which tells how the rain was obtained (Summers, p. 144): *"Tunc pater puellam per manum ad torrentem deduxit. 'Fac,' inquit, 'sed tantummodo super agrum nostrum.' Tunc puella manum in aquam misit et in nomine sui magistri iuxta doc-*

supplemented by the authority of Scripture and by practical instances attested by people worthy of all credence, are surely calculated to vanquish the most obstinate incredulity! [1]

205. Godelmann imparts various ways in which witches, schooled

trinam matris movit. Et ecce tantummodo pluvia agrum illum perfudit. Quod cernens pater, 'Fac,' inquit, 'et grandinem, sed tantummodo super unum ex agris nostris,' " and so on.

The other example reported by Del Rio is a story taken from Pontano, of a city besieged by the King of Naples, which ran short of water and obtained it by rains provoked by magic and sacrilege. Del Rio may have had before him other passages from the *Formicarius* or the *Malleus:* for example, as regards the latter, the incident recounted in *Pars* II, *quaestio* I, *cap.* III (Summers, pp. 104, 107): "As to the manner in which they [witches] are transferred physically from one place to another." A witch had not been invited to a wedding banquet. "Enraged and thinking to avenge herself, she conjured up the Devil, stated her grievance and asked him to be good enough to make a hail-storm and scatter the company at the dance. Consenting, he lifted her up and in full view of certain shepherds bore her through the air to [the top of] a hill near the town. As she afterwards confessed, there was no water there for pouring into her pit—a way they have, as will be seen, when they are getting hail. So she made a little hole and filled it with her urine in place of water, and stirred it with her finger, as her custom was, the Devil looking on. And straightway the Devil, raising the liquid high in the air, sent a violent storm with hail-stones, just upon the party at the dance and the people in the town. The guests were scattered. They were still talking together as to the cause of what had happened when the witch came home. That aroused their suspicions. But when the shepherds told what they had seen, the suspicion which had been strong became violent. [We laugh nowadays at such idiocy; but the sentiments it expresses have been the cause of untold sufferings to mankind, and countless deaths.] The woman was arrested and confessed that she had done those things for cause—probably because she had not been invited to the party. Then she was burned, in view also of many other acts of witchcraft [Probably as well authenticated as the above!] of which she had been guilty." Del Rio got this story from the *Daemonolatreia* of Remy, I, 25 (Lyons, pp. 158-62; Ashwin, pp. 74-75).

204 [1] *Op. cit.,* V, 16 (Vol. III, p. 99). In II, 11 (Louvain, Vol. I, pp. 152-54; Cologne, p. 136) he writes: "Thirdly . . . sorcerers can abate tempests, cause lightning and thunder, provoke hail-storms and rain-storms and like weather, and they can send them upon such lands as they choose." He rebukes people who do not believe such things and claim that only God can do them: "To be sure, God does do them as the prime, independent, universal efficient-cause; but his creatures do them as particular, dependent, and secondary efficient-causes. Wherefore the common opinion of theologians and jurists, which I stated as my thesis, is to be followed. It is proved, firstly, by Most Holy Scripture: for there Satan causes fire to fall from Heaven and destroy the servants and the flocks of Job; and he also causes violent winds. . . . Most Holy Scripture expressly states that the hail whereby the Egyptians were punished was sent by wicked angels. . . . Why, finally, are the demons so many times called by the Apostle 'princes of the air'? Far rather because of their great power over the air! The same is confirmed [secondly] not only by

of the Devil, can produce hail:[1] "They toss pieces of flint behind them, towards the west. Sometimes they throw sand from river-bottoms into the air. Often they dip a broom in water and make a sprinkling motion at the sky. Or they dig a little ditch, fill it with water or urine, and stir the liquid with a finger. Then again they boil hog-bristles in kettles, or set boards or timbers criss-cross on a river-bank. . . . Thus they make believe that the hail comes through their doings, whereas really it comes of the Devil, God permitting."

206. Weier denies that witches have any powers, but he concedes that the Devil has, God permitting. Such the interpretation he devised in striving to save the unhappy women who were being sent to the stake. He may have taken it seriously himself, and such deviousness may have been required in an age when law and custom cramped free expression of thought.[1] Few people went as far as

the ancient Law of the XII Tables . . . but by the decrees of Emperors and Popes. It is confirmed [thirdly] by all those Fathers whom I have quoted. . . . And fourthly, it is proved by history and by examples. Herodotus bears witness to the abating of winds and a storm by magicians at the time of Xerxes. [Not a word about the qualifying remarks of Herodotus (§ 193).] . . . Of the Finns and Lapps Olaus [Magnus] writes as follows [*Historia de gentibus septentrionalibus,* III, 16, p. 119 (Streater, III, 15, p. 47)]: "In olden times they put the winds up for sale to merchants, offering three knots on which a spell had been cast: untying the first they [the merchants] would get gentle breezes; untying the second, stronger winds, and the third, a whole gale.' " Just earlier, II, 9 (Louvain, Vol. I, p. 137; Cologne, p. 124), Del Rio tells the story of "Eric, King of the Goths, who could get a fair wind from any direction in which he turned his fur cap: and for that reason he was nicknamed 'Windy-Cap' (*Pileus Ventosus*)" [Magnus, *Ibid.,* III, 15, p. 116; Streater, III, 13, p. 45. In reading these passages in Magnus, Streater arbitrarily changes *"ventum venalem"* to *"vinum venalem,"* which gives a different cast to the anecdote, the game with the knots remaining a mere trick or curiosity.—A. L.]

205 [1] *De magis, veneficis, et lamiis,* II, 6, 21.

206 [1] *Histoires, disputes et discours,* III, 16 (Vol. I, pp. 357-58): "Furthermore, those poor old women are slyly tricked by the Devil. For as soon as he has seen and foreseen some tempest or change in the weather by watching the movements of the elements and the course of nature—a thing he does sooner and more readily than any human being could; or as soon as he has understood that someone is to receive some plague by the hidden will of God, whereof in such respects he is the executor, he besets the minds of those silly women, and fills them with all sorts of insane ideas, and shows them this or that opportunity for getting even with their enemies, as by clouding the sky, stirring up tempests, and making it hail." That rascal of a Bodin, however, has serious objections to Weier's theory: *De la démonomanie,* p. 235b: "As to what Wier says to the effect that witches cannot cause hail or thunder of themselves, I agree, and the same for killing people or

Tartarotti, who ascribes the phenomena of witchcraft to natural forces and leaves His High-and-Mightiness, the Devil, the mere credit of foreseeing them, so following a doctrine that had been current for centuries in the Christian Church (§ 213).[2] But he too appeals to the authority of Scripture, and judiciously balms the Holy Inquisition when he writes: "And here I could not, without blemish of grave injustice, dispense with paying a deserved tribute to the most revered and level-headed Tribunal of the Holy Inquisition of Rome, which on these matters is guided by such moderation and caution as unmistakably to manifest the spirit and motive by which it is inspired, regardless of the unjust insults and the groundless complaints that heretics keep hurling at it." [3]

207. In our time we may say what we please about witches, but not about sex; and just as in days gone by, whether out of conviction or from a desire to please people who in this connection can only be called ignorant fanatics, governments persecuted individuals who discussed the Bible freely, so in our day, and for similar reasons, governments prosecute individuals who discuss sex without due caution. Lucretius was free to speak his mind both on the religion of the gods and on the religion of sex.

208. In those days the heretic was called a criminal. So is the sex heretic today. To read what Bodin wrote of Weier is to read what

causing them to die by means of wax images and incantations. But what cannot be denied, and Wier himself agrees on that score, is that Sathan causes people, animals, and crops to die, if God does not keep him from it, and that that he does by way of the sacrifices, 'wishes,' and prayers of sorcerers, with the just permission of God, who uses His enemies to get even with His enemies." Bodin certainly knew a great deal about other people's business!

206 [2] *Del congresso notturno delle lammie*, II, 16, 7 (pp. 189-90): "There seems to be somewhat more persuasive force in the fact that these individuals boast, for example, of raising tempests or of causing the death of this person or that, and that there are trustworthy witnesses to the fact that things afterwards take place exactly as they predict. But that too can easily be explained on the assumption of illusion, by saying that the Devil, in order to give his followers a high opinion of his powers, loves to ascribe natural happenings to himself, foresees them, and incites witches to produce them; and thereupon they occur, not of his power, much less by the power of the witches, but because they were destined to occur according to natural course of nature."

206 [3] *Ibid.*, I, 10, 1 (p. 63).

Senator Bérenger and his brethren say today of people whose minds are not as narrow as their own.[1]

209. There is another analogy that sheds light on the nature of non-logical behaviour. As we noted in § 199, interpretations had to adapt themselves to popular prejudices, and so did law and penal procedure. The records of many many trials for witchcraft show that what happens is this: public rumour first designates the witch; public frenzy then assails and persecutes her; finally public authority is compelled to interfere. Here is one example among the countless that might be mentioned: In the year 1546, in the barony of Viry, a certain Marguerite Moral, wife of Jean Girard, complains to the châtelain of the barony that certain women have attacked and beaten her, at the same time calling her a witch (*hyrige*).[1] The châtelain proceeds against the defendants and learns from them that Marguerite is accused of having caused the deaths of certain children. Exactly as would be done today, he investigates in order to ascertain whether the charges made against Marguerite are true. At first the plaintiff, she is now the defendant! The charge next extends to Marguerite's husband. Many witnesses testify that the children died, presumably through practices by Marguerite. She and her husband are put to torture and of course say whatever they are asked to say. They confess to intercourse with the Devil, just as they would have confessed to administering poison, or anything else. Both accordingly are condemned to the stake and burned.[2]

208 [1] *Op. cit.*, p. 240b: "So then we are asked to condemn all antiquity as ignorant and mistaken, cancel all history, and draw a line through all laws human and divine as false, illusory, and based on false principles; and in place of all that set up the judgment of this man Wier and a few other sorcerers who are working hand in hand to establish and consolidate the empire of Sathan, as Wier cannot deny, if he has not lost all shame."

209 [1] [Bloodsucker, *cf.* Mistral, Canto I.—A. L.]

209 [2] Duval, *Procès des sorciers à Viry*, pp. 88-108: "Marguerite [Moral] . . . files complaint and criminal action before us, Claude Dupuis, châtelain of this barony, in due and proper form, against . . . [names of three women] alleging that on the twenty-ninth day of April at noontime, the said Marguerite coming from the fields from weeding her beans and being in her yard gathering greens, the said defendants came up each carrying a stick of wood in hand, and saying such words as 'Deceitful witch, you have got to go to Viry'; whereupon they began to beat the said plaintiff on her body with all their might and also tied her arms with a rope so that she could not move." The defendants are questioned and

210. In this instance interpretations play a very minor rôle. In the forefront stands the notion that death can be inflicted in some mysterious manner; and that concept works primarily on the minds of the plain people. The judges accept it too; but had it not been for the other notion that the truth can be ascertained by torture, one could not be sure what the outcome of the trial would have been. In a word, it is clearly apparent that public opinion is influencing the judges and that except for it they would have taken no action. So in our day governments have never taken action against sex heresy until after persistent agitation by that pestilential breed of individuals that forgathers in societies for the promotion of morality and conventions for the suppression of pornography; and our modern legislators, like our modern judges, for the most part accede

". . . declare that they know nothing, that they did in no way beat the said Marguerite, and would not have thought of doing so. They confess nevertheless that they said and called her a witch to her face, because many others so called her and almost everybody who knew her, especially since, after the death of the child of Pierre Testu, otherwise known as Grangier, the said Marguerite had fled, because people said that she had killed it." The trial continues, the châtelain hearing several witnesses. Some of them know nothing. Others testify corroborating Marguerite's charge that she had been beaten. But the châtelain and his jury are not convinced. And since the defendants accused of the assault and battery "have confessed that they said and rebuked the said Marguerite that she was a witch, which is a very serious charge," they order an investigation by criminal procedure (torture) to ascertain what truth there may be in it. So Marguerite the plaintiff becomes Marguerite the defendant. Several witnesses are heard. They mention a number of children who have died, they allege, because of Marguerite. One of them testifies that she had a quarrel with a certain woman named Andrée "and a little after one of her children died and also a child of her brother, Claude, under mysterious circumstances." In our day, there would have been an inquest to determine whether any poison had been administered. In those days it was not considered necessary that a material cause of death be shown. "Before the said children fell ill, the said Marguerite walked into the house of the witness, took a seat in the middle between the cradles of the said children, asking the said Andrée if she had a place where she could leave certain linen. . . . The said Andrée refusing, the said Marguerite was angry and wroth, and immediately afterwards the said children fell ill and died"—and the witness believed for that reason that they had been killed by Marguerite. Other evidence of the same kind is brought against Marguerite. One witness avers "that that was her fame and reputation in the village of Vers and everywhere where she was known, and that many people had said and charged to her face that she was a witch without her making any objection or taking any [legal] action."

reluctantly, and do their best to mitigate at least the hysterical frenzies of the sex-reformers.

211. Witches were being burned as late as the eighteenth century, and in doing such things governments and the Church were abetting popular superstition and so contributed to strengthening it; but they certainly were not the authors of it. Far from enforcing belief in such non-logical actions in the beginning, the Church found that belief forced upon it and sought to find logical interpretations for it. Only later did the Church altogether accept it, with the correctives supplied by its interpretations.

A writer who cannot be suspected of partiality to the Catholic Church says: "The slight attention paid in the thirteenth century by the Church to a crime so abhorrent as sorcery is proved by the fact that when the Inquisition was organized it was for a considerable time restrained from jurisdiction over this class of offences. In 1248 the Council of Valence, while prescribing to inquisitors the course to be pursued with heretics, directs sorcerers to be delivered to the bishops, to be imprisoned or otherwise punished [Labbe, Vol. XIV, p. 115, *cap.* 12]. In various councils, moreover, during the next sixty years the matter is alluded to, showing that it was constantly becoming an object of increased solicitude, but the penalty threatened is only excommunication. In that of Trèves, for instance, in 1310, which is very full in its description of the forbidden arts [Labbe, Vol. XIV, pp. 1450-51, *cap.* 79-84], all parish priests are ordered to prohibit them; but the penalty proposed for disobedience is only withdrawal of the sacraments, to be followed, in case of continued obduracy, by excommunication and other remedies of the law administered by the Ordinaries; thus manifesting a leniency almost inexplicable. That the Church, indeed, was disposed to be more rational than the people is visible in a case occuring in 1279 at Ruffach, in Alsace, when a Dominican nun was accused of having baptized a waxen image after the fashion of those who desired either to destroy an enemy or to win a lover. The peasants carried her to a field and would have burned her, had she not been rescued by the friars."[1]

212. People who see logical actions everywhere are therefore in error when they blame Catholic theology for the persecutions of witches. Such persecutions, incidentally, were as common among Protestants as among Catholics. Belief in magic belongs to all ages

211 [1] Lea, *History of the Inquisition,* Vol. III, pp. 433-34. Pertile is also of the same opinion. *Storia del diritto italiano,* Vol. V, pp. 447-48: "And the Church proceeded mildly, excommunicating practitioners of magic, subjecting them to canonical penances. . . . Nor did it abandon that system even later, when, in the thirteenth century, faith had been weakened by the reversion to paganism, and the spread of a neo-Manicheism in the sects of the Catharists ["Perfects"] and the Patarins, and older superstitions were coming to life again stronger than ever." But at this point the author, a man writing in our day, feels called upon to pass judgment on beliefs that he terms superstitious: "They were in truth very wicked notions not only involving belief in commerce with the Devil, in compacts with him in exchange for one's soul, and in powers obtained from him by calling on his name, consecrating oneself to him, worshipping him; but also involving something much worse—abuse of most sacred things." What this good soul calls "very wicked," others regard as objectively ridiculous and subjectively pathological! But such the power of certain sentiments! Here we have a man who is not a churchman writing towards the end of the nineteenth century, but who seemingly takes pacts with the Devil seriously, and calls them "wicked"; whereas many modern theologians are at least very sceptical, as witness the *Dictionnaire encyclopédique de la théologie catholique, s.v. Magie* (Wetzer, *s.v. Zauberei*): "The main question . . . is to determine whether demons can enter the special service of a human being. That question cannot be answered in the negative *a priori.* . . . Then a secondary question arises as to the manner in which the relationship of service between demon and human being is established. Popular belief answers [both questions] by assuming that the Devil can be 'conjured up' and thereby constrained to serve the human being. But that commonplace fancy cannot have our assent. . . . The stories that were so readily abused in a day gone by in that connexion . . . undoubtedly originated in the boastings or in the unhealthy imaginations of self-styled possessors of powers, and not one of them deserves the slightest credence.

"Another view, which was held by many theologians and played a part of some importance in the days of the prosecutions for witchcraft, held that the human being can strike a compact with the Devil and so bind him to certain services. The negotiation of the contract was regarded now as a literal objective procedure, now as subjective but no less literal, now as implicit, now as explicit. As for the objective reality, the contract may be thought of as made either by a person in possession of his right mind or by one in the sickly condition of the ecstatic. . . . As for direct commerce with the Devil . . . the notion is so vulgar that we may be excused from dwelling on it longer." The writer of this article recognizes that there may be such a compact in the ecstatic condition: "But it is readily apparent that such a pact could

and all peoples. Interpretations are the servants, not the masters, of the thing.[1]

Other writers, such as Michelet in his *Sorcière,* find the cause of the witchcraft superstition in feudalism. But where was feudalism when the Roman Laws of the XII Tables were penalizing people who laid curses on harvests? When people were believing in the witches of Thessaly? When Apuleius was being accused of using love-philtres to win the favour of the lady he married—not to mention countless other cases? The truth is, Michelet's interpretation is an exact counterpart of the Christian, except that the "great enemy" has changed his name: he used to be Satan; now he is Feudalism!

213. But to go back to the Christian interpretations. Even granting that the Devil had no power to produce storms, there was no adequate reason for eliminating him altogether from such phenomena on that account. He could be brought in in another way by saying that he could foresee storms and therefore predict them. That explanation has been current from the earliest days of Christianity down to our own. The idea, in brief, is that devils have aerial bodies, that they can travel with great speed, that being immortal they have had long experience and can therefore know and predict many

not be a contract in any ordinary sense. . . . Furthermore the alleged pact may be something altogether subjective, as is the case with the lunatics known as demonomaniacs. In such cases the patient imagines he has concluded a contract with the Devil, but there is absolutely nothing in reality corresponding to his illusion. . . . As for ways and means of binding a demon to the assistance of a human being in the exercise of magical powers, we assert that none such exist, and that if the demon enters the service of a person, he does so of his own accord under the lure of the elective affinity between his wickedness and the wickedness of the person. . . . The Devil, moreover, is not above the laws of nature. . . . He can do nothing that is not naturally possible in itself."

212 [1] Cauzons, *La magie et la sorcellerie en France,* Vol. III, pp. 63-65: "Of all Catholic publications, Del Rio's book was responsible for more victims than any other. . . . I say Catholic, for the Protestants had a generous share in prosecutions for witchcraft. If it might be hard to prove that they burned more witches than the Catholics, it would be just as hard to prove that they burned fewer. The certain thing is that persecution of unfortunates called witches raged violently in Germany and England, and more so than in Spain and Italy and even than in France, where witch-burnings were frequent, especially at certain times and in certain localities."

things in addition to predicting the things they are going to do themselves.[1]

We still do not know why it is that certain rites happen to attract devils. Never fear! There will always be as many explanations as are asked for! St. Augustine imparts that devils are attracted to physical bodies "not as animals are by food, but as spirits are by signs compatible with their pleasure or by various sorts of stones, plants, woods, animals, chants, rites." And, with all his weighty authority, St. Thomas agrees that this is so.[2]

214. From the very earliest days of demoniacal interpretation one very grave question kept coming up: Could magic practised with evil intent be met with magic practised with good intent? Constantine would permit such things, but Godefroi, in his commentary, disapproves of them, on the ground that evil things are not to be done in order to achieve legitimate purposes. Such also has been the doctrine of the Church.[1]

213 [1] St. Augustine, *De divinatione daemonum* (*Opera,* Vol. VI, p. 581), III, 7: "Demons are of such nature that with the senses of their aerial bodies they easily outstrip the senses of terrestrial bodies, and in view of the superior mobility of the same aerial bodies they incomparably excel in speed, let alone the legs of any human being or animal whatsoever, the very flight of birds. Endowed with those two things pertaining to the aerial body, to wit, sharpness of sense and swiftness of motion, they tell and foretell many things that are known to them before they are perceived by humans in view of the sluggishness of human senses. In view also of the long space of time over which their lives extend, demons acquire far greater experience than can be acquired in the short life of a human being." *Ibid.,* V, 9: "It should also be pointed out, while we are on this matter of foresight in demons, that many times they merely predict things that they are going to do themselves." Just as the physician foretells from external symptoms what the course of a disease is to be, "so in the trends and situations in the atmosphere that are known to him but unknown to us, the demon foresees approaching storms." Tertullian, *Apologeticus,* XXII, 10: "From living in the air close to the stars and in intercourse with the clouds, they have ways of knowing celestial forecasts (*habent . . . caelestes sapere paraturas*), so that they predict rains that they already know about."

213 [2] St. Augustine, *De civitate Dei,* XXI, 6, 1; St. Thomas Aquinas, *Summa theologiae,* Iª, *qu.* 115, *art.* 5 (*Opera,* Vol. V, pp. 545-46: *Utrum corpora caelestia possint imprimere in ipsos daemones*).

214 [1] *Codex Theodosianus,* IX, 16, 3 (Haenel, p. 868): "To what extent enchantments are prohibited or permitted: The Law of Constantine the Great: Deservedly to be dealt with and punished by the severest laws is the science of those individuals who, armed with art of magic, are found to have worked (*moliti, i.e., moliti esse*) to the hurt of human beings or to have turned chaste minds to lechery. Not action-

215. For that matter, there are plenty of legitimate recourses, quite apart from exorcisms and spiritual exercises, and all demonologists go into them at length. Sprenger and Krämer, for instance, give the following instructions (Summers, p. 190): "Against hail and storms the following remedy may be used in addition to the sign of the cross just mentioned. Throw three hail-stones into the fire, pronouncing the name of the Most Holy Trinity. Follow with the Lord's Prayer and the Angelic Salutation repeated two or three times. Then follow with *In principio erat Verbum* from the Gospel according to St. John, making the sign of the cross against the storm in all directions, backwards, forwards, and to the cardinal points; then, to conclude, repeat three times *Verbum caro factum est,* and say three times, 'In the name of this Gospel, let this storm cease.' Whereupon it subsides forthwith—provided it has been caused by witchcraft. These are held to be very sound practices and above suspicion [of heresy]. But if one throw hail-stones into the fire without invoking the divine Name, the action is held superstitious. If one should ask, 'Cannot the storm be quelled without hail-stones?' the answer is, 'Certainly, by using holy words in greater profusion.' In throwing the hail-stones into the fire the idea is merely to annoy the Devil while one is getting ready to undo his work by calling on the name of the Most Holy Trinity. It is better to throw them into fire than into water; for the sooner they melt, the sooner is his work undone. Nevertheless the outcome is all in the hands of the Divine Will." [1] More gibberish follows on the ways in which a

able by any prosecution, however, are remedies sought for human bodies, nor those rites which are practised (*adhibita suffragia*) in good intent in rural districts to allay fear of storms for the ripened vintage or damage from stoning by falling hail, such rites injuring no one in health or reputation and, if successful (*quorum actus*), serving only to prevent ruination of the gifts of God (*divina munera*) and the labours of men." The same law appears in the *Codex Justiniani,* IX, 18, 4 (*Corpus iuris civilis,* Vol. II, p. 595; Scott, Vol. XV, p. 32). This enactment was abrogated by the Emperor Leo, *Novellae,* 65, *Ad Stylianum, De incantatorum poena* (*Corpus iuris civilis accademicum Parisiense,* p. 1151; Scott, Vol. XVII, p. 262).

215 [1] *Malleus maleficarum, Pars* II, *quaestio* 2, *cap.* 7 (Summers, p. 188): "As to remedies against hail and lightning, and for spells cast upon cattle." The *Malleus* mentions other remedies besides. On being asked by a judge (Summers, p. 190) "whether hail-storms caused by witchcraft could be abated in any way," a witch

hail-storm can be caused or prevented. Del Rio lists numberless remedies, natural and supernatural, legitimate and illegitimate, whereby the mischief of witchcraft can be averted.

216. Here we can stop, not for lack of material, for of that there is enough to fill a good-sized library; but because what we have so far said suffices to show the essential traits of the family of facts that we have been examining, just as a certain number of plants suffice to show the characteristics of the family of Papilionaceae.[1]

217. The study just completed clearly shows the presence of the following characteristics in the family of facts considered (§ 514 [4]):

1. There is a non-logical nucleus containing, in simple compound, certain acts, certain words, that have specified effects, such as hurricanes or destruction of crops.

2. From this nucleus a number of branches, a number of logical interpretations, radiate. It is impossible not to observe that in general interpretations are devised for no other reason than to account for the fact that storms can be raised or quelled, crops protected or destroyed. Only in cases altogether exceptional is the opposite observable—the case, that is, where the logical theory leads to the belief in the fact. Interpretations are not always clearly distinguished from one another; they often interlock, so that the person accepting them may not himself know exactly what share is to be credited to each.

replied: "They can, and in the following manner: 'O hail, O winds, I abjure you by the five wounds of Christ, and by the three nails that pierced His hands and feet, and by the four Holy Evangelists, Matthew, Mark, Luke, and John, that ye melt into water ere ye fall.' " The *Malleus* also mentions the time-honoured custom of ringing bells. In our time bells have been replaced by "hail-cannon," with quite as good results.

216 [1] We shall have to prosecute many other investigations of this kind; we shall, that is, be called upon to examine many families of facts in order to find in each the elements that are constant and the elements that are variable, and then to classify them, dividing them off into orders, classes, genera, species, precisely as the botanist does. In this case I have thought it wise to set before the reader by way of illustration by no means a large, but at the same time a fairly appreciable, fraction of the facts that I have examined in arriving at the conclusions stated. Lack of space will prevent me from continuing to do that for all of the other investigations we shall have to make. The reader must bear in mind that I mention in these volumes only a small, oftentimes a very very small, portion of the evidence I have considered in making the inductions that I present.

3. Logical interpretations assume the forms that are most generally prevalent in the ages in which they are evolved. They are comparable to the styles of costume worn by people in the periods corresponding.

4. There is no direct evolution, such as is represented in Figure 5. Evolution takes the form shown in Figure 6. The pure non-logical

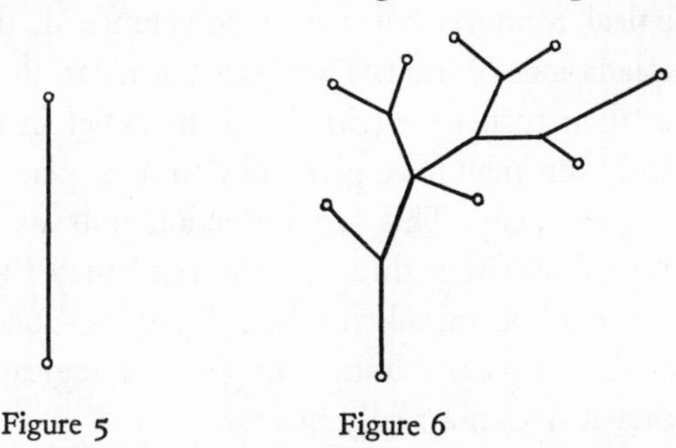

Figure 5 Figure 6

action has not been transmuted into an action of logical form. It is carried along with the other actions that are derived from it. It is impossible to determine just how the transformation has taken place —for example, trying to establish that from the mere association of acts and facts (fetishism) people went on to a theological interpretation, then to a metaphysical interpretation, then to a positive interpretation. There is no such succession in time. Interpretations that might be called fetishistic, magical, experimental, or pseudo-experimental are moreover often mixed in together in such a way that they cannot be separated, and very probably the individual who accepts them would not be able to separate them either. He knows that certain acts must have certain consequences, and he does not care to go beyond that and see how it all comes about.

5. In the long run, to be sure, degrees of enlightenment in people generally have their influence on the non-logical conduct in question, but there is no constant correlation in that respect. The Romans burned neither witches nor magicians, yet they were undoubtedly inferior in scientific development to the Italians, the French, the Germans, and so on, of the seventeenth century, who killed sorcerers

in large numbers. So, also, towards the end of the twelfth century and the beginning of the thirteenth, those unfortunates were not persecuted at all, though beyond all doubt that age was far inferior to the seventeenth century in intellectual and scientific development.

6. Belief in the non-logical conduct was not imposed by logical device of the Church, of governments, or of anybody else. It was the non-logical conduct that forced acceptance of the logical theories as explanations of itself. That does not mean that such theories may not in their turn have stimulated the belief in the non-logical conduct, and even may have given rise to it in places where it had not existed previously. This last induction puts us in the way of understanding how other things of the kind may have come about and how we may be mistaken when, knowing non-logical actions only under their logical coating, we give the logical aspect an importance that it does not really possess.

218. All the many cases we have examined in connexion with storms had something in common, something constant: the feeling that there are certain means by which storms can be influenced. There is besides a differing, a variable, element—the means themselves, and the reasons given for using them. The first element is evidently the more important; so long as it is there, people experience little or no difficulty in finding the other. It might well be, therefore, that as regards determining the form of society, elements similar to the constant element just discovered are of greater importance than the other, the variable elements. For the present we cannot decide the matter. Induction is simply pointing out to us one road that we shall find it advisable to explore.

As often happens with the inductive method, we have found not only the thing we were looking for, but another thing that we were not in the least expecting. We set out to discover how non-logical actions come to assume logical forms, and by going thoroughly into a special case, we have seen how that happens. But we have seen, in addition, that such phenomena have an element which is constant, or almost constant, and another element which is very variable. Now science looks for constant elements in phenomena in order to get at uniformities. We shall therefore have to make a special study of these different elements—and that we shall do in chapters following (§ 182[1]).

219. Meanwhile, other inductions loom before us, not yet as assertions, since they have been derived from too few facts, but rather as propositions that we must verify as we extend the scope of our researches:

1. If for a moment we consider the facts strictly from the logico-experimental standpoint, the policy of the Church with reference to magic is simply insane, and all those stories of devils are ridiculously childish. That much granted, there are people who infer from the premises that the religion of the Church is equally unsound and is therefore detrimental to society. Can we accept that inference? It is to be noted, in the first place, that the argument avails not only for Catholicism but for all religions, indeed for all systems of metaphysics—for everything, in fact, that is not logico-experimental science. It is impossible to concur in that opinion and regard as absurd the greater part of the lives of all human societies that have existed down to our time. Furthermore, if everything that is not logical is detrimental to society and therefore to the individual also, we ought not to find instances such as we have observed among animals (and are going to observe among human beings) in which certain non-logical behaviour proves beneficial, and even to a very high degree. Since the inferences are wrong, the reasoning must also be wrong. Where is the error?

The complete syllogisms would be: *a.* Any doctrine of which a part is absurd is absurd; that part of the Church's doctrine which deals with magic is absurd; therefore, *etc. b.* Any doctrine that is not logico-experimental is detrimental to society; the doctrine of the Church is not logico-experimental; therefore, *etc.* The propositions that probably falsify these syllogisms are: *a.* Any doctrine of which a part is absurd is absurd. *b.* Any doctrine that is not logico-experimental is detrimental to society. We must therefore examine those propositions closely and see whether they do, or do not, correspond to the facts. But in order to do that, we must first have a theory of doctrines and of their influence on individuals and society; and that is something that we are to attend to in the chapters next following (§ 14).

2. The questions just asked in connexion with doctrines also arise in connexion with individual human beings. If we consider the conduct of individuals from the logico-experimental standpoint, no name but "idiot" describes the man who wrote the absurdities with which Bodin stuffs his *Démonomanie*. And if we consider such conduct from the standpoint of the good or evil done to others, dictionaries supply only synonyms of "murderer" and "knave" for individuals who as a result of such idiocies have inflicted the cruelest sufferings upon many many human beings, and brought not a few of them to death.

But we at once observe that reasoning in that way we are extending to the whole what in reality applies only to the part. There are examples a-plenty to show that a man may be unbalanced in some things, level-headed in others; dishonest in some of his dealings, upright in others. From that conflict two errors arise, equivalent in origin, different in appearances. Both the following propositions are false—equally false: "Bodin has talked like a fool and done great harm to his fellow-men; therefore Bodin is an idiot and a rascal"; "Bodin was an intelligent and honest man; therefore the things he writes in his *Démonomanie* are sound and his conduct is exemplary." We see by that that we cannot judge the logico-experimental value and the utility of a doctrine by a facile consideration of the reputability of its author; that we must, instead, travel the rough and thorny path of studying it directly on the facts. And there we are back again at the conclusion that will be reached by an examination of doctrines themselves (§§ 1434 f.). All that we shall go into thoroughly later on. For the moment let us continue looking over the general field of non-logical conduct.

220. Worthy of some attention is the logical form that the Romans gave to their relations with the gods. In general it is the form of a definite and unequivocal contract that is to be interpreted according to the rules of law. If we stopped at that, we should see in the fact a mere manifestation of what has been called the legal-mindedness of the Romans. But similar facts are observable among all peoples. Even in our day the devout chambermaid who promises a few pennies to St. Anthony of Padua if he helps her to get back something she has lost is acting toward that saint exactly as the Romans acted towards their gods. What distinguishes the Romans, rather, is the wealth and precision of detail, the subordination of substance to form—in a word, the powerful cohesion of one act with other acts. And in that we glimpse a manifestation of the psychic state of the Romans.

221. The Athenian Plato takes no interest in these associations of ideas and facts which disincline people to separate facts logically. In the *Euthyphro* (17) he scorns the notion that sanctity can be regarded as the science of begging things of the gods.[1] For the Romans, and especially for Roman statesmen, the whole science of the relations of gods and men lay in just that. It was a difficult science. One had first to know to just what divinity to turn in a given emergency, and then to know its exact name. And since there might be doubts on such points, there were formulae for getting around the difficulty—for example, *"Jupiter Optime Maxime, sive quo alio nomine te appelari volueris"*—"Jupiter, Greatest and Best, or what ever you prefer to be called . . ."[2]

221 [1] Socrates speaking (Fowler, p. 55): "According to that definition, holiness would be the science of asking and giving." That, substantially, was the opinion of a great number of Greeks. We have already said that the difference between Athens and Rome lies more in the intensity of certain sentiments than in their substance.

221 [2] Macrobius, *Saturnalia,* II, 9: "It seems that all cities are protected by certain gods; and it was a secret custom of the Romans, unknown to many, that when they besieged an enemy city and thought they were on the point of conquering it, they 'called forth' its tutelary gods with a certain ritual. For otherwise they did not think it possible to take the city, or, had it been, they thought it impious to make captives of gods. For the same reason, the Romans were careful that the name of the patron god of Rome should remain secret, and even the Latin name of the city." Macrobius then gives a formula for addressing the gods of a besieged city and another for consecrating cities and armies after worshipping such gods. But he cautions that only dictators and generals-in-chief could use them effectively: "Dis, the Father, Veiovis, Manes, or by whatever other name it is proper to address thee . . ." The words of the formula had to be punctuated by specified acts: "When he says 'Earth,' he touches the earth with his hands. When he says 'Jove,' he raises his

222. Aulus Gellius, *Noctes Atticae,* II, 28, 2, remarks that no one knew what divinity to invoke in case of an earthquake—a most serious embarrassment. So "the ancient Romans, who in all the duties of life and especially in anything touching religious observance and the immortal gods were very scrupulous and circumspect, proclaimed public holidays whenever they experienced an earthquake or heard of one. But they refrained from naming the god, as their custom was, in whose honour the festivities were held in order that they might not bind the people to a mistaken rite by naming the wrong god."

223. When wine was offered to a divinity, one had to say, "Accept this wine *which I hold in my hands.*" These last words were added to avoid any possible misunderstanding, and the mistake in particular of offering the divinity by inadvertence all the wine in one's cellar.[1] "It is one of the principles of augural doctrine that imprecations and auspices of whatever kind have no value for those who, in starting out on an enterprise, declare they attach no importance to them; the which is one of the greatest bounties of divine gracious-

hands towards heaven. When he is acknowledging a vow, he touches his breast with his hands." Such things would be ridiculous if the idea were merely to make the gods understand. They are rational if words and gestures have an efficacy of their own. Virgil, *Aeneid,* II, v. 351: "The shrines and altars were deserted, for all the gods had gone away." And Servius annotates (Thilo-Hagen, Vol. I, p. 277): "Because, before the storming [of a city] the gods were 'called forth' by the enemy that sacrilege might be avoided. That is why the Romans would never let it be known under the tutelage of just what god the *Urbs* abided and the law of the pontiffs cautioned that the Roman gods should not be addressed by name lest they be tampered with (*exaugurari*). And on the Capitol there was a consecrated shield with the inscription: *Genio Urbis Romae sive mas sive foemina* (whether male or female). And the pontiffs prayed as follows: '*Jupiter Optime Maxime*—or whatever you prefer to be called; and he [Virgil] himself says, *Aeneid,* IV, vv. 576-77: 'Thee we follow, holiest of gods, whoever thou art.' "

223 [1] Arnobius, *Disputationes adversus gentes,* VII, 31 (Bryce-Campbell, p. 340). J. C. Orelli, the editor of Arnobius, annotates (Vol. II, p. 433): "In making an offering [to the gods] the ancients chose their words cautiously and exactly and always appended qualifications (*leges*) and conditions explicitly, lest they should bind themselves by some tacit obligation; and this is evident from not a few inscriptions." He gives an example.

ness." [2] All that seems ridiculous if one is disposed to argue the substance in logical terms. But it becomes rational if we premise certain associations of acts and ideas. If the sting of a scorpion is really to be avoided by pronouncing the number 2 (§ 182), is it not evident that when one comes upon an insect and would avoid its sting, one must first know exactly whether it is a scorpion or not, and then the number that has to be pronounced? If it is the act more than anything else that counts, obviously when one is offering wine to a divinity one must do exactly the right thing and not some other thing. In any event all such ratiocination, whatever its value, occurred *a posteriori* to justify conduct in itself non-logical.

224. Systems of divination in Rome and Athens differed no less than religions, and the differences lay in the same direction. Roman divination [1] was confined to "a simple question, always the same, and relating strictly to the present or to the immediate future. The question might be formulated thus: 'Do the gods favour, or not favour, the thing that the consultant is about to do, or which is about to be done under his auspices?' The question admits only of the alternatives 'yes' or 'no' and recognizes only positive or negative signs. . . . As for the methods of divination prescribed by the augural ritual, they were as simple and as few in number as possible. Observation of birds was the basis of it; and it would have remained the only source of auspices had not the prestige of the fulgural art of the Etruscans influenced the Romans to 'observe the sky' and even to attribute a higher significance to the mysterious phenomena of lightning. Official divination knew neither oracles, nor lots, nor the inspection of entrails. It refused to become involved in the discussion and appraisal of fortuitous signs, taking account of them only

223 [2] Pliny, *Historia naturalis,* XXVIII, 4 (2) (Bostock-Riley, Vol. V, p. 281). Cicero no longer understands these associations of ideas. In *De divinatione,* II, 36, 78, he says, speaking of Marcus Marcellus: "He used to say that whenever he was engaged on business of importance he made it his habit to travel in a covered litter, so as not to be interfered with by omens. That is very much like what we augurs do when we advise that all oxen about be ordered unyoked, in order to prevent 'marred omens' [by both oxen in a yoked pair dunging at the same time]."

224 [1] Bouché-Leclercq, *Histoire de la divination dans l'antiquité,* Vol. IV, p. 176.

as they occurred in the taking of auspices. With all the more reason it refrained from interpreting prodigies."

225. What the Romans could not find at home, they sought abroad in Greece and Etruria, where a freer imagination was creating new forms of divination. In the importance attached to the plain association of acts and ideas we must seek the explanation of one of the most extraordinary rules of Roman divination, the rule giving a counterfeit augury the same efficacy as a sign that had actually been observed. "He [the augur] could . . . rest content with the first sign, if it was favourable, or let unfavourable signs pass and wait for better ones. Then again, he could have the assistant augur 'renounce,' that is, 'announce,' that the expected birds were flying or singing in the manner desired—a practice, in fact, more trustworthy and which later became the regular procedure. This announcement, the *renuntiatio,* made according to a sacramental formula, created an 'ominal auspice' equivalent, for the purposes of the individual hearing it, to a real auspice."[1]

225 [1] *Ibid.,* p. 202. The same writer gives the following version of the ritual used at Iguvium, pp. 170-71: "The augur's assistant speaking from his station will propose as follows to the augur: 'I stipulate that you are to watch—a hawk on the right, a raven on the right, a woodpecker on the left, a magpie on the left, birds in flight on the left, birds singing on the left, being omens favourable to me.' The augur will stipulate as follows: 'I will watch—a hawk on the right, a raven on the right, a woodpecker on the left, birds in flight on the left and birds singing on the left, being favourable to me on behalf of the people of Iguvium in this particular temple.'" Cicero, *De divinatione,* II, 33, 71: "As regards fictitious signs taken as auspices (*ut sint auspicia quae nulla sunt*) those certainly which are customary with us, whether by the feeding of chickens or by lightning (*de caelo*), are mock-auguries (*simulacra auspiciorum*) and in no sense real ones." And continuing, 34, 71: "'Quintus Fabius, I beg you to be my augur.' And he answers: 'Gladly!' With our forefathers, an expert was used for such purposes—nowadays anybody will do. However, it does take an expert to know what 'silence' is—'silence' being the name given in the taking of auguries to the circumstance where there is no trace of blemish. It is the test of the perfect augur to be able to determine that. When the augur says to his assistant, 'Tell me whether there seems to be silence,' the assistant does not look up, he does not look around—he answers blithely (*statim*): 'There seems to be silence.' Then the augur: 'Tell me if they are eating.' 'They are eating.'" Livy, *Ab urbe condita,* X, 40, 11, records an instance where an augury, though invented, was taken as favourable from the simple fact of being "renounced." The consul Papirius is informed by his nephew, a pious lad, that his auspices have been fraudulently reported. Papirius replies: "Blessings on you for your conscientiousness

226. The Romans dealt with substance according to their convenience, at the same time paying strict regard to forms, or better, to certain associations of ideas and acts. The Athenians modified both substance and forms. The Spartans were loath to change either. Before the Battle of Marathon the Athenians appealed to Sparta for assistance. "The Spartan authorities readily promised their aid, but unfortunately it was now the ninth day of the moon: an ancient law or custom forbade them to march, in this month at least, during the last quarter before the full moon; but after the full they engaged to march without delay. Five days' delay at this critical moment might prove the utter ruin of the endangered city; yet the reason assigned seems to have been no pretence on the part of the Spartans. It was mere blind tenacity of ancient habit, which we shall find to abate, though never to disappear, as we advance in their history." [1]

The Athenians would have changed both substance and form. The Romans changed substance, respecting form. In order to make a declaration of war a member of the college of Heralds (Feciales) had to hurl a spear into the territory of the enemy. But how perform the rite and declare war on Pyrrhus when that king's states were so far away from Rome? Nothing simpler! The Romans had captured a soldier of Pyrrhus. They had him buy a plot of ground in the Flaminian Circus, and the herald hurled his spear upon that

and virtue! But if the augur makes a false announcement, the responsibility to the gods rests with him. I have the report that the corn danced [when the chickens refused to eat it] and that is a first-class omen for this army and for the Roman People!"

226 [1] Grote, *History of Greece,* Vol. IV, pp. 341-42. *Ibid.,* Vol. VII, pp. 66-67: The Argives took advantage of these traits in their neighbours, the Spartans. At the time of the war against Epidaurus, while the Spartans were sitting inactive for the whole month called Karneios, the Argives arbitrarily decreed the month shortened by four days and opened hostilities (Thucydides, *Historiae,* V, 54, 3-4). [Smith, Vol. III, p. 107: "The Argives set out on the twenty-seventh of the month preceding the Carneion, and continuing to observe that day during the whole time, invaded Epidaurus and proceeded to ravish it."—A. L.] On another occasion, they instituted a fictitious month of Karneios to keep the Lacedaemonians quiet. Knowing that he was to lead the Spartan army against Argos, Agesipolis went to Olympia and Delphi for an opinion as to whether he was bound to grant a truce. He was told that he was at liberty to refuse one (Xenophon, *Hellenica,* IV, 7, 2; Brownson, Vol. I, pp. 347-49).

property. So the feeling in the Roman people that there was a close connexion between a hurled spear and a just war was duly respected.[2]

227. Ancient Roman law presents the same traits that are observable in religion and divination; and that tends to strengthen our impression that it must be a question of an intrinsic characteristic of the Roman mind asserting itself in the various branches of human activity. Furthermore, in Roman law, as in Roman religion and divination, there are qualitative differences that come out in any comparison with Athens. Says Von Jhering,[1] "The written word or the word pronounced under circumstances of solemnity—the formula—strikes primitive peoples as something mysterious, and faith itself ascribes supernatural powers to it. Nowhere has faith in the word been stronger than in ancient Rome. Respect for the word permeates all relationships in public and private life and in religion, custom, and law. For the ancient Roman the word is a power—it binds and it loosens. If it cannot move mountains, it can at least transfer a crop of grain from one man's field to a neighbour's. It can 'call forth' divinities (*devocare*) and induce them to abandon a besieged city (*evocatio deorum*)."

226 [2] Servius, *In Vergilii Aeneidem,* IX, v. 52 (Thilo-Hagen, Vol. II, pp. 315-16): "Thirty-three days after service of the demands upon the enemy, the College of Feciales sent their spear. But in the case of (*temporibus*) Pyrrhus the Romans were to make war on a power overseas, and they could find no place to celebrate the ceremony of a declaration of war by the Feciales. They accordingly arranged for a soldier of Pyrrhus to be captured, and caused him to buy a plot of ground in the Flaminian Circus, that they might comply with the rite of declaring war on hostile territory. Then a column was erected on the spot at the foot of the statue of Bellona and duly consecrated." The commander-in-chief of an army had to keep his auspices in order, and that could be done only on the Capitol. But how do that when he was in a distant land? A very simple matter! An imitation Capitol was built on foreign soil, and the auspices were taken there. *Ibid., Aeneid,* II, v. 178 (Thilo-Hagen, Vol. I, p. 250): ". . . Or a site was chosen for a tent in which the auspices should be taken. But this practice [of taking the urban auspices] was observed by the Roman generals so long as they were fighting in Italy, in view of the nearness. But as the Empire was extended far abroad, that the general might not be too long separated from the army by returning to Rome from long distances to take the auspices it was ordained that a plot of conquered territory should be 'made Roman' in the district where hostilities were in progress, and the general could repair thither if his auspices had to be renewed."

227 [1] *Geist des römischen Rechts,* Vol. II-2, § 44, p. 441.

Von Jhering is only partly right; not words alone have such powers, but words plus acts, and in more general terms still, certain associations of words, acts, and effects that endure in time and are not easily disintegrated. In the often quoted example of Gaius,[a] where a man loses his case by calling his vines vines instead of trees, as they were called in the Law of the XII Tables, one cannot see that the word had any decisive power. Certain associations of ideas had grown up and the Romans were loath to dissolve them, and worked out their law in deference to them. Anything new in jurisprudence had to respect forms in the various *actiones legis*.

"Theories[2] as to the methods of voluntary transfers of property were very different in Roman and in Attic law. In Rome there were formal ceremonies for acquiring property—the *mancipatio,* and the *in iure cessio,* which had a translative efficacy in themselves independently of any physical transmission. Nothing of the kind is to be found in Athens. If in some other places in Greece a sale is attended by formalities reminding one of the *mancipatio,* a sale in Attic law remains a purely consensual contract, which *ipso iure* effects transfer of title *inter partes.* In Rome, furthermore, the act of transmission is of great importance as a method of transferring property. In Attic law it figures as a mere fact, devoid of any translative significance whatsoever. It appears as a simple means of discharging obligations, the transfer of title having previously taken place by virtue of the contract. Nor did Attic law, either, make the validity of a contract dependent on the observance of certain solemn forms. . . . Athenian law did not require any of the formalities commonly practised in other countries, such as sacrifices, or witnessing by a magistrate or by neighbours. Transfer took place in virtue of the mutual agreement, and there was no requirement of witnessing or of stipulation by written deed."

228. But the most striking trait in ancient Roman law is not so much its strict observance of the word, of the form, but rather the progress that it makes in spite of its adherence to associations of

227 [a] *Commentarii,* IV, 11 (Poste, p. 494; Scott, Vol. I, p. 185).

227 [2] Beauchet, *Histoire du droit privé de la république athénienne,* Vol. III, pp. 104, 151.

ideas all the way along. The fact was clearly apparent to Von Jhering, though that scholar was primarily interested in another aspect of Roman law. After reciting several cases where ancient jurists sacrificed meaning to the literal expression he adds, *Op. cit.*, Vol. II-2, § 44, pp. 458-59: "These examples seem to show that ancient jurisprudence adhered strictly to the letter in interpreting laws. Nevertheless, as I see the matter, that opinion is to be absolutely rejected; and in proof I will give a list of cases in which jurisprudence undoubtedly departed from the letter of the law."

Ancient Roman law was all form and mechanism and reduced freedom of choice on the part of litigants and magistrates to a minimum. Legal actions remind one of a grist-mill: grain was put in at one end and flour came out at the other. Says Girard:[1] "The rôle of the magistrate has to be clearly grasped. He does not judge. It would perhaps be an exaggeration to say that he formulates the complaint. His collaboration serves merely to lend an indispensable authenticity to the actions of the parties, especially to the action of the plaintiff. As in extra-judicial procedure, it is the plaintiff who is asserting his right in applying the *legis actio*. . . . As for the magistrate, his rôle is that of an assistant, and if it is not a purely passive rôle, it is at least almost mechanical.[2] He must be present, and he must pronounce the words that the law requires him to pronounce. But that is almost all. He cannot grant action when the law does not grant it, nor, in our sense, can he refuse it (*denegare legis actionem*) when the law accords it;[3] and if there is a trial, it is not he who passes judgment . . . the issue, formulated *in iure* before the magistrate, is decided *in iudicio* by a different authority. The task of the magistrate ends with the naming of the judge, a nomination made to a far greater extent by the parties than by him."

229. We could continue marshalling such facts; for in all departments of Roman law one can detect manifestations of a psychic state

228 [1] *Manuel élémentaire de droit romain*, pp. 973-74.

228 [2] The notion is Cicero's, *Pro Lucio Murena*, 12, 26.

228 [3] This is a controversial point which we need not go into for the purposes we have in view—namely, to show, without entering upon details, that the Roman magistrate played a virtually mechanical rôle.

A, that accepts progress while respecting associations of ideas. Detecting traces of it in the system of the *legis actio,* we also see traces of it in the formulary system, and it altogether controls in the whole department of so-called legal fictions. Legal fictions are to be noted among all peoples in certain stages of their history; but the extent of their development and their long survival are quite remarkable in the case of ancient Rome, as they are in the case of modern England.

230. Similar phenomena are observable in the various aspects of political life. As the result of an evolution common to the majority of Greek and Latin cities, the king was superseded by new magistrates in Athens, Sparta, and Rome. But in Athens both substance and forms were completely changed; in Sparta changes were less marked both in substance and in form; in Rome they were very considerable as regarded substance, and much less extensive as regarded forms.[1]

In deference to certain associations of ideas and acts, the sacerdotal functions of the king passed, in Athens to the archon-king, and in Rome to the *rex sacrorum;* yet neither of those offices had any importance politically. From the political standpoint the king disappears entirely in Athens. In Sparta he is kept, but with greatly reduced powers. In Rome he is remodelled with the fewest possible changes in forms. The supreme magistracy becomes annual and is divided between two consuls of equal power, each of whom can act independently of the other and can halt action by the other.[2] "The

230 [1] Mommsen, *Römische Geschichte,* Vol. I-1, p. 244 (Dixon, Vol. I, pp. 254-55): "Everywhere, in Rome, among the Latins, the Sabellians, the Etruscans, the Apulians, in all the Italic cities, in a word, as well as in the Greek cities, magistrates holding office for life gave way to magistrates appointed annually. Among the Greek cities Sparta of course is an exception. It is interesting that Rome and the Italic cities did not have an age of tyrants as Greece did; and the absence of such a stage in Italy was probably due, at least in part, to the psychic state of the Italian peoples, a psychic state more conspicuously noticeable in Rome. In Sparta, the two kings owed their royal dignity to hereditary succession; they presided at councils, administered justice, commanded the army, and served as intermediaries between Sparta and the gods."

230 [2] Traditions are all unanimous in showing that the consuls inherited virtually all the powers of the kings. Livy, *Ab urbe condita,* II, 1, 7: "You may set down

constitution[3] gave the consuls the right to expand their college, especially in time of war, by the addition of a third member exercising the more comprehensive powers of a dictator. Popular election of dictators did not come till a later date and by way of special exception. The dictator was named by one of the consuls, just as the king had probably been named in former times by the acting king [*inter-rex*]. This royal nomination had but one limitation—the fact, namely, that the consuls and their colleagues, the praetors, remained in office along with the dictator, although they deferred to him in cases of dispute."

231. It is a most surprising trait in the Roman constitution that the higher magistrates, though in reality named by the *comitia,* seem to be named by their predecessors. "The most ancient popular election was not a choice freely made from a number of eligible individuals. It was probably limited at first by the right of the magistrate directing the election to make nominations. It is likely that in the very beginning exactly as many names were submitted to the people as there were officers to elect, and that, in principle, the voters could do nothing beyond mere acceptance or rejection of a proposed person, exactly as was the case with a proposed law." [1]

Even in days more recent, under the Republic, the magistrate superintending an election could accept a candidacy (*nomen accipere*) or reject one (*nomen non accipere*). And later on it was further necessary for the presiding magistrate to consent to announce ("re-

the origins of our liberty rather to the fact that the consular authority was limited to a year than to any diminution of the powers the kings had held. The first consuls kept all the prerogatives and all the ceremony of the kings." Cicero, *De republica,* II, 32, 56: "The Senate, accordingly, held the State in the same balance in that period. . . . Though the consuls had a merely annual authority, in character and prerogative it was a royal authority." *Cf.* also Dionysius of Halicarnassus, *Antiquitates Romanae,* IV, 73-75 (Spelman, Vol. II, pp. 277-81). It is unimportant, for our purposes, whether these traditions be more or less authentic. In any event they reveal the psychic state of those who gave them the form they have or in part invented them, and that psychic state is the thing we are trying to stress.

230 [3] Mommsen, *Römisches Staatsrecht,* Vol. I, pp. 216-17.

231 [1] *Ibid.,* Vol. I, p. 470.

nounce," *renuntiare*) the successful candidate, and if he refused, no one could oblige him to.[2]

232. We find nothing of that sort in Athens. There was, to be sure, an examination (δοκιμασία) to decide whether archons (who were chosen by lot), *strategoi* (generals who were elective magistrates) and senators were fit to perform their duties; but that certification of prerogative was something very different from the *renuntiatio*. Athens makes forms consistent with substance. Rome changed from kingdom to republic by dividing the functions of magistrates. She went back to monarchy under the Empire by recombining them anew. In the long series of constitutional changes which took place between those two extremes, forms were as far as possible preserved even though substance changed.

233. Towards the end of his life Caesar seemed inclined to depart from that rule. To a people like the Athenians such a desire would have been considered reasonable enough. The few Romans still cherishing old-fashioned notions were incensed at the dissociation of ideas and acts implied in it. Only by mistaking the part for the whole has it been possible to imagine Caesar's ruin as due to the

231 [2] Valerius Maximus, *De dictis factisque memorabilibus,* III, 8, 3, tells how C. Piso refused to "renounce" M. Palicanus, a notorious trouble-maker whom he considered unworthy of the consulate: "In this situation, as lamentable as it was disgraceful, Piso was almost dragged to the rostrum by the tribunes; and they [the mob] crowded about him on all sides, demanding whether he intended to announce Palicanus as elected consul by the votes of the People. At first he answered that 'he did not think the Republic had so far lost its mind that things would ever come to such a shameful pass.' 'Well,' they pressed, insisting on an answer, 'if things do come to that pass?' 'I will not announce him!' he said." Aulus Gellius, *Noctes Atticae,* VII, 9, 3: "But the aedile who was presiding over the assembly said he would not accept the nomination and that it was not his pleasure that a recorder (*qui scriptum faceret:* a scribe) should become an aedile." The same incident is mentioned in Livy, *Ab urbe condita,* IX, 46, 2. There are many other examples of the kind. Livy, *Ibid.,* XXXIX, 39: "The consul, Lucius Porcius, was at first of the opinion that he [Fulvius Flaccus] should not be recognized as a candidate." The *Lex Iulia municipalis,* I, 132 (Girard, *Textes de droit romain,* p. 78), as reconstituted by Mommsen, expressly forbids "renouncement" of individuals reputed unfit: "Nor shall any of you take account of him from the *comitia* or the council, nor shall any of you announce anyone so elected by the *comitia* or the council against these things [*i.e.,* principles]."

extravagant honours that he arranged to have paid him. They were but one element in a whole array of things shocking to such Roman citizens as still lingered in the psychic state of the forefathers.[1] Augustus found ways to respect traditions better. He is prevaricating brazenly when he says in the Ancyra inscription: "In my sixth and seventh consulates, after ending the civil wars, I restored to the Senate and the Roman People the powers that I had received by universal consent; and in honour of that action a decree of the Senate gave me the name of Augustus. . . . Whereafter, though above all others in honours, I have held no greater powers than my colleagues."[2] Velleius Paterculus, who showers most lavish flattery on Augustus and Tiberius, says that Augustus "restored to the laws their former force, to the courts their old prestige, to the Senate its pristine majesty, and to the magistrates their time-honoured authority."[3]

234. There were still consuls and tribunes under the Empire, but those were no more than empty names. So under Augustus the *comitia* still met to elect public officials; and—what is more surprising still and still better demonstrates the attachment of the Romans to certain forms—even under Vespasian a law was passed by the *comitia* investing the Emperor with power! At first blush it would

233 [1] Cicero, *Philippicae,* II, 34; Dio Cassius, *Historia Romana,* XLIV, 1-3. Velleius Paterculus, *Historia Romana,* II, 56, 4: "Marc Antony, his colleague in the consulship and a man altogether ready for any act of daring, had brought great unpopularity upon him by placing the emblem of royalty upon his head as he sat on the rostrum for the festival of the Lupercalia, since he had rejected the offer in such a way that he showed he had not been displeased by it."

233 [2] Text as constituted by Franz: *"In consulatu sexto et septimo [postquam bella civili]a extinxeram, per consensum universorum [civium mihi tradita]m rem publicam ex mea potestate in Senatu[s populique romani a]rbitrium transtuli, quo pro merito meo Sena[tus consulto Augustus appel]l[at]u[s]sum, et laureis postes aedium mearum v[inctae sunt p]u[bli]c[e] su[pe]rque eas ad ianuam meam e[x]qu[erna fronde co]r[o]n[a ci]v[ic]a posi[ta ob servatos cive]s, qu[ique es] se[t pe]r [inscriptione]m [t]e[stis meae] virtutis, clementiae, iustitiae, pietatis, est p[osit]us clupe[us aureus in curia a Senatu populoque R]o[mano quo]d, quamquam dignitate omnibus praestarem, potestatem tamen nih[ilo] amplio [rem haberem quam] con[l]e[g]ae mei."*

233 [3] *Historia Romana,* II, 89, 3: *"Restituta vis legibus, iudiciis auctoritas, senatui maiestas, imperium magistratuum ad pristinum redactum modum."*

seem that those Romans must have had a deal of time to waste to be going through with such farces! "Just so [1] was Augustus made a tribune in the Roman year 718, and thereafter his successors. After a vote in the Senate, a magistrate, probably one of the consuls on duty, presented to the *comitia* a 'bill' (*rogatio*) designating the Emperor and specifying his powers and prerogatives. . . . So the Senate and the People both participated in the 'election.' . . . The form, therefore, was the form customary for extraordinary magistracies instituted under the Republic: first a special law, then a popular ratification. . . . The transfer of elections from the *comitia* to the Senate, effected in the year 14 of our era, changed nothing so far as the imperial *comitia* were concerned: it affected only nominations of ordinary magistrates, and had nothing to do with magistrates theoretically extraordinary."

235. In such things the fatuousness of some of the logical reasons human beings offer for their behaviour strikes the eye very forcibly. The Roman jurists were not joking, they were in earnest, when they said that "it has never been questioned that the will of the Emperor has force of law, since he himself receives his authority from a law." [1] But after all, the legions and the praetorians must have counted for something! The unlettered dame in the story was thinking straighter than the long-faced Ulpian when she said to Caracalla, "Knowest thou not that it is for an Emperor to give, and not to receive, laws?" [2]

234 [1] Mommsen, *Römisches Staatsrecht,* Vol. II-2, pp. 874-76.

235 [1] Gaius, *Commentarii,* I, 5 (Poste, pp. 25-26; Scott, Vol. I, p. 82): "An imperial 'constitution' is something that the Emperor has ordained by decree, edict, or notification (*epistula*). Nor has it ever been questioned that it has status as law, since the Emperor himself acquires his authority by law." Ulpian, in *Digesta,* I, 4, 1 (*Corpus iuris civilis,* Vol. I, p. 66; Scott, Vol. II, p. 227): "The pleasure of the Emperor has the force of law, inasmuch as by the royal law ratifying his *imperium* the People confers to him and upon him all its power and authority." The *Institutiones* of Justinian, I, 2, 6 (*Corpus iuris civilis,* Vol. I, p. 4; Scott, Vol. II, p. 7), repeat the same thing; but by Justinian's time all that was archaeology.

235 [2] Aelius Spartianus, *Antoninus Caracallus,* 10, 2: "It may be of interest to know how he is said to have married his step-mother, Julia. She was a toothsome dame, and was sitting about with her body quite largely exposed as though by oversight. Said Antoninus: 'I would, if the law allowed.' And she is said to have answered: '*Si libet, licet. An nescis te imperatorem esse et leges dare non accipere?*'" Aurelius

236. It is a familiar fact that the Greeks had no term corresponding exactly to the word *religio*. Ignoring questions of etymology, which after all would not get us very far, we may simply remark that even in the classical period *religio* in one of its senses undoubtedly meant painstaking, conscientious, diligent attention to duties.[1] It is a state of mind in which certain ties (§§ 126 f.) wield a powerful influence over conscience. If, therefore, we feel absolutely compelled to designate the psychic state in question by a word in common use,

Victor, *De Caesaribus,* XXI: "He [Caracalla] was like his father in his wealth and in the marriage he made; for enamoured of the beauty of Julia, his step-mother, whose crimes I have already recounted, he sought her for his wife. Frowardly she exposed her body to his gaze, as though unaware of his presence—he being very young; and when he said, *'Vellem si liceret uti!',* she, saucily enough, in fact stripping her shame of every veil, replied: *'Libet?* Then, by all means, *licet!'* " In this form the anecdote must be fictional in character. Actually Julia was Caracalla's mother, not his step-mother.

236 [1] Bréal-Bailly, *Dictionnaire étymologique latin, s.v. Lego,* derive *religio* from *lego: "Religio* meant 'conscientiousness,' and particularly conscientiousness in matters of piety. . . . From that first meaning all others are derived." Bréal's etymology is no longer accepted; but that is of scant importance, for neither in this case nor in any other do we intend to infer the character of a thing from the etymology of its name. Forcellini errs in representing as derived a meaning that more probably is primitive, but he states it very well: *"Religio:* . . . 10: figuratively, minute and scrupulous diligence and care: Italian *esattezza.* Cicero, *Brutus,* 82, 283: *'Eius oratio nimia religione attenuata* [His style was cramped by too great conscientiousness]'; *Idem, Orator ad Marcum Brutum,* 8, 25: 'It was the wise and sound conviction of the Athenians that they could listen to nothing that was not well-bred (*elegans*) and free from blemish; and if their orator was attentive to this fastidiousness on their part (*quorum religioni cum serviret*), he never dared utter a word that was insolent or distasteful': Italian *delicatezza.* 11: *Iusta muneris functio* [conscientious performance of duty]: Italian *puntualità.*"

One might caution, meantime, that the primitive meaning of *superstitio* was not at all what we mean by "superstition," but rather "excessive piety," something overstepping the orderliness, the regularity, so dear to the Romans. Aulus Gellius, *Noctes Atticae,* IV, 9, 1-3, quotes a line from an ancient poem, *"Religentem esse oportet, religiosus ne fuas,"* and the maxim means, he explains, that one should be "religious" (observant of one's pious duties) but not "superstitious" (not so observant to excess). And he cites Nigidius on the point: " 'That is the connotation of all words of the kind: *vinosus, mulierosus, religiosus, nummosus* ("overrich"), which suggest immoderate abundance of the quality alluded to. So a "religious" man was a man who had bound himself to an excessive, overconscientious observance of his pious duties (*religione*), so that the trait could be called a defect in him.' " Gellius continues: "But in addition to the sense mentioned by Nigidius, by another shade of meaning (*diverticulo*) a man of pure life scrupulously observing certain rules and keeping himself within certain limits may be called a 'religious' man."

the most appropriate term, without being strictly exact, would seem to be *religio.*[2]

237. An anecdote of Livy clearly brings out this scrupulous attachment to ties to the discomfiture of all other sentiments. A number of soldiers, not wishing to obey the consuls, began to consider whether they could be freed of the oath binding them to their obedience by killing them. After a time they came to the conclusion that a crime could not wipe out a sacred pledge, so they resorted to a sort of strike.[1] It matters little whether this be history or fiction. If it is fiction, the person who invented it knew that his hearers would consider it quite natural to wonder whether killing a person to whom one was bound by an oath were a means of getting rid of the oath; and natural also to answer in the negative, not from any aversion to homicide, but because homicide would not be the effective way of cancelling an oath. This whole discussion as to the way to escape the consequences of a vow belongs to *religio* in the Latin sense.

238. And as manifestations of the same *religio* we must regard the numberless facts that present the Romans as a conscientious, exact, scrupulous people, devoted—even too much so—to orderliness and regularity in their private lives. The head of every Roman family kept a diary, or ledger, in which he recorded not only income and expenditures, but everything of importance happening in the family circle—something similar to the day-books which Italian law requires merchants to keep, but also covering matters alto-

236 [2] Even if we stick to the Latin form of the word, some people will insist on understanding it in a sense altogether different from the meaning we wish to give it, whether because of its similarity to the word "religion" or because of other senses that the word has in Latin. It is my sad experience that no precaution can prevent people from taking terms in their ordinary meanings, and that no attention is paid to the definitions a writer gives, no matter how explicit and clear he makes them (§ 119).

237 [1] *Ab urbe condita,* II, 32, 2: "At first, it is said, it was debated as to whether they could be freed of their oath by slaughtering the consuls; but when they were told that no vow was ever cancelled by a crime, at the suggestion of a certain Sicinius they withdrew to the Sacred Mount [three miles from the city, across the Anio] in defiance of consular orders."

gether foreign to the mere administration of the family property.[1]

239. It might seem that the religion of the Greeks, in which reason and imagination played a more important rôle, should be more moral than the religion of the Romans, which comes down to a series of fictions in which reason played no part whatever. The contrary, however, was the case. We may ignore the scandalous adventures of the gods, and keep, rather, to the influence of religion on the conduct of daily life.[1] For the Romans the physical acts of the cult were everything, intentions nothing. The Greeks too passed through just such a stage in an archaic period of their history: a murder was expiated by an altogether external ceremony. But they, or more exactly their thinkers, soon outgrew this materialistic formalistic morality. "Even as there is no remedy for lost virginity," Aeschylus will cry, "so all the rivers of the world gathered into one avail not to wash the blood-stained hands of a murderer."[2] Cer-

238 [1] Cicero, *In Caium Verrem,* II, 23, 60: "We have heard of individuals not keeping books—that charge was made against Antony, but falsely, for his books were in the best of order. All the same there are some few examples of such reprehensible conduct. Then again we have heard of individuals whose books are missing for certain periods—and one might imagine reasons to justify that conduct. But what is unheard of and altogether ridiculous is the reply Verres made when we asked him to produce his books. He said that he had kept them up to the consulships of M. Terentius and C. Cassius, but had ceased doing so after that." On this passage Asconius annotates: "It was the custom for each Roman to keep his domestic accounts day by day over his whole life, so that it might be apparent for each day what he had laid aside from his income, what his earnings from trade, business, or money loaned, and what his expenditures or losses." To the demand on his client, M. Coelius, to produce his books, Cicero replies, *Pro Marco Coelio,* 7, 17: "A man who is still a junior in his family (*qui in patris potestate est*) is not required to keep books."

239 [1] Dionysius of Halicarnassus, *Antiquitates Romanae,* II, 19 (Spelman, Vol. I, p. 257): "One does not hear among the Romans of a Uranus castrated by his sons, of a Saturn devouring his children, of a Jove dethroning a Saturn and making him a prisoner in Tartarus; nor of divine wars and maimings, nor of gods in chains and made slaves of men. . . . (*οὐδέ γε πόλεμοι καὶ τραύματα καὶ δεσμοὶ καὶ θητεῖαι θεῶν παρ'ἀνθρώποις*)." According to Dionysius even rites of worship were more moral in Rome than in Greece.

239 [2] *Choëphorae,* vv. 71-74 (69-72):

Οἴγοντι δ'οὔτι νυμφικῶν ἑδωλίων
ἄκος, πόροι τε πάντες ἐκ μιᾶς ὁδοῦ

tainly one might expect to find a rectitude of conduct corresponding to such exalted thoughts. What we actually find is the opposite. In the end Rome got to be as immoral as Greece; but originally, and even in the fairly recent day of the Scipios, Polybius could write, *Historiae,* VI, 56, 13 (Paton, Vol. III, pp. 395-97): "So, not to mention other things, if a mere talent is entrusted to those who have charge of public monies in Greece, though they give bond to ten times the amount and there be ten seals and twice that many witnesses, you will never see your talent again; whereas with the Romans, magistrates or provincial governors who have the handling of large sums of money respect their given word out of regard for their oath." The sacred chickens may have been ridiculous; but they never caused the Roman armies a disaster comparable to the defeat that the Athenians suffered in Sicily through fault of their soothsayers.

240. Rome had no prosecutions for impiety comparable to the trials for ἀσέβεια in Athens, and, much less, to the numberless religious persecutions with which the Christians were to afflict humanity. Had Anaxagoras lived in Rome, he could have asserted to his heart's content that the sun was an incandescent mass, and no one would have paid any attention to what he said.[1] In the year

βαίνοντες τὸν χερομυσῆ
φόνον καθαίροντες ἰοῦσαν ἄτην.

Sophocles, *Oedipus Rex,* vv. 1227-28 (Storr, Vol. I, pp. 114-15): "I do not believe that the waters of the Ister and the Phasis could wash away the crimes committed in this palace." An epigram in the *Greek Anthology,* XIV, 71 (7) (Paton, Vol. V, pp. 62-63), gives an oracle of the Pythoness: "Stranger, enter a pure temple with a pure heart after touching the water of the Nymphs. The virtuous need only a drop, but a wicked man could not be cleansed with all the Ocean."

240 [1] According to Plutarch, *Nicias,* 23, 2-3 (Perrin, Vol. III, p. 291), Anaxagoras disclosed his theories of eclipses only to a few individuals. But at that time such speculations were not tolerated in Athens. "Protagoras was exiled. Anaxagoras was thrown into prison and extricated by Pericles with great difficulty. Socrates did not deal with physical sciences, but was none the less put to death because of his philosophy." *Idem, Pericles,* 32, 2 (Perrin, Vol. III, p. 93): "A law proposed by Diopeithes made it an actionable offence to deny the existence of the gods and discuss celestial things; and that brought suspicion upon Pericles because of Anaxagoras." Diogenes Laertius, *Anaxagoras,* II, 3, 12 (Hicks, Vol. I, p. 143), says that

155 B.C. the Athenians sent to Rome an embassy made up of three philosophers, Critolaus, Diogenes, and Carneades. Hellenophiles in Rome greatly admired the captious eloquence of Carneades; but Cato the Censor, mouthpiece for the spirit of the old Romans, viewed all such clever chatter as more than suspicious and urged the Senate to rush the business that had brought such individuals to Rome to the earliest possible close, "that they might go back to their schools and spout before the children of the Greeks, leaving young people in Rome to mind their magistrates and respect the laws as they had always done." [2]

Cato, mark well, does not care to discuss the doctrines of Carneades. He is not in the least interested in knowing whether or not their reasoning is sound. He is looking at them from the outside. All that captious hair-splitting seems to him to have no value. It can do no good and may do harm for young people in Rome to listen to it. Great would have been Cato's amazement had he known that some day people were going to kill each other to prove or disprove the consubstantiality of the Word or the second person of the Trinity—the Arian heresy; and rightly would he have thanked Jupiter Optimus Maximus for preserving the Romans from such folly (which, for that matter, in some instances, clothed a rational substance).

241. Athenian law, which was essentially logical and sought to settle questions on broad lines without embarrassments from a stupid formalism or too many fictions, should have been superior to Roman law. But everybody knows that the exact opposite was the case. "The Greek intellect,[1] with all its nobility and elasticity, was quite unable to confine itself within the strait waistcoat of a legal formula; and, if we may judge them by the popular courts of Athens, of whose working we possess accurate knowledge, the Greek tribunals ex-

Anaxagoras was accused of impiety by Cleon for having asserted that the sun was a molten mass. Plato, *Apologia,* 26, (14) (Fowler, p. 99), imagines Meletus as accusing Socrates of saying that the sun is a stone and the moon an earth. To which Socrates replies: "You must think you are accusing Anaxagoras, friend Meletus."

240 [2] Plutarch, *Cato Maior,* 22, 6 (Perrin, Vol. II, p. 371).

241 [1] Maine, *Ancient Law,* pp. 72-73.

hibited the strongest tendency to confound law and fact. . . . No durable system of jurisprudence could be produced in this way. A community which never hesitated to relax rules of written law whenever they stood in the way of an ideally perfect decision on the facts of particular cases, would only, if it bequeathed any body of judicial principles to posterity, bequeath one consisting of the ideas of right and wrong which happened to be prevalent at the time."

So far we agree with Sumner Maine; but we cannot agree when, *loc. cit.*, pp. 73-74, he ascribes the perfection of Roman law to the Roman theory of natural law. That theory was appended to the ancient fund of Roman law at a relatively recent date. Von Jhering comes closer to the crux of the problem. His description of the facts is excellent. As for the causes, what he calls "the rigorous logic of the conservative spirit" is nothing but the Roman psychic state, of which we have been speaking above, combining with logical and practical inferences that entail the fewest possible modifications in certain associations of ideas and acts.

I will transcribe Von Jhering's paragraph, putting in brackets the emendations that I consider appropriate:[2] "If Roman jurisprudence found a simple and logical law ready-made, it owes that advantage morally to the ancient Roman people, which, in spite of its spirit of liberty, had submitted for centuries to a relentless logic [to the logical consequences of associations—which they would not have anyone disturb—of ideas and acts]. . . . The truth of what we have just said is apparent in the peculiarly Roman manner—so familiar to all who know Roman law—of reconciling an embarrassing logic [certain associations of ideas and acts] with practical requirements by devices of all sorts: make-believe, roundabout detours, fictions. The moral aversion of the Romans to any violation of a principle once recognized [resulting from associations of ideas and acts] stimulates and, as it were, crowds their intelligence to exercise all its sagacity in discovering ways and means for reconciling logic and practical exigency. Necessity is the mother of invention. . . . The

241 [2] *Geist des römischen Rechts*, Vol. I, pp. 333-35 (Pt. I, § 20).

second national trait of the Romans mentioned above, their conservative spirit [conservative as regards forms, progressive as regards substance], worked in exactly the same direction, and it, too, was a powerful lever for their inventive talents in law. To reconcile the necessities of the present with the traditions of the past, to do justice to the former without breaking, either in form or in substance, with the latter, to discipline juridical intercourse and guide the progressive force of law into its proper channels—that for centuries was the truly noble and patriotic mission of Roman juridical science. [We can dispense with the mission, the nobility, and the patriotism.] Roman jurisprudence towered the greater in proportion to the difficulties that it encountered."

242. In statecraft there is better yet. We can only wonder how a system so absurd from the standpoint of logic could ever have survived. Magistrates with equal prerogatives, such as two consuls and two censors; tribunes able to halt the whole juridical and political process; *comitia* trying to work with the complication of the auspices; a Senate without any well-defined jurisdiction—such things seem to be loose parts of a ramshackle machine that could never have functioned. Yet it did function for century after century, and gave Rome dominion over the Mediterranean world; and when it finally broke down it broke down because it had been worn out by a new people that had lost the *religio* of the old. Thanks to ties of non-logical conduct and to forces of innovation, Rome found a way to reconcile discipline with freedom and strike a golden mean between Sparta and Athens.

243. The oration on the war-dead that Thucydides, *Historiae,* II, 35-46, ascribes to Pericles and Cicero's oration on the responses of the haruspices offer a striking contrast. The Athenian speaks like a modern. The prosperity of Athens is due to democracy, to just laws, to the good sense of her citizens, to their courage. These traits in the Athenians make Athens a better city than the other cities in Greece. The Roman does not bestow so much praise on the knowledge and courage of his fellow-citizens. "However highly we may esteem ourselves, O Conscript Fathers, we have not been superior in numbers to the Spaniards, in physique to the Gauls, in shrewdness to the Carthaginians, in the arts to the Greeks, nor even to the Italians and the Latins in the good sense native to our soil. But to all peoples and races we have been superior in piety, in religion, in that wisdom which has led us to understand that all things are ruled and directed by the immortal gods." [1] That seems to be the language of bigotry, and instead it is the language of reason, especially if the word "religion" be taken in the sense of the *religio* defined above. The cause of Roman prosperity was a certain number of ties, of *religiones,* which made the Romans a disciplined people. To be sure, Cicero was not thinking in just those terms—his theme was the power of the immortal gods—but the concept of the rule, of the tie, was not absent from his mind. He began by lauding the wisdom of the forefathers, "who thought that sacred rites and ceremonies were the affair of the pontiffs, and good auspices the affair of the augurs; that the ancient prophecies of Apollo were to be read in the Sibylline Books; and that the interpretation of prodigies belonged to Etruscan lore." [2] In truth, a genuinely Roman conception or order and regularity!

244. Among modern peoples, the English, at least down to the last years of the nineteenth century,[1] have more than any other

243 [1] Cicero, *De haruspicum responsis,* 9, 19: *"Quam volumus licet, patres conscripti, ipsi nos amemus, tamen nec numero Hispanos, nec robore Gallos, nec calliditate Poenos, nec artibus Graecos, nec denique hoc ipso huius gentis ac terrae domestico nativoque sensu, Italos ipsos ac Latinos, sed pietate ac religione, atque hac una sapientia, quod deorum immortalium numine omnia regi gubernarique perspeximus, omnes gentes nationesque superavimus."* In the *De natura deorum,* II, 3, 8, Cicero makes Balbus say: "And if we were to compare our national traits with those of other peoples, we would find ourselves their inferiors or at the best their equals in many things, but their superiors and by far in *religio,* which means worship of the gods." Note that *religio* is here defined as worship (*cultu*).

243 [2] *Op. cit.,* 9, 18: "*. . . qui statas solemnesque caerimonias pontificatu; rerum bene gerendarum auctoritates augurio; fatorum veteres praedictiones Apollinis vatum libris; portentorum explanationes Etruscorum disciplina contineri putarunt. . . .*" And see our § 182.[5]

244 [1] This qualification is necessary, for with the first decade of the twentieth century the government of England fell into the hands of Welsh and Irish fanatics. If that is not just a passing fancy but indicates a change in the character of the country as a whole, the England of the future will be nothing like the England of

people resembled the Romans in their psychic state. English law is still replete with fictions. The English political system keeps the same antiquated names, the same antiquated forms, whereas in substance it is constantly changing. England still has a king, as in the times of the Plantagenets, the Tudors, and the Stuarts; but he has less authority, less power, than the President of the United States. Under Charles I we see a civil war fought by the King in his Parliament against the King in his camp. No Roman ever devised a fiction so far-fetched! Even today the ceremonies connected with the opening of Parliament are archaic to the point of comedy. Before the Commons appears a pompous individual called the Gentleman Usher of the Black Rod, who invites them to proceed to the House of Lords to hear the Speech from the Throne. The Commons repair thither and then return to their own chamber, where the Speaker informs them with a perfectly straight face of something they have heard as distinctly as he. Immediately a bill has to be read, as a matter of mere form, to safe-guard the right of Parliament to be the first to discuss public business, without going into the reasons for the convocation. English political organization is adapted to the needs of the English people, just as the political organization of ancient Rome was adapted to the needs of the Roman people, and all modern peoples have sought to copy it more or less faithfully. That organization enabled England to issue victorious from the Napoleonic wars and has secured Englishmen greater liberties than the majority of European peoples have enjoyed. All this is now tending to change as a result of new customs and new habits that seem about to get a foothold in England.

245. In our discussion so far we have had to use terms of ordinary language, which are by nature not very strict in meaning. Keeping for the moment to the terms "Athenians," "Romans," and so on, used in the foregoing—exactly what do they represent? Among ancient peoples they designated citizens only, not slaves and not foreigners. But do our statements apply to all the citizens in ques-

the past. It is to the latter England, the only England very well known as yet, that I refer when I mention that country in these pages.

tion? From certain facts, acts, laws, customs, we have inferred the psychic state of the individuals who created those facts, performed those acts, accepted those laws and customs. Legitimate enough! But it would not be legitimate to pretend that they made up the whole nation, or even the numerical majority in the nation.

246. Every people is governed by an *élite,* by a chosen element in the population; and, in all strictness it is the psychic state of that *élite* that we have been examining.[1] We can, at the very most, go on and say that the remainder of the population followed the impulse given by it. An *élite* can change with changes in the individuals composing it or in their descendants, or even through the infiltration of extraneous elements, which may come from the same country or from some other country. When only children of Athenian citizens could be citizens in Athens, the Athenian *élite* could change only through changes occurring in its individual members, or through taking in new members from the Athenian citizenry at large.

247. Observable in Rome are not only changes of those same kinds, but also an infiltration of foreign peoples, now of Latins or Italians through an extension of the right of citizenship, now of miscellaneous elements of all sorts, even of Barbarians, by way of freed slaves and descendants of freedmen. Scipio Aemilianus was able to say to an unruly assembly of plebeians that they were not even Italians.[1] We must therefore be on our guard against drawing hasty conclusions from the examples we have been quoting. We have, to be sure, found the characteristics of certain *élites,* but we have not solved the problem of their composition.

248. These last considerations lead us to a point beyond which we begin to encounter a matter different in character from that so far

246 [1] The meaning of the term *"elite"* must not be sought in its etymology. It will be defined in Chapter XII.

247 [1] Velleius Paterculus, *Historia Romana,* II, 4, 4: "With all the assembly in an uproar he said: 'Many a time have I stood unmoved at the clamour of armed enemies! How then am I to be stirred by the clamour of men like you who have Italy for no more than a step-mother?' "

examined. It would be premature to go farther than we have gone, and dangerous to do so before we have finished what we have begun. Let us, therefore, retrace our steps. Our little excursion has served, however, to acquaint us with at least the existence of those other problems, which we shall come to in our later chapters.

CHAPTER III

Rationalization of Non-logical Conduct

249. The research just completed has called our attention—along with a number of incidental inductions—to the following facts:

1. The existence and importance of non-logical conduct. That runs counter to many sociological theories that either scorn or ignore non-logical actions, or else, in an effort to reduce all conduct to logic, attach little importance to them. The course we follow in studying the behaviour of human beings as bearing on the social equilibrium differs according as we lay the greater stress on logical or non-logical conduct. We had better look into that matter more deeply, therefore.

2. Non-logical actions are generally considered from the logical standpoint both by those who perform them and by those who discuss them and generalize about them. Hence our need to do a thing of supreme importance for our purposes here—to tear off the masks non-logical conduct is made to wear and lay bare the things they hide from view. That too runs counter to many theories which halt at logical exteriors, representing them not as masks but as the substantial element in conduct itself. We have to scrutinize those theories closely: for if we were to find them true—in accord with experience, that is—we would have to follow an altogether different course from the one we would follow were we to discover that the substantial element in the conduct lies in the things that underlie the logical exteriors (§ 146).

3. The experimental truth of a theory and its social utility are different things. A theory that is experimentally true may be now advantageous, now detrimental, to society; and the same applies to a theory that is experimentally false. Many many people deny that. We must therefore not rest satisfied with the rapid survey we have made so far, much less with the bald declaration in § 72. We must

see whether observation of the facts confirms or belies our induction (§§ 72-73).

4. As regards logical and non-logical conduct there are differences between individual human beings, or, taking things in the mass, between social classes, and differences also in the degrees of utility that theories experimentally true or experimentally false have for individuals or classes. And the same applies to the sentiments that are expressed through non-logical conduct. Many people deny such differences. To not a few the mere suggestion that they exist seems scandalous. It will therefore be necessary to continue our examination of that subject, on which we have barely touched, and clearly establish just what the facts have to say.

250. Meantime, our first survey has already given us an idea, however superficial, of the answers that have to be given to the inquiries suggested in §§ 13-14 as to the motives underlying theories, as to their bearing on experimental realities, and as to individual and group utilities—and we see that some at least of the distinctions that are drawn in those paragraphs are not merely hypothetical, but have points of correspondence with reality.

251. In the following pages we shall devote ourselves chiefly to running down non-logical actions in the theories or descriptions of social facts that have been put forward by this or that writer; and that will give us an approximate notion of the way non-logical conduct is masked by logic.

252. If non-logical actions are really as important as our induction so far would lead us to suppose, it would be strange indeed that the many men of talent who have applied themselves to the study of human societies should not have noticed them in any way. Distracted by preconceptions or led astray by erroneous theories, they may, "as they that have spent eyes," have caught imperfect glimpses of them; but it is hard to believe that they can have seen nothing where we find so much that is of such great significance. Let us therefore see just how the matter stands.

253. But for that purpose we have to take an even more general view of things: we have to see to what extent reality is disfigured in the theories and descriptions of it that one finds in the literature of thought. We have an image in a curved mirror; our problem is to discover the form of the object so altered by refraction.

Suppose we ignore, for the moment, the simplest case of writers who understand that the conduct of human beings depends, to some extent at least, on the environment in which they live, on climate, race, occupation, "temperament." It is obvious that the behaviour resulting from such causes is not the product of pure ratiocination, that it is non-logical behaviour. To be sure, that fact is often overlooked by the very writers who have stressed it, and they therefore seem to be contradicting themselves. But the inconsistency is now and again more apparent than real; for when a writer admits such causes he is usually dealing with what *is*—and that is one thing. When he insists on having all conduct logical, he is usually describing what, in his opinion, *ought to be*—and that is quite another thing. From the scientific laboratory he steps over into the pulpit.

254. Let us begin with cases not quite so simple but where it is still easy to perceive the experimental truth underneath imperfect and partly erroneous descriptions of it.

Here, for instance, is *The Ancient City* of Fustel de Coulanges. In it we read, p. 73 (Small, p. 89): "From all these beliefs, all these customs, all these laws, it clearly results that from the religion of the hearth human beings learned to appropriate the soil and on it based their title to it." But, really, is it not surprising that domestic religion should have preceded ownership of land? And Fustel gives no proof whatever of such a thing! The opposite may very well have been the case—or religion and ownership of land may have developed side by side. It is evident that Fustel has the preconceived notion that possession has to have a "cause." On that assumption, he seeks the cause and finds it in religion; and so the act of possession becomes a logical action derived from religion, which in its turn can now be logically derived from some other cause. By a singular coincidence it happens that in this instance Fustel himself supplies the necessary rectification. A little earlier, p. 63 (Small, p. 78), he writes: "There are three things which, from the most ancient times, one finds founded and solidly established in these Greek and Italian communities: domestic religion, the family, the right of property—three things which were obviously related in the beginning and which seem to have been inseparable."

How did Fustel fail to see that his two passages were contradictory? If three things *A, B, C* are "inseparable," one of them, for instance *A,* cannot have produced another, for instance *B:* for if *A* produced *B,* that would mean that, at the time, *A* was separate from *B.* We are therefore compelled to make a choice between the two propositions. If we keep the first, we have to discard the second, and *vice versa.* As a matter of fact, we have to adopt the second, discarding the proposition that places religion and property in a relationship of cause and effect, and keeping the one that puts them in a relationship of interdependence (§§ 138, 267). The very facts noted by Fustel himself force that choice upon us. He writes, p. 64 (Small, p. 79): "And the family, which by duty and religion remains grouped around its altar, becomes fixed to the soil like the altar itself." But the criticism occurs to one of its own accord: "Yes, provided that be possible!" For if we assume a social state in which the family cannot settle on the soil, it is the religion that has to be modified. What obviously has happened is a series of actions and reactions, and we are in no position to say just how things stood in the beginning. The fact that certain people came to live in separate families fixed to the soil had as one of its manifestations a certain kind of religion; and that religion, in its turn, contributed to keeping the families separate and fixed to the soil (§ 1021).

255. In this we have an example of a very common error, which lies in substituting relationships of cause and effect for relationships of interdependence (§ 138); and that error gives rise to still another: the error of placing the alleged effect, erroneously regarded as the logical product of the alleged cause, in the class of logical actions.

256. When Polybius stresses religion as one of the causes of the power of Rome (§ 313), we will accept the remark as very suggestive; but we will reject the logical explanation that he gives of the fact (§ 313[1]).

In Sumner Maine's *Ancient Law,* p. 122, we find another example like Fustel's. Maine observes that ancient societies were made up of families. That is a question of fact which we choose not to go into—researches into origins are largely hypothetical anyway. Let us accept Maine's data for what they are worth—just as hypotheses. From the fact he draws the conclusion that ancient law was "adjusted to a system of small independent corporations." That too is good: institutions adjust themselves to states of fact! But then suddenly we find the notion of logical conduct creeping stealthily in, p. 177: "Men are regarded and treated, not as individuals, but always as members of a particular group." It would be more exact to say that men are that in reality, and law, accordingly, develops *as if* men were regarded and treated as members of a particular group.

A little earlier, Maine's intromission of logical conduct is more obtrusive. Following his remark that ancient societies were made up of small independent corporations, he adds, p. 122: "Corporations *never die,* and accordingly primitive law considers the entities with which it deals, *i.e.,* patriarchal or family groups, as perpetual and inextinguishable." From that Maine derives as a consequence the institution of transmission, upon decease, of the *universitas iuris,* which we find in Roman law. Such a logical sequence may easily be compatible with a posterior logical analysis of antecedent non-logical actions, but it does not picture the facts accurately. To come nearer to them we have to invert some of the terms in Maine's previous remarks. The succession of the *universitas iuris* does not derive from the concept of a continuous corporation: the latter concept derives from the fact of succession. A family, or some other ethnic group, occupies a piece of land, comes to own flocks, and so on. The fact of perpetuity of occupation, of possession, is in all probability antecedent to any abstract concept, to any concept of a law of inheritance. That is observable even in animals. The great felines occupy certain hunting-grounds and these remain properties of the various families, unless human beings chance to interfere.[1] The ant-hill is perpetual, yet one may doubt whether ants have any concept of the corporation or of inheritance. In human beings, the fact gave rise to the concept. Then man, being a logical animal, had to discover the "why" of the fact; and among the many explanations he imagined, he may well have hit upon the one suggested by Sumner Maine.

Maine is one of the writers who have best shown the difference between *customary* law (law as *fact*) and *positive* law (law as *theory*); yet he forgets that distinction time and again, so persuasive is the concept that posits logical conduct everywhere. Customary law is made up of a complex of non-logical actions that regularly recur. Positive law comprises two elements: first, a logical—or pseudo-logical or even imaginary—analysis of the non-logical actions in question; second, implications of the principles resulting from that analysis. Customary law is not merely primitive: it goes hand in hand with positive law, creeps unobtrusively into jurisprudence, and modifies it. Then the day comes when the theory of such modifications is formulated—the caterpillar becomes a butterfly—and positive law opens a new chapter.

257. Of the assassination of Caesar, Duruy writes:[1] "Ever since the foundation of the Republic the Roman aristocracy had adroitly fostered in the people a horror for the name of king." In that the logical varnish for conduct that is non-logical is easily recognizable. Then he goes on: "If the monarchical solution answered the needs of the times, it was almost inevitable that the first monarch should pay for his throne with his life, as our Henry IV paid for his." In such "needs of the times" we recognize at once one of those amiable fictions which historians try to palm off as something concrete. As for the law that first monarchs in dynasties have to die by assassination, history gives no experimental proof of any such fact. We have to see in it a mere reminiscence of the classical *fatum,* and pack it

256 [1] On the shores of the Lake of Geneva one may see flocks of swans each of which occupies a certain area of the lake. If a swan of one flock tries to invade the territory of another flock, it is attacked, beaten, driven off. The old swans die, young ones are hatched and grow up, and the flock endures as a unit.

257 [1] *Histoire des Romains,* Vol. III, p. 411 (Mahaffy, Vol. III, pp. 398-99).

off to keep company with many similar products of the scholarly fancy.

258. Shall we banish from history the prodigies that Suetonius never forgets to enumerate in connexion with the births or deaths of the Roman Emperors, without trying to interpret them—for we shall see how mistaken such an effort on our part would be (§ 672)—and shall we keep only such of his facts as are, or at least seem to be, historical? Shall we do the same with all similar historical sources—for instance, with histories of the Crusades? [1]

In doing that we should be on dangerous ground, for if we made it an absolute rule to divide all our narrative sources into two elements, one miraculous, incredible, which we reject, and another natural, plausible, which we retain, we should certainly fall into very serious errors (§ 674). The part that is accepted has to have extrinsic probabilities of truth, whether through the demonstrable credibility of the author or through accord with other evidence.

259. From a legend we can learn nothing that is strictly historical; but we can learn something, and often a great deal, about the psychic state of the people who invented or believed it; and on knowledge of such psychic states our research is based. We shall therefore often cite facts without trying to ascertain whether they are historical or legendary; because for the use we are going to make of them they are just as serviceable in the one case as in the other—sometimes, indeed, they are better legendary than historical.

260. Logical interpretations of non-logical conduct become in their turn causes of logical conduct and sometimes even of non-logical conduct; and they have to be reckoned with in determining the social equilibrium. From that standpoint, the interpretations of plain people are generally of greater importance than the interpretations of scholars. As regards the social equilibrium, it is of far greater moment to know what the plain man understands by "virtue" than to know what philosophers think about it.

258 [1] [I read these sentences as interrogations. They are declarative in the original. Evidently the paragraph has been transferred to this point from some place in Chap. I, Pareto neglecting to establish connections.—A. L.]

261. Rare the writer who fails to take any account of non-logical conduct whatever; but generally the interest is in certain natural inclinations of temperament, which, willynilly, the writer has to credit to human beings. But the eclipse of logic is of short duration—driven off at one point, it reappears at some other. The rôle of temperament is reduced to lowest terms, and it is assumed that people draw logical inferences from it and act in accordance with them.

262. So much for the general situation. But in the particular, theorists have another very powerful motive for preferring to think of non-logical conduct as logical. If we assume that certain conduct is logical, it is much easier to formulate a theory about it than it is when we take it as non-logical. We all have handy in our minds the tool for producing logical inferences, and nothing else is needed. Whereas in order to organize a theory of non-logical conduct we have to consider hosts and hosts of facts, ever extending the scope of our researches in space and in time, and ever standing on our guard lest we be led into error by imperfect documents. In short, for the person who would frame such a theory, it is a long and difficult task to find outside himself materials that his mind supplied directly with the aid of mere logic when he was dealing with logical conduct.

263. If the science of political economy has advanced much farther than sociology, that is chiefly because it deals with logical conduct.[1] It would have been a soundly constituted science from the start had it not encountered a grave obstacle in the interdependence of the phenomena it examines, and at a time when the scholars who were devoting themselves to it were unable to utilize the one method so far discovered for dealing with interdependencies. The obstacle was surmounted, in part at least, when mathematics came to be applied to economic phenomena, whereby the new science of mathematical economics was built up, a science well able to hold its own with the other natural sciences.[2]

263 [1] Pareto, *Manuel*, pp. 145-46.

263 [2] Two very important books on mathematical economics are Osorio's *Théorie mathématique de l'échange*, and Moret's *L'emploi des mathématiques en économie politique*.

264. Other considerations tend to keep thinkers from the field of non-logical conduct and carry them over into the field of the logical. Most scholars are not satisfied with discovering what is. They are anxious to know, and even more anxious to explain to others, what *ought* to be. In that sort of research, logic reigns supreme; and so the moment they catch sight of conduct that is non-logical, instead of going ahead along that road they turn aside, often seem to forget its existence, at any rate generally ignore it, and beat the well-worn path that leads to logical conduct.

265. Some writers likewise rid themselves of non-logical actions by regarding them—often without saying as much explicitly—as scandalous things, or at least as irrelevant things, which should have no place in a well-ordered society. They think of them as "superstitions" that ought to be extirpated by the exercise of intelligence. Nobody, in practice, acts on the assumption that the physical and the moral constitution of an individual do not have at least some small share in determining his behaviour. But when it comes to framing a theory, it is held that the human being *ought* to act rationally, and writers deliberately close their minds to things that the experience of every day holds up before their eyes.

266. The imperfection of ordinary language from the scientific standpoint also contributes to the wide-spread resort to logical interpretations of non-logical conduct.

267. It plays no small part in the common misapprehension whereby two phenomena are placed in a relationship of cause and effect for the simple reason that they are found in company. We have already alluded to that error (§ 255); but we must now advance a little farther in our study of it, for it is of no mean importance to sociology.

Let *C,* as in Figure 3, § 166, stand for a belief; *D,* for certain behaviour. Instead of saying simply, "Some people do *D* and believe *C,*" ordinary speech goes farther and says, "Some people do *D because* they believe *C.*" Taken strictly, that proposition is often false. Less often false is the proposition, "Some people believe *C because* they do *D*." But there are still many occasions when all that we can say is, "Some men do *D* and believe *C*."

In the proposition, "Some people do *D* *because* they believe *C*," the logical strictness of the term "because" can be so attenuated that no relationship of cause and effect is set up between *C* and *D*. We can then say, "We may assume that certain people do *D* *because* they have a belief *C* which expresses sentiments that impel them to do *D*"; that is because (going back to Figure 3), they have a psychic state *A* that is expressed by *C*. In such a form the proposition closely approximates the truth, as we saw in § 166.

268. Figure 3 can be broken up into three others (Figure 7).

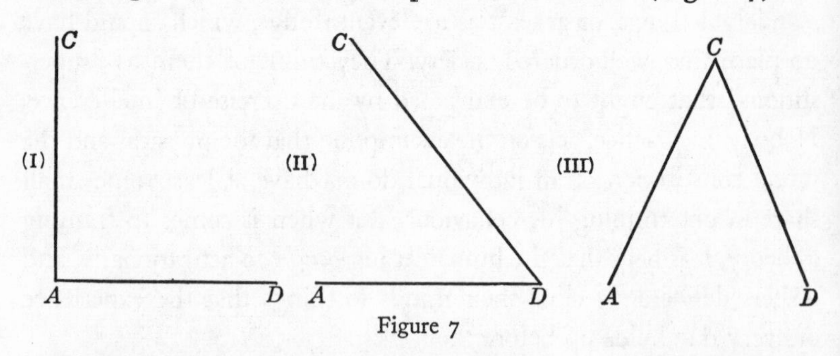

Figure 7

I. The psychic state *A* produces the belief *C* and the conduct *D*, there being no direct relation between *C* and *D*. That is the situation in the proposition, "People do *D* and believe *C*."

II. The psychic state *A* gives rise to the conduct *D*, and they both produce the belief *C*. That is the situation in the second proposition, "People believe *C* because they do *D*."

III. The psychic state *A* gives rise to the belief *C*, which produces the behaviour *D*. That is the situation in the proposition, "People do *D* because they believe *C*."

269. Although case III is not the only case, nor even the most frequent case, people are inclined to regard it as general and to merge with it cases I and II to which they preferably attribute little or no importance. Ordinary language, with its lack of exactness, encourages the error, because a person may state case III explicitly and be unconsciously thinking meantime of cases I and II. It often happens, besides, that we get mixtures of the three cases in varying proportions.

270. Aristotle opens his *Politics*, I, 1, 1 (Rackham, p. 3), with the statement: "Seeing that every city is a society (Rackham, "partnership") and that every society (partnership) is constituted to the end of some good (for all men work to achieve what to them seems good) it is manifest that all societies (partnerships) seek some good." Here we stand altogether in the domain of logic: with a deliberate purpose—the purpose of achieving a certain good—human beings have constituted a society that is called a city. It would seem as though Aristotle were on the point of going off into the absurdities of the "social contract"! But not so. He at once changes tack, and the principle he has stated he will use to determine what a city *ought* to be rather than what it actually is.

271. The moment Aristotle has announced his principle—an association for purposes of mutual advantage—he tosses it aside and gives an altogether different account of the origin of society. First he notes the necessity of a union between the sexes, and soundly remarks that "that does not take place of deliberate choice" [1]; wherewith, evidently, we enter the domain of non-logical conduct. He continues: "Nature has created certain individuals to command and others to obey." Among the Greeks Nature has so distinguished women and slaves. Not so among the Barbarians, for among the Barbarians, Nature has not appointed any individuals to command. We are still, therefore, in the domain of non-logical conduct; nor do we leave it when Aristotle explains that the two associations of master and slave, husband and wife, are the foundations of the family, that the village is constituted by several families, and that several villages form a state; nor when, finally, he concludes with the explicit declaration that "Every city, therefore, like the original associations, comes of Nature." [2] One could not allude to non-logical actions in clearer terms.

271 [1] *Politica*, I, 1, 4 (Rackham, p. 5): *καὶ τοῦτο οὐκ ἐκ προαιρέσεως . . .*

271 [2] I, 1, 8 (Rackham, p. 9): *Διὸ πᾶσα πόλις φύσει ἐστίν, εἴπερ καὶ αἱ πρῶται κοινωνίαι.*

272. But, alas, if the city comes of Nature, it does not come of the deliberate will of citizens who get together for the purpose of achieving a certain advantage! There is an inconsistency between the principle first posited and the conclusion reached.[1] Just how Aristotle fell into it we cannot know, but to accomplish that feat for oneself, one may proceed in the following fashion: First centre exclusively on the idea of "city," or "state." It will then be easy to connect city, or state, with the idea of "association," and then to connect association with the idea of *deliberate* association. So we get the first principle. But now think, in the second place, of the many many facts observable in a city or a state—the family, masters and slaves, and so on. Deliberate purpose will not fit in with those things very well. They suggest rather the notion of something that develops naturally. And so we get Aristotle's second description.

273. He gets rid of the contradiction by metaphysics, which never withholds its aid in these desperate cases. Recognizing non-logical conduct, he says, I, 1, 12 (Rackham, pp. 11-13): "It is therefore manifest that the city is a product of Nature and is superior (prior) to man (to the individual). From Nature accordingly comes the tendency (an impulse) in all men toward such association. Therefore the man who first founded one was the cause of a very great good." So then, there is the inclination imparted by Nature; but it is further necessary that a man found the city. So a logical action is grafted upon the non-logical action (§ 306, I-β); and there is no help for that, for, says Aristotle, Nature does nothing in vain.[1] Our best thanks, therefore, to that estimable demoiselle for so neatly rescuing a philosopher from a predicament!

272 [1] Similar contradictions are observable in metaphysical and theological disputes as to "free will," "predestination," "efficacious grace" (§ 280), and the like. Pascal well ridicules some of these incoherences; but, speaking as a metaphysicist and theologian himself, he replaces them with arguments that are worth but little more, and sometimes less. He had begun by saying, *Lettres à une provinciale,* I, p. 6: "I never quarrel over names, provided I am told what meanings they are given"; and with that he was almost taking his stand within the domain of logico-experimental science (§ 119). But he soon relapses, to go back to the domain of metaphysics, theology, sentiment.

273 [1] I, 1, 10 (Rackham, p. 11): *Οὐθὲν γάρ, ὡς φαμέν, μάτην ἡ φύσις ποιεῖ*: Rackham: "does nothing without a purpose."

274. In distinguishing the Greeks from the Barbarians in his celebrated theory of natural slavery, Aristotle avails himself of the concept of non-logical conduct. It is obvious, among other things, that logic being the same for Greeks and Barbarians, if all actions were logical there could not be any difference between Greeks and Barbarians. But that is not all. Good observer that he is, Aristotle notices differences among Greek citizens. Speaking of the forms of democracy he says, VI, 2, 1 (Rackham, pp. 497-98): "Excellent is an agricultural people; consequently one can institute a democracy where a people lives by farming and sheep-raising." And he repeats, VI, 2, 7 (Rackham, p. 503): "Next after farmers, the best people are shepherds, or people who live by owning cattle. . . . The other rabbles on which other sorts of democracy are based are greatly inferior." Here then we get clearly distinguished classes of citizens and almost a rudimentary economic determinism. But there is no reason for our stopping where Aristotle stops; and if we do go on we see that in general the conduct of human beings depends on their temperaments and occupations.

Cicero credits the ancestors of the Romans of his time with knowing that "the characters of human beings result not so much from race and family as from those things which are contributed by the nature of their localities for the ordinary conduct of life, and from which we draw our livelihood and subsistence. The Carthaginians were liars and cheats not by race but from the nature of their country, which with its port and its contacts with all sorts of merchants and foreigners speaking different languages inclined them through love of profits to love of trickery. The mountaineers of Liguria are harsh and uncouth. . . . The Capuans have ever been a supercilious people, because of the fertility of their soil, the wealth of their harvests, the salubriousness, the disposition, and the beauty of their city." [1]

274 [1] *De lege agraria,* II, 35, 95. In combating the Agrarian Law Cicero was trying to persuade his fellow-citizens that a colony established at Capua might become dangerous to Rome. For that reason he may not have been altogether convinced by his own argument. But we need not go into that. We are trying to ascertain not Cicero's personal views, but the opinions current in his time. And if he used the

275. In his *Rhetoric,* II, 12-14 (Freese, pp. 247-57), Aristotle makes an analysis, which came to be celebrated, of the traits of man according to age—in adolescence, in maturity, and in senility. He pushes his analysis further still, II, 12, 17 (Freese, pp. 257-63), and examines the effects on character of noble birth, wealth, and power—a splendidly conducted study. But all that evidently carries him into the domain of non-logical conduct.[1]

argument he used, it means that he thought it reflected the feeling of a larger or smaller element among Roman citizens.

275 [1] One may also detect a certain conception of non-logical conduct in the fact that Aristotle ascribes the virtues—temperance, justice, courage, and so on—to the non-rational part of the human being, *Magna moralia,* I, 5, 1 (Stock, p. 1185-b): "Foresight, intelligence (quickness of wit), wisdom, learning (aptitude for learning), memory, and other similar things arise in the rational part [of the soul]. In the non-rational one finds what are called the virtues: temperance, justice, energy, and all other moral qualities that are deemed worthy of praise." Aristotle's doctrine of the logical or non-logical character of conduct in general was perhaps not very clear—such doctrines rarely are. All the same he seems to have recognized non-logical elements, supplementing them with logical elements, and subordinating them to the logical. In the *Politica,* VII, 12, 6 (Rackham, p. 601), he says that three things make a man good and virtuous: *φύσις, ἔθος, λόγος*: "nature, habit, reason." As for the non-logical element, Aristotle admits that human beings act, in part at least, under the influence of external circumstances, such as climate, soil, and so on. In *Ibid.,* VII, 6 (Rackham, pp. 565-66), he clearly relates the conduct of human beings to such circumstances; and in *De partibus animalium,* II, 4 [An erroneous reference: read: *Historia animalium,* VIII, 28-29 (Thompson, pp. 606-07).—A. L.], he explains just how he thinks the relationship functions, in general, for living beings. The author (Aristotle ?) of the *Problemata,* offers, XIV (Forster, pp. 909-10), additional reflections on such relationships. So far we are within the domain of the non-logical. But the writer at once takes steps to be rid of it by a procedure that is general and which lies in subordinating it to logic: it becomes the material with which reason works. *Magna moralia,* I, 11, 3 (Stock, p. 1187-b): "Judgment, will, and all that is in accord with reason, constitute the principle of conduct, good or bad." Aristotle is not aware that in that he is contradicting what he said, in the *Politica,* that people who live in cold countries are courageous. In this case, the "principle" of courageous action, that is to say, the "judgment and will" to expose oneself to peril, is determined, according to Aristotle, by climate and not by "reason." He thinks he clears his traces by saying, *Magna moralia,* I, 11, 5 (Stock, *loc. cit.*), that first requisite is help from nature, and next will; but ignoring any metaphysical question as to the freedom of the will, which we choose not to go into, we still have the problem, first of knowing whether the two things that he considers independent are so in reality, and then in what proportions they figure in any concrete act. Going into that problem, one finds that there is conduct in which the first element, the non-logical, prevails, and other conduct in which the second element, the logical, prevails.

Aristotle was lured from the scientific path, aside from metaphysical considera-

276. Aristotle even has the concept of evolution. In the *Politics,* II, 5, 12 (Rackham, pp. 129-31), he remarks that the ancestors of the Greeks probably resembled the vulgar and ignorant among his contemporaries.

277. Had Aristotle held to the course he in part so admirably followed, we would have had a scientific sociology in his early day. Why did he not do so? There may have been many reasons; but chief among them, probably, was that eagerness for premature practical applications which is ever obstructing the progress of science, along with a mania for preaching to people as to what they ought to do—an exceedingly bootless occupation—instead of finding out what they actually do. His *History of Animals* avoids those causes of error, and that perhaps is why it is far superior to the *Politics* from the scientific point of view.

278. It might seem strange to find traces of the concept of non-logical conduct in a dreamer like Plato; yet there they are! The notion transpires in the reasons Plato gives for establishing his colony far from the sea. To be near the sea begins by "being sweet" but ends by "being bitter" for a city: "for filling with commerce and traffic it develops capricious, untrustworthy instincts, and a breed of tricksters." [1] Non-logical conduct has its place also in the well-known apologue of Plato on the races of mankind. The god who fashioned men mixed gold into the composition of those fit to govern, silver in guardians of the state (the warriors), iron in tillers of the soil and labourers. Plato also has a vague notion of what we are to call class-circulation, or circulation of *élites* (§§ 2026 f.). He knows that individuals of the silver race may chance to be born in the race of gold, or *vice versa,* and so for the other races.[2]

tions, by that great enemy of all social science: the mania for achieving some practical result. In the *Ethica Nicomachea,* II, 2, 1 (Rackham, p. 75), he says that he does not desire to confine himself to theory only: "For we study not to know what virtue is, but to become good; otherwise our study would be of no use." Aristotle had no other means of influencing others than logical argument; and so he was, as he had to be, inclined to make logic the controlling force in human conduct.

278 [1] *De legibus,* IV. Aristotle, *Politica,* VII, 5, also discusses the advantages and disadvantages of proximity to the sea.

278 [2] *Respublica,* III, 21, 415A. And *cf.* my *Systèmes socialistes,* Vol. I, p. 276.

279. That being the case, if one would remain within the domain of science, one must go on and investigate the probable characteristics and the probable evolution of a society made up of different races of human beings, which are not reproduced from generation to generation with exactly the same characteristics and which are able to mix. That would be working towards a science of societies. But Plato has a very different purpose. He is little concerned with what is. He strains all his intellectual capacities to discover what *ought* to be. And thereupon non-logical conduct vanishes, and Plato's fancy goes sporting about among logical actions, which he invents in great numbers; and we find him at no great cost to himself appointing magistrates to put individuals who are born in a class but differ in traits from their parents in their proper places, and proclaiming laws to preserve or alter morals—in short, deserting the modest province of science to rise to the sublime heights of creation.

280. The controversies on the question "Can virtue be taught?" also betray some distant conception of non-logical conduct. According to the documents in our possession, it would seem that Socrates regarded virtue as a science and left little room for non-logical actions.[1] Plato and Aristotle abandon that extreme position. They hold that a certain natural inclination is necessary to "virtue." But that inclination once premised, back they go to the domain of logic, which is now called in to state the logical implications of temperament, and these in their turn determine human conduct. Those

280 [1] Ritter, *Geschichte der Philosophie alter Zeit,* Vol. III, p. 305 (Morrison, Vol. III, pp. 262-63): "More interested in didacticism than in physic, Socrates sought the principle of all morality strictly in dialectic. So virtue, in his opinion, had no other foundaton than reason and knowledge. But Plato already had found that courage and moderation, two necessary phases of virtue, must pre-exist in the temperament of the human being, whose impulses lie in the heart, not in the head. Aristotle went even farther in that direction and clung more tightly still to physic, for which he had a temperamental predilection. As the first principle of virtue he takes not reason but natural impulse and the emotional states of the soul (πάθη)." Zeller, *Philosophie der Griechen,* Vol. III, p. 118 (missing in Alleyne): [For Socrates] "knowledge is not just an indispensable prerequisite, not just an auxiliary, to true morality: it directly constitutes all morality; and when knowledge is lacking, he is not content with the mere recognition of an imperfect virtue: he cannot see any virtue at all. Not till later on, in Plato, and more completely in Aristotle, will we find a correction of that narrow form of the Socratic doctrine of virtue."

old controversies have points of resemblance with the disputes which took place long afterwards on "efficacious," and "non-efficacious," grace.

281. The procedure of Plato and Aristotle in the controversies on the teaching of "virtue" is a general one. Non-logical actions are credited with a rôle that it would be absurd not to give them, but then that rôle is at once withdrawn, and people go back to the logical implications of inclinations; and by dividing those inclinations, which in fact cannot be ignored, into "good" ones and "bad" ones, a way is found to keep inclinations that are in accord with the logical system one prefers and to eliminate all others.

282. St. Thomas tries to steer a deft course between the necessity of recognizing certain non-logical inclinations and a great desire to give full sway to reason, between the determinism of non-logical conduct and the doctrine of free will that is implicit in logical conduct. He says that "virtue is a good quality or disposition (*habitus*) of the soul, whereby one lives uprightly, which no one uses wrongly, and which God produces within us apart from any action by ourselves." [1] Taken as a "disposition of the soul" virtue is classed with non-logical actions; and so it is when we say that God produces it in us apart from anything we do of ourselves. But by that divine interposition any uncertainty as to the character of non-logical conduct is removed, for it becomes logical according to the mind of God and therefore logical for the theologians who are so fortunate as to know the divine mind. Others use Nature for the same purpose and with the same results. People act according to certain inclinations. That reduces the rôle of the non-logical to a minimum, actions being regarded as logical consequences of the inclinations. Then even that very modest remnant is made to vanish as by sleight-of-hand; for inclinations are conceived as imparted by some entity

282 [1] *Summa theologiae*, Ia IIae, *qu.* 55, *art.* 4 (*Opera*, Vol. VI, p. 353): *"Virtus est bona qualitas seu habitus mentis qua recte vivitur et qua nullus male utitur et quam Deus in nobis sine nobis operatur."* The non-logical character of certain conduct is more clearly perceived in a following remark by the Angelic Doctor: "But it should be noted that of the active dispositions (*habituum operativorum*) some are always towards the bad, such as vicious inclinations; some are now towards the good, now towards the bad, much as opinion stands towards the true and the false."

(God, Nature, or something else) that acts logically (§ 306, I-β); so that even though the acting subject may on occasion believe that his actions are non-logical, those who know the mind, or the logical procedure, of the entity in question—and all philosophers, sociologists, and the like, have that privilege—know that all conduct is logical.

283. The controversy between Herbert Spencer and Auguste Comte brings out a number of interesting aspects of non-logical conduct.

284. In his *Lectures on Positive Philosophy* (*Cours de philosophie positive*) Comte seems to be decidedly inclined to ascribe the predominance to logical conduct. He sees in positive philosophy, Vol. I, pp. 48-49, "the one solid basis for that social reorganization which is to terminate the critical state in which civilized nations have been living for so long a time." So then it is the business of theory to reorganize the world! How is that to come about? "Not to readers of these lectures should I ever think it necessary to prove that ideas govern and upset the world, or, in other terms, that the whole social mechanism rests, at bottom, on opinions. They are acutely aware that the great political and moral crisis in present-day society is due, in the last analysis, to our intellectual anarchy. Our most serious distress is caused by the profound differences of opinion that at present exist among all minds as to all those fundamental maxims the stability of which is the prime requisite for a real social order. So long as individual minds fail to give unanimous assent to a certain number of general ideas capable of constituting a common social doctrine, we cannot blind ourselves to the fact that the nations will necessarily remain in an essentially revolutionary atmosphere. . . . It is just as certain that if this gathering of minds to one communion of principles can once be attained, the appropriate institutions will necessarily take shape from it."

285. After quoting Comte's dictum that ideas govern and upset the world, Herbert Spencer advances a theory that non-logical actions alone influence society. "Ideas do not govern and overthrow the world: the world is governed or overthrown by feelings, to which ideas serve only as guides. The social mechanism does not rest finally upon opinions; but almost wholly upon character. Not intellectual anarchy, but moral antagonism, is the cause of political crises. All social phenomena are produced by the totality of human emotions and beliefs. . . . Practically, the popular character, and the social state, determine what ideas shall be current; instead of the current ideas determining the social state and the character. The modification of men's moral natures caused by the continuous discipline of social life, which adapts them more and more to social relations, is therefore the chief proximate cause of social progress." [1]

286. Then a curious thing happens: Comte and Spencer reverse positions reciprocally! In his *System of Positive Polity,* Vol. IV, p. 5, Comte decides to allow sentiment to prevail, and expresses himself very clearly on the point: "Though I have always proclaimed the universal preponderance of sentiment, I have had, so far, to devote my attention primarily to intelligence and activity, which prevail in sociology. But the very real ascendancy they have acquired having now brought on the period of their real systematization, the final purpose of this volume must now be to bring about a definite predominance of sentiment, which is the essential domain of morality."

Comte is straining the truth a little when he says that he has "*always* proclaimed the universal preponderance of sentiment." No trace of any such preponderance is to be detected in his *Cours.* Ideas stand in the forefront there. But Comte has changed. He began by considering existing theories, which he wished to replace with others of his own make; and in that battle of ideas, his own naturally won the palm, and from them new life was to come to the world. But time rolls on. Comte becomes a prophet. The battle of ideas is over. He imagines he has won a complete victory. So now he begins proclaiming dogma, pronouncing *ex cathedra,* and it is only natural that nothing but sentiments should now be left on the field—his own sentiments, of course.[1]

285 [1] *The Classification of the Sciences,* Addendum, pp. 37-38.

286 [1] Comte is to an extent aware of the evolution he has undergone, *Système,* Vol. III, Preface, p. vii: "Comparing this volume with the historical portions of my fundamental treatise, it will be noted that my general system is deeper and more

287. Comte, moreover, began by hoping to make converts of people; and naturally the instrument for doing that was, at the time, ideas. But he ended by having no hope save in a religion imposed by force, imposed if need be by Czar Nicholas, by the Sultan, or at the very least by a Louis Napoleon (who would in fact have done better to rest content with being just a dictator in the service of Positivism).[1] In this scheme sentiment is the big thing beyond shadow of doubt, and one can no longer say that "ideas govern or upset the world." It would be absurd to suppose that Comte turned to the Czar, to Reshid Pasha, or to Louis Napoleon, to induce them merely to preach ideas to their peoples. One might only object that the ideas of Comte would be determining the religion which would later be imposed upon mankind; and in that case ideas would be "upsetting the world," if the Czar, the Sultan, Louis Napoleon, or some other well-intentioned despot saw fit to take charge of enforcing Comte's positivism upon mankind. But that is far from

complete, whereas my special demonstrations are less developed. From the latter point of view, this final elaboration of my philosophy of history is at variance with my original announcements, which promised more details and proofs in this volume than in my first outlines, to which, instead, I am now obliged to refer for such things. Brought to a clearer understanding of the true character of the philosophical régime, I have come to feel that systematic assertions, which I first regarded as something merely provisory, should be the normal rule of any truly systematic exposition. The progress I have made and the prestige it has won for me allow me in my advancing years to fall in with the free and rapid stride of my chief predecessors, Aristotle, Descartes, and Leibnitz, who simply formulated their thoughts, leaving the task of verifying and developing them to their readers. That division of labour in intercourse between minds is at once the most honourable for the initiated and the most profitable for founders." And in this last, Comte is unquestionably right! It is no little convenience if one can manage to be believed without being pestered for proofs!

287 [1] *Système,* Vol. IV, pp. 377-78: "To modify public life, it is enough for [the Priesthood of Humanity] that circumstances shall have brought to the fore some preponderant and responsible will. That condition has been fairly well provided for in France since the advent of the Dictatorship, which frees organized doctrine from the irksome obligation of deferring to legislatures that are ever disposed to perpetuate a revolutionary condition, even when they are reactionary. . . . Without having to convert either the public or its leaders, Positivism, therefore, in virtue of its fundamental truth and its utter seasonableness, can win a partial ascendancy adequate for realizing the final transition, even unbeknown to the principal supporters of the movement." An action that takes place unbeknown to the individual who performs it obviously belongs to the genus of non-logical actions.

being the meaning one gathers from the statements in the *Cours*.

288. Comte recognizes, in fact he greatly exaggerates, the social influence of public worship and its efficacy in education—all of which is just a particular case of the efficacy of non-logical impulses. If Comte could have rested satisfied with being just a scientist, he might have written an excellent book on the value of religions and taught us many things. But he wanted to be the prophet of a new religion. Instead of studying the effects of historical or existing forms of worship, he wanted to create a new one—an entirely different matter. So he gives just another illustration of the harm done to science by the mania for practical applications.

289. Spencer, on the other hand, after admitting, even too sweepingly, the influence of non-logical actions, eliminates them altogether by the general procedure described in § 261. Says he: "Our postulate must be that primitive ideas are natural, and, under the conditions in which they occur, rational." [1] Driven out by the door, logic here climbs back through the window. "In early life we have been taught that human nature is everywhere the same. . . . This error we must replace by the truth that the laws of thought are everywhere the same; and that, given the data as known to him, the primitive man's inference is the reasonable inference" (§§ 701, 711).

290. In assuming any such thing, Spencer puts himself in the wrong in his controversy with Comte. If human beings always draw logical inferences from the data they have before them, and if they act in accordance with such inferences, then we are left with nothing but logical conduct, and it is ideas that "govern or upset the world." There is no room left for those sentiments to which Spencer was disposed to attribute that capacity; there is no way for them to crowd into a ready-made aggregate composed of experimental facts, however badly observed, and of logical inferences derived from such facts.

291. The principle advanced by Spencer makes sociology very easy, especially if it be combined with two other Spencerian principles: unitary evolution, and the identity, or quasi-identity, of the

289 [1] *Principles of Sociology,* Vol. I, § 52.

savages of our time with primitive man (§§ 728, 731). Accounts by travellers, more or less accurate and more or less soundly interpreted, give us, Spencer thinks, the data that primitive man had at his disposal; and where such accounts fail, we fill in the gaps with our imagination, which, when it cannot get the real, takes the plausible. That gives us all we need for a sociology, for we have only to determine the logical implications of the data at hand, without wasting too much time on long and difficult historical researches.

292. In just that way Spencer sets about discovering the origin and evolution of religion. His primitive man is like a modern scientist working in a laboratory to frame a theory. Primitive man of course has very imperfect materials at his disposal. That is why, despite his logical thinking, he can reach only imperfect conclusions. All the same he gets some philosophical notions that are not a little subtle. Spencer, *Ibid.*, Vol. I, § 154, represents as a "primitive" idea the notion that "any property characterizing an aggregate inheres in all parts of it." If you are desirous of testing the validity of that theory you need only state the proposition to some moderately educated individual among your friends, and you will see at once that he will not have the remotest idea of what you are talking about. Yet Spencer, *loc. cit.*, believes that your friend will go on and draw logical conclusions from something he does not understand: "The soul, present in the body of the dead man preserved entire, is also present in preserved parts of his body. Hence the faith in relics." Surely Spencer could never have discussed that subject with some good Catholic peasant woman on the Continent. The argument he maps out might possibly lead a philosopher enamoured of logic to believe in relics, but it has nothing whatever to do with popular beliefs in relics.

293. So Spencer's procedure has points of similarity with Comte's procedure. In general terms, one might state the situation in this fashion: we have two things, *P* and *Q* (Figure 8), that have to be considered in determining the social order *R*. We begin by asserting that *Q* alone determines that order; then we show that *P* determines *Q*. So *Q* is eliminated, and *P* alone determines the social order.

294. If *Q* designates "ideas" and *P* "sentiments," we get, roughly, the evolution of Comte's theories. If *Q* designates "sentiments" and *P* "ideas," we get, roughly, the evolution of Spencer's theories.

295. That is confirmed by the remarks of John Stuart Mill on the controversy between Comte and Spencer. Says he:[1] "It will not be found, on a fair examination of what M. Comte has written, that he has overlooked any of the truth that there is in Mr. Spencer's theory. He would not indeed have said (what Mr. Spencer apparently wishes us to say) that the effects which can be historically traced, for example, to religion, were not produced by the belief in God, but by reverence and fear of Him. He would have said that the reverence and fear presuppose the belief: that a God must be believed in before he can be feared or reverenced."

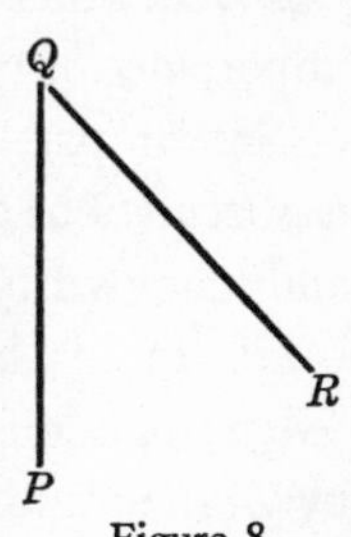

Figure 8

That is the very procedure in question! *P* is the belief in God; *Q*, sentiments of fear and reverence; *P* produces *Q*, and so becomes the cause determining conduct!

296. To a perfect logician like Mill it seems absurd that anyone could experience fear unless the feeling be logically inferred from a subject capable of inspiring fear. He should have remembered the verse of Statius,

"Primus in orbe deos fecit timor,"[1]

and then he would have seen that a course diametrically opposite is perfectly conceivable.[2] That granted, what was the course pursued

295 [1] *The Positive Philosophy of Auguste Comte,* p. 96 (London, p. 103).

296 [1] *Thebaid,* III, v. 661. The scholiast Lactantius [read Luctatius Placidus; see Knaack, *Rhenisches Museum für Philologie,* Vol. 56, p. 166.—A. L.] annotates [not very keenly] (Leyden, p. 406): "He says that the gods are worshipped for no other reason than the fear of mortals. As Lucan says, *Pharsalia,* I, v. 486: 'They fear inventions of their own devising' (*quae finxere timent*). Petronius [*Fragmenta,* XXVII] follows Statius: 'Fear first created gods on earth.' And Mintanor Musicus writes: '. . . the gods, whom humanity first invented under sting of pain.' "

296 [2] Holbach, *Système de la nature,* Vol. I, pp. 448, 456: "Mankind has ever derived its basic ideas on divinity from ignorance, fear, and calamity. . . . Man's earliest theology taught him first to fear and worship the elements themselves, and crude material objects."

in reality? Or better, what were the various courses pursued? It is for historical documents to answer, and we cannot let our fancy take the place of documents and pass off as real anything that seems plausible to us. We have to know how things actually took place, and not how they should have taken place, in order to satisfy a strictly logical intelligence.[3]

297. In other connexions, Mill is perfectly well aware of the social importance of non-logical actions. But he at once withdraws the concession, in part at least, and instead of going on with what is, turns to speculations as to what ought to be. That is the general procedure; and many writers resort to it to be rid of non-logical conduct.

298. In his book *On Liberty,* p. 16, Mill writes, for example: "Men's opinions . . . on what is laudable or blameable, are affected by all the multifarious causes which influence their wishes in regard to the conduct of others, and which are as numerous as those which determine their wishes on any other subject: sometimes their reason —at other times their prejudices or superstitions: often their social affections, not seldom their antisocial ones, their envy or jealousy, their arrogance or contemptuousness: but most commonly, their desires or fears for themselves—their legitimate or illegitimate self-interest. Wherever there is an ascendant class, a large portion of the morality of the country emanates from its class interests, and its feelings of class superiority."

All that, with a few reservations, is well said and approximately pictures the facts.[1] Mill might have gone on in that direction, and inquired, since he was dealing with liberty, into the relations of liberty to the motives he assigns to human conduct. In that event, he might have made a discovery: he might have seen that he was involved in a contradiction in trying with all his might to transfer political power to "the greatest number," while at the same time

296 [3] We noted Cicero's view of the practices of Roman divination in § 182 [3]: *De divinatione,* I, 3, 3: *"Atque haec, ut ego arbitror, veteres rerum magis eventis moniti quam ratione docti probaverunt."* That is very often the case: the fact, the non-logical action, comes first, then the explanation of the fact, the logical varnish.

298 [1] The reservations relate to Mill's not very exact use of terms such as "legitimate" and "illegitimate." But Mill cannot be specially blamed for that. It is a defect common to almost all writers who deal with such subjects.

defending a "liberty" that was incompatible with the prejudices, sentiments, and interests of said "greatest number." That discovery would then have enabled him to make a prophecy—one of the fundamental functions of science; namely, to foresee that liberty, as he conceived it, was progressively to decline, as being contrary to the motives that he had established as determinants of the aspirations of the class which was about to become the ruling class.

299. But Mill thought less of things as they are than of things as they ought to be. He says, *Ibid.*, p. 22: "He [a man] cannot rightfully be compelled to do or forbear because it will be better for him to do so, because it will make him happier, because, in the opinions of others, to do so would be wise, or even right. These are good reasons for remonstrating with him, or reasoning with him, or persuading him, or entreating him, but not for compelling him, or visiting him with any evil in case he do otherwise."[1]

299 [1] Mill, innocent soul, goes on to say, *loc. cit.*: "To justify that [such constraint], the conduct from which it is desired to deter him must be calculated to produce evil to someone else." He did not realize that sophistries are never wanting to show that the damage is there. Notice what happens in countries where people set out to enforce temperance and virtue in the holy name of "Progress": *Giornale d'Italia,* March 19, 1912: "Atlanta, Georgia, March 2. Last evening *Commendatore* Alessandro Bonci, who was stopping here temporarily in connexion with professional engagements, was arrested at the Georgian Terrace Hotel, together with his wife, his secretary, and his pianist, for violating the liquor law. It seems that Signor Bonci and his friends, like good Italians, who serve wine two meals a day at least, had adopted an ingenious device for doing so in spite of the law that forbids the use of wines and liquors in the State of Georgia. For several days the manager of the hotel had noticed that towards the middle of their meals the Boncis and their friends were in the habit of setting on the table four little bottles such as are used by druggists, with labels giving directions for using the presumptive 'medicines.' The regularity with which the Bonci party drank the contents of the bottles twice a day, as though each member of it were suffering from the same disease and required the same treatment, at length aroused the suspicions of the house detective. He mentioned the matter to a zealous policeman, who last evening, when the time for the 'treatment' came, confiscated the bottles. Each of them was found to have the capacity of a wine-glass and to contain nothing but excellent Chianti, with which, it seems, *Commendatore* Bonci travels well supplied in order to cope with the surprises of American law. Despite the lively protestations of Signor Bonci, the four offenders were put into an automobile and taken to the Court House, where Judge Ralendorf, after a summary inquiry, continued the case till this morning, fixing bail at $2,000. Then came the best, not to say the worst, of it. The celebrated

That may be a "good justice," but it is not the justice handed out to us by our masters, who each year favour us with new laws to prevent our doing the very things that Mill says people should be allowed to do. His preaching, therefore, has been altogether without effect.

300. In certain writers the part played by non-logical actions is suppressed altogether, or rather, is regarded merely as the exceptional part, the "bad" part. Logic alone is a means to human progress. It is synonymous with "good," just as all that is not logical is synonymous with "evil." But let us not be led astray by the word "logic." Belief in logic has nothing to do with logico-experimental science; and the worship of Reason may stand on a par with any other religious cult, fetishism not excepted.

301. Condorcet expresses himself as follows:[1] "So a general knowledge of the natural rights of man; the opinion, even, that such rights are inalienable and imprescriptible; a prayer voiced aloud for liberty of thought and press, for freedom of commerce and industry, for succour of the people . . . indifference to all religions—classified, at last, where they belong with superstitions and political devices [The good soul fails to notice that his worship of Progress is itself a religion!]—hatred and hypocrisy and fanaticism; contempt for prejudices; zeal for the propagation of enlightenment—all became the common avowal, the distinguishing mark, of anyone who was neither a Machiavellian nor a fool." Preaching re-

tenor found he had no more than $150 in his pocket, and he was faced with the prospect of spending the night in jail."

We may guess that if Signor Bonci had remembered that the ointment of St. John Goldmouth may be used on the hands of American reformers with as good effect as it had in Boccaccio's time on the hands of our virtuous Italian Inquisitors, he might have escaped such annoyance. In general terms: You happen to be in the dining-car when the train enters one of the abstemious states of the American Union, and the glass of wine that you were about to drink is snatched from the table in front of you. If you ask, "What harm am I doing to my neighbour by drinking this glass of wine?", the answer comes quick and prompt: "You are setting a bad example!" And the rabble that enforces its will upon you in that fashion speaks with indignation of Spanish Catholics who, to prevent setting bad examples, refuse to tolerate in Spain any public worship except the Roman Catholic!

301 [1] *Esquisse d'un tableau historique des progrès de l'esprit humain,* pp. 264-65.

ligious toleration, Condorcet is not aware that he is betraying an intolerance of his own when he treats dissenters from his religion of Progress the way the orthodox have always treated heretics. It is true that he considers himself right and his adversaries wrong, because his own religion is good and theirs bad; but that, inverting terms, is exactly what they say too.

302. Maxims from Condorcet and other writers of his time are still quoted by humanitarian fanatics today. Condorcet continues, p. 292: "All errors in politics and morals are based on philosophical errors, which are in turn connected with errors in physic. There is no religious system, no supernatural extravagance, that is not grounded on ignorance of the laws of nature." But he himself gives proof of just such ignorance when he tries to have us swallow absurdities like the following, p. 345: "What vicious practice is there, what custom contrary to good faith, nay, what crime, that cannot be shown to have its cause and origin in the laws, the institutions, the prejudices, of the country in which that practice, that custom, is observed, that crime committed?" And he concludes finally, p. 346, that "nature links truth, happiness, and virtue with chain unsunderable."

303. Similar ideas are common among the French *philosophes* of the later eighteenth century. In their eyes every blessing doth from "reason" flow, every ill from "superstition." Holbach sees the source of all human woe in error; [1] and that belief has endured as one of

303 [1] *Système de la nature,* Vol. I, pp. 398-409: *"The errors of mankind as to what constitutes happiness are the real source of its troubles. Inefficacy of proposed remedies.* . . . If we consult experience, we see that the real source of that multitude of woes that everywhere afflict the human race is to be sought in sacred opinions and illusions. Ignorance of natural causes first created gods for humanity: imposture clothed them with terror. The deadly thought of them pursued the human being without making him better, filled him with fears to no purpose, packed his mind with nightmares, blocked the progress of his intelligence, prevented him from seeking his own welfare. His fears enslaved him to deceivers who made pretence of working his weal. . . . Prejudices no less dangerous have blinded men as to their rulers. . . . A similar blindness we find in the science of morals. . . . So humanity's burden of woe has no whit been lightened, but has been made heavier rather by his religions, his governments, his education, his opinions, in a word by all the institutions that he has been persuaded to adopt [By whom persuaded? By someone

the dogmas of the humanitarian religion, holiest of holies, of which our present-day "intellectuals" form the priesthood.[2]

304. All these people fail to notice that the worship of "Reason," "Truth," "Progress," and other similar entities is, like all cults, to be classed with non-logical actions. It was born, it has flourished, and it continues to prosper, for the purpose of combating other cults, just as in Graeco-Roman society the oriental cults arose out of opposition to the polytheistic cult. At that time one same current of non-logical conduct found its multiple expression in the *taurobolium,* the *criobolium,* the cult of Mithras, the growing importance of mysteries, Neo-Platonism, mysticism, and finally Christianity, which was to triumph over rival cults, none the less borrowing many things from them. So, toward the end of the eighteenth century and the beginning of the nineteenth, one same current of non-logical conduct finds its expression in the theism of the *philosophes,* the sentimental vagaries of Rousseau, the cult of "Reason" and the "Supreme Being," the love of the First Republic for the number 10, theophilanthropy (of which the "positivist" religion of Comte is merely an offshoot), the religion of Saint-Simon, the religion of pacifism, and other religions that still survive to our times.

These considerations belong to a much more comprehensive order, properly relating to the *subjective* aspect of theories indicated in § 13. In general, in other words, we have to ask ourselves why and how individuals come to evolve and accept certain theories. And, in particular, now that we have identified one such purpose—the purpose of giving logical status to conduct that does not possess it —we have to ask by what means and devices that purpose is achieved. From the objective standpoint, the error in the arguments

not of the human species?] on pretence that his lot would be made more bearable. It cannot be too often repeated: In error lies the true source of the ills that afflict the human race. Not with Nature lies the responsibility for human unhappiness. No angry God ever willed that humanity should live in tears. No hereditary depravity made mortals wicked and miserable. Those deplorable consequences are all and exclusively due to error."

303 [2] Elie Reclus, *Les primitifs,* p. 161: "Since morality is measured, along its general lines at least, by intellectual development, no surprise will be occasioned by finding it very rudimentary here [among the Redskins]."

just noted lies in their giving an *a priori* answer to the questions stated in § 14, and in maintaining that a theory needs simply to be in accord with the facts to be advantageous to society. That error is usually supplemented by the further error of considering facts not as they stand in reality but as they are pictured by the exhilarated imagination of the enthusiast.

305. Our induction so far has shown from some few particular cases the prevalence of a tendency to evade consideration of non-logical actions, which nevertheless force themselves upon the attention of anyone undertaking to discuss human societies; and also the no mean importance of that tendency. Now we must look into it specially and in general terms.[1]

306. So let us now examine the various devices by which non-logical actions are eliminated so that only logical actions are left: and suppose we begin as usual by classifying the objects we are trying to understand.

CLASS A [1]

The principles [2] underlying non-logical actions are held to be devoid of any objective reality (§§ 307-18).

305 [1] Farther along, in Chapter IX, we shall have to consider a still more general subject—the variability of the arguments to which human beings are prompted by sentiments, and which provide logical exteriors for non-logical conduct. A strictly inductive course, such as we have been following, brings up the particular problem in advance of the general. That has the drawback of compelling us to examine the particular problem first, and to keep going back to things on which we have already touched. It has, on the other hand, the great advantage of making the materials we work with clearer and more manageable.

306 [1] [One need hardly remind the reader that these synoptic pictures of Pareto's classifications are unintelligible apart from the exposition *seriatim* of the various categories that he proceeds to make. They have to be continually re-read in connexion with the text that follows. This table is particularly obscure in itself, not only because of exceptionally opaque writing but because implicit in it is another classification that Pareto for some reason does not see fit to utilize. It is clear that the devices in Class A are used from a sceptical standpoint to discredit beliefs on logical grounds. The B-I and B-III devices are used by believers to represent their beliefs as logical. The other devices are "errors" commonly made by scholars in viewing the non-logical as logical. I use the term "device" for the sake of clarity; Pareto's term was "means." Whatever the term used, it has to be understood as not

306 [2] "Principle" here means the cause to which an action is to be ascribed.

Genera

Genus I. They are disregarded entirely (§§ 307-08)

Genus II. They are regarded as absurd prejudices (§§ 309-11)

Genus III. They are regarded as tricks used by some individuals to deceive others (§§ 312-18)

CLASS B

The principles underlying non-logical actions are credited with now more, now less, objective reality (§§ 319-51)

Genera and Subgenera

Genus I. The principles are taken as completely and directly real (§§ 319-38)

- Iα. Precepts with sanctions in part imaginary (§§ 321-33)
- Iβ. Simple interposition of a personal god or a personified abstraction (§§ 332-33)
- Iγ. The same interposition supplemented by legends and logical inferences (§ 334)
- Iδ. Some metaphysical entity is taken as real (§§ 335-36)
- Iε. What is real is an implicit accord between the principles and certain sentiments (§§ 337-38)

Genus II. The principles of non-logical conduct are not taken as completely or directly real. Indirectly, the reality is found in cer-

implying any intent to deceive on the part of a person using such a device or means. Pareto's classifications, which are taken over from botany, envisage classes, genera and subgenera (sometimes species and subspecies). I keep these terms in the tables of classification. In the text at large, to avoid a fatiguing technical atmosphere, I often render "genus" and "species" loosely as "type," "kind," "sort," or more generally "variety": the "Iβ variety," or "Iβ type" would be, in the tables, the "Iβ subgenus," and so on. Pareto makes but little use of the "genus" in the structure proper of his theories, the one exception perhaps being his analysis of the residue of asceticism (§§ 1163 f.). The "class," on the other hand, is essential to his theory of interdependence and intensities (Chapter XII). Since residues increase or diminish in intensities by "classes," and interdependences arise primarily within "classes," it is clear that the structure of the "class" has all along to be borne in mind.—A. L.]

tain facts that are said to be inaccurately observed or imperfectly understood (§§ 339-50)

IIα. It is assumed that human beings make imperfect observations, and derive inferences from them logically (§§ 340-46)

IIβ. A myth is taken as the reflection of some historical reality that is concealed in one way or another, or else as a mere imitation of some other myth (§§ 347-49)

IIγ. A myth is made up of two parts: a historical fact and an imaginary adjunct (§ 350)

Genus III. The principles of non-logical actions are mere allegories (§§ 351-52)

CLASS C

It is assumed that non-logical actions have no effect on "progress," or else are obstructive to it. Hence they are to be eliminated in any study designed solely to promote "progress" (§§ 353-56).

307. Let us examine these various categories one by one.

Device A-I: *Non-logical actions are disregarded.* Non-logical actions can be disregarded entirely as having no place in the realm of reality. That is the position of Plato's Socrates in the matter of the national religions of Greece.[1] He is asked what he thinks of the ravishing of Orithyia, daughter of Erechtheus, by Boreas. He begins by rejecting the logical interpretation that tries to see a historical fact in the myth (IIγ). Then he opines that such inquiries are as finespun as they are profitless, and falls back on the popular belief. On common belief the oracle at Delphi also relied when it prescribed that the best way to honour the gods was for each to follow the customs of his own city.[2] Certainly the oracle in no wise meant by that

307 [1] *Phaedrus,* 229-30 (Fowler, pp. 419-23).

307 [2] The fact is mentioned by Xenophon's Socrates. *Memorabilia,* IV, 3, 16: "Since thou seest that when the god of Delphi is asked how best to please the gods, he replies: *By following the custom of the city.*" Cicero, *De legibus,* II, 16, 40: "Our law shall further provide that of all our ancestral rites the best should be fostered. When the Athenians consulted the Pythian Apollo as to which rites they had better practise, they received the oracle: 'Those customary with the forefathers.' Then they came back again, saying that the custom of the forefathers had often changed, and

that such customs corresponded to things that were not real; yet actually they might as well have, since they were held to be entirely exempt from the verification to which real things are considered subject. That method often amounts to viewing beliefs as non-logical actions to be taken for what they are without any attempt to explain them—the problem being merely to discover the relationship in which they stand towards other social facts. That, overtly or tacitly, is the attitude of many statesmen.

308. So, in Cicero's *De natura deorum,* the pontifex Cotta distinguishes the statesman from the philosopher. As pontifex he protests that he will ever defend the beliefs, the worship, the ceremonies, the religion, of the forefathers, and that no argument, be it of scholar or dunce, will ever budge him from that position. He is persuaded that Romulus and Numa founded Rome, the one with his auspices, the other with his religion. "That, Balbus, is what I think, as Cotta and as pontifex. It is now for me to know what you think. From you, a philosopher, I have a right to expect some reason for your beliefs. The beliefs I get from our forefathers I must accept quite apart from any proof." [1] In that it is obvious that as pontifex Cotta deliberately steps aside from the realm of logical reality, which implies a belief either that traditional Roman beliefs have no basis in fact or else that they are to be classed with non-logical actions.[2]

309. Device A-II: *The principles of non-logical actions are regarded as absurd prejudices.* One may consider merely the forms of non-logical actions and finding them irrational, judge them absurd prejudices, at the most deserving of attention from a pathological

they asked which they should prefer of the various ancestral customs; and the god answered: 'The best.'" Cicero appends a logical consideration that has no logical force whatever: "And it is assuredly true that what is best should be taken as the most authentic tradition and the closest to God."

308 [1] III, 2, 5. *Cf. De divinatione,* II, 12, 28: "As regards divination, I think the custom should be cherished for considerations of state and common religion. But here we are in strict privacy and we surely have a right to discuss the matter quite frankly (*sine invidia*), and I in particular, since I have very grave doubts in not a few connexions."

308 [2] [Pareto wrote: "which means either that such [logico-experimental] reality does not exist or that it is of the genus of the principles of non-logical actions."—A. L.]

standpoint as veritable maladies of the human race. That has been the attitude of not a few writers in dealing with legal and political formalities. It is the attitude especially of writers on religion and most of all of writers on forms of worship. It is also the attitude of our contemporary anti-clericals with regard to the Christian religion —and it betrays great ignorance on the part of those bigots, along with a narrow-mindedness that incapacitates them for ever understanding social phenomena.

We have already seen specimens of this type of reasoning in the works of Condorcet (§§ 301-02) and Holbach (§§ 296 [2], 303). A more diluted type is observable in disquisitions purporting to make this or that religion "more scientific" (§ 16 [2]), on the assumption that a religion which is not scientific is either absurd or reprehensible. So in earlier times there were efforts to remove by subtle interpretation such elements in the legends and cults of the pagan gods as were considered non-logical. It was the procedure of the Protestants during the Reformation, while the liberal Protestants of our day are repeating the same exploits, appealing to their pseudo-science. So also for the Modernists in their criticism of Catholicism, and for our Radical Socialists in their demeanour towards Marxism.

310. If one regards certain non-logical actions as absurd, one may centre chiefly on their ridiculous aspects; and that is often an effective weapon for combating a faith. Frequent use of it was made against established religions from the day of Lucian down to the day of Voltaire. In an article replete with historical blunders, Voltaire says of the religion of Rome: "I am imagining that after conquering Egypt Caesar sends an embassy to China, with the idea of stimulating the foreign trade of the Roman Empire. . . . The Emperor Iventi, first of that name, is reigning at the time. . . . After receiving Caesar's ambassadors with typical Chinese courtesy, he secretly inquires through his interpreters as to the civilization, customs, and religion of these Romans. . . . He learns that the Roman People supports at great expense a college of priests, who can tell you exactly the right time for embarking on a voyage and the very best place for fighting a battle by inspecting the liver of an ox or the appetite with which chickens eat their barley. That sacred science was brought to the Romans long, long before by a little god named Tages, who was unearthed somewhere in Tuscany. The Roman people worship just one god whom they always call 'Highest and Best.' All the same, they have built a temple to a harlot named Flora; and most Roman housewives have little household gods in their homes, five or six inches high. One of the little divinities is the goddess Nipples, another the god Bottom. . . . The Emperor has his laugh. The courts at Nanking at first conclude, as he does, that the Roman ambassadors are either lunatics or impostors . . . but the Emperor, being as just as he is courteous, holds private converse with the ambassadors. . . . They confess to him that the College of Augurs dates from early ages of Roman barbarism; that an institution so ridiculous has been allowed to survive only because it became endeared to the people in the course of long ages; that all respectable people make fun of the augurs; that Caesar never consults them; that according to a very great man by the name of Cato no augur is ever able to speak to a colleague without a laugh; and finally that Cicero, the greatest orator and best philosopher of Rome, has just published against the augurs a little essay, *On Divination,* in which he hands over to everlasting ridicule all auspices, all prophecy, and all the fortune-telling of which humanity is enamoured. The Emperor of China is curious to read Cicero's essay. His interpreters translate it. He admires the book and the Roman Republic." [1]

310 [1] *Remarques pour servir de Supplément à l'Essai sur les mœurs,* Pt. IV (*Œuvres,* Vol. V, p. 48): "Contemptible customs in a nation do not always indicate that that nation is itself contemptible." Among the blunders mentioned are the following: 1. Cicero's essay *De divinatione* was written after Cæsar's death. But that is a small matter; if one is going to pretend that Cæsar sent ambassadors to China, one may also pretend that he was living when Cicero wrote the essay. 2. The Chinese pantheon was much better filled than the Roman pantheon. That error on Voltaire's part may be forgiven, since it was the error of all the *philosophes* of his time. With a little care, however, he might have avoided the following: 3. Wittingly or unwittingly, he confuses Roman divination with the Etruscan. The god Tages belonged only to the latter. 4. Jupiter Optimus Maximus was by no means the only god in the official cult of Rome. [I cannot believe that Voltaire did not know that. The very glaringness of the error calls attention to a sacrilegious parody of French Christianity in the allusions to Jupiter, Flora, and the Penates.—A. L.] 5. The Penates were not at all the gods of silly housewives. Servius, *In Vergilii Aeneidem,* II, v. 514 (Thilo-

311. In dealing with writings of this kind, we must be careful not to fall into the very error we are here considering, with reference to non-logical actions.[1] The intrinsic value of such satires may be zero when viewed from the experimental standpoint, whereas their polemical value may be great. Those two things we must always keep distinct. Moreover they may have a certain intrinsic value: a group of non-logical actions taken as a whole may be useful for attaining a given purpose without absolutely all of them, taken individually, being useful to that purpose. Certain ridiculous actions

Hagen, Vol. I, p. 298): "The Penates are all the gods worshipped in the home." Rome herself had her Penates. Voltaire would use Cicero against the silly housewives, but Cicero himself invokes the Penates, *Pro Publio Sulla,* 31, 86: "Wherefore, O ye gods of our forefathers, and ye, O Penates, who watch over this city and this country of ours, ye who during my consulship did confer your aid and your divine protection upon this state, upon the Roman People and its liberties, upon these homes, these temples, you do I invoke as witnesses to my integrity and honesty of purpose in appearing in defence of Publius Sulla." *Cf.* also *In Catilinam,* IV, 9, 18. 6. Whether he believed in such things or not, Caesar made a practice of consulting soothsayers. There is an allusion to that in *De divinatione,* I, 52, 119; II, 16, 36, which Voltaire quotes; and *cf.* Dio Cassius, *Historia Romana,* XLIV, 17, 18; Plutarch, *Caesar,* 63-64 (Perrin, Vol. VII, pp. 589-95); Suetonius, *Divus Julius,* 81; Pliny, *Historia naturalis,* XXVIII, 4 (2). To one of Cæsar's superstitions we have previously alluded in § 184 [2]. 7. Cicero does not dream of ridiculing all auspices. He was himself an augur, and speaks of auspices with the greatest respect, *De legibus,* II, 12, 31: "The office of augur stands very high and is of the greatest importance in the state [*i.e.,* in Cicero's ideal state] and it is clothed with the greatest prestige. And that I feel not because I am an augur but because we can think not otherwise." He had little or no regard for the intrinsic merits of augury; but he considered the institution useful to the state and consequently did not ridicule it (*cf.* the quotations in § 313 [1]). 8. Cato was speaking not of the augurs, but of the haruspices: Cicero, *De divinatione,* II, 24, 51: "Familiar the old jest of Cato, who used to express his wonder that one haruspex could ever look at another without laughing." For that matter it is a common error to confuse Roman augury with Etruscan divination by inspection of entrails. Only when they could not help doing so did the Romans appeal to Etruscan divination. Tiberius Gracchus, the father of the Gracchi, on being accused by Etruscan soothsayers, who were functioning at an election, of calling for a vote against the auspices, addressed them as follows: Cicero, *De natura deorum,* II, 4, 11: " 'You say that I am not in order, though I am putting this question as consul and as augur, and under good auspices? And you, Etruscans, you, barbarians—you presume to say what good auspices for the Roman People are? You presume to be interpreters for these *comitia?*' And he bade them to be gone from the Forum."

311 [1] Strictly speaking, this remark and the next following are irrelevant to the present chapter. I make them simply to warn anew of the habit people have of assuming that a writer says what he does not say (§ § 41, 74-75).

may be eliminated from such a group without impairing its effectiveness. However, in so reasoning we must beware of falling into the fallacy of the man who said he could lose all his hair without becoming bald because he could lose any particular hair without suffering that catastrophe.

312. Device A-III: *Non-logical actions as tricks for deceit.* After establishing, as in the two cases above, that certain actions are not logical, but still resolved to have them such in the feeling that every human act should be born of logic, a writer may go on and say that an institution involving non-logical conduct is an invention of this or that individual or group that is designed to procure some personal advantage, or some advantage to state, society, or humanity at large. So actions intrinsically non-logical are transformed into actions that are logical from the standpoint of the end in view.

To adopt this procedure as regards actions deemed beneficial to society is to depart from the extreme case noted in § 14, where it is maintained that only theories which accord with facts (logico-experimental theories) can be beneficial to society. It is here recognized that there are theories which are not logico-experimental, but which are nevertheless beneficial to society. All the same, the writer cannot make up his mind to admit that such theories derive spontaneously from non-logical impulse. No, all conduct has to be logical. Therefore such theories too are products of logical actions. These actions cannot originate in the sources of the theories, since it has been recognized that the theories have no experimental basis; but they may envisage the same purposes as the theories, which experience shows are beneficial to society. So we get the following solution: "Theories not in accord with the facts may be beneficial to society and are therefore logically *invented* to that end." [1]

313. The notion that non-logical actions have been logically devised to attain certain purposes has been held by many many writers. Even Polybius, a historian of great sagacity, speaks of the religion

312 [1] If one were to say "kept," or "preserved," instead of "invented" in the proposition in question, it would at times correspond to a greater or lesser extent with reality (§ 316).

of the Romans as originating in deliberate artifice.[1] Yet he himself recognized that the Romans succeeded in creating their commonwealth not by reasoned choices but by allowing themselves to be guided by circumstances as they arose.[2]

313 [1] *Historiae,* VI, 56, 8-12 (Paton, Vol. III, p. 395). After noting the great rôle of religion in Roman public life, Polybius adds: "That will seem strange to many. As for me, I believe that religion was established with an eye to the masses. In fact, if the city were made up entirely of educated people, such an institution might never have been called for. But since the masses everywhere are fickle and untrustworthy, full of lawless passions, unreasoning angers, violent impulses, they can be controlled only by mysterious terrors and tragic fears. It seems to me, therefore, that not by chance and not without strong motive did the ancients introduce these beliefs in gods and hells to the multitude." Strabo, *Geographica,* I, 2, 8 (Jones, Vol. I, p. 71): "Since neither women in the mass nor the utterly untutored mob can be influenced by philosophical discourse and preached into piety, reverence, and faith, superstition has to be called in." And then: ". . . myths being like that and turning out to the advantage of society, civilized living, and the continuity of the human race." *Cf.* Plutarch, *Adversus Colotem,* 31 (Goodwin, Vol. V, pp. 379-80). Then Livy, *Ab urbe condita,* I, 19, 4: "He [Numa] thought that fear of the gods should be instilled the very first thing, as a most effective measure for a populace that in those days was still crude and ingenuous (*imperitam*)." Here we are wholly within the realm of logical conduct, the masses being lured into religion by subterfuge. Cicero, *De legibus,* II, 13, 32 (Atticus, alluding to the different views of the two augurs Marcellus and Appius): " 'I have examined their writings and I find that according to the one, the auspices you mention were devised for purposes of state; while according to the other it would seem that you can actually foretell the future by your science.' " Cicero, *De divinatione,* II, 18, 43: "We find it written in our augural commentaries: 'It is sacrilege to hold *comitia* with Jove thundering or lightening.' That may have been devised for purposes of state, for our forefathers wanted to have some pretext for not holding *comitia.*" *Ibid.*, II, 33, 70: "Yet I believe that Romulus, who founded the city in obedience to auspices, must have thought that there was a science of augury for foretelling the future (antiquity erred in many matters) and we see that that belief has remained unshaken whether by experience, by learning, or by time. However, the custom and science of divination, the strict observance of it, and the prerogatives of the augurs and the prestige of their college, have been kept alive in deference to popular feelings, and in view of their great advantage to the state." A little later, II, 35, 75, he adds that he believed "the augural law to have been first established through belief in divination and to have been kept and preserved later on for reasons of state." That seems to have been

313 [2] VI, 11. He is comparing the republic of Lycurgus with the Roman Republic. He believes that Lycurgus was a real person and founded his state with preconceived purposes. Then he goes on: "The Romans achieved the same end in creating their own republic. Not through speculation (*οὐ μὴν διὰ λόγου*), but through their schooling in many struggles and vicissitudes and through their unfailing choice of what was best did they achieve the same end as Lycurgus and create the best of our governments."

314. We may take Montesquieu's view of Roman religion as the type of the interpretation here in question.[1] "Neither fear nor piety established religion among the Romans, but the same necessity that compels all societies to have religions. . . . I note this difference, however, between Roman legislators and the lawgivers of other peoples, that the Romans created religion for the State, the others the State for religion. Romulus, Tatius, and Numa made the gods servants of statesmanship; and the cult and the ceremonies that they instituted were found to be so wise that when the kings were expelled the yoke of religion was the only one which that people dared not throw off in its frenzy for liberty. In establishing religion, Roman law-makers were not at all thinking of reforming morals or proclaiming moral principles. . . . They had at first only a general view, to inspire a people that feared nothing with fear of the gods, and to use that fear to lead it whithersoever they pleased. . . . It was in truth going pretty far to stake the safety of the State on the sacred appetite of a chicken and the disposition of the entrails in a sacrificial animal; but the founders of those ceremonies were well aware of their strong and weak points, and it was not without good reasons that they sinned against reason itself. Had that form of worship been more rational, the educated as well as the plain man would have been deceived by it; and so all the advantage to be expected from it would have been lost."

315. It is curious that Voltaire and Montesquieu followed opposite though equally mistaken lines, and that neither of them thought of a spontaneous development of non-logical conduct.

316. The variety of interpretation here in question sometimes con-

Cicero's own opinion and it does not come far from the truth. Non-logical actions arise spontaneously. They may then be kept in deference to tradition or because of their proved usefulness. Of course any logical origin, by design of Romulus, is pure myth. *Cf.* Aristotle, *Metaphysica,* XI, 8, 13 (Ross, p. 1074b). After discussing the divinity of the stars, he adds: "The rest is a mythical adjunct, designed to influence the multitude and promote obedience to law and the common welfare." See further: Plutarch, *De placitis philosophorum,* I, 7, 2 (Goodwin, Vol. III, p. 119); and Sextus Empiricus, *Contradictiones,* IX, *Adversus physicos,* II, *De diis,* 14-16 (551) (*Opera,* Vol. II, pp. 539-40).

314 [1] *Dissertation sur la politique des Romains dans la religion,* p. 303.

tains an element of truth, not as regards the origin of non-logical actions, but as regards the purposes to which they may be turned once they have become customary. Then it is natural enough that the shrewd should use them for their own ends just as they use any other force in society. The error lies in assuming that such forces have been invented by design (§ 312). An example from our own time may bring out the point more clearly. There are plenty of rogues, surely, who make their profit out of spiritualism; but it would be absurd to imagine that spiritualism originated as a mere scheme of rogues.

317. Van Dale, in his treatise *De Oraculis,* saw nothing but artifice in the pagan oracles. That notion belongs with this group of interpretations. Eusebius wavers between it and the view that oracles were the work of devils.[1] Such mixtures of interpretations are common. We shall come back to them.

318. Likewise with this variety are to be classed interpretations that regard non-logical actions as consequences of an external or exoteric doctrine serving to conceal an internal or esoteric doctrine. That would make actions which are non-logical in appearance logical in reality. Consider a passage in Galileo's *Dialogue of the Greater Systems* (Salviati speaking):[1] "That the Pythagoreans held the science of numbers in very high esteem . . . I am well aware, nor would I be loath to concur in that judgment. But that the mysteries in view of which Pythagoras and his sect held the science of numbers in such great veneration are the absurdities commonly current in books and conversation, I can in no way agree. On the contrary, they did not care to have their wonders exposed to the ridicule and disparagement of the common herd. So they damned as sacrilegious any publication of the more recondite properties of the numbers and incommensurable and irrational quantities with which they dealt, and they preached that anyone disclosing such things would suffer torment in the world to come. I think that some of

317 [1] *Evangelica praeparatio,* V (*Opera,* Vol. III, pp. 307-402).

318 [1] *Dialogo dei due massimi sistemi del mondo, Giornata prima* (*Opera,* Vol. VII, p. 35).

them, to throw a sop to the vulgar and be free of prying importunity, represented their numeral mysteries as the same childish idiocies that later on spread generally abroad. It was a shrewd and cunning device on their part, like the trick of that sagacious young man who escaped the prying of his mother (or his curious wife—I forget which), who was pressing him to confide the secrets of the Senate, by making up a story wherewith she and other prattling females proceeded to make fools of themselves, to the great amusement of the Sentaors."

That the Pythagoreans sometimes misrepresented their own doctrines seems certain; but it is not at all apparent that that was the case with their ideas on perfect numbers. On that point Galileo is mistaken (§§ 960 f.).

319. Device B-I: *The principles are taken as completely and directly real.*[1] This variety is exemplified by non-logical actions of a religious character on the part of unquestioning believers. Such actions differ little if at all from logical actions. If a person is convinced that to be sure of a good voyage he must sacrifice to Poseidon and sail in a ship that does not leak, he will perform the sacrifice and caulk his seams in exactly the same spirit.

320. Curiously enough, such doctrines come closer than any others to a scientific status. They differ from the scientific, in fact, only by an appendage that asserts the reality of an imaginary principle; whereas many other doctrines, in addition to possessing the same appendage, further differ from scientific doctrines by inferences that are either fantastic or devoid of all exactness.

321. Device B-Iα: *Precept plus sanction.* This variety is obtained by appending some adjunct or other to the simple sanctionless precept—to the taboo (*cf.* § 154).[1]

319 [1] This extreme case recognizes non-logical actions for what they are and therefore ought not, strictly speaking, to be classified with procedures for giving non-logical actions the semblance of logic. However, we must consider it as the point of departure for many such procedures, and so glance at it here.

321 [1] The sanctionless precept is not of this variety because it does not evade but recognizes the fact that an action is non-logical—indeed it is in the sanctionless precept that non-logical actions can be most readily identified.

322. Reinach writes:[1] "A taboo is an interdiction; an object that is taboo, or tabooed, is a forbidden object. The interdiction may forbid corporal contact or visual contact; it may also exempt the object from the peculiar kind of violation involved in pronouncing its name. . . . Similar interdictions are observable in Greece and Rome, and among many other peoples, where generally it is explained that knowledge of a name enables a person to 'evoke' with evil intent the 'power' that the name designates. That explanation may have been valid at certain periods; but it does not represent the primitive state of mind. Originally it was the sanctity of the name itself that was dreaded, on the same grounds as contact with a tabooed object."

Reinach is right in regarding as an appendage the notion that knowledge of the name of an object gives a person power over it; but the notion of sanctity is likewise an appendage. Indeed, probably few of the individuals observing a taboo would know what was meant by an abstraction such as "sanctity." For them the taboo is just a non-logical action, just an *aversion* to touching, looking at, naming, the thing tabooed. Later on an effort is made to explain or justify the aversion; and then the mysterious power of which Reinach speaks (or perhaps his own notion of sanctity) is invented.

Reinach continues: "The notion of the taboo is narrower still than the notion of interdiction. The characteristic difference is that the taboo never gives a reason." That is excellent! The non-logical action has just that trait. But for that very reason Reinach should not, in a particular case, provide the taboo with a reason in some consideration of sanctity. He goes on: "The prohibition is merely stated, taking the cause for granted—it is, in fact, nothing but the taboo itself, that is to say, the assertion of a mortal peril." But in saying that he is withdrawing his concession and trying to edge back into the domain of logic. No "cause" is taken for granted! The taboo lies in a pure and absolute repugnance to doing a certain thing. To get something similar from our own world: There is the sentimental person who could never be induced to cut off a chicken's head.

322 [1] *Cultes, mythes et religions,* Vol. I, pp. 1-2.

There is no "cause" for the aversion; it is just an aversion, and it is strong enough to keep the person from cutting off a chicken's head! It is not apparent either why Reinach would have it that the penalty for violating a taboo is always a mortal peril. He himself gives examples to the contrary. Going on, he returns to the domain of non-logical actions, well observing that "the taboos that have come down into contemporary cultures are often stated with supporting reasons. But such reasons have been excogitated in times relatively recent [One could not say better.] and bear the stamp of modern ideas. For example, people will say, 'Speak softly in a chamber of death [A taboo that gives no evidence of having a "mortal peril" for a sanction.] out of respect for the dead.' The primitive taboo lay in avoiding not only contact with a corpse, but its very proximity. [Still no evidence of any mortal peril.] Nevertheless even today, in educating children taboos are imparted without stated reasons, or else with some mere specification of the general character of the interdiction: 'Do not take off your coat in company, for that is not nice.' In his *Works and Days,* v. 727, Hesiod interdicts passing water with one's face towards the sun, but he gives no reasons for the prohibition. [A pure non-logical action.] Most taboos relating to decorum have come down across the centuries without justifications" [and with no threats of "mortal peril"].[2]

323. With taboos may profitably be classed other things of the kind where logical interpretation is reduced to a minimum. William Marsden says of the Mohammedans of Sumatra:[1] "Many who profess to follow it [Mohammedanism] give themselves not the least concern about its injunctions, or even know what they require. A Malay at Marina upbraided a countryman, with the total ignorance of religion, his nation laboured under, 'You pay a veneration to the tombs of your ancestors: what foundation have you for supposing that your dead ancestors can lend you assistance?' 'It may be true,' answered the other; 'but what foundation have *you,* for expecting

322 [2] We have here been considering the sanction appended to taboos as a device for logicalizing non-logical actions. Farther along we shall examine them as devices for inducing observance of taboos.

323 [1] *History of Sumatra,* p. 250.

assistance from Allah and Mahomet?' 'Are you not aware,' replied the Malay, 'that it is written in a Book? Have you not heard of the Koraan?' The native of the Passumah, with conscious inferiority, submitted to the force of this argument."[2] That is a seed which will sprout and yield an abundant harvest of logical interpretations, some of which we shall find in the devices hereafter following.

324. Something like the taboo is the precept (§§ 154, 1480 f.). It may be given without sanction, "Do so and so," and in that form it is a plain non-logical action. In the injunction, "You *ought* to do so and so," there is a slight, sometimes a very slight, trace of explanation. It lurks in the term "ought," which suggests the mysterious entity Duty. That is often supplemented by a sanction real or imaginary, and then we get actions that are either actually logical or else are merely made to appear so. Only a certain number of precepts, therefore, can be properly grouped with the things we are classifying here.

325. In general, precepts may be distinguished as follows:

a. Pure precept, without stated reasons, and without proof. The proposition is not elliptical. No proof is given, either because no proof exists or because none is asked for. That, therefore, is the pure non-logical action. But human beings have such a passion for logical explanations that they usually stick one or two on, no matter how silly. "Do that!" is a precept. If it be asked, "Why should I do that?" the answer is, let us say, "Because . . . !" or, "Because it is customary." The logical appendage is of little value, except where violation of custom implies some penalty—but in that case the penalty, not the custom, carries the logical force.

326. *b. The demonstration is elliptical.* The proof, valid or not, is available. It has not been mentioned, but it may be. The proposition is a precept only in appearance. The terms "ought," "must," and the like may be suppressed, and the precept reduced to an experimental or pseudo-experimental theorem, the consequence deriving from the act without any interposition from without. This type of precept runs, "To get *A*, you must do *B*,"; or, negatively, "To

323 [2] For other examples of the kind see §§ 1430 f.

avoid *A*, you must refrain from doing *B*." The first proposition can be stated thus: "When *B* is done, *A* results." Similarly for the second.

327. If both *A* and *B* are real things and if the nexus between them is actually logico-experimental, we get scientific propositions. They have nothing to do with the things we are trying to classify here. If the nexus is not logico-experimental, they are pseudo-scientific propositions, and a certain number of them are used to logicalize non-logical actions. For instance, if *A* stands for a safe voyage and *B* for sacrifices to Poseidon, the nexus is imaginary, and the non-logical action *B* is justified by the nexus that connects it with *A*. But if *A* stands for a safe voyage and *B* for defective ship-building, we get just an erroneous scientific proposition. A mistake in engineering is not a non-logical action.

328. If *A* and *B* are both imaginary, we are wholly outside the experimental field, and we need not consider such propositions. If *A* is imaginary and *B* real, we get non-logical actions, *B*, justified by the pretext, *A*.

329. *c. The proposition is really a precept, but a real sanction enforced by an extraneous and real cause is appended to it.* That gives a logical action: the thing is done to escape the sanction.

330. *d. The proposition is a precept, but the sanction is imaginary, or enforcible only by an imaginary power.* We get a non-logical action justified by the sanction.[1]

331. The terms of ordinary speech rarely have sharply defined meanings. The term "sanction" may be used more or less loosely. Here we have taken it in the strict sense. Broadly speaking, one might say that a sanction is always present. In the case of a scientific proposition the sanction might be the pleasure of reasoning soundly or the pain of reasoning amiss. But to go into such niceties would be just a waste of time.

332. Device B-Iβ: *Introduction of a divinity or of personified abstractions.* A very simple elaboration of the taboo, or pure precept, is involved in the introduction of a personal god, or of personifications such as Nature, by will of which non-logical actions are re-

330 [1] For fuller explanation see Chapter IX (§§ 1480 f.).

quired of human beings and are therefore logicalized. How the requirement arises is often left dark. "A god (or Nature) wills that so and so be done." "And if it is not done?" The question remains unanswered. But very often there is an answer; it is asserted that the god (or Nature) will punish violators of the precept. In such a case we get a sanctioned precept of the species *d* above.

333. When the Greeks said that "strangers and beggars come from Zeus,"[1] they were merely voicing their inclination to be hospitable to visitors, and Zeus was dragged in to give a logical colouring to the custom, by implying that the hospitality was offered either in reverence for Zeus, or to avoid the punishment that Zeus held in store for violators of the precept.

334. Device B-Iγ: *Divinities plus legend and logical elaboration.* Rare the case where such embellishments are not supplemented by multiple legends and logical elaborations; and through these new adjuncts we get mythologies and theologies that carry us farther and farther away from the concept of non-logical conduct. It may be worth while to caution that theologies at all complicated belong to restricted classes of people only. With them we depart from the field of popular interpretations and enter an intellectual or scholarly domain. To the variety in question here belong the interpretations of the Fathers of the Christian Church, such as the doctrine that the pagan gods were devils.

335. Device B-Iδ: *Metaphysical entities taken as real.* Here reality is ascribed not to a personal god or to a personification, but to a metaphysical abstraction. "The true," "the beautiful," "the good," "the honest," "virtue," "morality," "natural law," "humanity," "solidarity," "progress," or their opposite abstractions, enjoin or forbid certain actions, and the actions become logical consequences of the abstractions.[1]

336. In interpretations of the B-Iβ variety, the personal god can inflict a punishment because he chooses to. In the case of "Nature" the punishment is an automatic consequence of the conduct. Those

333 [1] *Odyssey,* VI, vv. 207-08: πρὸς γὰρ Διός εἰσιν ἅπαντες ξεῖνοί τε πτωχοί τε.
335 [1] For the detailed argument see §§ 1510 f.

interpretations, therefore, are respectably logical. In the case of metaphysical abstractions, however, the logic is flimsy indeed. You tell a person, "You must do that because it is good," and he replies, "But I do not choose to do what is good." You are checkmated, for milord Good, estimable worthy that he may be, does not wield the thunderbolts that Zeus wields. So our latter-day Christians keep the God of the Old Testament but strip Him of all His weapons. There could be no trifling with the God of the Hebrews, who fiercely avenged transgressions of His laws, or with the God of St. Paul, who was no whit less quick to wrath. But, armed with the abstractions of their pseudo-science, with what can the neo-Christians threaten the unbeliever? Or what can they do for the believer to make his belief worth while? The answer is, "Nothing." The conduct they recommend is simply non-logical conduct. That does not mean that it may not be as beneficial to individual or society as any other, or even more so. It may or may not be. But in any event it is certain that it is not the logical inference from a principle, like the inference from the existence of a divine power and will that unbelievers will be punished and believers rewarded.[1]

336 [1] As for the God of the Hebrews, see Piepenbring, *Théologie de l'Ancien Testament*, pp. 98-99: "The holiness of God is intimately bound up with His jealousy, His wrath, His vengeance. . . . In the 'Old Canticle' (*Ex.* 15:7) Moses cries out to the Lord: '. . . In the greatness of thine excellency thou hast overthrown them that rose up against thee: thou sentest forth thy wrath, which consumed them as stubble.' [Can any neo-Christian abstraction say as much?] The wrath of God breaks out in the form of dire punishment every time His will is crossed, disregarded, transgressed." These milk-and-water Christians are inclined to think that all that changed with the coming of Christ, but such is not the case. The early Church Fathers discourse without mincing words on the punishments that will be visited on unbelievers. As for the God of St. Paul, one of the many passages will suffice: I Cor. 10:8: "Neither let us commit fornication, as some of them [the Israelites] committed, and fell in one day three and twenty thousand [Num. 25:1-9]." Can the abstraction concocted by the pseudo-science of the neo-Christians pretend to do as much? No! Well, in that case the precept will be obeyed by those who are already good Christians, and no one who is not will pay any attention. But that is the essential characteristic of the principles (§ 306 [1]) of non-logical actions. The Apostle continues: "Neither let us tempt Christ, as some of them also tempted, and were destroyed of serpents [Num. 21:4-9]. Neither murmur ye, as some of them also murmured, and were destroyed of the destroyer [Num. 11:16]." And later on, 22, he asks: "Do we provoke the Lord to jealousy? are we stronger than He?" Every

337. Device B-Iε: *What is real is the accord between the principles and certain sentiments.* This manner of envisaging facts is implicit rather than explicit. So for certain neo-Christians the reality of Jesus seems to come down to an accord between their conception of Him and certain sentiments they hold. They abandon the objective field, deny the divine nature of Christ, and seem not to care very much about His historical reality. They are satisfied with asserting that Christ is the most perfect type of humanity, which means that their notions of Christ happen to coincide with what, according to their sentiments, is the most perfect type of human being. Once on that road they finish by throwing all theology, all rites, overboard and end with the assertion that "religion is a manner of living."[1]

338. Along that line they might seem to be approximating the concept of non-logical conduct; but they are still radically at variance with it, since they are thinking not of what is, but of what ought to be, and rob the "ought" of the subordinate character

sensible man will answer no if the being in question is an omnipotent God; but many sensible men will answer yes if it is a question of an abstraction that some few individuals have distilled from their own sentiments.

337 [1] Auguste Sabatier, *Les religions d'autorité et la religion de l'esprit,* pp. 440-41 (English translation, pp. 281-82): "The letter, the alphabetic sign, characterizes the Mosaic religion in accordance with the form of its appearance in history, its manner of being and action. . . . The letter kills. Spirit, instead, characterizes the religion of the Gospel in accord with the very nature of the inner moral relationship that it sets up between God and man, in accord with the manner of being of the Gospel and the principle of its action. . . . In view of that you must surely understand what the religion of the spirit is. It is the religious relationship realized in pure spirituality. It is God and man conceived both as spirit and as reciprocally permeating each other to the point of attaining complete communion. Physical bodies are by definition impenetrable to each other. . . . Quite otherwise the relationship between spirits. Their inward tendency is to live each other's lives mutually and to combine in a higher common life. What the law of gravitation is to the physical world as regards the maintenance of its harmony, so love is and so love does in the spiritual and moral world. [The conception this gentleman has of the law of gravitation would make a story.] . . . Ultimate force in the moral development of the human being, the spirit of God no longer constrains him from without but determines, animates, him from within, and is the source of his life. . . . The fulfilment of natural duties, the regular exercise of all human faculties, the progress of enlightenment as well as of justice—that is the perfection of the Christian life. Becoming an inner reality, a fact of conscience, Christianity is now nothing more than conscience raised to its highest power."

(§ 326) it might well have in the case of some few individuals, and give it an absolute status that altogether transcends the experimental field. Their theories, in a word, have no other purpose than to decorate non-logical impulse with a logical rouge.

339. B-II: *The reality is no longer direct;* that is to say, it is no longer held that there is a god, a personification, an abstraction, or the like, from which non-logical actions may be logically inferred. *It is assumed that such actions have arisen spontaneously, by reasonings good or bad based on facts well or badly authenticated.* The difference between this variety and the B-I group is a radical one; for whereas the B-I devices ascribed reality to entities foreign to the experimental field, the entities posited in this variety arise within the experimental field, and the only questions are whether they have actually been observed and whether the assumed consequences are real consequences. "Beggars come from Zeus" is an interpretation of the B-I variety. I create the entity Zeus, which I assume to be real, and from its existence I draw certain inferences. "Whoever is hospitable to beggars will be happy" is an interpretation of the B-II variety. I pretend that I have observed that people who have been hospitable to beggars have been happy, and I draw the inference that if they continue to be hospitable to beggars they will continue to be happy. I have not created any entity; I am using real facts, combining them as I see fit.

340. Device B-IIα: *Observation imperfect, inferences logical.* This method of reasoning aims to throw back upon the premises a logico-experimental insufficiency that cannot be disputed. We have certain assertions that are manifestly in contradiction with logico-experimental knowledge. We may assume that the contradiction arises because the reasoning which produces the conclusions is not logical, and we are thereby carried into the domain of non-logical conduct. Or else we may hold that the reasoning is logical, but that it starts with premises inconsistent with experimental knowledge and so leads to conclusions where the contradiction is likewise apparent. In that way we are able to remain within the field of logical conduct. Typical of this variety are the theories of Herbert Spencer (§§ 285,

289-95). The rôle ascribed to non-logical conduct is reduced to a minimum and may even be eliminated. Underlying certain phenomena are certain observations of fact. It is assumed that from such alleged observations human beings have drawn inferences, reasoning very much as any thinker would reason. So we get the doctrines of those human beings and the reasons for their conduct.

341. Concepts of this kind figure to a greater or lesser extent in almost all theories dealing with the "origins" of social phenomena such as "religion," "morality," "law," and the like. Writers are driven to admit the existence of non-logical actions but are careful to push them back into the past as far as they can.

342. There may be some truth in such theories in so far as they call attention to certain simple types of complex phenomena. They go astray in trying to derive the complex phenomenon from the simple type, and still farther astray when it is assumed that that process is logical.

343. Ignoring for the moment the complex character of social phenomena, let us assume that certain phenomena *P*, observable at the present day, have an actual origin *A* (Figure 9). If the development took place along a continuous line *ABCDP*, it would be possible, in a sense, to take one of the intermediate phenomena *B*, *C* . . . as the origin, or cause, of *P*. If, for instance, going as far back as our historical knowledge permits, we found a thing *B* of the same nature as *P*, though much simpler, we should not go too far wrong in regarding it as the origin, or cause, of *P*.

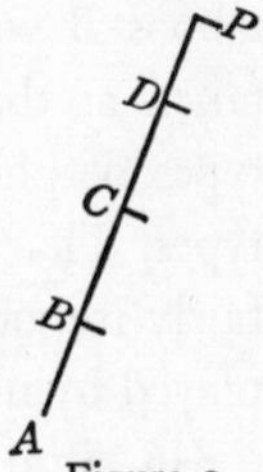

Figure 9

344. Unfortunately the assumption of development along a continuous line does not at all conform with the facts as regards social phenomena, or even as regards not a few biological phenomena. The development, rather, seems to take place along a line with many branches (Figure 10), even still ignoring the complex character of social phenomena, which hardly permits us to dissociate the social phenomenon *P* from other social phenomena (§ 513). Facts *B*, *C*, *D* . . . (Figure 10) are no longer located along a straight continuous line, but stand at the extremities or intersections of branch lines; and we cannot, even as a hypothesis very remotely approximative to the facts, assume that *C*, for example, or *E*, or any other similar fact observable in the past, is the origin, the cause, of *P*, observable in the present.

345. To take a concrete example: Reinach sees in taboos the origin of religion. In so doing, he seems to take the position pictured in Figure 9, *B* standing for the taboos, *P* for present-day religions. But even assuming that religion is unconnected with other social phe-

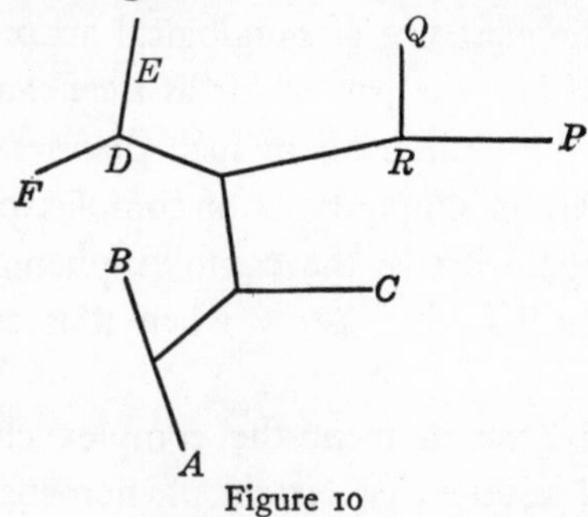

Figure 10

nomena, the situation is actually as represented in Figure 10, and the taboos *B* would be the extremity of a by-path. Taboos cannot be taken as the origin of religion. They may be regarded as simple types of phenomena, of which the religions *C*, *Q*, *P* are complex types. That is all the truth there is in the theories of Reinach, a fairly important truth, for that matter, since it emphasizes the part played by non-logical actions in religious phenomena.

346. Studies in origins in social matters often proceed very much after the manner of old-fashioned etymology.[1] The intermediate

346 [1] Brachet, *Grammaire historique de la langue française*, pp. 293-94 (Kitchin, pp. 195-96): "Before attaining the degree of exactness that it possesses today, etymology, like all the sciences and perhaps more notably than any other, traversed a long period of infancy, of gropings, of uncertain efforts, during which arbitrary associations, superficial analogies, reckless combinations, made up virtually its whole patrimony." Here Brachet quotes from Réville, *Les ancêtres des européens:* " 'Abidingly famous the day-dreams of Plato in the *Cratylus*, the absurd etymologies of Varro [*Etymologiae*, Dordrecht, Part III, pp. 165-176] and Quintilian among the Romans, the philological fancies of Ménage in France in the seventeenth century. People saw nothing strange about connecting *jeûne*, "fast," with *jeune*, "young." Is not youth the morning of life, and is one not fasting when one gets up? Most often two words

steps *C, D* . . . (Figure 9) are assumed or guessed at, in getting from *B* to *P;* and the temptation is to ask how things ought to have gone rather than how they actually went. Investigations, in such a case, lie outside the domain of experimental reality. Yet, historically speaking, they have not been altogether wasted: for they have served to open a breach in the ethical and *a priori* theories that have been explaining *P* by imaginary principles. That task accomplished, it is now time for them to give way to purely experimental theories.

347. Device B-IIβ: *Myths have a historical basis or else are imitations of other myths.* Origins and evolution being discarded, it is assumed that every myth is the deformed reflection of something real. Of this variety were the euhemeristic theories, so called, as to the origin of the pagan gods (§§ 682-708). Nothing is more certain than that there have been cases where human beings have been deified. The euhemeristic error lies, first of all, in generalizing a particular fact, and then in confusing the point *B* in Figure 9 with the point *B* in Figure 10, in assuming, that is, that because one fact precedes another fact in time, it is the origin of it. The theories of Palaephatus (§ 661) also belong to this variety.

348. In general, interpretations of this kind are very easy to work out. One arbitrarily changes in a myth anything that needs to be changed to produce a picture that is real. Take, for example, Astolfo's hippogriff in the *Orlando furioso* of Ariosto. The wingèd horse can be made a real horse by interpreting the story in the sense that the hippogriff was some very swift horse that was therefore spoken of as having wings. Dante sees Francesca and her brother-in-law lashed by "the hellish hurricane." The hurricane can be interpreted as a symbol of the carnal passion that smites the two lovers

of entirely different forms were derived from each other, the gulf between them being bridged by fictional intermediaries. That was the way Ménage got the French *rat* from the Latin *mus,* "mouse": "People must have said first *mus,* then *muratus,* then *ratus,* finally *rat.*" It was courageously assumed that an object could get its name from a quality opposite to its own, affirmation provoking negation, so that Latin *lucus,* "grove," came from *non lucere,* "not to be bright," because on entering a grove one finds it shady.' " Brachet continues: "From such a mass of erudite nonsense how could one of the leading sciences eventually arise in our day? By the discovery and application of the comparative method, which is the method of the natural sciences"—and the method we are trying to follow in these volumes.

like a hurricane. In such a procedure not the slightest difficulty will ever be encountered (§ 661).

349. With this variety we may class theories that explain the non-logical actions observable in a given society as imitations of non-logical actions prevalent in other societies. To tell the truth, not all non-logical actions are eliminated by this device; they are merely reduced in number, several of them being taken as duplicates of one.[1]

350. Device B-IIγ: *Myths taken as historical fact plus a fictional appendage*. In this variety we come a little closer to reality. In every myth the legend is assumed to have a nucleus of historical fact covered over by an alluvium of fiction. One removes the accretion, and finds the nucleus of fact underneath. Many books have been written from that point of view. Not so long since all the legends that have come down from Graeco-Roman antiquity were treated in that way.[1]

Our variety B-IIβ, above, is often the present variety, B-IIγ, carried to the extreme. There may be something historical in a myth, a something more or less extensive. As it is reduced to a minimum and finally disappears, we get the B-IIβ variety.

351. Device B-III: *The principles underlying non-logical actions are allegories*. The actions, it is held, are in reality logical. They seem to be non-logical only because the allegories are taken literally. A further assumption locates the source of such errors in language by an allegorical interpretation. Max Müller writes:[1] "There are many myths in Hesiod, of late origin, where we have only to replace a full verb by an auxiliary, in order to change mythical into logical language. Hesiod [*Theogonia,* vv. 211-12 (White, pp. 94-95)], calls Nyx (Night) the mother of Moros (Fate), and the dark Kêr (Destruction), of Thanatos (Death), Hypnos (Sleep) and the tribe of the Oneiroi (Dreams). . . . Now let us use our modern expressions, such as: 'the stars are seen as night approaches,' 'we sleep,' 'we dream,' 'we die,' 'we run danger during the night' . . . and we

349 [1] For examples see §§ 733 f.

350 [1] For several such interpretations see Chapter V.

351 [1] *Chips from a German Workshop,* Vol. II, p. 64. [The French translation which Pareto used for this passage has a number of errors.—A. L.]

have translated the language of Hesiod . . . into modern forms of thought and speech."

352. On that basis all myths would be charades. It seems incredible that a theory so manifestly absurd could have gained such wide acceptance. Müller's disciples did even worse than their master, and the solar myth became a convenient and universal explanation for every conceivable legend.

353. Class C. In this class, really, non-logical actions are not interpreted in such a way as to make them logical. They are eliminated, so that only logical actions are left. That serves just as well to reduce all conduct to logic. Such opinions are widely current in our time, and are an article of faith with a great many people who worship a powerful divinity known to them as "Science." Not a few humanitarians are of the same tribe.

354. Other people reason more soundly; and after noting a thing that is true enough—that science has contributed greatly to the advance of civilization—they go farther still and try to show that nothing that is not science can be useful. As the type of such theories one might quote the celebrated argument of Buckle: [1] "It is evident, that if we look at mankind in the aggregate, their moral and intellectual conduct is regulated by the moral and intellectual notions prevalent in their own time. . . . Now, it requires but a superficial acquaintance with history to be aware that this standard is constantly changing. . . . This extreme mutability in the ordinary standard of human actions shows that the conditions on which the standard depends must themselves be very mutable; and these conditions, whatever they may be, are evidently the originators of the moral and intellectual conduct of the great average of mankind.

"Here, then, we have a basis on which we can safely proceed. We know that the main cause of human actions is extremely variable; we have only, therefore, to apply this test to any set of circumstances which are supposed to be the cause, and if we find that such circumstances are not very variable, we must infer that they are not the cause we are attempting to discover.

354 [1] *History of Civilization in England,* Vol. I, pp. 179-82.

"Applying this test to moral motives, or to the dictates of what is called moral instinct, we shall at once see how extremely small is the influence those motives have exercised over the progress of civilization. For there is, unquestionably, nothing to be found in the world which has undergone so little change as those great dogmas of which moral systems are composed. . . .

"But, if we contrast this stationary aspect of moral truths with the progressive aspect of intellectual truths, the difference is indeed startling.[2] All the great moral systems which have exercised much influence have been fundamentally the same; all the great intellectual systems have been fundamentally different. . . . Since civilization is the product of moral and intellectual agencies, and since that product is constantly changing, it evidently cannot be regulated by the stationary agent; because when surrounding circumstances are unchanged, a stationary agent can only produce a stationary effect. The only other agent is the intellectual one; and that this is the real mover may be proved."

355. Buckle's reasoning is sound provided one add that all human conduct is logical and derives from moral and intellectual principles. But that proposition is false. In the first place, many very important actions are non-logical. Secondly, the things designated by the terms "moral principle" and "intellectual principle" are wanting in exactness: they cannot be taken as premises in a rigorous argument. Thirdly, Buckle's reasoning has the general defect of arguments by elimination in sociological matters—the enumeration is never complete.[1] He omits things of great importance. Theoretical principles of morality may be the same, and moral practices very different—for instance, the peoples who all preach the Christian ethics by no means all behave in the same way in practice.[2]

356. Buckle's argument reduces the practical rôle of moral the-

354 [2] Buckle quotes James Mackintosh, Condorcet, and Kant, in support.

355 [1] Pareto, *Manuale,* Chap. I, § 18.

355 [2] [Fielding, *Tom Jones,* IX, iii, 2: ". . . purposes . . . which though tolerated in some Christian countries, connived at in others and practised in all . . . are expressly forbidden . . . by that religion which is universally believed in in those countries."—A. L.]

ories to very small proportions, and in that it accords with the facts. But what it takes away from morals ought not be handed over to an "intellectual principle" (whatever that may be), but to the patrimony of non-logical actions, economic progress, improvements in communications, and the like. It may well be that something has to be assigned to scientific progress all the same, and therefore to the said "intellectual principle"; but there is a big difference between such indirect, non-logical influence, and a direct action by way of logical inference from a given principle.[1]

357. We need carry our study of this special classification no farther. It has already shown that existing doctrines may be broken up into two different elements: certain sentiments, and inferences from those sentiments. It opens, in other words, a path that it may or may not be profitable to follow to the end. We shall see as we go on.

358. Many statesmen, many historians, recognize non-logical actions without giving them that name and without going to the trouble of finding their theory. Just a few examples taken here and there from the works of Bayle,[1] implicit in which are several theories of non-logical conduct—and it is indeed surprising to find in a writer who lived two centuries and more ago certain truths that are unappreciated even today. Bayle declares and repeats that "opinions are not the rule of conduct"; and that "man does not regulate his conduct by his opinions. . . . The Turks hold certain tenets of that doctrine of the Stoics [fatalism], and they carry the business of predestination to extreme lengths. Nevertheless they may be seen

356 [1] Here and there in his work Buckle himself ends by making at least implicit allusion to non-logical actions. Trying to account for the differences between the Puritan Revolution and the French Fronde, he suggests, Vol. II, p. 150, "that in England a war for liberty was accompanied by a war of classes, while in France there was no war of classes at all"; and further, Vol. II, p. 162, that "the object of the [French] nobles was merely to find new sources of excitement, and minister to that personal vanity for which, as a body, they have always been notorious." Now whatever the route that is tried in order to get from such facts to logical inferences from an "intellectual principle," it is certain that the facts depend on natural inclinations, which cannot be regarded as resulting from any differences between the scientific and intellectual attainments of the English and the French at that period. No such differences existed.

358 [1] *Pensées diverses,* § 138.

to flee danger as other men do, and they are far from charging in battle with the courage of the French, who do not believe in predestination." The existence and importance of non-logical conduct could not be recognized in plainer terms. Find a general form for this observation of particular fact, and we get the starting-point for a theory of non-logical conduct.

359. Bayle further observes, *Ibid.,* § 139: "It cannot be said that people who fail to live according to the precepts of their religion do not believe in a God"; and he presses the point, *Ibid.,* § 136: "Man does not act according to his principles. He may be as rational a creature as you like, but it is none the less true that he almost never acts according to his principles. [In other words his conduct is non-logical.] He has indeed the strength, in speculative matters, not to draw wrong conclusions; for in such reflections he sins rather in his readiness to accept false principles than in drawing mistaken conclusions from them. But it is quite another matter when good morals are in question. [A particular remark that is true in general.] In morals he almost never hits on false principles. Almost always the ideas of natural equity are present in his conscience. Nevertheless he is always deciding in favour of his uncontrolled desires. [The usual vague phraseology, but the substance accords with fact.] . . . The true principle of human conduct . . . is naught but temperament, the natural inclination to pleasure, the taste for certain things, the desire to please, the habits acquired in intercourse with friends, or some other disposition arising from the depths of human nature, whatever the country in which one is born [This contradicts the preceding and is to be deleted.] and whatever the knowledge that has been instilled in the mind."

That comes very close to the facts. If we tried to give greater precision to Bayle's language, and establish a stricter classification, would we not have a theory of non-logical actions—their great importance so becoming more and more apparent?

360. Bayle quotes with approval a passage from Nicolle: " 'When the time comes for human beings to pass from speculation to action, they do not follow consequences; and strange it is to see how the human mind can stop at certain speculative truths without going on to their logical consequences in practice, which seem so bound up with those truths as to be in no way separable from them.'"[1]

361. Bayle soundly enough observes, *Ibid.*, § 51, that "the pagan religion was satisfied with an external rite" (§ 174); but he went wrong in believing, *Ibid.*, § 122, that it "had no influence on morals." He failed to perceive that ritual practices intensified sentiments (non-logical actions) and that such sentiments were in turn sources of morality.

362. He goes to some pains to prove that atheism is preferable to idolatry. To understand him aright we have to take account of the times in which he was living and the perils to which he was exposed. Just as in our time there are persons who give perpetual chase to "immoral" books, so in Bayle's time there were those who kept open season on books against Christianity. Unable to whip the horse, Bayle whips the saddle, and belabours idolatry with criticisms that apply just as well to all religions. At bottom his argument tends to show that since the majority of human actions are non-logical, forms of belief are of no great importance.

363. Montesquieu did not get that point, and his reply to what he calls "Bayle's paradox" is of little or no value. He is solving the problem by restating it when he says: "A prince who loves religion and fears it is a lion surrendering to the hand that caresses it, or to the voice that quiets it; the prince who fears religion and hates it is like the wild beast biting at the chains that keep it from attacking passers-by; the prince who has no religion at all is the terrible beast that never feels his freedom till he is rending and devouring."[1] Underlying all this declamation, which is mere fustian, is the proposition, evidently, that human beings act logically in accord with their beliefs. But that is the very thing Bayle denies; and proofs, not

360 [1] *Continuation des Pensées diverses,* § 139.

363 [1] *L'esprit des lois,* XXIV, 2: *Paradoxe de Bayle.* Montesquieu was right in saying that "in order to attenuate the horrors of atheism" Bayle was "too severe on idolatry"; but he should have recognized Bayle's artifice in doing that. It was a trick he used himself on other occasions.

mere asseverations of the opposite, were required to refute him (§ 368).

364. Taking his stand on logical conduct, Montesquieu says that "even if it were useless for subjects to have religions it would not be useless for princes to have them." Starting with the premise of non-logical conduct, we are carried to a conclusion directly opposite: the person in command needs rational combinations particularly, and the person who obeys needs more particularly an unreasoned rule independent of his scant knowledge.

365. The weakness in Bayle's argument is not the one that Montesquieu criticizes. It lies in an altogether different direction. After noting and amply demonstrating that human beings do not act according to logical inferences from principles, from opinions, and that a great many human actions of great importance are non-logical, Bayle should have centred his attention upon such actions. Then he would have seen that they were of many kinds; and he would have had to decide whether they were independent or influenced one another mutually. He would readily have seen that they do exert reciprocal influences, and therefore that the social importance of religion lies not at all in the logical value of its dogmas, its principles, its theology, but rather in the non-logical actions that it promotes. He was actually on the road to that conclusion when he asserted that "a religion has to be judged by the cult which it practises"; and when he stated that the pagan religion stopped at a purely external ritualism, he could hardly have been closer to experimental truth. One step more and he would have had the truth entire. But unfortunately he turns aside. Instead of judging religions, which are non-logical actions, by their social influence, he loses his way in questions as to their moral value, or better, as to their relation to what he is pleased to call "morality"; and in that we have a counter-attack by logic, which is again invading territory from which it had been expelled.

From that point of view one might repeat of Bayle what Sumner Maine says of him in commenting on the writings of Rousseau:[1]

365 [1] *Ancient Law,* p. 84.

"It [Rousseau's] was the first attempt to re-erect the edifice of human belief after the purely iconoclastic efforts commenced by Bayle, and in part by our own Locke, and consummated by Voltaire." But that goes to show how, in view of the indefiniteness of ordinary language, utterly different concepts may be expressed in the same words. Maine is thinking not of science or theory but of practice, as is clearly apparent from what immediately follows: "and [Rousseau's system has], besides, the superiority which every constructive effort will always enjoy over one that is merely destructive." It is not the function of theory to create beliefs, but to explain existing ones and discover their uniformities. Bayle took a great step forward in that direction in exposing the vacuity of certain interpretations and opening the way for the discovery of others more consistent with the facts. From the standpoint of theory, his work, far from being inferior to Rousseau's, is as superior to Rousseau's as the astronomy of Kepler is superior to the astronomy of Cosmas Indicopleustes. He may be blamed only for stopping too soon on a road which he had so splendidly opened.

366. Why he did so is hard to guess. The case is not rare. It would seem as though in science it is often necessary to destroy before building can begin. It may also be that Bayle was deterred from a complete expression of his ideas by the moral and religious persecutions common in his time, that the atmosphere of persecution affected the thinker not only materially but intellectually also, and constrained him to disguise his thought under certain forms. Just so in our own time persecutions and annoyances of all sorts emanating from votaries of the religion of sexual virtue have created an atmosphere of hypocrisy in speech and thought that influences writing. And so, if in some future age the expression of human thought comes to be liberated from sex "ties" just as it has already been freed of the ties requiring deference to the Bible, people desiring to understand the thought of writers of our day will have to take account of the masks with which it is disguised in deference to contemporary prejudices. Another cause may have been the scientific inadequacies of ordinary language. If Bayle had not had at his disposal such terms as "religion" and "morality," which seem to be exact but are not, he would have been compelled to deal with things instead of with words, sentiments, fictions; and in that case perhaps he might not have lost his way (§ 114).

367. But his case is merely typical of a vastly populous class of cases where error in argument is directly proportionate to defects in language. Anyone, therefore, desirous of remaining in the logico-experimental field and concerned not to be led astray into the domain of sentiment, must ever be on his watch against this the greatest enemy of science (§ 119). In social matters, human beings as a rule use language that lures them away from the logico-experimental domain. What does such language really mean? We have to be clear on that question before we can go farther, and to it we shall devote the chapter next following.

CHAPTER IV

Theories Transcending Experience

368. We are still with our induction. There are phenomena to which certain names are given in ordinary language: there are narrations, theories, doctrines, that refer to social facts. How are we to take them? Do they correspond to anything exact (§ 114)? Even when suitably retouched in form, can they be classed as logico-experimental theories (§ 13), or are they to be taken as non-logico-experimental? Even when grouped with the latter, do they correspond to something, at least, that is definite?

The study here in hand relates exclusively to the logico-experimental validity that certain arguments may (or may not) have. For the time being we deliberately ignore all questions as to the sentiments they hide, their persuasive force, the possible social utility of the underlying sentiments, and hence of the things that provoke them. Here, in a word, we are considering theories strictly from the objective standpoint (§ 13).

Interesting and very important for sociology are the phenomena designated in ordinary language by the terms "religion," "morality," "law." For centuries people have quarrelled about those terms, and so far they have reached no agreement even as to what they mean. They have been defined in many many ways, and since the definitions do not coincide, people have come to designate different things by the same names—an excellent means for never coming to an understanding. What is the cause of that? And should we try to add other definitions to the many already given? Or would it not be better to try to get at the character of such phenomena in some other way (§ 118)?

369. We have narratives, such as the Gospel according to St. John, that many have taken and still take to be historical narrative. Others say that it is just allegory; others that it is allegory combined with history; while still others claim to have a formula for separating what is historical from what is allegorical. Similar opinions were once current with regard to the myths of polytheism, and the procedure seems to be general. What are we to think of these various opinions? Should we select one from among them? Or is some other path open to us? There are no end of theories on morality, law, and so on. If we could find that one among them was true in the sense that it fits the facts, our task would be appreciably easier. But if we can find none such, how are we to proceed?

370. Induction may put us in the way of recognizing certain experimental uniformities. If we succeed in finding them, we can then proceed in the opposite direction, that is, deductively, and compare our inferences with the facts. If they are in agreement, we can accept the hypotheses we have been using—the experimental principles obtained in our induction. If they are not in agreement, we must reject those hypotheses, those principles (§§ 52, 69).

371. Suppose we stop for a moment and examine the term "religion"—and what we say of religion will apply by analogy to other terms of the kind, "morality," "law," and the like, which will frequently be crossing our path. To admit *a priori* the existence of religion (morality, law) leads to seeking the definition of it; and *vice versa,* the search for the definition presupposes the existence of the thing for which a definition is sought. It is a most impressive fact that all attempts so far made to find definitions of that kind have failed. Before going farther, we must recall the distinction between real movements and virtual movements (§§ 129-30). At present we are studying real movements only. We are, in other words, dealing with what *is:* we are not trying to discover what *ought to be* in order that this or that end may be attained.

372. Now a confusion is usually present in the use of the words "religion" ("morality," "law"). Not only are the investigations of real movements and virtual movements often confused, but even when they are distinguished and a writer declares he is keeping to real movements, two, or, to be more exact, many aspects of real movements are not kept distinct, or are not kept clearly distinct.

373. In fact, theory has to be kept distinct from practice. In a given people at a given period of history there is a theoretical religion (morality, law) and a practical religion (morality, law). We say *a* religion, *a* morality, *a* law, for the sake of brevity: really there are more than one, many many more than one, even where there is apparent unity (§§ 464 f.). These facts are undeniable, but they are usually stated in such a way as to minimize their importance as far as possible.

374. We observe, accordingly, that a certain religion (morality, law) is assumed to exist. For the believer it is the one he calls "true." Of it the theoretical religions observable are deviations, and practical religions are in their turn deviations of the theoretical religions. For a parallel, there is a given theorem in geometry. It may be demonstrated more or less well—and so we get theoretical deviations; it may be understood more or less well—and so we get practical deviations. But all that does not lessen the strict truth of the theorem as stated.

375. If the comparison held to the very end, the meaning of the term "religion" ("morality," "law") would be as exact as one might wish. The term would designate a certain type that might even be inferred from existing facts—a thing not possible with a theorem in geometry—by stripping the facts of incidentals and keeping to essentials, or else, as the evolutionists would have it, by determining the limit towards which the facts tend.

376. Unfortunately that is not the situation. Everybody is firmly convinced that *his* religion (morality, law) is the *true* type. But he has no means of imparting his conviction to anyone else. He cannot appeal to experience in general nor to that special kind of experience represented by logical argument. In a dispute between two chemists there is a judge: experience. In a dispute between a Moslem and a Christian, who is the judge? Nobody (§§ 16 f.).

377. In our times there are people who think they can evade this dilemma by abandoning the supernatural; they imagine that divergences can arise only in that domain. But they are wrong, just as the various sects of Christianity were wrong in a day gone by in believing that differences of opinion arose only from varying interpretations of the Scriptures which themselves were above discussion.

378. From the logico-experimental standpoint nothing is gained by replacing supernatural beings with metaphysical principles; for the metaphysical principles can be affirmed or denied as readily as the existence of a god, and there is no judge to settle the dispute (§§ 16 f.).

379. It is of no avail to appeal the issue to public indignation. Certainly, at the time of the quarrels between Lutherans and Catholics, to have asserted that from the logico-experimental point of view the Scriptures had the same value as the *Theogony* of Hesiod would have been to arouse general, not to say unanimous, indignation in Europe. And in the same way to dare question in our day the dogma that the sole purpose of society is the "good of the greatest number," and that it is the strict duty of every individual to sacrifice himself for the good of the lowly and the humble, would be to arouse if not universal at least fairly general indignation. But scientific problems are solved by facts, not by the holy horror of the few, the many, the all.

380. Along that route, therefore, we can never get to sharply defined meanings for our terms. Yet that is the first thing to be done if we would discuss matters of science fruitfully; whereas if the same term is used in a different sense by each individual, rigorous argument becomes impossible (§§ 442, 490, 965).

381. That manner of reasoning, moreover, has the very serious defect of bringing into the matter of definition disputes that should not arise until, owing to clear definitions, we can state exactly what the argument is about (§§ 119, 387, 963).

382. If one sets out to define what the "true" religion is, or the "type" religion, or the "ultimate" religion, it is evident that such a definition cannot be left to the choice of one's adversary, since the term contains a thesis: it asserts that the thing defined is the thing that corresponds to the truth, the type, the limit. That is the chief reason why physicists never dream of quarrelling over the name to be given to X-rays, chemists over the term "radium," or astronomers over the names for any one of the countless asteroids (except in cases where the personal vanity of some discoverer may be involved); whereas no end of breath is still being wasted over the definition to be given to "religion" ("morality," "law") (§ 119).

383. Here is Salomon Reinach, writing a book called *Orpheus: A General History of Religions* and which might be better called *A General History of Religions, as Viewed in the Light of the Dreyfus Case*. He believes that the dogmas of the Catholic, in fact of the Christian, religion are false, whereas the dogmas of his humanitarian-democratic religion are true. He may be right. He may be wrong. We are not going to argue that point; nor do we think that experimental science can be of the slightest service in solving such a problem. At any rate, the problem ought to be treated independently of definitions, whereas Reinach tries to make his readers accept a definition that will help him to establish his thesis. His adversaries are getting support from Catholic beliefs; so he tries to show that that religion is, substantially, nothing more nor less than the tabooism of the backward peoples. For that reason he has to eliminate from the very definition of "religion" everything corresponding to a higher intellectual grade. That he does quite skilfully, for his definition does not after all go very far wide of the facts (§ 1032).[1] But his theses, be they true or false, ought to be stated as theses—as proposi-

383 [1] *Orpheus,* Chap. I, § 5 (Simmonds, p. 3): "I intend to define religion as a 'sum of scruples that interfere with the free exercise of human faculties.' . . . The scruples in question . . . are of a special kind. . . . I will call them 'taboos.'" He goes on to explain that the scruple involved in the taboo "is never based on any rational consideration of a practical order, such as fear of getting pricked or otherwise hurt, in the case of a tree-taboo." Just previously (§ 1), Reinach had said: "Mythology is an assemblage of concocted stories—not invented, but capriciously combined and embellished—where the characters are beyond all verification in positive history. Religion, primarily, is a sentiment, plus the expression of that sentiment by acts of a special kind, namely, rites." Reinach is here considering mythology not as in process of formation, but as a thing ready-made and fully developed, perhaps even in the first stages of decadence—at a point, at any rate, where without scruple poetical elaborations may be appended to popular beliefs (§§ 1086-88). Accepting for the moment that very special standpoint, it is evident that in what he says Reinach takes account, though in no very specific terms, of both logical and non-logical conduct. Religion would be essentially non-logical, made up of what we are to call *residues* (Chapter VI). Mythology would, essentially, be a matter of literary and logical embellishments, of what we are to call *derivations* (Chapter IX).

tions subject by their very nature to controversy—and not tucked into a definition, which is, in part at least, at the arbitrary discretion of the author.

384. But here, on the other side, rises Father Marie-Joseph Lagrange, who believes that the Catholic dogmas are *true* and who naturally cannot, on pain of suicide, accept Reinach's definition. He says: "M. Reinach seems to think that a good definition has to apply to the full breadth of meaning which a term has acquired even by abuse."[1] In that we get, fundamentally, the concept of the "type" religion: once you depart from the type, you fall into an "abuse." Father Lagrange ignores the fact that what is for him a type is for someone else an abuse, and *vice versa.* He continues: "Because people speak, abusively—the figure is called catachresis in rhetoric—of a 'religion of honour,' that definition has to be accounted for in the definition of religion in general!" Yes and no! Yes—it has to be included if one is trying to define "what people call religion," just as the definition of the conjugation of an irregular verb has to be accounted for in a general definition of conjugation, if one is trying to define "what grammarians call conjugation"; and there is no point in debating whether the irregular conjugation is abusive or whether the regular conjugation is the abuse. Or no—the particular definition need not be accounted for in the general definition if one has *previously* and *explicitly* excluded facts of a certain order—a thing that Father Lagrange is not at all inclined to do. I can say that in Latin the active verbs of the first conjugation form their future in *-abo, -abis, -abit* . . . ; because when I specify "active verbs of the first conjugation," I previously and explicitly exclude all other verbs. But I could not give those endings for verbs in general and then, when I am shown the future forms *legam, leges,* for the verb *lego,* get out of my predicament by saying that *legam* is an abuse. I can say (it might not be true) that "originally" the active endings of the principal tenses of Greek verbs were -μι, -σι, -τι . . . because I have explicitly and in advance specified that I am dealing with *original*

384 [1] *Quelques remarques sur l'Orpheus de M. Salomon Reinach,* pp. 8-9 (Martindale, p. 11).

forms, a qualification which permits me to disregard verbs in -ώ by holding (rightly or wrongly) that they are not primitive or original. But I could not state sweepingly, without specific qualification as to origins, that Greek verbs ended in -μι, -σι, -τι . . . and then try to be rid of the verbs in -ω by calling them an abuse. In short, what is Father Lagrange trying to define? What people *call* religion (a linguistic question)? Or something else? And in the latter case, just what is the something else? Unless he tells us, we cannot decide whether his definition is good or bad.

385. Father Lagrange continues: "And we wind up with this definition of religion: *a sum of scruples that interfere with the free exercise of human faculties!* One would think it a question of a bet; for, with triumphant ingenuousness, Reinach proceeds to observe that his definition eliminates from the fundamental concept of religion everything that people commonly regard as the proper object of the religious sentiment!"

386. So it would seem that Father Lagrange is looking for what is *commonly* designated by the term "religion." That would take us back to the linguistic question. But look out for that word "commonly"—for in it treachery lies! What does it mean—"commonly"? Are we to compile statistics of the opinions of mankind? And only of people living today, or also of people who have lived in times past? Of Europeans only, or of all human beings who are living or have lived on the face of the earth? And are we to *count* opinions, or are we to *weigh* them (§ 595)? If we weigh them, with what scales? It would seem as though Father Lagrange were inclined to weigh them, since he calls some of them abusive; but in that case we may rest assured that if he selects the scales, they will register the weights he wishes them to register; and that if his adversary selects them, they will show an entirely different weight. Then again, besides religion in general there are religions in particular. What are we to do with them? In order to bar them, we have to go back to the theory of the type religion.

387. Father Lagrange adds: "It is another way of saying that M. Reinach's definition is contemptible. Logicians undoubtedly grant that a word has only the sense that is given it; but to define a traditional term in a sense counter to the general acceptation is a childish jest or a trap for fools."

But, just a moment! Can we be so sure? The thing that chemists call water is not what is commonly called water; nor is the gold of the chemists the gold of ordinary language. For the multitude a five-dollar gold-piece is made of gold; for the chemist it is a mixture of gold and copper with traces of many other elements. It was not at all a "childish jest" to define chemical bodies in a manner counter to "general acceptations"; on the contrary, that was the only thing to do to elevate chemistry to dignified status as a science (§ 115). Reinach is perfectly free to define the term "religion" counter to "general acceptation," provided: (1) that he gives a definition that is clear and exact; (2) that he does not confuse the thing which he is defining with some other thing that bears the same name; and (3) that there is some advantage in his new definition to compensate us for our trouble in remembering that the "religion" of Reinach is not the "religion" of other people. To spare us that trouble and avoid all danger of misunderstandings, it would be well if, instead of employing a term already in use, he were to use some other (§ 117), saying, for example: "I will call *X* the sum of scruples that interfere with the free exercise of human faculties." After that, but only after that (§ 381), he might formulate a thesis such as this: "*X* will be found present in everything that human beings call religion, and nowhere else." It would then be possible to verify on the facts the truth or falsity of the proposition (§ 963).

388. Suppose we do that now. From no other standpoint can experimental science envisage such questions. The chemist tells us that water is a compound of hydrogen and oxygen. The first of the conditions that we laid down is satisfied. The second is also satisfied, because in no treatise on chemistry is chemically pure water ever confused with the thing commonly known as water. And likewise satisfied is the third, because the advantage of knowing the exact composition of the thing called water is self-evident (§§ 108, 69 [5]). Then we are told that chemical water is the principal ingredient of the thing commonly called water that is found in wells, lakes, rivers, the sea, the rain. We verify the proposition and see that it is true. If someone went on and said that chemical water is not the principal ingredient in things not commonly known as water, the verification would not turn out so well; for water is the principal ingredient in wines, beers, syrups, and the like.

389. To avoid ambiguities, suppose we give a name to the thing defined by Reinach and call it religion-α. If we find that religion-α is identical with ordinary religion, so much the better for Reinach's religion. We are in no way disparaging his religion by calling it religion-α. The latter is simply a label we append to the thing to help us keep track of it (§ 119).

390. Certain it is that many religions which are and have been the religions of millions and millions of human beings—for instance, Indo-European polytheism, the Judao-Christian and Moslem religions, fetishism—contain religion-α. But all those religions—with the exception, partial at least, of fetishism—contain another thing which we may call religion-β (§ 119), and which, to use words of Father Lagrange, is "a belief in higher beings with whom it is possible to establish relations."[1] But now, which is the principal element in the things commonly known as religion, religion-α, or religion-β? In order to answer, we have to know the exact meaning of the term "principal." When we were comparing chemical water with river water, by "principal element" we meant the element having the greatest weight. Chemical analysis of river-water showed that the chemical water contained in it weighed more than all other ingredients. But how are we to *analyze* religions, and how are we to *weigh* the elements in them?

391. It may be said: "The principal element in religions is the belief in higher beings, since it is from that belief that the scruples

390 [1] *Etudes sur les religions sémitiques,* p. 7: "Everybody agrees at least that there is no religion apart from belief in higher powers with whom relations may be established." But "everybody" is in no such agreement. "Everybody" includes Reinach, and Reinach seems not to agree! But why do those two gentlemen insist on giving the same name to different things? Simply because they have an ax to grind on the sentiments the name arouses!

mentioned by Reinach logically emanate." To which the answer may be made: "The principal element in religions is the scruples, since the fact of their existence provoked in human beings the belief in higher powers"—the Romans had two sayings: "If there are gods, there is divination," and "If there is divination, there are gods."[1] In the theorems mentioned the word "principal" seems to mean "anterior in time." But even though it were demonstrated that belief in superior powers came first and scruples afterwards, it would by no means follow that at some later time the scruples were not the whole thing in religion, or the more active element in it. And if it were demonstrated that the scruples antedated the belief, it would in no wise follow that at some later date they had not yielded first place to belief in higher powers.

392. If one asks, then, "Are the religion-α and the religion-β present in all phenomena called religions?", the answer has to be no. On the one hand religion-α is more wide-spread than religion-β. In fetishism and tabooism in whole or in part, in modern free-thought, in Comte's positivism, in the humanitarian religion, in the metaphysical religions, there are scruples but no higher powers —at least no such powers are distinctly present. It is true that Comte ends by creating fictitious entities, but in theory they remain fictitious throughout. That fact merely shows that where there are such scruples, there is a propensity to explain them by a resort to higher powers.

393. On the other hand, there are some few cases where if religion-β is defined strictly as recognition of the existence of higher beings, it may be said that religion-β exists apart from religion-α, or at least, without any dependence of the latter on the former. Take,

391 [1] Cicero, *De divinatione,* I, 5, 9: "My opinion is that if those sorts of divination which we have inherited and practise are true, there must be gods; and that *vice versa* if there are gods, there must be people to know their will"—*i.e.,* there must be divination. *Idem, De natura deorum,* II, 3, 7: "What else do prophecies and presentiments of the future mean except that things that are to be are portended, 'signed,' predicted to men? That in part is why they are termed 'signs,' 'portents,' 'prodigies' "—[*i.e., prodigium* from *praedicere.*—A. L.]

for example, the religion of the Epicureans.[1] If we are told that we must not consider it because it is a scandalous thing, the reply is that we are not investigating the composition of *praiseworthy* religions, but the composition of all beliefs that are or have been called religions. And if it were said that the Epicureans too had scruples, we should reply that if the term "religion-α" is to be defined as broadly as that, then religion-α is everywhere present, for there is not and there has never been a human being in the world who does not have, or has not had, some scruple or other. In that case the term "religion-α" defining everything would define nothing.

394. There is, again, a sect of Buddhism that shows no trace of the second half of the definition of religion-β—of relations established with higher beings. In fact that half is explicitly rejected, as witness the conversation between Guimet and three Japanese theologians:[1]

"*Q.* My first question bears on the origin of the heavens, the earth, and everything about us. How do you explain their formation, according to the principles of the Buddhist religion?

"*A.* The Buddhist religion ascribes the existence of all things to what it calls In-En [Cause-Effect]. Each thing is only a combination of infinitely minute atoms. Those atoms combine to form moun-

393 [1] Cicero, *De natura deorum,* I, 19, 51. Explaining views of Epicurus he says of the nature of a god in a passage that is celebrated: "He does nothing. He has no worries or preoccupations. No exertion is required of him. He rejoices in his knowledge and virtue; and he can look forward to an eternity of infinite beatitude." *Cf.* Diogenes Laertius, *Epicurus,* X, 139 (Hicks, Vol. II, p. 663): "Such a one is immortal and blissful. He has no worries of his own, nor does he create them for anyone else."

394 [1] *Annales du Musée Guimet,* Vol. I, pp. 307-44: *Notes abrégées sur les réponses faites dans le Hioun-Kakou . . . par MM. Simatchi, Atsoumi et Akamatsou aux questions de M. Emile Guimet:* "The *Sin-siou sect,*" says M. Guimet, "is one of the strongest, as regards membership, in Japan." Note that Guimet and others call the thing here in question a religion. Anyone accepting the thesis of Father Lagrange might deny that such a thing could be called a religion, saying that such a name would be an abuse. But if one can get rid of facts contrary to a theory simply by calling them an abuse, it is obvious that no theory will ever fail of verification, and that it is a waste of time to go on investigating. We are here examining the peculiarities of things that have been called religions, not the traits of things that one writer or another would like to have called by that name.

tains, rivers, plains, metals, stones, plants, and trees. Such objects come into being from the natural relationship of their In and their En, exactly as all living beings are born by virtue of their In-En.

"*Q*. Is there no creator of the heavens, the earth, and all other things?

"*A*. No.

"*Q*. What is this thing which you call In-En?

"*A*. Nothing is formed naturally and of itself. It is always the relation of a this to a that that constitutes a thing. . . .

"*Q*. . . . I now ask you whether the conduct of human beings depends in any way on God.

"*A*. A man is responsible for his own conduct. It in no way depends on God. [No trace so far of any relations with higher beings, which, according to Lagrange, *everybody* recognizes!]

"*Q*. Do you not admit that God exerts an influence on humanity and guides us in the performance of our various acts of invention or improvement?

"*A*. The Buddhist religion admits of no creator. It ascribes everything to the In-En. It thereby declares that every human act is performed on the individual's initiative without any interference on the part of God.

"*Q*. It is evident that the term God is not the proper one. Nevertheless your religion does recognize a higher being, Amida, which it venerates and devoutly worships. Well, does not the power of Amida have some influence on human conduct?

"*A*. The differences prevailing among individual human beings, as regards their personal value and the value of what they do, depend more or less on the education they have received, and not at all on the will of Amida. . . .

"*Q*. I would readily admit that knowledge may be increased by effort . . . but, at the same time, in the domain of ethics, in the distinction between right and wrong, between what is just and what is unjust, does it not seem that there must be a higher being who rewards or punishes us for our conduct, much as the social authority punishes us for infractions of the rules of public order?

"*A.* Every good and every evil act has as its consequence a blessing or a sorrow. That results from the altogether natural conception of the In-Goua [synonym of In-En]."

395. Farther along: "*A.* In Buddhism at large, one often hears of prayers to the divinity that have been answered. Our sect absolutely forbids such prayers." If we choose to regard the two parts of the definition of religion-β as forming an inseparable unit—that is, the belief in higher beings plus the belief that it is possible to establish relations with them—we should have to conclude that religion-β is not present in the two religions just mentioned; and we would hardly know where to place them, for they do not fall, either, under the definition of religion-α.

396. We can only conclude, therefore, that as usual the terms of ordinary language do not lend themselves to rigorous classifications. Chemistry, physics, mechanics, and the other natural sciences were never built up by studying and classifying the terms of ordinary language, but by studying and classifying facts. Let us try to do the same for sociology.

397. Meanwhile, and still by way of induction, we discover that the definitions of Reinach and Lagrange are of a different character. Their authors may not have been aware of it, but they aim at classifying quite different orders of facts: Reinach's, certain states of mind; Lagrange's, the explanations that are given of them. Can it be that those two orders of facts are in general profitably to be distinguished, classified, examined? We shall see. Here at any rate there is a substantial difference, not a mere difference in the forms of ordinary parlance. For the moment let us go on with the inquiry in hand.

398. The difficulties encountered in efforts to define the terms "law" and "morality" have proved quite as serious as was the case with the term "religion." No way has yet been found even to distinguish law from morality. At one extreme we get a definition that is grossly empirical. We are told that law consists of a body of norms that are sanctioned by a public authority, and that morality consists of a body of norms imposed only by conscience. Such a definition is satisfactory enough for the practical purposes of lawyer and judge; but it does not have the slightest scientific value, since it assumes for criteria elements that are secondary and changeable—it is like classifying birds by the colours of their feathers. An action passes from law to morality or from morality to law according to the will or caprice of the legislator. The classification therefore may register such will or caprice, but not, as our purpose was, the intrinsic character of the act. Moreover, such a classification becomes useless when, as was the case in epochs remotely past, no public authority interferes to proclaim or enforce private law. Modern civilized countries have written codes, and it is an easy matter to determine whether a given act is or is not regulated by law. The definition in question is experimental, clear, exact; but that does not help very much, since it fails to classify the things which we were trying to understand.

399. If, furthermore, we try to consider things intrinsically, we are brought to considering "essences," and are so lured gradually away from the experimental field to go wandering about among the clouds of metaphysics, eventually arriving at the other extreme, where all objective reality goes by the board.

400. There are some who are candid enough to admit as much. Adolf Franck says:[1] "The idea of law, considered in itself, independently of the applications of which it is susceptible, and of the laws more or less just that have been made in its name, is a simple, absolute idea of reason and is therefore beyond any logical definition." At last! That unequivocally recognizes the fact that the concept of law belongs to a category within the domain of non-logical conduct; and unless some other theory, some theory of *innate* ideas, comes to our rescue, we have to admit that such a concept varies according to times, places, and individuals. To deny that, we should have to attribute an objective existence to "simple ideas"—the kind of existence once enjoyed by the gods of Olympus.[2]

400 [1] *Dictionnaire des sciences philosophiques, s.v.* "Droit."

400 [2] Others try to hide the conflict with reality under ingenious subtleties, the way people ordinarily do in trying to logicalize non-logical conduct. With that matter we have already dealt in Chapter III.

401. Theories of "natural law" and the "law of nations" are another excellent example of discussions destitute of all exactness. Many thinkers have more or less vaguely expressed their sentiments under those terms, and have then exerted themselves to link their sentiments with practical ends that they desired to attain. As usual, they have derived great advantage in such efforts from using indefinite words that correspond not to things, but only to sentiments. We are now going to examine such manners of reasoning for such correspondence as they may (or may not) have with experimental reality. But the conclusions we reach must not be carried over into any other field (§ 41). The question of their experimental validity is independent of any question of their social utility; and a theory may be as beneficial as one could wish under certain circumstances and in this or that period of history without having any bearing at all on experimental realities. "Natural law" is simply that law of which the person using the phrase approves; but the cards cannot be ingenuously laid on the table in any such terms; it is wiser to put the thing a little less bluntly, supplement it by more or less argument.

402. The objections that might be raised against any assertion of natural law are met in the following way: "Why must I subscribe to your opinion?" "Because it is in accord with reason." "But I am using reason too, and my idea is different from yours." "Yes, but my reason is *right* reason" (§§ 422 f.). "How comes it that you who are blessed with this right reason are so few?" "We are not so few: our opinion enjoys universal consensus." "And yet there are some who think differently." "I should have said the consensus of the good and the wise." "Very well! It was you then, the good and the wise, who invented this natural law?" "No, we got it from Nature, from God."

403. The resources on which defenders of natural law rely are chiefly: right reason; nature, with its appendages, rational nature, state of nature, conformity with nature, sociability, and the like; the consensus of all mankind, or of some essential part of mankind; the divine will.

404. Two questions especially are envisaged: (1) the authorship of natural law, and (2) the manner of its revelation.[1] God may be the author of natural law either directly, or else indirectly by means of Right Reason or of Nature, His servants. Nature may be the author of natural law either directly or, preferably, indirectly, by having engraved on the human mind a picture of natural law (or merely of *law*), which is forthwith discovered by right reason, or else by observing either general opinion or the opinion of the best-qualified individuals. It is possible also to speculate as to what humanity would be like in a "state of nature," a state that, to tell the truth, no one has ever seen, but with which metaphysicists are so well acquainted that from that state (so well known to them, to other people entirely unknown) they derive their knowledge of things which the rest of us have before our very eyes and might therefore know directly. Finally, Right Reason can command observance of natural law on its own unsupported authority.

405. Natural law may be revealed to us directly by God through writings inspired by Him—but that is a very rare case. Direct observation of the consensus of mankind, or of a part of mankind, might also reveal natural law directly; but that method, in point of fact, is seldom if ever followed. Really the function of revealing natural law belongs properly to Right Reason, either as its own production, or as deriving from Nature, or from God; or from universal consensus or some more limited consensus.

406. It is quite generally asserted, in substance, that the concept of natural law is inherent in the human mind. Some indication as to the source of the concept is often added, with further support of the consensus of all mankind, or of the best-qualified individuals. Ordinarily, almost all such weapons are used at the same time, because it is better to appeal to the greatest possible number of sentiments; and the various manners of revelation are themselves declared to be in accord with one another, again for the same reason.

407. The subjective argument by accord of sentiments seems to be as follows: It is perceived that existing laws are not an arbitrary,

404 [1] We encounter here, in a particular case, general methods of logicalization that we shall treat in Chapters IX and X.

nor even an entirely logical, creation—that they contain a substratum not due to any volition but subsisting by itself. That induction is in accord with the facts, and it ought to be stated in this form: "There are certain principles of non-logical conduct from which human beings deduce their laws. Such principles of non-logical conduct (or 'residues,' Chapter VI) are correlated with the conditions under which human beings live, and change with those conditions."

408. But in that form, which emphasizes the relative, subjective, non-logical character of the principles, the argument is repulsive to metaphysicists and theologians, and even to a large number of mere students of social matters. What they want is something absolute, objective, logical, and they invariably find it by using indeterminate words and defective reasonings ("derivations," Chapter IX). In the case in hand, the absolute and objective is sought in the consensus of the many or the all, in conformity with Nature, in divine will. Of all those things, or of some of them, they have most favourable opinions. They must therefore be in accord with that other thing, natural law, of which they have an equally high opinion: and logic must supply us with the nexus that brings the two excellences together (§ 514). In such theories, ever peeping out from under the various disguises, is the notion of a contrast between something that is constant and good ("natural" law) and something else that is variable and not so good ("positive" law); and that contrast is chiefly responsible for their conviction, and the conviction of those who agree with them (§ 515).

409. Whether the one or the other of these procedures occupies the forefront is altogether a matter of individual preference. Christians, of course, cannot do without God; but it is interesting that they make His interposition not so much direct as indirect. That may be because the metaphysicist overbalances the Christian in them. But pure metaphysicists are satisfied with Right Reason.

410. Aristotle finds it characteristic of natural law that it has the same force everywhere. That does not mean that it is always the same in every place, since there may be natural variations.[1] He uses that reservation to answer the denial of natural law on the ground of variations in the law of nations. In the *Rhetoric,* I, 13, 2 (Freese, p. 139), he expresses himself thus: "I say that law is peculiar or common (*ἴδιον καὶ κοινόν*). That law is peculiar which some ordain for themselves, and it may be written or unwritten. Common is that law which is in accord with Nature, since there is a just and an unjust by nature, which all people divine, though neither communication nor understanding exist between them."[2] Such really would be principles of non-logical actions, which are common to human beings everywhere, varying according to the conditions under which they live. Aristotle's theory would seem, therefore, to give first place to Nature. Universal consensus would be the means by which that origin according to Nature manifests itself.

411. Just how the things that have the same force everywhere are to be distinguished from those which do not is hard to imagine. Aristotle thinks he can show how, and he gives the example [*Ethica Nicomachea,* V, 7, 2 (Rackham, p. 295)] of a law prescribing that a goat and not a sheep should be sacrificed to Zeus. In fact, at first sight, it would seem evident that such a law must be arbitrary; but a slight modification in terms is enough to endow the prescription with the trait of pseudo-universality required by natural law. We need only say: "In every locality local customs must be observed. In our country it is customary to sacrifice a goat, and not a sheep; hence a goat must be sacrificed."

412. In one and the same treatise Cicero sways back and forth between the various demonstrations, so betraying the fact that it is not

410 [1] Aristotle, *Ethica Nicomachea,* V, 7, 1-4 (Rackham, p. 295): "Of political law a part is natural, a part legislative. That law is natural which everywhere has the same force and does not depend on opinion." *Idem, Magna moralia,* I, 33, 19 (Stock, p. 1194b, l. 30): "Some just things are so by nature, some by legislation." He goes on to say that natural things too can change; and he gives as an example the fact that one could use the right hand and the left hand indifferently, but that that would not preclude our still having a right hand and a left hand. Then he adds: ". . . the law that endures is most often just according to nature." And then: "Justice according to nature is therefore better than justice according to law."

410 [2] He says further, I, 10, 3 (Freese, pp. 105-07): "I call . . . that [law] common which, though not written, seems to be recognized by all."

the conclusions that follow from the demonstration, but that the demonstration is selected for the purpose of obtaining the conclusions. In his essay *On Laws, De legibus,* I, 6, 20, he says: "I will seek the origin of law in Nature (*repetam stirpem iuris a Natura*), who must be our guide in this whole matter." Here the appeal is to Nature directly; but a few lines above, I, 6, 18-19, she was brought in indirectly, and first place was given to a Supreme Reason, and Cicero continues: "Law is Supreme Reason implanted in Nature (*lex est ratio summa insita in Natura*), who bids us do the things we ought to do and forbids us their contraries. When this reason has been established and elaborated (*confirmata et confecta*) in the minds of men, it becomes law. . . . If that is well said—and I am of opinion that on the whole it is—right has its origin in law; for law is the force of Nature; it is the mind and the reason of the wise man, and the measure of what is just and what is unjust."

413. In this enumeration of highly estimable things divinity was missing—but not for long; II, 4, 8: "I observe that it has been the opinion of the wisest that law is not devised by human intelligence nor is it the decree of peoples, but something eternal that governs the whole world with the wisdom of its prescriptions and interdictions. Wherefore it has been said that law is the primal and ultimate mind of God, who prescribes and prohibits in all matters through reason. Rightly to be praised therefore is a law that the gods have bestowed upon the human race: for it is the reason and the thought [mind] of a wise being qualified both to command and to dissuade."

414. Elsewhere, I, 7, 23, right reason is said to be the law; and since right reason is common to gods and men, the latter stand in partnership with the gods—no more, no less: "Since nothing is better than reason and since it exists both in man and in God, a first partnership of reason exists between man and God. But those who have reason in common have also right reason in common, and since right reason is the law (*quae cum sit lex*) we must consider ourselves as brought through the law into partnership with the gods."

415. Then we are back with Nature again, II, 5, 13: "Law, then, is the distinction between what is just and what is unjust, modelled on that most ancient Nature, the beginning of all things." That blessed Nature is like an elastic band: it can be stretched to any length required, I, 8, 25: "Virtue is nothing but Nature perfect in itself and carried to its limit."

416. One cannot read all that without seeing that Cicero has a clear conception of a law that is not conventional. It comes out when he says, I, 10, 28, that "not by opinion, but by Nature was law constituted (*Neque opinione sed Natura constitutum esse ius*)." But then his ideas as to the origin and nature of such a law grow confused. He goes groping about to find every perfection he can think of to piece together with the high conception he has of law.

417. Little or no progress has been made since Cicero's time; and writers on natural law continue to make all possible combinations of the same concepts; save that the God of the Christians replaces the pagan gods, a scientific varnish is applied, and a pseudo-science is invited to reveal just what Milady Nature would have us do.

418. Roman jurists often put their theories under the protection of a certain natural law (*ius naturae, naturale*) common to all men and even to animals. They have been defended in that on the ground that human beings and animals have in fact certain mental traits in common. But it is not in the least with such traits that we are concerned; nor do they in any sense assume any authority as principles of law such as the champions of natural law envisage. So, in the very same fashion, from the fact that certain good or bad traits in a parent affect the character of his progeny, people have tried to conclude that it was "just" that the children should be punished for the sins of their fathers (§§ 1979 f.). Such reasoning involves a confusion between a state of fact and a state of "right," between what happens and what one should try to have happen. It is one thing to say, "The progeny of a syphilitic parent have certain diseases," and quite another thing to say, "The syphilitic father should be punished in his child, by inoculating the latter with diseases he does not have."

So also the term "solidarity" has been given to correlations between animals and human beings, or between human beings, with an inference from that fact of something altogether different—a certain "obligation" or "law" of solidarity (§§ 449-450).

419. In the proemium of the *Institutes* of Justinian, I, 2 (*Corpus iuris civilis,* Vol. I, p. 3; Scott, Vol. II, p. 5), we are told: "Natural law is that which Nature imparts to all animate creatures; for this law is not peculiar to mankind, but is shared by all animals that live in the air, on the earth, and in the sea. Hence comes the union of male and female that we call matrimony, the procreation and education of offspring. We see, in fact, that the animals have knowledge of this law." If we strip off the trappings of sentiment which disguise this passage it becomes frankly comical. The compilers of the *Institutes* are not content with saying "all animals"; they hammer on the point, so that every doubt may be dispelled and their period turn out more rhythmical: it is a question, no more, no less, of "all animals that live in the air, on the earth, and in the sea." So we get a natural law of earthworms, fleas, lice, flies, and in our day we might add, of infusoria. And not only does this pretty law exist; the animals know it—a thing, in truth, marvellous beyond words!

420. And in proof—the institution of matrimony is brought forward! Among certain species of spiders the male seizes the moment in which the female is not looking to rush upon her and copulate. He then flees as fast as his legs can carry him because the female will devour him if she gets her claws on him. Strange indeed how these animals *know* the natural law of matrimony—and use it!

421. To make law accord with the facts, the compilers of the *Institutes* use a method that is a very common resort: they introduce sly alterations in the meanings of terms. They say (*Corpus iuris civilis,* Vol. I, p. 3; Scott, Vol. II, p. 5): *"Hinc descendit maris atque feminae coniugatio* (variant, *coniunctio*), *quam nos matrimonium appellamus."* ("Hence comes the union of male and female that we call matrimony.") But this they contradict later on when they say,

I, 10, 12 (*Corpus,* Vol. I, p. 6; Scott, Vol. II, p. 15): *"Si adversus ea quae diximus aliqui coierint, nec vir, nec uxor, nec nuptiae, nec matrimonium, nec dos intelligitur."* ("If some unite in ways different from those specified, they cannot be known as husband and wife, nor is there either wedlock or marriage or dowry.") In one place they say that simple copulation, as in the case of animals, is what they mean by *matrimonium.* In the other place they withhold that name from unions which do not have certain other traits. Of the two contradictory propositions, one has to be eliminated—and better the first, since it is certain that in the language of law *matrimonium* is something more than simple copulation.

422. The law of nations (*ius gentium*) is declared to be imposed by natural reason (*naturalis ratio*). This natural reason is a beautiful creature to whom one may resort in distressing predicaments and use to demonstrate many fine things. It is also called right reason (ὀρθὸς λόγος), true reason, just, honest reason, and the like. It is not explained how the reason worthy of these exalted epithets is to be distinguished from the reason which has to go without them. But at bottom the former is always the one that meets the approval of the writer who bestows the laudatory epithet.

423. A person whom we shall call Primus observes that $A = B$. A person whom we shall call Secundus denies it. Primus thinks he proves his assertion when he says that $A = B$ because right reason will have it so. But why is the reason of Primus "right" reason, while the reason of Secundus is not? Who is to pass judgment in the dispute? If now a Tertius comes forward and says that to his mind the reason of Primus is right reason, that only proves that on the subject in hand Primus and Tertius happen to think alike; and what has that got to do with the other fact that $A = B$? If not only Tertius, but several individuals, many individuals—all men—agree with Primus, that fact continues to have no bearing on the objective proposition that $A = B$, except for people who take such consensus as proof of the theorem. But if we are going to reason in that fashion, it would be as well, and in fact much better, to bring on the consen-

sus in the first place, without dragging in right reason for the pleasure of chasing it away again! All that, of course, from the logico-experimental point of view. As an appeal to sentiment the introduction of right reason is a very helpful thing; for it enables one to insinuate that the person who does not accept the demonstration is somehow a poor sort of person. The procedure is general, and we shall return to it hereafter (§§ 480 f.).

424. At a later period we come upon an elect company of jurists who formulated the theory of natural law and the law of nations, and who are greatly admired by people who are so fortunate as to understand them: Grotius, Selden, Pufendorf, Burlamaqui, Vattel, and so on.[1]

425. Grotius says that "natural law is made up of certain principles of right reason which teach us that an action is morally proper or improper according as it is in accord or disaccord with a rational and sociable Nature, and that, consequently, God, who is the creator of Nature, commands or prohibits such actions."[1]

424 [1] Lack of space prevents us from examining all their definitions here; but that is no great loss, for they are all more or less alike and all equally hazy.

425 [1] *De jure belli ac pacis,* I, 10, 1 (Pareto used Barbeyrac's French translation): *"Pour commencer par le Droit Naturel, il consiste dans certains principes de la Droite Raison, qui nous font connoître qu'une Action est moralement honnête ou déshonnête selon la convenance ou la disconvenance nécessaire qu'elle a avec une Nature Raisonnable et Sociable; et par conséquent que Dieu, qui est l'Auteur de la Nature, ordonne ou défend une telle action."* The Latin original reads: *"Ius naturale est dictatum rectae rationis indicans actui alicui ex ejus convenentia aut disconvenentia cum ipsa natura rationali inesse moralem turpitudinem aut necessitatem moralem, ac consequenter ab auctore naturae Deo talem actum aut vetari aut praecipi."* (See Campbell, p. 21.) Grotius goes on to observe, § 2, that "the actions in regard to which Nature supplies such principles are obligatory or illicit in themselves, so that they are conceived as necessarily ordained or forbidden by God"—and that is what distinguishes it from human law. Noticeable here, as usual, is a perception that there is in law a something that is not arbitrary; and that something is "necessarily" connected with God, Nature, Right Reason, and other similar entities. Notes by Barbeyrac to French translation: "Grotius wrote: 'morally necessary,' but the term I use, 'morally proper,' is clearer and the contrast is more exact. I write 'reasonable *and sociable* nature,' following the author's regular formula, as witness § 12, No. 1; II, § 12, No. 3; III, § 1, No. 3. The copyist, or the printer, would seem to have overleapt the two words without the author's noticing, as has happened in other passages."

Pufendorf comments that that is reasoning in a circle, because natural laws are defined as what is proper and then to learn what is proper we have to resort to natural laws.[2] But Burlamaqui washes Grotius clean of any such blemish: "I cannot see any circle there; for the question as to the source of the natural rectitude or turpitude of proscribed or forbidden actions Grotius does not answer in the manner represented. He would say that the rectitude or turpitude arises from the necessary harmony (*convenance*) or discord (*disconvenance*) of our actions with a rational and sociable nature."[3] That is the usual method of defining one unknown by another unknown. From natural laws we are remanded to "rectitude," from rectitude to harmony; to say nothing of a certain "rational" nature which is not clearly distinguishable from a nature that is not such.

426. All the same, let us do the best we can. We have been referred to a "harmony"; let us see if we can discover what on earth it may be. Burlamaqui, *Ibid.*, II, 7, 2, gives us a lead: "As for the *harmony* finally, it is something approximate to order itself. It is a relation of conformity among several things, the one of which is in itself essential to the conservation and perfection of the other, and does its share in maintaining it in a good and advantageous state." It would seem, then, that the "rectitude" in question is something that stands in the relation indicated to a "rational and sociable nature." But our unknowns, far from getting fewer, are increasing in number. In addition to discovering what "rational nature" is, we now have to learn the meaning that the author gives to the words "conservation," "perfection," "good and advantageous state."

427. All this twisting and turning amounts in the end to saying that "natural law" is a phrase that arouses in the mind of the author an atmosphere similar to the atmosphere aroused by the words "rational nature," "conservation," "perfection," "good and advantageous state"—all of which are essentially undefinable. Why, then,

425 [2] *De iure naturae et gentium,* I, 1, 10 [Wrong reference. Pufendorf regarded I, 2, 6, as his basic comment on Grotius: Frankfurt, pp. 27-29; Kennett, pp. 18-20; Barbeyrac, Vol. I, p. 30.—A. L.]

425 [3] *Principes du droit naturel,* Pt. II, Chap. 5, Sec. 6.

instead of going so far afield, does not the author say it that way and have done with it? [1]

428. For Pufendorf "natural law is that law which is so invariably in accord with the rational and sociable nature of man that unless its norms were observed an honest and peaceful society could not exist among men." [1] He would seem here to be depending on experience alone; and if he continued along that line, natural law would simply be a law that governs societies in such a way that they are able to survive. But unfortunately experience shows that many are the societies which subsist, and each with a different set of laws; so we cannot know which of the latter is the natural law except by determining what they have in common—and that takes us into another field.[2]

427 [1] Here induction leads us to consider a general phenomenon with which we shall deal at length in Chapter IX. For the present let us continue examining the relations of these theories to experimental facts.

428 [1] *De officio hominis et civis,* I, 2, 16 (Oxford, Vol. I, p. 18; Vol. II, p. 16): *"Illa est quae cum rationali ac sociali natura hominis ita congruit ut humano generi honesta et pacifica societas citra eandem constare nequeat."*

428 [2] Burlamaqui, *Eléments du droit naturel,* Pt. III, Chap. 13, Sec. 1: "As regards natural law, the proofs based on the consensus and practices of the nations or on the sentiments of philosophers are not adequate for establishing that this or that thing is part of natural law. The extent to which even the wisest and most enlightened nations have gone astray on the most important matters is only too well known." Pufendorf also rejects the evidence of universal consensus. Pufendorf-Barbeyrac, *Le droit de la nature et des gens,* II, 3, 7 (Vol. I, p. 179; *De iure,* Frankfurt, p. 179; Kennett, pp. 124-25): "Others take for the basis of natural law the consent of all mankind, or of all nations, or of most nations, or of the more civilized nations, to recognize certain things as proper or improper. But for one thing, that is only, as the phrase goes, an *a posteriori* proof [In other words, an experimental proof, and therefore repugnant to every good metaphysicist.] and fails altogether to explain why this or that thing is prescribed or prohibited by natural law. Then again it is not a very sure method and is fraught with countless difficulties; for if one appeals to mankind as a whole, two annoying embarrassments arise, as Hobbes well shows, *De cive,* II, § 1. In the first place, on that assumption it does not appear that any human being actually using his reason could ever sin against natural law; for the moment one individual belonging to the human race embraces an opinion differing from the general, the consensus of mankind is impaired. In the second place, it seems manifestly absurd to take as the basis of natural laws the consent of those who break them more often than they observe them." Pufendorf defines natural law, *De iure naturae et gentium,* I, 6, 18 (Frankfurt, p. 109, Barbeyrac, Vol. I, p. 113; Kennett, p. 76), as "a law standing in such a necessary relationship to the reasonable and sociable nature of man that without observance of it no honest

429. But Pufendorf does not understand the matter in that way, really. He dismisses experience without further delay, adding that the law in question can be discovered with the sole aid of natural reason, by mere contemplation of human nature in general. Know ye, therefore, that[1] "to discover entirely and convincingly the distinguishing trait of natural law . . . it is sufficient to examine attentively the nature and inclinations of man in general." And so, with this blessed Nature, we are thrown back once more into full metaphysics, to land at a place where the "fundamental principle of natural law" dwells, the law that[2] "each individual should do his utmost to further the welfare of human society in general." That does not help us very much, for we now have to quarrel as to the character of that welfare. One person will say, "The welfare of society lies in an aristocratic system"; another will retort, "The welfare of society lies in a democratic system." And how are we going to settle the dispute on the principles of natural law? Pufendorf adds that "natural law has God for its author"—and that, in truth, must be the case![3]

430. Burlamaqui departs but slightly from Pufendorf. He says:[1] "By natural law is meant a law that God lays down for all men and which they can discover and know by the unaided light of their reason, considering attentively their nature and their state." Here there is no trace of the animals that made up such a fascinating menagerie in the *Institutes* of Justinian.[2] But a new entity has come

and peaceful society could exist in the human race. Or if one wish, it is a law that has, so to say, a natural goodness [The usual vagueness. Metaphysicists simply cannot hit on a notion that is exact.], in other words, an inner capacity of its own for procuring the welfare of mankind. The law is called natural because it can be known through the natural lights of reason, and by the contemplation of human nature in the large."

429 [1] *De officio hominis et civis,* I, 3, 1 (Oxford, Vol. I, p. 18; Vol. II, p. 17).

429 [2] *Ibid.,* I, 3, 9 (Oxford, Vol. I, p. 21; Vol. II, p. 19).

429 [3] *Ibid.,* I, 3, 11 (Oxford, Vol. I, p. 22; Vol. II, p. 19): ". . . *esse autem Deum legis naturalis autorem.*"

430 [1] *Principes du droit naturel,* Pt. II, Chap. 1, Sec. 2.

430 [2] Cruel to the poor animals, Pufendorf absolutely will not let them have a natural law in common with man, *De iure naturae et gentium,* II, 3, 3 (Frankfurt, p. 172; Barbeyrac, Vol. I, p. 171; Kennett, p. 119): "There have been people, apparently more minded to display their brilliancy than to sustain their thesis in

on the scene—God; though we are not told whether He be the God of the Christians, the God of the Moslems, or some other God. God has made a natural law common to all men, who, however, do not have the same God! It all sounds like a puzzle.

431. In Burlamaqui's proposition there are two definitions and a thesis. Natural law is twice defined, first as given by God, second as known through reason. The thesis lies in the assertion that the two definitions are in accord. It is not very clear how people who have different Gods, and especially atheists who have no God at all, can all agree. As for the conclusions reached by "attentively" considering the nature and estate of mankind, those are merely things that the author finds in accord with his own sentiments; and of course if anyone fails to reach Burlamaqui's conclusions, he must accuse himself of not having considered the nature and estate of men with sufficient attention. But if this person should persevere in his stand and assert that despite his "attentive" consideration of the nature and estate of man he arrives at different conclusions, on what basis could one decide which of the conclusions ought to be accepted (§§ 16 f.)? In a "consideration" of "nature" one can find anything one chooses. The author of the *Problems* (attributed to Aristotle) discovers in nature the reason why man of all animate creatures should be the one to have, in proportion to size of body, the shortest distance between the eyes, and he asks: "Can it perhaps be because more than others he is according to nature?" [1]

The "experience" of believers in natural law is on a par with our

earnest, who have marshalled from all hands any evidence tending to establish such an alleged law common to human beings and animals. Scholars, however, have long since rejected all the arguments put forward on that score. I might mention briefly here such as are derived from Holy Writ." And he proceeds to argue at length that the penalties laid on animals in the Bible involve no presupposition of a law of animals.

431 [1] *Problemata,* X, 15 (Forster, p. 892a): Ἢ διότι μάλιστα κατὰ φύσιν ἔχει τῶν ἄλλων. The writer continues: "It is the nature of sensation that it takes place in front; since, in motion, it is necessary to see objects in advance. The greater the distance between the eyes, the more is the gaze cast sidewise. So, to conform with nature, the distance must be the shortest possible, since in that way one can the better walk straight ahead." O blessed Nature, what wondrous revelations dost thou not vouchsafe us!

modern "Christian experience." In neither case is there anything that resembles the experience of the natural sciences; and the term "experience" serves only to dissemble the fact that the person who uses it is merely expressing his own feeling and the feeling of people who happen to share his views (§ 602).

432. In the Preface to his treatise *De officio hominis et civis* Pufendorf epitomizes his ideas, saying that there are three distinct sciences:[1] "Natural Law common to all men; Civil Law, which is or may be different in different countries; and Moral Theology. . . . Natural Law prescribes this thing or that because Right Reason compels us to judge it necessary for the preservation of human society in general." Take it for granted that the reason which fails to prescribe as our author wishes is not right reason; but we cannot know that it is not until we have a clear and exact definition of what it is.

433. Such a definition Barbeyrac, adapting Pufendorf, tries to give:[1] "From that it becomes apparent how we must judge of the rightness of reason in our inquiries into the foundations of Natural Law; in other words, how we are to recognize that a maxim is in conformity with or contrary to Right Reason. For the maxims of Right Reason are *true* principles, principles, that is, which accord with the nature of things as we know that nature after careful examination, or which are accurately deduced from some first principle true in itself. Those, on the contrary, are maxims of corrupt reason [*pravae rationis*] which are founded on false principles, or which are faultily deduced from principles true in themselves."

434. Underneath all this pretentious verbiage it is not difficult to recognize a principle dear to metaphysicists, whereby experimental truths may be discovered through introspection into the "human mind" (§ 493). So right reason must necessarily be in accord with experience, or with Nature, as these gentlemen say.

435. Pufendorf continues, II, 3, 14: "If, then, what is represented

432 [1] Oxford, Vol. I, pp. [2]-[3]; Vol. II, pp. viii-ix.

433 [1] Pufendorf-Barbeyrac, *Le droit de la nature et des gens,* II, 3, 13 (Vol. I, p. 190; Frankfurt, p. 192; Kennett, pp. 133-34).

as a maxim of Natural Law is really founded on the nature of things, one may safely regard it as a true principle and consequently as a principle of Right Reason; for the nature of things reveals to us only that which really exists."[1] If he were following the experimental method he would invert his terms and say, "What really exists reveals the nature of things." But following the metaphysical method, he tries to learn what really exists not from the observation of facts, but from "principles in accord with the nature of things." Of this accord Right Reason remains judge. Hence we go round and round in a circle: to know right reason we are referred to the nature of things, and to know the nature of things we are referred back to right reason.

436. Reasoning in that convenient fashion, the author can convince us of anything he chooses; and so it is that, without much trouble (according to him), one comes upon the discovery that the basis of natural law is sociability (sociality).[1] Sociability always

435 [1] Barbeyrac notes in his French translation (*loc. cit.;* Kennett, *loc. cit.*): "This sentence did not appear in the first edition. Since it did not fit in very well with the context I have altered connexions slightly but without in any respect departing from the author's meaning." He then executes the usual manoeuvre for crippling his adversaries by barring them from the list of individuals competent to judge of the issues in question: "The assumption here always is that one's adversaries are not Pyrrhonians [sceptics] or persons disposed to attach little importance to the true or the false; otherwise it would be useless to try to enlighten them." From the experimental standpoint an argument that will allow objections only from people who accept it is no argument. From the sentimental standpoint an argument by accord of sentiment can be accepted only by people who already entertain the sentiment, at least partially. Barbeyrac continues: "There has always been the question as to whether the just were just by nature and not by fiat of some arbitrary will—*φύσει, οὐ θέσει*: in other words, as the result of essential relationships between our conduct and its objects or the nature of things." The dilemma exists only for metaphysicists. Experimental science offers a third solution: It holds that the word "just" merely expresses certain sentiments, and is therefore not a little vague, as are the sentiments themselves.

436 [1] Pufendorf, *De iure naturae et gentium,* II, 3, 15 (Frankfurt, p. 197; Barbeyrac, Vol. I, p. 194; Kennett, pp. 136-37): "We shall have no great difficulty in discovering the true foundation of natural law. . . . Every individual is prompted to cooperate to the full measure of his capacities with other individuals, in the formation and maintenance of an orderly society in conformity with the constitution and purposes of all humanity without exception. [That will be Kant's "universal law."] And since anyone requiring a certain purpose also requires the means essential for achieving it, it follows that anything necessarily contributing to universal

figures in these systems, either overtly or in disguise, because they are designed to induce people not to injure but rather to help one another; and they therefore need the support of the sentiments, so called, of socialibity (sociality).

437. Burlamaqui throws still other sentiments into the fray, rightly judging that the greater the array of the favourable sentiments he can muster, the better off he is. When he is addressing Christians, he wants to have their religion on his side. Egoists he tries to convince that altruism is a good policy for egoists (§§ 1479 f.). With the result that he gets three principles for his natural laws:[1] "Religion, self-love, and sociability, or goodwill to other men."

438. The inadequacy of the definitions of metaphysical entities that writers use in the study of natural law in many cases does not escape them; and each exerts himself—with little success, alas!—to find better ones.

439. Burlamaqui protests that he is trying to follow the experimental method and says:[1] "People often speak of *the useful, the just, the honest,* of *order,* of *propriety* (*convenance*), but most often these different notions are not defined with exactness. . . . This lack of precision cannot fail to leave a certain amount of confusion and embarrassment in a discussion. If we are trying to get light, we must distinguish carefully, and define sharply. [Excellent! We are now all ears for a few clear and exact definitions!] A useful action is one that tends of itself to the conservation and perfection of man." Note the ambiguity in the impersonal "man." Had Burlamaqui said "of a man," we could say that what tends to the conservation and perfection of a thief is to know how to pick a pocket dextrously. But that cannot be said of man in general. It has still to be shown that what is advantageous for man in general is also advantageous for man in particular, since it is always to a particular person that the argument is addressed. But the author does not bother with that detail!

sociability must be regarded as prescribed by natural law, and anything disturbing to such sociability as prohibited by natural law."

437 [1] *Principes du droit naturel,* Pt. II, Chap. 4, Sec. 18.

439 [1] *Ibid.,* Pt. II, Chap. 7, Sec. 2.

An action is said to be honest when it is considered as "conforming with the principles of right reason [How is right reason to be distinguished from the reason that is not right?], with the dignity of human nature [What is this new entity?], deserving therefore of the approbation of men [And supposing some approve and some disapprove?], and consequently winning for the man who performs it consideration, esteem, and honour." Among warrior races such distinctions go to those who have slain most enemies, among cannibals to those who have eaten most. Order is "the disposition of a number of things with reference to some specified end and proportioned to a desired effect."

And at last we come to propriety. "Propriety (*convenance*) approximates order itself. It is a relationship of conformity [What is this conformity?] among several things, each of which is in itself promotive of the preservation and perfection of the other [And what this perfection?], and does its share in maintaining it in a good and advantageous estate." Good for whom? Advantageous for whom? A poison that leaves no trace "is promotive of the preservation and perfection" of the man who wants to murder a neighbour, and maintains him in an estate that is "good and advantageous" for him; but it cannot be said to be "promotive of the preservation and perfection" of the victim, or that it maintains the victim in a "good and advantageous estate." There is no such thing as a general propriety, in the sense given the term by Burlamaqui. The standpoint from which the propriety is viewed has to be specified.

440. Burlamaqui, instead, talks of everything objectively, as though his entities had an independent existence of their own (§ 471). And how he uses his definitions! *Loc. cit.,* sec. 3: "So we must not confuse the just, the useful, the honest. . . . But those ideas, though distinct from one another, contain nothing incompatible the one with the other. They are three relations which can all be appropriate and can all be applied to one and the same action considered from different points of view. And if they be traced back to their origin, they will be found to derive all from a common source, or from one and the same principle, as three branches from the same tree-trunk. That general principle is the *approbation of reason.*" Really now, was there any good excuse for taking such a roundabout route just to pay a call on Milady Reason, a lady already charged so many times with originating natural law?

441. Vattel gives right reason a rest; but it is of little relief to us, for in its stead another actor comes on the scene, a certain "happiness," which is even more of an unknown. Says Vattel:[1] "Natural law is the science of the laws of nature [Of a class therefore with chemistry, physics, astronomy, biology, and so on, which are certainly sciences of the laws of nature? No, because Vattel soon changes tack], of those laws which nature lays down for men, or to which they are subject for the very reason that they are men; a science, the first principle of which is that truth of sentiment [Here is a new one!], that incontestable axiom [And what if some blackguard did contest it?] that 'the great object of every being endowed with intelligence and sentiment is happiness.'" But what kind of happiness? The happiness of the "destroyer of cities" is certainly not the happiness of the citizens he slays. The happiness of the thief is not the happiness of his victim. The happiness mentioned here is a particular happiness, and we are not told how it is to be distinguished from the thing that commonly goes by that name. Such particular happiness is often called "true" happiness; but that adjective is of no great help in getting nearer to experimental realities. Nor are we greatly helped either by aspersions cast upon those who refuse to recognize it. "There is no man, whatever his ideas on the origin of things, and even though he have the misfortune of being an atheist, who ought not to recognize the laws of nature. Those laws are necessary to the common happiness of men. The man who would reject them or manifest contempt for them would by that fact declare himself an enemy of the human race and deserve being treated as such" (§ 593). To imprison or burn a man is not, unfortunately, a logico-experimental demonstration.

442. All these definitions and others of their kind present the following characteristics: 1. They use indeterminate words, which serve

441 [1] *Le droit des gens,* Vol. I, pp. 39-40.

to arouse certain sentiments, but which do not correspond to anything exact (§§ 380, 387, 490). 2. They define unknowns by unknowns. 3. They combine definitions with theses unproved. 4. Their purpose, in substance, is to arouse the hearer's sentiments as far as possible in order to lead him to a pre-established conviction.

443. Selden begins by noting that the writers who have dealt with natural law have derived it from four different sources: (1) from that which is common to all animate beings or, (2) to all nations, or most nations; (3) from natural reason accurately used; (4) finally, from the will of the Divine Majesty, author of nature, and therefore of natural reason.[1] He rejects the first three sources and accepts only the fourth, limiting natural reason, however, to the natural reason of the Hebrews and divine will to the authority of the Hebrew God.

444. The Talmud gives instructive details as to the manner in which the various nations were enabled to have knowledge of the Law given by the Hebrew God. The manner described is after all no less credible than that of Right Reason, while it has the advantage of being more effective, and Bertinoro quite properly observes that in view of it the nations could not excuse themselves by saying: "We had no way of learning the law."[1]

443 [1] Selden, *De iure naturali et gentium*, I, 4 (Strassburg, p. 43; Venice, p. 225): *"In designatione atque definitione Iuris Naturalis quae apud scriptores solet diversimode occurrere, alii ex Aliorum Animantium actibus ac usu Iura hominibus aliquot Naturalia petunt; alii Iuris naturalis Corpus e Moribus omnium seu plurimarum Gentium communibus; ex Naturali Ratione, seu recto eiusdem usu alii; et demum alii e Naturae ideoque Naturalis rationis Parentis, id est, sanctissimi Numinis Imperio atque Indicatione."*

444 [1] *Talmud of Babylon, Tract Sabbath,* IX (Pavly, pp. 27-28; Rodkinson, Vol. I, p. 163): "Each word issuing from the mouth of God on Sinai made itself heard in seventy different languages and filled the universe with an agreeable perfume. The voice of God was so powerful that at each word the Israelites retreated twelve leagues." *Talmud of Jerusalem, Tract Sotah* (The Suspected Adulteress), VII, 5 (Schwab, Vol. VII, pp. 305-06; Danby, pp. 300-01): "Then stones were brought and an altar erected. It was faced with mortar and the words of the Law were inscribed on it in seventy languages, as it is written [Deut. 27:8 [*i.e.,* 31:9]]." Commentary (Gemara): "Contrary to the Mishnah it has been taught that the said words were inscribed on stones at the place where they passed the night [Josh. 4:3], according to an opinion of Rabbi Juda. Rabbi Yossé says that they were written on the stones of the altar. According to people professing the first opinion,

445. If we keep strictly to forms, all these disquisitions on natural law look like a mass of nonsense. But if we disregard forms and consider what it is they hide, we discover inclinations and sentiments that exert a powerful influence in determining the constitution of society and therefore are worthy of closest study. Demonstrations given in such forms are not to be accepted because of their accord with certain sentiments, nor rejected because they are in patent discord with logic and experience: we should consider them simply as not existing (§ 463), turn our attention upon the matter which they conceal, and examine it directly for its intrinsic characteristics. So our induction once more leads to the discovery that we must separate doctrines, as we find them stated, into two parts, and that of the two parts one is far more important than the other. In the course of our study, therefore, we shall have to try to separate those two parts; and then not stop with the reflection that a certain argument is inconclusive, idiotic, absurd, but ask ourselves whether it may not be expressing sentiments beneficial to society, and expressing them in a manner calculated to persuade many people who would not be at all influenced by the soundest logico-experimental argument.[1]

446. The good sense of a practical man like Montaigne is antidote enough for all these wild declamations on natural law: but it does not go far enough to locate the error where it really lies or discover

holding that the Law was inscribed on the walls of an inn, it is conceivable that the nations of the world could have sent their scribes any day to copy the texts, since the Law was written in seventy languages. . . . But how accept the view (which is the view of the Mishnah) that the Law was inscribed on the stones of the altar? In that case must it not have been a question of some temporary structure, of which everything pertaining to worship must afterwards have been buried underground, before their departure? And how then could the pagans have profited by it? It was a miracle, of course! During the short space of time that the altar was standing, the Lord quickened the wits of the various nations, so that they could make rapid copies of the text of the Law written in seventy languages." Mishnah, *Sotah,* VII, 5 (*De uxore adulterii suspecta*) (Surenhuis, Vol. III, p. 262): (Bartenor [read Bertinoro]): ". . . in the script of seventy nations, that anyone desirous of knowing the Law could do so, and that the nations might have no excuse by saying, 'We had no way of knowing.' "

445 [1] For the moment it is sufficient to have seen that a path opens out before us here. The following of it will be a task for a later portion of this work.

the sentiments which such arguments conceal. Says he: "Certainly they are amusing, these people, when they try to lend a certain amount of authority to their laws by saying that some of them are fixed, perpetual, immutable, which they call natural laws and which are imprinted upon human beings by the requirements of their very nature." [1]

447. There are plenty of other theories neither better nor worse than these disquisitions on natural law, and they all arise in a desire to give a semblance of absoluteness and objectivity to what is relative and subjective. Here, for example, are the Physiocrats, who have certain ideas as to social organization, political constitution, freedom of trade, and the like. They might propound them directly, as others —to an extent at least—have done: but no, they prefer to derive them from some imaginary "natural and essential order of political societies"—the title, in fact, of a famous book by Le Mercier de La Rivière.[1] So back we go to battles of words. "The *absolutely just* may be defined as 'an order of duties and rights arising from a physical and consequently absolute necessity.' The absolutely unjust, therefore, is all that is contrary to that order. The term 'absolute' is not used here in contradistinction to 'relative' for only in the relative can the just and the unjust arise. But a thing which, strictly speaking, is only relatively just becomes nevertheless absolutely just because of its relation to the absolute necessity we are under of living in society." Then there is a certain "essential order" that is "the order of reciprocal duties and rights, the establishment of which is essentially necessary to the greatest possible increase of production, to the end that mankind may achieve the greatest possible amount of happiness and the greatest possible increase in numbers." This, it would seem, is all quite axiomatic, as is also the notion that the order in question is a branch of the physical order: "If any man were to object to recognizing the natural and essential order of society as a branch of the physical order, I should regard him as a

446 [1] *Essais,* II, 12

447 [1] *L'ordre naturel et essentiel des sociétés politiques,* pp. 11, 28, 38-39 (1910 ed., pp. 8, 21, 28-29).

person determined not to see, and studiously eschew any effort to cure him of his blindness" (§§ 379, 435[1]). Le Mercier de La Rivière has one notion that is in accord, substantially, with experience, the notion that "the social order is in no way arbitrary"; but the proof he gives of it is the worst imaginable.

448. As is usual with this sort of disquisition, the author believes that his ideas have to be accepted by everybody the moment they are stated (§§ 591 f.). "The simplicity and the obviousness of this social order are manifest to anyone willing to devote the slightest attention to it." But along comes the Abbé de Mably, who certainly gave the subject a great deal of attention, but was not in the least persuaded of this and other "obvious truths" alluded to in the first two parts of Le Mercier de La Rivière's work. He says:[1] "The author talks a great deal about obviousness, and I find nothing obvious about it. I have read and re-read his book, and far from finding my doubts diminishing in numbers, I have found them multiplying." At times Mably does not reason at all badly; and he is following principles of logico-experimental science when he observes, for instance, that a given order cannot be considered necessary to societies if we find actually existing societies that do without it. Le Mercier de La Rivière argues, p. 21, 1910 ed., p. 15, to show the necessity of private property in land. Mably comments: "If one were to stop at asking merely that every society should embrace a certain amount of real property, I would not feel embarrassed, for I readily see that it is indispensable that a society should have a domain by which its citizens may be assured of a living. But that one should regard as a matter of absolute necessity and justice a thing which civilized and prosperous societies have done without—that confounds my reason and upsets all my ideas." Ignoring, for a moment, public property in land and Madame Absolute Justice, a lady with whom we have no close acquaintance, the rest of the argument is sound. The author, moreover, mentions the case of Sparta, an example not so well chosen, for though Sparta had no private landownership of the

448 [1] *Doutes proposés aux philosophes économistes sur l'ordre naturel et essentiel des sociétés politiques*, 1768, pp. 4-9 (*Œuvres*, 1790, Vol. XI, pp. 3-7).

Roman type, the Spartans did know a sort of real property. But altogether to the point is the example of the Missions in Paraguay: "Even the Jesuits, sir, refute your arguments; and in Paraguay they are treating themselves to the privilege of defying the essential law of your natural order with impunity."

But the Abbé de Mably, like Le Mercier de La Rivière, has a preconception of his own to defend. He appeals to experience to suit his convenience in defending his pet idea of collective property, just as Le Mercier de La Rivière called on a "natural order" to help him defend private property in land. That explains Mably's failure to notice that the very same objection may be made to the first part of his argument that he raises in its second part. As a matter of fact nomadic peoples have no landed property, either collective or private. Mably might answer that the nomadic peoples are not to be counted among "civilized and prosperous societies"; but to take that line would militate against his own example of Paraguay for the very same reason. And if Le Mercier de La Rivière would only abandon his vagaries as to a "natural and essential order," he might adduce many a sound example to show that the most "civilized and prosperous" societies have been those very ones in which private property in land has existed. But to give the discussion such a turn would be to remove it from the field of sentiment and metaphysics, to which our authors often betake themselves, and transfer it to the field of logico-experimental science.

Quesnay quotes a number of opinions on natural law and finds an element of truth in all of them;[2] but "our philosophers have stopped at the paralogism, the incomplete argument, in their investigations into this important matter, which is the natural principle of all the rational duties of man." So he then sets out to complete their work. First he deals with justice: "If I am asked what justice is, I answer that 'it is a natural and sovereign rule recognized by the light of reason [If the "reason" of some individuals "recognizes" one rule, and the "reason" of other individuals another, how are we to pick the good one?], which clearly determines what belongs to one-

448 [2] *Le droit naturel,* pp. 42-43, 52-53.

self and what to someone else.'" After a good deal of rambling, he arrives at this conclusion: "Men living together in a society must therefore be subject to natural laws and positive laws. . . . Natural laws are either physical or moral. By physical laws is here meant 'the regulated course of every physical event of the natural order, which is obviously the order most advantageous to mankind.' By moral law is here meant 'the rule of every human action of the moral order consistent with the physical order, which is obviously the order most advantageous to mankind.' The sum of such laws makes up what is called 'natural law.' All men and all human powers must be subject to these sovereign laws instituted by the Supreme Being. [So Quesnay increases by one the very considerable number of individuals who have thought they knew the will of the Supreme Being in question and who, unhappily, are not in very close agreement.] They are immutable and irrefragable, and the best possible laws." To reason in such fashion is to reason in a circle; for if natural law is defined as that "which is obviously the most advantageous to mankind," it would be difficult to understand how "the sum of laws making up natural law" could contain anything but "the best possible laws." It is indeed surprising that these "immutable and irrefragable" laws should not have been discovered before Quesnay's time, and that they should not have been universally adopted once he had discovered them and revealed them to an eager world.[3]

448 [3] Daire, in his *Observations,* in *Physiocrates,* Vol. II, pp. 438-39, finds these theories of Quesnay and his commentator, Le Mercier de La Rivière, altogether admirable: "Instead of looking to the nature of man and his relations to the external world for the immutable laws that establish and maintain order within societies, our publicists and theologians have imagined that they were called upon to invent such laws; and the institutions at present prevailing in Europe bear witness to the success with which, in this connexion, they have replaced the views of the Creator with their own." But the Creator could not have foreseen any such substitution; otherwise He would have prevented it. Daire observes that Le Mercier de la Rivière goes counter to Rousseau's doctrines: "Instead of asking the legislator to create an order, Le Mercier de La Rivière urges him to conform to the order that is, and to seek a basis for it nowhere else than in the sentiment and reason that have been bestowed upon man that he may recognize the immutable laws on which his existence and his happiness here below depend." In this there is a timid effort to escape from the fog of metaphysics, but it is not a successful one. Never mind the appeal to the Creator and his

449. Interesting the analogy between such theories and that contemporary metaphysical dream known as the theory of solidarity. In the latter, as in one of the theories of natural law, the starting-point is—or rather, is alleged to be—experience. The theory of natural law recognizes a law common to human beings and animals. The theory of solidarity goes that one better and recognizes a law of interdependence among human beings, animals, plants, and minerals. If natural law was good, this law of solidarity is perfect.[1]

450. But these estimable metaphysicists have little patience with experience; so they are soon rid of it through one door or another. Natural law eventually allowed its animals to go to the dogs. The doctrine of solidarity does even better. It repudiates its own origin to the point of setting up a solidarity-fact in contradistinction to a solidarity-duty.[1]

451. How are we to find this latter? After all that we have been saying the canny reader cannot have a doubt. What in the world else are such things as "right reason," "nature," "the just," "the honest," good for? Just as they yielded the theory of natural law in a day gone by, so will they yield a theory of solidarity now, and as

views, which transports us to the domain of theology. "Immutable laws that establish and maintain order," and "the sentiment and reason *bestowed* on man that he may recognize" those laws, transport us far afield into the domain of final causes, or, in any event, remove us from the experimental field, where "immutable laws" designed for one purpose or another do not exist, but just plain facts and uniformities between them (§ 99).

449 [1] Bourgeois, *Essai d'une philosophie de la solidarité,* p. 3: "In the first place, what is objective solidarity, considered as a fact? Kant said: 'What makes up an organism is the reciprocity between its parts.' In that lies the germ of all biology. [This fanatic of "Science" might have quoted a biologist rather than a metaphysicist on a point of that kind.] . . . So the idea of life is identical with the idea of association. And the doctrine of evolution has shown the law by which this interdependence of parts contributes to the development, the progress, of each individual, each group of individuals."

450 [1] Bourgeois, *Ibid.,* p. 13: "So here we are very far removed from a solidarity-fact and very close to a solidarity-duty. Let us never confuse them; they are opposites. But it was necessary to establish the existence of the former in order to perceive the moral necessity of the latter." Milady Science has tripped rather hastily across the stage to vanish through the wings! Solidarity-fact has, however, found a champion in one Dr. Papillaut, *Ibid.,* p. 25: "I would make a demand in the name of natural solidarity, to which, in my judgment, too little attention is being paid." *Cf.* Bentham's attitude towards morality.

many other similar theories as writers of some moderate talent are pleased to devise (§ 1557).[1]

452. In the theories that we have just been examining three elements are distinguishable: (1) an experimental element, which is rarely absent but is often more apparent than real; (2) a metaphysical trans-experimental element, which is often dissembled but is never absent; (3) a theological element—and one therefore beyond experience, which is present in certain theories and absent in others. These last two elements are usually chosen from among the doctrines that enjoy greatest prestige in the society in which the author of the theory is living. Theology was not enforced in ancient pagan society, and the theological element is therefore missing in many theories which arose in those days. It is seldom absent, however, in

451 [1] Bourgeois, *Op. cit.*, pp. 8, 62-65, 72-75, 242: "When we ask what conditions a human society must satisfy in order to maintain its balance, we are forced to recognize that only one word can state them: 'Justice must be!'" But a query suggests itself. The societies that have hitherto existed in history—have they had their balance or not? If they have, they must have had justice already; and in that case why should M. Léon Bourgeois be trying to get it now through solidarity? If they have not enjoyed such balance, what is a "balance" that has never yet been known of men? "I am well aware that another purpose has been assigned to society, which is nothing less than happiness assured to each of its members. . . . Happiness is not material, divisible, externally realizable. The ideal of society is justice for all." Exactly what such a justice would be, M. Léon Bourgeois seems not to know, or at least he chooses not to tell. The objection had been raised: "M. Léon Bourgeois has declared that the origin of the idea of justice is of no importance, the moment one agrees that justice is necessary. All the same, very important practical consequences follow from the conception one has of justice." The reply is: "M. Léon Bourgeois . . . has not seen fit in this exposition to go into the question of the origins of the concept of justice. [He was not asked to discuss origins but to define the thing he calls justice.] However one try to explain them, the idea of and the hunger for justice are present in the human heart. That is a fact, which need simply be determined as a fact and with which we can start, and all the better since if theoretically there may be disagreement as to the first principles from which it is derived, practically everybody is in substantial agreement as to the meaning, significance, and content of this notion of justice." And so we find creeping in our never-sufficiently-praised friend and old acquaintance, Universal Consensus (§§ 591 f.). And miracle indeed had it failed to materialize! And Mademoiselle Raison? Patience! She too will soon be coming to the rescue of M. Léon Bourgeois! In his *Solidarité*, p. 76, one reads: "If the primal notion of good and evil is a necessity [What does that mean?], if the sentiment of moral obligation constitutes a 'categorical imperative' within us, the intellectual activity whereby the human being strives to define good and evil and determine the

theories originating in Christian societies, in which theology has been enforced. But of late, poor Theology has been driven from her throne and Science has taken her place—not experimental science, observe, but a certain metaphysical entity on which the name of science has been foisted.

453. Burlamaqui called religion to his support (§§ 430 f.). If he had lived in our times he would have appealed to Science. M. Léon Bourgeois resorts to Science. Had he lived in Burlamaqui's time he would have resorted to religion. The reader must not imagine that such a thing embarrasses those estimable gentlemen in the slightest. They know what they are driving at, and they are not unaware that all roads lead to Rome! [1]

premise of the moral obligation belongs to the domain of reason. . . . Everything in man's environment has evolved in proportion as the moral idea, the supreme function of the reason, has evolved within him." May Mademoiselle Raison be blessed with a long and prosperous life, that metaphysicists of the future may find her the loyal helpmeet she has proved to be to their predecessors! And a little place has been kept for Dame Nature too! *Essai,* p. 10: "In the first place Nature has designs of her own [The wicked hussy!], designs which are not our designs. The special aim of man in society is justice [Even in slave-holding societies?], and justice has never been the aim of Nature. Nature is not unjust, she is a-just. There is nothing in common therefore between the purposes of Nature and the purposes of society." And yet, certain predecessors of M. Léon Bourgeois, to wit, the Stoics, assured us that the supreme principle of morality was to live according to Nature (§ 1605)! How are we to know whether Bourgeois is right, or the Stoics? Metaphysicists have so long been inquiring into the purposes of Nature that by this time they should have discovered what they are. But each of them is still going his own road, and we, poor wretches, do not know whom to bet on. And the principle of sociability (sociality), which was of service to Pufendorf in his time, does not fail M. Léon Bourgeois. Implicitly it is present in everything Bourgeois writes. It appears here and there explicitly: Xavier Léon, *Le fondement rational de la solidarité,* p. 242: "Reason does not know individuals as such. Reason is realized by individuals in the mass, by all humanity [What a lucky man to know what "to realize reason" means!]. Reason is essentially human reason. . . . This eminently social trait in reason is the foundation of solidarity. It is that trait which confers on solidarity a moral value that one would strive in vain to extract from the empirical determination of a biological or social fact, or from the implications of a more or less tacit contract." (The passage is continued in the next foot-note.)

453 [1] Bourgeois, *Solidarité,* p. 25: "The scientific method is today making its way into all orders of knowledge. The most refractory minds, grudgingly it may be, are one by one submitting to it." That was written for the benefit of the French anti-clericals. As we read on, p. 73, we see what the science of M. Léon Bourgeois is: "The idea of right and wrong is, in itself, an ultimate idea: it is a primal fact,

454. It is understandable that Christian philosophy should look to the will of God for the origin of natural law. It might well be satisfied with that; and we should then have a theory consisting of a purely theological element. But it prefers also to have the aid of the metaphysical element, and perhaps of an experimental element—further proof that the form of such theories depends not so much upon their subject-matter as upon the concepts that are most in repute in the society in which they circulate. Most men refuse to be shut up within mere theology, and to win their assent the support of metaphysics and experience has to be procured.

455. We are told that "natural law is implanted and written in the heart of man directly by God Himself and that its purpose is to guide man, who aspires to his goal as a free being capable of good and evil."[1] Granted that God has "implanted and written" natural law in the heart of man, how are we to discover it? If by revelation exclusively, we would have an exclusively theological theory. But metaphysics interposes and even, it would seem, experience.

456. St. Paul in his time said, Rom. 2: 14-15: "For when the Gentiles, which have not the law, do by nature the things contained in the law, these, having not the law, are a law unto themselves: which shew the work of the law written in their hearts." Experience, therefore, might lead to the discovery of it in the hearts of men. But we are soon warned that we are not to trust exclusively to conscience, since it has been corrupted, *Loc. cit.:* "The primordial faculties of man have been enfeebled by original sin; so it is natural that the implications [of natural law] should not ever be drawn in their full

an essential attribute of humanity." But metaphysicists had said that two thousand years ago and more. It was hardly necessary to drag in science to repeat it. His "science" and the old metaphysics are as alike as two peas. Why then give two different names to the same thing? For no other reason than to play on certain sentiments now widely prevalent that are favourable to Milady Science. Xavier Léon, *Le fondement rational de la solidarité,* p. 245: "Solidarity is therefore justified as an exigency of reason. It is in substance the principle of intelligibility in our conduct, the prerequisite to the realization of unity of reason in humanity." If that is not metaphysics, what is metaphysics?

455 [1] *Dictionnaire encyclopédique de la théologie catholique, s.v. "Droit"* (Wetzer, *s.v. Recht*). The author quotes St. Paul, Rom. 2:15: ". . . Which shew the work of the law written in their hearts."

perfection by any man, and that often they should be drawn incompletely and erroneously. And that is why human laws, which are not and ought not to be anything but consequences of natural law, are always imperfect, often defective, and sometimes false." This "law of nature" turns up again in ancient Irish law, with postscripts by the Church and learned Irish doctors.[1]

457. St. Thomas identified: (1) an eternal law, existing in the divine mind; (2) a natural law, existing in men and partaking of the eternal law, and by which men discern good and evil; (3) a law devised by men, whereby they make provision for what is contained in the natural law; and finally (4), a divine law whereby men are infallibly led to the supernatural goal—supreme beatitude.[1] Her Ladyship Right Reason is absent from all this, but we soon see her putting in an appearance; and the Saint tells us that "it is certain that all laws, in so far as they partake of right reason, are derived from the eternal law." [2]

456 [1] Maine, *Early History of Institutions,* pp. 24-25: "It [the *Senchus Mor,* one of the ancient Irish law-books] describes the legal rules embodied in its text as formed of the 'law of nature,' and of the 'law of the letter.' The 'law of the letter' is the Scriptural law, extended by so much of the Canon law as the primitive monastic church of Ireland can be supposed to have created or adopted. The reference in the misleading phrase 'law of nature' is not to the memorable combination of words familiar to the Roman lawyers, but to the text of St. Paul in the Epistle to the Romans. . . . The 'law of nature' is, therefore, the ancient pre-Christian ingredient in the system, and the *Senchus Mor* says of it: 'The judgments of true nature while the Holy Ghost had spoken through the mouths of the Brehons [ancient doctors of Irish law] and *just* [italics mine] poets of the men of Erin, from the first occupation of Ireland down to the reception of the faith, were all exhibited by Dubhthach to Patrick. What did not clash with the Word of God in the written law and the New Testament and the consciences of believers, was confirmed in the laws of the Brehons by Patrick and by the ecclesiastics and chieftains of Ireland; for the law of nature had been quite right except as to the faith, and its obligations, and the harmony of the Church and people. And this is the *Senchus Mor.*' "

457 [1] *Summa theologiae,* Iª IIªᵉ, *qu.* 91 (*Opera,* Vol. VII, pp. 153-58: *De legum diversitate*).

457 [2] *Ibid.,* Iª IIªᵉ, *qu.* 93, *art.* 3 (*Opera,* Vol. VII, p. 164): *"Quoniam, teste B. Augustino, in temporali lege nihil est iustum ac legitimum quod non sit ex lege aeterna profectum, certum est omnes leges, inquantum participant de ratione recta, intantum a lege aeterna derivari."* [In the form above this text is the *conclusio* of the argument *Utrum omnis lex a lege aeterna derivetur* in the 1570 edition. It figures only in substance in the Leo XIII edition.—A. L.]

458. The *Decretum* of Master Gratian defines natural law in practically the same terms as Roman law (§ 419), so taking us back to a pseudo-experimental notion. The concession, however, is of little avail, as it is still necessary to consider what is required by Scripture and Catholic tradition.[1]

459. When Nature is taken as the direct source of natural law, concepts of the latter may be regarded as *innate ideas* and so take on an absolute character—which in no way spares us the trouble of resorting to divine activity in order to account for the innate ideas.

460. Denying innate ideas, Locke is logically required to reject the theory of natural law deriving from them. But that is of little gain to science, for we at once go back to the domain of right reason. Says he:[1] "I would not here be mistaken, as if, because I deny an innate law, I thought there were none but positive laws. There is a great deal of difference between an innate law and a law of nature; between something imprinted on our minds in their very original, and something that we being ignorant of may attain to the knowledge of, by the use and due application of our natural faculties." This is still the metaphysical method, which presupposes the existence of abstract entities; and it is probable that even had Locke desired to part from it, he would have been restrained from doing so by the consideration that he could not, without serious mishap, change the destination at which his argument had to arrive at all costs—the existence of a natural law.

458 [1] *Decretum Gratiani, pars* I, *distinctio* 1, *canones* 6-7 (Friedberg, Vol. I, p. 2): "Law is either natural law, or civil law, or the law of nations. . . . Natural law is the common law of all peoples, since it arises by instinct of nature (*instinctu naturae*) and not by any legislative act (*constitutione*)." And *cf.* Isidore, *Etymologiae,* V, 4, 1. But as Lancelotto cautions in his *Institutiones iuris canonici, lib.* I, *tit. ii,* (p. 11): "The above must be taken as applying to such customs as are not in conflict with divine law and canonical legislation; for if anything be found at variance with Catholic faith, it is to be regarded not so much as custom as long-standing error (*vetustas erroris*)." Isidore, *Ibid.,* II, 10, 3: "If law is based on reason, everything will be law that is based on reason, provided it be consistent with religion, in harmony with [Church] teachings (*disciplinae conveniat*) and promotive of salvation through reason."

460 [1] *Essay Concerning Human Understanding,* Bk. I, Chap. II, § 13 (*Works,* Vol. I, p. 44).

461. Grotius posits the metaphysical element *a priori,* the experimental element *a posteriori.*[1] His French translator, Barbeyrac, perceives the weakness of the demonstration *a posteriori;* but instead of observing that natural law is beyond experience and therefore to be regarded as scientifically non-existent, he grasps at the metaphysical demonstration and judges it valid.[2]

462. Hobbes, *Libertas,* I, 2, denies that natural law is given by universal consensus, or even by the consensus of the wisest and most civilized nations, sensibly asking who is to judge of the wisdom of a nation (§ 592). There can, he thinks, *Ibid.,* II, 2, be no other law of nature except reason, nor any precepts of reason save such as point the way to peace, if peace be attainable, or in default of that, to the means of defence by war. As usual religion and morality are eventually called in (*Ibid.,* IV, 1). The laws that are said to be of nature because prescribed by natural reason are moral laws, since they relate to conduct, and divine laws, since God is their author. They cannot therefore run counter to the divine word as revealed

461 [1] *De iure belli ac pacis,* I, 1, 12 (pp. 5-6—translation from Barbeyrac's French translation): "There are two ways of proving that a thing is part of natural law, the one *a priori* . . . [by reasons derived from the intrinsic nature of the thing]; the other *a posteriori* [by reasons derived from something external]. The first, the subtler [and more abstract], lies in showing the necessary accord or disaccord of the thing with a rational and sociable nature such as that of man. [So there are other such natures? What are they?] Following the other more vulgar line [Science is vulgar, metaphysics sublime.], it is inferred, if not with certainty at least with great probability, that a thing belongs to natural law because it is regarded as so belonging among all nations, or at least among the more civilized (*moratiores*) nations; for a universal effect presupposing a universal cause, an opinion so general can hardly have any other source than what is called common sense." [Barbeyrac's rendering is very free. His additions are printed in brackets. The Latin of Grotius begins: *"Esse autem aliquid juris naturalis probari solet tum ab eo quod prius est, tum ab eo quod posterius, quarum probandi rationum illa subtilior est, haec popularior."* And see Campbell, p. 24.—A. L.]

461 [2] Barbeyrac, note to his word "certainty," § 461[1]: "This manner of proving natural law is not very generally used, because only the most general principles of natural law are accepted at all widely among the nations; and of some of the most self-evident principles the contraries have long been regarded as matters of indifference in the most civilized countries, as witness the horrible custom of exposing infants."

in Scripture. All of which is proved with an impressive array of quotations.[1]

463. Epicurus, in his time, had sought the definition of natural justice in the pact, or contract.[1] Hobbes makes the contract one of the cardinal principles in his system, as do Rousseau with his famous social contract and the *solidaristes* of our day—all of them drawing different conclusions from the same premise. That is not surprising, since the principle is lacking in any exact meaning and the arguments based upon it derive their force not from logic and experience but from accords of sentiments. All such theories are infected—and therefore sterilized—with the same lack of exactness. From the logico-experimental standpoint they are neither true nor false: they are simply meaningless (§ 445).

464. So far we have been speaking of *a* religion, *a* law, *a* morality; but, as we cautioned above (§ 373), not even such unity can be assumed. In point of fact not only are there various religions, various moralities, various laws; but even if one may say that there are types of such entities, we have to pay due attention to the deviations from them which are met with in the concrete. Let us assume for a moment—though the assumption is in general contrary to fact—that, in a restricted group of people at least, a certain theoretical type prevails from which actual beliefs and actual conduct may be regarded as deviations. In a group having a civil code, for instance, it may be assumed—though the premise would not be altogether true to fact—that court decisions, as dictated by the jurisprudence which has developed side by side with the code (sometimes in opposition

462 [1] See also *Leviathan,* XV. Hobbes draws a distinction between natural *right* which is every individual's right to defend himself, and natural *law,* which is the norm in deference to which the individual refrains from doing what may be harmful to himself. *Leviathan,* XIV (Latin version): *"Jus et lex differunt ut libertas et obligatio";* English version: "Law and Right differ as much as Obligation and Liberty."

463 [1] Diogenes Laërtius, *Epicurus,* X, 150 (Hicks, Vol. II, pp. 673-75): "Natural justice is a symbol or expression of expediency, to prevent one man from harming or being harmed by another. Since animals are incapable of making covenants with one another to the end that they may neither inflict nor suffer harm, they are without either justice or injustice. And so for peoples which have been either unable or unwilling to form mutual covenants to the same end."

to it), or as formulated through error or ignorance on the part of magistrates, or for other reasons, are mere deviations from the norms of the code.

465. Suppose, for a hypothesis, it be a Catholic group. Three types of deviation will be observable:

1. The believer is perfectly sincere, but sins because the flesh is weak; he repents and detests his sins. In that we get a complete separation of theory and practice. It is the situation represented in the well-known lines of Ovid, *Metamorphoses,* VII, vv. 20-21:

> . . . *video meliora proboque—*
> *deteriora sequor.*

Practice does not in the least presume to become theory. All confessors know that in this connexion there are very considerable differences between individuals. Some fall frequently into the same sin, others relapse more rarely. It is evident that two collectivities having precisely the same theoretical faith may differ practically, according as one of them has more individuals of the first kind than of the second kind.

2. The believer is of lukewarm faith. He more or less disregards the precepts of his religion, and feels little or no remorse. Here we already get the germ of a theoretical divergence. Certain believers are merely indifferent; in their case the theoretical deviation is very slight. Others think they can atone for their religious shortcomings in some way. Still others do not even consider them shortcomings—they argue, split hairs, resort to casuistry. So theoretical deviations arise, and they grow like parasitic plants on the orthodox faith. In that way practical deviations go hand in hand with theoretical deviations, though these are not carried to the point of schism.

3. Theoretical differences become accentuated. Schism, heresy, partial or complete denial of the type-theory, ensue. On reaching that point, the deviation ceases to be a deviation, and we get an actually new type of theory.

As usual, transitions from one sort of deviation to another take place by imperceptible degrees.

466. To neglect these deviations and consider the type-theories only is the source of serious errors in sociology. Nothing can be more mistaken than to evaluate the influence of a given religion by its theology. We should be going very far wide of the truth were we, for example, to reason: "The Christian religion enjoins forgiveness of offences; hence the people of the Middle Ages, who were very good Christians indeed, always turned the other cheek." It would be erroneous to the same degree to appraise the social value of a morality by the theoretical statement of it.

A lesser error, but still quite a serious one, is to assume that court decisions in a given country are made in accord with its written laws.[1] The constitutions of the Byzantine emperors were often a dead letter. In our day, both in Italy and in France the written laws of the civil code may supply at least an approximate picture of practical legislation; but the penal code and its written laws do not in the least correspond with practical decisions, and the divergence is frequently enormous. We need say nothing of constitutional law. There is no relation whatever between theory and practice, except in the minds of a few silly theorists.[2]

466 [1] *Liberté,* July 25, 1912: "*Moulins.* The Court of Criminal Sessions at Allier has dealt with the case of Louis Auclair, 18, travelling salesman of Moulins, indicted for the murder of his father. Since the death of his mother at Cosne-sur-l'Œil last year, young Auclair had been on bad terms with his father. The latter had sold his property for some 20,000 francs and purchased at Montluçon, ave. Jules Ferry, a drinking-place that he began operating with his son. Shortly he took to drinking heavily, and young Auclair became uneasy as to his share in his father's property. Violent quarrels took place between father and son. One day the young man stole 1,000 francs from the barman, and left home, going to live at Moulins. On April 6 last he went back to Montluçon, and a new quarrel with his father resulted. About midnight, on the evening of the seventh, he broke into his father's establishment. The barman, hearing a noise, hurried down to the bar, and found the young man working at the till. Louis Auclair now pleads that he had gone there just to dare his father, not for purposes of robbery. In any case, there was a scuffle and the young man shot his father through the stomach, killing him. The jury handed in such a mild verdict that the Court sentenced the man responsible for such an abominable crime to one year in prison." If such a news item came not from France but from some little-known country, one might conclude that the written laws of that country dealt leniently with parricide—and that might be a mistaken inference.

466 [2] Here is an example chosen at random. It is typical of many other cases not only in France, but in Italy and other countries. *Liberté,* Mar. 23, 1912 (article

A practical fact is the result of many other facts, some of which give rise to theories and may therefore be learned through them. Take, for example, a penal decision following the verdict of a jury. Distinguishable among the factors entering into such a sentence are

by G. Berthoulat): "*Sabotage of Justice:* In spite of the conspiracy of silence, public attention is fixed on political interference in the Rochette case. Quite aside from the facts that have already come to light, ordinary horse-sense is enough: how could a man like Rochette, with such a retinue of pontiffs of the Bloc in his debt, whether public attorneys or otherwise, have failed to provide himself with a parliamentary body-guard? One need not hesitate on the point: Rochette *did* demand such protection! . . . That is why, in deference to an order from higher up, the Attorney General was compelled to move for the scandalous adjournment of the Rochette case, a motion in which M. Bidault de L'Isle docilely acquiesced and which M. Fabre himself, in his report, calls 'the one humiliation of my career.' Along with this case of sabotage of the courts, the Abbot of Launay, speaking before the Senate yesterday, gave the proofs of another no less serious in that astonishing case of the Chartreuse which, even more than the Duez episode, is the jewel of the liquidations in which the famous 'billion' went up in smoke. The Chartreuse was worth fifty millions. Why was it knocked down at five hundred thousand? Because it had depreciated! . . . But there again there have been political influences: and they were so effectively employed that the liquidator suddenly became the guardian of the individual named in his complaint. And the Court at Grenoble, though the case had been regularly brought before it, ruled in 1906, 1908, and 1909 that the papers in the case were to be held 'non-existent.' But they existed all the same, and so certainly that the Senate was asked to take official cognizance of them yesterday. However, politics having decided to 'get out the life-boats' for the plunderers of the Chartreuse, the Court and full bench of Grenoble did not shrink from that extraordinary miscarriage of justice. To fill out the trio of sensational acts of sabotage, what about this one: the pardon of the incendiaries of Ay obtained on February 11 by M. Bourgeois at the instance of his 'control,' M. Vallé? Those rascals had been sentenced to relatively insignificant terms in the reformatory, for had they not been clients of M. Vallé they would have gone to the penitentiary. They had been captured in the act of chopping holes in roofs, pouring gasoline inside and setting fire to the buildings. The town of Ay will have to foot bills that run into the millions on the single account of the arson and depredations of those individuals."

Then come the verdicts of the "kind-hearted juries" and other court decisions equally fantastic. A woman kills her husband and her aunt without serious provocation. Here is an account of her trial. *Liberté,* May 12, 1912: "Mme. P—— appeared before Criminal Sessions this morning gowned in deep mourning. She did not cease sobbing once during the whole session, her hysterics causing a suspension of her examination several times. Presiding Justice: 'Why did you kill your husband?' *A.* 'I was carried away by a power beyond me. If, at that moment, anyone had come and stopped me and said, "What are you doing, crazy?" I would have come to myself—nothing would have happened.' President: 'You were so little out of your head that when you reached the Gare d'Austerlitz, you went to the

the following: 1. Written law—the part it plays in criminal cases is often insignificant. 2. Political influences—in certain cases very important. 3. Humanitarian inclinations in judges and jurymen—these are knowable from humanitarian theory and literary sources.

toilet and reloaded your revolver.' *A.* 'I would have reloaded ten revolvers at that moment. I was out of my head. I was so little aware of what had happened that I thought I was going to surprise my husband and my aunt at Savigny. I did not remember what I had just done in the rue Sedaine.' President: 'After your second crime you returned to Paris, took your daughter in your arms and said: "Forgive me, I am a murderer!"' At this allusion the defendant bursts into hysterical sobs. Recovering a little she cries time after time: 'My child, my child, forgive me, please, please, forgive me!' Witnesses are called. The defence asks permission to call the little Paquerette, nine years old, the defendant's daughter. The prosecution and the presiding justice object, describing such an examination as an 'impropriety.' The defence insists. The defendant has hysterics again, requiring four policemen to hold her. She screams: 'My darling! My little girl! Forgive your mother!' The girl testifies in a barely audible childish voice that her mama told her always to remember her father in her prayers at night, and that her mama had never said anything unkind of her father. The moving scene deeply affects the spectators. After a recess, State's Attorney Wattinne closes with a severe arraignment of the defendant. The jury brings in a verdict of not guilty and the Court releases Mme. P——."

This is merely typical of a situation that is general. Says M. Loubat, Attorney-General at Lyons in a letter to the *Temps,* August, 1912: "Juries should be made up with a view to social defence and not to the occasional and fairly rare political cases that may come before Criminal Sessions. The results of the present system speak for themselves. Our highest criminal jurisdiction, which ought to approximate something like absolute justice in view of the tremendous and at times irreparable punishments that it has within its powers, is the least reliable, the most capricious, the most unpredictable imaginable. Certain verdicts are acts of downright aberration: parricide is condoned by a jury; in one same session defendants will be condemned to death, others equally guilty will be acquitted. If a court of judges indulged in such insanities there would be a public revolt. Such scandals would be impossible if the jury contained more men who were less credulous and less responsive to emotional stresses in the court-room."

Interested in a practical reform, the Attorney-General was here confining his attack to the point where the evil seemed greatest. But looking at the facts theoretically, decisions by judges are on the whole no better than jury verdicts. The services rendered the French Ministry by the Court of Appeals in the Dreyfus case are a matter of common knowledge. A very competent individual writes to the *Gazette de Lausanne* from Paris, Sept. 4, 1912: "You may be surprised that [for the Court of the Seine] we have not more than three or four Assistant Presiding Justices out of the dozen that are at all capable. For my part I am surprised that there are that many. They are not chosen for ability, but in view of their political affiliations. If they are competent jurists, that is just a matter of chance; and if they are independent, it is by oversight. On that bench we have at present a some-

4. Emotional, socialistic, social, political, and other inclinations on the part of jurymen—all knowable from theories and literary sources. 5. The general notion common to all despotisms, whether royal, oligarchical, or democratic, that the law does not bind the "sovereign," and that the "sovereign" may substitute personal whims for enacted law. This notion, too, is knowable through theories. In our day it is the fashion to say that "what we need is a 'living' law," a "flexible" law, a law that "adapts itself to the public conscience." Those are all euphemisms for the caprice of the individuals in power. 6. Numberless other inclinations, which are not perhaps generally operative, but which may chance to be preponderant in the minds of the twelve individuals—usually of no great intelligence, no serious education, no very high moral sense—who are called upon to serve on juries. 7. Private interests of the citizens in question. 8. The temporary impression made upon them by some striking fact—so after a series of startling crimes juries are inclined to be severe for a time.

In a word, it may be said that court decisions depend largely upon the interests and sentiments operative in a society at a given moment; and also upon individual whims and chance events; and but slightly, and sometimes not at all, upon codes or written law.[3] All

time Radical Senator who was beaten for re-election. He was appointed to the bench because he was a Radical and because he was regarded as a victim of the 'Reaction.' Now it happens that he is a first-class jurist, and so much the better. But had he not known how to serve a summons he would have been appointed with no more hesitation." That is France. In Italy things are worse, and by far.

466 [3] It would take a volume to quote some very small fraction of the facts adducible to this point. A writer in *Liberté*, Jan. 11, 1913 (L. Latapie), declares that the French magistrate today stands "helpless, spineless, in the face of an avalanche of crime and law-breaking. He defends society by waving a perfumed handkerchief at the dirk and brass knuckles of the bandit. Yesterday, in the Goutte-d'Or section, a mob all but lynched a burglar who was run down after being surprised on a 'job.' His record showed twenty-three convictions for house-breaking! Twenty-three times the police had discovered and arrested that particular rogue; and twenty-three times the courts had turned him loose with insignificant penalties! Nevertheless there is a law covering cases of incorrigible criminals. The magistrates do not enforce it, doubtless in fear of weakening their support among the 'advanced' parties. If Paris were suddenly purged of the fifty thousand professional criminals who could be in jail as well as not but who are left free to disturb the public peace, the Army of the Revolution would lose its

such factors, provided they be general and strongly influential, give rise to theories; and that is why we are studying now one theory, now another, not so much to become familiar with them in themselves as to attain through them a picture of the tendencies in which they originate.

467. In § 12 we noted the necessity of distinguishing between the subject-matter of a theory and the nexus by which the matter was drawn together to constitute the theory. In connexion with any given theory, therefore, two general and two particular problems arise. *In general:* 1. What are the elements utilized by theories? 2. What is the nexus that combines them? *In particular:* 1. What are the elements utilized by a *particular* theory (§ 470)? 2. What is the nexus that combines them (§ 519)? Our solution of those problems in § 13 yielded, in fact, a classification of types of theories. Now we must go deeper into that matter, which at the time we barely signboarded for future investigation.

most reliable troops. Our judges are getting along on the best of terms with the Revolution. Outrages against persons and property find an indefatigable spirit of forgiveness in the courts so long as the culprits hide behind some political pretext. Thieves and gunmen are so well aware of that that they never fail any longer to affiliate with the Anarchist party before setting out on a 'job.' If they shoot down a bank messenger and take his bag it is 'to vindicate democracy.' And if they take a shot at a policeman it is 'to improve social conditions.' The judge blanches white at mention of such dreadful social issues, and he draws his conscience down into his red robe the way a snail draws its head into its shell. Who knows? The courts may be largely responsible for the wave of crime that is today sweeping France. They are failing to inspire respect and fear for the law anywhere. They have so accustomed the professional agitator to getting off scot-free that he is considering himself intolerably persecuted if any gesture is made towards applying the laws to him. The governmental press, which is for ever flirting with the revolutionary parties, contributes not a little towards increasing uneasiness and hesitation among the judges. Their defence is well known: 'After all,' say they, 'why demand courage of us only? We follow the lead of the Government. Let the Government display a little energy against revolutionary law-breaking. Let it dissolve its alliance with institutions that are avowedly making war on the country and on organized society. Then we'll see about restoring the majesty of the law.' "

This last thrust is tucked in for polemical purposes. In reality, courts, Government, and public are moved by the same interests and sentiments. Outraged by some crime the public will strike down a law-breaker and then turn to feed anew on the inanities of humanitarians of every breed. Courts and governors follow the course the public approves.

In December, 1912, a Mme. Bloch came up for trial before Criminal Sessions in

468. Suppose we glance at an analogous case. Similar inquiries arise with reference to language. Grammar answers the general questions. Morphology yields the elements of language—substantives, adjectives, verbs, and so on. Syntax shows how they are combined. The grammatical and the logical analysis of a given passage answer the particular questions arising in it. Grammatical analysis yields the elements (substantives, verbs, and the like); logical analysis shows how they are combined and the significance they acquire through the combination. Carrying the analogy further, we might say that rhetoric deals with the passage more especially under its subjective aspect (§ 13).

469. The analogy extends also to the relations between theory and practice. Theory never gives a perfect picture of practice. Language is a living organism even today in our Western countries, where there is a continuous effort to crystallize it within specified forms, through which it is always breaking, much as the roots of trees split the ledges in the crevices of which they grow. In remote ages lan-

Paris for killing her husband's paramour, a certain Mrs. Bridgeman. The latter, as is usual with emancipated women on the American side of the Atlantic, was amusing herself with men while her husband devoted all his energies to money-making. Mme. Bloch was acquitted, and so far, nothing extraordinary—acquittals in such circumstances occur by tens and hundreds. What was not so commonplace was to hear a public ministry, which was supposed to be conducting a prosecution of crime, inciting to homicide. The State's Attorney delivered himself of the following: "The crime of this defendant was inexcusable. She had a legitimate victim in her own house—her husband. Had she smitten him, we could only nod in approval." The correspondent of the *Journal de Genève* usually has good things to say of the worst humanitarians. Of this detail, however, he wrote, Dec. 28, 1912: "The remark has caused an uproar, all the press protesting. But it would take more than that to keep the courts from discrediting themselves. The people at the Palais are playing to the galleries in a perfectly shocking manner. They seem to be less independent than ever as regards the higher powers, and more accessible than ever to the temptations of a cheap publicity. A great effort would be required to restore justice to the serenity, earnestness, and independence that are essential prerequisites to its effective functioning and prestige. The Rochette affair has not contributed to the good name of the French courts. It will be remembered that that high-flying captain of big finance disappeared at the very moment when he was to surrender to the authorities."

But all that results from the sentiments prevailing in the public at large and from the political system resulting from them. The causes are general and cannot be laid at the door of this or that individual.

guage developed freely like trees in a virgin forest—even in times not very long past spelling was still arbitrary in part. There is no reason for believing that the situation is, or has been, different with other similar products of human activity—with law, morality, religion. Indeed, facts in huge numbers constrain us to hold that they have developed much as language developed. In remote ages they were blended in a single mass, like the words in ancient Greek inscriptions, which were written without spaces between them, such contact modifying the last letter of one word and the first letter of a following word. The analytical process of separating one word from another, so simple in itself, was never carried out for Sanskrit, and was not effected for Greek till fairly recent times, traces of the original unions surviving even in classical literature.[1] So the analytical process of separating law, morality, religion, from each other, though evidently far advanced in modern civilized countries, has by no means been completed, and it has still to be carried out among the more backward peoples. Greek inscriptions, as well as the history of Graeco-Roman origins, present language, law, morality, religion, as a sort of protoplasm from which, by a process of scission, parts are sent off to develop as distinct, and finally as separate, en-

469 [1] Reinach, *Traité d'épigraphie grecque,* pp. 237-38, 245: "Spelling, especially in private documents beyond the control of the People's secretaries and the Senate, is even more individual than the script. It reflects not only the general habits of the period, but the caprices or manias of each stone-cutter. . . . The word *orthography* awakens in us moderns an idea of rules that was long stranger to the ancients. For us orthography is a fixed manner of writing words, oftentimes regardless of the way they are pronounced. For the ancients down to the Alexandrine era, as for the French down to the sixteenth century, no orthography, properly speaking, existed, and words were written much as they were pronounced. Writing was a living organism with them. It is a matter of schooling with us. . . . Countless examples of the variable spelling of the ancients could be quoted from inscriptions. There is an Athenian decree in which the forms ἐς and εἰς, ἀεί and αἰεί, appear just a few lines apart. . . . Curtius has shown from inscriptions that the normal state of the more ancient Greek as regarded final consonants was one of absolute mobility—the same situation that prevailed down to the end as regarded the consonants of prepositions in elision (ἀφ' οὗ). Later on a struggle for survival developed between the different forms, and the spelling that prevails in the classical language was the victor in that competition."

tities.[2] Studying the facts of the past with the ideas of our own day, we give body to abstractions created by ourselves, imagine that we find them in the past, and then when we come upon facts at variance with our theories, we call them deviations. So in our fancy we create a natural law from which positive laws would be deviations, and conjugations of regular verbs, from which the conjugations of irregular verbs would be deviations. The historical study of law and the historical grammar of the national languages have shattered that beautiful and well-ordered edifice—yet not to such an extent that it cannot still offer cosy refuge to our metaphysical sociologists. It is impossible to study history experimentally and not be impressed by the contingent character of law and morality. For a long time the grammar and vocabulary of Cicero and Caesar were *the* Latin grammar and *the* Latin vocabulary. Other writers showed deviations—if one did not go so far as to call them errors. Italian was the language of the "authorities" of the Crusca, and the person who spoke otherwise fell into error. At last scholarship has come to realize that there is not *a* Latin grammar, *a* Latin vocabulary, but many such. If Plautus and Tacitus write a Latin different from Cicero, it is somewhat ridiculous on our part to presume to correct them as if they were so many schoolboys who have not done their exercises with sufficient care. Even in our parts of the world, where law is crammed

469 [2] We have another analogy in the fact that scientific philology is a modern science unknown for centuries upon centuries even to men of great talent, and that it came into being and prospered through use of the experimental method. Greek grammar, for example, is much better known to modern scholars than to the scholars of ancient Greece. It seems impossible that Aristotle, or whoever it was that wrote the *Poetica,* could have written (20, 8, Fyfe, p. 77): "Since we do not ordinarily give a meaning to each part of a compound noun, so in *Θεόδωρος*, *δῶρον* has no meaning." The "critical" edition, obtained by the comparative, the experimental, method, is a modern thing—the humanists had no interest in it. The fanciful conjecturings of hypercriticism of texts must not be mistaken for scientific philology. The conjecture, after all, is nothing new. The alterations and suppressions to which not a few modern philologists presume to subject ancient Greek and Latin texts are in all respects kindred to the mutilations to which the Homeric poems fell victim at the hands of the Alexandrians. The justifications put forward by the moderns are comparable in ingeniousness, and oftentimes in absurdity, to the ancient.

into legislation and language into grammatical rules, evolution has ceased neither for the one nor for the other, and unity is an abstraction of which no trace is to be found in the concrete.

470. *The elements in theories.* Carefully observing the matter of which theories are constructed, we see that it is of two distinct kinds. Theories utilize certain things that fall within objective experience and are susceptible of objective observation (§ 13), or which may be logically inferred from observation and experience; and then again certain other things that overstep objective experience and observation—among them such as result from introspection or subjective experience (§§ 94-95). Things of the first kind we elect to call *experimental entities;* things of the second kind, *non-experimental entities* (§ 119).[1]

471. Certain entities seem to be experimental but are not, entities such as "heat," "cold," "the dry," "the moist," "depth," "height," and other similar conceptions of which ancient writers on the natural sciences made lavish use. To them may be added the "atoms" of Epicurus, "fire," and other such things. The poem of Lucretius may seem experimental as a whole; but it is not, for the entities with which it deals lie outside the experimental field.[1]

470 [1] As explained in § 6, we use the term "experimental" to designate not merely experience but objective experiment and observation.

471 [1] Davis, *The Chinese,* Vol. II, pp. 263-64 (1836, pp. 284-85): "The Chinese physiologists expressly call man a *Seaoutien-ty,* a 'little universe,' or 'microcosm,' and they extend to this the same doctrine of the *Yin* and *Yang,* or of the dual principle . . . maintaining the order and harmony of the natural world. They suppose that on a due proportion between these, or between *strength* and *weakness, heat* and *cold, dry* and *moist,* &c., consists the health of the human body; and that different degrees of excess or defect produce disease, and ultimately death. There is a great pretension to harmony and consistency throughout the whole system of physics, which perhaps might be called *beautiful,* were it only *true,* and based upon something better than empty speculation." Those interesting people are so well versed in science that "they do not even know the distinction between arteries and veins, and certainly not a syllable of the function of the lungs." They call the heart the "husband" and the lungs the "wife." "Without the practice of dissection, it would be singular indeed if they *did* know much." Of just that character were disquisitions on natural science in Western countries not so long ago, and such even today are many disquisitions on social "science."

Condillac well says:[2] "When philosophers use the words 'being,' 'substance,' 'essence,' 'genus,' 'species,' we must not imagine that they are designating by them certain aggregates of simple ideas derived from sensation and reflection. They mean to go farther than that and see specific realities in each of them. Indeed, if we go into greater detail and review the names of the substances 'body,' 'animal,' 'man,' 'metal,' 'gold,' 'silver,' and so on, we see that they all reveal to the eyes of our philosophers entities that are hidden from the rest of mankind.

"A proof that they regard such words as signs of some reality or other is the fact that when a substance has undergone some alteration they never fail to ask whether it still belongs to the same species to which it was referable before the change, a question that would become superfluous if they put concepts of substances and concepts of their species in different collections of simple ideas. When they ask if 'ice' and 'snow' are 'water'; if a 'foetal monstrosity' is a 'human being'; if 'God,' 'spirits,' 'bodies,' and even 'void' are 'substances' [All questions that logico-experimental science regards as meaningless, inconclusive, fatuous], it is evident that the question is not whether these things are in accord with the simple ideas gathered under the terms, 'water,' 'man,' 'substance' [That is a lapse into metaphysics. Really such problems are solved only by accords of sentiments.]—such a question would answer itself—but whether such things contain certain 'essences,' certain realities, which the words 'water,' 'man,' 'substance,' are supposed to designate."

Sometimes it is explicitly recognized that such entities are non-experimental—that fact, indeed, is taken as investing them with a higher majesty. At other times there is an effort to pass them off as experimental. Then again, there is a wavering between one conception and the other, and oftentimes no very clear idea at all regarding them—the case especially with politicians and other men of affairs who use such entities to express their thoughts. All that does not affect the manner in which they have to be regarded from the

471 [2] *Essai sur l'origine des connaissances humaines.* sec. V, § 7.

logico-experimental standpoint. However they are defined, and even if they are left undefined, they are, and will always remain, foreign to the experimental domain.[3]

472. Between the two kinds of matter just mentioned three combinations are possible: I. Experimental entities may be combined with experimental entities. II. Experimental entities may be combined with non-experimental entities. III. Non-experimental entities may be combined with non-experimental entities.

473. From the standpoint we are at present taking—the matter of accord with experience—it is evident that we can consider only combinations of the first variety, for the other two are not susceptible of any sort of experimental verification. To settle any dispute a judge is necessary (§§ 17, 27), and experience disclaims jurisdiction in disputes arising under combinations II and III.

474. In the treatise commonly entitled *De Melisso*[1] the following proposition is ascribed to a philosopher: "God being everywhere the same, He must be spherical."[2] That sets up a relationship between a non-experimental entity, God, and an experimental entity, the shape of a sphere. There is no experimental criterion for passing judgment on such an issue. And yet an apparently experimental reason is offered to prove that God is spherical: it is said that He is one, that He is absolutely similar to Himself, that He sees and hears on all sides.[3] The author of the *De Melisso* is not convinced and remarks that if everything that is similar to itself throughout has to be spher-

471 [3] Here, remember, we are considering theories objectively, quite apart from the inner thought of the persons who framed them. We are dissociating them from their authors and considering them in themselves.

474 [1] It is attributed to Aristotle, and the philosopher in question is alleged to be Xenophanes. Neither assertion seems to be substantiated. The question, however, is of no importance to us. We are interested in types of reasoning. We do not care whom they belong to.

474 [2] *De Melisso, Xenophane, Gorgia,* III (Bekker, p. 977b; Diels, p. 20): *πάντῃ δὲ ὅμοιον ὄντα, σφαιροειδῆ εἶναι.* Farther along, IV, 6, 7 (Bekker, p. 978; Diels, p. 27), a similar dictum of Parmenides is noted [and denied: *οὐδὲ τὸν θεὸν ἀνάγκη εἶναι διὰ τοῦτο σφαιροειδῆ*]; and in the fragments of Parmenides, *Carmen,* vv. 101-03 (Karsten, p. 38), one reads: "Since he [God] is perfect to the very extremities everywhere, he is like unto the globe of a round sphere, all of which is equidistant from its centre."

474 [3] *Ibid.,* IV, 6, 7 (Bekker, p. 978; Diels, p. 27).

ical, white lead, which is white throughout, should also be spherical. And he gives other arguments of the kind. All that very evidently overreaches the domain of experience, and if we would keep within the experimental field, we can neither endorse nor disavow either party in the controversy. Any siding with the one or the other would be due to some sentimental inclination on our part and not to any experimental consideration.

475. But we happen on another dispute in the same treatise. Xenophanes holds that the Earth and the air are infinite in extent, and Empedocles denies that.[1] The entities here are experimental, and experience can pronounce judgment. It has in fact rendered judgment—in favour of Empedocles.

476. Now most theories on social matters that have been current down to our own time tend to approximate the type of theory that is made up of non-experimental entities, but usurps the form and appearance of experimental theory.

477. Taking our stand on formal logic and disregarding validities of premise, the strongest position for us is provided by combinations of the type III, and the next strongest by combinations of the type II. If, in the proposition "$A = B$" both A and B are non-experimental entities, the person who would keep strictly to the experimental field can raise, obviously, no objections of any kind whatsoever. When St. Thomas asserts that angel speaks to angel, he sets up a relation between things about which the person keeping strictly to experience can say nothing. The case is the same when the argument is elaborated logically and one or more inferences are drawn. St. Thomas is not content with his mere assertion; he is eager to prove it, and says: "Since one angel can express to another angel the concept in his mind, and since the person who has a concept in his mind can express it to another at will, it follows that one angel may speak to another."[1] Experimental science can find no fault with the argument. It lies altogether outside its province. Many meta-

475 [1] *Ibid.*, II (Bekker, p. 976; Diels, p. 16). *Cf.* Artistotle, *De coelo,* II, 13, 7 (Hardie-Gaye, Vol. II, p. 294a).

477 [1] *Summa theologiae,* I[a], *qu.* 107, *art.* 1 (*Opera,* Vol. V, p. 488: *Utrum unus angelus alteri loquatur*).

physical arguments are of just that type, and many others differ from it only in taking over some term from the experimental sphere.

478. We are given the following definition: "All beings capable of some degree of activity—or one might simply say all beings, since absolute inertia is equivalent to non-being—tend to an end towards which all their efforts and all their faculties are directed. That end, without which they would not act—in other words, not exist—is what is called 'the good.'"[1] So one thing unknown and lying outside the experimental field ("the good") is defined by another thing even more unknown and likewise lying outside the experimental field ("the end"). On such an argument we can have nothing to say. For its part, unfortunately, the argument does not stay at home; it is soon intruding upon the experimental world, where it necessarily comes into collision with experimental science.

479. The first class of combinations comprises all scientific theories; but it also contains others—exceedingly interesting ones—that are pseudo-scientific in character. Pseudo-scientific theories arise through the elimination of some non-experimental entity that has been used merely to establish certain relations, not otherwise demonstrable, between experimental entities. The person, for example, who gives the definition of "the good" quoted above, has not the remotest intention of remaining in the high and nebulous regions whence he takes wing. Sooner or later he intends to return to this lowly earth of experience—it is too important, after all, to be entirely ignored. Similarly, to the assertion that the Scriptures are inspired by God the person who insists on remaining within the limits of experience can make no objection. But those who assert divine inspiration intend to use it eventually to set up this or that relation between experimental entities—to assert, for example, that there are no antipodes. Such propositions logico-experimental science has to judge intrinsically, without reference to the non-experimental considerations on which they are based. So again, the metaphysical theory of "solidarity" is immune to rebuttal from logico-experimental science; but those who invented that non-experimental phan-

478 [1] Franck, *Dictionnaire des sciences philosophiques, s.v. Bien.*

tom intend to avail themselves of it to establish relations between experimental entities and, specifically, between their pockets and their neighbour's money. Such experimental relations and operations logico-experimental science must judge intrinsically, disregarding the fancies and vagaries of the Holy Fathers of the Church of Solidarity.

480. These particular cases fall under the following general formula. Let *A* and *B* stand for two things lying within the experimental domain, and *X* for another thing lying outside that domain. A syllogism is drawn with *X* as the middle term. *X* eventually disappears, and just the relation between *A* and *B* is left. Experimentally, neither the major nor the minor premise can be accepted because of the term *X*, which transcends experience; and therefore the relation between *A* and *B* cannot be accepted (or rejected) either, for it is a relation that is experimental only in appearance. In *the logic of sentiment* (§ 1416), on the other hand, in a reasoning developing by accord of sentiments, the syllogism may be as sound as sound can be; because, in reality and taking due account all along of the indefiniteness of terms in ordinary language, if the sentiments aroused by *A* accord with the sentiments aroused by *X*, and the sentiments aroused by *X* with the sentiments aroused by *B*, it will follow that on the whole the sentiments aroused by *A* will accord with the sentiments aroused by *B*. Farther along (§ 514) we are to examine this argumentation from the standpoint of its persuasive force. Suppose just here we begin by considering it from the experimental standpoint.

481. We must be on close guard against two mistakes that may be made in inverse directions: (1) the mistake of accepting the relation between *A* and *B* arising from the elimination of *X*, on the strength of the syllogism, without a strictly experimental verification; (2) if it be experimentally verifiable that the relation between *A* and *B* exists, the mistake of concluding from that fact that, according to experimental science, *X* exists; or conversely, if it be experimentally ascertained that the alleged relation between *A* and

B does not exist, the mistake of concluding that, according to experimental science, *X* is non-existent (§§ 487, 516, 1689).

482. For that matter, our reason for rejecting on experimental grounds the relation between *A* and *B* arising from the elimination of *X* is in part purely formal; and we may ignore it if the relationship between *A* and *B* has been experimentally established. The test of that relationship is, after all, the purpose of the theory. Of what importance the means by which it is realized?

483. In such a problem we have to keep three researches distinct:

a. The investigation of *what is*—in other words, the study of real movements

b. The investigation of what *would happen* under certain conditions—in other words, of virtual movements

c. The investigation of what *ought* to be.

484. *a.* As for what really is, experience has passed its judgment. Reasonings of the type mentioned almost never yield relationships that are verifiable on the facts (§ 50).

485. Let us go back to the matter of the antipodes already alluded to (§ 67). Are there people called antipodes on the face of the earth? Good sense and prudence ought to have counselled people to leave the task of solving that problem to experience. St. Augustine chooses to solve it *a priori*—and, after all, his reasoning is no worse than many others that are accepted in our time, since it has, if nothing else, the merit of being intelligible. The Saint says:[1] "There is no reason for believing that, as some fancy, there are Antipodes, that is to say, people on the opposite side of the earth, where the sun rises when it sets on our side, people who tread with their feet that part of the earth which is opposite to the soles of our feet." There is no historical proof of the fact, the Saint continues. The part of the earth opposite to ours may be covered with water, and therefore be uninhabited. But then, even if it is not covered with water, "it is not at all necessary that it be inhabited. For Holy Writ makes no mention of such a thing and Scripture justifies its accounts through the fact that, in the past, things that it predicted have come to pass. And

485 [1] *De civitate Dei,* XVI, 9.

it is moreover exceedingly absurd to say that some men could have sailed across the vast Ocean, gone from this part to that part of the earth, and founded a new branch of the human race." The argument is well knit and, if one will, even sound; but unfortunately it is at war with the facts; nor have the many similar arguments designed to prove that there were and could be no antipodes enjoyed a better fate.

486. Lactantius Firmianus says: "Can anyone possibly be so stupid as to believe that there are men who walk with their feet up and their heads down? Or that there [at the antipodes] all that which with us lies on the ground is upside down? That crops and trees grow downward? That rain, snow, and hail fall upward to the earth?"[1] The error here may be of theological origin, but it is metaphysical in form at least. Lactantius reasons like a Hegelian. He

486 [1] *Divinae institutiones,* III, *De falsa sapientia,* 24, 1 and 7-9, 10-11 (*Opera,* Vol. I, pp. 254-56; Fletcher, Vol. I, pp. 196-97): *"Quid illi qui esse contrarios vestigiis nostris antipodas putant? Num aliquid loquuntur? Aut est quisquam tam ineptus qui credat esse homines quorum vestigia sint superiora quam capita? Aut ibi quae apud nos iacent inversa pendere? Fruges et arbores deorsum versus crescere? Pluvias et nives et grandines sursum versus cadere in terram?"* Lactantius replies to the "philosophers" the way our Hegelians answer the physicists. He says that from the movement of the sun and the moon the "philosophers" have concluded that the sky is round: "From this roundness of the heavens it would follow that the earth was contained in the centre of its interior; and if that were so, the earth itself would be globe-shaped; for nothing embraced by a round globe could help being round itself. But if the earth were round it would have to offer the same face [*i.e.,* the same sort of surface] to all parts of the sky, raising mountains, that is [*i.e.,* in the nether hemisphere as well as in the upper], spreading out its plains and its flat seas. And if that were so, this extreme consequence would also follow, that there would be no part of the earth which is not inhabited by men and other animals. So the roundness of the heavens [*i.e.,* the theory that the universe is a globe] would leave the Antipodes hanging head downward. And if you ask the people who sustain such marvels why everything does not fall into the nether part of the heavens, they answer that, in the nature of things, heavy things are carried towards the centre and are connected with the centre like spokes in a wheel, whereas light things, such as clouds, smoke, or fire, are repelled from the centre so that they rise towards the sky. What I am to say to that I am sure I do not know, unless it be that having uttered one foolish thing, they have to go on and defend it with another." That sounds like Hegel taking Newton to task! Lactantius, good soul, concludes: "I could prove with many arguments that it is in no way possible for the sky to be lower than the earth [Still the Hegelian method of arguing from concepts—here the concept "lower."], were it not time for this book to come to a close." A great pity! What we have missed!

finds, and everybody will find with him, that the concepts of "high," "low," "upwards," "downwards" (as known in our hemisphere), are incompatible with the existence of antipodes. He is right, in fact: it *is* ridiculous to imagine people walking with their heads down and their feet up. However, if a person reasons not on concepts but on things, and considers names merely as labels serving to keep track of things (§ 119), he readily sees that when we move on to the part of the earth opposite to ours we have to shuffle our labels about, exchanging the tag "upward" for the tag "downward." Then belief in antipodes ceases to be ridiculous. Though errors such as Lactantius made have vanished, or all but vanished, from the natural sciences, they are still very common in the social sciences, where many people continue reasoning in that fashion. Anyone not afraid lest his conclusions stand in a similar relation to the facts may go on reasoning like Lactantius or the Hegelians. If he would, as far as his ability will allow, have his conclusions stand to the facts in the relations observable in the physical sciences, he must try to reason after the manner now customary in those sciences (§§ 5, 69, 71).

487. Many have turned, and many, I believe, are still turning, the errors of the Fathers with regard to the antipodes to the discredit of Christianity, or, at least, of Catholicism. But really religion is in no wise responsible for such errors, and sufficient proof of that is the fact that many pagans also gave the earth a form other than spherical and ridiculed believers in antipodes.[1] Lucretius, the atheist, reasons no better than Lactantius. He deems absurd the view that the earth holds together because all bodies tend toward the centre. "Can you believe," he says, "that bodies can hold themselves up all by themselves, that the heavy bodies under the earth all tend upward and then stick to the opposite part of the earth upside down, like the reflections we see on our side in water? On similar grounds it is

487 [1] Plutarch, *De placitis philosophorum,* III, 10 (Goodwin, Vol. III, p. 155). *Idem, De facie quae in orbe lunae apparet,* 7, 2 (Goodwin, Vol. V, p. 243): "We must not heed philosophers when they try to refute paradox with paradox. . . . And what absurdities do they not put forward? Do they not say that the Earth is spherical, though it has such great cavities, heights, inequalities? That it is inhabited by Antipodians, who crawl like worms and lizards, upside down?"

maintained that animals go about head downwards, and that they cannot fall from the Earth into the nether spaces of the heavens any more than our bodies can rise to the higher regions of the sky." [2]

488. The best that can be said is that a strong faith of whatever kind, be it religious or metaphysical, saves a person from the prudent scepticism of the experimental sciences through the pride one takes in knowing the absolute. But that is an indirect cause of error. The direct lies in trying to reason on concepts rather than on facts, and in using introspection instead of objective observation.[1]

489. Amusing indeed is Cosmas Indicopleustes. His second prologue is entitled "Christian Topography, Embracing the Whole Universe, and Proved from Holy Writ, wherewith Christians Must Not Disagree." [1] First he takes a fling at "those who though Christians believe and teach with the pagans that the sky is spherical." He has proofs, excellent in truth, that the Earth is not spherical. "Considering its incalculable weight how can the Earth hang suspended in the air and not fall?" [2] Whereas from Scripture we learn that the world has the shape of an oven and that the earth is quadrangular. The tabernacle built by Moses is the image of the world. Needless to say, the existence of antipodes is a ridiculous myth; and to show just how ridiculous it is, Cosmas gives a drawing in which very large men are shown standing feet to feet on opposite sides of a very small globe, 131 D (Migne, p. 130; Winstedt, p. 92): "As for antipodes, Scripture does not permit us to utter or heed such nonsense. For it says [Acts 17:26]: '*and* hath made of one blood all nations of men for to dwell on all the face of the earth.' . . . It does not say on all the *faces,* but on the *face.*" And other arguments just as decisive follow.

487 [2] *De rerum natura,* I, vv. 1056-63. Lucretius, however, has one thing in his favour: he did not dream of persecuting those who differed with him.

488 [1] Here, as elsewhere, we contrast concepts with facts, the subjective with the objective, not in any metaphysical sense, but in an experimental sense, as explained in §§ 94-95.

489 [1] *Topographia Christiana,* Prologue B (Migne, p. 58; Winstedt, p. 41): Χριστιανικὴ τοπογραφία περιεκτικὴ παντὸς τοῦ κόσμου, ἀποδείξεις ἔχουσα ἐκ τῆς θείας Γραφῆς, περὶ ἧς ἀμφισβητεῖν Χριστιανοὺς οὐ δέον.

489 [2] *Ibid.,* 65A (Migne, p. 66; Winstedt, p. 46): τὰ τοσαῦτα ἀμύθητα βάρη τῆς γῆς, πῶς δυνατὸν ὑπὸ ἀέρα χρεμᾶσθαι καὶ ἵστασθαι, καὶ μὴ καταπίπτειν;

490. Even writers who are otherwise keen enough have theories no better when they set to reasoning metaphysically. Aristotle demonstrates at length in his *De coelo* that the movement of the heavens has to be circular. He begins by asserting that every movement in space must be either rectilinear, or circular, or else a combination of the two (I, 2, 2; Hardie-Gaye, Vol. II, 268 b). He follows with another declaration: that only rectilinear and circular movements are *simple*. Then he says, I, 2, 4: "I call those bodies simple which have in themselves naturally the principle of motion, such as fire, earth, and the like."[1] That is a definition, and no objection could be made to it if it were clear. Unfortunately it is not, and that is a defect common to all the definitions of the metaphysicists, since these inevitably contain terms that correspond to nothing real. "Have in themselves naturally the principle of motion!" What on earth can that mean? Nothing whatever! It is a verbiage that acts solely upon a reader's sentiments.

491. Those meaningless assertions and definitions eventually serve for reasonings that are professedly exact, I, 2, 5 (Hardie-Gaye, Vol. II, p. 269a): "So then, since there is a simple motion, and circular motion is simple; and since a simple body has a simple motion, and a simple motion belongs to a simple body (if it were compound it would move according to its preponderant constituent), there must be a simple body which by nature moves in a circle." That dazzling argument is reinforced by the following, I, 2, 9: "This motion, therefore, must necessarily be the first. The perfect by nature precedes the imperfect. Now the circle is perfect, whereas the straight line is not. . . . Hence if the primary motion is of that body which is first in nature, and if circular motion is superior to the rectilinear, which is proper to simple bodies (for fire rises in a straight line, and terrestrial bodies fall towards the centre), circular motion must necessarily belong to a simple body."[1] Obviously, there is nothing

490 [1] *λέγω δ' ἁπλᾶ ὅσα κινήσεως ἀρχὴν ἔχει κατὰ φύσιν, οἷον πῦρ καὶ γῆν καὶ τὰ τούτων εἴδη καὶ τὰ συγγενῆ τούτοις.*

491 [1] *'Αλλὰ μὴν καὶ πρώτην γε ἀναγκαῖον εἶναι τὴν τοιαύτην φοράν. Τὸ γὰρ τέλειον πρότερον τῇ φύσει τοῦ ἀτελοῦς, ὁ δὲ κύκλος τῶν τελείων, εὐθεῖα δὲ γραμμὴ οὐδεμία.* Τέλειος, "perfect," in Greek has two meanings: "finished," "complete," and also "with-

experimental about this argument. Its whole force lies in sentiments that are aroused by suitably chosen terms, and it persuades because those sentiments are in apparent accord with one another, or at least do not stand in overt conflict. Following that course one may find anything one wishes, just as one can look at the clouds in the sky and make out the shapes of any sort of animal. So Plato considers the circle and the sphere "divine." And why not? He is at liberty to call them "divine," just as a schoolboy baffled by the problems of spherical trigonometry is at liberty to call them "hellish." Such are mere expressions of sentiment, with no relation whatsoever to any objective reality.[2]

out fault," "the best possible." Aristotle, *Ethica Nicomachea,* V, I, 15 (Rackham, p. 259), uses the word in the latter sense to designate a virtue that is the "highest" "most exalted": τελεία ἀρετή. This ambiguity in the meaning of τέλειος helps to conceal the inanity of the argument in the *De coelo*. The circular movement is "finished" (complete) because it returns upon itself, because it can go on indefinitely on the same curve; and when in that way the adjective τέλειος has gained acceptance, it follows, by virtue of the double sense, that circular motion is better than any other motion (§§ 1556 f.).

There is still another play on ambiguity in *De coelo,* II, 4, 2 (Hardie-Gaye, Vol. II, p. 286b-87). There the reasoning on the "perfect" circle is repeated. The circle is said to be perfect as compared with the straight line because something can be added to the straight line, nothing to the circle. Then Aristotle goes on: "Therefore if the perfect is anterior to the imperfect, for that reason too the circle is first among figures." This argument is as valid for any closed curve as for the circle. So Aristotle says, *De generatione et corruptione,* II, 10, 8 (Joachim, p. 337a): "When air comes from water, and fire from water, and, again water from fire, we say that the process takes place in a circle, since it comes back upon itself." If the passage in the *De coelo* were to be interpreted in that sense, the contrast in the passage would be between a movement that returns upon itself and a movement extending indefinitely along an unclosed line. But that is in no wise the case: a geometric circle, no more, no less, is in question, for in II, 4, 6 Aristotle bars not only irregular polygons, but any curved figures where the radii are not all of equal length, such as egg-shaped or lens-shaped figures. It is therefore evident that the phrase "circular motion" has now one sense, now another; at one time it is just motion along a closed curve, at another, motion around a geometric circle.

491 [2] Plato, however, is speaking of circle and sphere as such. He lays down that some sciences are truer than others. He takes the case of a man who has a true knowledge of justice, and then tries to show how that knowledge mingles with other knowledge less perfect. *Philebus,* 62A: "Will such a man be sufficiently wise if he knows the nature (λόγον) of the divine circle and sphere (. . . κύκλου μὲν καὶ σφαίρας αὐτῆς τῆς θείας τὸν λόγον ἔχων) and does not know the nature (λόγον) of the human circle and sphere?"

492. Aristotle, *De coelo,* II, 13, 19 (Hardie-Gaye, Vol. II, p. 295b), explains how the immobility of the Earth used to be demonstrated according to Anaximander: There is no reason why a body placed in the centre and equidistant from the extremities should be moved upward rather than downward or obliquely; and since it is impossible for a body to move in opposite directions at one time, it must necessarily remain motionless. And here are words of one of the greatest scientists of our modern times: "A body at rest cannot set itself in motion, since it has within itself no reason for moving in one direction rather than in another. . . . The direction of rectilinear movement evidently follows from the lack of any reason why the body should move to the right rather than to the left of its original direction."[1]

Anaximander's proposition is contradicted by experience; the propositions of Laplace are confirmed by experience. In both cases the demonstrations are without the slightest value.

493. The argument is framed on the following model: "Anything that to me and other men seems impossible will certainly not happen. I see no reason why *A* should be *B*. Therefore *A* cannot be *B*." That is the usual introspective syllogism (§§ 43, 69, 111, 434).

494. The fallacy in the argument is less evident because what ought to be stated in subjective form is stated in objective form. Laplace said: "There is no reason why the body should move to the right rather than to the left." Had he chosen to state his thought exactly, he would have said: ". . . it seems to me that there is no reason why . . ." But in that form the fallacious character of the proof would have been more strikingly apparent. Laplace might have replied that he did not use the revised form because the thing seems as it seems not to him only, but to all men. Another of the great sources of error in such reasonings! It simply is not true that things seem to all men as they seem to him. Most men have never

492 [1] Laplace, *Traité de mécanique céleste,* Vol. I, p. 14: *"Un point en repos ne peut se donner aucun mouvement, puisqu'il ne renferme pas en lui-même de raison pour se mouvoir dans un sens plutôt que dans un autre. . . . La direction du mouvement en ligne droite suit évidemment de ce qu'il n'y a aucune raison pour que ce point s'écarte plutôt à droite qu'à gauche de sa direction primitive."*

given a thought to the subject! But never mind that. Even if they had, the universal consensus of mankind would not enhance the value of the proposition by a jot and would have no power to make a thing that is subjective objective (§ 502).

495. As usual, reasonings of this type are lacking in any exactness—a fact we have often had occasion to stress and shall continue stressing. What can it mean to say that a body "has within itself no reason for moving in one direction rather than in another"? And how can we know whether really it has no such reason within itself? In no other way than by observing whether it remains at rest. The Laplace proposition therefore amounts to saying that a body is at rest when it is at rest—a thing as true as it is useless to know.

496. To say that "force" is the "cause" of motion is to think one is saying something and to say nothing—to define an unknown by an unknown.[1] What would this thing called the cause of the movement be? It is difficult to imagine any other reply than that the cause is a force; so that the proposition comes down to saying that a force is a force. A ban has been laid on such methods of reasoning in the science of modern mechanics.[2] In these volumes we were trying to follow that good example for sociology.

497. "Natural," "violent," "voluntary" movements play an important part in ancient philosophy. To see how much nonsense can be emitted on such matters, one has only to read the tenth book of Plato's *Laws*. Aristotle, too, unfortunately allowed himself to be

496 [1] Poisson, *Traité de mécanique,* Vol. I, p. 2: "In general the term 'force' is applied to any cause of motion in a body." Physicists eventually became aware of the inanity of such a definition. Barré de Saint-Venant, *Principes de mécanique fondés sur la cinématique,* p. 65: "From our strictly practical point of view, we do not stop to consider whether 'mass' has any bearing on the *quantities of matter* in the various heterogeneous bodies . . . nor whether 'force' has any bearing on the *efficient-causes* of movement in such bodies."

496 [2] Picard, *La mécanique classique et ses approximations successives,* p. 6: "In the study of constant fields, force has been successively defined in two different ways, first by static measures, then from a dynamic standpoint, in terms of the accelerations corresponding to the fields. No relation between these two evaluations was *a priori* necessary, and we must regard it as an experimental result that the numbers representing forces considered from the dynamic and from the static standpoint are proportional." This last remark should be pondered with the greatest care. The conception it voices is fundamental to science.

lured into similar lucubrations, and so was in a position to be used against Galileo when the latter was laying the foundations of experimental physics. In that science the work of Galileo already belongs to a historic past. An achievement as significant is as yet barely on the horizon for sociology, even in our day.

498. Cicero puts into the mouth of Balbus an argument to prove that the stars move of their own volition. According to Aristotle, says Balbus, everything that moves is moved either by nature, or by force, or by choice. How then do the Sun, Moon, and stars move? "Whatever is moved of nature is borne either downward by its weight or upward by its lightness. No one of those things is the case with the stars, since they move in circular orbits. Nor can it be said that the stars are moved against nature by a greater force, for what force could be greater? It results, therefore, that the motion of the stars is voluntary."[1]

499. Theories of that kind are evolved in great numbers when thinking is based on concepts and words rather than on facts.[1] And when the error becomes manifest, when it can no longer be decorously denied, instead of abandoning the method of reasoning that led to it, people obstinately try to preserve it and merely seek ways of adapting it to the data of experience.

500. If experience has in advance established a relation between two experimental facts *A* and *B,* the theological or metaphysical thinker rearranges his words in such a way as to picture that relationship as closely as possible. But, unfortunately, if a person is in the habit of thinking in theological and metaphysical terms, he does not readily adapt himself to the exactness of scientific reasoning, with the result that the experimental relation existing between *A* and *B* is not reproduced as closely as is desired, and very often is grossly distorted.

501. Long protracted in science was the reign of the notion that

498 [1] *De natura deorum,* II, 16, 44: *"Quae autem natura moverentur, haec aut pondere deorsum aut levitate in sublime ferri: quorum neutrum astris contingeret propterea quod eorum motus in orbem circumque ferretur. Nec vero dici potest vi quadam majore fieri ut contra naturam astra moveantur: quae enim potest maior esse? Restat igitur ut motus astrorum sit voluntarius."*

499 [1] The matter will be dealt with at length in Chapter IX.

celestial bodies, being perfect, had to move in circles. It finally came to be recognized that that idea was false, or better, nonsensical; and the discovery was made by a method altogether different from Aristotle's—by the empirical observations of Kepler.

502. Now that metaphysicists know—or think they know—that planets move in ellipses with the Sun at one of the foci (§ 69 [5]), they do their best to arrive by their methods of reasoning at that conclusion, which is—or rather, which they imagine has been—established by experience.[1]

Says Hegel: "A circle is the curve the radii of which are all equal —that is to say, it is completely determined by the radius. It is a unity that can be added to itself, and therein lies its whole determinability. But in free motion, where the determinations of time and space are differentiated and a qualitative ratio is established between them, that same ratio has to be introduced into space as a *differential* producing two determinations in it. Consequently the essential form of planetary revolution is the ellipse." [2]

503. Hegel's demonstration, *Ibid.*, § 270, of Kepler's third law is wonderful indeed: "As root, time is only an empirical magnitude. As quality, it is nothing but an abstract unity.[1] As an aspect of the developed totality, it is, in addition, a determined unity, a reflected

502 [1] For the statement to be true, the motions of the planets have to be referred to a sun that is assumed to be stationary, at the same time assuming that the masses of the planets as compared with the Sun's, as well as the reciprocal attractions of the planets, may be ignored.

502 [2] *Naturphilosophie,* Pt. I, Chap. III, § 270 (p. 130). [As a check on Vera's exceedingly free and at times inaccurate translation Hegel's original is prefixed to Pareto's note.—A. L.]: *"Der Kreis ist die in sich zurückkehrende Linie, in der alle Radien gleich sind: d.h. er ist durch den Radius vollkommen bestimmt; es ist diess nur Eine, und zwar die ganze Bestimmtheit. In der freien Bewegung aber, wo räumliche und zeitliche Bestimmungen in* Verschiedenheit, *in ein qualitatives Verhältniss zu einander treten, tritt nothwendig diess Verhältniss an dem Räumlichen selbst als eine* Differenz *desselben hervor, welche hiermit zwei Bestimmungen erfordert. Dadurch wird die Gestalt der in sich zurückgehenden Bahn wesentlich eine* Ellipse;—*das* erste *der Kepplerischen Gesetze."* Vera is a Hegelian of great repute. He must have understood what his master meant in the passage quoted. I transcribe below certain of the notes that he appended to his translation of Hegel; they add light to a text that is already clarity itself.

503 [1] Hegel: *"eine bloss empirische Grösse, und als qualitativ nur eine abstrakte Einheit."* Vera, Vol. I, pp. 296-97: "It appears in that form in the fall (*chute*—the completed act of falling)."

totality.[2] It produces itself, and in producing itself it does not transcend itself.[3] But as it has no dimensions, in producing itself it attains only to formal identity with itself, to the *square;* and space, on the contrary, which constitutes the positive principle of external continuity,[4] attains to the dimensions of the concept, to the *cube*. Thus their primitive difference subsists in their realization. That is Kepler's third law concerning the ratio of the cube of the distance to the square of the time." Indeed! Who would ever have thought it! What a prodigious mind to understand all that! [5]

503 [2] Hegel, *"für sich."* Vera: "'In itself': here, that is, 'complete.'" Alas, the very interesting things called "reflected totality, in itself complete" are still unknown to us!

503 [3] Hegel: *"producirt sich, und bezieht sich darin auf sich selbst."* Vera: "The square, that is."

503 [4] Hegel: *"als das positive Aussereinander."* Vera: "As continuing positive exteriority."

503 [5] Hegel's German: *"Als Wurzel ist die Zeit eine bloss empirische Grösse, und als qualitativ nur abstracte Einheit. Als Moment der entwickelten Totalität aber ist sie zugleich an ihr bestimmte Einheit, Totalität für sich, produciert sich und bezieht sich darin auf sich selbst; als das in sich Dimensionslose kommt sie in ihrer Production nur zur formellen Identität mit sich, dem Quadrate: der Raum dagegen, als das positive Aussereinander, zur Dimension des Begriffs, dem* Cubus. *Ihre Realisirung behält so den ursprünglichen Unterschied derselben zugleich bei. Diess ist das dritte Kepplerische Gesetz, das Verhältniss des* Würfels der Entfernungen zu den Quadraten der Zeiten."

The most remarkable of Vera's notes, Vol. I, p. 297, relates to a sentence of Hegel immediately following the passage quoted in his translation: ". . . a law that is profound merely because it is so simple and expresses the intimate nature of the thing." [Hegel's original: ". . . *ein* Gesetz, das darum so gross ist, weil es so einfach und mittelbar die *Vernunft* der Sache darstellt."] It is too long to quote entire. This titbit will suffice, however—Vol. I, p. 297: "Now by the very fact that the fall (*chute*) is only an aspect (*moment*) of finished mechanics, time, space, and matter are present in it only in an abstract and incomplete manner: in other words, all the elements constituting them are not present in it in their fully developed form, their unity. Time figures only as a root, space as a square, and as a purely formal square." My heart-felt sympathy for that poor "fall" in which time figures only as a "root." I do not deny that this manner of stringing words together haphazard may lead to some "simple" and "profound" law that "expresses the intimate nature of the thing," for I have no idea of what such an estimable nature may be. But in the present volumes on sociology I am not looking for any such "intimate nature," and I therefore try, as best I know how and can, to keep clear of disquisitions of that kind (§ 20). The day may come when sociologies to be written in the future will stand in the same relation to those now in vogue as the celestial mechanics of Gauss stands to Plato's ramblings or the vagaries of the astrologers.

504. But there is better yet! What is a diamond? "The diamond is the typical crystal, that product of the earth at sight of which the eye rejoices because it sees in it the first-born of light and weight. Light is abstract and completely free identity. Air is the identity of the elements. The subordinated identity[1] is an identity passive to light, and that is the transparency of the diamond [*read,* crystal]."[a] Having understood the transparency of the diamond, you might now consider metal: "Metal, on the other hand, is opaque, because in metal individual identity is concentrated into a more profound unity by a high specific gravity."[2]

505. A reminiscence of that exalted and luminous thinking is doubtless to be seen in the following passage from a philosopher of our day.[1] "What is the movement of a body through space? It is mechanics realizing itself. What is the formation of a crystal in the bosom of the earth? It is geometry making itself visible to the eye." Similar reasonings are current among all metaphysicists regardless of their country of origin. The Chinese had long since observed the influence of the Moon on the tides and given an explanation of it worthy of a Hegel.[2]

504 [1] Hegel: *"unterworfene"*; Vera, Vol. II, p. 21: " 'Subjugated,' 'subdued,' as contrasted with the individual identity (*individuelle Selbst*) of metal, which is not passive to light."

504 [a] *Ibid.*, § 317 (p. 306): *"Der Urkrystall ist der Diamant der Erde dessen jedes Auge sich erfreut, ihn als den erstgebornen Sohn des Lichts und der Schwere anerkennend. Das Licht ist die abstracte, vollkommen freie Identität,—die Luft die elementarische; die unterworfene Identität ist die Passivität für das Licht, und das ist die Durchsichtigkeit des Krystalls. Das Metall ist dagegen undurchsichtig, weil in ihm das individuelle Selbst durch hohe specifische Schwere zum Fürsichsein concentriert ist."*

504 [2] The density of the diamond is about 3.5. Certain crystals have the following densities: glass, 3.3; various flints, from 3.6 to 4.3. Aluminium, however, has (melted) a density of 2.56. Following Hegel's system, therefore, aluminium ought to be more transparent than diamond or glass. It is the hard luck of the metaphysicists that the contrary happens to be true. But they are never terrified by such disasters and always find ways to reconcile the yes and the no. Their repeated errors and absurd theories have so discredited them in the physical sciences that no one takes them seriously any longer; but they continue to swagger about in the literature improperly denominated social science.

505 [1] Fouillée, *Critique des systèmes de morale contemporains,* p. 22.

505 [2] Davis, *The Chinese,* Vol. II, p. 283 (1836, p. 307): "M. Klaproth remarked, that in an encyclopaedia, written before the close of the ninth century, it is said

506. St. Thomas also knows how some bodies come to be opaque and others transparent:[1] "For light being a quality of the first alterant, which is the most perfect and formal in bodies, those bodies which are in the highest degree formal and mobile are lucid in act; those that are most like them, such as transparent bodies, receive light; and those that are most material neither have light in their nature nor receive light, but are opaque. This is manifest in the elements, for fire has light in its nature, but its light is visible only in extraneous matter, because of its subtlety. Air and water are less formal than fire and are therefore merely transparent. But the Earth, which is in the highest degree material, is opaque." The Angelic Doctor was a great saint, but not a great physicist.[2]

The terms "just," "equitable," "moral," "human," "socially-minded" (*solidal*), and the like, which are today current in the social sciences, are of the same character as the terms "hot" (§ 871), "cold," "heavy," "light," and so on, which were formerly used in the natural sciences. They often lead astray and give the impression that an altogether fantastic argument is of an experimental character (§§ 965, 1551).

507. It is a curious thing that in examining the theories of his predecessors, Aristotle was aware of the source of their errors:[1] "The

that 'the Moon, being the purest principle of water, influences the tides.'" Hegel, *Op. cit.*, § 279 (p. 177): "The Moon is a waterless crystal striving to complete itself, to quench the thirst of its rigidity in our oceans, so producing the tides. The sea swells upward and is on the point, as it were, of leaping toward the Moon, and the Moon in its turn seems eager to take possession of the sea." Metaphysical sociologists write on social questions today in just such terms. Hegel's German: *"Der Mond ist der wasserlose Kristall, der sich an unserem Meere gleichsam zu integriren, den Durst seiner Starrheit zu löschen sucht, und daher Ebbe und Fluth bewirkt. Das Meer erhöht sich, steht im Begriff, zum Monde zu fliehen, und der Mond, es an sich zu reissen."*

506 [1] *De natura luminis* (*Opuscula*, 51, *Opera*, 1570, Vol. XVII-2, p. 36, 1B).

506 [2] And yet he had begun with an acute remark, noting that ordinary language is misleading as to the nature of light: "Some have said that light is corporeal, led into that error by certain locutions that people use in speaking of light. We ordinarily say that a ray of light darts through the air, that rays of light are reflected, that rays of light intersect—all such things being apparently corporeal."

507 [1] *De generatione et corruptione*, I, 2, 10 (Joachim, p. 316a).

cause of their seeing the things that we know[2] less clearly [than we do] was their lack of experience; for people who have spent their lives observing nature are best qualified to make hypotheses as to the principles that bring great numbers of facts together." Had Aristotle remained faithful to the principle he stated so well, he might have hastened the progress of humanity in science by many centuries.

508. Bacon's case is even more curious. It has been frequently remarked that he thought soundly enough on the experimental method, but then practised it badly. Here, for example, is one of his admonitions:[1] "There is nothing sound about our notions whether in logic or physic. 'Substance,' 'quality,' 'action,' 'passivity' [Devey: "passion"], 'essence' [Devey: "existence"], are not sound [Devey: "clear"] notions: and much less 'weight,' 'levity,' 'density,' 'rarity' [Devey: "tenuity"], 'moistness,' 'dryness,' 'generation,' 'corruption,' 'attraction,' 'repulsion,' 'element,' 'matter,' 'form,' and the like. All are fantastical and indeterminate." But later on, (II, 5), he considers bodies "as a 'throng' (*turma*) or 'conjugation' of 'simple natures'";[2] and it does not occur to him that such "simple natures" are among the "notions" that he disavows.

509. In these pseudo-experimental arguments the terms *A, B* . . . which are brought into some relation or other, are usually indeterminate. We have noted ambiguities in Aristotle (§ 491). They are nothing as compared with the absolute indefiniteness of the terms used by some metaphysicists (§ 963).

510. Says Hegel: "In general one cannot deny the influence of comets. I set Mr. Bode shrieking some time ago by remarking that experience now proves that comets are attended by a good vintage, as happened in the years 1811 and 1819, and that that twin observation

507 [2] Τὰ ὁμολογούμενα: literally, "things on which we are agreed" [Joachim: "admitted facts"].

508 [1] *Novum Organum,* I, 15.

508 [2] "The rule or axiom for the transformation of bodies is of two kinds. The first regards a body as a throng (*turmam*) or union (*coniugationem*) [Devey: "aggregate or combination"] of simple natures; as, for example, in gold, the following properties [Devey: "circumstances"] are combined: yellowness, heaviness . . ."

is worth as much as the observations of the returns or comets, and even more."[1] Here he is stating a false proposition and betraying gross ignorance of astronomy by assuming that the uniformity in the "returns" of comets is a matter of merely empirical observation; but at least he uses clear and exact terms that correspond to concrete things. That, in fact, is why we see so readily that his proposition is false. But the clearness fades when he adds: "What makes cometary wine so good is the fact that the aqueous process abandons the earth, and so brings on a change in the state of the planet."[2] "What in all creation is that "aqueous process" which "abandons" our earth? Who has ever seen or heard of it?

511. The vagueness and absurdity are far greater in what Hegel says of the Moon and the tides (§ 505 [2]). In strict fact, we know what he means by "crystal," "water," "thirst," "rigidity." It is his manner of combining them that makes them hard to understand. But even that glimmer of comprehensibility vanishes when Hegel says, § 279 (p. 177): "Light is simple thought itself, existing under form of nature. It is understanding in nature, or—what amounts to the same thing—the form of understanding present in nature."[1] Or again, § 277 (p. 168): "Light as constituting universal physical identity is first positable as a differentiated term and consequently as forming here a distinct and external principle in matter qualified according to another determination of the notion that constitutes the negation of light, namely, darkness."[2]

510 [1] *Naturphilosophie,* § 279 (pp. 179-80): *"Einflüsse der Kometen sind durchaus nicht zu verneinen. Herrn Bode habe ich einmal zum Seufzen gebracht, weil ich gesagt, die Erfahrung zeige jetzt, dass auf Kometen gute Weinjahre folgen, wie in den Jahren 1811 und 1819, und diese doppelte Erfahrung sey eben so gut, ja besser, als die über die Wiederkehr der Kometen."*

510 [2] 180: *"Was den Kometen-Wein so gut macht, ist, dass der Wasserprocess sich von der Erde losreisst, und so einen veränderten Zustand des Planeten hervorbringt."*

511 [1] *"Es [das Licht] ist der einfache Gedanke selbst, auf natürliche Weise vorhanden. Denn es ist Verstand in der Natur; d.h. die Formen des Verstandes existieren in ihr."* Vera comments, Vol. I, pp. 378-79: "Understanding, rather than speculative reason, is predominant in light, precisely because light is an abstract identity."

511 [2] *"Das Licht verhält sich als die allgemeine physicalische Identität zunächst als ein* Verschiedenes (§ 275), *daher hier Aeusseres und Anderes, zu der in den*

512. If all such verbiage were nothing but a reflection of the psychic state of given individuals, there would be no more occasion for bothering with it than with the ravings of a lunatic. But it has been admired by many people, and its equivalents in the social sciences continue to enjoy great prestige. For that reason they deserve consideration as a social phenomenon of great importance (§ 965).

513. The psychic state of people who imagine they understand arguments of that kind is not so very different from the psychic state of the people who thought they understood the abstractions of the old mythology and theology. In that we get another proof of the fact that evolution does not take place along a continuous line (§ 344). The three psychic states, *A, B, C* of Figure 11 stand in such succession that they may be supposed to form a continuous unit; but there are branches which lead to experimental cognitions *p, q, r* . . . or to other mystical, theological, or similar vagaries, *M, N* . . .

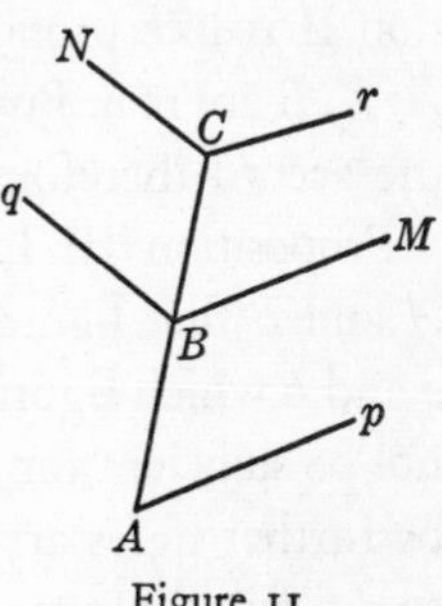

Figure 11

514. Those considerations carry us into the field of the *logic of sentiments* (§ 480). Ordinary thinking confuses the three propositions following:[1]

I. $A = X, X = B$, therefore $A = B$.

II. The name *a* of the thing *A* arouses in a person sentiments equivalent to the sentiments aroused by the word *X;* these are equivalent to the sentiments aroused by the name *b* of the thing *B;* therefore sentiments aroused by the name *a* are equivalent to the sentiments aroused by the name *b*.

anderen Begriffs-Momenten qualificirten Materie, die so als das Negative des Lichts, als ein Dunkles *bestimmt ist."* Vera comments, Vol. I, pp. 360-61: *"Hier Aeusseres und Anderes:* That is to say: light is first positable as a phase opposite and exterior to another phase." P. 365: *"Das Dunkele:* the obscuring principle."

514 [1] For the sake of brevity we use the form of the mathematical equation, such as "$A = X, X = B$, therefore $A = B$." In that way we avoid secondary questions as to the character of the premises in the syllogism. This is not a treatise on logic. We are trying merely to indicate the chief point in the problem. What was said of the syllogism in § 97 also applies to arguments in equation form.

III. The premises are the same as in II, but the conclusion is: therefore $A = B$.

From the experimental standpoint, proposition I is in accord with experience if *A, X, B* are real and well-defined things, and that accord is the closer, the more exact the definitions of *A, X, B* are made. On the other hand the accord may break down if the terms are ill-defined. If *X* is not real, or, in general, if one of the three things *A, X, B* is not real, there can be no question of any accord with experience (§ 480).

The sentiments aroused by *a, X, b* are real things; hence proposition II is like proposition I and, like it, accords with experience if *A, X, B* are real. But *a, X, b* are ordinarily very vaguely defined, and the accord therefore is usually not very close.

Proposition III has no logical value whatever, since the things *A* and *B* that figure in the conclusion are different from the things *a* and *b* which figure in the premises. To acquire such value it would not be sufficient for *A, X, B* to be real, well-defined things; it would be further necessary for the accord of the concepts *a, X, b* to correspond exactly to the relation between the things *A, X, B*. Just there, in fact, lies the essential difference between metaphysics and logico-experimental science; the former assumes such accord *a priori*, the latter subjects it to experimental verification.[2]

514 [2] Metaphysicists reply that every reasoning, whether experimental or not, is on concepts. We concede the point, since we are never willing to argue over names. Using that jargon (§ 95), we will say that the difference consists in the number of the concepts and in the way in which they are used. To learn the movements of celestial bodies Hegel uses a very few concepts, picked up here and there, and through them arrives at conclusions already known, which someone else has devised to represent those movements approximately and which he in his ignorance imagines represent them exactly. Hence if in computing the positions of heavenly bodies the concepts he obtains in this fashion were compared with the concepts observed through a telescope, great discrepancies would appear. Astronomers contemporary with Hegel, on the other hand, availed themselves of large numbers of concepts that they called astronomical observations, combined them with other large numbers of logico-mathematical inferences, and from the combination derived concepts as to the positions of stars that had the singular merit of fitting in fairly well —at least much better than Hegel's concepts—with the concepts derived by the astronomical observations of the time, and with those which were later derived from astronomical observations future from the standpoint of those days, past from ours. If, therefore, one would have concepts that like Hegel's are at variance with the

In the logic of sentiment proposition III is the type of all reasoning, substantially, and is held to be certainly "true." That type can be reshaped to fit the various types of syllogism. For one example, we may say: "The sentiments that the word *a* arouses in me are the same as the sentiments aroused in me by the word *X*, which stands for a general class; these are the same as the sentiments aroused by the word *b;* therefore the thing *A,* which corresponds to the word *a,* has the attribute *B,* which corresponds to the word *b.* But in that there is still too much exactness, and the type becomes substantially: "The sentiments aroused in me by *a* are *not incompatible with* the sentiments aroused in me by *X,* and these are not incompatible with the sentiments aroused in me by *b;* therefore *A* has the attribute *B.*" The argument, moreover, is in the form of a perfectly logical syllogism, and it is obtained by translating the propositions above in the following ways: "The sentiments aroused in me by *a* accord with those aroused in me by *X*" becomes "*A* is a member of the class *X*"; and "The sentiments aroused in me by *X* accord with those aroused in me by *b*" becomes "All *X*'s have the attribute *B.*" Hence, without any breach of formal logic, the conclusion is reached that "*A* has the attribute *B.*" This sort of reasoning is very widely used and, apart from the logico-experimental sciences, may be said to be the general rule. It is used by the masses at large and is almost the only one that carries conviction to them. It predominates especially in political and social discussion (§§ 586 f.).[3]

concepts yielded by observation, one should follow Hegel's lead. Those, on the other hand, who would have concepts which better approximate the concepts supplied by observation should follow the course pursued by astronomers, physicists, chemists, and the like. Here we are trying to discover sociological concepts of the latter kind, and for that reason we are following the latter course, which alone can provide us with them. We have absolutely no other reason for following it.

514 [3] Sensini, *La teoria della rendita,* pp. 201-02: "Literary economists of an extraordinary productivity indulge in inquiries that may be summarized in this fashion: 1. You treat a subject *X* without in any respect defining the terms you use. That allows you to play indefinitely on the ambiguity of the terms. 2. You never state a problem with the necessary definiteness, since by doing so it would be evident in the vast majority of cases that the problem stated does not exist or else is unsolvable because badly stated. 3. You make liberal use of metaphysical and in general vague expressions, which, since they mean nothing, can mean anything, and

From the experimental point of view the causes of error are the following: 1. The translations cannot be experimentally accepted even if *A, X, B* are real things. 2. There is no way of knowing to what, exactly, the terms *a, X, b* correspond. The best chance for experimental verification—though not for persuasion through sentiment—is offered by a proposition in which those terms correspond without too much vagueness to real things. In that case the translations are more or less readily adaptable to realities, and the conclusion is, roughly, verified by experience. But the correspondence between *a, X, b* and real things may be very uncertain and even fail if one of the things proves not to be real. That is not noticed in the argument, which is conducted around the words *a, X, b*—they are there even if real things corresponding to them fail to materialize. That is the most important cause of error, and it vitiates every reasoning of the kind. 3. The accord or mere compatibility of certain sentiments with certain others is a vague relation lacking altogether in exactness. "The sentiments that *a* arouses in me accord with the sentiments aroused in me by *X*" is a proposition in great part arbitrary.

In ordinary logic, finally, the conclusion follows from the premises. In the logic of sentiment the premises follow from the conclusion. In other words, the person who makes the syllogism, as well as the person who accepts it, is convinced in advance that *A* has the attribute *B,* and merely wishes to give his conviction an appearance of being logical. So he goes looking for two premises that can justify the conclusion, the premises, namely, that "The sentiments which *a* arouses accord with the sentiments *X* arouses" and "The sentiments *X* arouses accord with the sentiments *b* arouses." He has little trouble in finding them, in view of the vagueness of the terms and the indefiniteness of what is meant by "accord." [4]

so stand secure against every objection. 4. You appeal more or less covertly to sentiments in general and to those most in vogue at the moment you are writing." The vast majority of literary works on economic problems that are making fortunes for their authors today are of the kind Sensini describes.

514 [4] It is therefore evident that the proposition *"A* has the attribute *B"* is the constant element in the syllogism and the element of greatest social importance. The premises leading to that conclusion are the variable and less important element. In our example of storm-compelling (§ 186-216), the conclusion of the syllogism—

515. Again in contrast with what takes place in logico-experimental thinking, where the value of a term increases in proportion to its exactness, the terms of a reasoning by accord of sentiments are more effective in proportion as they are vague and indefinite. That explains the abundant use such reasonings make of terms such as "good," "beautiful," "just," and the like (§ 408). The more indefinite the concepts corresponding to *a, X, b,* the easier it is to establish, by way of sentiments, the accord between the concept *a* and the concept *X,* between the concept *X* and the concept *b.* If *X* is the concept "perfect," it is so indeterminate that it can be easily made to agree with the concepts *A, B,* determinate or indeterminate as these may be. "The motion of celestial bodies is perfect." And why not? Sentiment suggests no conflict between the two concepts (§§ 491 [1], 1556).

516. So we have now arrived inductively, by examining concrete facts, at the point suggested hypothetically in § 13: we see, in other words, that there are many subjective, sentimental considerations of great potency which prompt people to evolve and accept theories independently of their logico-experimental validity (§ 304). We shall therefore have to deal with that subject at some length (Chapter IX).

Meantime let us note another common error to which we have already alluded (§§ 16-17), and which lies in carrying outside the logico-experimental field conclusions that are valid only within it. After the elimination of a non-experimental term *X* has established a relation between the experimental terms *A* and *B,* proof or disproof of such a relation can in no wise serve to prove or disprove the "existence" of *X.* The experimental and non-experimental worlds have nothing in common and nothing touching the one can be inferred from the other. For a long time people tried to derive scientific propositions from the Bible, those, for instance, relating

the constant element—was that tempests, hail-storms, winds, can be caused or averted by certain rites. The variable element was the explanation of such power—the premises, in other words, from which the conclusion (the belief) resulted. Induction led us to note the fact, and we stated it in general form (§ 217). Now we are going a step farther, noting the causes of the fact, bringing it into relationship with other facts.

to the movements of the Earth and the stars. Nowadays the reverse reasoning is fashionable: from the fact, that is, that such scientific propositions are false, people try to infer that biblical theology is false (§ 487). Of those two methods of reasoning neither can be accepted by anyone who insists on remaining within the experimental field (§ 481). The scientific errors of the Bible merely show that we must not go to theology for the relationships obtaining between experimental facts; just as Hegel's scientific errors merely show that metaphysics is no better prepared than theology to supply those relationships. And that is all. The errors in question prove nothing as to any doctrines that metaphysicists and theologians may be pleased to set up outside the experimental field.

517. *b.* (§ 483). Inquiries into virtual movements when the movements belong to the experimental field are just a way of considering experimental relations; and therefore what has been said above applies to them also. If some term towards which virtual movements tend lies outside the experimental field, we need not deal with it here, unless an attempt should be made to return to experience by eliminating that term; but in that case we should again be going back to relations between experimental facts.

518. *c.* (§ 483). There remains the inquiry as to what *ought* to be done, the *precept* (§§ 325 f.). This is a class of relations that may lie entirely beyond experience, even when the related terms are experimental. What takes it out of the experimental field is the term "ought," which does not correspond to any concrete reality.[1] The question may still be asked, "And if an individual does not do what it is said he *ought* to do, what will happen?" That question leads to a consideration of virtual movements (*b,* § 483).

519. *Nexuses by which elements in theories are combined* (second problem stated in § 467). Let us begin with a few examples.

There is the case of chemistry when the atomic theory was in full vigour. Chemists worked on certain hypotheses and succeeded in explaining the facts of chemistry that were known and in foreseeing facts that were unknown and which experience eventually verified.

518 [1] *Manuale,* Chap. I, §§ 39-40.

Such are all scientific theories, and they have unmistakable characteristics.

520. But here now, for another example, is one of the so-called moral theories. It is of an entirely different character. There is no trace of any experimental verification of any sort. People ask how things ought to be, and they conduct the inquiry in such a way as to find certain relations that exist, or which they would like to have exist, among things. Imagine a chemist saying: "It is a pity that when mercury protochloride is exposed to light it should change spontaneously into mercury bichloride, a virulent poison. I shall therefore look for a chemical theory that will render such a thing impossible." Yet there you would have a widely cultivated type of moral theory.

521. Even apart from that type the difference between theories that allow themselves to be guided strictly by the facts and theories that try to influence the facts, is striking. Compare, for example, the atomic theory of modern chemistry and the atomic theory of Lucretius. The difference lies more in the character of the researches than in the greater or lesser experimental validity of the data and the conclusions.

522. In former times theories of natural facts were like modern moral theories. Later on they changed completely in outlook and became our modern scientific theories. Aristotle's treatise *De coelo* may be classed with modern treatises on morals. It cannot be classed with Newton's *Principia,* much less with Laplace's *Traité de mécanique céleste*. Anyone willing to read those three books one after the other will observe at once that Aristotle's is altogether different from the others in character and in the purpose of the investigation. There is no seeking the cause of such a difference in the ability or scholarship of the respective authors. Newton wrote a commentary on the Apocalypse well worthy of a place beside Aristotle's *De coelo.*

523. If, therefore, we set out to arrange theories according to the character of their demonstrations, we have to distinguish two types. In one the nexus consists entirely of logical implications of facts; in the other there is an added something that transcends experience

—some concept of necessity, duty, or the like. Finally, to complete our survey, we must further consider propositions in which the logical nexus is reduced to little or nothing—which are mere descriptions or narrations. In that way we get the three following classes:

Class 1. Descriptive propositions (§ 525)

Class 2. Propositions asserting experimental uniformities (§ 526)

Class 3. Propositions that either add something to experimental uniformities, or ignore them (§ 574).

524. Scientific theories consist of propositions of the first and second classes. Sometimes propositions of the third class are appended; and they may do no harm provided the non-experimental adjunct be superfluous; but they may impair the scientific character of the theory if the non-experimental adjunct affects conclusions. Sociological theories and many economic theories have hitherto made liberal use of propositions of the third class so affecting results. Such propositions must be eliminated if we would have a sociology or an economics of a truly scientific character.

Suppose we now examine the logico-experimental sciences with reference to the classes just mentioned. Here, however, we have to deal with them only in a very incidental way, since our main interest is in theories dependent upon social facts.

525. Class 1: *Descriptive propositions. Examples:* "I tried to find the density of pure water under an atmospheric pressure of 760 mm. of mercury; and I observed a maximum density at 4°." "Roman marriage was between one man and one woman at a time." The description may be extended to any length one wishes; but when it becomes at all protracted there is a danger that propositions of another class will creep in. The human being finds it very difficult to stop at mere description; he is always tempted to add explanation. To say, "The Greeks were hospitable to beggars," is a description; but to say, "The Greeks were hospitable to beggars *because* they thought that beggars came from Zeus," adds an explanation to the description. We could get back to pure description by saying, "The Greeks were hospitable to beggars, and there were some who said that they ought to be because beggars came from Zeus." The distinction may seem fine-spun, but it is a very helpful one; for slipping explanation covertly into description is a favourite device for obtaining acceptance for explanations devoid of a logico-experimental basis.[1]

526. Class 2: *Propositions asserting experimental uniformities.* In any statement of a uniformity there is something more than a description of happenings in the past; there is a forecast, more or less probable, of future happenings (§ 1068). If I say, "Under pressure of 760 mm. of mercury, water attains a maximum density at 4°," I say something more than I said in the description stated above (§ 525). I assert that if anyone puts water under those conditions he will observe a maximum density at 4°.

Note further that the last proposition contains a number of implicit assertions. It asserts that pressure and temperature are the sole determinants of density. If, for example, the electric tension of the atmosphere were also a determinant, the descriptive proposition would be *incomplete,* because I ought to have noted the atmospheric condition; but the proposition asserting the uniformity would be *false,* for if I were to make another experiment under different electrical conditions, I should not find the maximum density at 4°.

527. Suppose, instead of a hypothetical case, we take a real one. "I placed a thermometer in pure water, and I observed that the water began to solidify at 0°." My proposition is *incomplete.* I should have noted other circumstances—atmospheric pressure, for example. If I say, "Pure water solidifies at 0°," with no specifications as to other conditions, my proposition is *false.* James Thomson found that under a pressure of 16.8 atmospheres, pure water solidifies at a temperature of 0.129°. The proposition noted above, though false in the strictest sense, is customarily used by physicists because it is understood that the experiment is to be performed under the normal atmospheric pressure of 760 mm. of mercury and under other conditions well known to physicists. In that case there is no harm in

525 [1] This is not just the place to stop and consider how far the generic term "the Greeks" may be taken as exact.

such language; but if the conditions that are presumed are not accurately determined, if they are in the least respect uncertain, the proposition would have to be rejected. Of just such obscurities people avail themselves when they introduce conditions that cannot be taken for granted explicitly.

528. Metaphysicists imagine that experimental science deals with absolute propositions (§ 97), and on that hypothesis they reasonably conclude that in the statement, "Water solidifies at 0°," there must be something more than a mere epitome of experiments—there must be some principle of *necessity*. But that edifice crumbles—its foundations are weak. The scientific proposition, "Water solidifies at 0°," merely indicates that that fact has so far been observed and that *very probably* therefore it will be observed in the future (§ 97).

529. Someone might say: "That statement does not take into account the positions of the Sun and its planets in space. It is true that so far those conditions have not been known to influence the temperature at which water solidifies; but how can you be sure they will not do so in the future?" We can only say, "We are not sure." And we should have to give the same answer if someone were to assert that some day the Sun in its swift course will carry us into a four-dimensional space, or to a place where the laws of physics and chemistry will no longer hold. Every scientific proposition has to be understood as prefaced by the reservation "within the limits of time and space known to us." Beyond those limits lie probabilities, now slight probabilities, now great probabilities, but nothing more (§ 69-5).

530. It is laughable to reflect that though it is indispensable to state such reservations in sciences as advanced as chemistry and physics, there are people who think they are not necessary in a science as backward as sociology. But in any event we have no intention of quarrelling with them. Blessed indeed are they in knowing the essences of things (§ 19) and the necessary relations between facts. We, much more modest, are simply trying to discover such relations as experience discloses (§ 69-4); and if those good souls are right, it only means that we shall be discovering with great effort and after laborious investigation things that were revealed to them by metaphysical enlightenment. If the relations they talk about are really *necessary,* we cannot possibly find different ones.

531. Metaphysicists are still maintaining that one well-conducted observation is enough to establish a uniformity in chemistry and physics, and that therefore what is needed is a "higher principle" enabling us to draw just that inference—which certainly does not owe its existence to any great number of facts, since it has been drawn from only one. They are entirely wrong. Those many other facts are there. They are all the other similar facts that have been previously observed. Why is just one chemical analysis sufficient to determine the proportions in which two elements are combined in a compound? Because that fact falls into a group of incalculably numerous facts that have permitted recognition of the uniformity (law) of definite proportions. Why is one accurate observation enough to establish the gestation period of a female mammal? Because that fact is one of a very large group of facts which show that the period is constant (§ 556).

532. For that reason when a fact is referred to the wrong group, the conclusion is false. If one infers from the fact that there is a male and a female Phylloxera that all Phylloxeroi are born of males and females, so classing the Phylloxera with cases of sexual generation, one's inference is mistaken, for the case happens to belong to a category where parthenogenesis occurs. There is no "higher principle" to guide us. There is nothing but experience; and it shows that along with cases of sexual generation among Phylloxeroi there are cases of parthenogenesis.

533. Among propositions asserting uniformities, some give experimental "explanations" of facts. The explanation consists solely in putting the fact that is to be "explained" in relation with other facts. So one science, to wit, thermodynamics, "explains" why there are bodies (such as water) where the melting point lowers as pressure increases, and others where it rises. Such an "explanation" amounts to nothing more than placing that property in the substance in question in a relationship of uniformity with other properties in the same substance. Scientific explanations other than that do not exist.

534. It is inexact phrasing to say that celestial mechanics "explains" the movements of heavenly bodies by universal gravitation. Celestial mechanics has put forward the hypothesis that the movements of heavenly bodies satisfy the equations of dynamics; and down to our time the positions of heavenly bodies as calculated by dynamics have been the same, allowing for possible errors, as the positions obtained by observation. So long as that correspondence holds the hypothesis will be held sound. If it should fail to obtain some day, it will be modified.

535. What use can be made of facts in sociology, and how can uniformities be deduced from them? [1]

536. *Facts.* Facts are known through various sources that historical criticism sifts and appraises.[1] With the problems of historical criticism we are not called upon to deal specially here. We need concern ourselves merely with certain particular subjects that are of special importance to sociology.

537. *Numbers of facts.* It is evident that the greater the number of facts we have at our disposal, the better, and that perfection would be attained if all the facts of a given kind could be utilized. That, however, is altogether impossible, and therefore it is simply a question of a more or a less.

In assembling any great number of facts of a given variety two obstacles of differing nature are encountered. As regards antiquity, the sources yield facts in scant numbers. For modern times too many

535 [1] To find uniformities is really the purpose of this whole study; and step by step as we seek and find them we shall distinguish methods appropriate to the purpose from methods that are not. Actually, then, we might simply refer to the rest of these volumes as a whole. But it is helpful to have a general view of a subject and grasp it in its broad outlines. That is the purpose of the remarks following.

536 [1] De Morgan, *Les premières civilisations,* pp. 29-30: "The documents that constitute the foundations of history properly so called are of four different varieties: 1. Documents contemporary with events, inscriptions, coins, medallions, histories, annals, memoirs. 2. Archaeological documents, monuments, objects of one kind or another found on the ground or underground. 3. Narratives posterior to the events they describe. 4. Results of the various sciences . . . geology, zoology, botany, anthropology, ethnography, sociology, philology, which it is wise to supplement with data relating to industries, arts, commerce, scientific development, and so on."

are available to allow all to be sought out and quoted. To get them all together would in itself be a long and not very fruitful task. Then once they were assembled, no publisher could print the huge folios that would be required to hold them, and no reader would care to read them. What profit would there be in collecting all the accounts of all the strikes, big and little, that have occurred in all the countries of the world, and printing them in a large library of volumes?

Since records surviving from antiquity are relatively few, the modern custom is to quote all or nearly all writers who mention a given subject. That is well enough, and nothing else could be done, it would seem, in works of scholarship. That was more or less the method of the manual of Roman antiquities of Marquardt and Mommsen, of the dictionary of Greek and Roman antiquities of Daremberg and Saglio, and of other works of the kind. For the Middle Ages, the same may sometimes be done as regards literature proper; but many mediaeval sources still lie unpublished in European archives. For modern times materials are overabundant and no such thing is possible. A selection has to be made.[1]

537 [1] Critics at no great cost to themselves can always find some fact that has been omitted; and there are those who avail themselves of such omissions to condemn books which they could not by any means have written themselves. "You have omitted such and such a fact," they say, or, "You have used such and such an edition, and it is not the best." All that would be justifiable if the critic could add, "and the fact you omit is important for or against your theory," or, "The best reading of the best edition is equally important to you." Without that supplement the criticism is childish and betrays the mere fatuity of a pedant, sometimes well read, more often ignorant. That good soul M. Aulard, being too much in a hurry to find fault with Taine, had a comical adventure that reminds one of the proverb of the cat that, through too great haste, had blind kittens (see Cochin, *La crise de l'histoire révolutionnaire: Taine et M. Aulard*). Even as regards an insignificant detail deriving from Clement of Alexandria, Aulard's criticism is wholly wrong. Pareto, *"Un petit problème de philologie," Indépendance,* May 1, 1912: "After all, as regards the history of the French Revolution, it does not matter very much whether Taine gave an accurate or an inaccurate translation of a passage from Clement of Alexandria. M. Aulard could have overlooked the matter without the slightest embarrassment. But if he was bent on going into it, he should have done so with the time and attention required . . . and then he would have seen that the comparison drawn by Clement was exactly parallel with the comparison Taine wanted to draw, and so have abstained from a criticism destitute of any foundation." It is first-class comedy to catch M. Aulard condemning Taine for errors in

538. *Weight of facts.* The significance of facts is more important than their number. A single fact well observed and well described is of greater value than a very large number of facts carelessly observed and inadequately described.[1]

The pedantic custom of "complete bibliographies" has nowadays come into great vogue. A writer must quote all the writers who, well or badly, sensibly or stupidly, have touched on his subject.[2] As a rule he merely quotes them—he does not read, and much less master, them, and for the good reason—if for no other—that he would not have time for such a feat. But he transcribes the titles in an attractive index, and the more of them he gets in, the more he is admired by pedants and cephalopods. In determining the relations between facts or scientific laws, it would be better for him to master the principal authors and pay no attention to the others. Not even for knowing the history of a doctrine is it useful to read all the writers who have written on it; it is sufficient to centre on the chief types. It is laughable to see a person making a "complete bibliography" of the writers who have written on "income" and showing himself entirely ignorant of the phenomena known by that name and even more ignorant of their relations to other economic phenomena.

539. As usual, scholarship has gone to that extreme to avoid an-

transcription and making similar ones himself in quoting from Taine: *cf.* Taine's 10th ed., Vol. III, with Aulard's quotations: Taine, *tissus,* Aulard, *tissés;* Taine, *en chantant,* Aulard, *et chantant;* Taine, *et soulève,* Aulard, *il soulève.* Three errors in eleven lines! M. Aulard will say that they are insignificant, that they do not in any way change the meaning, that they do not affect his criticisms, that it is the part of a pedant to call attention to them. Excellent! That is just my point! And that is why I did not specify such errors in my review. But why did M. Aulard forget that golden rule and go carping at Taine? *Medice, cura te ipsum!*

538 [1] It is well known that in modern palaeography all manuscripts deriving from an archetype count as one only. The *Codex Ambrosianus* of Plautus, for instance, counts for more than all the other Plautan manuscripts.

538 [2] In *Indépendance,* Feb. 15, 1912 [wrong reference ?] Georges Sorel concludes the review of a book with a remark that applies to many similar cases: "This study, grounded on the strictest principles of the Sorbonne, and utilizing four hundred and twenty-two authors in its composition, affords an interesting example of the insignificance of the results that are achieved by the methods imparted by Lanson."

other, where it was a question of reasoning without giving facts. Of the two evils the lesser, and by far, is to give too many facts rather than none at all, and it is also better for the number of facts to be larger rather than smaller than is required for proof. Better even a "complete bibliography" of writers hastily read than complete ignorance of the literature of one's subject.

540. Leaving aside absolute certitude, which does not exist for the experimental sciences, and speaking only of greater or lesser probabilities, we have to recognize that for many historical facts such probability is slight, for others great, and for still others so great as to be equivalent to what in ordinary parlance is known as certainty. In that sense many facts are certain in general but uncertain in their details. It seems certain that the Battle of Salamis took place, but it is not at all certain that the details were just as Herodotus reports them. Indeed, to judge by analogy with other accounts of the kind, it is very probable that some of the details he gives are wrong. However, we do not know which. Even in times far closer to ours, it is "certain" that the Battle of Waterloo took place, but various details of it are still matters of dispute.

Following a method that will be explained in § 547, it is easy to see for oneself that when there are several accounts of a given episode, they often differ in particulars. In some of them it is possible to prove that particulars are wrong (§ 649), and any interpretation treating them as accurate would certainly lead to error. In that connexion, two pitfalls have to be avoided: on the one hand, the danger of basing theories primarily upon disputable facts—an error often made in investigations of origins; on the other hand, the temptation to reject any theory that is not supported by absolutely authenticated facts, as certain pedants nowadays seem inclined to do; on that basis all theories would be rejectable. We must find a just mean, framing our theories cautiously, sifting and selecting the facts and using them warily, always bearing in mind that the best of theories may show some small margin of error (§ 69 [5]).

What is said above is nothing peculiar to sociology: it applies to all the sciences, even the most exact. In using a table of logarithms to seven places one must know that beyond that point the logarithm cannot be guessed. Not so long ago the atomic weights of chemical elements were known only approximately. Now they are known with relative exactness, but absolute exactness we shall never have. From the days of Tycho Brahe down to our own, measurements of stellar distances have been brought closer and closer to perfection, but they were still very imperfect in Newton's time. Should scientists, on that account, have refrained from framing the theories of celestial mechanics, just to please a few pedants? Or indeed, to state the full truth, should they not rather forbear from theory now and forever? Absolutely exact measurements are not yet available, and they never will be.

We can go even farther. It was a fortunate circumstance for the foundation of celestial mechanics that in Kepler's time observations of the planet Mars were not very exact. If they had been he would not have detected an ellipse in the curve traversed by that planet and so would not have discovered the laws of planetary movement. It was also fortunate that he elected to study the movements of Mars rather than those of the Moon, which is subject to greater disturbances.[1]

540 [1] Bertrand, *Les fondateurs de l'astronomie moderne,* pp. 146-47: "Kepler was in a position to say, it is true, that an error of eight minutes was impossible on his part. That self-confidence saved the day. Had he been able to say as much of an error of eight seconds, all would have been lost. . . . Kepler was mistaken, in fact, in regarding the important advantage he had won over the rebellious and stubborn planet as one of those decisive victories that for ever end a struggle. Those great laws, eternally true [Bertrand might have dispensed with this discursion into metaphysics.] within reasonable limits, are not strictly mathematical. [They are a first approximation, the approximation of the elliptical movement so called.] Numberless perturbations are constantly deflecting Mars from his course, gradually freeing him from the frail bonds in which the fortunate astronomer thought he had shackled him for ever. For anyone going more deeply into the matter [Successive approximations], such irregularities once accounted for and become predictable bring a startling confirmation to the theory of attraction, which they enhance in importance in proportion as they make it clearer. But any premature acquaintance with them, which would necessarily have resulted from more accurate observations, would have wrapped the truth in unfathomable complications, and perhaps long have retarded progress in knowledge of the mechanics of the universe. For in that case Kepler would have had as good reason to reject the elliptical orbit as the circular orbit, and would have been forced to hunt for the laws of the irregular movement directly, at the risk of wearing out his stubborn patience and exhausting all his keen resourcefulness on insuperable obstacles." Whereas knowledge of the elliptical

What at that time was the work of chance must now be done by the method of successive approximations (§ 69-9). Every now and then the scientific theories of economics and sociology are challenged as disregarding certain particulars. That, instead, is a merit. One must first obtain a general concept of the thing one is studying, disregarding details, which for the moment are taken as perturbations; and then come to particulars afterwards, beginning with the more important and proceeding successively towards the less important.[2]

541. Suppose we have before us a text, or a number of texts, of a given writer. It (they) may be considered from three points of view: 1. As to what the writer thought, his psychic state, and how he came by it. 2. As to what he meant in a given passage. 3. As to how people of a given group at a given time have understood him. From the standpoint of the social equilibrium the importance of the queries increases from No. 1 to No. 3. From the objective standpoint No. 2 is virtually the only one to be considered, provided it be possible to establish a moderately exact relation between the writer's testimony and something objectively real. No. 1 is personal to the writer. No. 2 is impersonal, objective—the passage may be considered independently of the person who wrote it (§ 855). No. 3 relates to the writer's audience.

1. The ideas of a writer do not always present consistent unity,

movement led to the notion that the movements of the planets might be due to solar attraction. Then the theory of attraction was extended to the reciprocal influences of the planets upon each other and upon the Sun; and so the successive approximations of astrophysics were obtained.

540 [2] Deliberate disregard of certain particulars in a first approximation is oftentimes called an error, and those who make that criticism no more than confirm the old saw that "the silence that is golden never gets into lead." There are those who condemn one branch of social science for keeping distinct from other branches and imagine that to ignore one branch while dealing with another is to be either ignorant concerning it or neglectful of it (§ 33 f.). That criticism is different from the other, but it has an identical origin in a presumptuous ignorance of the character of scientific theories and the need of arriving at them by analysis. All the same, those good souls have to be thanked for not extending their censures beyond the limits of the social sciences. They might just as well censure an economist for not including cooking in his science, for cooking, as no one will deny, also contributes very considerably to joyous living (Pareto, *Cours,* §§ 2, 34).

not only because they vary with time, as may be seen in St. Augustine's *Retractationes* (*Opera,* Vol. I, p. 583) and other books of the kind, but also because in matters pertaining to sentiment an author may express differing and even contradictory ideas in the same text without being aware of it. When, therefore, one tries to ascertain his ideas on a certain matter, one may be looking for something that does not exist. Yet doing just that has now become the vogue. We have a pest of "psychological" studies of writers, which are, after all, mere collections of anecdotes and gossip serving as materials for the lectures and the light reading so especially dear to ladies of fashion who imagine that they are following the scientific movement in devouring them (§§ 858-59). It is also in style to wonder why a writer wrote what he wrote; and if one can somehow manage to discover that he wrote it in a moment of rage at a betrayal by a mistress, one thinks one has discovered America.

Beyond question, an author's views have some relation to the sentiments prevailing in the group in which he lives, and it is therefore possible, within certain limits, to gain from his views some light as to those sentiments, which, meantime, are elements in the social equilibrium. But it is curious that that is more especially the case with commonplace writers of mediocre talents than with eminent authors, those of great genius. The latter in virtue of their very qualities rise above the commonalty and stand apart from the mass of people. They therefore reflect less reliably the ideas, beliefs, and sentiments actually prevailing.[1]

2. When we know what a writer intended to say in a given text,

541 [1] Sorel well says in *"Quelques prétentions juives,"* pp. 217 f.: "Most often when we are trying to determine the historical rôle of a group of human beings, we study individuals to whom we think we can ascribe a capacity for representing, more or less perfectly, the spiritual force of the group at large; we note the sentiments, aspirations, philosophical conceptions, which those exceptional people have voiced. We construct from individual elements, in a word, that consciousness of rights and duties which according to our estimate prevailed in the group. Now and again historians have chosen to deceive themselves as to the reliability of the results obtained by that method, holding that 'representative men' are altogether determined by environment. Then again other writers, admiring the originality that not a few of such representative men evince, have seen creative geniuses in them. . . . Evidently, the truth lies somewhere between those two extreme views."

and provided we have reason to believe his testimony moderately veracious, we say that the text establishes certain facts. All documents called historical are substantially of that kind.

3. In addition to the facts usually made available in that way there are others which it is important for us to know. We have already seen, and we shall see more clearly as we go on, that the sentiments manifested in the beliefs and ideas of human beings are important factors in determining social phenomena; and it follows from this that sentiments and expressions of sentiments are "facts" as important for sociology as the "facts" that are actions. Even if the Battle of Marathon had never taken place, the conception the Athenians had of it remains a fact of great significance as regards the form of Athenian society. Thucydides, *Historiae,* I, 20, says that it is not true that, as the Athenian masses believed, Hipparchus was the tyrant when he was murdered by Harmodius and Aristogiton; but as regards the form of Athenian society the fact itself is less significant than the conception that the Athenian masses had of it. And among the forces exerting a powerful influence in determining that form was certainly the sentiment which found expression when the Athenians sang the praises of Harmodius and Aristogiton for killing the tyrant and making Athenians equals before the law.[2] So we arrive at the conclusion—it seems paradoxical but is not—that to understand the form of Athenian society it is much less important to know whether Hipparchus was really a tyrant, or even whether the whole story was not just a legend, than it is to know the ideas of the Athenians on the matter.

Does the famous oration on the war-dead of Athens that Thucydides puts into the mouth of Pericles repeat even approximately the words that Pericles actually delivered? We do not know, and for purposes of determining manners of feeling and thinking at Athens at the time, we little care. In all probability Thucydides

541 [2] Bergk, *Poetae lyrici Graeci,* Scolia, 9, 11, pp. 1019-20: "Mid branches of myrtle will I bear my sword even as Harmodius and Aristogiton when they slew the tyrant and made the Athenians equal before the law." "Mid branches of myrtle will I bear my sword, even as Harmodius and Aristogiton when they slew Hipparchus the tyrant at the Panathenaia."

wrote the oration in the spirit of the environment with which he was thoroughly familiar. It would be strange indeed that, inventing the oration out of whole cloth, he should have written it in such a way as to clash with attitudes with which his readers were as well acquainted as he (§ 243).

Nowadays there are people who say that Christ was a solar myth. Grant the point for the moment. Will the tremendous rôle played by Christianity, or rather by the sentiments manifested under Christian form in European society, be any the less important on that account? Sorel well says:[3] "As for the stigmata of St. Francis, we do not need to know just what those sores were like; but we do have to find out what conception the Middle Ages had of them. The conception was what influenced history, and that influence is independent of the physiological problem."

So, as regards a given country at a given period, the significance of what an author wrote lies not so much in what he meant as in what the people who read his book in that country at that time thought he meant.[4] There is a radical difference between a text considered as evidence of what a writer witnessed or thought—and used for the purposes of getting at the things he witnessed or thought—and a text considered as influencing its readers and used for purposes of determining the ideas and conduct of those individuals. When a text is considered from the biographical standpoint it is very important to know what the author intended to say. When a text is considered from the social standpoint such an inquiry is virtually irrelevant. The important thing is to know how the text was taken, even if it was taken upside down.

That point is not appreciated by people who think a text has an

541 [3] *Le système historique de Renan,* Vol. I, p. 37.

541 [4] Sorel, *"Quelques prétentions juives,"* p. 231: "Renan's judicious remarks are quite to the point here: 'In religious history, the significance of a text lies not in what the author meant but in what the requirements of the time made him mean. The religious history of mankind is a history of misunderstandings.' [And in a note he quotes Renan, *Histoire du peuple d'Israel,* Vol. IV, p. 193.] The remark also applies very well to secular history. The [German] Social Democracy has had to perform miracles of misinterpretation in order to pretend it was following Hegel" (§ 1101 [1]).

absolute meaning and has to be understood in its "true" meaning only. So they go hunting for that "true" meaning, and it turns out after all to be the one they like best—which gives them a chance to quarrel with anyone who does not see it as they see it.[5]

542. And in certain cases it is easier to know with certainty (very great probability) facts relating to expressions of thought than to know facts relating to conduct. There may, of course, be doubt as to the correctness of a text at our disposal; but once that doubt is removed, we have the fact itself before us and are not obliged to discuss it at second hand. Our knowledge of what Cicero says about Catiline is much more reliable than our knowledge of much of Catiline's conduct.

543. Literary compositions—works of the imagination, stories, legends, and the like—are generally of little value as sources for historical and geographical information. All the same, scarcity of documents sometimes forces us to depend on them for ancient times or for periods not extensively studied; but we must do so with great caution. To comprehend the situation more clearly, we might illustrate a method that we are to elaborate in § 547.

544. I have before me a short story by Alphonse Karr that contains allusions to Lausanne, Montreux, and Geneva.[1] Suppose we are faced by a problem such as ancient Greece presents to scholars of our day. Suppose some two thousand years hence Karr's story is the only surviving document in which Montreux is mentioned, and the scholars of that time are trying to ascertain the location of Montreux in respect to Lausanne and Geneva. Criticism shows that Karr is worthy of all confidence: he lived at a time when Montreux was still flourishing, and in a neighbouring country, France. Almost all wealthy and educated Frenchmen of his time made frequent

541 [5] Another point: Critical editions enable one to get back, with greater or lesser probability, to the archetype of manuscripts that have come down to us; but they cannot show the relations of the archetype to a writer's thought. We might not be able to get his thought altogether even if we had the original autograph. One need only think of what happens in our day of the printing-press. In reading proofs a writer often notices imperfections that escaped him when he was reading his original, especially if it has been dictated to someone else; and he makes changes in it.

544 [1] *"Pour ne pas être treize,"* pp. 8, 9, 78.

visits to Switzerland. It is very probable that Karr had personal knowledge of Montreux. He could have had, furthermore, no conceivable motive for concealing the truth. What he says may therefore be taken as the testimony of an eyewitness—better testimony than his could not be desired. A scholar ransacks libraries, studies, meditates, and he finds that one of Karr's characters passed through Montreux on his way from Lausanne to Geneva. Of course one has to be on one's guard against typographical errors—much like the miscopyings of scribes in the manuscripts of the old days. But no—that danger is dispelled by the author's own words: "I arrived at Montreux at about four o'clock. It is a village to the right of the highway bordering the lake as one comes in from Lausanne and stands some hundred paces back from the road. It is reached by a climb up over a narrow path that bristles with stones." No doubt therefore! It is really the road from Lausanne to Geneva, the road that has the lake to the left and the hills to the right as one comes in from Lausanne. Then comes another passage that confirms the others and dispels any suspicion of scribal error or textual interpolation. The same character in the story is returning from Geneva to Lausanne. "A half-hour later, the two friends departed for Lausanne. As they passed through Montreux, which stood on the height to the left, Eugène expressed a wish to go up to the village for a moment." Our future scholar will write a learned thesis, and deliver it before a society of scholars, showing that Montreux must have been located between Lausanne and Geneva; and who knows but what some archaeologist, following that lead, may even find the ruins of Montreux in the region so designated! And yet if one thing in this world is certain, it is that Montreux lies beyond Lausanne as one comes in from Geneva, and that in going from Lausanne to Geneva or returning from Geneva to Lausanne one does not pass Montreux.

Not a little of the information we have, or think we have, about antiquity has no firmer foundations than the inferences I have just drawn from Karr's story: and the certain error in his case shows the possibility of similar errors in classical scholarship.

545. Purely literary compositions, works of the imagination, stories, legends, are often valuable sources for knowledge of sentiments; and oftentimes indirect testimony of that kind is worth more than any amount of direct testimony. In his *Mimiambi* Herondas gives a parody of a counsel's plea before an Athenian court. The orator says, in substance, that if his opponent has prevented a famine by bringing grain into the city (or else, if he, the orator, has not performed such a public service) the fact ought not to militate against him in the eyes of the judges.[1] It is evident from the passage that it must have been a common opinion that judges were influenced in their decisions by considerations of benevolence or malevolence of the kind mentioned, quite aside from the merits of a case—otherwise the parody would lose all meaning. Its testimony therefore is worth more than any number of direct assertions (§ 572).

So many novels record prevalent opinions, and the opinions often correspond to certain facts and give synthetic conceptions of them that are much more valuable than anything that might be had from any amount of miscellaneous direct testimony.[2] When a book has many readers, it is highly probable that it reflects their sentiments and may therefore prove helpful in discovering them.[3] However, one has to make haste very slowly along such a path, for if we are too facile with our interpretations we may fall into serious blunders.

546. *Interpretations.* For the very reason that first-hand knowledge of facts is rarely available, interpretations are indispensable, and any-

545 [1] *Mimiambi,* II, 16: "If, then, piloting a ship from Achaea, he brought grain and put an end to the fierce famine . . ." Variant rendering (by Blass): "If I have not, piloting a ship from Achaea, brought grain and put an end to the fierce famine . . ." (Knox: "Perhaps he will say to you: 'I have come from Acre with a cargo of wheat and stayed the accursed famine.' ")

545 [2] Zola's *L'argent,* for example, gives a fairly accurate synthetic conception of life at the Paris stock exchange in the days of the Union Générale. Maupassant's *Bel Ami* gives a picture hard to match of the financial speculations of the politicians at the time of the occupation of Tunis by France, and of the part played by the press in those intrigues. Similar phenomena were observable later on at the time of the conflict between France and Morocco, following the Agadir affair.

545 [3] In great vogue towards the end of the eighteenth century in nearly all civilized countries, and in France in particular, was the doctrine that accounts all conduct logical and every non-logical action a "prejudice." The spread of the doc-

one resolved to do absolutely without them might as well not bother with history and sociology. But it is important to decide when, how, and to what extent they may, with a fair degree of probability, be trusted. That question, like all questions in the experimental sciences, has to be answered on the basis of experience.

547. There is one method that gives good results in many cases. Let *A* stand for a fact of the past. We do not know the "explanation" of it. So we find one—that is to say, we establish a relation between *A* and another fact *B,* by way of a certain interpretation. Now we have to ascertain whether the interpretation leads to plausible re-

trine may readily be judged from the fact that it affected even light literature—love-stories. For example, the younger Crébillon, *La nuit et le moment,* pp. 19-21:

"*Cidalise:* Truly now, Clitandre—you do not love Araminte? . . . (*Clitandre shrugs his shoulders.*) All the same—you have had her!

"*Clitandre:* Oh, that's different!

"*Cidalise:* So they say! It does seem to be different these days.

"*Clitandre:* Not just these days! The old days too!

"*Cidalise:* You astonish me! I thought this modern philosophy had changed all that.

"*Clitandre:* Well, I think myself that in such matters, as in many others, it has improved our thinking, but less by changing the things we do than by giving us a clearer understanding of why we do them. Now we seem not to be acting so much by chance. Before we learned to reason so well, we used to do the very things we do today; but we did them under stress of temptation, without knowing what we were doing, and with all the qualms of conscience that prejudice inspired in us. We were not any more virtuous than we are today, but we wanted to seem so, and there is no doubt at all that in those days a ridiculous prejudice spoiled many a good time. But at last we have been lucky enough to see the truth [Milord True and Milady Truth are the great divinities of emancipated religions.], and what a relief it is! Women have never been so care-free in society. There has never been so little affectation of virtue. You like her? Well, you take her—and she you! You are bored? You separate with as little ado as you began! You are right in saying that love figures very little in all that. But what was love but a desire that people chose to exaggerate in importance in their own minds—a sensuous impulse that they had been silly enough to represent as a virtue? [Less frivolous writers had said the same of the religious and other instincts.] Now we have come to see that pleasure is the only thing . . . and I take it that on the whole it has proved the height of wisdom to substitute so many pleasures for a few outworn prejudices that net very little esteem and a great deal of annoyance [for] those who take them as their rule of life." For a good understanding of the French Revolution such a passage is worth more than no end of direct description. Victor Hugo's *Les Misérables,* combined with, let us say, the novels of George Sand, gives a clear and exact conception of the epidemic of humanitarianism that swept all civilized countries during the nineteenth century.

sults. So if we can find in the present a fact *a* similar to *A*, connected in a manner well known with another fact *b*, also well known and similar to *B*, we use the parallel to "explain" *a*. If we do find the actual "explanation" *b*, the result is favourable to our method, and if we can find numerous examples, we may conclude that it gives fairly probable results. But if in trying to explain *a* we do not find *b*, that fact warrants suspicion of our method—there is one exception, there may be others. If we find even relatively few exceptions, little probability remains.[1]

548. In general the unknown has to be explained by the known, and the past is therefore better explained by the present than the present is by the past, though the latter method was followed by the majority of writers in the beginnings of sociology and is still followed by many (§ 571).

549. A certain amount of interpretation is nearly always necessary. A person reporting a fact does so in his own language, adding little or much to it from his own sentiments. To get at the fact we have to divest what he says of such accessories. That will be sometimes easy, sometimes difficult; but we must never forget the necessity, or at least the utility, of doing it. Travellers translate the notions they hear expressed in the languages of the countries they visit into words and ideas of their own. Their accounts oftentimes are now more, now less, at variance with the facts; and it is necessary, when such a

547 [1] We shall make frequent use of this method in the course of this work, so that we may here dispense with giving examples. We have already made some use of it, however, in § 544. We used it also, implicitly, in investigating the relations of the metaphysical method to experimental facts. Can that method lead, or can it not, to results verifiable by experience? Suppose we apply it to cases such as physics, celestial mechanics, or chemistry, where the experimental results are well known—or better yet, suppose we let Hegel do the applying, since he is so much admired by metaphysicists. If the metaphysical method leads to conclusions that are corroborated by long experience in those sciences, we shall have reasons for hoping that it will prove equally successful in other connexions—in social science, for instance, where experimental verifications are less practicable. If on the other hand, in physics, celestial mechanics, chemistry, it leads to conclusions that experience proves to be senseless, fantastic, idiotic, we shall have reasons for fearing that it will yield no better results in the social or historical sciences (§§ 484 f., 502 f., 514 [2]).

thing is possible, to retranslate in the inverse direction to get at the real states of mind of the people the traveller is describing.[1]

550. Similarly, it is in many cases unsatisfactory to get facts for sociology from translations, and if possible one should refer to the original texts. As usual, one need not go from one extreme to another. There are cases in which, let alone a translation, even a mere abstract is sufficient. It all depends on whether conclusions are based on the exact meaning of one or more terms; if they are, reference to originals is indispensable.[1]

549 [1] Reviewing Junod's *The Life of a South African Tribe,* Vol. I, *Social Life,* in the *Journal de Genève,* Aug. 25, 1912, the distinguished Egyptologist Édouard Naville writes: "One of the aspects of M. Junod's book that may prove most useful to students of very ancient philology is language. Primitive peoples almost always express themselves through metaphor. Anything even distantly approximating the abstract has to be rendered by something susceptible of sense-perception. On the other hand some altogether crude or commonplace act may be designated by the religious or ritualistic significance attached to it. Anyone not holding the key to such riddles is in danger of going completely wrong in his interpretations of words or phrases. I note, for instance, a custom that has also been observed in Egypt—the burial of broken vases or other objects with bodies in tombs. The Bantus do the same. On the grave of a man who has died they break all objects of no further value that belonged to him—old pottery, especially, and the handles of *zagaïes.* Everything his must die with him. That ceremony is called 'showing one's anger to the dead.' Now if we found such an expression as 'to show one's anger to the dead' in an Egyptian or Assyrian document, I doubt very much whether the most learned philologist would ever guess its true meaning: 'to break a dish.' I am afraid that, unfortunately, our translations may contain serious errors due to such ignorance. I believe that it is owing to such mistakes that many Egyptian texts, such as those in the Pyramids or the *Book of the Dead,* seem often so strange and so childish. We have not found the key to the metaphors that abound, especially in religious language. M. Junod's book is packed with such expressions. There are some on every page. I will mention two: 'to eat oxen' means to accept the purchase price, the *lobola,* of a wife, who may be bought for two, three, or even ten such animals. 'To eat two herds' is a legal term for wrongfully charging two *lobola.*"

550 [1] I have been very cautious in these volumes in quoting from languages I do not know. Such, for example, would be the case with the Talmud; though I hope the translations that I have used reproduce the text at least approximately. In any event, I refrain from any conclusion that might depend too much upon the strict meaning of some term. It would be very useful if some person who knows the oriental languages, Arabic, Sanskrit, Chinese, Japanese, and so on, would publish *literal* translations with philological notes of passages of texts serviceable to sociology. Until that is done, we shall have to feel our way along in the use we make of documents in those languages. Sumner Maine, *Early History of Institutions.*

551. The more important difficulties in understanding facts from other periods of history or other peoples arise from our coming to them with the mental habits of our own countries and our own times. We live, for instance, in countries and times in which there are written laws with a public authority to enforce them. It is hard for us, therefore, to understand the conditions prevailing among peoples who have not laws like ours, but unwritten customs with no public authority to enforce their observance.[1] By the very nature

pp. 8-9: "There is, however, another more permanent and more serious cause of embarrassment in drawing conclusions from these [old Irish] laws. Until comparatively lately they were practically unintelligible; and they were restored to knowledge by the original translators. . . . The translations have been carefully revised by the learned editor of the Irish text; but it is probable that several generations of Celtic scholars will have had to interchange criticisms on the language of the laws before the reader who approaches them without any pretension to Celtic scholarship can be quite sure that he has the exact meaning of every passage before him. . . . In what follows I attempt to draw inferences only when the meaning and drift of the text seem reasonably certain, and I have avoided some promising lines of enquiry which would lead us through passages of doubtful signification." [One might note, à propos of this passage, that in actual practice, Pareto used translations very much as he found them, and, in the cases of the modern languages, they were as often erroneous as not. Even a writer in his own language, Casati, he quotes in a garbled French translation. In the days when these volumes were in formation, scientific philology and textual criticism, as represented by the schools of Paul Meyer, Lanson and Bédier, were enjoying a virtual primacy in European university life. Pareto's efforts at textual criticism, especially in the classics, were made largely in deference to philological eminences which everyone, to use a phrase of Casanova, was ready to concede rather than go to the trouble of reading their books to see if their reputations were deserved. Pious enough in their intentions, those efforts were rarely prosecuted to decisive results and they remain, in the *Trattato* as well as in the *Cours* and the *Manuale,* as somewhat of a pedantic pose. This is said in no spirit of irreverence for Pareto's truly exceptional and marvellously assimilated culture, especially in the classical literatures, but just to keep certain aspects of this work in the light in which they belong.—A. L.]

551 [1] Maine, *Ibid.*, p. 286: "The learned Editors of the various Introductions prefixed to the official publications of Ancient Irish Law are plainly of opinion that such jurisdiction as any Irish Courts possessed was, to use the technical phrase, voluntary. The Law of Distress, in this view, was clearly enough conceived by the Brehon lawyers, but it depended for the practical obedience which it obtained on the aid of public opinion and of popular respect for a professional caste. . . . (pp. 38-39) Now, the want of a sanction is occasionally one of the greatest difficulties in understanding the Brehon law. Suppose a man disobeyed the rule or resisted its application, what would happen? The learned writer of one of the modern prefaces prefixed to the Third Volume of the Ancient Laws contends that the administration of the Brehon system consisted in references to arbitration; and I certainly

of their work scholars live partly in the past, their minds gradually acquire some of the habits of those periods, and so they are better able to understand the facts than people without that advantage. In our time, likewise, in certain cases there is a complete separation between fact and law—between, for instance, the fact of ownership and property right. There have been peoples and periods where fact and law in ownership were one and the same. In course of time the two were gradually divorced by a slow process of evolution, and now we find it difficult to picture one of the intermediary stages clearly to ourselves.

552. But all that is insignificant as compared with the difficulties arising from intrusions of sentiments, aspirations, interests, and non-experimental entities of a metaphysical or theological character. The fact, indeed, that we simply must not rest satisfied with the appearances, often very misleading, that such things give to facts, but must get back somehow to facts themselves, is what is guiding us in these volumes and constraining us to follow such a long and fatiguing road.

553. *Probability of conclusions.* Here we are called upon to find a solution for a problem of the kind solved by the calculus of probabilities, under the name of *probabilities of causes*. Take, for example, an urn containing a hundred balls, some of which are white, the others black—we do not know in what proportions, but we do know that all proportions are *a priori* equally probable. We draw a white ball. We are thereupon certain that all the balls are not black, but that all combinations allowing at least one white ball are possible. The probability that all the balls are white is 2/101—very small, therefore. The probability that the white balls may number at least

think myself that, so far as the system is known, it points to that conclusion. The one object of the Brehons was to force the disputants to refer their quarrels to a Brehon, or to some person in authority advised by a Brehon." *Idem, Ancient Law,* pp. 7-8: "It is certain that, in the infancy of mankind, no sort of legislature, not even a distinct author of law, is contemplated or conceived of. Law has scarcely reached the footing of custom; it is rather a habit. . . . It is of course extremely difficult for us to realise a view so far removed from us in point both of time and of association."

fifty is 765/1010—about three to one, that is. Now let us assume that according to some hypothetical law all the balls should be white. The drawing of a white ball corroborates the law in one instance. That verification gives the law a very small probability—about .02. The probability that the law will be verified more often than not is not very great either, being only about three to one.

554. When the calculus of probabilities first began to be studied, there was hope that it might yield exact formulae for finding probabilities of causes. The hope proved groundless because we have no means of establishing any likeness between practical cases and drawings of one or more balls from an urn. We have no knowledge whatever as to the number of balls in the urn, and little or none as to the *a priori* probabilities of the various combinations. Any help we might have hoped for from the calculus of probabilities fails, therefore; and we are reduced to evaluating probabilities approximately in other ways.

555. An extreme case would be the law of chemical combinations (§ 531). In that case we have an urn that very probably contains balls all of one colour. A single drawing is enough to determine the colour with great probability. We know, for instance, that all elements very probably combine in definite proportions (the proportion would be the colour, in the case of the balls). One experiment is enough to determine the proportion—one drawing, that is, to determine the colour (§§ 97, 531).

556. When a fact, *A,* can be classed with other facts, it is *a priori* probable that it follows the laws they follow. A single verification therefore yields a high probability that that is so (§ 531). The method, in other words, is first to observe similarities—then to verify. That is one of the methods most generally used for discovering experimental laws. Just so Newton, by way of hypothesis, extended to the heavenly bodies the laws of motion established for terrestrial bodies. He then verified the assumption on the movements of the Moon around the Earth, and so discovered the law for celestial bodies. His successors continued making verifications, all with good results. Now, therefore, his laws have a very high degree of probability.

Modern etymologists were able to observe in the fact the successive changes in a Vulgar Latin word that had developed into a modern French or Italian word. On the principle of *assimilation* (similitude) they extended the supposed laws they had discovered to other words, made verifications, and so constituted the science of Romance phonology.

The difficulty lies in establishing likenesses, because there is always something more or less arbitrary about them. In this as in other matters we have to appeal to observation and experience, which alone can yield trustworthy data. One of the characteristic errors of ancient writers was to infer similarities in things from similarities in names.

557. The principle of assimilation may yield apparently paradoxical solutions to some problems. Here is one such. Says Bertrand:[1] "Does not an uncertain event always have a definite probability, known or unknown?—By no means! What is the probability that it will rain tomorrow? There is none. . . . The King of Siam is forty years old: what is the probability that he will be living ten years hence? It is different for me than for someone who has talked with his physician, different for the physician than for someone who has received his personal confidences." Bertrand's inference would be that a person betting on the death of the King of Siam within the year would in no way be guided by probabilities, since none exist; and that is correct up to a certain point. In fact to issue an insurance policy on the life of one person alone would simply be gambling; but to issue insurance, as insurance companies do, on large numbers of people is to base a financial operation on the laws of probabilities. It may very well be that keeping to strict probabilities nothing can be decided as to the King of Siam. However, supposing Bertrand found himself behind the bars and were told: "You will not get out till either *A* or *B* dies. *A* is twenty years old, *B* sixty. Choose the man upon whose death you will have your liberty depend." We may guess that

557 [1] *Calcul des probabilités*, pp. 90 f.

Bertrand would choose *B* rather than *A*. Ought we say that he is choosing by chance, disregarding probabilities? In general if a happening *P*, assumed to be recurrent, is more probable than *Q*, shall we say that we are acting haphazard if, in the light of an interest, we elect a particular *P* in preference to a *Q*? Bertrand would say yes, because we are making but one choice and cannot have another chance. "Whether the King of Siam live or die, you have but one bet." But we can have other chances on other men of the age of the King of Siam, or on other similar cases of eventual happenings.

Let us assume that P_1 and Q_1, P_2 and Q_2, P_3 and Q_3 . . . are entirely different happenings, but that P_1 P_2 . . . are alike in the one respect that they have a greater probability than Q_1 Q_2 . . . on the assumption that the test may be repeated. I may now state the problem: In case I have only one choice between P_1 and Q_1, between P_2 and Q_2, have I a greater probability of winning by choosing P_1 P_2 . . . or Q_1 Q_2 . . . ? The answer is not doubtful: It is better to choose P_1 P_2. . . . Of course Bertrand might perhaps have done better by staking his release on the death of the twenty-year-older. All the same, if he did that in all similar situations, if in every act of his life he selected the less probable outcome as the more favourable, in cases where the test might be repeated, he would end by doing worse than he would have done by choosing the more probable outcome.

Bertrand solves the problem differently. For him there are objective probabilities and subjective probabilities. The type of the objective would be an urn containing known numbers of black and white balls, from which one ball is to be drawn at a time. The type of the subjective would be an event such as the death of the King of Siam, which depends upon circumstances only partially known. Bertrand bars subjective probabilities from his calculations.

558. That would amount to saying that it is just as well never to bother with probabilities and to act blindly in any event; for all probabilities are subjective, and the distinction that Bertrand would draw holds only as between a greater or a lesser amount of knowledge.

Says Bertrand, p. 90, "It will or will not rain [tomorrow]; one of the two events is certain right *here and now,* and the other impossible. The physical forces on which rain depends are as rigidly determined and are subject to laws as inflexible as the laws governing the planets. Would one dare inquire as to the probability of there being an eclipse of the Moon next month?" [1] Well—the same thing might be said of the drawing of a ball from an urn. The movements of the drawer are no less determined than the movements of the stars. The only difference is that we know how to calculate the latter but not the former. The regularity of certain movements depends upon the number of forces operating and the manner of their operation; and what we call manifestations of chance are the manifestations of numerous effects that are interwoven one with another. Bertrand himself gives the proof for that, p. xxiv: "The stamp of chance [That expression is wholly wanting in exactness.] is often imprinted, sometimes very curiously, on numbers that are inferred from the most rigorous laws. A table of logarithms is a case in point. For the 10,000 successive numbers in Vega's ten-place tables, I take the seventh figure in the logarithm. In this choice nothing is left to chance. Algebra governs everything; an inflexible law shackles all the figures. Nevertheless if one computes chances one should get, approximately, out of the 10,000 figures, the figure 0 1,000 times, the figure 1 1,000 times, and so for the rest of them: the formula conforms to the laws of chance [Interaction of causes]. Verification made, the seventh figure of the 10,000 logarithms was found 990 times to be 0; 997 times to be 1; 993 times to be 2; 1,012 times to be 4." However, that would not happen for the last figures of a table of squares, which not only bar certain numbers but also succeed each other in a definite order—the following: 0, 1, 4, 9, 6, 5, 6, 9, 4, 1. The eclipse of the Moon, which Bertrand mentions, may be compared to this latter case—the determination of the last figure

558 [1] And why not? Two men have no almanacs or calendars handy. One says to the other: "If it rains next month, you will give me ten dollars. If there is an eclipse of the Moon, I will give you ten." No one would accept such a wager; because *ordinarily* in our parts of the world it is more probable that it will rain during a certain month than that there will be an eclipse of the Moon.

in squares; but the comparison holds only if the person who is trying to forecast the eclipse is adequately equipped in astronomy. If he is not, the eclipse of the Moon is a fortuitous happening the uniformities of which he does not know. Drawing a ball from an urn may be compared to the first case, the seventh figure in Vega's logarithms; but naturally, only for a person who has a fairly advanced knowledge of mathematics. A person who does not know what logarithms and squares are can foresee nothing.

559. If a fact is certain (very probable) and is described with very great exactness, a theory developed with rigorous logic from it is also certain (has very great probability). Oftentimes the facts that sociology has to use have no high degree of probability and are, especially, not exact. Hence even though a rigorous logic be followed, a theory based on a single fact is not very probable; and it is even less so when strict logic gives way to inductions in which sentiments, "good sense," customary maxims, and the like, play a part. The remedy is to eliminate such inductions as far as possible, and then to consider not one but as many facts as possible—always judiciously, of course, as we have so many times cautioned (§§ 538 f.).

560. To increase probabilities nothing is quite so effective as the ability to make direct verification—experience in the strict sense of experiment. That is the chief reason why the laws of chemistry and physics, and even of astronomy, are overwhelmingly probable. For astronomy the experience lies in the verification of the actual location of the stars in the positions assigned them by theory. To a lesser but still very considerable degree, the probability of laws not susceptible of verification is enhanced if it can be shown that they are at least similar to other laws of which verifications occur.

561. The number of persons from ancient times down to our own who have asserted that they have seen ghosts is enormous. If probabilities increased with the mere number of observations, the existence of ghosts would have to be considered highly probable. Yet few people now believe in them. And why not? We must not answer the query by referring to alleged natural laws that would be violated by the existence of ghosts. That would be reasoning in a circle.

If the existence of ghosts could be proved, the laws would no longer stand. Nor can we say that apparitions are to be denied because they cannot be "explained." People who believe in ghosts or in other things just as mysterious can make the excellent rejoinder that neither can light (or electricity or magnetism) be "explained." Yet that in no way affects the reality of the facts that are assumed to prove their existence. The reality of a fact does not depend on the "explanation" that may be given of it.[1]

562. There are two cogent reasons why we do not believe (why we find very scant probability) in the existence of ghosts:

1. Direct experiment very frequently fails. If a person does not believe in wireless telegraphy, he need only purchase a little apparatus—they are for sale even in toy-shops—and he will see the thing take place before his eyes. There is no reason, therefore, for his believing in it in advance. But if he wants to see a ghost, conjure up the Devil, or make some other experiment of that nature, he will succeed or fail according to the state of mind he is in. "Out with unbelievers!" cries thaumaturgy. "Look, ye unbelievers!" says logico-experimental science.

2. There is no group of experimental facts with which apparitions can be identified. If, for example, it were experimentally shown that the Devil can be conjured up, there would be a certain probability in favour of ghosts, and *vice versa.* But unfortunately none of the categories of the ghost variety are susceptible of experimental verifications; so, for the present, the existence of ghosts has a probability that is exceedingly scant.

563. Following Newman, who was a cardinal of the Church, many authors have attached a great deal of importance to the cumulation of great numbers of independent slight probabilities as productive of a conviction of high probability.[1] There is some truth in

561 [1] The terms "explain" and "explanation" are here taken as indicating the *cause, origin, law* of a thing. If, as sometimes happens, by "explain" or "explanation" we mean relating a fact to other similar facts, we should not be in the situation here in question, but in the case examined in §§ 556-58.

563 [1] Newman, *An Essay in Aid of a Grammar of Assent,* p. 288 (quoted by Mansion, *Calcul des probabilités,* p. 77): "It is plain that formal logical sequence

that. That is the advantage of basing a theory on many different facts. But it is also partly false, in that it does not take account of the cogent persuasiveness of the mere possibility of making verifications.

564. Newman thinks that an Englishman believes his country an island simply because of a cumulation of little probabilities.[1] No, there is a more cogent reason, to wit, the *possibility* of a verification. It is not imperative that the person who believes England is an island should have made the verification himself, nor that he should know someone who had. The possibility of making one is enough, for then one could reason in this fashion: "What a reputation a man could make by proving that England is not an island! How much money that news would bring him! If no one has ever done such a

is not in fact the method by which we are enabled to become certain of what is concrete [So far Newman is in accord with experimental science in the sense that experimental premises are necessary. Logic of itslf gives nothing.]; and it is equally plain, from what has been already suggested, what the real and necessary method is. It is the cumulation of probabilities, independent of each other [There is much truth in that.], arising out of the nature and circumstances of the particular case which is under review [And the nature of our researches, experiments, and observations.]; probabilities too fine to avail separately, too subtle and circuitous to be convertible into syllogisms, too numerous and various for such conversion, even were they convertible" [That is true in some cases, untrue in others].

564 [1] *Ibid.*, pp. 294-96 (Mansion, *Op. cit.*, p. 79): "We are all absolutely certain beyond the possibility of doubt, that Great Britain is an island. We give to that proposition our deliberate and unconditional adhesion. . . . We have no fear of any geographical discovery which may reverse our belief. . . . Yet are the arguments producible for it (to use the common expression) in black and white commensurate with this overpowering certitude about it? Our reasons for believing that we are circumnavigable are such as these:—first, we have been so taught in our childhood, and it is so in all maps; next, we have never heard it contradicted or questioned. [He should have added: "yet the doubt was permissible by law and by custom."] . . . However, negative arguments and circumstantial evidence are not all, in such a matter, which we have a right to require. They are not the highest kind of proof possible. Those who have circumnavigated the island have a right to be certain: have we ever ourselves even fallen in with anyone who has? [An argument of scant value. The things we know directly or by direct testimony are very few as compared with the things we know indirectly.] . . . I am not at all insinuating that we are not rational in our certitude; I only mean that we cannot analyze a proof satisfactorily, the result of which good sense actually guarantees to us." [The French translator, P. Mansion, rendered "satisfactorily" by *manière complète*. Pareto: "And what can ever be done completely?"—A. L.]

thing, it is reasonably safe to conclude that it cannot be done." Suppose a prize of $10,000,000 has been offered to the man who could find a wolf on the Isle of Wight and that during the last hundred years no one has won the prize. That alone, and without any cumulation of scant probabilities, would convince one offhand that there were no wolves on the Isle of Wight. Suppose, on the other hand, the death-penalty awaited a man who said that England was an island or made any investigation in that direction. All of Newman's little probabilities would not dispel the doubt as to whether England were really an island.

565. Newman's followers have a purpose. They are trying in that indirect way to build up a case for the truth of historical traditions, and especially of religious traditions. But belief in such traditions is in no way similar to belief that England is an island. The traditions have no possibility of verification. The other thesis has. It has been known for centuries that England is an island, whereas a hundred and fifty years ago many things in Roman history were considered true that are now considered mere legend; and if the conclusions of Ettore Pais, the Italian scholar, are sound, we shall have to drop many other things from Roman history.

566. In finding out what Roman customs were like no cumulation of little probabilities, however large, is worth one relic discovered at Pompeii that anyone can see with his own eyes and make sure of.

567. According to Thucydides many Athenians were wrong as to the murder of Hipparchus (§ 541). Who could say how many other cases of the kind there must be, how many historical fictions we accept as true? But there is no such doubt as to the existence of the United States, even for people who have never been there and do not know anyone who has—there is always the *possibility* of verification. That is enough, considering the great profit there would be in proving the common belief mistaken.

568. From that it follows that before a theory can be considered true, it is virtually indispensable that there be perfect freedom to impugn it. Any limitation, even indirect and however remote, imposed on anyone choosing to contradict it is enough to cast suspicion upon it. Hence freedom to express one's thought, even counter to the opinion of the majority or of all, even when it offends the sentiments of the few or of the many, even when it is generally reputed absurd or criminal, always proves favourable to the discovery of objective truth (accord of theory with fact). But that does not prove that such liberty is always favourable to good order in a society or to the advancement of political and economic prosperity and the like. It may or may not be, according to the case; and that is a problem we still have to go into.

569. As far as establishing the experimental truth of a doctrine is concerned, there is no difference between the direct enforcement of acceptance of such a doctrine and the enforced acceptance of certain principles from which the doctrine follows. A constituted authority requires you to believe that 20 is equal to 24. Another comes along and says: "I am much more 'liberal'; I merely ask you to believe that 5 is equal to 6." It amounts to the same thing, for if 5 equals 6, two equal numbers multiplied by the same number giving equal products, it follows that the products of 5 and 6 multiplied by 4 are equal, and 20 therefore is equal to 24.

570. From the standpoint of scientific freedom, accordingly, Catholicism, which enforces acceptance of doctrine directly, and Protestantism, which requires merely that it be derived from Scripture, have the same value. "Liberal Protestantism" nowadays believes that it has taken a step in the direction of scientific freedom by dispensing with belief in the divine inspiration of Scripture; but it still clings to belief in a certain ideal of perfection, and that is enough to keep us out of the logico-experimental field. Nor can an exception be made for humanitarian dogmas, nor for the dogmas of the sex religion so dear to Senator Bérenger and other geniuses of the same magnitude. Let us keep the point strictly before us: There is no scientific liberty unless everything is open to doubt—even Euclid's geometry and three-dimensional space. It is ridiculous to say that one is disposed to grant liberty for "truth" but not liberty for "error"; for the point at issue is none other than to discover where the "truth" lies and where the "error"; and it cannot be settled if "error" cannot be defended by every possible reason that can be advanced in its favour. Only after such reasons have been validly refuted is judgment of error affirmed—pending further investigation. Many people fail to understand that, because in judging of truth or error they substitute a criterion of sentiment for the logico-experimental criterion.

571. The possibility of direct verifications, of new observations, is another reason for explaining facts of the past with facts of the present, which we are able to observe at our leisure (§ 548).

572. Take, for example, the following thesis: "In Athens political considerations and interests exerted a powerful influence upon judges in private litigations" (§ 545). We have direct proofs in the few pleas of counsel that have come down to us. Probability that the thesis is sound is increased by certain indirect evidence, such as allusions by Aristophanes (*Wasps*), and Herondas (§ 545 [1]). But it increases enormously in view of similar things going on in our day in Italy and France. If a person is still in doubt, he may, in a certain sense, make experiments. He can read the newspapers carefully and note cases in which such influence appears. He will find a goodly number of them every year and also see that for one reason or another not all of them get into the papers. He can then question people experienced in such matters and so placed as to be willing to tell the truth; and in that way, his direct induction will be confirmed by an indirect method.

573. Another example: There are those who say that witnesses in ages past to miracles or other supernatural happenings testified in bad faith. But what is the situation in our own time? Let us make an experiment! It will not be difficult to find among our acquaintances persons whom we know to be altogether honest yet who none the less assert that they have been in communication with spirits. Our age is sceptical. Past ages were credulous. The same thing must therefore have been the case, and even more easily, in the past.

574. Class 3 (as outlined in § 523): *Propositions that either add something to experimental uniformities or ignore them.* The problem is to determine the manner in which non-experimental principles influence theories, which, therefore, considered from the objective standpoint belong to Class II (§ 13). It is helpful to distinguish the case *A,* in which the introduction of non-experimental elements is explicit, from the case *B,* in which they are merely implicit. We are thinking of principal elements, of course. In concrete cases there may be a mixture of experimental and non-experimental elements. Just here we are considering cases where something is added to experimental uniformities, or where they are ignored.[1] *Authority,* for example, is here considered from the standpoint of what it adds to experimental uniformities.[2] The same may be said of *universal consensus,* the consensus of the majority, of the best-qualified individuals, and so on.

575. Under the aspect which we are now considering, we may classify types in the following manner:

TYPES OF CLASS 3

A. The abstract entities are explicitly introduced and are known independently of experience. Such knowledge is superior to experimental knowledge (§§ 576-632)

- A-α. Experience is given little or no place (§§ 582-612)
  - A-α1. Authority: divine authority, known through one or more individuals; authority of one or more individuals (§§ 583-90)
  - A-α2. Consensus of a number of individuals who are counted or weighed, or of mind in the abstract ("the mind") (§§ 591-612)
- A-β. Abstractions and principles determined independently of experience are incidentally and secondarily supported by experience (§§ 613-30)
- A-γ. Great importance is attached to experience, or there is a

574 [1] We shall meet with some of these types again in Chapters IX and X, and there examine the methods whereby, quite apart from logico-experimental inferences, certain conclusions are arrived at (§ 1397).

574 [2] In Chapters IX and X we shall consider the use that is made of authority in forcing acceptance of certain conclusions.

pretence of doing so. However, it is always in a subordinate rôle (§§ 631-32)

B. The extra-experimental origin of the abstract entities that are introduced is not explicitly stated. Either they are mere abstractions arbitrarily deduced from experience, or else they have an independent existence that implicitly may be non-experimental (§§ 641-796)

B-α. Myths, religious narratives, and other legends of the kind are historically real (§§ 643-61):

B-α1. Myths and the like taken literally without change (§§ 650-60)

B-α2. Myths and the like with slight and easy alterations in literal meanings (§ 661)

B-β. Myths and the like have a historical element combined with an unreal element (§§ 662-763):

B-β1. Myths and the like have historical origins, and the stories have undergone alterations in course of time (§§ 681-91)

B-β2. Myths and the like are made up of experiences wrongly interpreted and fallacious inferences from real facts (§§ 692-719)

B-β3. Historical facts are deviations from a type, or constitute a series with a limit or asymptote (in the mathematical sense) (§§ 720-32)

B-β4. Myths and the like are imitations of other myths. Two or more similar institutions are imitations of each other (§§ 733-63)

B-γ. Myths and the like are entirely non-real (§§ 764-96).[1]

576. A: *Abstract entities are explicitly introduced and are known independently of experience. Such knowledge is superior to experimental knowledge.* In that we have the chief characteristic of the

575 [1] We are to study the category A in this chapter; category B in the chapter following.

type. If, for instance, the thesis of unitary evolution be derived from experience we get a theory of Class I (§ 13). If the thesis be assumed *a priori,* we get a theory of Class II (§ 13). Generally in this case the principle is not deliberately removed from the experimental field. It is taken as self-evident, and one goes on from there, slipping unwittingly into a type B theory (§ 575). If, on the other hand, a "natural law" required by "natural reason" be assumed, one may talk about experience as much as one pleases: the theory will still remain in our group A above, because the *naturalis ratio* is superior to experience, and experience is allowed to confirm its dictates but never to contradict them.

577. At a given moment the centre of the Earth is at a certain distance from the centre of the Sun. Since the distance does not vary greatly, one can define (an arbitrary procedure) a roughly average distance and call it the distance between the Earth and the Sun. It may be hard to find such a thing, but it undoubtedly exists, and one can look for it experimentally.

578. But suppose we set out to discover who Jupiter is. The suspicion at once arises that the thing we are looking for may not exist. And even if we try to find what conception the Romans had of Jupiter, we may still be looking for something that never existed—there may have been more than one such conception. We can, indeed, following the method used above, outline a roughly average conception, and such a Jupiter, in part an arbitrary creation of our own (§ 103), can then be sought and found.

579. The belief that certain abstract entities exist independently of experience, and are not products of a partially arbitrary abstraction, is so self-evident, and so deeply rooted in the minds of most human beings, that the non-logical sentiment underlying it must be a very powerful one indeed. So we glimpse thus early one principle that may serve to guide us in a classification of social facts with reference to the determination of the social equilibrium. Moreover, since the belief has gone hand in hand with the progress of human societies, we are justified in surmising that however false it may be experi-

mentally, it may play a rôle of some practical advantage in social life.[1]

580. In dividing the theories of category A into genera, we may take as criteria the varying proportions of experimental inferences that they contain, starting from an extreme, A-α, in which there is little or none, going on through an intermediate genus, A-β, in which experience is mixed with other considerations, and arriving at another extreme, A-γ, in which, apparently at least, experimental considerations predominate.

By "experience" (§ 6) we here mean *direct* experience and observation. A person might say that he is going by experience (or observation) when he tries to find out from the Bible whether touching the Ark of the Lord leads to death and accepts that testimony without daring to doubt it or criticize it. Be it so—we are not going to argue over names. But just to prevent misunderstandings, we warn the reader that that is not the sense which we attach to the word "experience" (or "observation"), which here means either direct observation, or observation at second hand through testimony that has been sifted, discussed, criticized, as to whether people who touch the Ark of the Lord die or live on (§ 1482).

581. The motives we have for accepting an opinion are either external or "inner." The external motives, in addition to rigorously scientific experience, which we are not considering here, are chiefly authority and the consensus of other human beings, whether real or imaginary, with an appeal to "the mind"—to mind in the abstract. So we get our two genera A-α1, A-α2. The inner motives come down to accords with sentiments. They yield phenomena in which experience plays no part whatever, such as "living faith," which goes so far as to declare that it believes a certain thing because it is absurd. We are not going to deal with them just here, since we are now examining nothing but the means of logicalizing the non-logical. The living faith just spoken of is non-logical, but no attempt is made

579 [1] For the moment we can come to no conclusion on the point; but we are tempted to call attention to the possibility, in order to forestall the hasty inference that because we were rejecting the belief from the experimental standpoint we were intending to condemn it also from the social standpoint (§§ 72 f., 311).

to disguise it as logical. In the concrete case of a taboo without sanction there is, in a first stage, a preponderant element of living faith by virtue of which one believes without asking for reasons. It is possible, in a later stage, to discern the germ of a logical explanation, which is purely verbal and comes down to the bare statement: "We must do so and so because that is what we must do." [1]

Inner motives present other phenomena in which experience seems to play a part, and so we get the genera A-β and A-γ, and in addition, an element, primary or secondary, of category B. The semblance of experience is obtained either by assuming that what is really a product of sentiment is confirmed by experience, or else by effecting a confusion between objective experience and the expression of sentiment. This reasoning when pushed to the extreme gives us the introspection of the metaphysicists, which is nowadays assuming the new name of "religious experience"—the experience of the neo-Christians. In that way the person who frames the theory becomes judge (§ 17) and pleader at one time. The theory is judged by the sentiment that creates it, and the accord therefore cannot be other than perfect, and the judgment other than favourable (§ 592). But things are different when the judge is objective experience, which can, as it often does, deny the theory built up on sentiment—the judge is different from the pleader.

582. A-α: *Experience is given little or no place.* This substantially is the position of theologies and systems of metaphysics. The extreme case is the sanctionless taboo just mentioned, when one says, "You must do so and so, because you must." Then pseudo-logical fringes are appended in greater and greater abundance, until long legends or disquisitions are elaborated. As means of demonstration these pseudo-logical developments make lavish use of authority and universal consensus.

583. A-α1: *Authority.* Just here we are considering authority merely as an instrument for logicalizing non-logical actions and the

581 [1] Viewed under this aspect we might make casual note of this case under category A, leaving a more thorough study of it for Chapter IX, where we shall consider in their general aspects the explanations that human beings give of their conduct.

sentiments in which they originate.[1] Divine revelation, in so far as it is not considered a historical fact (B-α), belongs to this subvariety, as do also the divine injunction and the divine prophecy. After all, such things emanate strictly from human beings; and if we look closely we see that the point about divine will is made merely to justify the concession of authority to the individual represented as an interpreter of that will.[2] The Mohammedans accepted the authority of Mohammed just as educated people at a certain period in our history accepted the authority of Aristotle. The Mohammedans explained their acceptance on the basis of Mohammed's divine inspiration. The Christians pointed to the profound knowledge of the Stagirite. The two explanations are of an identical character. So it is easy to understand how they could be combined in periods of unenlightenment, and how the Virgil admired as a poet could become the wonder-working magician of the Middle Ages (§§ 668 f.).

584. Authority is frequently presented as an adjunct to other demonstrations. Its meaning, in such a case, is roughly as follows: "The facts we mention are so well known, the arguments we put forward so convincing, that they are accepted by everyone, or at least by all educated and intelligent people." That method of reasoning was

583 [1] To the general discussion of authority we shall return in Chapter IX.

583 [2] St. Augustine does, it is true, make a distinction between divine and human authority; but he goes on to point out that divine authority is known to us only through human beings and their writings. *De ordine* (*Opera,* Vol. I, p. 977), II, 9, 27: "Authority is partly divine, partly human; but the true, the fixed, the supreme authority is the one called divine." But those infernal demons are always on hand to lead us astray! "We must always be on our guard against the wondrous deceptions of aerial creatures, which are wont to deceive [human] souls—and very readily—by certain powers they have, notably their ability to foresee things within reach of the senses of their [aerial] bodies. . . . That authority, therefore, is to be called divine which not only transcends all human faculties in its sensible signs, but by its influence upon man (*ipsum hominem agens*) shows him how far it has deigned to stoop (*quo usque se depresserit*) on his account. Human authority, however, is often mistaken." But how are we to recognize the authority that is divine? *De vera religione* (*Opera,* Vol. III, p. 121), 25, 46: "God has seen fit that His intentions with the human race (*quid agatur cum genere humano*) should be made known through history and prophecy. But the credibility (*fides*) of temporal things past or future is a matter rather of faith than of knowledge; and it is our affair to decide to what individuals or what books we shall pin our faith for the proper worship of God, in which alone salvation lies."

widely used to prove the existence of witches, ghosts, and the like.[1]

585. The Protestant who sincerely accepts the authority of the Scriptures and the Catholic who defers to the Pope pronouncing *ex cathedra* are both doing the same thing under different forms. So also the humanitarian who swoons over a passage of Rousseau; so the socialist who swears by the Word of Marx or Engels as a treasure-store of all human knowledge; and so, further, the devout democrat who bows reverent head and submits judgment and will to the oracles of suffrage, universal or limited, or what is worse, to the pronouncements of parliaments and legislatures, though they are known to house not a few politicians of unsavoury reputation.[1] Each of such believers of course considers his own beliefs rational and other beliefs absurd. The man who admits the infallibility of universal suffrage as manifested by somewhat moth-eaten politicians flames with scorn at the mere thought that anyone can believe in the infallibility of the Pope, and demands that Catholics be deprived of the right to teach in the schools because their judgments are not "free." On the other hand, the judgment of a person who changes

584 [1] We shall revert to this matter in §§ 1438 f.

585 [1] One example from the host available: In Italy there was a great deal of opposition to a proposed bill giving a monopoly in life insurance to the State. It was alleged, among other things, that the mortality statistics used by the Government were not accurate. That was a scientific controversy, exactly parallel to Galileo's quarrel with the Inquisition as to the rotation of the Sun. The law being passed by the parliament, all controversies, the scientific included, were assumed to be settled, and on Sept. 16, 1912, the *Giornale d'Italia* published the following editorial: "As is well known, this newspaper has not been in favour of the insurance monopoly, basing its opposition on the economic theories of which Deputy Nitti has always been the avowed champion, on self-evident considerations of justice, and, finally, on considerations of expediency that, unfortunately, had to be given great weight in view of the hostility of European finance to Italy during the [Libyan] war. But our opposition ended the day the insurance monopoly was voted by the two houses of the parliament, because of our great and never disputed deference to the laws of the State. Now the Istituto Nazionale delle Assicurazioni has become a fact, as a state property, as a possession of the nation at large. All Italians who love their country must therefore hope that it will actually realize the purposes for which the law has established it, that it may extend the practical benefits of insurance to the people generally and become a potent factor in the economic progress of our country." One can detect not the slightest difference between that attitude and the attitude of the Catholic who, once the Pope has spoken *ex cathedra,* submits judgment and will to the Pope's decision.

views not from personal conviction, but in deference to the oracles of a political assembly, enjoys, it would seem, the quintessence of "freedom."

586. A person interested in arguments only as regards their logico-experimental force might suppose that when people are stocking up with such postulates they would see to it that they be as exact as possible and lend themselves to strictly logical development. But experience has shown that that is not the case, nor ought the fact seem surprising to anyone mindful of the logic of sentiments (§ 514). For purposes of persuasion postulates that may mean anything simply because they mean nothing exact are the best imaginable. And it is a matter of observation that different and sometimes opposite conclusions are often drawn from them. Oftentimes, besides, postulates of our A-α1 variety are combined and confused with postulates of our A-α2 variety. The logical element is often better in A-α1 than in A-α2.

587. An example or two of opposite conclusions drawn from the same principle.[1] There is a wide-spread belief that water and fire are pure and sacred. From it the Hindus conclude that the bodies of the dead ought to be either burned or thrown into the Ganges. The Parsees conclude, to the precise contrary, that neither fire nor water should be defiled through contact with a corpse.[2] It seems that in India cremation was not the absolute rule. It has, however, remained the principal means of disposing of the dead. The corpse is

587 [1] We shall be meeting others from time to time as we go on, for example, in § 873.

587 [2] Henry, *Le parsisme*, p. 16: "The Persians, as is well known, reject cremation after death as a horrible profanation. Here again let us stress the identity of standpoint underlying an altogether superficial antagonism. The common epithet of the Vedic Agni is *pàvaka*, 'the purifier.' Fire, say the Brahmans, is a thing essentially 'pure.' The dead body therefore must go through fire and leave all its impurities there, that the deceased may enter the eternal realm of Yama thoroughly cleansed. Thereafter the fire that has been so contaminated can be relieved of its noxious properties by a rite of lustration. Fire, reply the Mazdeans, is a thing essentially pure. Who, then, would dare violate its sanctity by thrusting upon it the abominable task of devouring the most loathsome thing in the world, a corpse in process of putrefaction? Arguments carried to extremes that touch are common enough in mystical systems."

laid on a pyre that has been reared in the midst of three fires kindled from the three sacred fires of the deceased (in case he has kept them burning). There it is burned with certain ceremonies that need not concern us here. "As fire watches over the Hindu's birth, so it watches over the fundamental phases of his life."[3] Corpses are still burned in India in our times. Says Sonnerat:[4] "As soon as the pyre has burned out, milk is sprinkled over the ashes, and the bones that have been spared by the fire are gathered up, put into urns, and kept till occasion offers to throw them into some sacred stream, or into the Ganges. The Hindus are convinced that the man whose bones get into a sacred river will enjoy infinite bliss for millions of years. Those living on the river-banks often throw corpses into the water whole, after hastening death by making the sick drink all the water they can hold, since they attribute miraculous properties to it."[5]

Herodotus, *Historiæ,* I, 140, discourses on the Persian, or at least the Magian, custom of having dead bodies devoured by birds or dogs. An epigram by Dioscorides says:[6] "O, burn not Euphrates, nor defile the fire in my person, O Philonimes. I am a Persian, yea, O my master, of the native Persian stock. To pollute fire is for us more bitter than grievous death. But wrap me in a shroud and give me to the earth. Nor do thou sprinkle my body with water, for I worship, O my master, the streams also."[7] Chardin describes the cemetery of the Parsees at Ispahan in Persia where bodies are exposed to ravens and birds of prey.[8]

587 [3] Oldenberg, *Religion des Veda,* p. 338.

587 [4] *Voyage aux Indes orientales,* Vol. I, p. 92.

587 [5] On p. 85 he remarks: "The Brahmans who worship Vishnu believe that the fire purifies them of their sins. Devotees of Siva (*Chiven*) claim that since they have been consecrated to the service of the god they do not need to go through fire, the sins they may have committed not being imputable to them. It is sufficient if they be sprinkled with lustral water, of which they make lavish use."

587 [6] *Greek Anthology,* VII, 162 (Paton, Vol. II, p. 91).

587 [7] Pliny relates that Tiridates refused to go to Rome by sea in order not to pollute the water by his physical necessities, *Historia naturalis,* XXX, 6 (Bostock-Riley, Vol. V, p. 428): *"Navigare noluerat, quoniam expuere in maria aliisque mortalium necessitatibus violare naturam eam fas non putant."*

587 [8] Sir John Chardin, *Voyage en Perse,* pp. 9 f.: "I shall describe a cemetery they have half a league outside the city of Ispahan in a very out-of-the-way locality. It is a circular tower made of heavy rough-hewn stones, and about thirty-five feet

588. Lack of definiteness in the premises explains how different conclusions may be drawn from them, but it does not explain why they are drawn; and in many cases we have no way of knowing whether the authority is the source of belief, or the belief (or rather, the sentiments underlying it) is the source of the authority. In many many other cases it is apparent that there has been a sequence of actions and reactions. Certain sentiments lead to the acceptance of a certain authority, and the latter in its turn reinforces the sentiments or modifies them; and so on over again.

589. The authority may be of one or more individuals; and if it

high and ninety in diameter. There is no door or other entrance. . . . When a body is to be placed in that tomb three or four of their priests climb to the top of the wall with ladders, hoist the corpse up with a rope and let it down inside along the upper shelf. . . . There is a sort of trench in the middle, which I saw to be full of bones and garments. The dead are laid fully clothed on little stretchers and placed side by side, so close as to touch, all around the tower and close up to the wall. . . . I could see bodies recently arrived, and still intact as to the feet and hands, which were naked; but much disfigured about the face, because the crows which flock about the cemetery and live by hundreds in the immediate neighbourhood attack that part of the body first. . . . Some fifty paces from the tower stands a little stone house . . . whence the high-priest watches to see in just what manner and on what part of the body the crows begin their work. . . . He does not have to wait long, for at least some bird will soon alight on the corpse and begin at the eyes. . . . In order not to frighten the scavenger the priest performs his observation through a little hole, noting which eye is first attacked and under what circumstances, basing thereon conjectures as to the status of the deceased in the other world and the future of his children and heirs in this. The right side is supposed to be the good one. . . . So I was told generally in all the countries where there are Parsees; but then again I have met individuals who denied all such magic or superstition."

If a man who does not know how to swim or is unable to do so is thrown into the water, he sinks and is drowned. However, in a day gone by it was held that if he floated it was because he was innocent. It was also held that it was because he was guilty (§ 956). Father Le Brun, in his *Histoire critique des pratiques superstitieuses,* Vol. II, pp. 256 f., notes the striking contradiction. He mentions cases where innocent people floated: "The defendant, a woman, was tied the way victims used to be tied for the cold-water test, and hurled from the top of a very high bridge into the river; but by the intercession of the Holy Virgin she remained afloat and the current bore her safe and sound to the shore. . . . It is quite clear that such miracles stand in conflict with the cold-water test. They kept the innocent afloat through a visible protection of God that has been made manifest in a hundred other such miracles. But by a surprising whimsicality that caused the adoption of the cold-water test, some were of opinion that innocent people sank in the water, while only the guilty kept afloat."

is confirmed by direct observation, it does not overstep our subvariety A-α1. Yet oftentimes the consensus is not based upon direct observation, but is merely taken for granted on the basis of certain sentiments held by the person asserting it; and then we get an instance of our subvariety A-α2. That is the case when there is an appeal to "universal consensus." It is certain that no one has ever been able to establish any such consensus by consulting all the human beings who have lived or are living on earth, and that the majority of them would not even understand the questions to which they are presumed to have given all the same answer. Such a claim, therefore, has to be translated somewhat in this fashion: "The thing, *in my opinion,* ought to enjoy universal assent," or else, ". . . the universal assent of people whom I consider wise, sensible, well-informed," and the like. The second assertion is by no means the same as the first.

590. The principle of authority holds even in our present-day societies, not only for the ignorant, and not only touching matters of religion and morality, but even in the sciences, especially in those branches with which a person is not directly familiar. Comte made this point very clearly, though he later drew erroneous consequences from it.

591. A-α2: *Consensus of a number of individuals who are counted or weighed; or of mind in the abstract* ("the mind"). The consensus may be invoked to show that certain things are inconceivable—an "infinite" straight line, for example. That is the situation in scientific or metaphysical abstraction, and we are not concerned with it here. On the other hand, the consensus may be alleged with reference to propositions the contraries of which are perfectly conceivable—the existence of gods, for instance. That situation does lie within our province.

If universal consensus, or the consensus of a majority or even of a few, is explicitly adduced as testimony to experience, we get the narrations of experimental science or, if the testimony overreaches experience, narrations of our group B. Here we are to deal with those cases only in which the consensus operates in and of itself and is put above experience. It may involve two things foreign to the experimental domain: (1) the fact of consensus; (2) the implications of the fact.

592. 1. *The fact of consensus.* It might be proved by statistics—a certain number of individuals are questioned and their answers noted. In such a case the fact would be experimental. But generally that is not done; the consensus is taken for granted, or at the most verified by some hasty experimental or pseudo-experimental investigation. When the consensus is alleged to be of "all men," experimental proof is absolutely out of the question, even when the "all" is limited to living persons without reference to the dead. It is impossible to question all human beings living on earth, or to make many of them even understand the questions for which an answer is desired. The same applies to a consensus of majorities, even if totals are confined to a specified territory.

To avoid such embarrassments, epithets are commonly resorted to: the consensus invoked is the consensus of all "intelligent," "rational," "honest" men, or the majority of them (§ 462). Then directly or indirectly one recognizes as intelligent, rational, honest, only people who share the opinion that has been decorated with the universal consensus (§ 1556); and so, by a splendid reasoning in a circle, it is undeniable that the opinion enjoys that consensus in fact.

To avoid the circle, it would be necessary for the qualities required in the people consulted to be independent of the opinions and determined only by general considerations, such as competence in given connexions. So one might invite the opinion of a farmer as to a given crop, and the opinion of a scientist on a problem in science; and that would be taking us from the question of consensus back to the question of authority. To remove the embarrassment of statistics not possibly obtainable and still to escape falling into the circle, the appeal is made to an abstract, undefined, and undefinable "mind," which is, after all, the mind of the person claiming the consensus, presuming the latter from the assent of his own mind, which he baptizes as "mind" in the abstract. So we get the introspection of the metaphysicists and of their successors, the neo-Christians. From the counted vote, which it is impossible to obtain, we move over to the assent that is weighed with loaded scales, and the number of the votes gradually comes down to the single vote of the person who started the voting in order to prove his theory (§§ 402 f., 427). All that takes us outside the domain of experience, which could alone show the alleged consensus either of all men or of the majority of men, or even of certain individuals selected for qualities independent of the opinion desired.

593. 2. *The consequences of the fact.* Let us assume the hypothesis most favourable for the purpose in view and suppose that the fact of consensus has been substantiated by experience to a fair degree of probability.[1] It is ordinarily inferred that the idea expressed in the consensus must all of itself correspond to reality; in fact for some metaphysicists it *is* reality. Even if they no more than assert a *necessary* correspondence with experimental reality, they are overstepping the bounds of experience. Experience by no means shows that when a very large number of people have an opinion that opinion corresponds to reality. All the way along from the belief that the Sun plunged into the ocean at night down to the countless beliefs in magic, we have examples of manifest errors that have been regarded as truths by vast numbers of people. When therefore one asserts that the opinion of the majority is in accord with experience, one is quitting the domain of experience. Such an assertion can be accepted only on non-experimental grounds (§ 42).

Here, again, the reasoning in a circle helps. If the objection is raised that human beings in large numbers have believed in witches, we answer that such people were neither intelligent nor well informed; and if we are asked how the intelligent and the well-informed are to be recognized, we reply that they are people who believe only in things that are real. After that we are in a position to assert in all confidence that the opinions of intelligent and well-informed people always correspond with realities (§ 441).

593 [1] As we have already said (§ 591), we are here ignoring the scientific case in which the probable existence of such an experience is inferable from the consensus.

If, to avoid the circle, we resort to the consensus of "competent" individuals, the competence being determined independently of the opinions desired, we are still left outside the domain of experience if we assert that their opinions are in accord with reality. Experience shows that the opinions of the "competent" are oftentimes wholly at variance with realities, and the history of science is the history of the errors of experts. Such opinions may therefore be used only as indicating a greater or a lesser probability of an accord between a theory and reality, the chances varying with the state of knowledge and the competence of the individuals expressing the opinions—never as an experimental proof of the theory, which can be furnished only by direct or indirect experience—and if that fact is not taken into account, we depart from the logico-experimental field. In the logico-experimental sciences the prerogative of judging (§ 17) belongs to experience. In certain cases it may be delegated to "competent" experts, provided they be chosen in a manner independent of the character of the reply desired; provided the problem submitted to them be stated with adequate clarity; provided they be truly acting as representatives of experience and not of this or that creed; and provided, finally, their decision may always be appealed to the supreme tribunal of experience.

594. When, again, the method chosen is to assert that universal consensus is itself reality, "creates" reality, it is generally understood that such consensus is not of human beings of flesh and blood, but of a certain ideal man; not of the minds of individuals taken one by one, but of an abstraction called the "human mind," or "the mind." And since the metaphysicist fashions the abstraction to suit himself, it is obvious that in gratitude to its creator it will eventually assent to anything he pleases.[1] Thence, in due course, arise such formulas

594 [1] Controversies as to the correspondence of concepts to objective reality are nowadays confined to metaphysics and its appendages in the social sciences. In days gone by they were very common in the natural sciences. Even geography was affected by that disease, as witness Strabo, *Geographica,* I, 4, 7-8 (Jones, Vol. I, pp. 245-47). He quotes Eratosthenes, who was claiming that disputes as to the precise boundaries of the continents were a waste of time because, there being no exact boundaries, such territories could not be divided off exactly. But Strabo comes back, saying among other things: "Who, in speaking of three parts and calling

as that the "inconceivable" does not exist, or that to know a thing one has to "think" it. The correspondence between the notions of the abstract mind (which in the end proves to be the mind of the author of the theory) and reality becomes self-evident, either because such ideas are in themselves reality, or because, if some little room is graciously made for experience, the mind creating the theory appears as both pleader and judge (§ 581).

595. In the concrete cases of arguments appealing to universal or majority consensus, experience is overreached in the two ways mentioned: by presuming an assent that is not experimental, and by drawing from it inferences that are not experimental either. All reasonings of the kind are further wanting in the trait of definiteness. Anything calculated to lend precision or strictness to the theory is left unexpressed. Much is made of universal or majority consensus without any inkling being given as to how it has been obtained, whether opinions have been counted or weighed, how and why it is presumed. Commonly, one gets vague formulas such as: "Everybody knows . . ." "Every honest man admits . . ." "No intelligent person denies . . ." The most patent contradictions are purposely disregarded. Universal consensus is adduced to prove the existence of God to an atheist, overleaping the fact that the very existence of the atheist who is to be converted, or controverted, destroys the universality of the assent.

The theory that the conceptions of "mind" in the abstract must necessarily accord with experience is explicitly stated only by some rare metaphysicist. Ordinarily it is slipped in implicitly. When one asserts that "everybody knows," that "nobody denies," that $A = B$, it is insinuated or suggested, rather than shown, that experimentally A and B will prove to be equivalents (§ 493).

each of them a continent, has not first had the idea of the whole that he is dividing into such parts?" He then goes on with an argument that forces a smile: "If there are two princes, one of whom claims all Libya and the other all Asia, how decide which of them is to get Lower Egypt?" Poor Strabo must have been momentarily out of his mind! He lived at the time of the Roman Empire, and he might have remembered that such disputes were settled not by the arguments of geographers but by force of arms.

596. All that is left loose and indeterminate; for if it were made definite and positive, the fallacy in the reasoning would become apparent. When it is asserted that human beings and animals have a certain law in common (§§ 419, 421, 449), we are not told exactly to what thing or things the term "law" is applied; whether by "human beings" and "animals" all men and all animals are meant, or only some, and how they are selected; on what observations of fact the assertion is based; and what conclusions are to be drawn, scientifically, from the supposedly established existence of such a law common to men and animals. All that is, and is left, wrapped in fog, and the argument in which such indefinite terms figure can appeal only to sentiments.

597. If the facts are considered in themselves, it may seem strange that educated and intelligent people could ever have imagined that experimental uniformities were to be discovered in any such way; stranger still that they should have had so many disciples, and their theories been admired—I do not say understood—by hosts and hosts of people; and strangest of all that there should be those who think they understand disquisitions on the "one" and the "multiple," formulas such as the "Being creates beings" of Gioberti, or abstractions such as that "goodwill" of Kant which *"is esteemed to be good* not by the effects which it produces, not by its fitness for accomplishing any given end, but *by its mere good volition—i.e.,* it is good in itself" (Semple translation).[1]

598. But since, far from being singular, strange, extraordinary, such cases are common, ordinary, the rule, they must obviously all be effects of some cause as cogent as it is general; and we begin to suspect that the cause is to be sought not so much in the value of the arguments, which is exactly zero, as in the strength of the sentiments that they disguise. If that should prove to be the case, the main thing in metaphysical theories would be the sentiments and not the arguments; and so, to stop at the arguments and judge a

597 [1] *Metaphysik der Sitten,* p. 12 (Semple, p. 4): [For the phrase of Gioberti, see his *Introduzione alla filosofia,* Vol. II, p. 204; and for a similar phrase, "being produces being," p. 194.—A. L.]

metaphysical system by its theories would be not unlike judging the strength of an army by the uniforms of its soldiers. It might also prove that this again was one of the many cases in which erroneous theories have their social usefulness, a fact that would contribute, in a subsidiary way at least, to their long survival, the influence of the underlying sentiments still continuing to be the main thing.[1]

599. Proof by consensus is often dissembled under a mask that is ostensibly, but not actually, experimental. That is the general rule in introspection. In experimenting on oneself, one assumes, without explicitly stating as much, that the experiment will be valid for all other people, or at least for all reasonable, intelligent, "thinking" people. Descartes begins his experiment on himself by assuming that everything that he has hitherto believed is unreal, false.[1] Then he runs on: "But shortly, as I was so trying to think everything unreal, I became aware that I, who did the thinking, had to be real; and observing that the truth 'I think, therefore I am' was so solidly grounded and so certain that all the most extravagant hypotheses of the sceptics were not able to shake it, I concluded that I could accept it without misgiving as the first principle of the philosophy I was seeking." It is evident from the whole essay that Descartes's purpose is not just to exhibit his personal sensations. He is trying to establish a thesis that will hold for others too. On close inspection, his argument is seen to contain several implicit assumptions: 1. That his thesis, "I think, therefore I am," has a meaning for others as well as for himself. 2. That others will accept the thesis. 3. That the thesis when so accepted will be something more than a collective illusion. Moreover, he crosses swords in advance with possible critics, and that betrays his conviction that his thesis has to be accepted by all who understand and reason aright. That is the usual procedure with metaphysicists: they have some thought or other and then, be-

598 [1] This is not just the place to deal with the question. Here we are considering theories primarily as to their accord with experience. However, we have often had occasion to wonder why and how they came to have such wide-spread appeal, and we shall see the answer more clearly as we proceed (Chapters IX and X and specifically § 1468).

599 [1] *Discours de la méthode,* IV (*Œuvres,* Vol. VI, p. 32).

cause the thing seems thus and so to them, they presume that every intelligent human being has to be of their opinion; and that for them is equivalent to the assent of all rational beings, or at least of a very engaging abstraction that they call the "human spirit," and which no mortal man has ever seen or knows anything about.

600. To conceal a fallacy it is often helpful to adopt an impersonal mode of expression. Descartes, for an example right at hand, says, *Ibid., loc. cit.,* p. 39 (italics mine): "But if *we* did not know that all within *us* that is real and true comes from a perfect and infinite being, however clear and distinct *our* ideas might be, there would be nothing to assure *us* that they had the perfection of being true." The pronoun "we" designates people impersonally; but who are those people—those "we's"? All the same, Descartes must have known perfectly well that the majority of people living on earth had never heard of his theory, that of those who did know of it many could make neither head nor tail of it, not a few denied it, and only a very very few agreed with it. And the question still stands: Why should a person not agreeing accept the thesis? If an experimental proof were possible, Descartes would have made haste to answer, "In view of the proof!" But there is no such proof; and there can be no question, either, of any consensus, whether universal, or of a majority, or even of any great number. It only remains for Descartes and his disciples to say, "We are right because we are right."

601. Spinoza is looking for a "first and general cause" for motion (blessed was he to know what that meant!). He observes that we must admit nothing that we cannot clearly and distinctly perceive (again italics mine); [1] "and since *we* clearly and distinctly perceive no other cause except God—that is to say, the Creator of matter—it becomes manifest that no general cause is to be admitted except God." But who, pray, are the people designated by the pronoun "we"? Assuredly not all human beings—for the reasons already given; and since not all, how is one to go about selecting the few, the many, who are to be blessed by inclusion among the "we," and

601 [1] *Renati Descartes principia philosophiae,* II, 11-12, and *Scholium a* (p. 60).

separating them from the reprobates who are to be left in the outer darkness? Spinoza "clearly and distinctly" sees God as the "cause" of motion—and what luck! But there are plenty of people who not only do not "clearly and distinctly" see God as the "cause" of motion, but who do not even know what "God" or "matter" can possibly be.

602. What has been said above may be repeated for any number of metaphysical propositions, and it also applies to what is known nowadays as Christian experience, which is merely a new name for a thing many many centuries old—and to wit, introspection (§§ 43, 69-2, 431).

603. What we have been saying attacks only one aspect of the problem we have set ourselves with reference to the numerous propositions of the type. It is undeniable that many such propositions have been accepted by learned, intelligent, and sensible people; and if one insists on sticking to a theory of logical conduct, it is all the more difficult to understand how such a thing could happen, the more clearly it is demonstrated that such propositions are destitute of any foundation whatever in experience and logic. We have to look in some other direction for the solution to the problem, therefore.[1]

604. In practice the subvarieties A-$\alpha 1$ and A-$\alpha 2$ seldom appear entirely separate: ordinarily they are combined, and lend each other mutual support; and they may even be re-enforced by arguments of our category B. A thing that is accepted mainly on authority is taken as further confirmed by the accord of "reason" and experience plus consensus. Introspection, for instance, yields a principle; the principle is assumed to be confirmed by the authority of the individual performing the introspection; then by the assent of others as determined in the ways just described, and sometimes further by pseudo-experimental arguments.

605. We have another example in Catholic doctrine. The Vatican

603 [1] We are not yet ready for the solution (§ 598). Suffice it for the moment to understand clearly that we are here considering just one aspect of the problem, and the aspect which from the social standpoint is perhaps the least important: the accord of such theories with experimental reality.

Council unequivocally asserts that "God, the beginning and end of all things, may be known of certainty from created things through the natural light of human reason. . . . Nevertheless it has been pleasing to His wisdom and goodness to reveal Himself and the eternal decrees of His will to the human race through another, the supernatural, channel."[1] Here A-α1 and A-α2 are closely conjoined, and in such a way that no conflict can arise between them. Experience is not asked whether faith can show one thing and reason another, for the answer would have to be in the affirmative, and a negative answer is desired. The method used to make the answer negative is the method used by all metaphysics—by all beliefs which try to get along without reference to experience. It lies in a declaration that the answer has to be negative, and that only the reason that agrees with faith is fit to be called reason. An unimpeachable demonstration is thus obtained, since every tautology is unimpeachable.[2]

605 [1] *Acta et decreta Sacrosancti et Oecumenici concilii Vaticani, cap.* II, § 1 (Schaff, Vol. II, p. 240): *"Eadem sancta mater Ecclesia tenet et docet Deum, rerum omnium principium et finem, naturali humanae rationis lumine e rebus creatis certo cognosci posse; . . . attamen placuisse eius sapientiae et bonitati alia eaque supernaturali via se ipsum ac aeterna voluntatis suae decreta humano generi revelare."*

605 [2] *Ibid., cap.* IV, §§ 1-4 (Schaff, pp. 247-49): *"Faith and Reason.* It has all along been and still is the consensus of the Catholic Church that there are two orders of knowledge to be distinguished both as to the principle and the matter (*objecto;* Schaff: "distinct both in principle and also in object.") As regards the principle, we know on the one hand by natural reason, and on the other by divine faith. As regards the matter (*objecto*), in addition to such things as natural reason may attain, mysteries that lie hidden in God are set before us for our belief, which, unless they were divinely revealed, could never be known. . . . (§ 3) And even if faith is higher than reason, there can never be any real conflict (*vera dissensio*) between faith and reason." There is an *a priori* reason why things have to be that way: "The same God that reveals the mysteries and inspires the faith has bestowed the light of reason upon the human soul; and God cannot deny Himself, nor can the true ever contradict the true." And there we are back with our tautologies again! Nobody is saying that the true can contradict the true. The claim is that one of the things called true is not true. Furthermore, all the argumentation is beside the point, once it is granted that God is omnipotent. All that need then be said is that God has willed things in that way. Why, then, all the palaver? Because the human being will have his logic, and he has to be humoured in one way or another! "And (§ 4) not only are faith and reason never in conflict, but they mutually support each other, since right reason shows the foundations of faith and in the light of faith perfects our knowledge of things divine." *Canones et*

606. St. Thomas works out a proof that is substantially the one adopted by the Vatican Council. He equates the processes of reason and faith with "truth," and thence concludes that they must be equivalents, since two things equal to a third are themselves equal.[1]

607. It is interesting to note that in their disputes with the pagans the Fathers of the Christian Church base proofs of their religion on the accord existing between it and the principles of morality, especially sex morality. If one forgets for the moment that logic is pointless outside the experimental field, and then reasons logically, it would seem that where there is an Omnipotent Being a thing should be moral because it is willed by Him, and not that He should exist because He wills what is moral. But thinking not of logical but of persuasive force, one sees at once that, especially in a debate with pagans, the persuasive force may lie in the dependence of the existence of God on morality. The pagans had certain moral principles in common with the Christians. Hence the expediency of starting with them to demonstrate the existence of the Christian God.[1]

608. Heckling the pagans on the matter of their gods Tertullian says, *Apologeticus,* XI, 11, "I ask you therefore whether they [the men who you say became gods] deserved to be exalted to the heavens or hurled into the pit of Tartarus, which, you now and then say, is the place of infernal punishments." And he mentions the various sorts of rascals who are in torment there and who, he asserts, are perfect replicas of the pagan gods. That is a sound and most dev-

decreta concilii Tridentini, sessio III, *De fide,* 3 (Schaff, Vol. II, p. 253): "If anyone shall maintain that divine revelation cannot be corroborated by external evidence (*externis signis*) and that the human being can be brought to faith only by inner personal experience and inspiration, let him be anathema."

606 [1] *De veritate Catholicae fidei contra Gentiles,* I, *proemium,* 7, 1 (*Opera,* 1570, Vol. IX, pp. 6-7): "It results that those things which are naturally inherent in the reason are true, in as much as it is impossible to conceive of them as false. [The basic principle of all metaphysical systems. Without it metaphysicists would go out of business.] Nor can one believe that the dicta of faith are false, since it is divinely confirmed in so obvious a manner. [But what the unbeliever denies is that the faith of the believer is obviously confirmed by God.] Since, therefore, only the false is opposite to the true, as is manifest if one consider their definitions, it is impossible for the aforesaid truth of faith to be contrary to those principles which the reason knows of nature."

607 [1] See, further, Chapters IX and X.

astating demonstration if the appeal is to sentiment, since the sentiments associated with the idea of a divine being and those associated with the idea of a rascal are absolutely repugnant to each other. But it is a demonstration devoid of the slightest logico-experimental value; for if it is asked why the pagan gods are rascals, it is hard to know what answer to make, unless it be that they violate some divine command. But along that road we bring up, as usual, on a tautology.

One can prove as much on the very authority of the sacred doctors. Christian writers blame the pagan gods for fornications. But why is fornication a crime, or if you prefer, a sin? Says St. Thomas: "If among the heathen simple fornication was not deemed illicit because of the corruption of their natural reason, the Israelites, enlightened by divine law, considered it illicit."[1] But if it is divine law that makes it illicit, how can fornicaton serve to demonstrate that the law declaring it illicit is divine? That is reasoning in a circle.

609. Just so reason the Holy Fathers of the Humanitarian Church in our day. They begin by calling "good" anything that is beneficial, and "bad" anything that is detrimental, to the greatest number, the People, the proletariat. Then they conclude that it is "good" to work for the advantage of those estimable souls, "bad" to work against them.

610. Christians could have adopted one of two courses to be rid of the pagan gods: they could have held them to be entirely imaginary, or have conceded them a reality that had its place in the new religion. There was no question of explaining the conceptions of the gods on the basis of non-logical conduct, not only because science was far from being sufficiently advanced for doing such a thing, but also because it would have struck a serious blow at the general principles of the Christian faith itself. In point of fact, the Christians pursued both the courses mentioned, and preferably the second—a thing not difficult to understand, since the second is more acceptable

608 [1] *Summa theologiae,* II^a^ II^ae^, *qu.* 104, *art.* 2 (*Opera,* Vol. X, p. 219, *Utrum fornicatio simplex sit peccatum mortale*): *"Quia apud gentiles fornicatio simplex non reputababur illicita propter corruptionem naturalis rationis, Iudaici autem ex lege divina instructi eam illicitam reputabant."*

to a living active faith that sees doings of God, angels, and devils everywhere. That is why, not so very long ago, Van Dale's book on the pagan oracles was considered offensive to the Christian religion, and Fontenelle's polished paraphrase of it even more so. For similar reasons, in our day many Christians shut their eyes to the quackeries of spiritualism and telepathy.

Christians perceived instinctively that if they took the view that the pagan oracles had nothing supernatural about them, they ran a danger of seeing the same theory extended to their own prophets, and that one of the best proofs which they thought could be offered of the truth of their religion would in that way be seriously shaken. To regard oracles, instead, as doings of devils had decisive advantages. It respected a principle common to Christianity and paganism—that there could be prophets and oracles—and furthermore drew a distinction between good ones and bad ones. The good ones, we hardly need add, were the prophecies, the bad ones the oracles, the ones being works of God, the others, of the Devil.

The same is to be said of miracles. Neither paganism nor Christianity denied that they were possible, but each called its own miracles true and the miracles of the other false—and the Christians added, for good measure, that the Devil often mimicked the miracles of God. For many long centuries mankind fed on such reasonings, which after all are no worse and no better than many current in our own time.

611. Nowadays a new belief, which retains the name of Christianity, is trying to replace traditional Christianity, rejecting the supernatural that for centuries was a prominent element in it and was also prominent in the Gospels.[1] It finds its main expression in

611 [1] Piepenbring, *Théologie de l'Ancien Testament,* pp. 22-24: "If the idea that Jehovah was the only god of Israel and that the Israelites were not to worship any other gods can be carried back as far as Moses, we cannot go that far back with absolute monotheism, which does not appear definitely in Israel till a much later date. . . . Not only the people but the kings, and Solomon himself, who had built a temple to Jehovah, either were addicted to cults of foreign gods or else favoured them—which proves that they regarded such gods as real. . . . Schultz rightly observes that in view of the vivid realism of the ancients, the first impression could never have been that the gods of other peoples were mere figments of

so-called Liberal Protestantism and to a lesser degree in Catholic Modernism. Just as primitive Christianity kept the principal traits of pagan morality, changing the theology, and indeed took advantage of the common morality in order to justify the change, so this neo-Christianity keeps the morality of traditional Christianity, changes the theology, and justifies the change by the common morality. Just as Jove was dethroned by the God of the Christians, the Divinity of Christ is now disappearing to make room for the Divinity of Humanity, Jesus being worshipped only as the exemplar of the "perfect man." Instrument of this transformation is universal consensus as revealed by the inner experience of the Christian. The good souls who resort to it are not aware that they get out of the Gospels only what they read into them themselves, and that they might just as well get their theories out of Virgil's *Aeneid* or any other book of the kind.

612. That delicious Plato has a simple, easy, and effective method for obtaining universal consensus, or if you will, the consensus of the wise. He has it delivered on call by one or another of the speakers in his dialogues, with the result that the consensus, at bottom, is only Plato's assent, though it is readily swallowed by people whose fanciful palates are tickled by such things. In the *Theaetetus*, 153, Socrates asks: "So then—motion you take to be good for soul and body, and the opposite not?" Theaetetus, at a nudge from Plato, replies: "It would seem so."[1] But had there been a third party to the argument, he might have answered, "I do not know, O Socrates, what on earth you are talking about!" And in that case, good-bye to your consensus, whether universal, or of the wise, or of human reason, or of any other conceivable brand.

Plato, however, does not appeal his theories to universal consensus

the imagination." It is easy to see that for Piepenbring the one true God is the God of Israel, and that all other gods are false; but it is less easy to see how he can prove such a point by rejecting the supernatural origin of the Bible. If we are to trust to inner experience, why is Piepenbring's better than somebody else's that leads to opposite conclusions?

612 [1] Σ. Τὸ *μὲν ἄρα ἀγαθὸν κίνησις κατά τε ψυχὴν καὶ κατὰ σῶμα, τὸ δὲ τοὐναντίον*; Θ. *Ἔοικεν.*

directly. He seems in fact to despise judgments by large numbers of men, counted, but not weighed.[2] The assent that he puts into the mouths of his characters represents the assent of mind in the abstract, and serves but indirectly to build up the theory—it is the rough mass of marble from which the artist in due time will extract the statue.[3] In that way he manages to create a confusion between consensus and the assent of the abstract mind, which is after all his own mind.

613. A-β: *Abstractions and principles, determined independently of experience, are incidentally and secondarily supported by experience.* As noted above, people find it difficult to abandon the experimental field altogether, and sooner or later they try to get back to it, for after all practical life more than anything else is the thing that counts. Theology and metaphysics do not wholly disdain experience, provided it be their servant. They take great pride in showing that their pseudo-experimental inferences are verified by the facts; but the believer and the metaphysicist already knew, prior to any experimental investigation, that the verification would turn out wonderfully, since a "higher principle" would never permit it to do otherwise. In their explorations in the realm beyond experience they satisfy a hankering that is active and even tyrannical in many people

612 [2] *Crito,* 44. Speaking of the *hoi polloi,* Socrates alleges that "since they cannot make sure whether anybody is wise or witless, they prefer to act at random." If the *Laches* is not by Plato, it voices Platonic ideas, and that is all that concerns us here. In that dialogue, 184, Socrates asserts point-blank that the majority view is to be disregarded:

"*Socrates.* What, Lysimachus—you would assent to anything a majority of us approved of?

"*Lysimachus.* What else could I do, O Socrates?

"*Socrates.* And you, too, Melesias, you would do the same? If you wanted advice as to the proper training for your son, would you follow the majority of us here, rather than a person who had been taught and trained under good masters?

"*Melesias.* I should follow the latter, O Socrates. . . .

"*Socrates.* . . . because, I suppose, if we would have a sound judgment, it could better be obtained from knowledge than from numbers."

612 [3] Ritter, *Geschichte der Philosophie alter Zeit,* Vol. II, p. 257 (Morrison, Vol. II, p. 227): "It was his [Plato's] advice that one should adopt such portion of [common] opinion as seemed plausibly sound and then subject it to severe examination as a basis for philosophy. He regards the formulations of [common] opinion as good points of departure for philosophical research."

for knowing not only what has been and is, but also what ought, or must necessarily, be; and, meantime, in professing to have taken experience into account—whether well or badly matters little—they escape the opprobrium of going counter to the scientific current, or even to plain good sense. But the facts that they take into account are facts selected for a definite purpose, and serving no other purpose than to justify a theory preconceived—not that it needs any justification, but just for good measure! The part assigned to experience may now be insignificant, then again very considerable; but, large or small, it is always within those limits and under those conditions. The doctrines of Comte and Herbert Spencer are types of this class.

614. The disciples of such doctrines regard them as perfect—and how could it be otherwise? They are at one with their masters both in thought and in sentiment, and they cannot see how any objection can be raised against a doctrine that in addition to satisfying both intellect and soul-hunger also has the support of such "experimental" verifications.

615. Viewed from a standpoint not strictly experimental, but didactic rather, and as contributing to the progress of science, such doctrines may be useful. They represent a transitional stage between theories based wholly on blind faith—between strictly theological, metaphysical, or ethical notions—and a definitely experimental state of mind.[1] The chasm between the two worlds is too great to be taken

615 [1] The theories of Lucretius, which are borrowed from Epicurus, have little if any experimental value; but there is an element of truth in what Lucretius says of them, especially if his remarks be applied not to the Epicurean system only, but to philosophical doctrines in general: *De rerum natura,* I, vv. 62-63, 66-67, 78-79:

> "*Humana ante oculos foede quom vita iaceret*
> *in terris oppressa gravi sub religione . . .*
> *primum Graius homo mortalis tollere contra*
> *est oculos ausus primusque obsistere contra . . .*
> *quare religio pedibus subiecta vicissim*
> *obteritur, nos exaequat victoria coelo.*"

("When human life was lying foully on the ground, oppressed by a deadening religion . . . a Greek, a mortal man, was the first who dared lift his eyes against it and resist. . . . And lo! religion, lying now under our feet, is in its turn trampled to dust, and the victory exalts us to the skies.")

at one leap; a bridge has to be provided. It is already something that people should be making a little room for experience and not standing exclusively on what they find or think they find in their inner selves. Even when experience is recognized merely for purposes of verification *a posteriori,* a very important forward step is being taken —a step so important that it has not yet been taken by many people, beginning with those who think they can get their lottery numbers from dreams and ending with our liegemen of the "categorical imperative."

616. Once experience is admitted (it matters little how) within the theological edifice, the latter begins to crumble—such portion of it, of course, as stands within the experimental domain, for the other wings are safe from any attack by experience. And the dismantling would become root-and-branch complete but for the interposition of a factor of great moment—the social utility of certain theories that are experimentally false.[1] So great is the need of such things which human beings feel that if one structure happens to collapse, another is straightway reared of the same material. That was the case with Positivism, which was, at bottom, just one of the numerous varieties of metaphysics: the old metaphysics fell for a brief moment, and then at once came to life again in positivistic form. Positivism is now threatening to crumble in its turn, and another metaphysical structure is in process of erection to take its place. That happens because people obstinately refuse to separate what is in accord with experience from what is beneficial to individual or society, and obstinately insist on deifying a certain entity to which they have given the name of Truth. Let *A* stand for one such thing that is useful to society; it is recommended to us, or required of us, by a certain doctrine of faith *P,* which is not experimental and often cannot be if it is to be accepted by a majority of the people in a given country. The doctrine holds sway for a more or less extensive period of time. Then if

616 [1] We shall deal with this matter thoroughly in Chapter XII. It is extraneous to the subject at present in hand. But this passing allusion was in point to explain why it is that the theological and metaphysical structure has collapsed completely, or virtually so, within the natural sciences, while it has held together longer in social theory and may perhaps never disappear in social practice.

experimental science has or acquires some prestige, there will be people to step forward and assert—inspired, though they do not always realize as much, by considerations of utility—that the doctrine or faith in question *must* be in conformity with experience; and other people will come forward to combat and ridicule that view. But since society cannot do without the thing *A,* some of the defenders of the old faith *P* will merely replace it with a new faith *Q,* no less discordant with experience. So years, centuries, go by; peoples, governments, manners and systems of living, pass away; and all along new theologies, new systems of metaphysics, keep replacing the old, and each new one is reputed more "true" or much "better" than its predecessors (§ 2340). And in certain cases they may really be better, if by "better" we mean more helpful to society; but more "true," no, if by the term we mean accord with experimental reality. One faith cannot be more scientific than another (§ 16), and experimental reality is equally overreached by polytheism, Islamism, and Christianity (whether Catholic, Protestant, Liberal, Modernist, or of any other variety); by the innumerable metaphysical sects, including the Kantian, the Hegelian, the Bergsonian, and not excluding the positivistic sects of Comte, Spencer, and other eminent writers too numerous to mention; by the faiths of *solidaristes,* humanitarians, anti-clericals, and worshippers of Progress; and by as many other faiths as have existed, exist, or can be imagined. Equally remote from the field of experience are Jupiter Optimus Maximus and the Jehovah of the Bible; the God of the Christians and Mohammedans and the abstractions of the neo-Christians; the categorical imperative, and the goddesses Truth, Justice, Humanity, Majority; the god People and the god Progress, and as many other gods as people in such infinite numbers the pantheons of theologians, metaphysicists, positivists, and humanitarians. That does not mean that belief in some of them or even in all of them may not have been beneficial in its time, or may not still be. As to that nothing can be said *a priori*—experience alone can decide.

The metaphysical ethics of the European *bourgeoisie* has of late been assailed and weakened by the metaphysical ethics of Socialism, which in its turn is now under fire from the metaphysical ethics of Syndicalism (§ 2002). Out of all this battling one thing has developed to draw people closer to an experimental attitude towards all such ethical systems: more or less distinctly people have become aware of their contingent character. *Bourgeois* morality, in view especially of the support it had in religion, was assuming a pose of absolute truth and that pose it has lost in the course of the past century after its many brushes with those fortunate rivals.

617. In the natural sciences the religious and metaphysical disintegration is still going on, with mere oscillations backward or forward, due to the fact that scientists too live in society and are more or less swayed by the opinions, beliefs, and prejudices prevailing in it. Experience, which once began timidly to lift its voice in the natural sciences, is now lord and master within them and ruthlessly banishes any *a priori* principles that try to assert themselves against it. Such scientific freedom seems to us an altogether natural thing because we are living in an age in which it is almost everywhere unrestricted. But we must not forget that down to two centuries ago, and less than that, a scientist could not discuss his science without first protesting that he was using experience only on matters irrelevant to faith. At that time it was wise on his part to take that subordinate position, since it was the only way to get a foothold within the fortress that was soon to fall.

618. The freedom enjoyed in the natural sciences is not yet enjoyed in sciences that have any bearing on social life. Save in the case of the religion of sex [1] the secular arm no longer reaches the heretic and the unbeliever—at least directly. But he is handed over to popular indignation and hostility, which ever rise to safeguard this or that principle or prejudice—a thing oftentimes promotive of the well-being of society. Indirectly public authority still makes the weight of its hostility felt by those who depart from the dogmas of existing governments even on strictly scientific matters.[2]

618 [1] *Cf.* Pareto, *Le mythe vertuiste*.

618 [2] For such reasons many Italians have had to live in foreign countries. In Prussia Socialists are barred from teaching in universities. In France dissidents from the Radical-Humanitarian religion are persecuted in every way—so the chair

619. The "historical" method opened the door for experience to make its way into some of the sciences from which it had been barred, and so served as a transition, beneficial from the strictly logico-experimental point of view, for bringing sociology closer to the level already reached by the natural sciences. Curious the confusion still obtaining in the minds of many people as to the "historical" and "experimental" methods.[1] The historical method, when it is—as it seldom is—genuinely historical and has no intermixture of metaphysical, sentimental, patriotic, and other similar reflections, is just a part of the experimental method. Its object is to study some

of Assyriology was refused to Father Scheil, one of the foremost authorities in that field. Of him De Morgan writes, *Les premières civilisations,* p. 36: "In Europe today hardly four or five scholars of real authority are to be counted in the field of Assyriology, and among them is Fr. Scheil. . . . His name will always be associated with his masterly translation of the laws of Hammurabi and his deciphering of the Elamite texts, a feat he accomplished without the help of a native interpreter." A chair at the Collège de France was withheld from Father Scheil on the pretext that as a priest he would lack the impartiality required for dealing with subjects connected with biblical history. But then, with no regard whatever for the glaring inconsistency, that excuse was tossed aside when it came to providing a chair in the history of religions for the ex-priest Loisy, famous for his bitter attacks on Catholicism. One may suspect that in the two parallel cases it was a question first of punishing an enemy and then of rewarding a deserter from the hostile camp. Mme. Curie was rejected by the Académie des Sciences for considerations in no wise scientific.

619 [1] Maine, *Ancient Law,* pp. 2-3, asserts that the Homeric poems contain hints as to the primitive forms of concepts of law (italics mine): "If by any means we can determine the early forms of jural conceptions, *they will be invaluable to us* [a]. These rudimentary ideas are to the jurist what the primary crusts of the earth are to the geologist [b]. They contain, *potentially,* all the forms in which law has subsequently exhibited itself [c]. The haste or the prejudice which has generally refused them all but the most superficial examination, must bear the blame of the unsatisfactory condition in which we find the science of jurisprudence [d]. The inquiries of the jurist are in truth prosecuted much as inquiry in physics and physiology was prosecuted before observation had taken the place of assumption [e]. Theories, plausible and *comprehensive* [f], but absolutely *unverified,* such as the Law of Nature or the Social Compact [g], enjoy a universal preference over *sober* research into the primitive history of society and law [h]; and they obscure the truth not only by diverting attention from the only quarter in which it can be found, but by that most real and most important influence which, when once entertained and believed in, they are enabled to exercise on the later stages of jurisprudence [i]."

The passage contains a mixture of sound and unsound assertions. It may be in-of the relations arising in the experimental domain; in other words, it deals with "evolution," with the manner in which certain facts succeed other facts in time. But still to be discovered are the relations obtaining at a given moment between simultaneous facts, and the uniformities in those relations; often also the relations between facts successive in time and their uniformities; and almost always, finally, the interdependences of all the elements.

When I know that grain comes from the wheat-plant, and the history of the wheat-plant, and also know the origin of man and the history of mankind, I still have to find out how much wheat the human being raises on an acre of land in a given territory at a given time, and the countless relationships arising between the growing of wheat under those conditions and the other facts of human life. When I know the history of money, I have no very exact idea as to the functions of money in economic life and much less as to the correlations between the use of money and other economic and

structive to separate them, since the example will serve for other similar cases. a. [Pareto's remark is based on a free translation of Maine by Courcelle Seneuil (p. 3), who rendered "they will be invaluable to us" by *ce sera au moyen de ces poèmes*. The remark as a whole, however, applies to Maine's general position. —A. L.] Doubtful statement. The Homeric poems are extensively rewritten. There are now people who claim that they are not archaic at all. See Bréal, *Pour mieux connaître Homère*, p. 5: "I am trying to show that the Greek epic belongs to an age of humanity that is already far beyond childhood and represents a civilization in no sense primitive." I confess that I am not at all convinced by Bréal's argument, but someone else might be. On what shaky foundations, therefore, would Sumner Maine erect the whole science of jurisprudence! This objection is of general bearing and valid for all cases where there is an effort to explain the well-known by the little-known. b. Granted. But the analogy has to be carried further. The complete history of the Earth would not give us the composition of a rock—the help of chemistry is needed. c. The expression "potentially" is purely metaphysical: it serves merely to adulterate an argument that the author would have strictly experimental. d. Very true, and equally valid for economics and sociology. e. *Idem*. f. [Pareto's remark falls. It is based on a mistranslation by Seneuil of "comprehensive" as "comprehensible" (*intelligible*).—A. L.] Comprehensible, yes, because in accord with sentiments—but not in accord with experience. Maine would have stressed this important distinction if, instead of thinking strictly of the historical method, he had given a thought to the experimental method. g. Not only is verification wanting; the language in those theories corresponds to nothing real. The same error as in f. h. For "sober research" one should say "experimental research." i. Very true, provided the remark refers to the experimental method. [The Homeric idea in (*a*) belongs not to Maine but to Vico, *Scienza nuova*, I, 2, 20.—A. L.]

social factors. If I have a thorough knowledge of the history of chemistry, it may help me to learn, but it will never directly yield, the chemical properties of new chemical combinations (§§ 34, 39).

In political economy or sociology, the so-called historical method, even if by some rare chance it be genuinely so, cannot be thought of as antithetical to the metaphysical method. The experimental method can.

620. Theologies not seldom offer prophecies and miracles as pseudo-experimental proofs, each religion, of course, considering its own prophecies good and its own miracles genuine, while holding the prophecies of other religions disastrously unreliable and their miracles frauds.[1] One need hardly observe that even if the facts were historically verifiable, as they never are, they would prove nothing from the experimental standpoint as to the supernatural portions of a religion. The reason why prophecies, even when they can be said to have come true by a prodigiously far-fetched interpretation, and miracles, even when unsupported by any valid historical proof whatever, serve so effectively to corroborate faith, lies not at all in their logico-experimental probability, but rather in the increased prestige that such things, be they fact or fable, confer upon their alleged authors.[2]

620 [1] Tertullian, *Apologeticus,* XX, 1-3: "And further . . . we offer the majesty of the Scriptures, if we fail to prove their divinity by their age, or if their age be doubted. [Authority guaranteed by antiquity.] . . . The evidence stands before our eyes—the world, all humanity, all history (*mundus et saeculum et exitus*). Whatever now happens was foretold of yore; whatever we now see with our eyes was then heard of human ears [As usual, no proof is given; for proofs, certainly, the generalities following can hardly be called.]: the fact that the earth swallows up cities; that the seas steal islands away; that wars civil and foreign destroy; that nation clashes with nation; that famine, pestilence, earthquakes (*locales quaeque clades*) and great slaughters devastate; that the lowly are exalted to high places, and the mighty abased." It took no special powers to predict such things, which were of everyday occurrence in those times. Apollo in his day had been much more definite: he told Croesus and Pyrrhus flatly that they were going to be whipped, and he hit many other nails squarely on the head.

620 [2] Draper, *History of the Conflict between Religion and Science,* p. 66: "Of this presumptuous system [Christian dogma], the strangest part was its logic, the nature of its proofs. It relied upon miracle-evidence. A fact was supposed to be demonstrated by an astounding illustration of something else! An Arabian writer, referring to this, says: 'If a conjurer should say to me, "Three are more than ten,

621. Miracles have always been common and are still common in our own day, as witness telepathy and similar arts. Nor is there any lack of contemporary religious prophets, especially in England and the United States. On a less exalted plane, the fourth pages of Italian newspapers often carry the predictions of certain prophets who, out of ardent love for their fellow-men and not without an eye to personal gain, make known to the public the numbers that are going to be drawn in coming lotteries. Such advertisements have been appearing for a good thirty years to my knowledge, and there must still be people who believe in them; for it costs money to print them, and if receipts did not at least cover expenditures, those estimable seers would certainly go out of business.

622. We are living in a rather sceptical age. Prophecies of lottery drawings, further, do not admit of ingenuities in interpretation, and the time elapsing between utterance and failure or fulfilment is very short. If in spite of these very unfavourable circumstances faith in such prophecies still endures, with all the more reason should a similar faith have flourished active and strong in ages of superstition, when prophecies were uttered in obscure terms allowing of any conceivable interpretation and when fulfilments could be deferred till Kingdom Come (§ 1579).

623. Says Galluppi in his *Natural Theology:* "If God really sends men of His choice to preach to others in His name truths that He has revealed to them directly, He does not fail to give such apostles and envoys all the means necessary for demonstrating the genuineness of their mission [Principle of authority]. God owes that much to Himself who sends them, to the apostles whom He sends, and to the people to whom He sends them. [Proof by general conformity of sentiments; Galluppi thinks so, hence everybody else must think so, and so it must be]. But what are those means? They are prophecies and miracles. . . . Prophecy is the certain prediction of future events

and in proof of it I will change this stick into a serpent," I might be surprised at his legerdemain, but I certainly should not admit his assertion.' Yet, for more than a thousand years, such was the accepted logic, and all over Europe propositions equally absurd were accepted on equally ridiculous proof."

that cannot be foreseen by men from natural causes. . . . God can therefore bestow on His apostles the gift of prophecy, and the gift of working miracles in His name. When those who announce themselves as apostles of God reveal to men dogmas that are not contrary to the principles of right reason [Right reason here serving as a shield against the pagans, who also had miracles and prophecies in plenty; but theirs were contrary to the principles of right reason, the Christian are not. Why? Ask Old Mother Hubbard.], and which tend to the glory of God and the happiness of mankind, and perform miracles to vouch for the truth of the doctrine they proclaim, they have abundantly proved their mission, and the people to whom they preach are in duty bound to receive them as divine and to hearken to the truth that they reveal. . . . Strictly speaking, prophecy itself is a miracle, for it is not natural knowledge, but a knowledge transcending the natural powers of the human spirit. But the prophecy may relate to events far distant in the future, and the prophet may lack the gift of other miracles. Prophecy alone is not therefore always sufficient to prove divine mission. But the miracle with which a divine apostle promises men to prove his mission divine is always conjoined with more or less prophecy. . . . The signs of divine revelation are therefore three: the one, intrinsic, and it is the truth and the sanctity of the doctrine that it teaches [Accord with certain sentiments]; the two others extrinsic [Pseudo-experimental], and they are miracles and prophecies." [1]

623 [1] *Elementi di filosofia,* Vol. VI, pp. 100-03. Says the *Dictionnaire encyclopédique de la théologie Catholique, s.v. Foi* (Wetzer, *s.v. Glaube*): "What then is the series of facts, what the cumulation of reasons, what the army of witnesses, that establish the Christian's conviction when he asserts that Jesus of Nazareth was the Sent of God, nay, God Himself? They are prophecies, miracles, the personal experience of each Christian [Tautology: the believer proves merely that he believes.], the general history of the world [The proof by prophecies and miracles is a concession to experience.] Meantime, the faith of the Christian has a further foundation that surpasses any other in depth and scope [The metaphysical proof superior by nature to experience.]: the inner experience of truth that comes to any human being who follows evangelical doctrine and the heavenly commandments." And lo, along come the Modernists and turn that very argument against the Catholics, who, to defend themselves, have to appeal to tradition and history! The "categorical imperative" is likewise a product "of the intimate experience that comes to any human being who follows the Kantian doctrine and the commandments of

624. Calvin will have it that Scripture bears within itself every evidence of divine inspiration. In other words he seems to appeal only to faith; and if he held to that ground, experimental science could raise no objections to his doctrine on the intrinsic side.[1] Extrinsically, however, it proves nothing and can be accepted only by people who already believe in it. From the experimental standpoint Calvin's yes exactly balances the no of any one of his opponents.[2] But he, good soul, does not see it that way, and he is soon reclaiming what he has given away.[3] That is customary with theologians and

Pure Reason"; but it proves nothing to a person who cares not a fig for Kant and his "pure reason." Here we have another very pretty tautology: *"History:* the limit of the Christian's certitude is the unity of Christian doctrine, a unity established over a period of two centuries and in the face of countless obstacles." The certainty of certainties is that there have been differences of opinion among Christians at all periods of history. If we call one such opinion orthodox and the others heretical, we can assert the continuous unity of the faith, having barred in advance everything that made it multiplex.

624 [1] *Institutions de la religion chrestienne,* I, 7, 5 (Allen, Vol. I, p. 85): "So let this point be considered settled: that only he whom the Holy Spirit has enlightened can rely on the Scriptures in wholeness of trust; for though it carries its credibility within itself for being accepted without rebuttal and without proof or argument [Here we are outside the experimental field, and with a vengeance.], it is nevertheless by its own testimony that Holy Writ possesses the certainty it deserves. Albeit of its own majesty [But suppose someone fails to see the majesty?] it has enough to command reverence, it begins, nevertheless, really to stir us when it has been sealed in our hearts by the Holy Spirit. [Without so much beating about the bush he might have said that those who believe it believe it.] So enlightened of the Holy Spirit, we believe that Scripture is of God, not by any judgment of ours or of anyone else, but above and beyond all human judgment we decide indubitably that it has been given us from the very mouth of God through the agency of men. . . . And then we no longer look for arguments or plausibilities on which to base our judgment, but subordinate our intelligence and judgment to it as to something exalted above the necessity of being judged." What a talkative soul! Calvin could have said all that in many fewer words. But he talked and talked, because it was a music altogether to the liking of his public.

624 [2] Gousset, *Théologie dogmatique,* Vol. I, p. 156: "First Rule: Scripture must be interpreted not just by reason, as the Socinians and modern rationalists contend; not by direct revelations, as enthusiastic believers have imagined; and not by special personal succour of the Holy Spirit lent to each individual, as Lutherans and Calvinists insist; but following the teaching of the Catholic Church." In other words, the metaphysical principle is replaced by authority. They both lie outside the province of logico-experimental science.

624 [3] Calvin, *Op. cit.,* I, 7, 4 (Allen, Vol. I, p. 84): "All the same, those who insist on trying to support the trustworthiness of Scripture by disputation are

metaphysicists. They quit the experimental world when experience blocks the path they are bent on following to establish their beliefs; but once they have done that, back they come to it; for after all it is as important to them as to anybody else, their pretended disdain for it being only an artifice for ridding themselves of objections that they cannot face.

625. Calvin was annoyed at the glimmer of experience that Catholics found in the consensus of the Church Fathers, and he gets rid of it by pretending that every man must believe in Scripture by inner persuasion. And if someone is not so lucky? He will roast him for you at the stake, as he did poor Servetus, or, if he can do nothing better, vilify him.[1] These may be excellent methods of persuasion, but their logico-experimental value is exactly zero.

perverters of good order. There will, to be sure, always be enough to answer our enemies with; and for my part . . . if I were called upon to join issue with the slyest despisers of God one might imagine, with all those who would fain be thought of as clever and entertaining hair-splitters to the overthrow of the Scriptures, I should hope I would not find it difficult to quash all their cackling; and if it were worth while to refute all their lies and insincerities, it would be no great trouble for me to show that the conceited nonsense which they put forward in bad faith is so much humbug." Just earlier he had said: "If I saw fit to debate this issue by reasons and arguments, I could adduce not a few things to prove that if there is a God in Heaven, the Law and the Prophets have come of Him. Even if all the scholars, and the cleverest in the world, were to rise on the other side and apply all their wits to assert themselves to the contrary, they could be forced to admit—unless they were hardened to a desperate impudence—that it is evident from manifest signs that God doth speak through the Scriptures." In that way one can prove anything one pleases. People who do not see things as Calvin does are "hardened to a desperate impudence." People not so impudent as that, therefore, see things as he does. And there are plenty of people who applaud arguments of that kind.

625 [1] In the one chapter above quoted, I, 7 and 8 (Allen, pp. 81-82, 84, 94-95): ". . . those sacrilegious villains (*vileins sacrilèges;* Latin version: *sacrilegi homines*) who have no other purpose than to erect an unlimited (Latin: *effrenatum*) tyranny under the fair name of the Church. . . . It is a silly dream on the part of those muddlers (*brouillons; eiusmodi rabulae*) that the Church has the power to pass judgment on Scripture. . . . As for those rascals (*canailles; hominum maledictis*) they ask how and by what we are persuaded that Holy Writ emanates from God. . . . It is easy to see how silly and wicked (*sotte et perverse; quam perferam et calumniose*) such an application is. . . . But even after we have upheld the sacred Word of God against all the protests and disparagements of these wicked people . . . I am well aware that this or that muddler (*brouillon; nebulones*) is forever cackling (*gazouiller; obstrepant*) to the effect that . . . A point these rascals make on the authority of the Book of Maccabees." In just such terms

626. Neo-Christianity nowadays seems inclined to put these extrinsic elements more or less, or perhaps entirely, aside and to pin its faith to the intrinsic elements strictly. In so doing it would be greatly improving its logical position, provided, after once deserting the experimental field, it did not try to get back to it again and begin dictating norms for the regulation of social life. On that basis proof is nothing more than mere accord with the sentiments of the preacher; but no one explains why and how dissenters have to listen to him. As a matter of fact, the success of neo-Christian doctrines is due altogether to their accord with democratic sentiments; they are the garb in which certain people—not so very many—see fit to disguise humanitarian sentiments.

627. In such doctrines there is a sincere belief, or in some cases a pretence, that great importance is being attached to experience. But in reality there is simply a shift from our A-α1 variety to A-α2.[1] Authority is dropped because it is too apparently in conflict with experience, and replaced by inner assent because its conflict with experience is less apparent—though not less profound.

Senator Bérenger denounces to the public prosecutor in France adversaries whom he is not the man to silence by argument.

627 [1] Fulliquet, *Les expériences du chrétien,* pp. 202-03: "The needs of the Reformation period, and their being forced to join issue with the Catholics, led the Reformers to lay great stress on the value of the Bible, as the only authority at all widely recognized on the other side capable of being set up against the traditonal authority of the Church. [Here Fulliquet is remaking history a little to suit himself.] Ostensibly the Reformers halt at replacing the Church with the Bible without changing the Catholic conception of faith—the acceptance and support of doctrine by trust, not in the Church now, but in the Bible. . . . But faith is no more trust in the Bible than it was trust in the Church. Faith is not acceptance of dogma. Faith is the trust of the heart in God and in Christ. Save that, as regards faith, the Bible has a fundamental rôle to play: the Bible places religious experience within our reach in the persons of servants of the Lord who have had it in the past. The Bible remains for ever, not authority, which in this domain means nothing, but the supreme influence in matters of faith. The Bible has no authority whatever in matters of belief [So Fulliquet is rid of the discrepancies, great and numerous, alas, between Scripture and the facts.], for belief never is and never can be anything more than an expression of the experiment of faith, of the life of faith." Fulliquet's persistence in calling "experiment" a thing that has nothing to do with the experiment of the natural sciences is designed, unwittingly it may be, to take advantage of the sentiments of approbation that attach, in our day, to the physical sciences.

628. Piepenbring, for instance, after admitting and illustrating errors in the Bible, thinks none the less that there is a divine element in it; and to distinguish the divine portion from the non-divine he is constrained to appeal exclusively to inner consensus. Says he:[1] "Is it possible to distinguish human elements in the Bible from divine elements, human errors from divine truth? Is it possible to say that such and such a word in the Bible or such and such a biblical reading is inspired and that another is not? No! That procedure would be quite mechanical and superficial; it would, furthermore, be impracticable. It is not in the dead letter, as that doctrine would have it, that we are to seek inspiration and revelation, but in the direct action of the spirit of God upon human hearts. [A good illustration of the shift from our A-$\alpha 1$ to A-$\alpha 2$.] . . . We have just shown as an undeniable fact that that part of Scripture contains errors. Anyone applying himself exclusively to textual criticism, instead of essaying, as we have done, a historical reconstruction of biblical teaching as a whole, would be able to find errors far more numerous than the ones casually noted here. . . . The fact that we have put forward is therefore fully established. But there is another fact that, as it seems to us, is no less fully established, namely, that the better elements in the Hebrew nation, foremost among whom stood the Prophets, the Psalmists, and the sacred writers in general, were under the influence of the spirit of God, which imparted to them a higher life and light, of which we have the expression, the translation, imperfect but real, in the Old Testament."

629. It may well be that the two facts are equally certain, but it is also certain that the proofs which may be offered for them are essentially different in character. For the first fact, that is, for the historical and physical inaccuracy, objective proofs may be adduced that may be verified by anyone; for the second fact, the only proofs available are subjective, and they are valid only for those few individuals who happen to share the writer's sentiments. Anyone inclined to go to the trouble may prove that Jacob's method of pro-

628 [1] *Théologie de l'Ancien Testament,* pp. 307-08.

ducing speckled lambs with his many-coloured coat[1] does not work, and it is not necessary to be blessed with certain sentiments to find that biblical zoology does not square with the facts. On the other hand there are any number of people who in no way share Piepenbring's admiration for the prophets of Israel and who consider "lower" the enlightenment that he deems "higher." How are we to decide who is right—in fact, what does "being right" mean in such a case?

630. Apparent from all that is the magnitude of the error of regarding these modern doctrines and others of their kind as "more scientific" than, for instance, Catholic doctrines based on authority (§§ 16, 516). In reality it is a question of different ways of appealing to what is presumed to be—and is not—science. The difference is a general one, and appears in many other theories. Some ask their verification of historical reality and twist it about to mean anything they wish it to mean. In one sense they may be said to be paying tribute to the importance and dignity of historical reality in that they invoke its aid. In another sense, they may be said to be disrespectful to it in—not deliberately, but unwittingly—interpreting and distorting it. Other theories disregard verification by history, and place their whole reliance on inner conviction. In one sense they may be said to be belittling the importance of historical reality by ignoring its force as proof. In another sense, they may be said to be respecting it, in that they do not presume to interpret and distort it.

631. A-γ: *Great importance is attached to experience, or there is a pretence of doing so. However, it is always in a subordinate rôle.* The transition from our A-β variety to A-γ is by imperceptible degrees. In A-γ experience is apparently sovereign—but it is the sovereignty of a constitutional king and amounts to very little. In the concrete, theories generally have elements belonging to both the

629 [1] [Pareto apparently confused in memory the striped rods of Jacob (Gen. 30:37-43) with the many-coloured coat of Joseph (Gen. 37:3). Having bargained with Laban for the spotted lambs, Jacob made the sheep conceive among hazel, chestnut, and poplar rods "pilled" with "white strakes," and they "brought forth cattle ringstraked, speckled, and spotted."—A. L.]

A group and the B group, and it is difficult to separate them because a writer may not disclose, in fact oftentimes does not himself know, whether this or that of his principles is superior or subordinate to experience. To avoid a double examination of the same theory we shall therefore speak of this variety A-γ in the next chapter, where we are to study B theories.

632. We do that for practical reasons only, and it in no way impairs the theoretical value of our criterion of classification. It might seem that the mere fact as to whether the sovereignty assigned to non-experimental principles be explicit or implicit were not sufficiently important to warrant a distinction by genera. Instead, the fact is of capital importance, for if the sovereignty in question is stated explicitly, the doors are shut against experience, whereas they stand open if it is left implicit. In Spencer's ethical system, *a priori* principles figure; but they are left implicit, and there is nothing therefore to hinder us, in following Spencer's lead, from rectifying them and so arriving—after a long detour, it is true—at a scientific theory. On the other hand, in the system of ethics that our humanitarians are trying to set up, there are principles which explicitly transcend experience—the principle, for instance, that everything must be sacrificed for the "good of the greatest number." It is impossible to imagine how a proposition of that kind could be verified by experience. Experience, therefore, can in no wise serve to correct it. It is an article of faith that transports us to a field entirely alien to experience.

CHAPTER V

Pseudo-scientific Theories

633. B (§ 575). The interposition of non-experimental principles, which was patent and explicit in group A, is more or less dissembled and implicit in group B. Theories are not logico-experimental, but there is an effort to make them appear so. There are cases, to be sure, where they may actually be—cases where the non-experimental element can be eliminated without materially altering results. If that is not possible, the theory cannot be classed, even in amended form, with the logico-experimental variety.

634. Here we are considering the B theories chiefly, for the purpose of segregating the logico-experimental element from the non-logico-experimental. The inquiry is important in two respects: 1. Such theories overlie facts that have been distorted; if we can manage to isolate the logico-experimental element, we ought to be able to get at the facts in their real form. 2. In case perchance the non-experimental element in a theory proves to be merely incidental, we can eliminate it and so get a logico-experimental theory.

635. Suppose, then, we have before us the statement of a theory, the text of a narration. We may envisage the two following problems:

1. Assuming that in the statement a part, small or large, is played by metaphysical or arbitrary inferences, by myths, allegories, and so on, can we get back from the author's language to the ideas he was really intending to express, to the facts he meant to describe, to the logico-experimental relations he was trying to formulate—and if so, how?

2. What possible procedures are there to arrive, through the use of such metaphysical or arbitrary inferences, myths, allegories, and the like, at certain conclusions that are desired in advance?

636. The situation can be better visualized in form of a graph. Case 1: We have a theory *T* (Figure 12), which is assumed to picture certain facts *A*—a statement *T* presumably originating in the facts *A*. *T* we know. Our purpose is to determine *A*. If our effort is successful, we shall be following the line *TA:* starting with the statement *T*, we get to *A*. But, if our venture—quite without design on our part—chances to fail, we get not to *A*, but to *B*, and imagine, though mistakenly, that *B* is the source of *T*. A procedure quite analogous is followed by modern scholarship in trying to reconstitute an original text from a variety of surviving manuscripts. The desired original would be *A*. The various manuscript versions form the complex *T*.

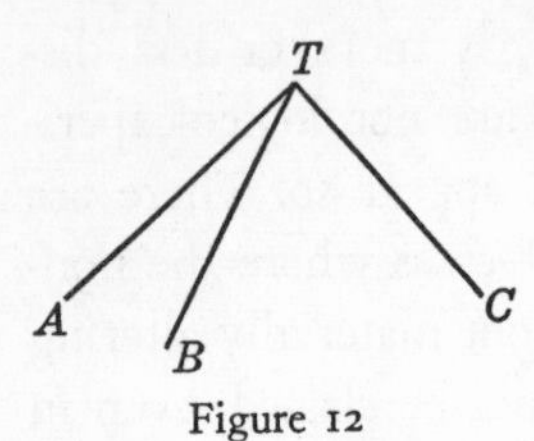

Figure 12

Case 2: From the statement of a theory, or a text, *T*, the idea is to draw certain conclusions, *C*, which are generally known in advance. One starts with *T* and through inferences of a non-logico-experimental character, one gets to *C*.

In the first case the quest is for *A;* in the second case, the quest is not for *C* (*C* being already known), but for a way of getting to *C*. Sometimes that is done deliberately: A person knows perfectly well that *C* does not follow from *T*, but he thinks it desirable to make it seem to. That would be a deceit, a trick, a logical action—one person trying to persuade another of a thing he knows to be untrue. But more often, much more often, the search for a road that will lead from *T* to *C* is not consciously premeditated. The investigator believes in *T* and keenly aspires to the ideal *C*. Quite without conscious design he brings the two sentiments together over the path *TC*. In that case we get a non-logical action. The person who is trying to persuade others has first of all persuaded himself. There is no trickery.

In the first case (the quest for *A*), though accords of sentiment are often exploited, there is the assumption at least that logico-experimental deductions are being used; and they are really used in the sciences. The route *TA* (or, in case of a mistake, *TB*) is therefore assumed, or at least is ostensibly assumed, and the search is for *A*. In the second case, where the search, deliberately or unconsciously, is for the route *TC*, though it is the pretence, and very often the sincere belief, that the logico-experimental method is being used, what more often is actually used is an accord of sentiments. The search is for a route *TC*, which will have the double advantage of leading to the desired goal *C*, and of being palatable to the people one is trying to win.

All that is seldom apparent. The two problems are not explicitly differentiated and the search for the path *TC* is represented in all sincerity as a quest strictly for *A*. As usual the non-logical action is given a varnish of logic. Suppose *T* stands for the text of the Gospels. We may seek the facts *A* that gave rise to them—and that would be a task for historical criticism. But the person who is not using historical criticism, or not using it strictly, is trying to derive from the Gospels certain principles of his own morality, or of the morality which he has in some way or other made his own, and therefore is using an *interpretation TC* suitable for getting him to the desired goal. He knows in advance that he is to believe in *T* and in *C*. Those two termini are fixed. The problem is simply to find a way to bring them together.

637. In the present chapter we shall deal chiefly with the first case (the quest for *A*), dealing with the second in Chapters IX and X. We say chiefly, and not exclusively, because in concrete cases elements corresponding to both problems are usually combined in varying proportions, and we should therefore be involving ourselves in long and wearisome repetitions if we tried to keep such elements strictly segregated in each concrete case and dealt exclusively first with one and then with the other.

638. In the logico-experimental sciences we first follow the line *AT* and formulate a theory from the facts; and then the line *TA*, deducing predictions of fact from theory. In literary productions involving departures from the logico-experimental method, the line *TB* is on occasion followed, but nearly always it is the line *TC*. *T*, moreover, is ordinarily indeterminate and will yield almost anything desired. Often, also, the line *TC* has very little to do with logic. In a word, from a sum of indefinite sentiments *T* one infers anything that happens to be desired—*C*.

639. Following the line *AT*, we proceed from the thing to a verbal term for designating it. Along the lines *TA, TB, TC* the procedure is from the verbal term to the thing. A sentiment prompting us to objectify our subjective sensations tempts us also to believe that in every case there must be some real object corresponding to any given term of language, *T*, and that therefore all that is needed is to find a way for locating it. There is the term "justice." There must therefore necessarily be something real corresponding to it; and people have sought high and low to find it. As a matter of fact, there are many terms *T* corresponding to sentiments held by one or more persons, but nothing more. Starting from *T* we may find those sentiments, but certainly not objects that have no existence.

640. A situation of very frequent occurrence is the following. From the sentiments *A* present in many people an indeterminate expression, *T*, is derived. Then a writer comes along and tries to draw certain conclusions, *C*, from *T*. *T* being indeterminate, he sees anything he chooses in it (§ 514), and then believes, and makes others believe, that he has attained an objective result, *C*. In reality he is accepting *C* only because *C* accords with his sentiments, *A*. But instead of following frankly the direct line *AC*, he follows the indirect line *ATC*, often a very circuitous route, in order to satisfy the need of seeming logical that he and other human beings feel.

Returning to our examination of theories as classified in § 575, let us see whether, and how, one can get back from them to the facts which they are assumed to represent.

641. B: *The extra-experimental origin of the abstract entities that are introduced is not explicitly stated.* For that matter, we must be resigned to finding metaphysical *a priori* principles explicit in this class, as well as in the A group, and rest satisfied with reducing them to as slight a rôle as possible. If we were to bar them altogether, we should have nothing, or almost nothing, left to put into the class we are here considering. In social matters such principles will creep in by hook or by crook. That is the case not only because they correspond to very powerful sentiments in human beings, but also because such matters are almost never studied for the exclusive purpose of discovering uniformities, but in behalf of some practical purpose, some propaganda, some justification of an *a priori* belief.

642. *They are sometimes mere abstractions arbitrarily deduced from experience.* This is characteristic of the experimental sciences; and the ear-mark by which we can recognize such abstractions is that they may be dispensed with whenever we so desire. The whole science of celestial mechanics can be expounded without resort to the concept of universal attraction. The hypothesis that astronomers are trying to verify on the facts is that celestial bodies move in such a way as to satisfy the equations of dynamics. The whole science of mechanics can be expounded without reference to the concept of "force," the whole science of chemistry without once mentioning "affinity." As for political economy, we have shown that the theories of the economic equilibrium can be stated without resort to my term "ophelimity" (§ 61), to the term "value," or to the abstraction "capital" (§§ 117 f.). In these volumes on sociology we could substitute plain letters of the alphabet for the terms "non-logical actions," "residues," "derivations," and the like, and the argument would stand just as well without the slightest alteration. We are dealing with things and not with words, nor with the sentiments associated with words (§§ 119 f.).

We shall go no farther here into the character of these logico-experimental theories, the better to confine ourselves to the theories more or less at variance with them that have so far constituted social science.

643. B-α: *Myths, legends, and the like are historically real.* This is the simplest and easiest solution of the problem of getting from *T* to *A*—of getting back from a text to the facts in which it originated. It may be accepted in virtue of a fervid, unreasoning faith that prides itself on believing even *quia absurdum*. With that procedure, as explained in § 581, we need not concern ourselves. Then again, it may be accepted on the same basis as any other historical account, and therefore as the consequence of a pseudo-experience, which would be identical with experience proper were the story subjected to severe historical criticism and to all the other experimental verifications required. The theories yielded by this solution differ from the theories of group A (§ 575) in that in the A theories the narration is enforced as an article of faith by some non-experimental power which generally is known on the authority of some individual (§ 583), and it is the interposition of such a power that provides the desired "explanation." In the present case, B-α, the theories are believed on their own pseudo-experimental evidence. From the scientific standpoint such a distinction is a vital one (§ 632). If a narration is presented as an article of faith, that alone is enough to banish it from the field of logico-experimental science, which has no longer any business with it as regards either acceptance or rejection. But if it is presented as vouching for itself on its own authority and obviousness, it is wholly within the domain of experimental science, and it is faith that loses all jurisdiction over it. That distinction, however, is seldom made by the person who believes such a narration, and it is very difficult to tell whether he is considering it merely as history or is believing it on some other ground. For that reason a great many cases, in the concrete, present mixtures of A theories and B theories. For instance, the authority of the writer himself is seldom missing, and it is a non-experimental element.

644. If the text we are trying to interpret were a historical narrative, we might in fact consider it as an at least approximative record of the facts with which it deals (§§ 541 f.).

645. Even in such cases, however, there are always some differences. Any account even of a very simple occurrence rarely represents it exactly. That has been shown over and over again by a favourite experiment of professors of criminology. Something is made to happen in the presence of witnesses, and they are asked to give an account of it in writing. As many slightly differing narratives are received as there are witnesses. A boy and an adult of lively imagination are made to witness something. If they are asked to tell what they have seen, it will be found that each adds something to it, and in the direction of making it more striking or interesting than it was in reality.[1] The same thing is true when a person is repeating a story he has heard (§ 1568).

Another curious thing: Since it is the general practice to make such embellishments, people habitually discount what they hear, so that an incident has to be somewhat overdrawn in order to make an impression at all corresponding to reality. If you see nine people out of ten laughing, and you wish to convey to someone an accurate impression of such great hilarity, you say, "Everybody laughed." If you were to say, "Nine of them laughed and one did not," the impression would fall short of the truth.

646. To be altered, a story need not pass from mouth to mouth. It is altered even in a repetition by the same person. A thing once said to be large will become larger in successive accounts, and a small thing will become smaller. The dose is constantly increased, and always under pressure of the same sentiment.

647. Exact data are available to show how deceitful certain impressions are. Singular indeed our common illusions as regards quotations from certain authors. I have often heard Italians quote Dante (*Inferno,* III, v. 51) to the effect: *"Non ti curar di lor, ma guarda e passa."* Dante wrote:

Non ragioniam di lor, ma guarda e passa.[1]

645 [1] [In his *Memoirs,* published in 1823, Lorenzo da Ponte, describing the hardships of an ocean voyage, says that he crossed the Atlantic in eighty-six days. In his *Compendium,* published in 1807, he says he crossed in seventy days. I have shown on the documents that he crossed on the *Columbia* in fifty-seven days (*Memoirs of Lorenzo da Ponte,* Philadelphia, 1929, p. 353). The point is this. Interpreters of Da Ponte, such as Fausto Nicolini (*Archivio storico italiano,* No. 1, 1930), enumerate such inaccuracies in the *Memoirs* to prove that Da Ponte was a liar and general reprobate (logical conduct: misstatement with intent to deceive). And to the extent of that intrusion of moralistic attitudes, they are doing a sentimental gymnastic and producing pseudo-scientific criticism. I view Da Ponte, instead, as merely manifesting, as Pareto would say, the residue here in question (non-logical conduct: unawareness of realities through stress of a sentiment—§ 888, residue I-β2), and so I come closer to a scientific interpretation of the facts.—A. L.]

647 [1] ["Let us not speak of them, but look and pass" (Fletcher translation); "Let us not speak of them, but look and go" (Anderson translation).]

Many Frenchmen, says Fournier, think they are quoting Molière when they say,

Il est avec le ciel des accommodements.[a]

"The verse is perfect, but Molière did not write it. In fact to get such a verse we have to take the substance of two lines in Act IV, Scene V, of *Tartuffe:*

Le ciel défend, de vrai, certains contentements;
mais on trouve avec lui des accommodements."[2]

Mirabeau's famous phrase, "Go tell your master," *etc.,* he never uttered. The Marquis of Dreux-Brezé rectified the facts in the Chamber of Peers at its session of March 10, 1833. "Mirabeau said to my father: 'We are assembled here by the will of the nation, and we will not leave except by force.' I ask M. de Montlosier if that be not so."[3]

648. A national author is often less accurately quoted by his

647 [a] "There are ways of coming to terms with Heaven."

647 [2] *L'esprit des autres,* pp. 374-75. *Ibid.,* pp. 104-05: "I know people who would blush red with anger if I were to tell them . . . that the celebrated verse

'La critique est aisée et l'art est difficile'

is not in the *Art poétique* of their darling, Despréaux. . . . They will go over the verses of the four cantos of the poem, and indeed through all the works of the poet; and not only will they not find the line they are looking for but incidentally they will find quite a few to the opposite effect. . . . Never mind—they will not be beaten so easily. They will still hold that their beloved line is by Boileau and that it is in the *Art poétique* . . . because it ought to be there." [So nine people out of ten will say that the celebrated definition of comedy, *"Castigat ridendo mores,"* is by Horace in the *De arte poetica,* as in fact it "ought" to be. Instead it is by Santeul, a Frenchman of the seventeenth century. So the Lord's curse on Adam and Eve (Gen. 3:19) is regularly quoted "by the sweat of thy brow" instead of "in the sweat of thy face." For another example from Pareto himself, see § 1397[2]. —A. L.]

647 [3] Quoted by Fournier, *L'esprit dans l'histoire,* p. 229. Fournier says further in a note: "According to the report in the *Journal des débats* of that same day, Mar. 10, 1833, M. de Montlosier nodded in the affirmative. Bailly's *Mémoires,* published in 1804, Vol. I, p. 216, report Mirabeau's words neither as they are ordinarily quoted nor [as rectified in the House of Peers]. On the other hand, Noël's *Éphémérides,* June, 1803, p. 164, establishes the version of M. de Dreux-Brezé [thirty years before his time]." [The passage, however, is missing in the third edition of the *Éphémérides.*—A. L.]

fellow-countrymen, who generally repeat from memory, than by foreigners who take the pains to verify quotations on his text. Something similar may have happened with ancient Greek writers in quoting Homer.[1] Such quotations are often different from the texts of Homer that have come down to us, and the differences are commonly explained as due to textual variants in the original. All the same, there remain cases in which the divergences seem due to quotation from memory. Ancient writers did not feel the need of accuracy of which some writers, at least among the moderns, make a point. Even a few years back many passages were being quoted from authors without indications as to where they were to be found, and what is worse, opinions were credited to them without textual references. As late as 1893 Gomperz wrote his elaborate *Greek Thinkers* without a single quotation—everything had to be believed, like the Delphic oracle, on his unsupported say-so. The general custom in historical works nowadays is different. The works of Fustel de Coulanges, Marquardt, the *Manual* of Mommsen and the *Roman History* of Ettore Pais, are models in that sense. In each of them the author's object is to be as accurate and objective as possible and to support his assertions with sound proofs.

649. Divergences between facts and accounts of them may be slight or insignificant. But they may also increase, multiply, and become so elaborate as to end in stories that have virtually nothing in common with the facts. So we get fantastic tales, legends, romances,

648 [1] Dugas-Montbel, *Observations sur l'Iliade,* Vol. I, p. 139 (*Iliad* III, vv. 8-9): "Plato quotes v. 8 in his *Respublica* [III, 389e] with a slight change. . . . It is probable that Plato was quoting from memory, but it is also conceivable that at that time Homer's text was not what it is today. However Strabo [*Geographica,* XII, 8, 7; Jones, Vol. V, p. 495] quotes v. 8, and Aulus Gellius [*Noctes Atticae,* I, 11; Rolfe, Vol. I, p. 55], vv. 8 and 9, in texts identical with our modern editions." *Ibid.,* Vol. I, p. 213 (*Iliad,* IV, v. 431): "I have already remarked that in quoting Homer, doubtless from memory, Plato tied the beginning of this line to the eighth of Canto III of the *Iliad*. . . ." Vol. I, pp. 402-03 (*Iliad,* IX, vv. 591-94): "In quoting this passage [*Rhetorica,* I, 7, 3; Freese, p. 81] Aristotle does not give the exact text that appears in our editions. . . . Aristotle's Homer may have been different in some respects from ours. . . . All the same, my guess would be that the difference here . . . is due to the fact that Aristotle was quoting from memory, as we suspected in the case of Plato."

in which there is no telling whether there is any basis in fact, and, if so, what the facts were. Even writings that are not considered legendary and pass as historical may be so widely at variance with reality as to bear a very scant resemblance to it.[1]

If we follow in this connexion also the method indicated in § 547, we shall find examples in great abundance to show how cautious one has to be in accepting details in stories that are on the whole altogether historical. In the year 1192 Conrad, Marquis of Tyre, was assassinated in that city. His subjects, needing a lord and protector, insisted that Isabelle, Conrad's widow, should straightway marry Henry, Count of Champagne, even though she was with child. An Arab, Imad ed Din, tells the story thus, in the *Book of the Two Gardens* (Vol. V, pp. 52-53): "On the very night of the murder, Count Henry married the princess, widow of the Marquis, and consummated the union even though she was with child. But in the religion of the Franks that circumstance is not an obstacle to marriage, the child being ascribed to the mother. Such the law with that nation of infidels."

If nothing but that were known of the Franks, one might infer that they traced lineal descent through the female line and would so increase by one the number of peoples with a matriarchal system. Very likely not a few facts adduced in support of the general theory of matriarchy have no better foundations.

650. B-α1: *Myths and the like taken literally without change.* We get the type of this variety in the blind faith with which biblical narrative was for so long accepted, the Bible being regarded as simple history—for when it is taken as inspired of God, and the fact of

649 [1] One example from the hosts available—Hagenmeyer, *Peter der Eremite,* p. 2: "When one is confronted on the one hand with documents on the Crusades attributed to writers of the eleventh and twelfth centuries, and which must be taken as sources emanating from eyewitnesses, and on the other hand with narratives of the same events written at later periods, a comparison is sufficient to show that oftentimes the tradition has been completely changed in character. It is a thing that anyone can verify for himself. Nor is it rare even to find that the primitive narrative is hardly recognizable under the legendary frills with which the modern account has been decorated, so that if one had to depend on the latter alone, it would be hard to determine just how much history it contained."

inspiration is the reason for its acceptance as history, we get a theory of Class III-A.[1] Of the same type are the many legends that have been taken as history, such as the tales connected with the founding of Rome.

651. For many centuries every statement by an ancient writer was accepted as high-test gold. The more ancient the author, the more trustworthy the fact. Says Dante of Livy:

Come Livio scrive, che non erra.[1]

Today we stand dumbfounded that so many absurd stories could have passed for history for so many generations; and the fact that they did so serves to demonstrate the value of that universal consensus on which the metaphysicists so pride themselves.

652. Not less amazing is it to see men of great ability lending their credence to old wives' tales and prophecies—and that goes to show the scant importance that is to be attached to authority in such matters. It seems incredible—yet there stands the fact—that the great Newton could have written a whole book to show that the prophecies of the Apocalypse had been fulfilled. How ever could the founder of celestial mechanics have harboured such childish idiocies![1] But the case, however extreme, is not exceptional. Many

650 [1] [Pareto's cross-references grow a little complicated: Class III is isolated in § 523 (theories adding something to experimental reality). Of it the genera A and B, as distinguished in § 574 and analyzed in § 575, are subvarieties, the extra-experimental element being explicit in A, and in B, disguised or implicit.—A. L.]

651 [1] *Inferno,* XXVIII, v. 12: "As Livy writes, whose word we cannot doubt" (Anderson translation).

652 [1] *Observations upon the Prophecies of Daniel and the Apocalypse of St. John,* pp. 14, 46-48. Newton finds Daniel a most lucid seer: "Amongst old Prophets, Daniel is most distinct in order to time and easier to be understood." Daniel clearly prophesies the fall of the Roman Empire "on the ten kingdoms represented by the horns of the fourth Beast (Rev. 13). Now by the war above described the Western Empire of the Romans, about the time that Rome was besieged and taken by the Goths, became broken into the following ten kingdoms. . . ." He mentions the kingdoms of the Vandals and the Alans in Spain and Africa; the Suevians in Spain; the Visigoths, the Alans in Gallia; the Burgundians, the Franks, the Britons, the Huns, the Lombards; and the kingdom of Ravenna. And he concludes: "Seven of these kingdoms are thus mentioned by Sigonius . . . add the Franks, Britons, and Lombards, and you have the ten: for these arose about the same time with the seven."

people think soundly enough on certain subjects and as badly as can be on others, being sages in one sphere, idiots in others. Numberless the chronologies extant "from the year of the Flood," "from the year of the foundation of Troy," and so on. Glance, if you please, at the histories of Orosius, and see how he brings all sorts of stories together and presents them as veracious history—giving the exact dates for good measure! Everything is grist for his mill whether it come from the Bible or from the mythologies of the pagans, against whom meantime he is writing.[2]

653. Such chronologies were appearing as late as the year 1802, when, in long and erudite notes to his translation of Herodotus, Larcher records the dates of no end of legendary happenings. He devotes a whole chapter to fixing the exact year of the fall of Troy, prefacing it, Vol. VII, p. 290, with the remark: "I lay it down as an actual fact that that city was taken in the year 3444 of the Julian period, 1,270 years before the common era; and I will prove it in my chapter on that epoch."[1]

654. To some extent in ancient times, more frequently in the Middle Ages and even later, many peoples were tracing their origins back to the peregrinations of the Trojans. Guillaume le Breton relates in all seriousness:[1] "As we have learned from the chronicles

652 [2] *Historiae adversus paganos,* I, 2, 1: "*Item.* In the year 775 *ante u. c.* [What a pity he does not give the day and the month!] fifty parricides were committed in one night among the children of Danaus and Aegyptus, brothers." [The legend in its commoner form was that the fifty sons of Aegyptus were married to the fifty daughters of Danaus, who slew their husbands at their father's command. See Harper, *s.v. Danaides.*—A. L.] *Ibid.,* I, 17, 1: "In the year 430 *ante u. c.* come the rape of Helen, the conspiracy of the Greeks, and the assembling of the thousand ships, whence the ten years' siege, eventuating in the famous fall of Troy, is foretold." Clement of Alexandria, *Stromata,* I, 21 (*Opera,* Vol. I, p. 826B; Wilson, Vol. I, p. 423), along with other interesting information and chronology, locates at the time of Lynceus [*i.e.,* of the Argonauts] the rape of Proserpine, the foundation of the Temple of Eleusis, the invention of agriculture by Triptolemus, the arrival of Cadmus at Thebes, and the reign of Minos in Crete.

653 [1] In the same translation of Herodotus, Vol. VII, p. 576, Larcher notes for the year 1355 B.C.: "The women of Lemnos, enraged at the preference of the Lemnians for their concubines, make a general slaughter of their husbands." For the year 1354 B.C.: "Oedipus, son of Laius, marries Jocasta, without knowing that she is his mother, and ascends the throne."

654 [1] *Vie de Philippe Auguste,* pp. 184-85.

of Eusebius, Idacius, Gregory of Tours, and many others, and from the testimony of all the ancients, Hector, son of Priam, had a son called Francion. Troilus, son of the same Priam, King of Asia, also had, it is said, a son called Turcus. After the fall of Troy, the Trojans, most of whom had escaped, became divided into two peoples, the one of which chose Francion king and so came to be called Franks. The other named Turcus their chief, whence the Turks derived their name." [2]

654 [2] Guillaume continues, p. 185: "Leading his people, Francion reached the Danube, where he built a city called Sicambria, and there he reigned. . . . Two hundred and thirty years having passed [No more, no less!] twenty-three thousand of them [No less, no more!] left under the leadership of Hybor . . . and came to Gaul. Arriving at a very pleasant and convenient spot on the Seine, they built a city there and called it Lutetia, because of the mud (*lutum*) that filled the place, and they called themselves Parisians, from Paris, son of Priam; or rather [For Guillaume has a flair for historical criticism.], they were so called from the Greek word *parrhesia,* which means 'boldness.' And there they dwelt one thousand two hundred and sixty years." Dugas-Montbel, *Observations sur l'Iliade,* Vol. I, p. 298 (*Iliad,* VI, vv. 402-03): "The famous poet Ronsard went even farther [in the *Franciade*] than Racine [in *Andromaque*]; for he assumes that this very Astyanax went to Gaul, came to be called Francion, and founded the line of the Kings of France. . . . The story seems to originate in an alleged passage of Manetho (*Manethone sacerdote egittio*) quoted by Annio da Viterbo, the latter in his notes, p. 33, referring to the historian Vincent de Beauvais (*Vincenzo historico francese*) as his authority. Vincent claims that on the fall of Troy Astyanax wandered to the Gauls, married the daughter of the king, and succeeded his father-in-law on the throne. Many poets are far from basing their plots on such secure historical foundations." The story may go as far back as Lucan, *Pharsalia,* I, vv. 427-28: "The Arvernians [Gauls] have dared to pretend themselves blood-kindred to the Latian [Roman] as a people of Iliac [Trojan] stock." In the *Fragmenta* of Fredegarius, *Epitomata,* II (Migne, LXXI, p. 577c), the legend is well knit and already full grown. As late as the sixteenth century, a scholar of Étienne Pasquier's calibre hesitated to deny such nonsense, *Recherches de la France,* I, 14 (p. 37): "As regards the Trojans, it is certainly surprising that all the nations, as it were by common consent, consider themselves highly honoured to derive their ancient origins from the destruction of Troy. So the Romans call their first founder an Aeneas, the French, a Francion, the Turks, a Turcus, and the people of Great Britain, a Brutus, while the first inhabitants of the Adriatic call themselves after Antenor. . . . For my part, I should not dare flatly to contradict that opinion, nor for that matter assent to it without reservation. It seems to me a very ticklish business to argue about the remote origins of peoples; because they were so small in their first beginnings that the ancient writers took no pains to establish the facts, so that gradually the memory of them vanished utterly, or else took the form of pleasant and frivolous tales." [There is no reference to the adventures of Francion in the half-witted *Chronicon* of Idatius, at least in the text of that work published in the *Maxima bibliotheca* of Bigne.—A. L.]

655. In the year of grace 1829, at a time when Niebuhr's work had gone through three editions, the Saint-Simonians were still swearing by Numa.[1]

656. But specialists in Roman antiquities had for years been voicing their doubts. Clüver in 1624, Perizonius in 1685, Beaufort in 1738, Charles Lévesque in 1807, and finally Niebuhr in 1811, had gradually been drawing nearer to the point where the historical unsubstantiality of the ancient legends became apparent. Mommsen, and finally the Italian Ettore Pais, banished them from history for good and all. By that time Grote had done the same for Greece.

657. But human beings are not readily brought to discarding their legends. They try, at least, to save as much of them as possible. The method most generally used is to alter meanings in the parts that seem irreparably unacceptable in order to divest them of traits too conspicuously impossible.

658. Available in exceedingly large numbers are examples of words transformed into things or properties of things; and oftentimes a whole legend is built up around a single term loosely interpreted.[1] In the languages in which names of things have gender, male personifications come from masculine nouns, female from feminine nouns (§§ 1645 f.). It may chance to be possible in some

655 [1] *Doctrine Saint-Simonienne, Exposition*, 1854, p. 19: "Moses, Numa, Jesus—they all fathered peoples that are dead or are dying today."

658 [1] Taylor, *Words and Places*, pp. 264-70 (quoted by Menzerath, *L'Einfühlung, et la connaissance du semblable*): "Men have ever felt a natural desire to assign plausible meanings to names. . . . How few children, conning the atlas, do not connect some fanciful speculations with such names as . . . the ORANGE River or the RED Sea . . . [which are] supposed to denote the colour of the waters, instead of being, the one a reminiscence of . . . the house of Orange, and the other a translation of the Sea of Edom. . . . [In a note]: FLORIDA is not the flowery land, but the land discovered on Easter Day (Pasqua florida). . . . No cause has been more fruitful in producing corruptions than popular attempts to explain from the vernacular . . . names . . . known only to the learned. . . . [In a note]: A groom used to call Othello and Desdemona—two horses under his charge—Old Fellow and Thursday Morning. . . . The citadel of Carthage was called BOZRA, a Phoenician word meaning an acropolis. The Greeks connected this with *βύρσα*, an ox-hide, and then, in harmony with the popular notions of Tyrian acuteness, an explanatory legend was concocted, which told how the traders, who had received permission to possess as much land as an ox-hide would cover, cut the skin into strips with which they encompassed the spot on which the Carthaginian fortress was

cases to get back from the name to the thing; but we must take care to do that only when we have adequate proofs of the development from the thing to the name. To be sure, when we are looking for the meaning of a term there is always the temptation to alter it slightly and give evidence of our ingenuity by bringing out hidden implications and so drawing name and thing together. But past experience shows that that course has almost always led to error (§ 547), and the more certainly, the greater the talent and learning of the interpreter, who is tempted by his very endowments to try unbeaten paths. Going from the name to the thing is to retrace the path that has led from the thing to the name. The return trip may be made in some confidence only when our knowledge of the original development is more or less thorough.[2]

659. There is an analogous situation in etymology. The ancients derived their etymologies from verbal similarities that were often very superficial, and nearly always they went wrong. Modern philologists accept no etymology that fails to accord with the laws of phonetics: they refuse, that is, to retrace the path from word to etymon unless they are certain of the original development from etymon to word.

660. So we are left in doubt when someone suggests going back from the name Saint Venise to Venus, until we have some other

erected." (Menzerath: "The classic example is *Romulus,* as the founder of *Rome,* a form philologically impossible.") Taylor continues, p. 269: "The name of ANTWERP denotes, no doubt, the town which sprang up 'at the wharf.' But the word Antwerpen approximates closely in sound to the Flemish *handt werpen,* hand throwing. Hence arose the legend of the giant who cut off the hands of those who passed his castle without paying him black mail, and threw them into the Scheldt, till at length he was slain by Brabo, eponymus of Brabant. The legend of the wicked Bishop Hatto is well known. . . . At a time of dearth he forestalled the corn from the poor, but was overtaken by a righteous Nemesis—having been devoured by the swarming rats, who scaled the walls of his fortress on the Rhine. The origin of this legend may be traced to a corruption of the name *mautthurm,* or customhouse, into the MÄUSE-THURM, or Mouse-tower. . . . Near Grenoble is a celebrated tower, which now bears the name of LA TOUR SANS VENIN, the tower without poison. The peasantry firmly believe that no poisonous animal can exist in its neighbourhood. The superstition has arisen from a corruption of the original saint-name of San Verena into *sans venin.*"

658 [2] We shall discuss the matter at length in Chapter IX.

proof than the mere resemblance of the words. But the suggested relationship will become the more probable in proportion as we get surer evidence of the direct development from Venus to Venise. That is exactly the way Maury goes about it:[1] "The legend of Saint Venise, as recounted in the *De cultu vineae Domini* of Pierre Subert (1513), in a fragment attributed to Liutprand of Cremona, a tenth-century writer, and in the Dexter Chronicle, establishes her pagan and entirely 'aphrodisiac' origin, though we should look for her name in vain in the *Acta.*"

We are not, for a contrast, able to accept the explanations of the birth of Orion offered by certain ancients, until we get better proofs of the original development.[2]

661. B-α2: *With slight and easy alterations in literal meanings.* Typical of this variety of interpretation is the method of Palaephatus in explaining legends—a method so easy and convenient that it can be used by anyone without the slightest difficulty.[1] We have

660 [1] *Croyances et légendes de l'antiquité,* p. 349.

660 [2] Clavier, *Bibliothèque d'Apollodore,* Vol. II, p. 49: "The story of Orion's birth is told at greater length by Homer's scholiast following Euphorion (*Iliad,* XVIII, v. 486; Dindorf, Vol. II, p. 171); Palaephatus, *De incredibilibus historiis,* 5 (Leipzig, pp. 36-39, Περὶ Ὠρίονος); Ovid, *Fasti,* V, vv. 493-536; and Hyginus, *Fabulae,* 195 (*Orion*), and *Poeticon astronomicon,* II, 34, 12 (Chatelain, p. 38). Jupiter, Neptune, and Mercury having been well entertained by Hyrieus, son of Neptune by Halcyone, daughter of Atlas, at Tanagra in Boeotia, where he was living, desired to give him evidence of their satisfaction. Hyrieus suggested the gift of a son. They therefore took the hide of the ox he had just sacrificed to them, went to one side, and into it did what, to use the words of Ovid, modesty forbids specifying further. They sewed up the hide, buried it, and at the end of ten months Orion came forth. He was first called by that name from the manner [ἀπὸ τοῦ οὐρῆσαι] of his engendering by the gods in the skin (*Etymologicon magnum,* 823). That bad etymology may have been the only basis for the story mentioned, which was an invention of fairly late poets. Hesiod, who was probably the source of Pherecydes, called him a son of Neptune and Euryala, daughter of Minos (Eratosthenes, *Catasterismi,* 3 [read 32, Schavbach, pp. 25, 58]; Hyginus, *Poeticon astronomicon,* II, 34)." And see § 691 [1].

661 [1] Our friend Larcher, in his notes to Herodotus (§ 653), takes what Palaephatus says quite seriously, *Op. cit.,* Vol. III, p. 494 (on Herodotus, IV, 75): "Medea introduced the use of hot baths into Greece (Palaephatus, *De incredibilibus historiis,* 44). Her use of cauldrons and fire gave the impression that she rejuvenated people by boiling them, and all the more readily in that she kept her method secret so that the doctors would not learn of it. Pelias was suffocated by the steam in his bath."

already alluded to it as one of the means for dissembling non-logical conduct (§ 347). The legend is kept, literally, but the meaning of the terms is altered just enough to eliminate everything implausible.

Familiar to everyone is Hesiod's vivid description, *Theogonia,* vv. 617-735, of the battle between the descendants of Cronus and the Titans, and there can be no question of his intending to do anything more than tell a simple story. The gods had Briareus, Cottus, and Gyges on their side. Each of these giants had a hundred hands and fifty heads. Palaephatus gets out of the hole as follows: "It is said of them that they had a hundred hands, though they were men. How else but call that nonsense? But the truth is this: they lived in a city named Hundredhands, situated in the region now called Orestis. Hence people called Cottus, Briareus, and Gyges the Hundred-handers. On appeal of the gods, they drove the Titans from Olympus." [2] The legend of Aeolus is readily turned into history by making him an astrologer who furnished weather forecasts for Ulysses.[3] It was said that the Chimaera was a lion in front, a goat about the middle, a dragon behind. But that would be impossible: a lion and a goat could not get along on the same fodder! The truth was that the Chimaera was a mountain. On the front slope lived a lion, on the rear slope a dragon, and in between them, goatherds.[4] If you do not find that explanation to your liking you might sample another by that Heraclitus who wrote the treatise *De incredibilibus* (15): "The form of the Chimaera is described by Homer [*Iliad,* VI, vv. 179-82], as: 'lion in front, dragon behind, and goat about the middle.' The truth must be as follows. A woman who was queen of a country had two brothers named Lion and Dragon as co-regents." And if you are still not satisfied, make a try yourself! Diodorus Siculus [*Bibliotheca historica,* III, 56, 5 (Booth, Vol. I, p.

661 [2] *Op. cit.,* 20 (Leipzig, pp. 84-86): Περὶ Κόττου καὶ Βριάρεως · Φασὶν οὖν περὶ τούτων ὡς ἔσχον ἑκατὸν χεῖρας, ἄνδρες ὄντες. πῶς δὲ οὐκ εὔηθες τὸ τοιοῦτον; τὸ δὲ ἀληθὲς οὕτως · τῇ πόλει ὄνομα Ἑκατονταχειρία, ἐν ᾗ ᾤκουν. ἦν δὲ πόλις τῆς νῦν καλουμένης Ὀρεστιάδος. ἔλεγον οὖν οἱ ἄνθρωποι: Κόττος καὶ Βριάρεως καὶ Γύγης οἱ Ἑκατοντάχειρες, βοηθήσαντες τοῖς θεοῖς, αὐτοὶ ἐξήλασαν τοὺς τιτᾶνας ἐκ τοῦ Ὀλύμπου.

661 [3] *Ibid.,* 18 (Leipzig, pp. 79-80): Περὶ τοῦ Αἰόλου.

661 [4] *Ibid.,* 29 (Leipzig, pp. 114-21): Περὶ Βελλεροφόντου.

197)], sees in Uranus a king of the Atlantides, who dwelt on the shores of the Ocean. He had forty-five sons by one woman or another. Eighteen were called Titans from the name of their mother, Titaia. Uranus and Titaia were worshipped as gods after their deaths, the former as Heaven, the latter as Earth. Incredible as it may seem, Palaephatus has found writers even in our day to take him seriously; and traces of his interpretations may be detected in modern theories on totemism and the origins of the family.[5]

662. B-β: *Myths and the like have a historical element combined with an unreal element.* This is one of the more important varieties. Explanations of the kind were widely current in the past and have not yet fallen into desuetude. For many people this has the advantage of reconciling love of legend with a desire for a certain amount of historical verity. It is convenient, furthermore, in that in general it admits of a lavish use of written documents, and in particular enables a writer to draw any inference he chooses from them. The norms for distinguishing what is historical from what is legendary are anything but exact. Everybody therefore twists them—very often without meaning to—in the direction that best serves the purpose in hand.

663. Nowadays ethical and aesthetic appendages are also introduced. That gives, it is claimed, a "living" history as contrasted with a "dead" history, which would be a history aiming strictly at accord with the facts.[1] This procedure, at bottom, substitutes the

661 [5] Grote, *History of Greece,* Vol. I, p. 418 (note 1): "The learned Mr. Jacob Bryant regards the explanations of Palaephatus as if they were founded upon real fact. He admits, for example, the city Nephelê alleged by that author in his exposition of the fable of the Centaurs. Moreover, he speaks with much commendation of Palaephatus generally: 'He [Palaephatus] wrote early, and seems to have been a serious and sensible person; one who saw the absurdity of the fables upon which the theology of his country was founded' (*Ancient Mythology,* Vol. I, pp. 411-35). So also Sir Thomas Browne, *Pseudoxia epidemica or Enquiry into Vulgar Errors,* Book I, Chap. VI (1835, p. 221; 1686, p. 17), alludes to Palaephatus as having incontestably pointed out the real basis of the fables."

663 [1] Renan, *Vie de Jésus,* Preface, p. lv: "In such an effort to bring lofty spirits from the past to life again a certain amount of divination and conjecture has to be allowed. A great life is an organic whole that cannot be translated through a mere agglomeration of little details. A deep feeling has to embrace that whole and create unity. The artistic sense is a trustworthy guide in such matters. The exquisite tact

writer's imagination for history. From the didactic standpoint the substitution may, conceivably, give a reader an image of the past that imprints itself on the mind more vividly than would be possible with a more accurate method. So illustrated histories may prove helpful to children and even to grown-ups by re-enforcing rational with visual memory. But such things are of no concern to science proper.[2]

664. Though Niebuhr rejected the traditional legends of Rome, he saw fit nevertheless to draw to some extent upon them, stepping, that is, from our III-B-α variety to III-B-β. But Duruy is much less scientific than Niebuhr. He simply cannot bring himself to bid farewell to tradition, and seizes every pretext to get back to III-B-α. "It was not," he suddenly bursts out,[1] "that we were intending to deny the existence of Romulus; only, the hymns that were still sung at the time of Augustus and which preserved the poetic history of the first king of Rome we now have to regard as mere legends such as all ancient peoples possessed." [2] In that we are getting pretty close

of a Goethe would there find a task worthy of it. The essential trait of creations of art is that they form living systems, each element depending on every other and determining it." That would be a definition of the historical novel. Renan, *Les Évangiles,* Preface, p. XXXIII: "In this volume, as in its predecessors, my idea has been to follow a golden mean between a criticism marshalling all its resources in defence of texts long since discredited, and an exaggerated scepticism rejecting *in toto* everything that Christianity has to say of its earliest origins." On this method of writing history see Sorel, *Le système historique de Renan,* an essay that deserves attentive reading and mastery. Reinach, *Orpheus,* Chap. VIII, § 27 (Simmonds, p. 226): "Is it even possible to extract the elements of a biography of Jesus from the Gospels? It is contrary to sound method to compose, as Renan did, a life of Jesus, eliminating the marvellous elements of the Gospel story. It is no more possible to make real history with myths than to make bread with the pollen of flowers." Golden words! But why, alas, does Reinach forget them when he sets out in his turn to make true history out of legends, and especially of legends which he imagines have something to do with totemism?

663 [2] We shall return to the matter of historical writing in §§ 1580 f.

664 [1] *Histoire des Romains,* Vol. I, p. 62 (Mahaffy, Vol. I, p. 64).

664 [2] Duruy had remarked earlier, Vol. I, p. 1 (Mahaffy, Vol. I, p. 1): "We have no intention of discussing the legends of the period of the kings. For that the reader interested in such speculations can turn to the first volumes of Niebuhr. . . . For our part such hypotheses, however ingenious and learned they may be, will always be as unreliable as the traditions they combat, and less significant than the admirable narratives of Livy, if not as truth, at least as colouring (*tableaux*)." We must first come to an understanding as to what we are doing. If the idea is

to the method of Palaephatus. How can Duruy cling to the historical existence of Romulus while regarding as legendary the only documents in which the memory of him has come down to us? Only in deference to the non-experimental principle that legend originates in history; and by following a method still less scientific whereby such origins may be recognized under a cloaking of legend.[3]

665. These *a priori* assertions experimental science cannot meet with *a priori* denials. One has to determine by experience, and experience only, whether a proposed method is or is not capable of uncovering the historical reality underlying the legend (§ 547).

666. For such a test we have, fortunately, a series of parallels with history on the one side, legend on the other: we know, that is, a historical fact and also the legend to which it has given rise. Assuming that only the legend is known, we can try to derive the historical fact from it by one method or another, and then we are in a position to determine whether the fact we get in that way is the real fact.

to get a literary effect, a writer may choose his "colouring" where he pleases; and someone else, for reasons equally good, may prefer Ariosto's *Orlando furioso* to the legends chosen by Duruy. If the idea is to write history, a writer's preferences as to colouring are of no importance whatever. The one thing that matters is to determine which account comes closest to the facts.

664 [3] Duruy notes, however, *Ibid.*, Vol. I, pp. 62-63 (Mahaffy, Vol. I, pp. 64-65), that "it would be easy to find resemblances to the Romulus legend in other national traditions. Like Romulus, Semiramis was the offspring of a goddess; like him, and like Cyrus, who was exposed in a forest and reared by a bitch, she was left to die in the desert, supplied with food by doves, and finally rescued by a shepherd of the king." In that Duruy was on the way to a natural classification of legends (§ 675), and he had one of the basic elements already—the fact that eminent personages have to have something extraordinary about their births or origins. Had he gone on, he would have found others. Very soundly he says: "Such legends, which are to be found on the far-away banks of the Ganges in the story of Chandragupta, made up, with others, the common patrimony of the peoples of Aryan extraction." But he soon gets off the track, going back to his historical interpretation, which he has himself barred in deciding that the Romulus legend formed part of a cycle of legends common to the Aryan races: "Romulus may be attached, if one will have it so, to the royal house of Alba. For us he will be just one of the military chieftains familiar in ancient and modern Italy alike, a leader who chanced to become king of a people on which fortunate circumstances and the location of Rome bestowed empire over the world." No, Romulus, Semiramis, Cyrus, and so on, are just names wherein the sentiments that gave rise to the many similar legends noted by Duruy himself attain concrete form.

If it is, the method is good; if not, it is worth little or nothing (§ 547).

667. The reconstruction of the fact must, of course, amount to something more than the mere assertion that certain persons about whom we otherwise know nothing, not even their names, once lived. That would be saying virtually nothing. If we know nothing about Romulus, where do we get by believing, with Duruy, that there was such a person? And why is the legend required, to know that much? The ancient Romans must have had military chieftains, just as all other peoples have had. That is a safe guess—it amounts almost to a certainty; but analogy is enough to tell us that, without requiring any legend of Romulus. The real problem has to be stated, therefore, as follows: Given a legend, have we any means of identifying in it a historical element, small though it be? [1]

668. Virgil is a historical character. On the other hand he is also a legendary character. Thanks to Comparetti's excellent book on Virgil in the Middle Ages, our knowledge of the legend, or, better, the legends about him, is very complete. Could we get at the Virgil of history if we had only the legends to go by?

Comparetti distinguishes two orders of legend: (1) Virgil in literary tradition; (2) Virgil in popular lore. We need concern ourselves here only with the second. The outstanding feature in the legends in mediaeval times is that Virgil is a magician. In many of them the sole points of contact with historical reality are that Virgil is a Roman citizen, and is somehow connected with an Emperor—very little indeed! Comparetti reprints among other legends a tale called "The Marvellous Feats of Virgil." The chapter headings give a fair idea of its character: "I. How Romulus slew Remus, his brother, and how the son of Remus slew Romulus, his uncle. [From the text]: It so happened that Remus, who was Emperor, died, and a son he had became Emperor after him. And that knight who had married the Senator's daughter started a great war which was a heavy burden to him and caused him much expense. That knight

667 [1] Lack of space forbids our treating the problem in the full wealth of its materials, but we must consider at least one example.

had a son by his wife, and he was born with great travail. For he refused to be born, and there was great to-do to make him issue from his mother's womb. But in the end he was born, and he required attentive watching for a long time, and that was why he was named Virgil [*vigilare,* to watch]. . . . II. Of the birth of Virgil, and how he was put to school. . . . And when Virgil was born the whole city of Rome shook from one end to the other. . . . Virgil had gone to Tollette to school, for he was a willing scholar, and he was very wise in the arts of necromancy. . . . III. How Virgil came to Rome and complained to the Emperor. . . . IV. How the Emperor of Rome assailed Virgil in his castle. . . . V. How Virgil shut up the Emperor and his army inside a wall. . . . VI. How the Emperor made peace with Virgil. . . . And it came to pass that Virgil fell enamoured of a damsel . . . and he besought her love through an old witch." The damsel gets word to Virgil *"que se vouloit coucher avec elle,* he must come very quietly (*tout quoy*) to the foot of the tower where she slept, after all the people were in their beds, and she would let down to him a basket tied to a rope, and he should get into the basket, and she would raise it up to her chamber. . . . VII. How the damsel left Virgil hanging in the basket." The damsel makes a fool of Virgil, but he gets even: "Virgil took his books and brought it to pass that all the hearth-fires in Rome went out, and there was no one who could bring fire into Rome from outside the city. . . . VIII. How Virgil extinguished the fires of Rome." The Emperor and his barons ask Virgil how they can get fire, and he replies: "You will build a scaffold in the market-place, and cause this damsel who left me hanging in the basket the other day to mount thereon naked in her shift, and you will have it cried through all Rome that whosoever would have fire shall come to the scaffold to get it lighted *à la nature dicelle damoiselle;* otherwise shall they have none. . . . IX. How the damsel was placed on the scaffold and how each person went there to light his candle or his torch as said. . . . X. How Virgil made a lamp that never went out. . . . XI. Hereinafter of the orchard that Virgil caused to grow [around the spring that fed the pond]. . . . XII. The image that

Virgil made of his wife." The image "was of such virtue that every woman who had seen it lost all desire *de faire le peché de fournication.* Whereat the women of Rome who loved for love's sake were exceeding wroth." They complain to Virgil's wife, and she upsets the image and breaks it. "XIII. How Virgil repaired the image and tripped his wife [so that she fell, like the image], and how he built a bridge over the sea." One of the Sultan's daughters falls in love with Virgil, and he brings her back to Rome (*chez lui*) on "a bridge in the air over the sea. . . . XIV. How Virgil took the damsel back to her country. . . . XV. How Virgil was arrested together with the damsel, and how he escaped, carrying the damsel off with him. . . . XVI. How Virgil escaped and carried the damsel back and founded the city of Naples. . . . XVII. How the Emperor of Rome besieged the city of Naples. . . . XVIII. How Virgil had the city peopled with scholars and traders (*marschandises*). . . . XIX. How Virgil made a serpent in Rome. . . . XX. How Virgil died."[1]

668 [1] *Virgilio nel medio evo,* Vol. II, pp. 282-300 (missing in Benecke). *Les faictz merveilleux de Virgille.* Several incidents in this legend are told of other persons in other tales. In the story of Joseph of Arimathea, the hero of the basket incident is Hippocrates, the only difference being that the vengeance ensues in a different form. Paulin Paris, *Les romans de la Table ronde,* Vol. I, pp. 246-71: "The history of the philosophers bears witness that Hippocrates was the most highly skilled of all men in the arts of physic. He lived long years in no special renown; but a thing he did in Rome spread the fame of his incomparable wizardry everywhere." He comes to Rome at the time when Gaius, nephew of the Emperor Augustus Caesar, was being mourned as dead. He perceives that the young man is not really dead, and heals him, whereat he is greatly honoured and petted by the Emperor. He falls enamoured of a lady who came to Rome from Gaul. She feigns consent and induces him to enter a basket that he may be drawn up to her chamber. "The lady and her maid were on watch at their window. They pulled the cord to the height of the room that Hippocrates thought he was to enter; but then they continued pulling, so that the basket was raised more than two lance-lengths above their window. Then they tied the cord to a hook in the wall, and cried: 'A good time to you, Hippocrates! That is the way to treat philanderers (*musards*) like you!' " The next morning Hippocrates is the laughing-stock of the city. But he takes measures to get even. He gives a certain herb to an uncouth and crippled dwarf. When the lady is touched with the herb, she falls in love with the dwarf, marries him, and is left to live with him. The writer, who seems not to have had a very fertile imagination, repeats the adventure once again to encompass the death of Hippocrates. Dardanus, nephew to Antonius, King of Persia, is given up for dead. Hippocrates heals him and in company with Antonius visits the King of Tyre, and receives his daughter in marriage. But the princess is contemptuous of such a match. After

669. Now suppose we knew nothing about Virgil except this long legend. How much historical fact could we get from it? None whatever! The story may be as interesting, amusing, or lively as one pleases, but it has no bearing on fact at all.

670. If we choose to go sailing out on the high seas of interpretation, we may get what we please from the legend by inferences that look persuasive enough, but which lead to nothing in any way according with historical realities. One might see in it a reminiscence of a great war between Rome and Naples, just as the *Iliad* is supposed to record a war between the Greeks and Asiatics. The erotic adventures of Virgil might tempt one to class him among the gods of generation, of whom he would be a Roman, or shall I say a Neapolitan, form. His difficulty in getting into the world might lead us to regard him as one of the manifestations of Hercules, or if you prefer, of Bacchus; and Naples being a Greek colony, such hypotheses would have a basis in history; and a pretty and very sizable monograph could be written to show that the legend is one of the many

many attempts on her husband's life have been checkmated by his wizardry, she finally takes advantage of his very science to poison him. King Antonius is in despair and asks whether there be no remedy. " 'There might be one,' [Hippocrates answers.] 'It would be to have a woman heat a big slab of marble burning hot by being stretched out on it entirely naked.' 'Well, let us try: and since your wife is the cause of your death, she will be the one we shall stretch out on the marble.' . . . So the lady was stretched out on the marble, and the cold of the stone gradually taking possession of her, she died in cruel pain an hour before Hippocrates." These stories simmer down to certain sentiments that are elaborated in forms more or less attractive and ingenious, the stories thus constructed being thereupon attributed to some well-known individual. The chief sentiments in this case are three: 1. The sentiment associated with the fact that the wise or the powerful can be brought to ruin by insignificant causes. It is a sentiment arising from the ups and downs commonly observable in life. 2. A misogynic sentiment, whereby a woman becomes the instrument of ruin for the wise or the powerful. 3. The sentiment of vengeance. The amount of fiction that originates in such sentiments is prodigious. Agamemnon, bravest of warriors, conqueror of the Trojans, is slain in his bath by a weak woman, but he is avenged by his son. Virgil the magician is tricked by a silly woman; but he more than evens the score. The wizard Hippocrates is able to raise the dead; but he cannot keep his wife from poisoning him. In the end he repays her. The names Agamemnon, Virgil, Hippocrates, or others equally famous are altogether incidental and may be replaced by others at will. The episodes themselves are of little importance. They vary at the fancy of the person who invents the legend or copies an old one.

associated with the invasion of Roman soil by the gods of Greece. And we could point to the *senatus consultus* against the Bacchanals (§ 1108) and connect Virgil's obscene device—he would now be a manifestation of Bacchus—for relighting the hearth-fires of Rome with the obscenities of the Bacchic mysteries. Many interpretations of legends rest on proofs much weaker than this, which we know to be entirely false.[1]

671. Some legends may have been elaborated otherwise; but it is also possible that they may have been developed like the one above; and unless we have some historical authority for deciding we can infer nothing, absolutely nothing, of a historical character from them.[1] Such legends one may find to one's heart's content in antiquity, in the Middle Ages, and even in modern times, and all along romance may be seen combining with history in an unmistakable manner. So when only the mixture is known, we have no way of telling how it was compounded.[2]

670 [1] Other methods of interpretation would yield other results; but they would all be foreign to reality (§ 789).

671 [1] Sorel, *Le système historique de Renan,* Vol. I, p. 41: "The interpretation of apocalypses was to play a great rôle in the labours that Renan was intending to undertake in 1848. We have seen that such a method could only eventuate in a discovery of history as underlying legend. I do not believe there is any fallacy more dangerous than the one involved in such an enterprise. Legend may throw invaluable light on the manners of thinking of a people. But it cannot give historical facts; and it was facts that Renan was intending to ask of his apocalypses."

671 [2] Chassang, *Histoire du roman . . . dans l'antiquité grecque et latine,* pp. 432-33: "One need merely glance at the Byzantine chroniclers to discover reminiscences of the old romances everywhere. . . . Zonaras, for instance, knows the stories of Cyrus according to Herodotus (*Historiae,* I) and according to Xenophon, and he prefers the latter, because, he says [*Epitome historiarum,* III, 26; Migne, Vol. 134, p. 311], 'he is writing a compendium and need only give the most plausible accounts.' For Cicero the *Cyropaedia* was just a story [*Epistulae, Ad Quintum fratrem,* I, 1, 8, 23]. Thanks to Zonaras it makes its bow as history. Cedrenus [*Historiarum compendium,* I, 136-37; Bekker, Vol. I, pp. 239-41], on a happier impulse, follows Herodotus, but stirs into the narrative of the historian of Halicarnassus a number of Jewish or Christian legends [notably that of the relations of Cyrus to one Daniel, who converted him to belief in the Jehovah of the pre-Christians]. Those stories appear in still ampler elaboration in Malalas [*Chronographia,* VI, 201 (158); Migne, p. 259]. Malalas, to be sure, has his authority, and a very imposing one: Julius the African, no less, who notes among the sources he used a *History of the War between Cyrus and the Samians,* written by the sage Pythagoras of Samos!"

672. A common method of interpretation lies in eliminating apparently fictional elements from a narrative and keeping the rest as history (§ 258). Used not as interpretation but as a mere device for eliminating incidental elements from texts that on the whole have their status as history, this method is not only helpful but in many cases indispensable. Few the texts of antiquity in which history is not interspersed with marvels; and if we were to reject them as history because of the miracles, we would know nothing whatever of antiquity—or even of times more recent.

673. But let us not overlook the two essential conditions (§ 258): The fiction has to be incidental, and the part held to be historical must have additional traits, and sufficient corroboration, to make it evidently historical. If the legendary element predominates, if the historical element is without corroborating testimony, or at least a fair amount of probability, the method becomes mere interpretation and is entirely misleading. In short, the reasons for accepting the testimony of a writer must be intrinsic to his person and his work, and not lie in any extrinsic principle that what is plausible has to be distinguished from what is not. The fact that a thing is plausible is not enough to make it true.

674. That is not all. There are cases where, if we eliminate elements suspected of being fictional and keep such as are apparently historical, we eliminate the very element that, if not true, has a chance of being true, and keep what is certainly false. A mediaeval story-book of Roman history [1] says: "We read in the chronicles that in the twenty-second year after the foundation of Rome, the Romans erected a marble column in the Capitol of the city, and on the column they placed the statue of Julius Caesar, and on the statue his name was inscribed. But this Caesar had three marvellous signs before dying. The hundredth day before his death the lightning struck in front of his statue, obliterating the first letter of his name. The night before his death the windows of his bedchamber flew open so violently that he thought the house was falling. On the very day

674 [1] *Le violier des histoires romaines*, pp. 229-30 [*Gesta Romanorum*, Dick ed., no. 80, p. 50].

he was killed, as he was entering the Capitol, some letters of warning were handed to him. They foretold his death, and had he read them, he would have escaped his murder and death." If we were to keep such parts of this story as seem to be historical and eliminate the apparently fanciful, we should have to keep the statement that Caesar was living in the year 22 A.U.C. and that in that year a column bearing his name and topped by his statue was erected in his honour in the Capitol. All of which would be entirely false. Meantime we would have to eliminate the three portents that preceded Caesar's death, and which, by the writer's own admission, are in the nature of miracles. But the portents are the things best corroborated in the histories most nearly contemporary with Caesar. They may be false: but they also may be true, at least in part.[2]

675. In the Virgilian legend mentioned we get an illustration of the way in which myths in general develop. It is something like the formation of crystals. Drop a grain of sand into a saturated solution of alum, and a number of large crystals will be seen to form about it. So around a story that has no basis in fact, but is a mere objectification of a sentiment, other stories of the same kind with various ornaments cluster, and form an agglomerate with it. Sometimes the characters are left imaginary; then again they are chosen from among historical characters whom the adventure seems best to fit. Once the character, historical or otherwise, is so chosen, he oftentimes becomes a type and is given a part in other imaginary adventures. Such characters, and even the adventures, are obviously incidental elements in the story, the chief element being the sentiments that it expresses. Ordinarily literary historians invert those relations: they stress the characters and the adventures, and disregard the sentiments to express which the stories were invented.[1] So

674 [2] Suetonius, *Divus Julius,* 81, 3-4: "And suddenly the doors of his bedroom opened of their own accord. . . . About eleven o'clock (*fere quinta hora*) he set forth, and a letter warning of the plot against him was handed to him by a chance passer-by. He mixed it in with other letters he was carrying in his left hand, as though intending to read it later." And *cf.* Dio Cassius, *Historia Romana,* XLIV, 18; Plutarch, *Caesar,* 65 (Perrin, Vol. VII, p. 595).

675 [1] The theories and manners of thinking current in society are generally treated in the same way. First prominence is given to the accessory elements—logi-

artificial classifications are obtained, all stories dealing with a given character, and resembling each other only in that subordinate respect, being grouped together. Whereas a "natural" classification would put into one class all stories expressing the same sentiments and therefore resembling one another in a major respect, the names that are used to give concrete point to the expression being disregarded, or virtually so (§ 684 [2]). So, again, around a historical fact so insignificant as oftentimes to amount to no more than a mere name (Virgil), a rank tanglewood of fiction flourishes, that has nothing absolutely to do with history. When, then, we examine such legends with a view to their origins, we cannot expect to find these in the pseudo-historical element, but only in the principal element—in the sentiments that are expressed.

676. So it is that around a single name a motley agglomerate of adventure gathers. That was the case with the gods of paganism. When later on, in the early days of criticism, it was seen that all those adventures could not possibly be assigned to a single person, a way was sought to account for the legend. The manner of development just described not being known, scholars preferred to see two, three, or even more persons in the god or hero to whom the many adventures had been attributed. So, as in the interpretations of Palaephatus, the letter of the legend was respected while its meaning was changed. Cicero enumerates three Jupiters, five Vulcans, three Aesculapiuses, and so on.[1]

677. There is no denying that in some cases divinities of different peoples were fused into one and given one same name. Of that the assimilation of Greek to Roman divinities would be sufficient proof.

cal expositions and pseudo-experience, non-logical conduct, which is the principal element, being relegated to the background or entirely ignored. These present volumes on sociology aim at restoring those elements to their natural relative position. That is why we began with a study of non-logical conduct. That is why we have given, are here giving, and will continue to give examples of inversions in the order of those elements. Later on, after we have distinguished them, and evaluated them according to their importance, we shall study them each in particular (Chapters VI to X). Until we have finished that task, we shall not have the real elements in the social equilibrium.

676 [1] *De natura deorum,* III, 22, 55-60.

The error lies in the assumption that all legends must have originated in that way.

678. As usual, let us revert to experience to determine how such legends are formed (§ 547). In plenty of cases it is apparent that the name of a person to whom a variety of adventures have been ascribed is not a name for two or three persons who have been blended into one. An amusing story, for instance, is told of Mme. de Talleyrand. But if we look into the facts it develops that the story was current long before Mme. de Talleyrand was born or thought of. She had the reputation of being a stupid woman, and she was therefore credited with incidents befitting the woman she was supposed to be.[1]

Her husband, on the other hand, was famous as a witty, shrewd, intelligent man; and in the same way he was credited with all the witty stories that came along. Fournier alleges that Talleyrand often appropriated the jests he read in the *Improvisateur français* and adds:[2] "But oftentimes he was provisioned with wit with even less effort on his part. He gathered them in from all hands without meaning to, even without knowing. Every jest to the point took his name for its flag, and so recommended enjoyed only the greater vogue in virtue of the careless habit talkers have, as Nodier says, of

678 [1] Lacombe, *La vie privée de Talleyrand,* p. 197: ". . . as witness this other story which made Napoleon burst into a laugh every time he thought of it at St. Helena (O'Meara, *Napoleon in Exile,* Vol. I, p. 435): Talleyrand had invited Denon, the Egyptologist, to dinner. With the idea that his wife should have a subject of conversation handy, he suggested that she read one of Denon's books. Going to the library, she picked up, by mistake, a copy of *Robinson Crusoe,* which she devoured at one sitting. At table that evening, still thrilling with the tale, she could hardly wait to take up Denon's marvellous adventures with him. 'Oh, Monsieur Denon, what a strain it must have been! Your ship wrecked! That desert island! But I'll guess you looked funny in that pointed hat!' The scholar gazed at her in amazement; nor did the mystery clear till Mme. de Talleyrand began on the subject of his man Friday. . . . The trouble with the story is that it is told now with Denon, now with Humboldt, now with a certain Sir George Robinson as hero; and worse yet, it was not invented for Mme. de Talleyrand. Years before her day, it seems, society wags were peddling it about, with just one variant: the mistake was ascribed to a priest. It would take a volume to accommodate all the anecdotes current on the Princesse de Bénévent [Mme. de Talleyrand]."

678 [2] *L'esprit dans l'histoire,* p. 267.

attaching all they know to well-known names.[3] A jest of his sometimes did not get to his ears until after it was worn out and become altogether stale. Hearing it then when it was an old story with everyone else, he would still be ingenuously laughing at it as the latest hit, though everybody had long since tired of it."

679. Another historical character, but one of ancient times, is credited with many implausible adventures: Laïs the courtesan. As usual, to remove incongruities in the story two Laïses were called in. "The conjecture," says Bayle,[1] "that there were two courtesans by the name of Laïs is based on the fact that it is chronologically impossible to attribute all that is reported of Laïs to one woman." But that is not the end of it; Bayle shows that to reconcile all details in the narrative, three different Laïses have to be assumed. It is preferable, he rightly adds, to imagine that Laïs has been credited with adventures of other courtesans.[2]

678 [3] Fournier notes, *Questions de littérature légale,* p. 68: "According to the *British Review,* October, 1840, p. 316, the person thus chosen as responsible for the jest of the day is to the dandies of the Parisian Mayfair what the statue of Pasquino is to the idlers of Rome: a sort of common bill-board on which anybody feels free to paste up his jests good or bad."

679 [1] *Dictionnaire historique, s.v.* Laïs.

679 [2] Bayle says in full: "There is a conjecture that there were two courtesans named Laïs. The lady here in question was carried to Corinth at the time when Nicias was in command of the Athenian army in Sicily, in other words, in the year 2 of the 91st Olympiad. She was then seven years old, if we are to believe the scholiast of Aristophanes [*Plutus,* v. 179; Dübner, pp. 334, 550, 662]. Now since Demosthenes did not dare to go to Corinth to visit Laïs except by stealth, he could not have been a stripling schoolboy, but a man already of some reputation. Let us make him at least thirty. That would make Laïs sixty-seven. There is no probability therefore either that Demosthenes cared much about seeing her, or that she would have held out for an exorbitant price. So then, it must have been another Laïs who had her eye on the wallet of Demosthenes. If we say that Demosthenes made the trip to Corinth at about twenty, Laïs would still be well on toward sixty. Speaking of Laïs, Plutarch expressly states that she was a girl from Hyccara in Sicily and that she had been carried away from there as a slave. So, according to Plutarch [*Alcibiades,* 37], the Laïs the Younger mentioned by Athenaeus was the Laïs born in Sicily before the 91st Olympiad; so that if the Laïs who asked the money of Demosthenes is a different Laïs, there have to be three courtesans by that name. . . . For my part, instead of assuming two Laïses, I should be inclined to imagine that the Greek writers, who were not strong on chronology, attributed to the famous Laïs an adventure of Demosthenes which concerned another woman." [The confusions about Laïs do not stop there. Villon, in his "Ballade of the Fair Dames

680. Some legends have a historical origin. The *Chanson de Roland* studied by Gaston Paris is one such.[1] One historical detail seems authentic: "On the fifteenth of August, 778, the rear-guard of the army that Charles, King of the Franks, was leading back from Spain after a half-successful expedition, was ambushed and destroyed in the Pyrenees by Basques of Navarre with whom the Franks were not openly at war." The King turned back, but was unable to avenge the massacre of his soldiers and had to proceed on his way. "Such the version given in the royal *Annales* and in Eginhard's *Life of Charlemagne*. It is the version adopted by all our historians. The Arab version is quite different. According to Ibn-al-Athir, 'it was the Mussulmans of Saragossa, the very people who had called Charlemagne to Spain, who inflicted that serious defeat on the Franks at a time when they were off Arab territory and were thinking themselves altogether safe.' "

On that scanty historical foundation a spacious edifice of legend was built up without any extrinsic trait to justify one in going back from the legend to history. After attempting a reconstruction of the true story of the battle, Gaston Paris observes: "Of the fight as we are able to picture it to ourselves very little is left in our poem." And he concludes: "We may infer from all that . . . that the *Chanson de Roland* certainly rests, in the beginning, on direct knowledge of events, people, and places, and that in certain respects it even shows very remarkable accord with the information supplied by history. But the form in which it has come down to us, a form three centuries posterior to the primitive form, is widely at variance with the latter, and that is due very largely to successive inventions by amplifiers and rewriters who were thinking only of literary effects and who, moreover, had no other source of information on the events celebrated in the *Chanson* than the poem itself." But what is the good of knowing that the legend has a historical background

of Long Ago," makes Alcibiades a female prostitute, first cousin to Thaïs: *"Achipiada ne Thaïs—Qui fut sa cousine germaine."* That is a confused reminiscence of Plutarch's description of Laïs as daughter to a concubine of the famous Athenian statesman.—A. L.]

680 [1] *Légendes du moyen âge,* pp. 3-4, 53-54, 61-62.

if we have no means of identifying the latter under the legendary trappings? The *Chanson de Roland* had a basis in historical fact. By a false analogy, are we to extend that conclusion to all the legends of the Carlovingian cycle? That would be a grave mistake, because for many of them no such historical background exists.[2] The principle of considering anything smacking of the supernatural as fictional may therefore, as proofs in abundance show, work more or less well with documents that are mainly historical; but it nearly always leads amiss when applied to legends. From legends lacking in extrinsic historical adjuncts we can therefore infer little or nothing that is historically real—nothing rather than little.

681. B-$\beta 1$: *Myths and the like have historical origins, and the stories have undergone alterations in course of time.* The remarks just made for our variety B-β apply also to the subvariety B-$\beta 1$. A type of this species is a euhemerism that we will call old-fashioned to distinguish it from the neo-euhemerism of Spencer.

682. Little is known about the *Sacred Anagraphs* of Euhemerus. From accounts of the work given by other writers we may distinguish two elements in it: first an interpretation, and then the proofs that are given of it. The interpretation, which views the gods as nothing but deified human beings, is partly sound, if not in the cases

680 [2] Many legends of the Carlovingian cycle have nothing to do with reality. We read, for instance, in Ménage, *Menagiana,* Vol. I, p. 110: "One of the greatest ingenuities ever written is the story in the 'Tale of Galien Restored' of the reception given by King Hugon, Emperor of Constantinople, to Charlemagne and his peers, and what followed from it. Charlemagne and his Twelve Peers stopped at Constantinople on their way back from the Holy Sepulchre, and were entertained in the palace of King Hugon. After a magnificent banquet, attended by his wife the Queen, his two sons, the princes Henry and Tiberius, and his daughter, the fair Jacqueline, he led them into a magnificent hall where they were to pass the night." Before falling asleep Charlemagne and his peers amuse themselves by boasting of imposible feats at arms. Such swaggering coming to the ears of King Hugon, he compels Charlemagne and his peers to make good their boasts. Heaven helping, Charlemagne cuts a fully armoured man in two at one stroke—and the story runs on. Suppose a story of that kind were found in Suidas, instead of in the *Menagiana,* and suppose the characters were Greek heroes. We may be certain that there would be no end of commentary to a thousand different purports in an effort to discover underneath it some historical basis, which it surely does not have. Strip the legend of everything marvellous, reduce it to the bare fact of Charlemagne's visit to Constantinople—and we get a fact that is altogether false!

mentioned by Euhemerus, at least in other similar cases. The proofs are worth nothing. Euhemerus asserts that he arrived, in the course of his travels, at an island called Panchaea, which was wholly consecrated to the gods, and that he saw there a temple to Zeus Triphylius, which had been built by that god in person while he was still living on earth. In the temple stood a golden column commemorating achievements ascribed to Uranus, Cronus, and Zeus, all three of whom had lived on earth and sat on thrones. Euhemerus filled a whole book with the deeds of men who had become gods.

After all, we do not know whether the travels in question were offered as proofs or whether they were a mere literary device for developing a theory which had, for that matter, different and better proofs. Several ancient writers considered the stories of Euhemerus downright lies. Strabo was of that opinion. After mentioning certain stories that he considers inventions, he adds:[1] "All that is not so very different from the hoaxes of Pitteas, Euhemerus, and Antiphanes. But those writers may be forgiven them. These charlatans are merely feathering their nests." Polybius too seems to have considered Euhemerus a deliberate liar. But it was only the testimony of Euhemerus that he rejected. As regards the interpretation, he too held that the gods were once men. He says, for a sample:[2] "Aeolus taught navigators how to manoeuvre in the Straits [of Messina], which are winding and difficult of egress because of the ebb and flow; and that was why he was called a dispenser of winds and held to be king thereof." He mentions other similar cases, and concludes, *loc. cit.*, 8-9: "So in each of the gods we see homage rendered to the inventor of some useful thing."

683. Polybius was familiar with real facts that showed how human beings had been deified. He notes, X, 10, 11 (Paton, Vol. IV, p. 125), that there were three low hills near New Carthage: "The one to the east is called the hill of Hephaestus. The one next to it bears the name of Alestus, who, it is said, came to be honoured as a god for

682 [1] *Geographica,* II, 3, 5.

682 [2] *Historiae,* XXXIV, 2, 5 (Paton, Vol. VI, p. 299). Polybius is criticized by Strabo, *Geographica,* I, 2, 15 (Jones, Vol. I, pp. 85-87).

having discovered the silver mines. The third is known as the hill of Cronus."

684. The Fathers of the Church, who in general did not make any great use of historical criticism, could be expected to offer favourable welcome to the theories and proofs of Euhemerus, which fitted their bill to perfection. St. Augustine holds it the most credible opinion that the gods were men, each of them succeeding, according to his abilities, manners of living, conduct, and various fortuities, in being deemed a god by his flatterers and in winning worship and rites.[1] Just previously, VII, 7, he had said: "What did they think of Jupiter, no less—they who placed his nurse in the Capitol? Do they not bear witness for Euhemerus, who, not as a teller of tales, but as a diligent historian, wrote that all those gods had been men and mortal?" Lactantius takes seriously what Ennius, following Euhemerus, says about the reigns on earth of Uranus and Saturn.[2] Says Minucius

684 [1] *De civitate Dei,* VII, 18.

684 [2] Lactantius Firmianus, *Divinae institutiones,* I, *De falsa religione,* XI, 33, and 45-47 (*Opera,* Vol. I, pp. 42, 44-45; Fletcher, Vol. I, pp. 30-32): "Euhemerus, a writer of the old days, who came from Messene, collected the biographies of Jupiter and other men who are considered gods, and compiled a history from the titles and inscriptions that were preserved in sacred temples of most ancient date, and especially in the shrine of Jupiter Triphylius, where a title on a certain column of gold indicated that it had been erected by Jupiter himself, and in it he had recounted his deeds, that it should be a reminder of his life to posterity. . . . Having described in his [Latin version of the] *Sacred History* [of Euhemerus] everything Jupiter had done in his lifetime, Ennius concludes [Fragment 725, Giles, p. 68]: 'Having five times gone about the whole earth, Jupiter divided his realms among relatives and friends, left laws and customs for men, taught them agriculture, and did many other good things. Eager not to be forgotten, yearning for undying glory, he left abiding memorials to his people. In the utter fullness of age he died (*vitam commutavit*) in Crete and went away to the gods; and the Curetes, his sons, cared for his body (*eum*) and clothed it with royal raiment (*decoraverunt eum*) [This may also mean: "paid worship to him, and decked his shrine with garlands." —A. L.]; and his tomb is in Crete in the town of Cnossus; and it is said that Vesta was the founder of that city; and on his tomb is written in ancient Greek characters: ZAN KRONOU, which is to say in Latin: "Jupiter [son] of Saturn." And these things are handed down to us not by fanciful poets, but by scholars (*antiquarum rerum scriptores*).'" Lycophron, *Cassandra,* v. 1194 (Mair, pp. 591-93), mentions the region where Zeus was born. In comment on the verse Tzetzes (Potter, p. 123) says that scholars know that kings bore the name of Zeus and were called gods and that Zeuses were born in Crete, Arcady, Thebes, and a thousand

Felix, *Octavius,* 21, 1-2 (Randall, p. 373; Freese, pp. 62-63): "Read the writings of historians or philosophers, and you will agree with me that men have been made gods because of their merits or their philanthropies, as Euhemerus relates; for he tells the manner of their birth, their native towns, and the location of their tombs, designating the places [to which they belong], such as the Dictaean Jupiter, the Delphic Apollo, the Pharian Isis, the Eleusinian Ceres. Prodicus says that those men were made gods who, travelling about the world and finding new things of use, brought them home to their peoples. Of that opinion is Persaeus, and he adds that their names were given to the things they found, whence the savoury proverb: 'Apart from Liber and Ceres Venus droops.'"[3]

685. Very numerous in times present and past are interpretations of this variety that are used to strip a story of its less credible elements in order to save the rest. So, for example, miraculous births are transfigured into natural births, and, as Dante says:

. . . e vien Quirino
Da sì vil padre che si rende a Marte.[1]

other places—καὶ ἐν ἑτέροις μυρίοις τόποις—where they had inscriptions. The usual case of similar sentiments finding expression in various ways (§ 675). *Cf.* Arnobius, *Disputationes adversus gentes,* IV, 14 (Bryce-Campbell, pp. 195-97). St. Cyprian, *De idolorum vanitate,* II, says (*Opera,* p. 567; Wallis, Vol. I. p. 444): "A cave of Jove may be visited in Crete, and his tomb is pointed out to one." St. Epiphanius, *Ancoratus,* 106 (*Opera,* Vol. III, p. 210), says of Zeus that "his grave is known to not a few, since even in our day it is shown on Mount Lasius in Crete." *Cf.* Clement of Alexandria, *Protrepticus* (*Exhortation to the Greeks*), II, 32 (Butterworth, p. 79). Non-Christian writers also mention the tomb of Zeus: Cicero, *De natura deorum,* III, 21, 53; Lucian, *De sacrificiis,* 10 (Harmon, Vol. III, p. 165); Statius, *Thebaid,* I, vv. 278-79; Lucan, *Pharsalia,* VIII, v. 872. In his *Hymnus in Jovem,* vv. 6-9, Callimachus brands stories of the kind as lies: "Zeus, some say that thou wert born on Mount Ida in Crete, others in Arcady. Which, O Father, are the liars? The Cretans are perpetual liars, for they have built a tomb they say is thine, O King. But thou art not dead: thou art eternal."

684 [3] [Randall drops his knitting to render the proverb daintily: "Venus without Liber and Ceres is a-cold." It goes better, however, in American: "Venus without Liber and Ceres is a-frost."—A. L.]

685 [1] "From such base lineage doth Quirinus come, who is hailed the son of Mars." *Paradiso,* VIII, vv. 130-31. [Romulus was son of Rhea by father unknown. Legend made Mars the parent.—A. L.]

686. To the present variety belong theories that derive the nature and properties of a thing from the etymology of its name.[1] The premise of such theories is, implicitly at least, that each thing was originally given a name corresponding exactly to its nature. That premise metaphysicists, still implicitly, may supplement with others; things being as the human mind imagines them, to reason from the name of a thing is tantamount to reasoning from the thing. This, in a word, is one of the many cases in which subjective sentiments are endowed with objective reality. The theory attains its maximum absurdity in Plato's *Cratylus.*

687. However, ignoring such *a priori* considerations, let us, as usual, appeal to experience. It may well be that in our day scientists try to name new things in such a way as to indicate some of their properties. In such a case etymology might be of use in discovering, if not the actual properties of a thing, at least the notion its discoverer had of it. So the name "oxygen" indicates not that that body is the sole generator of oxides, but that those who gave it the name (Scheele, Priestley, Lavoisier) thought that it was. The names given by people at large, and therefore most of the terms of ordinary language, do not have even that modified significance. They depend upon accidental circumstances which have often little or nothing to do with the nature of the thing.[1]

688. Among rigorously etymological interpretations one has remained famous. It was long believed that *servus,* "slave," came from *servare,* "to save," *i.e.,* to keep safe or sound; and a very pretty

686 [1] See Chapter X.

687 [1] Darmesteter, *La vie des mots,* pp. 41-42. Speaking of the quality of an object that serves to give it a name, Darmesteter says: "It is interesting that the quality need not at all be essential and really denominative. The French word *cahier* is, etymologically, a group of four things (O.F. *caier, caern, cadern,* Lat. *quaternum,* 'group of four' ['sheets,' understood]). . . . *Confection* is just a 'preparation' (Lat. *confectio*). *Chapelet* is just a 'little crown' (*chapel,* 'garland')." Töpffer, *Nouveaux voyages en zig-zag,* p. 6 (trip to the Grande Chartreuse): "Let a group of people live together, travel together, just for a few days, and you will inevitably see words and acceptations of words growing up which are strictly peculiar to the group, and this so certainly and so naturally that, just the reverse of what the scholars say, it seems much harder to explain how a language could fail to develop wherever human beings are consorting together than to imagine how it actually arises."

theory of slavery was derived from the etymology. The *Institutes* of Justinian say, I, 3, 3: "Slaves were called *servi* because the generals ordered that prisoners of war be sold, and therefore were wont to 'save' and not to slay them."[1] But that etymology is no longer accepted. *Servus,* it now seems, means "guardian of a house," and our pretty theory of slavery goes by the board.[2] A pity indeed! But if anyone is anxious to deliver himself of a theory of slavery based on the new etymology, he ought to attend to it at once, before the etymology is changed on us again.

689. In Italy and countries where there are any great numbers of Italian labourers, the name *crumiro* is used to designate a man who works while his comrades are on strike—a "scab." If this word were Latin or Greek, we might derive many pretty etymological theories from it: *crumiro,* or *krumiro* (as many write it) from κρούω, "to knock" or "beat," whence κροῦμα, "blow," "stroke," the etymology so indicating that the *crumiri,* or *krumiri,* were "beaten" by their fellow-workers. Many etymologies that have been and still are current are more far-fetched than that. As a matter of fact we know where the word comes from. The Krumiri were a tribe in Tunis, and the French took imaginary depredations by that tribe as a pretext for invading Tunis. The displeasure occasioned in Italy by the episode led to an association of the name Krumiri with unpleasant sentiments. When Italian working-men came to feel other unpleasant sentiments for men who they thought were betraying them in times of strike, they forthwith labelled them *crumiri* (§ 547).

690. This case is typical of a very wide-spread class. Every day we see new words and phrases originating in associations of ideas that

688 [1] *Corpus iuris civilis,* Vol. I, p. 4; Scott, Vol. II, p. 8: *"Servi autem ex eo appellati sunt quod imperatores captivos vendere jubent, ac per hoc servare nec occidere solent."*

688 [2] Bréal-Bailly, *Op. cit., s.v. Servus: "Servus* literally means 'guardian' . . . the slave being considered as the guardian of the house." James Darmesteter, *Notes sur quelques expressions zendes,* p. 309: "That origin of the word being gradually forgotten, *servus* came to mean simply 'slave,' and that sense is the only one that figures in derivatives such as *servio* and *servitus.* The etymology of *servus* understood as a prisoner of war whose life has been 'saved' is therefore to be rejected."

are frequently quite fortuitous.[1] If, in some period in the distant future, someone tries to discover what they mean by going directly from word to thing, he will certainly miss the mark. It is evident therefore that if we, in our time, use that method to get at things of the remote past, we may sometimes hit the truth, but may just as easily go astray.

691. The direct etymological procedure derives the name from the properties of the thing; the inverse procedure ascribes certain properties to the thing simply because of its name. This latter seems to have played a considerable rôle in mythology, and it is probable that many mythological episodes were invented because of names.[1] In many cases, however, it is a question of mere probabilities, and conclusive proofs are lacking.[2]

692. B-β2: *Myths and the like are made up of experiences wrongly*

690 [1] *Liberté,* Dec. 10, 1910 (from the *Cri de Paris*): *"Elle sait où est le compteur* —'She knows where the gas-meter is'—is the latest fad in the way of slang. It is going the rounds of the cabarets and vaudeville houses. You do not say of a woman: 'She is being seen about town with Monsieur X.' You say: 'She knows where his gas-meter is!'; and everybody understands. All the same, very few know how the expression started. . . . It seems that one of our playwrights, a young man and rich, invited a number of very pretty actresses and a few gentlemen to attend a reading of a new play of his in a studio which he prefers on certain occasions to his official residence. The company made their way in a body into a room shrouded in blackest darkness. The dramatist struck a match, turned on a gas-jet, and cried: 'Dear me—my franc has run out!' Without a moment's hesitation, though the room was dark, one of the young ladies opened a panel and pointed to the gas-meter. Light dawned in the room and in the wits of the company. The elect of the moment had betrayed herself. 'Oh, so she knows where the gas-meter is!' And the phrase took Paris by storm."

691 [1] Dugas-Montbel, *Observations sur l'Iliade,* Vol. II, p. 145 (*Iliad,* XVIII, v. 486): "As for Orion, he became, eventually, the hero of a very unpleasant adventure that Voltaire relates in the crudest terms in the article on allegory in the *Philosophical Dictionary* (*Œuvres,* Vol. VII, pp. 54-55), believing it to be an allegory. But the offensive tale did not originate in any desire to find an allegory. It was due to a mere association of the name Ὠρίων with οὖρον, 'urine.' Nor was Orion's name, either, derived from the adventure, as the little scholia say. The adventure was invented to account for the name. The proof is that all those vulgarities did not come on the scene till after Homer's time, for Homer knew the name." The proof is not very strong, but the conjecture has probabilities in its favour (§ 660).

691 [2] Etymology also plays a part in another variety of interpretations—B-γ. See §§ 780 f.

interpreted and fallacious inferences from real facts. This variety differs from the preceding, B-β1, in that, apparently if not actually, it assigns a more important rôle to experience, and its pseudo-experimental inferences are longer drawn-out and more ingenious and fine-spun.

693. The theory of "animism" belongs to this variety. It appears under several forms. In the more definite, it asserts that primitive peoples are convinced that human beings, animals, plants, and even non-living things have souls; and religious phenomena accordingly owe their origin and development to logical inferences from that conviction. In a less definite form it runs: "We can be sure that children and savages are animists, that, in other words, they project the volition acting within themselves upon things without and so people the world, and especially the creatures and objects immediately about them, with life and sentiments similar to their own."[1]

Inferences are evidently drawn out longer in the first form of animism than in the second, but there is no lack of them in the second. To reduce the second to sentiments corresponding to non-logical conduct, we have to change our language and say that the child and the savage in many cases, and even civilized man in some cases, act in the same ways towards the human beings, living creatures, and even objects with which they stand in contact.

694. When there is an effort to give a logical colouring to the non-logical conduct, inferences are appended. A person may say: "I do as I do *because* I believe that the animals, plants, and objects connected with me have a will such as I and other human beings have." Or the inference may be lengthened by giving the will in question a cause, attributing it to an entity called "soul," and asserting that other beings have souls just as human beings have.

693 [1] Neither here, nor anywhere else, do we intend to solve the problem of "origins" from the chronological standpoint (§§ 885 f.). Documents for any such research are wanting, and so it becomes a mere exercise of the imagination. We are going to try simply to reduce complex phenomena to simpler ones, and examine the relationships between them. It may be that the simple phenomena have preceded the composite in time, or the reverse may be the case. For the present we are not interested in the question.

Tylor goes even farther. Says he:[1] "The sense of Spiritualism in its wider acceptation, the general belief in spiritual beings, is here given to Animism." And he adds: "Animism characterizes tribes very low in the scale of humanity, and thence ascends, deeply modified in its transmission, but from first to last preserving an unbroken continuity, into the midst of high modern culture." Tylor must therefore be describing an evolution of those non-logical sentiments, or of their expressions. To tell the truth, it is surprising to hear that "tribes very low in the scale of humanity" should already have developed so subtle a theory as belief in the existence of spiritual beings. Their language has to be highly enough perfected to express abstractions such as "being" and "spiritual." It also has to be very well known to travellers, if they are to translate such terms accurately into ours.

695. Meantime there are plenty of doubts even with languages that are very well known.[1] One writer says of Chinese morals:[2] "Noth-

694 [1] *Primitive Culture,* 1871, Vol. I, p. 385; 1873, Vol. I, p. 486.

695 [1] We cannot give a definite translation even of the term ψυχή in the Homeric poems. In Greek writings of a later date it may be translated as "soul"; but in Homer it has a number of meanings that are not sharply defined. Theil, *Dictionnaire complet d'Homère, s.v.* Ψυχή: "Ψυχή, properly, 'breath,' and since breath is the sign of life, 'spirit,' 'life,' 'vital force,' 'soul': *Iliad,* V, v. 696: τὸν ἔλιπε ψυχή, 'the spirit left him': that is to say, 'he fainted'; but it may also mean 'he died,' as in *Odyssey,* XIV, v. 426, where it is a question of animals. It is, further, more often phrased with such words as μένος [soul and strength]: *Iliad,* V, v. 396; αἰών [life and soul]: *Iliad,* XVI, v. 453; and θυμός [soul and spirit]: *Iliad,* XI, v. 334. In *Iliad,* I, v. 3, it appears in the plural; and in *Odyssey,* III, v. 74, one notes: ψυχὰς παρθέμενοι, 'exposing their lives.' This vital principle was conceived as an actual substance. When a man dies it goes out through his mouth: *Iliad,* IX, vv. 408-09; or through a wound: *Iliad,* XIV, vv. 518-19. Whence, the 'souls of the dead' in the other world, 'soul,' 'spirit,' 'shade': ψυχὴ 'Αγαμέμνονος, Αἴαντος, 'the soul of Agamemnon,' 'of Ajax.' Such a soul was, actually, without body, but it kept the shape of the body: *Odyssey,* XI, vv. 204-09; it had no φρένες [mind, or perhaps vitals]: *Iliad,* XXIII, v. 103; therefore it was only a 'ghost,' εἴδωλον: *Odyssey,* XI, v. 601. The two words are often conjoined (ψυχὴ καὶ εἴδωλον): *Iliad,* XXIII, v. 103, *Odyssey,* XXIV, v. 14; and in that sense ψυχή is contrasted with the 'body,' which the ancient Greek thought of as his 'ego,' his personality (αὐτός): *Iliad,* I, v. 3; *Odyssey,* XIV, v. 32 [Wrong reference--perhaps XIV, v. 134, or XXIV, v. 35]. Ψυχή is never used in Homer to designate states of mind." When we have explanations equally detailed of the terms that are used by savages, we may have some conception of the words that travellers and missionaries arbitrarily translate by our word "soul."

695 [2] Farjenel, *La morale chinoise,* p. 20.

ing is easier for the translator than to yield to the temptation of making a text say what he wishes it to say, and that temptation is of course very great in dealing with works on philosophy or morals." It is therefore legitimate to wonder whether the missionaries and travellers through whom we get our knowledge of savage or merely backward peoples have not altered meanings of terms thus rendered.[3] But, after all, any mere presumption, however reasonable and probable, has to bow to the facts. To them, therefore, let us look for our solution.

696. In the first place the things we observe in our children cannot be grouped with the phenomena of animism. Children talk to their dolls and the house-dog as though dog and dolls were able to understand them long before they have any such notions as are expressed by the terms "beings" and "spiritual." We can go farther still. Even among adults, a hunter talking to his dog would be astounded were he asked whether he thought he was conversing with a "spiritual" being. In reality, in all such cases we are dealing with non-logical actions, with expressions of certain inclinations, and not with results of logical processes.[1]

695 [3] Even scholars who have perfect mastery of their subjects may in moments of inattention use terms not corresponding to the texts before them. Maury, *Histoire des religions de la Grèce antique,* Vol. I, p. 336: "The Elysium, or better the Elysian Fields (Ἠλύσιον πεδίον) is described in the *Odyssey* as 'a land where the just man leads a happy life in peace under a sky that is ever cloudless.'" Maury is referring to *Odyssey,* IV, vv. 561-69. Now for that passage the term "just" does not serve. There is no reference whatever to "just" men. It is a question of Menelaus, who is to go to the Elysian Fields not because he has been "just," but "because (v. 569) he has Helen to wife and is in the eyes of the immortals a son-in-law of Zeus": *οὕνεκ' ἔχεις Ἑλένην, καί σφιν γαμβρὸς Διός ἐσσι.* The line cannot be otherwise translated, and all the translations agree—the Latin, for instance: *"quoniam habes Helenam et ipsius Jovis gener es."* The verse (561) quoted by Maury, Σοὶ δ'οὐ θέσφατόν ἐστι, Διοτρεφὲς ὦ Μενέλαε, with the lines following, alludes to the fact for which the cause is given in v. 569; namely, that Menelaus is not to die but will go to the Elysian Fields because, *etc.* If we knew the passage only from Maury's version of it, we would conclude that it asserts a moral principle which really is not there.

696 [1] On Jan. 25, 1910, a great crowd was gathered in the Piazza d'Armi in Turin waiting for the Sun to go down in order to see the comet. The comet not appearing at once, many people began to hoot and whistle as Italians do in a theatre. Yet certainly not a person in the crowd imagined that the comet had a "soul." There was nothing to it except one of those impulses whereby we treat human beings, animals, and things alike. In his *Journal of a Cruise Made to the Pacific Ocean,* Vol. II, p. 31, Admiral Porter describes the pleasure and admiration evinced

697. But that proves nothing as to primitive peoples. We have to go on and examine the facts about them directly. Tylor cautions that his researches were conducted on two principles:[1] "First, as to the religious doctrines and practices examined, these are treated as belonging to theological systems devised by human reason, without supernatural aid or revelation; in other words, as being developments of Natural Religion. Second, as to the connexion between similar ideas and rites in the religions of the savage and the civilized world."

698. The first principle aims at solving *a priori* a problem that ought to get its solution strictly from observations of fact. There is nothing to justify our seeing in religious doctrines and practices mere products of reason, so excluding non-logical conduct; and it is evident that if we exclude them *a priori,* we shall not be able to find them afterwards in the facts. What follows substantiates that criticism: "What the doctrine of the soul is among the lower races, may be explained in stating the present [the animistic] theory of its development." The sentence exemplifies the usual errors of that method of reasoning: 1. The metaphysical abstraction "soul" is taken as a real thing. Every man that has eyes sees the Sun; one may therefore ask what notion—often it is a very hazy one—he has of it. But before we can find out what notion he has of the soul, we must know whether he has in mind any concept at all correspond-

by the natives of Madison Island on seeing a cannon fired: "They hugged and kissed the gun, lay down beside it, and fondled it with the utmost delight, and at length slung it to two poles and carried it toward the mountain"—as they had been ordered to do by Porter. The natives had no idea that the cannon was an animate being. They were merely expressing certain feelings of admiration provoked by its power. See, further, Erman, *Aegyptische Religion,* p. 7 (Johns, pp. 7-9). Noting the great discordance of Egyptian views about the cosmos, Erman adds: "Later on the Egypt of the historical period made up its picture of the world out of all these different features, mixing them together more or less haphazard, indifferent to the inconsistencies and impossibilities to which it was calling public attention. The sky is represented as a cow, with the bark of the Sun sailing on its belly. The sky is an ocean, yet the Sun was engendered by it. The Sun-god is a scarab and at the same time the scarab's eye. The names and images that are made to fit these different conceptions are jumbled together in a thorough-going mixture." Something of the sort is observable in Greek mythology.

697 [1] *Primitive Culture,* 1871, Vol. I, pp. 386-87; 1873, Vol. I, pp. 427-28.

ing to such a term. 2. The attempt to reconstruct theories held by primitive peoples on the basis of our present-day ideas as civilized people. In that way we get not the theories of primitive peoples, if any they have, but—a wholly different matter—the theories that we would evolve were we to put aside certain ideas we hold, a certain part of our knowledge, and then to work, with our logic, strictly on the concepts and knowledge remaining.

699. In fact, Tylor continues: "It seems as though thinking men, as yet at a low level of culture were deeply impressed by two groups of biological problems. In the first place, what is it that makes the difference between a living body and a dead one; what causes waking, sleep, trance, disease, death? In the second place, what are those human shapes which appear in dreams and visions? Looking at these two groups of phenomena, the ancient savage philosophers probably made their first step by the obvious inference that there is in every man two things belonging to him, namely, a life and a phantom. These two are evidently in close connexion with the body, the life as enabling it to feel and think and act, the phantom as being its image or second self; both, also, are perceived to be things separable from the body, the life as able to go away and leave it insensible or dead, the phantom as appearing to people at a distance from it."

700. That method of approaching phenomena, though slightly better, starts with the same principles that are used by Rousseau (§ 821)—putting facts aside, and trusting wholly to imagination. Of course if primitive peoples ever had their Aristotle, he may have managed to think with that rigorous logic on the metaphysical abstractions in question; but we may well wonder whether such an Aristotle ever was. Furthermore, after once reasoning so well mankind must have forgotten the art; for in historical times we find a thinking that is far from being as logical and luminous as the thoughts gratuitously ascribed to our savage ancestors.

701. We are not asking how savage or backward peoples *must* have reasoned, but rather how they actually reason. We are not trying to brush the facts aside, as is done in the method dear to Rousseau (§ 821) and his imitators: we are trying, instead, to put imagination aside as far as we possibly can and stick as close to the facts as we possibly can. Now there is an exceedingly large body of fact which goes to show that savage or backward peoples have little or no inclination towards abstract thinking, that they are very far from presuming to solve metaphysical or philosophical problems, or even problems to some little extent abstract, and that often they evince virtually no curiosity regarding them.[1]

702. Of a Negro tribe called the Mandingos, Mungo Park writes:[1]

701 [1] *Cf.* Captain Cook, *Account of a Voyage to the Pacific Ocean,* Vol. II, p. 310. Of the natives of Nootka (North America) Cook remarks: "Their other passions appear to lie dormant, especially their curiosity. Few expressed any desire or inclination to see or examine things with which they were unacquainted; and which, to a curious observer, would have appeared astonishing. If they could procure the articles they knew and wanted, they were perfectly satisfied; regarding everything else with great indifference. Nor did our persons, dress, and behaviour (though so very different from their own), or even the size and construction of our ships, seem to excite their admiration or attention." [Cook's texts show so many formal variants as to read like different writings. We follow the edition of 1784.—A. L.] Pruneau de Pommegorge, in Hovelacque, *Les Nègres de l'Afrique sus-équatoriale,* p. 29: "Not being able to imagine that, as I had been informed, they [the Sereres] had no religion, and finding myself one afternoon at sunset on the seashore with five or six men well on in years, I asked them through an interpreter if they knew who had made that Sun which was about to disappear . . . finally if they knew the sky and the stars that would be visible an hour thence. At my question the old men looked at each other as though nonplussed and made no answer. However, after a moment's silence, one of them asked me if I knew all those things." Pommegorge is not aware that from the standpoint of experimental science the knowledge he thinks he has of Him who made the Sun is worth less, much less, than the so frankly manifested ignorance of those Negroes. Of a Madison Island chief, Admiral Porter observes, *Op. cit.,* Vol. II, pp. 27-28: "After he had been a short time on deck, I endeavoured to impress him with a high opinion of our force; and for this purpose assembled all of my crew. It scarcely seemed to excite his attention. I then caused a gun to be fired, which seemed to produce no other effect on him than that of pain: he complained that it hurt his ears. I then invited him below where nothing whatever excited his attention until I showed him some whales' teeth. . . . I asked him if he had seen anything in the ship that pleased him—if he did to name it and it should be his. He told me he had seen nothing which had pleased him so much as one of the small whales' teeth." Hovelacque, *Op. cit.,* p. 456: "Abstraction is altogether outside his [the Negro's] powers of conception. There are no abstract words in his language. Only tangible objects are able to catch his interest. As for any generalizing, as for getting any sort of systematization from the mass of material phenomena, they should not be expected of him."

702 [1] *Travels and Recent Discoveries in the Interior Districts of Africa,* London, pp. 271-74; New York, pp. 306-09.

"I frequently enquired of some of them what became of the sun during the night, and whether we should see the same sun or a different one in the morning; but I found that they considered the questions as very childish. The subject appeared to them as placed beyond the reach of human investigation: they had never indulged a conjecture nor formed any hypothesis about the matter." Park asserts, however, that "the belief of one God and of a future state of reward and punishment is entire and universal among them." But one may wonder whether he has not to some extent credited them with ideas of his own, for he proceeds to note things not quite consistent with such a belief: "If they are asked for what reason then do they offer up a prayer on the appearance of the new moon, the answer is that custom has made it necessary: they do it, because their fathers did it before them. Such is the blindness of unassisted nature!" And farther along: "When interrogated in particular concerning their ideas of a future state, they express themselves with great reverence, but endeavour to shorten the discussion by observing *'Mo o mo inta allo!'* [No man knows anything about it!] They are content, they say, to follow the precepts and examples of their forefathers through the various vicissitudes of life; and when this world presents no objects of enjoyment or of comfort, they seem to look with anxiety towards another, which they believe to be better suited to their natures, but concerning which they are far from indulging vain and delusive conjectures." [2]

703. All that by no means precludes there having been peoples

702 [2] Similar observations are to be found in Burchell, *Travels in the Interior of Southern Africa,* Vol. II, p. 427: "I found no difficulty in making him [a Bachapin] sensible of a future state of existence, as the Bachapins seemed to possess some confused notions of this kind; but of their belief in retributive justice after death, I never could gain any clear account. [Of course one cannot discover what is not there!] Neither did it appear to me that they had any very sublime idea of the soul or of immortality [Or of solid geometry either, one might guess]. Of the worldly superintendence of a Supreme Power, they are not ignorant; but their knowledge is so mingled with superstition, that this can be of little practical benefit to their moral conduct or religious feelings. These superstitious notions could only have been the offsprings of the weakest mind; and the respect which continues to be paid to them proves, better than any argument, how low is the state of intellect and reason among these people."

with a theory of animism such as Tylor outlines (§ 694). Indeed, there certainly have been such peoples. But it is not in the least proved, either, that animism is the "origin" of religion or a simple form of more evolved religions.[1]

704. Herbert Spencer's refutation of animism has the same defects as the theory itself. He marshals facts to show[1] that "in the ascent from low to high types of creatures, the power of distinguishing the animate from the inanimate increases." The tests used to distinguish them are at first very vague and then gradually become more precise. First they are very general; then they are specialized; finally the classification becomes less often erroneous. "First *motion,* then *spontaneous* motion, then *adapted* spontaneous motion are the successive tests used as intelligence progresses." These observations are true in substance, erroneous in form—and unhappily, the form prevails in the bulk of Spencer's argument. What Spencer calls "classification" is a classification for us, but not for the animals that make it.

705. Let us go back for a moment to Fabre's experiments on the Cerceres (§ 155). In order to provide their grubs with living but paralyzed prey, those insects "select" certain species of Coleoptera. The term "select" has to be explained. If we say that the Cerceres select those particular Coleoptera, we are describing the objective end (§ 151), and in that sense the statement is true. But no one would grant that Cerceres use classifications like ours and that they select their Coleoptera the way an entomologist classifying insects might select them. We do not know how or why the Cerceres make their

703 [1] Tylor, *Ibid.,* 1871, Vol. I, pp. 377 f.; 1873, pp. 418 f., rejects the testimony of several travellers that certain peoples had religions, in the light of the contrary testimony of other travellers. [I suspect a misprint, the dropping of a *non* before *avevano* in Pareto's text. What Tylor rejects is the testimony that certain peoples had *no* religion.—A. L.] He is right in some instances. He may be right in others, and wrong in still others; for there is no way of showing that the negative testimony is always more credible than the positive. The fact stands in any event that savages in general are little prone to abstract thinking; and it is not at all certain that the concept "soul" which travellers attribute to them is identical with our "soul." The authenticated case of the Greek ψυχή is sufficient warning as to the ease of one's going wrong in such interpretations (§ 695 [1]).

704 [1] *Principles of Sociology,* Vol. I, § 64.

choices; but we can be certain that they do not make them by the rational, scientific methods of the entomologist. Similar facts are observable for human beings, and their non-logical conduct must not be confused with such logical actions as are involved in a scientific classification.

706. Spencer extends logical conduct to animals. Says he, § 63: "Yet a further test used by intelligent animals to discriminate the living from the not-living is the *adaptation* of motion to ends. Amusing herself with a mouse she has caught, the cat, if it remains long stationary, touches it with her paw to make it run. Obviously the thought is that a living thing disturbed will try to escape, and so bring a renewal of the chase. Not only is it expected that there will be self-produced motion; but it is expected that this motion will be away from danger." Roughly the facts are as stated; the description of them is entirely misleading, and the error lies in assuming that the cat thinks like a logical human being.[1] 1. Animals do not have the abstract concepts of "living" and "not-living." One need only watch a dog attentively to be sure of that. Much less can they know what an "end" and an "adaptation" are. 2. There is nothing to warrant belief that the cat thinks that a living thing disturbed will try to escape. It is a habit of cats to touch any little object with their paws to make it move if possible; and it matters little, from that standpoint, whether the object be, for example, a pen-holder well known to them, or a mouse, or an insect. If anything is certain it is that they act as if they did not have the abstract notions of "living" and "not-living" with which Spencer credits them. 3. Similarly, they have none of the abstractions required for designating a mouse's movement as away from danger. To be convinced of that one need only tie a piece of paper to a string and drag it either towards the cat or away from it. The cat jumps at the ball whether it moves in one direction or the other. Leave the paper at rest in the middle of the room, and after a time the cat will approach it and stir it with its paw exactly as it does in playing with a mouse. There is not the

706 [1] On this point see Martello, *L'economia moderna e la odierna crisi del darwinismo.*

slightest difference, and yet we cannot say with Spencer that the cat is arguing that "a living thing disturbed will try to escape." In case one should object that the cat thinks the paper ball a living thing, that would only mean that it is incapable of distinguishing the living from the not-living, and Spencer's whole argument crumbles. In any case it is clearly apparent that Spencer has merely translated the non-logical conduct of the cat into terms of logical conduct. Others translate the non-logical conduct of human beings in the same way.

707. Spencer himself moves on from animals to human beings. "Shall we say," he asks, § 65, "that the primitive man is less intelligent than the lower mammals, less intelligent than birds and reptiles, less intelligent even than insects? Unless we say this, we must say that the primitive man distinguishes the living from the not-living; and if we credit him with intelligence higher than that of brutes, we must infer that he distinguishes the living from the not-living better than brutes do." That method of reasoning would be sound enough if conduct were all strictly logical; but it is not of the slightest value as regards non-logical actions. It proves too much, and therefore proves nothing. If it were valid, it would follow that since the human being is certainly more intelligent than the Cerceres, he ought to recognize kinds of Coleoptera on which the Cerceres prey better than they do. But go to the most intelligent individual you know, someone even who is up to date in all the sciences except entomology, and ask him to find one of those Coleoptera for you. He will be absolutely unable to do so.

708. Spencer has another animistic theory, which involves him in a neo-euhemerism, the point of arrival being the same as in the ancient, but the proof different. Ancient euhemerism had pseudo-historical proofs (the *ego ipse vidi* of Euhemerus). This new system rests on the implications of certain facts that *seem probable to us*—something analogous to the evolution in religious theory which substitutes inner experience for external authority (§ 627).

709. Spencer assumes that the savage interprets dreams, trance phenomena, death, with rigorous logic. By a series of ingenious inferences primitive man arrives at the conclusion that human beings have doubles which may separate themselves from the body, and then extends that conclusion to plants and inanimate objects. Since syncope and catalepsis are mere temporary states, the savage, reasoning as Spencer, *Ibid.*, § 99, thinks he ought to reason, believes that death also is temporary, or, if permanent, is so because the double is kept away from the body too long: "Belief in re-animation implies belief in a subsequent life." Hence, with the same logic, arises the idea of another world, *Ibid.*, § 114: "The transition from a mountain abode to an abode in the sky, conceived as the sky is by primitive men, presents no difficulties." So now we have the sky peopled with the doubles of human beings. "But . . . besides the above origin, carrying with it the belief that departed souls of men live on the mountain-tops, or in the heavens, there is another possible, and indeed probable, origin, not carrying such a conclusion; but, contrariwise, restricting this heavenly abode to a different race of beings." It is "an invading race which, bringing knowledge, skill, arts and implements, unknown to the natives, were regarded as beings of superior kind, just as civilized men now are by savages." These conquerors established themselves on the heights near the clouds, and became inhabitants of the sky, divinities.

710. The origin of the gods once determined in this manner, the rest of religion comes easily. Says Spencer, § 162: ". . . the worship of the fetich is the worship of an indwelling ghost, or a supernatural being derived from the ghost." § 164: "Propitiation of the dead, which, originating funeral rites, develops into the observances constituting worship in general, has thus among its other divergent results idol-worship and fetich-worship." [1]

711. Spencer's theory is neither better nor worse than other similar theories. They all have one trait in common: Certain conjectures roughly compatible with observable fact are taken as premises; then this or that conclusion is drawn, reasoning as one *thinks* primitive man *must* have reasoned. That tells us the way things went in times on which we have no historical, no experimental, data of any kind.

710 [1] Spencer also explains totemism and myths such as the solar myth by his theory. See our § 793.

712. These theories undoubtedly contain a certain amount of experimental truth. They go wrong in leaping from the particular to the general, like a person seeing a forest of pine-trees and concluding that all forests are of pine. In totemism the experimentally true part is very considerable. Salomon Reinach suggests stating the code of totemism as follows:[1] "1. Certain animals are neither killed nor eaten, but some few specimens are raised and cared for. 2. The accidental death of such an animal is regularly mourned and it is buried with the honours customarily accorded to human members of the clan. 3. Sometimes the alimentary interdiction applies only to some part of the animal's body. 4. When animals ordinarily exempt from slaughter are killed in view of some urgent necessity, excuses are offered to them and efforts are made in various ways to mitigate the violation of the taboo—the slaughter of the animal. 5. After a tabooed animal has been sacrificed according to ritual it is mourned. 6. The skins of certain animals are worn by human beings, especially in religious ceremonies. Where totemism prevails, such animals are totems. 7. Clans and their individual members have animal names. Where totemism prevails, such animals are totems. 8. Some clans decorate their banners and weapons with pictures of animals and certain individuals paint or tattoo them on their bodies. 9. It is assumed that totem animals of species dangerous to human beings spare members of the totemic clan, but only provided they are such by birth. 10. Totem animals help and protect members of the totemic clan. 11. Totem animals reveal the future to their worshippers and guide their conduct. 12. Members of a totemic clan often believe themselves related by blood-descent to the totem animal."

713. This code is too particularized, too definite. It would be truer to the facts to say that totemism, as understood by one writer or another (§ 718 [1]), is a state of mind in which certain animals are respected, honoured, revered, human beings considering themselves bound to them by certain ties, doing them favours, and expecting favours in return.[1]

712 [1] *Cultes, mythes et religions,* Vol. I, pp. 17-26.

713 [1] More recently in his *Orpheus,* Chap. I, § 28 (Simmonds, pp. 13-14), Reinach does not press the complete code: "It is difficult to define totemism. We may say,

714. Many writers have dealt with these phenomena, usually trying to prove general what is strictly particular. Totemism has been regarded as nothing less than the "origin" of religion, and whenever some fancy even remotely suggesting totemism has been found, it has been taken as proof of the existence of totemism in that locality. Reinach uses such proofs in large numbers and Frazer is more extreme still, taking the slightest allusion to an animal as proof of the presence of totemism.

715. Unwittingly, doubtless, such writers reason after the manner of the palaeontologist who, given a few fossil bones, is able to reconstruct the whole animal from which they came. But the two cases are very different. The animal is an individual unit where the parts stand in necessary relations—dentition with feeding, for instance. Nothing of the kind obtains in the arbitrary complex to which the term "totemism" has been applied. A lion's jaw cannot belong to a herbivorous animal; but it is quite possible for the fact that honours are paid to an animal to have no connexion with any of the other characteristics said to be peculiar to totemism.

716. Let us, as usual, see what experience has to say (§ 547). Suppose some centuries hence only a few isolated facts are available as to the Florentine Republic. It will be evident that the Republic kept lions, that the street where they lived was called the Via dei Leoni, a name it bore for centuries. Excavations conducted on the site of Florence yield any quantity of little stone lions called *marzocchi*. It is further known that when the Republic conquered a place a column topped by a *marzocco* was erected there. And what not? There are legends to show that lions respected Florentine citizens

subject to more detailed definition hereafter, that it is a sort of worship that is paid to animals and plants considered as allies and kindred of the human being." Frazer, *Totemism*, pp. 1-2: "A totem is a class of material objects which a savage regards with superstitious respect, believing that there exists between him and every member of the class an intimate and altogether special relation. . . . The connexion between a man and his totem is mutually beneficent: the totem protects the man, and the man shows his respect for the totem in various ways, by not killing it if it be an animal, and not cutting or gathering it if it be a plant. As distinguished from a fetich, a totem is never an isolated individual, but always a class of objects, generally a species of animals or of plants, more rarely a class of inanimate natural objects, very rarely a class of artificial objects."

exactly as the code of totemism requires. So one could marshal a mass of evidence far more impressive than is required to satisfy the champions of totemism in such cases; and if we are to follow them in their reasoning, we are forced to admit that the lion was the totem of the Florentines in the days of their Republic. And yet we are certain that that was not the case; nor is there the slightest probability that the *marzocco* was the Florentine totem in times more ancient, say in the days of the Roman Republic, or in some epoch still more remote. If such a mass of fact does not prove totemism in this case, how are proofs fewer in number and less significant to do so in similar cases? [1]

717. At Muri (near Berne) in Switzerland a group design repre-

716 [1] Villani, *Cronica,* Bk. VI, Chap. 69: "At the time of the People of Florence, a very handsome and mighty lion was presented to the Commune, and it was caged in the Piazza di San Giovanni. It came to pass that through the remissness of its guard, the lion escaped from its coop and began running through the streets, whereat all the city was terrified. And it chanced to come to the Orto San Michele and there it seized a child and lay holding him between its paws. The child's cries were heard by his mother, who had no other child and had been with this child when the father died; and she ran upon the lion as if mad, wailing and tearing her hair, and snatched the child from the lion's paws. And the lion did no harm either to the woman or to the child; he only looked on, and did not stir. [All in strict obedience to Article 9 of Reinach's totemic code (§ 712).] There was a great question as to what chance it was, whether the gentleness of the lion's nature, or Fortune, which preserved the life of said child that he might grow up and avenge his father, as he afterwards did." What Villani calls the "gentleness of the lion's nature" was evidently the benevolence of the totem for its clan. One need only compare any number of totemistic explanations with this one to see that their proofs are not as strong, but that they are accepted in all conviction. If one had time to waste on such investigations, other documents could readily be found to support our totemistic interpretation of the Florentine *marzocco*—for example, Bayle, *Dictionnaire historique, s.v. Delphinus* (quoting Mabillon): "The inhabitants of Arezzo had torn down a stone lion (note by Bayle: "The coat-of-arms of the city of Florence.") that stood on the tower of the cathedral and thrown it into a well. When the French entered the city under Charles VIII, the lion was taken out and placed in the middle of the main street and all the inhabitants of the city who passed that way were obliged to kneel down before it and ask forgiveness for their revolt." If that were the only document known, what a pretty totemistic theory might be derived from it! The lion in question was a *marzocco,* and the episode is just one of the many historical instances of the compulsory saluting of a flag that has been insulted. Bayle's note makes everything clear. Without it, a person not knowing that the *marzocco* was the emblem of Florence might have imagined anything except a compulsory salute to a flag.

senting a goddess and a she-bear has been discovered—that, and nothing more. It has been taken as proving the existence of a totemic clan with the bear as totem.[1] If that is all the proof we need, why could we not just as well conclude that Venice was inhabited by a totemic clan with the lion as totem? In Venice we have something better than a single group. Designs representing a man and a lion can be seen there almost anywhere! We know that the man is St. Mark; but if we did not, we might take him for a god, just as the Swiss figure has been taken for a goddess. And if the goddess and her she-bear prove a totemic clan, why should not St. Mark and his lion serve the same purpose?

If the argument in the case of the Berne group were designed merely to suggest a line of inquiry, it might be considered, for in that case it would work equally well for Florence and Venice. As regards Berne, the investigation can go no farther for lack of documents, and we give up without reaching any conclusions. As for Florence and Venice, historical evidence is abundant, and we go on—to the conclusion that there is no trace of totemism there.

718. Totemism as understood by not a few writers presents a number of characteristics, *A, B, C, D*. . . . We have just seen that if *A* is present in a certain people, we can by no means infer that *B, C, D* . . . are present also. Conversely, if *A* is not present, we cannot conclude, either, that *B, C, D* . . . are not present.[1]

719. This latter consideration vitiates certain criticisms that Foucart makes of totemism. He observes, for example,[1] that "all the members of the Indian tribe call themselves descendants and relatives of the totem animal. Among the Egyptians only the chief is a descendant of the animal god. The Pharaoh of historic times is the only person who is a child of the Sparrow-hawk, who bears its name and is, in view of that, heir to the realm of the Sparrow-hawk,

717 [1] Reinach, *Cultes, mythes et religions,* Vol. I, pp. 55-58.

718 [1] One must not forget that there is no such thing as totemism in the sense in which there is such a thing as an animal called the elephant. What exists is a number of states of mind that certain writers have seen fit to gather into one class which they then proceed to designate as "totemism." How such a class is to be made up is within certain limits a matter of arbitrary choice.

719 [1] *La méthode comparative dans l'histoire des religions,* pp. 72-73.

and the latter's high-priest. The other individuals in the nation are not and do not pretend to be Sparrow-hawks." It is quite conceivable that the chieftains may have usurped something that formerly belonged to everyone and made it exclusively their own. But apart from that objection and others of the kind, Foucart's thesis would only prove that there are totemisms with the traits he indicates. It would prove nothing against totemism in general. Before it could prove anything in that direction totemism would have to be a single indivisible unit. The same thing might be said for his other strictures. What Foucart shows, in a word, is that, possibly, the totemic code of Reinach does not hold for Egypt as we know Egypt. He has by no means shown that the Egyptians did not have relations with animals similar to those described as totemism.[2] Similar objections may be made to the theory that religion originated in magic.

720. B-β3: *Historical facts are deviations from a type, or constitute a series with a limit.* Oftentimes in the view of their authors such theories contain a principle superior to experience, and ought therefore to be classified in A-γ (§ 575); but they are represented strictly as experimental theories and therefore belong here.[1]

719 [2] Foucart's argument, pp. 52-54, runs: "These animal-cults, which are so constant, so unvarying, in their characteristic traits, seem to be as ancient as Egyptian religion itself. They go back to its very origins, if one may presume to speak of times that we shall never know directly. . . . So there we have, in Egypt, the [essential] traits of zoolatry: gods of animal form, and human leaders who are their direct descendants. How did such a notion come into being? It must have derived from beliefs of the Egyptians, and from conceptions they had of the sensible world in which they moved. [So they began, good souls, by framing a theory of the sensible world and went on from there to invent their gods! The usual mania for logical interpretations! And what a complicated theory they worked out, according to Foucart!] . . . In their eyes everything in nature was alive, even what we call inanimate objects. Nature was made up of two elements [They even knew elements!]: a material wrapping, the body, and another element, subtler, invisible, but likewise material, to which they gave various names—soul, spirit, double. The combination [of the two elements] was indispensable if a body was to be alive." If Foucart had only added that those primitive peoples, living in times "that we shall never know directly," also invented algebra, his picture would be complete. See §§ 701, 695 [1].

720 [1] The contrast between the two varieties comes out very strikingly in certain passages in the *Doctrine Saint-Simonienne, Exposition, 2me séance,* 1854, pp. 82, 68 (Bouglé-Halévy, pp. 179-80, 158) (italicized words are so printed in the original French): "It is our task to show to an age that claims to be above all else *rational*

721. We find, for instance, the hypothesis of a primitive state of religious perfection. That state reappears in some contemporary religion, and the latter, naturally, is the "true" religion. Other religions exemplified in history are deviations, or degenerations, from the type. We also find the opposite hypothesis: The various historical religions are imperfect efforts gradually approximating perfection. The perfection here is located at the limit approximated through the deviations. In the other hypothesis it lay in the original religion and the deviations represented departure from it. Controversies as to primitive states of religious perfection are interesting primarily to attackers or defenders of Hebrew-Christian beliefs. They lie, therefore, in part, outside the domain of sociology.

722. For long centuries in Europe the primitive state of perfection was a dogma that could not be questioned without peril. Eventually the reaction came, and the dogma was superseded by another, not as yet enforced by the secular arm, which locates the state of perfection at the end of the evolution.

723. We must hold aloof from the controversy and keep strictly to the domain of experimental science. Believers also can stick to that domain, provided they are willing to distinguish faith from experience. That is what Father Marie-Joseph Lagrange does in his studies on Semitic religions, and what certain worshippers of the god Progress fail to do—notably Messrs. Aulard, Bayet & Co.[1]

that our *beliefs* as to the future of mankind, which have been revealed to us by a keen *sympathy* and an ardent *desire* to contribute to human happiness, are justified by the most rigorous *examination* of the facts. . . . We stated at the outset that Saint-Simon's conception was *verifiable* by history. Do not expect from us, however, any discussion of partial facts or any elucidation of details that are buried away in forgotten chronicles. [The usual procedure: experience is accepted in pretence, but then at once discarded.] We are to consider only the general laws that control (*dominent*) all such facts, laws as simple and as constant as those that govern the organization of the human body (? *de l'homme*). . . . It was Saint-Simon's mission to discover those laws, and he left them to the world as a sublime legacy. Our mission, as his disciples, is to carry on his revelation, to develop and propagate his noble ideas."

723 [1] *Etudes sur les religions sémitiques,* published with the *imprimatur* of the Archbishop of Paris. Says Father Lagrange, p. 1: "Our intention in studying Semitic religion has been simply to elucidate certain dark areas in the religions of the peoples that were neighbours or relatives of Israel. That domain has been so

724. Keeping strictly to the facts, we see that the development in religion does not show a uniformly progressive movement, *ab* (Figure 13), but follows an undulating line, *pqrst,* now rising, now falling.

far but scantily explored, and meantime discoveries in epigraphy are daily extending it. The wiser part, therefore, would surely be to halt at merely collecting the new facts and drawing the more certain conclusions from them. For our part, we have done our best to banish all preconceived ideas from our mind. We do not consider ourselves called upon to deal with the original Revelation, since the Scripture that transmits it to us also explains that it has been obliterated. [Theory of decadence from the type.] We have never yielded to the temptation of stressing the symptoms of religious degeneration more than was required." We need not decide here how far Father Lagrange succeeded in keeping his promise. It is evident enough from his book that it was made in all good faith. Compare his programme, now, with the programme of the official historiographer of the French Revolution, M. Aulard, in *Histoire politique de la révolution française,* Preface, p. v: "In this political history of the French Revolution, I intend to show how the principles of the Bill of Rights were carried out in institutions between the years 1789 and 1804, or interpreted in the speeches, writings, and acts of [political] parties and in the various manifestations of public opinion." M. Aulard is probably not aware that he is imitating Bossuet, who sets out in his *Discourse on Universal History* to show how the institutions and cultures of mankind have been governed by designs of Providence. Says Bossuet, *Discours,* Pt. III, Chap. I: "So all the great empires that have been seen on earth have contributed in one way or another to the welfare of religion and the glory of God, as God Himself declared through His prophets." M. Aulard continues: "The logical consequence of the principle of equality is democracy. The logical consequence of the principle of national sovereignty is the republic. [O unhappy Logic, how many stupidities are uttered in thy name!] Those two consequences were not drawn at once. [Because, unluckily for them, the people of those days did not have an expert logician handy, such as M. Aulard.] Instead of democracy the men of '89 set up a bourgeois system based on property qualifications; instead of the republic, they organized a limited monarchy." In the Aulard collection, M. Bayet published a little handbook for French elementary schools entitled *Lessons on Morals, Intermediate Grades* (*Leçons, etc.*). He apprises us, Preface, pp. i-ii, that his aim is to stress "the difference between scientific truths, which only the ignorant can refuse to recognize, and religious or metaphysical beliefs, which each of us has the right to accept, reject, or modify as he pleases." That is the mere metaphysics of "science," failing as it does to recognize the essentially contingent character of "scientific truths." If M. Bayet had any knowledge whatever of experimental science he would know that science is in process of continuous change and that it progresses precisely because scientists "refuse to recognize" certain principles that have always been regarded as "scientific truths." Among the "scientific truths" of M. Bayet one notes a very handsome theory of religion and another almost as pretty of the origin of religion. Says he, p. 155 (capitals and italics his): "Since we cannot know, scientifically, what takes place after death, men have tried to GUESS, and they have put forward no end of SPECULATIONS on the subject. Some

725. The mythologies of Hesiod and Homer are certainly less abstract, less fine-spun, than Plato's religion, which is also more abstract and subtle than the religion of the Gospels and the early Church Fathers. It seems probable that after an archaic period of high civilization ancient Greece experienced a Middle Ages followed by a Renaissance—something analogous to what took place in Europe between the days of the Roman Republic and our own.

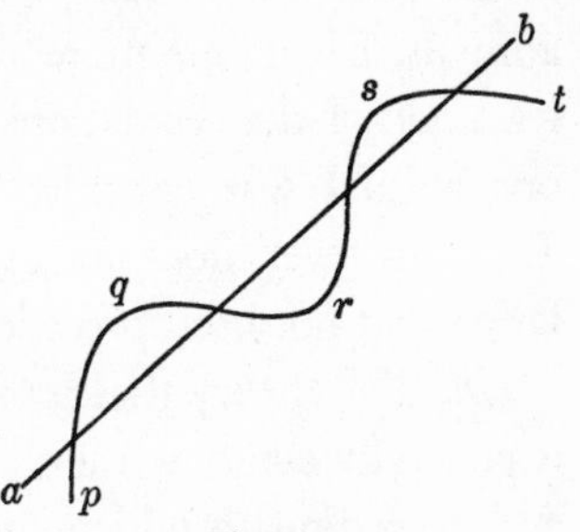

Figure 13

726. Our data on Egyptian religion seem to lead to similar conclusions. This shows a number of oscillations. In a study of the later religion of Ancient Egypt, Erman writes:[1] "Anyone who has followed the development of Egyptian religion thus far might imagine that it was advancing towards complete disintegration and an early end. Thoroughly exhausted, seeming as it were to survive itself, the Egyptian people had fallen prey to foreign conquerors. Nevertheless that aged people rose again and with it its religion took on a new life, if not a new youth. Towards the end of the eighth century [B.C.] we stumble on the remarkable symptom of a reversion towards the ideas of the people. . . . By that return to the old Egyptian spirit, religion itself acquired new strength, and to a greater degree than ever before permeated all branches of people's lives, as though it were their sole object in living. . . . But it was right there,

have said that after death NOTHING HAPPENS AT ALL. Others have thought that after death men stand in the presence of an *eternal being,* supremely good, supremely just: GOD. They have believed that God *judged* men, rewarding or punishing them. On that account they have said that men should *honour* and *worship* God, and they have fixed on the *prayers* with which He should be addressed and the ceremonies that should be performed in His honour. So a certain number of religions came into being." Bayet should have read an elementary text-book on the history of religions himself. Before setting out to teach other people, it is a credit to a man to have learned something on his own account. These estimable gentlemen, not being able to persuade others by argument, are now prosecuting anyone who fails to pay due respect to their profound science.

726 [1] *Aegyptische Religion,* pp. 169-70 (Johns, pp. 169-70).

under those conditions, that the strange side of the Egyptian faith, such as the worship of animals, attained its most exaggerated development."

727. Reasoning *a priori* one might be inclined to suppose that animal-worship in Egypt began by embracing a whole species of animals, becoming more restricted later on. But in the case of at least one of the oscillations accessible to observation the worship of one animal was extended to embrace all animals of the species. That, however, does not in the least prove that that particular oscillation had not been preceded by another in the opposite direction.

728. The theory that locates perfection at the end of an evolution is generally conjoined with another to which we have often alluded, and according to which present-day savages would be very similar to the prehistoric ancestors of the civilized peoples (§ 291). Two fixed points are thus obtained for determining the line of evolution, and by prolonging it sufficiently people obtain, or think they obtain, the limit that the evolution will approximate in the future.

729. Spencer, for instance, would combat the theory that attributes ancestor-worship to inferior races. It is surprising, he objects,[1] "that adherents of the Evolution-doctrine should admit a distinction so profound between the minds of different human races. . . . Those who believe in creation by manufacture, may consistently hold that Aryans and Semites were supernaturally endowed with higher conceptions than Turanians. If species of animals were separately made with fundamental differences, varieties of men may have been so too. But to assert that the human type has been derived from lower types, and then to deny that the superior human races have been evolved, mentally as well as physically, from the inferior, and must once have had those general conceptions which the inferior still have, is a marvellous inconsistency."

730. That is metaphysical and not scientific thinking. In the first place, the relations between facts of the present and facts of the past cannot be confined within the alternative of either creation or unitary evolution (§ 344). In the second place, accepting for the moment

729 [1] *Principles of Sociology,* Vol. I, § 150.

the doctrine of a unitary evolution, it is not proved that the backward races of our day are identical with our prehistoric ancestors. The probability, rather, is that they differ greatly, for the reason—if for no other—that they were lacking in those qualities which resulted in civilizing our races. Nor is there any proof, either, that mental evolution has to run parallel with physical evolution. Finally, even if it did, why might it not have sent off two branches, *A* and *B,* from a common trunk, *M,* one of which has ended in ancestor-worship, the other in a different belief? Just such an evolution has certainly taken place on the physical side, on the assumption of a common trunk, *M,* since we now have at least three racial branches, the white, the black, and the red.

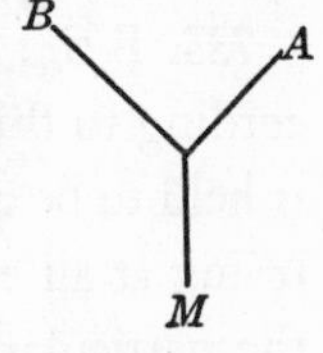

Figure 14

731. The theory that contemporary savages are identical with, or at least similar to, the prehistoric ancestors of civilized peoples has many opponents nowadays. But as usual people have gone from one extreme to the other and now assert that savages represent the senility rather than the infancy of the human races. That, evidently, is a consequence of the belief that locates the perfect state at the beginning of evolution instead of at the end. But the facts elude such *a priori* syntheses. If the ancient Gauls as they stood before the Roman invasion have to be compared either with savages or with the Frenchmen of our day, it is clear that they stand closer to the former than to the latter; and, conversely, one could not admit that the savages of our day are less like the ancient Gauls than like modern Frenchmen.[1]

731 [1] De Morgan, *Les premières civilisations,* p. 45: "The Homo (Pithecanthropus) alalus . . . still unable to speak, Haeckel's Homo stupidus, Mortillet's Anthropopithecus Bourgeoisi and Ribeiroi, are hypothetical creatures whose existence rests on nothing but guesswork devoid of definite scientific basis. That theory implies the original unity of the human species, which seems to be true of the races living today but may not have been for others that have disappeared. Those theories are altogether gratuitous, beyond any doubt; but they have nevertheless acquired status as axioms in the minds of many people and have served during recent years as foundations for a number of theories in which fancy takes the place of scientific thinking. [Note by De Morgan: "Élisée Reclus, among others, carries things to a ridiculous extreme in his *L'homme et la terre*. He goes so far as to regard domestic ani-

732. If the "historical series" of the Saint-Simonians be considered from the standpoint of the experimental demonstration that they think they can give of it, it belongs in this present category, B-β3, as does also Comte's theory of the "three phases" and further, Spencer's theory of "pre-morality." Spencer tries to derive morality from experience. He encounters facts that are not in accord with his ideas, and to be rid of them says that they belong not to moralitv but to "pre-morality." [1]

733. B-β4: *Myths and the like are imitations of other myths.* According to this principle, whenever two institutions are similar, one is held to be a copy of the other. Here again the error lies merely in trying at all costs to generalize a fact that may be altogether true in the particular case, and in so overstepping experience.

734. As usual, let us fall back on the method suggested in § 547. We have remarkable instances of almost identical institutions that seem really not to have been copied from one another. Describing a custom at Marseilles Petronius writes: [1] "Whenever the Marsilians were harassed by plague, some beggar used to volunteer to be supported in the greatest luxury at public expense for a whole year. Then clad in sacred vestments and decked with vervain, he was

mals (in view of improvements they have made) as 'candidates for humanity.' "] Not a few scientists, or self-styled scientists, regard the Pithecanthropus as our ancestor. There is no proof of any such descent. Not a single fact justifies the assertion that he was an ancestral form of man, or related even in a very remote way to our species. [Note by De Morgan:] Another theory tends to regard the simians as degenerate branches of the human race. *Cf.* J. H. F. Kohlbrugge, *Die morphologische Abstammung des Menschen,* Stuttgart, 1908."

732 [1] [An allusion apparently to Spencer's theory of an "intuitive moral sense." *Cf. Social Static,* pp. 17-19.—A. L.] For the historical series of Saint-Simon see *Doctrine Saint-Simonienne, Exposition,* 1854, pp. 18-19; Bouglé-Halévy, pp. 92-93 (italics and capitals as in the original): "But what is this new manner of envisaging *history,* of, as it were, asking the *past* to foretell the *future* of humanity? What is the value of the *proof* we offer in support of our dreams for that future? A new science, a science as *positive* as any other deserving of that title, was conceived by Saint-Simon —the science of the *human species.* His method is the method used in astronomy or in physics. Facts are classified by series of homogeneous terms and related in the order of *generalization* and *particularization,* so as to bring out their TENDENCY, show, in other words, the law of *increase* and *decrease* to which they are subject."

734 [1] *Fragmenta,* I (Buechler, p. 109). The fragment was preserved by Servius, *Ad Vergilii Aeneidem,* III, v. 57 (Thilo-Hagen, Vol. I, p. 346).

borne about the streets of the city [saluted everywhere] with curses that all the city's woes might fall on him, and finally he was thrown [into the sea]."

735. The Aztecs in Mexico observed a similar ceremony every year. They chose a young man from among their prisoners. "So designated for sacrifice a year in advance," writes Lucien Biart,[1] "the youth was dressed like the idol [of the god Tezcatlipoca]. He was free to walk the streets of the city, though always under guard, and was paid the same worship as the image of the supreme divinity. Twenty days before the god's festival the unlucky youth was married to four girls, and on the last five days efforts were made to procure him every possible enjoyment. On the morning of the ceremony he was escorted to the temple with great pomp. Just before arriving thither he bade his wives adieu. He then walked beside the idol in the procession. . . . When the hour for the sacrifice was at hand, he was stretched on the altar, where the high-priest, in a most reverent manner, cut open his breast and crushed his heart."[2]

736. The common conception of a whole year's enjoyment followed by death was not transmitted from the ancient Marsilians to the ancient Mexicans, nor *vice versa.* It arose spontaneously in both places. The same conception figures in another more general one in which human beings have ever delighted—the desire to bring

735 [1] *Les Aztèques,* pp. 125-26.

735 [2] And *cf.* Réville, *Les religions du Méxique,* pp. 135-36: "He was clothed in the vestments and decorations of Tezcatlipoca, and when he appeared about the town with an escort of eight pages in royal livery he was worshipped by the people as the divinity itself. The most attentive care was taken of him. He was bathed and perfumed and provided with a head-dress. His divine uniform was ever new. He was given four young wives chosen for their beauty. They bore the names of goddesses and were instructed to overlook nothing that might make their divine husband as happy as possible. During the three weeks preceding the ceremony these honorific distinctions were multiplied. . . . But on the next to the last day of the festival Tezcatlipoca's substitute was placed aboard a royal barge with his eight pages and his four goddesses and rowed across the lake. That evening the goddesses left their unlucky god and the eight pages escorted him to a lonely *teotcali,* some six miles farther along. He mounted the steps, breaking his flutes one by one. Reaching the top, he was seized by the priests who stood there waiting, stretched without warning on the sacrificial stone, cut open, and his quivering heart was proffered as a sacrifice to the Sun."

contraries, opposites, together (§§ 910 f.). From it numberless branches radiate.

737. Reinach, following Frazer's *Golden Bough,* Vol. III, p. 197, notes one such branch, which in its turn, forks into others [1]—"a periodic custom similar to the Roman Saturnalia and characterized by the temporary suspension of civil and moral laws. . . . The characteristic trait of the Saturnalia was the licence permitted to slaves, who became for a time masters of the house. [There we have the contrast. In the Middle Ages there will be another contrast similar, though not identical, in All Fools' Day—the *fête des Foux.*] . . ." [2]

737 [1] *Cultes, mythes et religions,* Vol. I, pp. 332-34.

737 [2] Le Bibliophile Jacob, *Curiosités de l'histoire de France,* pp. 14-31. Beleth, *De quadam libertate decembris* (in his *Divinorum officiorum rationale,* pp. 125-26), calls All Fools' Day " 'December freedom,' on the model of the pagan Saturnalia. The 'freedom' lay in an inversion of rôles and ranks in the clergy, who played all sorts of pranks inside the churches during the Christmas holidays and at Twelfth-night. Clerks, deacons, and subdeacons said mass in place of the priests. The priests danced, shook dice, played at ball, bowls, and other games of chance in front of the altar. The choir-boys masqueraded in costume and occupied the stalls of the canons. On Holy Innocents' Eve they elected one of their number bishop, clothed him in episcopal robes, anointed him, and paraded him about town to the ringing of bells and with bands of music. At the Feast of the Circumcision the churchmen appeared at mass, some in female attire, some dressed as clowns or street-performers, others with their capes and cassocks inside out [Principle of contrast.], and almost all wearing grotesque false faces. They then proceeded to elect a 'Bishop,' or 'Archbishop of Fools.' . . . At Antibes . . . the actors in the festival rushed into the stalls in the choir with their sacerdotal robes inside out [Again the contrast.] or in tatters, and capered about like people who had lost their minds. They held their prayer-books upside down, pretended to read through spectacles with orange-skins in place of lenses, and dusted each other with ashes or flour." Du Cange, *Glossarium ad scriptores mediae et infimae Latinitatis, s.v. Kalendae,* quotes a letter of Charles VII, King of France, dated Apr. 17, 1445: "Our beloved and loyal councillor, the Bishop of Troyes, has represented and complained to us that although . . . by decree of the Council of Basel [*Anno* 1431, *Sessio* XX, *Cap.* 11: Labbe, Vol. XVII, p. 322], it is expressly forbidden to ministers and attendants of the Church to participate in a certain mocking and scandalous festival that is called the 'Festival of Fools,' which is usual during the Christmas octave and holidays in not a few churches, cathedrals, and other chapter-houses, wherein said churchmen commit irreverences and mockeries towards God the Creator and His holy and divine services, to the grievous discredit and disrepute of the ecclesiastical calling at large, nevertheless, said churchmen in all churches and holy places during divine service, as well as outside, continue to utter great insolences, mockeries, and irreverences, with public spectacles and masquerades, using indecent attire unbecoming their state and profession, such as the raiment and garb of clowns, soldiers, and other secular occupations, some wearing female raiment, masks, false faces. . . ."

In the provinces things were the same but, if I may so put it, with more archaic traits. [Perhaps, but Reinach gives no proof of any such archaism.] We know the details of the Saturnalian festival from a troop of Roman soldiers encamped on the Danube, at Durostolum [ruins of Drst-Ostrov, Bulgaria], during the reigns of Maximian and Diocletian—they are recorded in an account of the martyrdom of St. Dasius published by M. Cumont. [Such a source is in itself suspect. The *Acta* of the martyrs often contain more piety than historical truth.] Thirty days before the festival the soldiers picked a good-looking young man by lot. They dressed him up as a king and pretended that he was the good king Saturn. He paraded the streets attended by a brilliant escort and had the right to use and abuse his power. On the thirtieth day he was obliged to kill himself on the altar of the god Saturn whom he had been impersonating. . . . In the classical period the King of the Saturnalia in Rome was no more than a vaudeville king—an inoffensive dolt. But the story of St. Dasius seems to prove that in more ancient times the king lost his life with his crown." The usual error of assuming that evolution can take place only along a continuous line (§ 344)! Accepting the story of St. Dasius as true, why should that episode, which took place *after* the institution of the Saturnalia in Rome, have to represent something that took place *before* the Saturnalia and of which they, the Saturnalia, would be a consequence? And at just what point on such a continuous line are we to locate the Mexican rite? It is more probable that the rite of Tezcatlipoca, the orgy at Marseilles, and other similar things, are like the points *A, B, C, D* . . . on branches shooting off from a common source, *T*, among which there may be some, such as the Roman Saturnalia, *E*, and the French All Fools' Day, *F*, which in fact represent an evolution in a continuous line. Reinach adds, p. 334: "Customs similar to the Roman Saturnalia prevailed in Crete, Thessaly, Olympia, Rhodes, and other places. . . . More curious still was the festival of the Sacaea, in Babylon, which lasted five days. As was the case in Rome, the slaves

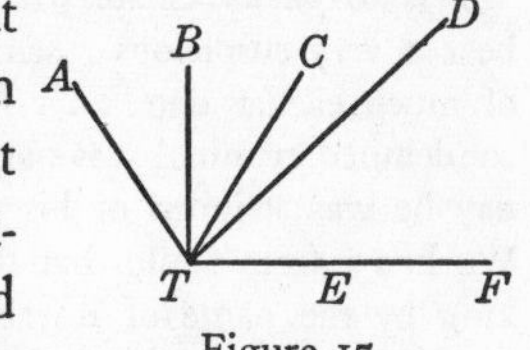

Figure 15

became masters, and in each household a slave dressed as the king and bearing the title of Zoganes wielded an ephemeral power. Moreover a condemned criminal was dressed as the king and was authorized to conduct himself accordingly, to the point of frequenting the royal concubines. At the end of the holiday, he was stripped of his fine vestments, flogged, and either hanged or crucified." Reinach further notes the resemblance between these cases and the story of Esther and another festival that was celebrated in Persia; and he goes on to describe a historical episode reported by Philo as having occurred at Alexandria. These resemblances to accounts of the Passion of Jesus tend, according to Reinach, to show that the latter was a myth.[8]

738. Reinach might have carried his analogies much farther, and he would readily have found any quantity of episodes, stories, legends, in which contrasts are set up between extreme felicity on the one hand and extreme misery on the other, or in which, ironically or otherwise, the semblances of power are conferred upon the wretch, and *vice versa*. The literatures of all lands draw liberally on

737 [8] *Orpheus,* Chap. VIII, § 36 (Simmonds, p. 229): "The details of the Passion bear a very suspicious resemblance to rites that were common in certain festivals of much earlier date. . . . At the feast of the Sacaea in Babylonia and Persia, a condemned criminal was paraded in triumph in royal robes. At the end of the holi day he was stripped of his fine raiment, scourged, and then hanged or crucified. We know from Philo that the populace of Alexandria called one such momentary king by the name of Karabas, overwhelming him with mock honours and then mistreating him. But Karabas means nothing, either in Aramaic or Greek. We must read Barabbas, which means in Aramaic 'son of the father.' . . . These collations indicate that Jesus may have been put to death not in preference to Barabbas but *as a* Barabbas. The authors of the Gospels understood neither the ceremony they were describing nor the character of the mock honours paid to Jesus." [The story appears in Philo, *In Flaccum,* VI (Cohn, Vol. VI, pp. 127-28; Yonge, Vol. IV, pp. 68-69). Journeying from Rome to Palestine whither he has been appointed as "King of the Jews," Agrippa decides to stop at Alexandria, where anti-Semitic sentiment is rife. Flaccus, the procurator, grudgingly accords him royal honours, the populace joining in with enthusiasm in turning the celebrations into a mockery, so absurd does it seem to them that there could be a "King of the Jews." Among other things they take a half-wit named Karabas, crown him as "King of the Jews" and escort him with mock-royal honours about the city. Philo upbraids Flaccus for anti-Semitism and for doing nothing to interfere with these insults to a guest of the city.—A. L.]

that inspiration and, without the least regard to historical fact, supply legend and story to the heart's content. There is, for instance, the story in the *Arabian Nights* where poor Abu-Hassân enjoys all the delights of a sovereign one day and is beaten as a lunatic the next.[1] A commonplace in the Greek novels was the plot designed to play on just that sentiment of contrast, and it served Boccaccio for the tales of his fifth day, which dealt with "fortunate outcomes for this lover or that after some cruel and unhappy mischance."

Reviewing Reinach's data, Father Lagrange saw clearly[2] that the Sacaea and other festivals of the kind may have had common origins, but do not stand in any direct relationship that would make one derive from the other either by imitation or otherwise.

739. So far it is a question of mere imagination. But human beings like to translate their fictions into reality so far as is possible and be it only under vain semblances—whence the development of various theatrical spectacles, invariably harmless in our time, though in ancient Rome they inflicted real sufferings on their actors and shed blood. In such things the human hankering for contrasts, which underlay the sanguinary spectacles both of Rome and Mexico, are caught as it were in the act of transforming themselves into realities.[1]

740. All these stories, mock facts, facts, have a nucleus in com-

738 [1] Burton, "The Sleeper and the Waker" in *Supplemental Nights,* Vol. I, pp. 1-35.

738 [2] *Quelques remarques sur l'Orpheus de M. Salomon Reinach,* pp. 39-52 (Martindale, pp. 30-32).

739 [1] Friedländer, *Sittengeschichte Roms,* Vol. II, pp. 386-87 (English, Vol. II, pp. 73-74), discusses theatrical spectacles in the Roman arena in which condemned criminals figured: "They were specially trained and rehearsed for their parts, in which they suffered torture and death not in play but very much in reality. They appeared in the arena clad in sumptuous gold-embroidered tunics . . . but suddenly the magnificent raiment would burst, like the robes of Medea, into violent flames that roasted the unhappy victims to death amid untold sufferings. . . . Christian men were obliged to submit to martyrdom clad as priests of Saturn, Christian women as priestesses of Ceres. Scarcely a form of torture or execution shiveringly alluded to in history or literature but was called upon for the amusement of the throngs at such spectacles. . . . As a rule executions took place in Rome in the early morning, and we know from Philo that that was the case in Alexandria." See further Martial, Lucian's *Ass* (*Lucis*), and *Metamorphoses,* X, of Apuleius.

mon.[1] But in addition to the common trait they have other characteristics that differentiate them from one another and make them susceptible of a variety of classifications, according to the criterion we select.

741. There might be, first, the criterion of reality, and in that case pure fictions, such as Boccaccio's tales, might go into a group *a.* Another group, *b,* would comprise theatrical representations of imaginary episodes—tragedies and dramas where the action is not in earnest, the Alexandrian custom reported by Philo, the French All Fools' Day, and the like. A group *c* would comprise representations that have an element of reality, the action being in earnest—on the one hand, such representations as the Roman Saturnalia, on the other, the bloody spectacles of the Roman circus. Finally would come a group *d,* where the reality is thorough-going, the sentiment of contrast supplying the forms only—and here the rites of Marseilles and Mexico.

The criterion might well be different—the extent, for instance, to which the contrast is carried. Along that line in a group, *1,* the contrast would halt at ascribing to persons or things characteristics that are in strident conflict with reality: the Alexandrian celebration, All Fools' Day, the countless stories where the fool is represented as a wit (or *vice versa*), and so on (§§ 668 [1], 737 [2]). In another group, *2,* the contrast is carried to an extreme: a state of felicity is followed by the greatest misfortune, or *vice versa.* The Greek tragedies present notable features belonging in this category. It is the power of this sentiment of contrasts, more than anything else, that gives the Greek plays their quality of sublime awe. In the same group we would also place the customs of Marseilles and Mexico. At bottom, the sentiments of contrast involved in the case of the powerful and glorious Agamemnon falling under the ax of Clytemnestra and the case of a youth who enjoys all the delights of life for a full year and is then led to slaughter, are not essentially different. Other criteria might be

740 [1] They constitute another illustration of a process that we met with above and which our next chapter will show to be general. There again we shall encounter the nucleus mentioned here (§§ 913 f.).

chosen, and they would yield different classifications, always from the standpoint of sentiments or non-logical conduct.

Considering these same materials from the standpoint of logical actions or of experimental reality, we should be carried into a quite different field. Then situations that belong to the same category from the standpoint of non-logical conduct would have to be distinguished. The tragedy of Agamemnon, for instance, and the Mexican sacrifice would belong to different classes.

742. Concrete situations may present combinations of these various types, along with other sentiments, other logical inferences, rhetorical ornaments, and so on.[1]

743. It is apparent, meantime, and it will be more so as we proceed (§§ 746-63), that little or nothing is to be inferred from resemblances between certain facts as regards their being imitations the one of the other or their originating one in the other by some other similar process of direct transformation. Nor are such resemblances to be pronounced artificial or imaginary. They may very well be real, the single sentiment underlying them finding different expressions in them.

744. Lagrange[1] is therefore right in rejecting the argument by which Reinach would prove (*Orpheus,* Chap. VIII, § 28) that the account of Christ's Passion in the Gospels is a mere reproduction of a pagan legend or rite. Reinach gives a number of examples of unfortunates who are first showered with pleasures and honours and then tormented. One of them, the Alexandria incident reported by Philo, has to be eliminated as not conforming to the groups *c* and *d* (§ 741) on which Reinach would rely to prove that the story of the Passion of Jesus is a myth devised in imitation of pre-existing festivals. The remaining examples prove very little. In fact they merely prove that the Passion of Jesus manifests the sentiment of contrast that figures in numberless other cases (§§ 913 f.).

If Reinach's reasoning were sound, why should the story of the

742 [1] For such composite types see Chapters VI and VII. We are not interested in them here, where we are merely illustrating our contention that many different branches may radiate from the trunk of a single sentiment.

744 [1] *Quelques remarques,* pp. 28-47 (Martindale, pp. 29-34).

Passion of Jesus be the only one copied from other narratives, and why should not some of these be copies of others still? If, furthermore, all episodes in which the sentiment of contrast figuring in the Sacaea or in other similar ceremonies appears are to be considered mythical, little indeed that is real would be left in the greater part of history. I am not in the least presuming here to solve the question as to the historical verity of all these facts. I am merely saying that the resemblances between them show nothing that can serve to prove some of them false and others true.[2]

745. Many other examples of similar institutions that are not imitations of one another might be mentioned. Herodotus alludes to an Egyptian lantern festival that parallels a festival of the Chinese, and which may also be regarded as a counterpart to the celebration in

744 [2] Lagrange makes the following points: The Karabas episode must not be confused with the Sacaea: "When the young king, Agrippa I . . . called at Alexandria, the people of that town decided to make fun of him. . . . They made a prisoner of a poor half-wit named Karabas—not being a convert, Philo could not have mistaken the name. . . . The unlucky idiot was dragged to the Gymnasium and made to stand in a conspicuous place. . . . He was clothed in royal robes, 'after the manner of actors on a stage,' and a number of young men appointed themselves his body-guard. . . . The mobs began acclaiming him as Marin, which, in Syriac, means 'master,' to make it clear that they were having their fun with Agrippa. It was, evidently, a piece of buffoonery failing in the respect due to a human unfortunate, but without flogging, without shedding of blood. [The incident, as recounted by Philo in the *Flaccus,* seems in fact irrelevant to the argument Reinach tries to build up.] All the same, it will be said, the affair is very like the body-guard scene at Jerusalem. Of course it is! That is why it has been going the rounds of the commentaries ever since Grotius called attention to it in 1641! [Grotius' note is reprinted in *Annotationes in Evangelium secundum Matthaeum* (Matt. 27: 28), in his *Opera theologica,* Vol. II-1, p. 269.—A. L.]. Nothing, in fact, could better serve to place the conduct of Pilate's soldiers in its proper historical setting. The idea, in both cases, was to ridicule the Jews and the aspirations of a Jew to the crown. [In other words, two branches from one same trunk, as in our Figure 14.] At Alexandria Agrippa is abused, so to speak, only in effigy, in the person of Karabas, said to be Barabbas. At Jerusalem a pretender to the throne is handed over to the soldiers at a time when such pretence is a capital offence; he is condemned in advance. It is all in fun at Alexandria. At Jerusalem the jest ends in blood." The Sacaea, on the other hand, does serve Reinach's purposes. Says Father Lagrange: "The festival is known to us through Berosus (Athenaeus, *Deipnosophistae* (*Banquet of Scholars*), XIV, 44). It lasted five days in an atmosphere of carnival. Masters were obedient to slaves. An individual robed as a king was paraded about in solemn pomp. Though Berosus is chary of details, he chances, interestingly, to mention the name given to the mock king: that Barabbas was called Zoganes! . . . At a later date, Strabo, *Geographica,* XI, 8, 4-5 (Jones, Vol. V, pp. 261-65), repre-

Florence known as the *rifocolone* (Festival of Jack-o'-Lanterns). There is no question of any imitation in these cases.[1]

746. The Vestal Virgins in Rome are in all respects similar to the Virgins of the Sun in Peru. In Rome the Vestals were chosen by the Pontifex Maximus. In Peru that function belonged to a woman who was dean of the virgins. Both in Rome and in Peru the Virgins chosen kept a sacred fire burning and were sworn to the strictest chastity. If they broke their oath, they were buried alive. Of course, people who explain everything by logic have long known and still know the reasons for that particular kind of punishment, as well as the explanations of all the other details in the two parallel institutions!

747. In the first place, why virgins? Several explanations are available, and we may choose among them at our pleasure. Dionysius of Halicarnassus relates that Numa erected a temple to Vesta and entrusted the cult to virgins in accord with Latin custom. "There are," he says, *Antiquitates Romanae,* II, 66 (Spelman, Vol. I, p. 343), "doubts as to what is guarded in the temple and why its custody is

sents the Sacaean festival as intimately associated with the worship of the Persian goddess Anaitis." As Father Lagrange points out, this may be the festival which Diogenes, according to Dio Chrysostom, *De regno,* IV, 66-67, described to Alexander: " 'The Persians take a condemned criminal and seat him on the royal throne in royal regalia. He is allowed to order everyone about, drink, have a good time, have his way at his leisure with the royal concubines. No one restrains him from doing anything he pleases. Then he is stripped, flogged, and hanged.' Dio's text was referred to in a marginal note to Wetztein's Gospels in 1752. No one exaggerated the significance of the parallel at that time. What recently brought it to life was the publication by M. Cumont of the *Acta* of St. Dasius. In this case, a Christian soldier refused to play the part of king in the Saturnalia, and was obliged on that account to suffer martyrdom. Now the mock king impersonated Saturn, and if, over a space of thirty days, he was free to indulge any whim, he was expected to sacrifice himself on the altar of the god on the day of the festival."

745 [1] Says Herodotus, *Historiae,* II, 62: "When the people assemble in the city of Sais to offer sacrifices on a certain night, they all light lamps in the open air around their houses. The lamps are little vases full of salt and oil, with a floating wick that burns all night. This celebration they call the Feast of the Lighted Lamps." Larcher comments on the passage, Vol. II, p. 297: "This festival is very like a lantern festival that has been customary in China from time immemorial. It tends to corroborate the view of M. de Guignes, who was one of the first to suspect that China was just an Egyptian colony." One of the many mistaken notions based on the principle that similar things must have common origins!

entrusted to virgins. Some say there is nothing there save the fire which everyone can see and that care of it is entrusted to virgins rather than to men by way of similitude, fire being undefiled even as the virgin is uncorrupted, and because to the most chaste of the divinities the purest of mortal things is pleasing." Ovid poses the question: "Why does the goddess have virgins as the ministers of her cult?" And he answers, because Vesta is a virgin: "Is it strange that a virgin should delight in virgin ministers and insist that the ceremonies of her cult be performed by chaste hands? Nor shalt thou see in Vesta aught but a living flame, and ne'er hast thou seen bodies born of flame! Seemly is it therefore that she who neither receiveth nor giveth forth any seed, should be a virgin and have virgin associates."[1] Cicero is much more practical:[2] "Let Vesta's cult be administered by virgins to the end that watch may be more readily kept of the fire, and that women may perceive how much chastity their nature can bear."[3] Plutarch has explanations in surfeit. In *Numa*, 9, 5 (Perrin, Vol. I, p. 339), he relates that that king assigned the everlasting flame to the care of the Vestals "either be-

747 [1] *Fasti*, VI, vv. 283-294. The Latin reads:

> *"Quid mirum, virgo si virgine laeta ministra*
> *admittit castas ad sua sacra manus?*
> *nec tu aliud Vestam quam vivam intellige flammam,*
> *nataque de flamma corpora nulla vides.*
> *iure igitur virgo est, quae semina nulla remittit*
> *nec capit et comites virginitatis habet."*

747 [2] *De legibus*, II, 12, 29.

747 [3] [Pareto's rendering is somewhat free. Cicero's meaning seems to be: "that women may know through them that strict chastity is compatible with (*pati*) female nature."—A. L.] The passage reads, in Latin: *"Virgines praesint ut advigiletur facilius ad custodiam ignis et sentiant mulieres in natura feminarum omnem castitatem pati."* There is a variant: *peti* for *pati*. If one reads *peti*, the meaning would be that women ought to be chaste because chastity is pleasing to the gods. Duruy, *Histoire des Romains*, Vol. I, p. 103 (Mahaffy, Vol. I, p. 107), seems to incline to that view: "The religious idea which had originally determined the conditions imposed upon the priestesses had, as a consequence, been supplemented with a moral idea. That undying flame symbolized the very life of the Roman People. Virgins only could keep it alive! The institution of the College of Vestals was therefore an instinctive glorification of chastity, and in times of deep faith the belief must have had a good influence on morals." Written in that fashion, history becomes a mere collection of moralizing fairy-tales for the edification of children.

cause he thought a pure and uncorrupted substance such as fire should be entrusted to persons who were chaste and pure, or because he judged the sterility and barrenness of fire consonant with virginity." Then again, in *Camillus,* 20, 4-5 (Perrin, Vol. II, p. 143), we get a different story. According to some, says Plutarch, Numa instituted the cult of fire because fire is the principle of all things and an image of the eternal power that governs the all. According to others, the Romans, like the Greeks, kept fire burning before sacred objects because of its purity.

748. But the fact that the Vestals were virgins is far from being an isolated case, and all such logical explanations fall of their own weight. A current of sentiment—not of logic—establishing a relation between sexual purity and the service of gods (or of God) makes itself felt from ancient times all the way down to our own. The Pythia had to be a virgin. Of course there is no dearth of logical explanations of the fact—when have they ever been wanting? Indeed, for any single case we always find several, the one better than the other. "It is said," writes Diodorus Siculus, *Bibliotheca historica,* XVI, 26, 6 (Booth, Vol. II, p. 101), "that the prophetesses of old were virgins because they were undefiled and because of their resemblance to Artemis [who was a virgin] and because they were most likely to keep the secrets of the oracle." But eventually a Thessalian, Echecrates by name, abducted and violated a Pythia of whom he had fallen enamoured; whereupon the people of Delphi made a law that the prophetess should be not a virgin but a woman over fifty. Later on, it seems, the office was restored to young women. That at least is what may be gathered from a passage in Plutarch.[1]

749. In the days of Pausanias a temple to the Artemis Hymnia

748 [1] Plutarch, *De Pythiae oraculis,* 22 (Goodwin, Vol. III, pp. 93-94): "So the Pythia who now serves the god must come of a good and law-abiding family and have herself lived above reproach." He goes on to say that the young woman described meets the ideal of Xenophon, who thought that a bride should go to her husband having seen and heard as little as possible of life. That may explain why Bouché-Leclerc, *Histoire de la divination dans l'antiquité,* Vol. III, p. 93, writes: "The god, who was thenceforth to be her only husband, wanted her beautiful and chaste. Any pollution would have made her unworthy of the mystic union that Christian propagandists took too much delight in ridiculing with their indecent allusions." A new logical explanation, for the mere asking!

still stood on the confines of the land of the Orchomeni, near Mantineia. The priestess at one time had been a young virgin, and a certain Aristocrates, historically a somewhat hazy figure, violated her, though she had taken refuge in the temple under protection of Artemis. The Arcadians put her to death by stoning and then decreed by law that "instead of a virgin, the priestess of Artemis should be a woman who had had commerce with men."[1]

750. Another temple to the Artemis Hymnia had, says Pausanias (*loc. cit.*, 13, 1), a priest and a priestess who were obligated to live in chastity, and a similar duty devolved upon the Essenes who presided at the suppers in the temple of Artemis at Ephesus. Their term of service, however, was only a year. In the temple to the Earth, near the river Crathis (*Ibid.*, VII, *Achaia*, 25, 12-13), the priestess could have lived with one man before assuming the post, but was obligated to remain chaste thereafter.

751. In other cases (*Ibid.*, VII, *Achaia*, 19, 1, and II, *Corinth*, 33, 2), priestesses could serve in the temple so long as they were maids, but had to resign on marriage. The Tegeans were more cautious still, giving Artemis a priestess who retained office only until she reached the age of puberty (*Ibid.*, VIII, *Arcadia*, 47, 3). At Athens the wife of the archon-king had to be a virgin at the time of her marriage.[1] Familiar the fact that among the Israelites the priest had to marry a virgin.[2]

752. Virginity was not the only quality required in a Vestal. She could not be a deaf-mute, nor have any physical defects. At the time when she was "taken" by the pontifex to serve as a Vestal, her parents had to be still living—or, as the Latins said, she had to be *matrima* and *patrima*. She had to come of a free-born and reputable

749 [1] Pausanias, *Periegesis*, VIII, *Arcadia*, 5, 12: Αντὶ γὰρ παρθένου διδόασι τῇ Αρτέμιδι ἱέρειαν γυναῖκα ὁμιλίας ἀνδρῶν ἀποχρώντως ἔχουσαν. Strange logic! As though a grown woman could not be misled as readily as a virgin! [Pareto seems to overlook ἀποχρώντως. Jones translates: "A woman who had had enough of intercourse with men," *i.e.*, too old for intercourse with men.—A. L.]

751 [1] Demosthenes, *In Neaeram*, 1370 (Auger, Vol. X, pp. 408-09): . . . Τὴν δὲ γυναῖκα αὐτοῦ νόμον ἔθεντο ἀστὴν εἶναι, καὶ μὴ ἐπιμεμιγμένην ἑτέρῳ ἀνδρὶ ἀλλὰ παρθένον γαμεῖν.

751 [2] Lev. 21: 13.

family.[1] Just so victims offered to the gods had to be perfect; and a feeling that persons and objects in the service of gods, or offered to them, have to be perfect persists all the way along from antiquity down to our own days.[2]

753. It is obvious that the causes of such things are not to be

752 [1] The conditions are stated by Aulus Gellius, *Noctes Atticae*, I, 12, 1-6, following Labeo: "Those who have written on the 'taking' of vestal virgins—Antistius Labeo most authoritative of them all—say that it was unlawful to 'take' a girl less than six years old or more than ten; that her father and mother had still to be living (*patrima et matrima*); that she could not have any defects of speech or hearing or be marked by any other bodily defect; that she could not be emancipated [from paternal control, through crime] nor daughter of a man who had been, even if she were under the authority of her grandfather (*in avi potestate*) with her father still living; that she was ineligible if either or both of her parents had ever served as slaves or engaged in any degrading occupation (*negotiis sordidis*)."

752 [2] Well known the fact that a Catholic priest is required to live in chastity and be free of any considerable physical defects. Lancelotto, *Institutiones iuris canonici, lib.* I, *tit.* 25 (p. 100): "A man who has married twice (*bigamus*) or has married a widow, a divorced woman (*eiectam*), or a prostitute, cannot be ordained." *Ibid.*, p. 102: "A man defective in body, unless the injury be of no importance, cannot be ordained." [And the heading reads: *Modica laesio non impedit ordinandum.*] *Decretum Gratiani, pars* I, *distinctio* 33, *canon* 2 (Friedberg, Vol. I, p. 123): "A man who, after baptism, has been the husband of two wives cannot be ordained a cleric, nor a man who has had but one woman, but as a concubine not as a wife; nor a man who has taken in marriage a widow, or a divorced wife, or a prostitute; nor a man who has mutilated himself in any part of his body in disdain [of the flesh] or at the promptings of a fear, justified or unjustified [of carnal sin]; nor a man proved to have received usury, or known to have played on the stage; nor a man who shall have repented of some mortal crime by public penance; nor a man who has at any time been insane or obsessed of devils (*afflictione diaboli vexatus*), nor a man who out of vainglory (*ambitionem*) shall have taken money in imitation of Simon Magus." *Ibid., distinctio* 32, *canon* 12: "No one shall be allowed access to a sacred order unless he be virgin and of proved chastity and down to the time of his subdiaconate shall have had but one wife herself a virgin" [The requirement made of the archon-king in Athens!]: Rabbinovicz, *Législation criminelle du Talmud,* p. 190: "Mishnah. Subject to the penalty of flogging are . . . a high priest who marries a widow (Lev. 21: 14); a priest who marries a divorced woman or a woman who 'has loosed the shoe' [*i.e.*, a widow refused in remarriage by her deceased husband's brother], Deut. 25: 9." *Decretum Gratiani, pars* I, *distinctio* 55, *canones* 4-5 (Friedberg, Vol. I, p. 216): "If anyone has mutilated himself, *id est, si quis amputavit sibi virilia,* he may not be a cleric, for he is a murderer of himself and an enemy of God's profession (that is, the priesthood—*Dei conditionis inimicus*). . . . If a man already a priest shall mutilate himself, let him be altogether damned, for he is a murderer of himself. . . . Those who mutilate themselves not knowing how otherwise to combat carnal temptation are not eligible to the priesthood." The priests of Cybele, on the other hand, were eunuchs.

sought in logical explanations of this kind, and that we shall find them only as we turn our attention to certain sentiments which account both for the things and for the explanations given of them.

754. An identical punishment was inflicted upon the Roman Vestals and the Virgins of the Sun in Peru if they broke their vows of chastity. In Rome, says Marquardt,[1] the guilty Vestal was carried "on a bier to the Campus Sceleratus near the Porta Collina. There she was flogged and then buried alive. The Romans dared not kill her, for they considered it *nefas* to cause a person consecrated to the gods to die a violent death." If the explanation is not to your liking, here is another. The dead are cremated. Would it not be inappropriate to burn a woman who has not faithfully tended her fire? Or will you have still another? The guilty woman was handed over to the gods, and her punishment left to them.[2]

755. If your appetite is still not sated, we will look around for something else. Réville has produced the following, which may serve both for Rome and Peru:[1] "Is it not astonishing that the punishment held in store for violators of the vow of chastity was exactly the same as the one inflicted on unchaste Vestals in Rome? They were buried alive![2] The parallel arises in the fact that in both countries the culprit was held to be hateful, after such a crime, to the divinities of the Day, of Light. She had provoked their wrath. The sight of a being worthy of their resentment could no longer be inflicted upon them. She could only be dedicated to the nether

754 [1] *Römische Staatsverwaltung: Sacralwesen,* p. 328.

754 [2] For both explanations see Plutarch, *Quaestiones Romanae,* 96 (Goodwin, Vol. II, p. 254).

755 [1] *Les religions du Méxique,* p. 367.

755 [2] Festus, *De verborum significatione,* XIV, *s.v. Probrum virginis Vestalis* (London, Vol. VI, p. 644): "Inchastity in a Vestal Virgin was punished capitally, and the man who had led her astray was flogged to death. According to M. Cato, in his oration entitled *De auguribus,* the law was posted in the atrium of the temple to Liberty, the exact text being lost along with that of many other laws when that temple was burned. Cato adds that when Vestal Virgins were convicted of profaning their priesthood by inchastity they were buried alive as having defiled the sanctity of Mother Vesta. Though criminals, they were not buried outside the city, but in a field near the Porta Collina, called the Field of Impurity (*Campus Sceleratus*)."

gods of Darkness, of Death, whose handmaiden she had elected to become."

756. The Romans themselves had different reasons for punishing Vestals. Their chief aim, it seems, was to escape impending misfortunes. "There are several signs," says Dionysius of Halicarnassus, "when divine service has not been in due form, chief among them the going out of Vesta, a thing that the Romans fear more than any catastrophe, for whatever the cause, they believe that it presages disaster for the City."[1]

757. There is a story[1]—whether it be history or legend matters little—that in Rome, about the year 481 B.C., a series of prodigies made it clear that the gods were angry. Investigation revealed that the Vestal Opimia was no longer a virgin. She was buried alive. Thereupon the sacrifices became favourable again, and the wrath of the gods was evidently appeased. Eleven years later, in 470 B.C.—still a very hazy period historically—a pestilence broke out among women in Rome causing many deaths.[2] No one knew which way to turn till a slave informed the high-priests that the Vestal Urbinia was no longer a virgin and that she was offering sacrifices for the City with impure hands. She was buried alive. One of her two lovers killed himself, the other was slain. "The pestilence among the women and the frequent deaths ceased as soon as these things were done." Another legend supplies an etymology for the name of the Campus Sceleratus. In the year 334 B.C., says Livy, *Ab urbe condita,* VIII, 15, 7-8, "the Vestal Minucia was reported to the priests by a slave informer. She had first fallen under suspicion by being more fashionably dressed than was seemly in the performance of her duties (*propter mundiorem iusto cultum*). She was at once ordered to abstain from the rites and to hold her slaves in her own possession [that they might be tortured to extract evidence against her]. After a trial she was buried alive in the Field of Impurity (*Campus Sceleratus*) next to the paved road at the Porta Collina. That

756 [1] *Antiquitates romanae,* II, 67 (Spelman, Vol. I, p. 348).
757 [1] *Ibid.,* VIII, 89 (Spelman, Vol. III, pp. 432-34).
757 [2] *Ibid.,* IX, 40 (Spelman, Vol. IV, pp. 74-75).

name was given to the place, I believe, because of her crime."

758. In times historical, and to wit, just after the defeat at Cannae (216 B.C), direful prodigies appeared. The Romans were terrified by the fact that within a year's time [1] "two Vestals, Opimia and Floronia, had been convicted of violating their vows. One of them had been buried alive, according to custom, near the Porta Collina, the other had committed suicide." Their lovers were flogged to death. But all that was not enough to dispel the terror. So the Sibylline books were opened, and they were found to prescribe extraordinary sacrifices. "Two Gauls, a man and a woman, and two Greeks, a man and a woman, were buried alive in the Forum Boarium in a place marked off by stones, where other human sacrifices had been performed. The which is unworthy of the Roman religion (or Foster: "which was rather a Greek than a Roman rite")."

759. It cannot be said that human beings, Greeks and Gauls, were buried alive in this case because they were considered objects of loathing to the divinities of Day or of Light. The character of the non-logical conduct expressed in those sacrifices and in the punishment of the Vestals is evident enough. It was the instinct of self-preservation, insisting on matching extreme misfortunes with extreme remedies (§§ 929 f.). It was the same instinct that impels people to make human sacrifices in order to ensure success in rites of magic (§ 931).[1]

760. The Vestal was buried in a little vault with a few provisions: a little bread, some water, milk, and oil.[1] That manner of death was not peculiar to guilty Vestals. There is an allusion to something similar in a tragedy of Sophocles.[2] According to certain traditions

758 [1] Livy, *Ibid.*, XXII, 57, 2-6.

759 [1] [A cross-reference to §§ 1092-93 would have been in point here also.—A. L.]

760 [1] Plutarch, *Numa*, 10, 5 (Perrin, Vol. I, p. 343). Plutarch explains the procedure on the ground that it would be sacrilegious to allow persons duly consecrated to the most sacred ceremonies to perish of hunger.

760 [2] *Antigone*, vv. 773-80 (Storr, Vol. I, pp. 374-75). Creon says of Antigone: "I shall lead her to a deserted place without trace of human being, and there will I shut her up alive in a cave, with enough food to spare me a sacrilege and the city a crime." The scholiast notes that that was an ancient custom, "that she might not seem to be killed by starvation, for that would be impious."

condemned Vestals were not always executed in the same way. The law prescribing burial alive is attributed by Zonaras to Tarquinius Priscus.[3]

761. Under the Empire the old laws were not always observed. Suetonius says of Domitian, *Domitianus,* 8, 4, that "he curbed immorality among the Vestal Virgins, which had been ignored by his father and brother, with a variety of severe penalties, at first with death, then with punishments according to the ancient custom.[1] He permitted the Oculata sisters and another Vestal, Varronilla, to choose their mode of death, sending their accomplices into exile. The Vestal dean, Cornelia, who had been acquitted at previous trials, was again indicted and found guilty. He caused her to be buried alive and her accomplices to be flogged to death, with the exception of one, a former praetor, against whom proofs seemed insufficient. He was exiled. Caracalla, too, had Vestals buried alive.[2]

762. By a fortuitous coincidence, the Virgins of the Sun in Peru were allowed to have commerce with the Incas, who were sons of the Sun; while in Rome, the Emperor Elagabalus, himself a priest of the Sun, went so far as to marry a Vestal and say: "I have done this that divine children may be born of me, a high priest, and of her, a supreme Vestal." [1]

760 [3] *Epitome historiarum,* III, 8 (Migne, Vol. 134, p. 566). Relating how Tarquinius caused an unchaste Vestal to be buried alive with a cot, a lantern, and a table with food, Zonaras adds: "From that time on it became the rule to punish in that manner such of the priestesses as failed to keep their vows."

761 [1] See also Dio Cassius, *Historia Romana,* LXVII, 3 (he has a slightly different slant on Domitian's crusade against the Vestals); and the younger Pliny, *Epistulae,* IV, 11: "He had set his heart on having Cornelia, the dean of the Vestals, buried alive, as though he thought that his reign would be glorified by an example of that sort."

761 [2] Dio Cassius, *Ibid.,* LXVIII, 16. And *cf.* Herodian, *Historiae,* IV, 6: "He had Vestals buried alive, on charges that they had not preserved their chastity." [Herodian, that is, doubting their guilt: ὡς μὴ φυλαττούσας τὴν παρθενίαν—A. L.]

762 [1] Dio Cassius, *Ibid.,* LXXX, 11; Herodian, *Historiae,* V, 4. He defended his conduct in a letter to the Senate on the grounds that "it was but a human sinne, that he was enchanted with the magicke of her beauty, and that it was no incongruitie for a priest to marry a priestesse, which could only be a seemlie and sacred thing." Réville, *Les religions du Méxique,* p. 366: "The Virgins of the Sun were cloistered in absolute seclusion, cut off from any connexions with the rest of society, especially as regards men. Only the Inca and his principal wife, the Coya,

763. Another coincidence is remarkable indeed. In Peru the Virgins of the Sun made certain loaves of bread of a very pure flour, which were offered to the Incas during a certain festival of the Sun. In Rome the Vestal Virgins prepared a dough of flour called *mola salsa* to be used for offerings to the goddess Vesta.[1] All these examples serve to show that, as we saw in § 743, resemblances between certain rites in no way prove that the one is derived directly from the other.

764. B-γ: *Myths and the like are entirely non-real.* In this group we find the numerous and important theories of allegory, including the theories of the solar myth and others of the same brand. All of them, widely current in the past, still have their adherents. They are dear to ingenious, subtle, imaginative minds, eager for unexpected discoveries. They represent, further, a salutory transition stage between blind faith and scientific scepticism; what can be no longer

were at liberty to enter the convent. These visits were not altogether disinterested, for the Inca ordinarily recruited his harem from the girls there. A son of the Sun and able to marry his sisters, he was merely choosing within his family. All the same, the young virgins were held to the strictest chastity and took oath never to depart from it. But the vow came down to a promise that they would belong to no husband save the Sun or 'him to whom the Sun should give them.'"

763 [1] Garcilaso de la Vega, *Comentarios reales que tratan del origen de los Incas,* Vol. II, pp. 182-84: "Of the four feasts of the Sun celebrated by the king-Incas, the chief one was the Raymi, coming in the month of June. . . . The priest-Incas, who were to perform the sacrifices, prepared the sheep and lambs that were to be used, the day before, as well as the food and beverages that were to be proffered to the Sun. . . . The 'wives' of the Sun spent that same night in grinding the flour for a dough called *cancu,* which they moulded into little loaves of bread about the size of an apple. . . . The chosen Virgins were the only ones allowed to grind the flour for the loaves, especially for those which the Inca and the princes of the blood were to eat. They also prepared all the other foods; for the notion was that on that day the Sun was host to his children." Servius, *In Vergilii Bucolicon,* VIII, v. 82 (Thilo-Hagen, Vol. III, p. 106): *"Sparge molam:* 'Flour and salt.' The term is derived from religion. 'Sacred flour': *mola casta, mola salsa* (for they both mean the same), is made in the following manner: Taking turns each day between the nones of May and the day before the ides [May 7-14: the same date, virtually, as that of the Peruvian ceremony, for they were both spring festivals.], the three eldest Vestals filled harvest baskets with spelt, and themselves roasted, crushed, and ground the grain, making a flour of it. Three times a year, at the Lupercalia, the feast of Vesta, and the ides of September, the Virgins made dough of the flour, adding cooking-salt and rock-salt."

defended has to be dropped, but there is an effort to salvage as much as possible of the old myths.

765. However, what often happens is that little or nothing really is saved. Past experience shows that little is gained by trying to logicalize an outworn belief. Often, in fact, that is the way to hasten its ruin. Abstract, ingenious, finely drawn reasonings have no great influence as regards fostering the non-logical sentiments that make up the substance of beliefs.[1]

766. It might be well, at this point, to recall in the particular the remarks as to the purpose of this immediate research that we made in general terms on the diagram in §§ 635 f. Given a piece of writing in which myths, allegories, and the like, are assumed to play a part more or less extensive, our main concern is to determine whether and in what manner we can get back from the text to the writer's ideas or to the facts that he meant to describe.

767. Grote has passed an excellent judgment on allegorical and historical interpretations of ancient Greek myths. Says he:[1] "The doctrine, supposed to have been originally symbolized and subsequently overclouded, in the Greek mythes, was in reality first intruded into them by the unconscious fancies of later interpreters. It was one of the various roads which instructed men took to escape from the literal admission of the ancient mythes, and to arrive at some new form of belief, more consonant with their ideas of what

765 [1] Sorel remarks in *"Quelques prétentions juives,"* pp. 292-93: "Catholicism has very appreciably strengthened its situation in the course of the nineteenth century by pursuing a policy quite different from the one advised by men of talent: the Church has stressed its theology, multiplied its monastic institutions, and attached to miracles an importance they had not enjoyed since the Middle Ages. . . . Bernard Lazare was terribly mistaken when he wrote, *L'antisémitisme,* pp. 359-60 [English, p. 327]: 'Christianity is disappearing like the Jewish religion, like all the religions that we can see very gradually perishing. It is succumbing to the blows of reason and science. . . . We are daily losing the feeling for the absurd, the need of it, and consequently the need of religion, especially the practical need; and those who still believe in the Divinity have ceased to believe in the necessity, and above all in the efficacy, of acts of worship.' Bernard Lazare was merely paraphrasing Renan in all that, without going into the question personally. In any event, things have changed greatly since 1894." The assertion quoted from Lazare is absolutely and completely at variance with the facts.

767 [1] *History of Greece,* Vol. I, pp. 439-40.

the attributes and character of the gods ought to be. . . . The same conflicting sentiments which led the philosophers to decompose the divine mythes into allegory impelled the historians to melt down the heroic mythes into something like continuous political history, with a long series of chronology calculated upon the heroic pedigrees. The one process as well as the other was interpretative guesswork, proceeding upon unauthorised assumptions, and without any verifying test or evidence: while it frittered away the characteristic beauty of the mythe into something essentially antimythical, it sought to arrive both at history and philosophy by impracticable roads."

768. A commentary on the Homeric poems written by Heraclides of Pontus [or Heraclitus of Alexandria], *Allegoriae Homericae,* may be mentioned as typical of the allegorical interpretation. The critic's purpose is to make Homer's stories rational, moral, and pious. So with reference to the passage in the *Iliad,* I, vv. 396-411, that speaks of an intention on the part of the gods to put Zeus in chains, Heraclides remarks, *cap.* 21, that "for those verses alone Homer would deserve to be banished not only from a republic of Plato but beyond the farthest pillars of Hercules and the inaccessible Ocean"; and he goes on, 22: "After all, there is only one way to excuse such impiety: we shall prove, namely, that the myth is allegorical." He therefore proceeds to explain in lengthy disquisitions, 24-25, that Zeus is the ether, Hera the atmosphere, Athena the Earth, Poseidon water, Thetis Providence. When Homer says that Thetis rescued Zeus when Hera, Poseidon, and Athena set out to put him in chains, he is representing a disturbance of the elements that is averted by Providence.

769. The *Odyssey,* V, v. 121, says that rosy-fingered Dawn abducted Orion. According to Heraclides [Heraclitus], *cap.* 68, that was Homer's way of saying "that a young man in the flower of his youth was carried off by Fate. Indeed it was a custom of the ancients when a man died not to move his body either at night or in the heat of the day, but at dawn, when the Sun's rays were not yet warm. So when a youth well born and distinguished for handsome physique died, his early-morning funeral was most happily called an

abduction by Dawn, as though he had not died but had been snatched away by an amorous yearning." Allegories of this kind have no sounder basis in fact than the interpretations of Palaephatus. Indeed it would serve just as well in this case to read that a queen by the name of Aurora misled a young man by the name of Orion.

770. There is no end to allegorical explanations of Homer's poems, and new ones have kept appearing every so often from ancient times down to our own. Eustathius already has a number, and eventually we get to a certain Hugon, who saw a prophecy of Christ's Passion in the Homeric poems; and to one Gerard Croese, who regarded them as an allegorical history of the Jews.[1]

771. In the same way and for the same reasons Virgil had his allegorical interpretations too. Comparetti notes that the works of Virgil were supposed to contain a prophecy of the coming of Christ:[1] "The most elaborate interpretation of the kind appears in an address delivered by the Emperor Constantine before a church assembly. . . . The translation of the eclogue [the fourth] into Greek verse as we read it today in the imperial lecture shows traces of the ancient plague of occultism. In not a few places it departs arbitrarily from the original, altering meanings with the obvious purpose of adapting things to the Christian interpretation propounded. The Emperor examines Virgil's composition in its various parts and finds hints of the advent of Christ in a number of particulars: the returning virgin is Mary; the new Heaven-sent progeny is Jesus; and the 'serpent which shall be no more' is the age-old Tempter of our forefathers." And that is not all.

772. Another fine specimen is Fulgentius. Says Comparetti farther along: "The *De continentia Virgiliana,* in which Fulgentius elucidates the content, or rather, the hidden content, of Virgil's poem is one of the strangest and most curious documents of the Latin Middle

770 [1] Hugon, *Vera historia Romana, seu origo Latii vel Italiae ac Romanae Urbis, e tenebris longae vetustatis in lucem producta,* Rome, 1655. Ὁμήρος ἑβραίος, *sive historia Hebraeorum ab Homero hebraicis nominibus ac sententiis conscripta in Odyssea et Iliade, exposita illustrataque studio ac opera Gerardi Croësi,* Dordrecht, 1704.

771 [1] *Virgilio nel medio evo,* Vol. I, pp. 134 f. (Benecke, p. 100).

Ages. . . . The writer makes haste to declare in a preamble that he is to confine himself to the *Aeneid* alone, since the *Bucolics* and the *Georgics* contain mystical significances so recondite that there is virtually no skill great enough to divine them fully. They constitute, at any rate, a burden too heavy for shoulders of his size, 'forasmuch as they would require too great knowledge, since the first meaning of the *Georgics* is wholly astrological, the second physionomical and medical, the third relative entirely to "haruspicinics" [art of divination].' "[1]

773. In the same way, and for the same reason, people have sought and found allegories in the Bible and in the Gospels. Immense the amount of work that has been done along this line by the Church Fathers and their successors, Catholic, Protestant, Modernist. Philo the Jew wrote *Allegories of the Sacred Laws,* which stand on a par with the allegories the ancients found in Homer and Virgil and those the Modernists have of late been discovering in the Gospels. Strange that these last should vaunt a mere reversion to antiquity as *modern*. That is something like discovering America in the twentieth century!

774. Says the Bible, Gen. 2:25: "And they were both naked, the man and his wife, and were not ashamed." Would you know what that means? Philo will enlighten you. It means that "the mind did not think and that the senses did not perceive, that the man was without thought, the woman without perception."[1] Clearer and more definite than that one could not be! Or would you know the

772 [1] *Ibid.*, pp. 144 f. (Benecke, p. 108). The opening verse of the *Aeneid, Arma virumque cano Troiae qui primus ab oris,* Fulgentius, *De Virgilliana continentia* (Müncker, Vol. II, p. 147), imagines Virgil as explaining as follows: "There is a threefold progress (*gradus trifarius*) in human life: first comes 'to have,' second, 'to manage what one has,' third, to 'beautify what one manages.' Those three steps you must regard as stowed away in that one verse of mine: *arma,* in other words, power, relates to corporal substance; *virum,* that is to say, wisdom, relates to intellectual substance; *primus,* that is, prince [*i.e.,* princely], relates to beautifying substance. Whence the following sequence: 'to have, to manage, to beautify.' So, under semblance of a tale, I have portrayed the whole lot of human kind: first nature, then learning, then happiness."

774 [1] *Sacrarum legum allegoriae,* II, 16 (Cohn, Vol. I, p. 103; Yonge, Vol. I, p. 96): *Οὔτε ὁ νοῦς ἐνόει, οὔτε ἡ αἴσθησις ᾔσθάνετο, ἀλλ' ἦν ὁ μὲν τοῦ νοεῖν ἔρημός τε καὶ γυμνὸς, ἡ δὲ τοῦ αἰσθάνεσθαι.*

meaning of the miracle of the water changed into wine, or of the blind man restored to sight, or of the man raised from the dead? This time the Rev. Father Loisy will tell you in terms as clear and definite as Philo's.[2] The change of the water to wine means the replacement of the Law by the Gospels. The blind man made to see and the man raised from the dead represent humanity called to the "true" light and the "true" life of the Incarnate Word. M. Loisy takes vigorously to task anyone not accepting such lucid interpretations out of hand. Says he: "The theologians of our day are so far removed from the ways of thinking of the Evangelist [John], and at the same time have so little sense of the possible and real in matters of history, that we must give up hope of making them understand that accounts such as the story of the miracle of Cana, the healing of a man congenitally blind, the raising of Lazarus from the dead—unintelligible, absurd, or ridiculous as matters of faith, unless they be regarded as bold tricks of a sleight-of-hand performer—are of easy and simple interpretation if we avail ourselves of the keys supplied by the Evangelist himself, and see in the miracle of the water changed to wine the Law replaced by the Gospel and in the blind man restored to sight and the man raised from the dead, humanity called to the true light and the true life by the Incarnate Word, who is Himself the Light and the Life."[3] Unfortunately that is the trouble with all allegorical interpretations of mythology. It is very difficult to make a choice, accepting this or that and rejecting the others.[4]

774 [2] *Simples réflexions sur l'encyclique Pascendi,* pp. 52-53.

774 [3] Further along, p. 55, M. Loisy complains that his meaning has been misrepresented by the Holy Office: "I say that John could call himself a witness to the Christ since he was the witness to His life in the Church. The Holy Congregation makes me say that John should not have offered himself as a witness to the Christ since he was only a witness for the Christian life. Under similar forms of expression the two ideas are different." To avoid such misunderstandings, M. Loisy should have expressed himself more clearly. "Pliny the younger is a witness to Trajan, Suetonius to a number of Emperors, John to Christ." From a historico-experimental point of view that really would seem to mean that Pliny knew Trajan, saw Trajan, Suetonius other emperors, John Christ. If one's meaning is something else, one should say so in unmistakeable terms.

774 [4] Another Modernist has tried his hand at allegorizing the wedding-feast at Cana: D'Alma: *La controverse du Quatrième évangile,* pp. 59-62: "Six stone jars

775. Are there allegories in the Gospel according to St. John? There may be—in fact, it is very probable that there are. But we have no means whatever of distinguishing the allegorical element from the historical element, and it is even possible that the writer of the Gospel did not distinguish them very clearly himself.[1] Nor is that all. Even assuming that we could determine for a certainty that a given story is allegorical, we are still nowhere as regards knowing exactly what allegory the writer had in mind. On that point the Apocalypse is evidence enough. It is certainly allegorical; but as for what the allegory is, people have been investigating for centuries and nothing certain has come of it.

776. M. Loisy has a strange way of understanding the significance of historical proofs. Says he:[1] "Remove from the Gospels the idea of the great Advent and the idea of the Christ-king, and I defy you to

stand on the floor according to the manner of purification among the Jews. They hold about two or three measures each. If one chooses to inquire further as to the meaning which the spiritual Gospel attaches to that symbol, the marriage feast at Cana has to be taken in connexion with the feast of which Jesus partook after he had gathered his first five apostles at the house of Levi-Matthew. There, answering a question of the Pharisees as to the difference between his rule of life and that of the disciples of John, he compares himself to the bridegroom who feasts with his friends and does not put his wine into old bottles (Mark 2: 22). Now the five disciples he has just assembled, and who make six if we count the bridegroom, are not leathern gourds but jars of stone, foundations of the Church. [If there had been six disciples the bridegroom would not have been counted, and the jars would have stayed at six. Had there been four disciples, there would still have been no difficulty: we count the bride as well as the groom and again get our six.] . . . Such, says the Evangelist, was the first of the miracles of Jesus. . . . It would have been strange indeed that Christianity should have had a grossly material miracle of that kind as its starting-point." With arguments of that sort one can prove anything one pleases.

775 [1] D'Alma agrees, *Op. cit.*, pp. 25, 19, that history is interwoven with allegory in the Gospel according to St. John: "His prologue complete, the Evangelist enters straightway upon the drama he has just outlined. There is a first encounter between darkness and light [John 1: 5: And the light shineth in darkness; and the darkness comprehended it not.] Not that John is the light: he was a witness [to the light, John 1: 8], a flaming, shining torch. He baptizes. From Jerusalem the Jews send him their official supervisors of religion—priests and Levites. Is that story to be taken literally? Or is it altogether allegorical? It may be both at once." D'Alma is right; but for that very reason it is futile to try as he does to sift the history from the allegory, and, one may add, from the fiction and the imagination.

776 [1] *Autour d'un petit livre*, p. 70.

prove the historical existence of the Saviour; for you will then have stripped His life and death of all their historical significance." So it would follow that it is the "idea" implied in a narrative which proves its historical veracity!

777. It is the ordinary confusion between subjective proofs and objective proofs (§ 1567). One has to make up one's mind: Either a story is a matter of faith, in which case objective proofs are superfluous, or it is a matter of history with an experimental substance, in which case subjective proofs, "ideas," beliefs, have no status as evidence. The same objection may be raised against neo-Christians, such as Piepenbring in his *Jésus historique,* who try their hardest to eliminate the supernatural and the miraculous from the Gospels. If the Gospels are to be taken as strictly historical texts, "Christian experience"—their accord, in other words, with the sentiments of this or that person—has no status as proof. The mistake these people make lies in their believing that their humanitarian inspirations have a greater objective force than mere faith in miracles.[1]

777 [1] Piepenbring bestows high praise on Loisy. He tries to conjecture what the primitive Gospels may have been and does not notice that in his own work, which is entirely hypothetical, he finds in them only what he chooses to put into them. So he is able to conclude, *Op. cit.,* p. 181: "If now we cast a glance in retrospect upon the ministry of Jesus, we are forced to recognize that in the sources of our Gospels miracles play a very insignificant rôle, coming down to a few cures worked by Jesus. Preaching was by far the important element in His ministry. The situation is quite different in the recent portions of the Gospels. An attentive comparison of them with their original sources proves that the miracles kept gradually increasing in evangelical history, becoming more and more extraordinary all along." What are the "sources" in question? Piepenbring himself confesses that they simmer down to the *Logia,* of which he says, p. 40: "The *Logia* have evidently come down to us in a disconnected state. A number of the texts are not strictly original but already bear the imprint of apostolic theology"; and then to a Proto-Mark, which no one has ever seen and of which many doubt the existence. Yet Piepenbring rears his whole edifice on those tottering foundations, p. 75: "Since it is not to be assumed that no other authentic element figures in our synoptic Gospels aside from the *Logia* and the Proto-Mark, they should be carefully scanned for such of those elements as are really there." People have tried to do just that with the *Iliad* and other legendary narratives, and to little or no purpose. There is no method for solving such riddles.

Among the prettiest transformations of a known text into an allegedly primitive text must be reckoned the feat of Bascoul in rewriting Sappho's ode. He asserts that the text we know is a parody—and so far, so good; but then with no other document than the text itself, he discovers the primitive text so parodied, and it

778. From the standpoint of objective reality, one cannot imagine what M. Loisy means when he says further along, p. 93: "This Christ [of the Gospel according to St. John] is undoubtedly not a metaphysical abstraction, for He is alive in the soul of the evangelist." Every metaphysical abstraction at all vivid is "alive" in the mind of the metaphysicist. Loisy would take the side of historical and scientific criticism as against the Roman Church; but then he is himself a theologian more metaphysical, more abstract, more abstruse, than the theologians of the Curia.[1]

779. In order to get at least something that is real into their allegories etymology has been called to the rescue, and etymological methods of interpretation keep turning up all the way down to our day. One of them, the system that leads to the solar myth, has enjoyed wide-spread acquiescence. As regards sociology, the intrinsic value of the method is of less significance than the fact of its wide acceptance, as indicating an influential mental state and the con-

proves to be something entirely different from the text we know! One can only hope that Bascoul will now go on and give us the "primitive *Iliad*," which will tell the true history of the Trojan War, and so bring to a triumphant conclusion the audacious emprise vainly essayed by Thucydides, Dio Chrysostom, and no end of other writers. Bascoul, *La chaste Saphos de Lesbos*, p. 30: The ode is not an erotic poem, but ". . . a description of the emotions caused by the rise of a poet-musician as a rival to Sappho and her school, and by his songs. Here history points to Stesichorus. [What a blessing to be able to guess what history is so easily!] As a great poet and a reformer of lyric poetry he must necessarily [When one knows what necessarily happens one also knows what happens.] have made a profound impression on Sappho, when she met him in Sicily, where she was in exile with her daughter. [What a pity we are not told the exact day and hour!] It was to rouse her daughter from her indifference that Sappho sang to her that masterpiece in the natural and sublime description of the emotions, which were provoked first by the appearance of the gods, then by inspiration, and finally by enthusiasm."

778 [1] The dispute today has become primarily political. It is a question not of historical criticism, but of attacking or defending the Roman Church. Reinach, *Orpheus*, Chap. VIII, § 20 (Simmonds, p. 223): "Collation of our Gospels, and the distinguishing of the successive strata of which they are made up, prove that even the legend of Jesus as taught by the Church is not corroborated in all its particulars by the texts cited in evidence." That is true; but Reinach accepts Loisy's interpretations, which are of no greater value. They are as wanting in proof as the interpretations of Homer by Heraclides [Heraclitus]. Now we are by no means caught in the dilemma of either accepting the *Iliad* as historical narrative or substituting the interpretations of Heraclides for it.

tinued prevalence of an anti-scientific attitude towards the traditions and institutions of the past.[1]

780. Max Müller and his followers carried the method of allegorical etymology to the extremest limits. Their procedure is to use for purposes of proof uncertain and very comprehensive meanings of certain words, which Müller generally derives from the Sanskrit. From them, by reasonings that are not a little loose and vague, sharply defined and positive conclusions are reached.

781. Here is an example. Müller is trying to interpret the legend of Procris.[1] He breaks it up into its "elements." "The first . . . 'Kephalos loves Prokris.' Prokris we must explain by a reference to Sanskrit, where *prush* and *prish* mean to sprinkle and are used chiefly with reference to rain drops. For instance, in the *Rig-Veda,* I, 168, v. 8: 'The lightnings laugh down upon the earth when the winds shower forth the rain.' The same root in the Teutonic languages has taken the sense of 'frost'; and Bopp identifies *prush* with the Old High-German *frus, frigere.* In Greek, we must refer to the same root πρώς, πρωκός, a dew-drop, and also Prokris, the dew. Thus the wife of Kephalos is only a repetition of Herse, her mother —Herse, dew, being derived from Sanskrit *vrish,* to sprinkle; Prokris, dew, from a Sanskrit root *prush,* having the same sense. The

779 [1] Foucart, *La méthode comparative dans l'histoire des religions,* pp. 18 f.: "In the course of the past century the discovery of the Vedic literature aroused an excitement in the learned world that is hard to imagine today. People thought they had come into possession of the songs that the shepherds of early humanity sang in honour of their gods as they led their flocks to pasture, songs faithfully transmitted by tradition. Those shepherds were believed to be the ancestors of the Aryan races, and the monuments [of their culture] were to supply the key to all the languages and all the religions of the Indo-European peoples. Knowledge of Greek and Greece were to suffer especially from such illusions. For half a century the etymological methods that claimed to be revealing the true nature of the Hellenic gods as solar myths and phenomena of weather held up all serious progress. The solar myth, especially, seems to be a sort of inescapable measles that growing sciences of religion have to suffer in early childhood. Egyptology is still infected with the hazy reveries of that early school, the mystical nonsense of which can be found still going the rounds in this late day. As regards the Hellenic religions, treatises recently published are still steeped in the time-worn errors propagated by Max Müller and his disciples." Unfortunately, Foucart's "comparative" method also has its faults, as every *a priori* method must have.

781 [1] *Chips from a German Workshop,* Vol. II, pp. 86-88.

first part of our mythe, therefore, means simply: 'The Sun kisses the Morning Dew.' The second saying is: 'Eos loves Kephalos.' This requires no explanation: it is the old story repeated a hundred times in Aryan mythology, 'the Dawn loves the Sun.' The third saying is: 'Prokris is faithless'; yet her new lover in a different guise is still Kephalos. This we may interpret as a poetical expression for sunbeams, the rays of the sun being reflected in various colours from the dew-drops—so that Prokris may be said to be kissed by many lovers; yet they are all the same Kephalos, disguised, but at last recognised. The last saying was, 'Prokris is killed by Kephalos,' *i.e.*, the dew is absorbed by the sun. Prokris dies for her love to Kephalos, and he must kill her because he loves her. It is the gradual and inevitable absorption of the dew by the glowing rays of the sun which is expressed, with so much truth, by the unerring shaft of Kephalos thrown unintentionally at Prokris hidden in the thicket of the forest." That may be the way people reason in dreamland, but what is certain is that one can prove nothing—or rather prove anything—in such a manner. Müller's etymologies of Procris and of Herse were impugned. In defence he says, *Ibid.*, pp. 86-87, note: "*Prishat,* feminine *prishati,* means 'sprinkled,' *guttatus* in Latin, and it is applied to a speckled deer, and to a speckled cow." When one has at one's disposal a term which of itself means a "rain-drop," a "dew-drop," "frost," "speckled cow," and a few terms equally definite, it is never difficult to extract from it anything one wishes. We must not forget meantime that interpretations of this sort have been accepted and admired by hosts and hosts of people.[2]

782. It would be too simple to see in the Centaurs products of the human imagination, which created those monsters just as it has created so many others. There must be some great mystery about such a conception. Etymology offers a choice among many interpretations. The term "centaur" may indicate [1] "a population of neatherds; for the name is derived from κεντεῖν, 'to goad,' and ταῦρος,

781 [2] I do not know Sanskrit and can therefore say nothing as to Müller's etymologies. I accept them with eyes closed. But the trouble is that even when they are unconditionally accepted, the reasonings based on them are worth little or nothing.

782 [1] Maury, *Histoire des religions de la Grèce antique,* Vol. I, p. 12, note.

'bull.' It refers to the custom of neatherds of driving their cattle with pointed sticks." If that etymology is not to your liking, you might sample another:[2] "Another etymology, modern this time, associates the word αὖρος, 'hare,' with the word κεντεῖν. That would make centaurs 'hare-drivers.'" If you are still not satisfied: "Comparative mythology, assuming an Asiatic origin for the Centaurs, has compared them with the Gandharvas of India, gods that were hairy like monkeys and, like the Centaurs, lovers of wine and women, and practising medicine, divination, and music, as did the Centaurs of Hellenic mythology. The comparison with the Gandharvas (the name means 'horse' in Sanskrit) would tend to make the Centaurs (*i.e.*, men-horses) personifications of sunbeams, pictured as horses in the imagination of the Aryans, or, as has also been said, as clouds, thought of as riding horses about the sun." If you are dubious about that, suppose we make them sons of Ixion and Nephele: "Some have seen in Ixion and his wheel an image of the sun sweeping along in its everlasting movement; others a personification of the hurricane and the waterspout. The Centaurs are either sunbeams or clouds surrounding the sun. They may also be taken as demons of the tempest, unless one prefers to regard them as symbols of the torrents that come rushing down from Pelion."

783. This method of reasoning by gross approximation should be carefully considered, for it is typical: a wheel revolves; the Sun revolves; therefore Ixion's wheel is the Sun. In general terms, the method is as follows. We set out to prove that $A = B$. We try, by appropriate selection of terms, to make A and B arouse more or less similar sentiments in people of our time. We then draw the inference that A was exactly equal to B in the eyes of people of ages long past. To attain that end, it is important not to make the statement too succinct. It must be drawn out long enough to give the sentiments in question time to come into play and gain momentum, burying the fatuity of our reasoning, meantime, in our many words.

784. Maury sees in the Centaurs "the metamorphosis that the

782 [2] Daremberg-Saglio, *Dictionnaire, s.v. Centauri.* So for the two following etymologies.

Gandharvas underwent in Greece. . . . The Gandharvas, in fact, are sunbeams, flames of the sacred hearth-fire in which gaudy reflections play, waves of the Soma, in which those flames are mirrored and which the Aryan imagination pictured as horses." [1] Those blessed Gandharvas are all that; and if it is not enough, fix it up to suit yourself. The Gandharvas are also Centaurs. Uhlenbeck, for his part, *Wörterbuch, s.v. Gandharvás,* does not believe that the Gandharvas have anything to do with the Centaurs. Victor Henry comes back at him and floors him with the following argument: [2] "In Vedic mythology the Gandharvas pass for prodigiously powerful and lascivious beings. Those are the epithets which precede their name, the attributes which everywhere follow them. . . . What do we know of the history of the Centaurs? Very little, after all. If descriptions of them abound, there are no legends, properly so called, about them. Nevertheless, in this incredible dearth of facts a single story stands out, and it is exactly to the purport that the Vedic portraitures led us to expect. Invited to the marriage of Pirithous and

784 [1] *Op. cit.,* Vol. I, p. 202. Bergaigne, *Les dieux souverains de la religion Védique,* p. 65: ". . . it seems legitimate to infer that in the eyes of the author of the hymn [in the Rig-Veda] at least, Gandharva is the same person as Savitri. . . . One may also wonder whether Gandharva, like Tvashtri, does not figure as an enemy of Indra. . . . In such a myth Gandharva can figure hardly otherwise than as the guardian of the Soma or as the Soma itself; and in the latter case he would be duplicating the rôle of Kutsa. . . . According to IX, 113, v. 3 [Griffith, Vol. IV, p. 104], the Gandharvas, already identified with sacrificing priests in Hymn III, 38, v. 6 [Griffith, Vol. II, p. 47], have received the bull (Soma) that has been reared in the clouds and have extracted from it the juice of the soma (the plant of the earthly Soma). In that guise they play a beneficent rôle by distributing the Soma to men. . . . In a word, the Gandharva is unquestionably an example of the confusion that has often taken place under a single name, of attributes belonging to a father and a son." Oldenberg, *Religion des Veda,* p. 244: "The Gandharva as a type goes back, along with its Vedic name, as far as the Indo-Iranian period; but it is all very very obscure. [In a note: "Manhardt and others have rejected, and rightly I believe, any identification of the Gandharvas and the Centaurs."] The Rig-Veda mentions the name in both the singular and the plural, but it gives only the vaguest and most incoherent hints as to what the name stands for. The features of Gandharva have been obliterated or greatly changed, probably as the result of the blending of all sorts of mythical beings under a single name. In a word, there is nothing definite or certain that we can even guess."

784 [2] *Nouvelles études de mythologie,* pp. 22-26.

Hippodamia, they tried to ravish the bride, but were overcome by Theseus and the Lapithae."[3]

785. Interesting, besides, is the way Henry brings grist to his own mill. If the adventures of the Centaurs and the Gandharvas were somewhat alike, they might serve to prove the identity of those mythical creatures. But they are altogether different; never mind—while there is life there is hope! . . . "To my mind," says Henry, p. 26, "the capital consideration is that *their stories are not the same!* The case with the stories is the case with the names. If the names were identical, the etymologist would scent some borrowing. If the stories were alike, the mythographer would suspect them of having travelled. Far from that! The Hindus know things about the character of the Gandharvas that the Greeks forgot. To even the score, the Greeks tell a story about the Centaurs of which the Hindus do not know the first word; and the character trait in question and the stories fit into each other like two fragments of a broken vase, and evidently derive from the same fund of ideas. Reducing that fund to its simplest expression, one has only to formulate the basic conception, or, if you will, the naïve riddle that was pregnant with this whole myth: 'Who are those formless male monsters who are forever going about scattering fertility?' And the least informed person in the world will at once answer: 'The clouds.'"

But now—in point of fact—of all the characters in Greek mythology the Centaurs are the least reproductive. They are lascivious, but sterile, or virtually so. A better answer to Henry's riddle would be Zeus. He is a male, he is "formless," in the sense that he is forever changing forms the better to seduce goddesses and mortal females, and as for reproductivity, he has no equal in Heaven or on Earth. Greek mythology speaks of little else than his sons and daughters.

786. Whenever a person turns up in history of whose existence we cannot be certain and who seems to be legendary, someone even-

784 [3] If that is the only story that survives, it is because Henry will have it so. Anyone minded to take the trouble will find plenty of Centaur stories of no less significance—for example, the adventures of Hercules in the land of the Centaurs.

tually makes a solar myth of him. That, for example, was the fate of Lucius Junius Brutus, the slayer of Tarquin.[1]

787. Let us resort here again to the method suggested in § 547. A Greek writer—for the present we will not say who—speaks of a certain Lamprocles, Λαμπροκλῆς. The name is made up of λαμπρός, "shining," and of κλέος, "glory," "fame." But who is—*par excellence*—shining, glorious, famous? The Sun, of course! On the other hand we know that Lamprocles was the son of a "gold-red mare"; and is it not evident enough that he must be the Sun, which appears just after dawn in crocus-coloured garb—κροκόπεπλος? A solar myth more certainly than many one might mention! But there is one difficulty—and it is a big one. The Greek writer whose name we have been holding up our sleeve is Xenophon. Lamprocles (*Memorabilia,* II, 2) was the son of Socrates and of Xanthippe (Ξανθίππη) from ξανθός, "gold-red" and (ἵππος, "horse"); and, in fact, neither the Sun nor the Dawn had anything to do with him.

788. Well known the fun that our grandfathers had at the expense of the solar myth by showing that Napoleon Bonaparte could also be accounted a myth of that sort.[1]

789. One might easily see a solar myth in our legend about Virgil (§ 668). Virgil's aerial journey and the fire that is extinguished and

786 [1] Pais, *Storia di Roma,* Vol. I, p. 477: "Some importance must be attached, however, to the fact that Junius Brutus, for the very reason that he was a hero identified with the cult of Juno, was likewise identified with the cult of Apollo, in other words, of the Sun. . . . Zaleucus, also, the lawgiver of Locris, had become famous for his severity. . . . Something of the same sort was told of the lawgiver Charondas, in fact the same adventures in general are ascribed to Charondas and Zaleucus. . . . But the circumstance that Zaleucus, who was reputed to have received his laws from Minerva, never existed deprives the accounts of all historical value. . . . Zaleucus was a divinity, and what kind of divinity is made clear by his very name, which means 'he who is wholly luminous.' In a word, Zaleucus was the Sun, and in his putting out one of his own eyes and one of his son's eyes we have symbols of the new Sun and the old." [A little slip in the text: Brutus did not kill Tarquin, but merely overthrew him.—A. L.]

788 [1] A pamphlet published on the subject has remained famous. The first edition, anonymous, was entitled: *Comme quoi Napoléon n'a jamais existé—grand erratum, source d'un nombre infini d'errata, à noter dans l'histoire du XIXe siècle,* Paris, 1827. The fifth edition, posthumous, bears the name of the author, J. B. Pérès, *bibliothécaire de la ville d'Agen.* A tenth edition appeared in 1864 and a critical edition

then rekindled suggest the idea of the Sun, which runs its course in the heavens and each day is extinguished at sunset and rekindled at dawn. The identity becomes the more evident as we stress the manner of Virgil's death:[1] ". . . he climbed into a boat, and the fourth in the company, put out to sea; and as they went thus chatting over the water, there came a gust of wind. . . . So were they swept away out upon the high sea, and thereafter was no one seen or heard of more." For the inhabitants of Naples the Sun in fact sets in the sea. And as for the boat, who can fail to see that it is a detail derived from Egyptian mythology, which has the Sun run its course in a boat?

790. Not in jest, but in all earnestness has one writer tried to show that the Gospel story of the life of Jesus is a solar myth drawn along the lines of Hebrew and Babylonian legends.[1]

791. All this by no means implies that there have never been solar myths. We say merely that they have to be identified as such by historical proofs, and not by the similarities prevailing between vague details in a story arbitrarily interpreted and the general traits of solar movements.

792. To speak in terms still more general, there have certainly

by Gustave Davois, with biographical and bibliographical notes, in 1909. The arguments used in the little pamphlet follow the lines of the interpretations of mythology as solar myths, pp. 15-17, 25. "It is held that his mother's name was Letitia. But Letitia means 'joy,' and the name is simply a designation for the Dawn, whose morning light spreads joy throughout all Nature. . . . It is noteworthy further that, following Greek mythology, Apollo's mother was named Leto, or Létô, Greek Λητώ. But if the Romans saw fit to change Leto into Latona, mother of Apollo, our age has preferred to make Letitia of it, because *laetitia* is the substantive form of the verb *laetor* (more rarely *laeto*), which means 'to inspire joy.' It is certain therefore that both mother and son were borrowed from Greek mythology. . . . It is said that this modern Apollo had four brothers. Now those four brothers can only be the four seasons of the year. . . . It is said that Napoleon put an end to a devastating scourge that was terrorizing all France and which was called 'the Hydra of Revolution.' Now a hydra is a snake—what kind of a snake does not matter, since we are talking mythology. That is an allusion to the Python, an enormous reptile that was an utter terror to Greece. That terror Apollo relieved, by killing the monster." The pamphlet concludes that Napoleon was Apollo, in other words, the Sun.

789 [1] Comparetti, *Virgilio nel medio evo,* Vol. II, pp. 299-300 (missing in Benecke).

790 [1] Jensen, *Das Gilgamesch-Epos in der Weltliteratur.*

been allegories, and not only allegories that are artificial products of scholarly minds but also allegories arising spontaneously among the people. Oftentimes, for that matter, the development is the reverse of the one assumed when the allegory is taken as coming from the name, whereas it is the name that comes from the allegory. A girl child is called Aurora not because she has rosy fingers: the fact of dawn has suggested the allegory of the rosy fingers (§ 794).

793. Herbert Spencer is not of that way of thinking. He extends his theory of the imperfect inferences from experimental facts to totemism and the solar myths. The worship of animals, he thinks, springs from the fact that the human being and the animal become blended in the mind of the savage. The habit of using names of animals as surnames for children or adults facilitates such identification of men and animals:[1] "We cannot wonder if the savage, lacking knowledge and speaking a rude language, gets the idea that an ancestor named 'the Tiger' was an actual tiger." From such confusion of the descent of the man bearing an animal name with the descent of that animal, all the characteristics of totemism are eventually obtained by a fine set of logical reasonings: "A second sequence is that animals, thus conceived as akin to men, are often treated with consideration. . . . Naturally, as a further sequence, there comes a special regard for the animal which gives the tribal name, and is considered a relative. . . . If the East Africans [as Livingstone tells us] think the souls of departed chiefs enter into lions and render them sacred, we may conclude that sacredness will equally attach to the animals whose human souls were ancestral. If the Congo people, holding this belief about lions, think 'the lion spares those whom he meets when he is courteously saluted,' the implication is that there will arise propitiations of the beast-chief who was the progenitor of the tribe. . . . So that misinterpretations of metaphorical titles, which inevitably occur in early speech, being given, the rise of animal-worship is a natural sequence."

794. This theory envisages nothing but logical conduct. It also applies to plants and inanimate things: "Now if an animal regarded

793 [1] *Principles of Sociology*, Vol. I, §§ 171-73, 181, 186, 188-91.

as original progenitor, is therefore reverentially treated; so, too, may we expect, a plant-ancestor will be. . . . One way in which a mountain comes to be worshipped as ancestor is here made manifest. It is the place whence the race came, the source of the race, the parent of the race: the distinctions implied by the different words here used being, in rude languages, inexpressible. Either the early progenitors of a tribe were dwellers in caves on the mountain; or the mountain, marking conspicuously the elevated region they migrated from, is identified as the object whence they sprang." Everything is explainable in that fashion: "That belief in descent from the Sea as a progenitor sometimes arises through misinterpretation of individual names, is likely. . . . It may be that sometimes Dawn is a complimentary metaphorical name given to a rosy girl; though I can give no evidence of this. But that Dawn is a birth-name, we have clear proof." Spencer mentions many instances to show that the name of Dawn (Aurora) was given to human beings by savages; and besides, many women have the same name in modern countries: "If, then, Dawn is an actual name for a person—if it has probably often been given to those born early in the morning; the traditions concerning one of such who became noted, would, in the mind of the uncritical savage, lead to identification with the Dawn; and the adventures would be interpreted in such manner as the phenomena of the Dawn made most feasible." This manner of reasoning by accumulating hypotheses and plausibilities should be attentively remarked; and also the fact that the long road leads to a goal which we might reach in one bound by saying that a woman named Aurora abducted a youth named Orion (§ 769).

Spencer continues: "Is there a kindred origin for the worship of Stars? Can these also become identified with ancestors? This seems difficult to conceive; and yet there are facts justifying the suspicion that it has been so. . . . Has identification of the Moon with persons who once lived, been caused by misinterpretation of names? Indirect evidence would justify us in suspecting this, even were there no direct evidence. . . . Even were there no direct evidence that solar myths have arisen from misapprehensions of narratives respecting actual persons or actual events in human history, the evidence furnished by analogy would warrant the belief. But the direct evidence is abundant." This so-called direct evidence is, instead, just a series of mere interpretations of Spencer's own, and they are on a par with other interpretations we have met with.

795. All such simple *a priori* explanations take us outside the realities of the very complicated situations underlying mythical narratives. Mingled in varying proportions in such myths are products of mere fancy, reminiscences of actual facts, and among peoples with literatures reminiscences of literary productions. And such things are further embellished by metaphors, allegories, and one theory or another, now childish, now exceedingly ingenious. Nor should we forget, either, the spontaneous clustering of legends around primitive nuclei of sentiment (§ 740), nor the frequent simultaneous presence of different processes of construction or formation.

796. The proposition, for instance, that Apollo is a solar god is a mixture of error and truth—of error in the sense that in a cycle such as the *Iliad* Apollo is not a solar god; of truth, in that in other cycles solar myths come to be combined with the not-yet-solar myth of Apollo and finally gain such predominance over the latter that Helius comes to be confused with Phoebus and Apollo.

797. Let us pause for a moment now and consider just where our induction has brought us. It has not only confirmed the wide-spread prevalence of non-logical conduct, which we noted as early as Chapter II, but has shown in addition that such conduct constitutes the substance of many theories which, judged superficially, might seem to be exclusive products of logic.

798. Our detailed examination of one theory or another has in any case led to our perceiving that theories in the concrete may be divided into at least two elements, one of which is much more stable than the other. We say, accordingly, that in concrete theories, which we shall designate as *c*,[1] there are, besides factual data, two

798 [1] To keep as far as possible from reasoning on words rather than on things, we shall begin in our usual manner (§ 119) by using letters of the alphabet to designate the things with which we are dealing, substituting names for this inconvenient method of notation in the next chapter.

principal elements (or parts); a substantial element (part), which we shall designate as *a,* and a contingent element (part), on the whole fairly variable, which we shall designate as *b* (§§ 217, 514 [4]).

The element *a* directly corresponds to non-logical conduct; it is the expression of certain sentiments. The element *b* is the manifestation of the need of logic that the human being feels. It also partially corresponds to sentiments, to non-logical conduct, but it clothes them with logical or pseudo-logical reasonings. The element *a* is the *principle* (§ 306 [2]) existing in the mind of the human being; the element *b* is the explanation (or explanations) of that principle, the inference (or inferences) that he draws from it.

799. There is, for example, a principle, or if you prefer, a sentiment, in virtue of which certain numbers are deemed worthy of veneration: it is the chief element, *a,* in a phenomenon that we shall study further along (§§ 960 f.). But the human being is not satisfied with merely associating sentiments of veneration with numbers; he also wants to "explain" how that comes about, to "demonstrate" that in doing what he does he is prompted by force of logic. So the element *b* enters in, and we get various "explanations," various "demonstrations," as to why certain numbers are sacred. There is in the human being a sentiment that restrains him from discarding old beliefs all at once. That is the element *a* in a phenomenon that we examined some distance back (§§ 172 f.). But he feels called upon to justify, explain, demonstrate his attitude, and an element *b* enters in, which in one way or another saves the letter of his beliefs while altering them in substance.

800. The principal element in the situation, the element *a,* is evidently the one to which the human being is most strongly attached and which he exerts himself to justify. That element therefore is the more important to us in our quest for the social equilibrium.

801. But the element *b,* though secondary, also has its effect upon the equilibrium. Sometimes the effect may be so insignificant as to be accounted equivalent to zero—as when the perfection of the number 6 is ascribed to its being the sum of its aliquots (1, 2, 3). But the effect may also be very considerable, as when the Inquisition burned people guilty of some slip in their theological calculations.

802. We have said (§ 798) that the element *b* is made up, in variable proportions, of sentiments and logical inferences. It is well to remark at once that in social matters its persuasive force depends as a rule chiefly on sentiments, the logic being accepted principally because it chances to harmonize with such sentiments. In the logico-experimental sciences, in proportion as they are brought to greater and greater perfection, the part played by sentiment tends to decrease towards zero, and the persuasive force lies altogether in the logic and in the facts. When it reaches that extreme the element *b* evidently changes its character, and we shall designate it by *B*. At another extreme there are cases in which the logical inference is not clearly manifested, as in what jurists call "latent principles in law." [1] Psychologists explain such phenomena as effects of the subconscious, or in some other way. We do not choose to go quite so far back here; we stop at the fact, leaving the explanation of it to others. All concrete theories fall between those extremes, approaching the one or the other to a greater or lesser extent.

803. Though sentiment has no place in the logico-experimental sciences, it nevertheless invades that field to some degree. If, overlooking such considerations for the moment, we designate as *C* the concrete theories of logico-experimental science that constitute the second group in § 523, we may break them up into an element *A* made up of experimental principles, descriptions, and experimental assertions, and an element *B* made up of logical inferences, along, further, with experimental principles and descriptions used for drawing inferences from the element *A*.

802 [1] Von Jhering, *Geist des römischen Rechts,* Vol. I, pp. 29-30 (Pt. I, § 3): "Despite the great skill of the classical jurists of Rome, there were, even in their time, rules of law that remained unknown to them and which were first elucidated by the efforts of the jurisprudence of our own day. I call them 'latent' principles of law. But, someone will ask, can such a thing be possible? To apply such a rule, must it not be known? For an answer we need simply point to the laws of language. Thousands of persons daily apply [linguistic] laws that they never heard spoken of [Non-logical conduct.], laws of which philologists themselves are not always clearly aware. The deficiencies of the understanding are made up for by sentiment, by grammatical instinct."

The theories *c,* in which sentiment plays a part, which add something to experience, which lie outside experience, and which constitute the third group in § 523, likewise break down into an element *a,* made up of manifestations of certain sentiments, and an element *b,* made up of logical reasonings, fallacies, and sophistries, along, further, with other manifestations of sentiment used for drawing inferences from *a.* There is, accordingly, a certain correspondence between *a* and *A,* between *b* and *B,* and between *c* and *C.* In these volumes we are dealing strictly with *c* theories, ignoring experimental scientific theories, *C.*

804. In trans-experimental and pseudo-experimental theories, *c,* writers seldom distinguish the elements *a* and *b* with the clearness required. As a rule they more or less confuse them.

805. *Example:* One of the principles of Roman law is the property-right. Once the principle is admitted, many consequences are logically inferable from it and they make up a very considerable portion of the theory of Roman civil law. There is a celebrated instance, the case of *specification,* in which the principle is not adequate for solving the problems that arise in practice. Girard, a very competent authority on Roman jurisprudence, writes:[1] "The theory of specification assumes that a person has taken a thing, and, notably, a thing belonging to another person, and given a new form to it by his own labour, so creating a *nova species* (*speciem novam fecit*): he has made wine out of grapes, a vessel out of metal, a boat out of lumber, and so on.[2] The question is to determine whether the object so manufactured is still the old object, and therefore lawfully belonging to the former owner, or a new object conceivably belonging to a new owner." That manner of stating the problem already to some extent confuses the elements *a* and *b* in the law of property. To keep them distinct one would have to say: "The problem is to

805 [1] *Manuel élémentaire de droit romain,* pp. 316-17.

805 [2] In a note: "The case does not arise when he has merely dyed a piece of cloth, or, Justinian to the contrary notwithstanding (*Institutiones,* 2, 1, 25 [*Corpus iuris civilis,* Vol. I, pp. 12-13; Scott, Vol. II, p. 37]), merely taken the wheat from the kernels that contained it."

determine the owner of a single object in which two property-rights have become blended."

806. A person considering nothing but legal constructions, *c,* ought in this case simply to confess that the principles supplied by element *a* in the law are not adequate for solving the problem, and that therefore others are needed. The new principle asked for might be that an *old* object always belongs to the old proprietor and that a *new* object may have a new proprietor. In that case Girard's framing of the issue would be perfect, but we would be avoiding one difficulty only to fall into another; for now we would need some principle for determining how flatly and squarely the new object is to be distinguished from the old, not in general terms, be it remembered, but as regards ownership. We would, in short, be no nearer a solution of the problem.

807. Law, *a,* may furnish the principle that ownership of the thing takes precedence over ownership of labour. That, we may conjecture, may have been the archaic principle, because on the one hand ownership of material substance is something more concrete than ownership of labour, and in general, the concrete takes precedence over the abstract; and on the other hand labour enjoyed no very high esteem in ancient Roman society.

808. Says Girard: "Very probably the ancient jurists, without going into theoretical niceties, regarded the object as remaining the same." That would be describing the evolution of the form rather than of the substance. The ancient jurists probably had in their minds a non-logical inclination that prompted them to give ownership of material substance precedence over ownership of labour. In a later phase they, or their successors, desiring to give a logical reason for their ruling, came out with the consideration that the object remained the same. But any other pretence might have served just as well.

809. The development of Roman civilization produced a corresponding development in capacities for abstraction and in the esteem in which labour was held. We might foresee, therefore, that in course of time the law, *a,* would supply other non-logical principles more favourable to labour.

810. Speaking of specification, in fact, Gaius says: "In other species appeal is made to natural reason."[1] This *naturalis ratio* is an old acquaintance of ours. Strange, indeed, had it not turned up! Under the wing of that authority the Roman jurists sheltered their expressions of sentiment, which corresponded to non-logical instincts in the society in which they lived. Gaius states that the writing done on a piece of parchment is held to belong to the owner of the parchment, the contrary being true of a picture painted on a canvas; and he comments:[2] "The reason given for this inconsistency is hardly adequate." As usually happens when people set out to explain non-logical conduct logically!

811. Girard continues: "Later on, in virtue of a nicer analysis, the Proculians maintained that it was a new object and should belong to its maker, on the ground either that the workman had acquired it by tenure, or perhaps simply that a thing should belong to its maker." Here again we get the evolution of the form rather than of the substance. It is not a case of "nicer analysis" yielding new principles; analysis has merely produced new logical justifications for new non-logical sentiments that had developed in the minds of the Romans and their jurists.

812. "In the face of this doctrine, the Sabinians—probably without denying that it was a case of a new object—refused to admit that the maker acquired the product of his labour, and held that the new article belonged to the owner of the old." As usual, the solution of the Sabinians was dictated by sentiments that they held and which they sought to justify by logical argument.

813. Gaius, quoted in *Digesta,* XLI, 1, 7, § 7 (*Corpus iuris civilis,* Vol. I, p. 737; Scott, Vol. IX, p. 157), gives a sample of such arguments: "In the case where a person makes a new thing in his own name out of material belonging to another, Nerva and Proculus

810 [1] [*Commentarii,* II, 79 (Poste, p. 200; Scott, Vol. I, p. 120): *"In aliis quoque speciebus naturalis ratio requiritur:* Poste: "On a change of species also we have recourse to natural law to determine the proprietor."—A. L.]

810 [2] *Commentarii,* II, 77-78 (Poste, pp. 199-200; Scott, Vol. I, p. 120).

opine that the owner of the thing is the person who has made it, because before that the thing made belonged to no one. More in accord with natural reason, Sabinus and Cassius rule that the owner of the material is the owner of the thing made from it, because without material nothing can be made." Benevolent, indeed, Dame Naturalis Ratio, who never withholds her assistance from anyone, and lends herself so readily to the proof of both the yea and the nay. These arguments are devoid of sense and simply express certain sentiments.

814. In the end a compromise solution was adopted on grounds no sounder. When the thing made could be restored to its original form the view of Sabinus and Cassius was followed. When that was not possible the view of Nerva and Proculus prevailed.

815. Returning to the general case: Ordinary parlance is nearly always synthetic and has its eye on the concrete situation. Usually, therefore, it confuses the elements *a* and *b,* which scientific analysis has to distinguish (§ 817). Practically it may be useful to consider the elements *a* and *b* together. If the principles, *a,* were definite, anyone accepting them would also be bound to all their logical implications, *b*. But the principles, *a,* being devoid of all precision, one may infer anything one chooses from them, and the implications, *b,* are therefore accepted only in so far as they accord with sentiments, which are in that manner called in to sift the logical inferences.

816. The abuse often heaped on moral casuistry or legal quibbles is chiefly due to the fact that the principles, *a,* have been designedly used, in view of their lack of definiteness, to support consequences that are repugnant to sentiment.

817. From the scientific standpoint, any progress in theory is strictly bound up with progress in distinguishing between the elements *a* and *b*—a point on which one cannot insist too emphatically. It is all very well that the function of art is to study the concrete phenomenon, *c,* synthetically and must therefore not separate the elements *a* and *b;* and to do that, moreover, is an effective method of persuasion, because nearly all human beings are in the habit of thinking synthetically, and find it hard to grasp, in fact are quite unable to grasp, a scientific analysis. But such analysis is indispensable to anyone trying to frame a scientific theory. That is all very difficult to get into the heads of people who have no aptitude for scientific thinking, or who divest themselves of it the moment they turn to matters pertaining to sociology. They obstinately insist on considering situations synthetically (§§ 25, 31).

818. When, therefore, a writer is read with the idea of passing a scientific judgment on his theories, it is essential first of all to do a thing that he almost never has done for himself: to distinguish the elements *a* and *b*. In general, in every theory it is necessary to distinguish carefully the premises—in other words, principles, postulates, sentiments—from the inferences that are drawn from them.[1]

819. Oftentimes in the case of theories adding something to experience (§§ 803, 523), the premises are at least partially implicit, that is to say, the element *a* is not declared or is not fully and clearly declared. If we would know what it is, a search has to be made for it.[1]

820. From the logico-experimental point of view, the fact that a premise is left implicit, or even just partially so, may give rise to very serious errors. The mere declaration of a premise raises the question as to whether and how far it is to be accepted; whereas if

818 [1] Sumner Maine was well aware, as regards law, of the antagonism between the metaphysical concepts of a perfect ideal and the study of the facts, which he identifies with the "historical method." Says he, *Ancient Law,* p. 87: "I believe . . . that it [the philosophy founded on the hypothesis of a state of nature] is still the great antagonist of the Historical Method; and wherever (religious objections apart) any mind is seen to resist or contemn that mode of investigation, it will generally be found under the influence of a prejudice or vicious bias traceable to a conscious or unconscious reliance on a non-historic, natural, condition of society or the individual." But Maine forgets all that when it comes to morality. He seems to think that morality is a model of perfection more nearly attained by the morality of the present than by the morality of the past. He says, for example, that English jurists regard English equity as founded on moral rules, and adds, *Op. cit.,* p. 66: ". . . but it is forgotten that these rules are the morality of past centuries . . . and that, though of course they do not differ largely from the ethical creed of our day, they are not necessarily on a level with it."

819 [1] To that search we were led in an incidental way in Chapter II (§§ 186 f.), and then again in Chapter IV and in this Chapter V (§ 740). We shall deal with it expressly in the chapters next following.

it is left implicit we accept it without being fully aware of what we are conceding; and we assume it to be definite and exact, whereas it is so far from being so that we would be put to it to find any meaning in it whatever.

821. Often a writer will say nothing at all about his non-experimental premises, and often, also, when he does declare them, he will try to create a confusion between them and scientific principles resulting from experience.

An interesting example of such a confusion is to be found in the theory stated by Rousseau as a preface to his discourse on the origin of inequality:[1] "Let us therefore begin by setting all facts aside. They have no bearing on the question. Such investigations as we may make in this connexion must not be taken as historical truths, but simply as hypothetical and contingent reasonings, calculated rather to elucidate the nature of things than to show their actual origin, something similar to the reasonings that our physicists are making every day as to the formation of the world."[2] So then, Rousseau's prospective research is essentially an experimental research; but the experience is a special kind of experience—something like what is nowadays called "religious experience"—having nothing whatever to do with the experience of the physical sciences, in spite of the confusion that Rousseau tries to create and which merely serves to prove his prodigious ignorance. He continues: "Religion requires us to believe that since God Himself removed men from the state of nature immediately after the Creation, they are unequal because He has willed that they be so; but it does not forbid our

821 [1] *Discours sur l'origine et les fondements de l'inégalité parmi les hommes.*

821 [2] Here, unwittingly, Rousseau brings the hammer down on his own thumb. He is right: his investigations are in fact like the idle speculations that sought the origin of the world in "damp," in "fire," and the like. His theories stand towards social science, properly so called, exactly as those physical speculations stood towards astronomy, as astronomy was even in Rousseau's day. He says further in the same preface: "Ignoring therefore all those scientific books that teach us only to know men as men have made themselves, and pondering the elementary and simplest operations of the human soul, I seem to perceive two principles anterior to reason." And Rousseau is the Holy Father of a church that pretends to represent reason and science as against a Catholic Church which, those gentlemen say, stands for superstition!

making conjectures, based solely on the nature of man and the creatures about him [Here the pseudo-experience.] as to what the human race might have become had it been left to itself. That is the question which is set me, that the subject which I propose to examine in this essay. Since my subject concerns mankind in general [An abstraction designed to get rid of experience after the pretence of accepting it.], I shall try to use a language suitable to all nations [Some of which were absolutely unknown to this shrewd rhetorician.], or rather, forgetting times and places, and thinking only of the human beings I address, I shall imagine myself as speaking in the Lyceum at Athens, with Platos and Xenocrates's for my judges, and mankind for my audience." So he goes chattering on, and discovers, starting from the "nature" of things, how things *must* have been, without being put to the trouble of verifying his fine theories on the facts, since he began by stating that he was ignoring them. There are still hosts and hosts of people who admire such prattle. That is why it has to be taken into account when one sets out to study human society.

822. Many other writers who none the less pretend to be using strictly scientific, even "materialistic" methods, follow more or less covertly the path blatantly trodden by Rousseau. Engels, for example, confesses that direct evidence as to a certain inferior stage traversed by humanity is not available; but he demonstrates the existence of such a stage *a priori* from the fact that man has evolved from the animal. It is fun to write history in that fashion, describing times altogether unknown on the basis of hypotheses altogether uncertain. People who admire that manner of thinking pride themselves on being more "scientific" than those who used to admire the holy Fathers of the Catholic Church when they disproved the possibility of antipodes (§ 16).[1]

822 [1] Engels, *Der Ursprung der Familie,* pp. 2-4: "First Inferior Stage: It is the childhood of humanity. Human beings were still living in their primitive homes in the tropical or subtropical forests, and partly at least in trees—which explains their managing to survive in the face of the great beasts of prey. Fruits, nuts, and roots were their food. The working out of an articulate language is the main achievement during this period. . . . We are likewise unable—though it may have lasted thou-

823. Amusing the case of Burlamaqui (§ 439). His theory of "natural law" is entirely metaphysical, and yet he writes:[1] "If strict attention be paid to our manner of establishing our principles of natural laws, it will be recognized that the method we have followed supplies fresh proof of the certainty and actual existence (*réalité*) of those laws. We have laid all abstract and metaphysical speculation aside to keep solely to the fact—to the nature and condition of things." But then, right away, and with the greatest ingenuousness, he contradicts himself: "We have derived our principles from the essential constitution of man and the relations in which he stands to other creatures." Essential constitutions, like all other considerations on "essences," lie outside the domain of experience. Burlamaqui so little comprehends what he is saying that he adds: "One cannot refuse to recognize natural laws or doubt their reality without repudiating the purest light of reason—a procedure that would eventually lead to mere scepticism (*Pyrrhonisme*)." In the experimental field what decides is the accord between theory and fact, not "the pure light of reason."

824. Given the element *a,* the element *b,* or better, *B,* may be built up deductively; and to study it therefore is very much easier than to study the element *a.* It has, in fact, produced the only social sciences that are today at all exact and well developed: the sciences of juridical constructions and pure economics (§ 2011).[1] Studies of

sands of years—to prove its existence by direct evidence; but once one grants that the human being came from the animal kingdom, such a period of transition has to be assumed. . . . Second Intermediate Stage: It begins with the use of fish (among which also are to be counted crustacea, shell-fish and other aquatic animals) as food, and with the use of fire. The two go together, fire alone making fish perfectly edible." What a lot of interesting things this man knows! Scientists are still arguing as to whether the human race has one or more origins and where, geographically, they are to be located. Engels knows that man came from the animal kingdom and that the development took place in the tropics or subtropics. He also knows that men began by eating fish; and that is not all, for "hunter-peoples, as pictured in the books, peoples living exclusively by hunting, that is, have never existed, the fruits of the chase being far too uncertain."

823 [1] *Principes du droit naturel,* Pt. II, Chap. 5, sec. 3.

824 [1] In this and the following paragraphs (as contrasted with its use in § 806) the term "juridical construction" is used not in the special sense it has in legal science (interpretation, "construing") but in the ordinary sense. Our term there-

the element *b* will be the more perfect, the nearer they come to being made up of logic only; and the less perfect in proportion as they assume, or allow to creep in, any great number of non-experimental principles that ought properly to remain in the element *a*. Moreover, since the element *a*, or even *A* (§ 803), is the part that gives rise, or may give rise, to doubts and uncertainties, the slighter it is, the sounder may be the science derived from it.

825. Pure economics has the advantage in fact of being able to draw its inferences from very few experimental principles; and it makes such a strict use of logic [1] as to be able to state its reasonings in mathematical form—reasonings having the further very great advantage of dealing with quantities. The science of juridical constructions also has the merit of requiring few principles; but it does not have the advantage of dealing with quantities. Quantity still remains the great stumbling-block in sociology; but we can at least be rid of the nuisance caused by intrusions of element *a* into element *b*.

826. Speaking in general terms, certain principles, *a,* may be arbitrarily assumed, and—provided they be definite—a body of doctrine, *c,* may be derived from them. But if the principles, *a,* are foreign to reality, it is evident that the part *c* will also have no bearing on the concrete. When, therefore, one would constitute a science, it is important to select one's principles, *a,* judiciously with a view to keeping as close to reality as possible, well aware as one may be that no theory, *c,* can ever represent reality in every particular (§ 106).

827. Other sociological theories have been used in efforts to constitute a rigidly scientific body of doctrine, but unfortunately with no success; and that because the principles on which the theoretical structure was based were too far removed from experience (§§ 2015 f.).

fore designates the framing, composition, creation, of a juridical theory. In this sense, celestial mechanics would be a mechanical *construction* based on the principle of universal gravitation.

825 [1] That merely by definition, to a certain extent arbitrary (§ 119). See *Manuale,* Chap. III, § 1: "We are to deal with the logical actions repeated many times over and in great numbers that human beings perform in order to acquire things satisfying to their tastes."

828. One such would be "social Darwinism." If it be granted that —apart from temporary oscillations—the institutions of a society are always those best suited to the circumstances in which that society is situated, and that societies not possessing institutions of the kind eventually perish, we get a principle susceptible of important logical developments that may well serve to constitute a science. That experiment was made, and for some little time there was reason to hope that a scientific theory, *c,* of sociology was at last within reach, since some of the inferences, *b,* were verified by the facts. But the doctrine declined with the Darwinian biological theory in which it originated. It was perceived that the explanations of facts that it yielded were too often merely verbal. Every form of social organization or life has to be explained by its utility, and to attain that end, arbitrary and imaginary utilities were brought into play. Unwittingly, the theory was just a return to the old theory of final causes. Social Darwinism still remains a well-ordered body of doctrine, *c,* but it has to be considerably modified before it can be reconciled with the facts. It determines not the forms of institutions but merely certain limits that they cannot overpass (§ 1770).

829. "Economic determinism" is another. If that theory be taken in the sense that the economic state of a society entirely determines all social phenomena arising within it, we get a principle, *a,* from which a wealth of inferences may be so drawn as to constitute a science. The economic interpretation of history was a notable forward step for social science, bringing out as it did the contingent character of certain phenomena, such as morals and religion, which many people regarded and still regard as proclaiming absolute verities. Undoubtedly, moreover, it contains an element of truth in that it takes account of the interdependence of economic and other social factors. Its error lies in representing that interdependence as a relation of cause and effect.

830. An incidental circumstance contributed to making the error much graver. Economic determinists saw fit to couple their theory with another, the theory of the "class struggle," from which it might just as well have been left entirely independent; and the classes, into the bargain, were reduced by a dichotomy somewhat cavalier to two. So the field of science was progressively deserted in favour of excursions into the domain of romance. For the historical materialists sociology becomes a very easy science. It is idle to waste time and energy discovering the relationships between facts—their uniformities. Any fact recorded by history, any institution described, any political, moral, or religious order exemplified, finds its cause in the "exploitation of the proletariat" by the *"bourgeoisie,"* and its remedy in the resistance of the "proletariat" to said exploitation. If the facts corresponded to such inferences, we should have a science as perfect as human science ever was, and more so. Unfortunately the theory goes in one direction and the facts in quite another (§ 1884 [1]).

831. Still another doctrine is the "theory of limits," which may well be called Spencerian or of the Spencerian school, if the writings of the master and his disciples could be purged of their numerous metaphysical accessories. It assumes, as its principle, *a,* that all social institutions tend towards a limit, are like a curve that has an asymptote (§§ 2279 f.). The curve known, the asymptote can be determined; known the historical evolution of an institution, its limit can be determined, in fact, more easily determined than the asymptote in the simpler case of the curve, for in mathematics knowledge of a few points on the curve is not enough to compute the asymptote—we must have its equation, know, that is, its intrinsic character—whereas, given a few points on the graph representing an institution, it is possible, or rather, it is believed to be possible, to determine the limit *ipso facto.*

832. This principle, *a,* lends itself to scientific inference, *b,* and so yields an extensive body of doctrine, which may be examined in Spencer's own *Principles of Sociology* and other works of that school. The doctrine—provided always we eliminate metaphysical intrusions—brings us close to the experimental method, since it is from the facts, after all, that the conclusions are derived. But, alas, facts are not all that count: the principle mentioned, that institutions have a limit, is always interfering, and that other principle, that the limit may be determined if a few successive stages of the institution are known. Furthermore, by a coincidence that would be strange indeed if it were truly fortuitous, the limit which a writer assumes to be determined strictly by his facts turns out to be identical with the limit towards which he is sentimentally inclined. If he is a pacifist, as Spencer was, most obliging facts show him that the limit towards which human societies are tending is universal peace; if he is a democrat, there is no doubt that the limit will be a complete triumph of democracy; if he is a collectivist, the triumph of collectivism; and so on. Hence a suspicion arises, and grows stronger as we proceed, that the facts are serving merely to conceal more potent motives of persuasion.

Be that as it may, the reasons advanced by these positivists to justify their inferences do not correspond to the facts, and that vitiates the whole structure. Then, finally, there is the serious difficulty (in time it might be corrected, of course) that we are at present far from possessing the historical knowledge which, strictly, would be indispensable for proper use of the method.

833. Different altogether in nature from the theory of limits are those theories which assume an indefinite, nebulous principle, *a,* utterly lacking in exactness and proceed to derive from it, with a logic apparently sound, conclusions that are after all mere expressions of sentiments, and gain no demonstrative force whatever from the reasoning that binds them to *a.* In fact it very frequently happens that from such a principle, *a,* one thinker will draw one set of conclusions and another a quite opposite set. There is generally little fault to be found with the reasoning in itself; but the principle does not lend itself to strict reasoning—like rubber, it may be stretched to any length desired.

834. The theories, *c,* cannot attain an even moderately scientific form unless the principles, *a,* are to some extent exact. From that point of view, an arbitrary definition is better than no definition at all. When we are dealing with matters of law, lack of definiteness may be corrected by fictions; and that method has its uses also in other sciences, when the purpose is to get simplified statements of theses. It is used even in mathematics. The theorem, for instance, that every algebraic equation has a number of roots equal to its power is useful and convenient in that form; but it is true only in virtue of the fiction that among such roots are to be counted not only real roots but imaginary ones.[1]

835. Well known the fact that in Rome the praetorian law modified the civil law not by alterations in the principles, *a,* which for a time retained all their formal strictness, but by interpretations and qualifications. The praetor serves notice that since according to civil law an obligation obtained by fraud is valid, he will make an *exception* for the non-enforcement of the obligation: that is to say, he inserts in the formula a clause (the *exceptio doli mali*) enjoining the magistrate to award judgment only *si in ea re nihil dolo malo Auli Ageri* (*i.e.,* John Doe) *factum sit neque fiat* (In case no fraud in the matter has been or is being committed by John Doe).[1] Whatever the theory accepted with reference to the *bonorum possessio,* it is incontestable that at a given epoch it served to introduce a praetorian inheritance more liberal than the inheritance of the civil law. The two modes of inheriting existed side by side. If the idea, for instance, was to emphasize blood-relationship, the civil law might have been amended, as was in fact done by the Emperors later on. The preference, instead, was to admit to the inheritance *unde liberi*

834 [1] I am using the term "fiction" here in a broad sense, as does Maine in his *Ancient Law,* pp. 24-25: "I employ the word 'fiction' in a sense considerably wider than that in which English lawyers are accustomed to use it, and with a meaning much more extensive than that which belonged to the Roman *fictiones*. Fictio, in the old Roman law, is properly a term of pleading, and signifies a false averment on the part of the plaintiff which the defendant was not allowed to traverse; such, for example, as an averment that the plaintiff was a Roman citizen, when in truth he was a foreigner. The object of these *fictiones* was, of course, to give jurisdiction, and they therefore strongly resembled the allegations in the writs of the English Queen's Bench and Exchequer, by which those Courts contrived to usurp the jurisdiction of the Common Pleas—the allegation that the defendant was in custody of the king's marshal, or that the plaintiff was the king's debtor, and could not pay his debt by reason of the defendant's default. But now I employ the expression 'Legal Fiction' to signify any assumption which conceals, or affects to conceal, the fact that a rule of law has undergone alteration, its letter remaining unchanged, its operation being modified." The meaning may be even more general, designating an assertion evidently false that is granted in order to leave a rule, a theory, a thesis, unchanged while changing its implications.

835 [1] Girard, *Manuel élémentaire de droit romain,* p. 40.

individuals whom the civil law would have called *sui* (relatives), in case they had no *minima capitis diminutio* (forfeiture of civil rights).

836. This procedure, we have seen (§§ 226 f.), was closely correlated with the Roman psychic state. But in addition, and quite unconsciously, we may guess, the Romans were realizing a most important purpose of giving stability to the principles, *a,* of law and, consequently, of finding ways to consolidate a body of legal doctrine, *c.* That was perhaps one of the chief reasons why Roman law became so superior to the Athenian (§ 241).

837. Legal construction of the Roman type appears in a large number of other instances. It was once believed that certain countries, such as England, which had only a customary law (in England the common law) had only one body of law, *a.* But that was an error which Maine did well to correct.[1] He pointed out the analogies between English "case law," supposedly derived from precedents, and the *responsa prudentium* of the Romans. The part *b* figures in the common law, but it is greatly inferior as regards theory to the parts *b* in other laws that have definitely accepted and framed their juridical systems.

838. Concrete juridical entities are made up of parts *a* and *b.* Descriptive law, *c,* catalogues those entities just as mineralogy catalogues rocks and minerals, leaving the question of their composition to chemistry.

839. Roguin has contributed treatises on *b* and *c,* with very scant reference to *a,* so that his work belongs in part at least to the general science of society. In his *La règle de droit* he is dealing with *b,* and he says (Preface, p. v): "This is an absolutely neutral study, that is to say, a study free from any appraisals. It shows not a trace of criticism from the standpoint of justice or morals. Nor is it, either, a study of natural law or philosophy in the ordinary senses of those terms. It has, furthermore, no bearing on the history of law: it does not try to link juridical institutions with causes, to show their effects. We are not even dealing with comparative law. Our purpose has

837 [1] In his *Ancient Law,* p. 32. See also Lambert, *La fonction du droit civil comparé,* Vol. I, pp. 180 f.

been to analyze the rules of law that have existed historically or which are merely imaginable, possible; to show the nature of the juridical relation as distinguished from relations of other kinds, and to determine the elements within it that are constant."

840. Later on Roguin deals with *c* in his *Traité de droit civil comparé,* adding a few *b* developments: "It is important to distinguish sharply between statements of fact and appreciations [A thing very rarely done in sociology!], between history, which records objective facts, and criticism, which passes judgment upon them."[1] Very few people are willing to do that, even in history!

841. The example of civil law is the easier to consider because it makes less of an appeal to sentiments. On the other hand, sentiments acquire great importance in criminal law, and that is one among many reasons why theories of criminal law have always been less perfect than theories of civil law. In morals and religion sentiments reign supreme, and therefore in those fields it is difficult to get theories that, let alone scientific, are even to any extent exact; what we get is an amorphous mass of metaphysical preconceptions and expressions of sentiments.

The Italian school of positive law might become scientific if it would only shed its useless appendages of democratic faith and be cured of its mania for immediate practical applications, which is the bane of all kinds of theory. At any rate it would seem that, following the trail it has been blazing, one might some day arrive at a scientific theory of criminal law.

Theology has a part *b* that, as in St. Thomas Aquinas, is sound and well developed; but its element *a* entirely transcends experience and therefore fails to interest us. Ethics, too, works from non-experimental principles and has in addition an element *b* that is truly chaotic and loses logical value almost entirely the moment ethics is separated from theology. Pseudo-sciences of that type take us altogether outside the logico-experimental field.

840 [1] Vol. I, p. 9. Roguin continues, pp. 10-11, *Le mariage:* "Now how ought we to evaluate those tendencies in legislation? We have not always been concerned to express any opinion. The present volume contains but very few critical judgments scattered here and there."

ment to analyze the rules of law that have existed historically or which are merely imaginable, possible [illegible] the nature of the juridical relation as distinguished from relations of other kinds and to determine the elements within it that are constant.

98. [illegible] adding [illegible] development [illegible] it is important to distinguish sharply between [illegible] [illegible] done in sociology between [illegible] positive facts, and [illegible] which passes judgment upon them [illegible]. Very few people are willing to do that [illegible].

99. The example of civil law [illegible] because it makes [illegible] on the other [illegible] definitions acquire great importance [illegible] many reasons [illegible] perfect than [illegible] requirements [illegible] [illegible] sentiment.

The [illegible] school of [illegible] law might become [illegible] would only [illegible] application, which is the [illegible]. At any rate [illegible] following [illegible] scientific theory of [illegible] natural law.

Theology [illegible] that [illegible] St. Thomas Aquinas [illegible] and well [illegible] and therefore [illegible] principles [illegible] is not [illegible] logical [illegible] strictly theo[illegible] is [illegible] from theology [illegible] outside [illegible] natural [illegible].

The Mind and Society

A TREATISE ON GENERAL SOCIOLOGY

by Vilfredo Pareto

Volume Two: Theory of Residues

CONTENTS

VOLUME II

THE MIND AND SOCIETY

Volume II: Analysis of Sentiment
(Theory of Residues)

CHAPTER VI[1]

Residues: Combinations and Group Persistence

842. Since social phenomena appear in complex form in the concrete, we saw at once that it would be helpful to divide them into at least two elements, distinguishing logical from non-logical conduct; and that gave us a first conception of the nature of non-logical conduct and of its importance in human society. But at that point a question arose: If non-logical conduct plays such an important rôle in human life, why has it been so generally neglected (§ 252)? We found in reply that almost all writers on social or political subjects have indeed observed such conduct, or at least caught glimpses of it. Many elements, therefore, of the theory we are framing in these volumes are to be found scattered about here and there in the works of various writers, though often under hardly recognizable forms.

843. But we saw that all such writers had ideas of their own to which they very expressly attached capital importance—ideas on religion, morality, law, and the like, which have been battle-grounds for centuries. So, if they did recognize non-logical conduct implicitly, explicitly they glorified logical conduct, and most of them regarded it as the only conduct worth considering in social phenomena. We were therefore called upon to see what truth there was in theories of that type, and to decide whether we were to abandon the course on which we had set out or take heart and push on.

We then proceeded to examine those various manners of considering social phenomena, and we saw that from the logico-experimental standpoint they were devoid of all exactness and of any strict accord with the facts; though from another standpoint, we could not deny the great importance that they had had in history

[1] Had we been following the deductive method, this chapter would have been placed at the beginning of Vol. I. I may find it desirable to follow that method in treatises to come. Here I have preferred the inductive approach, that my reader might follow the road I have myself traversed in arriving at the theories with which we shall hereafter be dealing.

and in determining the social equilibrium. That discovery lent force to a suspicion which had already occurred to us, and which will acquire greater and greater prominence in the course of these volumes: that the experimental "truth" of certain theories is one thing and their social "utility" quite another, and that the two things are not only not one and the same but may, and often do, stand in flat contradiction (§§ 1682 f., 1897 f.).

844. We found that it was as important to separate those two things as it had been to distinguish logical from non-logical conduct, and our inductive survey showed that the failure to make such a distinction had been the main cause of error, from the scientific standpoint, in most social theories.

845. So we looked at them a little more closely and saw how and why they went astray, and how and why, though fallacious, they enjoyed and still enjoy such great prestige. In the course of that investigation we came upon things which we had not thought of at the outset. But we went on analyzing, distinguishing, and soon we observed another possible distinction that struck us as being quite as important as the others we had made—on the one hand an instinctive, non-logical element that was constant, on the other, a deductive element that was designed to explain, justify, demonstrate, the constant element. Arriving at that point, we found that induction had given us the elements of a theory.

846. Here, now, we are called upon to frame it, that is to say, we must now drop the inductive for the deductive method, and see what consequences result from the principles that we have found, or think we have found. After that we shall have to compare our inferences with the facts. If they fit, we shall keep our theory. If they fail to fit, we shall discard it.

847. In this chapter (and since the subject is a vast one, in the next two) we are to study the constant element *a* (§ 798), going on, after that, to the deductive element *b*. But we are dealing with a very difficult matter, and a few more remarks in general on the elements *a* and *b*, and their resultant *c*, will not come amiss.

848. We saw in § 803 that in the theories of the logico-experimental sciences one may discern a basic element *A,* and a deductive element *B,* which in some respects are analogous to, in some respects different from, the elements *a* and *b* in theories that are not strictly logico-experimental.

The social sciences as hitherto cultivated show elements that bear a closer resemblance to *a* than to *A,* through their failure to avoid intrusions of sentiments, prejudices, creeds, or other predilections, tendencies, postulates, principles, that carry the thinker outside the logico-experimental domain.

849. The deductive element in the social sciences as hitherto cultivated sometimes comes very close to *B,* and there are cases where the logic is so adequate that the coincidence with *B* would be exact were it not for a lack of definiteness in the premises *a,* which deprives the reasoning of strict validity. But oftentimes in the social sciences the deductive element stands very close to *b,* as containing many non-logical and non-experimental principles and showing great susceptibility to inclinations, bias, and the like.

850. So let us make the elements *a* and *b* our main concern. The element *a* corresponds, we may guess, to certain instincts of man, or more exactly, men, because *a* has no objective existence and differs in different individuals; and it is probably because of its correspondence to instincts that it is virtually constant in social phenomena. The element *b* represents the work of the mind in accounting for *a.* That is why *b* is much more variable, as reflecting the play of the imagination.[1]

851. But if the element *a* corresponds to certain instincts, it is far from reflecting them all; and that is evident from the very manner in which we found it. We analyzed specimens of thinking on the look-out for a constant element. We may therefore have found only the instincts that underlay those reasonings. There was no chance of our meeting along that road instincts which were not so logicalized. Unaccounted for still would be simple appetites, tastes, in-

850 [1] As we have already seen (§ 802), the part *b* has in its turn to be subdivided, since it varies all the way from one extreme, where it is pure logic, to another extreme where it is pure instinct and fancy. We shall deal with that situation at length in Chapters IX and X.

clinations, and in social relationships that very important class called "interests."

852. We may also have found only a part of one of the things *a*, the other part being a mere appetite. If the sex instinct tended only to unite the sexes it would not figure in our investigations. But that instinct is often enough logicalized and dissembled under guise of asceticism; there are people who preach virtue as a way of lingering, in their thoughts, on sex matters. Examining their thinking, we accordingly find an element *a* corresponding to the sex instinct, and an element *b* that is the reasoning under which it hides. Diligent search might reveal similar elements corresponding to the appetites for food and drink. But in those cases the rôle played by simple instinct is far more considerable, at any rate, than in the case of sex.

853. The fact of being provident or improvident depends upon certain instincts, certain tastes, and from that point of view it would not figure in *a*. But in the United States the improvident instinct has fathered a theory that people ought to spend all they can earn; and so analysis of that theory yields a quantum *a*, which will be improvidence.

854. A politician is inspired to champion the theory of "solidarity" by an ambition to obtain money, power, distinctions. Analysis of that theory would reveal but scant trace of his motives, which are, after all, the motives of virtually all politicians, whether they preach white or black. First prominence would be held by principles *a* that are effective in influencing others. If the politician were to say, "Believe in 'solidarity' because if you do it means money for me," he would get many laughs and few votes. He therefore has to take his stand on principles that are acceptable to his prospective constituents.

If we stopped at that, it might seem that in the case before us the *a*'s were located not in the principles that suggested championing the theory to the politician, but in the principles that inspired acceptance of it by his hearers. But going a little deeper, such a distinction is seen not to hold. Oftentimes the person who would persuade others begins by persuading himself; and even if he is moved in the beginning by thoughts of personal advantage, he comes eventually to believe that his real interest is the welfare of others. Unbelieving apostles are rare and ineffective, but ubiquitous and ubiquitously effective is the apostle who believes, and he is the more effective, the more sincere his belief. The element *a* in a theory *c* is present both in the persons who accept and in the persons who propound it, but not to be overlooked in either case are the advantages accruing from the theory *c*, to the ones and the others.

855. In analyzing a theory *c*, we must keep the objective standpoint sharply distinguished from the subjective (§ 13). The two researches are very very often confused, and so two errors, in chief, arise. In the first place, as we have so often cautioned, the logico-experimental value of a theory is not kept distinct from its persuasive force or its social utility. Then again—and this is a peculiarly modern error—the objective study of a theory is replaced by a subjective research as to how and why it was evolved or adopted by its author. This second research certainly has its importance, but it ought to supplement the other, not replace it. Whether a theorem of Euclid is true or false, and how and why he came to discover it, are two separate questions, and the one does not preclude the other. If the *Principia* of Newton had been written by an unknown writer, would that in any way affect the value of the book? So two of the aspects under which a writer's theory may be considered (§ 541) become confused: (1) his manner of thinking, his psychic state, and how he came by it; (2) what he meant in a given passage. The first aspect, which is personal, subjective to him, is mixed in with the second, which is impersonal, objective. A factor in the confusion oftentimes is regard for the writer's authority. In deference to that sentiment it is assumed *a priori* that everything he thinks and believes must necessarily be "true," and that to determine his thought is tantamount to testing the "truth" (or when the logico-experimental sciences are concerned, the accord with experience) of what he thought.

856. Long prevalent was an inclination to consider theories exclusively from the standpoint of their intrinsic merit (sometimes their logico-experimental soundness), which, much more often, was determined with reference to the sentiments of the critic or to certain metaphysical or theological principles. Nowadays the tendency is to consider them exclusively from the extrinsic standpoint (aspects 1 and 3, § 541), as to the manner of their genesis, that is, and the reasons for their acceptance. Both methods, if used exclusively, are equally incomplete and to that extent erroneous.

857. The second error (§ 855) is the opposite of the first. The first considered only the intrinsic merit of the theory (aspect 2, § 541); the second only its extrinsic merit (aspects 1 and 3, § 541). It appears in the abuse of the historical method, which is frequent enough nowadays, especially in the social and economic sciences. In the beginning, in their eagerness to free their science of contingencies of time and place, the fathers of political economy made the mistake of viewing their findings as absolutes. It was a salutary reaction, therefore, when just such contingencies came to be taken into account, and from that point of view the historical method was a notable contribution to the progress of science. And a forward step no less important was taken when the effort to derive the forms of social institutions from dogmatic absolutes was abandoned in favour of historical studies that made it possible to learn how institutions had developed, and their bearing on other social phenomena. We are altogether within the domain of logico-experimental science when we ask not what the family ought to be, but what it has actually been. But the historical study is to be thought of as supplementing, not as replacing, our inquiry into the relations between the constitution of the family and other social phenomena. It is useful to know how, historically, theories of income have been evolved; but it is also useful to know the relations of such theories to the facts—their logico-experimental value.

858. However, this latter type of research is much more difficult than the mere writing of history; and there are plenty of people who are utterly incapable even of understanding, let alone of creating, a logico-experimental theory in political economy, yet who blithely presume to write histories of that science.

859. In the literary field historical studies often degenerate into mere collections of anecdotes that are easy to write and agreeable to read. To find out what a writer ate and drank, how he slept, the clothes he wore, is intellectually and scientifically easier than to deal with the relations between his theories and experimental realities. And if a critic can find something to say about a writer's love-affairs, he is certain to make a very entertaining book indeed (§ 541).

860. To study the element *b* is to study the subjective element in a theory. But the subjective element may be further subdivided into two: the general causes and the special causes that account for the genesis and success of a theory. General causes would be causes operative over fairly extensive periods of time and affecting considerable numbers of individuals. Special causes operate in an essentially contingent manner. If a theory comes into vogue because it serves the interests of a social class it has, in that fact, a general cause. If a writer invents a theory because he is paid to do so or because he wants to spite a rival, the cause is special.[1]

861. Things that exert powerful effects upon the social order give rise to theories, and we shall find them, therefore, in the course of our quest for *a*'s. In addition to such *a*'s there are, as we have just seen, appetites and interests. Taking them all together we have the sum of the things that operate to any appreciable extent towards determining the social order (§ 851), bearing in mind of course that the social order reacts upon them, so that we are all along dealing not with a relationship of cause and effect, but with an interrelation or a relationship of interdependence. If we assume, as in fact seems probable, that animals have no theories, they cannot have an element *a* of any kind and perhaps not even interests—all that is left in their case is instincts. Uncivilized peoples, however close to animals they may seem to stand, do have theories of one sort or another, and an element *a* has to be considered in dealing with them. And beyond

860 [1] In our study of *b* theories that is to follow (Volume III) we are to deal strictly with general causes. The study of special causes is of minor importance and can come later.

a doubt they have instincts and interests. Civilized peoples have theories for very very many of their instincts and interests. An element *a* figures through virtually the whole range of their social life.

862. In this volume we are to go looking for the element *a*. In many cases already (*e.g.*, §§ 186 f., 514, 740) we have distinguished *a* elements and *b* elements that we found combined and confused in some single phenomenon, *c*. That was in itself a start towards finding a norm for making such analyses. Suppose we get a still clearer view of the method from an example or two and then proceed with our systematic study.

863. *Example I.* Christians have the custom of baptism. If one knew the Christian procedure only one would not know whether and how it could be analyzed (§§ 186, 740). Moreover, we have an explanation of it: We are told that the rite of baptism is celebrated in order to remove original sin. That still is not enough. If we had no other facts of the same class to go by, we should find it difficult to isolate the elements in the complex phenomenon of baptism. But we do have other facts of that type. The pagans too had lustral water, and they used it for purposes of purification. If we stopped at that, we might associate the use of water with the fact of purification. But other cases of baptism show that the use of water is not a constant element. Blood may be used for purification, and other substances as well. Nor is that all; there are numbers of rites that effect the same result. In cases where taboos have been violated (§ 1252), certain rites remove the pollution that a person has incurred in one set of circumstances or another. So the circle of similar facts widens, and in the great variety of devices and in the many explanations that are given for their use the thing which remains constant is the feeling, the sentiment, that the integrity of an individual which has been altered by certain causes, real or imaginary, can be restored by certain rites. The given case, therefore, is made up of that constant element, *a,* and a variable element, *b,* the latter comprising the means that are used for restoring the individual's integrity and the reasonings by which the efficacy of the means is presumably explained. The human being has a vague feeling that water somehow cleanses moral as well as material pollutions. However, he does not, as a rule, justify his conduct in that manner. The explanation would be far too simple. So he goes looking for something more complicated, more pretentious, and readily finds what he is looking for.

864. The nucleus *a,* now that we have found it, is seen to be made up of a number of elements: first of all an instinct for combinations; people want "to do something about it"—they want to combine certain things with certain acts. It is a curious fact, also, that the ties so imagined persist in time. It would be easy enough to try some new combination every day. Instead there is one combination, fantastic though it be, that tends to prevail and sometimes does prevail over all competitors. Discernible, finally, is an instinct which inclines people to believe that certain combinations are suited to attaining certain objectives.[1]

865. *Example II.* We have seen many cases (§§ 186 f.) where people believed that they could raise or avert tempests. If we knew only one such case, we could make little or nothing of it. However, we know many cases and can identify a constant nucleus in them. Ignoring, for the moment, the element in the nucleus that relates, as in the case of baptism, to the persistence of certain combinations and the faith in their efficacy, we find a constant element, *a,* corresponding to the feeling, the sentiment, that a divinity exists and that, by a variable means, *b,* he (or "it") may be made to interfere and influence the weather. And then, right away, there is another sort of belief, the belief that it is possible to produce the desired effect by certain rites or practices, which mean nothing in themselves —the practice, for instance, of tearing a white cock asunder and carrying the two halves around a field to protect it from drought (§ 189). So the circle widens, and another constant *a* appears: an

864 [1] As for "causes" or "origins," we might guess that actually effective combinations, such as striking a flint to get a fire, may have led people to believe in the efficiency of imaginary combinations. But we need not, for the present, concern ourselves with that explanation or any other. We can rest content with establishing the fact, and stop at that. In some other connexion we might try to go further and explain the fact by other facts, then the latter by others still, and so on.

instinct for combinations, whereby things and acts designed for producing given effects are brought together haphazard.

866. *Example III.* Catholics believe that Friday is a day of evil omen as—so it is averred—the day of the Passion. If we knew just that, and nothing else of the kind, it would be difficult to determine which of the two facts, the evil omen or the Passion, was the main, and which the secondary, fact. But we do have other facts of the kind, many of them. The Romans had their "black" or "vicious" days (*dies atri* or *vitiosi*), which were days of evil omen—for instance, the eighteenth of July, the anniversary of their defeat by the Gauls at Allia, A.U.C. 365. That is one kind of *a*—the feeling that the day which is associated with some catastrophe is a day of evil omen. But there are other facts. Both the Romans and the Greeks had days of evil omen and days of good omen without there being any special causes in the nature of public successes or disasters. Hence there has to be a more comprehensive class of *a*'s, which includes the *a* just mentioned and expresses an impulse to combine days (and other things too) with good or evil omens (§§ 908 f.).

867. These examples give us an inkling as to how a composite situation, *c,* may be broken up into *a* elements and *b* elements.[1]

868. Before going any farther it might perhaps be advisable to give word-names to the things we have been calling *a, b,* and *c.* To designate them by mere letters of the alphabet in a measure embarrasses our discussion and makes it harder to follow. For that reason, and for no other (§ 119), suppose we call the things *a, residues,* the things *b, derivations,* and the things *c, derivatives.* But we must always and at all times remember that nothing, absolutely nothing, is to be inferred from the proper meanings of those words or their etymologies, that they mean respectively the things *a, b,* and *c* and nothing else.[1]

867 [1] We shall perform many other similar analyses in the course of this chapter.

868 [1] [Pareto makes no very extensive use of the term "derivative," probably because its functions are filled just as well by the term "theory," or better, "non-logico-experimental theory." Etymologically, a "residue" would be "what is left" (the constant element) when the variable elements have been eliminated from an action or a reasoning by a comparative analysis. It is always reducible to the synonymous phrase: "principle underlying a non-logical action or reasoning."—A. L.]

869. As we have already seen, the residues *a* constitute a multifarious mass of facts, which have to be classified according to the mutual analogies they present. In that way we get "classes," "genera," and "species." And so for the derivations *B*.[1]

870. Residues correspond to certain instincts in human beings, and for that reason they are usually wanting in definiteness, in exact delimitation. That trait, indeed, nearly always serves to distinguish them from scientific facts or principles *A,* which otherwise bear some resemblance to them. Many times *A*'s have come out of *a*'s as a result of making the *a*'s more exact. The term "warm" is indefinite. Using it, it has been possible to say that well-water is "warm" in winter and "cold" in summer. But as used by physicists the term "warm" corresponds to certain degrees of heat as registered by a thermometer; it is definite. That made it evident that the water in wells is not in that sense warmer in winter than in summer, for a thermometer lowered into a well registers about the same temperature in winter as in summer, or if anything a lower one.

871. Curious the number of different meanings the term "warm" has in Macrobius, *Saturnalia,* VII, 6-8, all of them showing as their residue the sentiments that the term "warm" awakens in the minds now of this, now of that, individual (§ 506). The doctors say that wine is warm; but a character in the *Saturnalia* disagrees, finding wine by nature cold. A woman's body, says another, contains a large amount of cold. No, answers a companion, the female body is naturally warmer than the male—it is so warm, in fact, that when it was the custom to dispose of dead bodies by cremation, a female corpse was commonly burned with each ten males so that the latter might more quickly be consumed. Women have so much heat in their bodies that they are able to wear light clothing in winter. Heat, moreover, is the principle of conception. All that is disputed by another, except as regards conception, the cause of which seems really to be heat. Why is it that in a very hot country wine has the property of cold instead of heat? The reason is that when the air

869 [1] [The classification of "derivatives" having already been given under "theories" in Volume I, §§ 523, 525, 526 f., 574 f.—A. L.]

is hot it drives the cold into the ground. The air is always hot in Egypt, so the cold permeates the soil and reaches the vine-roots, imparting its own properties to the wine. And we are told why a fan cools.[1]

872. That is the type of the metaphysical reasoning, whether ancient or modern. The premises contain terms altogether devoid of

871 [1] Says Macrobius, *loc. cit.:* "I have heard doctors say all the same thing, that wine should be reckoned among the warm substances; and only just the other day, in a discussion on the causes of drunkenness, Eustathius was preaching the warmth of wine. [The reásoning is clear: a drunken man feels hot, therefore wine is hot.] But pondering frequently on the matter myself, I have come to the conclusion that wine by nature stands closer to cold than to warmth." Heat, however, is not substantial to ("inborn in") wine but an incidental attribute (*accidens*): *"Dabo aliud indicium accidentis magis vino quam ingeniti caloris."* The proof alluded to is that all warm things stimulate sensuousness: ". . . *omnia calida Venerem provocant*"*:* but not wine, for "after abundant drinking of undiluted wine *fiunt viri ad coitum pigriores."* Here then warmth would be associated with degrees of amorousness. "Is anything colder than vinegar, which is only soured wine (*quod culpatum vinum est*)?" Not only vinegar: "The fruits of trees are coldest when their juices taste most like wine, such as the ordinary apple, the pomegranate, or the quince (*cydonia, cotonia*) described by Cato." In that case, warmth would have something to do with tastes. How explain the fact [which is not a fact] that women are harder to intoxicate than men? One suggestion is the abundance of damp in the female body (so that the wine is diluted?): *"Mulier humectissimo est corpore."* Another of the disputants points out that the wine the woman drinks gets chilled inside her by her natural cold. That statement brings a sharp retort: "It is no use, Symmachus, for you to go on saying that the female is cold by nature. I can show you easily, if you will allow me, that she is hotter than the male. . . . How can you say women are cold when it is undeniable that they are full of heat, being full of blood [*i.e.,* in menstruation]? Then there is another thing. In our day, of course, it is no longer the custom to cremate the dead. But the books tell us that in the days when it was considered an honour to the dead that they should be given to the flames, if occasion arose to burn a large number of bodies all at one time, the ministers of the rites used to add one female corpse to every ten of males. With the help of that one, which was as it were inflammable by nature and therefore burned rapidly, all the others caught fire. So you see, female heat was not unknown even to the ancients." Furthermore, don't we see women going around lightly clad in cold weather, and not at all bundled up as men are, so offsetting the cold in the air by their natural warmth? The argument seems weak to another in the party: "If they stand the cold better than men, it is because of their own cold: *similibus enim similia gaudent.* They are used to cold from the fact that they have a colder nature. That is why their bodies do not mind it." Macrobius, of course, does not fail to mention the usual story about well-water: "You know yourself, Albinus, from your own experience, that water drawn from deep wells or springs steams in winter and is cold in summer."

exactness, and from the premises, as from mathematical axioms presumably trustworthy, conclusions are drawn by strict logic. They serve, after all, to probe not things but the notions that given individuals have of things.[1]

873. The Macrobius example again shows how inexact terms may readily be used to prove both the pro and the contra. Women can wear lighter clothing than men because of the heat in their bodies. No, someone objects, it is because of the cold in their bodies.

874. In general terms, it is the indefiniteness of the residues *a*, chiefly, that unsuits them to serve as premises in strict reasonings, whereas *A* propositions can be and are constantly being so used in the sciences.

875. The residues *a* must not be confused with the sentiments or instincts to which they correspond (§§ 1690 f.). The residues are the manifestations of sentiments and instincts just as the rising of the mercury in a thermometer is a manifestation of the rise in temperature. Only elliptically and for the sake of brevity do we say that residues, along with appetites, interests, etc. (§§ 851 f.) are the main factors in determining the social equilibrium, just as we say that water boils at 100° Centigrade. The completed statements would be: "The sentiments or instincts that correspond to residues, along with those corresponding to appetites, interests, etc., are the main factors in determining the social equilibrium." "Water boils when its calorific state attains the temperature of 100° as registered by a Centigrade thermometer."

876. It is only by way of analysis and for the sole purposes of study that we distinguish various residues *a1, a2, a3*. . . . What is at work in the individual is sentiments corresponding to the groups (a_1, a_2, a_3); (a_1, a_3, a_4); (a_3, a_5); and so on. These are composites, as compared with the residues *a1, a2* . . . which are simpler. We might go on and break up *a1, a2* . . . as well into simpler elements; but we must know how to stop in time, because if made too general

872 [1] Some people are willing as an extreme concession to bar that type of reasoning from the physical sciences, but insist on retaining it for the social sciences. If we keep within experimental limits, however, there is nothing to justify any such distinction.

propositions end by meaning nothing. So the multifarious circumstances conditioning life on our globe may, in general, be reduced to solar light, the presence of an atmosphere, and so on; but the biologist needs conditions that are much less general than that as a basis for a greater number of biological laws.

877. It sometimes happens that a derivative, *c,* reached from a residue, *a,* by way of a derivation, *b,* becomes in its turn the residue of other phenomena and itself subject to derivations. The bad omen, for instance, that is associated with the presence of thirteen persons at a table may be a derivative from a sentiment of horror at Judas's betrayal followed by his suicide; but that derivative has become a residue by this time, and people feel ill at ease at a table of thirteen without the least thought of Judas.

878. All the pointers just given must be kept in mind at all times in the investigations following. Anyone forgetting them will get everything askew (§ 88).

879. This research as so far outlined has certain points of analogy with the ordinary researches of philology that deal with the roots and derivatives in which the words of a language originate. The analogy is not altogether artificial. It arises in the fact that products of the mental activity of the human being are involved in both cases, that their processes are the same. Take, for instance, Greek. The words in that language may be grouped in families, each family having its own root. There are the nouns meaning "anchor" (ἄγκυρα), "fish-hook" (ἄγκιστρον), "curved object" (ἀγκάλη), "bent arm" (ἀγκαλίς), "bend of the arm" (ἀγκύλη), "elbow" (ἀγκών); the adjectives "curved" (ἀγκύλος) and "hook-shaped" (ἀγκιστρωτός,-ή-όν); the verbs "to fish with a hook" (ἀγκιστρεύω) and "to bend" (ἀγκυλῶ). They all have the same root (residue) ἀγκ, which originates in, and expresses, the rather vague notion of something curved, hooked, crooked. By processes of derivation, which have their rules, words are derived from these roots, just as the derivatives, *c,* are derived from the residues, *a.* We find combinations of roots just as we find combinations of residues. The adjective "biting a hook" (ἀγκιστροφάγος) has ἀγκ and φαγ for its roots, the first referring to something vaguely hook-shaped, the second to eating. There are some very common derivations in Greek. The suffix ματ, for instance, combining with various roots, gives large numbers of words designating the effects of the actions indicated by the roots. So in social phenomena, certain derivations are very very common. The Will of the Divinity, for instance, serves to justify no end of prescriptions. Combined with the residue of filial love, it yields the precept: "Honour thy father and thy mother, for God so ordains."

880. Actually observable in society are certain derivatives, *c*, that derive from residues, *a*, by way of derivations, *b*. Other derivatives (γ) may be as regularly deducible from the residues as the *c*'s but are not observable in the concrete.

881. That situation has its philological counterpart in regular and irregular verbs. In point of fact such terms must not be taken literally. A so-called irregular verb is as regular as any other. The difference lies in the differing methods of derivation. A process of derivation used for certain roots gives a class of verbs that actually occur in the language. Used for other roots, it gives verbs that do not occur in the language. Conversely, the process of derivation used for these second roots yields verbs that occur in the language, but non-existent verbs when used for the other roots.

882. Derivatives treated as residues have their counterparts in language. The word ἀγκιστροφάγος ("biting a hook") was not derived directly from the roots ἀγκ and φαγ, but from ἄγκιστρον and φαγεῖν. Inflections, conjugations, comparatives, superlatives, locatives, to mention only a few, are all examples of derivations based on other derivations.

883. That is not all. The philologists of our time know that language is an organism which has developed according to its own laws and is not an artificial invention. Only a relatively few technical terms, such as "oxygen," "meter," "thermometer," and the like, are products of logical activity on the part of scholars. Such terms would correspond to "logical actions" in society. The majority of the words in ordinary usage correspond in their formation to "non-logical" actions.[1]

884. We have noted these analogies merely to facilitate a clear comprehension of the theories that we are expounding. They of course are not and could not be offered as proofs. Proof must come from direct examination of the facts and in no other way. The method that relies on analogies is a very bad method.

885. Investigations into the "origins" of social phenomena, which have so far concerned sociology in the main, have oftentimes been, though their authors were not aware of the fact, searches for residues. It was taken for granted, more or less vaguely, that the simple must have preceded the complex—that the residue must have been anterior to the derivative (§ 693). When Herbert Spencer locates the chronological origin of religion in the deification of human beings, he thinks he has found the residue of all religious phenomena, the simple phenomenon from which the complex religions observable in our day derive.

886. Two criticisms are to be made of that view. 1. No proof is offered of the hypothesis that knowledge of the residue is chronolog-

883 [1] It is high time that sociology were making some progress and trying to get to the level that philology has already reached. Many other analogies between the two sciences might be noted—to mention just one, the analogy between the abuse of the historical method in sociology and of hypercriticism of texts in philology. Reinach, *Manuel de philologie,* Vol. I, § 3, p. 48: "Boeckh has very properly called attention to a vicious circle to which philological criticism is not immune. In order to explain a text it has to be read under a certain form, and to read it under that form *without change* one has to be able to understand it and explain it. Hence a tendency in many scholars to correct or suppress all passages they do not understand. [That is a way also with writers interested in the "origins" of (social or historical) phenomena.] Says Nauck, in Schneidewin's edition of Sophocles: 'The conjecture that can claim plausibility is the conjecture that best realizes from every point of view what the most exacting mind would like to find in a Greek tragic author.' Boeckh seems almost to have been writing for Nauck's benefit when he said: 'The Athenians, at the suggestion of Lycurgus, had forbidden any alteration in the texts of the tragic authors. One could almost wish the ancient classics were protected by a similar law today.'" Nowadays, in the quest for "origins" everybody takes account of the facts that agree with his notions, and nothing else. Show me if you can the humanitarian who will accept an account of facts that runs counter to his beliefs, or the Marxian who does not test all facts by his doctrine of capitalism!

ically anterior to knowledge of the derivative. That has been the case in some instances, but certainly not in others. So in chemistry certain chemical compounds have been discovered later in time than the elements of which they are compounded, but many other compounds have been known earlier in time. In sociology the "latent" principles of law (§ 802 [1]) are an excellent example of derivatives that were known before their residues. An illiterate peasant woman in the mountains around Pistoia knows the conjugations of many Italian verbs by practice perfectly well and much better than any number of educated people; but she has not the remotest idea of the rules that govern the derivation of those conjugations from their roots.[1] 2. Even if knowledge of the residue is anterior in time to knowledge of the derivative, it is better to follow a course directly opposite to the one that has so far been followed. A chronological quest for the residue *a* is difficult, often impossible, because there are no documents for times so remote from ours; and it is illegitimate to take the imagination and the "common sense" of the modern man as substitutes for them. Imagination and common sense may, to be sure, yield fascinating theories, but they have little or nothing to do with the facts. To try to discover in primitive periods the residue, *a,* from which the phenomena, *c,* observable today, are derived is to try to explain the known by the unknown (§§ 548, 571). To the precise contrary, the less well known must be inferred from the better known; one must try to discover the residues, *a,* in the phenomena, *c,* that are observable today and then see whether there are traces of *a* in documents of the past. If in so doing we find that *a* existed before *c* was known, we might conclude that *a* is anterior in time to *c,* and that, in the particular case, the *origin* is one and the same with the *residue.* Where such proof is lacking no such identity can legitimately be assumed.

887. So far in these volumes we have tried, and we shall continue

886 [1] [In Pareto's 1916 edition in place of the Pistoian peasant woman one finds: "The good Athenian housewife who recognized Theophrastus for a foreigner the moment she heard him speak (Cicero, *Brutus,* 46 . . .) knew the conjugation of a certain number of Greek verbs perfectly well by practice and much better than many modern scholars."—A. L.]

at all times trying, to explain facts of the past by other facts that we are able to observe in the present (§ 547); and in any event, we shall always be at the greatest pains to work from the better known to the less known. We are not dealing with "origins" here, not because origins are not important historically, but because the question of origins has little or no bearing on the inquiry into the conditions determining the social equilibrium with which we are at present engaged. Of great moment, instead, are the instincts and sentiments that correspond to residues.

888. Suppose we begin by classifying residues.[1] Present also, of course, in social phenomena, in addition to the sentiments manifested by residues, are appetites, inclinations, and so on (§ 851). Here we are dealing strictly with the element that corresponds to residues. In that element many, sometimes indeed a great many, simple residues figure, just as rocks contain many simple elements that can be isolated by chemical analysis. In the concrete, one residue may prevail over others in given phenomena, so that they may be taken roughly as representing that residue. The present classification is made from the objective standpoint (§ 855); but we shall be called upon, here and there, to add some few subjective considerations.

CLASS I

INSTINCT FOR COMBINATIONS (§§ 889-990)

- I-α. Generic combinations (§§ 892-909)
- I-β. Combinations of similars or opposites (§§ 910-43)
  - I-β1. Generic likeness or oppositeness (§§ 913-21)
  - I-β2. Unusual things and exceptional occurrences (§§ 922-28)
  - I-β3. Objects and occurrences inspiring awe or terror (§§ 929-31)
  - I-β4. Felicitous state associated with good things; infelicitous state, with bad (§§ 932-36)
  - I-β5. Assimilation: physical consumption of substances to get effects of associable, and more rarely of opposite, character (§§ 937-43)

888 [1] For our classification of derivations, see § 1419.

I-γ. Mysterious workings of certain things; mysterious effects of certain acts (§§ 944-65)

I-γ1. Mysterious operations in general (§§ 947-57)

I-γ2. Mysterious linkings of names and things (§§ 958-65)

I-δ. Need for combining residues (§§ 966-71)

I-ε. Need for logical developments (§§ 972-75)

I-ζ. Faith in the efficacy of combinations (§§ 976-90)

CLASS II

GROUP-PERSISTENCES (PERSISTENCE OF AGGREGATES) (§§ 991-1088)

II-α. Persistence of relations between a person and other persons and places (§§ 1015-51)

II-α1. Relationships of family and kindred groups (§§ 1016-40)

II-α2. Relations with places (§§ 1041-42)

II-α3. Relationships of social class (§§ 1043-51)

II-β. Persistence of relations between the living and the dead (§§ 1052-55)

II-γ. Persistence of relations between a dead person and the things that belonged to him in life (§§ 1056-64)

II-δ. Persistence of abstractions (§§ 1065-67)

II-ε. Persistence of uniformities (§ 1068)

II-ζ. Sentiments transformed into objective realities (§ 1069)

II-η. Personifications (§§ 1070-85)

II-θ. Need of new abstractions (§§ 1086-88)

CLASS III

NEED OF EXPRESSING SENTIMENTS BY EXTERNAL ACTS (ACTIVITY, SELF-EXPRESSION) (§§ 1089-1112)

III-α. Need of "doing something" expressing itself in combinations (§§ 1092-93)

III-β. Religious ecstasies (§§ 1094-1112)

CLASS IV

RESIDUES CONNECTED WITH SOCIALITY (§§ 1113-1206)

IV-α. Particular societies (§ 1114)
IV-β. Need of uniformity (§§ 1115-32)
  IV-β1. Voluntary conformity on the part of the individual (§§ 1117-25)
  IV-β2. Uniformity enforced upon others (§§ 1126-29)
  IV-β3. Neophobia (§§ 1130-32)
IV-γ. Pity and cruelty (§§ 1133-44)
  IV-γ1. Self-pity extended to others (§§ 1138-41)
  IV-γ2. Instinctive repugnance to suffering (§§ 1142-43)
  IV-γ3. Reasoned repugnance to useless sufferings (§ 1144)
IV-δ. Self-sacrifice for the good of others (§§ 1145-52)
  IV-δ 1. Risking one's life (§ 1148)
  IV-δ 2. Sharing one's property with others (§§ 1149-52)
IV-ε. Sentiments of social ranking; hierarchy (§§ 1153-62)
  IV-ε 1. Sentiments of superiors (§ 1155)
  IV-ε 2. Sentiments of inferiors (§§ 1156-59)
  IV-ε 3. Need of group approbation (§§ 1160-62)
IV-ζ. Asceticism (§§ 1163-1206)

CLASS V

INTEGRITY OF THE INDIVIDUAL AND HIS APPURTENANCES (§§ 1207-1323)

V-α. Sentiments of resistance to alterations in the social equilibrium (§§ 1208-19)
V-β. Sentiments of equality in inferiors (§§ 1220-28)
V-γ. Restoration of integrity by acts pertaining to the individual whose integrity has been impaired (§§ 1229-1311)
  V-γ1. Real subjects (§§ 1240-95)
  V-γ2. Imaginary or abstract subjects (§§ 1296-1311)
V-δ. Restoration of integrity by acts pertaining to the offender (vengeance, "getting even") (§ 1312)

V-δ1. Real offender (§§ 1313-19)

V-δ2. Imaginary or abstract offender (§§ 1320-23)

CLASS VI

THE SEX RESIDUE (§§ 1324-96)

889. Class I. *Instinct for combinations.*[a] This class embraces the residues corresponding to the instinct for combinations, which is intensely powerful in the human species and has probably been, as it still remains, one of the important factors in civilization. Figuring as a residue in vast numbers of phenomena is an inclination to combine certain things with certain other things. The scientist in his laboratory makes combinations according to certain norms, certain purposes, certain hypotheses, for the most part rational (at times he combines at random). His activity is primarily logical. The ignorant person makes combinations in view of analogies that are mostly fantastic, absurd, childish (and often also by chance[1]). In any event they are in large part non-logical acts. There is an instinct that prompts to combinations in general, for reasons which are fleeting, momentary, undetectable. It deserves a separate classification as our genus I-α. Similar things often, less often opposites, are combined. That gives us a genus I-β. If the similarities or contrasts are generic, we get a species I-β1. Unusual things are often combined with important occurrences (I-β2); or things and happenings alike impressive are brought together (I-β3). A felicitous state attracts good or

889 [a] [Pareto seems to have adopted the term "combination" (*combinazione*) from the use made of it in Frazer's *Golden Bough*. However, the term is much more comprehensive in Italian than in English. In English, and especially in slang, we use many particular terms to cover the ground for which *combinazione* suffices for the Italian: for example, "deal," "happy inspiration," "idea," "big idea," "scheme." The term "combination" itself has a certain use in American slang in this sense. Unsatisfactory as it is, I have followed Mr. Bongiorno in transferring the Italian term as "combination," but Pareto's explanations must be borne in mind at all times. Synonyms of "the instinct for combinations" in one connexion or another might be "the inventive faculty," "ingeniousness," "originality," "imagination," and so on. The "instinct for combinations" is the progressive element in human society, as contrasted with the "myth-making instinct," or "instinct of group-persistence," which is the conservative force (see Chapter XII).—A. L.]

889 [1] The term "by chance" means simply that the causes underlying such acts are unknown.

praiseworthy things, and *vice versa* (I-β4), whereas an infelicitous contingency attracts bad, unpleasant, horrible things, and *vice versa.* In a genus I-γ we place combinations of things and acts that have something mysterious about them, and that genus falls into two species: mysterious operations in general (I-γ1), and mysterious linkings of names with things (I-γ2). The human beings feels a need for combining various residues (I-δ). Then again, we note a need that is the more keenly felt the higher the degree of civilization in a people: a need for cloaking acts that are in themselves non-logical with a logical veneer, for devising theories that may be altogether imaginary so only they be logical. We make a special genus for that: I-ε. Finally we have to provide for the belief in the efficacy of combinations (I-ζ). Taking Class I as a whole, one notes: (1) a propensity for combinations; (2) a search for the combinations that are deemed best; (3) a propensity to believe that they actually do what is expected of them.

890. There are, moreover, passive and active aspects to combinations. On the passive side the human being is subject to them; on the active side he interprets, controls, or produces them. The propensity, too, is a vague generic sentiment that operates passively and actively. It may be seen in vigorous action in games of chance among all peoples. There the quest for the best possible combinations is conspicuous and eager. As for the propensity to believe in the efficacy of combinations, it also has a passive and an active aspect. On the passive side, a person may believe that *A* is necessarily conjoined with *B* so that if *A* occurs, *B* must ensue. On the active side, the idea is that if one can manage to produce *A,* one can get *B* as a consequence (§§ 976 f.).

891. In the concrete case residues from other classes also figure, notably residues from Class II. Were it not for the persistence of certain relations, the combinations in Class I would be ephemeral insubstantial things. One might compare the situation to a building. The instinct for combinations, the quest for the best possible one, the faith in its efficacy, provide the materials. Persistence of associations gives stability to the structure; it is the cement that holds it together. Then faith in the efficacy of combinations again interposes to incline people to use the building. In many phenomena, especially among civilized peoples, one notes mixtures: logical actions, scientific inferences, non-logical actions, effects of sentiment. Here we are segregating by analysis things that occur in a compound form in concrete reality.

892. I-α: *Generic combinations.* There are reasons for generic combinations, just as there are reasons for specific combinations such as I-β; and if there were any point in doing so, one might subdivide our α variety into a number of subvarieties corresponding to the various reasons. Thousands and thousands of persons play the lottery assigning numbers to things they have seen in their dreams or to happenings that have impressed them.[1] One can imagine why the number 1 has been assigned to the Sun. It is a case of a $\beta 1$ residue (similarities); there being only one Sun, it goes very well with the number 1. But why does the Moon get the number 6, a pair of scissors, the number 7, a white cat, 31, a black cat, 36? We hope no one will try to tell us that experience has led to the belief in such correspondences. That may have happened in some few cases; but one need only glance at a "dream-book" to see that it would never have been possible to record enough experiments to justify all the assignments of numbers there made. It would take a maniac for logic to believe that the meaningless rigmaroles used in magic were chosen by experience—that Cato, for example, or someone acting in his behalf, put first one word and then another to the test before fixing on the ones he recommends in his magical recipe for sprains (§ 184 [2]).

893. It is all the other way round. One begins by believing in this

892 [1] See, for example, *The Book of Dreams, or Echo of Fortune* (*Il libro dei sogni* . . . Florence, A. Salani, n.d.). It contains 672 pages. In France, in the days when the lottery still flourished, publications of that type were abundant: for instance, *La Liste générale des rêves* . . . Paris, 1787—*General Catalogue of Dreams . . . With the Names of Things That Are Dreamed and the Numbers That Correspond to Them in the Drawings of the Royal Lottery of France,* translated from the Italian of Fortunato Indovino ("The Lucky Guesser"), illustrated with numerous cuts similar to said lottery. New edition, revised, corrected, and enlarged, with tables of drawings in the same lottery."

or that combination. Not till later on does someone come along who tries to justify the belief by logic and experience. The Greeks believed in dreams long before any Artemidorus volunteered to show by experience that dreams came true.[1]

894. No reader of Pliny's *Natural History* can fail to be struck by the vast numbers of combinations that have been tried for curing one disease or another. It would really seem as though every combination conceivable had been thought of! Take epilepsy, for instance. First we get laser-juice (distilled from the root of *laserpitium chironium*) with sea-calf's rennet, taken in doses of three parts juice and one part rennet, then plantain, betony, or agaric, mixed with oxymel (XXVI, 70, Bostock-Riley, Vol. V, pp. 196-97). Pliny mentions twelve plants in this one paragraph, in addition to rennet from the milk of the seal and the beaver. Then come remedies for epilepsy derived from the animal kingdom, XXVIII, 63 (Bostock-Riley, Vol. V, p. 353): bears' testicles, wild boars' testicles, wild bores' urine (which is more effective when allowed to evaporate in the animal's bladder); hog's testicles dried, triturated, and beaten in sow's milk; hares' lungs taken with frankincense and white wine. In all, nineteen combinations in the paragraph—not counting gladiator's blood (XXVIII, 2)! Another paragraph, XXXII, 37 (Bostock-Riley, Vol. VI, p. 46) mentions eight more combinations from the animal kingdom; another, XXX, 27, twenty-nine. Adding, we get sixty-nine combinations for epilepsy, and there must certainly have been others that Pliny failed to mention. For jaundice, Pliny recommends wine in which chicken's feet, previously cleansed in water, have been washed. He adds that the chicken's feet must be yellow (XXX, 28). That seems to indicate a residue of our I-β variety (similarities). But when one is told, XXX, 30, that to cure the ague one must wear the longest tooth of a black dog as a charm, no reason, however fantastic, is discernible for the treatment. Similar

893 [1] One of my critics has contended that non-logical actions arise from "excogitation" (which means logic all the same, no more, no less) and that only when the logical reasons have been forgotten do people invent explanations that make their conduct seem non-logical!

prescriptions are to be found not by the hundreds but by the thousands all over the face of the globe, and in our Western countries they have held their own down to very recent times. Cardinal Richelieu was once treated with horse-dung steeped in white wine. One treatment for fever was to wear around one's neck a live spider shut up in a nutshell.[2] Snakes and toads long played an important part in pharmacy. Absurdities all, one may say; yet if those absurdities had never been, experimental science would never have been either.[3]

895. Du Chaillu relates an incident that is characteristic.[1] On his killing a leopard, the natives asked him for the tip of the tail to use as an erotic amulet. They also wanted the brain; it promoted courage and good luck in hunting. Finally they begged him carefully to destroy the gall-bladder, since it was poisonous. The first of the combinations was of our I-α variety (generic); the second may have been of the I-β1 species (generic similarity), the leopard being a good hunter. Both were certainly ineffective. The third may conceivably have been effective in view of the ptomaines originating in putrefaction.[2]

896. When one is trying to discover the ways in which great events have come to pass in human society it may seem ridiculous to waste a paragraph on the tip of a leopard's tail. But if one is to argue in that fashion one ought not to worry either over the spittle of a patient in diagnosing tuberculosis, or bother with a rat in trying to fight the bubonic plague. So at one time philology disdained mere dialects and confined itself to the language of "recognized authors." That time is long since past in philology. So it should be in sociology (§ 80). The instinct for combinations is among the major forces determining the social equilibrium; and if it sometimes manifests itself in ridiculous and absurd ways, that fact detracts no whit from its importance.

894 [2] For no end of particulars, see Gallier, *Les mœurs et la vie privée d'autrefois.*

894 [3] It has been suggested that civilization originated in games of chance. There is an element of truth in the notion, in the sense that games of chance figure among the many manifestations of the instinct of combinations, which has been and remains a most significant factor in progress.

895 [1] *Explorations and Adventures in Equatorial Africa,* pp. 202-04.

895 [2] [Pareto is here following the outline in § 151.—A. L.]

897. Scientists interested in the origins of things have exerted themselves to discover how animals could ever have come to be domesticated; and they have met with very serious difficulties, especially when they were overeager to regard all human conduct as logical. We need not go into all the various hypotheses that have been advanced. Let us consider one, a theory of Reinach. It happens to suggest reflections pertinent to the matter here in hand.

898. Reinach begins by eliminating simple combinations:[1] "There may be domesticable animals about, but of that man knows nothing. Experience alone, long experience, could have enlightened him in that regard. But how and why would he even venture on such an experiment when he has no conception of domestication? Chance may reveal a flake of gold to primitive man, a mineral such as copper or iron, but chance could never show him a domestic animal! There can be no domestic animal except as a result of training received from man."

899. The reasoning would be excellent if all human conduct were logical, if—except in the case specified by Reinach, where pure chance throws in the savage's way the one completed object that he needs and can use—the only road to discovery were first to know what one wants, and then to look around for the best means of obtaining it. That in fact is the route which is followed in making scientific discoveries by rational processes. There is a demand for a source of power, light in weight and of high productive capacity. People hunt and they eventually find the gasoline engine. But most discoveries, especially in times past, were not made in that way. There is another way, and it lies precisely in the instinct for combinations, which impels the human being to put things and acts together without pre-established design, without knowing exactly what he is driving at—much as a person rambles about in a forest for the mere pleasure of rambling about. Even when design exists, it oftentimes has nothing to do with the result actually achieved. Very frequently the thing that was sought was not the thing that was discovered. What the alchemists wanted, for a decisive example,

898 [1] *Cultes, mythes et religions*, Vol. I, p. 88.

was a way for making gold. What they found was a variety of chemical compounds. It occurred to someone to allow a quantity of human urine to putrefy, then to mix the product with fine sand, and then to distill the mixture. The outcome of that weird and complicated process was the discovery of phosphorus. In many other cases the combination did not result in anything useful. One gropes blindly forward. Sometimes one finds. More often one does not.

900. In the case of domesticating animals human beings may have had some vague notion of the purposes of certain things they did. It happens every day about us that children will pick up a young bird that has fallen from its nest, and raise it. If the bird happened to be of any particular use, it would surely end by being domesticated. Children are not dreaming of any such purpose. They are just trying to amuse themselves by humouring their instinct for combinations, just as they do when on a romp they make the strangest combinations of the things at their disposal. In rural districts people will often raise young rabbits they happen to catch alive in the fields. They rarely become tame rabbits. The only purpose in raising them is the fun of raising them. Why in the world might such a thing not have been done with a rabbit in some earlier period of history? Why may not the rabbit have first been domesticated in some such way?

901. But there is better yet. Cowper Rose reports an incident in which the simple instinct for combinations may be seen at work in domesticating animals:[1]

"In Hinza's territory, a Kaffer, whose possessions excited envy and dislike, was accused of keeping a wolf, which, though confined during the day, roamed about the country at night, and destroyed the cattle. On this plea he was seized and deprived of everything, half of the cattle being taken by Hinza, while the other half was distributed among the councillors. The man was banished the country; and on leaving it, seized on the cattle of another, and carried them with him to Voosani, a neighbouring chief of Tambooki's. Hinza

901 [1] *Four Years in Southern Africa*, pp. 142-43.

sent to complain of the robbery, to demand the cattle, and to inform the chief of the crime of the man, whom he had protected. The cattle were returned, and great horror expressed at the crime. The missionary, who told me the story, in speaking to Hinza on the subject, said: 'You have plenty of cattle, why did you ruin the poor man?' when the chief turned to him with a peculiar smile which marked that he was not deceived, and, with a tone of mock seriousness, said: 'Yes, but it is a shocking thing, you know, to keep a witch-wolf.' "

902. Prominent here are two residues: the residue of combinations, in the man raising the wolf; and then the residue of neophobia (IV-β3) in the people who drove him out of town. Two residues can both work side by side in the same person; the man who raised the wolf might himself have been horrified at other novelties, just as those who considered raising a wolf a crime may have had practices of their own that involved strange combinations.

903. According to Reinach the animals that have been domesticated were ancient totems; and he goes on from there, heaping hypothesis on hypothesis and telling all about things of which he knows nothing as though he had seen them with his own eyes. That is the procedure of Spencer and many other sociologists. An ingenious, intelligent, well-read author advances a hypothesis, infers things from it in the light of his logic, his learning, his sentiments, and then imagines he is reconstructing the past of lethargic, uneducated savages who were endowed with little native intelligence, and who into the bargain lived under conditions entirely different from the ones surrounding the scientist-creator of the hypothesis and its implications.

904. "Imagine," says Reinach, *Op. cit.,* p. 93, "a race of savage huntsmen living in ancient France, a country where bulls, horses, deer, bears, wolves, not to mention other animals, were indigenous. The hunters are split up into clans or little tribes, each of them claiming a different animal for its ancestor. The wolf-clan thinks it is descended from the wolf, that it has made a pact of alliance with the wolves, and that, save in cases of legitimate self-defence, it must not kill wolves. . . . Each of the clans will refrain from hunting and killing this or that species of animal, but it will not stop at that. Since the animal is the protector of the clan, guides it in its wanderings, raises alarms in times of danger by crying and signs of uneasiness, there must always be two or more of its species living with the clan to act as its sentinels." The facts do not stand just that way. We know of many clans that have totems but do not use the totem animals as sentinels. However, suppose we let that pass; other clans may have used them that way. But why "two or more" such animals? Would one not be sufficient? One would be enough to act as watch-dog for the clan. But not enough to reproduce the species! That is the point Reinach has to get to! "These animals, captured young, get used to human beings, grow tame. Their young, born in contact with members of the clan, become their friends." So, you see, that is why there had to be two or more totem animals. But that is not all: one had to be male, the other female! If a clan's totem is a rooster (a rooster crows in time of danger) the rooster has to have a hen—one or more hens! But in the realm of hypotheses everything can readily be accounted for. We may guess that since those ancient Frenchmen worshipped Chantecleer they must surely have been French enough to provide him with the ordinary comforts of home.

905. The discovery of certain plants that are specific remedies for certain diseases is as difficult to explain as the domestication of animals. How could mere chance ever have led the Peruvians to discover that cinchona bark is a specific for malaria? Are we to say that the cinchona was the totem of a clan, and that out of reverence for its totem the clan elected to use its bark in cases of sickness? But in that event the same explanation would have to serve for other cases of the kind, and we would need as many totems as there have been folk-remedies for diseases. But there are infinite numbers of such remedies, so that we should have to assume, contrary to fact, the same infinite number of totems.

906. One may doubt whether there is a plant that has not been considered suitable for curing not just one but any number of diseases. How many ills the radish can cure, according to Pliny! Which all goes to show what scant resemblance such combinations bear to the experiments that are nowadays made in our laboratories. The idea would be that a plant was tried first for one disease, then for another, and that its use was eventually retained just for diseases for which it had shown itself effective. But the fact is, Pliny's prescriptions were kept even though ineffective, and many of them have been handed down to our day. What really underlay them was the instinct for combinations, and the same instinct is asserting itself even in our civilized day when in case of illness people say that "something has to be done" (residues, Class III) and medicines are administered catch as catch can (residues, Class I).

907. It may well be that at the time when animals were first domesticated cases such as Reinach imagines occurred—indeed more probably than not they did occur. The fact that an animal was a totem may have been one of any number of reasons that inspired combinations from which the domestication of animals resulted. Reinach's error lies chiefly in his giving as the only reason a reason that may have existed simultaneously with others. We know nothing of those early times. We cannot therefore deny a thing that is in itself possible. But neither can we affirm it; and it is to reason fallaciously to assert that because it was possible for a thing to be thus and so, thus and so it must have been. We may go even further. Even if we, now in our time, could see only one way in which a thing can have occurred, that might warrant the presumption that the thing took place in that way. But it may still have happened in some other way, of which we, *now* in our time, cannot conceive.

908. In the instinct to regard certain days as of good or of evil omen many residues may figure. Sometimes there is the residue of mere combination (I-α); it is difficult to see any others in certain of the correspondences noted by Hesiod. Sometimes present may be a residue of the I-β variety (similarities and opposites). But even in such a case, one can, as we have already seen (§ 894), get back in the long run, to our I-α variety. So the plain man in Rome ended, as Aulus Gellius notes, *Noctes Atticae,* IV, 9, 9-11, by confusing *religiosi dies,* which originally commemorated baleful events, with mere *dies nefasti,* on which the praetor was forbidden to sit in judgment or convoke the *comitia.*[1] In addition to the public holidays there were private holidays and certain families had special holidays of their own. Individuals, then as now, celebrated birthdays and kept other personal holidays on one account or another.[2] The Greeks also deemed it unlucky to work on certain days. In a diatribe against one Timarchus, Lucian says that the Athenians applied the term ἀποφράδες to baleful, abominable, unpropitious, unlucky days when "neither do magistrates sit in judgment, nor are cases brought before the courts, nor are religious ceremonies performed, nor anything of good omen. . . . That is the custom for a variety of reasons: whether because of great battles that have been lost, their an-

908 [1] *Loc. cit.,* 5: " 'Religious days' (*'dies religiosi'*) are days of mourning, of accursed memory (*infames*) or of inhibiting omens. Limitations are placed on celebrating divine services and beginning new enterprises on such days. The ignorant masses mistakenly and reprehensibly call them *dies nefastos*" [as it were, "court holidays," or just "holidays"]. Says Varro, *De lingua latina,* VI, 29 (Goetz-Scholl pp. 68-69): "On 'court days' [*i.e.,* days of good omen, *dies fasti*] praetors can utter any words at all without pollution. Their opposites are called 'court-holidays' [*i.e.,* days of bad omen, *nefasti*] and a praetor must not pronounce the words *do, dico, addico* ["I give, award, adjudge," in which he registers his judgments]. Court actions cannot therefore be prosecuted, for it would be necessary to pronounce one of those words." It may have been the other way round, in the beginning. Roman writers of the historical period did not know why certain days were of good omen, others of bad. A praetor who inadvertently uttered the words *do, dico, addico* on a court holiday had to atone for the slip by expiatory sacrifices. Quintus Mucius held that no atonement was possible for a praetor who had uttered them in deliberate violation of the interdict [and therefore that he had to resign]: Varro, *loc. cit.,* 30: ". . . *si imprudens fecit, piaculari hostia facta piatur; si prudens . . . eum expiari ut impium non posse.*"

908 [2] Macrobius, *Saturnalia,* I, 16: "There are, in addition, holidays peculiar to families, such as the Claudian, the Aemilian, the Julian, the Cornelian, clans, and each family observes such holidays as it has by domestic gatherings and processions (*domesticae celebritatis*). And there are individual holidays, such as birthdays and the days when [personal] auspices are taken, the death anniversaries [of relatives] and days of [personal] expiations. Among the ancients anyone naming the goddesses Salus [of public safety], Semonia [of crops in general], Seia [of sowing], Segetia [of reaping], or Tutilina [of protection of wheat] had to keep holiday. Every time a member of the Flaminian gens heard thunder, he kept holiday until he had made a propitiatory offering to the gods."

niversaries being decreed holidays inappropriate to any legal action; or indeed in honour of Zeus. . . ."[3]

909. Such combinations—such superstitions, as Christian writers call them—survived for long periods of time. Muratori notes that "Egyptian days" were observed and even registered in public calendars from a remote antiquity down to the sixteenth century of the Christian era.[1] This is one of the most tenacious of residues; we find it in every age of history, in every country, and no more among the ignorant than among the educated, even the highly educated, and whether they are temperamentally superstitious or the reverse.[2]

908 [3] *Pseudologista, De die nefasto, contra Timarchum*, 12-13 (*Opera*, Vol. VIII, pp. 66-67). The sentence was broken off by Lucian himself, as though he thought it hardly worth while to list things so well known.

909 [1] *Dissertazioni sopra le antichità italiane*, LIX (Vol. III, pp. 227-29): "Also to be counted among superstitions is the 'observance of times,' or 'of days' (*observatio temporum, dierum*). This one was very general in former times, the pastors and Fathers of the Church preaching against it in vain. . . . How tenacious this impious observance was even among Christians is apparent from the fact that 'Egyptian days' were scrupulously observed by many people from a remote antiquity down to the sixteenth century of our era, and even registered in public calendars. . . . Two days were so marked (*suis sedibus indicati*) in each month, and they were supposed to be so unlucky and of such bad omen that anyone doing anything on them could only look forward to an unpleasant outcome. Not only the plain people but gentlefolk of politer education stood scrupulously on guard against such days, judging that a tradition so ancient must rest on very trustworthy foundations. All the same it was fabricated nowhere save in the clouds, or else in the ingenious imaginations of impostors. [The usual mistake of regarding non-logical conduct as logical.] Of course, we have no great right to be surprised at such customs in our forefathers, nor at their unintelligent credulity and superstition, since not a few people in our time, and people more pretentious about their learning than minds of the darker ages ever dared to be, will not start out on a journey on Friday in fear of becoming the examples that prove the truth of a certain Spanish adage: 'Never start a wedding or a journey on a Tuesday or a Friday.' There are also people who shiver if they discover that they are sitting at table with twelve other guests, in the firm conviction that a whole year will not pass without one of the thirteen dying in some unexpected manner. And there are those . . . who think some misfortune is impending if they see salt accidentally spilled on the table." These latter superstitions, or rather combinations, have held on down to our time.

909 [2] Of the Emperor Augustus Suetonius remarks, *Divus Augustus*, 92, 2: "He observed certain signs and omens, trusting them implicitly. . . . He also observed certain days. He would never start out for any destination on the day after a *nundina* (market-day) nor begin any important business on the nones [fifth or seventh of the month], for no other reason, as he wrote to Tiberius, than the *δυσφημία*, the unfavourable omen, of the name." [Apparently a number 9 superstition—residues

910. I-β: *Combinations of similars or opposites.* Similarity or contrast in things, no matter whether real or imaginary, is a potent cause of combinations. The reason is at once apparent if one but consider the associations of ideas that such things provoke. Non-logical reasonings are often reasonings by association of ideas.

911. It is important to note that if *A* and *B* are similar things, and *C* and *D* their opposites, the phenomenon opposite to the combination $A + B$ is not the combination $C + D$, but the absence of any combination. The opposite of belief in God is not belief in the Devil, but absence of belief in either. The state of mind of the person who is continually dwelling on matters of sex has its opposite in the state of mind, not of the person who is continually alluding to sex with horror, but of the person no more concerned with it than with any other bodily function. The novelists have long been telling us that the opposite of love is not hate, but indifference (§ 957 [1]).

912. The homoeopathic principle, *similia similibus curantur,* combines similars. The opposite principle, *contraria contrariis,* combines opposites. Antithetical to both is experimental science, which entertains no *a priori* principles but allows experience to pass judgment in every case.[1]

I-α; and *cf.* § 892. Rolfe explains the feeling as due to the resemblance of *nonis* (on the nones) to *non is:* "You do not go."—A. L.] Busch, *Tagebuchblätter,* Vol. II, p. 239 (English, Vol. I, p. 473), May 1, 1871: "As I saw later, Jules Favre telegraphed that he would be in Frankfort on Friday, and the Chief [Bismarck] replied that he would arrive there on Saturday, perhaps because he considers Friday unlucky." That may have been a diplomatic pretext; but the fact that Bismarck used it shows that there were people to take him seriously. [In the case of Busch's diary, the English translation from Busch's first manuscript takes precedence both over the published German text and over the French translation. The latter shows considerable adaptation to French sentiments. As for the German, it was not published for many years after it was written and suffered much reworking at Busch's senile hands and at the hands of others.—A. L.]

912 [1] Heim, *Incantamenta magica Graeca Latina,* pp. 484-85, *Similia similibus:* "Belief in the potency of similars, which may be briefly stated in the adage *similia similibus,* had a great and universal vogue in magic and medicine. Superstitious writers of ancient times wrote and raved extensively on the subject, as, for instance, the physicists Democritus and Nepualius, whose works *On Sympathies and Antipathies* have survived to our time. It was believed that actual evils could be banished by certain fancied similitudes, people choosing deliberately to be so deceived. [A logical explanation of the instinct for combining similars or opposites.] Kopp

913. I-β1: *Generic likeness or oppositeness.* Residues of this variety are of very frequent occurrence. They oftentimes figure in magic —similar things and similar operations are combined, a human being, an animal, a thing, are influenced by working on some small particle that has been removed from their bodies; and in that there is the twin similarity of things and procedures.[1] Contraries are also associated, and active in many cases apparently are sentiments that prompt a deliberate search for contrasts (§§ 738 f.).[2]

mentions many examples, *Paleographia critica,* Pt. III, §§ 511-16 f.; Wuttke, § 477. Amazing the comments that superstition and fatuous thinking have provoked in this regard (*hic*), as, for instance, *Geoponicon,* II, 42, 2. . . . I have already dealt with the portrayals of Hercules strangling the lion that are frequently to be found on medallions and jewellery." [The Wuttke reference I fail to solve.—A. L.]

913 [1] Réville, *Les religions des peuples non-civilisés,* Vol. I, pp. 152-53: "The Kaffir is not as addicted to fetishes . . . is, therefore, not so much of an idolator, as the Negro, but he has, if such a thing be possible, even more charms and amulets of all varieties and names. . . . The idea is that the qualities or defects of a given object are transmitted by simple contact, and that the similarity between two facts, the one already accomplished, the other desired, is tantamount to a relationship of cause and effect. [The usual error of assuming rational processes of thinking where none such exist. Imagine a Kaffir indulging in metaphysical reflections on cause and effect! What really is there is a non-logical sentiment inspiring a belief that things and acts go in pairs with other things and acts of the same sort.] A Kaffir's string of beads contains a sheep-bone, an iron ring, a lion's claw, a shrike's claw. Why? That the wearer may fly with the speed of the shrike, have the strength of a lion, the hardness of a bone, the resistance of iron. Under threat of death the Kaffir will fasten to his chest an insect that lives a long time after being pierced with a pin: he wants to borrow its endurance. If he would soften the heart of a man of whom he is to buy some cattle or a daughter, he chews at a piece of wood till he has reduced it to pulp."

913 [2] It is interesting just here to note that the inductive and the deductive methods get us to the same point. Some distance back (§§ 733 f.) we made a direct study of cases involving similar facts, and we wondered whether the resemblances were due to imitation. Our answer was in the negative. We saw that there were cases where imitation was out of the question, and we were therefore led by induction to consider some other cause for the resemblances, namely, sentiments inclining human beings to put certain things together. Following the deductive method, we would have begun by recognizing, as we do here, the existence of the sentiments. From that we would have inferred that human beings entertaining the same sentiments would be likely in certain cases to act in similar ways without any reciprocal imitation whatever. In that case the facts we presented back there, instead of serving for purposes of induction, would have served for purposes of verifying conclusions already reached. Whether we proceed in the one way or the other, the method is strictly logico-experimental, since the facts remain at all times sovereign over the whole discussion.

914. Says the witch in Theocritus, *Idyllia,* II, vv. 24-31: "Delphis [her lover] has tormented me. A laurel-branch I burn upon Delphis. Even as this crackles aloud when it is kindled, and burns in a flash so that not even its ashes do we see, so may the flesh of Delphis be consumed by the fire. . . . Even as I melt this wax with the help of a god, so may Delphis the Myndian be likewise melted by love; and as I turn this rhomb of bronze, so may he [Delphis] be turned by Aphrodite towards my threshold." She works moreover on an object that has belonged to her lover, *Ibid.,* vv. 53-54: "This fringe from his mantle has Delphis lost, and, lo, I rend it and cast it into the unrelenting flame." [1] It was once and still is believed that a person can

914 [1] The scholiast notes (Dübner, pp. 20, 125-26): "As the laurel vanishes straightway when thrown into the fire, so may Delphis be consumed in body in the fire of love." Farther along, v. 58, the witch speaks of crushing a lizard for Delphis, and says that she will carry him a curse in a potion. There is no trace of any similitude in all that. It is just a residue of generic combination (I-*a*). Virgil imitates Theocritus in *Eglogae,* VIII, vv. 79-81, and adds a few items derived from popular superstitions:

> *"Ducite ab urbe domum, mea carmina, ducite Daphnim.*
> *Limus ut hic durescit et haec ut cera liquescit*
> *uno eodemque igni, sic nostro Daphnis amore."*

("Bring Daphnis home from town, bring him, songs of mine! Even as this clay hardens and this wax melts in the same fire, so may Daphnis in love of me.") Servius explains (Thilo-Hagen, Vol. III, p. 105, note): "She had made two images, one of clay which hardens in the fire, the other of wax which melts in the fire: in other words, that the heart of her lover might harden towards the woman he was at the time loving and all other women, the way clay hardens in the fire, but might soften and melt toward her as wax melts in the fire." In short, she would have her lover hardened to other women as clay in fire, and like wax melted by her love. Virgil continues, *loc. cit.,* vv. 82-83:

> *"Sparge molam et fragilis incende bitumine laurus.*
> *Daphnis me malus urit: ego hanc in Daphnide laurum."*

("Sprinkle sacred meal [on the fire] and burn these frail laurels in tar. The cruel Daphnis consumes me in fire; I burn this laurel for [on] Daphnis.") Servius notes, *loc. cit.: "In Daphnide laurum:* Either it is a case of an archaism for *in Daphnidem,* or we must understand that she is burning the laurel upon an image of Daphnis, in view of the similarity of the names." It is better to understand: *"in hac lauro uro Daphnidem."* The similarity becomes more exact in Virgil because the incantation is performed on relics of Daphnis. The witch buries them under her threshold, that they may bring Daphnis to her door, v. 92:

> *"Pignora cara sui, quae nunc ego limine in ipso,*
> *terra, tibi mando! Debent haec pignora Daphnim."*

("These mementoes [of the traitor] on my threshold, O Earth, I commit to thee. These pledges make Daphnis my due."—Fairclough).

be harmed if one tortures a wax figurine made in his image.[2] Tartarotti writes:[3] "Jean Bodin, one of the greatest writers ever for magnifying the powers of witches, sorcerers, and the Devil, alluding to people who make wax figurines and burn them or pierce them with needles in hopes so of wreaking vengeance on their enemies, cannot but confess, *De la démonomanie,* II, 8, that 'the incantation rarely works, since out of a hundred people perhaps not more than two are ever harmed, as has been learned from confessions by sorcerers.'" The judges who sat at the trial of La Môle, who was accused of making a wax image of Charles IX and piercing it with pins, believed, or feigned to believe, in such practices, as did the judges who tried the wife of the Maréchal d'Ancre.[4]

915. Here, as usual, we get a nucleus with a number of amplifications concentrated about it—one residue with a variety of deriva-

914 [2] Ovid, *Epistulae, Hypsipyle Iasoni,* VI, v. 91 (Ehwald, Vol. I, p. 92):

"Devovet absentis simulacraque cerea figit
et miserum tenues in iecur urget acus."

("She makes waxen images of the absent one, and lays a curse upon him, driving sharp needles into the quivering liver.")

914 [3] *Del congresso notturno delle lammie,* II, 17, 2 (p. 192).

914 [4] Hayem, *La maréchale d'Ancre: Léonora Galigai,* p. 280. The Maréchale (Eleonora Dori Galigai) testifying: "She [*i.e.,* the witness] does not know what wax images they are talking about, that that is the business of witches, she having never been aught but a Christian, and that they will never find out any such thing about her. *Q.* What did you use the images for? Answers that God might strike her dead if she knew anything about any wax images. *Q.* In the house, when it was broken into, pillaged, and torn down, there was a high room, like a garret, and in said room (*maison*) a coffin on a table and on the table a wax image covered with a shroud of black velvet, with four candlesticks with white candles at the corners. Answers that she would rather die than see a thing like that." *Registre criminel du Châtelet de Paris,* Vol. II, p. 287: "Prosecution of Jeanne de Brigue, *anno* 1390: And then witness asked said Jehennete whether she knew who the woman was who was causing him to suffer such torment; and she replied that it was the said Gilete . . . that she [Gilete] had made a wax face and put on it hair belonging to witness, and that every time he was sick in that way it was because she was putting the said face on the fire in a copper pan and turning it with a copper spoon, which spoon and pan he had himself given her. And then witness asked her [Jehennete] how she knew that, and she answered that she knew it because she had talked of his case (*à ses choses?*) and that never had anyone been so cruelly 'faced' (*envoulté,* bewitched, in the manner described) and that she had had a great deal of trouble in trying to cure him, more trouble than she had ever had in her life before."

tions. In Theocritus and Virgil there is an ungarnished resemblance between a wax image that is melting and a man burning with love. That seed sprouts, grows, and blossoms into an ample legend that is told [in Hector Boece's *Croniclis,* XI, 4] about one Duffus, King of Scotland. Said king was suffering from a disease unfamiliar to his physicians. He perspired every night and was unable to rest during the day. After numerous vicissitudes, it came to light that at Fores, in the nearby township of Murray, certain witches were in possession of a wax figure of the King. Whenever they set the image in front of the fire, the King began to sweat; and it was the incantations they recited before it that kept him from sleeping. All that, of course, was the work of the Devil, a derivation not available for Theocritus and Virgil, but which is never missing in Christian times. Theocritus, it is true, had a derivation of the same sort: thanks to Aphrodite the whirling of a rhomb is to bring the straying lover back. John Weier was a doctor and had a smattering of that experimental art which was so distasteful to metaphysicists and theologians, as it still is.[1] Weier takes no stock whatever in the story of the Scottish king. But it was swallowed whole by the Boutroux's and William Jameses of those days, seeming doubtless to them to possess a "truth" far superior to experimental truth and far more majestic.[2]

915 [1] In his *De operatione daemonum,* 14 (*Opera,* p. 851), Michael Psellus censures physicians who refuse to recognize works of the Devil and resort to experimental explanations of facts. Says he: "Small wonder that doctors think as they do, for they refuse to see anything that does not fall under the senses, and attend only to the body." Metaphysicists who adore Hegel and Kant, or the sublimities of a law of nations, are still finding the same fault today with scholars who insist on keeping within the limits of experimental realities.

915 [2] Weier, *Histoires, disputes et discours,* III, 14 (Vol. I, pp. 339-43): *"Ie proposerai en cest endroit une esmerueiable histoire . . . laquelle a esté escrite par Hector Boece. Le Roy Dussus* [sic] *tomba en vne maladie, laquelle de soy mesme n'étoit si dangereuse que dificile à conoistre par les plus doctes medecins. . . . Car il suoit toute nuit et ne pouuoit dormir, et de jour il se reposoit, à peine soulagé de la douleur qu'il auoit enduree toute la nuit."* Finally people in Scotland get an inkling, we are not told how, *"que le Roy estoit detenu par vne si longue espace de temps en langueur . . . non par maladie naturelle mais au moyen de l'art diabolique des sorcieres, lesquelles exerçoient contre luy l'art de Magie et sorcellerie en vne ville de Morauie* [sic] *nommee Forres."* The King investigates in that town, and discovers that soldiers there already had their suspicions, due to the talk of a mistress of one

916. It was, and still is, a trick of magicians for swindling simpletons to persuade them to bury gold or jewels in a certain place, with the idea that more gold and jewels will be attracted by them, the enchanter, in due course, appropriating the "bait." The newspapers report some instance of the use of this trick every so often.

917. If some incompatibility, real or imaginary, exists between certain things, the one can be used for getting rid of the other. The *Geoponicon* of Cassianus Bassus, II, 42, explains how a garden may be saved from the ravages of a parasitic weed called *orobanche,* "broom-rape," which destroys vegetables. The plant was also called "lion-grass," and that was enough to justify the assumption that anything believed to be at outs with the lion would be at war with that weed: "If you would have this grass appear not at all, take five shells [*variant:* or pieces of broken crockery] and thereon with chalk or some other white substance draw Hercules strangling the lion. Place one shell in each of the four corners of the field and one in the centre. Another cure has been found, physical and by antipathy, and it is vouched for by Democritus. He says that since the lion is stricken with terror at sight of a cock and runs away, if one takes a cock in one's hands and resolutely walks the round of the field, the lion-grass straightway departs and vegetables grow the better, the lion-grass fearing the cock." Present here are residues of two varieties: 1. A residue of the I-γ2 type links the name with the thing.

of them who happened to be the daughter of a witch. The soldiers go to her house by night: "*Lesquels entrans de force en la maison fermee trouerent vne sorciere qui tenoit vne image de cire representant la figure de Dussus, laquelle estoit faicte, comme il est vraysemblable, par art Diabolique et attachee à vn pau de bois deuant le feu, là où elle se fondoit, ce pendant que vne autre sorciere en recitant quelques charmes distilloit peu à peu vne liqueur par dessus l'effigie. Ces sorcieres doncques estant prises . . . et interroguees . . . elles respondirent que le Roy Dussus fondoit en sueur pendant que son effigie estoit devant le feu; et que tandis que l'on prononçoit les charmes il ne pouuoit dormir, tellement qu'à mesure que la cire fondoit il tomboit en langueur, et qu'il mourroit incontinent qu'elle seroit du tout fondue. Elles dirent aussi que les Diables les auoyent ainsi apprises.*" The witches are burned, and "*ce pendant que ces choses se faisoyent . . . le Roy commença à se reuenir, et passa la nuict sans suer, si bien que le iour suyuant il reprit ses forces.*" Weier concedes that the Devil may have done all that, but later qualifies: "I say that, on the assumption that the story is true, which I do not believe." [Pareto follows Weier.—A. L.]

Since the weed is called lion-grass, it has the characteristics of the lion. 2. A residue of the variety here in hand (I-β1) sets up an oppositeness between the cock and the lion.[1] Cleisthenes, tyrant of Sicyon, desired to abolish the cult of Adrastus in his city as constituting a bond between his people and the Argives with whom he was at war. Accordingly, says Herodotus, *Historiae,* V, 67, he began by asking the Pythia if he might not simply throw Adrastus out. On receiving a scornful negative, he devised a plan for being rid of the god indirectly. He asked the Thebans for Melanippus and having obtained him, dedicated a chapel in the Prytaneum to him. That he did because Melanippus had been a mortal enemy of Adrastus, and he assumed that if he paid honour to Melanippus and held in his name the feasts that had formerly been dedicated to Adrastus, the latter would withdraw of his own accord.

918. The act of parodying the rites of a religious cult shows a residue of this same variety, I-β1. The purpose of such travesties, which were frequently practised in ages past among the Catholic peoples, was to obtain things contrary to religion and morality. The "black masses" were of this type.

919. Sacrifices in Graeco-Roman antiquity are often determined by arbitrary, strange, absurd resemblances, being obtained from religious residues by derivations in which a residue of our I-β1 variety plays the principal part. In Greece the victim's head was turned towards the sky when the sacrifice was to the Olympian gods, towards the ground when it was to the nether gods. As a general rule, with many exceptions for that matter, male animals were sacrificed to male divinities, female to female. Likeness was the determining

917 [1] A variant shows how legends arising from the same residue grow more and more complicated. Instead of saying "one" or "someone," one of the manuscripts of the *Geoponicon* reads: "A virgin of marriageable age, barefoot, nude, wearing nothing about her loins, her hair hanging loose, holding a cock in her hands," *etc.* That gives another residue of our I-β2 variety (unusual things): one unusual thing, a virgin circling a field naked, is associated with an exceptional occurrence, the vanishing of the broom-rape. Note that she has to be of marriageable age—*ὥραν ἔχουσα γάμου*. If she were a child there would be nothing unusual in her going about naked.

factor in many cases; but in many others the reasons are either unknown or seem childish and extravagant.[1]

920. Resemblances appear in interesting ways in many other connexions. In Rome "the bride was girdled with a sash, which was loosed by the groom in the nuptial bed. The sash was made of sheep's wool, to the end that just as the wool when sheared in tufts is tangled and intertwined, so the husband might be bound and attached to the wife. The husband unties the Herculean knot in the sash as an act of good omen, that he may be as lucky in begetting offspring as was Hercules, who left seventy children." [1]

919 [1] Arnobius, *Disputationes adversus gentes,* VII, 19 (Orelli, p. 240; Bryce-Campbell, p. 326): " 'You are in error and apostasy (*erras et laberis*),' he said, 'for the reasons why female animals are sacrificed to female divinities and male to male are abstruse and recondite, lying beyond common knowledge.' " For the sacrifices of Aeneas, and the comment of Servius, *In Vergilii Aeneidem,* III, vv. 118-20, see above, § 192 [1]. Schoemann, *Griechische Alterthümer,* Vol. II, p. 208: "Goats were offered to Hera nowhere save in Sparta. Athena also disapproved of them and it was thought that her animosity came from the damage they did to olive-trees. [Derivation to explain a I-α residue.] For the same reason goats could not be taken to the Acropolis for purposes of sacrifice to any of the divinities who were neighbours of the tutelary goddess of the city. Dionysus must have reasoned the other way round [A common thing with derivations, one argument serving two opposite purposes.]; for he was supposed to take peculiar delight in offerings of he-goats in view of their ravages in the vineyards." Constant in all this the residue of combinations (I-α); variable, the reasonings that serve to logicalize the residue—the derivations. Daremberg-Saglio, *Dictionnaire, s.v. Sacrificium:* "As for the reasons given by the ancients for the preference or repugnance of this or that divinity for this or that victim, they are at times quite fatuous [residue I-α]. In any event they by no means derive from a single principle. At times it is a question of a mere play on words [residue I-γ]. Perch were offered to Hecate, says Apollodorus [*De diis,* XX, *Fragmenta,* 16 (p. 431)], and after him, Athenaeus, *Deipnosophistae,* VII, 92, *s.v. Mainides,* because the word for perch (τρίγλη) was associated with current epithets of the goddess: τρίμορφος, τριοδῖτις, τρίγληνος. The pig, suggests the Megarian of Aristophanes [*Archanenses,* v. 739], was a suitable victim for Aphrodite because its name, χοῖρος, was also the word for the female organ of sex. At other times the reason was sought in some resemblance more or less real between the temperaments of the god and the victim. . . . Now the alleged hostility of a god or goddess towards a certain species of animal is taken as a reason for sacrificing that species to them. Then again the same antipathy serves to prohibit such victims. . . . In sacrifices to the dead, the victim (when a victim was offered) seems ordinarily to have been a sheep; and the sheep was also the sacrifice for heroes, save in the case of warriors killed in battle. They were accorded heroic honours, with sacrifices of bulls (residue I-β1).

920 [1] Festus, *De verborum significatione,* III, *s.v. Cingulum* (London, Vol. I, pp. 156-57): *"Cingulo nova nupta praecingebatur quod vir in lecto solvebat, factum ex lana ovis, ut sicut illa in glomos sublata coniuncta inter se sit sic vir suus secum*

921. The I-β1 residue, combined with others from Class V (personal integrity), figures in a custom observed by Augustus in going begging once a year (opposites, contrast), and more generally in the various devices that were used for evading the "envy of the gods" (§ 1986).[1] It is present also in the complex of sentiments that leads people to treat inanimate objects as animate, and animals and things as if they were rational beings. In general it figures to a greater or lesser extent in the human inclination to reason by analogy (similars); and we shall therefore meet with it again when we come to derivations (§§ 1614 f.).

922. I-β2: *Unusual things and exceptional occurrences.* The instinctive feeling that rareties and exceptional happenings are connected with other rareties and exceptional happenings, or merely with things eagerly desired, serves also to sustain faith in the efficacy of such combinations. For the very reason that the things (occurrences) are unusual, the many proofs and counter-proofs that might show the fatuity of the belief are not provided. That fact, however, is not the cause of the belief, for observation proves that experiences to the contrary, even if exceedingly frequent, fail to shake faith in the combinations to any great extent, if at all. In Southern Italy many people wear horns on their watch-chains as infallible preventives against the evil eye, and experience has nothing whatever to do with the case.

923. The rarity of the object (occurrence) may be intrinsic or extrinsic, that is to say, it may belong to a class of objects (acts) that are rare in themselves, or the interest may derive from some accidental circumstance, even imaginary. Talismans and relics often belong to this latter category.[1]

cinctus vinctusque esset. Hunc Herculeaneo nodo vinctum vir solvit ominis gratia, ut sic ipse felix sit in suscipiendis liberis ut fuit Hercules qui septuaginta liberos reliquit."

921 [1] Suetonius, *Divus Augustus,* 91, 2: "He saw an apparition one night, and after that he went begging alms in public on a certain day every year, holding out cupped hands to those who offered coins." And *cf.* Dio Cassius, *Historia Romana,* LIV, 35, 3.

923 [1] Suetonius, *Nero,* 56: "Nero was seized by another superstition and clung to it most stubbornly. From a man of the people whom he did not know he had received an ordinary doll, such as a girl might use (*imagunculam puellarem*). He

924. Omens very often yield residues of the I-$\beta 2$ variety. They are often invented after the fact. Sometimes they are announced beforehand, and then some sort of verification is recognized. Expectation of an occurrence may even contribute to its happening. Omens derive their main appeal from belief in the efficacy of combinations (§§ 926 f.).

925. Suetonius never neglects to report the prodigies that presaged future ascents of Emperors to the throne and strange happenings that foretold their deaths. He always finds them in plenty. There is, for instance, the pretty story of the white hen that an eagle dropped into Livia's lap, Livia being Augustus's wife. The hen was holding a laurel-branch in its beak. There is no doubt about the unusualness of such a happening, and it naturally had to be associated with something equally extraordinary (§ 988). And that, in fact, was the case, at least in the fancy of the person who invented the story. Livia kept the hen and reared its chickens, and planted the sprig of laurel. The shoot grew into a tree and from the tree the Caesars cut the branches of which they made the crowns for their triumphs. Then it became customary to plant such branches all in the same place, and it was observed—such the value of experience [1] —that after the death of a Caesar, the laurel that he had planted withered away. During the last years of Nero the whole grove of laurels withered up to the very roots, and likewise all the descendants of the hen perished. All that, evidently, presaged the end of the

regarded it as a charm against plots on his life. Straightway a conspiracy chanced to be discovered, and he insisted on worshipping the image as a supreme divinity by triple sacrifices each day, trying to give the impression that he knew the future from warnings the doll gave him." The rarety in this case was the exceptional coincidence. In the following the object is rare in itself: Ollivier, *L'Empire libéral,* Vol. II, p. 55: "Among the effects left by his mother, Louis Napoleon [the future Napoleon III] found a variety of precious mementoes, one especially from which he could never be separated—'the talisman.' It was a jewel set with a piece of the True Cross, which had been found in Charlemagne's tomb about his neck and sent to Napoleon I at the time of the coronation. Great importance was attached to the possession of it in the family as a guarantee of divine protection. Josephine coaxed it from her husband with some difficulty and after the divorce she was not deprived of it. Eventually it went to Hortense."

925 [1] It is the experience of our theologians and metaphysicists nowadays; it yields exactly what has been put into it.

line of Caesars, which in fact became extinct in Nero.[2] Why should the birth of a colt from a mule necessarily presage some great event? One can find no other reason save that one rare event has to go with some other rare event. That particular omen among the Romans was adjudged baneful.[3] Just before the consul Lucius Cornelius Scipio set sail for Asia, the high-priests kept their eyes peeled for prodigies, and notable among them was the fact that a mule had had a colt.[4] Once upon a time a thunderbolt fell on the walls of Velitrae (Vellitri), and that incident was taken as a presage that a citizen of that city was to hold supreme power. Strong in that faith the Velitrians made war on the Romans, but with little success. "Not till years later did it become manifest that the presage had foretold the advent of Augustus," who came of a family of Velitrae.[5] That is one of the many prophecies—when they are not outright invention—that are not comprehended till after the fact (§ 1579).

Though Christians attribute everything to God, they often have their omens without reference, explicit at least, to divine interposition, so natural does it seem that rare things and exceptional occurrences should go together. The legend of Charlemagne records the "signs" that presaged his death. The Sun and the Moon were darkened, and the name of Charlemagne vanished of its own accord from the wall of a church that he had founded. No less than five such signs in all! [6]

925 [2] Suetonius, *Galba,* 1; Pliny, *Historia naturalis,* XV, 40 (Bostock-Riley, Vol. III, p. 336); Dio Cassius, *Historia Romana,* XLVIII, 52. Pliny and Dio do not mention any withering of the laurels. Pliny in fact says that some of them were still flourishing in his day.

925 [3] Pliny, *Ibid.,* VIII, 69: "Our annals record many instances of mules having colts, but it was taken to be a prodigy"—*i.e.,* in the bad sense. (Bostock-Riley, Vol. II, p. 325: "But such cases must be looked upon only as prodigies.")

925 [4] Livy, *Ab urbe condita,* XXXVII, 3.

925 [5] Suetonius, *Divus Augustus,* 94, 2.

925 [6] Pseudo-Turpin, *Les fais et les gestes le fort roy Charlemaine,* pp. 285-86: *"Plusieurs signes avindrent par trois ans devant qui apertement signifioient sa mort et son deffinement. Le premier fu que le soleil et la lune perdirent leur couleur naturelle par trois jours, et furent ainsi comme tous noirs, un pou avant ce qu'il moumst."* The fifth was that "one day while he was riding from one place to another on his horse, the sky suddenly darkened and a great sword of fire (*brandon*) waved across the heavens in front of him moving from right to left."

Taken as manifestations of divine activity presages and divination are derivations from I-β residues and more especially from those of the I-β2 species. Anything exceptional might correspond to the residue. Divine intervention was then introduced to explain the correspondence.

926. Constant over many centuries is the ascription of divine origins to heroes and great men. Every individual, be he real or imaginary, whose name appears at all prominently in history or legend owes his birth to some divine act, or it is at least attended by prodigies.[1] We must not confuse legends of divine origins with the fre-

926 [1] The conception of Buddha was attended by so many that it would be a long and not very profitable task to recount them even in brief proportion. Kern, *Histoire du bouddhisme,* Vol. I, pp. 23-24: The virtuous queen Maya dreamed that "the four divine sovereigns, the Cardinal Points, gathered her up with her bed and transported her to the Himalayas, where they set her down in the shade of a wide-spreading tree. . . . The Bodhisatva assumed the form of a white elephant, departed from the Golden Mount on which he dwelt, ascended the Mount of Silver, entered the Golden Grotto with a terrible thunder and, bearing a white water-lily in his trunk, marched thrice about the bed where Maya was resting, moving to the right as a sign of courtesy, opened the right side of the queen, and so entered her body. . . . At the moment of the Bodhisatva's conception in his mother's womb all nature was set in motion, and thirty-two presages were observed: an incomparable radiance encompassed the Universe. . . ." Latins do not indulge in these Oriental extravagances. Suetonius, on the authority of Asclepias Mendes, recounts the conception of Augustus by Atia as follows, *Divus Augustus,* 94, 4: "She had entered the temple of Apollo in the middle of the night to perform a sacrifice. Her litter was set on the floor and the other matrons went home (*domi irent:* also *dormirent:* went to sleep). She fell asleep. A serpent suddenly made its way to her side, and soon after departed. Awaking, she purified herself as was her custom after her husband's embrace. And at once on her body appeared a spot of the shape and colour of a serpent, and she could never remove it, and in view of it abstained from the public baths." Serpents, be it said in no disrespect to the reptile that tempted our Mother Eve, seem to have had a peculiar predilection for relations with women. One of them, whether on its own account or in behalf of Zeus, was responsible for Olympia's becoming the mother of Alexander the Great. Justin, *Historiae Philippicae,* XII, 16 (Clarke, p. 126): "The night in which his mother, Olympia, conceived him, she dreamed in her sleep that she lay with a huge serpent. Nor was the dream a mere illusion, for assuredly she was not fertilized by any mortal man." [So Pareto; literally: "She bore in her womb a work too great for human mortality."—A. L.] In XI, 11 (Clarke, p. 105), Justin tells how Alexander "hastened to the oracle of Jupiter Amon for light on his future and on his origin; for his mother had confessed to her husband Philip that 'she had conceived Alexander not of him but of a serpent of gigantic size.' Thereafter, being come almost to the end of his days, Philip proclaimed openly that 'her son was not his' and therefore divorced

quent cases where the appellative "divine" is bestowed on individuals merely to indicate their eminence in admirable, venerable, or excellent qualities—so Homer, *Odyssey,* XIV, v. 413, calls a swineherd divine (δῖος ὑφορβός).

Olympia as proven guilty of adultery." The legend grows and grows. Plutarch, *Alexander,* 2, 3-4 (Perrin, Vol. VII, pp. 227-29), relates that Philip saw a serpent near his sleeping wife (adding, 6, that according to one story Olympia kept tame serpents). Philip, he goes on, lost an eye, the eye "which he had applied to the chink in the door in order to see the god in the form of a serpent in embrace with his wife." [In reality Philip lost the eye at the siege of Methone.] [In reality, Plutarch (Clough, Vol. IV, pp. 3-4) merely records a prophecy that Philip *would* lose the eye.—A. L.] New embellishments finally evolve the story of Alexander's birth that is given by the Pseudo-Callisthenes, *Historia fabulosa Alexandri Magni,* I, 1-13 (Budge, pp. 1-13). It matters little for our purposes just what share in it is to be ascribed to naïve credulousness and what to sheer artifice, or whether there may have been some real basis for the legends, such as the fact that is vouched for by Lucian, *Pseudomantis,* 7 (Harmon, Vol. IV, p. 185), that Macedonian women often kept pet snakes. The mere fact that the legends existed, and more especially the fact that they met with a favourable reception, show that they corresponded to certain sentiments; and that is the one point we are concerned to establish. Here too and as usual, we get a nucleus with a fog of derivations extending around it. Publius Scipio, the first Africanus, also had a serpent for a father, an unusually big one, of course, and, of course also, divine: Livy, *Ab urbe condita,* XXVI, 19: Scipio's manner of living led to the belief that "he was a man of divine lineage, and so revived the story that was earlier told of Alexander the Great and was equally fatuous and fictional, that he was conceived of intercourse with a huge snake, and that the semblance of that prodigy [*i.e.,* something shaped like a snake] was time and again seen in his mother's bed, suddenly crawling away at the approach of human beings and vanishing from sight." And *cf.* Aulus Gellius, *Noctes Atticae,* VI, 1, 1-3. Servius Tullius could not be allowed to remain the son of a slave. Livy, *Ibid.,* I, 39, 5, assigns a less marvellous origin to that legendary character, suggesting that his mother was already with child by her husband, headman at Corniculum, at the time when she was made a prisoner. That is also the story told by Dionysius of Halicarnassus, *Antiquitates Romanae,* IV, 1 (Spelman, Vol. II, pp. 144-45). But for so great a man our present residue could be relied upon to provide something more and better. And in fact, Dionysius himself relates, IV, 2, that in the annals of Corniculum and in many Roman histories he has found another family-tree that smacks more of the legendary; and he tells a long story, which is later repeated by Ovid and Pliny, according to which Vulcan is to be held responsible for Servius Tullius and in a somewhat fantastic manner. Pliny, *Historia naturalis,* XXXVI, 70 (Bostock-Riley, Vol. VI, p. 384), tells the story as though he believed it, but robs Vulcan of the fatherhood and bestows it on the god of the hearth: "I must not omit one episode (*exemplum*) involving the hearth-fire that is famous in Roman letters. The story goes that while Tarquinius Priscus was on the throne, genitals of the male sex arose from the ashes in the flame of his hearth [*i.e.,* the sacred home-fire] and that the woman who was tending it, a slave, Ocresia, maid to queen Tanaquil, arose from her work with child. So was born Servius Tullius, who succeeded the Tarquin as king." Ovid,

In concrete cases of divine generations a number of residues figure. The central nucleus is made up of: (1) residues of group-persistence (Class II) whereby gods and spirits become projections of the human personality;[2] (2) sex residues (Class VI), that satisfy the

Fasti, VI, vv. 627-34, hands the paternity back to Vulcan, the latter functioning as in the miracle recounted by Pliny:

> *"Namque pater Tulli Vulcanus, Ocresia mater,*
> *praesignis facie Corniculana, fuit.*
> *Hanc secum Tanaquil sacris de more paratis*
> *jussit in ornatum fundere vina focum.*
> *Hic inter cineres obscaeni forma virilis*
> *aut fuit aut visa est—sed fuit illa magis.*
> *Iussa loco captiva fovet: conceptus ab illa*
> *Servius a coelo semina gentis habet."*

("Tully's father was Vulcan and his mother, Ocresia, a beautiful girl from Corniculum. Having prepared for the rites according to custom, Tanaquil bade her assist in pouring the wine upon the hearth, which had been adorned for the ceremonies. There among the ashes an unsightly shape of male form was visible—or they thought it was (and my belief is that it was). At the command of her mistress, the slave Ocresia leaned upon the hearth, and since she there became his mother, Servius has his lineage of heaven.") Whatever Ovid's inner thought, he leaves the impression (*sed fuit illa magis*) of believing that it was not an illusion on the part of Ocresia. Arnobius, *Disputationes adversus gentes,* V, 18 (Bryce-Campbell, pp. 241-42), is impressed only with the obscenity of the story and charges it to the account of the pagans. Divine origins may be found even for philosophers when they are very very great. Origen says, *Contra Celsum,* I (Augsburg, p. 30): "Some writers—not in ancient or heroic histories, but in books dealing with matters of very recent date—have seen fit to assert as a fact altogether possible that Plato was born of his mother Amphiction [Perictione], . . . Ariston [her husband] having been forbidden to have knowledge of her until she should have borne fruit of Apollo. But such are mere tales born of a belief that men esteemed superior to others in wisdom must have sprung of some divine seed, as would befit natures greater than human." And so it is, but without going such a long way round. It is simply because in the human mind sublime things are associated with sublime things and bad things with bad.

926 [2] Grote, *History of Greece,* Vol. I, pp. 80-81: "And thus the genealogy was made to satisfy at once the appetite of the Greeks for romantic adventure, and their demand for an unbroken line of filiation between themselves and the gods. The eponymous personage, from whom the community derive their name, is sometimes the begotten son of the local god, sometimes an indigenous man sprung from the earth, which is indeed itself divinized. It will be seen from the mere description of these genealogies that they included elements human and historical, as well as elements divine and extra-historical. . . . In the point of view of the Greeks . . . not only all the members were alike real, but the gods and heroes at the commencement were in a certain sense the most real; at least, they were the most esteemed and indispensable of all."

human hankering to dwell on procreative acts; (3) residues of the variety here in hand (I-β2) whereby a thing in itself remarkable must have a remarkable origin—and that is achieved in two ways: either by going back from a real thing to an imaginary origin, or by coming down from an imaginary origin to a thing equally imaginary.

927. Divine generations fall into two groups: 1. Divine beings unite with other divine beings and produce a divine progeny. Such the source of the many theogonies current among different peoples. This class, further, has a number of appendages. Instead of being strictly divine the entities may be merely spiritual; or they may so far depart from personification as to become mere metaphysical abstractions (§§ 1070 f.). In another direction, another residue of our present variety (I-β2) also comes into play. If divine procreation is the rule, the unborn one becomes the exceptional being, the eternal, "increate" being, and so too the person with one parent only, such as Minerva, engendered of Jupiter without female cooperation, or Vulcan born agamogenetically of Juno.[1] 2. Divinities unite with human beings or, very rarely, with animals. Unions of gods and women are more frequent among our Western races than unions of female divinities with men; and that because the myths were

927 [1] Ovid, *Fasti*, V, vv. 231-32:

"Sancta Iovem Iuno, nata sine matre Minerva,
officio doluit non eguisse suo."

("On the birth of Minerva motherless, holy Juno complained of Jove that he had not done his duty by her.") Flora instructs her as to how she may become a mother independently of a male, and tells of a flower someone had given her, *Ibid.*, vv. 253-56:

"Qui dabat, 'Hoc,' dixit, 'sterilem quoque tange iuvencam—
mater erit. Tetigi. Nec mora mater erat.'
Protinus haerentem decerpsi pollice florem:
Tangitur—et tacto concipit illa sinu!"

("He who gave it to me said: 'Touch a fallow heifer with this flower and she will bear a calf. I touched her, and in a trice she was a mother.' I plucked the clinging flower in my fingers forthwith and touched her [Juno], and at the touch on her body she conceived.") The myth of Hephaestus (Vulcan) goes back as far as Hesiod, *Theogonia*, v. 927; but Homer, *Iliad*, I, vv. 572, 578, makes him a son of Zeus and Hera. Apollodorus, *Bibliotheca*, I, 3, 5 (Frazer, Vol. I, p. 21), follows Hesiod: "Hera bore Hephaestus without embrace."

composed chiefly by men among peoples where the patriarchal family prevailed. So only can we account for the fact that in the Bible male angels fall enamoured of the daughters of men, never female angels of the sons of men.[2] This group like the preceding has its variations and postscripts, till step by step one gets to the point where the wind is fertilizing mares and, for that matter, women.[3] Here again I-β2 residues pile up one on the other. Procreations by divine commerce with human beings becoming common-

927 [2] Gen. 6:1-4: "And it came to pass, when men began to multiply on the face of the earth, and daughters were born unto them, that the sons of God saw the daughters of men that they were fair; and they took them wives of all which they chose. . . . There were giants in the earth in those days; and also after that, when the sons of God came in unto the daughters of men, and they bare children to them, the same became mighty men which were of old, men of renown." Kahn, *La Bible . . . traduite par les membres du rabbinat français,* Vol. I, p. 6: "Now when men had begun to multiply upon the earth and daughters were born to them, the sons of divine lineage found that the daughters of men were beautiful and chose as their wives such as were pleasing in their sight." In his *Quaestiones sive traditiones hebraicae in Genesim* (*Opera,* Vol. III, pp. 947-48) St. Jerome remarks (Gen. 6:2) ("saw the daughters of men that they were fair"): "The Hebrew word *eloim* is both singular and plural (*communis est numeri*) and God and gods may of course be rendered by the same word. That is why Aquila [a reviewer of the Septuagint] made bold to say 'sons of gods' in the plural, meaning divine holy creatures, in other words, angels."

927 [3] In his edition of Ovid, Vol. VIII, pp. 327-28, Panckoucke quotes a note of Saintange on *Fasti,* V, vv. 231-56 (see above, § 927 [1]): "If one feels any temptation to ridicule the mythical tale that Ovid has handed down to us, one should remember that in the eighteenth century a strait-laced English physician published a pamphlet called *Lucina sine concubitu* or *Lucina Freed from the Laws of Competition,* which was designed to show that a woman may conceive and bear offspring apart from any male commerce, like the mares in Virgil's *Georgics,* III, vv. 265-283, which were fertilized by no other stallion than the west wind—Zephyr. . . . There are women in fact who have found the charm of the west wind more delectable than any vulgar pleasure; as witness a formal decision of the superior court (Parlement) of Grenoble, Feb. 13, 1637, declaring legitimate a son born to a certain Mme. d'Aiguemère in the absence of her husband. . . . [The woman testified that] she had been sleeping on a summer's night with the windows of her room open to the west, and her coverlets in some disarray. She had dreamed that her husband had returned from Germany and been with her. She had been exposed to the west wind and had breathed deeply of it." Burette adds, and he seems not to be jesting: "Certainly there are occult mysterious forces in nature of which science has not yet mastered the secret. There are powers in the human imagination to which the wonders of magnetism have strikingly called attention." The decree of Grenoble was of 1637; but Panckoucke's edition of Ovid appeared in the year of grace 1835.

Pliny, *Historia naturalis,* VIII, 67 (Bostock-Riley, Vol. VI, p. 322): "It is well

place, other exceptional circumstances supervene. It is not enough that a man have a god for a father: he must also have a virgin mother, and bearing the child she still remains a virgin. It is not enough that Zeus engender Hercules: he must devote three nights to the task. Three is generally, though not exclusively, specified as the number of nights. In that a sacred-number residue, the three superstition, figures (§ 960 [8]). This whole process is just a particular case of a fact that is general: the re-enforcement of the principal residues in a legend by a cumulation of secondary residues.[4]

known that in Lusitania, near the city of Olysipo [Lisbon] on the Tagus, mares standing against the west wind (Favonius) conceive thereof and become gravid. The colts so born are very swift of foot but live not longer than three years." Aristotle, *Historia animalium,* VI, 18 (Thompson, p. 572a), records the belief that mares may be fertilized by a wind, but refuses to go bond for the fact. Varro, *De re rustica,* II, 2, 19 (Leipzig, p. 211; Harrison, pp. 191-92), notes the same thing as true of hens and says that the fact is well known: "In this matter of conception there is something incredible in Spain, though it is true enough. On the sea-coast in Lusitania, in the neighbourhood of the town of Olysippo and Mount Tagrus, mares at certain times are fertilized by the wind, just as hens are in our part of the world, their eggs being known as *ὑπηνέμια* ("wind-eggs"). However, the colts born of such mares never live longer than three years." Pausanias, *Periegesis,* VII, *Achaia,* 17, 9-14, gives a detailed account of the birth of the god Attis. To begin with, and making a long story very short, Agdistis was born of Zeus in an unusual manner, springing from seed that Zeus had dropped on the ground. Eventually from a part of the body of Agdistis that had been cut off and thrown away an almond-tree sprouted. Finally, a daughter of the river Sangarius placed some almonds from the tree in her corsage. They mysteriously vanished, and she gave birth to Attis. Here we get a series of strange procreations and strange details leading up to a single birth. There are many other such examples. The literature of divine procreation could be quoted to indefinite lengths. All of the stories involve a nucleus of residues with a nebula of poetic, or merely fantastic, embellishments gathering about it.

927 [4] As a descendant of Perseus, too, Alcmene was of Jovian lineage. According to Apollodorus, *Bibliotheca,* II, 4, 6 (Frazer, Vol. I, pp. 171-73), Electryon, Alcmene's father, gave her to Amphitryon along with his kingdom, but stipulating that Amphitryon should keep her virgin until Electryon's return from an expedition on which he was about to set out against the Teleboans. Electryon dying, Amphitryon himself, after various adventures, undertook the expedition against the Teleboans. Zeus outstripped him on his way home, assumed the guise of Amphitryon to make his way into his house and enjoyed Alcmene for a night, tripling it [in length] (*καὶ τὴν μίαν τριπλασιάσας νύκτα*). That was why Lycophron, *Cassandra,* v. 33 (Mair, pp. 496-97), calls Heracles the "lion of the three nights." Apollodorus, *Epitome,* 23 (Frazer, Vol. I, p. 172, note): ". . . *τὴν μίαν νύκτα πενταπλασιάσας ἢ κατά τινας τριπλασιάσας* (quintupling or, according to others, tripling the one night)." Palladas, *Greek Anthology,* IX, 441 (Paton, Vol. III, pp. 246-47), applies

As regards early classical antiquity, it would be easier to give the list of famous persons of human origin than those of divine. The divine seems actually to be the normal rule. Proof of the enduring permanence of the residue over long periods of time is the fact that in deference to it the Christians also made extensive use of legends about unions of spiritual beings with women in the genealogies of exceptional persons, merely substituting Christian demons for the pagan gods. To tell the full truth, the service of devils for purposes of generation has been abused rather than used by the Christian peoples. Merlin the magician was a child of the Devil, and there

the epithet τρισέληνος ("three-mooned," *i.e.*, "three-nighted") to Heracles. Statius, *Thebaid*, XII, v. 299 (Juno addressing the Moon):

> *"Da mihi poscenti munus breve, Cynthia, si quis*
> *est Iunonis honos: certe Iovis improba iussu*
> *ternoctem Herculeam: veteres sed mitto querelas."*

("Give me a brief favour, O Cynthia, I beg you, if you have any regard for Juno! Surely that matter of the Herculean thri-night at the bidding of Jupiter was not to your credit, but we can let bygones be bygones.") Commenting on the lines, Luctatius Placidus explains (Leyden, p. 781): "That oncoming day might not cut his pleasure short, Jupiter ordained that the night be lengthened thrice, the Moon traversing her course three times. It is said that Hercules was born of that union with Alcmene. Very aptly he [Statius] says 'Herculean thri-night' for the night on which Hercules was conceived." Diodorus Siculus brings out the residue very clearly, *Bibliotheca historica*, IV, 9, 2-3 (Booth, Vol. I, p. 225): "When Zeus deceived Alcmene he made a night of triple length, foreshowing by the labour spent in the procreation how great the might of the progeny was to be." Diodorus further notes that Zeus sought Alcmene not of lecherous desire, but for the purpose of begetting a son. Servius, *In Vergilii Aeneidem*, VIII, v. 103 (Thilo-Hagen, Vol. II, p. 213): "Amphitryon was king of Thebes. Jupiter fell enamoured of his wife Alcmene, and while he was absent at the siege of the town of Oechalia, possessed her for a night which he tripled in length. Alcmene thereupon gave birth to two sons, the one by Jove, Hercules, the other, Iphiclus, by her husband." For Iphiclus less effort was required than for Hercules. The scholiast of the *Iliad*, XIV, v. 323 (Dindorf, Vol. II, pp. 50-51), remarks that Amphitryon also begat a son by Alcmene on the same night as Zeus, and Apollodorus makes Iphiclus the junior of Hercules by one night. Latin writers more especially limit the conception of Hercules to two nights instead of three: *e.g.*, Ovid, *Amores*, I, 13, vv. 45-46; Propertius, *Elegiae*, II, 22, vv. 25-26; Martianus Capella, *De Nuptiis inter Mercurium et Philologiam*, II, 157 (Berne, p. 64); Seneca, *Agamemnon*, vv. 814-15. St. Jerome also mentions two nights: *Adversus Vigilantium*, X (*Opera*, Vol. II, p. 348; Schaff-Wace, p. 421): "Jupiter spent two nights in adultery with Alcmene that Hercules might be born a man of great strength." And see Hyginus, *Fabulae*, XXIX, *Alcumena*. But on the whole the Church Fathers are much more generous, allowing Zeus nine nights for his escapade: *e.g.*, Clement

have been those to ascribe a similar parentage to Luther. Nowadays regard for great men has fallen off considerably and such genealogies are things of the past.[5] [6] (For footnote 6 see page 551.)

928. Legends are first built up by residues and then explained by derivations. So long as the divine or merely spiritual entity which is brought into being by group-persistence (Class II) remains not far removed from its human origin, no difficulty is experienced in conceiving its copulation with other beings of its own kind or with human beings. From that trunk a branch shoots off which also occasions no great difficulties: divine beings are more or less transformed

of Alexandria, *Protrepticus* (*Exhortation to the Greeks*), II, 28 (Butterworth, pp. 67-69). Says Arnobius, *Disputationes adversus gentes,* IV, 26 (Bryce-Campbell, pp. 208-09): "Are you not uncomplimentary to your Jupiter, king of the world? . . . It is you who aver that he spent nine continuous nights with Alcmene. . . . And I must say you gained a precious deal if you have been blessed with a god, Hercules, who at such lubricious business outstrips a father who took nine nights to compile, compress, compound, an infant and then hardly had enough!" And *cf.* St. Cyril, *Contra impium Julianum,* VI (*Opera,* Vol. IX, p. 799).

927 [5] As for the theoretical question, see Del Rio, *Disquisitiones magicae,* II, 15 (Louvain, Vol. I, p. 180; Cologne, pp. 160-61): "We assert therefore that at times it is quite possible for offspring to result from commerce of a devil (*incubi*) with a woman, though in such cases the real father of the child would not be the demon but the man of whose seed the demon has made wicked abuse. This has been denied by Plutarch in his *Numa* [4] . . . but it is affirmed by the Egyptians, according to Plutarch, and by the Scholastics as a whole—and they were excellent philosophers. . . . And then we have instances in great numbers reported now by one writer, now by another, and if they are true they are doubtless to be accounted for on the hypothesis above. Antiquity offers its demigods, its Herculeses, its Sarpedons, its Aeneases, its Servius Tulliuses; England her Merlin, Pannonia her Huns, born of Arluns [*Arlunis*], Gothic witches, and fauns . . . nor is there any lack of people to place Luther in this same class. [See our note next following.] Six years ago, in the leading city of Brabant [Brussels] a woman was punished for having had a child by the Devil. Coming down to the present time, Louis Molina, one of the theologians of our Society, has stated that the thing has occurred, and many other writers of different nationalities have corroborated him, citing examples." For the "Huns" of Pannonia, *cf.* Jornandes, *De rebus Gothorum,* 24, 8 (p. 67): "Filimer, King of the Goths . . . who also invaded Scythia with his hordes, found among his people certain females, witches, whom he himself designated in his own tongue as 'Aliorumnas.' Suspecting them, he drove them in a body from his midst (*de medio sui*), and forced them to live in out-of-the-way parts of the land, keeping far from his soldiers. Unclean spirits wandering through the desert places laid eyes on them and mingled with them freely in carnal commerce, whence they brought forth that very fierce race of people." A people so savage and so hated had to have had some such origin. St. Augustine, good soul, knows quite as much about demoniacal gen-

into metaphysical abstractions that copulate with one another. Group-persistence facilitates the transition from cases where, for instance, heat and damp combine to produce grain, to other cases in which metaphysical principles procreate real or imaginary beings. But along another branch the difficulties seem rather to increase, in the case, namely, where the spiritual creatures remain personifica-

eration as he does about the antipodes and other such matters (§ 1438). Says he, *De civitate Dei,* XV, 23: "It is a matter of general knowledge, and many people claim to know of experience or to have heard from trustworthy persons who have had the experience, that sylvans and fauns, which are commonly called *incubi,* have often appeared in their wickedness to women and sought and consummated intercourse with them. Many persons, also, and of such merits that it would be the part of impudence [Just so: nothing less than impudence!] to dispute them, assert that certain demons which the Gauls call 'Dusii' attempt such impurity assiduously [Healy: "tempt others to impurity"] and succeed in it." Bodin inquires, *De la démonomanie,* II, 7, "Whether witches have carnal commerce with devils." "I have read," he says, "extracts from the examinations of the witches at Longny-en-Potez, who, I may add, were burned alive, with which Lawyer Adrian de Fer, Lieutenant-General at Laon, has supplied me. I will introduce some of their confessions here in regard to this matter. . . . [A number of confessions of women to carnal knowledge of the Devil follow.] Similarly we read in Meyer's book, XVI . . . that in the year 1459 large numbers of men and women were burned in the city of Arras, on mutual accusations, and on their own confessions, that they had been transported at night to 'dances' and had there had commerce with the devils. . . . Jacob Sprenger and his four colleagues on the Inquisition on witchcraft write that they have prosecuted no end of witches and executed very large numbers of them in Germany and that all of them in general and without exception confessed that the Devil had had criminal intercourse with them. . . . Henry de Coulongne . . . says that nothing is more commonly known in Germany, and not only in Germany, it being notorious all through Greece and Italy [*i.e.,* ancient Greece and Rome]; for fauns, satyrs, sylvans, are nothing but demons and evil spirits. Proverbially the word 'satyrize' means 'to act the [licentious] rogue.' . . . We read, further, in the history of St. Bernard, that there was once a witch who was regularly attended by the Devil at her husband's side without his perceiving it. The question as to whether such copulation be possible, and notably as to whether anything can come of it, was debated before the Emperor Sigismund; and it was decided, against the brief of Cassianus, that such copulation was possible, and conception likewise. . . . We also read in the *Histories of the West Indies,* Bk. I, Chap. XXVII, that those peoples took it as a fact that their god, Cocoto, cohabited with women, the gods of those countries being nothing but devils." For the remainder of the passage see § 928 [1]. A modern writer, in a book published in the year of grace 1864, refers to and believes in the endless amount of trash that has been concocted on the subject of generation by demons and concludes that the objective fact of intercourse between demons and human females cannot be denied: Des Mousseaux, *Les hauts phénomènes de la magie,* p. 297: " 'To deny these strange facts,' says a distinguished

tions and the gap between them and human beings widens. The Greeks did not feel in the least called upon to decide just how the seed of Zeus managed to fertilize the many women of whom he had carnal knowledge; whereas the Christians felt an irresistible compulsion to solve that problem in the case of relations between devils and women.[1]

jurist of unquestioned integrity [In a note: "A. de Gasparin, *Surnaturel,* Vol. II, p. 154." Another fine specimen!], the learned and widely experienced De Lancre [who caused the deaths of hundreds of men and women on charges of witchcraft] 'would mean to undo what all antiquity and *our own* court *procedures* [italics Mousseaux's] have shown.' And I repeat that it would also mean undoing what flesh and blood have shown of old and *in our own day,* what medical examination and theological science have established, each by its own peculiar methods." A fine example of the experimental value of that universal consensus which has of late been transfigured into universal suffrage. It may be, of course, that this latter-day divinity is immune to the blunders into which its predecessor was forever stumbling!

927 [6] For the genealogy of Luther, see Del Rio, *Op. cit.,* II, 15 (Louvain, Vol. I, p. 180; Cologne, p. 161) and *cf.* § 927 [5] above. Del Rio quotes Simon Fontaine, *Historia ecclesiastica nostri temporis* [For Pareto's strange title see Index.—A. L.]. It was not enough that the Devil should have figured in the birth of Luther; he also had to have a hand in his death. Del Rio himself writes, *Ibid.,* III, 1, 7 (Louvain, Vol. II, p. 76; Cologne, p. 429): "It was indubitably observed [at the age-old refuge for the insane] at Gheel [Geila] in the Brabant that the demons left the victims they obsessed and flew to Luther's funeral." Luther many times averred during his lifetime that he had seen devils. There is nothing strange therefore in the attendance of those estimable creatures at his funeral. In his *Histoires disputes et discours,* III, 25 (Vol. I, pp. 418-20), Weier tells a long story about the diabolical conception of Luther and then remarks: "The Catholic history of the state of religion in our time, written in French by a certain S. Fontaines, doctor in theology, says that an opinion which appears in print in many books is well founded, and to wit, that Marguerite, Luther's mother, conceived him of the Devil, who had had her company before that at a time when she was not married to John Luther." Maimbourg feels called upon to refute these fabrications, *Histoire du Luthéranisme,* Vol. I, pp. 22-24: "Luther was born at Islebe [Eisleben], a town in the county of Mansfeld, in the year 1483, and not of a devil (*incube*) as some have written without shadow of truth in order to whet the hatred against him, but the way other men are born; and that fact was never questioned until after he turned heretic."

928 [1] The question as to whether and how demons could fertilize women was answered in various senses by the Fathers of the Church. St. Thomas disserts learnedly on the point in the *Summa theologiae,* I[a], *qu.* 51, *art.* 3 (*Opera,* Vol. V, p. 19): "If, however, offspring sometimes results from intercourse with demons, the fact is due not to any seed deriving from them or from the bodies they assume but through the seed of some man, which has been assumed for that purpose (*ad hoc acceptum*), the same demon first becoming a woman to a man and then a man to a woman (*utpote quod idem daemon qui est succubus ad virum fiat incubus ad mulierem*), just as they take up the seed of other things for purposes of propagating those

Anti-clericals condemn the Christian religion on the basis of these absurd stories. But Christianity did not invent them, it inherited them from antiquity; and after all they are not more extravagant than others that are still enjoying wide currency. Judged by strictly logico-experimental standards, a person believing in the dogmas of universal suffrage may just as well believe in the divine origins of heroes, there being no great difference in the intellectual effort required for adopting either position. From the standpoint of social utility both those ancient absurdities and their modern counterparts may have had or may have a utility great, small, zero, zero minus. Nothing can be said on that point *a priori*. It all depends on times, places, circumstances.

929. I-$\beta 3$: *Objects and occurrences inspiring awe or terror*. This residue appears almost always by itself in certain situations of which the following is typical. Speaking of the Cataline affair, Sallust relates, *Bellum Catilinae,* XXII: "There were those at the time who said that after Catiline had finished his address he pressed his comrades in crime to an oath, and passed around bowls of human blood mixed with wine, whereof after they all had tasted, with imprecations upon traitors, as is the custom in solemn sacrifices, he made known his design to them, saying that he had done as he had to

things, as Augustine says; with the result that the child that is born is not the child of the demon but of the man whose seed has been utilized." The passage of St. Augustine alluded to, *De Trinitate,* III, 8-9 (*Opera,* Vol. VIII, pp. 875-79; *Works,* Vol. VII, pp. 90-96), is full of interesting information—among other things: "Bees certainly do not conceive the seed of their offspring through copulation, but seem to find it scattered about on the ground and collect it in their mouths." Continuing the Bodin quotation in our § 927 [5], *De la démonomanie,* II, 7: "The Doctors are not in agreement on the point, some of them holding that the devils called 'hyphialtes' or 'succubi' [first] receive seed from men and [then] utilize it with women as 'ephialtes' or 'incubi,' as Thomas Aquinas says—a thing very hard to believe. In any event, Sprenger writes that the Germans, who have had the most experience with witchcraft, having had sorcerers from most ancient times and in greater numbers than people in other countries, hold that such copulation at times results in children who are called *Vechselkind* [*sic*], or 'changelings.' They are heavier than other children and are always lean, and they will suckle three nurses dry without growing any fatter. The others are devils in the guise of children; and they copulate with nurses that are witches and oftentimes [vanish] without one's ever knowing what becomes of them."

the end that each having such a great crime to the charge of the other, they would be the less likely to betray one another. Some hold that these and many other stories were invented by certain individuals who thought to mitigate the unpopularity that later arose against Cicero by stressing the enormity of the crime of the men who had been punished."[1] Whether this story be true or a fabrication, the fact of the association of two terrible things remains: a drinking of human blood and a conspiracy to destroy the Roman Republic. This residue also appears in certain cases where human sacrifices are substituted for animal sacrifices. Animals will do under ordinary circumstances. Human sacrifices come to the rescue in extraordinary, terrifying situations.

The oath of Catiline and his accomplices is not reported in the same way by all historians; but whatever the form, the same residue transpires. Of Catiline and his accomplices both Plutarch says, *Cicero,* X, 3 (Perrin, Vol. VII, p. 107): "To bind themselves mutually by oath, they killed a man and tasted of his flesh." Says Dio Cassius of Catiline alone, *Historia Romana,* XXXVII, 30: "He killed a boy and took an oath on his entrails; then both he and the other conspirators confirmed the oath, their hands on the entrails."[2] We saw the working of this same residue in the human sacrifices that were offered in Rome after the defeat at Cannae (§ 758). Dio Cassius, *Historia Romana,* XLIII, 24, tells how Caesar's soldiers mu-

929 [1] Simpler the account of Florus, *Epitoma de Tito Livio,* II, 12, 3-5 (IV, 1, 3-5; Forster, p. 263): "A pledge of comradeship in conspiracy was also taken: human blood was passed around in cups and drunk. The greatest of crimes, had not the crime for which they drank been greater!" The last sentence formulates the ungarnished residue.

929 [2] The exact meaning of Dio's text has been disputed. It reads: *Παῖδα γάρ τινα καταθύσας καὶ ἐπὶ τῶν σπλάγχνων αὐτοῦ τὰ ὅρκια ποιήσας, ἔπειτα ἐσπλάγχνευσεν αὐτὰ μετὰ τῶν ἄλλων.* Gros, in the notes to his French translation of Dio, Vol. III, p. 219, remarks very soundly on the words *ἔπειτα ἐσπλάγχνευσεν*: "Xylander's rendering, 'he then tasted of them in company with the others,' has been repeated by Reimar and Sturz, by Wagner and Tafel. But that is not the meaning of *ἐσπλάγχνευσεν*, as Mérimée well points out in a note to his *Histoire de la conjuration de Catiline,* p. 113. The true meaning was indicated by Henri Étienne: *Σπλαγχνεύω*: 'I take these entrails in hand and touch them,' that is, as an oath binding conspirators in a plot." *Cf.* Duncan, *Novum lexicon Graecum, s.v.;* Eustathius, *Commentarii ad Homeri Iliadem,* Vol. I, p. 111 (*Iliad,* I, v. 464).

tinied because they had not received their wages, Caesar having spent all his money on certain games. Caesar seized one of the mutineers and had him put to death. "So he," says Dio, "was punished for the reason stated [as a mutineer]. But two other men were slain in guise of a sacrifice. The reason for that I could not imagine." The reason is to be sought, in part at least, in the residue here in question. The crime of the mutineers seemed an unheard-of thing, and could be expiated only in some terrible manner. Doubtless logical pretexts for justifying the sacrifice were afterward evolved in plenty.[3]

930. And just so the *ver sacrum* of the Romans. In ordinary times it was sufficient to promise the gods animal sacrifices, games, temples, a tithe of the war-booty, and so on. But when some extraordinary, some very critical, situation arose, the gods were promised all the living creatures that should be born during a specified spring season. It would seem that in remote ages the Italic peoples included human beings among the creatures in question, but in historical times the Romans made exceptions of children.[1] A *ver sacrum* was

929 [3] Marquardt, *Römische Staatsverwaltung: Sacralwesen,* p. 254, develops one such pretext: "Caesar had one of the mutineers put to death. Two others were sacrificed in the Campus Martius by the pontiffs, assisted by the *flamen* of Mars, and their heads were exposed at the Regia [headquarters of the state religion]. If the facts were really as reported, the sacrifice celebrated on that occasion was a *piaculum,* or atonement, necessitated by the selfish opposition of the soldiers to the offering to the gods of the sacrifices and thanksgivings due them. But why should the *piaculum* take the form of a human sacrifice? That is the surprising thing, in Caesar's time, whatever one may otherwise think of human sacrifices in Rome." The answer to Marquardt's question is simple. Whether the sacrifice was or was not a *piaculum,* whether the story be true or a fabrication, those who ordered the men slain or those who invented the story felt the appropriateness of matching with some terrifying act a case of insubordination on the part of Caesar's soldiers, who owed him such great gratitude.

930 [1] Festus, *De verborum significatione,* XIX-XX, *s.v. Ver sacrum* (London, Vol. III, p. 1002): "The Italians had the custom of vowing the 'sacred spring.' Under pressure of great perils they took a vow to sacrifice such living creatures as should be born among them during the spring season next ensuing. But since it seemed a cruel thing to slaughter innocent boys and girls, they waited till they grew up (*perductos in adultam aetatem*), then veiled them, and banished them across the borders." And *cf. Ibid.,* XI, *s.v. Mamertini* (London, Vol. I, pp. 378-79, and again with variants in a *Fragmentum,* Vol. III, pp. 1031-32); Strabo, *Geographica,* V, 4, 12 (Jones, Vol. II, p. 465); Dionysius of Halicarnassus, *Antiquitates Romanae,* I,

pledged, for instance, in the days when Rome was being hard pressed by Hannibal.[2] The contract with the gods was drawn up with the minute formalistic definiteness characteristic of the Roman People (§§ 220 f.).[3] The gods kept their compact loyally, but the Romans renegued. Not till twenty-one years later did they make up their minds to fulfil their vow,[4] and even then they did not comply with it very strictly, so that the sacrifices had to be repeated again.[5]

931. The same residue recurs in the sacrifices of children that are connected with certain rites of magic. Well known the allusions that Horace, *Epoda,* 5 (Canidia's incantation), and Juvenal make to such sacrifices.[1] In Europe accusations, true or false, in the premises, are frequent down into the seventeenth century. A child sac-

16 (Spelman, Vol. I, p. 38); Servius, *In Vergilii Aeneidem,* VII, v. 796 (Thilo-Hagen, Vol. II, p. 196); Nonius Marcellus, *De compendiosa doctrina,* 12 (Mercier, p. 522).

930 [2] Livy, *Ab urbe condita,* XXII, 9, 10; 10, 1.

930 [3] With what ingenious circumspection the compact was drawn is evident from some of the terms as given by Livy. It is a question of the animals that are being kept for sacrifice: "If an animal being kept for sacrifice (*quod fieri oportebit*) shall die, it shall be profane [not available for sacrifice] but no defilement shall result. If one shall be accidentally maimed or killed, no evasion shall stand. If one shall be stolen, no defilement shall result to the Roman People or to the individual robbed. If a sacrifice shall unknowingly be offered on a 'black day,' it shall stand as valid."

930 [4] [Pareto seems not to notice that according to the passage in Festus, which he read in Latin, the twenty-one years' delay would be the time required for the children born during the *ver sacrum* to grow up.—A. L.]

930 [5] Livy, *Op. cit.,* XXXIII, 44; XXXIV, 44.

931 [1] Juvenal, *Saturae,* VI, vv. 551-52:

> *"Pectora pullorum rimabitur, exta catelli*
> *interdum et pueri—faciet quod deferat ipse."*

("He will probe the breasts of a chicken, the entrails of a pup or even of a child—he will do things of which only he could tell.") Another allusion can be found in Cicero, *In Publium Vatinium,* 6, 14: "What depravity was ever so great in you, what madness so extravagant, that you should ever have undertaken such unheard-of, such criminal rites, as to evoke souls from the other world, and sacrifice to the dead with the entrails of boys?" And *cf.* Quintilian, *Declamationes,* 8 (*Gemini languentes*) (Leyden, pp. 103-19); Lucan, *Pharsalia,* VI, v. 558; Lampridius, *Antoninus Heliogabalus,* 8 (Magie, Vol. II, pp. 121-23); Eusebius, *Historia ecclesiastica,* VIII, 14, 5 (Lake, Vol. II, pp. 304-05); IX, 9, 3 (Lake, Vol. II, pp. 358-59); *Idem, De vita Imperatoris Constantini,* I, 36 (English, p. 492); Ammianus Marcellinus, *Res gestae,* XXIX, 2, 17; Theodoret, *Ecclesiastica historia,* III, 21 (*Opera,* Vol. III, p. 1119; Jackson, p. 106).

rifice seems to have been performed in behalf of Madame de Montespan in her efforts to retain the affections of Louis XIV.[2]

932. I-β4: *Felicitous state associated with good things; infelicitous state, with bad.* When a given state *A* is considered a happy one, there is an inclination to associate anything that is deemed good with it. When a state *B* is considered bad, the tendency is to associate all bad things with it. This residue often goes in company with another residue from Class II (group-persistences). So we get a nucleus, with many notions of good or evil things clustering about it, and so, by a process of abstraction, the way is opened for a personification of the whole nebulous complex whereby it becomes an entity by itself, first existing subjectively in the minds of people, but eventually by the usual procedure (§§ 94 f.) acquiring an objective existence.[1] [2]

933. For a long time in Europe everything good was placed under the aegis of the "wisdom of the forefathers." Nowadays everything

931 [2] Funck-Brentano, *Le drame des poisons,* pp. 171-72: "On the day fixed, they met at Villebousin: Mme. de Montespan, the Abbé Guibourg, Leroy, a 'lady of high rank,' who was certainly Mlle. Desœillets, and an unidentified person said to have been a representative of the Archbishop of Sens. In the chapel of the château the priest said a mass over the body of the favourite, who lay naked on the altar. At consecration, he chanted the formula of conjuration, the text of which he later surrendered to the Commissioners of the Chamber: 'Astaroth, Asmodea, princes of friendship, I conjure you to accept the sacrifice I here offer of this child [in exchange] for the things which I ask of you, namely, that the favour of the King and the Dauphin, my lord, be continued unto me and honoured [recognized] by the princes and princesses of the Court, so that nothing shall be denied me of what I shall ask of the King in behalf of my relatives and servitors.' According to Reynie, Guibourg bought the child who was sacrificed at the mass for £1—15 francs in our money. . . . The details of the mass were divulged by Guibourg, and for that matter corroborated by the testimony of Madame de Chanfrain, his mistress. The second mass celebrated over the body of Madame de Montespan took place two or three weeks after the first. . . . The . . . third was held in a house in Paris."

932 [1] For instance, "Progress": Georges Gaulis, *"La révolte des Albanais":* "There are steps towards progress that can be forced only at the point of the bayonet upon ignorant masses for whom the word 'progress' does not have the almost mystical significance that we attach to it." That is true of the Albanians. In France, Italy, England, Germany, "the ignorant masses" have a profound and mystical sense of progress!

932 [2] Just here we are interested in the nucleus, the residues, only; but it should not be forgotten that the process is extended by imperceptible degrees to the whole sum of residues and derivations.

good is credited to "progress." To have a "modern sense" of this or that is to have sound and solid sense. In the old days a man was praised for his "time-honoured virtues." Now he is praised for being a "modern man," or—to use, as some do, a neologism—for having an "up-to-date" outlook on things. It was once to one's credit to act "like a Christian"; today it is praiseworthy to act "like a human being," or better, "in a spirit of broad humanity"—when, for instance, one is defending a thief or a murderer. To succour one's neighbour was formerly a "charitable act"; today it is an "act of humanity." To suggest that a man was dangerous or prone to wrongdoing, he was once called a "heretic" or "godless man"; today it is enough to label him a "reactionary." Everything good is nowadays "democratic"; everything evil, "aristocratic." The high-priests of the god Progress and their communicants in Europe seethed with indignation when Abdul Hamid suppressed the Armenian rebellion, and they named him "the red-handed Sultan." But after such an outgiving of holy horror, they of course had none left when, in 1910, the Young Turks suppressed the Albanian rebellion in the holy name of Progress. The criterion of such people would seem to be something like this: A government has a right to suppress an insurrection if it stands in better favour with the god Progress than its rebels; otherwise it has no such right.

934. The adversaries of an institution hold it responsible for all the bad that happens. Its friends credit it with all the good. "It is raining—what a crooked administration!" So says the Opposition. "The weather is fine—what a blessed government!" So the Majority. What denunciations were hurled at the governments of the past in Italy on the matter of taxes, though they were light indeed as compared with taxes that are cheerfully tolerated today! The old Tuscan "liberals" inveighed against the Grand Duke for permitting "the immoral lottery"—see what the poet Giusti wrote on the subject in his ironical "Defence of the Lottery." But stepping into power themselves, they found it altogether natural and moral that an Italian government should run lotteries too. In France, in the days of the Empire, the Republicans raged against "official candidacies." When they came into power, they used "official candidacies" on a wider scale and in a more thorough-going fashion than the Empire had ever dreamed of doing.[1] The same Englishmen who assert that political crimes in Russia are due exclusively to bad government are convinced that identical crimes in India are due to outbursts of criminal brutality in their Hindu subjects.

935. The ancient Romans credited the gods with the successes of their Republic. Modern peoples attribute their economic betterment to corrupt, ignorant, altogether contemptible parliaments.[1] Under the old monarchy in France the king partook of the divine. When something bad occurred, people said: "If the King only knew." Now the republic and universal suffrage are the divinities.[2] "Universal suffrage, the master of us all." Such the slogan of our Deputies and Senators who are elected by the votes of people who believe in the dogma, *"Ni Dieu, ni maître!"* When an evil cannot be denied, the blame is laid on some circumstance or other that is not seldom quite incidental. There are people who really believe that all the evils observable in countries enjoying parliamentary government are due to the Australian ballot, or the list ballot, or the majority vote, and they recommend proportional representation as the cure-all. Such people are cherishing the illusion that they can remedy evils of substance by tinkering with forms. Their eyes are blind to the funda-

934 [1] Their predecessors in 1848 had followed the same policy, which for that matter had been the policy of the monarchical governments that they had succeeded. See in evidence Dugué de la Fauconnerie, *Souvenirs d'un vieil homme,* pp. 299-330.

935 [1] And to these add considerations with which we shall deal in §§ 1070 f.

935 [2] Failing of re-election in the general elections of May, 1910, M. Paul Doumer wrote to his constituents: "In taking my leave of the Parliament after devoting all my strength and such knowledge of public affairs as I may have exclusively to the service of the country, I prefer to utter no word of bitterness or recrimination. Universal suffrage is sovereign and its will is to be respected, whatever the sentiments that dictate it, and even when it is expressed through a balloting system which deforms and debases everything and tends to make of the winning candidate not the representative of the general interest, but the prisoner of private interests often of the least defensible kind." And those are the people who ridicule Catholics because they submit to the will of the Pope! And yet a Catholic does not say that "the will of the Pope must be respected whatever the sentiments by which it is motivated." He simply believes that the Pope's will is inspired of God; and that is why he defers to it.

mentals because they will not, or cannot, think counter to a sentiment that allows them to see nothing but good in universal suffrage and democracy.[3]

936. In France a justice of the peace had ruled that a man who was an idiot in the medical sense of the term could not be a voter. The High Court of Appeals (*Cours de Cassation*), in an opinion handed down on April 8, 1910, reversed the decision and ruled that "feeble-mindedness, when it has not been itself the cause of the interdiction, is not incompatible with enjoyment of the right to vote, as regulated by the decree of February 2, 1852." Mme. Marguerite Durand forthwith presented an idiot as a candidate at a public meeting and remarked, "Women cannot vote, but idiots can, and are even eligible for office"—so putting her finger on the absurdity not only of electoral inequality between men and women, but of the very principle of universal suffrage. For that matter, an idiot is not out of place as a voter among panderers, criminals, and other such people, who on election day vote early and often. By that, remember, we are in no way showing that on the whole and at a given historical moment universal suffrage is detrimental to society. We are merely showing that the halo of sanctity which is thrown about it is, from any experimental standpoint, ridiculous; and bringing to the surface the sentiments that find their expression in worship of that divinity. Nor have we shown either that such suffrage worship is not promotive of social welfare. That may or may not be one of the

935 [3] In March, 1910, a number of French scientists and university professors published a manifesto containing the following: "We demand an electoral reform as a means of strengthening the Republic and ameliorating our parliamentary system. . . . The count by districts has resulted in electoral and political immoralities that are intolerable: official candidacies, arbitrary acts in administration, arbitrary decisions in the courts, displacements of justice by favouritism, disorders in the public services, deficits in budgets in which private and clique interests prevail over the general interest. Deputies to the parliament must be freed of a slavery that obliges them to satisfy appetites in order to retain mandates. More dignity, more morality, must be introduced into the exercise of the right of suffrage." It never once occurs to those gentlemen that universal suffrage and democracy may have something to do with the political evils they are complaining of. Those divinities are essentially good, in fact, they are "the good" itself and can therefore never in any way do wrong.

many instances in which a belief intrinsically false is socially advantageous. In an objective study such as ours, we have to adhere strictly to the terms of a proposition and never overstep them (§§ 41, 73-74, 1678 f.).

937. I-β5: *Assimilation: physical consumption of substances to get effects of associable, and more rarely of opposite, character.* Human beings have often believed that by eating certain substances one may come to partake of the properties of those substances. On rare occasion such phenomena may imply belief in some form of mysterious communion between a man and his totem or divinity; but more often those are different things.

938. Zeus had received a prediction that Metis would one day bear him a child who would become Lord of Heaven. He swallows Metis, the latter being pregnant with Athena. A line of Hesiod, *Theogonia,* v. 899, adds: "to the end that the goddess might impart to him a knowledge of good and evil."[1] Pindar, *Olympia,* I, 62 (Turner, p. 10), says that Tantalus made bold to steal from Zeus the nectar and ambrosia with which he had himself been made immortal and to give them to his own comrades. Elsewhere, *Pythia,* IX, 63 (Turner, pp. 88-89), he says that the Hours bestowed immortality on Aristeus by pouring nectar and ambrosia between his lips. Familiar the important part played by the "soma" in the Vedic religion.[2]

938 [1] *'Αλλ' ἄρα μιν Ζεὺς πρόσθεν ἑὴν ἐγκάτθετο νηδύν,*
ὥς οἱ συμφράσσαιτο θεὰ ἀγαθόν τε κακόν τε.

The verse may be an interpolation, but that has no bearing on the matter in hand. Thereafter, as is well known, Athena emerged from the head of Zeus. And *cf.* Apollodorus, *Bibliotheca,* I, 3, 6 (Frazer, Vol. I, p. 25).

938 [2] Oldenberg, *Religion des Veda,* pp. 175-76, 181, *Soma, der Göttertrank:* "The drink that gives Indra the strength to execute his mighty feats is a juice pressed from the soma plant. The notion of an intoxicating beverage belonging to the gods seems to go back to Indo-European days. A liquor that instils a mysterious vigour, an ecstatic exhilaration, in the human being must be divine by nature and an exclusive perquisite of the gods. So among the American Indians tobacco was called a 'sacred plant' as a source of supernatural inspiration, and they believed that the gods smoked it in order to taste the same ecstasy. So the Indo-Europeans in their time located the home of the sacred drink in heaven. . . . But the liquor was carried off by a bird from the celestial repository where it lay under the eye of a vigilant demon. . . . Poets laud the wisdom, splendour, sub-

939. In view of and considering the strength, courage, and fleetness of foot of Achilles, some were pleased to assume that in his childhood he had been fed on marrow from the bones of lions and stags, and others specified bear's marrow and the viscera of lions and of wild boars.[1] The residue in that case is apparent enough, unless the fanatics of totemism are to insist that the lion, the bear, the wild boar, the stag, were all and at one time totems of Achilles. New Zealanders eat their enemies to become possessed of their strength. As usual, there is no lack of wide-roaming logical explanations (derivations), but the residue remains easily recognizable. Dumont d'Urville explains that the New Zealanders devour the "souls," the *waiduas,* of enemies whom they have slain.[2] The diet of Achilles

limity, of the soma, but rarely ascribe human form and conduct to it. . . . It is praised, Rig-Veda, VIII, 48, v. 3 (Griffith, Vol. III, p. 265), for the joy it brings to men: 'We have drunk of the soma, and, lo, we are immortals: we have ascended to the light and found the gods! What have we now to fear, O deathless ones, from the hatred or malice of men?' "

939 [1] Apollodorus, *Bibliotheca,* III, 13, 6 (Frazer, Vol. II, p. 71). For further dietary particulars, see Bayle, *Dictionnaire historique, s.v. Achille.*

939 [2] *Voyage de la corvette l' "Astrolabe,"* Vol. II, pp. 524-27 (royal edition): "The New Zealanders think that the soul, or spirit, which they call *waidua,* is an inner breath or puff of air, entirely distinct from the bodily substance. Upon death the two substances hitherto united separate. The *waidua* lingers hovering for three days about the body and then departs for the famous rock of Reinga (the word means 'departure'), which we have mentioned as the Cape Tenares of those savages. Thence an *atua* carries the *waidua* off to an abode of glory or shame, while the body, the impure part, vanishes into the dark. [The account so far is offered as an explanation of what follows. It is not a very good one, for "devouring" an "inner breath" or "puff of air" is at best a very strange procedure. It is evidently all an invention to get some sort of logic into the custom.] With such superstitious ideas it is only natural that they should think of eating the bodies of their enemies. In so doing, they believe, they will be absorbing the souls of their foes, adding them to their own and growing that much stronger. The more enemies of distinguished rank a chieftain has devoured in this world, the happier and more enviable will his triumphant *waidua* be in the next. This future bliss, moreover, is just one round of fish-and-potato banquets and of stubborn combats in which the chosen *waiduas* always come off victorious. The New Zealanders think the *waidua* is located in the left eye. On overwhelming a rival, therefore, a warrior never fails to dig out that eye and swallow it. . . . He also drinks the blood of his enemy to avoid the wrath of the swallowed *waidua;* for the blood being so imbibed, the *waidua* gets back some of the food that formerly sustained it and is so dissuaded from doing any harm thereafter." As usual the residue (the eating of a portion of the enemy's body) remains constant. The derivations are variable (inner breath, food).

as a child might be described in exactly the same terms. The idea, we may say, was to have him eat the *waidua* of lions, bears, stags, boars; and since the *waidua* resides in the marrow or viscera, those portions of the animals were given him to eat. Many customs of savage peoples analyze into the residue we are here considering, and which, for that matter, appears in somewhat disguised forms among civilized peoples.[3]

940. The eating of totems by savages is just a particular instance of the general custom of eating things held to be beneficial; but as a result of the now fashionable abuse of totemism, this totem "communion" has been represented as the "primitive fact" from which other "communions" have been derived. That in no wise results from our present knowledge. What we have is simply a series of communions showing one common residue—the residue of assimila-

939 [3] Frazer, *The Golden Bough,* Vol. II, pp. 353-55: " 'The savage commonly believes that by eating the flesh of an animal or man he acquires not only the physical but even the moral and intellectual qualities which were characteristic of that animal or man. . . . Thus, for example, the Creeks, the Cherokees, and kindred tribes of North American Indians, believe that nature is possest of such a property as to transfuse into men and animals the qualities either of the food they use or of those objects that are presented to their senses. He who feeds on venison is, according to their physical system, swifter and more sagacious than the man who lives on the flesh of the clumsy bear or helpless dunghill fowls, the slow-footed tame cattle, or the heavy wallowing swine' (James Adair, *History of the American Indians,* p. 133). . . . The Namaquas abstain from eating the flesh of hares, because they think it would make them faint-hearted as a hare. But they eat the flesh of the lion, or drink the blood of the leopard or lion, to get the courage and strength of these beasts (Theophilus Hahn, *Tsumi-Goam, the Supreme Being of the Khoi-Khoi,* p. 106). . . . The flesh of the lion and also that of the spotted leopard are sometimes cooked and eaten by native warriors of South-eastern Africa, who hope thereby to become as brave as lions (Macdonald, *Light in Africa,* p. 174; and *Idem, Superstitions and Religions of South African Tribes,* p. 282). . . . Sometimes if a Zulu has killed a wild beast, for instance a leopard, he will give his children the blood to drink, and will roast the heart for them to eat, expecting that they will thus grow up brave and daring men. . . . When a serious disease has attacked a Zulu Kraal, the medicine-man takes the bone of a very old dog, or the bone of an old cow, bull, or other very old animal, and administers it to the healthy as well as to the sick people, in order that they may live to be as old as the animal of whose bone they have partaken." Chardin, *Voyage en Perse,* Vol. VII, p. 115: "The Persians rate the sheep higher than all butcher animals, claiming that it has no bad habits and that none, therefore, can be contracted by eating its flesh; for their doctors hold unanimously that a man comes to resemble the animals on which he feeds."

tion. The residue also transpires in what Justin Martyr says of the Eucharist, *Apologia,* I, 65-66 (Migne, p. 427a; Davie, pp. 50-51): "Then bread and a cup of watered wine is brought to the presiding elder. He takes these things, praises and glorifies the Father of the Universe in the name of the Son and the Holy Spirit, and then makes a long thanksgiving [Eucharist] for all the favours we have received from Him. . . . After the presiding elder has offered thanks and all the people have responded, those whom we call deacons give of the consecrated bread, and of wine and water, to each of those present, and carry of it to absent ones. . . . We call this 'Eucharist food.'[1] . . . For we do not partake of it as of common bread or common beverage; but even as, through the word of God, Jesus Christ our Saviour became incarnate and assumed flesh and blood for our salvation, so through the words of His prayer are we taught that the consecrated food, whereof our blood and flesh by transmutation are nourished, is flesh and blood of the incarnate Jesus."[2]

941. As is well known, derivations without end have been appended to that simple fact, and theologians—and detractors of Christianity as well—have quarrelled copiously and fiercely on the subject. That is no concern of ours here. Let us note simply that to have identified the sentiment that figures as the residue in all communions does not in the least impair Catholic doctrine or the teaching of any other theology. If it did, to recognize the sentiment of love for a powerful and beneficent Being as the residue underlying the Christian's love of God would impair every religion inspired by that love. Whatever the faith may be, it can be expressed only in the language spoken by human beings and through the sentiments pres-

940 [1] Εὐχαριστηθεῖσα τροφή is, properly, the consecrated food that bears the grace of the Lord within it.

940 [2] A freer rendering would be: ". . . through the words of His prayer do we know that the consecrated food is the flesh and blood of the incarnate Jesus and that our flesh and blood are fed on that food by transmutation." Justin continues: "Evil daemons have imitated this institution in the mysteries of Mithras, wherein initiates are offered bread and a cup of water and are addressed with certain words that you know, or can know [if you choose]." The usual error of assuming that two similar derivations from one residue must be imitations one of the other. They are really parallel expressions of one same residue.

ent in them. To study such modes of expression in no way affects the things that are expressed (§ 74).

942. Disputes such as have raged about the Eucharist might have arisen in connexion with other cases of the kind. Had Graeco-Roman paganism survived down to our own day and the Eleusinian mysteries enjoyed continued popularity, people might have quarrelled just as vociferously over the cyceon, and sent just as many heretics to the stake. Initiates in the Eleusinian mysteries repeated the formula: "I have fasted; I have drunk the cyceon (*κυκεών*); I have drawn from the box; I have seen; I have put into the basket, and then from the basket into the box."[1] The cyceon that the initiates drank was evidently no ordinary cyceon, such as was commonly drunk; it acquired mystical properties from the ceremony in which it was used. Demeter had drunk the cyceon when, in sorrow, she was hunting for her daughter (Homer, *Hymnus in Cererem*, vv. 208-09; White, p. 303). According to her recipe it was made of water, flour, and grated mint-leaves. The recipe for the potion seems subsequently to have changed, wine being added, though Demeter herself had refused to drink wine. In the *Argonautica,* one of the Orphic compositions, vv. 323-30 (Leipzig, pp. 53, 525), the Argonauts seal their oath by drinking a still different cyceon made of flour, bull's blood, sea-water, with a touch of olive-oil.[2]

943. Of little interest to sociology is the rich harvest of derivations that is eventually garnered from these facts. Its concern rather is

942 [1] Clement of Alexandria, *Protrepticus* (*Exhortation to the Greeks*), II, 18. (Butterworth, p. 43): *'Ενήστευσα ἔπιον τὸν κυκεῶνα ἔλαβον ἐκ κίστης· ἐργασάμενος ἀπεθέμην εἰς κάλαθον, καὶ ἐκ καλάθου εἰς κίστην*. The word *ἐργασάμενος*, "having done" does not yield a satisfactory meaning. Migne proposes *θεασάμενος*, that is, "I have then inspected the sacred *ῥῶπον*, and the secret wares." That would be satisfactory. Arnobius renders in Latin, *Disputationes adversus gentes,* V, 26 (Bryce-Campbell, p. 251): "*Ieiunavi atque ebibi cyceonem: ex cista sumpsi et in calathum misi: accepi rursus, in cistulam transtuli.*" (Butterworth: "I fasted; I drank the draught; I took from the chest; having done my task, I placed in the basket, and from the basket into the chest.")

942 [2] And *cf.* Hesychius, *Lexicon, s.v.* Κυκεῶ: "A beverage made of a mixture of wine, honey, water, and flour." The scholiast of the *Odyssey,* X, v. 290, adds cheese.

with the residue, which is at work in many social phenomena and helps to explain them. In the incident described in the *Argonautica* we have passed, as frequently happens, from a special to a general—from a I-β5 to a I-α—residue. Observable among many peoples is a custom of having the sick swallow pieces of paper inscribed with certain symbols, certain letters, or else the ashes from such bits of paper, or water in which the ashes have been mixed.[1]

944. I-γ: *Mysterious workings of certain things; mysterious effects of certain acts.* This residue figures in many rites of magic, in amulets, in oaths taken on certain objects, in ordeals, judgments of God, and the like. It is also the principal element in taboos, with or without sanction. It corresponds to a sentiment whereby things and acts are invested with an occult power that is often vague and not clearly explained.

945. If we had nothing but the mediaeval "judgment of God" to go by we might be left in doubt as to whether the principal element in it were the alleged interposition of the Divinity. But ordeals appear more or less everywhere, often with judgments by a divinity, and often without. In the Middle Ages the "judgment of God" itself was forced upon a reluctant Church by popular superstition. It is evident, therefore, that the main element is the instinct for combinations, and that the introduction of a supposedly divine judgment is a derivation designed to explain and justify that instinct.[1]

946. We shall find it helpful to distinguish from our general case,

943 [1] Davis, *The Chinese,* Vol. II, p. 135 (1836, pp. 142-43): "The written spells which the Chinese sometimes use consist of mystical compounds of various characters or words, in which astrology is generally introduced, with the eight diagrams of Fo-by, the twenty-eight lunar mansions, the five planets, and so on. Some of these spells are kept about the person, others are pasted on the walls of rooms. 'Occasionally,' observes Mr. Morrison, 'they are used as cures for sick persons, by being either written on leaves which are then infused in some liquid, or inscribed on paper, burned, and the ashes thrown into drink which the patient has to swallow.'" [A favourite Italian story of a day gone by was that "Of the simple-minded rustic who gets a prescription from a doctor, thinks it the medicine, eats it, and gets well." Sagredo, *L'Arcadia in Brenta,* Venice, 1667, p. 60. But the jest is as old as Poggio and Domenichi (1574).—A. L.]

945 [1] The ordeal would be a subject for a "special"—as opposed to a "general"—sociology. Here we need go no farther than to note it as a case in which the instinct for combinations figures.

I-γ1, a special case, I-γ2, in which the names of things are supposed to have occult powers over them.

947. I-γ1: *Mysterious operations in general.* Cases are exceedingly numerous. Here we shall mention just a few. The residue often comes out strikingly in little incidents in themselves of scant moment. On May 2, 1910, a certain Muff was beheaded at Lucerne for arson and murder. One newspaper carried the following details:[1] "The last sacraments were administered. On the march to execution Muff carried on his person a genuine piece of the True Cross which Mme. Erica von Handel-Mazzetti had sent him, with a consoling message." Logically, a place for that relic in any judgment which God may pass on the man's crimes or on his repentance would be hard to find. We have to conclude that a sort of mysterious power was ascribed to it, something like the emanations from a bit of radium sealed in a glass tube.

948. The residue is more commonly observable under the disguise of one of its derivations. Feeling better if their attitudes are logical (residue I-ε) people wonder: "How do these things, these acts, come to have the effects they have?" And the answer is: "Through the interposition of a spirit, a god, the Devil." That is like explaining that opium induces sleep because it contains a sleep-inducing property.

949. An anecdote related by St. Gregory of Tours, *Historia ecclesiastica Francorum,* VIII, 16 (*Opera,* p. 460; Dalton, Vol. II, p. 342), lays bare both the residue and the derivation. A man had been accused of setting fire to a neighbour's house. Said he: "I shall go to St. Martin's Church, and taking oath upon my faith I shall return innocent of this crime." St. Gregory's informant declares: "Now it was certain that the man had set fire to the house. As he was on his way to take the oath, I turned to him and said: 'According to what our neighbours are saying you are not innocent of this crime. Now God is everywhere, and His power is the same outside [the church] as inside.[1] If therefore you are nursing the illusion that God or His

947 [1] *Gazette de Lausanne,* May 3, 1910.

949 [1] "*. . . sed tamen Deus ubique est, et virtus eius ipsa est forinsecus quae habetur intrinsecus.*"

saints will take perjury lightly, here is the church—swear, if you wish, but outside! For you will not be allowed to step foot across the threshold.'" He swears, and straightway falls dead, blasted by celestial fire! It is clear that the narrator wavers between two notions that are not easily reconcilable: a feeling that an oath is just as effective in one place as another, and then a feeling that it is more effective in some places than in others.[2] It was for daring to take oath in very front of the Church of St. Martin that the perjurer was struck dead; for the witness adds: "That was an object lesson to many [rascals] that they had better not take any false oaths *in that place* again!"[3]

950. Marsden[1] explains how oaths are administered in Sumatra and upon what strange objects: an old sword (kris), a broken gun-barrel, a rifle, sometimes the earth, the witness stooping to lay a hand upon it. As usual thinking in terms of logical conduct primarily, Marsden observes, p. 243: "It is a striking circumstance that practices which boast so little of reason in their foundation, which are in fact so whimsical and childish, should yet be common to nations the most remote in situation, climate, language, complexion, character, and everything that can distinguish one race of people from another."[2]

949 [2] Pertile, *Storia del diritto italiano,* Vol. VI, Pt. I, p. 372: "Such solemnities and precautions notwithstanding, perjuries were still very frequent. With the idea of protecting sacred objects from such misuses, King Robert ordered that oaths be administered upon reliquaries that were either empty or filled with counterfeit relics."

949 [3] "*Multis haec causa documentum fuit ne in hoc loco auderent ulterius periurare* (misprint: *peierare*)."

950 [1] *History of Sumatra,* pp. 240-43.

950 [2] Says Marsden: "The place of greatest solemnity for administering an oath is the *krammat,* or burying ground, of their ancestors, and several superstitious ceremonies are observed on the occasion. The people near the seacoast, in general, by long intercourse with the Malays, have an idea of the *Koran* and usually employ this in swearing, which the priests do not fail to make them pay for. But the island people keep laid up in their houses certain old reliques . . . which they produce when an oath is to be taken. The person who has lost his cause, and with whom it commonly rests to bind his adversary by an oath, often desires two or three days' time, to get ready his swearing apparatus, called on such occasions *sumpalian,* of which some are looked upon as more sacred and of greater efficacy than others. They consist of an old rusty *kris,* a broken gun barrel, or any ancient

951. Ordinarily, in fact, human beings try to fortify their faith in the occult powers of things in just such ways. In the *Iliad,* III, vv. 271-91, Agamemnon sacrifices victims to make his oath with Priam valid and formal. He cuts tufts of hair from the lambs' heads, and the hair is distributed among the Trojan and Achaian optimates. He then cuts the lambs' throats and utters an oath, to which Priam responds with a similar oath. Years, hundreds of years, after that legendary episode, acts of the same sort are being daily repeated. Forms alone change. It matters little whether the oath be taken upon sacrificial victims, upon the relics of saints, or upon other objects; whether the power invoked be Zeus, Helius, the Rivers, the Earth, the God of the Christians and His saints, a devil, or some other being. The essential point is that people believe that they can mutually and effectively bind each other by virtue of certain acts in part mysterious. The residue is that belief, and it is observable among all peoples from the earliest periods of history. Even today there are countries where oaths must be taken by laying a hand on the Bible or the New Testament; and the hand must be bare. One cannot imagine any logical reason why an oath should be less binding for the presence of a layer of leather between the hand and the Book. What evidently is working is a vague, indefinite feeling that the layer of leather may somehow impair the mysterious action of the Book, much as a non-conductor impedes the transmission of an electric current. However, the feeling is not expressed in any such definite form. It remains just an instinct whereby certain things are accepted and others rejected, and which can well be described in terms of this residue.

trumpery, to which chance or caprice has annexed an idea of extraordinary virtue. These they generally dip in water, which the person who swears drinks of, after having pronounced the form of words before-mentioned. The most ordinary *sumpalian* is a *kris,* and on the blade of this they sometimes drop lime-juice, which occasions a stain on the lips of the person performing the ceremony—a circumstance that may not improbably be supposed to make an impression on a weak and guilty mind. Such would fancy that the external stain conveyed to the beholders an image of the internal." The formula for the oath: "If what I now declare, namely . . . [Here the testimony is recited.] is truly and really so, may I be freed and clear from my oath: if what I assert is wittingly false, may my oath be the cause of my destruction."

952. A similar sentiment underlies conceptions as to the virtues of relics. As for objects deemed beneficent, it is important to distinguish between the mysterious powers they have intrinsically and the feeling of veneration for them, for the powers may exist independently of the veneration and *vice versa,* and things may be venerated that are not deemed beneficent. Both elements, however, may be present simultaneously. That is the situation with relics. Numberless the cases where an object belonging to a saint operates apparently in and of itself. In general terms, people may believe in the efficacy of certain rites of a religion without believing in the religion, a fact that emphasizes the non-logical character of the conduct (§§ 157, 184 [2]). Logically, one ought first to believe in a given religion and then in the efficacy of its rites, the efficacy, logically, being the consequence of the belief. Logically, it is absurd to offer a prayer unless there is someone to hearken to it. But non-logical conduct is derived by a precisely reverse process. There is first an instinctive belief in the efficacy of a rite, then an "explanation" of the belief is desired, then it is found in religion. This is one of the many cases where the residue figures as the principal element and the derivation as the secondary. In the particular, there are numberless instances where objects connected with saints function of and by themselves upon anybody who comes into contact with them.[1]

We read in Acts 19: 11-12 that "God wrought special miracles by the hands of Paul: So that from his body were brought unto the

952 [1] Chardin, *Voyage en Perse* (*Nouvelle bibliothèque,* Vol. VII, p. 11; Vol. VIII, p. 149): "The Persians believe that the prayers of all men are good and have their effects, and in cases of sickness and other troubles they accept and even court the devotions of the faithful of different religions, as I have seen them do on numberless occasions. . . . They make lavish use of magical and other such remedies when they are sick, and seek help not only of all their own saints but of the saints of all religions—pagan, Jewish, Christian, anything. Christians read the Gospel according to St. John over the sick—the Gospel that is used in the mass. Missionaries of the Roman, to an even greater extent than those of the Eastern, Church make a practice of such readings and for the benefit of men, women, and children alike. That can only be regarded as magic, for, as you can well imagine, the Persians understand Latin about as much as Europeans understand Persian. But, in addition, it must be accounted downright sacrilege, for those Mohammedans do not believe in the Word proclaimed in the Gospel, but believe ours the falsest and most damnable of all religions." Chardin argues throughout from the logical

sick handkerchiefs or aprons, and the diseases departed from them, and the evil spirits went out of them."[2]

953. Magic furnishes mysterious acts in countless numbers. If we were acquainted with Christian magic only, where "powers" invariably are ascribed to the Devil, or only with magics where "powers" are ascribed to some supernatural being, we could never determine whether the belief in the magic were a I-γ1 residue or a derivation—a consequence, that is, of beliefs in the Devil or other supernatural beings.

954. But the doubt is dispelled the moment we find cases of magic where no interference on the part of supernatural beings is presupposed. That shows that the constant element in magic is not the divine intervention, but the belief in mysterious operations, and that the introduction of the supernatural entity is a derivation designed to explain and justify the combinations showing the residue. There are many cases, moreover, where magic or quasi-magic is mixed in with religion inadvertently, unconsciously, without trace of evil intent. The Catholic Church has found itself obliged to con-

standpoint. In his *Travels and Adventures in the Persian Provinces,* J. Baillie Fraser tells a story of an old man who wore a copper box hanging about his neck (translation from the French translation in the *Bibliothèque universelle des voyages,* Vol. XXXV, p. 469): "It contained two small figures, the one a copper Lama, the idol usual in worship of the Grand Lama, and which is presented to pilgrims visiting His temple; the other a small Chinese image, painted on porcelain or terra cotta. The two relics were wrapped in a piece of yellow silk. He said he had received them from the Grand Lama at the Hassa, whither he had gone on a pilgrimage some years before. The man was a Hindu by religion, and worshipped idols in the Hindu manner. Nevertheless the relics came to him from the high-priest of another faith whom he had doubtless visited with a religious purpose. The man offered an interesting example of tolerance and ignorance at the same time."

952 [2] And *cf. Dictionnaire encyclopédique de la théologie catholique, s.v. Reliques* (Wetzer, *s.v. Reliquien*): "If the handkerchiefs and linen of St. Paul, which were things external to his person, cured diseases, that virtue should with all the more reason be ascribed to the very bodies of the saints that housed the souls from which such powers emanated. In his homily on St. Julitta [of Tarsus] St. Basil says: 'Her body now rests in the sumptuous vestibule of a church in that city and sanctifies the place where it lies and those who visit it.' 'Under the old dispensation,' he says elsewhere, *Homilia in Psalmum* CXV, § 4 (*Opera,* Vol. II, p. 111), 'the bodies of the dead were deemed unclean things. That is not the case under the new dispensation. Whosoever touches the bones of saints obtains by that contact somewhat of the sanctifying grace which dwells in saintly bodies.' "

demn misuses of holy water, of the Host, of this or that rite—any number of superstitions, in short.[1] St. Thomas does his best to save both the goat and the cabbages and justify the residue by the derivation. Speaking of the practice of carrying relics (scapularies) about

954 [1] *Decretum Gratiani, pars* 2, *causa* 26, *quaestio* 5, *canon* 3 (Friedberg, Vol. I, pp. 1027-28): "It shall not be lawful for Christians to keep to the traditions of the heathen. . . . 1. Nor shall they use rites (*observantia*) or incantations in collecting medicinal herbs, save only with the divine [*i.e.,* the Apostles'] Creed (*cum symbolo divino*), or the Lord's Prayer, that so honour be paid only to God the creator and lord of all men. . . . 3. Nor shall Christian women, either, perform false rites (*vanitatem observare*) in their spinning and weaving (*lanificiis*) but rather pray for the help of God who has given them the skill they have in that art (*texendi*)." Ferraris, *Bibliotheca canonica juridica moralis theologica, s.v. Superstitio:* "49. The 'health-rite' (literally 'observances of healths': *observantia sanitatum*) is a superstition whereby fatuous and ineffective agencies are applied to the preservation or recovery of health for human beings and animals. They become guilty of this superstition who use meaningless names (*ignota nomina*), certain prescribed words, certain characters, certain scripts, wrappings, signs, certain numbers of prayers and signs of the cross (*certum numerum crucium*), and other ineffective things of the sort for curing illnesses, healing wounds, stopping pains, staunching blood, or for making themselves or others invulnerable to spears, swords, cannon-balls, so that they may be immune to injury from the enemy and exempt from any misfortune or sickness; since all the said things and their like have never been appointed, whether by God, by Nature, or by the Church, to such purposes. . . . 54. Guilty of superstition are they who change seats or packs of cards while at play in order to avoid bad luck; who touch some particular wood in order to win at play; who refuse to sit down at table when their doing so would bring the number to thirteen . . . women who pray on St. John's Night [June 24] that they may see in their dreams the men they are going to marry; men who believe that if a fire has been covered with ashes in their presence they will not marry within the year; persons who stand brooms upside down so that if the woman whom they suspect of being a witch (*saga*) is one, she may be able to walk in no wise save backward, like a crab; persons who paste certain notes on door-posts that thieves may be forced to come thither; who think that when a hen crows like a cock some misfortune impends; who think that somebody's death or bad luck is foretold when a bird sings mournfully, when a crow caws, or a rabbit crosses their path; who fear some grave disaster if they see two priests raising the Host at the same time at mass; who think hens become safe from hawks if their first eggs are given to the poor; who keep eggs laid by hens on Saturday (*die Parasceves:* 'day of preparation for the Sabbath') for putting out fires; and so on for countless other superstitions almost infinite in number." All that is but an infinitesimal proportion of the countless ways in which the residues of combination assert themselves in such connexions. I will add just one more example—a discussion of the uses of holy water, from Thiers, *Traité des superstitions* (Avignon, Vol. II, pp. 20-21; Amsterdam, *Superstitions anciennes et modernes,* Vol. II, Pt. II, Bk. I, 2, 6, pp. 5-6): "Remarking that there is an element of superstition in using holy objects for purposes other than those to which they were appointed, Cardinal Cusa mentions the instance

one's person he says:[2] "If they are worn as evidence of faith in God and the saints whose relics they are, it is not illicit; but if some fatuous thing be held in view, for instance the triangular shape of the container (*quod vas esset triangulare*), or some other thing of the sort not pertaining to veneration of God and the saints, it would be superstitious and illicit."[3] As for scripts that may be worn on the person, one must be careful "that they contain no unknown words, lest some illicit thing be concealed therein."[4] In such a case evidently the sin would be involuntary.[5] Superstitions abide, while religions change: in other words, the residue endures and the derivations vary. The Christians did not invent the magic "spell"—the *fascinum*. They did not derive it from the fact that there was a Devil. They merely explained it, finding it ready-made in pagan society.

955. Tertullian says that "among the heathen there is a dreadful thing called the *fascinum*, 'the spell,' which comes as the unfortunate result of excessive praise and glory. This we sometimes believe

of holy water, which is drunk in order to recover lost health, sprinkled on lands and fields to make them more fertile, and given to animals to drink to cure them of this or that malady. . . . But in calling those three practices superstitions the learned Cardinal did not pay due attention to the words that the Church uses in blessing the water. It is stated very definitely that holy water is very good for casting out devils, driving away diseases, dissipating unhealthy air and bad winds, purifying houses and all other places where it is sprinkled and freeing them of anything disturbing to the peace and tranquillity of the faithful dwelling in them. . . . There is nothing superstitious, therefore, in giving human beings and animals holy water to drink, nor in sprinkling it about the houses and on the lands of Christians, provided such things be done in a pure faith and in perfect trustfulness in the goodness and omnipotence of God."

954 [2] *Summa theologiae*, IIª IIªᵉ, *qu.* 96, *art.* 3-4 (*Opera*, Vol. IX, pp. 334-35: *Utrum suspendere verba divina ad collum sit illicitum*).

954 [3] The Saint draws the general conclusion, *loc. cit., art.* 4: "The wearing of divine words about the neck, unless they contain something false or doubtful, is in no wise illicit, though it would be the more praiseworthy part to abstain from such things."

954 [4] *"Similiter etiam videtur esse cavendum si contineat ignota nomina, ne sub illis aliquid illicitum lateat."*

954 [5] [I wonder whether Pareto states the Saint's position quite adequately. St. Thomas seems to mean that scapularies may be worn as acts, signs, of faith (*per*), but not for purposes of magic. The presence of meaningless rigmaroles (*verba ignota*) would be *prima facie* evidence of magical intent and therefore sinful.—A. L.]

to be the work of the Devil, because he hates whatever is good, sometimes the work of God, for of Him comes judgment on pride in an exalting of the lowly and a humbling of the haughty."[1] Two things in the passage are noteworthy: first, the variability of the derivations, which go from one extreme to the other, from the Devil to God; and, second, God's humbling of the vainglorious, which is something similar to the "envy of the gods" of the pagans. St. Basil observes[2] a belief that envious people could harm others by a mere glance—"as it were by a maleficent emanation gushing from their eyes, harming and blasting."[3] That notion he rejects as ignorant folk-lore and an old wives' tale (*fabulam . . . popularem*): the truth is that the devils hate the righteous, and use the eyes of the envious to harm them. Del Rio bows to such holy authority, and, rejecting all other causes, holds the spell to be the work of the Devil. As usual the derivation sprouts, branches out, thrives luxuriant. Del Rio—lo, what wisdom!—knows just how the Devil goes about it:[4] "The spell is a pernicious capacity acquired by contrivance of demons in pursuance of a compact, tacit or explicit, between a man and the Devil. The pernicious property is spread generally about by the Devil in the ambient air. The man breathes in this polluted air in his immediate neighbourhood and it is drawn to the heart through the arteries thereof, so that shortly disease and corruption are distributed to every part of the body."[5] Ingenious explanations of the

955 [1] *De virginibus velandis,* XV (*Opera,* Vol. III, p. 24; English, Vol. III, p. 177): "*Nam est aliquid etiam apud ethnicos metuendum quod fascinum vocant, infeliciorem laudis et gloriae enormioris eventum. Hoc nos interdum diabolo interpretamur, ipsius est enim boni odium; interdum deo deputamus, illius est enim superbiae iudicium, extollentis humiles et deprimentis elatos.*"

955 [2] *Homilia de invidia,* 4 (*Opera,* Vol. II, p. 132).

955 [3] . . . *οἷον ῥεύματός τινος ὀλεθρίου ἐκ τῶν φθονερῶν ὀφθαλμῶν ἀπορρέοντος, καὶ λυμαινομένου καὶ διαφθείροντος.* [Garnier: *exitioso quodam quasi fluento . . . tabefaciente atque corrumpente.*]

955 [4] *Disquisitiones magicae,* III, 1, 4, 1 (Louvain, Vol. II, pp. 25-26; Cologne, pp. 379, 388), *De fascinatione.*

955 [5] Del Rio's definition is really more prolix. It began: "The spell, as properly so called in common parlance, is something not natural but of an imaginary superstitious character, as has been excellently shown by Léonard Vair, Lorenzo Annania, Francisco Valles, and Julius Scaliger. . . . It [this thesis] is further proved by the authority of the great Basil, who alludes to the belief contemptuously,

same sort had long been familiar. Plutarch, *Symposiaca,* V, 7 (Goodwin, Vol. III, pp. 327-33), discusses the spell at length. That there is such a thing is, he says, certain; but it is so hard to account for it that many people do not believe in it. And he goes on to show how the spell can arise in natural course. Another naturalistic explanation is given by Heliodorus, *Aethiopica,* III, 7.[6] It would be idle to go into such nonsense in detail. For our purposes we need simply remark this interesting example of derivations varying about a constant residue. Of course, once the disease is diagnosed, there is a scamper for the remedy; and there will naturally be remedies of various kinds according to the temperament of the doctor, naturalistic, magical, religious.

956. While such branches are growing out from the central trunk, the trunk itself endures through the ages; and the simple notion of a mysterious influence due to the evil eye holds its own down to our very day. Says Hesiod, *Opera et dies,* v. 348: "You would not lose your ox if you did not have a wicked neighbour."[1] Columella, *De re rustica,* I, 3, strengthens the dose. He quotes Hesiod's proverb and adds: "And it applies not only to our ox but to all our possessions," so seeming to combine the evil-eye with the malicious-neighbour superstition (§ 185). Catullus, kissing his mistress, fears the evil eye of the envious,[2] and in the *Eclogues* Virgil too dreads the

Homilia de invidia, loc. cit., as female chatter (Garnier: *fabulam . . . introductam in muliereum coetum*). . . . The spell results from a pact when the Devil, in ways known to himself, harms the victim of the spell by the gaze or praise of the spell-binder (*aspiciente malefico vel laudante*)." Then follows the definition given in the text.

955 [6] Underdowne version, Boston, p. 83: "The ayre which is about us on every side, enteringe into us by our eyes, nosthrilles, mouth and other poares, carrying with it suche outwarde qualities as it is indued withal, doth ingrafte a like infection in them who have received it."

956 [1] Οὐδ' ἂν βοῦς ἀπόλοιτ', εἰ μὴ γείτων κακὸς εἴη. And *cf.* § 185.

956 [2] *Carmina,* V, vv. 12-13:

> *"aut ne quis malus invidere possit*
> *cum tantum sciat esse basiorum."*

(". . . or that no evil person may cast the spell of envy, knowing of so many kisses") [L. Beebe in F. P. A.'s "Conning Tower," New York *World,* Sept. 21, 1916, renders: "Lest we should know, or evil eye discover How many kisses Lesbia gave her lover."] Muret, *In Catullum commentarius* (*Opera,* Vol. II, p. 727), notes: "The

spell.[3] Pliny, *Historia naturalis,* VII, 2 (Bostock-Riley, Vol. II, pp. 126-27), relates that "in Africa according to Isigonus and Nymphodorus, there are families of spellbinders, a word of praise from whom kills the flocks, withers the trees, and brings death to children. Isigonus adds that among the Triballi and the Illyrii there are individuals of the same sort who cast spells with their eyes and kill those upon whom they fix their gaze for any length of time, especially if it be in wrath. Grown people, in particular, fall ready victims. Such spellbinders have two pupils in each eye. There are women of the same sort in Scythia, called 'Bythiae,' according to Apollonides. Philarchus places the Thibii and many other such people in the Pontus. They are recognizable, he says, from having a double pupil in one eye and the image of a horse in the other. They do not sink in water even if weighted down by clothes.[4] Damon mentions people not unlike these, the Pharnaces of Ethiopia. Their sweat induces consumption in any human body touched by them. Even among the Romans Cicero says that when women have double

spell was thought to be unable to injure things of which the names or the number were unknown. [As usual the instinct for combinations working.] Even rustics of our day and country make it a matter of religion [not] to count the apples on young trees."

956 [3] *Eglogae,* III, v. 103:

> *"Nescio quis teneros oculus mihi fascinat agnos."*

("I know not what evil eye has its spell on my young lambs.") And VII, vv. 27-28:

> *"Aut si ultra placitum laudarit, baccare frontem*
> *cingite ne vati noceat mala lingua futuro."*

("Or if he praise beyond the due, wreathe my brow with nard that his evil tongue harm not the future of your bard.") As for the "evil tongue," Servius interprets (Thilo-Hagen, Vol. III, p. 86): "the tongue that casts a spell in intent of harm." Horace, *Epistulae,* I, 14, vv. 37-78:

> *"Non istic obliquo oculo mea commoda quisquam*
> *limat, non odio obscuro morsuque venenat."*

("There where you live no one disturbs my peace of mind with leering eye nor poisons with bite of slinking hate.")

956 [4] In the Middle Ages, and for that matter later, the same peculiarity was ascribed to persons guilty of some crime, especially heresy, and most of all, witchcraft. Hence the belief that they could be detected by the "cold-water test." Father Le Brun, *Op. cit.,* Vol. II, pp. 240-41, 253, 271, 284: "The 'cold-water test' was conducted as follows: The suspect was stripped naked, his left hand tied to his right

pupils in their eyes their gaze is always baneful." [4a] People still believe in the evil eye in our day, without crediting the Devil with any share in it. One need only reflect that many very good Catholics were convinced that Pius IX was a *jettatore*. It is interesting that spellbinders are more often women than men, and almost invariably old and ugly women, or at the very least ugly. Young women, pretty girls, never have the evil eye. In that the determining factor is a residue of the I-β4 variety.[5]

957. Mysterious the disease, mysterious also the working of the remedies, though on occasion some sort of an explanation is sup-

foot, his right hand to his left foot, so that he could not move. He was then thrown into the water at the end of a rope. If he sank, as a man so bound and unable to make any movement naturally would, he was deemed innocent; if he floated and could not be made to sink, he was adjudged guilty." Then again a person who floated was assumed to do so because of divine protection (§ 587 [5]). Clearly apparent in such cases is the mysterious efficacy of certain acts. Floating is adjudged an unnatural circumstance. It must therefore be associated with ethical traits in the individual. It may, however, go equally well with innocence and with guilt. Whichever it is, "explanations" will be available in plenty. For innocence, God's help will serve: "Good Christians have always believed, and rightly, that a miracle is required to keep persons so thrown into the water afloat; and innocent and devout individuals, on appealing to God for help, have many a time been saved when thrown into the water to drown." For guilt, more ingenuity will be required. According to Hincmar [*De divortio Lotharii regis,* VI (*Opera,* Vol. I, p. 669)], "since the coming of Jesus Christ a number of things have been changed. Water, for instance, which has been hallowed by contact with the body of Jesus in the Jordan and appointed to sanctify men by baptism, must no longer receive the guilty in its embrace when information is sought as to their crimes." Adolphus Scribonius, a philosopher of repute, studied cold-water tests at first hand in the year 1583 [*De examine et purgatione sogarum per aquam frigidam*] and concluded "that sorcerers are necessarily lighter than other people, because the Devil, a being of spiritual volatile substance, permeates all parts of their bodies and communicates his lightness to them, so that they become less heavy than water and accordingly cannot sink."

956 [4a] [This text of Cicero is not otherwise known: Lemaire ed. of Cicero's *Opera,* Vol. XXV, p. 263 (*Fragmenta incerta*).—A. L.]

956 [5] Carefully examining how a given person, man or woman, comes to get a reputation for possessing the evil eye, one gets the impression that it is very much the case of seed scattered on the ground, some of it sprouting, some of it dying. A report goes abroad that the individuals *A, B, C* . . . have the evil eye. As for *A* and *B,* that is the end of the matter; but the charge sticks in the case of *C,* often on most idiotic grounds. I may mention a personal experience. A lady, old, of course, and of unprepossessing physique, was alleged to have the evil eye. At a ball where she was a guest a chandelier chanced to fall. And everybody, at once,

plied by other residues.[1] Taboos would be a good illustration, but we can deal more advantageously with them when we come to derivations (§§ 1481 f.).

958. I-γ2: *Mysterious linkings of names and things.* Names may be linked to things in two ways: either mysteriously, for no experimental reason; or else because they suggest certain experimental, or even imaginary, properties of things. We distinguish the first case under this category. The second case yields residues of group-persistence (Class II). From the scientific point of view a name is a mere label serving to designate a thing. The label may be changed at will whenever some advantage is to be gained by doing so. It is from this standpoint that definitions are chiefly to be judged (§§ 119 f.).

959. But matters are different when viewed from the two standpoints mentioned. The name is joined to the thing by certain mysterious ties, now abstract, now experimental, now pseudo-experimental, sentimental, imaginary, fantastic. In such linkings of names and things there is nothing arbitrary. In experimental science names are quite arbitrary.

"There, now, tell me she hasn't the evil eye!"—quite disregarding the fact that the same proof might have served just as well against every other individual present. In accord with the proprieties, all the guests, including the *jettatrice,* soon after paid their calls on the hostess. A few days later her children came down with the measles! That was a final proof that the woman was what she was said to be; and she was subjected to such general and such cruel mistreatment that she left town.

957 [1] As for other devices see Daremberg-Saglio, *Dictionnaire, s.v. Fascinum.* Most of those mentioned were used in ancient times, but not a few have continued popular down to our own day. Notable, in the same article, the following: "The Romans placed their children under the protection of a special divinity, Cunina, whose function was to stand guard over the cradle (*cuna*), and shield little ones from the influence of the evil eye. Finally it was imagined that wild animals too might suffer from the spell and that instinct prompted them to ward it off by placing plants and pebbles of secret properties known to them in their lairs. . . . The insect known as the praying mantis (*μάντις σέριφος*) passed for having the evil eye and casting the spell not only on human beings but on animals. On the other hand, by an association of ideas constant in all superstitions of this variety, images of the praying mantis were supposed to be very effective for warding off spells. Pisistratus had one carved on the Acropolis at Athens as a preservative." However, such inconsistency is by no means peculiar to "superstitions of that variety." It is the general case, a residue being equally valid pro and contra, and the opposite of the pro being not the contra but absence of action (§ 911).

960. An excellent illustration of the sort of residue involved in mysterious linkings of names and things is the so-called perfect number, and it emphasizes with peculiar clearness the contrast between the logico-experimental reasoning and the reasoning by accord of sentiments. For mathematicians the term "perfect" is just a label (§§ 119, 963), serving to designate a number equal to the sum of its aliquots. For the number 6, for instance, the aliquots are 1, 2, 3, and their sum, in fact, is 6. The "perfect" numbers so far discovered are 6, 28, 496, 8128, and others. They are all even numbers. "Perfect" odd numbers are unknown. We might designate such numbers by some other name than "perfect." We might, for example, call them "imperfect," and nothing, absolutely nothing, would be changed. Euler's formula for discovering "perfect" numbers would yield imperfect numbers, but they would still be numbers equal to the sum of their aliquots.[a] It is quite a different matter when we are reasoning on sentiments. Then the name is of great importance: "perfect" is the opposite of "imperfect" and traits that make a number "perfect" prevent it from being "imperfect." What, exactly, the word "perfect" means in such cases no one knows, any more than one knows the meaning of the kindred terms, "just," "good," "true," "beautiful," and so on. All that is clear is that all such terms are symbols for certain sentiments which this or that individual experiences as pleasurable. It would be a waste of time to go over all the nonsense of which the Pythagoreans have delivered themselves on the subject of numbers. Aristotle clearly perceived the fantastic and arbitrary nature of such chatter. Of their numerical theories he writes: "And if their theories were defective in some respect, they made heroic efforts to have results tally. For example: They say that since the decade is perfect, comprising the whole nature of numbers, the planets have to be ten in number. But since only nine

960 [a] [The allusion seems to be to Euler's *Tractatus de numerorum doctrina*, III, §§ 106-09 (*Commentationes*, Vol. II, pp. 514-15). Euler's formula for perfect numbers was $2^{n-1}(2^n - 1)$, where $n = 1, 2, 3, 5, 7, 13, 17, 19$, Euler remaining doubtful about 31, 41 and 47. Strictly, a perfect number would be a number equal to the sum of its aliquots (divisors without remainder) including 1 but excluding the number itself. The aliquots of 28 are 1, 2, 4, 7, 14, 28.—A. L.]

are visible, they add an 'anti-Earth.'"[1] It may even be that 10 *is* a "perfect" number! How are we to say yes or no unless we are told what, exactly, the word "perfect" means? Philolaus does not enlighten us any more than the rest of them, but lets go with a hymn to the decade:[2] "Marvellous to contemplate the efficiency and nature of numbers according to the power residing in the decade. Supreme is the decade, perfect. It is the creatrix of all things, the principle, the guide, the regulatrix of divine, celestial, and human existence. Without the decade all is purposeless, uncertain, obscure." His Serene High-and-Mightiness, Number 4, is also divine, and in the "Golden Verses" of the Pythagoreans, vv. 45-48, he is used to swear by.[2a] Commenting thereon, Hierocles asks:[3] "How does the Number Four come to be a god?" And he answers: "The decade is the interval which separates numbers. For if one counts beyond [10], one returns once more to the numbers 1 and 2 and 3, and counts the second decade as far as 20, doing the same for the third decade as far as 30, and so on until one has counted the tenth decade and comes to 100; and then again 110 is counted in the same fashion; and so one may go on forever by decades. [In humble prose, without so much palaver, 10 is the basis of Greek numeration.] The number 4 is the virtue [the hidden principle] of the decade, the reason being that the sum of the numbers 1, 2, 3, 4 is 10. Moreover the number 4 exceeds the number 3 by unity, and is itself exceeded by 3 by the number 7." Verily, as Hierocles assures us, "unity and the number 7 have most beautiful and excellent properties!" That blessed number 7 has had hosts of admirers, the illustrious Auguste Comte, almost of our day, among them. It may therefore be worth while to see what Hierocles thinks of it: "The number 7 being motherless and a virgin,

960 [1] *Metaphysica,* I, 5, 3 (Ross, p. 986a): *τέλειον ἡ δεκὰς εἶναι δοκεῖ*: "The decade seems to be perfect." Clement of Alexandria, *Stromata,* VI, 11 (*Opera,* Vol. II, p. 306A; Wilson, Vol. II, p. 352) says: *ἡ δεκὰς δὲ ὁμολογεῖται παντέλειος εἶναι*: "By unanimous consent the decade is perfect."

960 [2] *Fragmenta,* 18 (Chaignet, Vol. I, pp. 239-42; Newbold, pp. 177-78).

960 [2a] [Strictly the *Carmen* reads, v. 47: *Per eum certe qui nobis tradidit quarternarium*. Lowe: "This by his name I swear, whose sacred lore First to mankind explained the mystic four."—A. L.]

960 [3] *Commentarius in Aureum carmen,* vv. 45-48 (Lowe, pp. 223-24).

stands next after unity in dignity."[4] The expression "motherless" means that 7 has no factors, that it is a prime number. The epithet "virgin" means that no multiple of 7 is to be found between 1 and 10. Why those two properties should give one number greater dignity than any other remains a mystery. In any event plenty of other properties are mentioned that enhance nobility in the number 7.

We need not dwell on the marvellous properties the Pythagoreans found in other numbers; but it would be a shame not to pay our respects to that most celebrated of numbers, the number 3, which has played and is still playing so important a rôle in the worship of human beings. Know ye, therefore, that "as the Pythagoreans also say, the universe and all things are based on the number 3; for the end, the middle, and the beginning make up the number of the universe, that is, the triad. We use that number as a thing received of Nature according to her laws in celebrating sacrifices to the gods."[5] Other vagaries follow. Then: "In as much as the all, the universe, the perfect, differ from one another not in concept, but only in substance, in the attributes after which they are named, mass would seem to be the only perfect magnitude. For it alone is defined by 3, and 3 is the all." People talk like that when they are dreaming.

The term *τριττύς*, "perfect sacrifice," was applied by the Greeks to the sacrifice of three animals: a pig, a ram, and a goat.[6] It was the *suovetaurilia* of the Latins, where the victims were a pig, a goat,

960 [4] *ἡ δὲ ἑβδομάς ὡς ἀμήτωρ καὶ παρθένος τὴν τῆς μονάδος ἀξίαν δευτέρως ἔχει.* (Lowe: "A septenary being motherless and a virgin has secondarily the dignity of an unite.") In his *Commentarius in Timaeum Platonis,* 36 (Mullach, pp. 188-89), Chalcidius dwells at length on the marvellous properties of the number 7: "Noteworthy another property of the number 7 that other numbers do not have. Of all the numbers comprised within the limits of the number 10, some engender other numbers, some are engendered by others, some both engender and are engendered. Only the number 7 neither engenders any other number lower than 10 nor is engendered by any other. . . . That was why it was called 'Minerva' by the ancients, as having no mother and being itself forever virgin."

960 [5] Aristotle, *De coelo,* I, 1, 2-3 (Hardie-Gaye, Vol. II, p. 268a).

960 [6] Suidas, *Lexicon, s.v.* Τριττύς: *ἡ ἐντελὴς θυσία, ἐκ συὸς, κριοῦ καὶ τράγου, ἐκ τριῶν.* —"The perfect sacrifice: [a sacrifice] of three victims: a pig, a ram, a goat."

and a bull.[7] "Uneven numbers are pleasing to the gods," says Virgil;[8] and in his commentary Servius explains how the number 3, or any other odd number, is to be interpreted.[9] The fact that the number 3 was sacred must have had something to do with the divising of the number 333,333 1/3, for use in votive offerings in Rome.[10]

961. Auguste Comte[1] plagiarizes the Pythagoreans and makes their number nonsense his own. He credits the deification of numbers to fetishism, and talks of "certain numerical speculations which, though sound enough at first in days of fetishistic spontaneity, came eventually to be vitiated by metaphysical mysteries. They concern what may properly be called the philosophical or religious properties

960 [7] According to Festus, *De verborum significatione,* XVII, *s.v.* (London, Vol. III, p. 880), the term was *solitaurilia,* because the three animals had to be uncastrated. He derives the latter word from an Oscan *sollum,* "whole," "intact."

960 [8] *Eglogae,* VIII, v. 75: *"Numero deus impare gaudet."*

960 [9] Virgil's word *"deus"* Servius interprets (Thilo-Hagen, Vol. III, pp. 104-05) as "any one of the gods, following the Pythagoreans, who assign the perfect number 3 to the supreme Deity of whom are the beginning, the middle, and the end; or in particular, Hecate, who is said to wield a threefold power. For that matter, the powers of virtually all the gods are represented by threefold symbols, as the three-forked lightning of Jupiter, Neptune's trident, Pluto's three-headed dog; and so for Apollo, the Sun, and Liber." Of *"impare"* he says: "Odd, because everything goes by 3's, the Fates, the Furies. Hercules was conceived in a triple night. Muses go by 3's. Or else, any odd number at all, there being 7 strings [to a lute?], 7 planets, 7 days named after gods, 7 stars in the North, and so on. Furthermore the odd number is immortal, being indivisible [What a pretty reason!], whereas the even number is mortal, being divisible. To be sure, the Pythagoreans, according to Varro, considered the odd number as having an end, and the even number as infinite, and therefore used odd numbers for healing and many other purposes, the gods of heaven liking the odd numbers, the nether gods the even."

960 [10] Marquardt, *Römische Staatsverwaltung: Sacralwesen,* p. 255: "Public prayers were drawn up with the help of the pontiffs, and the offerings, games, and sacrifices that were vowed could be evaluated at certain sums while they were being written. . . . Livy, XXII, 10, 7: 'on account of the same things, great games were vowed, to cost to the amount of 333,333 1/3 in brass asses (*aeris*).' That was a sacred number. It is still current under the Empire, as witness an inscription from Ephesus, *Corpus inscriptionum Latinarum,* Vol. III-2, no. 6065 (p. 979), in which a Roman dedicates that amount, substituting one-half a sestertium [in silver] for the 'heavy copper' (*triens*) that was no longer in circulation."

It would take us too far afield to review the many divine trinities that have held and still hold sway over the minds of men. To just one, as of modern coinage, we will advert farther along (§ 1659)—the trinity of the Saint-Simonians.

961 [1] *Système de politique positive,* Vol. III, pp. 129-30.

of numbers, which are altogether unappreciated by our academic doctors. Their true evaluation, which has been left for sociology to make, rests on the logical aptness of the first three numbers. . . . Ingenious experiments have shown that in animals distinct numeration ceases after 3. But one would try in vain to claim a more extensive privilege for our species. . . . In both cases, however, one can consider only abstract coexistence, which is always confused after 3, whereas concrete coexistence may, with human beings and animals alike, be exactly measured beyond 3, objects there taking the place of words. It is upon such abstraction, strictly, that the philosophical character of each number, considered with respect to its logical functions, depends. Going more deeply into this intellectual process, one perceives the source of the mental properties that I above assigned to sacred numbers, 1 representing any kind of systematization, 2 always distinguishing combinations, 3 everywhere defining progression."

This "positivistic" metaphysics is identical with metaphysics stripped of that epithet. Why must a combination always be of two elements, and not of three, or more? It is all quite childish! And as usual Comte gets out of his predicament by reasoning in a circle, declaring, *loc. cit.*, p. 130, any non-binary combination "vicious."[2]

961 [2] Says he, *loc. cit.*: "Dynamically considered any given entity (*existence*) presents three successive stages, a beginning, a middle, and an end. [Comte might at least have mentioned a writer or two who had said as much before him (§ 960 [5]).] Considered statically, its constitution results from the permanent concurrence of two opposite but comparable elements. [A prize for anybody who can explain what that means.] Considered as a whole it always appears as a unit. [Tautology.] So any structure where unity of principle does not prevail, any more than binary combination (*composition*) and any succession going beyond three degrees, are necessarily vicious, the operation being badly conducted or being left unfinished. [So saith the high-priest of Positivism, and that is that!] Their fully subjective synthesizing enables people who think in fetishistic terms to feel these fundamental properties of the three numbers that alone can be conceived without symbols [The learned philosopher is in error: the number 4 is very readily conceived without symbols, and so are other numbers, according to the individual.], especially when a developing number-system is concentrating [general] attention on the rudiments of arithmetic. All philosophical speculations on numbers arise from the subordination of other numbers to those three. Such speculations must therefore especially concern numbers that, not being susceptible of division [It would have been nice of Comte to mention some predecessor here—Hierocles, say (§ 960 [4]).], are appropriately

If any combination containing more than two elements is not a combination, one can say, of course, that all combinations are of two elements. Comte apparently bars the number 4 from the sacred numbers, though the Pythagoreans regarded it as divine. When all is said and done, the feeling of a modern Positivist is as good as the feeling of a philosopher of old. No one can say who is right and who wrong, since there is no judge to decide the quarrel. Having exalted the number 7 to such great dignity, Comte forthwith sets out, *Synthèse subjective*, pp. 127-28, to force it upon the world as the basis for a numerical system: "Formed by two progressions followed by a synthesis,[3] or by a progression between two couples,[4] the number 7, coming next after the sum of the three sacred numbers,[5] determines the largest group that we can distinctly imagine. Reciprocally, it fixes the limits of the divisions that we can directly conceive in any given magnitude. [Arbitrary assertions on Comte's part. Like all metaphysicists he does not derive his theories from the facts, but moulds the facts to his theories.] Such a privilege should lead systematically to its adoption as the basis of final numeration, concrete as well as abstract." What connexion is there between the number 7's being equal to $3+3+1$ or to $2+2+2+1$ and its being chosen as the basis of a number-system? But the word "systematically" saves the situation! So "true" liberty stands in contrast to the liberty that has no adjective (§§ 1554 f.)! But there are other good reasons still: "Such a base must be a prime number [So saith the high-priest of Positivism. Mathematicians say that the number with the largest number of factors is the best, 12 therefore being preferable to 10], especially in view of the general need of irre-

called primes (*premiers*) as universal roots. That explains the spontaneous fondness they everywhere inspire. [Everywhere? Did Comte investigate to see?] Here we need merely think of the popularity of the number 7, which derives in two ways from the three radicals by taking now a couple of progressions, now a progression of couples, according as the purpose be static or dynamic, and adding a synthesis [*i.e.*, unity?] either before or after them." This gibberish seems to mean first that $7=3+3+1$, and second that $7=2+2+2+1$. A most striking example of a reasoning by accord of sentiments!

961 [3] [*I.e.*, $7=3+3+1$.—A. L.]

961 [4] [*I.e.*, $7=2+3+2$.—A. L.]

961 [5] *I.e.*, 1, 2, 3.

ducibility [It cannot be so general, for quite a few peoples have chosen the number 10], but also because of the special advantage deriving from a full periodicity in fractional transformations."

962. Hebrew and Christian writers might be expected to feel great reverence for the numbers 6 and 7, because of the number of days God spent on the Creation. Philo the Jew, who repeats not a few Pythagorean fancies about numbers, remarks:[1] "Since the whole world was completed according to the perfect nature of the number 6, the Father honoured the seventh day, praising it and calling it holy. For a holy day it is, not of one people nor of one country but of the universe, and it alone is really worthy to be called popular and the birthday of the world. I know not who could adequately celebrate the nature of the number 7, since it is more excellent than words could say."[2] All the same, Philo tries to find words for at least some of the many beautiful properties of that holy number. He returns more than once to a subject so important. In his *Allegories of the Holy Laws* he begins by glorifying the number 6.[3] It would be absurd to imagine that the world was created in six days, for time could not have existed before the creation of the world. The expression "six days" must therefore be taken not as a period of time but as a "perfect" number. The number 6 is "perfect" because it is the first that is equal to the sum of its factors. Furthermore it is the product of two unequal factors (2×3). Then comes an explanation that must be surpassingly inspiring to anyone able to understand what on earth it means: "The 2 and the 3 have overcome 1, which is incorporeal nature. Two is the symbol of matter, and, like matter, divisible and sunderable. Three is the symbol of mass, for mass has three dimensions." Other beautiful properties of the number 6 appear in animate bodies, which move in six directions, backwards, forwards, upwards, downwards, to right and to left.

962 [1] *De mundi opificio,* 30 (Cohn, Vol. I, p. 31; Yonge, Vol. I, p. 26).

962 [2] *Τὴν δὲ ἑβδομάδος φύσιν οὐκ' οἶδ'εἴ τις ἱκανῶς ἀνυμνῆσαι δύναιτο, παντὸς οὖσαν λόγου κρείττονα.*

962 [3] *Sacrarum legum allegoriae,* I, 2 (Cohn, Vol. I, pp. 61-62; Yonge, Vol. I, pp. 52-53). Strickly speaking, Philo deals with the "diad," the "triad," the "hebdomad," and so on, rather than with the numbers 2, 3, 7 in themselves.

It is also important to know that Moses "sets mortal things in correspondence with the number 6, immortal and divine things with 7."[4] Our old and estimable acquaintance, Dame Nature, loves the number 7 and rejoices in it.[5]

963. St. Augustine is in doubt as to whether the six days of Genesis are to be taken literally, but he has no doubt whatever as to the perfection of the number 6: "We have called the number 6 perfect because it is equal to the sum of its parts, and the parts are such that if they alone are multiplied together they give the number of which they are parts."[1] In other words, the parts are the factors of 6. Six is equal to the sum of its factors, namely, of 1, 2, and 3. That is an experimental fact. Mathematicians put a label (§ 119) on the numbers having that property. On the label they write "perfect number"; but they might just as well write "imperfect number," or any other name. People reasoning by accord of sentiments make a thesis of the definition. The feeling they have of the "perfect" accords, for reasons unknown, with the feeling awakened in them by the reflection that a number is equal to the sum of its factors. Hence such a number is "perfect"; and since 6 is a number of that kind, it is a "perfect" number. But as a matter of fact, reasonings by accord of sentiments are not as strict as that. There is a confused sum of sentiments originating in contemplation of the number 6; and that, roughly, accords with another indeterminate sum of sentiments originating in contemplation of the word "perfect." This latter sum of

962 [4] *Τὰ μὲν θνητὰ ὡς ἔφην καταμετρῶν ἑξάδι, τὰ δὲ μακάρια καὶ εὐδαίμονα ἑβδομάδι.*

962 [5] *Χαίρει δὲ ἡ φύσις ἑβδομάδι.* In his treatise, *De decalogo,* 5-7 (Cohn, Vol. IV, pp. 272-74; Yonge, Vol. III, p. 140), Philo discourses on the "most perfect number 10," as also in *De congressu quaerendae eruditionis gratia,* 16-22 (Cohn, Vol. III, pp. 89-97; Yonge, Vol. II, pp. 175-82). For the number 7 see his *De septenario et festis,* 23 (*De legibus specialibus,* II; Cohn, Vol. V, pp. 95-141; Yonge, Vol. III, pp. 264-91). St. Epiphanius, *De numerorum mysteriis,* II, IV, V, treats first of the mysteries of the number 3 (*Opera,* Vol. III, p. 510); then of the excellences of the double of 3, in plain English, 6 (p. 514); and finally demonstrates overwhelmingly that the number 7 is perfect (*quod et septenarius perfectus sit numerus*) by listing at great length the sacred or important things that are 7 in number (pp. 514-18).

963 [1] *De Genesi ad litteram* (*Opera,* Vol. III, p. 245 f.), IV, 2, 2: *"Proinde istum senarium ea ratione perfectum diximus quod suis partibus compleatur, talibus dumtaxat partibus quae multiplicatae possint consummare numerum cuius partes sunt."* Briefly, $6 = 1 + 2 + 3$, and $1 \times 2 \times 3 = 6$.

sentiments accords just as readily, depending on the individual case, with the sums of sentiments originating in other numbers, such as 4, 10, and so on. According to the definition mathematicians use, 10 is not a perfect number; but from the standpoint of sentiment it may very well be, since the word "perfect" stands for something altogether indefinite (§ 509).

From the logico-experimental standpoint it would be absurd to say: "Six is equal to the sum of its factors; therefore God had to create the world in six days." There would be no connexion between the premise and the conclusion. On the other hand, a reasoning by accord of sentiments establishes just such a connexion by virtue of the term "perfect," which, following a procedure that is general (§ 480), it goes on to eliminate. "The number 6 is perfect; the creation is perfect; therefore it had to be completed in six days." St. Augustine states unequivocally: "In a perfect number of days, to wit, in six, did God finish his handiwork" (§ 1546).[2]

964. It might seem to someone that we have been going into such fatuities too seriously, and that would surely be the case were we considering them strictly from the objective, logico-experimental standpoint. But if from the subjective standpoint we consider that

963 [2] *Op. cit.*, IV, 2, 6: *"Perfecto ergo numero dierum, hoc est senario, perfecit Deus opera sua quae fecit"*; and even more explicitly in *Ibid.*, 7, 14: "Wherefore we cannot say that the number 6 is perfect because God completed all his work in six days, but that God completed his work in six days because the number 6 is perfect. So even if God's work had not been done, the number 6 would still be perfect; but if the number 6 were not perfect, God's work would not have been perfect in respect of that number." Speaking of the Trinity in his treatise on the mysteries of numbers, *De numerorum mysteriis*, III (*Opera*, Vol. III, p. 510), St. Epiphanius advances the thesis "that even the very number of the Trinity as written in Scripture is of a marvellous and mysterious nature"; and facts without end he adduces to prove as much. Suffice the following specimens: three things are in us; mind, spirit, and reason; three the things that cannot be sated; hell, lust, fallow soil. Three the virtues, Faith, Hope, Charity. Jonah dwelt in the belly of the whale three days and three nights. The Saint then goes on to laud the number 6 and finds it perfect also. To show that we have no bias or favouritism against any number, we had better mention a *Theological Arithmetic* (*Theologoumena arithmeticae*) by Nicomachus of Gerasa, wherein tribute of just praise is paid to all the numbers from 1 to 10. Photius, *Myriobiblon*, 187 (Geneva, p. 459) dares aver that Nicomachus talks nothing but nonsense, quite arbitrarily taking numbers as gods and goddesses.

such nonsense has been taken seriously by huge numbers of people in all periods of history, it becomes apparent that it must correspond to wide-spread and very cogent sentiments and that it cannot be ignored in a study of the forms of society.

965. Our study of sacred and perfect numbers has achieved the following purposes:

1. It has given another example of a constant element (residues) and a variable element (derivations) in complex phenomena.[1] The constant element in this case is a sentiment that links "perfection" to numbers in some mysterious way. The number to which the attribute of perfection is ascribed varies according to individual inclinations, and more variable still are the fanciful reasons suggested to account for the perfection.

2. It has given a striking example of the reasoning by accord of sentiments—an example, in other words, of derivation.[2] To base an argument on the perfection of numbers is altogether parallel to basing an argument on "natural law," "solidarity," and the like. Men like St. Augustine held such arguments no less sound, in fact rather more sound, than other arguments by accord of sentiments. In our time, however, it is easier to find people who would not take "perfect" numbers seriously but who hold "natural law," and such things, in high esteem. Such people will grasp the general bearing of our criticism of "perfect" numbers more readily than they would any criticism of "natural law" or "solidarity." That is the chief reason why we have lingered on the subject.

3. It has given an excellent example of the difference we have so often stressed between the definition of logico-experimental science and the metaphysical, theological, sentimental assertion. People who continue asking whether a thing be "just," "good," and so on, (§ 1551) are not aware that to ask such a question differs little if at

965 [1] It is true that we had already given so many examples that another was hardly necessary to prove the point.

965 [2] The study of numbers therefore would belong, strictly, to our chapter on derivations—Chapter IX. However, it saves us some repetition to consider them here.

all from asking whether a given number be "perfect" (§§ 119, 387, 506, 963).

4. It has served to contrast the exactness of the logico-experimental sciences with the vagueness of metaphysical, theological, and sentimental speculations. One need only compare the mathematical concept of "perfect" numbers with the sentimental concepts of individuals who apply the term "perfect" to any number they happen to like.[3]

5. It has given an example of the non-logical action that has no apparent social utility. The non-logical actions corresponding to disquisitions on natural law often seem to have, and sometimes actually do have, their social usefulness. That makes it not so easy to see their absolute fatuousness from the logico-experimental point of view.

966. I-δ: *Hunger for combining residues.* The human being often feels prompted to combine certain residues that are present in his mind. That is a manifestation of a synthetic tendency which is indispensable to practical life. Disjoining residues by analysis is a scientific process of which few people are capable (§ 30). Ask some individual who is not familiar with scientific method (or even, at a venture, someone who is, or ought to be) to solve the problem as to whether $A = B$. It will be found that almost irresistibly he will be inclined to consider at the same time, and without the slightest effort to keep them separate, other questions, such as: "Is it a good idea that A should be equal to B? Is it better to believe that $A = B$? Does the identification of A and B meet with the approval of certain people? Or do they disapprove?" And so on and on. Take the question, "Will the man who follows the precepts of morality achieve material prosperity?" (§§ 1898 f.). It is, virtually, impossible for many people to consider such a question by itself.

967. The human being is loath to dissever faith from experience; he wants a completed whole free from discordant notes. For long

965 [3] We shall be meeting other examples arising under captions 2, 3, 4, above. Our present lengthy discussion of perfect numbers will enable us to be more brief in dealing with them.

centuries Christians believed that their Scriptures contained nothing at variance with historical or scientific experience. Some of them have now abandoned that opinion as regards the natural sciences, but cling to it as regards history. Others are willing to drop the Bible as science and history, but insist on keeping at least its morality. Still others will have a much-desired accord, if not literally, at least allegorically, by dint of ingenious interpretations. The Moslems are convinced that all mankind can know is contained in the Koran. The authority of Homer was sovereign for the ancient Greeks. For certain Socialists the authority of Marx is, or at least was, just as supreme. No end of felicitous sentiments are harmonized in a melodious whole in the Holy Progress and the Holy Democracy of modern peoples.

968. The ancient Epicureans absolutely divorced the residues associated with their gods from other sorts of residues. But that case stands by itself, or is at least very rare. In general, many varieties of residues are blended in concepts of divinity. A similar process of concentration also takes place among the various divinities. That is one of the main forces at work in the development from polytheism to monotheism.

969. The impulse to combine residues plays a not inconsiderable rôle in the use people make of certain words of vague indeterminate meanings but which are supposed to correspond to real things (§ 963). The term "good," and the kindred term "well-being," are quite generally taken as standing for real things. "Good," at bottom, is something pleasing to the sense of taste. Then the sense circle widens and "good" is anything pleasing to the taste and promotive of physical health, and from that, anything promotive of physical health alone. Then the sense-circle widens again to embrace moral sensations, and they come to dominate in what is considered "good," and in "well-being." In the end, among philosophers and moralists especially, moral sensations are the only ones considered at all. In other words, the terms gradually come to designate a sum of residues towards which the person who uses them chances to feel sentiments of attraction and not of revulsion.

970. In "intellectuals" the impulse to combine residues goes farther still. They make one general blend of "well-being," "the true," "the beautiful," "the good," and some of them add "altruism," "solidarity," "the human," or better yet, the "broadly human," thus forming a simple complex gratifying as a whole to their sentimentality. Then that complex (or any other like it) which rests merely on the need for combinations may, eventually, acquire in virtue of residues of group-persistence (Class II) an independent existence, and in certain cases even be personified [for example, Progress, Democracy, Reason].

971. Far from negligible among the differences obtaining between a scientific research and a piece of literature is the fact that the former separates residues while the latter combines them. Literature satisfies the human hunger for combining residues and that need is left unsatisfied by science. As for the demand for logic, to which we shall soon be coming (§ 972), one might guess that it should be better satisfied by science than by literature; and so it may be with some few individuals. But not so for the majority of men. Most people are entirely satisfied with the pseudo-logic of literary compositions. Literature is much better suited to their understanding and their tastes than the exact, rigorous thinking of the experimental method. A scientific work may therefore convince the few specialists who understand the subject with which it deals; but literature is always better able to influence mankind in the mass. That is one of the reasons why political economy has remained so largely literary; and it might just as well be left such for people who are inclined to preach—but not for anyone interested in discovering the uniformities prevailing in economic or social phenomena (§ 77).

972. I-ε: *Hunger for logical developments.*[1] The demand for logic is satisfied by pseudo-logic as well as by rigorous logic. At bottom what people want is to think—it matters little whether the thinking be sound or fallacious. We need only reflect on the tangle-wood of

972 [1] This variety might be considered a species of the preceding, since it involves a combination of the logical residue with other residues. In view of its great importance, however, we find it advisable to make a separate classification for it.

fantastic discussion that has flourished and still flourishes around such incomprehensible subjects as come up in the various systems of theology and metaphysics—wild speculations as to the Creation, the purposes for which human life was ordained, and such things—to gain some conception of the imperiousness of the need that is satisfied by such lucubrations.

973. Those who proclaim "the bankruptcy of Science" [1] are right in the sense that science cannot satisfy the insatiable need of pseudo-logical developments that the human being feels. Science can merely relate one fact to another. There is always, therefore, a fact at which it comes to a halt. The human imagination refuses to stop there. It insists on going on, insists on drawing inferences even from the ultimate fact, on knowing its "cause," and if it cannot find a real cause it invents an imaginary one.

974. We should not forget that if this insistence on having causes at all costs, be they real or imaginary, has been responsible for many imaginary causes, it has also led to the discovery of real ones. As regards residues, experimental science, theology, metaphysics, fatuous speculations as to the origins and the purposes of things, have a common point of departure: a resolve, namely, *not* to stop with the last known cause of the known fact, but to go beyond it, argue from it, find or imagine something beyond that limit. Savage peoples have no use for the metaphysical speculations of civilized countries, but they are also strangers to civilized scientific activity; and if one were to assert that but for theology and metaphysics experimental science would not even exist, one could not be easily confuted. Those three kinds of activity are probably manifestations of one same psychic state, on the extinction of which they would vanish simultaneously.

975. This residue explains the need people feel for covering their non-logical conduct with a varnish of logic—a point we have already stressed time and again and at length. It also accounts for that element in social phenomena which we have designated as *b* (§ 798)

973 [1] See Pareto, *Manuale,* Chap. I, § 48.

and which constitutes the whole subject of derivations.[1] The usual purpose of a derivation, in fact, is to satisfy with pseudo-logic the need of logic, of thinking, that the human being feels.[2]

976. I-ζ: *Faith in the efficacy of combinations.* As we have already noted (§ 890), one may believe that *A* is necessarily conjoined with *B*. That belief may be based on experience, on the fact, that is, that *A* has always been observed in conjunction with *B*. From such a fact, however, logico-experimental science infers merely that it is more or less probable that *A* will always appear in conjunction with *B* (§ 97). To ascribe an attribute of "necessity" to the proposition, one has to add to it a something that is non-experimental—an act of faith (§ 1531).

977. That much being granted, if imagination were equivalent to demonstration,[1] the scientist working in his laboratory would note the combinations *AB* without preconception. But that is not the case. In prosecuting his researches, imagining, inventing, he allows himself to be guided by guesses, assumptions, preconceptions—perhaps even prejudices. That does no harm in the case of the scientist. Experience will be there to rectify any error that may develop from the sentiments he feels.

978. For the person who is not grounded in the logico-experimental method, rôles are inverted. Sentiments now play the leading part. Such a person is chiefly moved by faith in the efficacy of combinations. Oftentimes he is indifferent to experimental verifications. Often again, if he does give them a thought he rests content with utterly insufficient, sometimes even ridiculous, proofs.

979. Such conceptions reign sovereign in the minds of the majority of men, and that is why the mind of the scientist sometimes succumbs to them. That will happen the more readily, the more closely, in the pursuit of his calling, the scientist keeps in touch with the population at large and to the same extent the less aware will he be that his sentimental results are in conflict with experience.

975 [1] See Volume III.

975 [2] We need dwell no further here on residues of this type because they are virtually the subject of this work as a whole.

977 [1] Pareto, *Manuale*, Chap. I, § 51.

That is why the student of the social sciences finds it more difficult to adhere to the logico-experimental method than, for instance, the chemist or the physicist.

980. But let us ignore the logico-experimental sciences for the present, and look at things from the standpoint of sentiments and residues. If the combination *AB* is a fact not of the laboratory, but of ordinary life, it will in the long run engender in the minds of people a sentiment linking *A* indissolubly with *B,* and such a sentiment is virtually indistinguishable from a sentiment originating outside experience or pseudo-experimentally.

981. If there is a cock in the hen-coop, the eggs will produce chicks. When a cock crows at midnight, someone dies in the house. For the person reasoning on sentiment, those two propositions are equally certain and, for that matter, equally experimental; and the sentiment that dictates them derives in the one case as in the other from direct experience and from indirect experiences reported by other persons. If one objects that a rooster has been known to crow at midnight without anybody's dying, there is the answer that an egg from a hen living with a rooster often fails to produce a chick. The scientist distinguishes the two phenomena not only by direct experience, but also by the check of likeness—(assimilation) (§ 556). The plain man is not equal to that; and even when he declares the belief about the cock crowing at midnight an absurd superstition, he can offer no better reasons than he could when he held it to be an undebatable truth.

982. Speaking in general, the ignorant man is guided by faith in the efficacy of combinations (§ 78), a faith which is kept alive by the fact that many combinations are really effective, but which none the less arises spontaneously within him, as may be seen in the child that amuses itself by trying the strangest combinations. The ignorant person distinguishes little if at all between effective and ineffective combinations. He bets on lottery numbers according to his dreams just as confidently as he goes to the railroad station at the time designated in the time-table. He thinks it quite as natural to consult the faith-curer or the quack as to consult the most expert physician. Cato the Elder hands out magical remedies and directions for farming with the same assurance.

983. As experimental science progresses, people try to give an experimental gloss to the products of their sentiments and assert that their faith in combinations derives from experience. But one need only examine the facts a little closely to see the fatuousness of such explanations.

984. If superstition has on the whole fallen off in the masses in our day, the fact is due not so much directly to the influence of the logico-experimental sciences as indirectly to the prestige of scientists—they meantime having introduced quite a number of new superstitions of their own. And it is partly due to the enormous development of industrial life, which is to a large extent an experimental life and has had the effect of disputing—in no very explicit way, to be sure—the dominion of sentiment.

985. The belief that *A* must necessarily be linked with *B* is strengthened and becomes stable in virtue of residues of group-persistence. For the very reason that it is rooted in sentiments it takes over from them the vagueness which is their distinguishing trait; and *A* and *B* are oftentimes not definite things, definite acts, but classes of things or acts, usually corresponding to our I-β and I-γ varieties (similars or opposites, mysteries). Hence a thing *A* is linked to anything *B* provided it be a similar or an opposite, or exceptional, terrible, propitious, and so on. A comet presages the death of some important person, but who the person is nobody very definitely knows.[1]

985 [1] Examples are available for the asking—the old chronicles are literally crammed with them: *e.g.*, Foulcher de Chartres, *Histoire des Croisades,* pp. 33, 155, 217, 233: "When we reached the city of Heraclea, we saw a prodigy in the sky. A great light suddenly appeared, brilliant, and of dazzling brightness. It was shaped like a sword with the point turned toward the east. What the sign portended for the future we did not know, but committed present and future alike into the hands of God. . . . In the year 1106 a comet appeared in the sky. That sign began to glow during the month of February, on the very day of the new Moon. It evidently foretold some future happening, but not presuming to draw any prognostic from such a prodigy, we committed ourselves for all that it might portend into the hands of God. . . . At that time Balak had revealed to him through a dream a misfortune that was to come upon him; for he thought he saw Josselyn tearing out his

986. Whatever the origin of the belief that *A* is linked to *B*, whether it be experimental, pseudo-experimental, sentimental, fantastic, or of some other character, once it exists and has been consolidated, stabilized, by the residues of group-persistence, it exerts a powerful influence upon sentiments and conduct, and that in two directions, the one passive, the other active (§§ 890 f.).

987. On the passive side, given one element of the combination *AB*, the individual is uneasy if the whole combination does not materialize. So, *B* being posterior to *A*, on observing *A* he looks for *B* (comets, and events announced by them—presages in general). *B* being given, there is the conviction that it must have been preceded by *A*, and the past is ransacked until a corresponding *A* is found (events that were supposed to have foretold the rise of Roman Emperors to the throne). If *A* and *B* both lie in the past, they are brought together even if they have nothing whatever to do with each other (presages recorded by historians, when they are not inventions pure and simple).

988. Oftentimes *B* is left undefined or is defined only to the extent of belonging to a certain class. Something has to happen—exactly what no one really knows (§ 925). Under pressure of group-persistences the combination *AB* has acquired a personality of its own, independent, within certain limits, of *B*.

989. On the active side there is a feeling that if one can get *A*, one can get *B*. In that way the passive science of divination (§ 924) becomes the active science of sorcery. The Romans already had introduced an active element into divination through their rules for accepting or rejecting presages. Not all

[Balak's] eyes, as he thereafter made known to his men. His priests [He was an infidel.], to whom he reported his vision at once, asking for an interpretation thereof, told him that that misfortune, or some other equivalent, would surely happen to him if ever chance should will that he fall into Josselyn's hands. . . . [Balak is eventually slain in battle with Josselyn and decapitated.] Josselyn ordered it [the head] to be carried forthwith to Antioch as evidence of the victory he had won. . . . So was the aforesaid dream fulfilled, which Balak, gloomy prophet of his own fate, had recounted at the time of Josselyn's miraculous escape from prison. At that time, in fact, he had seen Josselyn tearing out his eyes; and tear them out he did, and well, taking with them his head and the use of his bodily members."

combinations lend themselves to such transformation. In the first place, combinations in which *A* does not lie within human powers —thunder, for instance, or the appearance of a comet—are of course barred. But there are cases even when *A* does lie within human powers where there is no belief that *B* can be obtained by use of *A*. A superhuman being is born of a virgin, but no one believes that a virgin will always yield such a child. It took thirty-six hours or more to engender Hercules, but no one imagines that by exerting oneself to that same extent one will as a matter of course beget a son of Herculean stature. There are cases, then, where there is a mixture of the active and the passive—words of good omen, for instance. If they are heard accidentally, they presage good fortune. It is also a good idea to utter them deliberately, to facilitate the advent of good fortune. Similarly, but *vice versa,* for words of evil omen.

990. In general terms, the concept of the capacity of *A* to produce *B* adds something to the simple concept of the combination *AB*.[1]

991. Class II: *Group-persistences*[1] (Persistence of aggregates).

990 [1] This would be the place for a study of magic and kindred arts, which, however, being a special investigation must be referred to Special Sociology.

991 [1] [The Italian phrase is *"persistenza degli aggregati."* The aggregate is an aggregate (combination, association, group) of *sensations*. The tendency to consolidate such groups of sensations and make them permanent in time Pareto regards as one of the great and fundamental forces in society. Pareto likes to clarify some of his conceptions by showing that they are merely scientific definitions of the hazy concepts of ordinary parlance, such as one notes in the comparison of the ordinary concept of "heat and cold" with the scientific concept of "temperature." In this sense the concept of "group-persistence" would be a definition of the ordinary concept of "habit" or "custom." The concept of "group-persistence" is basic in Pareto's theories of the social equilibrium and class-circulation, and in general in his whole conception of history. It is therefore one of the most important technical phrases in this work. All the difficulties, syntactical, rhetorical, expositional, that we met in the expression "non-logical actions" recur with "the persistence of aggregates." I fix on the phrases "group-persistence," "residues of group-persistence," "group-persistences" (for the eleven shown in his table, § 888), after careful and painful experimentation with all possible other translations. The obscurity that arises (when it arises) in connexion with the concept is due to the fact that in ordinary language the "group-persistences" are widely different in appearances: "Uncle Sam," "the Devil," "Russia," "goodness," "honour," "Santa Claus," "the individual," "Vilfredo Pareto" (to include the word "God" among such examples would be to tear the veil from a studious reticence on Pareto's part). These, analytically and experimentally con-

Certain combinations constitute a group of elements closely united as in one body, so that the compound ends by acquiring a personality such as other real entities have. Such combinations may often be recognized by the fact of their having names of their own, distinct from the mere enumeration of their component elements. The presence of such a name in its turn gives greater consistency to the concept of the group as a personality (§ 1013), by virtue of a residue which assumes that a name always has a thing corresponding to it.[2] The sentiments associated with the group may remain virtually constant, but they may also vary in intensity and in diffusion. Such variation must be kept distinct from that other and much greater variability which affects the forms in which the sentiments express themselves—from variability in derivations, in other words. There is, briefly, first, a nucleus, which has a personality of its own but which may vary, much as a chick varies in becoming a hen, or a

sidered, are groups (aggregates, combinations, associations) of sensations that the mind consolidates into units abiding (persisting) in time, denotes with a name and then more or less personifies. Different as they seem, they are alike from Pareto's point of view, as groups of sensations abiding (persisting) in time. The tendency of the mind (the instinct, sentiment, impulse) that creates such units is the force now of first, now of second, importance in determining the social equilibrium. The intensity of the impulse or sentiment in individuals determines what we ordinarily call "character." In society at large it determines the type of civilization or "culture." Anyone who chances to dislike the phrase "group-persistences" can restore the original Italian by reading "persistences of aggregates" or, "persistences of associations of ideas and acts," or if one is a real Paretan enthusiast, by reading "persistences of associations of the sensations *P, Q, R. . . .*" As for some of the possible translations that I discard. To use the term "persisting aggregates" would involve a far-reaching misunderstanding of Pareto's thought. Not the aggregate or group of associations does the work, but the fact that it persists in time. The same associations by and large are shared by all members of a community. They endure however only in some of them, and the people in whom they endure are different sorts of people from the ones who take up new associations each day. "Persistence of combinations": I am conscious of one defect in Pareto's exposition of his "group-persistences." He seems to hesitate as to whether he should establish some organic connexion between Class I and Class II residues, whereby the function of the latter would be to make the combinations of Class I habitual and permanent in time. If that was his idea, he should have made it far more explicit. If it was not his idea, then it would seem that persistence of specific combinations should appear as a special genus among Class II residues. "Persistence of combinations" has at any rate to be discarded in the light of this ambiguity.—A. L.]

991 [2] See Chapter X (Verbal Proofs), and especially § 1544.

caterpillar in becoming a butterfly; and then, second, there are the manifestations under forms of derivations of that nucleus, and they would correspond to the capriciously varying conduct of the chick or the caterpillar.

992. After the group has been constituted, an instinct very often comes into play that tends with varying energy to prevent the things so combined from being disjoined, and which, if disintegration cannot be avoided, strives to dissemble it by preserving the outer physiognomy of the aggregate. This instinct may be compared roughly to mechanical inertia: it tends to resist the movement imparted by other instincts. To that fact the tremendous social importance of Class II residues is to be ascribed.

993. Combinations that disintegrate as soon as they are formed do not constitute groups of subsisting individuality. But if they do persist, they end by acquiring that trait. Not by abstraction only do they take on a sort of individuality, any more than by abstraction only do we recognize groups of sensations by such names as "hunger," "wrath," or "love," or a number of sheep by the name of "flock." The point must be clearly grasped. There is nothing corresponding to the noun "flock," in the sense that the flock may be separated from the sheep which constitute it. At the same time the flock is not a mere equivalent to the sum of the sheep. The sheep, by the very fact that they are members of the flock, acquire characteristics which they would not have apart from it. A male and a female thrown together at an age for reproduction are something different from the same male and female taken by themselves. Yet that does not mean that there is an entity *X* distinct from male and female which represents the male and the female coupled.[1]

994. To these considerations must be added another, to which frequent reference has already been made in these pages, namely, that though the abstraction corresponding to the group may not have an objective existence, it may have a subjective existence, and that fact is most important in its bearing on the social equilibrium.

993 [1] [The Spanish have a word for it: *un matrimonio,* "a married couple."—A. L.]

An example will make that clear. Let us imagine that certain people have taken a river for their god. The fact may be explained in a great variety of ways: *a.* It may be said that by a process of abstraction the people in question have distinguished from the concrete river an ideal river that they regard as "a force of nature" and worship as such. *b.* It may be said that they have ascribed human attributes to the river, assuming that it has a soul, just as a man is assumed to have a soul, and that that soul has been deified. *c.* It may be said that the river has given rise within the people in question to a variety of sensations to an extent at least not clearly defined, but very potent. These sensations persist, and their sum, their combination, their aggregate, constitutes, *for the subject* and *for those people,* a thing to which they have given a name, just as people give names to all other subjective things deemed worthy of their notice. This entity together with its name is attracted by other similar entities and may take its place in the pantheon of the people, just as it may take its place near the flag in the patriotic aggregate (the German Rhine), or a more modest place in the baggage-train of the poets. No one of these three manners of approach is to be barred; but the third explains a number of facts that are not accounted for by the other two, and which sometimes even stand in conflict with them. The residue underlying the third hypothesis is therefore much more generally used than the other two residues.

995. We came upon cases of this kind on a previous occasion in our discussion of the gods of ancient Rome (§§ 176 f.); and we saw that they corresponded to certain associations of acts and ideas. We now carry the analysis a step further, and see in those cases residues of Class I which have become permanent under pressure of residues of Class II. A cult of that type is a sort of fetishism where the fetish is not a thing, but an act. If we tried to explain it by hypotheses *a* or *b,* we should never succeed in understanding how the Roman, whose mind was undoubtedly more practical, less subtle, less ingenious than the Greek mind, could have come out with so many abstractions, seen everywhere about him so many "forces of nature" (probably not even having the remotest notion corresponding to that term!), and so shown himself more idealistic than the Greek. It would seem, indeed, that the opposite should be the case. On the hypothesis *c*, the facts are very readily explainable. Class II residues were much stronger among the Romans than among the Greeks.[1] Hence it ought to follow—and it actually has followed—that a larger number of aggregates would acquire independent individuality, and it is such aggregates, precisely, that have been passed off as "personifications of forces of nature" by rationalizing historians far surpassing in subtlety of mind the rough and rude people among whom the associations in question originated.

996. We find inscriptions to the goddess Annona (the year's crop).[1] It seems hard to believe that by a process of abstraction the Romans should have personified the victualling of Rome, and then have proceeded to exalt the personification to divine rank. One readily sees, however, how strong and deep-seated the sensations associated with the maintenance of a food-supply at once so important and so difficult must have been. They came to constitute a group, which by the fact of permanency acquired an individuality of its own—became a *thing*. That thing, eventually, under its name, Annona, took its place with many other things of the same kind in the Roman pantheon.

997. The *annona*, the food-supply, existed not objectively but

995 [1] That we showed by proofs in Chapter II *passim*, but especially §§ 226 f. [And Pareto will show it again in Chapters XII and XIII (Vol. IV).—A. L.]

996 [1] De Ruggiero, *Dizionario epigrafico, s.v. Annona* (*dea*): "From the Capital itself (*Corpus*, Vol. VI, no. 22; Orelli, *Inscriptionum . . . collectio*, no. 1810): *Annonae sanctae Aëlius Vitalio mensor perpetuus dignissimo corporis pistorum siliginiariorum d(ono) d(edit)*. ("To Holy Annona, Aëlius Vitalio, surveyor in perpetuity, by most reverent gift of the guild of millers and bakers (this tablet) inscribes.") From Russicade [in Numidia] (*Corpus*, Vol. VIII, no. 7960; Orelli-Henzen, *Inscriptionum . . . collectio*, no. 5320): *M. Aemilius Ballator praeter (sestertium) X m(illia) n(ummum), quae in opus cultumve theatri postulante populo dedit, statuas duas, Genium patriae n(ostrae) et Annonae sacrae urbis sua pecunia posuit*, etc. ("Marcus Aemilius Ballator, in addition to 10,000 sestertia in cash that he gave at the request of the people for the building and operation of a theatre, has erected at his own expense two statues [the one to the] Genius of our country and [the other] to Holy Annona of this city.") Her cult developed most notably in Rome and its vicinity under the Empire, at a time when Rome had come to be liberally and cheaply provided with victuals, as a result of a reorganization in storage and marketing (*curae annonae*)."

subjectively. If anyone had thought in the old Roman days of having such religious pseudo-experiences as are had in ours, he would have found the goddess Annona in the minds of the Romans, along with other gods like her, male and female. That would have proved that certain associations of sentiments and notions were present under certain names in the minds of the Romans; but it would not in the least have proved the objective existence of such groups. In a certain sense, if we chose to use poetic language, we might say that such groups were "alive" in the consciousness of the Romans; but we could not say that they had any "life" outside that consciousness.[1]

998. Phenomena of this kind differ the more widely the farther they stand removed from their residues. The Romans stuck close to residues, for the very reason that they were but slightly inclined to theological and philosophical speculation. Owing to their aptitude for such speculations, the Greeks were carried far afield from residues by derivations, and one such derivation results in the anthropomorphism of the Greek gods—which explains why the Greek gods are so much more "alive" than the gods of the Romans (§ 178).

999. Viewed from any logical standpoint, the apotheosis of the Roman emperors was an absurd and ridiculous thing; but considered as a manifestation of abiding residues, it seems natural and reasonable enough. The Emperor, no matter who he was, personified the Empire, orderly administration, justice, the *pax Romana;* and such sentiments did not in the least languish because one man died and another succeeded him. The permanence of that aggregate was

997 [1] Sorel, *Le système historique de Renan,* Vol. IV, p. 341; Pt. III, Chap. I, entitled: *"La vie posthume de Jésus et les traces qu'elle a laissées"*—in question, the Apostles, after the death of Jesus: "During this period they thought they had before them a Jesus as real as the Jesus they had known in Galilee and that they were going on with their former life with him. And there is no doubt that that was the situation for a long time, for the claim was that the rules for fasting and for the Christian Passover went back to the revelation made by the risen Jesus (*Didascalia,* XXI [Gibson, Vol. I, pp. 92-101]). That presupposes that, according to very ancient traditions, the posthumous life of Jesus lasted long enough for ecclesiastical laws to have had time to form. I believe it has to be considered as lasting down to the martyrdom of St. James the Apostle. The surmise rests on a number of details that are intelligible on no other basis."

the fact, the apotheosis one of the forms under which it found expression.

1000. Similar considerations hold for many other instances of the deification of human beings. The thing did not take place, as Spencer imagines, as a result of a logical analysis (§§ 682 f.). It is just one of the many manifestations of the permanence of groups of sensations. We shall see farther along (§ 1074 [1]) that in the first place, Rome is made a goddess; and not till afterwards does someone imagine that there was a woman who had that name and so came to be deified. Similar examples occur in great abundance. Sometimes the development is from a god to an imaginary person, and sometimes from a real person to a god. All such are derivations and essentially variable, whereas the sentiments which find expression in that manner are constant.

1001. It has been observed that customs sometimes endure after the circumstances in which they originated have disappeared, and the phenomenon has—not generally, to be sure, but in one particular case—been called a "survival." Says Tylor, *Primitive Culture* (1871, Vol. I, p. 62; 1873, Vol. I, p. 70): "When a custom, an art, or an opinion is fairly started in the world, disturbing influences may long affect it so slightly that it may keep its course from generation to generation." That is what Tylor calls a "survival," but it is just a particular case of a thing much more general. The persistence of a custom may be due to its meeting weak resistance, but it may also be due to its having found support in a force superior to any opposing force, considerable though this latter may have been. So the Christian Church certainly fought might and main against pagan "superstitions," but with varying success. Some of them were demolished and disappeared. Others could not be conquered, and held their ground. When the Church realized that the resistance was too great, it ended by compromising, and contented itself with giving a new garb—often a very transparent one—to an old superstition.

1002. In such phenomena one clearly detects the working of residues constituted by group-persistences. But we get something more and better than that simple observation: They enable us to explain many other phenomena. Says Monsignor Duchesne:[1] "The litanies were solemn supplications instituted to invoke heavenly protection upon earthly possessions. They were sung in the springtime, in the season of the late frosts so dreaded by farmers. It is not surprising that on a point of that kind Christianity should have found itself in agreement with religious customs of an earlier period. [Christianity did not "find itself in any agreement"; Christianity simply had to resign itself to accepting certain customs—an entirely different matter.] . . . The same needs, the same sense of this or that danger, the same confidence in divine aid, inspired very similar rites." It would seem, from that, that paganism and Christianity, each operating independently, happened by chance, or as the result of identical causes, to institute the same festival. Such a thing might at a hazard be granted as a rule; but it is devoid of any probability in the present case, the moment we consider that the two religions were in no wise independent, that the newer was superimposed upon the older, and that the details of the ceremonies are identical—as Monsignor Duchesne himself notes: "In Rome the holiday selected was the twenty-fifth of April, a traditional date on which the ancient Romans celebrated the festival of the Robigalia. The principal rite in that festival was a procession, which, issuing from the city through the Porta Flaminia, made its way toward the Pons Milvius. . . . The Christian procession that replaced it followed the same route to the same bridge."

1003. In other cases the Church offered a greater and more effective resistance to the continuance of ancient customs. It arranged matters so that the Christian Easter did not fall on the same date as the Hebrew Passover. It tried to put an end to the celebration of the pagan festival of the first of January, and partially won its point by replacing it with Christmas. We may guess, therefore, that had it been able, it would also have changed the date of the Rogations.

1004. Monsignor Duchesne (whom we quote because he cannot be suspected of hostility to the Catholic Church) gives other examples,

1002 [1] *Origines du culte chrétien*, Vol. I, pp. 293 f.

Vol I, pp. 283-84: "The [Philocalian] calendar of the year 336 contains, for the twenty-second of February, a feast called the *Natale Petri de cathedra.* Its purpose was to commemorate the inauguration of the episcopate, or apostolate, of St. Peter. . . . The choice of the day had not been dictated by any Christian tradition. We need only glance at the ancient calendars of the Roman religion (*Corpus Inscriptionum Latinarum,* Vol. I, p. 386) to see that the twenty-second of February was devoted to the most popular of all festivals, the festival of the family dead. The observance of that festival and the rites which accompanied it was considered incompatible with the Christian profession of faith. But it was very difficult to uproot habits so particularly dear and deep-rooted. That, doubtless, was the reason why the feast of the twenty-second of February was established."

In that Monsignor Duchesne is entirely in the right. The explanation he gives is the one that best harmonizes with the facts. The Catholic Church had no end of difficulty in putting an end to pagan banquets in honour of the dead, and often enough it had to be prudent and rest content with transforming what it could not abolish.[1]

1004 [1] In his *Epistolae,* XXIX, 8 (*Ad Alypium*) (*Opera,* Vol. II, p. 118; *Works,* Vol. VI, p. 89), St. Augustine tells how he tried to abolish the custom of holding banquets in the churches in honour of the dead. His hearers were not convinced. Said they: *"Quare modo? Enim antea qui haec non prohibuerunt Christiani non erant?"* ("How is that? Bishops heretofore have not prohibited such things. They were not Christians?"). The Saint had a moment of perplexity and was about to withdraw, when those who had disputed him came and called on him; and he therefore explained just why the Church had had to tolerate such banquets in the past: "When peace was at last made after such long and cruel persecutions, throngs of heathen were disposed to adopt the Christian faith, but they were restrained by the fact that along with their idol-worshipping they had been accustomed to spending their holidays in riots of drinking and feasting, and it was not easy for them to give up enjoyments that were as ancient as they were wicked. Our elders, therefore, in order to condone such weakness in part and for a time, thought that in exchange for (*post*) the festivals they were giving up there should be others which could be celebrated in honour of the Holy Martyrs with the same splendour, though not with the same sacrilege." And he exhorts his flock to imitate the churches overseas, which were doing away with such wrongful things. When he was met with the rejoinder that "banquets were held every day in the basilica of the blessed Apostle Peter," he replied that "it was well known that they had often been pro-

1005. Examples without number show the saints taking over cults of the pagan gods, and so make clear that, at bottom, it is a case of one identical thing assuming different forms.

1006. Says Maury:[1] "This substitution of Christian ceremonies for pagan rites occurred whenever the latter were of such nature as to be susceptible of sanctification. It was especially the case in countries like Gaul, Great Britain, Germany, and the northern lands, where the Gospel was not preached until a fairly late date and where pagan beliefs showed themselves vigorous and less docile. The Church herself enjoined this compromise with popular superstition on her apostles, and so we still find numerous traces of it today in our rural districts. In certain places [in France] Charon's penny is still placed in the mouth of the dead. The statue of the saint is plunged, as was the statue of Cybele, in a sacred bath. The fountain continues to receive in the name of a saint libations that were poured of yore to a divinity. Oracles are obtained in practically the same manner as our ancestors obtained them [And just as naturalistic paganism had obtained them before the advent of anthropomorphic paganism.], and there is nothing, down even to the cult of the phallus, which has not been sanctified under evasive forms."

hibited. However, they did occur in places far removed from the bishop's influence (*conversatione* [Pareto renders: *abitazione*]). In a metropolis such as Rome there were always many licentious people about, especially foreigners, who arrived in town every day and observed heathen customs with a fidelity proportionate to their ignorance. It had therefore so far been impossible to eradicate the evil altogether." In the *Confessions,* VI, 2, St. Augustine voices commendation of St. Ambrose for prohibiting offerings of victuals in honour of the saints in the churches in Milan, "so avoiding giving the intemperate occasion for indulging in strong drink, and because such things smacked of the superstitions of the heathen *parentalia."* In his *De moribus ecclesiae catholicae et de moribus Manichaeorum,* I, 34, 75 (*Opera,* Vol. I, p. 1342; *Works,* Vol. V, p. 47), the Saint says anent bad Christians: "I know that many worship tombs and paintings. I have heard that many drink most excessively at the graves of the dead, offering banquets to the corpses, burying themselves [in wine] over those who lie buried [in earth], and setting such gluttony and tippling to the account of piety." The persistence of ancient customs is manifest in another of his letters, *Epistolae,* XXII (*Opera,* Vol. II, p. 92; *Works,* Vol. VI, pp. 53-54): "The drunken and licentious banquets that are held in the cemeteries are believed by the ignorant and carnally-minded masses to be not only

1006 [1] *La magie et l'astrologie dans l'antiquité et au moyen âge,* pp. 157-59. *Cf.* Saintyves, *Les saints successeurs des dieux.*

1007. A residue built up of certain associations of ideas and acts in ancient Rome comes down to our time under successive guises (§ 178). It does not change with the invasion of Greek anthropomorphism, whereby the fountain becomes a personified divinity, nor with the rise of Christianity—the god or goddess merely becoming a saint. On a parallel line, a metaphysical transformation gives the residue abstract form as a "natural force" or as a "manifestation of divine power"; but such transformations are kept for the use of writers and philosophers, and are not very warmly welcomed by the masses at large. The power inherent in the residue becomes evident enough in the fact of its persistence in the face of so many and such varying vicissitudes; and so it is clear that as regards deter-

an honour to the martyrs but a great comfort to the dead," and he advises Aurelius to suppress them. It is clear enough that the Church was doing everything in its power to extirpate customs such as these and tolerated them only when it could do no better. On that point it would be well to read the whole of a letter by Gregory the Great to Mellitus, *Epistolae,* XI, 4, 76 (*Opera,* Vol. III, pp. 1215-16; Barmby, Vol. I, p. 85). Just an excerpt here: Gregory is giving directions as to the manner of dealing with the English. First of all, he observes, heathen temples may be retained: "Take holy water (*aqua benedicta fiat*) and sprinkle it about in such temples; then let altars be built and relics be deposited in them. If such temples are well constructed (*i.e.,* worth the trouble), they should be made over from the cult of devils to the worship of the true God; for when those people see that their shrines are not being destroyed, they will dismiss error from their hearts, and acknowledging and worshipping the true God, feel more at home in gathering (*familiarius concurrat*) at their accustomed places. [Here the Church is evidently trying to make capital out of the popularity of certain heathen shrines.] And in cases where it is the custom to slaughter many cattle in sacrifices to devils, that too must be turned into a certain solemnity for them. For instance, on days of dedication or on the birthdays of the Holy Martyrs whose relics are being deposited there, let them make shrines to them out of the branches of trees about those same churches that have been made over from temples, and let them celebrate such occasions with religious banquets. . . . For evidently not everything can be eradicated from such untutored minds all at once." Muratori, *Dissertazioni sopra le antichità italiane,* LXXV (Vol. III, p. 464): "And since sometimes in these reunions [of the confraternities] it is thought that feasts are more solemnly celebrated with some sort of banquet and good wine, the which not seldom gives rise to quarrels and enmities, it behooves us once more to hearken to Hincmar, who attests that the same thing was going on in his day, nay, his words seem to be describing the customs of our own: 'For,' says he, 'there are banquets and feasts which the Divine authority forbids, and of them come expense and undue levy, and wicked and silly pleasures are the rule, and quarrels, hatreds, and dissensions, and often, as we have observed, even murders. Wherefore we forbid them.' "

mining the social equilibrium, it is far more important to consider the residue than to consider the various ephemeral vestments that it assumes in course of time.

1008. And it is also clear that forms change more readily than substance, derivations more readily than residues. Banquets in honour of the dead become banquets in honour of the gods, and then again banquets in honour of saints; and then finally they go back and become merely commemorative banquets again. Forms can be changed, but it is much more difficult to suppress the banquets. Briefly (and therefore not very exactly) one might say that a religious custom or a custom of that general character offers the less resistance to change, the farther removed it stands from its residues in simple associations of ideas and acts, and the larger the proportion it contains of theological, metaphysical, or logical concepts.[1]

1009. That is why the Catholic Church won an easy victory over the major gods of paganism, but found it much more difficult to deal with the little secondary divinities. And that again is why it could gain the acceptance of Graeco-Latin civilization for the theological concept of a single God—or Trinity—but at the price of permitting the abiding residues of the old religion to continue expressing themselves in the worship of saints and in many customs that at bottom were not greatly at variance with those which had prevailed in the past. That, finally, is the reason why it is easier to change a people's form of government than its religion, manners and customs, and language. Even in changes of government under

1008 [1] In his *Narrative of a Voyage to the Pacific and Behring's Strait,* pp. 309 f., Beechey writes of the Indians who were being taught in the missions at San Francisco: "The neophytes being thus arranged, the speaker began, '*Santíssima Trinidad, Diós, Jesú Cristo, Espíritu Santo,*' pausing between each name to listen if the simple Indians, who had never spoken a Spanish word before, pronounced it correctly or anything near the mark. . . . They did not appear to me to pay much attention to what was going forward, and I observed to the *padre* that I thought their teachers had an arduous task; but he said they had never found any difficulty, that the Indians were accustomed to change their own gods, and that conversion was in a measure habitual to them. I could not help smiling at this reason of the *padre* but have no doubt it was very true; and that the party I saw would feel as little compunction at apostatizing again, whenever they should have an opportunity of returning to their own tribe."

its varying forms the substance remains but little changed. The prefect under the Third Republic in France is the twin brother of the prefect under the Second Empire, and the "official candidacy" under the two governments differs little if at all.

1010. The fanaticism and idiocy that inspired the old prosecutions for witchcraft are present point for point in modern prosecutions for offences against the sex religion. Offenders are no longer burned at the stake, to be sure; but that is because criminal penalties have been mitigated all along the line. When severity was the rule witches were burned and thieves were hanged. Today sex heretics and thieves alike get off with mere terms in prison. But the forms of the phenomenon and the principles that it betrays are the same. Procedure under the Inquisition deprived the defendant of guarantees he enjoyed in the episcopal and civil courts. Says Lea:[1] "The procedure of the episcopal courts . . . was based on the principles of the Roman law, and whatever may have been its abuses in practice, it was equitable in theory, and its processes were limited by strictly defined rules. In the Inquisition all this was changed."

1011. And lo! the same thing is now being done for crimes of sex heresy, for the crime, for instance, of printing stories that are, or are reputed to be, obscene or even merely "immoral," the crime of photographing women scantily clad, the crime of mentioning the embrace of Daphnis and Chloe—things that have always been done and will always be done so long as the human race endures. Civilized governments give asylum to political exiles even if guilty of homicide, but they hand over sex heretics to their prosecutors, sex heresy being a more serious crime than murder, as was the crime of heresy in Catholic countries in days of yore. In England, the land of the habeas corpus, and in the year of grace 1912 (June), the House of Commons approved on second reading a bill permitting the police to arrest without warrant any person suspected of being about to commit a crime connected with the "white-slave trade." If the term designated nothing more than the fraudulent and deceitful alluring of a woman to a house of prostitution, there would be no question

1010 [1] *History of the Inquisition,* Vol. I, p. 399.

of any sex religion; it would be a crime like any other crime involving fraud or deception, aggravated in some instances by the greater damage inflicted on the victim. But such is not the case. In many many instances seaport authorities have halted prostitutes who deliberately and in full awareness of what they were doing expressed intentions of sailing overseas for the simple reason that they hoped to make more money in some foreign country. Not the remotest suggestion of fraud or deception! The crime could only be viewed as a transgression of a special taboo. So at Basel in Switzerland the police on one occasion raided all lodging-houses in the middle of the night, roused the guests, and whenever they found a man and a woman in the same room, demanded that they give proof of legal marriage. In this case it was evident that whatever the name of the law applied in such fashion, there was no question of fraud, deception, or any other such crime, but only of a violation of a sex taboo, much like the sin of the Catholic in eating meat on Friday or the sin of the Moslem in eating, drinking, or having commerce with his wife between sunrise and sunset on a day of Ramadan.[1]

1011 [1] A correspondent writing in the *Journal de Genève,* July 11, 1913, declares himself in favour of "suppressing the white-slave trade," but is nevertheless forced to admit on the strength of the facts that there is an element of farce in the whole business. Reporting the Convention on the White-Slave Trade held in London, June 30-July 5, 1913, he comments: "This convention will certainly equal in importance the Madrid convention of 1910, which marked an epoch in the battle against this new scourge [The good soul finds "new" a thing that has gone on from the days when Greek hetairai were inspiring Greek poets and dramatists down to our own.], which was brought to world-wide attention less than fifty years ago by the sagacity of a few philanthropists and specialists in sex morality [Some such specialists are closer students than they need be.]. Those gentlemen had some trouble in convincing their contemporaries that there was any such thing as the abominable traffic which they had set out to combat. But when the genuineness of certain allegations was placed beyond dispute, there was a shift from excessive scepticism to excessive credulousness, the public being inclined to accept without investigation and with evidence of real appetite yarns that were as dramatic as they were without basis in fact. The 'movies' came to corroborate this sensation-mongering with the fabricated testimony of their films, with the result that educated people, in the habit of using their minds, are no longer so easily taken in and are beginning to move the previous question. That is why, in this domain as in any other, it is important to have trustworthy organs of information and investigation. Those organs now exist and they are gradually coming to cooperate through the central international

1012. Exceptional procedures are usually justified by the seriousness of a crime, which is deemed so great as to warrant the risk of punishing some few innocent persons provided no guilty person escape. Such, in fact, is the experimental justification of exceptional procedures, like the French *loi des suspects,* in times of war or revolution. The justification is sentimental in the case of procedures against religious heretics; and with these must in our day be classed dissenters from that sex religion which our Inquisitors on Purity are trying to force upon civilized societies.[1]

1013. In many cases where the permanence of groups of sensations is involved, a development of great importance arises. The residue originates in the permanence of certain facts, but then contributes to maintaining that permanence until there is a clash with some obstacle that disintegrates or modifies the group. It is a question of a series of actions and reactions (§ 991).

1014. Erroneous the idealistic theory that regards the residue as the cause of the facts. Likewise erroneous, but at times less so, is the materialistic theory that regards the facts as the cause of the residue.

bureau in London and national Committees on the White-Slave Trade, so called. The reports presented by the delegates make it clear beyond shadow of doubt that if the 'trade' is not flourishing to any such fantastic proportions as certain writers have claimed, there is in fact such a 'trade' and that it is operating everywhere. There is not a large city in the world that does not have its 'traders,' its secret organization, its 'girl-market.' Only—and that is what explains the negative or sceptical attitude of certain court authorities towards the presentments of the vice societies—the 'white-slave trade' is no longer, as a rule, carried on by brutal methods that fall directly under the penal code, but by a sequence of shrewdly manipulated and progressive influences, contacts, temptations, degradations, whereby the young girl, but yesterday unsullied and self-respecting, embraces her ruin ostensibly of her own choice." *Habemus confitentem reum!*

1012 [1] Taking due account of the general mitigation of punishments, which applies to thieves and murderers quite as well, very much the same things may be seen going on today as in the days of the Inquisition. To avoid scandal the Inquisitors recognized secret accusations and kept the names of witnesses confidential. *Cf.* Bernard Guidon, *Practica inquisitionis heretice pravitatis,* p. 189: "If the Inquisitors find that any danger to witnesses is involved in the publication of their names, they may mention the names of such witnesses in the presence of a certain number of persons, not publicly but confidentially. There is a ruling on this point in a letter of Pope Innocent IV to the Friars Inquisitors of the Order of Preachers, *Cum negotium fidei catholicae. . . .* 'We urgently order that the names of accusers of heresy and witnesses thereto be strictly withheld from publication in view of the scandal

In reality the facts re-enforce the residue, and the residue the facts. Changes occur because new forces come into play to affect either the facts or the residue or both facts and residues—new circumstances occasion changes in modes of life (§ 976).

1015. II-α: *Persistence of relations between a person and other persons and places.* This variety falls into three subvarieties presenting similar and closely related characteristics, so that the residues readily blend and they also compensate one for the other.[a] These residues are common to men and animals. It is said that certain animals have a sense of "property," which is just a way of saying that they have a permanent sentiment attaching them to places and things. Also persistent in them is a sentiment attaching them to people and to other animals. The dog knows not only his master, but other individuals and animals about the house. A dog kennelled in a garden will not harm the cats and the poultry that belong there. Once outside the gate he chases all the cats and hens he sees; and he will attack a strange cat that enters his garden. In a case I have in mind, a number of cocks hatched in the same brood and kept together did

or danger possibly resulting from such publication.'" In our day, actually if not legally, procedure against "immoral literature" and other crimes of the modern heresy is the same. Many individuals are eager enough to be informers, but they also desire to remain anonymous, and their charges are lodged at second hand through the chairman, or executive secretary, of some "society for the suppression of vice." Such societies induce complaisant newspapers not to print news of prosecutions of "immoral literature" or of trials relating to the white-slave traffic, and for the very reasons alleged by Pope Innocent IV: "in view of the scandal or danger possibly resulting from such publication." The consequence now as then of such secret procedures is that their crookedness is never brought to public notice. Says Lea, *Op. cit.*, Vol. I, p. 406: "Had the proceedings been public, there might have been some check upon this hideous system, but the Inquisition shrouded itself in the awful mystery of secrecy [As our high-priests of purity do today.] until after the sentence had been awarded." In our day not even verdicts are published by newspapers that are politically controlled; to find out about them one must hunt them up in special publications, so that they remain unknown to the public at large. The interesting thing is that many of these modern inquisitors and their admirers hate the mediaeval Inquisitors and regard them as very wicked men; thinking they have cleared their traces when they have said that the faith of the old Inquisitors was "false," while theirs is "true."

1015 [a] ["Compensate" is a technical term with Pareto. For his theory of compensation among residues, a subdivision of his theory of varying intensities, see §§ 1701 f., and Index.—A.L.]

not fight. One of them was taken away and kept apart for six days. It was taken for granted that he could be put back with the others as a matter of course, but he was immediately attacked and killed. The same thing happened with two male cats that were born together and lived together peacefully. They were separated for a short time. When they were again brought together they went at each other furiously. The human sentiments of family, so called, of property, patriotism, love for the mother-tongue, for the ancestral religion, for friends, and so on, are of just that character, except that the human being dresses his sentiments up with derivations and logical explanations that sometimes conceal the residue.[1]

1016. II-α1: *Relationships of family and kindred groups.* Among animals that rear their offspring there is necessarily a temporary union between one or both parents and the young, but no notable residues seem, as a rule, to develop from such association. As soon as the young are able to take care of themselves, they separate from their parents and cease to recognize them. Among human beings, probably because the young need their parents or foster-parents for a much longer time, interesting and sometimes very powerful residues develop.

1017. These correspond to the forms of family association prevalent in the given country, and they also serve to strengthen or modify such forms. The best known, or rather the only, literature we have comes from peoples who have had a patriarchal family system—and they, after all, are the civilized peoples; so the only residues with which we are at all familiar are residues corresponding to the patriar-

1015 [1] Davis, *The Chinese,* 1806, Vol. I, p. 248 (1836, pp. 260-61): "To the system of clubbing together in families—we might almost say in clans—is to be attributed that sacred regard to kindred which operates better than a public provision for the relief of the poor and serves as one of the best means for the *distribution* of wealth. . . . Hence, too, that regard for the place of his birth, which always clings to a Chinese through life, often making him apply for leave to quit the honours and emoluments of office and retire to his native village. The same feeling makes the colonists who venture abroad in search of gain return home as soon as they have acquired something like a competency, though at the risk of being oppressed under the forms of law for having left China. They have a popular saying, 'If he who attains to honours or wealth never returns to his native place, he is like a finely-dressed person walking in the dark'—it is all thrown away."

chal type. We find them all through Graeco-Roman antiquity, in the Bible, and in the literatures of China, India, and Persia. That fact gives grounds for the notion that the patriarchal type of family was the only one concretely existing, and that deviations from it, which had been noted even in ancient times, were of little or no account. Those good souls who dreamed of a "natural law" did not fail to conclude that the patriarchal family was part of that law. But the day came when it was discovered, to the extreme astonishment of the learned world, that not only were other types of family extant among uncivilized or barbarous peoples, but that these may have played a part in the family organization of our own prehistoric ancestors, leaving traces that were still discernible in historic times.

1018. As usual there came a leap from one extreme to the other. It was a day when the concept of unitary evolution reigned supreme. So the manufacture of theories began at once. Starting with a primitive stage of the family—according to some writers, sex promiscuity or community in women—and going on through various intermediate stages (they are duly described in all details, as though anyone had ever been able to observe them with his own eyes!) it was shown how all peoples had modified their family organizations in a uniform direction and how civilized peoples had come by the type of family that prevails at present among them.

1019. The very few and very faint vestiges of families differing from the patriarchal type that are to be found in classical literature were put under high-powered magnifying glasses and became the foundations of rounded theories which do honour to the mental ingenuity and lively imaginations of their authors, but fail to testify as eloquently in favour of their historical and especially their scientific sense. Engels, for his part, killed two birds with one stone (§ 822): He reconstructed a history unknown to anybody except to himself, and brought the infamy and hypocrisy of the *bourgeoisie* to clearer light along with the ideal beauty of that evolutionary limit which we are to reach through Socialism.

1020. Though scientifically erroneous, these new theories of the family were didactically useful in that they served to break the circle within which every study of the family had formerly been confined by the prevalence of a single concept of family type: the patriarchal. Even the story by Engels may have had its use as showing to many people who had no aptitude for scientific investigation the immense amount of fatuity, stupidity, and hypocrisy that lurked in certain forms of bourgeois idealism.

1021. Whatever the causes, groups came to be formed among many peoples. Presumably they were bound to the soil and endured in time, the dead being one by one replaced by successors. It also happened that the nucleus of such groups was constituted by individuals bound to one another by ties of kinship. The existence of such groups stands in a relationship of interdependence with the existence of sentiments tending to make the groups permanent and which manifest themselves in various ways, but chiefly through what is called religion. We do not know the "origins" of such groups. The historical documents at our command present them in an advanced stage of evolution, often indeed in decadence. That much certain, three principal explanations of the historical phenomenon have been suggested: 1. Considering the nucleus primarily, it was explained that the groups in question originated in the family and that if in historic times they were no longer mere families, the fact was due to deviations from the type or from the "origin," because of abuses that had altered the "primitive" institution. 2. Stressing primarily the sentiments that prevail in the group and strengthen it, it was explained that the origin of the groups lay in religious beliefs (§ 254), and the family nucleus was accounted for by the religious prescription that certain religious rites should be performed by persons bound by ties of kinship (§ 254). In this case, deviations are much less marked than in the first, and in historic times in the countries considered the religious tie coincides exactly with the tie binding the group. That does not in the least prove that the groups originated in religion. Only the mania for logical interpretations and the gravely mistaken notion that sentiments have to precede acts can lead to the conclusion that the religious tie is the "origin" of the tie binding the group. 3. It was once possible to imagine that the groups were altogether artificial things, devised by legislators, but that interpretation now enjoys very little consideration, and properly so.

1022. But there is a fourth hypothesis that explains the known facts much better. It considers the groups as natural formations growing up about a nucleus which is generally the family, with appendages of one sort or another, and the permanence of such groups in time engenders or strengthens certain sentiments that, in their turn, render the groups more compact, more stable, better able to endure.

1023. These general considerations apply in the particular to the Roman gens, the Greek *γένος*, and the Hindu caste. The difficulties encountered in early efforts to determine what the gens and the *γένος* exactly were arose partly from the fact that definiteness was sought where, at least in very ancient times, nothing of the kind existed. It was the usual error of imagining that crude people with little or no propensity for abstraction and scientific thinking reason with the strictness and exactitude of jurists living in far more civilized and better-educated communities. The jurists of a later day had to solve very complicated problems and solve them in clear, precise, and logical terms, in order to determine who belonged to gens or *γένος*, and who did not. But in primitive times the problems were much simpler and came down to questions of fact; which in no wise means that the fact was arbitrary, but merely that it was determined by any number of considerations that later on, when it became important to define and classify them, were reduced in numbers and even changed in their relative importance.

1024. It is certain that in historical times the family was the nucleus of the Roman gens; but it is just as certain that the tie of kinship was not the only thing that figured in making up the gens. We must not become involved here in the intricate question as to whether the gens was made up of one, or of more than one, family. In the historical period girls of one gens were given in marriage to men of another gens. To be rid of one difficulty we might assume that that did not occur in times more ancient, but there would still be the question of adoption and "adrogation," which admitted outsiders to the gens. We might ignore that too. But still insuperable difficulties would remain. Legitimate birth was not alone enough to make a male child a member of the gens. He was presented to the father soon after birth, and the father might accept or repudiate him (*liberum repudiare, negare*). That arrangement was common to Greece and Rome. It has not the slightest appearance of being a custom of late date. Indeed it has all the ear-marks of coming down from a remote antiquity, and it is sufficient all by itself to show that there is something more to the gens and the γένος than descent from a common ancestor.

1025. Then come the appendages to the family, and consequently to the gens and the γένος—they are considered "appendages" because it had been decided *a priori* that blood-descent had to be the sole origin of the family group. But can we be sure that such "appendages" were not really organic survivals of the more primitive group? So in India now the practice of admitting outsiders into a caste is regarded as an abuse, and an abuse it may well be today; but who can be sure that in ancient times that was not one of the ways in which a caste was formed? [1]

1025 [1] Sénart, *Les castes dans l'Inde,* pp. 94 f.: "There has always been a rank growth of sects in India, and that sort of vegetation is far from dying out today. New sects turn up from year to year—only to be absorbed very soon, to be sure, in the rising tide of orthodox Hinduism, so called in spite of its composite character. As a rule such religious movements are very circumscribed, coming down to mere handfuls of ascetics who decide to consecrate themselves to penitence and celibacy and therefore reject the basic premise of caste—heredity. They recruit their forces from voluntary applicants or from children borrowed from other castes. All the same a number of such brotherhoods have members from both sexes and themselves develop into castes that are more or less hereditary. The movements so arising in the castes and continually modifying their inner structure are either individual or collective. Now by favour of influential patrons, now by trickery, now by fraud, now by corruption, certain people find ways of getting into this caste or that as individuals. That is the frequent case in the frontier districts, where observances are less strict. There have been instances where individuals from all the different castes have been made Brahmans by caprice of some ruler. A caste, moreover, may not be very strict and may open its ranks quite readily under certain conditions. There are clans of nomads and criminals that make a practice of admitting new members on money-terms." Such things have always happened. It is the grossest of errors to imagine that reality always tallies exactly with the abstractions of law-makers and men of letters.

1026. The Graeco-Roman clientage is the most interesting example of such appendages to the family. It throws a vivid light on the character of the vital cell in those ancient societies, as constituted not merely by the nucleus of individuals of common descent, but by individuals living together in close association and bound together by ties of common rights and duties. In Athens the new slave was made a part of the family by a religious initiation. Under the law of Gortyna, when a family became completely extinct, its lands went to such of its serfs as were bound to the soil.

1027. All that being undeniable, the tie of common descent had to be supplemented with the tie of religion in order to account for family, gens, and *γένος*. And in that we do get a little closer to reality, since religion is indeed one of the forms in which the ties of fact that supplement the tie of blood find expression. But it is a dangerous procedure to substitute the sign for the thing, the manifestation of a thing for the thing itself. It might lead one to imagining that religion was the "origin" of family, gens, and *γένος*, and that would be to go wide of the mark.

1028. Fustel de Coulanges assigns that very office to religion. The only hypotheses he considers are the first (the family unit) and the third (legal artifice) (§ 1021). He has no difficulty in showing that the blood-tie is not sufficient to account for the gens and the *γένος*, and to that extent his demonstration serves to call attention to other ties too. He also shows that the gens and the *γένος* cannot have originated as devices of law-makers. But he gives no evidence to show that his argument, which designates religion as the "origin" of those groups, is anything more than the usual *post hoc, propter hoc*. And just that is the weak point in his theory.

1029. On the theory that the gens was an artificial creation, he says, *La cité antique,* p. 119 (Small, p. 141): "Another defect in that system is that it assumes that human societies can have been instituted by agreement, by artifice. Historical science can grant no such assumption."

1030. Quite so. But it is just as impossible to assume that beliefs can have preceded the facts to which they relate. At the most, it is conceivable that believers in a revealed religion may admit as much in the case of *their own* religion. A Christian may well believe that the dogmas of his faith antedate the facts to which they relate; but that same Christian will not grant as much for pagan rites. And even if one adopt the theory of the decadence and perversion of a revealed religion, it must further be admitted that that decadence and perversion must have been determined by the facts, and did not arise independently of them.

1031. The religion of Graeco-Roman antiquity stands in close relation to the constitution of the groups comprising the social cellules. It grew out of residues originating in the permanence of those organisms and in turn guaranteeing their existence and permanence (§ 1013).

1032. The residues were very much alike in Greece and Rome. They developed differing derivations owing to the different temperaments of the two peoples. The residues that built up the family religions became, with a few modifications and additions, the residues that built up the city-state religions. Small wonder that those religions should show the trait noted by Reinach (§ 383)—"a sum of scruples interfering with the free exercise of human faculties"; since those residues corresponded exactly to the sum of ties—of obstacles to the free exercise of the faculties—that gave being and strength to the social cellule. Every theory is inclined to overstress the importance of its own principles; hence religion, which was a manifestation of existing ties, created in its turn new ties, and sometimes absurd ones. It has been many times said and well said that religion embraced every act of ancient life; but it would be even better to say that religion was the manifestation of ties, whether spontaneous or artificial, that figured in every act of ancient life. The separation of religion and state may have some meaning for modern peoples; but it could have had none for Graeco-Roman antiquity, where it would have meant the separation of the ties of civic life from the ties of the state. The tolerance of the ancient Roman city for various religions provided they wrought no offence to the national worship corresponds exactly to the tolerance the modern civil state has for various systems of morality and certain personal individual codes, provided these involve no infringement on positive legislation.

1033. The city cults were largely patterned on the family cults, and the imitation was direct. The worship of the domestic hearth-fire became the worship of the sacred fire of the city, in the Greek Prytaneum and in the Roman Temple of Vesta. But there are cases where a public cult originates not in the domestic cult but in the same residues that engendered the latter, there being no direct imitation, or at least apparently none.

1034. The Roman Penates correspond, in part at least, to the notion of domestic food-supply. The importance attached to provisioning by ancient families, the precautions that had to be taken to avoid famine, the agreeable sentiments connected with abundance, all corresponded to a powerful residue that expressed itself in the religious status of the Penates, divinities which were also associated with other residues of the same sort.

1035. Similar, at a much later day, the origin of the deification of the harvest—Annona (§§ 996 f.). Yet in that, so far as we know, no direct imitation was involved; the deification of Annona was not a copy either of the household worship or of the public worship of the Penates. It originated in the very same sentiments that found expression earlier in the ascription of a religious status to domestic provisioning.

1036. The Greek tribes had eponymic heroes and Greek and Latin cities had founders more or less deified. Those facts have been regarded as copies of real facts of descent, family, gens, and γένος coming from a single ancestor. That may well be. It may also well not be, the original ancestor being as much of a fiction as the eponymic hero and the divine founder. We can come to no decision so long as direct proofs are lacking.

1037. The Middle Ages saw a recurrence in the Latin countries of Europe of circumstances in part similar to the conditions under which the ancient families of the Latin races came into being; and just as a confederation of independent families produced the ancient city, so the feudal hierarchy produced the monarchies of centuries past. The feudal group had a family nucleus with appendages of extraneous elements. Says Flach:[1] "A family grouped around its chief forms the kernel of a far more extensive comradeship, the importance of which seems not to have received sufficient stress from historians—the *maisnie,* the lord's house, his chosen body-guard, the centre of resistance in his army, his best counsel, his daily *entourage.* The *maisnie* fills out, apart from the natural family, with the children and relatives of the vassals or the more trusted allies, and even with foreigners."[2] As was the case in more ancient times, religion interposes to give expression to the ties binding the group and to reenforce them. But the circumstances were in part different. Ancient families built up their own religions and therefore deified the things that promoted the ties. Feudal families had a religion ready-made outside their circle, and the process of deification was already complete. They therefore created no new divinities, but applied those already existing to their own needs. After describing the rites of *commendation* and *homage,* Flach adds, *Op. cit.,* p. 522: "But the authority thus established over the person was so established only with a view to his becoming a member of the household, which was

1037 [1] *Les origines de l'ancienne France,* Vol. II, pp. 455-56.

1037 [2] Fustel de Coulanges, *Op. cit.,* pp. 96, 126-27 (Small, p. 116): "Thanks to the domestic religion, the family was a small organized body, a diminutive society with its leader and its government. [Drop the allusion to the domestic religion and the description serves just as well for the feudal *maisnie.* Amend the wording to read that religion strengthened the association and gave it new power, and the parallel becomes complete.] . . . But the family of those distant ages was nothing like as small as the modern family. In great societies the family is broken up and reduced in numbers. But in the absence of any other society, it spreads out, develops, ramifies, without dividing. A number of junior branches remain grouped about the elder branch [So far the description applies exactly to the feudal family, a difference appearing only in the following:] before a single hearth around a common tomb. Another element also entered into the composition of this ancient family [and of the feudal clan]. The reciprocal need that the poor man has of the rich man and the rich man of the poor man created servants. But in that sort of patriarchal régime servant is synonymous with slave. One can readily see, in fact, that the principle of free voluntary service to be ended at the will of the subordinate can hardly be consonant with a social situation where the family lives in isolation all to itself. [The remark applies to the feudal family also.] The servant must in some way become a member of the family, and an integral part of the family." And both the ancient family and the feudal *maisnie* made provision for that very thing.

embodied in the lord [As it was of yore, in the *paterfamilias*.[8]], to his affiliation with the family unit, along with the rights and duties which such association entailed. Now that initiation took place with the most earnest, the most solemn, ceremony known to human beings in primitive societies—the swearing of a religious vow. In pagan times the person so affiliated became a participant in the domestic worship: he delivered himself, 'devoted' himself, body and soul, to a new family, and if he failed to keep faith he drew upon his head the vengeance of the gods. [Those are derivations: in more ancient times, religion was itself the manifestation of those ties.] In the Christian era the vow by which the vassal engaged his person was a most formidable one. It made martyrs of individuals who sacrificed their lives to remain faithful to it, outcasts of those who violated it."

1038. Pertile rejects the theory that fiefs originated in the clientage of ancient Roman law or in the military benefices of the Empire:[1] "Just as there is no continuity in time," he says, "between those institutions and the fiefs, so there can have been no connexion between them." Pertile is right in the sense that there was no direct imitation, just as we saw above that the goddess Annona was not directly derived from the Penates. But it would be erroneous not to recognize their common origin. The same sentiments (residues), acting under circumstances of fact in large part similar, and in part also different, resulted in institutions in large part similar, and in part also different—ancient clientage on the one hand, and on the other "commendation," benefices, fiefs.

1039. Pertile says, *Op. cit.*, p. 203, that "in clientage . . . the real element is entirely missing." That is the common error of jurists, who are more inclined to consider forms than substance. In ancient clientage the real element was lacking in law, but not in the fact.

1037 [8] *Ulpian, Digesta, Lib.* L., *tit.* 16, sec. 195, § 2 (*Corpus iuris civilis,* Vol. I, p. 970; Scott, Vol. XI, p. 286): *"Pater autem familias appellatur qui in domo dominium habet, recteque hoc nomine appellatur quamvis filium non habeat."* ("The term 'paterfamilias' is applied to the man who has authority over the household, and he is properly so called even though he have no child.")

1038 [1] *Storia del diritto italiano,* Vol. I, p. 204.

Nor was the military element lacking in the fact, in the sense that the client stood by his patron even in quarrels involving violence.

1040. Consider, for example, the story of Eumaeus in the *Odyssey,* XIV, vv. 55-71. Eumaeus, a servant of Ulysses, says that his lord, were he to return, would give to him, Eumaeus, "the things that an affectionate patron giveth to a servant who hath laboured well," that is, a house, a piece of land, and a wife. In the house and the land we have, *in the fact,* the real element. Ulysses reveals his identity to Eumaeus, and the latter fights at his patron's side to defeat the suitors. From all of which it is evident that *in the fact* he stands towards Ulysses in the same relation as a vassal towards the feudal lord.

1041. II-α2: *Relations with places.* These residues often blend with residues of the preceding variety (family and group relations) and with II-β residues (living and dead). Even moderns speak of their "native land," their "old home," which is not necessarily the birth-place but the place where the family lives, or has lived, and where they have spent their childhood. Among the ancients of the Graeco-Roman world relations to places combined with relations of family and groups (*gens, γένος*) and with relations to the dead to form a unit sum of residues.

1042. Something similar takes place among modern peoples. Looking at things superficially, one might imagine that patriotism of the modern type is a matter of territory, since the modern nations take their names from the territories they occupy. But looking a little more closely, one perceives that in awakening sentiments of patriotism the territorial name suggests a sum of sentiments, language, religion, traditions, history, and so on. In reality patriotism cannot be exactly defined, any more than "religion," "morality," "justice," "the good," "the beautiful," can be exactly defined. All such terms merely call to mind certain cumulations of sentiments of no sharply defined forms and with very vague limits (§§ 380 f.), the various units being held together by the residues of group-persistence.

1043. II-α3: *Relationships of social class.* Living in a given group impresses the mind with certain concepts, certain ways of thinking and doing, certain prejudices, certain beliefs, which, as is the case with so many other entities of the kind, endure in time and acquire a pseudo-objective individuality. The residues corresponding to them have in the past often assumed the forms of residues of family relationships. It has been imagined that social classes and even nations were so many lineages each with some common ancestor, real or mythical, and each indeed with its own gods, who were enemies of the gods of other groups. But the latter is a mere derivation, and among modern peoples it has fallen into desuetude.

1044. The form of the caste in India is unique, but the underlying substance is very very general. Something similar is observable in all countries, and oftentimes with greatest intensity in countries that make a show of some principle of equality. The distance between an American millionaire and a plain American is greater than the distance between a German nobleman and a German factory-hand. It is something like the distance between the castes in India, which is nothing like the distance between whites and blacks in the United States.

1045. In Europe the propaganda of the Marxian "class struggle," or rather, the conditions that found their expression in that manner, served to awaken or intensify corresponding residues in the "proletariat," or to be more exact, in a part of the population; whereas the concern felt by business men (*entrepreneurs*) not to run counter to democratic sentiments, in fact to exploit them for purposes of money-making, weakened or destroyed certain residues of collectivity in the higher social classes.

1046. A number of traits observable in the Jews of our time, and which are ordinarily ascribed to race, are mere manifestations of residues produced by long centuries of oppression. And the proof is easy; one need only compare a Russian Jew with an English Jew. The Russian Jew is readily distinguished from his Christian neighbours; not at all so the English Jew. And then there are the intermediary types, corresponding to the longer or shorter duration of the oppression. It is a well-known fact that the various professions often develop distinct types of individuality—in other words, present different residues corresponding to the respective type of activity.

1047. The associations known as sects, when held together by strong and exclusive sentiments, have well-known traits that have been observed in all periods of history. The persistence of relations within the sect strengthens such traits and weakens the effect that conflict with other sentiments operating outside the sect would otherwise have upon them. Hence one of the outstanding characteristics of sectarians: They lose the perception other people generally have of the relative values of things. What others may regard as a very mild sin, the sectarian may deem a serious crime;[1] and *vice versa,* what the former consider shameful or criminal the sectarian may regard as honourable and above-board.[2] The spy, the informer, is generally considered a dishonourable person; but in the days of the Inquisition many people thought spying a duty, as contributing to the extermi-

1047 [1] Countess Lydia Rostoptchine, *Les Rostoptchine,* pp. 222-26: "I remarked above how my grandmother detested drunkenness, a very natural vice that is intensified in the Russian by the severity of our climate. She made no distinction between the inveterate drunkard and the man who had overtasted by mere chance—a matter of a good time or of forgetting. Both in her eyes were equally deserving of the knout and Siberia. . . . On another occasion painfully graven in my memory, we were again walking on the drive when a woman, her clothing torn and stained with blood, came running towards us as fast as she could, pursued by the hostlers. She had escaped from the stable where she had been receiving a flogging. The poor woman threw herself at my grandmother's feet sobbing. I shall never forget the horror of the scene . . . the prostrate victim, and the impalcable suzerain sternly inquiring as to the cause of the punishment that Timothy had ordered. At mention of the hated name of vodka, and deaf to the vehement prayers of my mother and my father's more timid protests, my grandmother, whom I was enraged at that moment to call by that name, turned her back without a word and resumed her walk. The hostlers approached, seized the woman by the wrists, and dragged her off to receive the remainder of her punishment. And the poor thing was with child!"

1047 [2] Cunningham, *Two Years in New South Wales,* Vol. II, pp. 257-58 (anent convicts deported to Australia): "Designations of individual character have among them a very different meaning to what is attached thereto in honest society. A *good fellow* is one who divides fairly with his companions whatever he thieves in partnership, and who never confesses a theft or gives evidence against an associate. A *clever fellow* is a bang-up, bold, thorough-going knave, an able 'actor of all work'; while a *great scoundrel* is one who will be *base* enough to acknowledge his crime, or inform upon his partner." So now in our countries, in the eyes of certain people, a "good judge" is a judge who rules against the law, a "bad judge," one who conscientiously upholds it.

nation of heretics of Catholicism. Today it is also considered honourable and obligatory by many persons, as contributing to the extermination of heretics of the sex religion of our high-priests of purity. Notorious, in Italy, the Camorra and the Maffia; but the basic principles of Camorra and Maffia are applied in various cases in other quarters, as when members of the parliament refuse to permit prosecutions of their colleagues for crimes or misdemeanours that are in no sense political, for private slanders, and even for violations of the traffic regulations: that certainly is a legislators' Camorra, no more and no less. To satisfy a humanitarian caprice a jury at Interlaken allowed Tatiana Leontieff to get off with a very light penalty for murdering an aged and harmless unfortunate. To humour another whim, whether humanitarian or merely half-witted would be hard to say, a French jury acquitted a young man who had killed his father. Such people really consider themselves superior to criminals and far, far superior to the "despots who rule unhappy peoples."

1048. Sentiments may become so cogent in sectarians as to impel them to any extreme of crime—the very term "assassin" is derived from the feats of a certain historic association of criminals. All that is very well known; but not so commonly realized is the fact that the difference between certain acts, from the abject delations of our paladins of purity down to a murder committed by a gangster, is a difference only in intensity of sentiments, and sometimes only a difference in the courage of the persons involved—the difference, let us say, between the murderer who poisons an enemy and the murderer who faces his enemy revolver in hand.

1049. The notion, widely prevalent among uncivilized peoples, that anything is permissible against a foreigner or an enemy, that the moral laws in force in relations between citizens of the same country cease to apply in dealings with outsiders and enemies, is another expression of the residues of class. Such notions have been entertained even by civilized peoples—the Romans, for instance—and have not entirely disappeared among our contemporaries (§ 1050 [2]). Modern civilized peoples, as was the case in ancient Greece, have mutual relations with one another not greatly at variance with the moral laws prevailing at home; but they feel no obligation to consider them in dealing with uncivilized peoples, or peoples whom they consider such.

1050. Aristotle's theory of natural slavery, *Politica,* I, 2, 3-23 (Rackham, pp. 15-31), is the theory put forward by modern civilized peoples to justify their conquests of peoples whom they call "inferior" and their dominion over them. Aristotle said that some men are naturally slaves and others masters, and that it is proper for the ones to obey and the others to command, the which is just and of benefit to all concerned. So say the modern peoples who decorate themselves with the title "civilized." They assert that there are peoples—themselves, of course—who were intended by Nature to rule, and other peoples—those whom they wish to exploit—who were no less intended by Nature to obey, and that it is just, proper, and to the advantage of everyone concerned that they do the ruling and the others the obeying. Whence it follows that if an Englishman, a German, a Frenchman, a Belgian, an Italian, fights and dies for his country, he is a hero; but if an African dares defend his homeland against any one of those nations, he is a contemptible rebel and traitor. So the Europeans are performing a sacrosanct duty in exterminating Africans in an effort to teach them to be civilized. And there are always plenty of people to admire such work "of peace, progress, and civilization," with mouths agape! With a hypocrisy truly admirable, these blessed civilized peoples claim to be acting for the good of their subject races in oppressing and exterminating them; indeed so dearly do they love them that they would have them "free" by force. So the English freed the Hindus from the "tyranny" of the rajahs. So the Germans freed the Africans from the tyranny of their black kings. So the Italians freed the Arabs from the oppression of the Turks. So the French freed the Madagascans and—to make them freer still—killed not a few of them and reduced the rest to a condition that is slavery in all but the name. Such talk is uttered in all seriousness, and there are even people who believe it. The cat catches the mouse and eats it; but it does not pretend to be doing so for the good of the mouse. It does not proclaim any dogma that all animals are equal, nor lift its eyes hypocritically to heaven in worship of the Father of us all.[1]

1051. The theory of the superiority of the civilized peoples is for the most part used only against non-Europeans. But Prussians use it

1050 [1] For example, the Belgian Congo. Besides the minutes and documents of official investigations see Conan Doyle, *The Crime of the Congo.* As for the Portuguese, I quote from *Liberté,* Aug. 9, 1912: "In answer to charges of cruelty made against Portuguese planters in Angola, one of them has published a large volume vaunting the good treatment that Negroes 'bonded under contract' have been receiving from his fellow-residents in the colony. In [? an article in] *France d'outre mer,* M. René Claparède, general secretary of the International Committee on the Congo Leagues, refutes such assertions. He claims that the Negroes bonded under alleged contracts are actual slaves, the contracts being automatically renewable. That transforms the contract into servitude for life. As for the good treatment boasted by the Portuguese, it is so effective that the mortality-rate among the blacks is more than 10 per cent on the Portuguese islands, whereas it is lower than 2.6 per cent in Jamaica and Trinidad. The unhappy Negroes therefore do their best to escape from the plantations and get into the woods. Then comes the man-hunt that M. Claparède describes, following an account given him by a planter who had taken part in one. "The hunters," says M. Claparède, "had been taken by guides to a place for which it was known the fugitives had started. They came to some huts that had just been deserted. An old Negro was found near by hiding in the grass. 'We took him,' said the planter, 'and forced him to tell where the other slaves were. At first we could get nothing out of him, but after a time, without uttering a word, he pointed with his hand towards the tallest trees. There they were, men and women, clinging to the branches like so many bats! It was not long, I can assure you, before we had brought them all down through the foliage. What a bag we made that day!' " Such criticisms were published against Portugal and Belgium because they were not very powerful countries; but nothing was said about things equally bad or even worse that the English, Germans, and French were doing. The Belgian Government made reparation to a large extent for the oppression practised in the Congo by King Leopold's "Administration"; and the Portuguese Republic made full reparation for the oppression tolerated by the monarchy; whereas the larger "civilized" countries continue conquering the lands of so called barbarous peoples or maintaining their former rule over them, spreading death, affliction, and ruin in all such territories. Even the ultra-civilized Americans are acting no differently in their treatment of the wretched natives of the Philippines and the remnants of the Redskins, whom they have robbed of their ancestral lands. I will quote in point a document published in *Liberté,* July 21, 1913: *"Le Sort des Peaux-Rouges"* ("The Lot of the Redskins"): "A recent investigation by the New York *Herald* specifies the misdeeds of the Yankee administration, and here is the opinion of a specialist, Robert G. Valentine, formerly Commissioner of Indian Affairs: 'It is astounding to note that the whites follow quite different moral codes according as they are dealing with other white men or with Indians. People who would never think of stealing from their white neighbours find it quite natural to swindle an

also against the Poles; and there are Germans who would use it against the Latin peoples, regarding them as barbarians in comparison with the surpassingly excellent, moral, virtuous, intelligent, civilized, and so on, Germanic stock. In England and North America there are those who arrogate the same outstanding superiorities to the divine breed of the Anglo-Saxon. Such people always consider themselves rigidly "scientific" and ridicule those who differ with them as victims of outworn prejudices.[1]

1052. II-β: *Persistence of relations between the living and the dead.* The sum of relations between an individual and other individuals persists, by abstraction, in the absence of that individual or after his death. That explains residues which figure in vast numbers

Indian. They know, furthermore, that in doing so they run no risks. The swindlers themselves are not so much to blame as the American public which encourages their crimes by its indifference. I have plenty of proof available, and the facts in my possession are so abominable that a jury could not fail to punish them as they deserve. . . . A device often resorted to to deprive Indians of their money is to induce them to deposit their funds in banks which shortly afterwards go into fraudulent bankruptcy, the dishonest bankers then dividing the spoils with government agents. They have nine chances out of ten of going unpunished. Worse yet, Indians resisting the demands of white intruders have been murdered. A case of that kind occurred last year in Johnston County, Oklahoma, where two Cherokees who were not willing to "come across" were mercilessly "executed." In this case the courts had to interfere, and it developed that the county judge was in league with a gang of criminals engaged in fleecing the Indians of the county. The judge was impeached, and three or four convictions were obtained. However, the courts are in general very lax, and prosecutions involving the tribes very long protracted. . . . Then there is the case of the Pimas. That tribe had shown itself very industrious and was making a comfortable living off its lands. The activities of white men have reduced the Pimas to idleness, pauperism, and ruin. Land speculators have so manoeuvred as to get possession of the timber, pastures, and mines of the Pimas for insignificant sums. Arizona had hardly been admitted to the Union before white speculators were at work on the Navajos, a peaceful self-respecting people, because their lands had risen in value. It was again a story of intimidation and seizure.'" Such things are nothing as compared with the lynchings of Negroes and other such trifles. American missionaries are at sedulous pains to note the motes in other countries. They would do well to attend to some of the beams lying about in their own.

1051 [1] Napoleone Colajanni has well shown the fatuity of all such race chatter in his *Latini e anglo-sassoni: razze inferiori e razze superiori.* Arcangelo Ghisleri has also deflated various balloons of racial hypocrisy in a number of publications: [*e.g., Le razze umane ed il diritto nella questione coloniale; Metafisica tedesca e mentalità italiana.*]

of phenomena.[1] They are in some respects similar to II-α residues, and that explains why they are found combined with them in many many cases, such as family, caste, patriotism, religion, and so on. In combination with IV-$\delta 2$ residues (§§ 1149 f.), which prompt sharing of possessions with the objects of one's love or goodwill, they appear in such complex phenomena as honouring or worshipping the dead, or banquets and sacrifices connected with funerals or commemorations.

1053. Those who will have logical explanations for all human beliefs imagine that such phenomena presuppose belief in the immortality of the soul, for without such a postulate they would not be logical. To refute that notion, one need merely observe, ignoring countless other proofs, that among the people right about us, materialists are not less punctilious than others in honouring their dead, in spite of their philosophy; and that in London and Paris, to say nothing of other cities, there are cemeteries for dogs where such pets are buried by people who certainly do not credit the dog with an immortal soul.

1054. Ghosts, apparitions of the dead, which have at all times been taken seriously more or less everywhere, are nothing but tangible forms given to residues of persisting relations between the living and the dead, which by analogy also figure to some extent in ap-

1052 [1] Describing the Tahitians in his *Account of a Voyage to the Pacific Ocean,* Vol. II, pp. 164-65, Captain Cook speaks largely in terms of derivations, but that does not altogether conceal the residue: "The only great privilege they seem to think they shall acquire by death is immortality; for they speak of spirits being in some measure not totally divested of those passions which actuated them when combined with material vehicles. Thus if souls who were formerly enemies should meet, they have many conflicts; though it should seem, to no purpose, as they are accounted invulnerable in this invisible state. There is a similar reasoning with regard to the meeting of man and wife. If the husband dies first, the soul of his wife is known to him on its arrival in the land of the spirits. They resume their former acquaintance in a spacious house called *Tourova,* where the souls of the deceased assemble to recreate themselves with the Gods. She then retires with him to his separate habitation, where they remain forever, and have an offspring which, however, is entirely spiritual, as they are neither married, nor are their embraces supposed to be the same as with corporeal beings." The derivations are illogical and absurd simply because they are so irrelevant, the residues being the important thing.

paritions of divinities, angels, devils, fairies, and other personified entities of the kind. In our day they are satisfied by "double personalities," telepathy, and other such trumpery.

1055. It is apparent, on close scrutiny, that the concept of the survival of the dead is at bottom merely the extension of another notion which is very powerful in the human being, the notion that the individuality of a person is a unit over the course of the years. In reality both the physical and the psychic elements in the human being change. Neither materially nor morally is an aged man identical with the child he was. And yet we feel that in him there is something which endures the same. Overstepping the experimental field, people call it a "soul," without being able to explain very clearly what becomes of such a soul in lunacy, for example, or in "second childhood," or just when, between the time when the human egg is fertilized and the first cry of the new-born babe, such a soul finds its way into the body. Such matters need not concern us here, since they transcend the confines of the experimental field within which we have chosen to remain. Our point is merely to show that one same residue is present in the belief in the unity of the living individuality and in the belief in survival after death.

1056. II-γ: *Persistence of relations between a dead person and the things that belonged to him in life.* The relations of a man to the things once belonging to him endure in the minds of the living after his death. Hence the widely prevalent custom of burying or burning such objects with a corpse, or otherwise destroying them, and that of killing his wives, his slaves, his animals.

1057. As usual a logical explanation of such customs puts in an appearance; and again as usual, they are regarded as corollaries of a belief in another life for the person who has died. If a man's weapons are laid in his tomb, it is in order that he may use them in a life to come. Libations are poured on his grave, and food left, that his soul may eat and drink. Living beings are sacrificed that he may find company and service over there.

1058. Such beliefs there certainly were; but they are derivations —that is to say, they are essentially variable; whereas the constant element in all that is the persistence of the relations between the dead person and the things that were once his.

1059. Read, for example, the account of the funeral of Patroclus in the *Iliad,* XXIII, vv. 65-98. The ghost of Patroclus appears in a dream to Achilles. He in no wise asks him for utensils or living beings for his service in another life. All he asks of his friend (vv. 83-84) is that their ashes may rest together in the same urn. There we have our residue, virtually without any derivation whatever; and it is a residue so powerful that it has stood intact over these many centuries and over so many changes in peoples and beliefs. It is usual enough in our day for people to provide in their wills that their bodies shall rest near the bodies of loved ones. Be they Christians or free-thinkers, there is nothing in their beliefs that logically can prompt them to do any such thing; they are merely inspired by the sentiments manifested in this residue. The Myrmidons of Achilles each consecrate their shocks of hair to Patroclus (vv. 135-36). What use could he have for such a gift in another life? Nor could the twelve Trojan prisoners who were slaughtered on his pyre have made very agreeable companions for him. Why should we think differently of the four horses and the two dogs that were likewise slaughtered? In any event there is nothing whatever in the poem to justify the assumption that they were to be of service to the soul of Patroclus. Champions of the logical explanation may object that, "originally," living creatures were sacrificed to attend on the soul of the dead, and that later on, the meaning of the tradition being lost, human beings and animals were slain more or less at random. But that would be a mere hypothesis not supported by any facts, nor even by any analogy with other facts; for in general, the non-logical act precedes the logical act, and the assumption there would be that the opposite was the case.

1060. The pyre on which the body of Patroclus has been burned is extinguished with wine (*Ibid.,* v. 250). The intention was to honour the hero with the use of that precious liquid (I-β2). Not the slightest hint in the poem suggests that Patroclus was to drink the wine. In the *Odyssey,* Ulysses pours libations of water, honey, and wine in honour of the dead, and sprinkles flour. The dead do not taste of any such offerings. They do come running to drink the blood of the victims! Elpenor requests Ulysses to burn his panoply with his body, but there is no indication that he is to use the weapons in another life. They are burned for the same reason that an oar is planted on the mound covering the body of Elpenor. What we have there is simply a persistence of the relations between a man and the things that belonged to him. The mother of Ulysses says: ". . . as soon as life has left the white bones, the soul flits hither and thither abroad like a dream." She makes no mention whatever of having with her the objects that were placed on her tomb or burned on her pyre.

1061. So cogent is the preconception in favour of logical explanations that a writer will often add one quite unconsciously to a description. In the more ancient tombs in Egypt objects that were once used by the living are found with their bones. We have no documents whatever to indicate just what relations obtained between such things in the eyes of the Egyptians of those days. Yet a very distinguished Egyptologist, Erman, no less, describes what he sees as follows (gratuitous logical explanations in italics): "In those ancient times, some object was placed in the hands of the deceased, *in the belief that it would be of service to him in death.* So one of the ancient cadavers in our collection still holds the large stone on which in his lifetime he was wont to grind the green pigment that he used for colouring his body. Another has a leathern purse in his hand. But a great many other things are placed near the corpse: pots, above all, and ladles, with food and drink, *in order that the deceased may not suffer from hunger;* harpoons and stone knives, *that he may hunt his food and defend himself against his enemies;* a chequer-board, *for his entertainment during leisure hours. . . .* There are other things too which can have had no use save in a supernatural sense. The little clay bark is to aid him in crossing the lakes that . . . surround the celestial fields of the blest. The clay bull will be slaughtered for him, and the hippopotamus, of the same material, will be his game. The clay maidservant in the large vat will knead barley-meal with her feet in preparing his beer for him. . . . To the other female figure, coy, composed, *the duty evidently falls of supplying her lord with the consolations of love;* and so she is painted in beautiful colours of varied hue, as though she were about to be decked and crowned with flowers; and her thighs and legs have that sinewy development which the African of our day still regards as the supreme ideal of feminine beauty." [1]

1062. It is certain that in later ages such logical explanations corresponded exactly with popular beliefs; but that in no way proves that there was the same correspondence in a much earlier period for which we have no documents. Yet these logical explanations assume just that.

1063. Finally, the fact of chronological evolution is one thing and the fact of residues and derivations quite another. There is no occasion for speculating as to how the first fact arose in ages about which we know nothing, when we are studying the second in times that we know very well, as witness the following example.

1064. In December, 1911, a band of thieves desecrated the tomb of

1061 [1] *Aegyptische Religion,* p. 116 (Johns, pp. 115-16). Naville, *La religion des anciens égyptiens,* pp. 45-47: "In historical times one notes in the Egyptians very positive ideas that inclined them to make mummies of their dead. They attached great importance to that rite, and it was so solidly grounded in their consciousness that the custom lasted down into the Christian era and even called forth severe reproof from certain of the Church Fathers. (*Cf.* § 1004 [1].) The mummy has become almost symbolic of the dead of the Land of Egypt, and that seems always to have been the case. Great, therefore, was the astonishment of the early excavators who found that in a very ancient period, prehistoric or primitive as one may choose to call it, things were not the same. Modes of burial at that time seem to have corresponded to quite a different conception than came to prevail later on. [Better: burial customs changed with changes in the concepts correlated with such customs.] In the necropolès of the native population that was eventually subjugated by conquerors from abroad, one finds little rectangular or oval graves. The corpses are buried in them intact without any trace of a mummification process. The knees are drawn up against the chest. . . . That has been called the embryonic position and has been interpreted as a posture preparatory to second birth, it being the one best adapted to a body about to be reborn to a new life. [The usual abuse of logical interpretation.] I find that explanation a little abstruse for such a crude people. Another much simpler one is suggested by the Father of History, Herodotus." The suggestion was, in brief (*Historiae,* IV, 190), that the custom came from such peoples as the Nasamones, who kept the dying in a sitting posture after the Oriental manner.

Mme. Lantelme for the purpose of stealing the very rare and very valuable jewels that had been buried with the actress some days previous. Their venture was not successful. The envelope that contained the jewels was found in the grave. Now in this case two things are as certain as certain can be: 1. That the jewels were buried with the dead actress. 2. That the persons responsible for that act did not in the least imagine that the jewels would be of actual use to the lady in some other life. Now supposing two or three thousand years hence that tomb were to be discovered with its jewels, just as we are nowadays finding other tombs of past ages containing weapons and jewels; and supposing the discoverers, reasoning as we do now, were to conclude that people of this age of ours believed that a dead person was to use the things that were buried with him in an after-life. Such a conclusion would be manifestly erroneous. Now we are drawing similar conclusions about peoples of the past in the same way from identical facts. Why are ours not just as far wrong? We are merely stressing the possibility of the error. We are not saying that it is necessarily so. But the mere possibility is enough to discredit a reasoning that may be summarized in the following terms: "To our way of thinking, certain facts have only one logical explanation. Those facts, therefore, necessarily arose in the manner indicated by our explanation." No, they may have taken place in some other way; and the choice between the various ways must be made in the light of direct proofs and not indirectly on the basis of inferences that facts have often proved to be fallacious. We must work from the known to the unknown, explaining facts with other facts, not with the impressions our minds have of them (§ 547).

1065. II-δ: *Persistence of abstractions.* After an agglomerate of relations has grown up, either in the manner described in § 991 or in some other, a corresponding abstraction appears that may persist in time; and then a new subjective entity comes into being.

1066. Such residues underlie theologies and systems of metaphysics, which might properly be defined as cumuli of derivations from such residues. Hence the great importance of theologies and metaphysical systems—not the importance they are supposed to have when considered as logical sciences, but as expressing residues that correspond to powerful social forces.

1067. From that standpoint past and present alike show remarkable uniformity. There is, however, a difference in the matter of personification of abstractions, which among our Western people was far more characteristic of the past than it is of more recent times. Let us glance at one or two abstractions that are so important as to deserve classification by themselves.[1]

1068. II-ε: *Persistence of uniformities.* An important instance of the persistence of abstractions is the common procedure of generalizing a particular uniformity or even a single, isolated fact. A fact is observed. It is stated in abstract language. The abstraction persists and becomes a general rule. The thing is a matter of everyday occurrence. We may even go so far as to say that that is the characteristic manner of reasoning of people not trained to scientific thinking and even of many who are. Very few people indeed state particular facts under particular forms, and are able to distinguish that form of expression from the other which states a general rule, and furthermore to distinguish the rule that is an instrument of research and subject to experimental verification from the rule that is assumed to be above such verification (§ 63). Going to extremes in the direction of abstractions superior to experience, we get metaphysical principles, "natural" principles, "necessary" relationships, and the like (§ 531).[1]

1069. II-ζ: *Sentiments transformed into objective realities.* Such residues are exceedingly numerous, so much so that they are rarely absent from any discussion that is not conducted with strictest scientific exactitude. They underlie all subjective proofs derived from sentiments, and they exert a powerful influence upon the considerations that inspire the production and acceptance of theories (§ 13). The introspection of the metaphysicist, the "inner experience" of the

1067 [1] To avoid repetitions we shall postpone our discussion of certain other abstractions till later on (§§ 1070 f.), when we come to the matter of personifications.

1068 [1] Of these as well as of the following residues (II-ζ) we need give no examples here, since we deal with them in great numbers in the whole course of these volumes.

Christian, and other similar manners of thinking, all involve transformations of sentiments into objective realities.

1070. II-η: *Personifications.* The lowest degree of personification lies in the naming of an abstraction, a uniformity, or a sentiment, and so transforming them into objective individualities. Thence, step by step, we mount to the highest degree, where the personification is complete and we get anthropomorphism.[1] Bringing in the sex residue we get male and female principles, or divinities in every respect similar to men and women. Places and things may also be personified, without there being on that account any deification. Such personifications arise spontaneously in the mind independently of any process of reasoning.[2]

1071. Language is a very effective instrument for lending continuity to such groups and for personifying them; and the mere bestowal of a name on a sum of abstractions is often sufficient to transform it into an objective individuality. Conversely, every name is supposed to have some such reality corresponding to it (§§ 1543-1686). Language also may play a part in endowing the abstractions with sex, but the sex residue is itself sufficient to account for that development. Language thereupon comes in to determine what the sex shall be.

1072. Anthropomorphism works in different ways among different peoples and in different periods of history. There was a great dif-

1070 [1] In his *Cultes, mythes et religions,* Vol. III, pp. 186-96, Reinach calls attention to a small figure published by Mommsen, bearing the inscription ΓΕΡΜΑΝΙΑ and then to a figure in mosaic with the inscription ΓΑΛΛΙΑ. In that mosaic, says he, "we are privileged to pay our respects to the first certain portrayal of [a personified] Gallia [Gaul] that Graeco-Roman art has handed down to us. The medallion that ornaments the bust is part of a very extensive mosaic dating from the reigns of the Antonines. . . . Already known were some few specimens of [personified] provinces or towns in mosaics of the second century. The tradition of topical personification of this kind was not lost during the high Middle Ages." Many examples of such personification of Rome are to be found on Roman coins and medallions.

1070 [2] Robiou, *L'état religieux de la Grèce et de l'Orient,* p. 22: "In Pindar [*Olympia,* VIII, 86; *Pythia,* X, 44 (Turner, pp. 81, 93)], and a little later in the *Electra* of Sophocles [v. 792], Nemesis is personified, but neither Aeschylus, nor even Herodotus in a work in which she plays an important part, make her an anthropomorphic creature properly so called. In other words, the conception seems to

ference between Greek anthropomorphism and the more archaic religion in Rome. There is also a very great difference between the anthropomorphism of Graeco-Roman antiquity and the religious notions of our own time. Yet we moderns have abstractions in plenty, and except for the one point of personification, they are very like the abstractions of old.

1073. It has often been said that Socialism is a religion. In the field of anthropomorphic derivations such a proposition is absurd; for surely nobody in our day has ever conceived of Socialism in a male form, the way the ancient Romans conceived of the goddess Roma in female form. But in the domain of residues the proposition corresponds quite to the facts, in the sense that the sentiments which in times past found their expression in worship of the goddess Roma, or the goddess Annona, and the sentiments which now find their expression in such faiths as Socialism, Progress, Democracy, and the like, are exactly similar.

1074. In the case of Rome sentiments begin by suggesting a mere image. They then develop in intensity to the point of a deification. They end by degenerating into objects of poetic or literary admiration, which endures down to our own very day. The Romans began by picturing Rome as a woman, and then made the woman a goddess. The vivid sentiment that found expression in the deification of the city persisted, in another form, even after the fall of paganism,

have been wavering at the time between the abstract and the mythological senses." According to the editor of *La sagesse de Jésus fils de Sirach,* pp. 390-91, the author of Ecclesiasticus "at times personified Wisdom, as the writers of his people had done before him; but he gradually slips back towards a more concrete representation, and one cannot be sure in many cases where he mentions Wisdom whether he is thinking of the metaphysical entity or of the practical virtue. His various statements are quite inconsistent. She is the first of creatures, eternal, omnipresent. Every man partakes of her. . . . God has bidden her to abide with Jacob and she has made Jerusalem her capital. She is more or less completely identified at times with the fear of the Lord and even with the Law." Toutain, *Les cultes païens dans l'Empire romain,* Vol. I (*Les cultes officiels*), pp. 415-16: "If we except the two goddesses Fortuna and Victoria, who deserve a special examination in view of their importance, the abstract divinities whose names we have remarked in [Roman] inscriptions are: Aequitas, Bonus Eventus, Concordia, Copia, Disciplina, Fama (?), Felicitas, Fides Publica, Gloria, Honos, Iuventus, Libertas, Mens or Bona Mens, Pax, Pietas, Prosperitas Deorum, Providentia, Salus Generis Humani, Sanctitas, Virtus."

eventually losing vigour and becoming a mere rhetorical expression. So we get a nucleus of sentiments persisting in varying intensity in time and expressing themselves under a variety of forms. The peoples who enjoyed the blessings of the *pax Romana* cherished, with regard to Rome, a sum of sentiments and concepts corresponding to the power of Rome and the benefits vouchsafed by Roman rule. In terms of the language then common among men the expression of such sentiments and concepts took the form of calling Roma a goddess and rearing temples to her. The same sentiments were expressed in worship of Rome and the ruling Emperor in common—*Romae et Augusto,* say the inscriptions; and a similar worship we find of Rome-and-Venus.[1] [2]

1074 [1] Daremberg-Saglio, *Dictionnaire, s.v. Roma: Rome personnifiée ou déifiée* (E. Maynial): "The most ancient portrayal of Roma as a symbolic personification of the state appears on the recto of the first denarii of the Republic beginning with the year 269 B.C. . . . In engraving that head on their coins the Romans had no idea whatever of representing Roma as a divinity, but intended merely to create an emblem for their city under guise of an armed woman, following in that the example of many Greek cities. The foreign peoples, in a spirit of flattery or gratitude, were the ones who endowed the personification of Roma with the status and attributes of a divinity. . . . While they were deifying Rome, the Greeks gave the new goddess a definite history and personality. The most ancient tradition relative to Roma is reported by Dionysius of Halicarnassus after the historian Callias [*Antiquitates Romanae,* I, 72 (Spelman, Vol. I, p. 165)]. It represents her as a Trojan. Under the Empire the cult of Roma became elaborate and fixed rites were established. . . . The Emperor Hadrian formally recognized the worship of the deified State and gave it official status in the capital." Toutain, *Les cultes païens dans l'Empire romain,* Vol. I, pp. 41, 74, 376: "Worship of the goddess Roma survived at one point or another of the Roman world during virtually the whole period of the high Empire. As distinguished from the worship of the Emperor it seems not to have been very wide-spread in the Latin provinces. . . . The worship of Roman power, under one or another of its various forms, was general in the Latin provinces. If the goddess Roma had fewer worshippers than she had in Greece and Asia during the last two centuries of the Republic, the imperial divinity at least received boundless homage. To say nothing of the Augustus himself, living or dead, a veritable worship was paid to his associates, his house, his qualities, his exploits." Toutain goes on to show that such worship was quite spontaneous and was never forced upon the masses. In the large, people worshipped Rome and the Emperor; in the detail—and sometimes a very petty detail—individuals and groups of individuals paid worship to anybody or anything that they thought might be in a position to help them: "The miller's guild at Guntia worshipped the god of that river because the river drove their millstones."

1074 [2] On being rescued by Titus Quintus Flaminius, the Chalcedonians consecrated the most beautiful buildings in their city to him. Plutarch, *Flaminius,* XVI,

1075. From the logical standpoint an engrossing admiration for Rome and a fact of deification of that city are different things; but from the standpoint of sentiment they are altogether similar, the second oftentimes being a mere translation of the first into the language current. Martial is expressing only popular sentiments when he exclaims: "Rome, goddess of the world and the peoples, without a peer and without a second!"[1]

1076. Such sentiments endure in time by mere force of inertia, even after the circumstances in which they originate have passed away. The abstraction becomes detached from the facts and lives a life of its own. St. Jerome will still be saying of Rome: "City powerful, city queen among cities, city praised of the Apostle, thy name,

3-4 (Perrin, Vol. X, p. 369), gives the text of two of the inscriptions on the edifices, one: "This gymnasium to Titus [Flaminius] and to Heracles the people [consecrates]"; the second, "To Titus and Apollo this Delphineon, the people." In Plutarch's time a "priest of Titus" was still being appointed, and still in use was a paean ending with the words: "We venerate the faith of the Romans, a faith we vow to cherish, and which we pledge ourselves to serve. Sing, O Virgins, to Zeus the great, and to Rome and to Titus, and therewith to the Faith of the Romans. *Io! Paian! Oh!* Titus, Saviour!" At about that time at Locris an altar was consecrated "To Jupiter Optimus Maximus, the immortal gods and goddesses, and eternal Rome": (Orelli, *Inscriptionum . . . collectio,* no. 1799): *"Iovi optimo maximo diis deabusque immortalibus et Romae aeternae Locrenses."* At Melos a statue and a bronze wreath were offered to Rome by the people. And *cf.* Livy, *Ab urbe condita,* XLIII, 6, 2: "The people of Alabanda [Asia Minor] urged the point that they had built a temple to the City of Rome and held annual games in honour of that goddess." Tacitus, *Annales,* IV, 56, 1, relates that in a competition of eleven cities for the privilege of building a temple to Tiberius, the people of Smyrna urged their long-standing fidelity to the Roman people and added that "they had been the first to rear a temple to the City of Rome, during the consulship of M. Porcius, at a time when the Roman People had done great things, to be sure, but had not yet attained its present supremacy, Carthage still flourishing and there being powerful kings in Asia." Dio Cassius, *Historia Romana,* LI, 20, 6: "Among other things which he set in order, Caesar [Augustus] permitted Ephesus and Nicaea to rear a temple to Roma, and to Caesar his father, whom he designated as the Hero Julius." Orelli mentions a number of individual priests of the cult of Roma and other gods: *Ibid.,* no. 155: *"sacerdoti Romae et Aug. P.H.C. [i.e., Provinciae Hispaniae citerioris]"*; nos. 488, 606: *"Romae et Augusto Caesari divi F. Patri patriae."* ("To Rome

---

1075 [1] *Epigrammata,* XII, 8, vv. 1-2:

> *"Terrarum Dea gentiumque Roma,*
> *cui par est nihil et nihil secundum!"*

[Pareto read: ". . . who is second to nothing."—A. L.]

O Rome, among the Greeks signifieth power and among the Hebrews sublimity."[1] And so on and on till nothing but the mere poetic reminiscence is left among the poets of our day.[2] But if today it is mere reminiscence, at one time it was a vital and influential sentiment.

1077. From the middle of the nineteenth century on the peoples of Western Europe witnessed a progressive improvement in their living conditions, the progress becoming more remarkably rapid towards the end of that century, and during the first years of the twentieth. Great prosperity engendered a group of agreeable sentiments and ideas that eventually came to cluster about nuclei known as Progress and Democracy. These powerful and beneficent entities are contemplated by people of our time with sentiments very like the emotions our ancestors felt for the power of Rome.

1078. Countless examples of this process might be mentioned, because, in general, any sentiment that is keenly felt tends to assume the form of faith in some abstraction or other. I will halt at the

and Augustus Caesar, son of the Divine [Julius] and father of his country"); nos. 732, 1800, 3675: ". . . *mun. L. restitutae in maiorum libert. Roma*" ("Roma [*i.e.*, a statue of the goddess Roma], by gift of the Lycians [Asia Minor] restored to their ancient liberties"); "*Iovei Capitolino et populo romano [virtutis]* M[*aximae*] *benivolentiae beneficiq. caussa.*" ("In recognition of its great valour, benevolence and generosity"); no. 5211: ". . . *sacerdos Romae et Aug.*; no. 7172: *in aede Romae et Augusti.*" From a later period, Rutilius, *Itinerarium*, I, vv. 47-50 (Paris, pp. 88-89):

> "*Exaudi, Regina tui pulcherrima mundi,*
> *inter sidereos Roma recepta polos:*
> *exaudi, genetrix hominum genetrixque Deorum,*
> *non procul a caelo per tua templa sumus.*"

("Hearken, O Queen, fairest of thy world, Rome now welcomed among the stars of heaven; hearken, O mother of men and gods: thy temples have brought us nigh unto heaven.")

1076 [1] *Adversus Jovinianum*, II, 38 (*Opera*, Vol. II, p. 337; Schaff-Wace, p. 415): "*Urbs potens, urbs orbis domina, urbs Apostoli voce laudata, interpretare vocabulum tuum, Roma, aut fortitudinis nomen est apud Graecos, aut sublimitatis iuxta Hebraeos.*"

1076 [2] Carducci, "Before the Baths of Caracalla" (*Poesie*, pp. 795-97):

> "*Religioso è quest' orror: la dea*
> *Roma qui dorme.*"

("A holy thing this awe: here sleeps the goddess Rome!")

single case of "pacifism." Says George Kemeny:[1] "It is of a doctrine, therefore, that I intend to speak, not of a religion, much less of a creed. The meanings of those two last terms have been so altered in the course of the ages, they have undergone so many reincarnations, that they have become quite disfigured and often serve today to express ideas that stand in direct conflict with the pacifist ideal. [So the religious idea is being thrown out through the door, but we will soon find it coming back through the window.] I trust that I am not falling into any sin of blasphemy when I declare that pacifism in the highest sense of the term is neither a means nor an end, but a belief based on a sort of revelation. [The salient feature in many doctrines called religions.] The moral substance of pacifism being of a higher order [There is no definition to enable us to distinguish a "higher" from a "lower" order.] and present in every universal conception of life [What can that wonderful thing be?], pacifism must be placed on a footing with Buddhism, Judaism, Islamism, Christianity [Why then did he begin by saying that it was not a religion?], though it is safe to say that it surpasses all these conceptions in that it is common to them all, is present in them all, unites them all."[2]

1079. The example is of special interest in that it is one of many in which the residues clearly transpire through the derivations. Stress of sentiment puts logic to flight. Kemeny began by banishing pacifism from the "religions." A few lines further on he puts it

1078 [1] *Le mouvement pacifiste, Correspondence bimensuelle du Bureau International de la Paix à Berne,* Apr. 15, 1912, no. 7, pp. 99-101.

1078 [2] The whole article is a sermon such as we find in other religions; in fact it seems to be a reminiscence of some sermon he may have heard in a church, p. 101: "There are no miracles without faith. Pacifism as a world-doctrine will work miracles only if it reigns in your hearts." The flexibility of derivations is well illustrated in the case of certain Italian pacifists who preached war in the name of peace (§§ 1705 f.)! There is an apparent contradiction, and the contradiction is real enough from the standpoint of logic; but not so from the standpoint of sentiment. The pacifists in question were attaching the term "pacifism" to a sum of sentiments of benevolence and brotherly love, and that same group of sentiments is one of the elements in patriotism. "Pacifism" and "patriotism" therefore become two names for one same thing, and one is conscious of no contradiction in following the various impulses of the group of sentiments. In just the same way, how many wars have been fought in the name of Christianity, which preaches peace!

"on a footing" with doctrines that beyond any doubt everybody calls religions. The contradiction is not apparent to him, since he is writing under the influence of a powerful sentiment, whereby pacifism "like an eagle soareth" over other religions—that must be why it is not one of them, though it is in other respects like them! He shows that pacifism does not conflict with any religion—the eagle is flying like a humble sparrow—but then he adds, pp. 100-01: "There is another analogy between religion and pacifism, an analogy expressed in words that are often uttered in jest: 'It is faith that saves!' Pacifism, too, encompasses salvation. All those who have worked in the pacifist movement consistently, sincerely, without selfish ulterior purposes, have certainly been conscious of being better men therefor. Pacifism destroys the germs of evil one by one. It purifies our thoughts, ennobles our instincts; and by that very fact exercises a regenerating influence on individuals and races." If one had a weakness for personification along with such notions, one would get an image of Pacifism, just as we got images of the pagan deities—something like the statues of the goddess Roma, or like the picture some people have of the God of the Christians, a rather handsome old gentleman with a long beard, sitting on a cloud.

1080. There have been—to be sure by way of exception—no end of modern derivations fashioned on the ancient pattern. Auguste Comte personified the Earth, rebaptizing it as "the Great Fetish"; and Humanity, too, for which he ordained a ritual of worship. Our present-day "humanitarians" are expressing not a few of Comte's ideas in a language of their own.

1081. The word "Socialism" has stood, and still stands, for something great, powerful, beneficent; and about that nucleus, again, no end of hopes, dreams, agreeable sensations, have come to cluster. Just as the ancient divinities multiplied, subdivided, competed, so in our day, alongside the godhead of Socialism, we have the godheads of Social Reform and Social Legislation—not to mention lesser gods such as Social Art, Social Hygiene, Social Medicine, and countless other things, which in grace of the affix "social" become partakers of the divine essence.

1082. Lyall classifies the various styles of deification among the Hindus, and they hold, with some slight modification, for many other peoples:[1] "1. The worship of mere stocks and stones and of local configurations, which are unusual or grotesque in size, shape, or position. [*Cf.* Class I residues.] 2. The worship of things inanimate, which are gifted with mysterious motion. 3. The worship of animals which are feared. 4. The worship of visible things, animate or inanimate, which are directly or indirectly useful and profitable, or which possess any incomprehensible function or property. [These, so far, have been groups of sensations of the simpler forms. The following involves a process of abstraction more remote from simple sensation:] 5. The worship of a *Deo,* or spirit, a thing without form and void—the vague impersonation of the uncanny sensation that comes over one at certain places. [Then come categories involving the persistence of certain sensations in time:] 6. The worship of dead relatives and other deceased persons known in their lifetime to the worshipper. 7. The worship of persons who had a great reputation during life, or who died in some strange or notorious way—at shrines. [From there we go on to abstractions of greater and greater complexity:] 8. The worship in temples of the persons belonging to the foregoing class as demigods or subordinate deities. 9. The worship of manifold local incarnations of the older deities, and of their symbols. 10. The worship of departmental deities. 11. The worship of the supreme gods of Hinduism and of their ancient incarnations and personifications, handed down by the Brahmanic scriptures."[2]

1083. So far Lyall's description is perfect; but thereafter he succumbs to the general weakness for logical explanations, assuming that the worship of certain inanimate objects is to be attributed to

1082 [1] *Asiatic Studies,* pp. 7-9.

1082 [2] Hovelacque, *Les nègres de l'Afrique suséquatoriale,* p. 397: "The religion of the superequatorial blacks is a fetishism of a most rudimentary character. Let the sight of some creature, object, or spectacle stir the individual to some unusual degree and he will attribute to that creature, object, spectacle, some special power. It is not spiritualism, or spiritism, that we get: there is so far no notion of immaterial being. It is something in the direction of animism."

the "intelligence, which argues that a stock or stone embodies divinity only because it has a queer, unusual form." He inadvertently refutes himself when he says: "Now the Brahmanic explanation of this reverence for curious-looking things, especially for things conical and concave, is always at hand and producible to the earnest inquirer after divine emblems and manifestations; but these interpretations appear to belong to a later symbolism, which is habitually invented by the more ingenious to account upon orthodox principles for what is really nothing but primitive fetishism rising into a higher atmosphere." [1]

1084. Examining the facts directly, Lyall was able to get at the underlying residues. If the residues are not always apparent, it is because we do not get the facts directly, but know them only under the gloss laid over them by poets, philosophers, theologians, and

1083 [1] The passage continues, pp. 9-10: "For the feeling which actuates the uninitiated Indian worshipper of stocks and stones, or what are called freaks of nature, is in its essence that simple awe of the unusual which belongs to no particular religion. It survives in England to this day in the habit of ascribing grotesque and striking landmarks or puzzling antiquities to the Devil, who is, or has been, the residuary legatee of all obsolete Pagan superstitions in Christian countries. In any district of India such objects or local configurations as the Devil's Quoits . . . would be worshipped. Similar things are actually worshipped all over Berar, and in every case some signification, either mythical or symbolical, has been continued or sanctioned by some expert Brahman to justify and authorize the custom. [The derivation, and admirably described!] Yet it seems certain that among the vulgar there is at first no *arrière pensée* in their adoration. [A good description of the residue.] The worshipper requires no such motive, he asks for no sign, offers no prayer, expects no reward. He pays reverent attention to the Unaccountable Thing, the startling expression of an unknown power, and goes his way. [Next come derivations.] It is not difficult to perceive how this original downright adoration [Residues.] of queer-looking objects is modified by passing into the higher order of imaginative superstition. [In other words, how derivations originate.] First, the stone is the abode of some spirit; its curious shape or situation betraying *possession*. Next, this strange form or aspect argues some *design*, or handiwork, of supernatural beings, or is the vestige of their presence on earth. One step further lands us in the world-wide regions of mythology and heroic legend, where the naturally remarkable features of a hill, a cleft rock . . . commemorate the miracles and feats of some saint, demigod, or full-blown deity. Berar is abundantly furnished with such fables, and beyond them we get, as I think, to the regarding of stones as emblems of mysterious attributes . . . and to all that class of notions which entirely separate the outward image from the power really worshipped. So that at last we emerge into pure symbolism, as when anything appears to be selected arbitrarily to serve as a visible point for spiritual adoration." The passage is continued in § 1090.

men of letters. Of the ancient religion of the Vedas, for instance, we know nothing but a literary-theological product passed on to us in religious hymns of a prolix vacuity that is truly remarkable, and which are quite as devoid of sense as of definiteness. And we have no other documents for determining the character of parallel forms of popular belief that in all probability existed then, as they exist now, expressing themselves in the facts studied by Lyall.[1]

1085. So the mythology of the Greek tragic poets, superior as their poems are to the Vedic hymns in meaning, definiteness, and clarity, is probably—one might say certainly—different from the popular mythology that we at least descry through the few documents known to us on the subject—the writings of Pausanias, for instance.

1086. II-θ: *Need of new abstractions.* Abstractions become outworn or untenable for one reason or another; they disappear or lose their appeal. But the need for them endures and new abstractions are required to take the places of those which disappear or weaken. So popular mythologies are superseded, among the educated, by scholarly, subtle, abstruse mythologies; ingenious theogonies become the order of the day—speculations as to the creation of the world, the primitive state of humanity, and so on. Then another onward step is taken: supernatural abstractions give ground to metaphysical abstractions; there are speculations as to the "essences" of things, and people expatiate in incomprehensible language on even more incomprehensible subjects. Finally these metaphysical abstractions are topped off with pseudo-scientific abstractions. Laplace's nebular theory was holding a prominent place in Socialist sermons a few years

1084 [1] There are many other cases like that—for instance, Pallas, *Reise durch verschiedene Provinzen des Russischen Reichs,* Vol. III, pp. 60-61: "The Ostiaks also manifest a sort of worship for certain mountains and trees that have struck their imagination or have been declared sacred by their priests. They never go by one such without discharging an arrow—a testimony of respect that they pay. What I have been saying applies to individual worship. Public worship is addressed to first-class idols, which their priests have blessed. . . . In days gone by the Ostiaks used to worship many trees in that particular forest, where they hung up the furs and hides of animals they had sacrificed. But the Cossacks began to steal the furs, so they resolved to cut down the trees. They cut them up into logs or large wheel-like blocks (*Klötze*), which they decorated with ribbons and signs and set up in safe places. It is to such places that they go with their offerings today."

back and supplying conclusive proof that Evolution, Holiest of Holies, was to lead the world to a Socialist golden age. People who have ceased worshipping the relics of saints turn to worshipping "solidarity." Those who cannot accept the theology of Rome turn to the theology of the Modernists as something more "scientific." Numberless the cases of this kind where forms change and the need of persisting abstractions endures.[1]

1087. To judge by the little we know of it, the primitive religion of the Roman people was deficient, to some extent at least, in this element of theological and metaphysical abstraction. That must have been one among the many causes that opened the doors to the invasion of Hellenism; nor could it have been altogether stranger to the vogue, later on, of the Oriental cults of Mithras and Christ, though in that the succession of new races to the ancient Roman stock was the most decisive factor. The meagreness of theological and metaphysical abstraction in present-day humanitarianism is impeding its progress as a religious creed; and the same is true of the closely kindred doctrine of Liberal Protestanism.

1088. Not only does the human being need abstractions: he also needs to develop them—he wants them alive in his mind, not dead. So it comes about that the more flourishing a religion is, the more vigorous and vital are the heresies arising within it. There is a static demand, and a dynamic demand, for abstractions.

1086 [1] A single individual can run this whole gamut in one lifetime. In July, 1913, a monument was unveiled in Paris to Father Hyacinthe. The inscription on it reads: "Father Hyacinthe, a priest of Saint-Sulpice, then a barefoot Carmelite, preached from the pulpit of Nôtre-Dame (1864-1869), then left the Church and married, September 3, 1872. For twenty years thereafter he preached the reform of Catholicism and the brotherhood of the churches (1873-1890). During the twenty years thereafter he rose above all churches and died as a monotheistic free-thinker." By no means an isolated case. It is a general rule that people begin by severing connexions with the Catholic Church on the claim that all they want is a better, more liberal form of Catholicism. But they very seldom stop there. They go on evolving. Their Catholicism becomes theism. Sometimes their theism becomes materialism. Sometimes, again, the evolution halts at a certain point, and there comes a retrogression, the individual dying in the Catholic faith of his childhood. [The American example might be the spiritual Odyssey of Henry James the Elder, who travelled leagues and miles in quest of truth and finally pounced on Swedenborgianism. That would be something like the monk's pursuit of Angelica in the *Orlando Furioso*.—A. L.]

CHAPTER VII

Residues: Activity and Sociability

1089. Class III: *Need of expressing sentiments by external acts.* Powerful sentiments are for the most part accompanied by certain acts that may have no direct relation to the sentiments but do satisfy a need for action. Something similar is observable in animals. A cat moves its jaws at sight of a bird; the dog twists and turns and wags its tail at sight of its master; the parrot flaps its wings.

1090. Says Lyall further:[1] "The present writer knew a Hindu officer of great shrewdness and very fair education who devoted several hours daily to the elaborate worship of five round pebbles which he had appointed to be his symbol of Omnipotence. Although his general belief was in one all-pervading Divinity, he must have something symbolic to handle and address." Notable in that is not merely the need for the symbol, but the need for "doing something," acting, moving the limbs, fixing the attention on something concrete—escaping, in a word, from a state of passive abstraction. In our day, Flammarion and other scientists hold a meeting at the spring equinox and watch a sunrise.

1091. The acts in which sentiments express themselves reinforce such sentiments and may even arouse them in individuals who were without them. It is a well known psychological fact that if an emotion finds expression in a certain physical attitude, an individual putting himself in that attitude may come to feel the corresponding emotion. The residues of this class, accordingly, stand conjoined with emotions, sentiments, and passions in a complex concatenation of actions and reactions.

1092. III-α: *Need of "doing something" expressing itself in combinations.* As regards combinations we come across residues of Class I again. It is a question really of a variety of compound residues. Few the cases in which, as in the Lyall example, combinations are

1090 [1] *Asiatic Studies,* p. 10 (concluding quotation in §§ 1082-83 [1]).

due to pure chance, or better, to vague or very complicated motives. In general some more or less fantastic rule determines the choice of the combination. The impulse to "do something" is overwhelming; the fancy sets to work, and finds a way to satisfy it. In such cases the III-α residue—in other words, the demand for action—is the chief factor; Class I residues, in other words, the combinations, are secondary. The norms governing the combinations—in other words, the derivations from the Class I residues—are incidental and generally of little importance.

1093. For that reason it is difficult, and not seldom impossible, to distinguish operations in magic from religious rites, with the result that the common mania for substituting the search for "origins" for the search for residues has led people to conclude that magic was the "origin" of religion. The demand for action, which corresponds to the III-α residue, gives rise to occult, magical, and religious rites. There is a transition by imperceptible degrees from the first variety to the last. Numberless the examples in procedures devised for healing the sick.[1]

1094. III-β: *Religious ecstasies.* One may feel a calm and thoughtful need for "doing something." But that sentiment may rise in intensity to the point of exaltation, exhilaration, delirium. There is a merely quantitative difference, therefore, between the III-α and the III-β types. Religious chants, contortions, dances, mutilations performed in states of delirium, belong to the III-β variety. However, mutilations and, more generally, voluntary sufferings often involve another kind of residues—the ascetic type of which we shall speak hereafter (§§ 1163 f.).

1095. Shamanism is an interesting case where our "action" residues come to light with relatively few complications. Says Sir John Lubbock:[1] "Wrangel, however, regarding Shamanism as religion in the ordinary sense, was astonished at this: 'It is remarkable,' he says (*Siberia and Polar Sea,* p. 123), 'that Shamanism has no dogmas

1093 [1] The great variety in the rites inspired by the need human beings have felt for averting or producing storms was noted in Chapter II (§§ 186 f.).

1095 [1] *Origin of Civilization,* pp. 222-23.

of any kind. It is not a system taught or handed down from one to another; though it is widely spread, it seems to originate with each individual separately, as the fruit of a highly excited imagination, acted upon by external impressions, which closely resemble each other throughout the deserts of Northern Siberia.' [Lubbock, like everyone else who has dealt with such matters, has the fixed idea of logical derivations, so he explains:] It is far from easy in practice always to distinguish Shamanism from Totemism on the one hand, and Idolatry on the other. The main difference lies in the conception of the Deity. In Totemism the Deities inhabit our earth. In Shamanism they live generally in a world of their own, and trouble themselves little about what is passing here. The Shaman is occasionally honoured by the presence of the Deity or is allowed to visit the heavenly regions."

1096. In that we get the usual mistake of assuming a development from the abstract to the concrete. In reality the route is the precise opposite. The idea would be that before there were any concrete cases of the kind, human beings began by evolving an abstract, logical conception of the Deity; thence inferring the rules that were to guide their conduct; and finally acting concretely in the light of that conception and those rules! In general the very opposite is the case. Theories that divinities inhabit the Earth or some other world are altogether accessory to the concrete facts of totemism and Shamanism. They did not produce the observed facts. They have been devised to explain them.

1097. Religious frenzy is not peculiar to any one religion or people. It appears in most religions and among most peoples, now in mild, now in very exaggerated, forms. It is not therefore a logical derivative of any one of the religions in which it is observable. To the contrary, the religious theory is devised to explain it. We are in a position to study it in cases that are taking place before our eyes, and so are enabled to proceed from the known to the unknown in dealing with phenomena more remote in place or more ancient in time. There is, for example, the Salvation Army, whose chief instrument of conversion is religious exhilaration. It considers itself a branch of Christianity, yet its procedures would be no whit different if it belonged to some other religion, the Mohammedan, let us say.

1098. The Welsh "revival" differs but slightly from the Salvation Army. The theological element is negligible: religious frenzy is the main thing. A Frenchman, M. Henri Bois, attended the Welsh revival of the year 1904-05. He was impressed by the fact that individuals in the throes of religious fervour shrank from arguments with unbelievers.[1] The Torrey Mission was to some small extent theological, the revival, not at all.[2] The meeting of April 11 was (p. 269) "a strange meeting! Fervid, passionate prayers, men and women boxing with their clenched fists! Several lapse into the *hwyl!*[3] . . . In a *hwyl* one loses all self-control—one is almost unconscious—the subconscious in fact comes to the fore. A little girl is sitting two seats to my right. She begins to pray along with others. They begin to sing, but that makes no difference to her. She continues praying. She catches their attention for a moment; they listen with cries of *Amen! Yes! Very good!* Then, apparently, the meeting has had enough of her. It breaks forth into a great hymn. The little girl continues praying. She has been praying now for a long time. She is in a *hwyl,* completely oblivious to everything about her. She sits with

1098 [1] *Le réveil au pays de Galles,* p. 147: "There were unbelievers in the galleries. Sidney Evans [the evangelist] advises 'Christian workers' not to argue with them but to 'bear witness,' exemplify, 'show forth,' the 'life that is in them'—to pray. In the front row at the meeting is a woman who would like to be converted but cannot make up her mind. A Christian sitting at her side begins praying for her in a loud voice. Still she cannot make up her mind. The meeting draws to a close. She does not stir. And the Christian also keeps his seat beside her, talking to her, exhorting her."

1098 [2] *Ibid.,* p. 129: "While the Torrey Mission is more dogmatic, more concerned with doctrines, the revival is all emotion, all excitement—it is stirring, vital. At the Torrey Mission the address is a long affair and a very important feature. Torrey is so much the schoolmaster that some of his hearers may be seen taking notes. The address is nothing at the revival. There everything comes down to singing and praying."

1098 [3] *Ibid.,* pp. 268-69: "If at times the Welsh 'pray singing' they also 'sing praying.' They call that the *hwyl* in Welsh." And *cf.* Rogues de Foursac, *Un mouvement mystique contemporain,* p. 140: "The word *hwyl* designates not a mere exercise in oratory, but a peculiar state of the soul of which the plaintive melopoeia in question is, or is supposed to be, a translation. Psychologically it is made up of an intense emotion that leads to unconsciousness of the outer world and a consequent amnesia." Shamanism could not be described in terms at all different.

her eyes closed as though possessed by an outer power which controls her utterly."

1099. This state of unconsciousness through emotional stress is identical with the exaltation trance of the Shaman, though the derivations with which the respective states are explained are so widely different. The Welsh fanatic, during a "revival" as described by Bois, offers the counterpart of well-known phenomena observable in all peoples in all periods of history.[1]

1100. One may claim that the cries of the Angekok are inspired of the Devil, while cries of the revivalists are inspired of God. That is a problem which experimental science cannot consider and which it could in no wise solve. What is certain, experimentally, is that the two cases are identical and manifest the same residues.

1101. Prophets of all eras seem to have had at least something in common with such enthusiasts. Modern democracy has chosen to seek its ancestors among the Hebrew prophets. That is one of those fantastic genealogies which pleasantly tickle the vanity of the *parvenus*. In attributing the inspiration of their prophets to God and the inspiration of pagan prophets to the Devil, the early Christians were coming pretty close to the truth, in the sense that they were to an extent aware that the two things were manifestations of the same residue. The old view that the prophets of both schools were

1099 [1] *Ibid.*, p. 227: "I saw a young man lying full-length on the steps leading to the platform. His face was distorted, his fists clenched. He delivered a vehement prayer in that posture, and did not rise even when he had finished praying. As the meeting was protracted and 'warmed up' I could see emotions gradually rise. Men would clench their fists and start boxing, as it were, in rhythm, keeping their seats and uttering not a word; or else they would begin beating their heads, or burying their faces in their two hands, or waving their arms wildly about, all in silence. I saw women and girls gradually succumb to the contagious nervous excitement and grow more and more unconscious of the outer world. They would sit there with flushed cheeks and vacant eyes or sometimes with their eyes closed. If the inner excitement became too strong, they would burst forth, men and women, and apparently quite unconsciously, into prayers or hymns." *Ibid.*, p. 241: "In addition to 'thanksgivings' there are prayers that amount to mere shouting: 'crying unto the Lord,' 'wrestling with God,' 'agonizing in prayer'—such in exact literalness are the expressions they use. One hears piercing shrieks from sinners who believe themselves lost and are appealing to God to have mercy on them: 'Lord, be merciful to *me, me, me!*' "

charlatans and rogues went farther astray, mistaking the exception for the rule.[1]

1102. In the same way the view that the Hebrew prophets were just degenerates and half-wits also goes wide of the mark. To be sure mental pathology must have played some part in such phenomena, but it does not account for them entirely; and to be persuaded of that one need only observe phenomena going on before our eyes (§ 547). In the United States there have been prophets, like the so-called Elias, who enjoyed perfect mental health and had the sole purpose—which they sometimes realized—of making money. Similar occurrences have been common in all countries at all times. Not long ago the Marconi investigation in England showed that certain politicians who stand high in the esteem of the Welsh fanatics and affect the language of the prophets of Israel in their public utterances do not forget their own interests nor scruple to speculate in the stock-markets. Such facts have no bearing on the phenomena we are here examining. But then again, in the ranks of the Salvation Army, among the enthusiasts of the Welsh revival, the fanatics of prohibitionism and purity campaigns, among humanitarians and prophets of the god Progress, and so on and on, there are undeniably individuals who vary little if at all from the normal type of the sane man; and if others do, that merely proves that exaltation may readily go hand in hand with a pathological state, but not that sane people are necessarily immune to it.[1]

1101 [1] Sorel, *"Quelques prétentions juives,"* pp. 230 f.: "The fact that leaders of popular insurrection have at one time or another, in the Middle Ages, or in earlier modern periods, pretended to base their revolt on words uttered by the prophets of Israel does not justify the inference that those prophets were revolutionaries. It is in point to recall a sage remark of Renan: 'In religious history a text means not what the author meant, but what the needs of the moment made him mean.' " (For the remainder of the quotation see § 541 [4].) That is all very true. The case is general and arises in the fact that the derivation is secondary and that as many derivations are always available as are required to justify residues, inclinations, interests. Renan used one of the usual phraseologies: the "needs of the moment." What can that new entity be? In order to keep within experimental limits, it has to be rectified to read: "what people get out of it in order to justify their sentiments, inclinations, interests, at a given moment."

1102 [1] Binet-Sanglé, *Les prophètes juifs,* pp. 76-77 (the ancient prophets of Israel in question): "The Jahvist *nabi* is a degenerate with an incompletely developed cere-

1103. Furthermore, the social significance of prophecy lies not so much in the prophets as in the people who believe in them; and when we find a genius like Newton among such people, we have to admit that our action residue plays no small part in social phenomena.

bral cortex that contains a limited number of mnesic neurones, in other words of frames for images and ideas. For that reason the field of his thinking is also limited. Furthermore, as a consequence of this arrested development of the neurones and the hypercontractibility that results from it, the *nabi* has a special disposition towards cerebral dissociation, to the formation of those independent groupings of neurones which constitute the theatre for those mnesic short-circuits which supply the conditions for hallucinations and obsessions." Not a few Protestant writers concede that there may have been something pathological about the ancient seers: *e.g.*, Piepenbring, *Théologie de l'Ancien Testament*, pp. 16-17: "The prophets have sometimes been regarded as lunatics or abnormals because all sorts of eccentricities crept into ancient prophecy. A thing that further contributed to their earning that reputation was their resort to in fact strange symbolic acts to give plastic expression to their thoughts. [But siding with the incendiaries as regards ancient prophecy, they turn fireman to save the prophecy of a later day, nor can they do otherwise, if they would keep the Gospels: *Ibid.*, p. 73 (the "new prophecy" in question):] It appears in its full purity, purged of the traditional usages that one meets in the other peoples of antiquity and which exerted a powerful influence upon the ancient prophets of Israel. The latter still practised the art of divination and their work was not immune to a more or less unhealthy exhilaration. The prophets of our period, instead, are preachers, speaking under divine inspiration but without losing consciousness of themselves, and following the trend of political events of which they are attentive observers. [So saving both the goat and the cabbages; believers will be satisfied with the divine inspiration, pseudo-experimentalists with the political outlook.] All that proves beyond dispute that the prophets of Israel manifested something similar to 'glossolalia'—that lower degree of Christian inspiration [Piepenbring, notice, does not reject inspiration outright, but merely demotes it to a lower grade.], and other similar phenomena that have been witnessed since that time in the Church, especially under the influence of American Methodism. But it does not prove that all [Some were, but not all!] of them were in that condition when they received the Divine Word. The two kinds of Christian inspiration described by St. Paul (I Cor., Chapter 14) are evidently something very similar to the two types of prophecy in ancient Israel. And just as the Apostle ranks plain evangelical preaching higher than 'glossolalia,' so we must give simple prophetic preaching under the inspiration of the Spirit of God a higher plane than ancient ecstatic prophecy." Piepenbring does not define what a "higher plane" of prophecy would be, so we can neither accept nor refute his thesis. He does not, and cannot, give a single experimental proof that such prophets were "inspired by the spirit of God." Such a thing can be believed only as an act of faith. Nor can one imagine why the act of faith should stop at the general proposition and not go on to accept as true all the particulars of prophecy, both old and new, no criterion being given for determining where faith is to halt and experimental research to begin.

1104. Only the mania for judging things by the incidental element in them, by derivations, can obscure the exact similarity of all phenomena of religious exaltation, or frenzies of kindred type.

1105. "Ecstasy," for example, the *manía* of the Pythia, had the same residue as other phenomena of religious ecstasy; and as far as good sense is concerned, the Pythia gave more signs of it than many a Hebrew prophet. Says Bouché-Leclerq:[1] "Intoxicated, it was said, by the vapours of the cave and utterly possessed by the god, the Pythia lapsed forthwith into an ecstasy that the poets have been pleased to depict in the loudest colours and which we shall not describe after them. Such nervous excitement was not always simulated, for in Plutarch's time one Pythia died of it" (*De defectu oraculorum,* 51; Goodwin, Vol. IV, pp. 62-63).[2]

1105 [1] *Histoire de la divination dans l'antiquité,* Vol. III, p. 101.

1105 [2] The prudish reticence of the author who cannot muster the courage to describe the ecstasy of the Pythia (in a scientific work in four volumes!) is characteristic of the fatuous sexophobia prevalent in our day. Van Dale lived at a time when scientists were not affected by that malady. He does not mince words when it comes to describing what took place. The idea, in two words, was that an evil spirit entered the body of the Pythia through her sexual organs and gave answer through her mouth. Such the great mystery that cannot be revealed without offence to our bigots of prudery! Sorry as I am for their discomfort, I am going to quote what Van Dale has to say, *De oraculis veterum ethnicorum,* pp. 153-54: "It is said not only that the 'Cacodaemon,' or Devil, was taken into the body of the Pythia while she was sitting on the Tripod, but that he entered thither through her female or private parts and gave out through her mouth answers which the heathen (*Ethnici*) called divine and the Christians diabolical. The pagan writers themselves make no mention of any such thing, and the numerous early Christians who assert it do so without giving any proof (*non nisi nuda assertatione*), many modern theologians carelessly following them. The first of Christian writers, to my knowledge, to make that assertion was Origen, *Contra Celsum,* VII (Augsburg, p. 343, Latin, p. 338), who writes: 'The Pythia was assuredly the most celebrated of soothsayers. It is said that that prophetess of Apollo squatted over a hole in the cave at Castalia and took in the spirit issuing from it through her private organs, until, entirely filled by said spirit, she gave forth those celebrated and divine utterances which the Oracles were supposed to be.' Chrysostom, *Homilia in I Cor.,* 22 [read, 29] (Gaume, Vol. X, p. 304; Chambers, p. 170) follows Origen, and just as hesitantly using *dicunt* (λέγουσι) where Origen has *narrant:* 'It is said that the Pythia, a certain woman, at times squatted on the Tripod of Apollo, her legs apart, and that an evil spirit entering her body from below (*inferne*) filled her with its frenzy (*furore*).' The scholiast of Aristophanes seems to have borrowed what he says (*sua*) from this latter, Chrysostom, since he uses virtually the same words." The scholium mentioned by Van Dale relates to the *Plutus,* v. 39 (Dübner, pp. 327, 545-46, 688).

1106. The phenomena of the Welsh revival enable us to understand phenomena observable in the days of the Crusades (§ 547). It is a mistake to see in the latter mere effects of "mediaeval superstition." They were products of many circumstances, some of which are still observable in our time, in the "revival trance" for example, and other such things. The important part played by children in revivals serves to show how crusades by children may have come about.[1]

1107. The English are a more level-headed people than the Welsh, and not a few were shocked at doings in the revival. One of them said to M. Bois, *Op. cit.*, p. 261: "Those hymns of praise are paeans! Why, they remind me of the Corybantes!" A remark not so far from the truth, after all, since the two phenomena have the same residue.[1]

1106 [1] Michaud, *Histoire des croisades*, 1877, Vol. I, pp. 28-29 (Robson, Vol. I, pp. 56-57): "In those days the pilgrim spirit, which became more violent as it passed from person to person and might be called, in line with a phrase of St. Paul, 'Cross-madness,' was a flaming, obsessing passion that overwhelmed all other feelings. . . . Women, children, clerics, branded crosses on their foreheads or other parts of their bodies as evidence of God's will. . . . A thing hardly believable, thieves, brigands, left their hidden retreats, came forward to confess their crimes, and on receiving the Cross promised to go to Palestine to expiate them." Exactly what happens nowadays at revivals and in Salvation Army missions. Then as now such conversions were ephemeral things. Lea, *History of the Inquisition*, Vol. I, pp. 147-48: "It was during the preaching of this crusade [against the Albigenses] that villages and towns in Germany were filled with women who, unable to expend their religious ardour in taking the cross, stripped themselves naked and ran silently through the roads and streets. Still more symptomatic of the diseased spirituality of the time [Lea might have observed a spirituality just as diseased in his own country. That harpy who went about dismantling barrooms with a hatchet [Mrs. Carrie Nation] was a modern sufferer from the crusader malady.] was the Crusade of the Children, which desolated thousands of homes. From vast districts of territory . . . crowds of children set forth, without leaders or guides, in search of the Holy Land . . . and the few who eventually found their way home again could give no reason for the overmastering longing which had carried them away."

1107 [1] Horace, *Odes*, I, 16, vv. 5-9:

> *"Non Dindymene, non adytis quatit*
> *mentem sacerdotum incola Pythius;*
> *non Liber aeque, non acuta*
> *sic geminant Corybantes aera,*
> *tristes ut irae."*

("Not so doth Dindymene (Cybele), not so doth the Pythian (Apollo) who dwelleth in the shrine, shake the minds of their priests, not so doth Liber (Bacchus), not so

M. Bois also records the opinion of a lady of Anglican affiliation to whom he was enthusiastically describing a revival meeting. Says he, *Op. cit.*, p. 137: "My admiration and enthusiasm found scant echo. My hostess belonged to the Anglican Church. She had attended a Welsh meeting and had been quite scandalized at the absence of orderliness, regularity, decorum. Think of it! She had taken her Anglican hymn-book with her, as one always does in attending a respectable service. She had not been able to use it once!"

1108. Such more or less must have been the sentiments of many Roman Senators when they voted the *senatus consultus* against the Bacchanals; and not greatly different the sentiments that Euripides puts upon the lips of Pentheus.[1]

1109. Livy's account, *Ab urbe condita,* XXXIX, 8-16, is obviously exaggerated. The rebukes for obscenity levelled at the Bacchanals are the usual insults that religious sects hurl at each other—so regularly, indeed, that there is no way of knowing how much truth there is in them. We cannot accept Livy's testimony as altogether trustworthy nor decide just to what extent the indictments laid

do the Corybantes, beat their ringing bronze, as black wrath doth [the human heart].")

1108 [1] *Bacchae,* vv. 215-28 (Coleridge, Vol. II, p. 94): "Sometime absent from this city, I now hear of new misfortunes that have befallen it. Our women have left their homes for a feigned inspiration, and are wandering the shady hills, hailing this new god, Bacchus, whoever he may be, with dances. Each revel-troop has its brimming wine-cups, and each and all depart to the solitudes to enjoy the embraces of men, pretending to be 'Maenads' performing sacrifices—but with more thought, I hear, to Aphrodite than to Bacchus. Such as my guards have been able to seize, they hold manacled in the public prisons. Those who have escaped will I capture on the hills and bring hither." Cicero, *De legibus,* II, 14, 35-36, expressed himself in terms no different. What he is condemning evidently is unruly chaotic ceremonies. Anything governed by public authority he is ready to allow:

"*Marcus*. We can hardly agree as to what comes next!

"*Atticus*. What would that be?

"*Marcus*. The matter of religious ceremonies conducted at night for women.

"*Atticus*. But I do agree [to the requirement that private worship should be performed with priests appointed by the state], especially since orderly (*solenni*) sacrifice in public you expressly except."

But Cicero sees fit to expatiate:

"*Marcus*. But if we prohibit night-time services, what about our Iacchus [the Bacchus of Eleusis], our Eumolpidae [his priests] and their rites—most majestic

against the Bacchanals were justified. Let us assume for the moment that they were true: the fact still stands that the Senate also prohibited mysteries celebrated in Magna Graecia that were not in the least held to be obscene. It is therefore clear that the Senate had quite other purposes in view than the mere safe-guarding of morals; and one has only to read a speech of the consul Postumius, which Livy quotes, 15-16, to see that political considerations were the chief ones. "No one would care, particularly," says Postumius, 16, 1-2, "if they had become mere perverts through these filthy acts which are a great disgrace to them, provided they had kept their hands clean of crimes and their minds of treason to the State. Never has there been so great an evil in the Republic involving either more individuals or more things. I assure you that all the roistering, all the cheating, all the corruption, that has gone on during these past years has originated in that sanctuary of crime. This conspiracy has itself not revealed the full measure of the wrongdoing: it has stopped at private crime merely because it has never yet been strong enough to destroy the state." [1]

ones? We are not legislating for the Roman People, remember, but for the [average] law-abiding, well-governed country.

"*Atticus.* Well, I suppose you would except the rites to which we were initiated ourselves.

"*Marcus.* Yes, I would."

All the same Cicero does not care to have such things going on in Rome. He concedes at the most that women may be initiated into the rites of Ceres but in clear light of day and according to Roman ritual, *Ibid.*, 15, 37: "*Marcus* . . . The sternness of our forefathers in such matters is evident from the ancient decree of the Senate against the Bacchanals, and the investigation and suppression [of those practices] by the consuls, with an army raised for that special purpose. If you find that rather severe of us Romans, you should remember that in the very heart of Greece Diagondas of Thebes prohibited all nocturnal rites by a permanent law." In a word every legitimate requirement of religion can be met by a cult that has been well organized by the state: "The public priest should absolve from fear [of prosecution] minor oversights [of a religious character: *imprudentiam*] that have been sanely (*consilio*) expiated [by sacrifices]; but any effrontery in the practice of obscene (*foedis*) rites he should condemn and brand as sacrilegious." [The text of Cicero is corrupt and his exact meaning obscure. For various reconstitutions and renderings see Keyes, ed. of *De legibus,* Loeb Classical Library, p. 417. Pareto read: *audaciam in admittendis religionibus foedis damnet.*—A. L.]

1109 [1] Reinach does not believe the accusations made against the Bacchanals. He well remarks, *Cultes, mythes et religions,* Vol. III, p. 269: "The charges spread

1110. The legends about enemies whom Dionysus meets and vanquishes betray the working in Greek sentiment of a certain resistance to religious frenzies. It was less effective among the Greeks than among the Romans, for Greek life was less earnest, less restrained, less decorous than Roman life.

1111. Before opening his biography of Epaminondas, Cornelius Nepos cautions the Roman reader that he must not judge foreign manners by the standards of his home country: "We know, of course, that according to our notions music does not become a person of distinction, while dancing we class frankly among the vices. Those things are enjoyed and held in high honour among the Greeks."[1] All the same, singing and dancing figure in the Roman cults of the Salii (cult of Mars) and the Arvales (cult of the Lares). In the Lupercalia the Luperci, perfumed, almost naked, raced around the Pomerium of the old Palatine City and lashed with goat-hide whips such women as they encountered, so stimulating fertility in them. That festival, curious to note, was one of the last to succumb to the pressure of Christianity. Residues of that sort, as we have already seen (§§ 1004, 1008), are much more stubborn than derivations.

1112. Religious exaltation frequently eventuates in the belief that certain persons are in communication with the Deity. Not infrequently excursions into the supernatural world also occur. Williams describes a case of that kind, which he witnessed in the Fiji Islands.[1]

abroad as to the immorality of the mysteries are all crude or ridiculous fabrications such as were circulated in that same Rome against the early Christians, then in the Christian world against Manicheans, Jews, Templars, and many others. Human malice is not very imaginative. Murder, sodomy, and rape always stand at the head of the list of complaints against sectarians whom hatred would destroy." But from then on Reinach gives free rein to his fancy, and describes the Bacchanalia in terms far overreaching the documents at our disposal. That is guessing, not writing, history.

1111 [1] *De excellentibus ducibus,* XV, 1-2.

1112 [1] Lubbock, *Origin of Civilization,* pp. 339-40 (quoting Williams, *Fiji and the Fijians,* Vol. I, p. 224): "Unbroken silence follows. The priest becomes absorbed in thought, and all eyes watch him with unblinking steadiness. In a few minutes he trembles; slight distortions are seen in his face, and twitching movements in his limbs. These increase to a violent muscular action, which spreads until the whole frame is strongly convulsed, and the man shivers as with a strong ague fit. In some

If that description be compared with what Bois says of certain occurrences at the Welsh revival it will be evident beyond shadow of doubt that the derivations are different in the two cases, but that the residue is the same.[2]

1113. Class IV: *Residues connected with sociality.* This class is made up of residues connected with life in society. Disciplinary residues might also be grouped here, if one agrees that the sentiments corresponding to them are strengthened by living in society. In that direction, it has been observed that with the exception of the cat all domestic animals when at liberty live in groups. On the other hand society is impossible without some sort of discipline, and therefore the social structure and the disciplinary structure necessarily have certain points of contact.

1114. IV-α: *Particular societies.* A need for particular associations is observable among the majority of peoples. They are of many different kinds. Some are for purposes of mere amusement, others for

instances this is accompanied with murmurs and sobs, the veins are greatly enlarged, and the circulation of the blood quickened. The priest is now possessed by his god, and all his words and actions are considered as no longer his own, but those of the deity who has entered into him."

1112 [2] Bois, *Le réveil au pays de Galles,* pp. 493 f.: "On reaching the platform, Evan Roberts rises at once, halts the singing and asks: 'Is there light in this place? I fear not! Have we come here just to see with our eyes, or to worship the living God? Have we come here for amusement's sake or to be sanctified?' A pause. 'No, there is no light in this place! And,' he asks savagely, 'what is the meaning of it, my friends?' He leans forward over the pulpit, his face flushed, red, congested, the veins bulging. 'There is something unusual here, something that will not do!' He shouts the words. Someone starts a prayer: 'If there is something here that is hurting . . .' 'Do not say yes,' cries Roberts, interrupting. 'Do not say yes!' And he falls into his chair, weeping and moaning: 'Restrain them, O Lord!' His heavy sobs are a terrible thing to hear. Dr. McAfee rushes to his side. 'O Lord,' cries Roberts desperately, 'it is greater than I can bear!' Then he turns to the audience: 'It is a greater burden than I have ever been called upon to bear!' He falls silent. The whole hall is now in prayer. Sobbing violently, Roberts cries: 'It is hard always to be obedient to God!' . . . He pauses, then: 'It is the same trouble as last evening! I have to give a message . . . !' And again he succumbs to his emotion. Finally, summoning all his strength, mastering himself, he says: 'God entrusted this message to me some days ago, but I was not to reveal it until this evening. This is the message. Do with it as you see fit. It comes directly from God. The foundations of this Church do not rest on the rock! . . .' A profound sensation in the hall!"

purposes of individual advantage. Still others have religious, political, literary, or other purposes.[1]

Alluding to the wide-spread prevalence of burial colleges in Rome, Renan observes that the members of such associations became closely united, almost as closely as blood-relatives.[2] The fact emphasizes the power that sentiments engendered by associations of the kind may acquire. Renan himself found similar sentiments among the Oriental Christians of his time, and they are little different from the sentiments readily observable in many religious, political, and social sets and sects today. The gilds of the Middle Ages were very like the colleges of ancient times. The fact that their patron was a Christian saint and not a pagan god certainly did not change their character. Also interesting is the fact that the activities of the gilds and the ancient colleges were very much the same—the banquets included. That is just another of the many instances in which forms are seen to change, substances remaining the same: derivations vary, the residue endures. The sentiments that prompt human beings to organize in particular societies are to be kept distinct from the sentiments which develop inside such societies: the latter correspond to all sorts of residues, notable among them the residues of the II-α3 variety (relations of class, §§ 1043 f.).

1115. IV-β: *Need of uniformity.* That need is felt also by animals that live in society. If a hen is painted red and returned to its flock, the other hens at once attack it. The need of uniformity is much more strongly felt among uncivilized than among civilized peoples.

1116. In human societies the uniformity desired may be general throughout a people, but it may also differ according to the various groupings of individuals within the people. We get a picture of the situation in the crystallization of salt solutions. Around a central nucleus successive stratifications cluster to form a thick crystal. But there is not one crystal only in the solution; there are a number of

1114 [1] This is not the place to give even a summary account of such societies. We are interested merely in noting the residues that, in general, are observable in them.

1114 [2] [Pareto seems to be referring to Renan, *Histoire des origines du Christianisme,* Vol. II, pp. 354-58. However, Renan deals repeatedly and *passim* with the Roman burial colleges, or gilds, in that work and in *Marc-Aurèle.*—A. L.]

crystals. In the same way there is not one centre of similarity in a given society, but a number of centres. Sometimes there is conflict between the different "sets," the one trying to extend its own particular uniformity to others. Then again there is no such conflict, each individual resting content with the uniformity of the group to which he belongs and respecting others.

1117. IV-β1: *Voluntary conformity on the part of the individual.* Imitation is of that variety. Imitation plays an important rôle in social phenomena: one individual imitates other individuals; one group, one nation, imitates other groups, other nations. We have of course seen (§§ 733 f.) how mistaken it is to regard similar institutions as necessarily imitations. The similarities may have evolved from similar circumstances. It may also happen that imitation serves to strengthen similarities. Laws against theft, for instance, grow up among various peoples out of similar circumstances; but when such peoples come to have mutual relations, they may to some extent copy each other's laws. So for political institutions and other branches of social activity.

1118. The imitation may have a purpose: to attain some result that is beneficial, or is deemed beneficial, by means which have been seen to yield those results when used by others. Such an imitation would be a logical action. But oftentimes no such purpose exists, at least no conscious purpose; and we then get non-logical actions, which, as usual, come to be tinted with logical colourings.

1119. The residue finds expression in virtually pure form in the temporary uniformities imposed by fashion. It is often impossible to find any imaginable utility in a style. For people to say, "We follow the fashion in order to do as others do," amounts to saying that they imitate because they imitate. It is true that the person refusing to fall in line would become a victim of public censure, but the censure would be merely the sanction of the general sentiment and with it we would be moving from our present residue (IV-β1) to the variety next following (enforced uniformities).[1]

1119 [1] On fashion in general, see Squillace, *La moda,* p. 24. Squillace rightly observes that "these collective currents or tendencies peculiar to periods of time

1120. The origins of things that come to be imitated are often obscure. How and why they are imitated frequently depends upon combinations of circumstances that are for the most part unknown and which we roughly designate by the term "chance." It is therefore altogether erroneous to insist on finding logical causes for the facts observable at a given moment, and the inferences drawn in that direction are oftentimes quite fanciful.

1121. In the year 1909 women in Europe were wearing huge broad-brimmed hats in the so called Merry Widow style. Suppose some traveller who knew nothing of European life had chanced to arrive in Europe just then. He might have sought a logical explanation for the custom just as European travellers seek logical explanations for the similar things they see among uncivilized peoples. In writing an account of his travels, he might have said that women in Europe believed they could make sure of a merry widowhood by wearing broad-brimmed hats of a peculiar shape. Another traveller might have held, instead, that such hats were preservatives against widowhood. Still another might have seen in the fad remnants of the customs of some other social state.

1122. What here is an arbitrary hypothesis on our part is reality itself in no end of studies on the customs of antiquity and uncivilized or barbarian societies. Anyone observing a taboo sets out forthwith to find a logical reason for it. It is not beyond the range of possibility that such a reason may have existed, but that case would be rare indeed. It may also happen that a reason may be discovered or at least divined, but that case would be rarer still. In the most frequent case, the logical reason never existed; or if it did, we have no way of knowing what it was; and we therefore guess at some other.

more or less brief may be grouped under the generic and comprehensive term of 'styles,' that is to say, modes of thinking and feeling, under certain circumstances, and at certain moments, in full uniformity with other individuals of the same society at the same historical moment." At times such "styles" have general causes operating on large numbers of individuals, many others adopting them by mere imitation. Then again, the whim of a single individual may give rise to a style and be imitated by others. Edward VII long set styles of dress for men in England.

1123. The Wahabis prohibit the use of tobacco. Tobacco is taboo for them. There is no question of running down any archaeological reason in this case, for the prohibition is of recent date. Palgrave went looking for a logical explanation for the taboo. He found one in the passion of sectarians for distinguishing marks—"the passion for sectarian discrepancy"; and there was some truth in that, in the sense that members of sects imitate customs that are peculiar to their "set." But then Palgrave strays farther from the facts, by ascribing the prohibition to a logical design on the part of leaders of the sect. If he had documents or direct testimony to substantiate his explanation, we could do nothing but accept it. But his theory is just an inference from an implicit premise that a taboo must have a logical cause, which one may find by considering the intentions of law-givers who established it.[1]

1124. That method is quite generally fallacious. Founders of religions are not shrewd hypocrites endeavouring surreptitiously to attain certain ends. The apostle, as a rule, is a man convinced of his own message—that, in fact, is an almost indispensable requisite if he is to win any following. So in cases where documents are lacking, to ascribe astute and knavish intentions to him carries one, in all probability, far from the truth. It may well enough be that after tobacco had been prohibited for any number of reasons unknown to us, the prohibition may have been retained because, as Palgrave observes, it was a convenient means for distinguishing Wahabis from other Mohammedans. The logical explanations which the Wahabis

1123 [1] *Journey through Central and Eastern Arabia,* Vol. II, pp. 14-15: "The early history of the Wahhabee sect, narrated in my first volume, may have, I think, sufficiently shown my readers that the idea of aggression and conquest was no less present to Mohammed-ebn-'Abd-el-Wahhâb and his disciple, the chief Sa'ood, than that of dogma or proselytism; both of these men, and the latter perhaps even more than the former, had in view not only to found a sect, but an empire; not only to convert their neighbours, but to subdue them. . . . Now, to embark on such a career, some decent pretext was wanted, while a visible and unequivocal badge was equally required to counterdistinguish their party from all others. The profession of the Unity of God, the regular performance of prayers almost identical with those of all other Mahometans . . . would not suffice for either one or the other end, would neither warrant the sword, nor sufficiently distinguish those who unsheathed it from those against whom it was unsheathed. . . . Something additional was requisite, and tobacco stepped in conveniently for the Wahhabee."

themselves give for the prohibition of tobacco are in the nature of derivations.

1125. Some customs connected with taboos are so strange that they defy any possible logical explanation. Consider, for example, what Frazer has to say, and anyone desirous of further instances may find them at will in the literature of travel.[1] But, without roaming afield from our own countries, there are the strange customs of many of our own sects such as the Masons or the Good Templars. In French-speaking countries the Good Templars are an anti-alcoholic society. In a secret convention recently held at Lausanne nothing could be seen except their usher, an individual dressed in a flaming red uniform. Discover if you can any possible relation between a flaming red uniform and total abstinence!

1126. IV-β2: *Uniformity enforced upon others.* The human being not only imitates to become like others; he wants others to do likewise. If a person departs from the uniform rule, his conduct seems to jar, and produces, quite apart from any reasoning, a sense of discomfort in the persons associated with him. An effort is made to eliminate the jar, now by persuasion, more often by censure, more often still by force. As usual, there is no lack of logical chatter to explain such procedures; but they originate not in the causes so alleged, but in great part at least in a sentiment of hostility to violations of uniformity, re-enforced by sentiments of asceticism and other sentiments of that type.

1127. The requirement of uniformity is particularly assertive in matters of logic. From the logical standpoint the maximum of absurdity would seem to be reached in condemning a man to the stake

1125 [1] *Golden Bough,* Vol. I, p. 327: "Thus, among the Creek Indians a lad at initiation had to abstain for twelve moons from picking his ears or scratching his head with his fingers: he had to use a small stick for these purposes. For four moons he must have a fire of his own to cook his food at; and a little girl, a virgin, must cook for him. During the fifth moon any person might cook for him, but he must serve himself first, and use one spoon and pan. On the fifth day of the twelfth moon he gathered corn cobs, burned them to ashes, and with his ashes rubbed his body all over. . . . While the ceremony lasted, he might touch no one but lads who were undergoing a like course of initiation. Caffre boys at circumcision live excluded in a special hut." Frazer gives no end of similar examples.

because he does not think as others think on some theological question that is incomprehensible to any rational human being. But that criticism is valid only for the derivation, for the logical reason devised to explain what has been done. The act itself is just the manifestation of a sentiment of hostility to a violation, regarded as particularly flagrant, of a uniformity. Today transgressors of that kind are no longer burned at the stake, because the whole scale of penalties has been lowered; but people who preach birth-control are sent to prison. One is allowed to deny the actual presence of Christ in the Host, but not to believe that if a man is not well enough off to support children, he would do better to keep them from coming into the world and use measures calculated to prevent conception.[1] But marvellous to relate, people who condemn and persecute the birth-controllers, who are heretics of the sex religion, speak with bleeding hearts of the heretics of the Church, loathing those who

1127 [1] On July 22, 1913, a police detective in Paris tried to kill a certain Mme. Roudier, with robbery in view. He was arrested and on being questioned confessed the crime. *Liberté*, July 23, 1913: " 'I am a wretch,' he cried, after stating his name and position. 'I had to get money somehow. Poverty drove me to it. I have a little boy a year old. My wife is expecting another. I was at the end of my resources, with just 13 cents in my pocket. I have been living on the rue Nationale for only a week. Moving expenses and then the rent took everything I had.' 'Why didn't you ask assistance of your superiors? They would certainly have helped you out.' 'I didn't dare. I was too young in the service. Besides, I was afraid such a step would get me a bad mark. . . . I met Mme. Roudier a year ago. In my predicament I at once thought of that woman, with the idea of going and asking a loan of 50 francs. Once in her presence I could not find the courage to make my request. I was just leaving when I suddenly thought of my little family, which would soon be without anything to eat. . . . A hellish idea came into my mind. . . . I saw red. . . . I rushed upon the woman. She screamed. I began to choke her to rid my ears of her piercing shrieks. Then I realized that I was lost and I took to my heels. . . . Oh, I'm guilty all right! But I swear to you it was just a moment's madness.' " Now the question arises: Was that man right or wrong in having two children whom he could not support? We are not here concerned with deciding the question either one way or the other; but evidently if the question is to be considered, people must be free to speak of birth-control, anti-birth-control, and even of contraceptive measures; for, after all, if one would have an end, one must accept the means. If that is forbidden, if such problems are not to be discussed, we go back to the times when it was forbidden to discuss the dogmas of the Catholic Church. Those who admire those times may, consistently, be willing to go back to them; but those who condemn them are ridiculously illogical when they try to imitate their procedures.

persecuted them, calling them ignorant fanatics, and saying and believing in all good faith that they themselves are wiser than they, know more than they, and are freer from superstition—that, no more and no less! There are people who think that in order to condemn Catholicism they have only to mention the Inquisition and the tortures it inflicted upon heretics, but at the same time admire English judges who condemn to the whipping-post a man guilty of no greater crime than selling pictures deemed obscene.[2]

Joinville relates how St. Louis, King of France, punished blasphemers against the Faith—and that is grievously shocking to our free-thinkers, who, for their part, deem it altogether proper that blasphemers against any one of their dogmas should be just as severely punished.[3] The fanatics of the goddess Science say that it is their veriest intention never to stray outside the field of logic and experience, nay, that is why they consider themselves so superior to believers in other religions. But really if one would keep strictly to that field, one could not prove that showing a picture of a naked woman is a greater crime than blaspheming the god of any religion,

1127 [2] Of the countless examples available suffice the following: *Liberté*, June 13, 1912: "Yesterday forenoon H. J. B., 22, appeared in court at Newington on a charge of persistent loafing on the sidewalks of Piccadilly, despite orders from the police to move on, and of offering obscene pictures for sale to passers-by. Magistrate Lowrie embellished his sentence with a few remarks: 'I am sorry I cannot give you the punishment you deserve. I shall however do the best I can. You will receive twenty-nine lashes from the cat-o'-nine-tails and serve nine months at hard labour in prison.'" We may expect from this exalted magistrate some day a *Malleus maleficarum* of his own, granted of course that he has the brains to write a book. Believers in metempsychosis might imagine that the soul of that Meletus who accused Socrates of corrupting Athenian youth, after making a short sojourn in the body of that Pierre de Lancre who had so many witches burned in the *"pays de Labourd"* (Gascony), finally ended up in the person of this estimable English magistrate.

1127 [3] *Histoire de Saint Louis*, CXXXVIII, 685: "The King had such affection for God and His Gentle Mother that all whom he could convict of uttering improprieties anent God and His Mother or vulgar oaths he caused to be severely punished. So at Cesarea one day he ordered a goldsmith to the stocks in his under-drawers and shirt-tail with the bowels and lights (*fressure*) of a pig about his neck, and so many of them that they came up to his nose. Since my return from overseas I have heard that he had a Parisian merchant branded on the nose and lips with a red-hot iron, for the same reason, though I did not see it myself. And the holy King said [on that occasion]: 'I would willingly be branded with a hot iron myself so only my realm were cleansed of all dirty oaths.'"

or that crimes of the one species do greater harm to society than crimes of the other. In fact, precisely because they cannot enlist the support of reason, fanatics of all times and countries are inclined to resort to force to impose on others the uniformities that they hold so dear. The same Joinville tells a story in which the resort to violence is candidly espoused without any dressing of hypocrisy. The Catholic clergy invite some Jews to a debate at Cluny. A knight on the Catholic side uses no other arguments than his fists, and the good King approves and blesses him.[4] "There you have Catholic superstition," many a contemporary of ours will say. But, after all, that knight had the high honour of being a predecessor of Senator Bérenger, who meets those who disagree with him not with arguments, but with complaints to the State Prosecutor, and who also finds himself in the precise situation in which King Louis held that force

1127 [4] *Ibid.*, X, 51-53: "The King told me that there had been a great conference of clerics and Jews at the monastery at Cluny. A knight was there and he asked that the leading cleric and the chief scholar of the Jews be called before him and so that was done. And he asked a question of the Jew as follows: 'Master,' said the knight, 'I ask you whether you believe that the Virgin Mary who bore God in her womb and in her arms had that child as a Virgin and whether she was Mother of God.' and the Jew replied that of all that he believed not a word. And the knight answered that truly he had acted the lunatic in entering her church and her house not believing in her, nor loving her; 'And forsooth,' said the knight, 'you shall pay for it.' Whereupon he picked up his staff (*béquille*) and struck the Jew a blow behind the ear and knocked him to the floor. And the Jews took flight carrying their master with them in a sorry state, and so the conference came to an end. Then the Abbot came to the knight and told him he had done a very crazy thing. And the knight replied that the Abbot had done a still crazier thing in getting such a conference together; for before it closed, any quantity of good Christians in there would have gone away unbelievers from not having understood what the Jews were talking about. 'So,' said the King, 'I tell you that nobody, unless he is a very good clerk, ought to argue with them; but when a layman hears someone speaking badly of the Christian law, he should defend the Christian law only with his sword, giving it to him in the belly and up to the hilt.'" Such disputes were frequent in the old days, and continued down to the Reformation. St. Gregory of Tours, *Historia ecclesiastica Francorum*, VI, 5 (*Opera*, p. 375c; Dalton, Vol. II, pp. 237-38), tells of a debate with a Jew that took place before King Chilperic. The Saint said some very beautiful things to the unbeliever, but was unable to persuade him; whereupon the King allowed him to go in peace, without receiving harm from anyone: *"Haec et alia nobis dicentibus, numquam compunctus est miser ad credendum. Tunc rex silente illo cum videret eum his sermonibus non compungi ad me conversus postulat ut accepta benedictione discederet."*

should be used; since a defective education, an obtuse mind, and an appalling lack of good sense prevent the Senator from effectively showing the faith that is in him in any other way.

1128. The requirement of conformity does not apply in the same way in all directions. The Romans were not at all theologically-minded, and required uniformity only as regarded external ceremonies of worship. The Chinese government tolerates all sorts of religions provided they remain subject to the state. Our modern governments confiscate newspapers printing pictures of naked women, and do not interfere with the sales of papers that preach pillage, arson, and slaughter of the *bourgeoisie*.[1]

1129. Such manifestations of the instinct of uniformity are, moreover, spasmodic and irrational, as are almost all manifestations of such instincts. There were few prosecutions for impiety in Athens but the impious were many. Roman persecutions of Christians were carried out by fits and starts without system or method. Persecutions by the Catholic Church were better systematized and logically more coherent because they were not manifestations of the instinct of uniformity pure and simple; the Church organized the business and

1128 [1] Many instances might be mentioned to point this contrast. We have already noted several. Add to them the following: *Corriere della sera,* Jan. 12, 1913: "At Boston the women who crowded the opera-house for the first production of Puccini's *Tosca* were scandalized at the so called sofa scene between Scarpia and the heroine in the second act. Suffice it to say that the chief of police interfered and gave orders that on moral grounds the scene should be either deleted or radically altered on following nights." The actors rebelled. "A telegram was sent to Puccini, who replied that the scene must be presented in its entirety, and that if that could not be done, the show should be suppressed without further ado." A compromise was arrived at: Tosca remained standing, "and the Bostonians, the chief of police included, were satisfied." That for the recto; here now is the verso: *Gazette de Lausanne,* Jan. 21, 1913: *"Sabotage and Digestion:* Mr. Ettor, one of the leaders of the I.W.W., who was recently acquitted of criminal complicity in strike violence at the textile factories in Lawrence, Massachusetts, advises hotel and restaurant waiters in New York to poison capitalists or at least to sabotage the meals they eat. 'If you are forced to return to work under bad conditions,' said Ettor, 'do so with the firm resolve to make it uncomfortable for the capitalists to eat meals prepared by your union.' Large hotels and restaurants in New York are engaging private detectives to supervise their kitchens and dining-rooms." According to the worthy legislators of Massachusetts less harm is done to a man by poisoning him than by allowing him to see two opera-singers, the one male, the other female, sitting on

added a pinch of logic. Logic vanishes again in the persecutions by modern governments of heretics of the sex religion, now become the official religion. The sale of most obscene books is permitted without trace of hindrance, while newspapers much less obscene are confiscated. Certain writers are prosecuted, others enjoy immunity, and one can discover not the slightest reason to justify such discriminations. Indictments are brought at crudest random, and one is reminded for all the world of one of those big flies that are caught in a room and go buzzing round and round because they cannot find a way out.

No less capricious the attitude of certain governments towards anti-militarism. In Germany that doctrine has always been suppressed; but in Italy and France it is now tolerated, now prosecuted. In France Hervé is put in prison, but school-teachers are allowed to preach anti-militarism in the class-room—what is more, the lay school is protected by threats of fine and imprisonment against anyone's criticizing it. In Italy a few years ago it was permissible to preach anti-militarism and insult the army. In 1912 a newspaper in Naples, the *Propaganda,* was brought to trial for publishing anti-

the same sofa on a stage. If we leave Massachusetts, we find things even better. In New York an association has been discovered that has burned more than a thousand houses in order to collect the insurance. While these praiseworthy things are going on, the police are busy keeping obscene or merely sensuous books from getting into the city from Europe. In Indianapolis, just south of Chicago, the trial of a number of criminals who had been dynamiting industrial plants and private homes and killing people gave Federal Judge Anderson occasion for declaring that if local authorities had done their duty, such crimes might have been avoided. It would seem, in fact, that there would have been a greater social advantage in doing that than in hunting down young men who are spooning with young women in the parks. The corruption of American Congressmen may well be called a "trade" if that name is to be applied to the corruption of willing women; with this difference, that Congressmen are selling other people's goods, such women their own. American virtuists are so deeply concerned with the "white-slave trade" that they have no time to think of the first, and it is well known that the "white Congressman trade" is prospering, blossoming, and bearing fruit in the United States. Even very recently a certain Mulhall publicly accused a great many legislators of corruption, and declared himself ready to prove his accusations with no end of documents referring to over twenty thousand letters and telegrams. The Congressional Labor Commission seems to have been the principal "victim" of this trade in white Congressman, victims, of course, in the sense in which most of the women involved in the so called white-slave trade are victims.

militaristic articles, one of which had been written by a high army officer and published in the *Riforma sociale* in 1887. The apparent contradiction disappears once one reflects that governmental policies follow and favour variations in derivations that partisan sentiment in the public will have uniform, the requirement of uniformity persisting through all such changes.

1130. IV-$\beta 3$: *Neophobia.* This is a sentiment of hostility to innovations that are calculated to disturb uniformities. It is very very powerful among uncivilized or barbarous peoples, and shows a very considerable strength among civilized peoples, being surpassed only by the instinct for combinations (Class I residues).

1131. In Paris in February, 1911, women who appeared on the streets in *jupes-culottes* ("bloomers") were attacked and beaten by mobs. Similar incidents took place in Italy and Spain, and more or less everywhere. Much the same things had happened previously when "picture hats" first came into vogue, and on occasions of other innovations in fashion.

1132. It is interesting that many individuals who suffer from neophobias in some departments of life may look with favour upon anything new in some other direction, say in politics or religion, and for the simple reason that it is new. They are shocked at innovations in tailoring and dressmaking, but fume at the mouth because the Pope does not take kindly to the innovations of the Modernists, and heap abuse on governments that make haste slowly in adopting "social reforms." Fresh proof that contradictory residues can function simultaneously in the mind of one same person! In the case just mentioned the conflict is between the residues of neophobia and the residues of the religion of Progress.

One might also consider the opposite of neophobia—eagerness for innovations; but one may doubt whether that be a sentiment by itself and not rather a product merely of the instincts for combinations and, in our time, also of sentiments of adoration for the god Progress.

1133. IV-γ: *Pity and cruelty.* These contrary sentiments are better taken together. As we observed some distance back (§ 911), the opposite of the two would be indifference. It is not easy to distinguish the sentiment of pity from many others that ape its forms. Undeniable the fact that for a century or more past the punishment of crime has grown progressively milder. Hardly a year goes by but new laws are passed in favour of criminals, while existing laws are applied by courts and juries with greater and greater leniency. It would therefore seem as though pity for criminals were increasing, and pity for their victims decreasing.

1134. On the other hand there are cases from which it would seem that pity in general is increasing, the difference just noted depending on the fact that the criminal brought to bar is present, while his victim is absent. Sentiments of pity at all intense are felt, chiefly, for people who stand before one's eyes. They are much weaker for the absent. The jury sees the murderer and pities him, and that is true of judges too. The victim is not visible—he has vanished. To think of him is just a painful duty. The juryman who acquits a murderer today will as likely as not join a mob to lynch a murderer tomorrow if the crime is committed before his eyes.

1135. Characteristic in this connexion is an anecdote related by Meng-Tseu, a Chinese writer. A king sees an ox that is being led to sacrifice. He is stirred to pity for it, and orders that a sheep be used its stead. He confesses that he did that because he could see the ox, but not the sheep.[1]

1136. Typical of a long list of examples is the case of Liabeuf, thief, panderer, and murderer, who was glorified by revolutionaries because he had slain a policeman, and mourned by society women and wealthy members of the French *bourgeoisie* who dally as a

1135 [1] Pauthier, *Confucius et Mencius*, p. 209. Meng-Tseu says to the King: "A tender heart inspired you to do that. The ox was there before your eyes. The sheep you had not yet seen. When a superior man has seen animals alive he cannot endure the thought of their dying. When he has heard their death-cries he cannot eat of their flesh. That is why the superior man locates his slaughter-house and his kitchen in out-of-the-way places."

There may be other cases where the murderer is absent and the victim remains. In that situation evidently what we have just said no longer applies.

sport with Tolstoian or some similar brand of pity.[1] With the revolutionaries such conduct may have been logical; they were enemies of the state, and it is quite natural therefore that they should applaud anyone fighting its police. It may also have been logical with certain members of the *bourgeoisie* who thought they might win votes or the favour of certain politicians by standing by Liabeuf. But still left would be persons for whom those considerations, or others of the sort, would not apply, who were acting sentimentally, non-logically. Such behaviour is very complex. It is motivated not only by the generic sentiment of pity, but also by a special sentiment of pity for the particular wrongdoer, a sentiment that is the more

1136 [1] The story is told in the *Journal de Genève,* July 3, 1910: "On Febuary 26, 1907, in the lower criminal court at Saint-Etienne, Liabeuf was sentenced to four months in prison for theft. On June 7, 1907, he received three months for the same offence in the same court. On August 14, 1909, in the lower criminal court of the Seine, he received three months in prison and was fined 100 francs for 'special vagrancy.' [A phrase from the jargon of a hypocritical age. Dante would have called a spade a spade and Liabeuf a pimp.] On May 14, 1910, he was sentenced to death in Criminal Assizes. . . . After sharing in the exploits of a gang of thieves and becoming entangled with professional criminals, Liabeuf left Saint-Etienne and went to Paris. There, far from mending his ways, he again began frequenting the haunts of vice and prostitution. On his conviction for 'special vagrancy,' he had sworn mortal hate against Detectives Vors and Maugras, whose sworn testimony had proved his undoing. With his vengeance in view he made himself a pair of arm protectors (*brassards*) and another pair of leather mittens bristling with nails. He set out from his favourite bar one evening with that formidable armament to hunt up the two detectives. But they were not the ones to fall under his fury. His victims were policemen whom the bandit had never seen before. The frightful butchery is still fresh in the public memory: Patrolman Deray mortally wounded from a bullet and stabs from a butcher's knife. His comrades Fournès, Février, and others literally cut to shreds. . . . Liabeuf to be sure protested all along against his conviction for 'special vagrancy.' But in the course of the debate before the jury, no new fact, no new circumstance came to light to cast any real doubt on the man's guilt on that charge." With the women who are fascinated by such criminals the poet Carducci dealt in his satire "On the Fadda Case" (*Poesie,* pp. 492-94). They turned up again at the trials of Musolino and other bandits. They may usually be seen at trials of exploiters of female vice. The verses of Juvenal still hold fresh, *Saturae,* VI, vv. 110-12:

> *"Sed gladiator erat—facit hoc illos Hyacinthos.*
> *Hoc pueris patriaeque, hoc praetulit illa sorori*
> *atque viro: ferrum est quod amant . . ."*

("But he was a gladiator! That fact makes them all so many Hyacinths! That she prefers to her children, her sister, her husband, her country! What such females

intense, the worse he is as a criminal. There were members of the *bourgeoisie* who at the urge of sentiment sought the acquittal of Liabeuf, sympathized with him, sided with him. Had their conduct been altogether determined by the generic sentiment of pity, that sentiment should have spoken as vehemently for the victim, or at least for his widow, as for the murderer. But not one of the individuals in question gave a thought to the wretched plight of Policeman Deray's widow.[2] Vigorous opposition was expressed, moreover, in many quarters to granting policemen the right to use arms in self-defence. It took the exploits of the ruffians Garnier, Bonnot, and Co. to strike a balance between humanitarian pity and fear of future mischief in the hearts of the French *bourgeoisie,* good souls, and induce the Government to allow the police to use their weapons against criminals bent on killing them.[3]

1137. In individuals sentiments are always more or less complex, sometimes very much so. In making a scientific analysis, therefore, we have to fix our main attention on sentiments, not on individuals. Examining the complex of sentiments involved in pity for

love is the bleeding steel!") The scholiast notes very soundly: *"Sed gladiator:* Cruelty lent charm to such beastliness and revealed him to her as something beautiful and fair."

1136 [2] Of her *Liberté* spoke as follows: "The innocent victim of the tragedy in rue Aubry-le-Boucher has led a cruel life since her husband met his death. Already smitten in her tenderest affections, Mme. Deray has been subject to daily insults from the underworld. Public discussion as to the fate of the murderer served to keep her grief and sufferings alive. What the poor woman has undergone since Liabeuf's execution is indescribable. She has been obliged to leave the home to which so many memories bound her. The police themselves advised her to leave. Fortunately she has found a modest situation in house-work, which will enable her to earn her living and support her little boy, who was heart-broken at his father's failure to come home, fell sick, and is hardly well even now." One writer went so far as to say that Liabeuf's victim deserved no sympathy, because it was part of the policeman's trade to get killed. That same writer, however, is agitating for a law to place the occupational risk of the employee on the shoulders of the employer. Another case of two contradictory residues working side by side in the same individual!

1136 [3] *Liberté,* May 6, 1912: "All the papers are commending the exploit of the patrolman at Bougival who shot a burglar as the latter made a motion to draw his revolver—all the papers except *Humanité*. The Socialist organ says: 'We consider that "courageous exploit" both execrable and dangerous.' Dangerous it undoubtedly is—for our crooks. But execrable? Hardly execrable!"

criminals, one is led to breaking it up along the following lines: 1. The sex residue. It figures in nearly all judgments on crimes of passion, so called. 2. Residues of sectarian, patriotic, and other group sentiments. We are inclined to great indulgence towards persons belonging to our "set." We are indifferent, when not actually hostile, to persons not of our "set." 3. Residues of Class II (group-persistences). Religious and political convictions tend to make us indulgent towards those who share them with us, ill-disposed towards those who do not.

Not to be overlooked, further, is the question of interest in cases where individuals give evidence of pity as a means to some personal end. Such would be logical conduct. The residues that are left over pertain strictly to pity; they fall into three varieties. In one, a sentiment of personal pain prevails, and it is extended to embrace pain in others (IV-$\gamma 1$). In the other two, the sentiment is less personal or not at all so. It leads to an instinctive repugnance to pain in others (IV-$\gamma 2$), or to a reasoned repugnance (IV-$\gamma 3$).

1138. IV-$\gamma 1$: *Self-pity extended to others.* If people are unhappy and are inclined to lay the blame for their woes on the environment in which they live, on "society," they are apt to view all who suffer with a benevolent eye. That is not a logical reasoning; it is a sequence of sensations. If we try to state them in rational form we deprive them of the very thing that gave them force and efficacy—their indefiniteness. Bearing that in mind, one may, roughly, state the reasoning corresponding to such sensations as follows: "I am unhappy, and 'society' is to blame. So-and-so is unhappy, and so 'society' must also be to blame. We are comrades in misfortune, and for my comrade I have the indulgence that I should have for myself; he has my pity."

1139. Something more or less of the kind figures in the humanitarianism of our time. People in poor economic circumstances are convinced that "society" is to blame. By analogy, the crimes of thieves and murderers are also felt to be chargeable to "society." So thieves and murderers come to look like comrades in misfortune worthy of benevolence and pity. "Intellectuals" are convinced that they are not playing a sufficiently important rôle in the social hierarchy; they envy people of wealth, army officers, prelates, in short all others in the higher social rankings. They imagine that criminals and the poor are also victims of the same classes. They feel that in that respect they are like them, and therefore feel benevolence and pity for them. While Mme. Tarnowska was on trial in Venice, she received a poem by a schoolmistress voicing a hope for her speedy liberation. The teacher in question may well have been an upright but unhappy woman. Unhappiness drew her close to the murderer, and filled her with pity for her. The novels of George Sand, Victor Hugo's *Les misérables,* sold widely to people harbouring just such sentiments. Certain women are vaguely conscious of how nice it would be if they had a husband to provide them with the necessaries and luxuries of life, and a number of paramours to satisfy their amorous yearnings. Certain men are likewise aware of the advantage of having other men support the women they enjoy. All such sentiments find expression in a theory that is called "the right to happiness." In plainer language, it might be called the right to adultery. Hence sentiments of benevolence for adulterers and to some extent even for panderers.

1140. Such sentiments may drive individuals to rebellion and murder. Just after the bandits Bonnot and Garnier met their death in a clash with the French police, many persons who thought they had been wronged by the authorities, even in respect of some minor traffic summons, raised one shout—"Good for Bonnot!" Attempts upon the lives of kings, presidents, or other eminent men are largely the work of unhappy individuals, more or less out of their heads, who vent their feelings by striking out haphazard at the first person of note who crosses their path.[1]

1140 [1] In its issues of July 5-6, 1912, the *Matin* published Garnier's diary. There the criminal may be seen voicing his various sentiments under the derivations brought into fashion by the literature of the day. Says Garnier: "Every being born into this world has a right to life. That is undeniable, since it is a law of nature. [Garnier must have got that from some newspaper, which must have got it from some hack writer, who, in turn, must have got it from some first-liner such as Victor Hugo, Anatole France, or Léon Bourgeois.] In my earliest childhood I came to know authority in the persons of my father and mother; and before reaching the

1141. The existence of such residues makes it probable that many who are seeking their own advantage, but claim to be working for the good of "society," do so in all good faith. It may therefore be that many people who are doing practical Socialism with profit to themselves really believe they are doing theoretical Socialism for the good of all, or at least of the greater number.

1142. IV-$\gamma 2$: *Instinctive repugnance to suffering*. This is a sentiment of disgust at the sight of all suffering, regardless of whether it

age of understanding, I rebelled against that authority as well as against authority in school. [Mere expressions of sentiment.] I was thirteen at the time, and just beginning to work. Awakening to reason, I began to understand what life and the social machine were like. I saw that individuals were bad. I said to myself: 'I must find some way to get out of this rot of bosses, workers, *bourgeois,* magistrates, police, and all the rest. [Another derivation taken from some Socialist newspaper.] All such people disgusted me, the ones because they did the bossing, the others because they were spineless enough to go through all those motions. Refusing either to exploit or be exploited, I began shop-lifting, but could not make very much at that. [All derivations, just to say that he wanted to enjoy life without working. At bottom he was neither better nor worse than other individuals, such as the Tarnowska woman, for whom our estimable humanitarians feel such exceptional pity.] I got caught, for the first time. For the first time—I was seventeen then—I got three months in jail. On being released I went home to my parents, and they gave me terrible scoldings. But my term in prison, my having had my taste of what is called justice, had made me more of a rebel than ever. It was then that I became an Anarchist. I was about eighteen. I did not want to go back to work again [The real reason for all the patter. People of that kind cannot live in a civilized society, but our kind-hearted humanitarians object to eliminating them.], so I returned to individual reprisal. [A derivation copied from some third-rate paper, which got it from some "thinker."] But no better luck than the first time! Within three or four months I was caught again. I got two months. . . . [He then goes on to tell how he came to hob-nob with Anarchists and to believe in their theories:] My mind was soon made up. I became what they were. [That is to say, he adopted that particular expression for sentiments he had all along held.] I resolved never again to work for other people. I also resolved to work for myself. But how go about it? I didn't have very much, but I had acquired a little more experience; and I was full of energy. I was determined to defend myself from that pack of wolves, so full of stupidity and iniquity, that present-day society is. [A derivation not unlike the derivation of the "thinkers" when they say they are trying to work towards "a better humanity with a little more justice." That is why they want the votes of the Garniers, to send them to parliament. The Garniers of course find it more expeditious and more rational to get the little more justice directly for themselves.] I left Paris when I was about nineteen and a half, for I looked forward to my term of military service with loathing. [People of that sort dislike civil discipline, but military discipline they loathe.] Will that sly, irresponsible mass change some day? It may! I hope so! Meantime, for my part, I am not going to

be beneficial or otherwise. It has provoked the proverb, "The merciful doctor aggravates the sore." The sentiment is often observable in weak, submissive, spineless individuals. If they chance to succeed in overcoming it, they are likely to show themselves exceedingly cruel. That explains a remark one sometimes hears to the effect that women are more tender-hearted and at the same time more cruel than men.[1]

sacrifice myself for it. Now is the time I am living on this earth. Now is the time I have a right to live, and live I am going to with all the means that science [The god of his religion.] puts at my disposal. I will meet trickery with trickery, force with force. . . . [He recounts various adventures in crime in Belgium. "Wanted" by the police in Brussels, he slips back to Paris,] where I took a job on *L'anarchie* and set to work with a will. I worked almost every day, and since the pay was rather small I joined some of my comrades in a number of burglaries, though the intake did not amount to very much. So I turned to counterfeiting, but that was not a success either. The risks were greater than in night-work and I made more at that. . . . [These estimable humanitarians may say what they will; but it is evident enough that if such people were eliminated from society, their exploits would come to an end. Mild punishments allow them to continue. Garnier joins a gang of criminals and tells about a large number of burglaries he carries out with them:] During the two months of September and October our chief job was the post office at Chelles, where we got 4,000 francs. There were others of less account. Finally, early in November we did another at Compiègne, which netted 3,500 francs. . . . [Garnier teams up with Bonnot and learns how to drive a car. He describes his "first big haul"—the murder of a bank messenger carrying funds:] I go up to about three yards from the boy. I pull my gun and coolly give him a first bullet, then a second. He falls, his companion taking to his heels, scared out of his wits. I pick up one bag. My pal gets the other, which that fool of a boy will not let go of, for he is not dead. But he ends by dropping it, for he loses consciousness. [Humanitarians pity poor wretches like Garnier but give not a thought to their victims. The second instalment of Garnier's "Memoirs" in the *Matin* recounts many other crimes. I will transcribe just one story—the murder of a chauffeur!] I picked up a big piece of wood . . . and gave it to him with all my might just over the left temple. The chauffeur dropped without a cry. He was dead or what amounted to that. To be sure he wouldn't come to, one of my pals went and got a jack weighing some hundred and fifty pounds and set it on his chest. Within a few moments he stopped moving. He was dead." Anatole France sells no end of books showing that such ghouls are unfortunates (§ 1638 [1]). It is instructive to set side by side the sentiments voiced by Garnier and the sentiments of people who buy such books and dote on them.

1142 [1] *Liberté,* May 8, 1912: "At Sceaux, 8 rue de Bagneux, stands a garden-lodge that goes with the mansion there. It is the home of Mme. Herbuté de Bute, 51, a gentlewoman. She is deaf and nearly blind. She lives there alone. She has always passed for a woman of some property and one of her former maids said as much to Gabriel Gaugnon, 18, a mechanic, living at Fontenay-aux-Roses. Gaugnon made up his mind to rob the lady, and suggested to friends of his that they join

1143. The fact that among the Greeks and the Romans heads of families were called upon to make animal sacrifices may have served to arrest the development of the sort of pity here in question. Such pity is often the mainstay of those who condemn wars of whatever description. They dwell chiefly on the sufferings of the killed and the wounded, never stopping to consider the advantages a war may have won. But not a few such sentimentalists of this type readily forget their declamations when other sentiments gain the upper hand. The sufferings of the killed and the wounded are important only so long as it suits the convenience of the pacifist (§ 1559). This variety of pity is widely prevalent in decadent ruling classes. In fact it may serve as an adequate diagnosis of such decadence.

1144. IV-γ3: *Reasoned repugnance to useless sufferings.* This sentiment is characteristic in strong, energetic people, who know what they want and are able to stop at the exact point that they consider it desirable to attain. In judging its government, a people instinctively understands the difference between this sort of pity and pity

him in the venture. They accepted. They are Fernand Le Bas, 17, from Bourg-la-Reine, and Fernand Léard, 21, of Sceaux. On January 10 last Léard presented himself at Mme. Herbuté's cottage under guise of a delivery man sent by a grocer in Paris to deliver an order. Léard made sure that the lady was deaf and so informed his accomplices. The three went back there the following evening, January 11, at six o'clock. Léard broke open the garden-gate, which was locked with a key. With the help of Gaugnon he then broke open the door of the cottage. Le Bas stayed outside on watch and the other two made their way into the house. Mme. Herbuté was reading the evening paper in her bedroom. She heard no sounds. Léard suddenly seized her by the throat with the idea of holding her and keeping her from making any outcry, while Gaugnon was going through the things in the room. But Mme. Herbuté tried to free herself. Falling to her knees, she managed to extract a knife she carried from her pocket and made a pass at Léard, who leapt back instinctively. The lady was so enabled to rush from the room and snatch up her revolver. She dashed out into the garden, where Le Bas fell upon her, threw her to the ground, and held her down. Mme. Herbuté did not lose her presence of mind. She fired one shot from her revolver in Le Bas's direction, calling meantime for help. The three rogues were arrested shortly after. This afternoon they appeared before Criminal Sessions, Department of the Seine. All three made a full confession, and Mme. Herbuté de Bute on giving her testimony begged for the jury's leniency in their favour. To the astonishment of everybody, the jury brought in a verdict of not guilty and the three toughs were dismissed from the bar. . . . The verdict is baffling only in appearance. It is explainable on the one hand in view of the terror that the Bonnot-Garnier gang and

of the preceding type. They respect, they esteem, they love the pity of a strong government; they ridicule and scorn the pity of a weak government. The latter they regard as cowardice, the former, as generosity. The term "useless" above is subjective; it reflects a feeling of the person who uses it. In certain cases it is possible to determine that a thing is objectively "useless" to society; but in many many others there is doubt, and sociology is far from being sufficiently advanced to dispel it. However, it would be a mistake to conclude, in the light of an eventual and remote chance of some advantage, that the infliction of suffering will prove beneficial. Decisions have to be based on the greater or lesser probabilities. It would be manifestly absurd, for instance, to say that it might be a good thing to kill a hundred or so people at random on the chance that a future murderer might so be disposed of. There was more room for doubt in the argument often advanced to justify prosecutions of witches, that many common criminals were to be counted among them. And the doubt would probably be insuperable were

its avengers are spreading on every hand; for it is only too certain, alas, that so far the people who ought to be executed are doing most of the executing. Then again, jurymen who are cowardly enough to be afraid find a further excuse in the fact that criminal legislation during these past years has been inspired exclusively by the increasing sympathy with which gunmen and Anarchists have been viewed by those in power; whence the conclusion, for that matter logical enough, that the maxim 'Be kind to animals' is a humanitarian watchword that altogether conforms with signs 'from on High.' Finally there is a third prime factor. The policy of 'No enemies to the Left' has also affected the jury system in the direction of increased incompetence. Criminal Sessions have been blessed with a new set of jurors and among these 'self-conscious proletarians' not a few, we may guess, have a real esteem for Bonnot, whom the 'unified' [Socialist] Hervé has described as a 'professor of energy.'" *Liberté,* May 9, 1912: "A Seine jury yesterday acquitted a trio of unusually distinguished rascals who broke into a little cottage one evening last January and did their best to kill, in the thought of robbing her, an elderly gentlewoman, deaf and half-blind, who was living alone there. They did not succeed in their twin and very laudable intent, but assuredly through no fault of their own. It was because their victim was ill-mannered enough not to let herself be plucked without raising an outcry. The jury however concluded that it was only fair to give these youths of such tender age a chance to return to their favourite studies in murder and theft. The astonishment is general. The lawyers [of the defence] have hardly got their breath back yet, and their clients much less. They in fact will not understand till some day in the near future they appear in court again between three other pairs of gendarmes. By that time they will have grown up and learned how to do a better job."

there no means of distinguishing between a poisoner and a hysterical female who thinks that she is having commerce with the Devil. There are such means, however, so the doubt vanishes, and the sufferings so inflicted may be judged objectively useless.[1]

1145. IV-δ: *Self-sacrifice for the good of others.* Life in society necessarily rests on a certain reciprocal goodwill between individual and individual. The sentiment may be weak or strong, but it cannot be entirely wanting. It is manifested in both animals and human beings in acts of mutual assistance and common defence—in other words, by the sufferings an individual takes upon himself for the good of others. Such phenomena are observable even among non-social animals in their relations to their young, which are fed and protected by one or both of the parents. The lioness shares her prey with her cubs, the hawk and its mate share their prey with their chicks. In our own homes male canaries may be seen feeding their mates and their little ones.

1146. All known facts incline one to the belief that the sentiment which prompts a man to help and protect his family and the group to which he belongs is, in part at least, similar to the sentiment observable in animals. The difference lies in the fact that the human being cloaks such conduct with a logical varnish. Very beautiful theories have been evolved to show that a man *ought* to love his country. However, the effect of such theories is virtually nil. It is insignificant at any rate as compared with the influence of the non-logical sentiment that inspires patriotism. One would really have to have the sickly brains of the day-dreamers of the "social contract," or of the "debt to society" of the "solidarists," to imagine that people fight for their countries the way a partner in a business concern pays in an assessment.

1147. Not only do the sentiments that inspire a man to self-sacrifice for the benefit of others influence the members of a society directly to perform certain acts and to approve of those who do them and admire them. They exert an indirect influence upon the

1144 [1] Such considerations are not strictly in point here, since they overstep the domain of residues and bring up questions of logical conduct.

individual who is encouraged to this or that behaviour, not only by a sentiment of his own favourable to such conduct, but also and often even more forcibly, by a desire to win the admiration of others or to avoid their censure. Conversely, as we shall see for the general case in § 1161, if we find that certain things are done to satisfy this desire for public approval, we may safely conclude that functioning in the group in question are sentiments corresponding to these IV-δ residues.

1148. IV-δ1: *Risking one's life*. People risk or even sacrifice their lives out of deep feelings of sociality, or from the importance they attach to the esteem of others. It would seem that in animals only the first sentiment figures. Polygamous males are wont to defend their females; it is a matter of everyday observation that the cock defends his hens, the bull his cows. Even domestic animals of different species defend one another when they are members of the same household. House-dogs have been known to defend the house-cat, and the house-cat a puppy. In human beings, in most cases, it is impossible to distinguish a sentiment of that variety from the desire to win the approbation of one's fellows. Tacitus records that among the Germans the chiefs were surrounded by liegemen who fought strenuously to defend them and who were forever disgraced if they returned alive from a battle in which their chief had fallen.[1] General

1148 [1] *Germania,* 14: "*Iam vero infame in omnem vitam ac probrosum superstitem principi suo* (surviving his prince) *ex acie recessisse.*" Similar sentiments prevailed in Sparta among the citizens. It was a disgrace for a man to return alone after his comrades had been slain. Herodotus, *Historiae,* VII, 229-31, tells of two Spartans, Eurytus and Aristodemus, whom Leonidas sent home from Thermopylae because of serious trouble with their eyes. They stopped at Alpene. The news coming that the Spartans were surrounded by the Persians, Eurytus had himself guided to the battle-field by his helot, and died fighting. Aristodemus lingered at Alpene. (According to another story, they had both been sent on a mission, Eurytus returning promptly, Aristodemus delaying.) "When Aristodemus returned to Lacedaemon he was branded with infamy and disgrace." Plutarch, *Lacaenarum apophthegmata* (*Sayings of Spartan Women,* 22, Babbitt, Vol. III, p. 467): "A man was telling his sister how her son had fallen gloriously in battle. She replied: 'I am as glad for his sake as I am sorry for you who played false to such valiant company.'" *Ibid.,* 6 (Babbitt, Vol. III, p. 461): "A man was describing to his mother the glorious death of his brother. 'Are you not ashamed,' she said, 'to have missed such company on such a journey?'" Herodotus, *Historiae,* V, 87, also tells how one man

Nogi, victor for the Japanese at Port Arthur, killed himself with his wife on the day of the Mikado's funeral. In that case the sacrifice of life had no direct utility. It was a pure manifestation of sentiments of sociality, subordination, hierarchy, combined with certain group-persistences of the old-fashioned Samurai, and with a desire for the approbation of people sharing those sentiments.

1149. IV-δ2: *Sharing one's property with others.* There are any number of shadings between the state of mind where one gives up one's life and this milder form of sentiment where there is a mere renunciation of certain enjoyments for the benefit of other individuals. Here too examples are exceedingly numerous among both animals and human beings.

1150. The little girl who dresses up her doll and offers it food is not merely imitating her mother; she is expressing a spontaneous sentiment of her own, as is the case with the swallow that has hatched a brood for the first time and carries food to her nestlings.

1151. Combining with Class II residues (group-persistences), the present residue accounts for sacrifices offered to objects inanimate or animate, to the dead, to gods. In the more complex cases other causes may also figure.

1152. At first blush one might imagine that this residue was at work in all individuals of the ruling class who sided with the subject classes. But that is not the case. As one looks more closely it is apparent that such persons may be classified in the following manner: 1. Persons who assume leadership of the subject classes to attain some political, financial, or other advantage. History is replete with the doings of such people. Aristocracies usually owe their falls to them. In a day gone by violence was the only recourse, and that limited their number. Nowadays, when there is a pacific instrument, the ballot, their number has increased inordinately, since revolutions are no longer necessary to assure them some measure of success. Democracy, moreover, affords outlets for all ambitions, from the

alone returned from an Athenian expedition against Aegina and how he was slain upon his return to Athens by the wives of those who had fallen, "indignant that he alone of all should have saved himself." Whether such tales be history or legend matters little for our purpose, which is merely to get at certain sentiments.

ambition of the political boss (Pareto: *grande elettore*) in a township to the ambitions of aldermen, councilmen, Deputies and Senators; and outlets from the modest "job" obtained through the influence of a Congressman, to the directorship of a department or the control of a treasury. In Europe today how many people are Socialists just to obtain such a post, just as tomorrow they would be conservatives if a conservative government should come into power! 2. Persons who, with an eye to their interests, tie the donkey where the "boss" directs. Under the Restoration in France the "level-headed young man" went to mass; under Louis Philippe he read Voltaire; under the Second Empire he found it highly praiseworthy to say that he was "uninterested in politics." Today, he has to be "interested in politics"—he has to be a *blocard,* a humanitarian, a Socialist.[1] He may have to be a Nationalist tomorrow. Today financiers and captains of industry have discovered that it is to their interests to abet the Socialists. Captains of industry and financiers of a wealth to be computed in millions are to be heard calling for "social legislation"; and one might believe that they were inspired solely by love of their neighbour, with whom they are passionately bent on sharing their worldly goods. But keep your eye on what happens after said "social legislation" has been passed. You will see that their wealth has not decreased, but increased, that they have given nothing away, but have rather received. The Caillaux-Bertaux ministry in France was made up largely of millionaires. In them even with a microscope you could detect no trace of a desire to share their goods with others. Giolitti's "democratic" majority in Italy was made up of people who understood "business" (and a very good business they did indeed);

1152 [1] The term *"blocard,"* now in common use, may perhaps be unintelligible a few years hence. I will explain, therefore, that M. Clemenceau once founded in France a newspaper called the *Bloc*. In it he exhorted all "republicans" to consolidate in one mass, one "block," to fight reaction. He was aped in France and Italy by hosts of good souls who clasped hands in order to clamber the more easily into control of the public weal and fatten thereon. The traditional terms for their kind—"Camorrist" in Italy or "grafter" elsewhere—fell into desuetude, the newly coined term *"blocard"* being used instead. [In these volumes we follow the late M. Clemenceau's own caprice in the spelling of his name. The usual form of the word is *Clémenceau*.—A. L.]

nor did his ministry lack the support of the "steel men" or the "sugar men"; yet one may doubt whether those estimable people were inspired by any desire to share their goods with others. They became Nationalists and fire-eaters (*guerrafondai*—militarists) when it turned to their interest to do so; and they passed the bill extending universal suffrage to illiterates the moment "the old man" assured them that that was a first-class device for securing "good elections," and therefore for "sitting pretty." [2] In England Lloyd George is quite willing to distribute the properties of the peers among "the poor"; but he keeps an eye on his own pocket-book, and does not disdain a risk on the stock exchange. And there is his team-mate, John Burns. No one can see what he has given to others; but anyone can see what he has received and the fat salaries he has been able to earn—assiduously striving for the welfare of others. 3. Persons who are sincerely inclined to give something to others because they instinctively feel that they will receive more than they give. They give away a sparrow in the hope that he will come home a capon. Working in them is

1152 [2] Fradeletto, *Dogmi ed illusioni della democrazia:* "Today we are witnessing most unexpected changes of heart, which—such the mysterious workings of chance!—never coincide with a sacrifice or a personal risk, but always, or almost always, coincide, with a striking 'clean-up' on Exchange. People who a short time since were shouting the war-slogans of sedition that they might elbow their way into public life with the applause of the revolutionary parties are now voicing counsels of prudence that they may hold their places by the votes of the reactionaries. . . . But a spectacle even more astonishing to the naïve must be these mass-conversions that are taking place, these descents of grace from on high which suddenly enlighten a whole Chamber and convert it. The proofs are close at hand in time and in space: *domestica facta!* Before the sixth of April, 1911, how many partisans of universal suffrage were there in the Italian parliament? Luzzatti's reform bill, which would have given the vote to anyone able to read and write and so would have increased the electorate by a little more than a million, seemed to a great many people premature, unseasonable, a thing not 'wanted by the country,' a dangerous concession to extremist parties on the Left. But since the sixth of April, since the descent of tongues of fire in the shape of a few words dropped by the Head of the Government, the devotees of universal suffrage have become legion, and among the warmest are those who voted against Luzzatti's cautious measure. But that is not all. In the summer of 1910, while the Daneo-Credaro bill was up for debate, illiteracy was solemnly proclaimed our worst sore, our shame, our ruin [It is not at all proved that those who expressed that opinion were right.], our abiding title to discredit in the eyes of foreign countries. Two years later, while the new electoral bill was before the parliament, we heard at times a sort of idyllic paean lifted to illiteracy, now held to constitute a presumption of instinctive good

the present residue combined with other residues looking to the advantage desired. 4. A few "intellectuals," defective in energy, knowledge, and good sense, who take the declamations of the types named above seriously. But they are few in numbers, and some who might seem to belong among them really belong to the other types. 5. It cannot be denied that conceivably there may be individuals of energy, knowledge, and good sense who propound social and "solidarian" doctrines out of a sincere desire to share their goods with others; but it is not easy to find examples of them. Saint-Simon was rich. He died poor and friendless. It might seem as though he could be mentioned as one. But his wealth he squandered in pleasure-seeking, and he was comforted in his friendless poverty by his pride in being a Messiah, the founder of a new religion. In such things the main motives of his conduct! All these types are to be found among those subscribing to the doctrine of "solidarity," which is more often invoked for purposes of receiving than for purposes of giving; and rare as white blackbirds are those who believe in it with-

sense, unsullied by 'fragmentary education.'" [It is not at all proved that those who expressed such sentiments were wrong.]

The explanation of such things is very simple. It was stated by Sir Edward Grey in regard to an exactly identical situation in international affairs. On Aug. 1, 1913, the House of Commons heckled him with questions on the Balkans. He was asked whether there were any principle of international law whereby Turkey might be restrained from repudiating the treaty of peace and reoccupying Adrianople and Thrace. He replied that there was not. He was reminded that on the outbreak of the Balkan War the Powers had pompously declared that, whatever the outcome of the war, the territorial *status quo* had absolutely to be maintained in the Balkans; and he was asked whether the Powers had any reasons, other than the victories of the Allies, for repudiating that solemn declaration. He replied that there was, in fact, no other reason. Finally after many other questions Sir Edward Grey had a moment of genuine frankness and said: "The questions that have been put to me seem all to be framed on the assumption that the policies of the Powers have been dictated by considerations of logic and international law. In point of fact each Power has been following the course indicated by its own special interests, and by a collective desire to preserve peace in Europe." His frankness, however, did not go so far as to mention the powerful financial interests that were guiding all the Powers, severally or collectively. The point of this long note might be summarized in a few words of Beaumarchais, in *Le Barbier de Séville,* Act IV, Scene VIII. Don Bartholo is astonished that Bazile has undergone a change of heart like the ones just mentioned: "*Bartholo:* What, Bazile? You signed? *Bazile:* What do you expect! That devil of a man always has his pockets full of unanswerable arguments!"

out ulterior motives. As we have already noted (§ 1147) and will note again (§ 1162), the existence of these various categories in no wise detracts from the social importance of the sentiments registered by these IV-δ2 residues. Indeed it emphasizes their very great significance, since they are resorted to and used, be it indirectly, in so many and such different ways.

1153. IV-ε: *Sentiments of social ranking (hierarchy).* Sentiments of ranking on the part of inferiors as well as superiors are observable in animals. They are very wide-spread in human societies. It would seem indeed that no human society at all complex could survive without them. Relationships of superiority and inferiority are changed in forms, but none the less kept, in societies that ostensibly proclaim equality for all individuals. A sort of temporary feudalism is the rule in such societies, with a progressive descent in rankings from the politicians at the top to the politicians at the bottom. Anyone doubting this need only try to obtain something, in Italy or France for instance, without the support of the local "boss," the Deputy in the parliament, the "powers that be" in art, science, or public service; or (at the bottom of the ladder) the "fixer." With sentiments of social ranking we may class the sentiment of deference the individual feels for the group of which he is a part, or for other groups, and his desire to have their approval or admiration.

1154. It is absurd to imagine that the old-style feudalism in Europe rested solely on force. It held its own in part by virtue of sentiments of reciprocal affection, which are observable in other countries also where feudalism prevailed or has prevailed—in Japan, for instance. The same may be said of Roman clientage, of the craft-gilds of the Middle Ages, of the monarchies, and in general of all social systems in which a social ladder exists. In fact, only when it is crumbling and is about to give way to another does a hierarchy cease to be spontaneous through becoming preponderantly or exclusively a matter of force. I say preponderantly, because the element of unmixed force is never missing.

1155. IV-ε1: *Sentiments of superiors.* They are sentiments of patronage and benevolence, supplemented oftentimes by domineering sentiments, or sentiments of pride. These last may coexist with sentiments of apparent humility, as one may observe in religious corporations and among ascetics. One may in good faith thrill with the pride of being humbler than another.

1156. IV-ε2: *Sentiments of inferiors.* They are sentiments of subordination, affection, reverence, fear. They are indispensable to the constitution of animal societies, to the domestication of animals, to the ordering of human societies. They are often observable *de facto* in individuals who call themselves Anarchists. Anarchists have their "leaders," even though they do not call them such, and there are plenty of Anarchists who show almost superstitious deference to the authority of physicians and medical practitioners who are not seldom quacks. Manifestations of the sense for authority are very very numerous and endlessly varied. It is common to accept the authority of a person who has, or presumes to have, some real or imaginary symbol of superiority.[1] Hence the reverence of the young for the old, of the novice for the expert; in a day gone by, of the illiterate for the learned, of the person who spoke only a modern language for one who spoke Latin; of the plebeian for the noble—in our day, of the non-union worker and many people of the *bourgeoisie* for the union man; of the weak for the strong (or reputed strong), of the man of one race for the man of another regarded as superior; of the woman for the man (when special circumstances do not make her the dominant party); of the subject for the sovereign; of the believer for the priest, the prophet, the ascetic, the man who pretends to be to a greater extent than others in the good graces of

1156 [1] From no end of examples the following: Landor, *In the Forbidden Land,* Vol. II, p. 167: Held prisoner in Tibet Landor was about to be slain when he was saved by a peculiar arrangement of the fingers on his hand. "The Lama . . . examined my hands and spread my fingers apart, expressing great surprise and astonishment. In a moment all the Lamas and soldiers came round and examined my manacled hands. . . . The Pombo, too, upon being informed, immediately came and inspected my fingers, and the proceedings were at once stopped. When some weeks later I was released, I was able to learn from the Tibetans the reason for their amazement. My fingers happened to be webbed rather higher than usual and this is most highly thought of in Tibet. He who possesses such fingers has, according to the Tibetans, a charmed life, and, no matter how much one tries, no harm can be done to him."

the Deity; of the voter for the politician; of the plain man for the man of mystery, the fortune-teller, the charlatan—and in our days, particularly, for the physician, the hygienist, the promoter of "reform measures," or the person who otherwise comes forward as a high-priest of the god Progress; of the poor in spirit for the emancipated woman, who, he thinks, is above sex appetites; of the old-time bigot for the first friar who came along; of the new bigot for the pontiffs of humanitarianism.

1157. In virtue of the persistence of abstractions (§§ 1065 f.) the sentiment of authority may to a greater or lesser extent become disengaged from the person and attached to the symbol, real or presumed, of authority. Hence the importance for those in authority of "keeping up appearances"—"prestige," the outward semblance of superiority. The detachment may be complete, and the sentiment of authority may attach itself to inanimate objects, as in the reverence felt by many people for anything that is written or printed, and in some countries for anything written or printed on paper bearing a seal or an official stamp (§ 1430). The residue also plays a more or less important part in other phenomena, such as fetishism, the worship of relics, and the like.

1158. A passage in Machiavelli's *Mandragola* well brings out the plain man's reverence for anyone speaking Latin.[1] Molière too makes sport of it, but time was when the best minds believed that historical truth was to be sought in Latin texts, and that a text deserved credence from the mere fact of being written in Latin. Not so long ago it was taken for granted that the older the manuscript, the better it was. Palaeography has shown that some ancient manuscripts are less correct than others more recent.[2]

1158 [1] Act II, Scene II: "*Callimaco. . . . Nam causae sterilitatis sunt aut in semine aut in matrice . . . aut in causa extrinseca. Nicia.* The most wonderful man that ever was!" Had Callimaco spoken in Italian, Nicia, who also knew Latin, would not have assented with the same extravagant admiration.

1158 [2] Paulin Paris, *Les grandes chroniques de France,* Vol. I, Preface, p. xv. Noting that the spurious chronicle of the Pseudo-Turpin was the first to be translated into French, Paris remarks: "It occurred to no one to dispute its trustworthiness. It is easy enough for us to do that today. How can it be authentic, we would say, when earlier historians make no mention of it, when Charlemagne's contempo-

1159. In England there used to be a curious privilege called benefit of clergy (*privilegium clericale*), whereby certain persons escaped punishment for crime, on a first offence at least. It applied not only to persons who had taken holy orders, but to anyone who could read. Trying to find a logical reason for the privilege, Blackstone says[1] that "everyone that could read (a mark of great learning in those days of ignorance and her sister superstition)" was "accounted a clerk or *clericus,* and allowed the benefit of clerkship, though neither initiated in holy orders, nor trimmed with the clerical tonsure." But the people of those days were not such dolts, after all, as to think that a man belonged to the clergy when they very well knew that he did not. The privilege, therefore, could not have had any such origin. It arose rather from the respect in which the clergy and other such classes of citizens were held. James I, by his Statute 21, article 6, extended benefit of clergy even to illiterate women convicted of thefts under 10 shillings in value. William and Mary (Statutes 3, 4, 5) extended to women without restriction any benefit of clergy enjoyed by men. It is evident, therefore, that in days not so remote from ours benefit of clergy was simply a privilege granted to certain classes of people deemed worthy of special consideration, among them persons able to read and write.

raries give the facts in an entirely different and far more plausible manner? But at that time no one in the world knew those contemporary historians. One thing only was known: Turpin's *Chronicle* was written in Latin and that was enough to justify the trust of the most fastidious." In another essay, *Op. cit.,* Vol. II, Preface, p. x, he says: "At the time when the monument constituted by the *Great Chronicles of Saint Denis* was being erected, anything of a certain antiquity that was written in Latin could claim by that very fact the acceptance of everybody." Davis, *The Chinese,* Vol. II, pp. 370-71 (1836, p. 163): *"The god's visit to the home of Yu-Kong."* The god is rebuking Yu-Kong, who has been saying that he has dutifully obeyed all the rules laid down for him: ". . . Among them was a rule commanding you to reverence written characters; and nevertheless your pupils and your colleagues tear leaves from ancient books and paper the walls of their rooms with them and wrap parcels. Some even use them to wipe off their tables, and then excuse themselves by saying that if they do soil the paper, they burn it afterwards at once. Such things are going on every day before your eyes, and nevertheless you never utter a word to prevent them. And you yourself if you chance to pass a piece of paper with writing on it in the street—what do you do but take it home and throw it into the fire?"

1159 [1] *Commentaries,* IV, 28.

1160. IV-ε3: *Need of group approbation.* This is one of the cases in which the difference between the sentiment and the manifestation of it which constitutes the residue comes out most clearly. The need that the individual feels for being well regarded by his group, for winning its approval, is a very powerful sentiment. On it human society may be said to rest. But it works in silence, oftentimes without being expressed. Indeed the person who most desires admiration —glory—from his group pretends to be indifferent to it. Strange as it may seem, he may really be indifferent to it, and then again unwittingly allow himself to be guided by the approbation or admiration of others. That is observable in ascetics who are such in good faith.

1161. The sentiments of sociality manifested by various sorts of residues are nearly always accompanied by a desire for the approbation of others, or for avoiding their censure. But it is not very usual for this latter sentiment to express itself in the residue corresponding to it. Conversely, the residue sometimes hides other residues. A person may say that he is prompted by a desire to win the esteem of others, whereas to some extent, however slight, he is also prompted by a desire to do the thing that after all merits such esteem. When a person does a thing and says, "It is good," or refrains from doing a thing and says, "It is bad," it is hard to say whether he means, "It is approved (or disapproved) by the group," or that it accords or disaccords with his own sentiments. The two considerations function simultaneously. As a rule the approbation or censure of the group reinforces a sentiment already present in the individual (§ 163). There may, of course, be the perfect hypocrite who is loath to do a thing but does it to win public esteem. There may be the coward who lets himself be killed in war to escape the stigma of cowardice. But such cases are not, after all, very frequent. In the commoner case, a person has a faint impulse to do a thing and does it to win public esteem, or the naturally brave man is inspired to heroism and gives his life in the thought of glory.

1162. The cases just noted where the individual is not at all, or not entirely, inspired by the sentiment corresponding to the residue that happens to be involved, but entirely or in part by the desire to win the approbation or escape the censure of his group, none the less shows the social importance of the sentiments corresponding to the residues in question. For if the residue is not acting upon the individual directly, it is doing so indirectly through the approbation or censure of the group; and only because that sentiment is influential in the group does the approbation or censure have its force. Even the ascetic who is a perfect hypocrite bears witness to the strength of the ascetic residue in the group whose opinion he values. He becomes a hypocrite and his hypocrisy is approved and admired in the group. If the group were indifferent to him his hypocrisy would serve no purpose.

1163. IV-ζ: *Asceticism.* Observable in human beings is a special group of sentiments that has no counterpart in animals. They are sentiments that prompt the human being to seek sufferings or abstain from pleasures without design of personal advantage, to go counter to the instinct that impels living creatures to seek pleasurable things and avoid painful things. They constitute the controlling nucleus in the phenomena known as asceticism.

1164. If we knew only one type of asceticism—the Catholic, for instance—it would be hard to distinguish the residue from the derivation. A man does penance because he believes that in so doing he is pleasing God and making amends for his sins. The religious feeling might well be the residue, and penance the logical consequence of it. There are, in fact, cases where matters seem to stand that way. But there are other cases where the variable element is the reason given for the penance, the penance itself coming down to mere renunciation of the pleasures of life, which would be the constant element. So long as the reasons vary with varying conceptions of the deity, we get for a constant element the religious concept in general. But lo, there are ascetics, such as the ancient Greek Cynics, who had no religious conceptions whatever, so that uniformity goes by the board. And there stand the Spartans, who practised asceticism as a means of maintaining strict discipline; and the Buddhists, who turned ascetics in order to stultify all vital energies. Among our own contemporaries we find ascetics in the name of the goddess Science who abstain, or pretend to abstain, from the use of alcoholic beverages; other ascetics who dare not look at a pretty girl in the name of a sex morality of their own, which—who can guess why?—regards the sexual act as the worst of crimes; others who cannot endure light literature; still others who make war on dramatic productions that are not altogether dull and fail to "solve some social problem." It is therefore apparent that the constant element is the self-infliction of sufferings, the variable element the reasons they have—or say they have—for doing so.[1]

1164 [1] Montet, *De l'état présent et de l'avenir de l'Islam,* pp. 59-61: "It has been observed that the Mussulman who aspires to status as a marabout and seeks distinction for his asceticism is inclined, once he has been proclaimed a saint, to relax quite readily from his acts of continence, which served merely as a ladder for attaining that status. . . . Licentiousness has more than once gone hand in hand with the most extreme austerity, as examples from the most widely differing religions show. . . . So there are obscene saints, immodest saints, immoral saints. There is plenty of trustworthy testimony as to the escapades and public scandals of such people. . . . There are degrees, furthermore, in filthiness and personal neglect. One frequently encounters marabouts who go about in tatters and never wash. Others make a boast of their uncleanliness and their lice . . . and affect the greatest contempt for the comforts of this world. . . . As may readily be imagined, continent saints, ascetic saints, antinomian saints, are veritably legion in Islam." Fraser, *Travels and Adventures in the Persian Provinces,* pp. 93-95: "In the course of two hours, my friend the dervish arrived, and recommenced his hints of information in a strain which I could not at all comprehend; for I endeavoured in vain to recollect his features or the place where I could have before seen him. At last I displayed so much impatience at his continued grimaces that being convinced of their further inutility he made himself known to me. He was, it appeared, a native of Shiraz, who, being a clever but a lazy fellow, had taken to a life of wandering idleness to avoid the miseries of occupation, and now lived by his wits. He had seen much of the world, had discovered that it was easy and profitable to gull it, and practised what his experience had taught him, to the extent of his ability. . . . My friend the dervish had now thrown aside the cant of his profession, and was beginning to be communicative, when Zein-ul-Abudeen, with some other persons, unfortunately entered, upon which he suddenly relapsed into grimace and jargon." The Church Fathers often complain of monks who usurped the semblance of asceticism in order to trick people. In the fourth century Joannes Cassianus, *Collationes,* XVIII (*De tribus generibus monachorum*), makes a veritable class of them as a "fourth order of monks" (*Caput* 8: *De quarto genere monachorum*), holding it to be of quite recent origin. Alluding to them in his *De monastica exercitatione,* VIII (*Opera,* p. 727), St. Nilus the Abbot describes them as shunning the hard life in the monasteries, which they could not endure, and besieging the wealthy like so many parasites.

1165. The main residue appears in that constant element. But it is not the only residue that figures in it. All social phenomena are complex mixtures of many elements involving many residues. In the ascetic, oftentimes, along with the residue of asceticism one notes the residue of pride (IV-ε1). He feels himself superior to the generality of mortals, and those who admire him recognize that superiority (§ 1161, IV-ε2). Active in him sometimes is a religious residue (§ 882) and then again a residue of uniformity (IV-β2), as when he sets out to force his asceticism on others, or a residue of a presumed utility, real or imaginary (§ 851). All such residues have to be put aside to get at the residue of pure asceticism.

1166. Now that we have found it, we still have to determine its affinities with other residues, in other words, its proper classification.[1] That is not an easy thing to do, and it would almost seem as though asceticism had to stand in a class by itself. But it is soon apparent that the facts of asceticism belong to a large class comprising acts of abstinence, renunciation of pleasures, voluntary self-sacrifice. Subvarieties may be distinguished in the class by considering the purposes of such sacrifices and their degrees of intensity. Two men voluntarily reduce their consumption of food, one in time of famine, that there may be a little bread for everybody, the other in time of plenty, just to inflict a pain upon himself. Those evidently are two different sorts of acts, even though the second may be regarded as a different manifestation of certain instincts that also figured in the first. Four men abstain from drinking wine: the first because he has discovered that wine is injurious to his health; the second in order to save the money he spends on wine for the benefit of his children; the third to set an example of abstinence for a drunkard who is ruining himself and his family; the fourth to inflict

1166 [1] We are not trying, remember, to determine "what asceticism is" (§ 118). We are merely asking whether there is a class of facts that possess such and such characteristics in common. To that group we then give the name of asceticism, but only by analogy, there being among such facts certain facts that in ordinary parlance are called ascetic. So the botanist does not ask "what Ranunculaceae are." He is looking for a genus of plants that possess certain common characteristics. He calls the group Ranunculaceae, because among them is the plant commonly called ranunculus. He might label the genus with any other name just as well.

a pain upon himself. There we get acts of four different kinds. The first involves self-interest and residues of personal integrity (Class V). The second and third arise out of regard for one's neighbour—residues of sociality (Class IV). The fourth is distinct from these last two; in the first place, because the purpose they were seen to have is missing, in part at least; then again intensities are different—in the fourth case intensities ordinarily are greater. We are therefore justified in grouping the last three sorts of actions together and in regarding the fourth type as a particular case of the instincts that give rise to the other two.

1167. So we are placed in the way of finding the proper location for acts of asceticism in a natural classification (§ 147). They appear as depending on the residues of sociality, the social purpose being attenuated, playing a slighter and slighter rôle, even disappearing, while intensities increase, assume gigantic proportions, overreach all bounds. In general terms, individual temperance, besides conceivably having some utility for the individual himself—a case that we are not considering here—may have its utility for others, for the group. In a case where there is a shortage of food, fasting becomes a public service. In conditions of general poverty, abstinence from voluptuous consumption is a benefit to the group. If every individual yielded to the sex-instinct at sight of any woman, human society would dissolve. Abstinence in this last respect is of very great utility, and that explains why sex asceticism has come to be so general; not that it was invented of design with that in view, but because as manifesting certain sentiments it encountered no obstacles in social utility. Next in order comes asceticism in food, as manifested in fasting and in taking poor and insufficient nourishment, because food-supply was one of the major problems of ancient societies, where famines were frequent. Residues of pride, admiration, and the like are also favoured by such circumstances, for abstinence in matters of sex and eating is evidence of no common will-power.

1168. From the standpoint of the group, providence, which means abstinence from a present with a view to a future advantage, has its utility, in fact is an indispensable prerequisite to progress in civilization. In the individual case economy is a useful thing. Carried to extremes it becomes miserliness. So with the group, abstinence from present enjoyments finds its hypertrophy in asceticism. Present enjoyment, furthermore, is oftentimes a matter of merely sensuous pleasure, whereas the future blessing resulting from abstinence and saving is often a matter of intellectual reflection. In that lies one of the many encouragements to the subordination of sense to intelligence. The ascetic goes farther in that direction and declares all sensuous pleasures vain. Then some go farther still in the same direction: sensuous pleasures are not only empty things; they are sins, crimes; one should spend one's life in mortifying the senses.[1] Now it is often of benefit to a group that the individual should sacrifice himself to his faith, and admiration for the martyr originates, partially at least, in an instinctive perception of that truth. The man who dedicates himself absolutely to a faith and apart from it sees nothing else in the world readily comes to look to sensible people as though he were not altogether sound of mind. Go far enough in that direction, and we get those Christian ascetics who simulated madness as an ascetic discipline.[2]

1168 [1] Many writings of prohibitionists consider nothing but the effects—all presumably bad—of wine and other alcoholic beverages on physical health and pay no attention to the pleasure a man gets from a temperate use of liquors. The idea apparently would be that a man should think of nothing but his health, that pleasure by itself is vanity. To think logically, as people never do in arguments addressed to the sentiments, that would mean giving up almost everything a human being does. One should not go out of doors because a brick might fall on one's head, or one might meet a mad dog or have some other accident. One should never go in swimming for fear of getting drowned, nor climb a mountain for fear of falling over a precipice; nor kiss a girl—and the point has been made in all earnestness—for fear of catching a germ; nor enter a theatre or any shut-in place because of the bad air. To say it in a word with the Latins, one should *propter vitam vivendi perdere causas.*

1168 [2] Besse, *Les moines d'Orient,* pp. 48-49: "There used to be a still more extraordinary form of monastic life in the East. . . . Its adepts, who were held together by sentiments of profound self-abasement, simulated madness. Father Or seems to encourage one such disciple to carry his contempt for the world to that extreme. 'Eschew the society of men by flight afar,' he said. 'Show thy contempt for the world and its ways by semblance of madness in this or that regard.' There was a recluse at Tabenna whom everyone regarded as a lunatic. Her comrades were inclined to take advantage of her, but she never dropped a word of impatience, exhibiting to them all a most inspiring example of humility and sisterly

1169. Admiration for the external evidences of asceticism to some extent rests on the utility that acts of abnegation may sometimes and within certain limits have. As a rule people do not go beneath the surface of things and they readily mistake the sign for the thing itself. Another element figuring in the admiration is envy, an inclination on the part of the individual who is kept from certain pleasures to wish that others were kept from them too. Those who are he comes to regard as his comrades, and those who voluntarily deprive themselves of things that he does without from harsh necessity he views with admiration. That partially explains the favour the mendicant orders have always enjoyed with the poorer classes, and the admiration for chastity that is very very general. With many men the favours of young and beautiful women are luxuries that they cannot afford. Male jealousy inclines them to hate anyone who can, and sentiments of common sacrifice fill them with admiration for the man who could, but voluntarily refrains. Many feminists hate men and persecute women who have lovers simply because they have been unable to find men of their own. In every period of history there have been people to disparage what they cannot have, and to hold such disparagement a praiseworthy thing in themselves and in others.

1170. There are acts that seem incapable in any respect of being directly beneficial to society. What social advantage can there be in a man's passing his life on top of a column? But it should not be overlooked that, indirectly, the sentiments which find expression in that way or others equally ridiculous may be of benefit in so far as they indicate a mastery of sensual and worldly instincts of which not everybody can boast. In such conduct and in other behaviour that

love. So she attained to a very high grade of sanctity. But that was an exceptional case. In the course of the century following there came to be quite a number of monks in Palestine who simulated madness. It was indeed the general rule for men well advanced in years and of accomplished virtue. They spent considerable periods of time in prayer and liked to attend to pilgrims and the care of the sick. Their austere living won them general esteem." These people, notice, practised their asceticism themselves. Our contemporary Paladins of Purity, who are as much lunatics as those ever were, try to force their insanity upon other people by dint of fines and sentences to jail.

may be of benefit to the group within narrow limits, but transcends them and sometimes by far, noteworthy both in human beings and animals is a tendency to continue certain acts even when their utility to the individual performing them has come to an end. When a cat has no mice to catch, it plays with a paper ball as if it were a mouse. Give a squirrel all the food it can possibly require and it will continue laying in provisions. A dog may be given all the meat it wants, but it will bury a left-over bone and later dig it up and eat it, though it has plenty of other bones at its disposal.

1171. Acts of asceticism are quite largely acts originating in residues related to life in society that continue functioning when they have ceased to have any utility and acquire an intensity which carries them beyond the point where they might be useful. The residue of asceticism must, in other words, be classified with residues of sociality, and frequently represents a hypertrophy of sentiments of sociality.

1172. This latter circumstance explains why ascetics are oftentimes exceedingly selfish people. Asceticism in expanding has absorbed all the individual's social instinct, so that he has none left for showing benevolence to others, not even to his own family oftentimes (§ 1187).[1]

1172 [1] Literature in all periods has exploited such contrasts in human nature. Dorens, who lived under Louis XIII in France, wrote in a satire:

"Gardez-vous bien de lui les jours qu'il communie."

("Look out for him on the days when he takes communion.")

Famous the verses that Molière puts into the mouth of Orgon, who has been converted by Tartuffe, Act I, scene 6:

"Il m'enseigne à n'avoir affection pour rien;
de toutes amitiés il détache mon âme;
et je verrois mourrir frère, enfans, mère et femme,
que je m'en soucierois autant que de cela."

("He teaches me to feel affection for nothing; he severs my soul from all friendship. I could see mother, wife, children, brothers die, and care no more than that!")

So there are many women among our contemporary uplifters who spend day after day trying to reclaim more or less repentant prostitutes, more or less reformed thieves, while they neglect the washing at home, keep their husbands and children in rags, and serve on the family table meals that a dog would refuse to eat. Sorbière, *Sorberiana, s.v. Dévot* (p. 80): "There is nothing more to be feared than a

1173. The instinct of sociality is much more highly developed in the human race than in animals, and that is why asceticism is a peculiarly human trait. In the same way insanity is a peculiarly human disease because the human intelligence is far superior to intelligence in animals.

1174. But if asceticism in its nucleus is a hypertrophy of certain instincts relative to sociality, it follows, as is the case in general with similar phenomena, that around that nucleus other manifestations foreign to sociality cluster. Abstinence from things of benefit to others brings on, by a process of imitation, abstinence from things that are of no benefit to others or even such that abstinence from them is harmful to others. Abstinence from useful things such as clothing, food, and the like, is often attended in ascetics by ridiculously useless doings, such as spending one's whole life erect on a column as the Stylites did, or by behaviour frankly prejudicial to society, such as uncleanliness, which often attends practices of asceticism.

1175. In our present-day societies such manifestations of asceticism as flagellations and mutilations have virtually, if not altogether, ceased. Such things, too, in a day gone by may have represented hypertrophies of instincts of self-sacrifice for the general good. That may well have been the case with the ritualistic flagellation of which examples abound in many countries at one time or another, the supporting derivations varying according to times and places (§ 1190).

1176. Oftentimes observable in the phenomena of asceticism is an element of hypocrisy. Indeed the perfect type of the hypocrite would seem to be the person who poses as an ascetic. Too much has been said on the subject to require a word from us here. But besides the case of the hypocrite, there are many other cases in which it hangs on in attenuated forms to the point of virtually disappearing, other residues claiming the leading rôle in the composite phenomenon.

devout man in anger: he becomes a vengeful snapping animal, because he thinks that God owes him tit for tat, that religion is offended in his person, that his wrath is divine." The same may be said of our contemporary humanitarian. There is nothing to match the rage of that animal when he considers that Progress, Democracy, Solidarity, have been offended in his person.

1177. Taking a given number of concrete cases of asceticism, all apparently identical, it is hard, not to say frankly impossible, to classify them even approximately into types.[1] Ordinarily it is as great a mistake to pass them all off for the genuine article as it is to take them all as mere examples of hypocrisy. There are honest, sincere ascetics, and even in them there is no telling how much influence we are to ascribe to the residue of asceticism, or to the derivation that, arising in the residue, goes on to produce the corresponding conduct even when the residue has lost its force. There are ascetics who are inspired by impulses of imitation, which are stronger than any others in many human beings. Then again there are ascetics who are inspired to a greater or lesser extent by motives of self-interest, or by any number of complex sentiments that have nothing to do with asceticism. Finally come the hypocrites, and even they are hypocritical to varying degrees: some are ascetics in part and hypocrites in part; some are pure or almost pure hypocrites.[2]

1178. Among the professional prudes of our day who are for ever persecuting what they call immorality, there are likewise some few who are really persons of conviction and are altogether stranger to sexual satisfactions. Then there are another few who are consistent in their conduct and actually repress carnal impulses in deference to "moral principles." There are quite a good few who find in militant morality a mere pretext for satisfying their interest in obscene things. Read an obscene book for pleasure? Not they! They read it to see

1177 [1] Intimate familiarity with certain particular cases may enable one, so far as those cases go, to give at least a hint as to a possible classification. Romolo Murri, in *Voce,* Dec. 7, 1911: "With regard to the matter of celibacy, the clergy of today may be divided into three categories. First, individuals whom a vocation athirst with idealism, a real calling to struggle and sacrifice, spiritually unfits for family life, silencing or anaesthetizing all cries of the flesh. Such priests are few; they may be counted on the fingers for any given generation. Second, individuals who accept celibacy as a prerequisite that is necessary, or is considered necessary, to a life of "piety," to priesthood as a profession, but whose piety and religious aspiration are strong enough to suppress any regrets for all that has been given up and to hold them to chastity. Such priests represent, I believe, not less than 10 per cent and not more than 20 per cent of the clergy. In the third group are the ones who fall. For them and through them the priesthood becomes, for a certain period of life at least, a hypocrisy and a sacrilege."

1177 [2] See Pareto, *Le mythe vertuiste.*

whether there is legal ground for suppressing it as a crime! Women who have had many lovers in younger days are prone to apply themselves in maturer age to reforming wayward girls. They enjoy lingering in thought on pleasures now materially beyond them. And that far the residue of asceticism has kept pace with others. But there is no trace of it in hypocrites; in persons who hate the opposite sex because they are too much attracted by their own; in persons who find compensation for lascivious conduct in purity of speech; in those poor in spirit who repeat parrot-like the things they hear others say. In a word, concrete acts that present appearances of identity may be due to widely differing causes.[1]

1179. Among the residues that are alien to asceticism but appear in concrete phenomena in combination with the ascetic residue, notably, are the residues of personal integrity (Class V). They manifest themselves in the ascetic's pride, and through them asceticism becomes a kind of sport. The ancient Athenian Cynics unquestionably enjoyed the astonished wonder that their antics aroused in other people. The story, truth or fiction, that was told of Plato as turning the tables on Diogenes when the latter taxed him with pride, reflects the attitude of many people towards the quaintness of the Cynics;[1] and the same may be said of Lucian's satire on the death of Peregrine (§ 1183 [2]).[2] When Daniel climbed up on his pillar (§ 1187 [5]), not a few believed that he was doing so out of vainglory.

1180. In all times and places, the ascetic life, genuine or partly genuine, simulated or partly simulated, has helped many individuals to honours and money at the expense of the plain man.[1] It should

1178 [1] What we say here of asceticism applies just as well to many concrete cases of behaviour resting on other residues.

1179 [1] Diogenes Laertius, *Diogenes,* VI, 2, 26 (Hicks, Vol. II, pp. 27-29): "Plato being host one day to a number of friends of Dionysius, Diogenes stamped on Plato's carpets and said, 'I stamp on Plato's vanity!' Plato retorted, 'What a lot of dust [pride] you raise—in seeming not to have any!' According to another version, Diogenes said, 'I am raising Plato's dust [pride]'; and Plato, 'Rather your own dust, O Diogenes!' "

1179 [2] *De morte Peregrini* (*Opera,* Vol. VIII, pp. 263-93; Fowler, Vol. IV, pp. 79-95).

1180 [1] Heber, *Journey through the Upper Provinces of India,* Vol. I, pp. 110-11, 99-100: "A few days since I saw a tall large elderly man, nearly naked, walking

not be forgotten either that not all men are to the same degree sensitive to pain, and just as in olden days there were those who could endure prolonged tortures while others immediately succumbed, so there are people who readily endure sufferings as ascetics that no one else could possibly withstand. The history of tattooing, of various types of mutilation, of the cruelties practised on prisoners of war

with three or four others, who suddenly knelt down one after the other and catching hold of his foot kissed it repeatedly. The man stood with much gravity to allow them to do so but said nothing. He had the string (*pectu*) of a Brahmin. Another man passed us on Sunday morning last hopping on one foot. He was a devotee who had made a vow never to use the other, which was now contracted and shrunk close to his hams. Lately, too, I saw a man who held his hands always above his head, and had thus lost the power of bringing them down to his sides. . . . The crowd on the Meidân was great and very picturesque. The music consisted chiefly of large double drums ornamented with plumes of black feathers, like those of a hearse, which rose considerably higher than the heads of the persons who played on them. . . . The devotees went about with small spears through their tongues and arms, and still more with hot irons pressed against their sides. . . . From time to time as they passed us, they laboured to seem to dance, but in general their step was slow, their countenances expressive of resigned and patient suffering, and there was no appearance, that I saw, of anything like frenzy or intoxication. . . . [The ceremony ends with a voluntary torture:] The victim was led, covered with flowers and without any apparent reluctance, to the foot of the tree: hooks were then thrust through the muscles of his sides, which he endured without shrinking, and a broad bandage was fastened round his waist, to prevent the hooks from being torn through by the weight of his body. He was then raised up and whirled round. At first the motion was slow, but by degrees was increased to considerable rapidity. In a few minutes it ceased; and the by-standers were going to let him down, when he made signs that they should proceed. This resolution was received with great applause by the crowd, and after drinking some water he was again spun round." Besse, *Les moines d'Orient,* pp. 496 f.: "Among the privations voluntarily undertaken by certain monks, St. Epiphanius makes special mention of abstention from bathing [*Panarium adversus haereses, lib.* III, *tomus* II, *Expositio fidei,* 33 (*Opera,* Vol. II, p. 830)]. . . . There were those who went farther still and spurned the most elementary precautions of cleanliness. . . . St. Hilarion was one of these, and Abraham the Recluse, who never washed his feet and hands. [The recluse Abraham may have been a great saint. He certainly was a dirty one. Let us hope and pray that no emulator of Senator Bérenger will ever take it into his head to force that type of virtue upon us.] St. Pachomus allowed a general anointing of the body with oil only in case of sickness. One had to have authority to perform such a service for a brother either by virtue of one's office or by obedience. . . . St. Ephraim enjoined on those performing such a duty to look carefully to their eyes, their hands and their tongues. . . . There were monks who condemned themselves never to cast their eyes about them, even to look at the furniture in their cells; to sleep a certain number of nights on briars; to live near pools of stagnant water; and so on. They resorted to these devices to be rid of be-among the American Indians and other peoples, corroborates these inferences.[2]

1181. Extraordinary cases of asceticism have been and are still to be witnessed in the East. Orientals have the endurance of savages and brute animals for physical pain, and it is no great wonder

setting temptations. Whenever Hammon was conscious of an importunity from the flesh, he treated his body with pitiless severity. One of his favourite measures was to burn himself with a hot iron. To banish an impure thought that was tempting him, St. Macarius of Alexandria threw himself naked into a quagmire. The stagnant water attracted quantities of mosquitoes to the place, some, avers Pallas, as big as wasps and able to pierce the hide of a wild boar. The Saint endured that new sort of sackcloth for six long months. One may imagine the state his body was in. He looked like a leper. Some thought of loading themselves down with chains and pieces of wood. That was an excellent means of subduing one's body." Examples of that type of penance are frequent enough in the West: St. Gregory of Tours, *Historia ecclesiastica Francorum,* VI, 6 (*Opera,* pp. 376-77; Dalton, Vol. II, p. 238): "In the city of Nice in those days was a recluse by the name of Hospitius, a very abstemious man, who wore iron chains next to his body and over them sackcloth and lived on naught but bread and a few dates. . . . Finding him in that condition in the pit of a tower, the Lombard invaders thought him a criminal. One of them was minded to slay him, but his arm was stiffened [in mid-air], nor did it become sound again till the holy man had made the sign of the cross upon it."

1180 [2] J. L. Burckhardt, *Travels in Arabia,* p. 259 (alluding to Hindu ascetics who pursue pilgrims to Mecca (*hadji*) begging alms): "The gates of the Mosque are always beset with them. Every coffee-house and water-stand is a station for some of them, and no *hadjy* can purchase provisions in the markets without being importuned by Indians soliciting a portion of them. I saw among them one of those devotees who are so common in the north of India and in Persia: one of his arms was held up straight over his head, and so fixed by long habit that it could not be placed in any other situation." Lafitau, *Mœurs des sauvages américains,* Vol. II, pp. 274, 280, 284-86: "Among the tribes of North America that are known, slaves are punished by roasting over slow fires, but the scene takes place with so many details of incredible barbarity that one shudders at the very thought of it. [A description follows.] . . . So the bloody tragedy came to an end—and I am at a loss to say which deserved the greatest wonder, the brutish ferocity of the inhuman savages who were treating poor slaves with such cruelty . . . or the endurance of the slaves themselves, who displayed in the face of the most frightful torments a greatness of soul, a heroism, that is altogether unimaginable. [Burned and tortured in a thousand ways] the prisoners sing their own great feats of arms and those of their tribes. Hurling curses at their tormentors, they try to intimidate them by threats, calling upon their friends to rescue or avenge them. They ridicule the executioners for not knowing their business, telling them how to apply the fire to inflict a bitterer pain, describing what they themselves did to prisoners who fell into their hands. If by chance they have ever dealt with a victim from the tribe of their captors, they enter into the greatest detail of the torments they inflicted, fearless of the consequences of such talk, which can only serve to enrage their

therefore if individuals are to be found among them who submit to cruel tortures for the sake of attracting attention, or at times for a price. Sonnerat gives a good description of the multifarious forms of asceticism in India and it may serve as typical of the thing in general.[1]

tormentors. Though the sheer violence of their anguish makes them foam at the mouth or stare with the wild eyes of madness, they never utter a word of shrinking. The women are as heroic as the men. I saw one have two finger-nails torn out in my presence. Not a cry, not a groan! The most I could catch on her face was an imperceptible expression of tedium. Some of them laugh under torture, take the whole matter as a jest, and amiably thank those who have hurt them most. The savages seem to train themselves for such exhibitions from earliest childhood. Children have been seen to clasp each other with naked arms, with a burning coal between them, wagering as to who could stand it longest and with the least show of pain. I myself saw a child between five and six years old who had been seriously scalded about the body by a vessel of hot water being accidentally upset upon him. Every time his wounds were dressed, he would strike up his death-song and sing it with incredible courage, though he was suffering the keenest anguish at the time."

1181 [1] *Voyage aux Indes orientales et à la Chine,* Vol. I, pp. 256-62: "The Sanjassi (or Sanachi) is either a Brahman or a Chouta. He dedicates himself exclusively to the divinity. He takes a vow to be poor, chaste, and sober. Owning nothing, with no interest in anything, he wanders from place to place, his head shaven, almost naked with a single strip of yellow cloth to cover his back. He lives altogether on alms and eats only enough to keep himself alive. [Those traits are typical of many ascetic associations.] The Pandaroons are not less revered than the Sanjassis. They are worshippers of Siva. They smear their faces, chests, and arms with ashes of cow's dung, and go about the streets carrying peacock-plumes in their hands, begging alms, and singing hymns of praise to Siva. . . . The Karé-Patré Pandaroon is a variation on the Pandaroon proper. He takes a vow of perpetual silence. [*Cf.* the Western Trappist.] He enters a house and claps his hands in begging alms, in order not to speak. His name is significant: *Karé* means 'hand,' *Patré,* 'plate.' . . . The Tadin goes begging from door to door, dancing and singing hymns of praise, and recounting the metamorphoses of Vishnu. . . . The Hindus, finally, have religious Penitents. The Penitents correspond among the Gentiles to the fakirs among the Mongols. They are inspired by their fanaticism to abandon family, property, and so on, and lead lives of utter misery. . . . The only articles they are allowed to possess are a lingam, to which they pay continuous worship, and a tiger's skin on which they sleep. They inflict on their bodies everything that a fanatical fury can suggest. Some tear their flesh with whips [*Cf.* the discipline of our Catholics.] or have themselves chained by the feet to trees to be released only when they die. Others take a vow to remain all their lives long in some uncomfortable position, keeping their hands always closed, for instance, so that their finger-nails, which they never cut, in the end grow through their hands. Some sit with their arms folded across their chests or raised above their heads, so that they have lost the power to bend them. Not a few bury themselves in the ground, breathing only through little

1182. Monks and ascetics have been known in India from most ancient times. The student of the Vedas had to live with his master, obey him, serve him. In that, evidently, residues of rank (IV-ε) are at work in combination with the ascetic residue, as is the case with monks in the Christian monasteries. He must, furthermore, be strictly chaste, temperate, humble, and live in poverty. Buddhism has a complete code for the ascetic life, in some respects very like the rule devised by St. Francis of Assisi—and that is another of the many cases where similar institutions have grown up spontaneously without any imitation (§§ 733 f.).[1] Just such practices, with minor

openings. Others, less fanatical, bury themselves no higher than their necks. Some have taken a vow to spend their lives standing, without ever lying down. They sleep with their bodies leaning against walls or trees, and to prevent themselves from slipping into comfortable postures, they wear frames of lattice-work about their necks. Others stand for hours at a time on one foot, staring open-eyed at the sun. To acquire greater merit still others stand with one foot off the ground, their weight resting on the great toe and their arms, into the bargain, raised above their heads. They stand between four cauldrons in which fires are burning and gaze at the sun with unwinking eyes. There are those who appear in public stark-naked to show that they have become insusceptible to any passion, that on abandoning their bodies to the Divinity they have returned to a state of innocence. The people are convinced of their virtue, look upon them as saints [Generally observable among many peoples.] and think they can get from God anything they ask for. In the belief that they are doing a very pious act, people assiduously provide them with food [Also very general.], put the morsels into the mouths of such as have vowed never to use their hands, and clean them. While the Penitent is sunk in his contemplation, there are women who approach, kiss his private parts, and pay worship to them. . . . Characteristic of the Penitents is an overweening pride; they have a very great esteem for themselves and believe in their own sanctity. They refuse to be touched by members of the lower castes and by Europeans, fearing pollution. They will not even allow their personal articles to be touched, and at once move on if anyone approaches them. They evince sovereign contempt for anyone not of their calling and look upon such as profane things. Everything about them is supposed to hide some mysterious property and to be worthy of devout worship."

1182 [1] Kern, *Histoire du bouddhisme,* Vol. II, pp. 3-5, 14-16: "One of his strictest obligations is to observe absolute chastity: he must not touch a woman or look at one, if there is any danger to his purity. He must strive incessantly and earnestly to control his tongue, his appetite, and his hands. Play, menial labour, the acquisition of objects that have not been offered to him, unkindness to living creatures, unkind words, are all strictly forbidden him, and likewise the use of wines and strong drinks (at least among the Brahmans). He must abstain from salt, honey, meat, spices. He must not sleep during the daytime. He must not use perfumes or ointments, nor wear smart clothes. He must in general avoid anything tending to encourage effeminacy, such as dancing, singing and instrumental music. . . . One

variations, are to be noted among many different peoples at many different periods of history. In our day there are people who admire them. Paul Sabatier drools unctuously over the ascetic practices, at times not so very hygienic, of St. Francis of Assisi.[2] It is evident therefore that the residue plays a far from negligible rôle in the senti-

of the most characteristic duties of the student is that he should each day beg alms for his maintenance." Each Veda had to be studied twelve years; but only one Veda was required, whereupon the student was free to return to life as a layman and marry. If he chose, he could remain a student all his life.

The mendicant monk, the Bhikshu, differs from the student in that he is not subject to a master: "The rules of conduct for the Bhikshu may be summarized as follows: He has no home and no personal property. He leads a roving life, save during the rainy season, when he has to have a fixed residence. He begs alms once a day in the village for his maintenance. He must renounce all desires, master his tongue, his eyes, his conduct, and observe the strictest continence. He may have one garment to hide his nakedness, or wear cast-off rags, first washing them. He must keep his head shaven, save for one tuft on the very top of the crown. [Such a person is hardly distinguishable from the Franciscan.] . . . Not to be confused with the mendicants properly so called, the Bhikshus, . . . are the hermits, who live lives of mortification in solitude in order to accustom themselves to renunciation of worldly things and prepare themselves for the hereafter. [As Christian hermits do.] Though they are allowed to beg alms for their support, it is exceptional for them to do so. . . . The hermit lives in the jungle, getting his own living from fruits and wild vegetables and practising asceticism. . . . The Buddhists have in the Dhûtangas a complete set of rules for the ascetic life. The Dhûtangas are thirteen in number among the Buddhists of the South, twelve in the north: I. To wear a garment made of rags gathered from a dunghill or a dump. (As a rule the monks are inclined to disregard this provision.) . . . II. To own three such garments. . . . III. To take no food save such as is received in alms. . . . IV. While begging alms for one's living to go systematically from door to door, to the poor as well as to the rich, neglecting no one. . . . V. To remain seated at the same place during a meal. . . . VI. To eat only from a single ladle or alms-plate. . . . VII. To take no second repast after the morning meal. . . . VIII. To live in solitude. . . . IX. To live at the foot of a tree. . . . X. To sleep out of doors. . . . XI. To live in a cemetery. . . . XII. To spend the night at the spot one happens to reach without design. . . . XIII. To sleep in a sitting posture. . . . In the Northern rule articles IV and VI are missing. It has, however, another provision . . . prohibiting the use of felt."

1182 [2] *Vie de Saint François d'Assise,* p. 165 (Houghton, p. 144): "One day Brother John . . . who had been placed in special charge over a leper, brought him on a walk to the Portiuncola, as though he had not been suffering from a contagious malady. He did not escape rebukes and hearing them the leper could not hide his distress and sorrow. . . . Francis easily perceived that and felt a sharp pang of remorse. The thought that he had pained 'one of the sick of the good Lord' he could not bear; and not only did he beg his forgiveness, but he had him stay for the repast, sat down beside him, and ate out of the same plate with him."

ments of certain people of our time. Derivations draw sharp distinctions between the dirty practices of Hindu ascetics, Athenian Cynics, the Franciscans, and similar sects; but identical residues underlie them all.

1183. People who are not victims of the sentiments corresponding to the ascetic residues either take towards ascetics of that brand the attitude voiced by Rutilius of old, in wonderment at their dislike for the good things life has to offer; [1] or else frankly ridicule them, as Lucian ridiculed Peregrine.[2] As a rule, moreover, people laud ascetics of their own faith and censure others. Christians deride Hindu ascetics and revere their own. Humanitarians cannot endure Christian asceticism, but glorify the asceticism of teetotallers and prudes. There are people who rave at the celibacy rule for the

1183 [1] *Itinerarium,* I, vv. 439-46 (Paris, pp. 138-39):

> "*Processu pelagi iam se Capraria tollit.*
> *Squalet lucifugis insula plena viris.*
> *Ipsi se monachos Graio cognomine dicunt,*
> *quod soli nullo vivere teste volunt.*
> *Munera fortunae metuunt dum damna verentur.*
> *Quisquam sponte miser ne miser esse queat?*
> *Quaenam perversi rabies tam stulta cerebri*
> *dum mala formides nec bona posse pati?*"

("And lo, as we proceed, Capraria rises from the sea, an island infested with men who shun the light. They call themselves by a Greek name, monks, because it is their will to live alone without companionship (*monachus* from *μόνος*). The gifts of fortune they fear in fear of damnation. What kind of person is this that makes himself wretched in order to escape wretchedness? What stupid madness of perverted minds—in fear of an evil, to spurn all blessings!")

1183 [2] *"De morte Peregrini,"* 1-2 (*Opera,* Vol. VIII, pp. 263-64; Fowler, Vol. IV, p. 79): "Poor dear Peregrine—or Proteus, as he loved to call himself—has quite come up to his namesake in Homer. We have seen him under many shapes: countless have been his transformations for glory's sake; and now—'tis his last appearance—we see him in the shape of fire. So vast was his ambition! Yes, Cronius! All that is left of the best of men is a handful of ashes. . . . I fancy I see you chuckling away at the old dotard; or rather I hear you blurting out the inevitable comment—'Mere imbecility, mere clap-trap, mere—everything else,' that we are accustomed to attribute to these gentry. But then, you are far enough off to be comparatively safe: now I made my remarks before a vast audience, at the very moment of cremation (and before it for that matter), exciting thereby the indignation of all the old fool's admirers, though there were a few who joined in the laugh against it. I tell you I was within an ace of being torn limb from limb by the Cynics, like Actaeon among the dogs." (Fowler.)

Catholic priest, yet would legislate against premarital relations between men and women, not perceiving, in their intellectual pauperism, that both attitudes are one and the same and arise from the same causes.

1184. "In the summer-time Diogenes rolled about [in his tub] on the burning sand, and in the winter went about hugging statues covered with snow, accustoming himself to all such hardships."[1] To chasten promptings of the flesh St. Francis once threw himself naked into the snow.[2] Be such stories fact or legend, the people who invented or retold them show, now through Diogenes and now through St. Francis, the working of a residue that prompts human beings to eschew the pleasures of life and seek out suffering, whatever the reason they give for their conduct. The Cynics degenerated, just as in later times the Franciscans degenerated; but the fact that they both continued to enjoy wide-spread popularity even in their day of degeneracy shows the great power the residue must have nad in the masses to sustain such popularity; nor did the ridicule of sensible people serve to weaken it.[3]

1184 [1] Diogenes Laertius, *Diogenes,* VI, 23 (Hicks, Vol. I, pp. 25-27).

1184 [2] Jacopo a Voragine, *Legenda aurea,* CXLIX (*De Sancto Francisco*): "And on a tyme as this holy man was in prayer, the deuyll called him thryes by his owne name, and whanne the holy man had answered hym he said: None in this world is soo grete a synner but yf he conuerte hym our lord wold pardone hym, but who that sleeth hymself by hard penaunce shall neuer fynde mercy. And anone this hooly man knewe by the reuelacion, the fallace and deceyte of the fende, how he wold haue withdrawen hym for to doo well. And whanne the deuyll saw that he myght not preuayle ayenst him, he tempted hym by greuous temptacion of the flesshe, and whan this holy seraunt of god felte that, he despoylled of his clothes and bete hymself right hard with an hard corde saying: Thus broder Asse it behoueth the to remayne and to be beten, and whan the temptacion departed not he went out and plonged hymself in the snow al naked, and made seuen grete balles of snowe and purposed to have taken them in to his body, and sayd, This gretest is thy wyf, and of these foure, two ben thy doughters and two thy sones, and the other tweyne, that one thy chamberer and that othir thy varlet or yeman, haste the and clothe them for they al deye for cold, and yf thy besynes that thow hast aboute them greue the sore, then serue our lord parfightely. And anon the deuyll departed from them al confused, and saynt Frounceis retournjd ageyne in to his celle glorifying god." (Caxton.)

1184 [3] The early day of Epictetus had its equivalent for the adage "The habit does not make the monk." Epictetus, *Dissertationes,* IV, 8, 4-5: "It is not easy to judge opinions from exteriors. . . . This man is a philosopher. Why? Because he

1185. Philo the Jew wrote a treatise on the contemplative life of the Therapeutae.[1] It has been a moot question whether the treatise is really Philo's, and also, on better grounds, whether the Therapeutae were men in the flesh or a mere literary invention. The point is of little importance for our purposes. The fact that a writer, be he who he may, described such things, be they real or imaginary, shows that at the time he wrote a strong current of asceticism prevailed. That is all that need concern us for the moment. Women were admitted into the sect, but they had to remain virgin. Horror for sexual relations is an obsession seldom missing in asceticism, especially in its intenser manifestations, where it approximates insanity.

1186. There is no doubt that the Essenes, on the other hand, were real people. They were like the Hindu ascetics, and the "Perfects" of the Albigenses were, in turn, like them. "To the westward of the shores [of Lake Asphaltides] and far enough away not to be harmed by its fumes, dwell the Essenes, a solitary people and marvellous beyond all others in the world. They live without any woman, for-

wears a coarse mantle and a long beard! Yet—the mountebanks, what do they wear? And so, if one of them is caught doing some shameful thing, there comes the cry forthwith, 'See what philosophers do!' Whereas, since the thing he does is shameful, one should rather say that he is not a philosopher." In *Ibid.*, III, 22, Epictetus contrasts the true with the false Cynic, accusing the latter of every vice. Cynics were still to be seen in the day of St. Augustine: *De civitate Dei,* XIV, 20: "Even now we see that there are philosophers who are Cynics, and not only go about in sheets, but also carry the Cynic's staff." Lucian is not sparing of invective against self-styled philosophers. In *Piscator,* 11 (Harmon, Vol. IV, p. 19), he says that he has found no trace of philosophy among men who go about wrapped in sheets [Harmon: "short cloaks"] and wearing unkempt beards. The scholiast remarks that the same may be said of the monks of his time. In the *Dialogi mortuorum,* X, 8 (*Opera,* Vol. II, pp. 170-71; Fowler, Vol. I, p. 121), Mercury requires a philosopher to draw aside his mantle and then, peering at him, exclaims: "O Zeus, what boastfulness he was hiding under there, what ignorance, what quarrelsomeness, what vainglory . . . ! And here? Bless us—gold, lechery, impudence, wrath, high living, effeminacy! Hide nothing, man, for I see everything!" On the exclamation "O Zeus! What a boastfulness . . ." the scholiast comments: *τὶ ταῦτα τοῖς καθ' ἡμᾶς μοναχοῖς ἁρμόδια* ("That goes for our monks.") An epigram, XVI, 19, in the Appendix of Maximus Planudes to the *Greek Anthology* (Paton, Vol. V, pp. 168-69) plays on the word *Irene,* which means "peace" in Greek and was also the name of a bishop's concubine. "Peace (Irene) be with you all!" says the Bishop, entering. "But how can she be with us all, if you have her in the other room all to yourself?"

1185 [1] *De vita contemplativa* (Cohn, Vol. VI, pp. 46-71; Yonge, Vol. IV, pp. 6-20).

swearing love, and without money, in the company of the palms. Their numbers are replenished day by day, because many who are weary of life and the fluctuations of fortune are attracted by their manner of living."[1] Flavius Josephus says that "property is held in common among them, the rich enjoying no more wealth than the poor. Such the custom of more than four thousand men, and they have neither wives nor slaves, because slaves are a cause of injustice and wives of discord." Josephus may be suspected of describing the causes for asceticism in those terms because he had no very clear conception of the real ones.[2]

1187. Among the countless follies of the ascetics not the least silly were the practices of the Stylites, a name given to certain devout Christians who spent portions of their lives on top of columns. The earliest known individual of this type was St. Simeon, called in fact, the Stylite, who lived in the fifth century.[1] He was born in Cilicia and entered a monastery in earliest youth. Moving on to a second, he remained there ten years, leading a life so excessively austere that, to believe the account of Theodoret, he ate only once a week, whereas the other monks ate every other day. He practised self-mortification in other ways that were deemed so extravagant by his superiors that he was expelled. He thereupon withdrew to a little cell near Antioch, where he continued his self-inflicted sufferings. After three years of that he betook himself to a mountain-top and walled himself up in a cramped cell fastened by a heavy iron chain about his foot (Garnier). Pilgrims flocked to him from all parts of the world, and he rewarded them with many a pretty miracle.[2] Annoyed,

1186 [1] Pliny, *Historia naturalis,* V, 17 (Bostock-Riley, Vol. I, pp. 430-31).

1186 [2] *Antiquitates Judaicae,* XVIII, 1, 5 (*Opera,* Vol. IV, p. 139; Whitson, Vol. IV, p. 59).

1187 [1] Theodoret, *Religiosa historia,* XXVI, *Symeones* (*Opera,* Vol. III, pp. 1463-84), claims to have seen St. Simeon personally. And *cf.* Theodorus Lector, *Excerpta ex ecclesiastica historia,* I, 12 (Migne, p. 171) and I, 18 (Migne, p. 174); Valois, [? *Theodoreti et Evagrii historia ecclesiastica* (notes), Vol. II, p. 565], Evagrius, *Ecclesiastica historia,* I, 13 (*Opera,* pp. 2454-59; English, pp. 24-28); Antonius (*Symeonis discipulus*), *Vita Symeonis Stylitae.*

1187 [2] Says Theodoret, *loc. cit.* (*Opera,* pp. 1478-79): "Not only was I present at his miracles, but I heard him prophesy the future. [On one occasion] he predicted a great drought and crop-failure, followed by famine and pestilence, two full years in advance."

finally, at so much bustle about him, he took to the top of a column, standing there erect. He first ordered one made six cubits high, then successively columns twelve, twenty-two, and thirty-six cubits high. "So great his desire to be near unto Heaven and far from this Earth!" And at that point, to silence critics who were ridiculing the Stylite, the good Theodoret recalls in his favour, *loc. cit.*, the penances of Isaiah, Jeremiah, Hosea, and Ezekiel. Perched on his column, St. Simeon converted no end of people who came to look at him. Theodoret says he saw them. Women were not allowed to enter the enclosure where the pillar rose. Simeon refused to see even his mother (§ 1172). Just how long he lived on the column is a moot question.[3] He had a spiritual successor, one Daniel, who also decided to live on top of a pillar.[4] These holy and silly

1187 [3] Baronio, *Annales ecclesiastici, anno,* 460, IV (note by Antoine Pagi): "In his supplement (*Auctarius*) to the works of Theodoret (*Dissertationes, lib.* II, *cap.* V, § 3, sec. 5-11; Theodoret, *Opera,* Vol. V, pp. 239-41) Garnier examines the celebrated question as to the year in which Simeon the Stylite mounted his column and the length of time he stood on it. He notes that Baronio mentions three things that are at variance not only with all the biographers of Simeon, including Theodoret, but with Baronio himself." He concludes that the Saint must have spent some forty years on the column.

1187 [4] Baronio, *Op. cit., anno* 460, XVII-XX: "But just as Elijah designated Elisha as the heir of his spirit and the imitator of his virtues, so Simeon seems to have made the monk Daniel the legitimate successor to his spiritual legacy, and to have exhorted him to take up that angelic manner of life by divine prophecies and visions. Like Elisha in assuming the mantle of Elijah, Daniel was found worthy to receive the cowl of Simeon shortly before the latter's death, he having sent it by his disciple Sergius to Leo the Emperor, who, however, had not accepted it. The which must evidently have been by divine plan, inasmuch as Daniel became the heir of the spirit and virtue of Simeon in the giving forth of signs, for it happened [that Daniel took the cowl] on the very day on which Simeon departed this life. In taking the cowl from Sergius, he revealed to the latter the death of Simeon, which had been revealed to him, and forthwith, in the greatest confidence, as though he were entering upon a paternal inheritance, he mounted a column that he had erected at Ostia in Pontus. It was his lot to be criticized among others by St. Gennadius, Patriarch (*antistes*) of Constantinople, who was shocked by the strangeness of his conduct and was apprehensive lest he were a man of overweening conceit (*inflatus superbia*), inspired by emulation of the great Simeon with a view to winning popular favour and so acquiring notoriety (*gloriolam*). But by signs divinely manifested the Patriarch was at length persuaded that Daniel was a lover of God, that he had made that effort not of human presumptuousness but supported by the counsel of God, governed by His authority, inspired by His spirit, sustained by His help." He lived on the column many years and worked no end of first-class miracles.

men had other emulators. They are still being mentioned as late as the year 806, when Theodore of Studa advises the Emperor Nicephorus in a letter to select the patriarch of Constantinople from among the "bishops, Stylites, and recluses."[5]

1188. If we had only the Christian Stylites to go by, we might be left in doubt as to whether such practices were logical consequences of Christian beliefs (§§ 184, 734, 829). But exactly identical cases are observable in places where there is no trace whatever of Christianity. We may suspect therefore that they all have a common cause, independent of beliefs. Not that beliefs may not have cooperated with such causes, but with them, I say, not replacing them. So in ascetic acts of penance, residues of personal integrity (Class V) are working in combination with residues of asceticism—since one among the penitent's motives is to purge himself of sin. But the residues of asceticism come to the fore again when the penance is served for the sins of others.

1189. Whoever the author of the *Syrian Goddess,* he was certainly not a Christian and was not describing customs of Christians. All the same in that document we find Stylites, temporary Stylites at least, and a type of asceticism that as far as concrete results are concerned is not so very different from the asceticism of St. Simeon. No less than four explanations of the conduct of the Stylites are given in the *Syrian Goddess,* nor are they so very different, after all, from the explanations given for Christian Stylitism.[1]

1187 [5] Baronio, *Op. cit., anno* 806, V: "*. . . ex praepositis et ex stylitis et ex inclusis.*"

1189 [1] Lucian, *De Syria dea,* 28-29 (Harmon translation, Vol. IV, pp. 379-80): "The place therinne the temple sytt is a hylle; and it liggeth wel in the myddes of the cytee, and two walles enviroune it. Oon of the walles is auncien, but the tother is not mocheles elder than oure tyme. The entree of the holy place maketh out toward the Septemtryon, well a 100 fadmes of largenesse; and in that entree stont tho yerdes that leet set, on heighte a 300 fadmnes. A man goth up the oon of thise yerdes twyes in the yeer and woneth at the cop of the yerde for the space of 7 dayes. And the cause of his goynge up, as men seyn, is this. Lewed folk trowen that he speketh with the goddes on highe and axeth bones for alle Surrye, and the goddes heren his preyeres fro there nyghe. [First derivation.] But othere wenen that this also is don be cause of Deucalioun in tokene and mynde of that tribulacioun, whan men wenten into montaynes and into the gret highe trees for fere of the flode. [Second derivation.] Now to me, that is not to beleven. I suppose wel that thei don this for worschipe of Bacchus, and I conclude it thus. Yerdes

1190. Ascetic flagellation is fairly wide-spread in terms of both time and space. Familiar the Spartan institution of flogging for young men at the altar of Artemis Orthia, and the flagellation of Christian penitents in the Middle Ages. Writers have collected similar cases and suggested various explanations for them. They have been taken as demonstrations of courage and indifference to pain—and there is some truth in that. Lycurgus has been credited with the intention of accustoming his fellow-citizens to courageous endurance of pain —and explanations of that kind always have scant probability. It has been suggested that flagellations were surviving remnants of older practices of human sacrifice—and that may well be, but proofs of any such thing are entirely lacking. It used to be said that flagellation served to drive out evil spirits. That is a derivation, probably with a residue lurking underneath. It has been explained that the victims acquired the strength and vitality of the instruments used in

that thei maken for worschipe of Bacchus, on tho yerdes ther setten alle wayes wodene men; but I schalle not seye whi. [Third derivation. Add now the fact that the Stylite is doing penance and we get a fourth derivation. That shows that the many derivations are the variable, secondary element in the case, the main, the constant, element being the residue that the derivations are designed to explain.] . . . The manere of his goynge up is this. He putteth a schort corde abouten himself and the yerde and thanne he climbeth on peces of wode ynaylled on the yerde, bigge ynow for to lette setten on his toon; and ther as he climbeth he throweth up the corde with bothe hondes right as he mighte schake the reynes of a charre. If ony ther be that hath not seen this thing but hath seen men that climben trees of palme in Arabye or in Egypte, or elles where, he understondeth whereof I speke. [The description apparently of an actual eyewitness.] Whan he is comen to the ende of his weye, he letteth falle an other corde that he hath, that is long, and draweth uppe what him list, wode and clothes and purveyaunce, of the whiche he frameth a sete lyk as a nest, theron he sytteth and abydeth for the space of the before seyde dayes. And manye comynge putten gold or silver or peraunter brasse, that thei usen for here moneyes, in to a vesselle that lyeth there neer, seyinge everychon his name. Than oon that stondeth there beside calleth it uppe; and whan that other resceyveth the name of eech, he preyeth for him, and in preyinge schaketh a thynge of brass that souneth gret and schrille when it is stered. [Significant the parallel: Crowds came from the world over to St. Simeon's column. The Emperor Leo had a monastery built near Daniel's pillar for that saint's disciples.] And he ne slepeth never. For if that ever he falle on slepe, a scorpioun goynge up awaketh him and doth him pitous harm; and that is the peyne that is leyde on him for slepynge. Now this tale that is told of the scorpioun is a holy tale and wel semynge, but wher it be trewe or non, I wot neer. Natheles, me seemeth that drede of fallynge avayleth moch to wakfulnesse."

the flogging; and that too is a derivation. Flogging was also interpreted as a purifying process for the victim—again a derivation. For the Christians flagellation was a way of doing penance.

1191. The totemic explanation of course could not fail to put in an appearance, since totemism nowadays has to have a finger in everything. Reinach adopts it, following Thomsen:[1] "The young men of Sparta were flogged with hazel rods, and the goddess presiding over the ceremony was the goddess of the hazel (Lygodesma, from the Greek *lygos,* 'hazel'). The Luperci lashed women in Rome with thongs of hide from a he-goat or a she-goat, and Luperca, the goddess presiding over the ceremony, partakes of both the she-wolf and the she-goat (*lupus, hircus*). The purpose of the flogging, therefore, was to transmit to the victim's body the strength and vitality of the tree or animal—undoubtedly, former totems." That "therefore" is truly splendid! At the very least, one might expect the conclusion to be tied to the premise somewhat more effectively! The explanation would not change, notice, whatever the material used in the flogging. Would it not serve just as well for the hide of any other animal? Strength and vitality were by no means confined to he-goats and she-goats! Worth a round of applause, also, the broad jump that is taken to reach the conclusion. Granting that the purpose of the flogging was to transmit to the victim the strength and the vitality of the material from which the whip was made, or which it symbolizes—must that material necessarily have been a former totem? When one is satisfied with proofs as tenuous and fragile as that, one can prove anything.

1192. As we have repeatedly suggested (§§ 23, 670), let us not go looking in this case for "origins" destined to remain obscure. Let us look for the sentiments that underlie the conduct. Let us not go guessing at possibilities in times for which we have no documents. Let us confine our attention to facts attested by documents that we can trust.

1193. First of all, cases of flagellation in the concrete are not necessarily all of the same kind. The lashes, surely not very painful, that

1191 [1] *Cultes, mythes et religions,* Vol. I, p. 180.

were inflicted on the women of Rome during the Lupercalia may have little or nothing to do with the very painful flagellation of the Spartans. So let us look about for some case of flagellation that is very simple, and calculated, therefore, to betray the residues more clearly.

1194. Casati happens to describe just such a simple case, and it is a matter of young men flogging one another to show their courage and win the admiration of young women.[1] Our totemists will of course say that since the whip was made of hippopotamus hide the purpose of the flagellation was to transmit to the young man the strength of the hippopotamus, a former totem. If a whip chanced to be made of the hide of some other animal *A,* or were a switch from some tree *B,* substitute *A* or *B* for the hippopotamus, and we still get the same explanation. Indeed it would always serve, for the whip has to be made of something! Disregarding such fanciful explanations, we find expressed in the case described by Casati sentiments that we know to be widely diffused among human beings; and probably therefore they figure in other cases of the kind.

1195. It would be surprising indeed that they should be missing in the floggings of the young men at Sparta, and that the Spartans, so eager in everything they did to show themselves contemptuous of the comforts of life, and scornfully indifferent to pain and death, were to lay them aside in the special case of flagellation, where they would seem to be most appropriate. The view of the ancients that

1194 [1] *Dieci anni in Equatoria,* p. 48 (Clay, p. 49). "The dances open the first day with a very curious and typical ceremony. The young folks, the girls on one side, the boys on the other, begin singing joyous love-songs. Then one of the girls rises, takes a whip of hippopotamus hide, and hands it to one of the boys, who accepts it with polite thanks. He looks about him crying: 'Who would be loved and admired?' 'I!' a companion answers, stepping forward with uncovered shoulders. The youth with the whip belabours his shoulders soundly—fifteen lashes in all, and applied with a will. To comply with the rules the welts must be distinctly visible. The two actors now invert rôles and repeat the game. Then they retire, proud of having displayed their physical and moral fortitude before the eyes of their fair ones." Compare with this account Plutarch's description of the flagellations at Sparta, just below. [There are substantial differences in Casati's various texts. The English version of his work seems to have been the first published.—A. L.]

flagellation was instituted by deliberate device of the legendary Lycurgus was mistaken. Very probably, however, flagellation was a manifestation of sentiments connected with training for endurance of pain and with self-sacrifice on the part of the individual to the group. Those sentiments were very powerful in Sparta. A country where people led lives of incredible hardship, and where mothers disowned sons who fled from battle or who alone escaped where their comrades perished (§ 1148 [1]), must necessarily have had boys who courted sufferings commensurate with their age. The fact that the floggings took place at the altar of Artemis Orthia is secondary, incidental. Had there been no such goddess, it would have been no great task to find another. The concrete case of Sparta and the concrete case described by Casati seem to differ in one respect. The residue, common to them both, endurance of pain (IV-ζ) is combined, in the case of Sparta, with a feeling that the pain is inflicted in behalf of the country and its gods—a sentiment of individual sacrifice (IV-δ), therefore.[1]

1196. In the Middle Ages voluntary flagellation turns up again. It would be altogether ridiculous to see any trace of totemism or of any device for acquiring physical strength in this mediaeval case. St. Dominic Loricatus first preached flagellation. His story is well known, and nothing, absolutely nothing, in it suggests either of those notions. St. Dominic Loricatus flogged himself as a penance for himself and for others—such the derivation covering the ascetic residue. It is not surprising that at a time when all imaginable austerities were being devised to satisfy the ascetic urge, flagellation should have been one of them. It would have been surprising had it not been thought of. Condemned by many people, that new mortification was defended by St. Peter Damian, who quite soundly re-

1195 [1] Plutarch, *Instituta Laconica*, 40 (Babbitt, Vol. III, pp. 443-45); and *Lycurgus*, 18 (Perrin, Vol. I, pp. 261-65); and Lucian, *Anacharsis*, 38 (Harmon, Vol. IV, pp. 63-65). Placidus, *Commentarii in Statii Thebaidem*, IV, 227 (Leipzig, 1671, pp. 425-26): "Why he mentions the Eurota he explains himself. The Laconians play a whipping-game (*vapulando contendunt*) on the banks of that river; and he is the prouder who has had the courage for more than the prescribed number of lashes; for when anyone dies under them, he is publicly crowned at his funeral."

marked that it could not be condemned unless the other mortifications of the Holy Fathers were to be condemned likewise. To the objection that Jesus, the Apostles, and the martyrs had been flogged by others but had not tortured themselves, Damian replies that we are quite able to punish ourselves and that, just as we fast of our own accord, so we may chastise ourselves with our own hands.[1]

1197. St. Dominic Loricatus (*i.e.,* of the iron armour) got that surname, according to his *Life* by St. Peter Damian, from at all times wearing an iron tunic. He observed scrupulous chastity to the day of his death and practised all sorts of corporal penances, spending his life reciting psalms, making genuflections, and flogging himself. Some years before his death he discovered that leathern whips inflicted greater pain than willow switches and therefore adopted them. His was a case of mental alienation. But just as megalomania is a mental disease taking the form of excessive pride, so the follies of St. Dominic betray an excess of the sentiment that induces the individual to abandon all thought of personal integrity (*cf.,* Class V residues). St. Dominic did penance for the sins of others, sacri-

1196 [1] *Epistolae,* V, 8, *Ad clericos Florentinos* (*Opera,* Vol. I, p. 75, col. 2, C-D). The Saint argues further: ". . . He performs excellent penance who makes up in pain, through flagellation of the flesh, for the gain he has lost through carnal pleasures, and inflicts a present healthful discomfort upon that which, through his noxious delight in it, was the cause of his sin. It matters little to what punishments the flesh of the penitent is subjected, so only the pleasure of the earlier allurement be exchanged for the vicarious pain of the punished body. If to those who do not practise it (*non facientibus*) the discipline of the rods seems strange and therefore reprehensible and is represented (*iudicatur,* misprint for *indicatur*) to the stupidity of envious belief as a destruction of the law and an undoing of the decretals, are we to say that the Venerable Bede is to be rebuked (*est,* misprint for *esse*) for asserting in the face of (*post*) ancient laws that certain penitents should be shackled in iron chains? And is that manner of living (*vita*) of the Holy Fathers to be spat upon which (*quem,* misprint for *quae*) bears witness that they did penance for their sins, some by standing for weeks and fortnights (*ogdoadas et pentadecas*) in [piles of] thorns, some by standing from sunrise to sunrise with their arms uplifted stiff above their heads, and some by hiding from view for long periods (*jugiter*) in caves they dug for themselves? And is the Blessed Macharius properly to be ridiculed because for six months at a time—not in penance for any sins he had committed himself (*dum se minimum quid admisisse poenituit*)—he exposed his limbs naked to the sharp beaks of mosquitoes (? *culicum*), which were fit to pierce the hide of a wild boar?" And see *Opuscula,* LI, 9, *De Dominico Loricato: De ratione disciplinae* (*Opera,* Vol. III, pp. 400-01).

ficing himself for the salvation of others (IV-δ). A pretty computation in arithmetic worked out by St. Peter Damian shows that a hundred years of penance could be offset by reciting twenty Psalms [*read* Psalters] accompanied by self-flagellation with switches or leathern thongs.[1] It seems that St. Dominic managed to perform that feat in six [*read* five] days' time. On one occasion at the beginning of Lent, St. Dominic begged St. Peter Damian to impose one thousand years of penance upon him, and he had paid almost the whole debt before the end of that Lent.[2]

1198. In his efforts to promote the practice of self-flagellation, St. Peter Damian reminds one, *mutatis mutandis,* of the ascetics of our time, who would deprive human life of all material pleasures and who so fiercely persecute the smile of woman and the warmth of wine. If it be objected that ours are mere pseudo-ascetics, the comparison nevertheless holds between their admirers and the admirers of the flagellations of the "Saint in Armour."[1]

1197 [1] *Idem, Opuscula,* LI, 8-9, *De Dominico Loricato* (*Opera,* Vol. III, pp. 400-01). P. 400, col. 1, D: "According to that same author [St. Dominic Loricatus] credit for a hundred years of penance could be obtained in that way. It is our regular procedure to count three thousand blows of the rod as the equivalent of one year of penance. However, as has often been tested (*probatam,* misprint for *probatum*) the recitation of ten Psalms allows opportunity for one thousand blows. Now since there is no doubt that the Psalter contains one hundred and fifty Psalms, accurate computation shows that there are five years of penance in this discipline of the Psalter. But whether you multiply 5 by 20 [Pareto rightly corrects *vices* to *vicies.*—A. L.] or 20 by 5, the result is 100. It follows therefore that anyone reciting twenty Psalters with flagellation (*disciplina*) may be sure he has won credit for a hundred years of penance." The Saint's arithmetic does not show a wrinkle. [Pareto misread "Psalteria" as "Psalms"—a difference between 20 and 3,000! St. Dominic, still according to St. Peter Damian, usually recited two Psalters every ordinary day, and at least three Psalters on days in Lent: *loc. cit.,* C.: *vix dies ulla praetereat quin duo Psalteria modulando utraque manu scopis armata nudum corpus allidat . . . quadragesimalibus circulis . . . ad minus tres Psalteria.* On the special occasion in question here he must have performed his stint not in six days, as Pareto says, but in five.—A. L.]

1197 [2] *Ibid.,* 9: *"Memini quoque quia cuiusdam Quadragesimae imminentis initio mille annos imponi sibi per nos ad poenitentiam petiit: quos certe omnes ferme antequam ieiunii tempus transigeretur explevit."*

1198 [1] A certain Mr. Cannon, an American, turned ninety-seven preachers loose upon his countrymen during the Christmas season of the year 1911 with the idea of persuading them to abstain from women and wine. No comparison is possible between Mr. Cannon and St. Dominic. The one makes money on the stock-market

1199. Record of the penances of St. Dominic chances to have survived in the works of St. Peter Damian. We may readily imagine that there were other cases of the kind, perhaps less severe, of which no record has come down to us. Be that as it may, towards the year 1260 an epidemic of flagellations broke out in Italy and raged for several years thereafter, now in one place, now in another, now abating and dying out, now flaring up again. Muratori believes that many of the modern brotherhoods and congregations originated in the flagellations of those days: "Forasmuch as the notion was fixed in the minds of people that flogging was a most salutary act of penance and since zeal of faith was strong with them, they came together in devout societies each with its own banners, marching about thereafter in public processions singing godly hymns, and repairing on holy days to their churches, where they practised flagellations, prayed for divine forgiveness, and performed other acts of Christian devoutness." [1]

(a place of no great repute as an abode of virtue), keeps the pleasure for himself, and presents the penances to others. The Saint lived in utter poverty and hardship, and inflicted penances upon himself to compensate for the enjoyments of others. A comparison is possible, however, between their respective followings, for these are in both cases inspired by an ascetic sense for eschewing the pleasures of life and seeking its sufferings.

1199 [1] *Dissertazioni sopra le antichità italiane,* LXXV (Vol. III, p. 468). And *cf.* his *Annali d'Italia,* Vol. VII, pp. 290-91: "The present year [1260] was further celebrated for a novelty in religion, which had its beginnings in Perugia, as some say with a child, according to others with a hermit who asserted that he had revelation of it from God. This man preached repentance to the people, representing a heavy scourge from Heaven as imminent unless they repented and made peace with one another. Wherefore men and women of all ages organized processions, lashing themselves and invoking the protection of the Virgin, Mother of God. This popular devotion moved on from Perugia to Spoleto, attended by a wondrous spirit of compunction, and thence into Romagna. The people in one town would gather in processions, sometimes ten and even twenty thousand strong, and march to a neighbouring town, and there in the cathedral flog themselves to the point of bleeding, crying to God for His mercy and for peace among men. [In that the residue of sociality comes into view in naked form.] Catching the spirit, the people of that town would then go to the next in the same way, so that by the end of the winter, the fashion had spread across the Alps, into Provence, Germany, and as far away as Poland. [The usual course of such epidemics, as was seen in our own times in the activities of the Salvation Army.] On October 10, the people of Imola brought the revival to Bologna. Twenty thousand Bolognese then

1200. The Roman Church, which has always been inclined to moderateness, condemned the excessive asceticism of the flagellants, just as in our day the Church of England preserved an attitude of hostility to the orgies of the Welsh revival. The flagellant epidemic of the year 1260 spread as far afield as Germany and aroused great excitement there. Rinaldi, who continued the *Annals* of Cesare Baronio, describes (following Stero) the penances practised by the German flagellants,[1] and also notes that the sect eventually turned to heresy. "This piety of the penitents," he says, *loc. cit.*, "later degenerated into loathsome heresy. Though it had a good beginning in great pomp of sanctity, it was changed by the acts of the Devil into wickedness and debauchery." Flagellants are again in the public eye in Germany in the year 1349, and this time they may be seen rising to appease the divine wrath manifested in a pestilence that

marched upon Modena, and an equal number of Modenese to Reggio and Parma. So from place to place the thing was carried on to Genoa and through the whole of Piedmont. [The Welsh revival spread in much the same way, though on a far smaller scale, in our day.] However, the Marquis Oberto Pallavicino and the Torriani refused to allow the processions to enter the territories of Cremona, Milan, Brescia, and Novara; and King Manfred also forbade them the March of Ancona and Apulia, fearing lest that pretence of piety dissembled some political stratagem. This harshness the Monk of Padua deeply deplores. As a result of this devout stirring of the people, numberless reconciliations were effected among hostile factions, and exiles were allowed to return to their homes. Numberless the confessions and communions—rites much neglected in those barbarous times; and the conversions, whether lasting I could not say, of prostitutes, usurers, criminals, and other wrongdoers." (The usual momentary effects of such epidemics, as may also be seen in the Welsh revival.) In *Dissertazioni,* LXXV above quoted, Muratori specifies further: "The rite spread from one town to the next adjoining. The people of a city, dressed in sackcloth and barefooted, formed in procession two by two, and with the crucifix at their head marched to the next city, imploring peace and the forgiveness of wrongs. Towards the end of October, for example, the Bolognese came to Modena, more than twenty thousand strong, headed by their banners, lashing themselves, and singing hymns of praise and other crude songs. The Modenese went out as far as Castello Leone to receive them and welcome them to their city. They repeated their flagellations, their prayers and wailings in the cathedral and then after service of refreshments by the citizens returned to their homes."

1200 [1] *Annales ecclesiastici, anno* 1260, VIII: "Henricus Stero claims—in that agreeing with the Monk of Padua—that the rite of the flagellants started in Perugia and spread to Germany. Their manner of supplication he describes as follows: 'That form of penance was a hard thing to bear and a horrible and pitiable thing to look upon. The flagellants marched with their bodies bared down to the middle,

was at that time ravaging those unhappy lands.[2] As usual superstition went hand in hand with asceticism, and again as usual, hypocrisy supplied the cloak for criminal doings. These German flagellants read the counterpart of a letter that had been delivered at the Church of St. Peter in Jerusalem by an angel, and which said that Jesus Christ was wroth at the sins of the world but that, in deference to prayers of the Virgin and the angels that He be merci-

then with a sort of skirt (*quadam veste*) reaching to their heels. Their heads and faces were hooded to prevent recognition. They marched in double or triple file, like priests, with a banner or a cross in front. They lashed themselves twice a day for thirty-three days in memory of the time Our Lord Jesus Christ spent in the flesh on this earth [Jesus figures here very much as did the Artemis Orthia in the flagellations of the Spartans. A devout people connects its institutions with its own gods.], the flagellations lasting for the duration (*quousque . . . compleverunt*) of certain chants that they had composed concerning the Passion and death of Our Lord, and which they sang either in the churches or outside them, with two or three leaders of the singing, and now prostrating themselves on the ground, now raising their naked arms to heaven, and regardless of mud or snow, cold or heat. Their pitiable gestures and terrifying flagellations moved many people to tears and to taking up the same form of penance.' "

1200 [2] *Ibid., anno* 1349, XVIII (quoting Albert of Strasburg, *Chronicon,* pp. 149-50): "The pestilence gradually spreading in Germany, people began marching about the country lashing themselves. In mid-June of the year mentioned [1349], two hundred came to Spires from Swabia. They had one man as leader and two other teachers, whose commands they obeyed implicitly. They crossed the Rhine at day-break. A great crowd gathering, they formed a vast circle in front of the minster in the city of Spires. Going into the circle, they stripped themselves of their garments and footwear, being left in a sort of shirt, in place of breeches (*in modum braccae*), that reached from waist to heel (*a femore ad talos*). Then as they marched about the circle they would throw themselves on their faces one after the other, their arms outspread as though crucified, the ones coming behind stepping over those prostrate on the ground and touching them lightly with their flails. Those who had been the first to prostrate themselves were the first to rise; and they would resume the march about the circle, lashing themselves with whips of four thongs tipped with iron nails, singing the Sunday doxology in German (*cantu vulgari invocationis dominicae*) with many prayers. Meantime three of them stood in the centre of the circle lashing themselves and singing in loud voices, and after them others sang. After some time, at a given signal, they all knelt and threw themselves on their faces with arms outspread like persons nailed to the cross, praying in loud sobs. The two masters walked round and round the circle exhorting them to pray to the Lord for mercy upon the people of Spires, and upon all those who had done them good or ill and upon all sinners and all souls in Purgatory. And there were many other things of the kind." [The *Chronicon* ascribed to Albertus Argentinensis seems really to have been written by Matthew of Neuburg (Mattaeus Neuburgensis). See Hamcke, *De M. Alberti Argentinensis Chronico,* n. p. [1866].—A. L.]

ful, He had prescribed that each of those persons should withdraw from the world for thirty-four days and do penance in flagellation.[3] In certain respects at least, the pseudo-scientific pronouncements that people in our time use to preach abstinence from the enjoyments of wine and women are just as silly as the letter from Jerusalem, though in a different way.

1201. The writer of a life of Pope Clement VI asserts of the flagellants of 1349 that "under guise of penance and good works, they slyly committed many crimes"; and that same Pope complains in a bull addressed to the Archbishop of Magdeburg that "under semblance of piety, they cruelly turn their hands to works of impiousness. The blood of Jews (to whom Christian pity gives shelter and protection, not suffering harm to be done to them in any way), nay, the blood even of Christians, do they shed; and to the undoing of good order they lay hold on possessions of clergy and laity alike." [1] The Pope accordingly orders that they be condemned and dispersed. Sentence was also passed against them by the University of Paris, and Philip, the king, forbade them entrance to the realm of France on pain of death.

1202. Flagellants appear again at Misura in 1414, and again they are persecuted and dispersed. This time they were saying that ordinary baptism by water did no good and had to be replaced with a baptism by blood through flagellation. Three years later, in 1417, they break out in Aragon (St. Vincent Ferrer), and Gerson writes a treatise against the abuse of flagellation, which he countenances only when exercised in moderation and at the direction of superiors. In the year 1582 Henry III of France founded congregations for flagellants; but in that case a new element creeps in—eroticism,

1200 [3] The Albert [or Matthew] in question summarizes, *loc. cit.*, the letter that was read on that occasion: *"Cuius literae tenor similis in sententia esse dicebatur in ecclesia S. Petri in Ierusalem per angelum praesentatae, in qua narrat angelus Christum offensum contra mundi pravitates, plurima exprimens crimina violationum diei dominicae, et quod non ieiunetur feria sexta, blasphemias, usuras, adulteria, Christumque rogatum per B. Verginem et angelos pro misericordia, respondisse quemlibet per triginta quatuor dies se debere exulando flagellare ut misericordiam Dei consequantur."*

1201 [1] Baronio-Rinaldi, *Op. cit.*, *anno* 1349, XXI.

the ascetic current going astray.[1] Even in later times, many very devout people were opposed to flagellation, on the ground that it often concealed erotic perversions. Such cases are entirely, or in large part, foreign to asceticism.

1203. Likewise to be distinguished from it are such acts as appear in the Lupercalia in Rome, which, on quite inadequate grounds, the totemists would classify with the flagellation of young men at Sparta. In Sparta the pain inflicted on the victims was an essential element in the rite. In the Lupercalia pain had no part, or at least no apparent part. In the Lupercalia the Luperci ran about the city streets with leather whips cut from the hides of sacrificial victims, and struck the women they encountered with them, the women thus being assured of children. That is just one of the many practices that have been invented by the human fancy to cure women of sterility, and it is of the same nature as the many practices equally numerous that have been devised to cure males of impotence. It may

1202 [1] Pierre de l'Estoile, *Registre-journal de Henri III,* pp. 159-60: "In this month of March of the present year 1583, the King decreed and established a new order, which he named the Order of Penitents, himself and his two favourites (*mignons*) joining the brotherhood; and he caused to enter it also several lords-gentlemen and others of his Court, inviting likewise the prominents of his parliament in Paris, his Exchequer, and other courts and jurisdictions, along with a goodly number of the outstanding burghers of the town. . . . On which day [March 25, 1583, the Feast of the Annunciation] a solemn procession of the said brotherhood of the Penitents took place, they coming about four in the afternoon to the Convent of the Augustinians . . . two by two, and accoutred like the flagellants of Rome, Avignon, Toulouse, and the like. . . . On Holy Thursday, the seventh of April, from about nine o'clock in the evening, the procession of the Penitents, in which the King with all his favourites (*mignons*) marched all night long about the streets and to the churches, in great magnificence of torches and excellent music, and masked (*faux-bourdonnée*). And there were some, even the royal favourites (*mignons*) it is said, who lashed themselves during the processions, their poor backs being all red from the blows they gave themselves." The public ridiculed such buffoonery. After the procession the following quip went the rounds:

> *"Après avoir pillé la France,*
> *et tout son peuple despouillé,*
> *est-ce pas belle pénitence*
> *de se couvrir d'un sac mouillé?"*

("After pillaging France and stripping her people clean, is it not fine penance to go about in a wet sack?")

be that among the fantastic reasons underlying these products of the imagination the reason given by the totemists may also have figured. In that case they would have made a good guess, as may sometimes happen in cases where one has no certain knowledge to go by. Pausanias, *Periegesis,* VIII, *Arcadia,* 23, 1, notes that at Alea, in Arcady, a feast was celebrated in honour of Bacchus: "At that festival," he says, "in obedience to an oracle of Delphi, women are flogged, as are the young men of Sparta at the altar of the Orthia." Trying to discover the reasons for a thing when we know so little about it is like trying to guess the numbers that will be drawn in a lottery—a sheer waste of time.[1]

1204. Among the civilized peoples of our day such manifestations of asceticism as fasts and flagellations have all but disappeared. As early as 1831 an *Instruction to Confessors* reads:[1] "The true and

1203 [1] On the Lupercalia see Ovid, *Fasti,* II, vv. 425-8:

> *"Nupta, quid exspectas? non tu pollentibus herbis*
> *nec prece nec magico carmine mater eris.*
> *Excipe fecundae patienter verbera dextrae:*
> *iam socer optati nomen habebit avi."*

("Bride, why waitest thou? Thou shalt become a mother not from potent herbs nor prayers nor magic chants. Submit in patience rather to the lashes of the fertilizing whip, and straightway thy husband's father will be the grand sire he yearns to be.")

He then recounts, vv. 441-48, an oracle of Juno and what came of it:

> *" 'Italidas matres,' inquit, 'caper hirtus inito.'*
> *Obstupuit dubio territa turba sono.*
> *Augur erat: nomen longis intercidit annis—*
> *nuper ab Etrusca venerat exsul humo.*
> *Ille caprum mactat: iussae sua terga maritae*
> *pellibus exsectis percutienda dabant.*
> *Luna resumebat decimo nova cornua motu:*
> *virque pater subito, nuptaque mater erat."*

(" 'A shaggy goat,' came the voice, 'will mate with Italic mothers!' The throng stood in awed silence at the ambiguous prophecy. But an augur was there (his name has been forgotten in course of the passing years, but he had lately come as an exile from Etrurian soil). He slaughtered a goat. At his bidding the women offered their backs to lashes from thongs cut from its hide. And the new Moon was again showing pointed horns in the tenth month, when the man became a father and his bride a mother.")

1204 [1] *Pratica del confessionale compilata da un provetto confessore,* Turin, 1831, Vol. III, p. 311.

direct manner of subduing the rebellious flesh is through the use of fasting or other mortifications, such as haircloth, the scourge, and the like; and those were the penances prescribed for the most part by the Holy Fathers. However, it is not always possible or expedient to require formal fasts of nothing but bread and water several times in the week, or over periods of years, according to Church practice or as specified in the Sacred Canons. What penitent in our day would accept them or observe them? According, therefore, to present regulations and to the actual usage of judicious confessors, fasts and all other mortification of the flesh should be used as moderately as possible." Now less than ever is there any question of hair-shirts, flagellations, and strict fasts in Italy, France, Germany, or England. It is said that some very moderate use is still made of them in Spain.

1205. So in modern European countries the Nazaritic vow among the Jews seems to have fallen into disuse. Nowadays Nazarites are, one may say, unknown, having been superseded in part by the prohibitionists of all religions (or of no religion). According to the Bible, the Nazarite was required to abstain from the use of wine and all other alcoholic beverages, vinegar, and all beverages obtained from the grape or raisin.[1] He could not cut his hair, and was obliged to observe other rules, to keep himself in a state of purity. A Nazareat lasted for thirty days, or for some other specified period, or it might even be perpetual. The Talmud dwells on it at length.[2]

1205 [1] Num. 6:4 (*Vulgate*): *"Cunctis diebus quibus ex voto Domino consecrantur, quidquid ex vinea esse potest, ab uva passa usque ad acinum, non comedent."*

1205 [2] Talmud of Jerusalem, Tract Nazir, III, 6, 1-3 (Schwab, Vol. IX, pp. 138-48; Danby, p. 287): "(Mishnah) Three things fundamentally are forbidden the Nazir: impurity, cutting of the hair, and consumption of any product of the vine. All things coming of the vine, grape-skins, for instance, grape-pits, or dried seeds, will be taken together in determining the regulation minimum, there being no violation of abstinence till a quantity of grape equal in bulk to an olive has been eaten." The "Commentary" goes into some very fine discriminations. The Nazir is forbidden to eat the flesh of an animal that has been quartered. Hence a problem: "Rabbi Yohanan and Rabbi Simon b. Lokisch debate the question of eating an ant that has been bitten in two in the mouth and then eaten, Rabbi Yohanan concluding in favour of a penalty, Rabbi Simon against one. Rabbi Mescha asked Rabbi Zura: 'Do Rabbi Yohanan and Rabbi Simon b. Lokisch rule on the question of a grapeseed which a Nazir has bitten in two in his mouth and then eaten?' [Yet teetotallers of our day have been known to refuse food they suspect of being flavoured

1206. Manifestations of asceticism under forms of mortifications of the flesh are still common among Mohammedans and Hindus, and in semi-civilized countries. They are also frequent among the more advanced savages, though much more rare among peoples living virtually on the plane of the brutes. In modern civilized countries asceticism has evolved into prohibitionism, a phobia for anything suggesting sex, the pathological humility of many sincere humanitarians. Occasionally, also, some manifestation turns up, such as the long fast that is nowadays prescribed in the name of Science Sacrosanct, after having for ages been recommended or required in the name of some other divinity.[1]

When the residues of asceticism are combined with the residues of the instinct for combinations (Class I), the result is a very elaborate code, which in any given variety of asceticism seems ridiculous to those who do not share the sentiments corresponding. But such persons usually have other sentiments of their own corresponding to other varieties of asceticism, so that they observe codes altogether similar to the ones they deride.

All these varieties of asceticism, when exacerbated by their codes,

with wine.] A person eating five ants [What a titbit!] even at one mouthful and whether wittingly or not, will be penalized for each insect so eaten, since each ant, in spite of its smallness, constitutes a separate item. But if the ants are crushed before being eaten, the Nazarite will be guilty but once, and even then the total amount consumed must be equivalent to an olive. . . . (Mishnah) Unless otherwise specified the Nazareat is a period of thirty days. A voluntary shaving during that period, or a forcible shaving at the hands of brigands, upsets the period, and it has to be begun over again. If a Nazarite has clipped his hair with scissors or shaved with a razor or pulled out any hair, regardless of the amount, he is guilty. He may rub himself and even scratch himself, but he must not comb his hair for fear of pulling one out." Failure to observe the prescriptions of the Nazareat has its penalties: "He said in the presence of Rabbi Yossé: 'The moment one has cut a single hair during a Nazareat period, one is subject to a flogging.'" People are much more humane today. One merely goes to jail, in a number of states in the American Union, for making a sly wink at a lady.

1206 [1] I am personally acquainted with a teetotaller who is an atheist and who gives not a thought to the Bible. He carries his hatred of alcoholic beverages to the point of abstaining from vinegar, seasoning his salads with lemon. He will not eat fish that has been seasoned with white wine, nor will he touch jugged hare—because of the red wine that is used in the sauce. The residue remains the same—derivations change.

and when efforts are made to enforce them upon others, are the source of huge amounts of suffering that have afflicted, and continue to afflict, the human race. The fact that people tolerate such sufferings, and sometimes even accept them voluntarily instead of rejecting them and stamping on those who promote them as on poisonous snakes, shows conclusively how powerful the sentiments corresponding to them are. Really they are perversions of the instinct of sociality, and without that instinct human society could not exist.

CHAPTER VIII

Residues: Individual Integrity and Sex

1207. Class V: *Integrity of the individual and his appurtenances and possessions.* This class is in a sense the complement of Class IV (sociality). To defend one's own things and strive to increase their quantity are two operations that frequently merge. So defence of integrity and development of personality are two operations that may differ little or even be one and the same. The sum of sentiments called interests is of the same nature as the sentiments to which the residues of the present variety correspond; hence sentiments of "interest" ought strictly to be put in it. But they are of such great intrinsic importance in the social equilibrium that they are best considered apart from residues.

1208. V-α: *Sentiments of resistance to alterations in the social equilibrium.* The equilibrium may be one actually existing, or an ideal equilibrium desired by the individual. But whether real or imaginary, if it is altered, or thought of as altered, the individual suffers, even if he is not directly affected by the alteration, and sometimes, though rarely, even if he gains by it.

1209. In a people that has the institution of slavery, the ancient Greeks, for instance, a citizen may not himself be a slave-owner, but he feels the wrong that is done to the slave-owner in taking the slave away from him—a reaction against an act that disturbs the existing equilibrium. Another citizen would keep the Barbarians slaves and make all Greeks free men; he is envisaging an equilibrium which for those times would be partially ideal. Still another citizen would abolish slavery altogether. He is contemplating an equilibrium which, for those times again, is altogether ideal.

1210. If an existing state of social equilibrium is altered, forces tending to re-establish it come into play—that, no more, no less, is what equilibrium means (§§ 2068 f.). Such forces are, in chief, sentiments that find their expression in residues of the variety we are here examining. On the passive side, they make us aware of the alteration in the equilibrium. On the active side, they prompt us to remove, repel, counteract, the causes of the alteration, and so develop into sentiments of the V-δ variety (§§ 1312 f.). The forces (or sentiments) that come into play when the social equilibrium is disturbed are nearly always perceived by the individual members of that society under some special form. Needless to say, they, as individuals, know nothing about any forces, nothing about any equilibrium. Those are just names which we, as scientists, apply to what is going on. They are conscious of an unpleasant disturbance—it may sometimes be painful, and very painful indeed—of their integrity as it was when the state of equilibrium was still being maintained. Ordinarily such sensations belong to the vague categories known as the "just" or the "unjust." When a person says: "That thing is unjust," what he means is that the thing is offensive to his sentiments as his sentiments stand in the state of social equilibrium to which he is accustomed.

1211. Where a certain kind of property exists it is "unjust" to take it away from a man. Where it does not exist it is "unjust" to bestow it on him. Cicero would have those who are in power in the state refrain from that type of liberality which takes away from the ones in order to give to the others. "Many are they," he says, "who, especially if they are covetous of splendour and glory, take away from the ones what they bestow with a free hand on others." [1] That principle, on the other hand, is fundamental to the so called social legislation that is so dear to the men of our time. Soldiers who are dividing booty taken from an enemy resent as "unjust" any alteration in the rules usually followed in making such partitions. A similar feeling prevails even among thieves in dividing their loot.[2]

1212. The various elements in the social equilibrium are very imperfectly distinguished, especially when the social sciences are at all

1211 [1] *De officiis,* I, 14, 43. And he adds: "The transfers of property made by Lucius Sulla and Gaius Caesar from its rightful owners to other parties should not be accounted liberalities, for nothing is generous that is not also just."

1211 [2] Other residues also figure in the nebulous things called "justice" and "injustice"; but this is not the place to go into them.

backward. So the sentiment that inspires resistance to alterations of equilibrium places alterations in insignificant matters on a par with alterations in very important matters, and people regard as equally "just" a sentence condemning an anti-trinitarian to the stake and a sentence condemning a murderer to death. The mere wearing of clothes different from the common fashion clashes with the sentiment as violently as other far more important transgressions against the social order. Even today, among peoples who call themselves civilized, a woman is not allowed to walk the streets in male attire.

1213. The residue we are here examining prompts a remark of great importance, though it may not appear so at first blush. Take a society in which murder is becoming a frequent occurrence. That society is evidently breaking up. To check the process of dissolution, the sentiment corresponding to our residue does not have to come into play. The immediate interest of the members of the society is enough. In ordinary parlance it will be said that the individual who opposes that state of things is not inspired by any "ideal of justice," but by his instinct of self-preservation, an instinct that he shares with animals and which has nothing to do with any "ideal" of "justice." Now take a very large community where the number of murders is very small. The probability that a given individual will be the victim of a murder is very slight, equal, let us say, to the probability of his succumbing to any number of other perils—of his being bitten by a mad dog, or killed in a railroad accident, things to which the individual pays little attention. The sentiment of direct self-preservation has but slight influence in this case. But another sentiment comes into play and functions vigorously: a sentiment of revulsion against anything disturbing to the social equilibrium as it has existed and is accepted by the individual.

1214. If that sentiment did not exist, every slight incipient alteration in the social equilibrium would meet little or no resistance, and could therefore go on growing with impunity until it came to affect a sufficiently large number of individuals to provoke their resistance from a direct concern to avoid the evil. That is what happens to a certain extent in every society, however highly civilized. But the extent to which it happens is minimized by the interposition of the sentiment of resistance to any alteration in equilibrium, regardless of the number of individuals directly affected. As a consequence the social equilibrium becomes much more stable, and a much more energetic action develops as soon as any alteration sets in.[1]

1215. Examples of such phenomena are exceedingly numerous. One of the most recent was provided by France in 1912. For many years criminals had been treated with ever increasing indulgence in the country. The lay school had become a pulpit for Anarchy, and the social fabric was breaking down in many other respects. The effects became apparent in cases of "sabotage" in the ship-yards and on the railways, and finally in the exploits of a gang of Anarchists, Bonnot, Garnier, and Co. Then some slight reaction occurred. Undoubtedly fear of direct danger on the part of inhabitants of Paris and the suburbs had something to do with it; but, after all, the probability of any given citizen's being struck down by such criminals was very very slight. What interposed with greatest effect was the sentiment of opposition to disturbance of the social equilibrium as it had been. That feeling, in human society, is somewhat analogous to the instinct in animals that makes them flee at perception of danger.

1216. It is readily understandable, therefore, that through a combination of this residue of equilibrium with the residues of our Class II (group-persistences) compound residues of great social importance are built up, corresponding to vigorous and powerful sentiments of the type very vaguely designated by the term "ideal of

1214 [1] An example taken from mechanics will make the matter clearer. Let us assume that a material point stands in equilibrium and that when it is moved from the position of equilibrium a force proportional to the displacement comes into play, tending to carry it back to its former position. If the displacement is slight, the equilibrating force will also be slight, and the point can move quite a distance from its position of equilibrium. Now let us assume that in addition to the force just mentioned, every displacement of the point from the point of equilibrium, whatever the degree, brings into play a constant force of considerable power. In that case the slightest displacement is immediately counteracted by a very considerable force, is unable to increase, and the point is immediately restored to the position of equilibrium. This, notice, is just an analogy—by no means an identity (§ 121).

justice." From the logico-experimental standpoint to say that an "injustice," whether done to one person or to many, involves an equal offence against "justice," is to say a thing that has no meaning. There is no such person as "Justice," and one cannot imagine what "offences" could possibly be offered her. But the wording only is faulty. At bottom what is expressed is a feeling, vague and instinctive to be sure, that it is a good thing that resistance to disturbances of the social order should not stand in direct ratio to the number of individuals affected, but should have a considerable force independent of any such number.

1217. Going back to the example of Bonnot, Garnier, and Co. A number of devotees of the goddess "Science"—the science that has nothing to do with logico-experimental science—observed in great anger that the reaction which developed at the time was absurd, that it could not be said that the criminals in question were products of any *one* of the causes against which the country was aroused. They repeated that argument for every one of the causes in point, with the usual sophistry of the bald-headed man pointing to his one hair; and added that criminals there had always been in all societies at all times in history.[1]

1217 [1] So in England, in 1913, outrages by the "suffragettes" provoked sentiments of bitter resentment in the public at large, people feeling instinctively that to grant the right of disturbing the peace to anyone desirous of using force would sooner or later bring about the dissolution of society. The fanatic humanitarian mystics who were then governing the country did not see matters in that light; nor is the fact to be wondered at, for it is characteristic of fanaticisms and mysticisms that they put people out of touch with all realities. The Prime Minister read statistics in the House of Commons which tended to show that the crimes of the suffragettes were to be counted on the fingers, and that therefore repressive measures could continue mild as in the past. A few days later the newspapers reported two incidents: the one, that one of the harpies in question, who had been in prison for her misdeeds, had been set free as a result of her going on a hunger-strike; the other, that the suffragettes had used paraffin to set fire to Treytom House at Englefield Green, near London, the mansion being completely destroyed (it belonged to Lady White, widow of General Sir George White, the defender of Ladysmith). The damage was estimated at £4,000 sterling. Near the ruins handbills were found bearing the inscription: "Stop tormenting our comrades in prison, and give votes to women." One cannot imagine just why the eminent Prime Minister neglected to state how many more such crimes would be necessary to induce humanitarian arithmetic to grant protection to law-abiding citizens and withdraw

1218. In all that, in so far as reaction had been determined not at all by logic, but by instinct, there was an element of truth. One might add that had logic been the determining factor, there would have been no reaction, for the very good reason that there would have been no action in the first place. A matter of instinct was the pity that allowed criminals to go scot-free, preached anarchy to schoolchildren, and dissolved every tie of subordination to authority. Instinctive, therefore, was the fear that prompted people to react against such outrages. Instinctive is the conduct of the animal in approaching the bait that is set to trap him; and instinctive also his flight if, when near the bait, he perceives signs, real or imaginary, of danger.

1219. The only inference that can be drawn from all that is that non-logical actions play a great part in social life and that sometimes they produce an evil, and then again the remedy for it.

1220. V-β: *Sentiments of equality in inferiors.* This sentiment is often a defence of integrity on the part of an individual belonging to a lower class and a means of lifting him to a higher. That takes place without any awareness, on the part of the individual experiencing the sentiment, of the difference between his real and his apparent purposes. He talks of the interest of his social class instead of his own personal interest simply because that is a fashionable mode of expression.

1221. Striking tendencies arise from the very character of this sentiment, and at first glance they might seem to be contradictory. On the one hand there is a tendency to make the largest possible number of persons share in the advantages that the individual asks for himself. On the other, there is a tendency to restrict that number as far as possible. The contradiction disappears the moment we consider that the tendency is to admit to the advantages all whose cooperation helps one towards obtaining them, so that their intro-

licence to commit crimes at pleasure from hysterical furies who gloated over the things they did. Meantime what the Government actually did was to take steps not to put said females in prison but to station firemen at the hydrants day and night that they might be ready wherever fires started by the suffragettes broke out.

duction yields more in profits than it costs; and to exclude all who do not help, or help less effectively, so that their participation costs more than it yields. Similarly, in a war it is a good thing to have as many soldiers as possible for the fighting, and as few as possible for the division of the spoils. Demands for equality almost always conceal demands for privileges.

1222. There is another apparent contradiction. Inferiors wish to be the equals of their superiors, but they will not allow their superiors to be their equals. From the logical standpoint two contradictory propositions cannot be true at the same time. If $A = B$, it follows necessarily that $B = A$. But the contradiction disappears on reflection that the demand for equality is nothing but a disguised manner of demanding a privilege. The member of one class who demands equality for that class with some other really intends to win it a privilege as compared with the other. If the proposition $A = B$ really means that $A > B$, it is in no way contradictory—in fact, it is the perfection of logic—to go on and say that $B < A$. People agitate for equality to get equality in general, and then go on to make countless numbers of distinctions to deny it in the particular. Equality is to belong to all—but it is granted only to the few.[1]

1223. The Athenians set surpassing store on being equals before the law—*ἰσόνομοι*, as they said—and they sang the praises of Harmodius and Aristogiton who had made them so. But that equality did not extend to foreigners or resident aliens or even to persons of whose parents only the father was a citizen. Among the citizens themselves it was by no means considered contrary to equality that the poor should oppress the rich. Citizens of Sparta who enjoyed full rights were the Equals, the *ὅμοιοι*, but in reality they constituted an aristocracy of very limited numbers, which were constantly decreasing. The bare fact that a person was not rich enough to partake of the communal repast deprived him of status as an Equal. Among the peoples of our day equality of all human beings is an article of faith; but that does not preclude great differences, in

1222 [1] Pareto, *Manuale*, Chap. I, § 50.

Italy and France, between "union" and "non-union" working-men, between plain citizens and citizens who have "influence" with Deputies, Senators, "grand electors" (local bosses), and the like. Before handing down decisions, judges look well to see with just whom they are dealing. There are gaming-resorts that the police dare not enter, because they would be sure to find law-makers and other important persons there. How many prominent people in Italy carry knives with blades more than four inches long? That privilege is denied (by an utterly fatuous piece of legislation) to plain citizens, but not to people who belong to the political aristocracy or enjoy its protection. So in a day gone by it was legal for the nobleman to carry arms, not so for serf or villein.[1]

1224. Such things are known to everybody. That in fact is why no attention is paid to them, why if some Simple Simon ventured to complain of them, people would laugh at him as at someone complaining of the weather. Yet that does not prevent them from believing, in all good faith, that they are enjoying equality. There are hotels in certain places in the United States where a person cannot have his boots polished because it is an offence against Holy Equality for one person to polish another's boots. But the very people who cherish that lofty doctrine of equality are eager to expel the Chinese and Japanese from the United States; are disgusted at the very thought of a Japanese schoolboy sitting at a desk near child of theirs; will not allow a Negro to be accommodated at a hotel that they frequent, or ride in a railway coach which has the honour of transporting them. The thing would seem incredible if it were not true—but there are those among these fierce believers in Holy Equality who

1223 [1] In *La Ragione,* June 16, 1911, the Italian Deputy, Pio Viazzi, writes: "Is it not a matter of common knowledge that every [Italian] court has its privileged attorney, who is called the 'prince,' usually the shrewdest intriguer in the lot? He is the lawyer who monopolizes the wealthiest clients, is unfailingly resourceful in securing last-minute evidence, is friends with all the judges, gets postponements that are denied to others; whose questionable witticisms in open court meet with considerate smiles, and whose clients always receive a benevolent consideration that is never useless even when it is not altogether unfair and iniquitous." [A magnificent portrait of such a person is drawn in the character named Malaguzzi, in Guglielmo Ferrero's *La terza Roma* (The Seven Vices), Vol. I.—A. L.]

hold that Jesus died to redeem all men (and they call them "brethren in Christ"), and who give their mite to missionaries to go out and convert people in Africa and Asia, yet who refuse to worship their God in an American church to which a Negro is admitted.[1]

1225. Both European and American democracies profess to be founded on principles of thorough-going equality between human beings. But the equality is strictly for men, not for women. "One man, one vote," cry our fanatics; and they hide their faces in holy horror if someone remarks that the vote of the educated man should not be equal to the vote of the illiterate, the vote of the delinquent to the vote of the honest citizen, the vote of the ne'er-do-well to the vote of the useful citizen. There must be perfect equality, because all human beings are equal. But that fine principle is forgotten when it is a question of women. By a neat trick of sleight-of-hand, equality of human beings becomes equality of males, nay, of certain males. The very persons who regard the principle of universal suffrage as a dogma above discussion, superior to every consideration of expediency or convenience, deny suffrage to women on grounds of expediency and convenience; because, they say, votes for women would strengthen clerical or conservative parties.

1226. We are not concerned here with the social utility of such measures. It may be great even if the arguments with which people try to support them are absurd. Then again, it may be nil. Just here we are examining these reasonings merely with reference to the sentiments that inspire them. If the reasonings are patently false but are nevertheless approved and accepted, the fact cannot be due to their logical force but simply to the strength of the sentiments that they hide. That is the fact which it is so important to grasp.

1227. The sentiment that is very inappropriately named equality is fresh, strong, alert, precisely because it is not, in fact, a sentiment of equality and is not related to any abstraction, as a few naïve "in-

1224 [1] In 1911 the United States repudiated a commercial treaty with Russia because the Russian Government was denying right of entry to Jews carrying American passports. That was regarded as an offence against equality. But the United States refuses entry to many Asiatics who are Russian subjects—and that is not at all an offence against equality!

tellectuals" still believe; but because it is related to the direct interests of individuals who are bent on escaping certain inequalities not in their favour, and setting up new inequalities that will be in their favour, this latter being their chief concern.

1228. The residues we still have to consider, the V-γ and V-δ varieties, have one trait in common, the following: Integrity having been somehow altered, the effort is to restore it, if possible, or else to obtain compensations for the alteration. If the restoration is effected by acts pertaining to the individuals who have suffered alteration in integrity, we get the V-γ variety, which subdivides into two species, V-γ1, where the subject is real, and V-γ2, where the subject is imaginary. If the restoration is effected by acts pertaining to the agent of the alteration, we get our V-δ variety, which subdivides into the species V-δ1 where the agent is real, and V-δ2 where the agent is imaginary.

1229. V-γ: *Restoration of integrity by acts pertaining to the individuals whose integrity has been impaired.* This variety embraces the purifications that were so generally used in ancient societies and which are still common among uncivilized or barbarous peoples. They have virtually or completely disappeared in the civilized societies of our day; and for that reason we might content ourselves with a bare mention of them, were it not that they provide excellent illustrations of the manner in which residues act and blossom out into derivations. Knowledge of them therefore helps indirectly to an understanding of similar phenomena and we are tempted to dwell on them at some little length here.

1230. The subject is a very complicated one; and it will help if we draw a few distinctions. We must consider the various cases first of all (*a*) from the standpoint of the persons or things, real or imaginary, that figure in them—that is to say, from the objective standpoint; and second (*b*), from the standpoint of the attitudes or feelings of the persons who participate in operations of purification or restoration of integrity—that is to say, from the subjective standpoint.

1231. *a: Objective standpoint.* Here three distinctions are in order:

1. *The subjects undergoing the alteration.* Here again a number of aspects present themselves:

Character of the subjects. They may be real or imaginary, a fact that yields our subdivision of the genus into the species V-γ1 and V-γ2. Further to be considered would be subjects that are abstractions of real subjects, for example, "the family," "the nation," and the like; but to avoid complicating our outline unnecessarily we shall consider them "unreal" and include them under species V-γ2. Someone accustomed to considering conduct from the logical point of view might imagine that the concept of alterations in integrity was first applied to human beings and then extended either by analogy or through group-persistence to things, abstractions, imaginary beings. But we have no proof of any such development, which may have occurred in certain cases and not in others. The development, furthermore, may sometimes have been in the opposite direction, the concept being carried over from things to people. But leaving origins aside and attending strictly to interdependences in facts, it seems obvious enough that analogy and group-persistence serve to maintain alterations of integrity in people, things, and abstract or imaginary beings in homogeneous masses; and it may often be said that, for those reasons, the concept of alteration passes back and forth from one such subject to another. Since the human being is the principal concern with human beings, it is understandable that the usual course is from the human being to other sorts of subjects. "Real" subjects would be human beings, animals, plants, things, buildings, cities, territories, societies, and groups such as armies, families, nations, and the like. They are exceedingly numerous and variegated.

Extension in space. Even here, without meaning to imply anything as to origins, we may say that the human being frequently appears as a nucleus in the various concepts, the alteration extending from him to the various groups of which he is assumed to form a part. Notable among such groups are the family, blood-relationships more or less far-reaching, ethnical groups, such as the tribe, the city, the nation, even the whole "human race." Group-persistences are of such effect that the individuals composing the groups are not alone considered, but the groups themselves acquire independent individuality. Alterations of integrity often follow the opposite course, being carried over from the group to individuals. Among many peoples non-logical feeling makes a unit of the family, which continues to figure as a unit in logical or pseudo-logical derivations. This trait, which was general among our Graeco-Latin ancestors, is still very conspicuous in Chinese society. That fact stands in close relation with another—the fact of "family responsibility," and with strange phenomena such as the Hebrew "levirate" or the Greek "epiclerate," whereby, within the limits of the possible, the integrity of an individual without offspring is restored, and the integrity of his posterity, or rather of the group that is called "the family," is maintained.

Extensions to animals, inanimate objects, and abstract or imaginary beings. The direct course, from the human being to these entities, is the usual one; but there are cases of the opposite. All such entities may be taken as persons and undergo alterations of integrity.

Extensions in time. This cannot fail to occur when the alteration is not materially subsistent at the moment of the restoration. The two operations being successive, it is implicitly assumed that the subject is continuous (§ 1055). If a man does penance for a sin that he has himself committed, it is taken for granted that the person who has sinned and the person who does the penance are one and the same. But extension in time takes place in many other situations. Alteration and restoration are extended in the direction of ancestry and in the direction of posterity. The former direction is preferred by the Chinese, the second by Europeans. Pushed to its extreme limit, the extension to posterity gives rise to the concept of original sin (§ 1288). Another extension in time oversteps the confines of earthly life, and we get such beliefs as metempsychosis, Nirvana, punishment or recompense for the souls of the dead, redemption, and so on.

2. *Alteration.* This may also be real or imaginary. It may be a material alteration, or a purely conceptual affair. The remarks just made on extensions in space and time apply to it.

Manners of transmitting the alteration. Transmission may result from contact; from certain relationships between the subjects involved—descent, for instance; from acts having effects now real, now imaginary. Ordinarily, thanks to group-persistences, notions and concepts applying to real manners of transmission are carried over to the imaginary.

3. *Means of alteration and restoration.* These too may be real or imaginary. The residues of combination interpose to supply an immense variety of practices that are deemed capable of altering integrity, and an even greater abundance of rites deemed suitable for restoring integrity—among them, magical practices and all sorts of religious rites. Partisans of logical conduct usually give first importance to the means and believe that the purifications take place by virtue of certain reasonings. Those who are aware of the important rôle played by non-logical conduct in human life give first prominence to sentiments, consider means as subordinate, and realize that reasonings are just cloaks for the sentiments that inspire the purification rites (§ 1239). Choice of means may be of great importance from the standpoint of social utility. The ancients purified themselves in times of epidemic with frequent baths, people in the Middle Ages with religious processions and penances, remaining in the same untold filth as when they started. The two means were different cloaks for the same sentiment, but the first was beneficial to society, the second useless, and even harmful, in view of the contacts between the healthy and the sick in the processions, and the violations of sound hygiene involved in the penances! [1]

1231 [1] A legendary episode that is typical of many historic cases of purification is mentioned in the *Iliad,* I, vv. 313-14. A pestilence was raging in the Greek camp. "The son of Atreus bade them purify themselves. They did so, throwing the filth into the sea." Eustathius remarks on the passage, *Commentarii,* Vol. I, p. 90: "Purification means cleansing with ablutions. And this among the ancients was

1232. There are a few considerations that apply in common to all the distinctions just made. For all of them we find real cases historically well authenticated. Not only may a man suffer material alterations of integrity, but he may suffer alteration in his reputation, and not only as an individual, but as a member of certain groups. Extension of alteration to the family becomes a fact when there are laws to impose it, but it may also take place without the interposition of any law. The man who gets rich brings prosperity to his family; the bankrupt, distress. There are hereditary diseases that visit the sins of parents upon their children. Peoples suffer from the mistakes of their rulers and gain by their wise policies. The means by which an alteration is transmitted *de facto* are not material only. The spoken word is a powerful instrument, and defamation may be worse than a bodily wound. The transition from the real to the imaginary is often imperceptible and cannot be accurately delineated even with the methods of modern science. There is still doubt, for instance, as to whether certain diseases are or are not hereditary, and doubts as to the manner of their transmission are far from being dissipated. It seems not to be true, as the Moslems think, that contact with a hog does any harm to a man. It is known,

a very appropriate expression, for the purifications were performed in connexion with sacrifices." And he continues: "Why into the sea? Because sea-water by its very nature is appropriate to washing. They threw the filth into the sea, where, it is said, there is no filth. Hence the proverb, 'The sea cleanseth men of all their ills.'" The proverb is a line in the *Iphigenia in Tauris* of Euripides, v. 1193 (Coleridge, Vol. II, p. 377). Diogenes Laertius, *Plato,* III, 6 (Hicks, Vol. I, p. 283), claims that the verse alludes to an incident in the life of Plato, who, falling ill in Egypt, whither he had gone with Euripides, was cured by some priests with sea-water. The whole scene in the *Iphigenia* is worth a reading, to see the way in which altogether fantastic notions are jumbled together with notions that might have some bearing on cleanliness or disgust at filth. Iphigenia declares, v. 1171, that the two strangers brought to her are defiled by murder of their mother and, v. 1177, she carries the image of the goddess out of doors to save it from contamination by contact with a murderer. She also says, v. 1191, that before she can sacrifice for them she must purify them. "At the fountain or in the water in the sea?" asks the King, v. 1192. It is then that Iphigenia replies that "sea-water cleanseth (washes) men of all their ills." Further along, v. 1199, she feels that she also has to "purify the image of the goddess." The King assents, v. 1200: "In truth, the stain of the matricide hath defiled it." That is not all. The two prisoners have to be veiled so as not to defile the sunlight, and to escape the same defilement no citizen must look upon them, and the King has to draw a veil over his eyes.

on the other hand, that rats are an important factor in spreading the bubonic plague. Beliefs, in the imaginary cases, might be attributed to observations presumably made in real cases; and that may sometimes have happened—but it is not to be accepted as the general rule, for it would oblige us to believe that human knowledge originated in rigorously logico-experimental science, which then proceeded to degenerate into imaginary beliefs. All known facts point to an opposite development. In the recipes that antiquity has bequeathed to us we find remedies that are really effective along with remedies that have no effect at all. It is certain that human beings did not first know the good remedies, then going on to apply the concept of efficacy to the bad ones. They devised them all hotchpotch, and in plenty of cases the bad ones came first, the good ones not being discovered till much later.

1233. Real cases contributed to engendering a general vaguely defined belief embracing the imaginary along with the real. That belief was strengthened both by observation of real cases and by supposed effects of imaginary cases, and also by certain instincts of repugnance to certain things—the origins of such instincts being as unknown as the origins of instincts in animals. Then derivations interfere on a lavish scale to enhance the complexity of the concrete phenomenon.

1234. *b: Subjective aspect.* As regards the sentiments of those who resort to restorations of integrity, we may distinguish: 1. The sense that the individual has of his own integrity and that of his dependents and possessions, with the various extensions in space and time above noted (§ 1231). 2. The feeling that if such integrity is impaired it may be restored. 3. The sentiments prompting the use of certain means to attain that end.

1235. Variability in such things increases from 1 to 3, while their importance as regards their bearing on the social equilibrium diminishes from 1 to 3. Let us look at them separately.

1. The sentiment of the alteration of integrity is at first vague, indistinct, as all such sentiments are. The different sorts of integrity, material, moral, political, and so on, are not distinguished or not

clearly distinguished. Nor are the integrities of the human being, the animal, and the thing clearly distinguished. Then gradually step by step the different kinds of integrity are recognized and give rise to various theories.

The same confusion exists as to the causes of alterations in integrity. At first little attention is paid to whether the cause lies in conduct on the part of those whose integrity has been altered or in the conduct of someone else. But those two cases are soon distinguished. Later on and with greater difficulty the voluntary cause is distinguished from the involuntary. In this latter consideration as to will or intent a trace of metaphysics figures.

1236. Other distinctions come to be made, and other forms of alteration are segregated. Important, for instance, the distinction between the permanent alteration and the temporary. The type of the permanent would be the stain on the murderer in Greece, in the days when he was required to purify himself; or the state of mortal sin in the Catholic. The type of the temporary would be the state of a person who lies under a spell, or of the Catholic tempted of the Devil.

1237. 2. The same confusions, and in due course the same distinctions, arise as to restoration of integrity. For example, taking the one extreme, restoration of integrity is exclusively a matter of external, mechanical acts (§ 1252), which may even be performed without the knowledge of the person who is to benefit by them. At the other extreme, restoration of integrity is exclusively a matter of inner voluntary acts on the part of the individual. In the intermediate cases, which are the commoner ones among civilized peoples, the restoration takes place by means of certain external, mechanical acts, supplemented by inner acts of will, with varying conceptions as to the relative importance of the respective types.

1238. 3. The sentiment that determines choice of means corresponds to the residues of combinations (Class I), which are fertile of no end of suggestions, the supply being further augmented by derivations. Sometimes there is a feeling that some means there must be, but what it is cannot be definitely determined. The purification then either is entrusted to some indeterminate act, or many different agencies are used in the hope that the good one may be among them.

1239. The forms of usage observed in purifications are of scant importance as regards the social equilibrium. Of great importance is the feeling that the violator of a rule, a taboo, suffers an alteration of integrity, and important also the feeling that the integrity can be restored. But after all, it matters very little whether the restoration be effected by touching a pewter plate (§ 1252 [1]), or in some other fashion. In the theory of logical conduct, that scale of importance is inverted. It is assumed that it is faith in the means that prompts people to the act of purification and inspires the sentiments involved in the rite (§ 1231).

1240. V-γ1: *Real subjects.*[1] The sense of integrity is among the most powerful sentiments human beings have. It has its roots in the instinct of self-preservation, though it radiates far afield from there. Often, also, alteration of integrity is felt instinctively and gives rise to concrete actions in numbers truly vast.

1241. What is known as "remorse" is a manifestation of the concept of altered integrity. The person who violates a certain norm that it has been his habit to observe feels ill at ease from that very fact. He is conscious of being somehow less than he was before. To escape from that painful state of mind, he looks about for some means of removing the stain, of restoring his former integrity; he finds it and he uses it. The rites that are used to escape the consequences of violating a taboo illustrate the situation in fairly simple form.

1242. When one insists on reducing everything to logical conduct, a sharp distinction is drawn between the remorse that follows violation of a norm of "true" morality or "true" religion and the remorse that follows transgression of a norm of "superstition." From the standpoint of non-logical conduct the two cases are identical. Every person, of course, believes his own morality the "true" moral-

1240 [1] In view of the complexity of the phenomena we shall have to make some mention of the next following residues (V-γ 2) in dealing with this species.

ity, his own religion the "true" religion.[1] The Moslem laughs at the Catholic's qualms at eating meat on Friday, and the Catholic laughs at the Moslem's remorse at grazing a hog with the hem of his garment. At them both laughs the atheistic teetotaller who cannot forgive himself a spoonful of wine. A case of remorse noted among the Australian aborigines has often been cited as something extraordinary, but substantially it is altogether on a par with the many remorses of civilized peoples.[2] Remorse, in part at least, is not a consequence of reasoning. It arises spontaneously, instinctively, from the feeling that a transgression has altered personal integrity. Many instances have been cited to show that dogs also feel remorse.

1243. What has been done cannot be undone, but one can meet one force with a counter-force of equal power and opposite tendency, so that the two will balance and effects will be neutralized. One fact can be counterpoised to another fact in such a way that the impression left by the second will cancel the impression left by the first. One can dry a man if he has been in the water, warm him if he has been out in the cold, clean him if he has been befouled. Through the persistence of abstractions these material acts, or others like them, are extended to the intellectual and moral sides of the human being, and there they sprout, leaf out, blossom, and yield a bounteous harvest of most variegated conduct.

1244. Integrity may be altered profoundly or just slightly, so that the restoration may involve regeneration of the whole personality

1242 [1] Brunet, *Les propos de table de Martin Luther,* p. 261: "Master Kinnick answered [to Luther]: 'If you say that the Holy Spirit is certainty of God, then all sectarians who have an unswerving certainty about their religion have the Holy Spirit.' Doctor Luther replied: 'They have no such certainty. Mohammed, the Papists, the sacramentalists, base their faith not on the Word of God, but on their personal convictions.'" All believers reason like that.

1242 [2] Sturt, *Two Expeditions into the Interior of Southern Australia,* Vol. II, p. 54: "The old men have alone the privilege of eating the emu; and so submissive are the young men to this regulation, that if, from absolute hunger or under other pressing circumstances, one of them breaks through it, either during a hunting excursion or whilst absent from his tribe, he returns under a feeling of conscious guilt and by his manner betrays his guilt, sitting apart from the men and confessing his misdemeanour to the chief at the first interrogation, upon which he is obliged to undergo a slight punishment."

or come down to a simple act serving to counterbalance another act defiling to him. The Catholic Church makes a distinction of that kind in its classification of sins as mortal or venial. An incantation alters the integrity of its victim but is not an indelible blemish, such as a murder committed by him would be. In general, but especially in cases of profound alterations, the restoration purports to restore the person to the state in which he was prior to the acts that have defiled him.

1245. The taint presumably contracted in such a manner may be considered as a material consequence of certain acts and therefore materially removable by certain other acts. Or, by the interposition of other residues or through derivations, the taint may depend on certain circumstances, among which oftentimes the intent of the person, and in that case too, identical or analogous circumstances have to be produced to remove the taint.

1246. So also to restore integrity strictly material instrumentalities may be used, exactly as though a material stain were to be removed. Then again, exclusively moral and intellectual means may do; [1] but in general the latter have to be supplemented by material agencies. Very very often an evolution seems to have taken place whereby material means have come to be supplemented by notions of a moral and intellectual character, these latter in the end coming to prevail exclusively, the material means figuring as mere symbols—something altogether secondary.[2] That gives rise to the common error of

1246 [1] St. Augustine, *De moribus ecclesiae catholicae et de moribus Manichaeorum,* I, 34, 76 (*Opera,* Vol. I, p. 1342; *Works,* Vol. V, p. 47): "Such as amend their ways of their own goodwill and with the help of God recover through repentance (penance) what they had lost through sin."

1246 [2] Oldenberg, *Religion des Veda,* pp. 317-18: "On the one hand . . . sin is a transgression of the will of the gods, which has provoked their wrath. The expiation, therefore, is addressed to them, it aims to satisfy and appease them. The suppliant brings them his gifts, humbles himself before them. But on the other hand, sin is a sort of fluid that sticks to the sinner like a glue. In that sense the expiatory rite involves magic practices calculated to dissolve the glue, destroy it, or remove it to a distance at which it can do no harm, so that the sinner is left free and pure again, much as a man reeking with sweat is relieved of his grime by a bath, or the way a feathered bird is freed of its egg. . . . This second point of view is not altogether inconsistent with a divine action. The elimination of the sinful matter may be conceived of not as the direct consequence of the incantation,

assuming that the material element has always been incidental, that it has never served any other purpose than to give external form to the moral and spiritual concept. Water removes material stains. It is therefore taken for granted that it can also remove moral stains.[3] Ordinarily used by human beings to remove material impurities, it becomes chief among the agencies for removing moral impurities. Water is now and again supplemented by other things, either actually or verbally, large numbers of combinations originating in Class I residues being available for the purpose.[4] Blood, sulphur, and

but as due to the power or ingenuity of the god whose succour has been invoked." The facts are well described. Some slight retouching would remove the inevitable varnish of logical processes.

1246 [3] Dubois, *Mœurs, institutions et cérémonies des peuples de l'Inde,* Vol. II, p. 257: "These hermits [the *vanaprasta*] made no distinction between soiling of soul and body. They were convinced that the soul communicated its stains to the body and *vice versa* and thought that the bath in washing the body also served to purify the soul, especially if the water came from the Ganges or from other reputedly sacred sources. Fire completed purification, and that was why the bodies of such penitents were burned when they departed this life."

1246 [4] First come the waters of springs, rivers, the sea. Philo the Jew wrote a whole book to explain just what victims could be offered according to the Jewish rite, which he regarded as an altogether rational rite but which, in point of fact, tallies in many respects with pagan rites. Says he, *De victimas offerentibus seu de sacrificantibus,* II (Cohn, Vol. V, pp. 40-41; Yonge, Vol. III, p. 212): "The victim must be whole, entirely free from blemish, of select quality approved by the unbiased judgment of the priests and by their critical scrutiny. [Pagan rules, as well.] . . . This is not a senseless rule, but accords with intelligence and reason. However, care must be exercised with regard not only to the victims but also to the sacrificial priests, to the end that they [the sacrifices] be not vitiated by any untoward circumstance. Indeed, as I have said, let him [the priest] purify his body with baths and aspersions, and once bathed and sprinkled, let him not venture beyond the precincts of the Temple even once, save he be commanded to remain without for seven days. . . . Almost all perform their ablutions with pure water, many with sea-water, some few with river-water, others still with spring-water fetched in jars." Just such aspersions were customary among the pagans. See Pollux, *Onomasticon,* I, 1, 8 (Dindorf, Vol. I, p. 5, and see note, Vol. IV, p. 18), and Hesychius, *Lexicon, s.v.* Δάλιον. The Ebionites, says St. Epiphanius, *Panarium adversus haereses, lib.* I, *tomus* II, *Haeresis* 30, § 2 (*Opera,* Vol. I, p. 407), were like the Samaritan Jews in that "every time they come into contact with some foreigner and every time they have commerce with a woman and have left her, they wash themselves with water, either sea-water or some other, according to the supply at hand. But if after they have so immersed themselves in water and washed themselves they chance to encounter any thing of evil omen, they hasten back and wash themselves over again, often in their clothes." Of the priests in Egypt, Plutarch says, *De solertia animalium,* XX, 4

other things have also been used in purifications. Interesting the extension of the idea of purification in the belief that the Flood was a purification of the Earth.[5]

1247. Among many ancient peoples material and moral taints, whether resulting from voluntary or from involuntary acts, were regarded as all on a par. Spots equally black result from uncleanness or crime, from homicide deliberate or accidental, from the impurity of childbirth in the case of a woman, or the impurity of guilt.

(Reiske, Vol. X, p. 57), that "to purify themselves they use water of which the ibis will drink, since the ibis will not touch water that has been polluted or is otherwise unwholesome." The Romans made extensive use of river (running) water: Virgil, *Aeneid* II, v. 719: *"donec me flumine vivo abluero"* ("till I shall have cleansed myself in a living (running) stream"). Servius remarks (Thilo-Hagen, Vol. I, p. 323): *"Flumine vivo:* That never dries up (*perenni*). It is a term used in augury." IV, v. 635: *"Dic corpus properet fluviali spargere lympha."* ("Tell her to make haste and sprinkle her body with river-water.") Servius annotates (Thilo-Hagen, Vol. I, p. 574): *"Spargere lympha:* In sacrificing to the nether gods, they sprinkled themselves with water," as also in VI, v. 230: *Spargens rore levi et ramo felicis olivae* ("Sprinkling light dew with a branch of the propitious olive"). So too they purified themselves in sacrificing to the gods of heaven, as in II, v. 719: *Donec me flumine vivo abluero.* However, just here he is sacrificing to the nether gods, as witness: *Sacra Iovi Stygio."* And *cf.* VI, vv. 635-36: *"Occupat Aeneas aditum corpusque recenti Spargit aqua."* ("Aeneas gains the threshold and sprinkles his body with fresh water.") Servius annotates (Thilo-Hagen, Vol. II, pp. 88-89): *"Recenti:* ever flowing. . . . *Spargit aqua:* Cleanses himself, as having been defiled either by his glimpse of Tartarus, or his hearing (*auditu*) of crimes and punishments. *Spargit:* because purifying for the nether gods." Ovid, *Fasti,* IV, v. 778: *"Et*

1246 [5] John Spencer, *De legibus Hebraeorum ritualibus,* Vol. II, Bk. III, § 2, pp. 783-84: "Generally current in a day gone by was the opinion that the Flood was no less than a great catharsis of the World, which God had sent that He might cleanse the land and wash away and make amends for the taint it had suffered (*haustam*) from the impure morals of earthly inhabitants. The ancient Hebrews, the philosophers, and not a few Christians clung stubbornly to that view. That the notion had its supporters among the ancient Hebrews may be legitimately inferred from the language used by Philo [? *De confusione linguarum,* 7]: 'When therefore the Supreme Creator decided to purge the earth with water . . .' That Christians were imbued with the same belief is evident from Origen, *Contra Celsum,* IV (Augsburg, p. 179; Latin, p. 177), when he says: 'I know not why Celsus thinks the overthrowing of a tower is like the Flood, with which Christians and Jews alike assert that the Earth was purged.' Origen, *Ibid.,* VI (Augsburg, p. 325; Latin, p. 320), likewise bears witness that philosophers were of that opinion: 'The destruction of the human race by the Flood was a purification of the Earth, as altogether reputable philosophers among the Greeks relate, in the words: 'When the gods bring on a flood to purge the lands with water' (Plato, *Timaeus,* 22)."

The material taint may arise from real uncleanliness, but also and just as well from imaginary. The taint contracted by an individual may extend, by contact or otherwise, to other persons, things, abstractions.[1]

in vivo perlue rore manus" ("Wash thy hands in living (fresh) dew"), and *Fasti,* V, vv. 431-35: "*Ille memor veteris ritus . . . Terque manus puras fontana perluit unda.*" ("Observant of the ancient rite . . . he thrice washes his hands clean in spring-water.") Propertius, *Elegiae,* III, 10, vv. 12-13, says to his beloved: "*Surge et poscentes iusta precare deos, Ac primum pura somnum tibi discute lympha.*" ("Rise and pray the gods who seek their proper due, but first banish sleep from thine eyes with pure water.") In *Ibid.,* III, 3, v. 51, Calliope sprinkles the poet with water from a spring. Tibullus, *Nemesis,* I, vv. 11-14, is speaking of the lustration of the fields, according to the ancient rite handed down from the forefathers:

> "*Vos quoque abesse procul iubeo: discedat ab aris*
> *cui tulit hesterna gaudia nocte Venus;*
> *casta placent superis: pura cum veste venite*
> *et manibus puris sumite fontis aquam.*"

("You also I bid depart! Away from these altars, you who last night enjoyed the pleasures of Venus. The gods love the chaste! Come with clean garments and in clean hands gather up the water in the spring.") In the *Argonautica,* III, v. 1030, of Apollodorus, Medea advises Jason to "wash himself in the living current of a river." The Greeks used sea-water also: *cf.* Aristophanes, *Plutus,* vv. 656-57, where Carius leads Plutus to the sea to purify him. And the scholiast remarks (Dübner, pp. 361, 577): "It was the custom of the ancients to purify there [in the sea] such as needed purification." Pausanias, *Periegesis,* IX, 20, *Boeotia,* 20, 4 (Dindorf, p. 459), says that the women of Tanagra bathed in the sea in celebrating the mysteries of Dionysus. To get lustral water, salt was sometimes added to fresh water, or burning brands were extinguished in it: *cf.* the scholiast of Aristophanes, *Pax,* v. 959 (Dübner, pp. 200, 475): ". . . since fire is good for purifying all things, as Euripides says in the *Heraclidae,* v. 928" ("His body burnt by the fire's fierce flame": Coleridge, Vol. I, p. 179). Besides fire, sulphur, tar, and like substances were used: Ovid, *Metamorphoses,* VII, v. 261: "*Terque senem flamma, ter aqua, ter sulfure lustrat.*" ("Thrice he sprinkles the old man with fire, thrice with water, thrice with sulphur.") Theocritus, *Idyllia,* XXIV, vv. 94-98 (Edmonds, p. 295): "But first purify the house with fire of pure sulphur. Then, as the custom is, place a crown on thine head and take a green branch and sprinkle about with pure water mingled with salt. Then sacrifice a male swine to Zeus the Most High." And *cf. Odyssey,* XXII, vv. 481-82; XXIII, v. 50. The custom of mingling ashes with water was also wide-spread (§ 1266). The well-known cult of springs and rivers may have had some connexion with the purifying properties ascribed to their waters. As late as Nero's time it was believed that the gods punished anyone failing of respect to springs. Tacitus, *Annales,* XIV, 22, 6, relates that Nero took a bath in the springs of the Aqua Marcia. That was considered a profanation "and a sickness [with which he was smitten] bore witness to the wrath of the gods."

1247 [1] Speaking in general terms, human beings show an extensive class of non-logical actions relating to cleanliness, quite similar to the instinct for cleanliness in

1248. Ordinarily concepts of alteration of integrity depend directly upon sentiments, and have only an indirect bearing on utilities of individuals and society—and that, indeed, by way of the sentiments. Those two manners of considering alterations of integrity are there-

certain animals. Pigeons, for example, wash every day, and the cat is for ever cleaning its fur. Such actions in human beings at times present fetishistic traits, as is usual with many other non-logical actions. Close kin to them are other actions that are similar in forms and appearances, or else are prompted by one derivation or another, but which have nothing to do with cleanliness. Well-bred people in civilized countries take baths in the morning, and that is a simple act of cleanliness. With the ancients the same act takes on a religious character. Virgil, *Aeneid,* VIII, vv. 67-70: On awakening Aeneas scoops water from the river in the hollow of his hands: *"Undam de flumine palmis sustulit."* Servius explains (Thilo-Hagen, Vol. II, p. 209): "Because night is said to pollute by the mere fact of sleeping. So Persius [*Saturae,* II, v. 16]: *Et noctem flumine purgat."* ("He washes the night away in the river.") (Actually the line in Persius reads *purgas* for *purgat.*) But then we find another notion creeping in that has nothing to do with cleanliness: *Aeneid,* IV, 6: *"Postera Phoebea lustrabat lampade terras."* ("The next day was purifying the Earth with the Phoebean lamp.") Servius explains (Thilo-Hagen, Vol. I, p. 461): "Purifying, because the night had somehow polluted the world." The Jews believed that the night spoiled the water in sacred vessels: Mishnah, Tract Yoma, III, 10 (Danby, pp. 165-66); Surenhuis, *Mischna,* Vol. II, p. 224 (comment by Sheringham): "It is a tradition of the Hebrews also that water in a sacred vessel is polluted by the night: and since the laver was a sacred vessel, they resorted to a device [So Danby; ? *machinam*] so that the water would not have to stay in the laver overnight. Maimonides in *Hilcoth Beth Habbechira:* 'They used a device (? *machinam*) to hold the water that was to be kept for any length of time (*iugiter*), and it was built outside the Temple (*prophana erat*) so that the water in it should not be polluted by the night; for the laver was a sacred vessel and sanctified [its contents]; but anything sanctified in a holy vessel is polluted if it is kept overnight.' . . . It is stated in the Gemara (commentaries) (*Sevachim,* f. 19) that the hands are polluted by the night . . . and therefore the Talmudists assert that it is lawful for priests to wash their hands and feet on leaving the Temple; but all the same when they return the next day they have to wash [again] even if they have not slept during the night . . . because the hands are polluted by the night." Surenhuis believes that the Jews took this superstition over from the Gentiles—the usual mistake of regarding products of the same sentiment as imitations (§§ 733 f.). Jews and Gentiles alike had other types of impurity, some of which at least may be connected with cleanliness. Leprosy was "unclean" among the Jews. That may be taken as something similar to the control of contagious diseases among modern peoples. Contact with dead bodies was "unclean." That prescription may have served to avert dangers of poisoning by toxins, or otherwise have been thought of as a measure of hygiene; however the notion had altogether fantastic embellishments. One might be tempted to pass the ascription of impurity to women in childbirth as a measure of hygiene; but when the Bible (Lev. 12:2) ascribes seven days of impurity to a woman who has a male child, and fourteen days (*Ibid.,* 12:5) if the child is a girl, any ra-

fore radically different. When phenomena are taken synthetically and first prominence is given to considerations of ethics or social utility, not only are there great differences but there is actual antithesis between phenomena that appear similar from the standpoint of residues and derivations. Thus from the botanical standpoint, parsley (*Carum petroselinum*) and the classic "hemlock"—("fool's parsley": *Aethusa cynapium*), are closely kindred species of the Umbelliferae; whereas from the medical or hygienic standpoint they have opposite properties, the former being a condiment, the latter a poison.

1249. In the Gospel according to St. Mark, 7:3 f., the Pharisees meet Jesus with the reproach that His disciples did not wash their hands before eating, as was the custom of all Jews. But Jesus answers them, and then explains to the disciples that not material things make a man unclean, but moral things such as evil thoughts, adultery, unchasteness, murder, and the like. For many many centuries Christians have plumed themselves on their ideal religion as contrasted with the material religion of the Jews, without observing that over bypaths devious they went back to the very practices which they laid to the charge of the Pharisees; and Catholics have believed, and still believe, that eating meat on Friday brings defilement upon a man, exactly as the Pharisees believed that one incurred a taint by partaking of food without first washing one's hands. Such the power of residues that they bring opposite doctrines to the same point, and such the power of derivations that few are they who are aware of the inconsistency! Jesus said (Mark 7:15): "There is nothing from without a man that entering into him can defile him; but the things which come out of him, those are they that defile him." It would be difficult to speak more clearly, and the further explanation Jesus gives to the disciples dispels any doubt whatever. And yet Catholics believe that meat, which surely is "without a man," defiles him if it is eaten on Friday and that certain rites are required

tional consideration of hygiene fails to explain the difference. Other forms of "uncleanness" we had better mention in Latin: *"Immundities menstruatae; concubitus coniugalis; somni seminis fluxum procurantes; ex alvo aut vesica levata."*

to cleanse him of the taint. And there are no end of derivations to show that there is not the slightest contradiction between the Saviour's declaration that nothing that is without a man can defile him by entering into him and the doctrine that the meat which he eats on Friday leaves him tainted. This is one of the many cases in which it is apparent that as regards their bearing on the social equilibrium residues far surpass derivations in importance. Residues are very very hard to modify. Derivations are stretched to any length required, like rubber bands.

1250. The case just noted in the Gospel of St. Mark is a particular case of a phenomenon that is general. When the residue of restoration of integrity is functioning alone, or virtually so, exclusively material agencies for restoring integrity may be accepted. But then other residues from the class of group-persistences come into play. In deference to them it is customary to regard individuals possessing certain traits as of a higher order; and that sentiment is shocked when material agencies of purification or other agencies lift to the higher order individuals not possessing the qualities which the persisting sensation associates with that order. Diogenes well expressed the feeling when he said:[1] "It is ridiculous that Agesilaus and Epaminondas should be left in the mire, while an abject rabble of initiates get to the Isles of the Blest."[2]

1250 [1] Diogenes Laertius, *Diogenes,* VI, 39 (Hicks, Vol. II, p. 41).

1250 [2] Plutarch, *De auditu poetarum,* IV (19), 21 (Babbitt, Vol. I, p. 113), reports the same remark in a different text. In question are the lines of Sophocles [*Fragmenta,* 58, 8, Musgrave, Vol. II, p. 274]: "Thrice blessèd they to whom it hath been given to be initiate [to the Eleusinian mysteries] ere they come to Hades, for they are they that alone shall live! The rest shall suffer all manner of evil." Then Plutarch quotes the comment of Diogenes as follows: "What? Because he is an initiate the thief Pataecion shall be better off after death than Epaminondas?" Diogenes Laertius, *Diogenes,* VI, 42 (Hicks, Vol. II, p. 45), relates of Diogenes that "seeing an individual purifying himself with water, he exclaimed: 'O unhappy man! Know you not that as you could not wash away a mistake in grammar with a purification, neither can you wash away a mistake in living?'" Euripides was conscious of the conflict between the ancient formalistic religion and the newer rationalism. He makes Iphigenia say of Artemis, *Iphigenia in Tauris,* vv. 380-86 (Coleridge, Vol. II, p. 350): "I approve not the wilful prescriptions of the goddess. If some mortal be defiled by a murder or by touching a corpse or a woman in childbed, she bars him from her altar as unclean. Yet she delights in human sacrifices! Latona, consort of Zeus, can in no way be guilty of such a stupidity!" And

1251. In the examples following, to avoid cumbersome and useless repetitions we shall consider cancellations of taints and agencies of cancellation together; but the reader will have no difficulty in keeping the two things separate in his mind.

1252. The violator of a taboo experiences sensations of degradation, fear. He rids himself of them—he restores his integrity—by performing certain acts (§ 1481). Sometimes violations of taboos are counterbalanced by certain mechanical acts devoid of any moral content.[1] That is one type. Bring in other residues and especially derivations, and other types in very large numbers result. The absence of any moral element, or at least of the moral element involved in repentance, in a resolve not to do wrong again, is char-

stupid it is, in fact, from the logical standpoint. But that sentiment is posterior to the sentiment which combines non-logical actions as simple acts of fetishism without any resort to logic whatever.

1252 [1] Domeny de Rienzi, *Océanie,* Vol. III, pp. 53-54: In the Tonga Islands, "any person who lays hands on a chief of higher rank is taboo, but the interdiction has no serious consequences if the *moë-moë* is used." He must perform that rite "before he can use his hands to eat. The ceremony consists of pressing first the flat of the hand, then the back of the hand, against the sole of the foot of a ranking chief, then in washing the hands in water or rubbing them with banana or plantain leaves. Then he can eat in all security. Anyone so unfortunate as to have eaten with tabooed hands must go and sit down in front of a chief, pick up the latter's foot, and press it against his stomach. That is to prevent the food he has eaten from doing him any harm. Otherwise his body would swell up and certain death ensue. Taboo is incurred also by eating in the presence of a relative of higher rank without turning one's back, and also by eating food a chief has handled. If taboo has resulted from touching the person or garments of the *toui-tonga,* he alone can remit the penalty, for there is no chief as high as he. For that purpose he keeps near his door a pewter plate which Captain Cook gave him as a present. It is sufficient to touch the plate to be freed of the taboo." In that the influence of combination residues (Class I) is apparent enough. The pewter plate reached the Tonga Islands long after the taboo had been established. It could therefore have had nothing to do with the original taboo. But it was a remarkable and precious object and so made its way into the rites (§ 922). Interestingly, theft too was regarded as a violation of the taboo, "and since it is thought that sharks attack thieves in preference to honest people, suspects are forced to bathe in waters infested by sharks, and if they are bitten or eaten they are adjudged guilty." Those savages regard a taboo as violated by eating certain foods, and also by stealing, and certain rites are in order. Catholics think it a sin to eat certain foods on certain days, and also to steal, and certain rites are in order. The native Tongan goes to his chief, the Catholic to his priest. For the Tongan, there are cases that have to go before the highest chief. For the Catholic there are cases with which only the Pope can deal.

acteristic in anticipatory purifications that are performed in advance of the act which they are designed to counterbalance. The prayer to Mercury that Ovid ascribes to the Roman merchants, imploring the god to absolve them of past and future sins, would, if authentic, be an example of an anticipatory purification.[2] The Catholic Church does not permit absolutions of future sins,[3] but it has its difficulties with an instinct in its faithful that inclines them to ascribe effectiveness to the material acts of Catholic worship independently of any moral element.

1253. At a certain period in Greece a custom of purifying homicide, voluntary or involuntary, comes to the fore. Let us not speculate here as to whether the custom was native to Greece or came from other countries. Certainly there is no trace of it in Homer, but that is not enough to solve the problem. At a later period, in any event, the custom is general. It is a question, at that time, of certain acts which have to be performed by some person other than the murderer. The person need not, necessarily, be the priest of a god, but neither can he be chosen at random. He had to be, it would seem, a person of prominence. The taint follows on the slaying automatically, regardless of the circumstances under which it occurs,

1252 [2] *Fasti*, V, vv. 681-88:

> " '*Ablue praeteriti periuria temporis,' inquit*
> *'Ablue praeteritae perfida verba die.*
> *Sive ego te feci testem falsove citavi*
> *non audituri numina magna Iovis,*
> *sive Deum prudens alium Divamve fefelli,*
> *abstulerint celeres improba dicta Noti,*
> *et pereant veniente die periuria nobis:*
> *nec curent superi si qua locutus ero.*' "

(" 'Purge me,' he said, 'of the pledges I have broken in the past, purge me of the deceits of a bygone day. If I falsely have called thee to witness or invoked the great divinity of Jove (who will not hear anyhow) (Frazer: "in the hope that he would not hear"), or if knowingly I have cheated any other god or goddess, let the swift winds waft my evil words away. And may the false oaths I shall tomorrow swear be not charged to my account (*pereant*). May the gods above ignore them, if I chance to utter them.' ")

1252 [3] Dante, *Inferno,* XXVII, vv. 118-20: "For not absolved can be one who repents not. Nor both at once can one repent and will, Because a contradiction there consents not" (Fletcher).

even if the provocation is deemed legitimate. In that we get the restoration residue in a pure form. Herodotus, *Historiae,* I, 35, tells of a man who came to Croesus to be purified: "Having come to the house of Croesus he begged him to purify him according to the rite of the land. Croesus did so, rites of purification being similar among Lydians and Greeks." Not till the ceremonies are over does it occur to Croesus to ask: "Who art thou, man, and from what part of Phrygia comest thou whom my hearth receiveth? What man or what woman hast thou slain?" The mechanical automatic character of the rite is strikingly apparent in this case. Whoever the man, whatever the murder, and be it a merit or a crime, it is all the same—the purification has to be vouchsafed, and it is performed in the same way in any event. The Phrygian gives his name, his father's, his grandfather's, and adds: "Unintentionally slew I my brother." So involuntary homicide, like voluntary homicide, leaves its taint. Herodotus, notice, makes no mention of the gods; their interference is a subsequent adjunct along with new residues clustering about the basic residue. In the *Bibliotheca* of Apollodorus, I, 9, 24 (Frazer, Vol. I, p. 115), for the Argonauts to know that they are being persecuted by the wrath of Zeus for the slaying of Absyrtus, their ship has to speak and warn them, with the further admonition that the persecution will not end till they have been purified by Circe. Apollodorus then remarks as naturally as can be: "They went to Circe as suppliants, and she purified them."

1254. Apollonius of Rhodes gives the particulars of the purification, *Argonautica,* IV, vv. 585-709, probably following ancient traditions, which he tries to embellish with logical explanations, bringing in Zeus. At first the Argonauts suffer many hardships at sea, exactly as happens to a violator of a taboo who has not been purified. Finally their ship, the *Argos,* speaks up, to the purport that "they should not escape long wanderings and great storms unless Circe should purify them of the cruel slaughter of Absyrtus." They reach Circe's isle after a difficult voyage. Jason and Medea go up to the palace of the goddess and sit down before the hearth according to the custom of suppliants, without uttering a word. Jason drives the weapon with which he had slain Absyrtus into the ground, whereat Circe understands what is being asked of her. She offers a prayer to "the Justice of Zeus of the Suppliants," and then performs, with ablutions, the sacrifices whereby, along with the ablutions, unclean suppliants are purified when they come and sit at her hearth. First she places an expiatory victim on the altar, a suckling pig, cuts its throat and sprinkles their hands with its blood.[1] And then she purifies them again with other libations, calling on the name of "Zeus the Purifier, who hearkeneth to prayers in appeasement of blood that hath been shed."

1255. Apollodorus seems to think of purifications as normal procedures after homicide. The daughters of Danaus who slew the sons of Egyptus are purified by Athena and Hermes, as representatives of Zeus (II, 1, 5; Frazer, Vol. I, p. 143). Heracles slays his children in a fit of madness and is purified by Thestius (II, 4, 12; Frazer, p. 183). He also has to be purified after slaying the Centaurs (II, 5, 12; Frazer, p. 233). In a new fit of madness he kills Iphitus, son of Eurytus, and then asks Neleus to purify him. But Neleus is a friend of Eurytus and refuses. Heracles then gets the purification at the hands of Deiphobus (II, 6, 2; Frazer, p. 239). It is interesting that in spite of the purification he is smitten with a serious illness in punishment for the murder of Iphitus, and is not cured of it till he sells himself as a slave and gives the proceeds to the youth's father (II, 6, 2; Frazer, p. 241). Evidently another tradition is here being grafted upon the first, without the author's even trying to make them agree. Legend supplies many other examples of purifications after involuntary homicide. Peleus is purified of two killings of that sort.[1] But there is better yet. In exterminating bandits Theseus

1254 [1] Literally, "the male offspring of a sow, her teats still bulging from the belly that hath borne." Of that particular victim, the scholiast remarks: "Λυτήριον means . . . 'that which purifies.' It is a suckling pig. Those who are performing a sacrifice of purification bathe the hands of the recipient in the blood of such a pig."

1255 [1] Apollodorus, *Bibliotheca,* III, 13, 2 (Frazer, Vol. II, p. 63): Peleus, purified by Eurytion, shoots at what he thinks is the wild boar of Calydon. The arrow strikes Eurytion and kills him. Peleus is purified by Acastus. Diodorus Siculus, *Bibliotheca historica,* IV, 72, 6 (Booth, Vol. I, p. 283): In a game Peleus accidentally kills a half-brother on his father's side and he is purified by Actor.

is performing a public service; yet he has to be purified of their blood.[2] Apollo himself has to be purified of slaying the Python. Living at an age later than the days when the legend originated, Plutarch thinks it ridiculous that a god should have to be purified.[3] Ajax purifies himself after killing some sheep in a fit of madness.[4] Some go so far as to require purification of hunters and dogs returning from the chase.[5] The strictly mechanical character of the taint of homicide and the ensuing purification comes out clearly in a story told by Pausanias, *Periegesis,* V, *Elis* I, 27, 10. A child at play strikes his head against a bronze bull and dies. The statue is felt to be tainted by homicide. "The Eleans thought best to remove the bronze from the Alteum as guilty of murder; but the god at Delphi prescribed that the bull be left where it was and be purified with the rites usual among the Hellenes for involuntary homicides."

1256. The legend of Orestes is one of the cases in which the wholly material purification can be seen in process of transformation, partial at least, into a moral purification. Orestes is purified at Delphi by Apollo. But that is not enough—well known his ensuing trial at Athens. Pausanias, *Periegesis,* III, *Laconia,* 17, 7-9, tells how the Spartan king Pausanias accidentally killed a girl named Cleonice. He tried all sorts of purifications, but they could not avail to cleanse the defilement contracted by such a misfortune. That was why he was the only one not saved by the refuge offered by Chalcioicus.

1257. Commerce between a man and a woman, whether legiti-

1255 [2] Plutarch, *Theseus,* 12, 1-2 (Perrin, Vol. I, p. 23): "So Theseus continued punishing the wicked." Proceeding on his journey, he comes to the river Cephisus. There he meets the sons of Phytalus. They welcome him. He begs them to purify him, and they do so with the customary rites.

1255 [3] The slaying of the serpent and the subsequent purification of Apollo were commemorated at Delphi: *Quaestiones graecae,* 12. In the *De defectu oraculorum,* 15 (Goodwin, Vol. IV, p. 21), Plutarch exclaims: "It is altogether ridiculous, my friends, that after killing the beast, Apollo should have fled to the borders of Greece because he needed purification."

1255 [4] Sophocles, *Ajax,* vv. 654-55 (Storr, Vol. II, pp. 56-57).

1255 [5] Arrian, *De venatione,* 32, 3: "After a fortunate chase a sacrifice must also be performed, and the first-fruits of the chase offered to the goddess as a purification for the dogs and hunters, according to the custom of our land."

mate or not, was considered a cause of impurity among the ancient Greeks as well as among other peoples. Here too we have a transition from a purely material uncleanness to a moral impurity. Theano, a woman of the Pythagorean sect, was once asked: "How many days after commerce with a man may a woman be considered pure?" and she answered, "If with her husband, at once; if with some other man, never."[1]

1258. Among many peoples, chiefly uncivilized or savage, not only the sexual act, but also menstruation, induces impurity.[1] Countless examples might be cited in point. Noteworthy the prescriptions

1257 [1] Diogenes Laertius, *Pythagoras,* VIII, 43 (Hicks, Vol. II, p. 359); Clement of Alexandria, *Stromata,* IV, 19 (*Opera,* Vol. I, p. 1331A; Wilson, Vol. II, p. 195); Stobaeus, *Florilegium,* LXXIV, 55 (Meinecke, Vol. III, p. 61); Theodoret, *Graecarum affectionum curatio, Sermo* XII, *De virtute activa* (*Opera,* Vol. IV, pp. 1143-46).

1258 [1] Hovelacque, *Les nègres de l'Afrique suséquatoriale,* pp. 311, 475: "During their monthly periods the women, as a rule, live apart, sometimes, as in certain districts along the Gold Coast, in huts appointed to such seclusion [Quoting "Bosman, II, 371," *i.e., New and Accurate Description of the Coast of Guinea,* Letter XVIII, p. 329]. 'Women in menstruation are regarded hereabouts [on the Slave Coast] as so particularly tainted that they would never during such a period dare to enter the house of the king or of any important person, and women who violate such orders are punished with death or at least servitude for life. . . . Letter XXI, p. 416, by one David Van Nyendael: They are not allowed to enter their husbands' houses or to touch the least thing whether in the preparation of meals or in house-cleaning.' " Lafitau, *Mœurs des sauvages américains,* Vol. I, pp. 262-63: "[Such seclusions during periods and purifications] are very strict in [South] America. The women are given cabins apart, much as lepers were segregated among the Jews. They are regarded as so unclean at such times that they are forbidden to touch any article of common use. On a first infraction of that rule they are separated for thirty days from the rest of the tribe, and the fire in the cabin that they have entered is put out and the ashes are dumped outside the village. Then a new fire is lighted, as though the first had been sullied by their presence. In tribes living along the Rio de la Plata, they are sewn up in their hammocks at such periods, like corpses, with just a little opening for them to breathe through. There they stay for the duration of the period, whereafter they are subjected to all the rites usually applied to girls who have reached the age of puberty. . . . Tavernier, *Voyages en Perse,* p. 85 (1630 ed., Vol. I, p. 396), says that among the Gaures 'as soon as the women or the girls feel their periods coming on, they promptly leave the house and go off by themselves to the country to little bamboo huts with cloths hanging over the entrances in place of doors. They are provided with food and drink daily throughout the period. When it is over, each of them according to her means sends a goat, a chicken, a pigeon, to the priest as an offering, thence proceeding to bathe.' "

in the Bible, which are no longer observed by Christians.[2] Parturition is regarded among many peoples as a cause of impurity. Births and deaths were alike prohibited on the island of Delos. Both in Greece and in Rome the new-born babe was purified.

1259. In Greece contact with a dead body or the mere sight of one induced impurity. A jar of water taken from another house was set in front of the house where a person lay dead that departing visitors might perform purification.[1] People who had attended funerals made purification.[2]

1260. Countless the forms of impurity, but they all corresponded to a single sentiment, real or imaginary, of alteration in personal integrity; and they were remedied by appropriate ceremonies of purification. In such a plethora of dreaded impurities the superstitious soul was afraid of everything. Theophrastus shows one such leaving the temple after washing his hands and sprinkling himself

1258 [2] Lev. 15:2 f. (Vulgate): *"Vir qui patitur fluxum seminis immundus erit. . . . Vir de quo egreditur semen coitus lavabit aqua omne corpus suum et immundus erit usque ad vesperum. . . . Mulier cum qua coierit lavabitur aqua et immunda erit usque ad vesperum. Mulier quae redeunte mense patitur fluxum sanguinis septem diebus separabitur. Omnis qui tetigerit eam immundus erit usque ad vesperum. . . . Omne vas super quo illa sederit quisquis attigerit lavabit vestimenta sua, et ipse lotus aqua pollutus erit usque ad vesperum. Si coierit cum ea vir tempore sanguinis menstrualis immundus erit septem diebus, et omne stratum in quo dormierit polluetur."* It is customary to explain these prescriptions as hygienic. If that were so, the state of uncleanness ought to end after the prescribed washing. Instead it continues (§ 1247 [1]).

1259 [1] Pollux, *Onomasticon,* VIII, 7, 65-66 (Dindorf, Vol. I, p. 131); Hesychius, *Lexicon, s.v.* Ἀρδάνια; Suidas, *Lexicon, s.v.* Ἀρδάνιον; Eustathius, *Commentarii ad Homeri Iliadem,* VIII, v. 187, Vol. II, p. 201.

1259 [2] Virgil, *Aeneid,* VI, vv. 229-30:

> *"Idem ter socios pura circumtulit unda,*
> *spargens rore levi et ramo felicis olivae."*

("Aeneas thrice purged his comrades with pure water, sprinkling a light dew with a branch of the auspicious olive.") Servius annotates (Thilo-Hagen, Vol. II, p. 42): *"Thrice:* either actually three times, or more often than that. For though they had incurred pollution from the burial, every purgation is addressed to the Higher Gods. That is why he uses an odd number, or else because that particular lustration required it. *Circumtulit:* 'purged.' It is an archaic word. Says Plautus, *Fragmenta,* 48 (68): *Pro larvato te circumferam:* 'I will purge thee as one bewitched,' the lustration taking its name from the fact that a torch, or [burning] sulphur, or in some cases, victims, were 'carried around.'"

with lustral waters and walking about all day long with a laurel-leaf between his lips. Every so often he purifies his house. He dares not go near a tomb or a woman in childbed. He goes down to the sea-shore for a sprinkling with sea-water. If he chance to encounter something reputed to be of evil omen, he purifies himself by pouring water on his head, and having someone carry a shrimp and a puppy in a circle around him.[1] On driving away the courtesans with whom she has surprised Propertius, Cynthia purifies the chamber.[2] Anyone stressing derivations primarily would find an abyss between purification for a crime and this love-game. But looking strictly to the constant and significant element in such phenomena, their perfect similarity is obvious. Juvenal ridicules the purifications of a superstitious woman who in early morning in midwinter goes to the Tiber, breaks the ice, plunges in three times, and shivering washes her head in the eddying current.[3]

1261. The impurity extends from the person who has incurred it to others who have been in contact with him or are otherwise re-

1260 [1] Theophrastus, *Characteres,* 16 (18), "The Superstitious Man" (Jebb, pp. 162-65). I have used the general expression, "something reputed to be of evil omen," to avoid entering on the problem of the exact meaning of this very corrupt passage. Coray thinks it is a question of the evil eye. Plutarch, *De superstitione,* III, 166 (Babbitt, Vol. II, p. 461), speaks of the superstitious individual who has had a bad dream. He goes to a quack, then turns to "the old crone who performs purifications, then takes a plunge in the sea, and finally spends one whole day seated on the ground." Apuleius, *Metamorphoses,* XI, 23, tells of a purification: "The time for it having come, as the priest said, he led me, in the press of a great crowd of the devout, to the baths near by, and first subjecting me to the usual ablution, then praying to the god for forgiveness and sprinkling [in a circle about] me in a very pure manner, he pronounced me clean (*abluit*)."

1260 [2] *Elegiae,* IV, 8, vv. 83-86: "She fumigates all the spots that the girls had touched . . . and washes the threshold with pure water. She bids me change all my garments, and thrice my head she circles (*tetigit*) with a sulphur flame." Tibullus, *Delia,* 5, v. 11, speaks of performing lustrations for his beloved, when she was ill, by circling three times with sulphur about her:

"Ipseque ter circum lustravi sulfure puro."

His "pure sulphur," is the καθαρὸν θεῖον of the Greeks—"purifying" sulphur.

1260 [3] *Saturae,* VI, vv. 522-24:

"Hibernum fracta glacie descendet in amnem,
ter matutino Tiberi mergetur et ipsis
vorticibus timidum caput abluet."

lated to him—from parents to children, from the individual to the group to which he belongs, to animals, material things, a whole country. To lend credence to the so-called *Institutes of Manu* the mere fact that a close relative has died is a cause of impurity, though the corpse has neither been seen nor touched.[1] Evidently, therefore, it is a question of a nebula extending to greater or lesser distances about a nucleus.

1262. When the family is felt to be the social unit it follows that any alteration of integrity in one of its members extends to the family as a whole, in space and in time, much as a wound inflicted on one part of the body of a living being affects the body as a whole. In the infliction of penalties upon a whole family for a crime committed by one of its members a logical action may figure: the design to influence the individual through the affection he may be assumed to have for his family: but also active is the residue underlying the conception of the family as the social unit. That is why such collective penalties disappear when the individual becomes the unit, as has been the case in Europe. They have persisted down to our own times in China, where the family remained the unit.[1]

1261 [1] Loiseleur-Deslongchamps, *Lois de Manou,* V, 74-77 (p. 382): "Such the [ten-day] rule of impurity caused by the death of a relative when one is on the spot. But in case of absence at a distance the rule laid down for *sapindas* and *samânodakas* prescribes as follows: If news of the death of a relative in a distant locality arrives within the ten days' period of impurity, the impurity holds for the remainder of the period. If the tenth day has elapsed, the impurity holds over three nights. If a year has passed, a bath is sufficient for purification. If news of the death of a relative or the birth of a male child arrives after the expiration of the ten days, one may be purified by plunging fully dressed into water." Those are not merely theoretical prescriptions. They are put into practice. Du Bois, *Mœurs, institutions et cérémonies des peuples de l'Inde,* Vol. I, p. 244: "Hindus regard themselves as sullied by mere attendance at a funeral. They take a plunge-bath immediately after the ceremonies, and no one would dare re-enter his house without having performed purification in that manner. The mere news of the death of a relative, be it a hundred leagues away, has the same effects, and makes the same purification obligatory on all members of the family who hear of it. The taint, however, does not extend to mere friends and acquaintances of the deceased."

1262 [1] Farjenel, *La morale chinoise,* pp. 243-44: "[In Chinese law] individuality is absorbed in the paternal powers of the head of the family, the magistrate, the prince, who theoretically are elder brothers and fathers of all Chinese subjects. The terrible principle of solidarity in penal law, so incomprehensible to Westerners, used to be manifest evidence of that concept of human personality. There were certain

1263. If a man has neither sons nor daughters, the family integrity is altered (daughters are not considered when the family is perpetuated through the male line) and something has to be done about it. Hence the various arrangements for permitting a man married to a barren woman to take another wife, now divorcing, now keeping, the first. If the man dies childless, that remedy no longer avails, and we get such institutions as the Athenian epiclerate, the Jewish levirate, and so on. Derivations eventually obscure such facts, but not to such an extent as to conceal their substantial traits from an attentive observer.[1]

crimes of such enormity that they could be avenged only by the decapitation of all ascendants and descendants of the guilty person, even though they had no knowledge of the crime and the crime were not actually perpetrated but merely plotted. It is the spirit of Chinese law that the family taken *in globo* is the only real individuality. That provision figured in Chinese written law down to April 25, 1905."

1263 [1] To give some idea of such phenomena certain provisions in the *Institutes of Manu* will suffice. A thorough treatment of them would be the province of a *special* sociology, which would follow this *general* sociology.

Loiseleur Deslongchamps, *Lois de Manou,* IX, 45 f. (pp. 422-56): "He alone is the perfect man who is made up of three persons combined—to wit, his wife, himself, and his son; and the Brahmans have propounded this maxim: 'The husband makes but one same person with his wife.' . . . 48. The owner of the male that has sired with cows, mares, sheep, female camels, buffalos, and goats, and slave-girls has no property-right over the offspring. The same it is with the wives of other men. . . . 58. An elder brother who cohabits with the wife of a younger brother, and a younger brother with the wife of an elder brother, are degraded even if they have been invited to do so by the husband or by relatives, unless the marriage be barren. . . . 59. When one has no children the desired progeniture may be obtained through the union of one's wife, on suitable authorization, with a brother or another relative (*sapinda*). . . . 60. Rubbed with liquid butter and observing silence, let the relative assigned that office approach at night a widow or a childless woman and beget a single son, but never a second. . . . 61. Considering the fact that the purpose of this arrangement may not be perfectly attained by the begetting of a single child, those thoroughly versed in this question are of opinion that women may lawfully have a second son in this manner. . . . 127. A man without a male child may bid his daughter rear a son for him . . . by *saying to himself,* 'Let the male child which she shall bear become mine and perform the funeral rite in my honour.' 128. So of yore the Pradjâpati Dakcha himself bade his fifty daughters give him sons for the increase of his line. [Hence the further prescription:] *Ibid.,* III, 11 (p. 353). The sensible man will not marry a girl who has no brother or whose father is not known, in fear lest, in the first case, she be given him by the father only in the intent of adopting the son that she may have; and lest, in the second case, the marriage so contracted be illicit [? as contracted with a bastard]." And *cf. Ibid.,* IX, 136 (p. 426).

1264. Biblical prescriptions, subsequently developed in the Talmud, yield a luxuriant harvest of prescriptions pertaining to impurities and purifications.[1] Impure and unclean objects are arranged in a series according to decreasing impurities on the plan of father and sons. At the top of the lists stands the "forefather" of uncleanness.[2] Next come the "fathers of uncleanness," and then, in four degrees of descent, the "sons of uncleanness." Contact with the "forefather" gives rise to certain "fathers." "Sons" in the first degree are objects made unclean through contact with "fathers"; "sons" of the second degree acquire uncleanness through contact with "sons" of the first, the third through contact with the second, the fourth through contact with the third. "Fathers" and "sons" may be according to law (*ex lege*), or according to the commentaries (*ex instituto scribarum*). The "forefather" of uncleanness is the human corpse. According to law there are thirty-two "fathers," to wit, "creeping things" (*reptilia*), the dead bodies of beasts or human beings, and so on.[3]

1264 [1] It would be a waste of time to go into them here at length; but some notion of them will prove useful, the particular case giving a bird's-eye view of the thing in general.

1264 [2] Surenhuis, *Mischna,* preface to Part VI (Tohoroth) (Vol. VI, p. C2): "The 'uncleanness of the dead' (*immundities mortui*) embraces nine fathers of uncleanness, and flesh from a corpse to the amount of an olive defiles with 'uncleanness of the dead'; so also flesh torn [by an animal, Lev. 22:8] from the corpse to the amount of an olive, and putrefied flesh to the amount of a spoonful, and that amount of bone and blood from a corpse. The corpse of a dead man taken as a whole is the 'forefather of uncleanness.' "

1264 [3] *Loc. cit.,* p. D: "The 'fathers of uncleanness' *ex lege* are thirty-two, to wit: a creeping thing (*reptile*), the corpse of an animal, a human corpse, a man polluted by a human corpse, vessels that have touched a man polluted by a human corpse, vessels polluted by a human corpse, vessels that have touched other vessels which have been polluted by a human corpse, a tent, a grave, *eiectio seminis,* expiatory water, a red heifer, bull-calves and he-goats appointed to sacrifice (*qui comburendi erant*), a scapegoat, *vir gonorrhea affectus, et foemina gonorrhea affecta, menstruosa, puerpera,* a saddle (*equitatio*) [see Lev. 15:9] and a chair (*sessio*) [Lev. 15:6] of either sex [? *i.e.,* whether used by unclean man or woman], anyone *qui cum menstruosa corpus miscuit,* the blood of an unclean woman, her saliva, urine, *profluvium seminis, eiectio seminis illius,* a leper on the days of his numeration [*i.e.,* quarantine, Lev. 13:4-5], a leper on days of undoubted leprosy [*i.e.,* positively diagnosed, Lev. 13:8], a garment contaminated by leprosy, and finally a house contaminated by leprosy [Lev. 14:34 f.]. These, I say, are called 'fathers of uncleanness *ex lege.*' "

The "creeping things" are listed in the Bible, and they are animals of one kind or another, though just which is not certainly known, the commentators giving different lists.[4] Champions of logical conduct may rustle about as much as they choose, but they will never succeed in finding just why those particular animals should be unclean and others not. According to the Scribes the "fathers of uncleanness" are twenty-nine.[5] The "sons" of uncleanness are also either by law or by institute of the Scribes. The first degree, as regards profane things, is unclean and induces uncleanness by contact. The second, however, does not. In sacred things the first three degrees are unclean and induce uncleanness, the fourth does not.

1264 [4] Lev. 11:29-32: (Vulgate) *"Haec quoque inter polluta reputabuntur de his quae moventur in terra: mustella et mus et crocodilus singula iuxta genus suum, mygale et chamaeleon et stellio et lacerta et talpa";* (King James version:) "These also shall be unclean unto you among the creeping things that creep upon the earth: the weasel and the mouse and the tortoise [Septuagint, κοκόδειλος, Vulgate, *crocodilus*] each after his kind, and the ferret and the chameleon and the lizard and the mole." Surenhuis, *loc. cit.*, p. C2: "By *reptilia* are meant the eight kinds of 'creeping things' mentioned in the Law, such as the weasel, the mouse, the turtle, the crawling weevil (*attelabus*), the lizard, the newt, the snail, and the mole. The blood of reptiles, their flesh and fat, have the same degree of uncleanness. The hides or skins of four of the *reptilia*, the crawling weevil, the lizard, the newt, and the snail, are of the same degree of uncleanness as the flesh. However, the bones taken from creeping things do not defile. Other creeping and loathsome things, such as the frog, toad, snake, viper, and the like, do not defile." Segond's French translation, p. 78: ". . . the mole, mouse, and lizard, according to their kinds; the porcupine, the frog, turtle, snail, and chameleon." Crampon's French translation: ". . . the weasel, the mouse, and all kinds of lizards; the shrew, the chameleon, the salamander, the green lizard, and the mole."

1264 [5] Surenhuis, *loc. cit.*, p. D2: "But if we compile the 'fathers of uncleanness' from the Institutes of the Scribes, we find that they are twenty-nine, such as bone from a corpse to the amount of a grain of barley, blood from a bruise, earth belonging to Gentiles, a cemetery (a field in which bones of dead bodies lie buried: *ager in quo cadaverum ossa latent*), a swelling (scab) over a bruise that has bled, a man polluted by those things, vessels that have touched them or been otherwise polluted by them, a man who has touched a [hallowed] vessel, [hallowed] vessels that have touched a man, vessels that have touched other vessels so polluted in the ways mentioned, a Gentile woman, a woman in irregular period, *foemina quae maculam sanguinis praepostere vidit, foemina quae in accessu menstruali se non visitavit praepostere, puerpera quae aliquod foetus membrum peperit,* her couch, saddle (*equitatio*), saliva, urine, *et immunditiei sanguis;* and further a *vir qui cum foemina immunda rem habuit quae gonorrhoea laborabat,* a male Gentile, an idolater, [objects pertaining to] an idolatrous worship, anything killed by a Gentile, and finally the dead body of a bird [otherwise] clean."

"Fathers" of uncleanness defile human beings and receptacles; "sons," only foods and beverages. "If a man has touched a 'creeping thing,' he contracts an uncleanness of the first degree, and contaminates oil, if he touches it; and if again such oil comes into contact with honey, it contaminates it . . . and if the honey comes into contact with water, it contaminates it, and in that way the oil, the honey, and the water each acquires an uncleanness of the first degree." [6] The uncleanness lasts for a greater or lesser length of time, and there are many prescriptions on the subject. The Talmud devotes an entire book to leprosy, adding many regulations to the by no means few that are laid down in the Bible (Lev., Chapters 13-15).

1265. Impurities being thoroughly identified, the next thing is to get rid of them. Luckily, washing in water happened to be lavishly recommended. That served at least towards cleanliness. However, minute prescriptions usually guided the believer in his purifications. The Bible gives numbers of them and the Talmud lengthens the list.

1266. As was the case with other peoples, Jewish purifications were performed with special waters and in special ways. Notable, among the Israelites, the sacrifice of a red heifer. It had to be undefiled and without blemish. After killing it, the priest "shall take of her blood with his finger and sprinkle of her blood directly before the tabernacle . . . seven times." So the Greeks purified with the blood of a suckling pig, and satirizing the custom Aristophanes, *Ecclesiasuzae*, v. 128, has his congress of women open with a sacrifice of the lustful weasel (§ 919 [1]). The heifer was burned in a manner prescribed, and the ashes were then gathered up and mixed in water to provide the "water of separation." [1] It was a custom of the Romans to sacrifice,

1264 [6] Surenhuis, *loc. cit.*, p. E.

1266 [1] Num. 19:19-22: "And the clean person shall sprinkle upon the unclean on the third day and on the seventh day: and on the seventh day he shall purify himself and wash his clothes and bathe himself in water and shall be clean at even. But the man that shall be unclean and shall not purify himself, that soul shall be cut off from among the congregation, because he hath defiled the sanctuary of the Lord: the water of separation hath not been sprinkled upon him: he is unclean. And it shall be a perpetual statute unto them that he that sprinkleth the water of separation shall wash his clothes; and he that toucheth the water of separation shall be unclean until even. And whatsoever the unclean person toucheth shall be unclean; and the soul that toucheth it shall be unclean until even."

about the middle of April, a heifer that was, as they said, *"forda,"* "fertile and with calf." The priests took the calf from the heifer's belly, and it was burned by the Dean of the Vestals (*Virgo Vestalis Maxima*), the ashes being kept to purify the people on the feast day of Pales (the Palilia or Parilia).[2] Already the blood of a horse, regularly sacrificed in October in the Field of Mars, had been set aside for the same purpose.[3] The Palilia were celebrated on the twenty-first of April. The people went in throngs to the altar of Vesta, got possession of the horse's blood, the ashes of the calves, and masses of dried bean-stalks. The crowd was sprinkled with water with a laurel-branch, there were fumigations with sulphur, fires were made of the bean-stalks and the people leapt over them.[4] A survival of this festival is to be seen in the bonfires that are still burned in several

1266 [2] Ovid, *Fasti*, IV, vv. 639-40:

> *"Igne cremat vitulos quae natu maxima Virgo est,*
> *luce Palis populos purget ut ille cinis."*

("The eldest of the Virgins burns the calves in the fire that the ash may cleanse the people on the morn of Pales.")

1266 [3] Festus, *De verborum significatione*, XIII, *s.v. October* (London, Vol. II, pp. 519-20): "The name *October* was applied to a horse that was sacrificed in the month of October in the Campus Martius. There was a great rivalry between the inhabitants of the Subura quarter and those living on the Sacra Via for possession of the head. If the Suburites won, it was nailed up on the Mamilian Tower, if the Sacravienses, on a wall of the Regia. The tail of the horse was rushed to the Regia that the blood in it might drip into the [sacred] fire there."

1266 [4] Ovid, *Fasti*, IV, vv. 727-28, 731-34, 739, 781-82:

> *"Certe ego transilui positas ter in ordine flammas,*
> *virgaque roratas laurea misit aquas. . . .*
> *I, pete virginea populus suffimen ab ara;*
> *Vesta dabit: Vestae munere purus eris.*
> *Sanguis equi suffimen erit vitulique favilla;*
> *tertia res: durae culmen inane fabae. . . .*
> *Caerulei fiant vivo de sulphure fumi. . . .*
> *Moxque per ardentes stipulae crepitantis acervos*
> *traiicias celeri strenua membra pede."*

("I myself have leapt over the bonfires burning in triple row while the laurel-branches sprinkled us with dewlike mist. . . . Run, O ye people, to receive your fumigation from the altar of the Virgins. Vesta will vouchsafe it: pure ye shall be by gift of Vesta. The blood of the horse will be your purification, and the ash of the calf, and a third thing, the pile of empty stalks of hard beans. . . . Let the blue fumes rise from the burning sulphur. . . . And you had better be limber and quick of foot as you leap over the burning piles of crackling tinder!")

districts in Italy. Catholics burn the palms of the previous year on Ash Wednesday and use the ashes to make the sign of the cross on the foreheads of the faithful.[5]

1267. But the cleansing power of water over persons or things is evidently lost sight of in such cases, for it is unclean to touch "water of separation," the imaginary trait taking precedence over the real. The Talmud as usual expatiates on these defiling properties of purifying water. A distinction is drawn between waters available in sufficient quantities for aspersion, and waters not available in such sufficiency. The first contaminate the carrier, the second only persons who touch them. And be sure not to forget that "if a string is attached to the unclean thing, and a man lifts the unclean thing by the string, he is defiled by the uncleanness of the weight, for the weight of the unclean thing touches him; and he in turn contaminates his garments, or all the garments and vessels that he touches, save only earthen vessels"! [1]

1266 [5] *Dictionnaire encyclopédique de la théologie catholique, s.v. Cendres* (*Mercredi des*) (Wetzer, *s.v. Aschermittwoch*): "The ash that is spread on the heads of the faithful comes from the burning of the palms of the preceding year. It is blessed just before the Ash Wednesday mass by a special ritual."

1267 [1] Mishnah, Tract Kelim (*De vasis*), I, 2 (Danby, p. 604; Surenhuis, Vol. VI, p. 16), comment by Bartenoro [read: Bertinoro]. And *cf.* also the following, *Ibid.*, I, 1 (Surenhuis, *loc. cit.*, pp. 15-16): "Fathers of uncleanness are: creeping things, seed of copulation, a man defiled by the dead, and a leper in the days of his numeration, and expiatory waters insufficient in quantity for the sprinkling. All these things defile persons and vessels by touch, and earthen vessels by air but not by weight." Bertinoro's comment: "*Semen concubitus:* only the seed of copulation of the Israelite and full-grown (*adulti viri*). The seed of copulation of the Gentile does not defile [For similar distinctions see §§ 1278 f.], not even by institute of the Scribes, for the seed of the Gentile is altogether clean. Nor does the seed of copulation of the adolescent defile. . . . Earthen vessels, foods, and beverages that have been in contact with the dead [in a house where a person has died] do not become fathers of uncleanness. Only an Israelite becomes a father of uncleanness by contact with the dead. A Gentile and an abortion delivered after eight days do not contract uncleanness from the dead. . . . *Expiatory waters insufficient for sprinkling:* they too defile by touch, and if in quantities sufficient for sprinkling, they defile by weight as regards the person and vessels, as appears from Num. 19:21. [The passage refers only to sprinklers.—A. L.] Our doctors, however, hold that the sprinkler is not defiled, the Law meaning simply to determine a measure for the carrier, and specifying (*nempe*) that there should be sufficient for aspersion. For the Law distinguishes between waters and waters, that is to say, between waters in sufficient

1268. Legislation on the material circumstances of cases is fulsome and fine-spun. A chicken swallows a reptile and eventually strays into an oven. If the chicken remains alive it does not defile the oven: if it dies, it does.[1] If milk drops from a woman's breast into an oven, the oven is unclean; and so if in sweeping an oven a woman pricks a finger and puts it into her mouth.[2] There are rulings on cases where weasels or cats go travelling about with *reptilia* in their mouths,[3] on spittles clean and unclean, semi-fluid and dry, in public places or in private.[4] As regards matters of sex there are disquisitions a-plenty that would hold their own with the obscenities with which modern anti-Clericals so bitterly taunt the Jesuits.[5] Manners of ablution are debated at length, and their effectiveness. There are, accord-

quantities for aspersion, which defile the person, he defiling his garments, and waters insufficient for aspersion, which defile the person so that he defiles foods and beverages, but not his garments. Superior to this are the dead body and expiatory waters in quantities sufficient for aspersion. They defile a man by weight, just as he defiles his garments by touch, and garments removed from the garment by touch (*et subtractas veste tactu*)." Maimonides: "*Defilement by carrying:* it means that if a man has lifted a weight of unclean substance, he is defiled, even if he himself has not touched the body that was unclean. . . . Of similar nature is [defilement by] *inclination,* a timber being laid over the top of a wall, with the uncleanness on one end of the timber. If by leaning one's weight on the other end one raises the end on which the uncleanness is located, one is defiled by the inclination of the timber." Bertinoro: "*Et subtractas veste tactu.* It means garments withdrawn from uncleanness. In this case contact results from carrying. For anyone in contact with the dead or the *menstruae aquas* but not carrying these does not defile the garments he has on."

1268 [1] Mishnah, *loc. cit.,* VIII, 5 (Danby, p. 615; Surenhuis, Vol. VI, p. 48).

1268 [2] *Ibid.,* 11 (Danby, p. 616; Surenhuis, Vol. VI, p. 51).

1268 [3] *Ibid.,* Tract Tohoroth, IV, 2, 3 (Danby, p. 720; Surenhuis, Vol. VI, p. 327).

1268 [4] *Ibid., loc. cit.,* IV, 6; V, 7-8 (Danby, pp. 720, 723; Surenhuis, Vol. VI, pp. 329, 330).

1268 [5] *Ibid.,* Tract Mikwaoth (*De lavacris*), VIII, 4 (Danby, p. 742; Surenhuis, Vol. VI, p. 381): "*Si gentilis eiecerit semen ab Israëlita immissum, immunda est. Si filia Israëlitae eiecerit semen a gentili iniectum, munda est. Si uxor domi coitum passa sit et postea se laverit sed pudenda non purgaverit, perinde est ac si non lavavisset se. Si is qui semen emisit se immerserit sed non prius minxerit, tum postquam urinam reddiderit, immundus est. R. Iose dicit: Aegrotus et senex immundus est, sed infans et sanus mundus est.*" Bertinoro: "*In iuvene et sano mundus est, quia fortissime emittunt semen ita ut nihil remaneat.*" There is even worse: *Ibid.,* VIII, 3 (Surenhuis, p. 380). A whole treatise, Tract Niddah (*De fluxu menstruo*), goes into all possible cases with the greatest fulness (Danby, pp. 748-57).

ing to the case, things that separate, and other things that do not separate, the water from the body.[6]

1269. If now we look down on all this, as it were in a certain perspective, disregarding minutiae as one does in making a map, we readily grasp the general outlines of the thing. The nucleus is an instinctive repugnance to dead bodies and to filth of one kind or another. That repugnance is in certain cases beneficial to the human being, just as it is beneficial to animals to abstain from poisonous foods.[1]

1270. How animals come by such useful instincts we do not know. That they do have them is certain. Cattle, goats, and sheep do not touch poisonous plants in the pasture. It is an interesting fact, on the other hand, that they will eat them in hay. Birds seem to avoid poisonous seeds. We might say with the Darwinists that by a process of selection animals not endowed with such instincts have perished. Some other explanation might be imagined. Whatever the causes, the fact is there, and at it we halt.

1271. In the case of the human being, the nucleus shows two supplements (§§ 1273 f.): first, an interposition of residues from Class I, which inspire numberless combinations, and their logical explanations. We have quoted the Talmud as offering a remarkable instance of such material combinations and their explanations, and all within a juridical sphere, with some very few metaphysical or theological reflections, the authority of the Bible being chiefly invoked very much as a jurist might point to a written code of law.

1272. The niceties of the Jews are not at all exceptional. Their

1268 [6] *Ibid.*, Tract Mikwaoth, IX, 1 (Danby, p. 742; Surenhuis, Vol. VI, p. 382): "*Haec in homine dividunt: fila lanae et lini, et corrigiae in capitibus filiarum. R. Iehuda dicit: fila e lana et e pilis non dividunt, quia ad illa perveniunt aquae.*" Fairly dirty remarks follow, in IX, 2. IX, 3 reads: "*Haec non dividunt: capilli, pili axillae, locus occultus in viro. R. Eliezer dicit: perinde se res habet in viro et in foemina, quidquid quis curat id dividit, sin minus, non dividit.*" Bertinoro: "*Et locus secretus in viro, nam vir istius loci non tam accuratam curam gerit, imo ne quidem foemina, nisi maritata sit, uti expositum est; si ergo quis talia loca non curat, ipsa nec dividunt, si nempe ea non sint in maxima corporis parte.*" And the commentaries keep it up.

1269 [1] It is one of the many cases of non-logical conduct that we came upon in Chapter II.

counterparts are to be met with among other peoples, especially among the Hindus and the Mohammedans. Many Hindu prescriptions tally almost word for word with the Hebrew.[1]

1273. The non-logical actions connected with uncleanness and purification supply excellent illustrations of the II-2 and II-4 varieties distinguished in §§ 151 f. They have a subjective logical purpose—obedience to certain religious injunctions. Some of them are without any objective logical end—refraining from lifting an unclean object with a string, for example. Those both belong to our II-2 variety. Some have an objective logical purpose contributing to hygiene—for instance, condemning as unclean a beverage into which a particle from a dead body has fallen. That purpose would be approved by the subject if he knew it, and we would have a non-logical action of the II-4α species.

1274. That has led people to represent such actions as logical

1272 [1] Dubois, *Mœurs, institutions et cérémonies des peuples de l'Inde,* Vol. I, pp. 245-52: "Menstruation and childbirth lend temporary uncleanness to women. The mother of a new-born babe lives a whole month apart from other people . . . and women are subjected to the same segregation for their periodic seasons of uncleanness. . . . When the days of expiation are over, the clothing such women have been wearing is given to the washerwoman. It is carefully kept from entering the house, and no one would dare let his eyes rest on it. However, to purify themselves of such uncleanness, the wives of Sivaites (*lingamistes*) merely rub their foreheads with ash of cow's dung; and that simple ceremony they hold sufficient. . . . Earthen vessels are by nature susceptible of irremediable pollution, a thing not true of metal-ware. To be purified the latter need simply be washed. The others, being no longer usable, have to be destroyed. It is the same with clothing as with dishes: some are susceptible of defilement, others are not. . . . A scrupulous Brahman must be careful where he puts his feet when he walks. He would be defiled and required to take a bath if, by oversight, he chanced to set foot on a bone, a bit of broken crockery, a rag, a paper napkin with which someone has eaten, a piece of hide or leather, a lock of hair—anything unclean. The place where he sits down also requires his careful inspection . . . nor is his manner of eating a matter of indifference. The Hindu has an insurmountable horror for saliva. It is not so much a concern with neatness that obsesses him in that regard as his everlasting dread of the unclean. Contact with one animal or another, the dog especially, defiles the person of the Brahman, and it is amusing to watch the capers they cut, the precautions they take, to avoid the intimate caresses of one of the most faithful comrades of man. If in spite of their efforts the dog manages to reach them, they have no recourse but to hurry away and plunge fully dressed into a bath 'to be free of the pollution that the touch of the unclean animal has brought upon their persons and their garments.' "

actions, and it has contributed to the extension of the label to actions not belonging to the II-4α species. But no such logic figures in them. One may insist that the rules on menstruation were rules of hygiene; but in that case, why distinguish the menstruation of a Jewess from the menstruation of a Gentile, and the corpse of a Jew from the corpse of a Gentile?

1275. The second element that appears in the human being but not in the animal (§ 1271) is a need for explaining, not the combinations as such, but the principles that give rise to them; in other words, a desire to logicalize conduct that is non-logical. Active in that are not only the residues that reflect the hunger for logic (residues I-ε), but also residues of persisting abstractions (II-δ, §§ 1065-67). This supplement falls into two aspects—pseudo-experimental explanations on the one hand, and, on the other, explanations that overstep experience.

1276. Typical of the pseudo-experimental variety is the explanation which long enjoyed wide acceptance that the prohibition of pork for Jews was a hygienic principle supported by a religious sanction.[1]

1276 [1] Maimonides, *Guide of the Perplexed,* III, 48 (Munk, Vol. III, p. 396; Friedländer, Vol. III, pp. 251-52): "So I say that all the foods which the Law forbids constitute an unhealthy diet. Of all that has been forbidden us only pork and lard are not generally regarded as deleterious; but that is a mistake, for pork is a moister and more exuberant food than is good for us. But the chief reason why it is held in abomination by the Law is that the pig is a very uncleanly animal and feeds on uncleanly things. . . . Thus the fat of the inner organs of the pig is over-nourishing and so harmful to good digestion and productive of phlegmatic blood. . . . As for the characteristic signs [of the clean animal], the cloven hoof and cud-chewing for quadrupeds, and the presence of fins and scales in fish, the fact is that the presence of those signs is not the reason why eating them is permitted, nor lack of them the reason for their prohibition. They are just signs enabling one to recognize the good species and distinguish it from the bad." Maimonides explains and justifies all the biblical prescriptions with reasons derived from experience and logic. In some very few cases he confesses his inability to find any, *Ibid.,* III, 47 (Munk, Vol. III, p. 394; Friedländer, Vol. III, pp. 249-50): "The reason why purification was performed with cedar, hyssop, crimson wool, and two birds has been indicated in the Midrashôt; but it does not serve our purposes, and so far I have not been able to account for any of those things. Nor can I see, either, why cedar, hyssop, and crimson wool are used in the red-heifer rite, nor why a bunch of hyssop is used for sprinkling the blood of the lamb at Passover. I can find nothing to justify the preference given to those species." Logical explanations of unclean-

1277. Totemism, which explains everything, of course also explains the aversion of the Semites to the pig, presumably an ancient totem and as such revered and not used as a food! That might be true, and there are facts in favour of such a theory. J. L. Burckhardt

animal prescriptions come down to our own day. Mills, *History of Muhammedanism,* pp. 311-12: "The nature of the climate of the East has rendered certain meats detrimental to health. Legislators have therefore either divided beasts into the clean or the unclean, that is to say, those that are proper, and those that are not proper food, or they have specifically prohibited some, and left the people to their discretion with respect to the use of the rest. [All that is purely fantastic, and arises merely in a desire to see logical conduct in everything.] Of the former description of lawgivers was Moses; of the latter, was Muhammed. That the flesh of the *ignavum animal* (as Tacitus so decently calls the hog) engenders cutaneous disorders, more especially in warm countries, is a well-known fact; the filthiness of the quadruped [Mills would doubtless have agreed with the dictum of another Englishman that "the swine was properly so called."—A. L.] is sufficient to give a distaste of it; and accordingly we find that the Egyptians, Arabians, and other oriental nations have always abhorred it. The necessity of the case dictated the prohibition." Reinach well demonstrates the fatuity of such explanations in his *Cultes, mythes et religions,* Vol. I, pp. 11-13: "Oftentimes the prohibition to kill animals of one or more species comes in the shape of a taboo, a non-motivated interdiction, that is, or an interdiction justified after the fact by considerations of an entirely different order, hygienic, for example. That is still observable among the Mussulmans and the Jews." But Reinach goes wrong in regarding such rules as consequences of totemism. He himself shows that they may have had a different origin when he says: "Even in our day the Russian peasant will not kill a dove because the dove is the bird of the Holy Spirit, and even in France children are taught not to harm the lady-bird, which is called 'God's little animal' (*bête-du-bon-Dieu*). [There is not the slightest indication that the lady-bird was ever a totem in France. Reinach goes on to say himself, *Op. cit.,* pp. 91-92:] One of the most ancient and most widely diffused forms of religion [He ought really to say, "of non-logical conduct."] is a scruple against killing or eating some animal. Such scruples are still common enough. Mussulmans and Jews will not eat pork. Russians will not eat pigeons. Europeans, as a rule at least, will not eat dog-meat, and many still feel for horse-meat an instinctive repugnance that goes back to some ancient religion." Perhaps, but there are other things of the kind for which no religious or totemic explanation is imaginable. Ram-mutton goes very well in France and England. There are Italians in Central Italy who refuse to touch it in any form. Is there any likelihood that the ram was their totem? If one say that it is a religious prescription, on what documents could such a contention be based? Many Englishmen stand aghast at sight of a Frenchman eating frogs' legs. In all countries there are plenty of people who have an absolute repugnance to oysters. The Arabs eat grasshoppers. I challenge anyone to offer one to a European. In all such cases, there is no trace of any totemic, religious, or if you will, hygienic reason. They are just non-logical actions like the hosts of others observable in the human race.

relates:[1] "Some years ago an English ship went ashore near Djidda [Arabia] and among various spoils obtained from the wreck by Sherif Ghaleb was a large hog, an animal probably never before seen at Djidda. This hog, turned loose in the town with two ostriches, became the terror of all the sellers of bread and vegetables; for the mere touching of so unclean an animal as the hog, even with the edge of the gown, renders the Moslem impure and unable to perform his prayers without previous ablutions. The animal was kept for six months, when it was offered by the Sherif to an American captain for fifty dollars; but such a price being of course refused, it soon after died of a surfeit, to the great satisfaction of the inhabitants."[2] Here one notes characteristic traits of reverence for the totem, and if all cases were of this kind, the explanation would acquire great probability. But there are cases where it does not fit. In the Bible the hog is not the only animal that cannot be used as food. Many others are in the same fix. If there were only a few such animals one might imagine they were all totems. But can so many many all have been—all aquatic animals, for instance, and most of

1277 [1] *Travels in Arabia*, p. 208.

1277 [2] It is well known that the dog also is reputed unclean by the Moslems. Says Burckhardt, p. 386: "It is not unworthy of remark, that Medina, as far as I know, is the only town in the East from which dogs are excluded; they are never permitted to pass the gate into the interior, but must remain in the suburbs. . . . The apprehension of a dog entering a mosque, and polluting its sanctity, probably gave rise to their exclusion." Mills, *History of Muhammedanism*, pp. 467-68: "The benevolence of the Muselmans extends to the animal creation, and it is an established article in the Moslem's belief that the irrational animals will be judged on the last day and have mutual vengeance for the injuries they have done each other in this life. From feelings of compassion, hunting is held in abhorrence by the Turks, and birds are seldom deprived of their liberty. . . . According to popular tradition Muhammed was kind to the domestic animal, the cat. Its gravity of deportment and independent indifference well accord with the sullen solemnity and pride of the Turks. Though they are far too cleanly to admit them to touch their persons, yet they are received in their houses; the dog is not treated with the same benevolent attention. . . . His touch is deemed contagious and his very name is the Turk's bitterest expression of contempt." Such differences between the cat and the dog cannot be explained by totemism. Mills quotes in a footnote a remark of Labat, *Mémoires du Chevalier d'Arvieux*, Vol. III, p. 227: "Cats are not unclean animals; therefore they may eat and drink of the same things as the faithful do. But if a dog drink in the vessel of a believer, it must be washed seven times (Mishat, Vol. I, p. 108)."

them unknown to the Hebrews—that have neither fins nor scales?[8] One might answer that the prescription not to eat totems was subsequently extended to other animals. But granting that, it has still to be shown whether the pig was the totem from which the interdiction sprang or an animal to which the abomination was extended from others that were totems—and on that point we have not the slightest information. The conclusion is that the hog may well have been an ancient totem, but that such a fact requires specific proof, which for the present is not available; while the general fact of aversion to the use of its meat or to contact with it proves nothing because it would be proving too much.

1278. Speaking of certain laws on uncleanness Rabbinovicz tries to explain the prescription that a dead Gentile is to be considered clean. But the derivations to which he resorts he refutes later on himself.[1]

1277: [8] Lev. 11:12: (Vulgate) *"Cuncta quae non habent pinnulas et squamas in aquis polluta erunt"*: (King James) "Whatsoever hath no fins nor scales in the waters, that shall be an abomination unto you."

1278 [1] *Législation criminelle du Talmud,* Preface, pp. xxxiii-xxxv. "The Jews never buried their dead along public highways; and they furthermore marked graves with a sign called *tzijon*. Gentiles did not do that. The result was, at a time when the Jews were everywhere surrounded by Gentiles, that the Jews were unable to observe the laws of uncleanness as regarded the Gentiles, being unable to recognize their graves; so that in the end they came to believe that such graves did not defile." Rabbinovicz himself supplies the means for refuting this conjecture by showing that it applies to a particular case of a theory that is general; and which it certainly does not fit. Trying to refute another theory, which he rightly regards as erroneous, he says: "So they had a tradition, which had grown up . . . that the grave of a Gentile did not defile. Following a habit of the Talmud, that tradition was tied to a word in the Bible. Scripture says that an *adam,* a man, who is dead is a cause of uncleanness. The word *adam,* it was held, meant a Jew and nobody else. ([In a note]: It was not observed that the word *ysch,* 'man,' also excluded Gentiles in connexion with another case of uncleanness.) The passage [where the word *adam* so figures] was badly comprehended by several commentators and was still being attacked by enemies of Judaism as late as the past century. . . . They did not know that the passage in question had not been found till centuries after the Jews had grown accustomed to applying the law of cleanness to the graves of Gentiles. So also the passage in the Song of Songs that forbade the Jews to revolt against Gentiles . . . was not discovered till after the last revolution of Bar Khokhbah, when any rebellion had become impossible." In his *Législation civile du Talmud,* Vol. V, p. 381, again adverting to the law that a dead Gentile was clean, Rabbinovicz adds: "Rab says: 'If, as regards certain rules of uncleanness, a dead

1279. Gentiles were considered clean in certain cases chiefly because the non-logical conduct related, in its basic nucleus, to members of the group, to Jews, that is, but later on was extended by a process of reasoning to non-Jews as well. Rabbinovicz says that the Hebrews could not distinguish the graves of Gentiles. But they could not distinguish the spittles of Gentiles either; and in that case the Talmud rules in a sense directly contrary to its ruling in the other. Rabbinovicz himself notes the fact: "If there be a Gentile woman within the city, the spittles are impure (as regards the *haberim,* who have pledged themselves to observe the Mosaic laws on purity, since the Gentile woman might chance to be in a period)."[1] So we get many other problems of the kind with varying solutions, which cannot always be brought down to considerations of convenience for the Hebrews at a time when they were forced to live in contact with Gentiles.[2]

man has to be taken as a living individual, that must have been to prevent his being considered dead in cases of merely apparent death.'" As usual, derivations are the variable element in the thing, residues the constant. See further § 1279 [2] below.

1279 [1] *Législation civile du Talmud,* Vol. V, p. 411.

1279 [2] We mentioned one such problem just above in § 1278 [1]. Add the following: Mishnah, Tract Tohoroth, V, 8 (Danby, p. 723; Surenhuis, Vol. VI, p. 335): "If there be in the city a half-witted woman, either a foreigner or a Cuthaean, then all spittles found in the city are unclean." Maimonides: "We have stated . . . that Gentiles are to be regarded as *seminiflui* in all respects. Further in our fourth article of the code *De menstruis* we stated that a Cuthaean woman must always be held open to suspicion of being in a period. But it is not to be overlooked that a half-wit does not take care of herself, nor observe the times of her periods as defined in the Law." *Ibid.,* Tract Niddah (*De fluxu menstruo*), IV, 3 (Danby, p. 748; Surenhuis, Vol. VI, p. 400): "The blood of a female foreigner, and the blood of a female leper in state of cleanness, are clean according to the School of Schammai. The school of Hillel rules that it is on a par with spittle and urine." Bertinoro: "According to the School of Schammai, the blood of a female Gentile is clean, though with respect to spittle and urine the Schools of Schammai and Hillel are in agreement." Maimonides: "We have already . . . remarked that Gentiles in no wise defile, according to the Law, but the Scribes have ruled that they are to be regarded as *seminiflui* in all respects." *Ibid., loc. cit.,* VII, 3 (Danby, p. 753; Surenhuis, Vol. VI, p. 415): "All spots coming from Raca are clean, but unclean according to Rabbi Jéhudam, because they are proselytes and prone to err (*quia proselyti sunt et errant*). Such as come from Gentiles are clean. Such as come from an Israelite and from the Cuthaeans are unclean according to Rabbi Meir, clean

1280. The purpose of the trans-experimental explanation is to account for a prescription in which people believe on faith and which requires certain practices. It begins with the simple assertion of the taboo and gradually goes on to the most abstruse metaphysical and theological hair-splitting. In Leviticus one meets a simple form of explanation: the regulation as to purity and purification is bluntly stated as coming from God. Then again the assertion is re-enforced with more or less exhortation.[1] Finally comes a type of explanation usual with taboos: it is said that the transgressor runs a risk of death, and a religious explanation is further added.[2]

1281. A new stratum of explanations was added by Christianity. The Hebrews performed sacrifices and used the blood of sacrificial victims for purifications, as other peoples did.[1] The Christians wanted to abolish the custom and, not satisfied with that, they wanted to explain why they abolished it. St. Paul says that the blood of the Christ shed once and for all is the most perfect of sacrifices

according to the Scribes because they are not suspect of blemish." Bertinoro: "Those who come from Raca, and their blood, are unclean, because the inhabitants of that place are foreigners." Maimonides: "We have several times stated that Gentiles do not defile by the *fluxu seminis vel sanguinis nec fluxu menstruo:* the Scribes ruled concerning them, but gave no ruling as to their blemishes." Bertinoro: *"From Raca:* In the Targum the words *inter Cades et Sur* are rendered as 'between Raca and Chagra.' *Because they are proselytes:* their blood being unclean. . . . *Are prone to err:* it is as though he said, they are not very neat, nor do they cover over their blood-spots. Therefore we may suspect that they may perchance be *foeminae menstruae maculae. Such as come from Gentiles are clean,* because the Scribes have made no rulings as to their blemishes, and according to the Law their blood is altogether clean." *Ibid., loc. cit.,* X, 4 (Danby, pp. 756-57; Surenhuis, Vol. VI, p. 424): *"Seminifluus, seminiflua, menstrua, puerpera,* and lepers who have died, defile if they are carried, until the flesh changes. A Gentile that dies is clean of defilement if he is carried."

1280 [1] Lev. 11:43: "Ye shall not make yourselves abominable with any creeping thing that creepeth, neither shall ye make your selves unclean with them, that ye should be defiled thereby."

1280 [2] Lev. 15:31: "Thus shall ye separate the children of Israel from their uncleanness, that they die not in their uncleanness, when they defile my tabernacle that is among them."

1281 [1] So in Ex. 29:18 the sacrifice of the ram is explained with the words: "And thou shalt burn the whole ram upon the altar: it is a burnt offering unto the Lord: it is a sweet savour, an offering made by fire unto the Lord." That, roughly, was the reason given for pagan sacrifices.

and supersedes the old.[2] Interesting in that the persistence of an association, whereby the Christians dare not do away with the notion of the sacrifice altogether, but stop at transforming it in such a way that it carries on, but under a different form.[3]

1282. Residues of restoration of integrity in persons and things figure in many other cases. The Catholic Church used to "reconcile" penitents. It still "reconciles" churches and cemeteries.[1]

1283. Group-persistences result in the extension of practices devised for human beings (such as juridical acts and restorations of integrity) to animals and things. But that does not mean that there has necessarily been any direct imitation. Imitation may figure to some

1281 [2] Heb. 10:5-14 represents the single sacrifice of Christ as sufficient for all sins. And *cf.* Heb. 9:12-14: "Neither by the blood of goats and calves but by his own blood he entered in once into the holy place, having obtained eternal redemption for us. For if the blood of bulls and of goats and the ashes of an heifer sprinkling the unclean sanctifieth to the purifying of the flesh, how much more shall the blood of Christ . . . purge your conscience from dead works to serve the living God?"

1281 [3] Really this whole subject is a matter of derivations, to which we shall come in our next chapter. We made this digression here in order to show by one more example how residues may be got at in the complex concrete case.

1282 [1] *Dictionnaire encyclopédique de la théologie catholique, s.v. Réconciliation des pénitents* (Wetzer, *s.v. Reconciliatio poenitentium*): ". . . An act whereby, in days when a severe discipline prevailed in the Church, public penitents were officially reconciled with the Church and formally admitted to its circle, after completing their penance. . . . Pope Innocent I writes to Decentius, Bishop of Gubbio, that penitents of the Roman Church receive absolution and are admitted to Church communion on Holy Thursday. . . . The admission was made with a solemnity fit to stir all hearts." *Ibid., s.v. Réconciliation des églises et des cimetières* (Wetzer, *s.v. Reconciliation der Kirche und des Begräbnisplatzes*): "When a church has once been appointed to divine worship and blessed, it can never lose its status as a sacred thing . . . but it can be profaned by acts affecting its sacred character. [A good example of altered integrity in things.] Neither church nor cemetery can continue to serve their hallowed purposes so long as they remain profane. To restore them to their proper condition a religious ceremony called 'reconciliation' [Restoration of integrity.] is required. That act has deep roots in the exigencies of religious sentiment [Quite so, owing to the residues here in question.] and in the conviction it inspires [Derivation.] that God withdraws from places where He has been insulted and that expiation is required to recall the Lord to such a sanctuary. . . . If a man who has defiled his soul, the hallowed temple of the Holy Spirit, through sin can be reconciled with God through penance, a church that has been profaned may likewise become the residence of God again as the result of a solemn rite."

extent, but in other respects it may be a question of the direct effects of a single sentiment.

1284. So the notion of purification is extensible in space. Certain signs indicate that some vague peril is impending over a group of people, a country, and steps have to be taken to avert it.

1285. The type of such phenomena would be the exorcism (*procuratio*) of prodigies by the Romans. A prodigy was a threat of oncoming disasters and something had to be done, and in a hurry, to avert them. A prodigy, moreover, involved a taint, and a purification was called for. When a man has unwittingly swallowed a poison he must find an antidote to counteract its effects. In descriptions of such cases that have come down to us, clearly apparent are, first, a feeling that *something has to be done,* and then, a breathless search for that something.[1]

1285 [1] Bouché-Leclerq, *Histoire de la divination dans l'antiquité,* Vol. IV, pp. 80-82: "Any prodigy, whatever it may have been and even if its meaning could not be divined, required expiatory ceremonies. When a man is frightened by a miracle it is natural for him to interpose sacrifices and prayers between himself and the danger he apprehends. [In general terms, he interposes some sort, any sort, of action. When an animal is frightened at the sight of some unusual object, he reacts physically: a dog barks, a horse rears and prances, the lion lashes his flanks with his tail.] The Greeks and Romans hardly overstepped such merely empirical exorcism (*procuratio*), which the most ignorant could understand. Instead of trying to discover what will had wrought the miracle and the purpose it was designed to fulfil [A lengthy derivation.], they called upon the 'gods who avert' evils [*θεοὶ ἀποτρόπαιοι, dii Averrunci*] and took courage in the thought that they had met enemies unknown with trustworthy friends. [A much shorter derivation.] Some ritual or other, a sacrifice, an offering, the recitation of a magical rigmarole, or some other external expression [The residue working unmixed.], completed the task of propitiation that had begun with the prayer. [More probably, the prayer came afterwards.] Numa had taught the Romans how to exorcise a certain number of so to say ordinary prodigies, and experience had enabled them to supplement the old ritual with some few empirical recipes. They had learned as far back as the day of Tullius Hostilius that a rain of stones was adequately 'taken care of' (*procuratio*) by nine days of holiday. [Whereas the haruspices came closer to the notion of purification:] As a rule they regarded prodigies less as warnings for the future than as complaints for the past. The abnormal character of the sign indicated, they thought, some imperious demand ordinarily inspired by some offence committed against the gods and not atoned for. The prodigy once recognized as such and, as the phrase was, 'accepted' (*suscipere prodigium*), the first problem was to determine which of the gods was the complainant. The prodigy once credited to its real author, it became easier to determine the cause of the complaint and the price for which it would be forgotten. Scrupulous investigation rarely failed

1286. In certain cases it was known exactly what the alteration in integrity had been. It was called a *piaculum,* and the same term was applied to the remedial rites. In case a sacrifice had not been performed in strict accordance with ritual, integrity was restored by repeating the sacrifice. For other sorts of violation one sacrifice or another served. Aulus Gellius, *Noctes Atticae,* IV, 6, relates that on learning that the spears of Mars had stirred in the sanctuary of their own accord, the Senate ordered a sacrifice to Jupiter and Mars, and that in case other victims should prove necessary—"*si quid succidaneis opus est*"—they should be sacrificed to Robigus (the god who averted mildew). Gellius ponders the term "*succidaneae*" at length and concludes that they are victims that served to "fill out" where previous offerings had proved insufficient. "For the same reason victims offered on the eve of solemn sacrifices were called *praecidaneae.* So the term *porca praecidanea* was given to the sow that was sacrificed by ancient custom to Ceres as a *piaculum* 'in advance of' a new harvest (*ante fruges novas captas*), in case someone had died in a family and the necessary purifications had not been, or had been inadequately, performed."

1287. The *lustratio* and the *piaculum* were often confused, since they both aimed at restoration of integrity. The *Arvales fratres* necessarily had to enter the sacred forest with cutting-knives in order to perform the sacrifices. On the other hand, it was forbidden to carry such instruments into the forest. The rule, therefore, being at all times broken, needed the support of a rite designed to restore integrity. Such a rite was performed by the Magister, or the Pro-Magister, who made an expiatory sacrifice of two pigs and a heifer in the morning and awaited the Arvals in the afternoon. That was the procedure at the annual ceremony, which fell in May or June. But then, in addition, whenever any work had to be done in the

to develop some oversight that had either not been noticed or had been inadequately repaired, and that was taken as the prime cause of the prodigy. If nothing of the kind came to light, the soothsayers were at liberty to conclude either that the inquiry had not been carried far enough or that the prodigy related to the future. To play the safer, the haruspices often looked in both directions, their findings showing mixtures of complaints and prophecies."

forest special expiatory sacrifices were required. In these customs of the College of the Arvals, which go back to very ancient times, the mechanical character of the restoration of integrity is clearly apparent. It was something very like sharpening an ax that has been dulled in cutting down a tree. Something has to be done. It is regularly done, and there is nothing wrong in doing it. All the same, it has to be offset by doing something else, to restore a certain balance that has been disturbed by the doing of it.

1288. The concept of altered integrity is extensible also in time, so leading to the notion that posterity may be held responsible for the sins of the forefathers. Hence the Christian doctrine of original sin, and other notions of the kind, such as the idea of the Orphics that the integrity of humankind had been primevally altered.[1] Such notions logically led to the belief that expiations and purifications are somehow required. Plato, in his day, mentions soothsayers who managed to persuade the rich that they held the secret of purification rites that could purge the crimes of men in general, and of their ancestors in particular.[2] Ovid retells the stories that were current in his time as to an original taint of the human race.[3]

1289. The type-case of a restoration of an integrity altered by orig-

1288 [1] Daremberg-Saglio, *Dictionnaire, s.v. Orphici:* "The Orphics believed in the divine nature of the soul and in a Fall, an original sin. Created in the first place by the gods, the soul had lived in Heaven, being exiled thence in consequence of a sin, the *παλαιὸν πένθος* of which Pindar speaks [*Fragmenta,* Boecke, Vol. II-2, p. 623], the *μεγάλα ἁμαρτήματα* alluded to by Jamblichus. Just what the sin was is unknown. Following the common explanation, humanity had sprung of the blood of the Titans, murderers of Zagreus. By birthright, therefore, man was an enemy of the gods, but at the same time there was something divine in him coming from the Titans. In addition to the general defilement attaching to all human beings, there was a particular defilement hereditary in certain families."

1288 [2] *Respublica,* II, 364 B-E. They used books of Musaeus and Orpheus and imposed not only on private individuals but even on the governments of cities.

1288 [3] *Metamorphoses,* I, vv. 155-62. Jupiter strikes down the Giants with his thunderbolts; but Earth gives life to their blood and "changes it into men, a race true to its birth in blood, being contemptuous of the gods, cruel, bloodthirsty, violent." To tell the truth, all such tales, all such derivations, in which the sense of an original taint finds its expression, are intrinsically of little significance. Yet with them many professed students of religion are chiefly concerned, quite disregarding the sentiments, the residues, that they manifest, and which are the prime factors in determining the social equilibrium.

inal sin would be Christian baptism. We are not called upon here to go into the numberless derivations that the dogma of baptism has inspired, and much less into the question of its spiritual value. Such subjects altogether transcend the experimental field in which we have elected to remain. However, from the standpoint of residues, it is impossible not to connect present-day Christian baptism with the baptism practised by St. John the Baptist, and with the ablutions that have been and are still in use among peoples and peoples without end. In Christian baptism the effect of one such ablution has acquired definite form as regards restoration of integrity: baptism removes not only original sin but all other sins that may have tainted the individual down to the precise moment of baptism. Numberless the passages in the Holy Fathers relating to the matter. They may be epitomized in the following declaration, which is usually included in the works of St. Augustine but seems to be really by an author unknown: "*Remission of sins:* Holy baptism entirely removes all sins, both original and one's own: sins of word, of deed, of thought; sins known and unknown—all are remitted. He reneweth man, who made him."[1]

1289 [1] St. Augustine, *De symbolo, Ad catechumenos sermo alius* (*a*), X, 10 (*Opera,* Vol. VI, p. 639). A *Decretal for the Armenians* by Pope Eugene IV rules: "The effect of the sacrament of baptism is the remission of all original and present sin, and of any penance that might be owing on the account of such sin. Therefore no satisfaction is to be required of recipients of baptism for past sins. Those who die before they have committed any sin advance straightway to the Kingdom of Heaven and the vision of God." St. Cyril of Jerusalem, *Catechisis tertia: De baptismo,* XV (*Opera,* pp. 446-47; Gifford, p. 17), makes specific mention of fornication and adultery among the sins so remitted. However, this status of Christian baptism is too well known to require any extensive documentation. A few opinions will suffice. St. Augustine states the Church doctrine over and over again: *e.g., Sermones,* LVI, *In Evangelium Matthaei,* 6:7-15, *De oratione dominica,* IX, 13 (*Opera,* Vol. V, pp. 377 f.): "Be ye baptized . . . and so shall ye enter! And be certain that you are forthwith forgiven all sins that you incurred from your parents in the fact of birth according to Adam in original sin, in view of which you hasten with your children to the grace of the Saviour, and all sins that you have added thereunto in the course of your lives—sins of word, of deed, of thought—all are forgiven you." The Saint sees in the Flood a symbol of baptism: *Contra Faustum Manichaeum,* XII, 17, (*Opera,* Vol. VIII, p. 265; *Works,* Vol. V, pp. 216-17): "It rained for forty days and forty nights, because every possible sin of a sinner is comprised within the Ten Commandments of the Law covering the whole Earth, which is in four parts, ten times four making forty. Both the sins which pertain to the day—to prosperity—and those pertaining to the night—to

1290. So, reasoning logically, one could infer that it was wiser to defer baptism until the very moment of death, so that, being cleansed of every sin by the rite, one would necessarily be saved; and support for that opinion could be found in the Gospels, where it is written, Matt. 20: 1-16, that the labourers of the eleventh hour shall be paid as those of the first. But, as everybody knows, logic has no place in such thinking—one same derivation can prove both the yea and the nay. The Church vigorously combated such interpretations, which in fact would have reduced all religion to a merely mechanical act at point of death.[1] On similar grounds the Church

adversity—are washed away in the sacrament of heavenly baptism." Gousset, *Théologie dogmatique,* Vol. II, p. 415: "This grace [of baptism] obliterates the original sin that the child bears in him at birth. In adults baptism erases all present sins that they may have committed before baptism and remits all spiritual penalties due on account of any sin whatsoever." *Canones et decreta Concilii Tridentini, sessio* V: *De peccato originali,* 5 (Richter, p. 14; Schaff, Vol. II, p. 87): "If anyone shall deny that the offence of original sin is forgiven by the grace of Our Lord Jesus Christ conferred in baptism, or assert that anything that has real and proper status as sin is not taken away, but holds that it is merely erased or not imputed, let him be anathema." The concluding remark on the notion that baptism does not obliterate original sin entirely, but merely cancels it so that it cannot be charged against one, is an allusion to a heresy that the Pelagians attributed to the Catholics. St. Augustine, *Contra duas epistolas Pelagianorum,* I, 13, 26 (*Opera,* Vol. X, p. 562; *Works,* Vol. XV, p. 256): " 'According to him, they hold that baptism does not give plenary remission of sins nor obliterate crimes, but shaves them off so that the roots of all sin still abide in a flesh that is evil.' Who but an infidel would ever sustain such a position against the Pelagians?" Calvin, *Institutions,* IV, 15, 1-3 (Allen, Vol. III, pp. 327-28): "Baptism is sent to us from Him as a letter patent signed and sealed, whereby it is enjoined, confirmed, and assured unto us that all our sins are so remitted, overwritten, abolished, erased, that they will never be considered by Him, never be refreshed in His memory, never charged by Him to our account. . . . Baptism promises us no other purification than by the aspersion of the blood of Christ, which is figured in the water through the similitude it has therewith in washing and cleansing. . . . And we must not imagine that Baptism is given to us only for times past, so that we must seek some other remedy for the sins into which we fall after Baptism. I am aware that that error arises from the fact that in olden times there were those who would not take Baptism till the end of their lives and on the point of death, that they might so have plenary remission for the whole of their lives [§ 1290]—a foolish fancy that has often been rebuked by the bishops in their writings. We must know instead that at whatever time we are baptized we are forthwith washed and purged for the whole course of our lives."

1290 [1] St. Gregory of Nazianzos, *Oratio* XL, 20 (*Opera,* Vol. II, pp. 383-86; English, p. 377): "But someone may say: 'What does it avail me to be bound earlier by baptism and by such haste deprive myself of the pleasures of life, when

condemned so-called Hemerobaptists. Also reasoning by strict logic, they baptized every day to be rid of moral blemishes, much as one might wash one's hands after the day's work.[2]

1291. Integrity before birth may be envisaged as well as integrity after death; but whereas the former has a bearing on a real subject, the living person, the subject in the latter case is abstract or imaginary.

1292. Time was when purifications with the blood of a bull (the *taurobolium*) or with the blood of a ram (the *criobolium*) became very frequent in Roman worship. The *taurobolium* was used either as a public sacrifice for the health of the Emperor or for the regeneration of a private person. A man went down into a trench over which a bull or a ram was slain by cutting the throat, and the blood of the animal dripped upon him, purifying him either forever, or for a certain period of time, after which the sacrifice had to

it is possible to enjoy them and receive divine grace at the last? For those who came early to labour in the vineyard had none the better wage, but received the same hire as those who came last.' " The Saint explains that the parable must not be interpreted in that fashion. In the first place it makes no mention of baptism. Furthermore, if the last did not work as long as the first, they were in no wise inferior in goodwill. A parable can mean anything one wants it to mean.

1290 [2] St. Epiphanius, *Panarium adversus haereses, lib.* I, *tomus,* I, *Haeresis* 17 (*Opera,* Vol. I, p. 255): *"Against the Hemerobaptists, fourth of Jewish heresies, seventeenth in order. . . .* Chiefly peculiar to this heresy is the doctrine that one should be baptized (βαπτίζεσθαι) daily at all seasons of the year, spring and autumn, winter and summer, whence the name of Hemerobaptists. They declare that there is no salvation for man save he baptize himself in water every day, washing himself and cleansing himself of every sin." St. Epiphanius assails that view, on the ground, in brief, that not all the waters in the ocean, nor all the water in the seas, rivers, and springs, nor all the water in the rain could, put together, wash away the sins of men, who must purify themselves by repentance. To which the heretic might have retorted: "Why, then, do you use water in your single baptism?" As a matter of fact, baptism involves an external act and an internal act, and now the one, now the other, takes the foreground according to the strength of the sentiments corresponding. Petau (Petavius), *Appendices geminae pro vindicandis ad Epiphanium animadversionibus,* 19-20: "That persons baptized while sick in bed are to be barred from the priesthood is the doctrine laid down in the *Canon Neocaesarensis* XII, and by Pope Cornelius, in a letter to Fabius, bishop of Antioch, quoted by Eusebius, Bk. VI, Chap. XXXV [read, *Historia ecclesiastica,* VI, 43, 14 and 17; Lawler, Vol. II, p. 123], in which he says of Novatus: 'It is unlawful to admit to the clergy anyone who has been baptized in bed because of sickness, as he [Novatus] was.' "

be repeated.[1] The Christians, naturally, resented the competition of such purifications with their own rites. Firmicus Maternus exclaims: "Why does the *taurobolium,* or the *criobolium,* cover you with blood in clots accursed? To wash away the taint that is upon

1292 [1] Daremberg-Saglio, *Dictionnaire, s.v. Taurobolium:* "The first *taurobolium* we can date belongs to the year 134 [A.D.] [It was devoted] not to the Mother of the Gods, but to the Celestial Venus of Carthage. Next in order of antiquity comes a *taurobolium* held at Lyons for the health of Antoninus Pius and his children and the welfare of the colony. The latest known was of the year 390, and it was taken by a Senator in his own behalf. In the meantime frequent public *taurobolia* must have been celebrated. . . . Private *taurobolia* can be traced, by inscriptions, from the second century down to the last days of paganism, but they were especially frequent after the reign of Julian." As Marquardt says, "at the end all pagan forms of worship seemed to converge on the *taurobolium.*" Some inscriptions: Orelli, *Inscriptionum . . . collectio,* no. 2352: ". . . *Taurobolio criobolioque in aeternum renatus* . . ." ("regenerate forever through a *taurobolium* and a *criobolium* . . ."); 2355: ". . . *iterato viginti annis ex perceptis tauroboliis VI aram constituit.*" ("this altar erected on the repetition of six *taurobolia* twenty years after their first taking [*ex perceptis*]."); 6032 (Henzen): "*Pro salute imp. L. Septimi Severi . . . taurobolium fecerunt. . . .*" ("They made a *taurobolium* . . . for the health of the Emperor L. Septimius Severus."). Prudentius, *Peristephanon, Hymni,* X, vv. 1011-50 (*Opera,* Vol. II, pp. 260-61). Vv. 1016-20 read:

> "*Tabulis superne strata texunt pulpita*
> *rimosa rari pegmatis compagibus:*
> *scindunt subinde vel terebrant aream,*
> *crebroque lignum perforant acumine,*
> *pateat minutis ut frequens hiatibus.*"

("Over [the trench] they build a platform of planks. It is full of cracks from the joints of a scanty framework. . . . Then they split the planks or pierce the floor with many borings so that it is thickly dotted with holes.") A bull is led up on the platform and his throat cut with the consecrated blade. The blood falls on the sieve-like floor. "Then through the numerous holes the blood rains as a dew infect, and the priest in the trench receives it, offering his vile head, his garments, the whole of his reeking person, to every drop." *Anthologia veterum Latinorum epigrammatum,* I, 57 (Vol. I, p. 33):

> "*Quis tibi taurobolus vestem mutare süasit,*
> *inflatus dives subito mendicus ut esses,*
> *obsitus et pannis modicis tepefactus, . . .*
> *Sub terra missus, pollutus sanguine tauri?*
> *Sordidus, infectus, vestes servare cruentas,*
> *vivere cum speras viginti mundus in annos.*"

("What bull-vendor enticed you into changing your clothes that you might turn in a flash from bloated Croesus to beggar, and be locked up, shivering in light garments, underground, to be dirtied with the blood of a bull till you reek with filth and grime and your garments are soaked with blood—and all in the hope of living clean for twenty years?")

you, you need a crystal spring, pure water you need, that after many stains the blood of Christ, with the Holy Spirit, may purify you."[3] Tertullian accuses the Devil of imitating sacraments of the Christian religion in the pagan mysteries (he may be right, for we do not know who the Devil is nor what his ways and morals).[4] "He sprinkles his believers and his faithful, and promises to wash away their sins with that ablution." And elsewhere vouching for the effectiveness of Christian baptism, he says:[5] "Even the heathen, who are strangers to all knowledge of spiritual powers, attribute the same capacity to their idols. But widowed of every virtue, their waters are deceptive. They initiate to an Isis or a Mithras with an ablution. They sprinkle even their gods. For the rest, they besprinkle round about their homes, their farms, their temples, and whole cities, and everywhere they expiate. During certain games of Apollo and at Eleusis they bathe, and presume to be regenerate and to have escaped punishment for their forswearing. So among the ancients those who had been tainted by homicide betook themselves to purifying waters."

1293. It is understandable that with such a great variety of rites to choose from the choice might prove perplexing. If the urge to purification rested on belief in a purifying power, that power would determine the consequences of the sentiment. What we observe instead is that the sentiment comes first; and then a means of satisfying it with some rite is sought; and sometimes the person desiring purification does not know to whom to turn.

1294. That is what happened in the famous purification of Athens executed by Epimenides.[1] "He took white sheep and black, led them to the Areopagus, and thence allowed them to go whither they pleased, enjoining on those who followed them to sacrifice them to

1292 [3] *De errore profanarum religionum*, 28-29 (Migne, p. 1043): ". . . *Quaere fontes ingenuos, quaere puros liquores, ut illic te post multas maculas cum Spiritu Sancto Christi sanguis incandidet.*"

1292 [4] *De praescriptionibus hereticorum*, 40 (*Opera*, Vol. II, p. 40; English, Vol. II, p. 48).

1292 [5] *De baptismo, adversus Quintillam*, 5 (*Opera*, Vol. V, pp. 161-62; English, Vol. I, p. 48).

1294 [1] Diogenes Laertius, *Epimenides*, I, 110 (Hicks, Vol. I, pp. 115-17).

the god of the place where they halted. Whereupon the plague ceased. That is why even now here and there in villages of Attica there are altars without names of gods that commemorate the expiations made at that time." Juvenal, *Saturae,* VI, vv. 511-68, satirizes a Roman matron who lends willing ear to all sorts of charlatans and pays good money to Jewess and Chaldean and to the priest of the Mother of the Gods.

1295. According to Zosimus, *Historia nova,* II, 29 (Reitemeier, pp. 150-51; Davis, pp. 51-52), Constantine decided in favour of Christianity because it offered purifying expiations for his particular crimes that he could not find in the pagan religion. That may not be the whole truth. Constantine may have had other reasons and stronger, such as the large number of Christian soldiers in his legions. All the same, superstition has its influences even on criminals! Bandits have been known to carry images of the Virgin on their persons. After ordering his mother's murder Nero, according to Suetonius, *Nero,* 34, 4, "had a sacrifice celebrated by magicians in an effort to evoke and propitiate her shade. In his journey through Greece he did not dare present himself for initiation into the Eleusinian mysteries because the voice of the herald holds the impious and the wicked afar off."[1] Eusebius says that, before advancing upon Maxentius, Constantine inquired as to the god to whom he should entrust himself in order to win the battle; and that he decided upon the God of the Christians because Emperors who had worshipped pagan gods had had bad luck.[2] The fact that Constantine inquired as to the religion best suited to his purposes is vouched for, therefore, both by a friend, Eusebius, and by an enemy, Zosimus, and they differ only in their manner of accounting for his choice. The story of Zosimus shows the residue of restoration of integrity. In the story of Eusebius the residue is a sentiment of personal in-

1295 [1] Dio Cassius, *Historia Romana,* LXII, 14, 4 (Carey, Vol. VIII, p. 161), says that Nero avoided going to Athens "because of the tradition about the Furies" (*διὰ τὸν περὶ τῶν Ἐρινύων λόγον*).

1295 [2] *De vita Imperatoris Constantini,* I, 27 (*Opera,* Vol. II, pp. 941-42; English, p. 489): *Ἐννοεῖ δῆτα ὁποῖον δέοι θεὸν ἐπιγράψασθαι βοηθόν*: ("inquires diligently as to which god he had better call to his aid.")

terest. Supplementary in both stories are combination residues (Class I).

Closely related to residues of restoration of integrity, so much so indeed as sometimes to be confused with them, are residues whereby men, animals, and things are endowed by certain rites with qualities that they do not have and so acquire a certain imaginary integrity. There is no question of restoring an altered integrity. The integrity is created by bringing something that was imperfect to perfection.

1296. V-γ2: *Imaginary or abstract subjects.* Here we get compounds, residues of our V-γ varieties uniting with residues of group-persistence (Class II). Suppose we begin with cases where the latter predominate. The persistence of an abstraction (II-δ) endows it with a personality, the integrity of which may be impaired; and any person with a deep feeling for the abstraction also feels the offence to its integrity, not only as a thing belonging to himself, but also as something belonging to his group, so that the II-δ residues are re-enforced by residues of the IV-β variety (sociality-uniformity).

1297. That explains the penalties which so many peoples in all periods of history have inflicted on offences offered to prevailing religions, popular customs, abstractions of all sorts. To preach that the Father came before the Son, or some other theological heresy of that sort, to utter an ill-calculated hurrah or an unfortunate hiss, to picture on a postcard the pretty figure of Paolina Borghese that Canova immortalized in marble, are deemed serious crimes and profoundly shock many people, not a few of whom are as indulgent as can be towards thieves and murderers. Numberless the cases in centuries past where mobs have risen against heretics, abused them, robbed them, put them to death. The Pan-Germanists of our time will not brook the slightest contradiction of the dogma that proclaims the Germans far superior to all the peoples that have been, are, and ever will be on this Earth of ours, or perhaps even in the solar system, modestly to say nothing of planets possibly gravitating around other suns and of the peoples that may inhabit them. Every now and then a newspaper will print a furious protest on the part of some Pan-Germanist who has turned wild beast (assuming that he was not already one) because a menu in some restaurant has been written in French. Others boil in holy wrath because a railway timetable reads "Genève" instead of "Genf." But then again there are people who lose their minds, again assuming that they once had minds, at the mere thought that a boy and girl may be exchanging love-letters through "General Delivery," when they hear the cooing of two turtle-doves, remark the absence of a fig-leaf "on a marble child exposing his male innocence to light of day"; or—moved by envy or some other form of hate—chance to reflect that somebody somewhere may be feasting his eyes on feminine beauty in the nude. (The conduct of such people, to be sure, often fails to coincide with the moral fury of their preachings.) Unfailingly, of course, derivations supervene to show that such ravings are logical, nay, the very essence of logic, that they hold the public welfare in view as their one and only end; and that those who "introduce new gods into the city" were justly and for the public welfare condemned of yore to drink the hemlock and in our time are justly put into prison or made to pay a fine.[1]

1298. The concrete case commonly shows the following elements:

1. Residues of group-persistence that make it possible for an abstract or imaginary subject to be taken as real (II-δ).

2. Some fact, real or imaginary, whereby it is believed, or assumed, that the integrity of some entity has been impaired.

3. Residues of restoration of integrity (V-γ) inspiring acts that are designed to compensate for the supposed offence.

4. Supplementary residues of hostility to alterations in the social equilibrium (V-α).

Derivations transmute imaginary subjects and acts into real subjects and acts, and replace the sentiments manifested by the residues with logical and pseudo-experimental inferences.

1299. In other cases the sentiments of group-persistence, though still playing an important rôle, are not altogether predominant. Among the many peoples in widely separated periods of history

1297 [1] [The literary allusion in the text is to Carducci, *A proposito del processo Fadda* (*Poesie*, p. 494).—A. L.]

who have had criminal codes of law, the factor determining the acceptance of the code has been a sentiment made up of the three kinds of residues just mentioned. In general when criminal codes do not exist and the personal vendetta is the rule, the residues of group-persistence are either absent or extremely weak; but they come into play again wherever the vendetta widens in scope and becomes a family or tribal duty. Here again there are derivations to show that the codes have strictly logical motivations—and these are sought now in the will of some deity, now in the wisdom of some semi-divine or very wise lawgiver; now in the sound sense of the forefathers; now in the will of the people; now in some metaphysical abstraction; now in purposes of social welfare, in some pretext of reform for criminals, or some other notion of the sort.

1300. It is interesting that oftentimes all these arguments, however varying and contradictory, work up to the same objective—a fact which clearly shows that the arguments are the secondary things, whereas the main thing is the objective, or rather the sentiment that determined its choice. A man kills another man under such circumstances as not to be justified by public opinion. He is made the target now of a vendetta by the family of his victim, now of the penalties decreed by a god, by a legendary lawgiver, by a sovereign, by the people, by the hair-splitting quibbles of the lawyers—but as the proverb says, all roads lead to Rome, and whatever road is chosen, it leads to the infliction of a certain penalty upon the murderer. Scholars have been trying for centuries and centuries to discover how and why such a penalty can or ought to be inflicted. They have not so far been able to agree on any single theory and continue disputing, each in favour of his own. It is obvious, therefore, that the conclusion precedes the premise not only historically but also logically; and that in turn proves that the conclusion does not follow from the premises, but that the premises are invented to give a reason for the conclusion.

1301. Illuminating in this connexion was a development in France in our day. The humanitarians had to all intents and purposes succeeded in abolishing the death-penalty; the President of France was pardoning as a matter of practice all murderers condemned to death. The parliament was regularly refusing to appropriate money for the fees of the public executioner. Under pressure of derivations, the death-penalty had gone out of existence. Then came the Soleilland affair, a case where a brute raped and cruelly murdered a little girl of humble family. He was condemned to death and then, duly, in line with the humanitarian theories prevailing, his sentence was commuted. But derivations are effective only when they are in harmony with residues, which are the real motors behind human conduct. In the Soleilland case no such harmony prevailed. Residues of personal integrity and group-persistence still functioning in the psychic state of the French people were not in accord with the humanitarian derivation. Events therefore followed a course contrary to the derivation and in accord with the residues.[1] The Presi-

1301 [1] "Scientists" spoke contemptuously of the morbid excitement that the crime aroused in the French public, representing the crime as a product of "prejudices" and of ignorance of their sublime theories. Hesse, *Les criminels peints par eux-mêmes,* pp. 146-47: "It was an impulsive, unpremeditated crime, committed by an individual who was predisposed by his antecedents and vices to just such outrages. That is the truth which the memoirs of Soleilland reveal. Debauchery, excesses, alcoholism, a natural inclination to violence, were all abetted by unfortunate circumstances. How many immoral crimes involving murder of children are committed under just such conditions by just such criminals! [An overstatement to some extent; statistics do not show any great numbers of murders of little girls after rape.] Yet somehow the Soleilland affair has made an unusual impression on public opinion. It is hard to say why. The dramatic discovery of the little girl's body in the parcel-room of a railway station; the fact that the hunt was for many days directed by the fiend himself; the fact that this is the off season for news and that the papers needed something to fill their empty columns—all that may have contributed to work up the sensation. . . . Soleilland's picture completes this gallery of abnormals, whose examinations show that they are fitter subjects for mental pathology than for the criminologist." If this writer, Hesse, really cannot understand why "the Soleilland affair made an unusual impression on public opinion," it can only be that the metaphysics in his theories has deprived him of all grasp over the realities of life. The conduct of the French public was instinctive, like the act of the hen in defending her chicks, of the bitch or the lioness in defending her young. The public did not intend to allow brutes like Soleilland to go on raping and murdering little girls under the wing of psychiatrists, with their dictionary of ten-syllabled terms, and the criminal lawyers allied with them. M. Hesse should be made to see that the reasons underlying the conduct of such fiends are of little or no importance. The important thing is to get them destroyed, the way rattlesnakes, mad dogs, and rats with the bubonic plague are destroyed. To fan Hesse's righteous indignation to white heat we must also tell him, and people like him, that

dent of France had to resign himself to signing death-warrants again. The parliament again began to vote appropriations for the public executioner; and the worst murderers again began to wend their way to the guillotine. Something very much the same occurred later on when the Bonnot and Garnier gang set out to spread destruction far and wide among law-abiding citizens. The instinct of self-preservation was again aroused in the public.[2] And something of the sort, though on a far smaller scale, took place in Switzerland. A well-meaning jury at Interlaken had inflicted an insignificant penalty upon the "heroine" Tatiana Leontiev. Logically enough the Russian Terrorists concluded that Switzerland was getting to be a favourable climate for their exploits; so before long they tried to "expropriate" a bank at Montreux, "executing," or in plain English murdering, such employees of the bank as resisted them. But the Swiss public reawakened to good sense, and the instinct of self-

the extenuating circumstances which he alleges, to wit, "debauchery, excesses, alcoholism, natural inclinations to violence," and let us add, as a special favour to him, atavisms from alcoholic and half-witted ancestors, are not extenuating but rather aggravating circumstances from the standpoint of social defence, since they increase rather than diminish the probability that the eminent individuals blessed with such traits of character will commit crimes of rape and murder. The French public understood instinctively that the one practical effect of all the chatter about "abnormals who are fitter subjects for mental pathology than for the criminologist" was to allow said "abnormals" to continue committing crimes to the damage of "normals," who, for their part, refused to tolerate any such thing, and rose in self-defence as does an animal when its life is threatened. If the metaphysics of our criminologists suffers in consequence, that is of course a great pity; but perhaps not so much of a pity as to allow little girls to go on being raped and murdered with impunity.

1301 [2] *Liberté,* May 6, 1912: "M. Herriot, mayor of Lyons, has also bidden good-bye to humanitarianism, born 1898, died 1912. He writes this morning: 'We demand that an end be put to this counterfeit sentimentality, which is just a caricature of self-respecting kind-heartedness. We demand that the presidential pardon shall cease to be what a courageous magistrate has called "a premium on murder." This business of extenuating circumstances is being carried too far. Reprieves are being carried too far, and the privilege-of-review period should be lengthened from five to eight years. Instead of heaping the graves of policemen killed in course of duty with flowers, more severity should be shown to those who shoot them.' One thing is clear. Yesterday's policy of turning the other cheek is going to lead in France to a policy of night-stick and cudgel."

preservation won out over the stupidities of the humanitarians.[3]

1302. In the matter of anti-militarism and anti-patriotism theories have not changed in France and in Italy during recent years. But for some reason or other Class IV residues (sociality), and especially δ residues of that Class (self-sacrifice), have changed in intensity; so that juries and judges have been convicting for anti-militaristic and anti-patriotic offences for which they formerly acquitted, and meantime there has not been the slightest change in the laws.[1] The Italian Government expelled Hervé, a man whom a few years before, during the period of benevolent indulgence for detractors of the army, it would at least have regarded with indifference. The wise change as times change! Here the facts are more striking than

1301 [3] Similar cases might be mentioned for all countries in all periods of history.

1302 [1] Colajanni, *Rivista popolare,* Dec. 31, 1911, p. 653: "In the preceding number of this review we called attention to the 'new spirit' that has come over the Italian courts since Nationalism has been on the rampage. . . . Optimists have been objecting that the instances mentioned in my article might very well be regarded as accidental idiosyncrasies of individual magistrates. Today that objection is left without a leg to stand on, because arrests, prosecutions, and convictions for incendiary editorials, incitements to striking and class-hatred, and other essentially political and essentially elastic crimes, are taking place everywhere. Convictions on such counts are reported from Ferrara. De Ambris and Zocchi are arrested at Parma. Giusquiano is under arrest at Pisa. A warrant is out for Lori at Florence. . . . This sudden outburst of reactionary fury has been ascribed to orders issued by the Minister of Justice and Pardons. I do not believe that. I happen to know that Signor Finocchiaro-Aprile, the minister in question, is a man entirely stranger to reactionary sentiments. The explanation is quite different. Our magistrates . . . showed special leniency to Socialists when they had reason to believe that the Socialists were all-powerful in high circles. Today they have reason to believe that the Government's outlook has changed. Now they are hoping to win promotions by siding with the Nationalists and Clericals. So there they are, arresting, prosecuting, convicting." Very well—but why did the "Government's outlook" change? Professor Colajanni himself reveals the secret: "Down to yesterday the Nationalists were satisfied with writing patriotic songs. Now they have an excited public on their side [The primary cause of the change.] and they are now resorting to violence in direct ratio to the amount of leeway accorded them by the police. . . . They spat upon Professor Bonfigli and beat him. They jeered a magistrate because he thought it his right to rise from his seat in a theatre when he saw fit. With the aid of police in uniform and in plain clothes, they lifted the critic of the *Avanti* bodily from his seat at the Scala and threw him out of the building because he refused to rise when the 'Royal March' was being played."

usual because a single cause and a single effect are involved, and because the change has taken place in such a short time. But they are in all respects similar to developments in criminal law where numbers of causes are mixed in together with many effects and which take place over longer periods of time. Criminal law reflects residues more directly than civil law. That is why civil law is oftentimes more logical than criminal law.

1303. Religions involving metempsychosis have souls reborn in human beings or animals for purposes of purification. Plato too speaks imaginatively of such a thing in the *Republic* and the *Timaeus,* books in which that illustrious dreamer, who still has his admirers among the people of our time, delivers himself of the grossest absurdities conceivable as to the manner in which this world of ours is made.[1] But even towards the person who is removed for good and all from this Earth, a sentiment of integrity endures that combines the many residues of Class II to determine the conduct of the living towards the dead.

1304. In the *Iliad,* XXIII, vv. 71-74, Patroclus asks Achilles to bury him promptly, that he may enter the abode of the dead.[1] So and for the same reason in the *Odyssey,* XI, vv. 51-56, the shade of Elpenor appeals to Ulysses. Virgil's Aeneas, *Aeneid,* VI, vv. 325-30,

1303 [1] *E.g., Timaeus,* 90-92: "Those among created men who were effeminate and led unholy lives were doubtless changed into women in their second existence." And the good soul goes on to impart "that then the gods set about creating a desire for copulation"—and explains at length how such union takes place. There are many other interesting things. He says for instance, 91E, that the simple and the naïve become birds, counting in that class anybody not altogether satisfied with his metaphysical poppycock. People ignorant of philosophy become four-legged animals and beasts of prey. The worst of them do not even get legs, but crawl on their bellies. Idiots and dullards (92B) generally become fish, because the gods did not deem them worthy of breathing a purer air.

1304 [1] "Bury me betimes that I may pass within the portals of Hades. The souls of the dead are keeping me off and allow me not to join their company beyond the river. So am I left wandering about Hades." On v. 73 the scholiast remarks (Dindorf, Vol. II, p. 250): "The [verse is marked with] a critical sign, because unburied souls remain without the river and mingle not with those who are in Erebus. The [same] critical sign also marks verses that are to be suppressed (*Odyssey,* XI, vv. 38-43)." The implication would be that the tradition was not Homeric. But that fact has no bearing on our study here. It is enough for our purposes to know that it was current in ancient Greece.

sees the souls of unburied bodies wandering about for a hundred years before they are allowed to enter Erebus.[2] Dante, *Purgatorio*, III, vv. 136-41, sees the souls of those who died in contumacy of Holy Church detained in the ante-Purgatory for thirty times as long a period as they spent in their presumption.[3] Residues remain the same, while derivations expand, diversify, change.

1305. This residue, again, underlies the Catholic derivation of Purgatory and the various liturgical devices for restoring the integrity of souls detained there. Jesting in the *Philopseudes*, 27 (Harmon, Vol. III, pp. 361-63), upon the superstitions of his time, Lucian has Eucrates describe the apparition of his wife, Demaenete, to him after her death: "On the seventh day after her death I was lying on this couch just as I am now. . . . And lo, Demaenete herself enters and sits down at my side. . . . At sight of her, I threw my arms about her and began to weep and moan. But she bade me dry my tears, and began upbraiding me because I had promised to offer her in sacrifice her whole trousseau, yet had I not burned one of her gold-embroidered sandals; and she told me that the sandal would be found under the chest, whither it had fallen—and for that reason

1304 [2] Lines 329-30 are an imitation of the passages in Homer:

> *"Centum errant annos volitantque haec litora circum,*
> *tum demum admissi stagna exoptata revisunt."*

("A hundred years they wander flitting about the shores [of Acheron]. Then, admitted at last, they come to see the pools they so long to reach.") The line preceding, v. 325, reads:

> *"Haec omnis quam cernis inops inhumataque turba est."*

("All these you see here are a throng of the poor and unburied.") Servius comments (Thilo-Hagen, Vol. II, p. 56): "People without legitimate, even symbolic, burial. Poor, without (*inopem*) [the rite of] throwing earth [upon the dead], *ops* meaning earth, in other words, without burial. He wants to show that symbolic burial [as in the cenotaph (*inanem*)] is as effective as plenary burial."

1304 [3]

> " 'Tis true who in contumacy hath died
> Of Holy Church, though he repent at last
> Still needs must wait upon this shore outside
> Full thirty-fold the time that obdurate
> He hath been in presumption, if such ban
> Do not indeed deserving prayers abate."

(Fletcher translation.)

we had not found it and so had burned only one. We had still a great deal to say when a bark came from a wretched Maltese terrier that was under the bed, and at that sound she vanished. We found the sandal under the chest, and made haste to burn it." In the same work, 31 (Harmon, *loc. cit.*, pp. 367-69), Lucian has Arignotus tell a story of a ghost who had been haunting a house but disappeared when the body was found and buried.

1306. That story has numberless counterparts among pagans and Christians alike. The person who has died appears as a ghost and haunts people until provision has been made, among the pagans for his burial, among the Christians for his burial plus masses, prayers, and other rites in his behalf. The origin of the derivation is apparent enough. Pliny the Younger, *Epistulae,* VII, 27, tells a story of a house in Athens that was haunted by a ghost. The philosopher Athenodorus rents the house at a bargain. A ghost in chains appears. He follows the ghost till it vanishes at a certain spot. On digging into the ground there, bones are found in chains. They are given honourable burial, and the ghost gives no more trouble.[1]

1307. Among Christians the ghost asks for prayers. But the derivation lengthens and lengthens, since there may be doubt as to whether the request is not made by a devil rather than by the soul of the dead.[1] Says Tertullian: "We make yearly oblations for the dead, and on the birthdays of martyrs. . . . If you ask Scripture for light on these disciplines and others of the kind, you find nothing. But it will

1306 [1] Suetonius, *Gaius Caligula,* 59: "His [Caligula's] body was secretly conveyed to the gardens of the Lamian family, half burned on a hastily constructed pyre, and covered with a little earth. Later on it was disinterred, burned, and buried by his sisters on their return from exile. It is well attested that before that was done, the custodians of the gardens were pestered by ghosts."

1307 [1] Calmet, *Dissertations sur les apparitions,* XLIII (pp. 129-30): *"One should beware of ghosts that ask for prayers.* Ordinarily apparitions of the dead ask for prayers, masses, pilgrimages, restitutions or payments of debts that they had not met, which would go to show that they are in Purgatory and need the help of the living in their sufferings. . . . But one must be on one's attentive guard against such apparitions and solicitations. . . . In his *De la démonomanie* (Bk. 3, cap. 6, p. 157) Bodin mentions more than one example of demons that have appeared in that manner, asking for prayers and even assuming the guise of persons praying over the graves of the dead to give the impression that the soul in question needed prayers."

be shown you that their authority is tradition, their evidence custom, and their observance faith." [2] That, really, tallies exactly with the known facts. The residue of restoration of integrity gives rise to this or that derivation which appears in tradition, is confirmed and modified by custom, and ends by becoming a matter of faith.

1308. In its doctrine of Purgatory the Catholic Church merely gives definite form to derivations from a residue that is as ancient as the history of our Western races, and of many other races too, and which has come down to our time from a day when libations were being poured on the graves of the dead in many countries in Europe.[1] The doctrine may have profited by the existence of the residue, as it may have profited by other social forces; but it cannot have created it, since it had existed for centuries and centuries before the Church was born. Dom Calmet therefore is altogether in the right when he says, *Op. cit.*, LXXX, p. 239: "Those who contend that all the talk about ghosts and apparitions of souls is a mere invention of members of the clergy selfishly interested in holding people to such beliefs, overlook the fact that the ancient pagans, who derived no advantage from such apparitions, and the Barbarians, for instance those of the North, who never went into subtleties in such matters, speak of spirits, apparitions, hobgoblins, demons, and good genii in virtually the same terms as Christians and churchmen." But a

1307 [2] *De corona militis*, 3-4 (*Opera*, Vol. IV, pp. 293-94; English, Vol. I, pp. 336-37): *"Oblationes pro defunctis, pro nataliciis annua die facimus. . . . Harum et aliarum eiusmodi disciplinarum si legem expostules scripturarum nullam invenies. Traditio tibi praetendetur auctrix, consuetudo confirmatrix et fides observatrix."*

1308 [1] The Annamites of China have rites for delivering the souls of the dead from torment. Diguet, *Les Annamites*, pp. 192-93: *"Rite of the 'Lam Chay,' or solemn fast for the delivery of souls in torment.* These rites have the sole purpose of getting out of Hell certain souls that may be detained there on one account or another and may as a consequence of their unhappiness become harmful to their former families. When a person has died on an unlucky day or his grave is located in an ill-chosen spot, or even if some one of the countless rules for ritual that govern funerals has been omitted, Annamite families are convinced that all their misfortunes are ascribable to that untoward circumstance. . . . Among the reasons that may bring a soul to distress must be counted sins of all sorts that have to be purged by sufferings in the other world. . . . Rites during the fast are directed by the magician, or Thay-phu-thuy ('Master-Wood-Water'), who gets his name from his use of a wand and of holy water during services. . . . The delivery of the dead is sometimes made the occasion for a great memorial festival to which hundreds of guests are invited."

further error is common enough. That is to conclude that since such phenomena are not fraudulent they must necessarily be genuine. No such dilemma confronts us. There is a third hypothesis that oftentimes accords with the facts, namely, that the phenomena in question merely manifest the subjective existence of certain residues, which persist in time and assume numerous and ever changing forms.

1309. The Council of Trent declares it to be the teaching of the Catholic Church that "there is a Purgatory and that the souls therein detained profit by the prayers of the faithful and especially by the very acceptable sacrifice of the altar." [1] If one chose to epitomize in similar language the beliefs of our Graeco-Roman and, more generally still, of our Indo-European ancestors on this subject, one might say that "there is a place (the abode of Ἅιδης, the abode of the *inferi*) where the souls are detained, and that such souls profit by the religious rites which the living perform in their honour and that each soul profits by the food which his descendants place on his grave." Ordinarily people who lay the prime stress on derivations feel that there is an abyss between the two beliefs. Those who regard the study of social phenomena as a mere pretext for preaching "virtue" or "progress" will be outraged that anyone should dare to compare a belief where the peace of the dead depends, in part at least, on their righteous behaviour on Earth with another belief in which it depends upon mechanical acts such as libations and offerings of food.

1310. Both are right if we look at things from the standpoint from which they are pleased to consider them. But there is another

1309 [1] *Canones et decreta Concilii Tridentini, sessio* XXV (*De Purgatorio*) (Richter, p. 391; Schaff, Vol. II, p. 198): *"Cum catholica ecclesia . . . docuerit purgatorium esse animasque ibi detentas fidelium suffragiis potissimum vero acceptabili altaris sacrificio iuvari."* And *cf. Ibid., sessio* VI: *De iustificatione,* 30 (Richter, p. 33; Schaff, Vol. II, p. 117): "If anyone shall say that after the acceptance of the grace of justification the sin of any penitent sinner is so remitted, and the guilt of eternal damnation is so obliterated, that no guilt remains [requiring] temporal [temporary] punishment to be paid in this world, or in the world to come in Purgatory, before entrance to the Kingdom of Heaven can be granted (*patere*), let him be anathema."

standpoint, the strictly scientific standpoint, from which social phenomena are studied much as the naturalist studies plants and animals. From that standpoint the two beliefs are in every respect similar. They are derivations from residues of group-persistence and residues of restoration of altered integrity.

1311. The integrity of the corpse as well as the integrity of the soul may be altered. There are many stories of the dead bodies of excommunicates rising from their graves and leaving the churches where they were buried at the words, read by an acolyte, "Let non-communicants retire."[1] There is another pretty story about the incorruptibility of bodies of excommunicates. Says Dom Calmet, *Op. cit.*, pp. 344-45: "There is a very ancient belief that the bodies of excommunicates do not decay. That appears in the life of St. Libentius, Archbishop of Bremen, who died January 4, 1013. That

1311 [1] St. Gregory (the Great), *Dialogi*, II, 23 (missing in Migne; Gardner, pp. 84-85): Two nuns were great gossips, and their sins were reported to St. Benedict: "On hearing this of them, the man of God sent to them at once, saying: 'Chasten your tongues, for if you do not mend your ways, I shall excommunicate you.' This sentence of excommunication he uttered not as a pronouncement but as a threat. But they in no wise changed from their original habits, and within a few days died and were buried in the church. And it came to pass that whenever masses were being celebrated in the church, at the customary words called aloud by a deacon, 'Let non-communicants retire,' their nurse, who had all along been making offerings to the Lord for masses in their behalf, would see them rise from their graves and leave the church. After remarking several times that they left the church at the summons of the deacon and were unable to remain within, she recalled the words that the Saint had said to them in their lifetime, that he would bar them from communion unless they mended their ways and words. When this thing was reported to the Saint, he was filled with great sorrow and straightway made an oblation in his own behalf with the words, 'Go, and have a mass said for them, and they will no longer be excommunicate.' And when the oblation had been offered in a mass, at the customary summons of the deacon that non-communicants should retire from the church, they were no longer seen to depart." Their integrity, in other words, had been restored by the oblation and their bodies were no longer constrained to leave their graves. In the same dialogues, II, 24 (Gardner, p. 86), Gregory tells of a monk who died in a state of disobedience to his abbot. He was buried, but every time his body was put under ground, the earth vomited it forth. St. Benedict ordered that a consecrated host be placed on the breast of the body, and it was never again cast forth by the earth. Admirers of mediaeval "science" should not forget that in those times so dear to them little stories such as the above were accepted as true by everyone. The judgment passed upon them in our day is more in conformity with the facts.

holy prelate had excommunicated a number of pirates. One of them died and was buried in Norway. Seventy years later his body was found whole and without trace of decay, and it fell to dust only when it had received absolution from Bishop Alvaredo. To win prestige for their schism and show that the gift of miracles and the episcopal prerogative of binding and loosing subsists in their Church more visibly and certainly than in the Latin and Roman Church, the modern Greeks maintain that with them too the bodies of excommunicates are incorrupt." [2] It is a matter of common knowledge that the bodies of saints are also incorruptible. As usual the same derivation proves now heads, now tails.

1312. V-δ: *Restoration of integrity by acts pertaining to the offender.* There is a sentiment that impels animals and human beings to hurt those who have hurt them, to return evil for evil. Until that has been done a person experiences a sense of discomfort, as if something were wrong with him. His integrity has been altered, and it does not recover its original state until he has performed certain acts pertaining to his aggressor. Typical are the sentiments underlying vendettas or duels.[1]

1313. V-δ1: *Real offender.* This is by far the most important variety, in fact virtually the only one we need to consider. The offence

1311 [2] Dom Calmet further states, p. 346: "The modern Greeks tell the story that under Manuel (or Maximus), Patriarch of Constantinople in the fifteenth century, the Turkish Emperor of Constantinople determined to know the truth as to the claims the Greeks made about the incorruptibility of people who died in their excommunication. The Patriarch ordered the opening of the grave of a woman who had had criminal commerce with an Archbishop of Constantinople. Her body was found intact, blackened and greatly swollen. The Turks enclosed the body in a coffin under the Emperor's seal. The Patriarch offered prayer, giving absolution to the dead woman. Three days later the coffin was opened, and the body was found to have fallen to dust." On such beliefs, Huet, Bishop of Avranches, comments (Lenglet-Dufresnoy, *Traité . . . sur les apparitions,* Vol. II, p. 175): "I am not considering whether the facts as reported are true or whether it is just a question of a popular error. Certain it is that they are vouched for by so many skilled and trustworthy writers and by so many eyewitnesses that one must be very careful in reaching a decision."

1312 [1] Cunningham, *Two Years in New South Wales,* Vol. II, p. 34: "In common with almost all savages, revenge with them is never satiated till quenched in the blood of an adversary. Like the Chinese, they are not particular about the person, but if a *white* injures them, they generally satisfy their rage upon the first of that colour they can conveniently meet with."

frequently affects more or less extensive groups even if it is done to one individual member. Relatives of the victim, his dependants, companions, fellow citizens, and even animals—the dog defending its master, for example—may feel the offence as done to them, that their integrity has been altered; and so the need of a restoration of integrity may arise in them and prompt them to react against the offender. Whence, in their many varieties, the obligation of vengeance and the right to blood-money, which are observable among barbarous or semi-civilized peoples. Such residues often blend with the residues of the V-α variety (social equilibrium). Even among civilized peoples of our day, if a citizen of one country is harmed in a foreign country his government often takes the offence as a pretext for exacting indemnity. That is a mere logical act. But many people are led to approve of it by the identical sentiment that in olden times made vengeance a duty. A European is murdered in an uncivilized country. A village where none of the guilty parties are to be found is bombarded and numbers of innocent people are killed. The integrity of the citizens of the civilized country is restored at the expense of the inhabitants of the uncivilized country. The sum of sentiments designated by the term "hatred" may be at least partially classed with this variety. Fear very often lies at the bottom of hatred both in men and in animals. In many cases when the fear goes, hatred turns to contempt. In general terms, hatred arises from a desire to repel an attack on one's integrity. Vigorous conviction is an element in integrity, and that explains the violence of theological hatreds. Hatred wanes when faith wanes, or when the individual no longer considers the faith an essential part of his personality. The artist, the writer, the poet, are led not only by vanity, but also by a profound feeling for their arts, to see an offence to their individual integrity in any contrary expression of opinion, or even in mere silence. Oftentimes any change in the existing state of things is deemed an offence and is repelled by attachment to tradition—neophobia.

1314. Tatiana Leontiev was let off with a light penalty by a very enlightened jury at Interlaken. She had killed an unlucky individual by the name of Müller, mistaking him for the Russian minister Durnovo, upon whose person the heroine had intended, so she averred, to wreak vengeance for the mistreatment of Socialists in Russia. Asked by the Court whether she were not sorry for her mistake, she replied in the negative: "Anyhow, this Mr. Müller was a *burjui* too!" The harpy's reasoning—it was accepted, notice, by those kind-hearted jurymen—may be stated as follows: A *bourgeois,* Durnovo, had offended the Russian Socialists. It was therefore "just" to kill a Mr. Müller who had not the remotest share in the doings of Durnovo, but was, however, a *bourgeois.*

1315. From the logical standpoint the reasoning is idiotic. But it gets its force not from its logic but from the sentiments that it expresses—and they correspond to residues of restoration of integrity. To avenge one of its subjects the Russian Government kills people who have in no way offended the subject, but are of the same nation as the offender. To avenge certain of her friends (among whom some were shown to have been very friendly indeed) Tatiana Leontiev murders an unlucky Müller who has had no imaginable part in the offences complained of, but who did belong to the same class as the offender—the *bourgeoisie.* In both cases the integrity of certain *A*'s has been altered, and it is restored by altering the integrity of certain *B*'s. As for the jurymen, they thought that the integrity of certain humanitarian beliefs of theirs had been impaired by the Russian Government and therefore regarded as excusable any act that had as its cause or pretext a design to restore that integrity.

1316. Why Tatiana Leontiev should have fixed upon Mr. Müller as the scapegoat remains a mystery. She might have chosen her own father. He was not only a *bourgeois* but actually an employee of the Russian Government. She might have chosen one of those jurymen, for they, good souls, were also *bourgeois.* Why, furthermore, should she have thought it proper to lead a life of luxury on the money that she received from a *bourgeois* father and which came from the Russian Government? Why, finally, should humanitarians be so particular about killing a mad dog when they are quite willing to leave the world at the mercy of the worst criminals or half-wits? However, it is altogether idle to look for logical reasons for non-logical conduct.

1317. An individual who is barred from a group finds that his integrity has been altered in that simple fact, and the alteration may be felt so keenly as to serve as a very heavy penalty indeed. Even though there is no actual exclusion, the mere declaration that a person's integrity no longer subsists may be equivalent to a penalty inflicted by force.

1318. That explains why in a number of primitive legal systems sentences without sanctions of any kind, and for the execution of which no public authority is designated, are quite the rule. Jurists who are surprised at such things need only reflect that in our own day we still have decisions by "courts of honour" which are of the very same nature. There is no force of public authority to execute such decisions. The mere statement of one may be a penalty much more severe than the day or so in prison inflicted by formal sentence of an ordinary court. There may be indirect sanctions for a sentence that has no direct sanctions, for the integrity of the individual upon whom it bears is altered by it, and in consequence of it he no longer stands on a par with other individuals previously his equals. But such a consequence is in any event accessory. The prime fact is that integrity has been declared altered by certain authorized persons. Caesar, *De bello Gallico,* VI, 13, observed that in Gaul sentences passed by the Druids derived their force from just such indirect consequences.[1] He might have compared that with the *nota censoria* of the Romans or with the *sacer esto* declaration of ancient Roman

1318 [1] "They [the Druids] rule on almost all disputes public or private. If a crime has been committed, a murder for instance, if there is some dispute about an inheritance or over property-bounds, it is they who decide, making awards and fixing punishments. If any one, be he a private individual or an official of state, does not abide by their decree, they bar him from the sacrifices. [Likewise the only weapon available to the Christian priesthood when their faith was still persecuted and had not as yet won the support of the secular power.] That penalty is a very serious one with them. A person under such interdict is classed with the impious and criminal. [Alteration of integrity, the main effect of the declaration or sentence.] He is shunned by everyone. No one will talk to him or be seen in his company, lest some untoward consequence be incurred from the contact. He cannot sue

law.[2] In the concrete case a number of different residues are usually operative. But outstanding in the instances mentioned is a residue whereby the wrongdoer is declared stripped of his integrity. He loses status: he is expelled from the group. The ancient laws of Ireland yield similar cases, which Maine appositely compares with others arising under Hindu law to which we have already alluded (§ 551).[3]

1319. The state of mind in which one alteration of integrity is met with another alteration of the same sort gives rise to the exceedingly numerous rules that determine the nature and amount of the compensatory alteration. As for the quantum, we start with the very simple rules of the old-time "head-money" (*talio*) and come down

for justice, nor obtain any public office (*honos*)." [Indirect consequences of the alteration of integrity.]

1318 [2] Jhering, *Geist des römischen Rechts,* Vol. I, pp. 279-81 (Pt. I, § 18): "The *homo sacer* lived in a state of religious and temporal proscription. Handed over (*sacer*) to the vengeance of the divinity he had outraged by his crime, barred as a consequence from all human intercourse, his property confiscated and sold for the benefit of the treasury of the gods, he could be killed by anybody at will. Did status as *sacer* carry any penalty with it? I believe not. Of course, if by penalty one means the troubles ensuing on a crime, to be declared *sacer* was the heaviest penalty imaginable. There was no terror that it did not involve. It represented the extreme degree of persecution and humiliation. The [public] enemy had no rights, but what made the situation of the *homo sacer* worse was the psychological element, his consciousness of being an object of loathing, horror, execration, to men and gods, of being a source of mortal contagion [The most extreme form of alteration of integrity.], of being shunned by everyone. [Consequences of the alteration.] Once existing, the declaration *sacer esse* was a resource the law may have used, but it was not established by legislation, any more than the infamy that went with it. [Residues provoke legislation. They never derive from legislation save in some few exceptional cases.] The lawgiver never thinks up such institutions as the penalty of the *sacer* or infamy, or if he does, as when the privilege of wearing the national cockade is withdrawn, he altogether misses fire. Institutions of that sort emanate from the very heart of the people and from nowhere else. They are a spontaneous expression of the moral sense of the public at large. [Drop the "moral" and that may stand.] They are a sentence of condemnation pronounced and executed by the people as a whole." [No, they express majority sentiments and nothing more.]

1318 [3] *Early History of Institutions,* p. 43: ". . . in ancient Ireland it is at least doubtful whether there was ever, in our sense of the words, a central government; it is also doubtful whether the public force at the command of any ruler or rulers was ever systematically exerted through the mechanism of Courts of Justice; and it is at least a tenable view that the institutions which stood in the place of Courts of Justice only exercised jurisdiction through the voluntary submission of intending litigants." That is true, translating ancient psychology into modern juridical terms. Using the language of the time, we would say that the pronouncements of the

to the "dosimetric" system—as Enrico Ferri styled it—of the Zanardelli code in Italy, a system as ridiculous as it is "scientific."[1]

1320. V-δ2: *Imaginary or abstract offender.* This residue is clearly apparent in cases where people pick quarrels with their fetish, or with some saint, spiritual being, or god. The countless examples that might be cited may be epitomized as follows:

1. Men treat the imaginary being as a real being. They praise him, blame him, glorify him, revile him, bargain with him, vowing him gifts if he gets them what they want, threatening him with harm if he fails to stand by them; decking his image with garlands if he satisfies them, neglecting him, insulting him, even thrashing him, if he disappoints them.

2. These simple associations of ideas and the non-logical actions corresponding to them are subsequently explained and justified by derivations. The imaginary being may be regarded as uniformly good. The pact then takes the form of a simple promise to show gratitude with gifts—for instance, the contract which the Romans used to make with Jupiter that he might bring them victory, or the vows of gifts made by modern Catholics to St. Anthony of Padua if he enables them to recover articles they have lost. He may be considered sometimes good and sometimes evil, and the effort then is to treat him in such a way that he will be good. Or he may be considered chiefly or exclusively evil, and the effort then is to humour him by treating him well, or to punish him by abuse. Finally he may be considered as essentially evil—the case of the

Brehons (Irish jurists) had the prerogative of declaring what a man was, of judging the character of his conduct. It was that declaration, supported by public opinion, which dealt the more or less serious blow to the man whose integrity was altered by it. Of the Brehons Maine writes, p. 52: "No authority of our day is possibly comparable with that of the men who, in an utterly uncritical age, simply said of the legal rule, 'So it has been laid down by the learned,' or used the still more impressive formula, 'It is written.'" But "courts of honour" in our time function in exactly the same way, and the most that they can say of the laws they follow is, "Such is the custom!"—a procedure no whit less arbitrary than saying, "It is written."

1319 [1] This is not the place to go into such questions. The situation is complicated, showing a substratum of residues of one sort or another overspread with derivations of greater or lesser complexity.

Devil of the Christians. He then deserves nothing but abuse.[1] So we go step by step from the simple association of ideas to the ingenious and complicated theology; but residues remain under the varying derivations essentially the same.

1321. Well known the fact that peoples who have fetishes discard or abuse them on proper grounds of dissatisfaction, and without, apparently, any great amount of thinking.[1] So it is with Italian peasant women of our day when they abuse the image of a saint who has not done them the favour asked, and with people who curse and swear not out of bad manners, but in the deliberate intent of insulting God or the Virgin—and the trait is by no means confined to illiterates. Ancient Greece admired the poems of Homer, which represent mortals as quarrelling and battling with gods. In more ancient times that does not seem to have been in the least shocking. Later on, Plato waxes wroth at the adventures of Homer's deities, and still later, in annotating the Homeric poems the Alexandrines try to reduce them to less impious readings. In the *Iliad*, XXII, v. 20, Achilles addresses Apollo exactly as Letourneau's Negro did his fetish when he says: "Surely I would avenge myself on thee

1320 [1] In *L'évolution religieuse dans les diverses races humaines*, pp. 70-71, Letourneau notes that the Kaffir *morimo* "is a general term serving to designate spirits and ghosts. . . . All calamities are ascribable to the *morimos*, and they are ordinarily heaped with abuse. The missionaries found it impossible to convince the natives that God, the Christian God, could disapprove of their insulting the *morimos*. The Kaffirs think of the *morimos* as invisible human beings, and they would be glad enough to kill them if that were possible. 'If I could only get at him, and run him through with my spear!' said a Kaffir chief in speaking of a *morimo*." The Kaffirs, according to Letourneau, have another term, *thiko*, which Moffat defines as a "malignant, devil-like spirit—sometimes Death. The Hottentots are thinking of the *thiko* when they shoot poisoned arrows at the sky during a storm, evidently hoping to hit him and kill him." [Surprising that Pareto did not comment that the *thikos* and *morimos* are variables—derivations. The theme of "shooting God" or "killing God" is trite in European folk humor. In Jean Aicard's *Adventures de Gospard de Besse*, an episode is entitled: *L'homme qui a tué Dieu*. A marksman misses a partridge on a point blank shot, attributes the humiliation to the Eternal Father, and shoots his remaining cartridge at the sky.—A. L.]

1321 [1] Letourneau, *Ibid.*, p. 95: "For that matter, unless a fetish is particularly feared it is dropped as soon as it fails to give satisfaction. The Negro in Guinea treats his fetish exactly like a human being. Before changing one he will give it a thrashing to teach it to obey. If he wants to conceal his conduct from a fetish, he hides the fetish inside his belt."

had I power in me!" Diomed, *Iliad,* V, vv. 383-402, assaults Aphrodite and afterwards Ares too. There is a show of justification, since Athena stands as counsellor and protector of Diomed, who may so be regarded as a tool that Athena uses in striking at Ares. To console Aphrodite, her daughter Dione reminds her that many gods have had to endure terrible sufferings at the hands of mortal men. Again in the *Iliad,* III, vv. 390-417, Helen gives Aphrodite a piece of her mind.[2] At a much later period we find a similar incident in the *Dionysiaca* of Nonnus of Panopolis, XLVIII, vv. 689-98, where, furious at her violation by Dionysus, the nymph Aura runs to the temple of Aphrodite and flogs the statue of the goddess.[3] From the standpoint of historical reality the two stories are equally imaginary. As indices of sentiments, the values are not quite the same. The popularity of the *Iliad* in the early days proves that Helen's blasphemy did not shock the Greeks of those times; the story of Helen therefore registered very general sentiments. The story of Aura in the *Dionysiaca* merely registered the sentiments of a limited number of lettered people, and may be nothing more than a poetic device.

1322. Plato's indignation at the poets for the stories that they tell of the gods[1] is a reaction of logic against such associations of non-logical ideas. But the people who believed such tales by no means drew from them all the logical implications they might contain, and their reverence for the gods was not in the least diminished by them. So in our day a woman may berate a saint for not granting her favours and still not lose her reverence for him; just as the revivalists in Wales lose none of their esteem for leaders who show themselves skilled gamblers in the stock-market; nor our "proletarians" theirs for leaders who coin money with their Socialism, or rate as "prole-

1321 [2] Aphrodite is trying to induce Helen to make up to Paris. Helen is unwilling and loses her temper with the goddess: "Go and sit by his side yourself! Withdraw from the pathways of the gods and never again set foot on Olympus!" Aphrodite replies: "Provoke me not, wench that thou art!" The scholiast, v. 395 (Dindorf, Vol. I, p. 162), finds Helen's rebuke blasphemous and the goddess's rejoinder unseemly.

1321 [3] In *Ibid.,* XXX, vv. 192-208, comes the story of the death of Alcimacheia, who had gone so far as to flog the statue of Hera.

1322 [1] *Respublica,* II, 17, 377D-78; III, 3-5, 389-92.

tarians" by the labels they flaunt but as wealthy *"bourgeois"* by their bank-accounts.[2]

1323. Pausanias, *Periegesis,* III, *Laconia,* 15, 10-11, mentions a statue of Aphrodite that had shackled feet and explains that according to one legend it was an allegory devised by Tyndareus to show that women ought to be subject to their husbands. According to another it was his revenge on Aphrodite for her share in the crimes of his daughters, Helen and Clytemnestra. Pausanias thinks it ridiculous to imagine that one could get even with a deity by punishing a wooden image of her in that manner. Arrian, *De expeditione Alexandri,* VII, 14, repeats a story, though without any great faith in it himself, that in his great sorrow for the death of Hephestion Alexander the Great ordered the temple of Aesculapius destroyed to punish that god for not saving his friend. On the day when Germanicus died, according to Suetonius, *Gaius Caligula,* 5, "mobs stoned the temples of the gods and demolished their altars, some families casting their household gods into the street and exposing all infants born on that day." [1] Weird as such sentiments may seem, they have their counterparts even in our time, and not only in the ignorant crowds in Naples who hoot at San Gennaro if the blood is slow in coming to a boil, but among the educated as well.[2]

1322 [2] When Bebel died in 1913, he left a fortune of almost a million francs. Even granting the reductions his friends insisted should be made, it still amounted to several hundred thousand francs.

1323 [1] *"Quo defunctus est die lapidata sunt templa, subversae Deum arae, Lares a quibusdam familiares in publicum abiecti, partus coniugum expositi."*

1323 [2] Consider, for example, the notion of some humanitarians that strict solidarity exists between man and God. But that is mild; one of them, a Protestant pastor, urges mankind to encourage God and bids Him have no fear: Monot, *Un athée,* pp. 36-37 (The preacher voices the opinion that if evil exists in the world, it is because God cannot prevent it): "Well, that vanquished God I hear speaking in my heart! . . . God strives to abolish evil and does not always succeed. . . . At such times, as we contemplate spectacles of iniquity or unexplainable unhappiness, we might use the following language for our faith, in a sublime talk with our heavenly Father: 'Fear not, I have no suspicion of Thee! I know that Thou hast not deceived us in these things. If I believed that, I should be in despair!' . . . All the same, to pray to the Father . . . is to ally our impotence with His impotence and say to Him: 'If we are defeated we shall fail together! Nothing is lost! I am still Thy child!' " A person who takes such gibberish seriously might just as well believe that Diomed struck Aphrodite with his sword.

1324. Class VI: *The sex residue.* Mere sexual appetite, though powerfully active in the human race, is no concern of ours here, for the reasons stated in § 852. We are interested in it only in so far as it influences theories, modes of thinking—as a residue. In general terms, the sex residue and the sentiments in which it originates figure in huge numbers of phenomena, but they are often dissembled, especially among modern peoples.

1325. Graeco-Roman antiquity thought of the sexual act as satisfying a bodily need, on a par with eating, drinking, adorning one's person, and the like; and all such things the ancients regarded with indifference, generally condemning abuses, and less frequently excessive refinements, in pleasures. A passage in an oration of Demosthenes against Neaera has remained famous: "We have," says he, "hetairae for our pleasures, concubines for the daily health of the body, wives to give us legitimate children and faithfully to attend to our households."[1] In Rome we get first a legal distinction between women who were obligated to chastity and women who were not. The law evidently had strictly civic objectives in view, enforcing certain duties that were considered beneficial to the state upon free-born women, but leaving men free in matters of sex so long as the exercise of freedom did not prejudice interests of the state.[2] For

1325 [1] *In Neaeram,* 1386 (Auger, Vol. X, pp. 448-49): Τὰς μὲν γὰρ ἑταίρας ἡδονῆς ἕνεκ' ἔχομεν, τὰς δὲ παλλακὰς τῆς καθ' ἡμέραν θεραπείας τοῦ σώματος, τὰς δὲ γυναῖκας τοῦ παιδοποιεῖσθαι γνησίως καὶ τῶν ἔνδον φύλακα πιστὴν ἔχειν.

1325 [2] Mommsen, *Römisches Strafrecht,* pp. 688-89: "The free-born woman in Rome was obligated by moral law to abstain from all carnal intercourse with men before marriage, and to keep to her husband after marriage. The man, on the other hand, was subject to the same moral code only to the extent of not impairing the chastity of a virgin or another man's wife in complicity with the woman." The Republic went to few pains in legislating on such matters, leaving crimes of that sort to domestic tribunals. Augustus and his successors instituted legal punishments under Imperial law, *Ibid.,* pp. 691-92: "The law took account of immorality only if it involved a free-born woman obligated to chastity (*matrona, materfamilias*); but in such cases the punishment always extended to the male accomplice. Female slaves were not subject to that law, nor were married or unmarried women who were not held to moral strictness by their manner of livelihood, namely: prostitutes, so long as they practised their profession; keepers of public resorts; actresses; keepers of places open to the public; women living in open concubinage. However, the mere fact of leading a dissolute life did not exempt the free-born woman in Rome from the legal consequence of her immorality. . . . [In a note:] Impunity could be

our Purity-campaigners today all love out of wedlock is illicit. For the Romans some forms were legitimate, some illegitimate.[8] They were not as tolerant of adultery in married women as sex-reformers of our day are, just as they did not have the sectarian rages of our moderns at amours with freed women or other women of the kind.

assured only by formal registration on the lists of prostitutes or by the fact of embracing a calling that implied the same looseness." The essentially civic character of the legislation comes out in that. Later on, towards the end of the Roman Empire, St. Augustine could write, *Sermones* (*Opera*, Vol. V), CLIII, 5, 6, that fornication and drunkenness were forbidden not by human but by divine laws: "You see the man enamoured of his carnal lusts . . . go seeking his pleasures on all hands in drunkenness and fornication, to mention no other things. And those things I mention because they may be committed under the law of man but not under the law of God. For what man is ever brought before a judge because he has entered the resort of the harlot, or who before a court because he has become (*defluxit*) licentious and unclean through his debaucheries (? *lyristrias*)? Who has ever been charged with crime (*crimen invenit*) because, though married, he has violated a slave? But so in the forum of man, not in the forum of Heaven, so in the law of the world, not in the law of the Creator of the world." In that the Saint draws a distinction, too soon to be forgotten, between law and morality. Custom came to establish a number of distinctions among public women. Nonius Marcellus, *De compendiosa doctrina*, 5 (Mercier, p. 423), mentions two such categories: "There is this difference between the *meretrix* and the common prostitute (*prostibulum*): the *meretrix* is of a more respectable place and occupation, being so called from the fact that she serves for pay, but only at night; the *prostibulum* is so called from her standing in front of her house by day and by night for purposes of gain." There were also categories corresponding to prices. Festus, *De verborum significatione*, IV, *s.v. Diobolares* (London, Vol. I, p. 224): "*Diobolares meretrices dicuntur quae duobus obolis ducuntur.*" Celius insulted Clodia with the epithet *quandrantaria*—"to be had for a fourpence."

1325 [8] Ovid is careful to state over and again that he sings only of legitimate passions. *Ars amatoria*, I, vv. 31-33:

> "*Este procul vittae tenues, insigne pudoris;*
> *quaeque tegis medios instita longa pedes!*
> *Nos Venerem tutam concessaque furta canemus!*"

("Hence, ye vapoury headbands, symbols of purity, and ye long skirts that half cover the feet! We are to sing to a harmless Venus, and of thefts within the law!") The *vittae* were worn by Vestals, matrons, and young girls: Servius, *In Vergilii Aeneidem*, VII, v. 403 (Thilo-Hagen, Vol. II, p. 156): "Fillets for the hair were worn only by matrons, never by prostitutes." Ovid repeats vv. 31-32 in *Tristia*, II, v. 247; then instead of v. 33 he writes, v. 249:

> "*Nil misi legitimum concessaque furta canemus.*"

("We sing of nothing but fair game and of thefts within the law.") And *cf.* his *Remedia amoris*, vv. 385-86, and *Ex Ponto*, III, 3, v. 51; Tibullus, *Delia*, 6, v. 67;

They were inspired not by sex residues, but by considerations of public utility. An inscription found at Isernia shows taverns posting in conspicuous places not only prices of victuals, but the tariffs for the women provided for public accommodation. A traveller spends one *as* for bread, two *asses* for the food served with the bread, eight *asses* for a girl and two *asses* for the hay for one mule.[4] Ulpian

Plautus, *Miles gloriosus,* ll. 789-93. In the *Ars amatoria,* III, vv. 57-58, 483-84, 613-16, Ovid repeats:

> *"Dum facit ingenium petite hinc praecepta, puellae,*
> *quae pudor et leges et sua iura sinunt. . . .*
> *Sed . . . quamvis vittae careatis honore,*
> *est vobis vestros fallere cura viros. . . .*
> *Nupta virum timeat, rata sit custodia nuptae:*
> *hoc decet, hoc leges iusque pudorque iubent.*
> *Te quoque servari modo quam vindicta redemit*
> *quis ferat? Ut fallas ad mea sacra veni!"*

("While still she [Cythera] inspires me, seek of me, O maidens, the precepts that modesty, the law, and your oaths, allow. . . . Even though you lack the honour of the headband, it must still concern you to know the arts of deceiving your men. . . . Let the bride respect her husband. Let every care be taken for the protection of the wife. That is all proper enough. That much the law, justice, decency, require. But who could tolerate that you, who have just been freed by touch of the praetorian rod, should continue a slave? Come to my oracles to learn the arts of deception!")

1325 [4] *Corpus inscriptionum Latinarum,* Vol. IX, no. 2689 (p. 251): "*'Copo* (*caupo,* innkeeper) *computemus.' 'Habes vini* [*sextarium*] *unum: panem, assem unum; pulmentarium, asses duos.' 'Convenit.' 'Puellam, asses octo.' 'Et hoc convenit.' 'Faenum mulo, asses duos.' 'Iste mulus me ad factum* (*sic.* ? that mule will be the ruin of me).'" The stone shows a carving of a traveller holding a mule by the halter and settling his accounts with a woman. Ulpian, in *Digesta,* XXIII, 2, 43 (*Corpus iuris civilis,* Vol. I, p. 370; Scott, Vol. V, pp. 251-52) (defining the word *palam*): "We regard as publicly prostituting not only a woman who has sold herself in a brothel but a woman who, as the custom is, has not spared her virtue in a public hostelry or some other such place. We also interpret the term 'publicly' quite generally in the sense of 'without love.' It applies not to the woman who has succumbed to an adulterer or ravisher but to the one who has played the rôle of prostitute [*i.e.,* for money]. . . . If a woman keeping a hostelry has mercenary women [in her employ], as the custom is with many women who keep prostitutes under guise of servants (*instrumenti cauponii*), it is to be ruled that such a woman comes under the term of procuress." *Codex Justiniani,* IV, 36, 3 (*Corpus iuris civilis,* Vol. II, p. 279; Scott, Vol. XIII, p. 117): "*Imperator Alexander. . . .* That said law be not evoked, such a woman [a slave sold for honourable purposes] must never have made money with her body nor practised prostitution in a public hostelry under guise of service." A law of Constantine distinguishes the proprietress of an inn from the women who serve the customers. The former may be accused of adultery; the

implies that many brothels were kept in places belonging to respectable people.[5] Later on, towards the end of the Roman Empire, and for causes that are still in part obscure, considerations of sex became a tyrannical obsession in the minds of men and assumed religious forms, often asserting themselves as a sort of religious horror. It is a curious fact that among the civilized peoples of our day the sex religion has survived as the last to which the support of the secular arm is still lent. One may blaspheme God and the saints with impunity, one may preach civil war, destruction, expropriation—but one cannot publish obscene books or licentious pictures. So the Wahabis (§ 1123) regard tobacco-smoking as the worst of crimes, something far more infamous than murder or theft. Such an inverting of the scale of seriousness in crimes—and an inversion it can only seem to a person not sharing certain religious sentiments —is an essential trait in the punishment of religious heresies and an index of the sway the persecuting instinct exerts over men who are playthings of their prejudices and feelings.

1326. In our Western races three abstinence taboos come down

latter not, because of their lowly estate. See *Codex Iustinianus,* IX, 9, 28 (*Corpus iuris civilis,* Vol. II, p. 588; Scott, Vol. XV, p. 15); Virgil, *Copa;* Philostratus, *Epistulae,* 32 (25), 33 (24), 60 (23). The distinction drawn in Justinian's law clashes with the Christian taboo, which is well formulated by St. John Chrysostom, *Homilia V, in I ad Thessalonicos,* I Thess. 1:1-4 (Gaume, Vol. XI, p. 533; Prevost, p. 344). That saint refuses to consider any distinction. According to St. Paul, he says, one must eschew commerce not only with the wife of a Christian brother "but with other women, both married and public. One must abstain from all fornication." In the *Digesta,* III, 2, 4, § 2 (*Corpus iuris civilis,* Vol. I, p. 98; Scott, Vol. III, p. 9) Ulpian writes: "Guilty of pandering is an individual who keeps female slaves for purposes of prostitution; but the person who makes a business of prostitution even with free-born women is in the same case. Whether that is done as the main business, or as an accessory to some other business (as the keeper of a tavern or lodging-house (*stabularius*) who has had such slaves as servants but practising prostitution on the pretext of such service; or again, the keeper of a bath-house, who keeps female slaves who ply that trade in said bath under pretext of taking care of the clothing of customers of said bath, as is commonly done in some of the country districts), said individual is to be held to the penalty for pandering." If prostitutes were available in all such places, there must have been a plenty of them.

1325 [5] In the *Digesta,* V, 3, 27, § 1 (*Corpus iuris civilis,* Vol. I, p. 149; Scott, Vol. III, p. 188): "Taxes that have been collected on rents of urban properties will be applied to that purpose, even if they have been collected from brothels, for brothels are kept on many properties belonging to reputable people."

across the ages, and in order of increasing virulence: abstinence from meat, abstinence from wine, abstinence from everything pertaining to sex. Abstinence from meat can be traced as far back as Pythagoras. Surviving from Plutarch are two tracts against the use of meat, *De esu animalium* (Goodwin, Vol. V, pp. 3-16), to say nothing of a whole treatise on the same subject by Porphyry. The Christians recommended abstinence from meat and enforced it in one form or another. Last in line come the vegetarians of our own day.[1] There was a great deal of talk in ancient times on moderation in the use of wine, but little or none on total abstinence. The early Christians advised a moderate use of wine, or indeed abstinence from it as well as from meat, first as a means of doing penance, but also and more especially as a means of attenuating impulses to carnal sin. There are plenty of prescriptions in such regards by the Church Fathers.[2] However, the Catholic Church has always aimed at a golden mean. Requiring abstinence from meat on certain days, it permitted the use of wine, so showing itself more liberal than many a modern pseudo-scientist. The prohibitionists of our time are re-enacting the feats of the religious fanatics of old. Abstinence from amorous indulgences and from everything even remotely calculated to suggest them is observable, in theory at least, among the early Christians,

1326 [1] Guérin, *Les conciles généraux et particuliers,* Vol. I, p. 55 (*Concile d'Ancyre en Galatie, l'an 314* [Labbe, Vol. I, p. 1503]): "Canon XIV orders priests and acolytes who were eschewing meat not to do so out of contempt for it as though meat were an unclean thing. It goes on to enjoin them to partake of meat and to eat it with vegetables that have been cooked with it, in order to show that their abstention from it was not due to any loathing for it or any idea that it was a wicked thing. . . . That ordinance by the council was a wise precaution against Ebionites, Manicheans, and some few other heretics, who were condemning the use of meat as wicked; for the faithful might have been led to imagine that the priests and acolytes in question in the canon were intending to favour the errors of such heretics. The use of meat is therefore not wrong in itself, though it may be meritorious to abstain from it in a spirit of penance, or as a matter of duty, at the times specified by the Church." Had the Church not safe-guarded personal freedom in the choice of foods in that manner, champions of purity might be going about in our time browbeating governments into putting people who eat meat into prison.

1326 [2] Fra Bartolommeo da San Concordio, *Ammaestramenti degli antichi,* 24, 3, 1: "The palate is a cause of sensuality. . . . (24, 4, 1) The use not only of food but also of wine must be temperate. . . . (24, 4, 5) Wine is beyond any doubt a breeder of sensuality."

and in our day, still in theory, it has again given rise to a pathological fanaticism of purity.

1327. Residues in these phenomena are compounds. At least three elements are discernible in them.

1. Least important is a residue of combinations, in view of which members of a sect have some sign or other to distinguish them from the generality of men, from outsiders, from members of other sects. Prohibitions of certain foods are observable among many many peoples. The Bible prohibits the flesh of the hare. No consideration of asceticism or the like can be detected in the prohibition (§§ 1276 f.)—it is a plain residue of combinations. That residue is often combined with another relating to personal integrity—to pride. The compound serves not only to distinguish, but to glorify.[1] Residues of that sort may very probably have figured in the effort of the Christians to keep themselves distinct from the heathen.

2. The element most important for the first two taboos (meat and wine), and of considerable importance for the third as well (sex), is a residue of asceticism. It manifests its presence in the fact that such taboos are accompanied by abstentions and mortifications that certainly belong to asceticism. That is strikingly apparent in the case of the Christians, less apparent in other abstainers, barely if at all perceptible in still others. The prohibitionists of our day pretend to be interested strictly in public welfare. But it is by no mere chance that they are also as a rule humanitarians, religious zealots, moralists, and champions of sexual purity. Not a few of them, though they may not be aware of it, may not be altogether unaffected by the ascetic residue.

3. Sentiments incidental to asceticism, such as conceit, envy of others who are enjoying what one cannot afford, eagerness for the esteem and admiration of this or that group, and so on.[2]

1327 [1] Renan, *Marc-Aurèle,* p. 570: "It is pleasant to think of oneself as belonging to a little aristocracy of truth-holders, to imagine that one possesses the treasure of the good with a few other privileged souls. Pride has its share in that attitude. The Jew and the Syrian *metuali,* humiliated, despised by everybody, are at bottom scornful, contemptuous creatures. No insult touches them. They are so proud to be of the chosen people!"

1327 [2] With those things we dealt in §§ 1169-71.

4. A need for expressing one's faith, in this case an ascetic faith, by external acts (Class III residues, § 888).

1328. Religious exaltation sometimes figures in the three taboos. The meat taboo assumes a religious form in India, not so in our Western countries. Scattered examples in connexion with the wine taboo are observable here and there among our contemporaries. With the sex taboo the fact is general all the way along from antiquity down to our own time.

1329. There are actually localities where the meat and wine taboos are more or less scrupulously observed, where, that is, groups of people actually abstain from meat and fermented drinks. For that matter, in such communities or countries the abstinence is at times merely apparent, as is the case in present-day Turkey. But as regards the sex taboo, differences in substance are negligible, there being notable differences only in forms. Prostitution is prohibited in Mohammedan countries, but it has substitutes in concubinage and in even worse practices. It was also prohibited in our parts of the world in days when morals were far from being better than they are at present. The sex taboo is one of the many cases in which sentiments are so powerful as to render substance virtually constant, admitting only of changes in forms. The contrast is so great that one is tempted to adopt the paradox that immorality is greatest there, precisely, where it is most severely condemned by morality and by law. Many indications lead to the belief that that is true of several states in the American Union—though one should not derive a general law from particular instances.[1]

1329 [1] It has been proved, of late, that there is much truth in Casanova's *Mémoires*. On the score of immorality, there were great differences as to forms, very slight differences as to substance, in the countries he visited. Salvatore di Giacomo, in *Giornale d'Italia,* Feb. 11, 1913: "Was Giacomo Casanova lying or telling the truth when, in his laborious solitude in the library which the good Count Waldstein had entrusted to his patient and learned reorganization, he told, among other things, the things that he had seen in Naples or which had happened to him during his sojourn there? Were the names of the people he knew in Naples really the names that he gives? And the Neapolitan society of those days—the people, the army, the clergy, our fatuous nobility, our attitude of frivolity, and that marvellous and almost inconceivable breath of noble ideas, of economic scholarship, of a new and inspiring philosophy in some few individuals, in whose austere ethical codes

1330. In the religion of sex, as in many other religions, inflexibility in forms gives rise to perversion and hypocrisy; the fable of the forbidden fruit is of all periods of history.[1] In the Middle Ages, and even somewhat later, when religious frenzies were rife, evocations

one already senses as it were a warning criticism of the times—were they as the observing adventurer describes them? We shall see. But meantime, if I may express in general terms an opinion that I have reached on the stories of Casanova which have to do with Naples, I can only say that he has surprised me not only for his having kept over so many years such a good memory of episodes and in their minute details, but for the literal accuracy of his account, which stimulated me to run down in our archives not the phantoms of an excited imagination, but persons and things that really existed, nay, that are almost alive today!"

1330 [1] Noting in his *Mœurs, institutions et cérémonies des peuples de l'Inde,* Vol. I, pp. 440-41, 437-38, how wide-spread and offensive he found incontinence to be among the Brahmans, Dubois adds: "And yet—who could imagine such a thing after what I have just been saying?—there is no country in the world where the outer semblances of decency, properly so called, are more generally observed. What we call *galanterie* is altogether unknown to them. That free, *risqué* chatter, those insipid allusions, that endless flattery, that boundless solicitude and attentiveness that is the stock in trade of our parlour 'dandy' would seem insulting to a Hindu lady, even to one not very strict in her morals, if she were offered them in public. If a husband ventured on any familiarities with his legitimate wife he would be set down as a ridiculous person of no very good taste." That may be repeated to the letter for many countries in Europe and America where words are hypocritically chaste and conduct unpleasantly indecent. So for another remark of Dubois: "Though adultery in a woman entails disgrace and is condemned by the rule of the Brahmans, it is nevertheless not punished in their caste as severely as in most others. If it is kept secret, little importance is attached to it. Publicity is the only thing that worries them, and in case of gossip, husbands are the first to contradict aspersions on the honour of their wives, in order to avoid the consequences of a public scandal." In one respect however, India is free of the hypocrisy observable in Western countries: "Relations with a prostitute or an unmarried person are not regarded as crimes by the Brahmans. Those men, who have associated notions of sin with violations of the most inconsequential rules, see no sin whatever in the extremest gratifications of sense. It was largely for their benefit originally that bayaderas and prostitutes were attached to service in the temples. They may often be heard reciting a scandalous line to the effect that 'commerce with a prostitute is a virtue that erases all sin.' "

Thinking of the pleasures of love Ovid observes, *Amores,* III, 4, v. 17:

"Nitimur in vetitum semper cupimusque negata."

(We strive for the forbidden and yearn for what is denied.) And he had said, *Ibid.,* III, 4, v. 9, that "she to whom erring is free, errs less": *Cui peccare licet peccat minus.* And, *cf. Ars Amatoria,* III, v. 603:

"Quae venit ex tuto minus est accepta voluptas."

(The pleasure that involves no danger is the least enjoyed.)

of the Devil and pacts with him were frequent. Who would dream of doing such things in our day, when the religious mania has, to a very large extent, abated? Many obscene expressions of lust may have, in part at least, very much the same origins as the old evocations of the Devil. Henry III of France was forever shuttling back and forth between rites of religious asceticism and offences against nature. He is just the type of a very large class of individuals. In our day, the very countries that lay greatest stress on purity reveal the worst cases of obscenities. Whenever the worship of Cythera is banned, the rites of Sodom and Lesbos come into vogue. The residue is constant. If its natural forms are interfered with, it assumes others.

When a person is under the sway of an all-absorbing idea, he is inspired to ridiculous conduct that provokes nothing but hilarity in those who are free of his impediment. That is why many rites of worship among savage and even civilized peoples seem fit subjects of mirth. Expressions of the sex residue are no exception to that rule. In England, Germany, and the United States in our day, instances of sex prudery, whether sincere or hypocritical, come to light every now and then that are as ridiculous as the most outlandish taboos.[2]

1330 [2] *Liberté,* Feb. 14, 1912: *Berlin,* Feb. 12: "Six years ago the widow of a captain in the Prussian army set up a little farm near her villa at Tetlow and living in peace there ever since have been two sheep, a pony, three ducks, a number of rabbits, and a flock of hens with a cock. For six continuous years quadrupeds and bipeds alike knew only the joys of a well-fed, happy existence. But the other day the thunderbolts of justice fell on their peaceful abode. It is quite a story. Across the way from the barnyard stands a primary school, and at recess-time the little Prussians had been in the habit of watching the antics of hens, ducks, and sheep. The schoolmaster chanced to follow his charges one day as far as the barn-yard fence and what he saw filled him with indignation. He took his most eloquent magisterial pen and addressed the burgomaster of Tetlow in part as follows: 'The daily spectacle of unaesthetic sexual inclinations on the part of the feathered tribe is exerting a most deleterious influence on the morality of the children in this school.' The conduct of the widow's enterprising rooster had shocked the good soul in his tenderest aesthetic sensibilities! Stranger still, the burgomaster, also best of souls, forthwith directed the lady *by police order* to shut up the cock behind closed doors. She, however, was deaf in that ear and sought an injunction of the courts. The Crown's attorney supported the mayor with a speech in which he roundly condemned the growing looseness of Prussian morals. The defence sought

1331. The sex residue is active not only in mental states looking to unions of the sexes or lingering on recollections of such things, but also in mental states that evince censure, repugnance, or hatred towards matters of sex. Strange as it may seem, there are data

to bring out the comic aspects of the case and made a motion that the 'Court proceed to an inspection of the farm and order the schoolmaster to present the rooster for a demonstration of immorality.' The court-room being in a tumult of laughter, the Court had the good sense to quash the police order issued by the mayor and to condemn the state to the costs." Another instance of soft-brained sex hypocrisy: *Gazette de Lausanne,* Jan. 1, 1913: "Is it lawful for a man to kiss his wife in a train in England? The Bavarian Government recently fined a man for just such an offence. Very properly stirred, a large English daily sent one of its best reporters to consult a high official of the British railways to determine whether travellers on trains in England were exposed to similar risks. The reassuring oracle emanating from that distinguished source was as follows: 'Patrons of the English railways have nothing to fear. A man may under most circumstances kiss his wife or any other duly authorized person on a station platform or in a train at a moment of arrival or departure or even during a journey. He may hold his companion's hand or even press it against his body. He may also allow his wife to rest her head on his shoulder whenever she feels fatigued.' These lucky Englishmen! At last they have their Charter of Necessary Liberties!" Stories of this kind are ordinarily taken as jests, but they are not jests; they are extreme manifestations of the sex residue, which assumes gigantic proportions in certain minds, fascinates and obsesses them, and deprives them of that sense of what is real and what is ridiculous which continues to function in minds not so seriously affected. Such things are observable in all times and places. They are the rule among the Christian ascetics and not rare among the Jews. Hosts of examples might be quoted from the Talmud. Suffice the following: Talmud of Jerusalem, Tract Taanith, I, 6 (Gemara) (Schwab, Vol. VI, pp. 149-50; Danby, p. 195): ". . . At the time of Noah's entry into the Ark, cohabitation was forbidden him, as it is written (Gen. 6:18) . . . but on coming out the privilege was restored to him in the words . . . (Gen. 8:16). . . . Rabbi Hiya b. Aba remarks: 'The expression "They left the Ark according to their families" means that it was for having preserved their lineage *sine coitu* that they were lucky enough to escape the Flood. The correctness of that interpretation is proved by the fact that the three who sinned against nature in the Ark, Cham, the dog, and the raven, were punished.'" Spicy details as to the misconduct of the raven in question are supplied by another Rabbi: *Commentarius Rasche* in *cap.* VIII, Genesis (8:7), (Scherzer-Abicht, *Selecta rabbinica-philologica,* p. 196): *"Exeundo et redeundo* ["And he sent forth a raven which went to and fro . . ."] He went to and fro about the Ark and did not fulfil his errand, because he had suspected Noah of designs on his wife *ne coiret cum illa in absentia."* That is pretty good, but there is better yet. Scherzer-Abicht translate (*Ibid.,* p. 18) a note by another Rabbi on Genesis. "Scripture teaches that Adam visited all animals and beasts and found his appetites unsatisfied by any of them"; and they add (pp. 66-67): "Reuchlin, *Cabbala,* I, f. 626 [Hagenau, f. VII, N] quotes Rasche as follows: 'Adam visited all animals and beasts of burden, but his senses were not inflamed till he came to his wife.' The last words are missing in my text. In this connexion Capnio, in person

a-plenty for showing that the very thought of chastity, when it assumes any prominent position in the mind, may have an underlying sex residue, and many individuals have been led over the road of purity to solitary vices.[1]

of Simeon the Jew . . . says that with those words, incarnate devils and fury-like spirits, rather than men, were preparing to raise the wrath of Christendom against us . . . for [the Christians] interpreted the line to mean that at that time Adam had foul commerce with all beasts and animals. But how could such a big man as Adam, and such a great one, have knowledge in a female way (*feminaliter*) of a flea, a fly, a cicada, a cimex?" It would seem impossible that the human being could sink to such depths of sottishness and that such a race of idiots could have survived to our day. Talmud of Babylon, Tract Berakoth, I, 5 (2) (Schwab, Vol. I, p. 260; Cohen, p. 59): "Suckling his mother's milk, he—David—perceives her breasts and breaks forth into song in these terms: 'Bless the Lord, O my soul, and forget not all His benefits' [Ps. 103:2]. 'What are those benefits?' 'His having,' answers Rabbi Abahou, 'placed the breasts of the mother in the seat of intelligence.' 'Why?' 'That the child,' answers Rabbi Juna, 'should not see nudity (as is the case with the females of animals),' or, according to Rabbi Matna, 'that the suckling of the child should not take place from an unclean part of the body.'" We are still

1331 [1] Renan, *Marc-Aurèle,* pp. 245-47: "One of the mysteries most deeply glimpsed by the founders of Christianity was the fact that chastity is a form of voluptuousness, and modesty one of the forms of sexual passion. Men who are afraid of women are, as a rule, the ones most attached to them. How often may we not say in all soundness to the ascetic: *Fallit te incautum pietas tua!*?" There is no mystery in the thing. It is nothing more than the "theory of veils," so called. Renan is well describing, but not so well interpreting, when he goes on to say: "That explains the strange mixture of timid modesty and sensuous languor that is characteristic of the moral sentiment in the primitive churches." A plain case of the sex residue. However, Renan feels in duty bound to append a bit of declamation: "Away with the base suspicion of the vulgar débauché who cannot comprehend such innocence! All was purity in those holy liberties! And furthermore, purity was essential to an enjoyment of them. [Renan of course was there in person and can testify that everything was purity itself.] Legend represents the pagans as jealous of the privilege of the [Christian] priest to see for a moment in her baptismal nudity the woman who was to become his spiritual sister as a result of that sacred immersion. What words to describe the 'holy kiss' which was the ambrosia of those chaste procreations?" All the same, those very Christians soon became aware that danger lurked in the "holy kiss" where men and women were involved. Athenagoras, *Legatio pro Christianis,* XXVIII: "If one kiss a second time for the pleasure of it [he sins] . . . so it is meet that we be cautious in the kiss, and more so in the salutation; for if our thought be defiled however so little or in any way, we are banished from eternal life." In the *Paedagogus,* III, 11 (*Opera,* Vol. I, p. 659; Wilson, Vol. I, p. 330), Clement of Alexandria would have the kiss not "immodest" but "mystical" and delivered "with chaste lips, closed" (διὰ στόματος σώφρονος καὶ μεμυκότος). With all due respect to Renan, this last prescription is not so terribly pure as purity goes. And *cf.* § 1394.

1332. The sex residue may figure in relations that are altogether innocent and chaste, and it is a manifest error to assume that wherever it is present relations of a physical character are necessarily envisaged. There are instances without end of women who have followed men at the bidding of a deep religious passion and treated them with great affection without hint of physical interest. That was apparent in the Welsh revival of 1904, where Evan Roberts was made the target of tenderest admiration on the part of women who seem really to have been pure of heart.[1] Such cases should put us on our guard against too ready acceptance of charges that adversaries hurl at one another on this score. It has been said that the Countess Matilda's feelings for Pope Gregory were those of a lover rather than a daughter. That seems not at all likely.

1333. On the other hand, the fact that the sex residue may be active in speech and writing that are altogether chaste, as well as in the frankly obscene, should serve to remind us that as regards stimulating physical passions the chaste may be as effective as the obscene and *vice versa.* It all depends on the individual. Some people

waiting for our respectable and brainy virtuists to pass a law ordering infants to close their eyes in drawing at their mothers' breasts. *Liberté,* Dec. 6, 1912: *"Purity in Australia.* At the instance of the Australian Government, the federal customs of Australia have just prohibited importation of indecently illustrated postcards, and so far, so good. But Australian customs agents have been instructed to interpret the term 'indecent' in the broadest sense to include anything of a blasphemous, indelicate, 'immodest,' or uncouth character. 'Immodest' is a very elastic term. Under it postcard prints of Rodin's 'Kiss,' of 'Alone at Last,' of 'Cupid and Psyche,' to keep to works of art, will be forbidden in Australia. One used to say 'Chaste Albion.' A prize for a word to give to Australia!" Gossip has it, meantime, that that well-chaperoned country knows all it might be expected to know of unnatural vices. *Journal de Genève,* Mar. 31, 1911: "A sentence just passed on Mr. X Y, editor-in-chief of a London weekly, is an indication of the vigour with which England is resolved to push her campaign against pornographic literature. Speaking for the Crown, Mr. Muskett declared to the Chief Justice, Mr. Marsham, that a number of the weekly edited by Mr. X Y contained an obscene paragraph. After a severe arraignment of Mr. X Y, the justice condemned him to a fine of ten pounds and costs." But absconders from the Continent find a safe refuge in England in view of the complications of extradition proceedings.

1332 [1] Bois, *Le réveil au pays de Galles,* pp. 437-38, 459. The story is told by Evan Roberts, the *dramatis personae* being as follows: "Mary, a Miss Mary Davies of Gorseinon, unrelated to the two better-known Davies girls, Annie and Maggie, who are sisters of Maestey; then Dan, Evan Roberts's brother. Says Evan Rob-are sensuously susceptible to talk and writing of the chaste variety, others rather to indecent literature. It has been said, and perhaps truly, that Guarini's *Pastor fido* has led more women astray than Boccaccio's *Decameron* ever did.[1]

1334. The sex residue figures actively in the vastly larger portion of literature. Tragedies, comedies, poems, novels, can hardly do without it. Moderns draw a distinction—along what lines is not quite clear—between a literature that is allegedly "moral" and a literature that is allegedly "immoral." The drawing of it oftentimes is a mere matter of hypocrisy, people shrinking at the word and not at the thing, and doing the thing but avoiding the word. At any rate, if it is not actually impossible to write an entertaining novel, comedy, or tragedy without the love-interest, successful ones in which love does not figure to some extent are as rare as white blackbirds—and that is enough to show the tremendous power of the sex residue. The public crowds in throngs to the criminal courts to listen to trials where passions are at issue and attention is the more greedy, the more obscene the matters discussed. Such audiences count no

erts: 'Just then a voice said to me: "You must observe silence for a whole week." The Davies sisters had just come in. When Mr. Mardy Davies had left the room, I asked them in writing to sing Newman's hymn "Lead, Kindly Light." . . . They did so. It was touching, solemn. When they came to the words "One step enough for me" there were tears in their eyes. Then they sang "I need thee every hour." Then one of them asked me, "What are we to do?" My answer was, "Wait until I get a definite message from Heaven." Heaven *suggests* [The word "suggests" was doubly underlined in the notebook in which Roberts wrote his responses.] that one of you go home and the other remain with me.' After a long time spent in prayer, my answer was ready: 'Annie is to stay here and take care of me. Mary will go home and rest or else go with Maggie and Dan.' " Annie Davies remains and Roberts hands her her instructions in writing: "No one but you is to see me during this coming week, not even my father and mother." And the girl nursed the prophet for a week without once hearing him utter a word. Bois comments: "One thing in all this might well surprise, not to say shock, a French reader—the assurance with which Roberts represents as a definite communication from Heaven an alleged command to keep a young girl all alone with him, while all others are sent away and he refuses to see anyone for a whole week. . . . The Holy Spirit had of course forbidden Roberts to speak, but he was still free to listen, write, and read. Many people besides Roberts might have seen in that suggestion rather a temptation than a divine command."

1333 [1] *Journal des Goncourt,* Vol. III, p. 6 (Jan. 1, 1866): "The French woman is more often led astray by the romantic in what she reads than by anything obscene."

end of men, and especially women, who in other places are energetic defenders of morality and wage frantic war on immorality.[1]

1335. We have had occasion time and again to note that the sex residues manifest themselves in phenomena quite similar to what is commonly called religion, and that they therefore as a whole may properly be classified with religious phenomena. The sex religion, like other religions, has its dogmas, its believers, its heretics, its atheists (a fact, also, to which we have made frequent allusion). But since that view is at variance with views more generally held, it will not come amiss if we add some further proof to those already given.

1336. Our single concern, remember, is to determine whether certain phenomena present, or do not present, certain specified traits—and not to evaluate their effects upon individuals or societies (§ 74). When we have recognized that the phenomena in question make up a group similar to the group known as religion, we still know nothing as to the good or the harm they may do. There are harmful religions, beneficial religions, religions that are neither the one nor the other; and nothing we have so far said will give any inkling as to the class in which the sex religion has to be located.

1337. In general religions do not admit their subjective character. They pretend to be objective, and hold that logico-experimental science confirms their dogmas throughout. In their primitive stages they are satisfied with their material elements. Becoming more advanced, they are inclined to take on intellectual, abstruse, and especially mysterious elements. Certain objects of worship are kept hidden from view, certain names are never pronounced, or if they are, only with holy reverence or holy horror. The Jews did not utter the name of their God. The Romans had a name for their city that was unknown to the public. The Athenians had severe punishments for anyone attempting to unveil the Eleusinian mysteries. Oftentimes in religions one gets a sentiment of mingled love and fear, even of terror, for the beings worshipped. Dogmas, like the prescriptions in taboos, are the premises, never the conclusions, of logical develop-

1334 [1] Carducci's poem, "*A proposito del processo Fadda*" (see §§ 1136 [1], 1297 [1]), is not a mere poem: it is a sound description of commonplace facts.

ments. The mere denial of them is a crime, or at least the index of a perverse nature. The ardent believer is shocked at objections to his faith, and often meets them not with arguments, facts, remarks, in rebuttal, but with a resort to force, either direct or through some public authority. As likely as not a prosecution for impiety will not be held subject to the general rules of legal process. The mere charge of a crime so serious is enough to deprive the accused of traditional guarantees that are never denied in cases of other crimes. Defence of a given religion becomes a defence of "morality," "justice," "decency," and must therefore be encouraged even by persons not holding that faith, so long as they are at least "moral" or "honest." "Moral" or "honest" no one not a Christian could be in the Middle Ages nor, in the view of many Mohammedans, can a non-Mohammedan be today. Now all of those traits, in their varying degrees, are recognizable in the mass of phenomena that go to make up the present day Religion of Sex. Not only that. The sex religion also adopts those time-honoured principles of conduct known as *raison d'état,* whereby the end is held to justify the means, so that when the end is of supreme importance, one need not scruple to smite the innocent, provided in so doing no guilty person escape (§ 1012 [1]).

1338. Among the peoples of antiquity and barbarous peoples of modern times, the sex organs and sexual acts are just part of a general fetishism. We moderns, judging things according to our own notions, distinguish the two types of fetishism, so that the sex fetishism endures, while other fetishisms have disappeared or lost most of their force. It would be beside our point to cite cases and proofs of sex fetishism among various races;[1] but since it is our duty to become acquainted with all the residues that have a bearing on the social equilibrium, we must mention a number of facts that go to show the importance and the continuity of the sex residue in our Western countries; and as usual let us devote our main attention to the civilization that has come down to us from Greece and Rome.

1338 [1] On the one hand the facts are well known, and on the other hand, they are a subject not for a general sociology, but for a special sociology dealing with fetishisms.

1339. We have seen that among the ancient Romans almost all the non-logical actions of life gave rise, by virtue of the residues of group-persistence, to concepts that eventually appear as minor deities (§§ 176 f.). There were little gods for all the acts of life, from conception to death. If we arrange such concepts in order, category by category,[1] we observe that for us moderns a considerable hiatus develops between certain points, whereas for the ancients the series is continuous.

1. Gods for acts occurring before the consummation of matrimony: Juno Juga or Juno Pronuba, who joins in marriage; Deus Jugatinus, who presides at the marriage union; Afferenda for the delivery of the dowry; Domiducus, who leads the bride to the husband's house; Domitius, who keeps her there; Manturna, who makes her stay with her husband; Unxia, who presides over the anointing with oil which the bride performs on the threshold of her new home; Cinxia, who presides over the removing of the bride's girdle; Virginiensis Dea, who keeps watch over the bride's virginity.[2] On all such matters the moderns speak freely, and even

1339 [1] I follow Marquardt's enumeration, *Römische Staatsverwaltung: Sacralwesen*, pp. 10-17.

1339 [2] Martianus Capella, *De nuptiis inter Mercurium et Philologiam*, II, 149 (Berne, p. 61. For the beginning of the quotation see our note next following, § 1339 [3]): "Thee [Juno] mortal brides should summon to their nuptials as Interduca [variant, *Interdua*] and Domiduca, Unxia and Cinxia, that thou mayest protect them on their way and take them to their longed-for homes and destroy evil omens [Marquardt suggesting *funestum* for *faustum*.] as they anoint the doorposts, and not desert them as they lay aside their girdles in their nuptial beds." Romans and Greeks alike attached a religious significance to the removal of the virgin's girdle. Festus, *De verborum significatione, s.v. Cinxiae* (Amsterdam, 1699, p. 150): "The name of Juno Cinxia was regarded as sacred in marriage rites, the girdle with which the new bride was girt being removed at the beginning of marriage." Suidas, *Lexicon, s.v.* Λυσίζωνος γυνή ["a girdle-loosing woman"]: "A woman having intercourse with a man, for on the point of consummation virgins dedicated their virginal girdles to Artemis." "Whence," as the scholiast on Apollonius, *Argonautica,* I, 288, remarks, "the temple in Athens to 'the girdle-loosing Artemis.'" And *cf. Orphica, Hymnus* 35 (36), 5 (Leipzig, pp. 299, 576-77; Taylor, pp. 85-86); Callimachus, *Hymnus in Jovem,* v. 21 (". . . *temporis quo Rhea zonam solvit*"); Homer, *Odyssey,* XI, v. 245 (though Zenodotus omits the verse and Aristarchus rejects it). Hence also the expressions *zonam solvere,* ζώνην λῦσαι "to loose the girdle," used of a woman having commerce with the opposite sex. A woman who had married but once could say that she "had loosed the girdle

with satisfaction. No fetishism has survived for any of the acts mentioned. The hiatus develops with the group next following.

2. Gods presiding over consummation. They are as numerous as the gods in the other groups. For the Romans this type of fetishism was in no sense different from any other fetishism; but it is the only one the moderns have kept—they have dropped the others. Bridging the hiatus, we get the following categories, of which, again, the moderns speak freely, the gods and goddesses of parturition forming a transition between the two groups.

3. Gods of birth: Juno Lucina, invoked by women in childbirth; Diespiter, who presided over birth itself; Candilifera, so called because a candle was lighted at birth; the two Carmentes, Prorsa and Postverta (relating to the manner of the child's presentment); then Egeria and Numeria.

4. Gods invoked just after birth: an Intercidona (who protected the house against Silvanus); a Deus Vagitanus, who opened the child's mouth that it might utter its first cry; a Cunina, who attended to the cradle, and so on—ten in all.

5. Gods of infancy. Potina and Educa taught the child how to eat and drink—thirteen in all (§ 176 [2]).

6. Gods of adolescence—twenty-six in all. Then come numberless gods and goddesses, dealing with all the occupations of life until with death Libitina and Nenia come on the scene.[3]

for only one man: *Greek Anthology,* VII, 324 (Paton, Vol. II, pp. 174-75): *μούνῳ ἐνὶ ζώναν ἀνέρι λυσαμένα.*" Theocritus, *Idyllia,* XVII, v. 60 (Edmonds, p. 215), uses the locution of a woman in childbirth.

1339 [3] The chief gods in the hiatus were: Mutinus, Subigus, Prema, Pertunda, Perfica, Janus Consivus, Liber and Libera, Fluonia, Nona, Decima, Partula Vitumnus, Sentinus. Ample information about them survives in the Church Fathers. To the passage quoted from St. Augustine in § 177 [3], the following may be added from the *De civitate Dei,* VII, 2-4, 11—the Saint is saying that the "chosen" gods of Varro are one and the same with others that were assigned to humbler offices [He is not, however, ridiculing the pagan gods altogether, but sustaining an argument for monotheism by analogy: since all the pagan gods come down in the end to one god, Jupiter, the pagans might just as well accept the one God of the Christians.—A. L.]—"In the first place Janus himself *aperit aditum recipiendo semini* at the time the infant is being conceived, all the business taking its beginning from that, each little thing being assigned to its respective little god. Saturn is there *propter ipsum semen,* and Liber *qui marem effuso semine liberat;* and there too Libera, who

1340. The hiatus appears in a distinctly religious guise in the writings of the Church Fathers; and as long as it remains of that character no judgment can be passed upon it by anyone who is concerned to keep to the experimental field and must therefore con-

is said to be Venus, and performs the same service for the woman *ut etiam ipsa emisso semine liberetur*. These are the only ones in the lot who are called 'chosen' gods. But the goddess Mena is also there to preside over the female period. A daughter of Zeus, she is none the less a menial (*ignobilis*) on that account! This province of the female period the same writer [Varro] assigns to Juno, no less, in his list of select gods, and she is even queen among them! And there also Juno Lucina presides over the same mess (*cruori*) with the same Mena, her stepdaughter. Two other gods are there, very vague individuals, Vitumnus and Sentinus, the one to bestow life, the other sense (*sensus*) on the child." And the Saint's argument is sound; it would have been very stupid of the Romans to assign such menial functions to the greater gods already existing. However, the Romans did not go from the gods to the acts: they went from the acts to the gods. The Saint is led astray by the preconception that essentially non-logical actions have to be logical: "Vitumnus, the life-giver, and Sentinus, the sense-giver, ought rather to be ranked among the chosen gods than Janus the introducer of the seed, Saturn its giver or sower, and Liber and Libera *seminum commotores vel emissores*, for [surely] it is a degrading thing to be concerned with such seed (*quae semina . . . cogitare*) before it has attained life and sense." The Saint goes on to say, IV, 11, that Jupiter may be everything that is claimed for him, but that all the same "he is the lowest in all that herd of menial gods. Under the name of Liber, *praesit . . . virorum seminibus* and under the name of Libera [*praesit seminibus*] *feminarum*. He is the Diespiter who leads the child to light of day, and the goddess Mena who has been put in charge of the female period. He is the Lucina on whom mothers in travail call. No other than he lends succour to the infant at birth in rescuing it from the bosom of the Earth, and so is called Opis (*opem ferat: Opis*). . . . He is called Paventia from the terror (*pavore*) of the child, Venilia from the hope of its coming (*de spe quae venit*), Volupia from the lust of procreation, Agenoria *de actu*, Stimula *de stimulis quibus ad nimium actum homo impellitur*, Strenia *strenuum faciendo*, Numeria *quae numerare doceat*. He it is in person of the god Jugatinus who unites bride and groom, and he it is in person of the *Dea Virginiensis* whose name is called when the girdle of the virgin bride is loosed. He is that Mutunus or Tutunus who is known as Priapus among the Greeks. All these things which I have mentioned, with due apology to chaste ears (*si non pudet*), and all the many things that I have not mentioned, for I think that some of them should not be—all these gods and goddesses in short come down to one god, Jupiter, or else they are, as some claim, parts of him, his powers." That treats on a par gods which later Christians were to sever with a hiatus. Tertullian, *Ad nationes*, II, 11 (*Opera*, Vol. V, p. 148; English, Vol. I, pp. 488-89): "They divide the whole life (*statum*) of man from his very conception in the womb into separate domains. A certain god Consevius presides over the amorous combat, and a certain Fluviona prevents miscarriage (*infantem in utero retineat*). Then Vitumnus and Sentinus, through whom the child first acquires life and sense, and then a Diespiter, who brings on birth. At the moment of birth there was a [goddess] Candilifera, for a candle was lighted

sider religious phenomena from the strictly extrinsic standpoint as social facts.

1341. Interesting from that standpoint is the fact that when the war on paganism was over, the religious character of the hiatus

at that time, along with other goddesses who derive their names from services connected with parturition. . . . They say it is the province of a Postverta to help a child if it is in wrong position, of a Prosa Carmentis if it is in normal position. . . . Speaking of the wedding itself, an Afferenda is placed in charge of providing the dowry [Never any trace of hiatus in that connexion!]; but, oh, for shame! there is a Mutunus and a Tutunus, a Pertunda, a Subigus, a Prema, a Perfica. [Now plenty of hiatus in Tertullian.] Mercy, ye gods of indecency: *Luctantibus sponsis nemo intervenit!*" Tertullian again in *De anima,* 37 (*Opera,* Vol. IV, p. 253; English, Vol. II, p. 498): "Roman superstition invented a goddess Alemona for nourishing the unborn child, a Nona and a Decima, so called from the critical months, a Partula to attend to parturition, and a Lucina to bring the child forth. We believe that those are divine functions belonging to angels (*Nos officia divina angelos credimus*)." Interesting this last remark. It is, after all, a mere question of competing theologies. Arnobius, *Disputationes adversus gentes,* IV, 7, and III, 30 (Bryce-Campbell, pp. 189, 171, 193-94) (proving that such gods do not exist): "Are we to count as one of the gods that Perfica who causes (*perficit*) those obscene and filthy enjoyments to proceed to the end with uninterrupted pleasure? Or that Pertunda who presides in the bedchambers over *virginalem scrobem effodientibus maritis?* Or that Tutunus, the wearing [*cuius . . . inequitare*: "whose riding of your matrons by"] of whose monstrous emblems and disgusting amulets (*fascino*) by your wives and matrons you regard as a favourable omen and insist on having (*optatis*)? . . . And does not an identical reasoning eliminate Juno from the list of the gods? For if Juno is the air (*aer*), as you commonly say in jest, transposing the letters of her Greek name [Ἥρα], no wife and sister of Jupiter the Omnipotent is any longer left [and with her go her special manifestations as] Fluonia, Pomona, Ossipagina [§ 176 [2]], Februtis [purification], Popolonia [fertility], Cinxia [§ 1339 [2]], or Caprotina [she who gave warning of the approach of the Gauls from a wild fig-tree]; and so it develops that there is nothing whatever behind that vacuous semblance of a name (*inanissima nominis fictio*) which has been made so famous by the fatuous beliefs of men." (The usual error of regarding non-logical conduct as logical.) Festus, *De verborum significatione,* VI, *s.v. Fluonia* (London, Vol. I, p. 270): "Women worshipped Juno Fluonia in the belief that she prevented hemorrhages in childbirth." Martianus Capella, *De nuptiis inter Mercurium et Philologiam,* II, 149 (Berne, p. 61) (invocation by Philology personified): "Beautiful Juno—though the heavenly fellowship would supply thee with another name, we call thee Juno because of the help thou dost give us (*a juvando*). . . . Or shall we call thee Lucina (or even Lucetia), from the light thou bringest to new-born babes? Do not expect me to call upon thee as Fluonia or Februalis or Februa, since I am undefiled of sex and have suffered no bodily pollution." The quotation is continued just above, § 1339 [2]. Lactantius Firmianus, *Divinae institutiones,* I, *De falsa religione,* 20, 36 (*Opera,* Vol. I, p. 77; Fletcher, Vol. I, p. 57): "A Cunina, too, is worshipped, as standing guard over infants in the cradle and keeping off the evil eye; and a Sterculus, who first established the custom of manuring the

seemed to be something quite incidental to the Christian faith; but while the conflict was acute the sex religion was called in to re-enforce Christianity and testify to its truth. Manifestly the idea of St. Augustine and others is that the pagan religion was false because it was obscene. The fact that sex sentiments could be appealed to as arbiters is evidence of their great strength. It is also manifest that the claim so often advanced down to our own time that the world owes its cult of purity to Christianity is untenable. Quite to the contrary, the cult of purity, sincere or hypocritical as it may have been, was a powerful factor in the triumph of Christianity. One need only read the Church Fathers to see at once and unmistakably that in defending their derivations they relied upon sentiments favouring chastity and hostile to sex indulgences, which were quite as current among the pagans as in their own circles. They used those sentiments, indeed, to reach minds which were closed to their theological dogmas, and persuade them that they ought to accept a religion that so well expressed sentiments of which they already approved. Such a thing will not strike the reader as surprising after the many proofs we have given that derivations follow, and do not precede, sentiments, though, of course, they may then serve to re-enforce them. Nor is it new for us to see sentiments of sex called in to judge competitions between religions and religious sects. This case is just one of a long long series of similar cases. Religions and sects are for ever accusing one another of obscenity and immorality. The pagans dubbed the agapes of the early Christians "obscene promiscuities of men and women," and at a later day orthodox Christians were to heap the same charges on the "meetings" of heretics. Protestants made effective use of the hackneyed charges of indecency and immorality against the Catholic clergy, and all Christians have with

fields; and a Mutinus, in whose naked (*pudendo*) lap brides seat themselves on the eve of their weddings [And see St. Augustine, *De civitate Dei,* VI, 9, who, etymologizing for Priapus, writes *prius sedent* for *praesident*], that he 'may be the first' to have impaired their purity." *Cf.* Arnobius, *Disputationes adversus gentes,* IV, 11, and Tertullian, *Apologeticus,* XXV, 3, 10-11 (Glover, pp. 137-39). Festus, *Ibid.,* XI, *s.v. Mutinus* (London, Vol. I, p. 445): "There was a shrine to Mutinus Titinus in Rome whither women went in broad-bordered togas to sacrifice to him."

one accord pressed it against atheists—time was when "liberal" and "libertine" were synonymous terms.[1] The philosophers of the eighteenth century used the sex weapon relentlessly against the Church, and the same blade, which has never yet grown rusty, is continually being brandished in France and Italy, where if not the only, it is at least the chief, argument put forward by many newspapers against the Church.

1342. How true or how false such charges may be or have been

1341 [1] Perrens, *Les libertins en France au XVIIe siècle*, pp. 5-10: "The sixteenth century applied the term 'libertinage' to the spirit of unbelief, which had been a very ancient thing in France. . . . The great heresiarch, Calvin, fought bold thinking, licentious habits, and the conservative party at large in his 'young ones of Geneva.' . . . Unluckily the opposition interpreted the word 'liberty' not only in a political sense but in the voluptuous sense so popular among young men. . . . Was there so much licence? Probably not, for fires were lighted about the stakes on the basis of doctrines. [So today our Inquisitors on Purity use imprisonment and fines in lieu of arguments they are unable to find in their wretched brains.] . . . Calvin now began to add moral accusations to charges of false doctrine. . . . His appointed victims became 'licentious Christians fallen from grace and given over to the demon of the flesh, Anabaptists, the abomination of despair.' [That could very well come from Senator Bérenger or some other idiot of the same breed.] . . . In his copious vocabulary of invective one finds the term 'libertine,' which he seems to have been the first to introduce into French. The word as an epithet for an adversary does not appear in any manuscript of the sixteenth century. *Libertin* and *libertinage* are words not to be found in the oldest French lexicons. The Jesuit Philibert Monet was the first to make up his mind to naturalize the two new-comers in ordinary French parlance (*anno* 1635). . . . Independence in religious thinking was the main thing that Calvin branded as 'libertinage.' To use it as he used it would have been an abuse. He had burned the bridges behind him. . . . But in the long run the bridges were rebuilt. Those who insist on crossing them in the seventeenth century are forcing the hand of their time. . . . As regards individual conduct, the honourable denotation is new, but there are cases of it. Mme. de Sévigné writes: 'I am such a libertine when I sit down to write that the first turn I take controls all the rest of my letter.' Whereas Furetière, who harks back to the regular usage, declares a 'libertine' the schoolboy who plays hookey from his classes or disobeys his teacher, the disobedient wife or daughter, the man who is restive under constraints and follows his own inclinations *without however departing from the rules of virtue or good manners*. He is as particular as Richelet is in stressing that significant qualification, for he adds that a woman may say of herself *in a good sense and with altogether proper connotations* that she was a born *libertine*. Voltaire too thinks of a libertine as a man who wants his independence [*Dictionnaire philosophique, s.v. Liberté*]. But it was inevitable that in an age of believers the independent spirit should be regarded as a scandalous thing if it was extended to matters of faith. Whence a derived meaning, which readily became the main one."

is not the question at issue here. We can stop at the fact that their regular recurrence in such great abundance in the whole course of so many centuries down to our own times bears incontestable witness to the great influence that sentiments of sex have upon human societies, a truth that is further corroborated by other facts in large numbers.

1343. Worship of the organs of sex has had its day in many lands. The fact should not seem surprising once we reflect that such cults were just a part of the general fetishism everywhere where the hiatus described above (§ 1339) had not developed. In Graeco-Roman antiquity phallic worship is observable not only among peoples of exuberant imagination, the Greeks, for instance, but even in earnest, unimaginative Rome. In Rome it appears as in no sense a product of decadence, but as a fetishism surviving others that had gradually died out. Triumphant Christianity found phallic rites still in full vigour; nor did it succeed in extirpating them altogether. They hung on throughout the Middle Ages. In the very times when Christian faith was most ardent obscene figures continued to be carved on sacred edifices and painted in miniature in sacred books, while certain Christian saints inherited the functions of the gods of generation and the Church had no little trouble in putting an end to these various kinds of obscenity.[1] [2]

1343 [1] An epigram of Antiphilus of Byzantium in the *Greek Anthology*, IX, 263 (Paton, Vol. III, pp. 138-41), shows a case of fetishism identical with the cults observable today among African Negroes: "When the old woman Eubule had something in mind, she was wont to regard the first stone that she found in her path as an oracle of Phoebus, and she would pick it up and weigh it in her hand. If she chanced to want nothing, she would find it heavy; if she had some wish, it would be lighter than a leaf. So she did whatever she pleased. But if things turned out badly she ever blamed Phoebus for the work of her own hands." Ancient

1343 [2] Cabanès, *Mœurs intimes du passé*, 3d ser., pp. 20-23, 110-11: "*The grotesque faun of the cathedrals:* So-called indecent figures come down very late even on religious monuments, and they have been noted in many places more or less mutilated but still so readily visible as to leave no doubt of their former existence. That they are still to be seen in fairly large numbers is indicated by the fact that in 1901 the Pope instructed the clergy to make a very careful examination of church buildings for the special purpose 'of destroying or rectifying all paintings either in the nude or insufficiently clothed.' The Sovereign Pontiff might have mentioned

1344. As usual, residues abide while derivations change. Nowadays it is the fashion to justify the hiatus that has developed in the series which was unbroken under the Romans with the pseudo-scientific arguments our times insist on having, so transmuting non-

heroes swore by their spears: Justinus, *Historiae Philippicae,* XLIII, 3 (Clarke, p. 302): ". . . In the beginning, our forefathers worshipped their spears as immortal gods, and we have a survival (*memoriam*) of that worship in our day, when spears are offered to the statues of gods." Aeschylus, *Septem adversus Thebas,* vv. 514-15 (529-30), says of a warrior: "He grasps a spear which in his assurance he holds in higher honour than a god and more precious than his eyes, and by it he swears an oath." [Smyth translation.] And *cf.* Virgil, *Aeneid,* XII, vv. 95-96; Valerius Flaccus, *Argonauticon,* III, vv. 707-11; Homer, *Iliad,* I, v. 234. The fetishisms in which Priapus figures were of the very same kind. Literature and inscriptions abound in allusions to him and there is nothing obscene about them: *Corpus inscriptionum Latinarum,* Vol. XIV, no. 3565 (p. 379): [On the top of a block of stone:] "To the genius of the god Priapus, powerful, mighty, invincible, Julius Agathemerus, freedman of Augustus [dedicates this stone in gratitude for] being warned in his sleep by the kindness of friends." (On the bottom:) "Hail, Holy Priapus, father of all things, hail. Grant me an untiring youth. . . . Grant me the power to charm fair maidens with the spell of wanton eye. Grant me to dispel soul-destroying cares in constant gaming and good times. Let me not fear old age too much nor be tortured by the fear of wretched death that is to bear me to the unwelcome mansions of Avernus where the King [Pluto] enchains (*coercet, sc. vinculis*) the vapoury (*fabulosos*) souls of the dead (*mortis quae ad domus trahet invidas Averni Fabulas manes ubi rex coercet*) and whence Fate allows no one to return. Hail, Holy Father Priapus, hail." (On one side:) "Come, all of you together, all you maidens [the Dryads and Naiads] who attend the sacred grove, all you maidens who worship the sacred waters." (On the other side:) "O Priapus, mighty, beloved, hail! Thy name chaste virgins invoke in prayer that thou shouldst loosen a girdle too long tied. Thee the bride invokes." (Here we follow the notes of De Ruggiero (*Syll. epig.* [?], Vol. II, pp. 23-24), who amends "*fabulas*" to "*fabulosas,*" modifying "*manes,*" and renders as "*inanes.*") Dessau, *Inscriptiones Latinae selectae,* no. 3581: "*Faustus Versenni P. ser. Priapum et templum d.s. peculio f.c.*" (Faustus, slave to Publius Versennus, had ["*f.c.: faciendum curavit*] this Priapus [*i.e.,* the statue] and temple reared at his own expense.") *Ibid.,* no. 3582:

---

sculpture as well as paintings; though it is only fair to state . . . that church buildings are not the only ones which reflect the manners and morals prevailing at one time or another in their ornaments. To say nothing of the winged Priapi on the Arena at Nîmes, or the sandstone monoliths in phallic form in the square at Préciamont (Oise), naturalia of a doubly inferior art have been observed more or less everywhere. The brush of the illuminator was neither more chaste nor more reticent than the chisel of the sculptor. There is a Bible with fairly skillful illustrations that were long attributed to John of Bruges. It portrays as naturally as can be the biblical episode of Lot and his daughters [Gen. 14:31-38]." *Cf.* § 1380. Such cases are not the few and the exceptional; they are the many and the commonplace. To describe them Witkowski needed three very fat volumes.

logical conduct into logical. Prosecutions of individuals who fail to respect a hiatus non-existent for the Romans are represented as necessary if we would have the younger generation strong and vigorous. But the younger generations in the Rome that conquered the whole

"Priepo Pantheo P.P. Aelii Ursio et Antonianus aediles col. Apul. dicaverunt Servero et Quintiano cos." ("Ursio and Antonianus, aediles of the colony of Apulia, dedicated this statue [*Pantheo for Pantheon*] to Priepus in behalf of [*P.P.*] Aelius during the consulship of Serverus and Quintianus.") St. Augustine, *De civitate Dei,* VII, 24: "In the rites of Liber a reputable matron placed a crown on the phallus in the presence of a throng of onlookers, among whom, blushing and sweating [we may imagine], if there be any shame (*frons*) in men, stood mayhap her husband. In the celebration of a wedding the new bride was bidden to sit down on a pyle of Priapus." But that is nothing compared to the indecencies in the mysteries of Cybele, the "Great Mother." In *Ibid.,* VII, 21, the Saint states that altogether respectable married women publicly crowned the phallus to obtain good harvests: "In the hamlets (*compitis*) of Italy certain rites of Liber are celebrated with such disgusting licence that male organs are worshipped in his honour and not [*nam* misprint for *non*] in a somewhat modest secret at least, but with a brazenness that shouts aloud in the public squares (*in propatulo exsultante*). On the holidays of Liber the obscene member was set up over every door in great honour and then carried about in parade, at first in the streets of small country towns, but eventually in Rome itself. In the town of Lavinium a whole month was dedicated to Liber, and on all those days everybody used obscene language until finally the image was paraded through the forum and restored to its accustomed place. It was necessary for a married woman of unimpeachable reputation to place a crown on the obscene object. For the god Liber apparently required so much placating for the sprouting of the seed, so much was needed to keep the evil eye (*fascinatio*) from the fields, that a respectable woman was forced to do in public a thing that a prostitute would not be allowed to do on the stage if married women were in the audience." All the same, in the more ancient times when those rites were customary "the altars on the Capitol glistened with trophies of Gallic and German kings"; while it was mystics of the Augustinian brand who "beckoned to barbarian swords to batter down the noble walls of Rome." [First allusion to Carducci, *"Agli amici della valle tiberina," Poesie,* p. 393. The second, ?—A. L.] Lactantius Firmianus, *Divinae institutiones,* I, *De falsa religione,* 21-25 (*Opera,* Vol. I, p. 83; Fletcher, Vol. I, p. 61): "At Lampsacus [on the Hellespont] the ass was the prescribed victim for Priapus," and Lactantius gives an obscene reason for the custom that very probably was invented to explain it. Arnobius cries, *Disputationes adversus gentes,* IV, 11 (Bryce-Campbell, p. 193): "If we did not bend the knee as suppliants to Mutunus and Tutunus, would that be the end of the world, would everything go topsyturvy?" And he is right; for if one thing is certain it is that worshipping or not worshipping one god or another was a matter of utter irrelevance to the welfare of Rome. And *cf.* Pausanias, *Periegesis,* VI, *Elis* II, 26, 2; and IX, *Boeotia,* 31, 1-2. Diodorus Siculus, *Bibliotheca historica,* IV, 6, 1-4 (Booth, Vol. I, pp. 222-23), states that Priapus was worshipped not only in temples but also in the open fields, as their guardian, and that he was thought to be effective against spells. The cult of the phallus had a long life. There are traces of it as late as the

Mediterranean basin—were they a race of weaklings?[1] The soldiers of Caesar conquered the Gauls and other peoples, to say nothing of the legions of Pompey—were they weaklings? Can it be that Senator Bérenger is more of a fire-eater than Julius Caesar?[2] Such perse-

sixth century. Evagrius, *Ecclesiastica historia*, I, 11 (Migne, p. 2451; English, p. 23): "A person might very properly laugh at the phalli of the heathen, their Ithiphalli, their Phallagogy, their grotesque Priapus and that Pan of theirs who is worshipped in the obscene member." Nicephorus Callistus also mentions the thing in his day, *Ecclesiastica historia*, XIV, 48; and *cf*. Suidas, *Lexicon, s.vv.* Ἰθύφαλλοι, Φαλλοφόροι, Φαλλοί; Hesychius, *Lexicon, s.vv.* Ἰθύφαλλοι, Εἰθύφαλλον, Φαλλός; Harpocratio, *Lexicon in decem oratores Atticos, s.v.* Ἰθύφαλλοι; Demosthenes, *In Cononem*, 1263 (Auger, Vol. VI, pp. 348-49); Athenaeus, *Deipnosophistae*, IV, 3; XIV, 16; Eustathius, *Commentarii ad Homeri Odysseam*, I, v. 226 (Vol. I, pp. 52-53). If we are to believe the author of the *Philosophumena*, V, 4 (Cruice ed., p. 237), Priapus figured largely in the Justine heresy, and got his name from the fact that he was "created before" (*priapus* from *prius*) anything else: "That is why he has a place in every temple, is honoured by all Creation, and has the fruits of the created world draped about him when he is carried about the streets, since he is the cause of creation." Well known the rôle of Priapus as the guardian of gardens: Virgil, *Georgics*, IV, vv. 110-11:

> *"Et custos furum atque avium cum falce saligna*
> *Hellespontiaci servet tutela Priapi."*

("Let the guardianship of the Hellespontian Priapus with his willow sickle serve as protection against thieves and birds.") *Eclogues*, VII, vv. 33-36:

> *"Sinum lactis et haec te liba, Priape, quot annis*
> *exspectare sat est: custos es pauperis horti.*
> *Nunc te marmoreum pro tempore fecimus, at tu*
> *si foetura gregem suppleverit aureus esto."*

("This cup of milk and these cakes are all you can expect, O Priapus, year after year. You are the guardian of a poor man's garden. For the present we have

---

1344 [1] As a measure for restoring discipline in his camp in Spain, Scipio expelled a large number of sutlers from it and prostitutes to the number of two thousand. Valerius Maximus, *De dictis factisque memorabilibus*, II, 7, 1: ". . . *nam constat tum maximum inde institorum* [pedlars] *et lixarum* [camp-followers] *numerum cum duobus millibus scortorum* [prostitutes] *abisse*." Xenophon did much the same for the Ten Thousand (*Anabasis*, IV, 1, 14), but as a measure for conserving food-supplies.

1344 [2] Suetonius, *Divus Julius*, 65: "He [Caesar] judged his men not by their good morals nor by their families, but by their prowess as soldiers, treating them all with the same strictness and the same indulgence." *Ibid.*, 67: "A merciless disciplinarian when it came to desertion and mutiny, he winked at other things. Sometimes after winning a great battle he would relax routine duties and give the men free rein in satisfying their lusts. It was a saying of his that 'his soldiers were fighters even when smelling from women.'" And *cf*. Dio Cassius, *Historia Romana*, XLII, 55.

cutions are held to be necessary to protect family virtues, as if those virtues were few or weak among the ancient Romans in the days when the image of the phallus was protecting children, men, and even victorious generals from the evil eye. And they are said to safe-

made you of marble, but you shall be of gold if the coming lambs fill out the flock.") And Ovid, *Fasti*, I, v. 415: *"At ruber hortorum decus et tutela Priapus . . ."* ("And ruddy-thighed Priapus, the ornament and guarantor of the gardens.") And *cf.* Tibullus, *Delia*, I, vv. 17-18; Columella, *De re rustica*, X, vv. 29-34 (Vol. I, p. 399); Horace, *Saturae*, I, 8 [Fairclough: "How Priapus put the witches to rout."]; *Greek Anthology*, XVI (The Planudean Appendix), 236-43 (Paton, Vol. V, pp. 300-05). The cult of Priapus appears in places where it cannot possibly have implied any obscene allusion. He was the guardian of tombs, for instance. Dessau, *Inscriptiones Latinae selectae*, no. 3585 (Now in Paris, found in Rome among the ruins of tombs along the Via Appia): *"Custos sepulcri pene destricto deus Priapus ego sum. Mortis et vitai locus."* ("I the god Priapus of the *penis destrictus* am the guardian of this tomb. This is a place of death and life.") *Ibid.*, no. 3586 (Verona inscription): *"dis manibus . . . Locus adsignatus monimento in quo est aedicla Priapi."* ("Sacred to the gods of the dead . . . A place devoted to burial which is the home of Priapus.") In the *Greek Anthology*, VI, 33 (Paton, Vol. I, pp. 314-15), Priapus is designated by the poet Maecius as protector of the sea-shore. And *cf. Ibid.*, VI, 89 (Paton, pp. 346-47); VI, 193 (Paton, pp. 398-99—the poet Flaccus); and X, 1 (Leonidas) and 2 (Antipater) (Paton, Vol. IV, pp. 2-5). This latter contains an exhortation to sailors to put to sea, and ends with the words: "This I say to you, I, the Priapus that stands in the harbour, son of Bromius." An image of Priapus is stamped on coins from Lampsacus. Strabo, *Geografica*, VIII, 6, 24 (Jones, Vol. IV, p. 205), speaks of a town that was called Priapus because that god was worshipped there. [This is a misapprehension on Pareto's part. Strabo says (Jones translation): "Orneae is named after the river that flows past it. . . . It was from Orneae that the Euphronius who composed the *Priapeia* calls the god 'Priapus the Orneatan.' "—A. L.] Lajard, *Recherches sur le culte de Vénus . . . en Orient*, pp. 51-54: "Significant the presence of the very organ of female generative capacity among the emblems that are grouped around the androgynous figure which I take to be the Assyrian Venus, or Mylitta. . . . Another cone even shows a priest dressed in an Asiatic costume and performing an act of worship before an altar visible on which are a *κτείς* and the star of Venus, or else the Sun. There the *κτείς* seems to be the emblem of the goddess herself. The presence of such an attribute on all these different monuments seems to me to characterize the cult of the oriental Venus with that same forcefulness, that ingenuous crudeness, which was doubtless stamped in the beginning on the religious doctrines current among the Assyrians and Phoenicians. Reaching over the centuries and over a long series of religious or political revolutions, those doctrines have left such deep imprints on the soil of Western Asia that on examining the manners and morals of the peoples living there today one gets the gloomy impression that despite the successive efforts of Christianity and Islam, worship of the *κτείς* has not disappeared in certain religious sects of the Near East and notably in a locality that was famous in a day gone by for the worship of Venus that was practised there. In our day, in fact, the Druses of the Lebanon district pay a real

guard the chastity of women, as though Roman matrons in the heyday of the Republic were any less moral than the emancipated women of the United States, which of all countries is the paradise of sex hypocrisy.[8]

worship to the female organ of sex in their secret vespers, and so worship every Friday evening, the day, that is, that was consecrated to Venus of yore, and also the day on which the Mussulmans are required by Mohammed's code to perform the double duty of going to mosque and attending their wives. . . . As regards these vespers . . . we are told that each initiate . . . is obliged to make a general confession and that the greatest of all sins is fornication with 'sisters' or female initiates. But the Nozaïrians, who have also kept the ceremonies of *κτείς* worship, regard carnal commerce as the only means by which perfect spiritual union is attainable." Athenaeus, *Deipnosophistae,* XIV, 56: "Μυλλοί: Heraclides of Syracuse says in his *De ritibus* that at Syracuse on the day of the Thesmophoria [festival in honour of Ceres] [cakes in the form of] female *pudenda* were made of sesame and honey and passed around in honour of the goddess. They [the cakes] were known throughout all Sicily as *mylli.*" *Cf.* Martial, *Epigrammata,* XIV, 69 [This epigram refers to a sweetmeat shaped like a Priapus. Pareto gives another reference to Martial, IX, 3, v. 3. This is mistaken. If he was thinking again of a Priapine pastry the reference might be to VI, 73, v. 2.—A. L.] And see further: D'Ansse de Villoison, *De triplici theologia mysteriisque veterum commentatio,* quoted by Sainte-Croix, *Mémoirs pour servir à l'histoire de la religion secrète des anciens peuples,* pp. 246 f.

1344 [8] On a line in Horace that deals with the symptoms of advancing age, *Epoda,* VIII, v. 18, *"Minusve languet fascinum?"* ("Is your spell any the weaker?") Porphyrio comments: "An allusion to the male organ, for it was customary to place that ugly object in front of things that were likely to be cast under a spell." Pliny, *Historia naturalis,* XXVIII, 7 (4) (Bostock-Riley, Vol. V, p. 290): "If a stranger enters the room, or if someone looks at a sleeping child, the nurse spits three times, though they (*illos,* the children) are already protected by the god Fascinus, who is the guardian not only of children but also of generals. He is worshipped by the Vestals as a god among other Roman gods and an image of him is hung from the floors of the chariots of generals as they ride in triumphal processions and protects them like a physician ever at hand against the evil eye of envy." Varro, *De lingua Latina,* VII, 97 (Goetz-Scholl, p. 119): "Obscene things are so called, perhaps, because of the indecent images (*obscaena, i.e., virilia*) that are hung about the necks of children to protect them from the evil eye." Daremberg-Saglio, *Dictionnaire, s.v. Fascinum, Fascinus:* "The phallus was carved in bas-relief on the walls of cities and all sorts of buildings public or private. An example unearthed at Pompeii also has an inscription, *Hic habitat Felicitas,* an assertion of good omen designed to bar the door to bad luck. The phallus was one of the commonest constituents in amulets worn on the person. Countless objects have been found ornamented with that design. Hardly a collection of antiquities is without one. Sometimes, to increase the effectiveness of a charm, several phallic designs would be grouped together to make up a sort of monstrosity. Then again the phallus would be given wings and legs. The licentious fancy of the ancients gave itself free rein in such grotesque compositions. . . . In cases of any immediate danger

1345. The United States mails refuse to carry an English novel because it is deemed too "sensuous"; but they carry without the slightest scruple publications that preach slaughtering the moneyed classes and robbing them of their property. But, really, can anyone keeping strictly to logic and experience consider such activities less harmful to individual and society than a little "sensuality" in print? [1]

from the evil eye, one could extricate oneself quite readily by making a gesture that is still familiar in Italy and other countries as 'the fig' (*far la fica*). . . . Inserting the thumb between the fore and middle fingers, one got a suggestion of the two sexes in union. To represent the two organs one by one was a very effective prophylactic." Of such things Pliny says, *Op. cit.*, XI, 109 (49) (Bostock-Riley, Vol. III, p. 92): "There is no difference between peoples in this respect, and universal also are such rites." After his allusion to the crowning of the phallus by respectable matrons (§ 1343 [1]), St. Augustine exclaims of Varro (*De civitate Dei*, VII, 21): "And he would call such acts of sacrilege sacred rites (*sacra*)!" Theodoret, *Graecarum affectionum curatio, Sermo* III, *De Angelis* (*Opera*, Vol. IV, p. 890): "At the festival of the Phallagogia, those who are celebrating the orgy pay honour to the little creature Priapus, with his *ingenti et exporrecto membro*, and so to the phallus of Liber, his father. In the same way the female *pecten* (*cf.* κτείς, § 1343 [1])—so the female organ is called—is worshipped with divine honours by female initiates to the Thesmophoria [of Ceres]."

1345 [1] *Liberté*, Jan. 9, 1913: "From the summer months of 1905 down to February 1912, when arrests took place on a large scale, unionist dynamiters had been trying by a 'nitro-campaign' to intimidate employers of non-union labour. Their activities spread terror in every shop and factory from New York to California. The Los Angeles *Times* building was blown up on Oct. 1, 1910, the deaths of twenty-two non-union type-setters resulting. That outrage required energetic action. It was then discovered that the International Association of Bridge and Structural Iron Workers was ordering the systematic destruction of shops, mills, and factories that disregarded the mandates of organized labour. The forty thousand exhibits that appear in the case, to say nothing of the oral testimony of witnesses, show that the Bridge and Iron Workers' Association had organized that agency of 'agitation' and that it was functioning with some efficiency. A secret budget of a thousand dollars a month was being devoted to purchases of dynamite. All the great industrial centres had information bureaus that kept the central committee supplied with the data required for prompt and direct action. When a company refused an increase in wages or took on 'yellow' help, when an employer undertook to guarantee the independence of non-union labour, when a non-unionized enterprise was competing with a unionized business in such a way as to lower wages and therefore had to be ruined, the dynamiters came on the scene; one of their delegates was sent to the place and a bomb exploded. One of these audacious terrorists, Ortie MacManigal, has told the story of his expeditions to the court in abundant detail. He has participated in fifty 'jobs,' most of them successful, in the five years since he began his propaganda by action. Let us give him the floor. 'In 1907,' says he, 'Herbert S. Hockin, secretary-treasurer of the Bridge Workers, came to see me in Detroit. "You are used to working in the quarries," he said, "so you know how to handle explosives. From now

Senator Bérenger goes around scrutinizing the costumes of chorus-girls with a view to safe-guarding morality. But he is also the author of a probation law that turns hosts of criminals loose upon the public to resume their former feats of prowess. Yet are crimes of violence really less reprehensible than a glimpse at a pair of legs, or even at a pair of thighs, on a stage? In some cities in the United States the authorities send policewomen about the streets to provoke "mashers" and arrest them, but they never hire detectives to provoke Anarchists to crimes of violence and then arrest them. Can logic and experience ever have shown them that a lewd remark to a woman on the street does greater harm to individual and society than a crime of arson, a murder, or a theft (§ 1325)? On March 28, 1913, the French Chamber debated an amnesty bill. It was proposed to vote pardons for all persons convicted of anti-militaristic agitation. The propa-

on you are in the pay of the union. It needs you." I tried to object, but he gave me to understand that if I refused the Executive Committee would black-list me and that I would be out of a job. In the end I gave in.' From that time MacManigal had a busy life. He started 'work' in Ohio, Illinois, Massachusetts, New York. He had a liberal expense allowance from the union heads. On occasions when his bombs failed to go off or were discovered in time to prevent explosion, he got only travelling-expenses. He communicated with headquarters only by telegrams of apparently insignificant content. When things went well he would simply send the newspaper item. . . . Ortie MacManigal tells his story in a matter-of-fact way. His confession, which is a real novel, is not less than seven hundred pages long. Here is a specimen from it. 'In June, 1908, I was on a job at Evanston, Illinois. Hockin paid me a visit. He had come to tell me that he had got hold of a new invention that would do wonders. It was a sort of clock device with a charge of nitroglycerin, which went off one hour, five hours, even ten hours after setting, according to the way you regulated it. It was very easy to work, and it gave you time to get far enough away to establish an alibi. He wanted me to start using it at once. I refused. "But we have tried it," he said, "at Steubenville, Cincinnati, Indianapolis. It works fine." ' " As regards police corruption in the United States, to say nothing of corruption in other public departments, there are documents without end. Here is one: *Journal de Genève*, Mar. 1, 1913: "Mayor Gaynor of New York, testifying before the commission investigating corruption in the police department, declared: 'At the time I came into office police inspectors were retiring millionaires. Some of them had town and country homes, yachts, automobiles. The police were collecting three millions annually in graft from disorderly houses alone. That situation no longer prevails today. There may be one or two exceptional cases of graft. But don't imagine the newspapers are altogether clean of graft. For twenty-five years they have been in it up to their necks.' "

ganda in question had urged citizens not to answer the call to arms, or if forced to do so, to fire on their officers rather than on the enemy. It had also given instructions for damaging a cannon so that it could not be used. The bill was defeated, after impassioned debate, by a vote of 380 to 171. At the same session a bill was introduced to grant amnesty to persons convicted of agitation for birth-control. That bill was defeated by a vote of 471 to 16. What are we to conclude? That betraying one's country, murdering army officers, destroying war materials, and handing the country over to an enemy are less important crimes than expressing one's opinion freely as to whether one should or should not take economic circumstances into account in bringing children into the world? Such a reasoning does not hold, and the non-logical, religious character of the whole procedure is evident enough.[2]

1346. Much less pretentious but no whit better is the argument which would justify the hiatus by the claim that it is designed to prevent minds from dwelling on loathsome things. But what more loathsome than a corpse in a state of decomposition, swarming with maggots, let us say? Yet one can speak of such a thing freely, and feel no compulsion to use Latin words or Greek letters for either the corpse, the decomposition, or the maggots. Obviously, therefore, the hiatus must have developed in response to some other sentiment than a feeling of revulsion for unclean things.

1345 [2] Frequent is a derivation that is designed to give a semblance of practical utility to prescriptions of a religious character. So the prohibition of pork among the Jews has been represented as a measure of hygiene. In the same way birth-control propaganda is said to be condemned only on patriotic grounds as tending to decrease the number of men available for a country's defence. If that argument were sound, the 471 French Deputies who condemned birth-control agitation ought *a fortiori* to have condemned an agitation designed to deprive the army of the weapons required for fighting an enemy. It is also somewhat ludicrous to be so fussy about increasing the number of men available for an army, just to have them killed by their comrades later on if they have brains enough to become officers. Much more consistent were those German women who, copying Lysistrata, preached a "mother's strike" to stop supplying the *"bourgeoisie"* with slaves and the Empire with soldiers. It is true that the considerations underlying a vote taken in a legislative body are very complex, and that logic is the last thing one should ask of them. In view of that, if the vote in France stood alone it would prove nothing. It acquires significance, however, from the fact that it is typical of an exceedingly large number of cases.

1347. The sentiment in fact is of a class with the sentiments that prompt people to have an element of mystery in their religions. The hiatus as it exists today is a reticence of form rather than of substance. It appears very much as an oscillation in the degree to which mystery is carried. Mystery was not unknown among the ancient Romans, but in our time it shrouds many things that were formerly left in the light of day.

1348. If we would keep to the logico-experimental field in dealing with such facts, we must not in any way share in the religious sentiments in which they originate, or at least must put our sentiments aside so long as we are dealing with them.

1349. These sentiments may be of great practical utility in the conduct of social life. They are certainly fatal to theoretical investigations conducted in the logico-experimental field. Anyone not feeling his mind altogether at ease would therefore do better to read no farther in this chapter, just as people who believe in the divine inspiration of the Koran do well in not reading historical criticisms of that book or of the life of Mohammed.

1350. A man may be a scientific sceptic in one field and a man of faith in another field; but he cannot, "because a contradiction there consents not," be a sceptic and a believer in the same field. The believer, precisely because he is one, can only regard his own religion as true and other religions as false. He therefore judges, as he has to judge, the facts by that standard. From the experimental point of view two actions may be in all respects similar, but he will judge them now good, now bad, according as they belong to his own religion or to some other. He readily sees the mote in his neighbour's eye. He cannot see the beam in his own.

1351. Like the believer in any other religion, the believer in the Religion of Sex rejects *a priori* every argument that runs counter to his faith; and he feels in duty bound to constrain others to assent to his faith, though he would complain bitterly enough if anyone tried to force some other faith upon him. Wherever he has the support of the secular arm he achieves by force what he cannot achieve by persuasion. In many Christian countries it is possible to blaspheme Christ as much as one pleases and no court of law will effectively intervene. But the same courts will condemn an obscene postcard with swift despatch.

1352. The Romans read without trace of indignation the verses (*Epoda,* VIII, XII) in which Horace alludes to organs of the female body under their exact Latin names; but the Romans would never have tolerated either anti-patriotic or anti-militarist utterances. Many moderns will tolerate these latter but cry aloud for dire punishment on anyone who writes as Horace wrote. When the high-priest, Caiaphas, heard words of Jesus offensive to his religious sentiments, he "rent his garments"—*scidit vestimenta sua,* wailing, "He hath uttered blasphemy." So Senator Bérenger, high-priest among our pedlars of purity, waxes wroth at the mere thought that Mme. Regina Badet should appear on the stage in skirts a little short. The Moslems hold the hog in horror and would not taste its flesh at any price; but they speak freely of sexual intimacies. Our sex-reformers feel, or pretend to feel, horror at such discourse, but eat pork with the best of appetites. Dubois relates:[1] "A European of my acquaintance had written a letter to one of his friends in favour of a Brahman whom I had recommended to him. On finishing the letter he sealed it with a sealing stamp, which he moistened with the tip of his tongue. The Brahman noticed it, refused to receive the letter, left in a bad temper as though he had been grievously insulted, and preferred losing the advantages he might have gained from the recommendation to being the bearer of a missive polluted in such a fashion." Our sex-reformers of the prolific breed that is so deft at finding the mote in a neighbour's eye would ridicule the stupidity of that Brahman, without remembering that their behaviour would be precisely the same if the stamp on the letter was engraved with an image of the phallus, which the ancient Romans used without trace of scruple in warding off the evil eye.[2]

1352 [1] *Mœurs, institutions et cérémonies des peuples de l'Inde,* Vol. I, p. 252.

1352 [2] The Catharists exchanged a kiss of peace; but their Perfects were not allowed to touch a woman, so they imparted the kiss by way of a copy of the Gospel: Guiraud, *Cartulaire de Notre-Dâme de Prouille,* Vol. I, Preface, pp. cxcix: "The Perfects kissed each of the faithful on both cheeks . . . and there was no difficulty about that so long as the ceremony was between men. It grew complicated when there were women in the congregation. A Perfect could in no case touch a woman

1353. The sex residue appears in combination with other residues in many social phenomena, and here therefore we have to repeat in part what we said of asceticism.

1354. Let us as usual ignore the case of plain hypocrisy, which is much rarer, after all, than is ordinarily supposed. Hypocrisy is oftentimes a device for executing certain logical purposes and therefore has no place among the residues.

1355. The sex residue figures in many religious effusions. At times it is recognizable out of hand, then again it is almost impossible to identify it as something apart from the strictly religious sentiment.[1] Enemies of the Roman Church have pretended to find it where it certainly was not. Friends of the Church have tried to deny its presence even where it was in striking evidence. Many of the priests who leave the Church are moved to do so, now consciously, now unwittingly, by interests of sex. The same urge is not without its influence on much of the criticism of the Modernists, just as in their disposition to play up to democracy lurks a hope of securing advantages thereby.[2]

even with the tip of a finger. With all the more reason was it forbidden him to kiss one. The rule was so strict that in the rite of the blessing, which involved the Perfect's resting his palms on the head of the convert [or invalid], he was directed, if the recipient was a woman, to hold his hands above her head without touching her—*tenendo manum super caput infirmi, non tamen tangendo si sit mulier*. The same difficulty had to be evaded in the rite of the kiss, and what the Catholic liturgy calls an 'instrument of peace' was used for the purpose. The kiss is deposited on some object of particular veneration, and then the individual who for one reason or another cannot be kissed goes and gets it there. . . . The Perfect in charge of a Catharist ceremony kissed a copy of the Gospels and handed it to the women to kiss. . . . They did so and then kissed one another." The sex-reformers of our day, who are the most perfect idiots of whom human history makes mention, differ from the Catharists in dogmas but not in the sex residue.

1355 [1] *Cf.* I Cor. 5. If all sex-reformers were Christians, one might have no certain means of distinguishing the sex residue from the purely religious residue; but free-thinkers sometimes go in for purity and the religious residue does not figure in that case. Says the good St. Ambrose in *De virginibus*, I, 8, 52 (*Opera*, Vol. II, p. 159): *"Castitas enim angelos fecit. Qui eam servavit angelus est, qui perdidit diabolus."* ("Chastity hath made angels; for he who hath preserved his chastity is an angel, he who hath lost it, a devil.") Free-thinkers have—or pretend to have—neither angels nor devils. They cannot take advantage of such a language.

1355 [2] Traditional pleasantries often state facts in vivid form. Take a story in Sorbière, *Sorberiana, s.v. Moine* (pp. 145-46): "A certain monk having put off

1356. The cult of woman figures explicitly or implicitly, openly or thinly veiled, in many religions—a thick book might be written on the subject. One should not forget the many genealogies of divine beings that all show a sex residue, nor allegories and personifications, male or female, of abstractions or other fantastic aggregates. All such things go to show how at all times thoughts of sex crowd into the human mind. Certain it is that forced chastity, especially when it is scrupulously observed, tends to introduce amorous sentiments into situations where there is, and can be, no question of erotic relations. That is already apparent, in germ, in the extreme fondness of a little girl for her doll, an animal, her friends, and sometimes, though she may be unaware of it, for her parents. The fact can be proved, for when the girl marries or comes into contact with a man in some way or other, such forms of affection either disappear or diminish in intensity. Cut off from men, a woman oftentimes entertains for a pet sentiments that have—though she may not be aware of it—an erotic element. Other women, in the same cir-

the frock applied for assistance to the late Prince Maurice of Orange. [The same story is often told with other names and so, probably, is fictional in character.]: *"Cuius causa huc venisti?"* asked the Prince. *"Religionis,"* answered the friar. *"Religio cuius generis?" "Foeminini!" "Ergo,"* the Prince concluded, *"tu huc venisti propter genere foemininum."* [The phrase *"religio cuius generis"*—in case the jest is not apparent to anyone—has a double meaning: "What sort of religion?" "Of what gender is the word religion?" The friar, thinking his Latin is being tested, answers: "Feminine gender." "I see!" concludes the Prince, "You came here looking for a woman."—A. L.] In the *Journal de Genève,* Sept. 17, 1913, a friend of Father Loyson (Father Hyacinthe) reports a conversation that took place in Rome between the ex-priest and Prince Baldassare Odescalchi: "Said the Prince (the details of the conversation I got both from M. Loyson himself and the Prince): 'But, Father, since you continue to call yourself a Catholic priest, why should you not return to the Roman fold?' 'Why, Prince Odescalchi . . . you forget that there are difficulties!' 'What difficulties?' 'Well, first of all, there is the question of infallibility!' 'Oh, infallibility!' said Prince Odescalchi. 'There are ways of coming to an understanding—there are interpretations! That could not be an insuperable obstacle.' 'But then there's the matter of my marriage.' 'Yes, your marriage, of course. There's some difficulty there, but not insuperable either. You are as well aware as I that Catholic priests of the oriental rites marry. You might be transferred to some oriental rite.' [The Pope, Leo XIII, appointed Father Vives, a Capuchin friar, to handle negotiations. Nothing came of them.] . . . M. Loyson has repeatedly asserted that the conferences failed primarily because of his inability to accept the dogma of papal infallibility. But the question of his marriage was a much more serious difficulty than Prince Odescalchi ever imagined."

cumstances, devote themselves to charities, social agitation, or religious activities. The so-called feminist is often just a hysterical woman in want of a mate.[1]

1357. Veneration and hatred for a given thing may likewise be forms of a religion which has that thing for its object of worship. The religious trait is eliminated only by indifference (§ 911). That is why the hiatus in the sex series is more of form than of substance. The Negro in maltreating his fetish, the Catholic in reviling his saint, are both manifesting a religious mood not shared by the man who is indifferent to fetish and saint alike. That is a matter of common knowledge as regards love. It was observed of old that love and hatred are kindred things, the opposite of both being indifference. It is also a trite remark that the men who most malign women are the ones who can least do without them.[1]

1358. We need therefore not be surprised that strong sex impulses often lead to loathing for the sexual act and, in the Christian saints, to misogyny. Often enough in their invectives one detects a combination of a sentiment of pure asceticism with a sentiment of unsatisfied sexual interest. The sex-urge may become so violent as to provoke hallucinations, and the Christian becomes convinced that the Devil is tempting him to sins of impurity. And the Devil in question was not altogether without his reality. He is actually present in the mind of the human being, though he is more effectively banished by a sexual act than by any rite of exorcism.

1356 [1] Bayle, *Dictionnaire historique, s.v. Junon:* "I would go so far as to say that the extremes to which the Christian went in regard to the Virgin Mary and which surpass anything the pagans ever invented in the worship of Juno [Because to a greater degree than the Christian their religion offered other channels for the expression of the sex residue.] came of the same source, from the habit, I mean, of honouring and courting women with more devotion and more respect than is paid to the other sex. [From the sex residue, in other words.] It is impossible to dispense with women either in civil or in religious life. Strip the Roman communion of its worship of female saints, and especially of the woman who is called Queen of Heaven or Queen of the Angels, and terrible gaps would be opened in it. What would be left would fall to pieces like *arena sine calce, scopae dissolutae.*"

1357 [1] Athenaeus, *Deipnosophistae*, XIII, 5: "Someone remarked to Sophocles that Euripides was a misogynist. 'In his plays, yes,' said Sophocles. 'But in his bed he is a philogynist.' "

1359. One needs to read only a portion of what the worthy Friar Bartolommeo da San Concordio has to say in disparagement of women, and the remarks the Church Fathers devoted to the subject would fill a fair-sized library.[1]

1360. Persons who feast on such exhortations may likely enough be brought to such a pass by the sheer ardour of unsatisfied senses as to have the female of the species constantly on their minds, to shun women in fear of the danger they represent, to hate them out

1359 [1] Says Fra Bartolommeo, *Ammaestramenti degli antichi,* 25, 10, 1-10: "To have converse with women is to expose oneself to the perils of sensuality. *Ecclesiasticus,* 42:12-13. 'Sit not in the midst of women, for from garments cometh a moth, and from women wickedness.' Jerome to Oceanus [Frankfurt, 1684, Vol. IV, p. 213: *Ad Oceanum, De vita clericorum*]: 'Especially do I warn thee to be watchful; for it is the clerk's temptation to go oft unto women. . . .' 'Converse with women is the door to the Devil, the road to iniquity, the sting of the scorpion. . . .' 'With a flaming fire doth woman singe the spirit of him who abideth with her.' 'Verily he cannot of his whole heart walk in the path of the godly who hath converse with women. . . . Art thou chaste? Lo, thou dost tell a great lie; for if thou seekest chastity, why goest thou with women? The woman of pleasing converse love thou of the mind and not of the body.' Gregory, in the third of the *Dialogues* [III, 7 (*Opera,* Vol. III, p. 229; Gardner, p. 113)]: 'Those who order the body to continence presume not to abide with women.' *Idem, In registro* [*i.e., Epistolae,* IX, 2, 60 (Migne, Vol. III, p. 997; Barmby, Vol. II, p. 85)]: 'It is written of the blessed Augustine that he refused to live with his sister, and he said, "The women who are with my sister are not my sisters." ' The caution of a man so great may well be a firm lesson unto us. Isidore, in *Synonima,* II [17 (4) (Migne, p. 849)]: 'If thou wouldst be secure against fornications, keep in body and in gaze aloof from woman; for dwelling near the serpent not long wilt thou hold off from him; abiding near the fire but in danger, not long shalt thou be safe; for thou shouldst be of iron, yet shouldst thou sweat of some heat.' Jean Plantavit, in his *Florilegium rabbinicum,* p. 458, relates that 'a certain wise man looking upon a small but pretty woman said: "Small is the beauty, but the evil is great." ' And he comments: '*The evil is great:* the wicked woman is worse than evil, as Chrysostom well said in words which Antonius Melissa quotes [in his *Sententiae*], II, 34 [Migne, p. 1090], and as we have elsewhere cautioned. For he says: "O Evil! A wicked woman is worse than any evil! Deadly are dragons and poisonous snakes, but the deadliness of a woman is deadlier than the poison of serpents. The wicked woman is never chastened: treat her sternly and she rageth, mildly and she runneth wild. Easier is it to melt iron than to tame a woman. He who hath a bad wife may know that he hath received the reward of his sins. There is on earth no wild beast to be compared to a bad wife. What quadruped is fiercer than the lion? None, save a bad wife! What serpent is deadlier than the dragon? None, save a bad wife!" ' " And *cf.* Athenaeus, *Deipnosophistae,* XIII, 6-10 [This, however, is a light-hearted treatment of the theme.—A. L.] Such the usual attitude of men who malign women out of morbid attachment to them.

of attachment to them, and to envy those who they see are enjoying them; and just such envy creeps into their glorifications of virginity, the praises they shower upon married couples who live in continence and their horror for fornication. They, meantime, seem to be in the utmost good faith—that, indeed, is the thing which sharpens and intensifies their sentiments.

1361. Others, too, may be in good faith. The zeal evinced by priests and moralists in safe-guarding women from "temptations" may express an unmixed religious or moral enthusiasm. But not seldom sex jealousies enter in. Such sentiments can function quite apart from any actual sex relation. Eunuchs, as is well known, are often susceptible to jealousy—they are usually jealous, in fact, and in our parts of the world the violence that jealousy may assume in the sexually impotent is a matter of common observation. Then there are the professional prudes of the humanitarian cult, and women who are aged or ugly and have no hope of romance in their lives. Such women are prone to jealousy and quite lose their heads if they see a young man looking at a young or pretty girl or going so far as to speak to one. All this may happen quite apart from any perception on the individual's part that the sex residue is influencing his conduct. So envy may be so intimately blended with the sex residue as to be indistinguishable from it even by the person who is experiencing the complex sentiment.

1362. Towards the end of the eighteenth century and the beginning of the nineteenth the view generally prevailed that Christian theologians were alone responsible for the efforts to deprive mankind of the pleasures of the senses and therefore of those sexual pleasures which "Nature" had vouchsafed to men. But developments after that time, and especially since 1900, show that the theologians of free-thought are no less valiant in repressive zeal than the theologians of Christianity, and that modern inquisitors of "heretical depravity" in the Religion of Sex are a good match for the old-time inquisitors of "heretical depravity" in the Catholic Church.[1]

1362 [1] The old misapprehensions arose from the fact that the free-thinkers of the time were trying to take advantage of the ever present and ever vigorous residues

1363. It is a curious fact that while the Christian, and especially the Catholic, Church denounces amorous pleasures, it is from them in the main that it derives the metaphors through which it expresses manifestations of faith. The Church is the Bride of Christ, to say nothing of the interpretations of erotic elements in the Song of Songs, which turn a love-song not a little coarse and not a little absurd, to tell the truth, into an epithalamium of the Church as the Bride of Christ. Christian nuns are "brides of Christ." To Him they

of sex in their battle with Christianity. Once they had won that fight, they did more and worse than their sometime adversaries. Not even as able a thinker as Buckle avoids the misapprehension alluded to. In his *History of Civilization in England*, Vol. III, pp. 270-72, he begins very judiciously: "The happiness derived from gratifying the senses, being thus diffused over a wider area, and satisfying, at any given moment, a greater number of persons than the other form of happiness is capable of, does, on that account, possess an importance which many who call themselves philosophers are unwilling to recognize. Too often have philosophic and speculative thinkers, by a foolish denunciation of such pleasures, done all in their power to curtail the quantity of happiness of which humanity is susceptible." But then he goes on to say: "If, then, we review the history of opinion in connexion with the history of action, we may probably say, that the ascetic notions of philosophers, such, for instance, as the doctrines of the Stoics, and similar theories of mortification, have not worked the harm which might have been expected, and have not succeeded in abridging, to any perceptible extent, the substantial happiness of mankind. . . . But, though philosophers have failed in their effort to lessen the pleasures of mankind, there is another body of men who, in making the same attempt, have met with far greater success. I mean, of course, the theologians, who, considered as a class, have in every country and in every age, deliberately opposed themselves to gratifications which are essential to the happiness of an overwhelming majority of the human race. Raising up a God of their own creation [That overlooks free-thinkers.], whom they hold out as a lover of penance [That overlooks at least some of the pagans.], of sacrifice, and of mortification, they, under this pretence, forbid enjoyments which are not only innocent but praiseworthy. For, every enjoyment by which no one is injured, is innocent. . . . The theologians, however, for reasons which I have already stated, cultivate an opposite spirit, and, whenever they have possessed power, they have always prohibited a large number of pleasurable actions, on the ground that such actions are offensive to the Deity." That [logic], however, is not the cause of their conduct—their conduct is non-logical: it is the derivation with which they justify their conduct; and that that is the case is apparent from the fact that free-thinkers who have no Deity to consider offended deport themselves in exactly the same manner, but using different derivations denouncing "offences" against "modesty" or "morality" or some other fetish of theirs. Buckle's remarks are therefore not in strict accord with the facts, if by "theologians" we understand the theologians of Christianity or any other religion. They come into exact line with the facts if by "theologians" we mean fanatics of every breed who take pleasure in annoying their neighbour.

consecrate their virginity, and for Him they nourish a passion in which the sacred blends with the profane. Nor is that the whole story. The Church Fathers are unable to speak for any great length of time without alluding, if only by metaphor, to sex. The vision of woman hovers before their eyes. Banished in one direction, back she comes from some other.

1364. Even in the Gospels there are passages in which the sex residue comes into view, in a very incidental way, to be sure. There is no apparent reason why in place of the parable of the ten virgins something else could not have been found less likely to fix attention on virginities and consummations. But woman dominates the later stages of Christianity more especially, till she is finally exalted to the splendours of a heavenly throne in the person of the Virgin Mary.

1365. Compare such things with Xenophon's *Memorable Sayings of Socrates*. For Xenophon sex is a physical need like any other, the satisfaction of it being condemned only in the excess. Xenophon is not greatly concerned with it, any more than he is with other physical needs—eating, for instance. It is not on his mind. His main concern very evidently is with something else. But it weighs like an incubus on the mind of the Church Fathers, provoking in them something like the hankering of the thirsty soul in Dante's *Inferno* for the water he longs for.[1]

1366. In a well-known passage St. Paul accepts matrimony as the lesser evil: it would be better for a person not to have commerce with the opposite sex, but if one is not of that fibre, marriage may be allowed. St. Paul was undeniably a misogynist. But we know too little about him to say whether that attitude sprang from some physical deformity, as in the case of Leopardi, from lack of success

1365 [1] *Inferno,* XXX, vv. 64-69:

> "The little brooks that down each verdant hill
> Flow into Arno from the Casentine
> Making their beds so fresh and cool, are still
> Ever before me, and not all in vain;
> For more their image parches than this plague,
> Howe'er the flesh from off my face it drain."
>
> (Fletcher translation.)

with women or some other such cause, or from pure mysticism.[1]

1367. Of truly celibate nuns St. Cyprian declaims: "Now we come to those who are virgins of body and in them our interest must be the greater in proportion as their glory is the more sublime. They are the flower of the ecclesiastical vine, the honour and ornament of spiritual grace. They are the character beautiful, the perfect and undefiled achievement of glory and of honour. They are the image of God that corresponds to the sanctity of Our Lord, that part of Christ's flock which is most glorified. Through them the glorious

1366 [1] I Cor. 7:1-2: "Now concerning the things whereof ye wrote unto me: It is good for a man not to touch a woman. Nevertheless, to avoid fornication, let every man have his own wife, and let every woman have her own husband." The passage was a hard nut for the Christians to crack. Some took it in an obviously false sense as addressed only to priests. Some toned it down, explaining that if virginity held first place, the married state came second. Others still observed that the old Law bade mankind to increase and multiply at a time when the Earth had not been populated. Now that it was covered with people, the injunction no longer held. But after all the passage could hardly be clearer: it is the dictum of a virtuist who abhors the carnal act and yields to marriage only as the lesser of two evils. St. Jerome notes on the passage, *Commentarius in epistolam I ad Corinthios* [Pareto quotes *Opera,* Paris, 1623-24, Vol. VIII, p. 199; missing in Migne]: "What I preached at the outset was the sound doctrine (*bonum*), to wit, that one should not touch a woman according to the habit of marriage. But since you tell me that many incontinents are violating that teaching, let a remedy be granted them that they die not in fornication. Virginity and continence are therefore preached as most desirable (*in primis*) following this example of the Apostle; but if anyone is not too ashamed to confess himself incontinent and demands the relaxation of incontinence, let the remedy of marriage not be denied to him, just as when the patient is restless and avers he cannot abstain from all fruit, the shrewd physician will allow him somewhat of it lest he take such as will do him harm. . . . But the lust-lovers commonly answer: 'Why then did God in his first blessing bid men to be fruitful and multiply?' That, of course, the Earth might be filled with people. But now that it has been so filled we must restrain ourselves from incontinence." St. Anselme of Laon [see § 1803 [5]], in his commentary, *In epistolam I ad Corinthios* (7:1-2), likens woman to a fire that burns at the touch: "Note the wisdom of the Apostle: he does not say that it is good not to have a wife, but that it is good not to touch a woman, as though the danger lay in the contact, as though he who touches a woman is lost. Just as one is burned on touching fire, so at the touch of man or woman one senses one's nature and becomes aware of the difference of sex. It is good not to touch! *But to avoid fornication* let each man have his *legitimate wife,* not a concubine, and each woman her husband. Nothing but the fear of fornication explains such a concession." *Canones et decreta Concilii Tridentini, sessio* XXIV, 10 (Richter, p. 216; Schaff, Vol. II, p. 197): "If anyone shall say that the conjugal state is to be preferred to virginity or celibacy and that it is not better and more holy to remain virgin and celibate than to marry, let him be anathema."

fecundity of our Mother Church rejoices. In them she flourishes the more bounteously, and the more virginity adds to its numbers, the greater is the Mother's joy." In penning those torrid lines the Saint probably imagined that he was responding to a purely religious sentiment; but it is more than probable that without his knowledge a sex residue was at work in him.[1]

1368. St. Augustine relates that he frequented women in his youth, but that after his conversion he became averse to all such contacts, even legitimate.[1]

1367 [1] *De disciplina et habitu virginum,* III (*Opera,* p. 443; Wallis, Vol. I, p. 336): *"Nunc nobis ad virgines sermo est, quarum quo sublimior gloria est maior et cura est. Flos est ille ecclesiastici germinis, decus atque ornamentum gratiae spiritalis, laeta indoles, laudis et honoris opus integrum atque incorruptum, Dei imago respondens ad sanctimoniam Domini, illustrior portio gregis Christi. Gaudet per illas atque in illis largiter floret Ecclesiae matris gloriosa fecunditas, quantoque plus copiosa virginitas numero suo addit tanto plus gaudium matris augescit."* St. Augustine, *De doctrina christiana,* IV, 21, 47 (*Opera,* Vol. III, p. 112; *Works,* Vol. IX, pp. 157-58), quotes the lines as an example of style. Many other equally vivid expressions of the kind are to be found in the Church Fathers. Coming upon them one thinks of an epigram of Rufinus in the *Greek Anthology,* V, 77 (Paton, Vol. I, pp. 166-67), and is tempted to suspect that the sentiment would be less colourful had the Fathers been better acquainted with the things they were raving about: "If women had such charm after the bed of Cypris, no man surely would ever be sated after love of his wife. For after Cypris all women are a bore." And *cf.* Tatius Achilles, *Leucippe et Clitophon,* IV, 8.

1368 [1] *Soliloquia,* I, 17 (*Opera,* Vol. I, p. 878; Starbuck, p. 543) (a dialogue between Reason and the Saint): *"Reason.* What about a wife? Are there not consolations in one that is beautiful, chaste, well mannered, well educated? *Augustine.* However attractive the colours in which you paint her, with whatever virtues you endow her, I have decided that there is nothing that I must more studiously shun than such intercourse. In my judgment nothing lowers a man's spirit farther from Heaven (*ex arce*) than the caresses and physical contact of a woman—and if one has a wife such things cannot be avoided." *Idem, Contra Julianum, haeresis Pelagianae defensorem* (*Opera,* Vol. X, pp. 641 f.), III, 24, 42: *"Concupiscentiae carnalis qui modum tenet malo bene utitur; qui modum non tenet malo male utitur; qui autem etiam ipsum modum sanctae virginitatis amore contempserit malo melius non utitur."* [This pious gibberish is unintelligible apart from its context. It is the mechanically constructed counter-thesis to a declaration of Julianus, who held that the sex instinct (*naturalis concupiscentia*) having been placed in man by the Creator must be a good thing, though conceding that the practitioners of ascetic chastity were essaying a "glorious emprise." Said he: *Concupiscentiae naturalis qui modum tenet bono bene utitur, qui modum non tenet bono male utitur, qui autem etiam ipsum modum sanctae virginitatis amore contempserit bono melius non utitur, confidentia quippe suae salutis et roboris contempsit remedia ut gloriosa possit exercere certamina.* This, with some goodwill, is intelligible: "He who (follows the way

1369. In St. Jerome the strength of sentiment in respect of everything pertaining to women and sensuous pleasures is something quite exceptional. The Saint is for ever counselling virgins and widows, comforting, advising, rebuking them. He is much less interested in married women and actually gives the impression of regarding husbands unconsciously as his rivals. He feels hurt that certain heretics were mean enough to accuse him of condemning matrimony; but one must say that he gave quite a few grounds for such charges.[1]

1370. In an epistle to the Virgin Eustochia he stresses the evils of matrimony from a worldly standpoint: the annoyance of pregnancy, the crying of children, the jealousy of a husband's mistresses, household worries; and he has his virgin express her unwillingness to fall under the sentence pronounced in Genesis: "In sorrow thou shalt bring forth children."[1] "That is a law for women, not for

of ?) natural concupiscence makes a good use of a good thing; he who eschews that path makes a bad use of a good thing; but he who spurns it altogether through love of holy chastity eschews the use of a good thing to better advantage inasmuch as in confidence as to his strength and security he has spurned legitimate remedies in order to essay a glorious emprise." Augustine states that his one difference with Julianus here is as to whether the sex instinct is a good or an evil, it being for him an evil. He accordingly adopts the form of statement of Julianus, but replaces the word *bonum* with the word *malum*.—A. L.]

1369 [1] *Epistolae,* 48, 10-12 (*Ad Pammachium pro libris contra Jovinianum*) (*Opera,* Vol. I, p. 499; Schaff-Wace, p. 40): "My opinions on the subject of those who are pure, on widows and married people, must be sufficiently clear from the passage in my Commentary on the Apocalypse [where I wrote] (*Adversus Jovinianum,* I, 40; *Opera,* Vol. II, p. 269; Schaff-Wace, p. 378): 'The pure are they who sing the new song which no one can sing save he be pure. . . . They are the first-fruits of the Lord, Lambs of God, without blemish.' And if virgins are the first fruits of the Lord, it follows that the widowed and those who are continent in marriage come after the first fruits in a second and third degree. I give second and third place to widows and married women, yet I am charged (*dicimus* misprint for *dicimur*) by heretical madness with condemning marriage!" And he goes on, *loc. cit.,* 12, to beg his reader's indulgence and claim extenuating circumstances: "A thoughtful and kindly reader should judge things apparently harsh from all that I say (*de caeteris*) and not accuse me of expressing different sentiments in one and the same book. For who could be so stupid, so unskilful in writing, as to praise and condemn the same thing?" [So failing to take due account of the predicament of the man who has a thought but cannot in view of this or that consideration express it in full.]

1370 [1] *Ad Eustochium de custodia virginitatis, Epistola,* XXII, 2 (Wright, p. 57): *"Nec enumeraturum molestias nuptiarum, quomodo uterus intumescat, infans vagiat,*

me!" she cries. In his qualms about pregnancy the Saint must be reckoned a predecessor of the birth-control advocates of our day, and Senator Bérenger, who has a mania for indictments, ought to have the French Attorney-General hale him into court. That being impracticable in view of the Saint's having been dead for so many centuries, his books at least might be expurgated. The Saint, however, might get some consideration from the fact that, though plain-clothes men were unknown in those days, he had other ways of dealing with people who tampered with the morals of virgins.[2]

1371. The thought of woman exacerbated by unsatisfied hankerings tormented the poor Saint and survived his practices of morti-

cruciet pellex [concubine], *domus cura solicitet, et omnia quae putantur bona mors extrema praecidat* [and in the end death cuts off everything that is called a blessing]." *Adversus Helvidium de perpetua virginitate Beatae Mariae,* XX (*Opera,* Vol. II, p. 204; Schaff-Wace, p. 344) (Married women are distracted from their religious duties by family worries): "Do you think it is the same thing to attend to your prayers and fasts by day and by night, and to stop what you are doing at the coming of your husband (*gressum frangere*) and brighten your face and simulate affection? Here the children are crying and the family is in an uproar. The children are calling for your kisses and for a word. The bills have to be figured up, the accounts settled. There are the army of cooks with their sleeves rolled up (*accincta*) grinding the meats. In the other room a group of seamstresses are making a noise. And there is your husband with his friends! The wife darts hither and thither like a swallow about the whole house, to see if the dining-couch has been set up, if the floors have been swept, if the wine-cups have been crowned, if the dinner is ready. Tell me, I pray you: Where in all that is there time to think of God? And I have described a happy home!" Striking the contrast between that civilization and the ancient Roman. The things the Saint disparages here were the pride and glory of the matron in the heyday of Rome.

1370 [2] *Epistolae,* V, *Ad Laetam de institutione filiae* (*Opera,* Vol. I, pp. 872-73; Schaff-Wace, p. 191): "At the command of her husband, Hymettius, who was grandfather to the virgin Eustochia, Praetextata, a very noble woman, changed the styles and ornaments of the virgin and redressed her unkempt hair in the worldly fashion, thinking so to thwart her designs and her mother's expressed wishes. And lo, on that same night an angel appeared before her, threatening woe unto her in dread voice, and crushing her to earth with these words: 'Hast thou the boldness to prefer a command of thine husband to the will of Christ? Presumest thou to lay impious hands on the head of God's virgin? Verily those hands shall soon wither, in punishment for what they have done, and finished this fifth month thou shalt be carried away to Hell; and if thou dost persist in this sin, thou shalt lose husband and children all.' And so it came to pass in due course, and the death of the unlucky woman bore witness to the too great delay in her repentance."

fication. Retiring to the desert, he relates, "to the society of scorpions and wild beasts," he "was frequently molested by troops of dancing girls. My face paled from fasts, but my mind flared hot in a cold body. In the dead flesh of a man there burned naught but the fires of lust."[1] Such hallucinations are familiar things in the writings of the Fathers. Demons were forever besetting the saints of asceticism and tempting them under female forms. St. Jerome mentions other instances in addition to his own, and in general the lives of the saints are replete with them.[2] It is readily comprehensible that harbouring a sex residue of such power, St. Jerome should have been accused of taking too much pleasure in the society of women—a charge that he, of course, indignantly and probably in all honesty denies. "Many virgins," he explains,[3] "oftentimes gathered about me, and to not a few of them I expounded divine Scripture to the best of my ability; and our readings inspired assiduity, assiduity familiarity, and familiarity confidence. Let them bear witness whether they ever found aught in me unbecoming to a Christian. Have I ever accepted money? Have I not spurned gifts, whether great or small? Has the coin of others ever clinked in my hand? Have I been immodest

1371 [1] *Ad Eustochium de custodia virginitatis, Epistola* XXII, 6 (Wright, pp. 67-69).

1371 [2] The case of St. Hilarion, which I choose at random: St. Jerome, *Vita sancti Hilarionis,* VII (*Opera,* Vol. II, p. 36; Schaff-Wace, p. 304): "Many his temptations, and ingenious the traps laid by the devils by day and by night. . . . How many times did naked women appear before him as he lay on his cot? How many times were luscious banquets spread before his famished eyes?" A young woman and a square meal would have done for all those demons. A great many saints were tempted in just such ways. The story of St. Anthony is even too well known. St. Francis also had his troubles (§ 1184 [2]) and his disciples as well as he. The Protestants were enemies of the Franciscans, of course; but they make a sensible remark anent a temptation of Brother Aegidius, though it is garbed in one of the inevitable derivations: *L'Alcoran des cordeliers,* II, 186: "While Brother Aegidius was at Spoleto he had a greater temptation than he had ever experienced before through hearing the voice of a woman. However, by prayers, flagellations, and divine rites he cast her forth from him and so was completely freed." The editor of the *Koran* comments on the vision itself: "Is it any wonder these presumptuous charlatans (*caphars*) are always stewing day and night in the secret fires of roistery, since they have rejected holy matrimony, which is the God-given cure for such temptations?" And on the flagellation: "Such thrashings are inventions of Satan and are nowhere approved by God."

1371 [3] *Epistolae,* 45, 2 (*Ad Asellam*) (*Opera,* Vol. I, p. 481; Schaff-Wace, p. 59).

either of speech or eye? I am reproached of nothing save my sex; and of that I am reproached only because of the journey of Paula and Melania to Jerusalem."

1372. All the same his conversation was inclined to tread dangerous ground, and his continuous harping on erotic pleasures was of a sort calculated to put chastity in peril. To the virgin Eustochia he writes:[1] "It is difficult for the human soul not to love something: to something our spirits must needs turn in affection. But carnal love is vanquished by spiritual love, desire is quenched in desire [Most suggestive language.]; and carnal love is certain to diminish as spiritual love increases. Repeat often as you lie on your pillows: *By night on my bed I sought him whom my soul loveth.*" The quotation is from the Song of Songs, 3:1. It refers—or rather, the Saint thought it referred—to a spiritual bridegroom. But, alas, it suggests, especially when a girl utters it on her pillows, the image of a physically real bridegroom. In all such utterances, even if they are uttered in all innocence, the sex residue figures, just as it figures in the piety of a certain French pastor who, out of loathing for pornography, goes to a show to measure the length of the ballet's skirts and the precise amount of ankle and thigh they leave exposed.[2]

1373. Heretics went as far as the orthodox in their worries over sex. As already suggested (§§ 1341 f.), the charges of indecency that are hurled back and forth by various religious sects are not to be taken too seriously; but they suffice to show the force of the sex

1372 [1] *Ad Eustochium de custodia virginitatis, Epistola* XXII, 17 (Wright, p. 89).

1372 [2] In the same letter to Eustochia, 25 (Wright, p. 109), the Saint makes a long comparison between the heavenly and the earthly bridegroom, with quotations from the Song of Songs: "Always let the secret of your chamber be your shelter and protection. Always may the Bridegroom sport with you within (*laudat* misprint for *ludat*). Are you in prayer? You are conversing with your husband. Are you reading? He is talking to you. And when you fall asleep, He will come to the door and put His hand through the hole in the door [Song of Songs, 5:3] and touch your breast [Exquisitely physical imagery for spiritual acts.]; and awakening you will arise and say: 'Thou hast ravished my heart' [*Ibid.*, 4:9 (?): Vulgate, *Vulnerata caritate ego sum*—"I am sick with love"]; and from Him you will hear: 'A garden enclosed is my sister, my spouse, a spring shut up, a fountain sealed' [*Ibid.*, 4:12]. . . . Jesus is a jealous husband (Wright, p. 111); He does not wish your face to be seen of other men" (*Zelotypus est Iesus: non vult ab aliis videri faciem tuam*).

religion, which is great enough to provide the weapons men need for their battles and to enable it to serve so many religions in all periods of history as the pretext for persecutions great and small.

1374. Not a few accusations of immorality are brought rightly or wrongly against heretics in St. Augustine's treatise on heresies, *De haeresibus ad Quodvultdeum* (*Opera,* Vol. VIII, p. 21). The Saint deals at length with the Manicheans or Catharists (Perfects), on the one hand describing them as finding evil present in all matter and therefore as very strict in rejecting everything carnal, and on the other hand accusing them of licentious depravities.[1] To judge them

1374 [1] To summarize the Saint's accusations at large: The *Simonians* taught the detestable depravity that commerce with women was a matter of scant importance. The *Saturnians* imitated the depravities of the Simonians. On being rebuked for too great love for his wife, a most beautiful woman, and desiring to purge himself of the charge, Nicolas, leader of the *Nicolaitans,* gave notice that anyone who chose might have her. The *Gnostics* were called *Borborites* (Greek, mud-lovers) because of their gross immoralities. The *Carpocratians* taught all sorts of depraved practices. The *Cerinthians* believed that after the Resurrection mankind would live a thousand years in Christ's earthly kingdom, spending the time in gluttony and all sorts of lusts. The *Secundians* differed from the *Valentinians* only in degree of depravity. The *Cainites* honoured Cain and the inhabitants of Sodom. The *Tatians* condemned marriage and held it to be on a par with fornication and other vices, nor would they admit married people to their sect, whether men or women. The *Kataphrygians* held a second marriage equivalent to fornication and were said to have celebrated licentious mysteries. The *Peputians* or *Quintillians* gave great authority to women. The *Adamites* imitated the nakedness of Adam in Paradise before the Fall. They condemned marriage on the ground that Adam had no commerce with his wife either before the Fall or before he had been driven from Paradise, and that therefore had no one ever sinned there would have been no marriage. They went naked to their meetings and listened to their sermons and took their sacraments naked, thinking of their church, in fact, as Paradise itself. The *Elcesaites* or *Sampsaeans* worshipped two women. The *Valesians* practised castration. The *Catharists* condemned second marriages. The *Apostolics* rejected married people. The *Origenists* practised unmentionable depravities. For the *Manicheans* or Catharists, see below, § 1374 [2]. The *Hieracites* admitted only celibates as members. The *Antidicomarians* denied the virginity of Mary, on the ground that after the birth of Jesus she had relations with her husband. The *Priscillianists* forbade the use of meat, and separated husband and wife on the ground that flesh was created by the Devil and not by God. The *Paternians* "think that the human body below the waist was created not by God, but by the Devil. They therefore allow all sorts of licence to the nether parts of the body and lead most impure lives." St. Augustine claims to have had personal knowledge of the *Abeloites:* "They had no commerce with their wives, yet the dogmas of their sect did not permit them to live unmarried. Man and woman, they lived together in continence, and adopted a boy and a girl who were to succeed them in their pact of comradeship."

by what we know of their successors in the Middle Ages, the Albigenses, it would seem probable that they practised an exceedingly rigorous asceticism entirely free of depravities. We can of course not be altogether sure. St. Augustine taxes them with believing that the holy virtues turned into males in order to attract the women of hostile sects and into women in order to appeal to males. True or fanciful as this picture of Manichean doctrine may be, the fact remains that the sex residue played an important part either in their thinking or in the arguments of their adversaries.[2]

1374 [2] Guiraud, *Cartulaire de Notre-Dâme de Prouille,* Vol. I, Preface, pp. cii-iii: "The norms of the Manichean ethics were very austere. In its absolute rule of celibacy and in the strictness of its abstinences, it went far beyond the severest monastic disciplines. It is easy to see why those who observed them readily gained reputations for sanctity in the easy-going moral atmosphere that prevailed in the South of France. . . . Not being able to deny the astonishing results, the Catholic preachers were reduced to declaring that such Puritanism was mere hypocrisy and that its grim outward semblances concealed only a more shameful viciousness. Catholic writers of our own day have adopted that thesis and also declared, without shred of proof, that Catharist virtue was an artificial pose designed to deceive the simple-minded. . . . There is no occasion for resorting to such gratuitous and facile speculations to explain the rigour of Catharist morals. It is sufficient to note that far from appealing to the crowd at large regardless of persons and conditions, the Manichean rule was practised only by a small *élite* that was carefully prepared to accept it and live up to it." Guiraud is a Catholic historian, hostile to the "Perfects."

See St. Augustine, *Ibid.,* I. As regards the asceticism of the Manicheans (Catharists): "They have divided their Church into those two professions, the Elect, that is, and the Auditors. In other people, and even in their own Auditors and especially in those who have children, they think that that element of good and divine substance which is mixed and combined into foods and drinks is present in a scantier (*artius* for *arctius*) and less pure mixture. . . . They do not eat meats . . . nor even eggs . . . nor do they partake of foods containing milk. . . . They do not drink wine . . . saying that it is the gall of the princes of darkness. Though they do eat grapes, they will not drink the fermented juice (*musti*) nor the fresh. . . . They regard trees and plants as so much alive that they feel the life that is in them and experience pain when they are hurt. . . . For that reason they consider it wicked to clear a field of brush. . . . They condemn marriage out of hand and prohibit it so far as they can, since they forbid the generation of children, which is the reason for marriage unions." And as regards Manichean (Catharist) abominations, the Saint says: "On that pretext, or rather under the constraint of an execrable superstition, their Elects are obliged to take as it were their Eucharist *conspersam cum semine humano,* that in that way, as is the case with the other food they take, it may be cleansed by a divine substance. But they deny that they do any such thing, asserting that other persons unnamed do it under pretence of being Manicheans." But the Saint points, in rebuttal, to the testimony of two girls who had confessed to participating in the obscene rite, and adds: "Not so very long ago, a num-

1375. St. Augustine derives some of his information from St. Epiphanius, who adds further indecent details, in the case of the Gnostics especially, quoting, in his turn, St. Irenaeus. It seems hardly possible that such particulars could be altogether true. Some of them at least must have been imagined by a brain fermenting with prurience.[1]

1376. A community in which sexual unions were altogether prohibited would soon disappear unless, as was the case with the Essenes, it were replenished by recruits from other communities. A religion that aspires to become universal or at all wide-spread, unless it preaches the extinction of its disciples or the human race must necessarily permit marriage and rest content with regulating it. St. Paul seems not to have thought of that. His idea in allowing marriage was merely to avoid the very serious sin of fornication. But such considerations figured to some extent in the policy of the Catholic Church towards marriage, the moment the Church became a force of importance in society and began aspiring to supreme leadership over the destinies of men. Small heretical sects might here and there rescind the concession made by the Apostle and condemn sexual commerce absolutely and for all; and here and there one of them might even go so far as to recommend or require castration as a surer guarantee that the abhorred union would be eschewed. The Church, however, managed to hit on the golden mean, taking the position that matrimony was a praiseworthy state though less

ber of them were discovered and taken to Church, according to the Bishop's report that you have sent to me. Under severe examination they confessed that [the rite in question] was not a sacrament but an incantation in witchcraft (*non sacramentum sed execramentum*)."

1375 [1] St. Epiphanius, *Panarium adversus haereses, Lib.* I, *Tomus* II, *Haeresis* 31, 3 (*Opera,* Vol. I, pp. 474-543). St. Irenaeus, *Contra haereses,* I, 6, 3 (Migne, p. 507; Keble, p. 20): "Some of them, insatiable devotees of their carnal pleasures, say that things of the flesh should be matched with things of the flesh, things of the spirit with things of the spirit. And some of them secretly corrupt the women whom they instruct in their doctrine, as many of their victims, on reconversion to the Church of God, have confessed, with all the rest of their error. Some indeed quite openly and without trace of shame make such women as happen to strike their fancy their brides, taking them away from their husbands. Others begin more modestly, pretending to be living with their sisters, till in course of time it all comes out, the sister being found with child of the brother."

saintly than virginity. Rulings on successive marriages were to vary: now they were permitted but not recommended; now they were permitted but under censure; then again they were flatly prohibited. That is the case with divorce, and many other subjects that we need not here go into.

1377. But all Christians—except for some few heresies, which are for that matter not very well authenticated—agree with St. Paul that unchasteness is among the gravest sins; and in that notion, which is shared also by many unbelievers and atheists of modern times, the sex residue is clearly manifest, the residue enduring, the religious derivations that cloak it changing.

1378. Has this reprobation of carnal sin proved very effective in suppressing it in the concrete? If one reads history with unprejudiced eyes, looking for the actual facts rather than for what one might wish the facts to be, one can only doubt that it has. In the first place, and in general, if we were to find that with the growth of faith in a given religion that disapproved of carnal sin there were a diminution in immorality, or *vice versa,* one might take the coincidence as a certain indication of the probable effects of moral theory upon conduct. But if we find that periods of eager faith are also ages of great immorality, we are obliged to conclude, not that faith fosters immorality, since it is evident enough that other causes have been functioning, nor that faith has done nothing to promote morality, since after all we cannot be sure that the immorality would not have been worse had there been no faith; but that the sex residues are so powerful that in many cases they are able to override the prescriptions of faith. In so concluding we should be doing nothing more than epitomizing a multiplicity of facts in a general statement, and the conclusion may also be accepted by ardent believers, by ardent Catholics, for example—only they would express it in different language: where we speak of the power of the sex residue, or, better, of the sentiments registered by the sex residue, they would speak of the power of a Devil who is going about *quaerens quem devoret.* Nor could they, if they were at all inclined to be logical, deny that the facts seem to show the scant effects of moral theories on conduct; for they assert that very thing in different words when they say that to escape the traps of the Devil the human soul needs the support of divine grace.

1379. There are facts without end to show that among certain peoples and in certain periods of history enthusiastic faith may go hand in hand with immorality. Have we, from the earliest centuries of Christianity down to times very near our own, heard aught else than complaints as to the moral laxity of Christians? Even making liberal allowance for exaggerations by our censors, and granting that the evil has loomed larger in their eyes than it has been in reality, we can hardly imagine that none of the complaints had any foundation in concrete fact. And then, leaving talk aside, there are the facts themselves. Granted that some of them have been fabrications, can they all have been? To assume such a thing would be to cast doubt upon every historical certainty. At no time has there been any lack of sophistries to disprove the truth. Some have contrasted the vices of the present with the virtues of a past that was never a present for any living soul and which has existed only in their imaginations. Some have contrasted the vices of their own countries with the supposed virtues of other countries. That was one of the motives of Tacitus in writing his *Germania,* and the same prejudice inspired the pious declamations of Salvian of Marseilles. Salvian goes to many words in contrasting the vices of the Romans with the virtues of the Barbarians. But if he spoke truth, we can only conclude that the Barbarian virtues must have lasted for a very short season; for hardly a century after Salvian's time the *History* by St. Gregory of Tours is portraying those same Barbarians as a blood-thirsty, avaricious, lustful crew.[1] [2] [3] (For footnote 3 see page 858.)

1379 [1] For that matter, Tacitus himself says, *Germania,* 15, that when the Germans were not engaged in warfare, they spent much time in hunting "but even more in idling, sleeping, and guzzling (*dediti somno ciboque*)." In *Annales,* XII, 27, 3-4, he tells how the Romans managed to surprise the Gauls because the latter were half-asleep after spending their booty in one round of carousals.

1379 [2] Says Salvian, *De gubernatione Dei,* III, 9 (Sanford, p. 92): "It is God's command that every Christian should keep even his eyes chaste. Yet how many are they who are not sunk in the mire of fornication? And what else? Grievous and painful is what I am about to say! The Church herself who should be the consoler

1380. Admirers of the Middle Ages in our day refuse in any way to grant that those were times of brutish immorality, and they will accept any sort of sophistry so only to escape the plain evidence of the facts. There is the argument, for instance, that the obscene paint-

of God in all things—what is she but an irritation to Him? With the exception of some few who shun evil things,what else is almost any foregathering of Christians than a cesspool of vice? How many men can one find in the Church who are not either drunkards or gluttons, either adulterers or fornicators, either seducers of maids or pursuers of women, either thieves or murderers? [Such things are not confined to the slave, the low-born, the soldier: they are sins of the well-born (III, 10; Sanford, p. 96):] Tell me whether any one of them is innocent of the two crimes that may be considered capital—murder and rape? Is there one of them that is not either dripping with blood or reeking with slimy impurity? . . . [IV, 5; Sanford, p. 107:] How many are there among the rich who keep their marriage sacraments, who are not swept headlong by lustful furies, who do not use their own homes and families as brothels, and who do not follow their mad impulses against whatever persons the flame of wicked lust has drawn them? Exactly as is written in the Scripture of such things: 'They are as fed horses in the morning, each one neighing after his neighbour's wife' (Jer. 5:8). What else does a man prove of all this except that it is true of him, when he tries to possess in intercourse whatsoever woman has caught his eye? It may seem unfair that anything should be said of concubines, for in comparison with the crimes I have mentioned concubinage is a sort of chastity—it is confined to a relatively few married men and serves to bridle lust among a certain number of husbands and wives. I say husbands and wives, because things have come to such a pass of thoughtlessness that many men think their housemaids are their wives. And if only they would stop at that! [Literally: would that just as they are thought of as almost wives, so they might be considered as the only wives.] [On the lookout, as usual, for antitheses, Salvian finds one in a contrast between the morals of masters and slaves (IV, 6; Sanford, p. 108):] The slaves taken on the whole are immune to such crimes or greater ones. Is there any slave that has a flock of concubines? Is any one of them disgraced with the evil of having many wives? Does any one of them—after the manner of dogs and swine—think he has a right to any woman whom he can induce to submit to his lust? [Salvian compares Romans and Barbarians (IV, 13; Sanford, p. 121):] There are two kinds of people among the Barbarians as a whole—either heretics or heathen. As regards the divine law we are incomparably their superiors, but as regards living and the conduct of life I am exceedingly sorry to say that we are worse. To be sure, as I have cautioned above, I do not say this of absolutely the whole Roman people. I except first of all the churchmen, and then not a few laymen who are the equals of the churchmen. But all or almost all the rest have far worse morals than the Barbarians. [However, Salvian concedes that the Barbarians are of no great account either (IV, 14; Sanford, p. 122):] The Barbarians are cheats, and so are we. The Barbarians are grasping, and so are we. The Barbarians are lecherous, and so are we. The Barbarians are full of all sorts of wickedness and impurity, and so are we. [Not worrying over his inconsistency, he returns to the charge: the Romans are worse than the Barbarians. He begins with a bitter thrust at the Aquitanians (VII, 3; Sanford, p. 193):] I am sure there is less wickedness in a brothel. The whores that

ings and sculptures that have come down from the Middle Ages (§ 1343 [2]) and the scurrilous language used in the romances and *fabliaux* and other mediaeval writings, far from revealing corrupt morals, show the healthy moral poise of people who can in all safety

are to be found in a brothel have never taken a marriage vow, and they therefore cannot be said to violate a sacrament they know not of. They are amenable to punishment for inchastity, but not for the crime of adultery. Furthermore, not many brothels are permanent things, and few the prostitutes who damn their unhappy lives in them. But among the Aquitanians, what city as regards its wealthier and nobler sections but has been virtually a brothel? Who of its rich and leading men but has lived in the mire of debauchery? Who has not taken his plunge into an abyss of filthiest sewage? Who has ever kept faith with his wife? [He accuses owners of ruining their female slaves (VII, 4; Sanford, p. 195):] One can gather from that what a filth of loathsome strumpets there must have been when a woman under a lecherous master was not allowed to be chaste even if she wanted to be. [It seems that in view of all these offences against chastity the Lord brought the Romans under Barbarian dominion (VII, 6; Sanford, p. 196):] Though God has handed them over to the Barbarians because of their corrupt lives, even under the Barbarians they have not abandoned their lecheries. [Again borne aloft on the wings of his mania for declamation, Salvian credits the Barbarians with all the virtues (VII, 7; Sanford, p. 196):] Among the chaste Barbarians we are the unchaste. I will go farther still: the Barbarians are disgusted at our lewdness! [He sounds something like Senator Bérenger—or some other person who has lost his mind—when he prattles on, in conclusion (*loc. cit.*):] It is not lawful among the Goths for a Goth to be a whore-monger. Among them lewdness is permitted only to the Romans, to the prejudice of their race and name. And what hope have we, I ask, before God? We love lechery, the Goths hate it. We abhor purity, they worship it. Fornication with them is a crime and a disgrace, with us it is a distinction." To make a long story short, Salvian lived at a time when morals were no worse than they had been in the past, when Rome was conquering the Barbarians. He disregards that fact, and imagines that the Romans had been conquered because of their immoralities.

1379 [3] The dissoluteness of the Frankish kings as recounted by Gregory of Tours is too well known to require detailed mention. Here are a few facts gleaned from the *Historia ecclesiastica Francorum* and from its sequel, known as the *Chronicles of Fredegarius,* II, 12 (*Opera,* p. 209C; Dalton, Vol. II, p. 56): "When Childeric, who was a dissolute man of excessive licence, became king over the Franks, he began lecherously to rape and mislead their daughters." Of Duke Victor Gregory writes, II, 20 (*Opera,* p. 216B; Dalton, Vol. II, p. 60): "He fled to Rome and trying to carry on a similar licence there, he was stoned to death." II, 42 (*Opera,* p. 238C; Dalton, Vol. II, p. 80): "At that time Ragnacharius was king at Camaracum. He was so bent on licence that he could hardly be brought to spare his close relatives. He had Farro for his counsellor, a man smirched with the same vices." Theodobert (III, 21-26; *Opera,* pp. 260-62; Dalton, Vol. II, pp. 103-05) takes up with a certain Deuteria who was occupying the Castle at Capraria: "Deuteria came forth to meet him, and he, seeing that she was a handsome woman, fell enamoured of her and joined her to his bed." After a time he marries her: then, "seeing that her daugh-

call a spade a spade. To believe some writers, one would imagine that men and women of the Middle Ages were so many Daphnises and Chloes. Arguments of that kind might be passed if the mere existence of obscene statues and pictures and the mere use of in-

ter was full grown, and in fear that her husband might lust after her and take her as a mistress, she had her placed in a litter to which two unbroken bulls had been hitched and pulled off a bridge." IV, 13 (*Opera*, p. 278C; Dalton, Vol. II, p. 125): "In those days Chramnus was in residence at Arvernum, and he did many irrational things. . . . He had no affection for any man of whom he might have had good or useful counsel, but gathered about him persons of low birth and still in the unstable years of youth, and gave all his favour to them, listening to their counsel, so that he ordered by royal decree that the daughters of Senators should be taken away from them by force." V, 21 (*Opera*, p. 340C and see p. 342C; Dalton, Vol. II, pp. 195, 197): Of two bishops he says that on attaining their posts they began to run riot "in invasions of property, massacres, murders, and adulteries." And he adds: "Nor was there any lack of women to connive with them in such corruption." VI, 36 (*Opera*, p. 403A; Dalton, Vol. II, p. 267): "There was a priest hailing from a city of the Cenomanni [Northern Italy] who was an exceedingly licentious man and a great lover of women, of the table, and other sensuality, and was addicted to every kind of vice. Having often frequented the wife of a certain individual, who was a harlot . . ." VI, 46 (*Opera*, p. 414A; Dalton, Vol. II, p. 279): Of Chilperic Gregory says that "No lust or license could be imagined in thought which he had not perpetrated in deed." VIII, 19 (*Opera*, p. 461C; Dalton, Vol. II, p. 344): "Though Dagulfus, an abbot, was often censured for his extravagances, since he had committed several thefts and murders, he was none the less dissolute in his adulteries. At one time when the wife of a neighbour had caught his fancy and he was intriguing with her, he sought various pretexts whereby he might entice the woman's husband inside the precincts of the abbey and do away with him. Finally the man replied to him that if he came near his wife again, he would be punished." IX, 13 (*Opera*, p. 492B; Dalton, Vol. II, p. 383): "The wife of Wiliulf himself was living with a third man, the son of Duke Beppolenus, and he himself, by common knowledge, had left two wives living. For he was a frivolous, sensuous man. In his inordinate fondness for women, he would leave his own wife and take up with her maids. Despising legitimate marriage, he was always on the look-out for something else." IX, 20 (*Opera*, p. 502A; Dalton, Vol. II, p. 394): The King had summoned a synod of bishops. Questioned as to his reasons for doing so, he answered: "Many improper things have been going on and have to be attended to—immoralities, for one thing." IX, 27 (*Opera*, p. 506A; Dalton, Vol. II, p. 398): "Duke Amalo sent his wife to another of his properties to look after matters there. While she was away, he fell enamoured of a certain girl, free-born; and one night, after an orgy of wine at table, he sent his sons to get possession of the girl and bring her to his bed." IX, 33 (*Opera*, p. 511A; Dalton, Vol. II, p. 404): A man complains to a bishop: "You carried off my wife with her maids. Now see, that is not becoming in a priest, for you have committed adultery—you with my maids and she with your men." Now from Fredegarius, *Chronicum*, 36 (p. 624B): King Theodoric pays frequent calls on Saint Columban: "And since he came very often, the man of God began to rebuke him for living in adultery with concubines and

decent language were to be taken as proving sexual immorality. It is true enough that severely impeccable modes of speech may go hand in hand with morals far more corrupt than anything connected with indecencies in speech. However, the argument is false. In the writings in question, not forms only are obscene; the substance is obscene. Translate the romances and the *fabliaux* into words as chaste as one may wish, couch in elegant periphrase the things they say with brutal frankness, and the substance is still there —and it is obscene in the highest degree.[1]

1381. In addition to literature, there are the facts, as reported in chronicles and other documents; and in truth nothing more is needed to assert in all assurance that the period of the Middle Ages was not more chaste than ours, and seems, indeed, to have been more corrupt. There are those who reject immorality in the clergy as proof of the general immorality of the times, and they lay it to the account of religion, "Catholic idolatry," or "Papism," to use terms of the Protestant reformers. But that is another fallacy which is at war with the facts. Immorality was not worse in the clergy than in the public at large—in fact it was not so bad. If there were the many bishops to match the many corrupt barons, there were clerics who set examples of virtue hardly to be matched in the laity. It is often apparent that when certain mediaeval chronicles speak of im-

not preferring the legitimate affections of his wife." *Ibid.*, 42 (p. 653C): King Clothaire is criticized "for betaking himself too assiduously to hunting and for too ready response to the advances of women and girls." *Ibid.*, 48 (p. 637A): "The Chuni went every year to pass the winter season among the Slavs, and made paramours of their wives and daughters." [Such the morals of the good Salvian's Barbarians in the mass!] *Ibid.*, 60 (p. 644B): King Dagobert "was exceedingly addicted to pleasure. He had three queens, in imitation of King Solomon, and no end of concubines. The names of the queens were [He gives them.] . . . but the names of the concubines would be far too many to include in this *Chronicle*." *Ibid.*, 70 (p. 650C): King Clothaire "was at all times roistering with concubines." Such the morals of the kings! One may imagine that the morals of their subjects could not have been much better!

1380 [1] To point the contrast—the *Malleus maleficarum* of Sprenger and Krämer contains obscene descriptions; but they are not essentially obscene in the intent of the authors. The *Roman de Renart* contains obscene terms (*e.g.*, vv. 12386-486). With some goodwill one may again grant that the indecency is primarily in the expression. No such excuse is possible with many *fabliaux*.

morality in the clergy, they take immorality in the laity for granted, and that the special wrath is due to the mere fact that the clergy is at fault.[1] The measures taken against immoralities by Church councils, lay rulers, and other authorities of every sort and description prove the prevalence of immoralities. A thing that does not exist is not for ever being prohibited. The taxes imposed on prostitutes in many places show that their numbers could not have been small, for in that case the tax would not have been worth the bother. We have records of many trials for "bestiality," and many animals so misused were publicly burned. On the immorality of the Crusaders a library of books might be compiled. It may well be that some of their doings have been represented as worse than they actually were; but they cannot all have been invented out of whole cloth.[2 3 4] (For footnotes 3 and 4 see page 862.)

1381 [1] This chapter would become far too long were we to document even in very small part the huge number of facts available to show the immorality in deed, as well as in word, that prevailed in the Middle Ages, to say nothing of times earlier and later. And it would be of little use to expatiate on things known to everybody and which only partisan passions can overlook.

1381 [2] As for decrees on immoralities, *cf.* Council of Arles (Eliberritanum), *anno* 309, 12 (Labbe, Vol. I, p. 994; and see addendum of Mansi, Vol. I, p. 128): "If a mother or any relative or any Christian shall have procured [for a female child], communion shall be withheld even *in extremis.*" 71 (Labbe, Vol. I, p. 999): "Communion shall be withheld to violators of boys even *in extremis.*" Council of Ancyra, *anno* 314, 15-16 (Labbe, Vol. I, pp. 1495, 1498): "Cohabitors with males, or cattle . . . : "Cohabitors with males or cattle are ordered by the Sacred Synod to do penance (*orent*) on a footing with persons bewitched (? *hiemantes*) or possessed by devils . . ." 20 (Labbe, Vol. I, pp. 1499, 1505): "Women who kill children born of fornication shall do penance for ten years." Council of Toledo, *anno* 693, 17 (3) (Labbe, Vol. VIII, p. 60): "Such as may be found guilty of acts of sodomy and have frequently permitted themselves such wickedness, in case they shall be bishops, priests, or deacons . . ." Council of Ratisbon, *anno* 742, VI (Labbe, Vol. VIII, p. 271): "Any servant of God or handmaid of Christ who shall fall into sin of fornication . . ." Council of Tours, *anno* 813, 41 (Labbe, Vol. IX, p. 355): "Many individuals have been found here who are guilty of incests, parricides, and murders, and some we have already excommunicated; but they take that very lightly and persist in the same crimes, wherefore may your mercy decide what henceforward is to be done with them." Council of Treves, *anno* 895, 43 (Labbe, Vol. XI, p. 650): "If anyone shall be guilty of fornication with a woman and without his knowledge his son or brother likewise unknowingly shall have fornicated with the same woman . . ." Council of Milan, *anno* 1565, *Decretum* 65 (Labbe, Vol. XXI, p. 73): "That harlots may be clearly distinguishable from

1382. It is one of the dogmas of the present-day religion of sex that prostitution is an absolute "evil," and like every other religious dogma, it is not debatable. But from the experimental standpoint it is still a question whether prostitution may, or may not, be the occu-

respectable women, let the bishops make provision that they wear some sort of conspicuous veil."

1381 [3] As for taxes on vices, *cf*. Pertile, *Storia del diritto italiano,* Vol. II, Pt. I, p. 435, note 51: "The public decrees of Lucca for the year 1351 (*Bandi Lucchesi,* no. 313) publish a rental contract for a brothel at 120 gold florins a year for that year. Sometimes there was a show of palliating the taint of such revenues by applying them to some purpose of public welfare. *Anno* 1404, Catherine, duchess of Milan, regent for her son Giammaria: 'We hear that the money deriving from taxes on resorts and harlotries in the commune of Milan and which have been paid have been specially appointed to the payment of expenses incurred in repairing the fortresses of that city and in payment of assignments for wolves and foxes [*i.e.,* "bounties" for people killing such animals] and for other such purposes'—and she orders that that arrangement be continued. . . . *Cf*. Osio, [*Documenti diplomatici,* Vol. I, p. 257]. In order to increase revenues from brothels it was ordered in Mantua (*Stat. iud. dac. Com. Man.,* f. 143) that [legal tariff restrictions on prices be abolished] and 'that the buyers of such taxes [*i.e.,* licences] should not have a price fixed by the commune which they may ask for their wares, but that it is allowed them by the commune to sell their wares for the best prices they can get and according as trade and customers shall be found.' "

1381 [4] As regards the morals of the Crusaders, there is the Mussulman testimony, which we may disregard as suspect of bias, *e.g.,* the *Book of the Two Gardens,* Vol. IV, p. 433. (While the Franks were besieging St. John of Acre, A.D. 1189-90, *anno* 585 of the Hegira): "a vessel brought them three hundred women of very unusual beauty. They had been recruited here and there among the islands [of the Mediterranean], having enlisted for that shameful service. Voluntary exiles for the consolation of those abroad, they had left their homes to become the mistresses of those wretches. Far from withholding their favours from monks and priests (*célibataires*), they offered themselves to them of their own accord, regarding the offering as the more meritorious and deeming that no sacrifice could be greater than theirs if the man to whom they gave themselves had the double status of foreigner and celibate. [A transparent invention.] Some of our Mamelukes deserted our camp [Something much more probable.] under the lash of carnal desire to follow that path of damnation, like the ignorant wretches they were." But the testimony of Christian writers is not to be tossed aside on the same grounds: *e.g.,* Gauthier le Chancelier, *Histoire des guerres d'Antioche,* pp. 104-05 (*anno* 1115-19). "Some, sworn enemies of fasting and followers of the pleasures of the table, did their utmost to imitate the rule of life not of those who live well but of those who feed well. Others, in addiction to lechery, frequented the resorts of harlots and overstepped the bounds of all decency. . . . They used the gold and precious stones of Arabie to make ornaments and coverings for *les parties sexuelles de leurs épouses,* and they so did, not to hide such parts from view nor to quench the flames of lust, but to the end that 'those who had lost their taste for lawful pleasures might be stimulated the more keenly by the unlawful, so intensifying crime with crime,

pation best suited to the temperaments of certain women, as being more congenial to them than any other that they might follow; and whether prostitution is, or is not, within certain limits beneficial to society as a whole (§ 1382[4]). Followers of the modern religion of

thinking, as we may suspect (*? ut praelibaremus*), that they were adorning (*? dealbare*) their women and satisfying them, since they were trying in that way to imitate their lusts.' The women had nothing saintly, nothing well-bred, in their manner of enjoying the pleasures of the senses. Scornful of their husbands' beds, they resorted to places of assignation to practice impurities there. They spent night and day in one round of pleasures, amusements, feastings." An age in which such a passage could be written could not, making all due allowance for fabrication, have been an age of such innocence as not to relish the flavour of obscene stories and pictures. Robert le Moine, *Histoire de la première croisade*, p. 407 (Jesus is speaking, having appeared in a dream to a priest to complain of the doings of the Christians): " 'I have permitted all these tribulations and hardships which they are facing because many things have gone on with women, Christian and heathen, that are grievously painful to my eyes.' " Foulcher de Chartres, *Histoire des croisades*, p. 40, also regards the sufferings of the Crusaders at Antioch as a punishment for their immoralities: "Numbers of them weakly and shamelessly gave themselves over to pride, licentiousness, and brigandage. A council was therefore called and all women, whether legitimate wives or concubines, were banished from the army, lest our men should bring the wrath of the Lord down upon themselves by their crimes of debauchery." The same detail is given by Guibert de Nogent, *Gesta Dei per Francos*, V, 17 (*Recueil*, p. 195; Migne, pp. 760-61). And *cf.* Jacques de Vitry, *Histoire des croisades*, pp. 271-72. Book II is entitled: *De la corruption des contrées de l'occident et des péchés des occidentaux*. ". . . Continence," says the author, "so beloved in the heavenly mansions and so pleasing to God, was despised as a worthless thing. The men turned indiscriminately and shamelessly to lustful pleasures, and like hogs wallowing in the mire took delight in such filth. . . . Marriage bonds became very flimsy between relatives and allies, and unbridled licence was not halted even by differences in sex." Ernoul, *Chronique* (Mas Latrie ed.), pp. 86, 91, 216-17, *anno* 1180-84): "Now I must tell you of his manner of life [of the Patriarch of Jerusalem]. When he returned from Rome he became infatuated with the wife of a merchant who lived at Neapolis, some twelve leagues from Jerusalem. And he often sent for her and she went. He gave her much property in order to stand well with her husband. It was not long before her husband died. Then the Patriarch came and took her to live with him in Jerusalem, and he bought her a fine stone house. [The morals of the Greeks were no better:] Now we shall tell you of Andronicus, who was emperor of Constantinople. There was not a pretty nun in the whole land, nor daughter or wife of gentleman or burgher so only she were pretty, that he did not take her and force her to be with him." Jerusalem is besieged by Saladin. The inhabitants pray for rescue, but "Our Lord, my Lord God, could not hear any plaint or prayer that was made in the city because the stench of lust and adultery and sins against nature which was in the city did not allow any prayer that was made before God to rise to Heaven." Evidently such things explain the general opinion prevalent at the time that a man came home from the Crusades worse than he went. In the days of St. Louis, Rutebeuf

sex offer no proof whatever in support of their answers to those questions. Their assertions have to be believed in just as one believed in Zeus in a day gone by and just as now the Mussulman believes that contact with a pig is a source of very serious blemish.

wrote a dialogue (*Œuvres,* Vol. I, p. 156) between a man who wanted to go on the Crusades and one who did not, and the Crusaders come in for some sharp criticism: *La desputizons dou Croisié e dou Descroisié:*

> *"Mult vont outre meir gent menue,*
> *sage, large, de grant aroi. . . .*
> *Si ne valent ne ce ne quoi*
> *quant ce vient à la revenue."*

("All sorts of people go overseas, the poor, the rich, the strict, the easy—but they are not worth *that* when they return.") Guillaume de Nangis, *Chronique* 7, *anno* 1120: "William and Richard, sons of Henry, King of England, the daughter and the niece of that king with a large company of lords and gentlemen of England, were lost at sea in trying to cross from Normandy to England, though the sea was calm and there was no wind. It was said, and in all truth, that they were almost all tainted with the crime of sodomy." Guibert de Nogent, *Vie . . . par lui-même,* III, 3 (pp. 5-7): "There was, in fact, a certain . . . Enguerrand de Boves, who was a generous, prodigal, exceedingly wasteful person. He affected limitless respect and munificence toward the Church, having learned to think that religion was a matter of such things and nothing else. But in another direction he was so fond of women that he always had about him a number of them, bought or borrowed, and in general did nothing except what their effrontery encouraged him to do. Having always failed in his efforts to get a wife, he began to chase the wives of others, managed furtively to seduce the wife of the Count de Namur, a relative of his, and after urging her secretly to crime, finished by living publicly with her as his legitimate wife. . . . The woman was a daughter of Roger, Count of Portian. . . . All those . . . who have known him agree that we should have too great cause for blushing not only in detailing the course of his escapades but even in adverting to them in this history." Regord (Rigot), *Vie de Philippe-Auguste,* p. 139: "In the year of Our Lord 1198, the Foulques here in question took a priest as his assistant to help him in his preaching. . . . Every day, in accompanying the various sermons, he saved some soul from the sin of usury and what is even more from the sin of lust. He even managed to bring back to conjugal continence women who had been living in places of prostitution, there giving themselves to all comers at negligible prices, not even choosing their accomplices." Mathieu Paris, *Grande chronique,* Vol. III, pp. 400-02 (*anno* 1229), gives an account of riots among the students in Paris. They were accusing Queen Blanche of an affair with the Papal Legate and an obscene song was going the rounds:

> *"Heu, morimur strati, vincti, mersi, spoliati:*
> *mentula legati nos facit ista pati."*

Muratori, *Antiquitates Italicae, Dissertatio* 20 (Vol. IV, pp. 251-53; missing in *Dissertazioni*): "During the tenth century of our era, which was the most corrupt that Christian Italy ever saw, licence was given such an inordinately free rein that

Such dogmas may, or may not, be useful to society under certain circumstances. Sacred prostitution has prevailed among many peoples. The fact may seem surprising to anyone labouring under the influence of the hiatus mentioned in § 1339; but not to one who is free of that influence and realizes that such a rite in no sense differs in character from the sacrifices of one kind or another—human sacrifice included—that were offered to the gods, nor from such consecrations as the *ver sacrum* of the Romans (§ 930).[1] Common prostitution is observable among all civilized peoples and in all periods of history. It prevailed among the Hebrews, a people chosen of God, and among the pagans. The Greeks and Romans regarded the harlot's profession as of a lower order than others, but no less necessary. The institution survived the Greeks and Romans. Christianity failed to suppress it. It has held its own down to our own day, and one may reasonably guess that it will live on in future ages despite the wrath

even the leading princesses openly treated themselves to every form of loose morals. Special notoriety for that sort of thing was acquired, around the year 925, among the Lombards by Hermengarde, wife of Adelbert, Marquis of Ivry (*Eporedia*) and among the Romans by Marogia, mother of Pope John XI and wife of the Marquis Alberico the Elder, her mother, Theodora, and another Theodora, her sister. The record of their vices has been transmitted to posterity in a rather free style by Liutprand, the historian of those days. In that same century the clergy likewise began to despise the continence that had been observed in the West from the foundation of the Church, and the unhealthy spirit went so far that priests, deacons, and subdeacons kept women as their wives under the public eye on the plea that what was in no sense unlawful among the Greeks should not be unlawful for them. Verily do the vices thrive more easily by far than the virtues. The pestilence in question gradually pervaded almost all the cities of Italy and the *Urbs* itself. The wicked leaders connived at the thing, the good ones resisted. . . . On the margins of a very ancient manuscript of sacraments owned by the Canonicate at Modena I note the following: 'I, Andrea, a priest, promise before God and all the saints, and before you, Bishop Guarino, that I shall not practise carnal intercourse, and if I should do so, may I lose my post and benefice in the Church.' And another similar oath follows: 'From this time on, I, Giovanni, archpriest, promise you, Guarino, my bishop, that in all the days of my life I shall not commit adultery with the wife of another man, nor fornication with an unlawful harlot, and if I should do so, I hereby declare myself in [mortal] danger.' "

1382 [1] The subject in itself does not properly concern us here. It is a matter for a special sociology. Nor are we interested in the question of the utility of prostitution. In these chapters we are concerned strictly with determining the character of the various residues and the intensities with which they function.

of some of our contemporaries who are often more chaste in theory than in practice. In view of the hypocrisy of ideas about sex, first in mediaeval and then in modern times, governments have now and again been induced to fight prostitution by law. Such efforts have had little or no success, and that is another indication of the power of the sex residues. Prostitution was rife among the devoutly Catholic peoples of the Middle Ages, as witness the many regulations that were made with regard to it and the threats of punishment that were incessantly addressed to prostitutes, the very fact of the constant reiteration proving their inefficacy. Prostitutes are already mentioned in the laws of the Barbarians. The *Capitularies* of the pious Charlemagne represent prostitutes as plying their trade in the very palace. They further allude to grave depravities that were threatening the welfare of the realm, and fix penalties for unnamable vices. The constitutions of the Kingdom of Sicily prohibit the forcing of harlots by violence.[2] [3] [4] [5] [6] [7] (For footnotes 3-7 see pages 867-871.)

1382 [2] As regards sacred prostitution, it is noteworthy that courtesans played a part even in Roman worship, which was very austere on the whole. In the *Fasti Praenestini* one reads (*Corpus inscriptionum Latinarum*, Vol. I, Pt. I, p. 236): "*Robigalia: Feriae Robigo via Claudia ad miliarum [quintum], ne robigo frumentis noceat. Sacrificium et ludi cursoribus maioribus minoribusq(ue) fiunt. Festus et puerorum lenoniorum, quia proximus superior meretricum est.*" (*Robigalia:* Holidays, Robigo, on the Via Claudia at the fifth milestone. A sacrifice to keep the rust from harming the crops, and games with major and minor races are held. Also the feast of panderers, because the feast next preceding [The Vinalia, coming on April 22, the Robigalia on April 25.—A. L.] is for prostitutes.") The feast of the Vinalia was celebrated by prostitutes: Ovid, *Fasti,* IV, vv. 865-68:

> "*Numina vulgares Veneris celebrate puellae:*
> *multa professarum quaestibus apta Venus.*
> *Poscite ture dato formam populique favorem;*
> *poscite blanditias dignaque verba ioco.*"

("Pay honour, ye girls of the public, to the divinity of Venus, the Venus who grants great profits to the business of her devotees. Make your offering of incense and then ask for beauty, and popularity, and the arts of love, and the gay words that go with your play.")

For the festival of Flora, see *Ibid.*, V, vv. 331-34, 349-50:

> "*Quaerere conabar quare lascivia maior*
> *his foret in ludis liberiorque iocus:*
> *sed mihi succurrit numen non esse severum*

1383. The good king St. Louis discovered that brothels had been established in his camp at Damietta near the royal pavilion. The many allusions to the "King of Harlots" mention the prostitutes who followed the French Court and others who were under

aptaque deliciis munera ferre Deam. . . .
Turba quidem cur hos celebret meretricia ludos
non ex difficili causa petenda subest."

("I was about to ask why there should be greater licence in these games and a freer speech; but it occurs to me that the divinity they celebrate wears no long face, that she has functions conducive to pleasures. . . . As to why these games should be celebrated by a throng of harlots, the cause is not hard to imagine.") Well known the fact that at Corinth the city's prayers to Aphrodite were offered by prostitutes, and supplications were addressed to that goddess at the time of the Persian invasion. A scholium on Pindar tells of a man who brought a hundred young courtesans to the sacred forest of the goddess to show his gratitude for a favourable answer to his prayers. And *cf.* Athenaeus, *Deipnosophistae,* XIII, 33. Athenaeus also gives, XIII, 31, a list of temples and festivals that were named after hetairae. [Pindar, **Trag. 122 (L. C. L., Sandys, p. 580).—A. L.**]

1382 [3] Prostitution among the Hebrews: For one thing, prostitution is explicitly prohibited in Deut. 23:17 ("There shall be no whore of the daughters of Israel"); and there are plenty of other allusions in the Bible to show that such a thing was not unknown among the Jews. To reconcile the law with the fact it has been claimed that the law in Deuteronomy referred to sacred prostitution only and the fact to common prostitution. John Spencer vigorously defends that view, *De legibus Hebraeorum ritualibus,* Vol. I, Bk. II, § 35 (p. 561). Quoting the passage in Deuteronomy, he observes: "What is prohibited in those words is not the common prostitute who gives her body for money or in mere quest of pleasure, but the so-called sacred harlot who is consecrated to some foul god of the heathen and practises all sorts of abomination in his honour." That may well be, but it may just as well be that, as is the case among all peoples in such matters, there was some divergence between a theoretical prohibition in the law and a practical toleration in the fact. In any event, prostitutes there were among the Jews, otherwise there would have been no sense in forbidding a priest to marry one (Lev. 21:7). In Judg. 11:1, there is mention of a Jew (Jepthah) who was the son of a harlot. The famous judgment of Solomon (I Kings, 3:16) was rendered in a dispute between two harlots (". . . There came two harlots unto the king"). The story of Tamar (Gen. 38), who traps Judah as a harlot after he had refused her as a wife, could not have been written in a society where prostitution was unknown. And it is told without trace of censure: "When Judah saw her, he thought her to be an harlot because she had covered her face," and he proceeded to cohabit with her. [Judah does say, "She hath been more righteous than I."—A. L.] One of the Proverbs (VI, 26) declares that "by means of a whorish woman a man is brought to a piece of bread." Samson went to Gaza (Judg. 16:1) and "saw there a harlot and went in unto her"; and there is no word of censure in Holy Writ. Many passages in the Talmud show the common divergence between theory and practice in the matter of chastity: Talmud of Jerusalem, Tract Berakoth,

the jurisdiction of that same official. When we come at a later date, the sixteenth century, upon a veritable outburst of corruption we must remember that it is not a thing appearing *ex novo,* but just one of many oscillations over a continuous curve. In a word, prostitution

III, 4 (Gemara) (Schwab, Vol. I, p. 65; Schwab, *Berakoth,* Vol. I, p. 67) (in question the *thebila* (*tefillah*)—a bath of purification taken after carnal pollution): "*Comment la thébila nous empêche-t-elle de pécher? En voici un exemple: Il est arrivé qu'un surveillant de jardins était prêt à commettre un péché avec une femme mariée; mais ils voulaient d'abord s'assurer de pouvoir se purifier immédiatement après* [Striking here the mechanical character of the purification. *Cf.* § 1257]; *pendant ce temps des étrangers arrivèrent et ils furent empêchés de commettre le péché. Un autre, ayant voulu séduire une esclave du Rabba, recut d'elle cette réponse et ce refus: 'Je ne puis prendre la thébila que quand ma maîtresse en prend.' 'Toi,* [*esclave*], *tu n'es considérée que comme une bête,' lui dit le séducteur, 'donc tu n'as pas besoin de thébila.' 'As-tu oublié,' répondit celle-ci, 'qu'il est écrit: Celui qui péche avec une bête doit être mis à mort* (*lapidé*)*?' Et ils ne péchèrent point.*" Talmud of Babylon, Tract Berakoth, III, 5 (Gemara) (Schwab, Vol. I, p. 313; Schwab, *Berakoth,* p. 67; Cohen, pp. 150-51), tells a similar story of the phylacteries worn by Jews: "*Les rabbins ont enseigné qu'avant d'entrer aux cabinets on retire ses phylactères à la distance de quatre coudées . . . il faut les tenir à la main ainsi enveloppés, puis les placer dans des trous à proximité des cabinets, mais ne donnant pas sur la rue, de crainte que les passants ne les prennent et ne donnent lieu à de faux soupçons; car il arriva ceci à un étudiant: ayant laissé ses phylactères dans des trous situés sur la rue, une femme de mauvaise vie vint les prendre et les apporter à la salle d'étude, en disant que cet étudiant les lui avait donnés pour récompense* (*de son libertinage*)*. Le jeune homme en entendant ces mots monta sur le toit et se jeta en bas par désespoir.*"

1382 [4] According to tradition (Athenaeus, *Deipnosophistae,* XIII, 26) Solon was the first to establish brothels in Athens, *διὰ τὴν τῶν νέων ἀκμήν*: "because of the exuberance of the young men in the city." Horace, *Saturae,* I, 2, vv. 31-35:

> "*Quidam notus homo cum exiret fornice, 'Macte*
> *virtute esto,' inquit, sententia dia Catonis.*
> *Nam simul ac venas inflavit tetra libido,*
> *huc iuvenes aequum est descendere, non alienas*
> *permolere uxores.*"

("On seeing a man he knew issuing from a brothel he said: 'Congratulations!'—an opinion of divine wisdom by Cato. 'For as soon as a noisome lust begins to swell the veins, it is a good idea for young men to come here and not go pestering other men's wives.' ") Pseudo-Acron, *Scholia in Horatium* (Paris, 1519, f. 175): "A certain individual came out of a brothel just as Cato was going by. The man took to his heels, but Cato called him back and commended him. But on seeing the man issuing again from that same brothel, he is reported to have said, 'Young man, I commended you for coming here, not for living here.' " The anecdote reflects the Roman's tolerance of the use, and reprobation for the abuse, of sex. Porphyrio, *Commentum in Horatium* (Paris, 1519, f. 175): "On seeing a respectable man issuing from a brothel, Marcus Cato, the Censor, commended him, deeming that there was nothing wrong in a man's satisfying his natural desires." In Athenaeus, *Op. cit.*, XIII, 26, the poet Zenarchus is made to rebuke young men for pursuing married women instead of contenting themselves with prostitutes: "Dreadful [dreadful and intolerable] things are the young men of this city doing. The brothels are full of most beautiful girls. There they stand in proper line, warming themselves in the sun, their breasts bare, their bodies naked." And he wonders that the young men can so soon be so forgetful of Draco's laws against adultery. In his oration *Pro Marco Coelio*, 20, 48, Cicero defends his client for frequenting prostitutes: "But anyone contending that a young man is forbidden commerce with mercenaries is altogether too strict. I cannot deny the fact [of the interdiction], but it is at variance not only with the licence of our times, but with the custom of our forefathers [A most interesting statement.] and the things they deemed allowable. When have such things not been done? When have they been rebuked, when not permitted? When, finally, has it ever been that a lawful thing was not allowable?" And *cf.* Marcus Seneca, *Controversiae*, II, 12, 10 (*Nepos ex meretrice susceptus*, Bouillet, p. 211): "He has done no wrong, he says. He is enamoured of a harlot—a quite usual thing. He is a mere boy! Wait a while! He will mend his ways, and take a wife." Terence, *Adelphoe*, *ll.* 102-03, and Prudentius, *Contra Symmachi orationem, Hymni*, I, vv. 134-38 (*Opera*, Vol. II, p. 138) [However the lines of Prudentius are not just to this point.—A. L.]. Roman law upheld the dignity of matrons but left broad liberties to courtesans and their patrons: Suetonius, *Tiberius*, 35: "To be free of the rights and obligations (*dignitate*) of matrons and evade the penalties imposed by the laws, women of compromised reputations began to enroll as prostitutes." Tacitus, *Annales*, II, 85: "In that year [A.D. 19] the Senate passed severe laws against profligacy among women and decreed that no woman whose father, grandfather, or husband had been a Roman knight could register as a prostitute. That was because a woman of praetorian rank named Vestilia had so registered with the aediles, as was permitted by the ancients, who deemed it a sufficient deterrent for a woman well born that she should make public declaration of her infamy." Papinian, in *Digesta*, XLVIII, 5, 10, § 2 (*Corpus iuris civilis*, Vol. I, p. 896; Scott, Vol. XI, p. 35): "A woman who has registered as keeper of a house of prostitution or hired out her services [as an actress] on a public stage for the purpose of evading the penalties of adultery can be indicted for adultery and condemned by decree of the Senate." Livy explains, *Ab urbe condita*, XXXIX, 9, how the Bacchanalian orgies came to be discovered: "A famous courtesan, the freedwoman, Hispala Fecenia, a person worthy of a better lot, continued practising the profession that she had practised as a girl slave even after she had won her freedom. She had established relations with one Aebutius because they were near neighbours, and doing no harm to him either in his property or reputation. She had loved him and sought him of her own accord, and since he was ever in need because of the niggardliness of his family, the courtesan had helped him, out of the kindness of her heart." Even Fathers of the Church recognized prostitution as a necessary evil. St. Augustine, *De ordine*, II, 4, 12 (*Opera*, Vol. I, p. 977), observes that there are necessary evils, such as executioners, prostitutes, panderers: "Can anything be called more loathsome, farther removed from decorum and more fraught with wickedness, than prostitutes, panderers, and other pests of that kind? Yet remove the prostitute from society and everything would be corrupted by lust. Give the harlot the ranking of the matron and you bring the matron into disrepute and defilement. That is why that class of women who are so exceedingly corrupt in their manner of living as regards their morals are assigned to the lowest station by the laws of social ranking." St. Thomas, *Summa theologiae,* IIa IIae, *qu.* 10, *art.* 11 (*Opera,* Vol. VIII, p. 93: *Utrum infidelium ritus sint tolerandi*): [Just as God suffers certain evils to avoid greater ones] "so those who preside over human governments properly tolerate certain wrongs lest certain good things have hurt or even worse evils be incurred, as Augustine says." And he quotes the lines just mentioned. The pagan Emperors taxed prostitutes in Rome and Christian Emperors did the same at Constantinople: Suetonius, *Caligula,* 40: "This strange and unheard-of tax Caligula first collected through the civil tax-collectors [publicans] and then through the centurions and the praetorian tribunes." He taxed the earnings of prostitutes to the amount of the proceeds from one venture, the law furthermore requiring registry of prostitutes and keepers of disorderly houses. Aelius Lampridius, *Alexander Severus,* 24, 3 (Magie, Vol. II, p. 223): "He would not allow the proceeds of the tax on disorderly houses, prostitutes, and mendicants [? *exoletorum;* Magie: "catamites"] to be paid into the sacred treasury, but assigned them to the public budget for the upkeep of the Theatre, the Circus, the Amphitheatre and the Stadium (*aerarii,* read *stadii*)." Zonaras, *Epitome historiarum,* XIV, 3 (Migne, Vol. 135, p. 54), states that the Emperor Anastasius laid a tax called the *crisagyrium* (gold and silver tax, Latin, *aurargenteum*) on "all paupers, mendicants, and courtesans." In his fourteenth *Novella* (III, 1), *De Lenonibus* (*Corpus iuris civilis,* Vol. III, pp. 94-98; Scott, Vol. XVI, pp. 78-80), Justinian complains that prostitutes were flocking to Constantinople from all parts of the Empire and "the place and its environs were full of brothels." He therefore enjoins on all his subjects to help remedy the situation by "conducting themselves chastely to the best of their ability." What a pulpit for that sort of sermon!

1382 [5] As for Barbarian legislation, *cf.* the *Codex legis Wisigothorum,* III, 4, 17 (Canciani, Vol. IV, pp. 97-98): "Matter of prostitutes whether free-born or slaves, or in case judicial authorities have been lax in prosecuting and punishing their crime. If a girl or woman free-born shall be shown to be a prostitute publicly practising her profession in a city and though frequently taken in adultery evinces no shame but is shown to have gone on soliciting many men through her evil habit, she shall be arrested by the Count (*Comes*) of such city."

1382 [6] As for the court of Charlemagne, *cf. Capitularium de minesterialibus palatinis,* 1: "Each attendant at court shall by a diligent taking of the roll (*discutiat*) first among his men and then among his peers see whether he can find hiding among them or at our court any unknown person or prostitute." *Capitularium regum Francorum,* VII, 143 (Canciani, Vol. III, p. 320): "But since with the help of God and through the merits and intercession of the Saints and servants of God whom we have at all times tried, as we still are trying, to honour and glorify, we and our successors have so far acquired realms and territories and won many victories, so it must henceforward be the concern of all of us that we should not be deprived of such things—which God forbid—because of the foul and unlawful vices that we have mentioned. For many lands which have practised encroachments, robberies, confiscations, invasions and abuses of church properties and oppressions of priests and other servants of God and other sorts of wrongs, or unlawful things such as adulteries, sodomies, or frequentings of prostitutes, have never long endured strong in secular war or abiding in faith. And in what measure the Lord has permitted avenging punishments to come upon and serve those who

prevails among almost all civilized peoples and in all periods of history. There are very considerable variations in forms, very few in substance.[1 2 3] (For footnote 3 see page 873.)

1384. So far we have been speaking of people in general. Let us

are guilty of such crimes now through the Saracens, now through other peoples, is apparent (*liquet*) to anyone reading their histories. And unless we beware of such things, we have no doubt that similar punishments will overtake us also, for God takes His vengeance for all such things." Virtually the same words are repeated in the Fourth Appendix (*Additio quarta*) to the *Capitularium,* sec. 160 (Canciani, Vol. III, p. 408), but with this adjunct: "Such immoral women, whether of the monasteries or of the laity, oftentimes and in large part kill the offspring they have conceived in sin, so sating the other world with unhappy souls and filling not the churches with adoptive children but the graveyards with dead. God grant that (reading *pereatis*) ye perish not from such things and that we fall not with our realm (reading *peccatis:* "that we fall not with our realm because of such sins")." As we shall see further along (§ 1391 [3]), Charlemagne notes that priests and clerics were frequent sinners with the women with whom canon law, assuming such contacts to be innocuous, permitted them to live. Morals in the people generally were no better. *Capitularium cit.,* VII, 336-56 (Canciani, Vol. III, 340-41): *"That concubines are unlawful:* A man who has a wife cannot at the same time have a concubine nor shall love of a concubine keep him apart from his wife. . . . On men who have had intercourse with animals (*pecorum*) or who after the manner of animals have committed incest with relatives within the limits of blood-relationship or have had commerce with males." And *cf. Ibid.,* Bk. VI, 27 (Canciani, Vol. III, p. 264).

1382 [7] As for the laws of Sicily, see *Constitutiones regni Siculi,* Bk. I, 20 (Canciani, Vol. I, p. 311): *"On forcing prostitutes* [*against their will*]: Laws of King William: Those unfortunate women who are distinguished by the nefarious trade of the prostitute shall have our favour, in response to their petition (*gratulantes*), to the extent that no man shall force them to do his pleasure against their will." *Ibid.,* Bk. III, 53 (Canciani, Vol. I, p. 372): *"On penalties for a mother who makes her daughter a public prostitute:* Laws of the Emperor Frederick: We ordain that mothers who publicly prostitute their daughters shall be subject to the penalty fixed by the late (*divus*) King Roger of having the nose cut off. We think it not so much unjust as severe that there should be penalties for other women who merely abet (*consentientes*) and offer to the pleasures of men daughters whom poverty prevents them from marrying off or supporting and who thereby earn livelihood or favours."

1383 [1] For conditions in the French camp at Damietta, read Joinville, *Histoire de Saint Louis,* XXXVI, 171: "The rank and file took to light women, so that the King banished all such individuals from the army in one sweep when we came back from taking the town [*prison*]. I asked him why he had done that, and he told me that he had discovered that the people whom he had sent away had set up their brothels within a stone's throw of his tent and that too at a time when the army was in the direst straits it had ever been in."

1383 [2] On the "King of Harlots" see Pichon, *Le roy des ribauds:* C. Fanchet, p. 25: "It is said that the light women who followed the court were obligated

now look at various classes of people in particular. If in so doing we were to find that immorality is not observable among individuals highly placed in religious orders that condemn carnal indulgence, an influence of doctrines upon conduct would be plausibly indicated. But if that is not the case, if morality is none the greater where faith seems greatest, we shall again conclude, as we have previously concluded, not that faith is a bad thing, nor even altogether without influence, but that in many cases it is not powerful enough to subdue the sex residues.

1385. Beginning with the reproaches addressed of old to the philosophers of Greece and Rome, coming on through the accusations brought against the Catholic clergy, or the Christian clergy in general, we finally reach our own time, when similar charges can be lodged against our virtuists.

during the month of May to make the bed of the Provost of the Mansion. They had come to be called *ribaudes* because of their bold impudence and immodesty." According to Bouteillier, an author writing about 1459, and who is also quoted by Miraumont (p. 37), the King of Harlots "collected a tax of two sous a week from all brothels and from the women in them." Du Tillet, quoted by Estienne Pasquier, *Recherches de la France,* VIII, 44 (p. 750), quoted by Pichon, *Op. cit.,* p. 78, repeats the detail of the bed-making: "The harlots who follow the Court are under the charge [of the King of Harlots] and are obliged to go and keep his room in order all through this month of May." Du Cange, *Glossarium . . . mediae et infimae Latinitatis, s.v. Ribaldi,* quotes the privileges of the King of Rogues at Cambray: "Said King may have, take, collect, receive from each woman who goes with a man, when she has earned her money and provided she has rented or is renting a house in the city, five sous of the Paris mintage for each time. 2. From all women coming under the law who enter the city for the first time, two sous of the mintage of Tours. 3. From each woman coming under the law who moves from one house or resort (*estuve*) to another to live, or who goes out of the city and stays one night, twelve pence." Criticizing the remark of Bouteillier, above, Gouye de Longuemare (pp. 96-97) [*i.e., Eclaircissemens, etc.,* pp. 223-24] none the less substantiates the prevalence of [Court] prostitutes: "As for what Bouteillier says of his [the "king's"] jurisdiction over 'brothels and the women in them,' one must understand that his function was to visit such places and enforce the observance of a certain orderliness. . . . The houses and the women who lived in them had to pay a tax of two sous a week. . . . Immorality would seem to have been permitted at the time in the retinue of our Kings. All the same it should be noted that it was only tolerated there, just as disorderly houses were tolerated in Paris. . . . It seems indeed that the purpose of the tolerance was merely to avoid still greater irregularities." [Whatever the motives underlying the fact, the fact remains a fact.] Le Bibliophile Jacob, *Curiosités de l'histoire de France,* pp. 163-64: "Rogues' Royalty went to the distaff on the passing of the good Lord of Gri-

1386. People who are inclined to attach great or exclusive importance to logical conduct are tempted to infer from the fact that a few or many believers in a given religion are dishonest that that religion is "false," useless, harmful. But those who understand the important rôle non-logical conduct plays in human life also understand that such a conclusion is not warranted. Philosophy is not to be condemned because there have been dishonest philosophers, nor the Catholic religion because there have been criminal priests, nor the religion of our Inquisitors on Purity because dissolute individuals are to be counted among them. Such religions, all religions, are to be judged by different standards. Even disregarding non-logical conduct and keeping strictly to the logical, the accusations in question are in many cases unjustified.

1387. The bitter censure that has been heaped upon the Jesuits

gneaux. 'A lady, and sometimes a great lady,' says Rabutaux in his interesting *Mémoire sur la prostitution en Europe,* 'had charge of policing the women at court. In 1535 her name was Olive Sainte, and she received an allowance of ninety pounds from Francis I 'to help her and said girls to live and meet such expenses as they should properly make in ordinarily following the court. . . .' Several ordinances of the same sort, issued between the years 1539 and 1546, have been preserved, and they show that every year during the month of May all the girls about the court were allowed the honour of offering the King the 'Spring bouquet' (*bouquet du renouveau*) or 'valentine,' which welcomed the return of spring and amorous pleasures." P. de Miraumont quotes (p. 41) an order of July 13, 1458, also referring to the superintendence by a woman. It "expressly enjoined and ordered upon all prostitutes and others not on the registers of the mistress in charge of said girls, to vacate the court forthwith on publication of said order, girls on the registers meantime being forbidden to go about in the villages, and carters, muleteers, and others to transport them out or back or give them lodging, and further to swear and blaspheme the name of God."

1383 [3] As for the success of repressive measures see Lamare, *Traité de police,* I, *Lib.* III, *tit.* V, ch. 6, pp. 521-22: "St. Louis set out to abolish prostitution: his Ordinance of 1254 begins with just that reform. It states that all prostitutes, girls or women, shall be driven from towns and villages alike. . . . But long and sad experience showed at last that prostitution could not be totally abolished without occasioning other irregularities incomparably more dangerous to religion, to morals and the state. . . . It then became the policy to tolerate those unhappy victims of impurity . . . An Ordinance of the Prefect of Paris, September 18, 1367, orders all women of dissolute life to go and live in the brothels and public places assigned to them . . . and other persons are forbidden to rent them houses in any other places on pain of confiscation of the rents; and the women themselves are forbidden to buy houses elsewhere on pain of losing them."

for discussing cases of conscience relative to sex in their treatises might be logically justified if it came of the conviction that neither morality nor law should interfere in matters of sex. It is not justified if it comes, as it usually does, from people who believe that morality and law ought to interfere in sex. Obviously it is impossible to regulate a thing without discussing it. The Jesuits, moreover, were far from being the only ones to harp on sex. They had predecessors in the Church Fathers and successors in all those who, believers and infidels alike, have since set out to regulate sex relations.[1]

1388. The "abolitionists" of our day who would abolish prostitution root and branch use language more indecent than the Jesuits ever did; and a language furthermore that is common to everybody, whereas the Jesuits used Latin. Our puritans also fight immorality, at times in such ways as to make one's mouth water for sin. I say nothing of those who under pretext of educating the young to chastity write books to impart all the details of the sexual act.

1389. The evidence that, as regards morality in individuals, theories and facts are far from always corresponding is exceedingly abundant, too abundant indeed. We must be on our guard against it and reject not a little of it. But meantime the evidence on the other side is also suspect, because it may, even when produced in good faith, express a mere ill will that takes advantage of the powerful weapon provided by the sex residue to vent its spleen. The evidence furnished by neutrals is also not always above suspicion, for the impression left upon our minds by the contrast between fine

1387 [1] There is no good reason for doubting the utter good faith of St. Alfonsus Liguori when, *Theologia moralis,* Vol. I, p. 228, he confesses his repugnance to dealing with violations of the Sixth and Ninth Commandments: *"Treatise on the Sixth* [*i.e.,* Seventh] *and Ninth Precepts of the Decalogue:* Reluctantly now we approach the consideration of a subject the very name of which corrupts the minds of men. Would that I could express myself more briefly and in a language more veiled. But since it is the more frequent and abundant topic in confessions and the thing that drags the greater number of souls to hell—indeed I do not hesitate to say that all who are damned are damned because of this one vice of impurity or at all events not apart from it—I have been obliged to express myself clearly (though as chastely as possible) and to discuss many many things in detail for the instruction of those interested in mastering moral science."

preaching and bad practice tends to magnify shortcomings in preachers of virtue. Not even the testimony of loyal believers in a religion against its priesthood is always to be accepted at face value. There is a natural inclination in the human being to exaggerate an evil the better to correct it, and to substitute preaching for impartial observation. As regards the neutral and the believer, such reservations apply more especially to comments upon the facts, little if at all to the bare facts themselves. Everything is possible, but it is not very probable that a believer will invent a fact outright for the mere pleasure of slandering people who hold the same faith as he. Nor is it very likely that an unbiased person interested in having an accurate record of facts would invent the things that he records. In a word, the causes of error that we have indicated have their influence on all historical documents. If we would reject absolutely everything in which they figure, we should have to give up all history of whatever kind as a hopeless business.

1390. St. Jerome betrays the fact that in his early day there were priests who for all the world resembled the cassocked "dandies" of the eighteenth century, as well as women very very like the petticoated sex-reformers of our day who for sheer love of purity cannot get their minds off prostitution. The allusions of the Saint, along with the laws that the Emperors had to proclaim against too close intimacies between women and clergy, remove any doubt we may have held that the remarks of Ammianus Marcellinus on the Roman pontiffs of his time may have been slanders. "Considering," he writes, *Res gestae,* XXVII, 3, 14, "the magnificence of that office in the city of Rome, I can understand the excessive eagerness some people manifest for obtaining it and why it is fought for with such bitterness. The person who secures it is sure of growing rich through the gifts of Roman matrons, of having a carriage to ride in in robes of the most elegant fashion, and of enjoying banquets that surpass the feasts of kings in splendour." [1]

1390 [1] St. Jerome, *Ad Pammachium adversus errores Ioannis Hierosalemitani* (*Opera,* Vol. II, p. 561; Schaff-Wace, p. 428): "Poor Praetextatus! He died just as he had been named consul! A sacrilegious soul and a worshipper of idols, he used to say playfully to the blessed Pope Damasus: 'Make me bishop of the city of Rome, and I'll turn Christian at once!' "

1391. The Theodosian Code had a law that forbade ecclesiastics and self-styled "continents" to frequent the homes of widows and female orphans, and to accept gifts from such women under pretext of piety. Another law forbade them to keep women in their houses when a scandal was likely to result. Laws of that kind are to be found in other codes, notably in Charlemagne's Capitularies. The battle the Popes waged all through the Middle Ages against a concubinary clergy is too well known to require documentation.[1 2 3]

1391 [1] As for the protection of widows and orphans, *cf. Codex Theodosianus,* XVI, 2, 20 (Haenel, pp. 1492-93): *Imperatores Valentinianus, Valens et Gratianus Augusti (AAA) ad Damasum Episcopum urbis Romae.* "Priests or ex-priests or those who choose to call themselves 'continents' shall not enter homes of widows and female wards, but they shall be banished by public sentence if hereafter relatives of such women or members of their families shall see fit to have them brought to trial. And we likewise ordain that such individuals shall not be allowed possession of anything from the liberality or last will of any woman to whom they may have secretly attached themselves under pretext of piety, and any legacy made by any such woman to any such person shall in all respects be null and void so that they shall receive nothing even through a third (*subjectam*) person from any gift or testament." Godefroi annotates (Vol. VI, p. 48): "'Continents' were individuals inspired by personal zeal for a better life, following a vow to live more austerely apart from the consolations of legitimate matrimony. The ἀποταττόμενοι practiced celibacy. The word ἐγκρατευόμενοι means 'the temperate.'"

1391 [2] As for priests keeping women in their homes, *Ibid.,* XVI, 2, 44 (Haenel, p. 1514), *anno* 420: "It is not becoming that a man who is ostensibly practising a rule of life before the laity should be compromised (*decolorari*) by any so-called sororial association. All persons whatsoever therefore who are supported by the priesthood of whatever grade or who are distinguished with the honour of the priesthood, should know that association with women not their kin (*extranearum*) is forbidden them. . . . *Interpretation:* All persons practising the profession of priest are forbidden to associate on terms of intimacy with women not their kin. Notice is served (*noverint*) that the attendance (*solatia*) of mothers, sisters, or daughters is all that is permitted them in their homes, for the law of nature does not allow that any wicked deed or thought should arise in connexion with such persons. Even of such women, however, they are to be chosen as attendants who have been married before service with a priest." And see the long note by Godefroi, Vol. VI, p. 86.

1391 [3] For the allusion to Charlemagne, *cf. Capitularium regum Francorum,* VII, 376 (Canciani, Vol. III, p. 343): *"That females shall not live with priests or other clerics nor act as their servants nor stay in their houses nor approach the altar."* Charlemagne bars women who were passed by the old canons, "because it is our experience that at the instigation of the Devil crime has frequently been committed with even those women." And *cf. Ibid.,* VII, 452 (Canciani, Vol. III, pp. 353-54). The Third Appendix (*Additio tertia*), 117, reads (Canciani, Vol. III, p. 386): *"On the introduction of women* [into homes of priests]: It shall be strictly for-

1392. It had been a long-standing evil, and one must say that if it is to be counted a degeneration of Christianity, the corruption set in at a very very early stage. St. Cyprian expatiated at length on the subject and he was a man of the third century. In a letter he writes to one Pomponius, *Ad Pomponium de virginibus,* conjointly with other priests, he expresses himself as follows: "Very dear Brother: We have read the letter that you sent us by our brother Pacomius, urgently requesting in answer our opinion as to those virgins who, despite their vows to remain in their state and observe continence, are found to have slept in the same beds with males, among whom, you state, a deacon, and who, though openly confessing to so sleeping with men none the less aver that they are still virgins." The Saint condemns that sort of household on the strength of biblical quotations: ". . . Virgins cannot be allowed to live with men—I do not say to sleep with men, but even to live in their houses. . . . How many the men who are ruined in that way, and how many the virgins who are corrupted by that illicit and dangerous contiguity to the supreme sorrow of our soul! . . . If they really will not, or cannot, persevere [in their state], it is better for them to marry than to fall into hell-fire by sinning." According to St. Jerome married women and widows who hobnobbed too intimately with priests behaved no better.[1]

bidden for any priest to have a woman with him in his house save as permitted by the canons."

1392 [1] St. Cyprian, *Epistolae,* 62, 1-2 (*Opera,* pp. 364-65; Wallis, Vol. I, p. 204). And *cf. Ibid.,* 62, 3 (*Opera,* pp. 367-69; Wallis, Vol. I, p. 206): *"Nec aliqua putet se hac excusatione defendi, quod inspici et probari possit an virgo sit cum et manus obstetricum et oculus saepe fallatur. Et si incorrupta inventa fuerit virgo ea parte sui qua mulier potest esse potuerit tamen ex alia corporis parte peccasse quae violari potest et tamen inspici non potest. Certe ipse concubitus ipse complexus ipsa confabulatio et osculatio et coniacentium duorum turpis et foeda dormitio quantum dedecoris et criminis confitetur!"* (See below, § 1394 [6]). More chaste and by far than such women was the Roman matron who used an image of the phallus to protect her children from the evil eye; nor would a paterfamilias of the better Roman days have allowed daughters of his to submit to such indecent inspections. To cap the climax Saint Cyprian adds a touch about divine jealousy which had better stay in Latin (*loc. cit.*): *"Si superveniens maritus sponsam suam iacentem cum altero videat nonne indignatur et fremit? Et per zeli livorem fortassis et gladium in manum sumit? Quid? Christus Dominus et iudex noster, cum virginem suam sibi dicatam et sanctitati suae destinatam facere cum altero cernit,*

1393. The censures heaped by the Fathers and dignitaries of the Church on immoralities in the clergy are usually met with the defence that they were not descriptions of literal fact, but assumed the existence of evils in order to point a lesson. That objection was raised against Cardinal Peter Damian for one among many others. But can we possibly imagine that St. Cyprian invented the letter of Pomponius, which he answers, out of whole cloth? Can everything he says be fiction? Even granting all that, it would still not be enough. The acts of the Councils and no end of other documents are there to vouch for the fact that women commonly lived with priests. But to defend the clergy it is unnecessary to brand all such evidence as false. It is sufficient to observe that, after all, the morals of the clergy were no worse, indeed they seem to have been on the whole better, than the morality generally prevailing at the time.[1]

quam indignatur et irascitur! Et quas poenas incestis eiusmodi coniunctionibus comminatur!" For Jerome's picture of the merry widows of those days see his letter *Ad Eustochium, Epistolae,* XXII, 6 (Wright, p. 85) (Widows affecting chastity in question): "Their houses are full of flatterers, full of guests. The very priests whose rôle would better seem to be that of the teacher who is feared kiss them on the foreheads, or hold out their hands—to bless them you might think if you did not know—to receive the rewards of the greeting. The widows, meantime, seeing that the priests need their help, become conceited and proud and to the rule of a husband that they have experienced they much prefer the freedom of widowhood, call themselves 'continents' and nuns and after equivocal suppers (*post cenam dubiam*) see Apostles in their dreams!"

1393 [1] As for the Damian incident: That saint had brought the immorality and vices of a number of ecclesiasts to the attention of the Pope: St. Peter Damian, *Liber Gomorrhianus ad Leonem IX, Romanum Ponteficem* (*Opera,* Vol. III, p. 73): "Argument: [St. Peter Damian] deplores the detestable, nay, unspeakable criminality into which men of his time who were consecrated to God were falling. He argues that they should be removed from the sacred orders as unworthy and begs the Roman pontiff Leo to restrain such foul sinners with all his authority." And *cf.* Burchard, *Diarium,* May, *anno* 1493 (Vol. II, p. 79): "[Pope] Alexander [VI] has carried on the policy of marrying his female progeny that Innocent began and has improved upon it. The whole clergy therefore is falling to with a will to the business of raising families. From highest to lowest they are living with concubines very much as wives and indeed publicly. Unless God forfend, this corruption will extend to the monks and friars, though virtually every monastery in the *Urbs* is already a brothel, with nobody objecting." Thuasne, Burchard's editor, comments (*loc. cit.*): "This comparison of brothels and convents is a common theme with writers of the fifteenth century"—and he mentions examples. Infessura, *Diario,* pp. 259-60: "Among other things also that may be ascribed to those times [*anno* 1490] is the fact that the Reverend Father, the Vicar of the Pope in the City and District, think-

1394. The women who live with the clergy were variously designated: *subintroductae* (*i.e.,* secretly), "strangers" (*i.e.,* not of one's kin), "sisters," "agapetes" (lovers in Christ), and there is frequent allusion to them in the acts of the Councils.[1] St. John Chrysostom has

ing as befitted a kind soul to shelter the lambs of the flock entrusted to his care, issued an edict prohibiting laymen and clergy of whatever rank or condition, and among other things, on pain of excommunication, suspension, and loss of benefices, from keeping concubines either privately or in public, since he had learned that that was being turned to the discredit of divine law and against the reputability of the clergy, there being many, in fact countless numbers of priests, both high prelates and ordinary clerics, who were keeping concubines, so that that was not judged a proper manner of living in them and they were diminishing the devotion and faith of the laity. When the Holy Father heard of that, he hastily summoned said Bishop and Vicar to him and sharply reprimanded him for issuing the interdict and bade him rescind it at once since, he said, the thing was not prohibited, because the manner of living of priests and attendants at the Curia had come to such a pass that hardly one could be found who was not keeping a concubine or at the very least a prostitute to the glory of God and the Christian faith. That may be the reason why, as competent authority avers, the number of prostitutes practising publicly in Rome at that time has been estimated at 6,800, not counting those who were living as concubines and those who were plying their trade not publicly but in secret with five or six others, each one of them having one or more procurers." In his *Diarium,* Vol. II, p. 400, Burchard mentions a service that took place in August, 1497: "Harlots and other disreputable persons were present everywhere between the altar and the Cardinals." And, *Ibid., anno* 1501 (Vol. III, p. 167), he describes the famous banquet with the fifty courtesans offered by Pope Borgia: "That evening fifty prostitutes, more chastely known as courtesans, had supper with Duke Valentine in his apartment in the Apostolic Palace, and after the meal they danced with the servants and the others there present, first in their costumes and

1394 [1] Speaking against Paul of Samosata in his *Historia ecclesiastica,* VII, 30, 12, Eusebius uses the term *συνεισάκτους*, " 'taken in with,' as the people of Antioch call them, and those of the priests and of the deacons who live about him . . . and we know how many [priests] have fallen as a result of allowing women near them." And *cf.* Nicephorus Callistus, *Ecclesiastica historia,* VI, 30. In his letter to Eustochia, *De custodia virginitatis, Epistola* XXII, 14 (Wright, pp. 81-83), St. Jerome cries: "I shrink from mentioning such profanity. Sad is it yet true! How did this pest of the 'agapetes' ["sisters in Christ"; Wright: "dearly beloved sisters"] get into the Church? How is it we have come to have another name for unmarried wives? Whence this new sort of concubine? I will speak more plainly: Whence this whore who keeps to one man, one house, one chamber, often indeed one bed! And they call us evil-minded if we suspect something (*suspiciosos nos vocant, si aliquid extimemus*)! Here a brother leaves an unmarried sister to her own devices. There a maid will have none of her unmarried brother. No indeed! She must have a 'brother' not her kin! And since they both pretend to be of one mind on that point, they seek the spiritual solace of 'strangers,' but for the purpose of carnal pleasure amid all the comforts of home (*ut domi habeant carnale commercium*)!"

two whole sermons against them. In the first [2] he says that the forefathers knew two reasons for a woman's living with a man: one of them was righteous and rational—matrimony; the other, more modern, was unrighteous and illegal—fornication, which was the

then naked. After dinner also the common candlesticks were taken from the table with candles lighted and set on the floor and chestnuts were strewn over the floor among the candlesticks set in line (*projecta*) and the harlots gathered them up scrambling on all fours among the candles, the Pope, the Duke, Milady Lucretia, the Duke's sister, being present and looking on. At length the last gifts were brought out, silk dresses, boots in pairs, caps, and other things for those *qui pluries dictas meretrices carnaliter agnoscerent quae fuerunt ibidem in aula publice carnaliter tractate arbitrio presentium,* the gifts being distributed to the winners." Thuasne notes: "The [story of the] banquet of the fifty courtesans is corroborated by Materazzo who, however, speaks of lords and ladies of the court instead of the servants and courtesans in Burchard's story [See *Archivio storico italiano,* Vol. XVI-2, p. 189]; by a letter of Silio Savelli . . . which Sanudo inserts in his diary, and finally by the Florentine orator, Francesco Pepi. . . . Early in the eighteenth century the French regent gave a series of twelve balls at the Little Luxembourg, where dancers male and female and entirely nude revived the gay festivities of the Vatican." Machiavelli, *Vita di Castruccio Castracani* (*Opere,* Milan, 1804-05, p. 153): (After the defeat which Castruccio inflicted upon the Florentines) "he halted with his people on the plain of Peretola . . . where he lingered for many days dividing the booty, celebrating the victory, and having medals struck in contempt of the Florentines and racing horses, men, and courtesans." Burchard, *Diarium,* Vol. III, p. 146 (June 19, 1501): "A place near the Acqua Traversa was appointed . . . for the lodging of attendants of the King of France on their way to Naples. . . . Fences were built about the place, and supplies of bread, meats, eggs, cheese, fruit, and all other necessaries laid in, and by special order sixteen harlots to provide for the needs of those people." Familiar the fact that concubinage was wide-spread among priests in the Middle Ages and that in many instances lay and religious authorities sold the privilege of keeping concubines at certain rates. It was an evil of long standing, and many chroniclers allude to it, *e.g.,* Mathieu Paris, *Grande chronique,* Vol. I, p. 293 (*anno* 1129): "That same year, on August 1, King Henry held a great Council in London to prohibit concubinage in the clergy. William, Archbishop of Canterbury, Thurston, Archbishop of York, and their followers attended. Thanks to an awkward blunder of the Archbishop of Canterbury, Henry fooled all the prelates roundly. He indeed got high justice on clerical concubinage, but the business was to end in a great scandal, for the King made a fortune by selling back to the priests the right to keep their concubines." Things are much the same in our day in places where sex-reformers have got purity into the law, the profits going to the police, who know how to tolerate immorality in practice. *Ibid.,* 286-87: "In the year of Our Lord 1125, Jean de Crème, Cardinal of the Holy Apostolic See, visited England with the King's permission and went from diocese to

1394 [2] Gaume, Vol. I, pp. 279-326: Πρὸς τοὺς ἔχοντας παρθένους συνεισάκτους. Gaume's editor, Savil, paraphrases: "*Adversus eos qui apud se fovent sorores adoptivas quas subintroductas vocant.*"

work of the Devil. In his own day another reason strange and paradoxical had come into vogue; for there actually were men who took girls into their houses without marrying them and apart from considerations of sex and lived with them to old age. The reasons alleged

diocese, from abbey to abbey, not without everywhere collecting bounteous presents. On the day of the Nativity of the Blessed Mary he held a solemn council in London, where he preached forcefully against concubinage among priests, declaring it an abominable crime to go from the arms of a courtesan to partake of the body of Christ. But after communing that day, he was found spending the evening with a courtesan." Similar mishaps have befallen sex-reformers in our day. The centuries roll by, human nature remains the same! There is a passage in Cornelius Agrippa that certainly oversteps the truth, but which no less certainly is in partial accord with the facts. Appearing in the Antwerp edition of 1530, the passage was deleted in the Lyons edition of the *Opera omnia.* On the point see Bayle, *Dictionnaire historique, s.v. Agrippa.* The copy at my disposal begins: *"Splendidae nobilitatis viri et armatae militiae Equitis aurati . . . Henrici Corneilii Agrippae ab Nettesheym De Incertitudine et Vanitate Scientiarum et Artium atque excellentia Verbi Dei Declamatio"*; for a colophon: *"Iona. Grapheus excudebat anno a Christo nato MDXXX, mense Septemb. Antuerpiae."* The pages are not numbered; but there is a register of the sheets. In the chapter *De arte lenonia* (sheet *z,* recto, last page) Agrippa fiercely declaims against the immorality of his age: "The jealous husband is pacified by gold, by gold is the heart of the relentless rival softened. Guards most scrupulous are vanquished by gold, for gold doth every door swing open. Every marriage-bed has its price in gold. The stoutest door-bar, the hardest rock, the unsunderable bonds of matrimony, are broken in twain by gold. What wonder that virgins, maids, matrons, widows, nuns (*vestales*), are venial, if Christ Himself is sold for gold? With gold the panderer as leader, countless are they who have risen from lowliest station almost to the supreme heights of nobility. This man prostitutes his wife and he is made a Senator, that one prostitutes his daughter, and lo, he is a Count. A third solicits the embrace of a married woman for his prince, and straightway he is a royal chamberlain deemed worthy of an ample salary. There are those who have become important men and been placed in charge of public bureaus by marrying royal mistresses. Many cardinals and Popes have won many rich benefices by those same arts nor is any road in the Church more expeditious. . . . [Agrippa turns to ancient examples of the use of religion for purposes of pandering, and then goes on:] Nor if I chose to mention them would I find any lack of modern examples. For priests, monks, friars, lay brothers, and the women they call 'sisters,' have the special prerogative of pandering, since under guise of religion they are free to go anywhere and to talk without witnesses to anybody as long, and as often, as they wish under pretext of visitation, consolation, and secret confession, so piously are their panderings accoutred; and there are those among them who call it a pain and a punishment to touch hand to money, but who are not at all stirred by the words of St. Paul: 'It is good for a man not to touch a woman' [I Cor. 7:1], and who time and again touch them and with unchaste hands, who stealthily slink to the brothels, corrupt consecrated nuns, seduce widows and the adulterous wives of those who offer them hospitality." Then (sheet *a,* p. 1, recto) comes the passage discussed by Bayle and which appears in a very free French translation in the 1603 ed., n.p., for such a practice the Saint deems ill-founded. He thinks the main consideration was that "a certain sensuous pleasure comes from living with a woman, not only in a conjugal relationship, but also quite apart from marriage or physical relations." [3] And that pleasure indeed he finds greater than the joys of marriage, since in marriage a man tires of his wife through frequent contact, and a wife ages sooner than a spinster. It would seem that those spiritual intimacies were carried a bit far; for, after quoting an apothegm stressing the danger of the kiss, the Saint adds: "I need hardly say as much to those who kiss and caress the women who live in their homes." [4] And he runs on at length to confute the various pretexts advanced in justification of such practices. In his second sermon [5] the Saint deals with the women involved. In general he thinks it wrongful for consecrated virgins to dress fastidiously. As for those who live with men, the Saint would have them buried alive. He flouts the shameless proofs they give of their virginity.[6] He confutes, preaches, groans, exhorts. Strange indeed if for so much smoke there were no fire whatever in actual life. As a matter of fact it is transparent proof that the scandal existed and was no small scandal at that; and there is plenty of other evidence to the same purport.

p. 394: "The laws and the canons are also enlisted in that army [of vice], and serve to foment immorality by working in favour of the powerful for the validation and legitimizing of wrongful marriage and in breaking up marriages that are legitimate and holy, and by forcing priests to cowardly secret lusts by forbidding them honourable marriage. The law-breakers have found it better that men of the Church should lead disgusting lives with concubines than respectable orderly lives with married wives, perhaps because the profits and conveniences that they derive from the concubines are the greater. For we read that a certain bishop made boast at a banquet that he had eleven thousand priests in his diocese who kept concubines and that they paid him every mother's son at the rate of a pound apiece a year."

1394 [3] *Δοκεῖ μοί τινα ἡδονὴν ἔχειν τὸ συνοικεῖν γυναιξὶν, οὐ νόμῳ γάμου μόνον, αλλὰ καὶ γάμου καὶ συνουσίας χωρίς.*

1394 [4] *'Εγὼ δὲ τοῦτο μέν οὐκ ἂν εἴποιμι ὅτι τὰς συνοικούσας φιλοῦσιν ἢ ἐπαφῶνται.*

1394 [5] Gaume, *loc. cit.:* Πρὸς τὰς ἐχούσας ἄνδρας συνεισάκτους: [Savil] "*Adversus eas qui viros introductorios habent.*"

1394 [6] The passage reads in Latin translation: "*Obstetricis enim ars et sapientia hoc solum potest videre: an congressum viri corpus tulerit. An liberum* [*sit*] *et adulterium ex osculis et corruptionum amplexibus effugerit, dies illa tunc declarabit quando verus Dei sermo qui occulta hominis in medium adducit et praesens nunc his quae clam fiunt omnia et exuta ante omnium oculos ponet: tunc sciemus bene an ab his sit purum et undequaque incorruptum corpus.*" (§ 1392 [2].)

1395. The nineteenth canon of the Council held at Ancyra in Galatia, in the year 314 (canon XX, Labbe, Vol. I, p. 1494), forbids virgins to live with men as "sisters." The Council of Nicaea eleven years later (*anno* 325, canon III, Labbe, Vol. II, p. 34) forbids the clergy to keep in their houses *subintroductae* other than mothers, sisters, aunts, or other women above suspicion.[1] Nor did the Church relax its battling in later times to prevent its priests from keeping paramours or concubines. But results were negligible. What serious proportions the task of suppressing a concubinary clergy in the Middle Ages assumed is a matter of common knowledge. There were, to be sure, Popes who attached little importance to sexual morality, but there were others who, no less certainly, did their utmost to enforce it. In the end, after great efforts public concubinage was abolished, but not much was accomplished as regards substance.[2]

1396. If one consider on the one hand the immense power that the Church held through the spiritual, moral, and material weapons it had at its disposal, and on the other the insignificance of the results achieved, one gets some conception of the tremendous power of the sex residue, and comes to realize how ridiculous certain fatuous pygmies of our day are in even dreaming that they can repress it.[1]

1395 [1] See Du Cange, *Glossarium . . . mediae et infimae Latinitatis, s.v. Subintroductae;* and *Idem, Glossarium . . . mediae et infimae Graecitatis, s.v.* Συνείσακτοι.

1395 [2] In a number of countries the clergy are more moral today than they ever were in times past; but that fact is due rather to the selection that is now exercised, all candidates who fail to give certain promise of genuine vocation being rejected.

1396 [1] [In his treatment of the sex residue Pareto is less objective than is his wont, and his exposition may be perfected in some important respects. For instance when he comes to the matter of the combination of the sex residue with other residues, one would have thought that he would follow his classification and show how the combination is effected with each class of residues in turn and the consequences of the combination. Some interesting analyses would have resulted. General: The general effect of the sex residue in combination with others is to intensify those others, so that if a sex slant can be introduced into a non-logical impulse, the latter flares on high. This is so true that one of the ways to gauge fluctuations of intensities of sentiments in history is to watch the effects that various transformations have on the status of women. Historians have commonly noted that one of the most striking results of the so-called Christian revolution was the abolition of the Graeco-Roman harem and a step toward the equalization of women with men. This can be stated in Paretan language in terms of a sudden intensification of Class V residues in the ruling classes. So a contrast between the treatment of women by the law before the eighteenth century and their modern status brings out the rapid development of humanitarian sentiments (Class IV and Class II residues). Particular: 1. Pure and generic manifestations of sex, so frequent in ancient and medieval times, nay, so unconscious, have been reduced to a sub-social level and are punished by law in all Western countries. Examples, the obscenities that are drawn or written on walls and bill-boards in public places. 2. Combinations with Class I residues. The chief manifestation here is in wit: the risqué story, sub-rosa and in art. The phenomenon presents wide variations in time and in space, and accounts for certain aspects of our Western national literatures. 3. Combinations with Class II residues. Important is the phenomenon of Platonic love. Not less than a dozen professorial chairs have been created to produce literary drool on this subject, and all to no scientific purpose, the Platonism, so-called, being nothing but a combination of the sex residue with certain persisting abstractions, God, Eternity, Virtue, and the like. 4. Combinations with activity residues. Example: obscene oaths, past and present. A subject to which not less than fifty doctoral dissertations in Germany have been devoted, to the great distress of bibliographers and librarians and to no corresponding scientific advantage.

One may wonder, further, whether, in a strictly sound Paretan classification, the sex residue would be a class by itself, or a genus of a much larger class, which I would define as residues connected with parts of the body and their functions. I will not go into this matter save to point out that apart from what I will call a "stercorary residue" German humor and French humor simply would not exist; that the juvenile literature of many continental countries would take far different forms, and that an American writer named Chick Sale would have had to find a different route to immortality. I am not sure that musical criticism would not be able to issue from its present theological stage (to use language of Comte) if it could be brought to consider certain "auditory residues." Oriental literatures have a veritable cult for the navel, Western literatures for visual residues, Papal encyclicals for the "olfactory." It is a gross mistake to reduce all these attitudes to sex, in the bad sense under the term "obscenity," and in the good sense under the term "beauty."—A. L.]